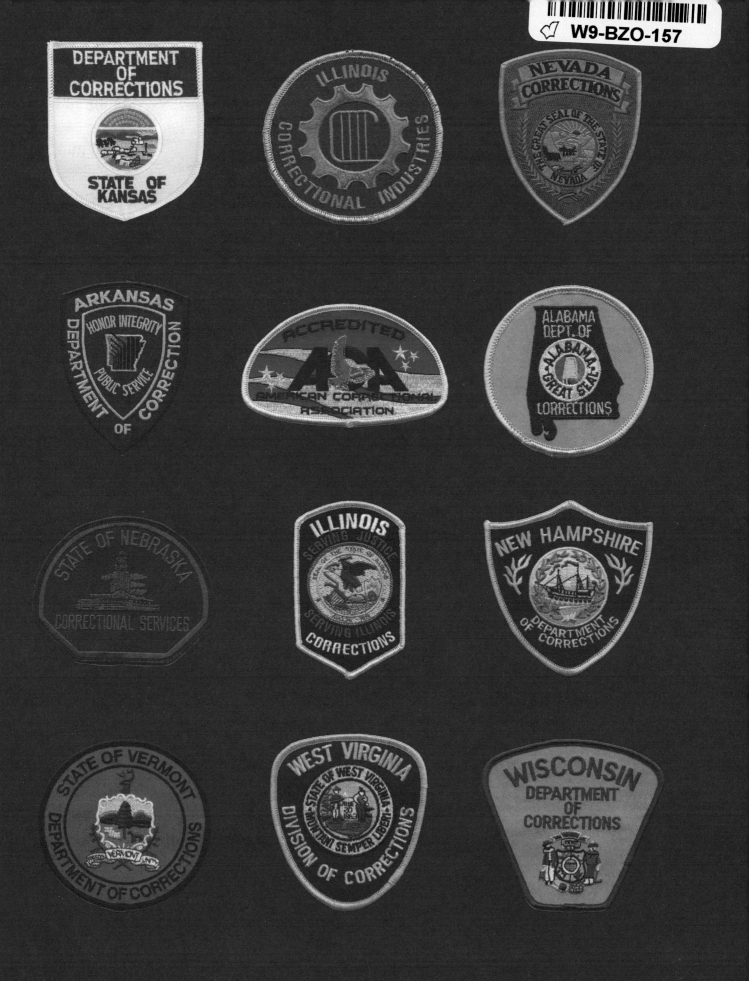

CORRECTIONS IN THE 21st CENTURY

CORRECTIONS IN THE 21st CENTURY

FOURTH EDITION

Frank Schmalleger, PhD
Distinguished Professor Emeritus
University of North Carolina

John Ortiz Smykla, PhD
Professor and Chair
Department of Criminal Justice and Legal Studies
University of West Florida

McGraw-Hill
Higher Education

Boston   Burr Ridge, IL   Dubuque, IA   New York   San Francisco   St. Louis
Bangkok   Bogotá   Caracas   Kuala Lumpur   Lisbon   London   Madrid   Mexico City
Milan   Montreal   New Delhi   Santiago   Seoul   Singapore   Sydney   Taipei   Toronto

Published by McGraw-Hill, an imprint of The McGraw-Hill Companies, Inc., 1221 Avenue of the Americas, New York, NY, 10020. Copyright © 2009, 2007, 2005, 2000. All rights reserved. No part of this publication may be reproduced or distributed in any form or by any means, or stored in a database or retrieval system, without the prior written consent of The McGraw-Hill Companies, Inc., including, but not limited to, in any network or other electronic storage or transmission, or broadcast for distance learning.

This book is printed on acid-free paper.

1 2 3 4 5 6 7 8 9 0 CCI/CCI 0 9 8

ISBN: 978-0-07-337502-1 (Student Edition); 978-0-07-332643-6 (Annotated Instructor's Edition)
MHID: 0-07-337502-0 (Student Edition); 0-07-332643-7 (Annotated Instructor's Edition)

Editor in Chief: *Michael Ryan*
Publisher: *Frank Mortimer*
Sponsoring Editor: *Katie Stevens*
Marketing Manager: *Leslie Oberhuber*
Developmental Editor: *Kate Scheinman*
Production Editor: *Paul Wells*
Production Service: *Ellen Brownstein*
Manuscript Editor: *Sharon O'Donnell*
Design Manager: *Preston Thomas*
Text/Cover Designer: *Preston Thomas*
Photo Researcher: *Editoral Image, LLC*
Production Supervisor: *Dennis Fitzgerald*
Composition: *10.5/12 Sabon by Newgen*
Printing: *45# Pub Matte Plus, Courier Inc.*

Credits: The credits section for this book begins on page CR-1 and is considered an extension of the copyright page.

Library of Congress Cataloging-in-Publication Data

Schmalleger, Frank.
    Corrections in the 21st century / Frank Schmalleger, John Smykla.
        p. cm.
    Includes bibliographical references and index.
    ISBN-13: 978-0-07-337502-1 (alk. paper)
    ISBN-10: 0-07-337502-0 (alk. paper)
    1. Corrections—United States.   2. Corrections—Vocational guidance—United States.   I. Smykla, John Ortiz.   II. Title.
HV9471.S36 2009
364.6023'73—dc22   2007030060

The Internet addresses listed in the text were accurate at the time of publication. The inclusion of a Web site does not indicate an endorsement by the authors or McGraw-Hill, and McGraw-Hill does not guarantee the accuracy of the information presented at these sites.

www.mhhe.com

For my granddaughters, Ava and Malia
—Frank Schmalleger

A mi esposa, Evelyn, con amor siempre
—John Smykla

ABOUT THE AUTHORS

Frank Schmalleger, PhD, is Distinguished Professor Emeritus at the University of North Carolina at Pembroke. He also serves as director of the Justice Research Association, a private consulting firm and think tank, based in Palm Beach, Florida, focusing on issues of crime and justice.

Dr. Schmalleger holds a bachelor's degree from the University of Notre Dame and both a master's and a doctorate in sociology from Ohio State University with a special emphasis in criminology. From 1976 to 1994, he taught criminal justice courses at the University of North Carolina at Pembroke, serving for many years as a tenured full professor. For the last 16 of those years, he chaired the Department of Sociology, Social Work, and Criminal Justice. As an adjunct professor with Webster University in St. Louis, Missouri, Dr. Schmalleger helped develop a graduate program in security management and loss prevention that is currently offered on U.S. military bases around the world. He taught courses in that curriculum for more than a decade, focusing primarily on computer and information security. Dr. Schmalleger also has taught in the New School for Social Research online graduate program, helping build the world's first electronic classrooms for criminal justice distance learning.

Dr. Schmalleger is the author of numerous articles and many books, including *Criminal Justice Today* (Prentice Hall, 2009), *Criminal Justice: A Brief Introduction* (Prentice Hall, 2008), *Criminology Today* (Prentice Hall, 2009), and *Criminal Law Today* (Prentice Hall, 2006). He is founding editor of the journal *Criminal Justice Studies* (formerly *The Justice Professional*) and has served as imprint advisor for Greenwood Publishing Group's criminal justice reference series.

Dr. Schmalleger is also the creator of a number of award-winning Web sites (including cybrary.info and crimenews.info) and founder and codirector of the Criminal Justice Distance Learning Consortium (cjdlc.org), a project of the Justice Research Association.

John Ortiz Smykla, PhD, is professor and chair of the Department of Criminal Justice and Legal Studies at the University of West Florida. Previously, he was professor of criminal justice at the University of Alabama, where he served as department chair for 10 years, and at the University of South Alabama, where he served as department chair for 3 years.

Dr. Smykla teaches courses in corrections and research methods. He teaches online, face-to-face, and using a blended format at the University of West Florida. He has taught two-way interactive corrections courses across several campuses of the University of Alabama system and has supervised more than 50 master's and doctoral students. Dr. Smykla earned the interdisciplinary social science PhD in criminal justice, sociology, and anthropology from Michigan State University. He holds bachelor's and master's degrees in sociology from California State University at Northridge.

Dr. Smykla has authored or edited four corrections books. His coauthored data set *Executions in the United States, 1608–2003: The Espy File* is one of the most frequently requested criminal justice data files from the University of Michigan's Inter-University Consortium for Political and Social Research.

Dr. Smykla has published more than 40 research articles on corrections issues, including "The Human Impact of Capital Punishment," "Effects of a Prison Facility on the Regional Economy," "Jail Type and Inmate Behavior," "Juvenile Drug Courts," and, most recently, "Correctional Privatization and the Myth of Inherent Efficiency." Dr. Smykla has delivered more than 50 conference papers in the United States and abroad. In 1986, he was a Senior Fulbright Scholar in Argentina and Uruguay.

Dr. Smykla is a member of the Academy of Criminal Justice Sciences and the Southern Criminal Justice Association. In 1996, the Southern Criminal Justice Association named him Educator of the Year. In 1997, he served as program chair for the annual meeting of the Academy of Criminal Justice Sciences. In 2000, he served as president of the Southern Criminal Justice Association. Dr. Smykla is a member of the Mobile County Metro Jail Planning Committee and a member of Friends of the Holman Prison Faith-Based Restorative Justice Honor Dorm, Atmore, Alabama.

BRIEF CONTENTS

EXPANDED CONTENTS

CHAPTER 3

SENTENCING: *To Punish or to Reform?*   68

PART 2   COMMUNITY CORRECTIONS   107

CHAPTER 4

DIVERSION AND PROBATION: *How Most Offenders Are Punished*   108

CHAPTER 5

INTERMEDIATE SANCTIONS: *Between Probation and Incarceration*   154

PART 3 INSTITUTIONAL CORRECTIONS   203

CHAPTER 6

JAILS: *Way Stations Along the Justice Highway*   204

CHAPTER 7

PRISONS TODAY: *Change Stations or Warehouses?*   250

CHAPTER 8

PAROLE: *Early Release and Reentry*   308

PART 4   THE PRISON WORLD   355

CHAPTER 9
THE STAFF WORLD:
Managing the Prison Population   356

CHAPTER 10
THE INMATE WORLD:
Living Behind Bars   390

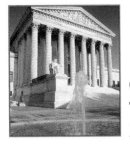

PART 5   ISSUES IN CORRECTIONS   495

CHAPTER 14

THE VICTIM: *Helping Those in Need*   540

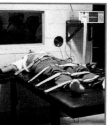

CHAPTER 15

DEATH: *The Ultimate Sanction*   574

CHAPTER 16

JUVENILE CORRECTIONS: *End of an Era?*   620

CHAPTER 17

PROFESSIONALISM IN CORRECTIONS   658

BOXED FEATURES

CAREER PROFILE BOXES

BOXED FEATURES

COMMISSION ON SAFETY AND ABUSE IN AMERICA'S PRISIONS BOXES

ETHICS AND PROFESSIONALISM BOXES

BOXED FEATURES

CORRECTIONS CONNECTIONS NETWORK NEWS BOXES

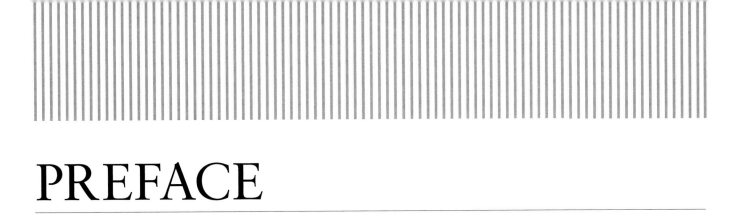

PREFACE

Corrections, when seen as the control and punishment of convicted offenders, has been an important part of organized society from the earliest days of civilization. It has not always had a proud past, however. In premodern times, atrocious physical punishment, exile, and unspeakable torture were the tools used all too often by those called upon to enforce society's correctional philosophies—especially the strongly felt need for vengeance.

Important changes in correctional practice began around the time of the American Revolution, when the purposes of criminal punishments were closely examined by influential reformers. More recently, corrections has become an important field of study in which scientific techniques are valued and reasoned debate is encouraged.

The best, however, is yet to come. It is only within the past 30 years that conscientious corrections practitioners have begun to embrace the notion of professionalism—wherein ethics, a sense of high purpose, a personal long-term career commitment, a respect for the fundamental humanity of those supervised, and widely agreed-upon principles and standards guide the daily work of correctional personnel. Corrections professionalism, although not yet as well known as police professionalism, has garnered support from policymakers and is winning respect among the public. It serves as this textbook's organizing principle.

Corrections in the 21st Century:

- provides an in-depth look at the past, present, and future of corrections;
- identifies the many *subcomponents* of modern-day corrections;
- highlights the *process* of modern-day corrections;
- focuses on the *issues* facing the correctional enterprise today;
- provides an appreciation for contemporary real-world correctional *practice*;
- examines the opportunities represented by new and developing corrections *technologies*; and
- points students in the direction of the still-emerging ideal of corrections *professionalism*.

It is our belief that a new age of corrections is upon us. It is an age in which the lofty goals of corrections professionalism will take their place alongside the more traditional components of a still-developing field. It is our hope that this textbook will play at least some small part in helping bring about a new and better correctional enterprise—one that is reasonable and equitable to all involved in the justice process.

THE FOURTH EDITION

The Fourth Edition of *Corrections in the 21st Century* contains a number of notable and exciting elements. Among these are feature articles provided by *Corrections Connection Network News (CCNN)* exclusively for this textbook, and *Reflections on the Future* essays written specifically for this text by well-known corrections practitioners and scholars.

The following changes have been made across the entire text to better focus reader attention on the key learning materials in each chapter:

- Correlation of end-of-chapter review questions to the objectives listed at the start of each chapter.
- The book's design has been streamlined to make key content more accessible to students at all levels.
- Some related materials have been moved to the Web to more clearly focus on the key points in each chapter, and to facilitate reader understanding of the text's main points.
- Some features, such as Live Links and Ethical Dilemmas, have been consolidated, putting them together at the end of chapter or on the Web.
- The photo program has been enhanced to better grab student interest and draw readers into the text.

Other general enhancements include:

- Important new material from the report of the Commission on Safety and Abuse in America's Prisons has been incorporated throughout the book.

- Ethics and Professionalism boxes have been created to highlight ethical issues in corrections, and author-created Ethical Dilemmas have been incorporated within each Ethics and Professionalism box.
- Evidence-based practices have been consistently integrated throughout the chapter material and the literature relating to such practices is now frequently cited.
- A number of new stories focusing on current events now open the chapters.
- The most recent data and literature have been reviewed and incorporated throughout.
- New Corrections Connection Network News (CCNN) boxes have been added to a number of chapters.

Significant chapter-specific content changes include the following:

Chapter 1

- "The Corrections Explosion" section has been updated.
- Considerable updates have been made to the "Measuring Crime" section.
- A box introducing the work of the Commission on Safety and Abuse in America's Prisons has been added.
- A new Ethics and Professionalism box has been added.

Chapter 2

- New materials describing the lives and the work of prison reformers Sanford Bates and George Beto have been added to this chapter.

Chapter 3

- A discussion of the Washington State Institute for Public Policy's econometric study is now included to show how incarceration rates can affect county crime rates.
- A brief discussion of *Cunningham* v. *California* (U.S. Supreme Court, 2007), in which the U.S. Supreme Court found that California's determinate sentencing law (DSL) violated a defendant's right to trial by jury because it placed sentence-elevating fact finding within the province of judges, has been added to "The Legal Environment and Sentencing Guidelines" section of this chapter.

Chapter 4

- Exhibit 4–6 now reflects the fact that the state of Michigan has a dual organization of probation with both state and local agencies providing probation services.
- The discussion of issues facing probation and parole officers has been expanded.
- A new section discusses the major sources of probation and parole officers' stress.
- The chapter now contains more research on those states with laws allowing authorities to collect supervision fees from probationers and parolees.
- An insert has been added about the importance placed by the American Psychological Association (APA) on the officer–offender relationship in the "what works" literature.
- The chapter includes new research from the American Probation and Parole Association on the ideal caseload for probation and parole.

Chapter 5

- Drug court material from throughout the text has been moved to this chapter and consolidated.
- The chapter now contains new material from the 2006 Washington State Institute for Public Policy assessing the effectiveness of the average intensive supervision probation program in reducing recidivism.
- The chapter now includes coverage of two important 2006 publications on drug court effectiveness from the National Institute of Justice and the Washington State Institute on Public Policy.
- The chapter contains new material on changing the focus of juvenile boot camps, especially in Florida law.

Chapter 6

- The chapter now contains new material on fourth-generation jails.
- Added coverage of a report from the National Institute of Corrections that is intended to help jail and prison administrators more effectively manage the women in their care.
- Additional coverage of public versus privately run jails, and a description of local jails that charge inmates a housing fee have been added.
- The chapter includes added discussion of research on how jails rapidly are becoming the

nation's default mental health system—including the consequences of inmate suicides and challenges facing small jails in dealing with the issue.
- The chapter now contains a new heading and new material on jail reentry strategies, including discussion of jurisdictions that tailor inmate work programs to local community needs.

Chapter 7
- The chapter now contains a new box discussing the report of the Commission in Safety and Abuse in America's Prisons.
- New material has been added on evidence-based research concerning correctional programs and services as they relate to recidivism.
- The chapter includes new research on faith-based programming and its effectiveness.
- The chapter now contains a new heading and added materials describing State Prison Industries.

Chapter 8
- The chapter now contains added material on state and federal governments' initiatives concerning prisoner reentry.
- Material on parole supervision programs that produce lower rates of recidivism has been added.
- The chapter also contains two new sections titled "Prisoner Reentry and Community Policing" and "Community-Focused Parole."

Chapter 9
- A box titled "Correctional Leadership" from the report of the Commission on Safety and Abuse in America's Prisons has been added.
- The chapter contains a new Ethics and Professionalism box, with author-created Ethical Dilemmas.
- Material about Zacarias Moussaoui has been added to the "Impact of Terrorism on Corrections" section.
- This section also includes added commentary on the new report by the Homeland Security Policy Institute at George Washington University and the Critical Incident Analysis Group at the University of Virginia—as well as a 2006 USDOJ Inspector General report critical of the BOP with regard to managing high-risk inmates who might have terrorist connections.

Chapter 10
- The chapter now mentions the role of prison-related themes in rap music.
- The number of inmate types discussed in the chapter has been expanded to 13 (with the addition of the "gang-banger").
- Four paragraphs have been added under the section "Characteristics of Women Inmates" describing the Julia Tutwiler Prison for Women in Alabama.
- In that same section, new material from BJS surveys has been added about the percentage of female prisoners who have previously experienced physical and sexual abuse.
- Under the "Social Structure in Women's Prisons" heading, new information about the culture of imprisoned women at the Central California Women's Facility has been added.
- More material on gender-responsive strategies has been added.

Chapter 11
- The chapter now further clarifies the central questions raised by those interested in the rights of prisoners.
- The coverage of relevant U.S. Supreme Court cases has been enhanced to include the 2006 case of *U.S.* v. *Georgia*, in which the Court held that, under the Americans with Disabilities Act, a state may be liable for rights deprivations suffered by inmates with disabilities held in its prisons.
- Added coverage has been provided on the 2006 U.S. Supreme Court case of *Beard* v. *Banks*, in which the Justices held that Pennsylvania prison officials could legitimately prohibit the state's most violent inmates from having access to newspapers, magazines, and photographs.

Chapter 12
- The chapter now contains a new box about the Commission on Safety and Abuse in America's Prisons' report on health care.
- The chapter contains a new section titled "Drug Use and Dependence," and another new section on the latest research from the White House Office of National Drug Control Policy.
- The chapter now provides a discussion of 13 principles of effective drug treatment.
- The chapter contains new material on peer-led counseling, which is a method for reducing high-risk behavior among incarcerated populations.

Chapter 13

- The chapter contains new material on California's use of sentencing guidelines to control prison crowding.
- The chapter now contains a new section titled "Jail Gangs: Security Threat Groups," in order to highlight the importance of the issue for jails.
- A box describing the Commission on Safety and Abuse in America's Prisons' report on limiting segregation within institutions is included.
- The latest U.S. Supreme Court rulings impacting supermax prisons, and the latest research relating to the market shares of private prisons has been added.

Chapter 14

- The chapter streamlines the coverage of significant events in victims' rights over the past few decades.
- There is added mention of the Violence Against Women Act of 2005, which was signed into law by President George W. Bush in 2006.

Chapter 15

- The chapter contains a new Exhibit 15–1 showcasing countries with and without the death penalty.
- The latest data on the number of people executed and on death row today have been added.
- Several new Web Informed Viewpoints describing the American Medical Association's position on physician participation in executions have been added.
- New material on court challenges to the constitutionality of lethal injection, including what's taking place in Florida, is now part of the chapter.
- New material has been added on the U.S. Supreme Court case of *Schriro* v. *Summerlin*, in which the Court held that its 2002 ruling in *Ring* v. *Arizona* did not apply retroactively to cases that already had been decided.
- New material has been added describing the cost of capital punishment in New Jersey.
- The chapter now includes a new Talking About Corrections feature on issues related to the possibility of televising executions, and a new Eye On Corrections feature about the likely future of lethal injection.

Chapter 16

- Added coverage has been provided on English Poor Laws as they contributed to the development of juvenile justice in this country and abroad.
- The chapter includes considerable coverage of today's juvenile correctional facilities, including restrictive facilities such as training schools and detention centers, and community-based programs such as probation, day treatment, and outreach initiatives.
- The chapter now describes the findings of the 2006 survey of juvenile correctional facilities undertaken by the Council of Juvenile Correctional Administrators (CJCA).
- The chapter now outlines findings from the Office of Juvenile Justice and Delinquency Prevention's most recent Juvenile Residential Facility Census.
- The coverage of peer and youth courts (also known as teen courts) has been updated.
- The chapter's coverage of youth gangs has been updated.

Chapter 17

- The coverage of professionalism in corrections has been enhanced and streamlined.
- A box titled "Culture and Profession" from the report of the Commission on Safety and Abuse in America's Prisons has been added.

ORGANIZATION

The Fourth Edition of *Corrections in the 21st Century* includes 17 chapters whose organization reflects aspects of the correctional process. Chapters are grouped into five parts, each of which is described in detail in the following paragraphs.

Part One, "Introduction to Corrections," provides an understanding of corrections by explaining the goals underlying the correctional enterprise and by describing the how and why of criminal punishments. Part One identifies professionalism as the key to managing correctional personnel, facilities, and populations successfully. Standard-setting organizations such as the American Correctional Association, the American Jail Association, the American Probation and Parole Association, and the National Commission on Correctional Health Care are identified, and the importance of professional ethics for correctional occupations and correctional administrators is emphasized.

Part Two, "Community Corrections," explains what happens to most convicted offenders, including diversion (the suspension of formal criminal proceedings before conviction in exchange for the defendant's participation in treatment), probation, and intermediate sanctions.

Part Three, "Institutional Corrections," provides a detailed description of jails, prisons, and parole. The reentry challenges facing inmates released from prisons are explained. Education, vocational preparation, and drug treatment programs that are intended to prevent reoffending also are explored.

Part Four, "The Prison World," provides an overview of life inside prison from the points of view of both inmates and staff. Part Four also describes the responsibilities and challenges surrounding the staff role. A special chapter, Chapter 12, focuses attention on special correctional populations, including inmates who are elderly, who have HIV/AIDS, and who are mentally and physically challenged. We have chosen to integrate our coverage of women in corrections—including information about the important NIC report titled "Gender Responsive Strategies: Research, Practice, and Guiding Principles for Women Offenders"—throughout the body of the text rather than isolating it in Chapter 12.

Part Five, "Issues in Corrections," explores some of the most controversial topics in contemporary corrections. Prison crowding, capital punishment, the conditional rights of prisoners, and juvenile corrections all can be found in this section of the text. Victims' rights and the role that correctional authorities can play in protecting and advancing those rights also are explored. Chapter 17, "Professionalism in Corrections," concludes the section.

PEDAGOGICAL AIDS

Working together, the authors and editor have developed a learning system designed to help students excel in the corrections course. In addition to the many changes already mentioned, we have included a wealth of new photographs to make the book even more inviting and relevant.

To this same end, our real-world chapter-opening vignettes give the material a fresh flavor intended to motivate students to read on; our photo captions, which raise thought-provoking questions, actively engage students in the learning process. Redesigned and carefully updated tables and figures highlight and amplify the text coverage. And chapter outlines, objectives, and reviews, plus marginal definitions and an end-of-book glossary, all help students master the material.

The Schmalleger/Smykla learning system goes well beyond these essential tools, however. As mentioned, *Corrections in the 21st Century* offers a unique emphasis on corrections professionalism, an emphasis that has prompted us to create a number of innovative new learning tools that focus on the real world of corrections:

- *Corrections Connection Network News*—exclusive feature articles from a popular Web site for corrections practitioners that lend a real-world air to the text.

- *Career Profiles*—enlightening minibiographies of corrections professionals, such as a parole officer, a victims' advocate, a corrections officer, a youth counselor, and a substance abuse manager.

- *Offender Speaks* and *Staff Speaks*—intriguing interviews with offenders and practitioners that provide a balance of perspectives and further expand on the text's real-world emphasis.

- *Commission on Safety and Abuse in America's Prisons*—a series of boxes throughout the text highlighting the findings of this important national commission that was formed to examine conditions in American prisons following the abuse scandals at the military-run Abu Ghraib prison in Iraq. Each box in the series focuses on a subset of the commission's findings, such as correctional leadership, security, oversight and accountability, and measuring correctional effectiveness.

- *Ethics and Professionalism*—boxes that highlight ethical codes and critical concerns from America's premier corrections-related professional associations. Included are features from the American Correctional Association, the American Jail Association, the American Probation and Parole Association, the International Association of Correctional Training Personnel, and others. Included in each Ethics and Professionalism box are author-created Ethical Dilemmas, which present students with ethical questions from the corrections field and guide them to an insightful resolution. Ethical Dilemmas are supplemented with Web-based resources maintained by the authors and specifically selected to help students navigate particular ethics-related issues.

- *Talking About Corrections*—Web-based on-demand audio features in which corrections professionals discuss important issues relating to today's correctional enterprise.

- *Two special chapters*: (1) Chapter 12, "Special Prison Populations," which brings focus to the discussion of special populations in corrections, and (2) Chapter 17, "Professionalism in Corrections," which draws together the book's professionalism theme.
- *Appendix: "Careers in Corrections"*—an appendix that presents the steps involved in planning a career, developing employability and job readiness, and finding the right job.

In addition to the features we have developed to further our goal of creating a uniquely practical, professionally oriented text, we also have included end-of-chapter review material to help students master the concepts and principles developed in the chapter:

- *Reflections on the Future*—contributed essays from some of the field's most respected scholars and practitioners that offer insights into the future of sentencing, jails, parole, and other institutions in American corrections.
- *Chapter Summary*—a valuable learning tool organized into sections that mirror the chapter-opening objectives exactly; the summary restates all of the chapter's most critical points.
- *Key Terms*—a comprehensive list of the terms defined in the margins of the chapter, complete with page references to make it easy for students to go back and review further.
- *Questions for Review*—objective study questions (exactly mirroring the chapter-opening objectives and summary) that allow students to test their knowledge and prepare for exams.
- *Thinking Critically About Corrections*—broad-based questions that challenge students to think critically about chapter concepts and issues.
- *On-the-Job Decision Making*—unique experiential exercises that enable students to apply what they have learned in the chapter to the daily work of correctional personnel.
- *Live Links*—important corrections-related full-text articles on the Internet.

SUPPLEMENTS

Visit our Online Learning Center Web site at www.mhhe.com/schmalleger4 for robust student and instructor resources.

For Students

Student resources include Internet links, chapter-specific multiple-choice self-quizzes, exercises, flashcards, crossword puzzles, and study aids.

For Instructors

The password-protected instructor portion of the Web site includes the instructor's manual, a comprehensive computerized test bank, PowerPoint lecture slides, and a variety of additional instructor resources.

IN APPRECIATION

Writing a textbook requires a great deal of help and support. We would like to acknowledge and thank the many individuals on whom we relied. Special thanks go to William W. Sondervan, Director of Criminal Justice, Investigative Forensics and Legal Studies at the University of Maryland, and Ania Dobrzanska, Program Coordinator with the Moss Group in Washington, DC, for their contributions to this book's final chapter; to Dennis Stevens at Sacred Heart University, Fairfield, Connecticut for his research on special features; to Jody Klein-Saffran at the Federal Bureau of Prisons and Gary Bayens at Washburn University for their contributions to our chapters on parole and juvenile corrections, respectively; to Erika Overall and Major William Hayes of the Kent Division of the King County (Washington) Jail, Regional Justice Center for the photograph and schematic of the fourth-generation jail; to the criminal justice and legal studies faculty and staff and the dean of the College of Professional Studies at the University of West Florida for their encouragement and for the resources they made available; to Dr. Richard Hough, University of West Florida, for creating many of the instructor and student supplements that appear on our book Web site; and to Laura Joyce for her help in Web and AIE development. We also gratefully acknowledge the contributions of the following individuals who helped in the development of this textbook.

Steve Abrams
California Department of Corrections and Rehabilitation
Santa Rosa, California

Stanley E. Adelman
University of Arkansas School of Law
Little Rock, Arkansas
University of Tulsa College of Law
Tulsa, Oklahoma

Tom Austin
Shippensburg University
Shippensburg, Pennsylvania

Ken Barnes
Arizona Western College
Yuma, Arizona

Jeri Barnett
Virginia Western Community College
Roanoke, Virginia

Kathy J. Black-Dennis
University of Louisville
Louisville, Kentucky

Robert Bohm
University of Central Florida
Orlando, Florida

David A. Bowers Jr.
University of South Alabama
Mobile, Alabama

Vicky Dorworth
Montgomery College
Rockville, Maryland

Carrie L. Dunson
Central Missouri State University
Warrensburg, Missouri

Hilary Estes
Southern Illinois University, Carbondale
Carbondale, Illinois

Robert Figlestahler
Eastern Kentucky University
Richmond, Kentucky

Lynn Fortney
EBSCO Subscription Services
Birmingham, Alabama

Don Drennon Gala
Federal Bureau of Prisons
Atlanta, Georgia

Donna Hale
Shippensburg University
Shippensburg, Pennsylvania

Homer C. Hawkins
Michigan State University
East Lansing, Michigan

Nancy L. Hogan
Ferris State University
Big Rapids, Michigan

Ronald G. Iacovetta
Wichita State University
Wichita, Kansas

Connie Ireland
California State University, Long Beach
Long Beach, California

James L. Jengeleski
Shippensburg University
Shippensburg, Pennyslvania

Brad Johnson
Atlanta, Georgia

Kathrine Johnson
University of West Florida
Ft. Walton Beach, Florida

Mike Klemp-North
Ferris State University
Big Rapids, Michigan

Julius Koefoed
Kirkwood Community College
Cedar Rapids, Iowa

Walter B. Lewis
St. Louis Community College at Meramec
Kirkwood, Missouri

Shelley Listwan
Kent State University
Kent, Ohio

Jess Maghan
Forum for Comparative Correction
Chester, Connecticut

Alvin Mitchell
Delgado Community College
New Orleans, Louisiana

Etta Morgan
Pennsylvania State University
Capital College, Pennsylvania

Kathleen Nicolaides
University of North Carolina, Charlotte
Charlotte, North Carolina

Sarah Nordin
Solano Community College
Suisun City, California

Michael F. Perna
Broome Community College
Binghamton, New York

Scott Plutchak
University of Alabama at Birmingham
Birmingham, Alabama

John Sloan
University of Alabama at Birmingham
Birmingham, Alabama

Anthony C. Trevelino
Camden County College
Blackwood, New Jersey

Sheryl Van Horne
Radford University
Radford, Virginia

Shela R. Van Ness
University of Tennessee at Chattanooga
Chattanooga, Tennessee

Gennaro F. Vito
University of Louisville
Louisville, Kentucky

John Vollmann
Florida Metropolitan University
Pompano Beach, Florida

Ed Whittle
Florida Metropolitan University at Tampa College
Tampa, Florida

Beth Wiersma
University of Nebraska at Kearney
Kearney, Nebraska

Robert R. Wiggins
Cedarville College
Cedarville, Ohio

Kristen M. Zgoba
Rutgers University
New Brunswick, New Jersey

Dawn Zobel
Federal Bureau of Prisons
Alderson, West Virginia

We greatly acknowledge the assistance and support of the many dedicated professionals who provided original written contributions for the *Reflections on the Future* boxes in this edition. They include:

Thomas J. Cowper, Police Futurists International

Richard S. Frase, University of Minnesota

Tara Gray, New Mexico State University

Edward A. Harrison, National Commission on Correctional Health Care

Herbert J. Hoelter, National Center on Institutions and Alternatives

Illinois Governor's Commission on Capital Punishment

Leslie W. Kennedy, Rutgers University

Ken Kerle, American Jail Association

Richard Kiekbusch, University of Texas–Permian Basin

James W. Marquart, University of Texas–Dallas

William L. Tafoya, University of New Haven

Morris L. Thigpen Sr., National Institute of Corrections, United States Department of Justice

Jeremy Travis, John Jay College of Criminal Justice

Mark Umbreit, University of Minnesota

Kathy Waters, Arizona Supreme Court

Alan C. Youngs, Lakewood, Colorado, Police Department (retired)

Finally, we want to acknowledge the special debt that we owe to the McGraw-Hill team, including publisher Frank Mortimer for his encouragement and support; senior sponsoring editor Katie Stevens for keeping the project on track; marketing manager Leslie Oberhuber for seeing value in this textbook; developmental editor Kate Scheinman for her attention to the many day-to-day details that a project like this entails; production editor Paul Wells; permissions editor Sheri Gilbert; production service Ellen Brownstein; production supervisor Tandra Jorgensen; design manager Preston Thomas; photo researcher David Tietz; copy editor Sharon O'Donnell; and indexer Kay Banning. The professional vision, guidance, and support of these dedicated professionals helped bring this project to fruition. A hearty "thank you" to all.

Frank Schmalleger
John Smykla

A GUIDED TOUR

Overarching Umbrella of Professionalism

Unique to our text, Frank Schmalleger and John Smykla craft the theme of professionalism into the framework of every chapter, focusing attention on the active and crucial role that professionalism plays in corrections today.

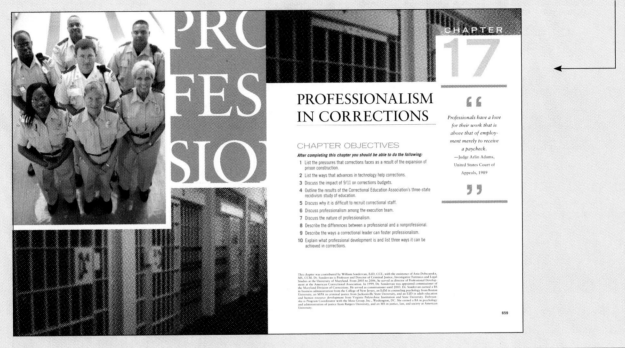

Latest Developments in Corrections

Cutting-edge topics in this new edition include:
- developments in prison mental-health care
- security threat groups (gangs)
- terrorism and corrections
- the corrections explosion
- women in prison
- correctional reformers
- fourth-generation jails
- stress on the job
- drug courts
- public versus privately run jails
- community service
- pay-to-stay jails
- prisoner reentry
- the latest Supreme Court cases
- drug abuse and treatment
- capital punishment
- juvenile correctional facilities

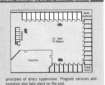

Up-to-the-Minute Data

The most recent FBI, Bureau of Justice Statistics, and Corrections Compendium sources appear throughout the text.

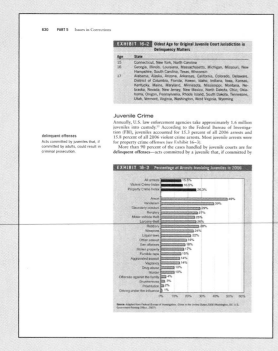

Innovative Learning Tools

NEW! Ethics and Professionalism boxes have been created to focus on ethical issues in corrections. Each box includes author-created Web-based ethical dilemmas.

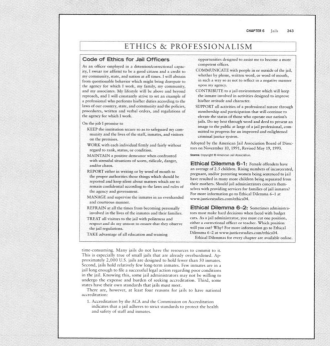

NEW! Commission on Safety and Abuse in America's Prisons boxes highlight important real-world material from the recent Commission report.

Chapter-Opening Objectives Are Keyed to End-of-Chapter Summaries and Questions for Review

This pedagogical development provides an integrated framework for objectives, summaries, and review questions, helping students absorb content throughout each chapter.

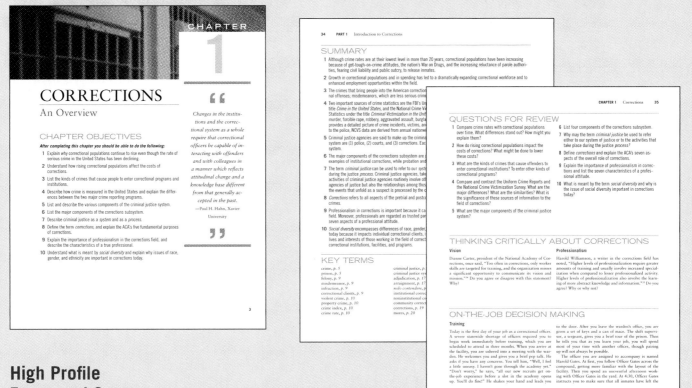

High Profile Faces and Cases

Taken from today's headlines, these chapter introductions provide timely corrections-related coverage and the background needed to understand the role of corrections in today's world.

Getting Personal

Offender Speaks and **Staff Speaks boxes** contain intriguing interviews with a variety of offenders and corrections professionals. These boxes provide a balance of perspectives and further expand the text's real-world emphasis.

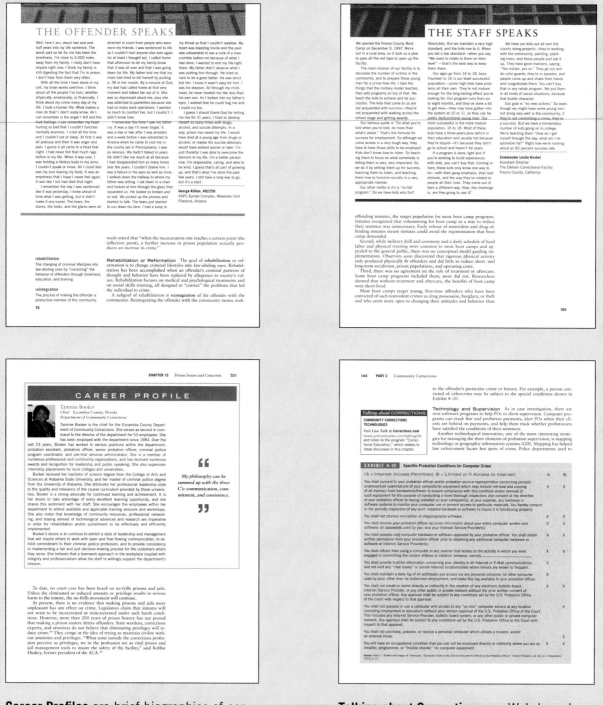

Career Profiles are brief biographies of corrections professionals, such as a community corrections chief, a youth counselor, a parole officer, a victim advocate, and a substance abuse manager.

Talking about Corrections are Web-based on-demand audio features in which corrections professionals discuss important issues relating to today's correctional enterprise.

Essays and Articles

Reflections on the Future essays, written specifically for this text by some of the field's most respected scholars and professionals, offer insights into the future of corrections.

Corrections Connection Network News (CCNN) articles, from a popular Web site for corrections practitioners, highlight practical issues facing corrections professionals in their day-to-day work.

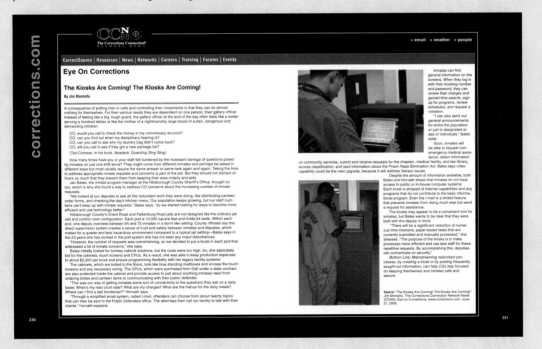

End-of-Chapter and End-of-Book Features

The end-of-chapter Review & Applications section includes clear, concise summaries, key terms, review and critical-thinking questions, on-the-job exercises, and Web-linked corrections-related articles.

KEY TERMS

special-needs inmates, p. 461
substance-abusing inmate, p. 461
therapeutic community (TC), p. 468
HIV (human immunodeficiency virus), p. 471

AIDS (acquired immunodeficiency syndrome), p. 472
tuberculosis (TB), p. 482
hospice, p. 484
syphilis, p. 486

gonorrhea, p. 486
chlamydia, p. 487
genital herpes, p. 487
Americans with Disabilities Act (ADA), p. 488

QUESTIONS FOR REVIEW

1 What is a *special-needs inmate*?

2 Summarize the management problems that special-needs inmates pose for corrections officials.

3 What criteria would you use to assess the impact that substance abusers have on the corrections system?

4 How would you design a system that makes it easier to treat HIV in prison?

5 What ideas can you add to the five essential elements of providing cost-effective management of HIV/AIDS inmates?

6 What evidence explains why there are so many inmates with mental illness in prison?

7 Suggest additional strategies for diverting persons with mental illness from the criminal justice system.

8 What should corrections do about the cost and health issues associated with older inmates?

9 Why is it important to understand the legal issues surrounding special population inmates?

THINKING CRITICALLY ABOUT CORRECTIONS

Aging Prison Population and Costs

As the prison population ages, the costs of incarcerating large numbers of older inmates will skyrocket. This, in turn, will strain correctional budgets and adversely impact correctional administrators' ability to provide essential services to the general prisoner population. Should elderly inmates be released from incarceration? Could services provided by other public agencies be tapped to meet the needs of elderly inmates? If so, which services might be invoked?

The Principle of Least Eligibility

Discussions of the principle of least eligibility invariably fire emotions. Should inmates receive free medical care that is not available to law-abiding citizens? Why or why not? Would you support a ballot proposal to formalize the principle of least eligibility as law in your state? Why or why not? If such a law were adopted, do you think it would withstand challenge through the state and federal court systems? Why or why not?

ON-THE-JOB DECISION MAKING

How to Use Personal Experience to Advance Correctional Training in HIV/AIDS

You are the warden of a state prison and on record as a supporter of the principle of least eligibility. Walter Edmunds is one of your most dependable correctional officers. Mature, calm, and unfailingly professional, Edmunds can be counted on in every crisis. You have come to rely on his leadership as a positive element among the correctional staff. Unfortunately, Edmunds has a young son dying of AIDS, which he contracted through a blood transfusion during an appendectomy.

Yesterday, your medical staff conducted training for your correctional officers on procedures for handling inmates

suffering from HIV and AIDS. About 10 minutes into the training session, Edmunds apologized for interrupting and then asked why the prisoners received top-notch medical treatment for free, treatment that ordinary law-abiding citizens can't afford.

From that single question, things quickly deteriorated, and Edmunds became increasingly agitated. Before long, the training room was in turmoil, as Edmunds's questions and angry comments whipped up the sympathy and anger of his fellow correctional officers.

Clearly out of his depth, the medical officer canceled the remainder of the training session and then bolted to your office. By the time he finished relating the incident, one of your correctional lieutenants appeared to report that the

unionized correctional staff was in an uproar and threatening to walk off the job. What would you do to defuse this situation? Once you contained the crisis, how would you handle Edmunds?

Deciding Legitimate Penological Concerns

You are a correctional lieutenant at a state prison that has a conjugal visitation program. Carl Packard, one of your inmates, was recently diagnosed as HIV-positive. During an interview with a member of the medical staff, Packard acknowledged recent illicit drug use during which he shared a needle with other inmates. He and the medic believe this needle sharing to be the source of Packard's HIV infection.

Yesterday, Packard applied for a conjugal visit with his wife. You summoned him to your office and asked if he had

advised his wife of his infection. Packard stated he had not and that he had no intention of "tellin' that bitch nothin'." This morning, you sought guidance from the prison's legal advisor and the warden. They informed you that infection with HIV did not prohibit an inmate's participation in the conjugal visitation program and that privacy policies prohibit you from informing Mrs. Packard of her husband's physical condition. You strongly believe that the threat to Mrs. Packard's health and safety outweighs what you consider to be ill-advised rules and policies.

1. What do you do?
2. What is your reasoning?

LIVE LINKS

at www.justicestudies.com/livelinks04

12–1 Mental Health Problems of Prison and Jail Inmates

The report compares the characteristics of offenders with a mental health problem to those without, including current offense, criminal record, sentence length, time expected to be served, co-occurring substance dependence or abuse, family background, and facility conduct since current admission. It presents measures of mental health problems by gender, race, and age. The report describes mental health problems and mental health treatment among inmates since admission to jail or prison. Findings are based on the Survey of Inmates in State and Federal Correctional Facilities, 2004, and the Survey of Inmates in Local Jails, 2002. Highlights include the following: Nearly a quarter of both state prisoners and jail inmates who had a mental health problem, compared to a fifth of those without, had served three or more prior incarcerations; female inmates had higher rates of mental health problems than male inmates (state prisons: 73 percent of females and 55 percent of males; federal prisons: 61 percent of females and 44 percent of males; local jails: 75 percent of females and 63 percent of males); over one in three state prisoners, one in four federal prisoners, and one in six jail inmates who had a mental health problem had received treatment since admission.

12–2 Crossing the Bridge: An Evaluation of the Drug Treatment Alternative-to-Prison (DTAP) Program

DTAP is a program that offers prosecutors the same kind of effective alternative to prison that has proved so successful for judges in drug courts. Significantly, DTAP shows

that coerced treatment can work for a most difficult population: drug-addicted offenders, including sellers, who have as many as five prior felony convictions and who have spent an average of 49 months in prison. The National Center on Addiction and Substance Abuse (CASA) evaluation found that individuals participating in the DTAP program, including those who did not graduate, were less likely to be re-arrested, reconvicted, and reincarcerated. DTAP participants remained in treatment six times longer than the overall median of individuals in long-term residential drug treatment programs. DTAP graduates are at least three times more likely to be employed than they were before their arrest.

12–3 Telemedicine Can Reduce Correctional Health Care Costs

Telemedicine, the remote delivery of health care through telecommunications, is promising for prison use. This report examines how prisons can use telemedicine to reduce health care costs and decrease security risks. Demonstrations of telemedicine in four federal prisons indicate that, in addition to cost savings, remote telemedical consultations can provide access to new specialists and improve the quality of care delivered to prison populations.

12–4 Correctional Health Care Addressing the Needs of Elderly, Chronically Ill, and Terminally Ill Inmates

This report discusses the management of aging and infirm prisoners. It focuses on what we know about elderly, chronically ill, and terminally ill inmates; effective evaluation for identifying the special needs of inmates; program, housing, and treatment considerations; ethical and policy

---

The Careers in Corrections appendix provides unique, step-by-step advice in career planning, developing employability and job readiness, and finding the right job so that students can move forward on the path to professionalism in corrections.

APPENDIX

CAREERS IN CORRECTIONS

Career development experts tell us that career development is a lifelong process that involves continual and consistent maintenance. Your interests, skills, and preferences change throughout your life. Thus, it is important that you know the steps involved in career planning, developing employability and job readiness, and finding the right job.[1]

CAREER PLANNING

Successful career planning is a continual process of self-assessment, occupational research, decision making, contacting potential employers, working at a job, and reevaluating your situation (see Exhibit A–1).

Self-Assessment

Career planning begins with **self-assessment**—learning who you are and what you can and want to do by evaluating your interests, skills, and values. Self-assessment tools, which pose a series of questions and identify potential career choices based on your answers, are available from most college and university career counselors as well as in bookstores and on the Internet. The questions involved pertain to (1) personal information—education, experience, achievements, personality factors, and interest in various activities; (2) skills—abilities in such areas as athletics, analysis, management, communication, and persuasion; and (3) values—ranking work-related issues (such as job location, pressure, security, responsibility, teamwork, and wages) in order of importance.

In addition, for a position in corrections, certain personal and physical attributes will be required by your employer. The California Department of Corrections (www.cdc.state.ca.us), for example, requires that a correctional officer candidate have a "history of law-abiding behavior" and "emotional maturity and stability, . . . leadership ability, tact, . . . alertness, integrity, dependability, good judgment, and the ability to work cooperatively with others." The Texas Department of Criminal Justice (www. tdcj.state.tx.us) requires, among other qualifications, that candidates in addition to not having any felony convictions not have had Class A or B misdemeanor convictions within the past five years.

In general, correctional officer applicants must:

- be at least 18 years old (in some states 21 years old);
- be a U.S. citizen;

self-assessment
Learning who you are and what you can and want to do by evaluating your interests, skills, and values.

A-1

Supplements for Students and Instructors

Visit our book-specific Online Learning Center Web site at www.mhhe.com/
schmalleger4 for robust student and instructor supplements.

- For students, we feature multiple-choice quizzes, Web-based exercises,
  links to articles and audio features, flash cards, and other student
  material.
- Our password-protected instructor center includes chapter-specific lesson
  plans, a comprehensive instructor's manual, a computerized test bank,
  PowerPoint Presentation slides, and other teaching tools.

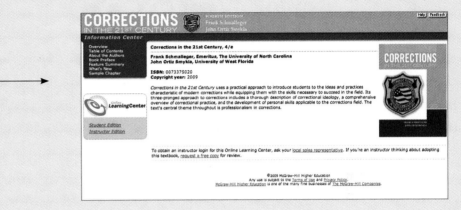

The Annotated Instructor's Edition is a special edition of the textbook for instructors only, featuring numerous instructional tools such as Web-informed
viewpoint exercises, teaching tips, and professional issues for discussion.

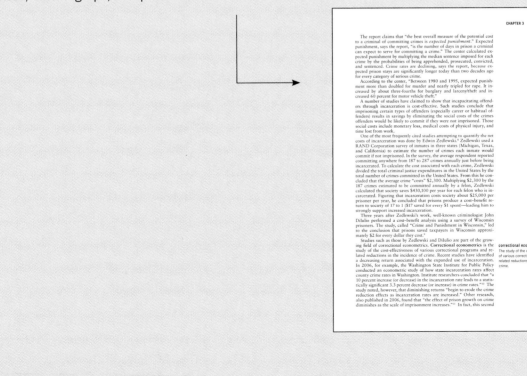

PART ONE
INTRODUCTION TO CORRECTIONS

Part One develops an understanding of cor-

rections by examining the purposes of correctional punishments and by exploring how offenders have been punished throughout history.

Today, crime rates are falling but the number of people under correctional supervision (on probation or parole or in jail or prison) is increasing. Get-tough-on-crime attitudes, the War on Drugs, and the reduction in the use of discretionary parole board release explain this increase.

Professionalism is the key to managing the growth in the correctional population. Standard-setting organizations such as the American Correctional Association, the American Jail Association, the American Probation and Parole Association, and the National Commission on Correctional Health Care offer detailed sets of written principles for correctional occupations and correctional administrators.

Nevertheless, professional credentialing in corrections is new. The seed was planted during the Enlightenment when reformers such as Cesare Beccaria and the Philadelphia Quakers shifted the focus of punishment away from the body and toward the soul and human spirit. Correcting the soul and human spirit required understanding the causes of crime and new reforms. To that end, the

National Prison Association (now known as the American Correctional Association) met in Cincinnati, Ohio, in 1870 to advance correctional theory and practice. The assembly elected then Ohio governor and future U.S. president Rutherford B. Hayes as the first president of the association. Today, the ACA remains the leader in advancing professionalism in corrections through education, training, and skills development.

The professional nature of corrections is also seen in the way sanctions are developed. From a time when theory and practice advocated indeterminate sentences to the legislatively mandated determinate sentences of today, correctional decision makers have had to use their knowledge of human behavior, philosophy, and law to construct sanctions that are fair and just. The correctional goals of retribution, just deserts, deterrence, incapacitation, rehabilitation, and restoration have produced the sanctions of probation, intermediate sanctions, jail, prison, and capital punishment.

What are the consequences of punishment? Choosing the best sanction means understanding the political, social, economic, human, and moral consequences of crime control. For that reason, corrections is a field in which complex decision making requires the skills of professional staff and administrators.

CO

REC

TIO

CORRECTIONS

An Overview

CHAPTER OBJECTIVES

After completing this chapter you should be able to do the following:

1 Explain why correctional populations continue to rise even though the rate of serious crime in the United States has been declining.

2 Understand how rising correctional populations affect the costs of corrections.

3 List the kinds of crimes that cause people to enter correctional programs and institutions.

4 Describe how crime is measured in the United States and explain the differences between the two major crime reporting programs.

5 List and describe the various components of the criminal justice system.

6 List the major components of the corrections subsystem.

7 Describe criminal justice as a *system* and as a *process.*

8 Define the term *corrections,* and explain the ACA's five fundamental purposes of corrections.

9 Explain the importance of professionalism in the corrections field, and describe the characteristics of a true professional.

10 Understand what is meant by *social diversity* and explain why issues of race, gender, and ethnicity are important in corrections today.

Changes in the institutions and the correctional system as a whole require that correctional officers be capable of interacting with offenders and with colleagues in a manner which reflects attitudinal change and a knowledge base different from that generally accepted in the past.

—Paul H. Hahn, Xavier University

In late 2006, the complete sixth season of the HBO hit series *Oz* was released on DVD. The show, about prison life, finished its six-year run in 2003, although episodes continue to air on HBO On Demand and other networks. *Oz* was HBO's first and longest-running fictional drama series. The *Boston Globe* once called it "the best written, hardest-edge drama on TV."[1] *Oz* was set in Emerald City, a prison within a prison at the fictional Oswald Maximum Security Prison somewhere in what might have been upstate New York. Among its characters, *Oz* featured "wise guys" and their Don, devout black Muslims, neo-Nazis, an Irish gangster, a white lawyer serving time for killing a young girl in a drunk-driving accident, various oddballs, and an old-timer who beat the electric chair during the 1965 East Coast blackout. At the show's center stood actor Ernie Hudson, who played the role of Warden Leo Glynn. Glynn's rock-solid strength was often called upon as he was forced to make hard decisions affecting both inmates and staff. Critics say that *Oz* will be remembered for the way so many of its actors brought humanity to their roles, sometimes turning even the most hardened long-term convicts into complex, deep men with their own code of violent justice. More recently, FOX Broadcasting Company's show *Prison Break,* starring Dominic Purcell (as Lincoln Burrows) and Wentworth Miller (as Michael Scofield), has brought the realities of prison life into American living rooms through weekly episodes. Even though both shows are fictional, and not necessarily representative of contemporary American correctional institutions, their popularity illustrates the significant role that prisons and the correctional enterprise hold in America today.

A scene from the award-winning HBO prison drama *Oz.* The popularity of shows like *Oz* and FOX Broadcasting Company's more recent series *Prison Break* illustrate the significant role that prisons and corrections have in American society. How would you explain that role?

Dominic Purcell and Wentworth Miller, stars of FOX Broadcasting Company's show *Prison Break.* The series, much of which is filmed at a former prison, has captivated viewers for the past three seasons. Why are television shows that depict prison life so popular with television audiences?

THE CORRECTIONS EXPLOSION

One amazing fact stands out from all the contemporary information about corrections: While serious **crime** in the United States consistently declined throughout much of the 1990s, and while such declines continued into the early years of the 21st century, the number of people under correctional supervision in this country—not just the number of convicted offenders sent to **prison**—has continued to climb. Crime rates are approximately 20 percent lower today than they were in 1980. They are near their lowest level in 25 years. But the number of people on probation is up almost 300 percent since 1980, the nation's prison population has increased by more than 400 percent, and the number of persons on parole has more than doubled. Exhibit 1–1 illustrates these trends.

Indications are that the trends identified in Exhibit 1–1 will not end anytime soon. In 2007, the Public Safety Performance Project of the Pew Charitable Trusts released a comprehensive report on the future of America's prisons. The report, a forecast of U.S. correctional populations based on 50 official state estimates and projections by the Federal Bureau of Prisons, concluded that by 2011, one in every 178 U.S. residents will be living in prison. "Imprisonment levels," says the report, "are expected to keep rising in all but four states, reaching a national rate of 562 per 100,000, or one of every 178 Americans. If you put them all together in one place," the report says, "the incarcerated population in just five years will outnumber the residents of Atlanta, Baltimore and Denver combined."[2]

The question is, Why? Why the steady increase in correctional populations in the face of declining crime rates? The answer to this question, like the answers to most societal enigmas, is far from simple. Pursuit of the answer is important, however. As Franklin Zimring, director of the Earl Warren Legal Institute at the University of California at Berkeley, points out, "The change in the number of inmates tells us . . . about our feelings about crime and criminals."[3]

The answer has a number of dimensions. First, it is important to recognize that get-tough-on-crime laws, such as the three-strikes (and two-strikes) laws that were enacted in many states in the mid-1990s have fueled rapid increases in prison populations. The conservative attitudes that gave birth to those laws are still with us. Noted criminal justice scholar John P. Conrad summarizes today's mood this way: "There is an unprecedented consensus on the necessity for strengthening criminal justice. This consensus can be summed up in one sentence. Criminals must be locked up and kept off the streets."[4] Conrad goes on to explain: "The vast expansion of corrections today has not come about without good cause. For the citizen on the streets, there is only one reasonable response to the violence he or she fears. Lock them up, and hang the expense."[5]

A second reason correctional populations are rapidly increasing can be found in the nation's War on Drugs. The War on Drugs has led to the arrest and conviction of many offenders, resulting in larger correctional populations in nearly every jurisdiction (especially within the federal correctional system). In Exhibit 1–2, compare the total number of individuals incarcerated for drug offenses with, for example, the total incarcerated for property offenses. Drug arrests continue to increase. Although they account for a large portion of the nation's correctional population, they do not figure into the FBI's calculations of the nation's rate of serious

crime

A violation of a criminal law.

prison

A state or federal confinement facility that has custodial authority over adults sentenced to confinement.

EXHIBIT 1–1 **Trends in Corrections Since 1980**

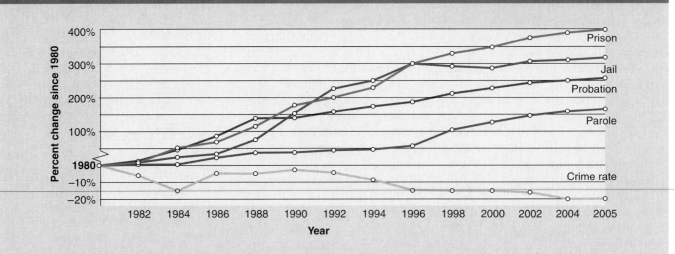

Sources: FBI, *Crime in the United States, 2005* (Washington, DC: U.S. Department of Justice, 2006); Paige M. Harrison and Allen J. Beck, *Prisoners in 2005* (Washington, DC: Bureau of Justice Statistics, 2006); and Lauren E. Glaze and Thomas P. Bonczar, *Probation and Parole in the United States, 2005* (Washington, DC: Bureau of Justice Statistics, 2006).

crimes. Hence, the War on Drugs goes a long way toward explaining the growth in correctional populations even while the rate of "serious crime" in the United States appears to be declining.

Third, parole authorities, fearing civil liability and public outcry, have become increasingly reluctant to release inmates. This has contributed to a further expansion of prison populations.

Fourth, as some observers have noted, the corrections boom has created its own growth dynamic.[6] As ever greater numbers of people are placed on probation, the likelihood of probation violations increases. Prison sentences for more violators result in larger prison populations. When inmates are released from prison, they swell the numbers of those on parole, leading to a larger number of parole violations, which in turn fuels further prison growth. Statistics show that the number of criminals being sent to prison for at least the second time has increased steadily, rising to 35 percent of the total number of admissions in 1995, from 17 percent in 1980.[7]

Historical Roots of the Corrections Explosion

Seen historically, the growth of correctional populations may be more the continuation of a long-term trend than the result of recent social conditions. A look at the data shows that correctional populations have

EXHIBIT 1–2 **Number of Prisoners by Offense, 2005**

Type of Offense	All	Male	Female
Violent offenses	650,400	621,600	28,800
Property offenses	262,000	237,100	24,900
Drug offenses	250,900	226,800	24,100
Public-order offenses	86,400	82,000	4,400

Source: Adapted from Paige M. Harrison and Allen J. Beck, *Prisoners in 2005* (Washington, DC: Bureau of Justice Statistics, July, 2006).

U.S. correctional populations have grown dramatically over the past 25 years, as this photo of male arrestees gesturing to the camera from a crowded facility shows. What factors led to a substantial increase in the use of imprisonment in this country beginning in the 1980s?

continued to grow through widely divergent political eras and economic conditions. Census reports show an almost relentless increase in the rate of imprisonment over the past 150 years. In 1850, for example, only 29 people were imprisoned in this country for every 100,000 persons in the population.[8] By 1890 the rate had risen to 131 per 100,000. The rate grew slowly until 1980, when the rate of imprisonment in the United States stood at 153 per 100,000. At that point, a major shift toward imprisonment began. While crime rates rose sharply in the middle to late 1980s, the rate of imprisonment rose far more dramatically. Today the rate of imprisonment in this country is about 490 per 100,000 persons, and it shows no signs of declining.[9] Exhibit 1–3 illustrates changes in the rate of imprisonment over the past 155 years. Probation statistics—first available in 1935—show an even more amazing rate of growth. Although only 59,530 offenders were placed on probation throughout the United States in 1935, more than 4.1 million people are on probation today.[10]

Correctional Employment

Growing correctional populations and increasing budgets have led to a dramatically expanding correctional workforce, and to enhanced employment opportunities within the field. According to historical reports, persons employed in the corrections field totaled approximately 27,000 in 1950.[11] By 1975 the number had risen to about 75,000. The most current statistics available show that the number of uniformed correctional officers in adult prisons alone has grown to more than 215,000.[12] When juvenile detention facility personnel, probation and parole officers, correctional administrators, jailers and other corrections professionals are added, the total number of persons employed in corrections today stands at more than 748,000.[13] Exhibit 1–4 shows some of the employment possibilities in corrections.

New prisons mean jobs and can contribute greatly to the health of local economies. Some economically disadvantaged towns—from Tupper

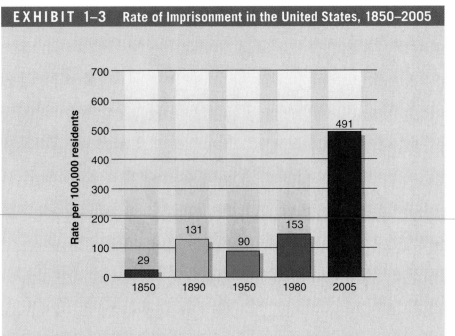

EXHIBIT 1–3 Rate of Imprisonment in the United States, 1850–2005

Rate per 100,000 residents

- 1850: 29
- 1890: 131
- 1950: 90
- 1980: 153
- 2005: 491

Sources: Margaret Werner Cahalan, *Historical Corrections Statistics in the United States, 1850–1984* (Washington, DC: U.S. Department of Justice, 1986); and Paige M. Harrison and Allen J. Beck, *Prisoners in 2005* (Washington, DC: Bureau of Justice Statistics, 2006).

EXHIBIT 1–4 Careers in Corrections

Academic teacher	Field administrator	Psychologist
Activity therapy administrator	Fugitive apprehension officer	Recreation coordinator
Business manager	Human services counselor	Social worker
Case manager	Job placement officer	Statistician
Chaplain	Mental health clinician	Substance abuse counselor
Chemical dependency manager	Parole caseworker	Unit leader
Children's services counselor	Parole officer	Victim advocate
Classification officer	Presentence investigator	Vocational instructor
Clinical social worker	Probation officer	Warden/superintendent
Correctional officer	Program officer	Youth services coordinator
Dietary officer	Program specialist	Youth supervisor
Drug court coordinator	Programmer/analyst	

Lake, in the Adirondack Mountains of upstate New York, to Edgefield, South Carolina—are cashing in on the prison boom, having successfully competed to become sites for new prisons. The competition for new prison facilities is reminiscent of the efforts states made some years ago to attract new automobile factories and other industries.

CRIME AND CORRECTIONS

The crimes that bring people into the American correctional system include felonies, misdemeanors, and minor law violations that are sometimes called *infractions*.

Felonies are serious crimes. Murder, rape, aggravated assault, robbery, burglary, and arson are felonies in all jurisdictions within the United States, although the names for these crimes may differ from state to state. A general way to think about felonies is to remember that a **felony** is a serious crime whose commission can result in confinement in a state or federal correctional institution for more than a year.

In some states a felony conviction can result in the loss of certain civil privileges. A few states make conviction of a felony and the resulting incarceration grounds for uncontested divorce. Others prohibit convicted felony offenders from running for public office or owning a firearm, and some exclude them from professions such as medicine, law, and police work.

Huge differences in the treatment of specific crimes exist among states. Some crimes classified as felonies in one part of the country may be misdemeanors in another. In still other states they may not even be crimes at all! Such is the case with some drug law violations and with social order offenses such as homosexual acts, prostitution, and gambling.

Misdemeanors, which compose the second major crime category, are relatively minor violations of the criminal law. They include crimes such as petty theft (the theft of items of little worth), simple assault (in which the victim suffers no serious injury and in which none was intended), breaking and entering, the possession of burglary tools, disorderly conduct, disturbing the peace, filing a false crime report, and writing bad checks (although the amount for which the check is written may determine the classification of this offense). In general, misdemeanors can be thought of as any crime punishable by a year or less in confinement.

Within felony and misdemeanor categories, most states distinguish among degrees, or levels of seriousness. Texas law, for example, establishes five felony classes and three classes of misdemeanor—intended to guide judges in assessing the seriousness of particular criminal acts. The Texas penal code then specifies categories into which given offenses fall.

A third category of crime is the **infraction.** The term, which is not used in all jurisdictions, refers to minor violations of the law that are less serious than misdemeanors. Infractions may include such violations of the law as jaywalking, spitting on the sidewalk, littering, and certain traffic violations, including the failure to wear a seat belt. People committing infractions are typically ticketed—that is, given citations—and released, usually upon a promise to appear later in court. Court appearances may be waived upon payment of a fine, which is often mailed in.

Measuring Crime

Two important sources of information on crime for correctional professionals are the FBI's Uniform Crime Reporting Program (UCR) and the Bureau of Justice Statistics' National Crime Victimization Survey (NCVS). Corrections professionals closely analyze these data to forecast the numbers and types of **correctional clients** to expect in the future. The forecasts can be used to project the need for different types of detention and rehabilitation services and facilities.

Uniform Crime Reports The FBI's crime reports are published annually. Individual reports are referred to by their official title, *Crime in the United States. Crime in the United States* contains information on eight major crimes: murder, forcible rape, robbery, aggravated assault,

felony
A serious criminal offense; specifically, one punishable by death or by incarceration in a prison facility for more than a year.

misdemeanor
A relatively minor violation of the criminal law, such as petty theft or simple assault, punishable by confinement for one year or less.

infraction
A minor violation of state statute or local ordinance punishable by a fine or other penalty, but not incarceration, or by a specified, usually very short term of incarceration.

correctional clients
Prison inmates, probationers, parolees, offenders assigned to alternative sentencing programs, and those held in jails.

violent crime

Interpersonal crime that involves the use of force by offenders or results in injury or death to victims. In the FBI's Uniform Crime Reports, violent crimes are murder, forcible rape, robbery, and aggravated assault.

property crime

Burglary, larceny, theft, motor vehicle theft, and arson as reported in the FBI's Uniform Crime Reports.

crime index

An annual statistical tally of major crimes known to law enforcement agencies in the United States. Note: The FBI suspended use of the term *crime index* in 2005, while the usefullness of the terminology is reviewed.

crime rate

The number of major crimes reported for each unit of population.

burglary, larceny-theft, motor vehicle theft, and arson. These major crimes, also traditionally known as *Part I offenses,* are divided into two subcategories: **violent crime** and **property crime.** Violent crime consists of murder, forcible rape, robbery, and aggravated assault. Burglary, larceny-theft, motor vehicle theft, and arson fall into the property crime category. Exhibit 1–5 summarizes the crimes reported to police in the eight major crime categories.

The data, gathered from police agencies across the country, include only crimes known to the police. Unreported or undiscovered crimes, which might outnumber those reported to the police, are not included in the crime reports.

The sum total of all major crimes provides a national **crime index** (useful in comparing the occurrence of major crimes over time. *Crime in the United States* also reports a **crime rate** each year. The rate of crime is calculated by dividing the total number of major crimes by the population of the United States. The result is expressed as the number of crimes per 100,000 people. Crime rate comparisons provide a more realistic portrayal of changes in crime over time—and of the likelihood of victimization—than do simple comparisons of crime index totals.

The FBI reported that a total of 11.4 million major crimes occurred throughout the United States in 2006. The 2006 crime rate of 3,808 offenses per 100,000 U.S. inhabitants was the lowest since 1984.[14] The violent crime rate in 2006 was 474 per 100,000, while the rate of property crimes was 3,334 offenses per 100,000.

If we look at Exhibit 1–5, we see that 17,034 murders were recorded in 2006. The murder rate was 5.7 offenses per 100,000 inhabitants. According to supplemental FBI data, 78.9 percent of murder victims in 2006 were male and 90.2 percent were 18 years old or older. Of victims whose race was known, 47.1 percent were white and 50.2 percent were black. Almost 91 percent of known murderers were male, and more than 90 percent were 18 or older. Of murderers whose race was known, 54.8 percent were black and 42.8 percent were white.

FBI data offer corrections personnel a glimpse of the background, makeup, and motivation of the offenders who may eventually become clients of the correctional system.

EXHIBIT 1–5   **Major Crimes Known to the Police, 2006**

Offense	Number	Rate per 100,000	Clearance Rate
Violent Crimes			
—Murder	17,034	5.7	60.7%
—Forcible rape	92,455	30.9	40.9
—Robbery	447,403	149.4	25.2
—Aggravated assault	860,853	287.5	54.0
Property Crimes			
—Burglary	2,183,746	729.4	12.6
—Larceny-theft	6,607,013	2,206.8	17.4
—Motor vehicle theft	1,192,809	398.4	12.6
—Arson[1]	69,055	26.8	18.0
U.S. Total	**11,470,368**	**3,834.9**	

1. Only fires determined through investigation to have been willfully or maliciously set are classified as arsons.
Source: Adapted from FBI, *Crime in the United States, 2006* (Washington, DC: U.S. Government Printing Office, 2007).

The FBI also provides data on the numbers of arrests in the United States for all types of crimes. Law enforcement agencies made an estimated 14.4 million arrests in 2006 for all offenses except traffic violations. The highest arrest count for a specific crime category was 1.9 million arrests for drug abuse violations. Simple assaults registered 1.3 million arrests, while arrests for driving under the influence numbered 1.46 million. In 2006 the nationwide rate of arrest was 4,832.5 per 100,000 people.

Solving and Clearing Crimes Most crimes reported to the police are not solved. Crimes that are solved are said to be *cleared*. For the UCR, a known offense is considered *cleared* or *solved* when a law enforcement agency has charged at least one person with the offense or when a suspect has been identified and located but circumstances have thus far prevented charging the suspect.

The *clearance rate* is the number of offenses cleared divided by the number of offenses known by police. Law enforcement agencies nationwide cleared 44.3 percent of violent crimes and 15.8 percent of property crimes in 2006. For major crimes, the clearance rate was highest for murder (60.7 percent) and lowest for burglary (12.6 percent). For many consensual crimes, such as prostitution, gambling, and drug abuse, rates of arrest are lower still. Exhibit 1–5 shows the clearance rates for major crimes reported in 2006. The clearance rates for individual crimes help corrections professionals know the types and numbers of clients to expect in the correctional system.

National Incident-Based Reporting System (NIBRS) The FBI is implementing a new crime reporting program called the *National Incident-Based Reporting System,* or NIBRS. Under the new system, many details will be gathered about each criminal incident. Included among them will be information on place of occurrence, weapon used, type and value of property damaged or stolen, personal characteristics of the offender and the victim, the nature of any relationship between the two, disposition of the complaint, and so on. The new reporting system gathers data on 22 general offenses: arson, assault, bribery, burglary, counterfeiting, vandalism, narcotic offenses, embezzlement, extortion, fraud, gambling, homicide, kidnapping, larceny, motor vehicle theft, pornography, prostitution, robbery, forcible sex offenses, nonforcible sex offenses, receiving stolen property, and weapons violations. Data will also be gathered on bad checks, vagrancy, disorderly conduct, driving under the influence, drunkenness, nonviolent family offenses, liquor law violations, "peeping Tom" activity, runaways, trespass, and a general category of all other criminal law violations.

The FBI began accepting crime data in NIBRS format in January 1989. Although NIBRS was intended to replace the old system by 1999, delays have been frequent. It will be a few more years before all police departments report their crime data to the FBI in NIBRS format.

National Crime Victimization Survey (NCVS) The nation's second crime measuring tool is the National Crime Victimization Survey (NCVS).[15] The NCVS was begun by the Bureau of Justice Statistics (BJS) in 1973. It provides a detailed picture of crime incidents, victims, and trends. The survey collects detailed information on the frequency and nature of the crimes of rape, sexual assault, personal robbery, aggravated and simple assault, household burglary, theft, and motor vehicle theft. It

Racial minorities are overrepresented among all segments of the correctional population in comparison with the ethnic makeup of America. What is the reason for this lopsided ethnic representation?

does not measure homicide or commercial crimes (such as burglaries of stores).

To gather data for the NCVS, U.S. Census Bureau personnel each year interview all household members at least 12 years old in a national representative sample of approximately 77,200 households. The total sample contains about 134,000 persons. The NCVS collects information on crimes suffered by individuals and households, whether or not those crimes were reported to law enforcement agencies. It estimates the proportion reported for each type of crime covered by the survey, and it summarizes the reasons that victims give for reporting or not reporting. For many types of offenses, the NCVS shows more crimes being committed than does the UCR. Exhibit 1–6 shows total victimizations reported by the NCVS for 2005. Compare the totals for similar categories in Exhibits 1–6 and 1–5. This comparison will help you understand the importance of knowing the source and the manner of compilation of the data you use to make corrections decisions.

The NCVS provides information about victims (age, sex, race, ethnicity, marital status, income, and educational level), offenders (sex, race, approximate age, and victim–offender relationship), and crimes (time, place, weapons, injuries, and economic consequences). Information also includes the experiences of victims with the criminal justice system, self-protective measures used by victims, and possible substance abuse by offenders. NCVS data are published annually under the title *Criminal Victimization in the United States*.

According to the most recent NCVS,[16] U.S. residents age 12 or older experienced approximately 23.5 million crimes in 2005. Seventy-seven percent of those crimes, or 18 million, were property crimes, and 23 percent (5.4 million) were crimes of violence. NCVS findings show that Americans age 12 or older experienced fewer violent and property crimes in 2005 than in any other year since 1973, when the NCVS began.

EXHIBIT 1–6	Criminal Victimizations, 2005
Type of Crime	**Number of Victimizations**
All Crimes	**23,440,710**
Personal Crimes[1]	**5,400,780**
Rape/sexual assault	191,670
Robbery	624,850
Assault	4,357,190
Personal theft[2]	227,070
Property Crimes	**18,039,930**
Household burglary	3,456,220
Motor vehicle theft	978,120
Theft	13,605,590

1. The NCVS is based on interviews with victims and therefore cannot measure murder.
2. Includes pocket picking, purse snatching, and attempted purse snatching.

Source: Adapted from Shannan M. Catalano, *Criminal Victimization, 2005* (Washington, DC: U.S. Department of Justice, September 2006), p. 2.

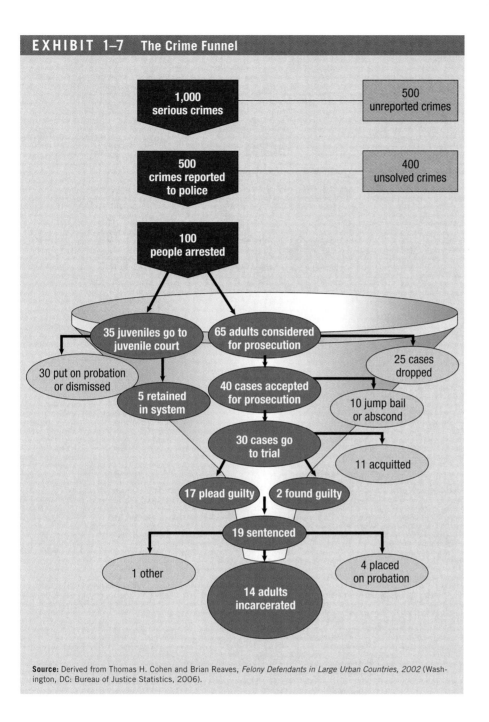

EXHIBIT 1–7   The Crime Funnel

- 1,000 serious crimes
  - 500 unreported crimes
- 500 crimes reported to police
  - 400 unsolved crimes
- 100 people arrested
  - 35 juveniles go to juvenile court
    - 30 put on probation or dismissed
    - 5 retained in system
  - 65 adults considered for prosecution
    - 25 cases dropped
    - 40 cases accepted for prosecution
      - 10 jump bail or abscond
      - 30 cases go to trial
        - 11 acquitted
        - 17 plead guilty
        - 2 found guilty
          - 19 sentenced
            - 1 other
            - 14 adults incarcerated
            - 4 placed on probation

Source: Derived from Thomas H. Cohen and Brian Reaves, *Felony Defendants in Large Urban Countries, 2002* (Washington, DC: Bureau of Justice Statistics, 2006).

The Crime Funnel

Not all crimes are reported, and not everyone who commits a reported crime is arrested, so relatively few offenders enter the criminal justice system. Of those who do, some are not prosecuted (perhaps because the evidence against them is insufficient), others plead guilty to lesser crimes, and others are found not guilty. Some who are convicted are diverted from further processing by the system or may be fined or ordered to counseling. Hence, the proportion of criminal offenders who eventually enter the correctional system is small, as Exhibit 1–7 shows.[17]

EXHIBIT 1–8   The Adult Criminal Justice System

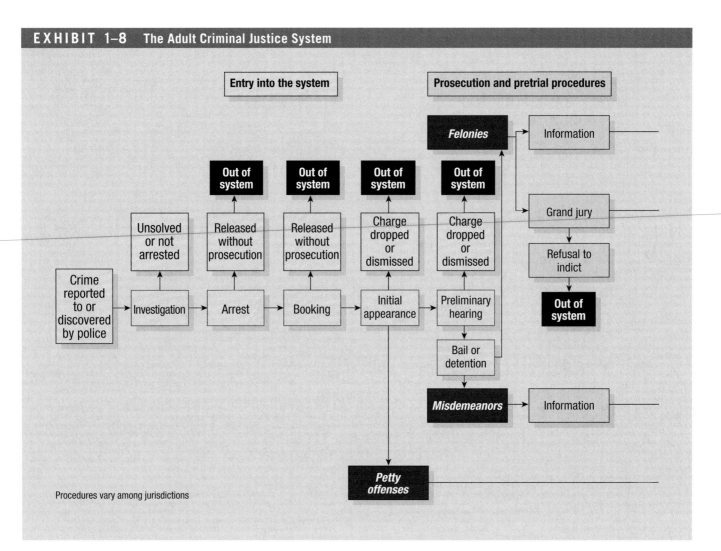

CORRECTIONS AND THE CRIMINAL JUSTICE SYSTEM

criminal justice

The process of achieving justice through the application of the criminal law and through the workings of the criminal justice system. Also, the study of the field of criminal justice.

criminal justice system

The collection of all the agencies that perform criminal justice functions, whether these are operations or administration or technical support. The basic divisions of the criminal justice system are police, courts, and corrections.

Corrections is generally considered the final stage in the criminal justice process. Some aspects of corrections, however, come into play early in the process. Keep in mind that although the term **criminal justice** can be used to refer to the justice *process*, it can also be used to describe our *system* of justice. Criminal justice agencies, taken as a whole, are said to compose the **criminal justice system.**

The components of the criminal justice system are (1) police, (2) courts, and (3) corrections. Each component, because it contains a variety of organizations and agencies, can be termed a *subsystem*. The subsystem of corrections, for example, includes prisons, agencies of probation and parole, jails, and a variety of alternative programs.

The *process* of criminal justice involves the activities of the agencies that make up the criminal justice system. The process of criminal justice begins when a crime is discovered or reported.

Court decisions based on the due process guarantees of the U.S. Constitution require that specific steps be taken in the justice process. Although the exact nature of those steps varies among jurisdictions, the description that follows portrays the most common sequence of events in

EXHIBIT 1-8 (*continued*)

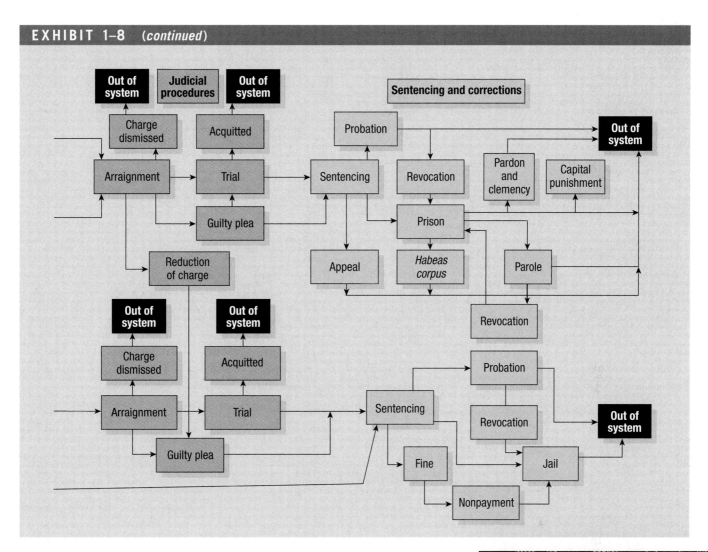

response to serious criminal behavior. Exhibit 1–8, which diagrams the American criminal justice system, indicates the relationship among the stages in the criminal justice processing of adult offenders.

Entering the Correctional System

The criminal justice system does not respond to all crime because most crimes are not discovered or reported to the police.[18] Law enforcement agencies learn about crimes from the reports of citizens, through discovery by a police officer in the field, or through investigative and intelligence work. Once a law enforcement agency knows of a crime, the agency must identify and arrest a suspect before the case can proceed. Sometimes a suspect is found at the scene; other times, however, identifying a suspect requires an extensive investigation. Often no one is identified or apprehended—the crime goes unsolved. If an offender is arrested, booked, and jailed to await an initial court appearance, the intake, custody, confinement, and supervision aspects of corrections first come into play at this stage of the criminal justice process.

Prosecution and Pretrial Procedure

After an arrest, law enforcement agencies present information about the case and about the accused to the prosecutor, who decides whether to file

Al Gore III, son of the former Vice President, pleaded guilty in 2007 in Laguna Niguel, CA, to two felony counts of drug possession and one misdemeanor count of marijuana possession. A judge ordered him to complete a drug rehabilitation program. Explain the stages of criminal processing from arrest through conviction.

THE OFFENDER SPEAKS

Very few of us do not think about beating the system. After all, the system deprives us of the freedom we cherish. It stands for all that we resent: lack of choice, restricted movement, denial of access to loved ones. We resent the walls, bars, uniforms, being told what to do, what programs we must take.

Moralists argue that we get exactly what we deserve, and many citizens believe that we are treated too well. Few of us can argue that we didn't know what we were getting into when we made the bad choices that landed us in prison. None of us arrived by accident, and if we are honest with ourselves, we'll acknowledge a whole series of destructive behaviors that preceded our committal to a "monastery of the damned."

In view of status and our chances of success upon release, the future doesn't look particularly bright. It's damn depressing to have to accept our collective reality. Hope is found in beating the system, the smart way. The smart way is not the path many of us have continually taken: defiance, conflict with "the man." AA members are familiar with the slogan "I can only change myself, not others." It is always easier to project blame for our inadequacies onto others. But until we come to terms with our individual reality, separate the crime from the man, decide that the "I am" is capable of much more than the label implies— we're doomed to failure.

The administration uses education statistics to create the illusion of massive programming. It is up to us to demand the delivery. Enroll in courses. Develop the thirst to learn. Ask for help from peer tutors. An education is the ultimate form of restorative justice. The entire population benefits when just one con becomes literate. Educated cons have reason to lift their heads in self-assurance. We are better able to articulate our needs, better able to negotiate collectively, better able to see a future for ourselves.

Whether "the man" wants to acknowledge it or not, educated prisoners get respect from everybody inside and outside the prison. Adult education and training at every level—whether basic literacy, high school, college or university—are vital. The positive skills we learn in prison can't be taken away from us at the gate.

Joseph E. McCormick
A prisoner

---

formal charges with the court. If no charges are filed, the accused must be released. The prosecutor can also drop charges after filing them. Such a choice is called *nolle prosequi;* and when it happens, a case is said to be "nolled" or "nollied."

A suspect charged with a crime must be taken before a judge or magistrate without unnecessary delay. At the initial appearance, the judge or magistrate informs the accused of the charges and decides whether there is probable cause to detain him or her. Often, defense counsel is also assigned then. If the offense charged is not very serious, the determination of guilt and the assessment of a penalty may also occur at this stage.

In some jurisdictions, a pretrial-release decision is made at the initial appearance, but this decision may occur at other hearings or at another time during the process. Pretrial release on bail was traditionally intended to ensure appearance at trial. However, many jurisdictions today permit pretrial detention of defendants accused of serious offenses and deemed dangerous, to prevent them from committing crimes in the pretrial period. The court may decide to release the accused on his or her own recognizance, into the custody of a third party, on the promise of satisfying certain conditions, or after the posting of a financial bond. Conditions of release may be reviewed at any later time while charges are still pending.

In many jurisdictions, the initial appearance may be followed by a preliminary hearing. The main function of this hearing is to determine whether there is probable cause to believe that the accused committed a crime within the jurisdiction of the court. If the judge or magistrate does not find probable cause, the case is dismissed. However, if the judge finds probable cause for such a belief, or if the accused waives the right to a preliminary hearing, the case may be bound over to a grand jury.

A grand jury hears evidence against the accused, presented by the prosecutor, and decides if there is sufficient evidence to cause the accused to be brought to trial. If the grand jury finds sufficient evidence, it submits an indictment to the court.

Not all jurisdictions make use of grand juries. Some require, instead, that the prosecutor submit an information (a formal written accusation) to the court. In most jurisdictions, misdemeanor cases and some felony cases proceed by the issuance of an information. Some jurisdictions require indictments in felony cases. However, the accused may choose to waive a grand jury indictment and, instead, accept service of an information for the crime.

Judicial Procedures

Adjudication is the process by which a court arrives at a decision in a case. The adjudication process involves a number of steps. The first is **arraignment**. Once an indictment or information is filed with the trial court, the accused is scheduled for arraignment. If the accused has been detained without bail, corrections personnel take him or her to the arraignment. At the arraignment, the accused is informed of the charges, advised of the rights of criminal defendants, and asked to enter a plea to the charges.

If the accused pleads guilty or pleads *nolo contendere* (accepts a penalty without admitting guilt), the judge may accept or reject the plea. If the plea is accepted, no trial is held and the offender is sentenced at this proceeding or at a later date. The plea may be rejected if, for example, the judge believes that the accused has been coerced. If this occurs, the case may proceed to trial. Sometimes, as the result of negotiations between the prosecutor and the defendant, the defendant enters a guilty plea in expectation of reduced charges or a light sentence. *Nolo contendere* pleas are often entered by those who fear a later civil action and who therefore do not want to admit guilt.

If the accused pleads not guilty or not guilty by reason of insanity, a date is set for trial. A person accused of a serious crime is guaranteed a trial by jury. However, the accused may ask for a bench trial, in which the judge, rather than a jury, serves as the finder of fact. In both instances, the prosecution and defense present evidence by questioning witnesses, and the judge decides issues of law. The trial results in acquittal or conviction of the original charges or of lesser included offenses. A defendant may be convicted at trial only if the government's evidence proves beyond a reasonable doubt that the defendant is guilty, or if the defendant knowingly and voluntarily pleads guilty to the charges.

Sentencing and Sanctions

After a guilty verdict or guilty plea, sentence is imposed. In most cases the judge decides on the sentence, but in some states the sentence is decided by the jury, particularly for capital offenses, such as murder.

To arrive at an appropriate sentence, a court may hold a sentencing hearing to consider evidence of aggravating or mitigating circumstances. In assessing the circumstances surrounding a criminal act, courts often rely on presentence investigations by probation agencies or other designated authorities. Courts may also consider victim-impact statements.

The sentencing choices available to judges and juries frequently include one or more of the following:

- the death penalty;
- incarceration in a prison, a jail, or another confinement facility;

adjudication
The process by which a court arrives at a final decision in a case.

arraignment
An appearance in court prior to trial in a criminal proceeding.

nolo contendere
A plea of "no contest." A no-contest plea may be used where a defendant does not wish to contest conviction. Because the plea does not admit guilt, however, it cannot provide the basis for later civil suits.

- community service;
- probation, in which the convicted person is not confined but is subject to certain conditions and restrictions;
- fines, primarily as penalties for minor offenses; and
- restitution, which requires the offender to provide financial compensation to the victim.

In many states, *mandatory minimum* sentencing laws require that persons convicted of certain offenses serve a minimum prison term, which the judge must impose and which may not be reduced by a parole board or by " good-time" deductions.

After the trial, a defendant may request appellate review of the conviction to see if there was some serious error that affected the defendant's right to a fair trial. In some states, the defendant may also appeal the sentence.

At least one appeal of a conviction is a matter of right. Any further appeal (to a state supreme court or in the case of federal court convictions, to the United States Supreme Court) is *discretionary,* which means that the higher court may or may not choose to hear the further appeal. After losing all their available *direct* appeals (also known as *exhaustion of state remedies*), state prisoners may also seek to have their convictions reviewed *collaterally* in the federal courts via a writ of *habeas corpus.* In states that have the death penalty, appeals of death sentences are usually automatic, and extensive federal *habeas corpus* review often takes place before the sentence of death is actually carried out.

The Correctional Subsystem

After conviction and sentencing, most offenders enter the correctional subsystem. Before we proceed with our discussion, it is best to define the term *corrections.* As with most words, a variety of definitions can be found.

In 1967, for example, the President's Commission on Law Enforcement and Administration of Justice wrote that *corrections* means "America's prisons, jails, juvenile training schools, and probation and parole machinery." It is "that part of the criminal justice system," said the commission, "that the public sees least of and knows least about." [19]

Years later, in 1975, the National Advisory Commission on Criminal Justice Standards and Goals said in its lengthy volume on corrections, "*Corrections* is defined here as the community's official reactions to the convicted offender, whether adult or juvenile." [20] The commission noted that "this is a broad definition and it suffers . . . from several shortcomings."

We can distinguish between institutional corrections and noninstitutional corrections. A report by the Bureau of Justice Statistics (BJS) says that **institutional corrections** "involves the confinement and rehabilitation of adults and juveniles convicted of offenses against the law and the confinement of persons suspected of a crime awaiting trial and adjudication." [21] BJS goes on to say that "correctional institutions are prisons, reformatories, jails, houses of correction, penitentiaries, correctional farms, workhouses, reception centers, diagnostic centers, industrial schools, training schools, detention centers, and a variety of other types of institutions for the confinement and correction of convicted adults or juveniles who are adjudicated delinquent or in need of supervision. [The term] also includes facilities

institutional corrections

That aspect of the correctional enterprise that "involves the incarceration and rehabilitation of adults and juveniles convicted of offenses against the law, and the confinement of persons suspected of a crime awaiting trial and adjudication."

Scott Peterson being escorted to prison following his 2004 trial in San Mateo County (California) Superior Court. Peterson was convicted of the 2002 murders of his pregnant 27-year-old wife, Laci, and the couple's unborn son, Conner, and is now on death row at San Quentin State Prison. Correctional clients are those who have been found guilty of crimes in a court of law. Who decides what happens to defendants following conviction? After they enter the correctional system?

for the detention of adults and juveniles accused of a crime and awaiting trial or hearing." According to BJS, **noninstitutional corrections**, which is sometimes called *community corrections,* includes "pardon, probation, and parole activities, correctional administration not directly connectable to institutions, and miscellaneous [activities] not directly related to institutional care."

As all these definitions show, in its broadest sense, the term *corrections* encompasses each of the following components, as well as the process of interaction among them:

- the *purpose* and *goals* of the correctional enterprise;
- jails, prisons, correctional institutions, and other *facilities;*
- probation, parole, and alternative and diversionary *programs;*
- federal, state, local, and international correctional offices and *agencies;*
- counseling, educational, health care, nutrition, and many other *services;*
- correctional *clients;*
- corrections *volunteers;*
- corrections *professionals;*
- fiscal appropriations and *funding;*
- various aspects of criminal and civil *law;*
- formal and informal *procedures;*
- effective and responsible *management;*
- community *expectations* regarding correctional practices; and
- the machinery of *capital punishment.*

When we use the word *corrections,* we include all of these elements. Fourteen elements, however, make for an unwieldy definition. Hence, for purposes of discussion, we will say that **corrections** refers to all the various aspects of the pretrial and postconviction management of individuals accused or convicted of crimes. Central to this perspective is the

noninstitutional corrections (also *community corrections*)

That aspect of the correctional enterprise that includes "pardon, probation, and parole activities, correctional administration not directly connectable to institutions, and miscellaneous [activities] not directly related to institutional care."

corrections

All the various aspects of the pretrial and postconviction management of individuals accused or convicted of crimes.

A Louisiana State Police SWAT team drives past flood victims waiting for rescue in New Orleans after powerful Hurricane Katrina made landfall in 2005 and flooded much of the city. The officers had been deployed to restore order in the stricken city after looters took advantage of the social disorder that followed in the hurricane's wake. What role does the criminal justice system play in the maintenance of social order?

recognition that corrections—although it involves a variety of programs, services, facilities, and personnel—is essentially a management activity. Rather than stress the role of institutions or agencies, this definition emphasizes the human dimension of correctional activity—especially the efforts of the corrections professionals who undertake the day-to-day tasks. Like any other managed activity, corrections has goals and purposes. Exhibit 1–9 details the purpose of corrections as identified by the American Correctional Association (ACA).

The Societal Goals of Corrections The ACA statement about the purpose of corrections is addressed primarily to corrections professionals. It recognizes, however, that *the* fundamental purpose of corrections "is to enhance social order and public safety." In any society, social order and public safety depend on effective social control. Some forms of social control take the form of customs, norms, and what sociologists refer to as *mores* ('mȯr-,āz). **Mores** are behavioral standards that embody a group's values. Violation of these standards is a serious wrong. They generally forbid such activities as murder, rape, and robbery. **Folkways,** in contrast, are time-honored ways of doing things. Although folkways carry the force of tradition, their violation is unlikely to threaten the survival of the group.

Societal expectations, whatever form they take, are sometimes enacted into law. The **criminal law,** also called *penal law,* is the body of rules and regulations that define public offenses, or wrongs committed against the state or society, and specify punishments for those offenses. Social control, social order, and public safety are the ultimate goals of criminal law.

The correctional subsystem is crucial in enforcing the dictates of the law because the rewards and punishments it carries out play a significant role in society's control of its members.

mores

Cultural restrictions on behavior that forbid serious violations—such as murder, rape, and robbery—of a group's values.

folkways

Time-honored ways of doing things. Although they carry the force of tradition, their violation is unlikely to threaten the survival of the social group.

criminal law (also *penal law*)

That portion of the law that defines crimes and specifies criminal punishments.

Offices of the American Correctional Association (ACA) in Alexandria, Virginia. The ACA is a leading proponent of professionalism in corrections. What does corrections professionalism entail?

PROFESSIONALISM IN CORRECTIONS

Only a few decades ago, some writers bemoaned the fact that the field of corrections had not achieved professional status. Happily, much has changed over the past few decades. By 1987, Bob Barrington, who was then the executive director of the International Association of Correctional Officers, was able to proclaim, in a discussion about prisons, that "correctional facilities . . . run smoothly and efficiently for one basic

---

EXHIBIT 1–9   **American Correctional Association**

Role of Corrections Policy Statement

The overall role of corrections is to enhance social order and public safety. Adult and juvenile correctional systems should:

- implement court-ordered supervision and the safe and humane detention of those accused of unlawful behavior prior to adjudication;
- assist in maintaining the integrity of law by administering sanctions imposed by courts for unlawful behavior;
- offer the widest range of correctional programs that are based on exemplary practices, supported by research and promote pro-social behavior;
- provide gender- and culturally-responsive programs and services for detainees and adjudicated offenders that will enhance successful reentry to the community and that are administered within the least restrictive environment consistent with public safety;
- address the needs of victims of crime;
- routinely review and ensure that correctional programs are addressing the needs of correctional employees, the community, victims and offenders; and
- collaborate with other professions to improve and strengthen correctional services and to support the reduction of crime and recidivism.

Source: Copyright © American Correctional Association.

reason: the professional and forward-thinking attitudes and actions of the correctional officers employed."[22]

Some writers on American criminal justice have said that the hallmark of a true profession is "a shared set of principles and customs that transcend self-interest and speak to the essential nature of the particular calling or trade."[23] This definition recognizes the selfless and ethical nature of professional work. Hence, "professionals have a sense of commitment to their professions that is usually not present among those in occupational groups."[24] Work within a profession is viewed more as a "calling" than as a mere way of earning a living. "Professionals have a love for their work that is above that of employment merely to receive a paycheck."[25]

Although it is important to keep formal definitions in mind, for our purposes we will define a **profession** as an occupation granted high social status by virtue of the personal integrity of its members. We can summarize the *attitude* of a true professional by noting that it is characterized by the following:

profession

An occupation granted high social status by virtue of the personal integrity of its members.

- a spirit of public service and interest in the public good;
- the fair application of reason and the use of intellect to solve problems;
- self-regulation through a set of internal guidelines by which professionals hold *themselves* accountable for their actions;
- continual self-appraisal and self-examination;
- an inner sense of professionalism (i.e., honor, self-discipline, commitment, personal integrity, and self-direction);
- adherence to the recognized ethical principles of one's profession (see the Ethics and Professionalism box in this chapter); and
- a commitment to lifelong learning and lifelong betterment within the profession.

Most professional occupations have developed practices that foster professionalism among their members.

Corrections professionalism today includes recognition of the importance of scientific studies of corrections, sometimes referred to as **evidence-based penology.** In any discussion of evidence-based penology (also known as *evidence-based corrections*), it is important to remember that the word *evidence* refers to scientific evidence, and not to criminal evidence. Corrections professionals who adhere to an evidence-based philosophy acknowledge the problem-solving potential of social science research methods, and keep abreast of the latest findings in their field. Evidence-based corrections is also discussed in Chapter 7.

evidence-based penology (also *evidence-based corrections*)

The application of social scientific techniques to the study of everyday corrections procedures for the purpose of increasing effectiveness and enhancing the efficient use of available resources.

Standards and Training

Historically, professional corrections organizations and their leaders have recognized the importance of training. It was not until the late 1970s, however, that the American Correctional Association (ACA) Commission on Accreditation established the first training standards. The commission did the following:

- specified standards for given positions within corrections;
- identified essential training topics;
- set specific numbers of hours for preservice (120) and annual in-service training (40); and
- specified basic administrative policy support requirements for training programs.[26]

ETHICS & PROFESSIONALISM

American Correctional Association Code of Ethics

1. Members shall respect and protect the civil and legal rights of all individuals.

2. Members shall treat every professional situation with concern for the welfare of the individuals involved and with no intent to gain personally.

3. Members shall maintain relationships with colleagues to promote mutual respect within the profession and improve the quality of service.

4. Members shall make public criticism of their colleagues or their agencies only when warranted, verifiable, and constructive.

5. Members shall respect the importance of all disciplines within the criminal justice system and work to improve cooperation with each segment.

6. Members shall honor the public's right to information and share information with the public to the extent permitted by law subject to individuals' right to privacy.

7. Members shall respect and protect the right of the public to be safeguarded from criminal activity.

8. Members shall refrain from using their positions to secure personal privileges or advantages.

9. Members shall refrain from allowing personal interest to impair objectivity in the performance of duty while acting in an official capacity.

10. Members shall refrain from entering into any formal or informal activity or agreement that presents a conflict of interest or is inconsistent with the conscientious performance of duties.

11. Members shall refrain from accepting any gifts, services, or favors that are or appear to be improper or imply an obligation inconsistent with the free and objective exercise of professional duties.

12. Members shall clearly differentiate between personal views/statements and views/statements/positions made on behalf of the agency or Association.

13. Members shall report to appropriate authorities any corrupt or unethical behaviors for which there is sufficient evidence to justify review.

14. Members shall refrain from discriminating against any individual because of race, gender, creed, national origin, religious affiliation, age, disability, or any other type of prohibited discrimination.

15. Members shall preserve the integrity of private information; they shall refrain from seeking information on individuals beyond that which is necessary to implement responsibilities and perform their duties; members shall refrain from revealing nonpublic information unless expressly authorized to do so.

16. Members shall make all appointments, promotions, and dismissals in accordance with established civil service rules, applicable contract agreements, and individual merit, rather than furtherance of personal interests.

17. Members shall respect, promote, and contribute to a workplace that is safe, healthy, and free of harassment in any form.

Adopted by the Board of Governors and Delegate Assembly in August 1994.

Source: Copyright © American Correctional Association.

Ethical Dilemma 1–1: In light of tight state budgets and overcrowded prisons, should governors use their authority to provide early release to some inmates? If so, under what circumstances? For more information go to Ethical Dilemma 1–1 at www.justicestudies.com/ethics04.

Ethical Dilemma 1–2: You are the warden of the only medium security prison in your state. Your nephew is sentenced to serve 10 years in your institution. Using the ACA Code of Ethics as a guide, determine what ethical issues you will face. For more information go to Ethical Dilemma 1–2 at www.justicestudies.com/ethics04.

Ethical Dilemma 1–3: One of your fellow correctional officers accepts candy and snacks from one of the inmates. She doesn't ask for the snacks, nor does she do any favors for the inmate. Should you report this activity? Will you report it? Using the ACA Code of Ethics, determine the ethical issues, if any, involved in this behavior. For more information go to Ethical Dilemma 1–3 at www.justicestudies.com/ethics04.

Ethical Dilemmas for every chapter are available online.

THE STAFF SPEAKS

Agencies such as the Palm Beach (Florida) County Sheriff's Office understand that 40 hours of training every four years is not sufficient to maintain the proficiency of skills or the continuous development of staff. The Palm Beach County Sheriff's Office requires all certified correctional officers to participate in a minimum of 40 hours in-service training annually. This program is designed to develop not only technical skills but also the overall well-being of the officer.

In most training situations there is not the need, time, or resources to transfer detailed knowledge of theoretical concepts. Required outcomes must apply a practical balance between understanding the reason an action is done in a particular way and having the ability to apply procedures correctly.

It is important to define performance indicators and targets against these objectives, which are acceptable and practical expected levels of achievement.

Knowledge assessment techniques need to be integrated into training to enable assessment of whether adequate competencies have been achieved by each officer.

The Palm Beach County Sheriff's Office mandates the attendance and curriculum for 24 of the 40 hours. This 24-hour block attended by all officers consists of firearms, defensive tactics, first aid/CPR and blood-borne pathogens, and CJSTC (Criminal Justice Standards & Training Commission)–mandated courses. The remaining 16 hours are chosen by the individual officer from a training catalog compiled each year by the Bureau of Training. The available classes for selection by the officer range from yoga, nutrition, and retirement planning to advanced handgun and pressure point controlling techniques.

The presented materials in these in-service classes are not intended to be a comprehensive course in technical development and skills. Rather the lessons

are meant to be a supplement that will give the officers an enhanced perspective on how to develop their skills and themselves. Not only do the lessons give the officers helpful tips and concepts, but they also are meant to provide them with insight on good methods to use.

There is no such thing as a common knowledge of an unstated objective. Objectives need to be defined to ensure accountability. When determining the objectives of training, training managers should also define the indicators by which they can judge whether training programs are successful. This will make evaluation of training considerably more relevant.

Captain Alan Fuhrman
Palm Beach County Sheriff's Office
Planning & Research Unit
West Palm Beach, Florida

Following ACA's lead, virtually every state now requires at least 120 hours of preservice training for correctional officers working in institutional settings; many states require more. Probation and parole officers are required to undergo similar training in most jurisdictions, and correctional officers working in jails are similarly trained.

Through training, new members of a profession learn the core values and ideals, the basic knowledge, and the accepted practices central to the profession. Setting training standards ensures that the education is uniform. Standards also mandate the teaching of specialized knowledge. Standards supplement training by doing the following:

- setting minimum requirements for entry into the profession;
- detailing expectations for those involved in the everyday life of correctional work; and
- establishing basic requirements for facilities, programs, and practices.

From the point of view of corrections professionals, training is a matter of personal responsibility. A lifelong commitment to a career ensures that those who think of themselves as professionals will seek the training needed to enhance their job performance.

Basic Skills and Knowledge

In 1990, the Professional Education Council of the American Correctional Association developed a model entry test for correctional officers.

Melanie Estes
Day Youth Counselor   United Methodist Family Services
Richmond, Virginia

Melanie Estes has been with the agency for only a few years and is currently one of two senior counselors. She completed a four-year degree in criminal justice in 1997 and is planning to attend graduate school in social work at Virginia Commonwealth University.

As a youth counselor, Estes assists in developing, implementing, evaluating, and modifying individual and group treatment plans. She ensures that daily routine and expectations are followed in the residential home. It is also her responsibility to plan, oversee, and evaluate daily and weekly schedules of agency program activities. She is the liaison between the agency and the residents' social workers, probation officers, parents, and any others that may be involved in the youths' treatment. She keeps all parties informed of residents' progress.

As a staff member, Estes's foremost duty is to act as a change agent for clients in the program. She believes that it is important that staffers learn that their interactions and interventions with one another are as crucial to the habilitative process as their interactions and interventions with youth. As a team member, she is asked to evaluate her coworkers' performance and to provide support, feedback, and training for other team members. Once a month, she is the chairperson and recorder for the weekly team meeting.

Working with troubled juveniles is challenging and rewarding, especially with abandoned and abused children. I'm not kidding anyone when I say that it is hard to maintain a healthy balance between friend and caretaker. But one of the greatest experiences I ever had is to help at-risk youth.

The test was intended to increase professionalism in the field and to provide a standard criminal justice curriculum.[27]

The council suggested that the test could act "as a quality control measure for such education, much as does the bar exam for attorneys." The standard entry test was designed to "reveal the applicant's understanding of the structure, purpose, and method of the police, prosecution, courts, institutions, probation, parole, community service, and extramural programs." It was also designed to "test for knowledge of various kinds of corrections programs, the role of punitive sanctions and incapacitation, and perspective on past experience and current trends."

More recently, Mark S. Fleisher of Illinois State University identified four core traits essential to effective work in corrections.[28] The traits are as follows:

- **Accountability:** "Correctional work demands precision, timeliness, accountability and strong ethics." Students may drift into patterns of irresponsibility during their college years. Once they become correctional officers, however, they need to take their work seriously.

- **Strong Writing Skills:** Because correctional officers must complete a huge amount of paperwork, they need to be able to write well. They should also be familiar with the "vocabulary of corrections."

- **Effective Presentational Skills:** "A correctional career requires strong verbal skills and an ability to organize presentations." Effective verbal skills help officers interact with their peers, inmates, and superiors.

- **A Logical Mind and the Ability to Solve Problems:** Such skills are essential to success in corrections because problems arise daily. Being able to solve them is a sign of an effective officer.

Talking about CORRECTIONS

WORKING IN TODAY'S PRISONS AND JAILS

Visit *Live Talk* at **Corrections.com** (www.justicestudies.com/talking04) and listen to the program "Working in Today's Prisons and Jails," which relates to ideas discussed in this chapter.

corrections professional

A dedicated person of high moral character and personal integrity who is employed in the field of corrections and takes professionalism to heart.

professional associations

Organized groups of like-minded individuals who work to enhance the professional status of members of their occupational group.

certification

A credentialing process, usually involving testing and career development assessment, through which the skills, knowledge, and abilities of correctional personnel can be formally recognized.

In sum, we can say that a **corrections professional** is a dedicated person of high moral character and personal integrity who is employed in the field of corrections and takes professionalism to heart. He or she understands the importance of standards, training, and education and the need to be proficient in the skills required for success in the correctional enterprise. The corrections professional recognizes that professionalism leads to the betterment of society, to enhanced social order, and to a higher quality of life for all.

Standard-Setting Organizations

A number of standard-setting **professional associations** in the field of corrections have developed models of professionalism. Among them are the American Correctional Association (ACA), the American Probation and Parole Association (APPA), and the American Jail Association (AJA).

Standard-setting organizations like these offer detailed sets of written principles for correctional occupations and corrections administration. The ACA, the APPA, and the AJA, for example, all have developed standards to guide training and to clarify what is expected of those working in corrections. Moreover, many professional associations have developed codes of ethics, outlining what is moral and proper conduct. Some of these codes will appear in later chapters.

Correctional associations also offer training, hold meetings and seminars, create and maintain job banks, and produce literature relevant to corrections. They sometimes lobby legislative bodies in an attempt to influence the development of new laws that affect corrections.

Future chapters will present ACA policies. The ACA policies are important because they guide the development of training and because they influence the work environment of many agencies and institutions.

In 1999, the ACA, through its national Commission on Correctional Certification, established a program for certifying correctional staff, from line officers to executive leaders. **Certification** is part of a process called *credentialing* that focuses specifically on the individual. Its counterpart is accreditation, a formal process that highlights the quality of a facility in an effort to ensure that it meets health, safety, and other correctional standards. Accreditation is discussed in more detail in Chapter 13. ACA certification began officially in January 2000 when the first Certified Corrections Executive (CCE) application was accepted by the ACA. The first CCE examination was administered in August 2000.[29]

There are four categories of ACA Certified Corrections Professional (CCP), extending from those who work at the highest organization levels to personnel employed at the line level, working directly with offenders. Those categories are: (1) Certified Corrections Executive (CCE), (2) Certified Corrections Manager (CCM), (3) Certified Corrections Supervisor (CCS), and (4) Certified Corrections Officer (CCO). Applicants for certification must pass a 200-item multiple-choice examination, document their corrections experience, show compliance with the ACA's Code of Ethics, and meet minimum requirements for formal education. Educational requirements increase with each certification level. While a high school diploma or equivalent is required of those seeking CCO certification, CCS and CCM certification seekers are required to hold two-year college degrees (or its equivalent), while those applying for certification at the CCE level must hold a four-year college degree (or equivalent). According to the ACA, the organization's certification program creates the *opportunity* for a lifetime of progressive professional achievement. Anyone successfully

Education is an important component of any successful profession. Shown here are three educational institutions offering undergraduate programs in corrections. What role does the American Correctional Association see for higher education in advancing the corrections profession?

completing the certification process is designated as a Certified Corrections Professional (CCP).[30] Recertification happens at three-year intervals and requires a specified number of continuing education contact hours.

The purpose of the ACA Professional Certification Program is "to uphold standards for competent practice." Moreover, certification provides an opportunity "for staff to be recognized as qualified correctional practitioners."

Like the ACA, the AJA, through its five-member Jail Manager Certification Commission (JMCC), offers a program for the certification of jail administrators, managers, and supervisory personnel. The first Certified Jail Managers (CJMs) were recognized in 1997.[31]

EXHIBIT 1–10   **American Correctional Association**

Higher Education Policy Statement

The field of corrections, in cooperation with higher education, should contribute to the improvement of the professional practice of corrections. Academic programs concerned with criminal justice, juvenile justice and corrections should:

- provide a pool of qualified candidates for correctional service, and assist in the delineation of dimensions of work responsibilities that may emerge as a result of changing social, economic, political and technological trends;
- promote understanding, both for correctional practitioners and for the public at large, of the complex social, ethical, political and economic factors that influence all areas of corrections;
- challenge assumptions about crime and corrections, and stimulate change when change is needed;
- partner with criminal justice, juvenile justice and corrections organizations to promote and support ethical standards in research, planning and evaluation in all areas;
- engage in public service related to corrections, including informational programs, volunteer programs and opportunities for training, such as internships and practicums to enhance the relationship between the academic community and correctional practitioners;
- support, through program and faculty development, the evolution of corrections as a distinct professional discipline;
- implement programs in corrections at the associate degree level that can serve as a minimum requirement for full professional status as a correctional employee, and as a minimum requirement for certification; and
- partner with correctional agencies to promote and facilitate all continuous learning initiatives for employees.

Source: Copyright © American Correctional Association.

Education

Education is another component, besides basic job skills and job-specific training, of true professionalism. Training, by itself, can never make one a true professional, because complex decision-making skills are essential for success in any occupation involving intense interpersonal interaction—and they can be acquired only through general education. Education builds critical-thinking skills, it allows the application of theory and ethical principles to a multitude of situations that are constantly in flux, and it provides insights into on-the-job difficulties.

Correctional education that goes beyond skills training is available primarily from two- and four-year colleges that offer corrections curricula and programs of study (see Exhibit 1–10). Courses in corrections are also typically found in undergraduate and graduate programs in criminal justice. The day will come when at least a two-year degree will be required for entry into the corrections profession.

SOCIAL DIVERSITY IN CORRECTIONS

The corrections profession faces a number of social issues that are of special concern to Americans today. Contemporary issues include questions about the purposes and appropriateness of punishment in general and the

Kathleen Dennehy (*left*), Massachusetts Commissioner of Corrections, and Dora Schriro (*right*), director of the Arizona Department of Corrections. In recent years, the number of women working in corrections has increased significantly. Do you think that gender bias exists within the correctional career field today?

acceptability of capital punishment in particular; the usefulness of alternative or nontraditional sanctions; the privatization of correctional facilities; and the rights and overall treatment of prisoners. At the forefront of today's issues are those involving concerns about gender, race, ethnicity, and other forms of social diversity.

While a number of these issues are discussed in later chapters, this brief section provides definitions of some of the terms that will be discussed and suggests some structure for what is to follow.

Some terms, such as *race,* are not easy to define. Historical definitions of race have highlighted some supposed biological traits, such as skin color, hair type, or shape of the skull and face. Eighteenth-century European physical anthropologists distinguished between white, black, and Asian (or "yellow") races. The notion of race, however, is now generally recognized as a social construct and is not seen as an objective biological fact. Moreover, racial distinctions have blurred throughout American society, which has long been characterized as a melting pot. Nonetheless, when asked, the majority of Americans today still identify themselves as members of a particular racial group.

To say that race is a social construct means that racial distinctions are culturally defined. It does *not* mean, however, that such distinctions are without consequences. On the contrary, great social significance is often attached to biological or other indicators of race, and race plays a crucial role in social relations. *Racism,* which is also socially constructed, can be the result. **Racism** has been defined as social practices that explicitly or implicitly attribute merits or allocate value to members of racially categorized groups solely because of their race.[32] In the field of corrections, as in other social endeavors, it is racism (rather than race itself) that is the real issue because it can lead to forms of racial discrimination, including inequities in hiring and promotion for those working in corrections, and to unfairness in the handling of inmates or other correctional clients because of their race.

Considerable overlap exists between the concept of race and that of *ethnicity.* In contemporary usage, both terms imply the notion of lineage,

racism
Social practices that explicitly or implicitly attribute merits or allocate value to individuals solely because of their race.

COMMISSION ON SAFETY AND ABUSE IN AMERICA'S PRISONS: FIGHTING PRISON ABUSE

" *What happens inside jails and prisons does not stay inside jails and prisons. It comes home with prisoners after they are released and with corrections officers at the end of each day's shift. . . . We must create safe and productive conditions of confinement not only because it is the right thing to do, but because it influences the safety, health, and prosperity of us all.* "

— Commission on Safety and Abuse in America's Prisons

In 2004 the world was shocked to see photos of mistreated prisoners at the American-run Baghdad Central Detention Facility in Iraq—a lockup formerly known as Abu Ghraib prison. The photos showed shackled and naked prisoners being threatened with dogs, piled on top of one another, and being taunted by their captors. At least one inmate died after being abused, and the Pentagon launched an investigation into alleged atrocities at the facility. Eventually a small number of soldiers were court-martialed, reduced in rank, or pleaded guilty to charges of abusing detainees.

The Abu Ghraib scandal highlighted the important role of good correctional practice and inspired top American corrections representatives to issue a statement saying that the "ill treatment and torture of incarcerated individuals whether by military personnel, intelligence personnel, or civilian corrections staff is condemned by corrections professionals."[1] The statement was signed by the presidents of the American Cor-

rectional Association, the Association of State Correctional Administrators, the International Association of Correctional Officers, and the executive directors of the American Jail Association, the American Probation and Parole Association, the National Sheriffs' Association, the North American Association of Wardens and Superintendents, and others.

The Abu Ghraib scandal led to the creation of the Commission on Safety and Abuse in America's Prisons. The commission, organized by the New York–based Vera Institute of Justice, and sponsored by private foundations and major law firms, was formed to examine conditions in U.S. correctional facilities. After a year of fact-finding public hearings throughout the country, the commission (also known as the Vera Commission) issued a comprehensive report in 2006. Excerpts from the commission's report are presented in boxes throughout this text.

Source: Adapted from the Commission on Safety and Abuse in America's Prisons, *Confronting Confinement* (New York: Vera Institute of Justice, 2006). 1. See "The State of Corrections," *Criminal Justice Washington Letter,* May 28, 2004.
Note: The full 126-page report, *Confronting Confinement: A Report of the Commission on Safety and Abuse in America's Prisons,* can be accessed on the Internet at www.prisoncommission.org.

The infamous Abu Ghraib prison near Baghdad, Iraq. Photos of prisoner abuse by American military personnel at the facility in 2004 highlighted the need for proper training and high correctional standards. How can better training improve standards?

EXHIBIT 1–11   Corrections Personnel by Gender and Rank

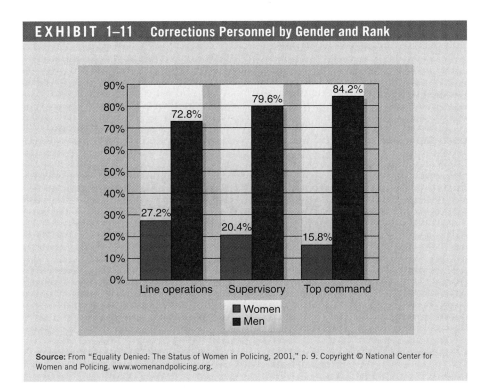

Source: From "Equality Denied: The Status of Women in Policing, 2001," p. 9. Copyright © National Center for Women and Policing. www.womenandpolicing.org.

or biological and regional as well as cultural background and inheritance. Of the two, however, ethnicity is most closely associated with cultural heritage. Members of an ethnic group generally share a common racial, national, religious, linguistic, and cultural origin. Hence, from an ethnic perspective, a person might identify himself or herself as Hungarian, even though he or she has never lived in Hungary, does not speak Hungarian, and knows little of the history of the Hungarian nation. Ethnic differences can lead to serious consequences, as prison gangs built around ethnicity demonstrate.

At first blush, the term *gender* seems more straightforward than race or ethnicity because it relates to differences between the sexes. In fact, many critical issues that concern correctional administrators today reflect a rapid increase in the number of women entering correctional service.

For many years corrections was a male-dominated profession. Although the correctional process has always involved some women, historically most women in the profession have attended to the needs of the small number of females held in confinement. It wasn't until the 1970s that women began to enter the corrections professions in significant numbers. Many went to work in facilities that housed males, where they soon found themselves confronting *gender bias* from an entrenched macho culture.

Today, women working in correctional facilities largely have been accepted, as evidenced by the fact their proportion is more than double the proportion of female law enforcement officers: Twenty-six percent of sworn correctional officers in the United States are women, while only 13 percent of police officers are female. As Exhibit 1–11 shows, however, women working in corrections tend to be concentrated in the lower ranks and are underrepresented in supervisory positions. According to the National Center for Women in Policing, women of color hold 12.9 percent of corrections positions, 9.7 percent of top command positions, and 9.1 percent of supervisory positions.[33]

Race, ethnicity, and gender are all aspects of social diversity—although diversity in society extends to many other areas as well, such as economics, religion, education, intellectual ability, and politics. Keep in mind, as you read through this textbook, that in the field of corrections diversity issues can be described from four perspectives: (1) as they impact individual correctional clients, (2) as they determine correctional populations and trends, (3) as they affect the lives and interests of those working in the field of corrections, and (4) as they change the structure and functioning of correctional institutions, facilities, and programs.

REVIEW & APPLICATIONS

REFLECTIONS ON THE FUTURE

Does Corrections Need to Look Ahead?

by William L. Tafoya
University of New Haven

Two decades ago mathematician Olaf Helmer observed: "Traditional piecemeal approaches [to problem-solving] have proven to be sterile." He went on to note, "What is needed is a new type of massive, imaginative, and interdisciplinary effort" (1983: 372). Inspired by Helmer's admonition I penned a book chapter in which I argued the need to apply the methods of the field of Futures Research to criminal investigations (Tafoya 1990). Here I offer the same suggestion to corrections professionals. The extrapolation of current crime statistics and incarceration rates strongly suggests it is highly probable that—absent a new type of massive intervention—America will continue to construct rather than dismantle correctional facilities over at least the next two decades. The Bureau of Justice Statistics, for example, reports that the incarceration rate in America rose from 139 per 100,000 in 1980 to 470 per 100,000 in 2001 (USDOJ 2003). Perhaps it is time for a massive, multidisciplinary, imaginative approach to alternatives to incarceration? While this is not a new proposal, the alternatives previously attempted appear to have been largely unsuccessful. Why?

Overall the literature devoted to the future of criminal justice is quite sparse. The good news is that the portion dedicated to corrections is actually quite impressive. The bad news is that the majority of these publications tend to focus on identifying ways to increase the methodological precision of projecting incarceration rates rather than on forecasting ways to more effectively identify reliable alternatives to incarceration that do not put the public at risk from recidivists and career criminals (AP 2003; HRW 2003a; HRW 2003b). A notable exception is the work of Criminologist Gene Stephens who attributes the reduced crime, reduced fear, and revitalized communities of the 1990s to the combined efforts of imaginative and interdisciplinary efforts such as Community-Oriented Policing and the Restorative Justice movement (1999: 34). Practitioner-scholar Bernard Levin and his colleagues (2002) have endorsed this contention. What does the discipline of Futures Research offer to corrections that will contribute to a safer, saner society?

Futures Research, like other academic disciplines, is based on historical fact, scientific methods, and

human values. To this mix, Futures Research adds vision, creativity, and innovation. Three essential ingredients set Futures Research apart from the traditional disciplines. Among its *principles* is the conviction of (1) the unity or interconnectedness of reality, (2) the crucial importance of time, and (3) the significance of ideas. Of the discipline's *premises*, consensus has solidified around three postulates: (1) the future is not predetermined, (2) the future is not predicable—but can be forecast, and (3) future outcomes can be influenced by individual choice.

The *priorities* of Futures Research include three goals: (1) the *possible*, to form perceptions of the future; (2) the *probable*, to study likely alternatives; and (3) the *preferable*, to make choices to bring about particular events. Further, futurists subscribe to six planning time frames: the Immediate (present to 2 years), Short-term (2–5 years), Mid-level (5–10 years), Long-range (10–20 years), Extended (20–50 years), and Distant (50 years and beyond). Futurists do not cling to the status quo, the supposedly tried and true beliefs of the past. Futurists explore divergent ways to deal with old problems and constructing unprecedented ways to anticipate new paradigms.

The tools for looking ahead include an array of forecasting methodologies. The U.S. Army Corps of Engineers commissioned SRI International to compile *The Handbook of Forecasting Techniques* (SRI 1975). Of the *quantitative* methods, the Monte Carlo technique is excellent for probability distributions, sampling, and random number generation. The procedure has been used effectively in cost-benefit studies. The Markov Chain technique is used to describe a process in which a set of states moves through a sequence of steps observing probabilistic rather than deterministic laws. The procedure has been used successfully to delineate organizational growth and personnel administrative matters. Bayesian statistics enable a planner to utilize actual, realistic variables to anticipate the unexpected. Well suited to small sample sizes, it is arguably the best mathematical approach to problem solving in which uncertainty is a major factor. Finally, the Box-Jenkins method of Autoregressive Integrated Moving Averages (ARIMA) is designed to handle complex time-series data in which there is no apparent pattern. Unlike other quantitative techniques, the Box-Jenkins method does not require a clear definition of the trend.

Of the *qualitative* methods, several stand out. The Delphi technique is a structured group process that maximizes the likelihood of reaching consensus and identifying disagreement. The method involves anonymous structured exchanges between members of an expert panel. Iteratively the facilitator provides controlled feedback to the panel who remains anonymous to each other until the procedure is completed. One of the most well-known techniques, it has been widely heralded as well as vilified. It is a procedure that should be reserved for truly long-range planning, as the conventional administration requires more than a year to complete.

Also well known, Scenario Writing is intended to expand the plausible (known facts) to identify the possible, probable, and preferable. It consists of four essential elements: hypothetical, summarized, multifaceted, and factually based. It is an excellent tool for addressing the question "What if?" Cross-Impact Analysis is a means by which the probability of one forecast event can be adjusted as a function of its potential interaction with all other forecast events. Relevance Trees present a hierarchical structuring of detailed relationships. The method is ideal for analyzing situations in which distinct levels of complexity are involved. The discipline of Futures Research and its forecasting methodologies are discussed in greater detail in a number of sources, many conveniently available online from the World Future Society, such as the CD-ROM "The Knowledge Base of Futures Studies" (Slaughter 2001). The Society of Police Futurists International (PFI) also provides data mining assessments in its listserv discussions as well as its online and hard copy newsletter, *Police Futurist* (www.policefuturists.org).

Three decades ago renowned futurist and social critic Alvin Toffler observed, "If we do not learn from history, we shall be compelled to relive it. True. But if we do not change the future, we shall be compelled to endure it. And that could be worse" (1972: 3). There is ample evidence to demonstrate that most past correctional practices work only in limited fashion and only in the short term, if at all. We pour money down a well of desperation hoping that if we lock up offenders long enough they will be too old to recidivate once they are released. That belief has not been fully substantiated.

Will the present generation of corrections professionals learn from the history of their field and blaze new trails? Or will they ignore those lessons and follow the path of the past? Will those who read these words embrace the stale status quo, enduring

the practices of the past? Or will they devise new, massive, imaginative, and interdisciplinary efforts to shape a brighter future for the field of corrections and American society? What if?

REFERENCES

Associated Press. 2003. "Incarceration rates of industrialized nations," www.zpub.com/un/prison1.html.

Helmer, Olaf. 1983. *Looking forward: a guide to futures research*. Beverly Hills, CA: Sage Publications.

HRW. 2003a. "Punishment and prejudice: Racial disparities in the war on drugs" *Human Rights Watch World Report*, www.hrw.org/campaigns/drugs/war/adult-male.htm.

HRW. 2003b. "U.S. incarceration rates reveal striking racial disparities." *Human Rights Watch World Report*, www.hrw.org/press/2002/02/race0227.htm.

Levin, Bernard H., et-al. 2002. "Social change, social policing: A consideration of trends," Presentation at the joint conference of the Society of Police Futurists International and the World Future Society, Philadelphia, PA, July 20–22.

PFI, Society of Police Futurists International, *Police Futurist*, www.policefuturists.org.

Slaughter, Richard A., ed. 2001. "The knowledge base of futures studies" CD-ROM. Bethesda, MD: World Future Society.

SRI. 1975. *Handbook of forecasting techniques*. Fort Belvoir, VA: U.S. Army Corps of Engineers.

Stephens, Gene. 1999. "Preventing crime: The promising road ahead," *The Futurist*, 33:9 (November): pp. 29–34.

Tafoya, William L. 1990. "Futures research: implications for criminal investigations." in James N. Gilbert, ed. *Criminal investigation: Essays and cases*, Columbus, OH: Merrill Publishing; pp. 197–218.

Toffler, Alvin. 1972. "Probing tomorrow." In Alvin Toffler, ed. *The futurists*. New York: Random House; pp. 3–10.

USDOJ. 2003. "Incarceration rates trend chart." Bureau of Justice Statistics, www.ojp.usdoj.gov/bjs/glance/d_incrt.htm.

About the Author

William L. Tafoya is professor in the School of Public Safety and Professional Studies at the University of New Haven, Connecticut. He teaches courses in two programs, forensic computer investigation and national security. A retired special agent of the FBI, he spent 11 years on the faculty at the FBI Academy in Quantico, Virginia. His PhD dissertation research (criminology, University of Maryland) is titled "A Delphi Forecast of the Future of Law Enforcement." He is founder of the Society of Police Futurists International (www.policefuturists.org).

SUMMARY

1 Although crime rates are at their lowest level in more than 20 years, correctional populations have been increasing because of get-tough-on-crime attitudes, the nation's War on Drugs, and the increasing reluctance of parole authorities, fearing civil liability and public outcry, to release inmates.

2 Growth in correctional populations and in spending has led to a dramatically expanding correctional workforce and to enhanced employment opportunities within the field.

3 The crimes that bring people into the American correctional system include felonies, which are relatively serious criminal offenses; misdemeanors, which are less serious crimes; and infractions, which are minor law violations.

4 Two important sources of crime statistics are the FBI's Uniform Crime Reports (UCRs), published annually under the title *Crime in the United States,* and the National Crime Victimization Survey (NCVS), published by the Bureau of Justice Statistics under the title *Criminal Victimization in the United States.* The UCR reports information on eight major crimes: murder, forcible rape, robbery, aggravated assault, burglary, larceny-theft, motor vechicle theft, and arson. The NCVS provides a detailed picture of crime incidents, victims, and trends. While UCR data are based upon crime reports made to the police, NCVS data are derived from annual nationwide surveys of American households.

5 Criminal justice agencies are said to make up the criminal justice system. The main components of the criminal justice system are (1) police, (2) courts, and (3) corrections. Each can be considered a subsystem of the criminal justice system.

6 The major components of the corrections subsystem are jails, probation, parole, and prisons. Jails and prisons are examples of institutional corrections, while probation and parole are forms of noninstitutional corrections.

7 The term *criminal justice* can be used to refer to our *system* of justice, or it can refer to the activities that take place during the justice *process.* Criminal justice agencies, taken together, make up the criminal justice system. Since the activities of criminal justice agencies routinely involve other agencies, the word *system* encompasses not only the agencies of justice but also the relationships among those agencies. The justice *process,* on the other hand, refers to the events that unfold as a suspect is processed by the criminal justice system.

8 *Corrections* refers to all aspects of the pretrial and postconviction management of individuals accused or convicted of crimes.

9 Professionalism in corrections is important because it can win the respect and admiration of others outside of the field. Moreover, professionals are regarded as trusted participants in any field of endeavor. This chapter also discussed seven aspects of a professional attitude.

10 *Social diversity* encompasses differences of race, gender, and ethnicity. Social diversity is important in corrections today because it impacts individual correctional clients, influences correctional populations and trends, affects the lives and interests of those working in the field of corrections, and may help determine the structure and functioning of correctional institutions, facilities, and programs.

KEY TERMS

crime, *p. 5*
prison, *p. 5*
felony, *p. 9*
misdemeanor, *p. 9*
infraction, *p. 9*
correctional clients, *p. 9*
violent crime, *p. 10*
property crime, *p. 10*
crime index, *p. 10*
crime rate, *p. 10*

criminal justice, *p. 14*
criminal justice system, *p. 14*
adjudication, *p. 17*
arraignment, *p. 17*
nolo contendere, p. 17
institutional corrections, *p. 18*
noninstitutional corrections, *p. 19*
community corrections, *p. 19*
corrections, *p. 19*
mores, *p. 20*

folkways, *p. 20*
criminal law, *p. 20*
penal law, *p. 20*
profession, *p. 22*
evidence-based penology, *p. 22*
evidence-based corrections, *p. 22*
corrections professional, *p. 26*
professional associations, *p. 26*
certification, *p. 26*
racism, *p. 29*

QUESTIONS FOR REVIEW

1 Compare crime rates with correctional populations over time. What differences stand out? How might you explain them?

2 How do rising correctional populations impact the costs of corrections? What might be done to lower these costs?

3 What are the kinds of crimes that cause offenders to enter correctional institutions? To enter other kinds of correctional programs?

4 Compare and contrast the Uniform Crime Reports and the National Crime Victimization Survey. What are the major differences? What are the similarities? What is the significance of these sources of information to the field of corrections?

5 What are the major components of the criminal justice system?

6 List four components of the corrections subsystem.

7 Why may the term *criminal justice* be used to refer either to our system of justice or to the activities that take place during the justice *process?*

8 Define *corrections* and explain the ACA's seven aspects of the overall role of corrections.

9 Explain the importance of professionalism in corrections and list the seven characteristics of a professional attitude.

10 What is meant by the term *social diversity* and why is the issue of social diversity important in corrections today?

THINKING CRITICALLY ABOUT CORRECTIONS

Vision

Dianne Carter, president of the National Academy of Corrections, once said, "Too often in corrections, only worker skills are targeted for training, and the organization misses a significant opportunity to communicate its vision and mission."[34] Do you agree or disagree with this statement? Why?

Professionalism

Harold Williamson, a writer in the corrections field has noted, "Higher levels of professionalization require greater amounts of training and usually involve increased specialization when compared to lesser professionalized activity. Higher levels of professionalization also involve the learning of more abstract knowledge and information."[35] Do you agree? Why or why not?

ON-THE-JOB DECISION MAKING

Training

Today is the first day of your job as a correctional officer. A severe statewide shortage of officers required you to begin work immediately before training, which you are scheduled to attend in three months. When you arrive at the facility, you are ushered into a meeting with the warden. He welcomes you and gives you a brief pep talk. He asks if you have any concerns. You tell him, "Well, I feel a little uneasy. I haven't gone through the academy yet." "Don't worry," he says, "all our new recruits get on-the-job experience before a slot in the academy opens up. You'll do fine!" He shakes your hand and leads you

to the door. After you leave the warden's office, you are given a set of keys and a can of mace. The shift supervisor, a sergeant, gives you a brief tour of the prison. Then he tells you that as you learn your job, you will spend most of your time with another officer, though pairing up will not always be possible.

The officer you are assigned to accompany is named Harold Gates. At first, you follow Officer Gates across the compound, getting more familiar with the layout of the facility. Then you spend an uneventful afternoon working with Officer Gates in the yard. At 4:30, Officer Gates instructs you to make sure that all inmates have left the classroom building in preparation for a "count." As you enter the building, you encounter a group of six inmates heading toward the door. Before you can move to the side, one of the inmates walks within an inch of you and stares at you. The others crowd in behind him. You can't move. You are pinned to the door by the men. The man directly in front of you is huge—over 6 feet tall and about 280 pounds. His legs look like tree trunks, and his arms are held away from his body by their sheer bulk. You're staring at a chest that could easily pass as a brick wall. With a snarl he growls, "What do you want?"

1. How do you respond? Would you feel more confident responding to a situation like this if you had had some training?

2. If you tell the inmates that it's time for a count and to move along, what will you do next? Will you ask anyone for guidance in similar future situations or just chalk up the encounter to a learning experience? To whom might you talk about it?

3. Suppose you are a manager or supervisor at this facility. How would you handle the training of new recruits?

Leadership

You are a correctional officer at the McClellan Correctional Facility. You and your coworkers have been following, with high interest, the events at Brownley, another correctional facility located approximately 35 miles away. Prisoner rioting at Brownley during the past four days has left four correctional officers and 19 prisoners seriously hurt. It now appears, though, that while tensions remain high, the riot has been contained and the prisoners at Brownley are settling back down. The uneasy truce, however, mandates resolution of the issues that led to the riot in the first place.

The main issue leading to the riot was the prisoners' claims of mistreatment at the hands of certain members of the Brownley correctional staff. State correctional administrators have determined that an essential first step in preventing future riots is replacement of certain members of the correctional staff at Brownley. You are called to your supervisor's office, where she informs you that you are being reassigned temporarily to Brownley, with a possibility that the reassignment may become permanent.

This news does not make you happy. The logistical impact alone is irritating, because it will mean a significant commute each day. More important, though, is that you will be leaving a cohesive team of skilled and dedicated correctional officers with whom you have developed a close bond. You trust each other, and you trust your leaders. There's no telling what you will encounter at Brownley.

Your worst fears are realized when you report for your first shift and your new sergeant takes you aside. "We can't let them win on this," he says. "You know the drill. Stay on 'em hard, and don't cut 'em any slack. We need to let them know from the get-go that things haven't changed—we're still in charge, whether they like it or not, and we ain't gonna take any guff from the likes of them!"

It is immediately apparent to you that your sergeant has a strong "us-against-them" perspective. Your experience tells you that such an attitude at the leadership level likely induces similar, often stronger attitudes at the correctional officer level, and your common sense tells you that this is probably the root of the problem at Brownley.

1. How do you respond to your new sergeant?

2. If you elect to keep this information to yourself, how will you establish yourself with the Brownley inmates as a CO who does not subscribe to the other CO's practices without appearing weak or exploitable?

3. If you elect to bring this information to the attention of someone higher up in the supervisory chain, how will you deal with potential adverse reactions from your new coworkers?

LIVE LINKS

at www.justicestudies.com/livelinks04

1–1   Correctional Populations in the United States

These tables present data on the growing number of persons in the United States who were under some form of correctional supervision. Begun in 1985, the tables offer the latest information in a series based on data from annual BJS surveys. They present jurisdiction-level counts of prisoners, probationers, and parolees by gender, race, admission type, release type, and sentence length. Data are also provided on persons under jail jurisdiction for the nation, as well as the 25 largest jurisdictions. Jail information includes the number of inmates by gender, race, juvenile status, and conviction status, and the total jail capacity and percentage occupied at midyear.

1–2   Justice Expenditure and Employment in the United States

This link provides selected data from the Census Bureau's Annual General Finance and Employment Survey. Data presented include police protection, judicial and legal services, and corrections expenditure and employment for federal, state, and local governments in 2003 and national trend data for 1982 to 2003.

PUNISHMENTS

A Brief History

CHAPTER OBJECTIVES

After completing this chapter you should be able to do the following:

1 Describe the types of punishment prevalent in ancient times.

2 List and describe the major criminal punishments used throughout history.

3 Explain the role of torture in the justice systems of times past.

4 Explain the ideas that led to the use of incarceration as a criminal punishment and as an alternative to earlier punishments.

5 Explain the role of correctional reformers in changing the nature of criminal punishment.

> *No man shall be forced by Torture to confesse any Crime against himselfe nor any other unlesse it be in some Capitall case, where he is first fullie convicted by cleare and suffitient evidence to be guilty. After which if the cause be of that nature, That it is very apparent there be other conspiratours, or confederates with him, Then he may be tortured, yet not with such Tortures as be Barbarous and inhumane.*
>
> —Massachusetts Body of Liberties of 1641, Section 45

Before the advent of prisons, corporal punishments were often imposed for serious crimes. Some, although not regularly administered, were especially gruesome. In 1757 Robert-François Damiens was sentenced to be quartered publicly in Paris for attempting to kill King Louis XV. As the executioners took their places, it was announced that

corporal punishments
Physical punishments, or those involving the body.

THE STOCKS.

An offender in the stocks in Colonial times. Early punishments were often both physical and public. What purposes did such punishments serve?

the flesh will be torn from his breasts, arms, thighs and calves with red-hot pincers, his right hand, holding the knife with which he committed said [crime], burnt with sulphur, and, on those places where the flesh will be torn away, poured molten lead, boiling oil, burning resin, wax and sulphur melted together and then his body drawn and quartered by four horses and his limbs and body consumed by fire, reduced to ashes and his ashes thrown to the winds.[1]

As it turned out, Damiens was a very muscular man. He remained conscious throughout the tortures, although a report tells us that he "uttered horrible cries." When it came time for him to be quartered, the four horses were unable to pull him apart—even after repeated attempts. Finally, six horses were used, and when they were still unable to disjoint the prisoner, his muscles had to be "cut through with knives."

Gruesome as this story may be, it illustrates the relative newness of our present system of corrections, which depends largely on the use of fines, probation, imprisonment, and parole. This chapter traces the historical and cultural roots of our present system.

PUNISHMENTS IN ANCIENT TIMES

Before the large-scale building of prisons began in 17th-century Europe, a variety of practices, based on the law and justice concepts of certain cultural groups, were used to punish wrongdoers and maintain civil order. We will briefly highlight some of these practices and the traditions that have influenced modern correctional practices.

Ancient Greece

In the cultural history of punishments, the Greek city-states provide the earliest evidence that public punishment is part of the Western tradition—and that its roots are in ideas of law and justice. Of all the city-states, the practices of Athens are the best documented. This documentation, which ranges from the writings of orators and philosophers to plays and poetry, tells us that many early crimes were punished by execution, banishment, or exile. Greek poets described stoning the condemned to death, throwing them from high cliffs, binding them to stakes (similar to crucifixion), and cursing them ritually. In many cases, the bodies of executed criminals were regarded as dishonored and were prevented from being buried. Their bodies were left to scavengers and the elements, serving as a warning to anyone contemplating similar crimes.

Other punishments in ancient Athens included "confiscation of property, fines, and the destruction of the condemned offenders' houses."[2] Public denunciation, shaming (*atimia*), imprisonment, and public display of the offender were also used. Criminal punishments in ancient Greece sometimes included civil penalties, such as loss of the ability to transfer property, to vote, and to marry.

Ancient Israel

The chief record of ancient Hebrew history is the Bible. It describes the law and civilization of the ancient Hebrews, including their criminal law and penology. Punishments used by the Hebrews mentioned in the Old Testament included banishment, beating, beheading, blinding, branding and burning, casting down from a high place, crushing, confiscation of property, crucifixion, cursing, cutting asunder, drowning, exile, exposure to wild beasts, fining, flaying, hanging, imprisonment, mutilation, plucking of the hair, sawing asunder, scourging with thorns, slavery, slaying by spear or sword, use of the stocks, stoning, strangulation, stripes, and suffocation.[3] Michel Foucault, the French historian, says that the purpose of physical punishments was primarily revenge. "It was as if the punishment was thought to equal, if not to exceed, in savagery the crime itself," he writes.[4]

A stoning in pre-Christian times. How do ancient punishments and the philosophies that influenced them contribute to today's understanding of the role of criminal punishment in society?

Early Rome

The Twelve Tables, the first written laws of Rome, were issued in 451 B.C. Conviction of some offenses required payment of compensation, but the most frequent penalty was death. Among the forms of capital punishment were burning (for arson), throwing from a cliff (for perjury), clubbing to death (for writing insulting songs about a citizen), hanging (for stealing others' crops), and decapitation. Not mentioned in the Twelve Tables were several other forms of capital punishment in vogue in ancient Rome. For killing a close relative, the offender was subjected to the *culleus*, which consisted of confining the offender in a sack with an ape, a dog, and a serpent, and throwing the sack into the sea. Vestal virgins who had violated their vows of chastity were buried alive. As an alternative to execution, offenders might choose exile. Offenders who went into exile lost their citizenship, freedom, and immovable property. If they returned to Rome, they could be killed by any citizen.[5]

PHYSICAL PUNISHMENTS

In Western societies the practice of corporal punishment carried over into the Christian era. Physical punishments were imposed for a wide variety of offenses during the Middle Ages. Physical punishments were also used in the American colonies: "The whole baggage of corporal punishments, as they existed in England, were brought to this country, and flourished, especially in New England where the precepts of Calvinism adorned them with pious sanctions."[6] The Puritans, for example, sometimes burned witches and unruly slaves; made wide use of the stocks, the pillory, and the ducking stool; branded criminal offenders; and forced women convicted of adultery to wear "scarlet letters."

As justice historian Pieter Spierenburg notes, many physical punishments during the Middle Ages and in "early modern Europe" were *theatrical punishments*.[7] That is, they were corporal punishments carried out

THE OFFENDER SPEAKS

The purpose of punishment is for someone to learn from what they have done wrong. For example, when you were a child and you got caught sneaking a cigarette from your father's pack, the punishment was a spanking and getting sent to your room until told to come out. Well, most kids learn from this. Then you have the hard-headed ones such as myself who did not learn. I had to do this over and over and over again. Repeat the punishment until I got it right. I beat my head against the wall too many times and it ended up hurting too much.

If there were no punishment it would be one place I would not want to live. There would be total chaos throughout the world. Back to the wild, wild west days. I also believe that the punishment should fit the crime. Myself, I've spent 10 years 3 months in prison which I deserved to do. I did wrong, and this is my example of how the punishment should fit the crime. I was convicted of 11 armed robberies which I said I did over 10 years. I've met people in prison who did one armed robbery and they have been in since the early 1970s. I do not feel that is right.

Gary James Campbell
Palm Beach Detention Center, Florida

Michael Fay, the American teenager who was caned in Singapore in 1994. Corporal punishments like caning, which involves whipping with a bamboo rod, are still used in more than two dozen countries as criminal sanctions. Fay, who was 18 years old when caned, had spray-painted some parked cars. Can corporal punishment be an effective criminal deterrent?

in public. Spierenburg divides punishments that were both physical and public into five degrees of severity: (1) whipping or flogging; (2) burning of the skin; (3) mutilation, or "more serious encroachments on bodily integrity"; (4) a merciful instant death; and (5) a torturous and prolonged death.[8]

Flogging

Flogging (or whipping) has been the most common physical punishment through the ages.[9] The code established by Moses, for example, authorized flogging, and Roman law specified flogging as a punishment for certain forms of theft. Flogging was common in England during the Middle Ages as punishment for a wide variety of crimes. In England, women were flogged in private, but men were whipped publicly.[10]

The construction of flogging whips varied greatly, from simple leather straps or willow branches to heavy, complicated instruments designed to inflict a maximum of pain. A traditional form of whip was the cat-o'-nine-tails, consisting of nine knotted cords fastened to a wooden handle.

Convicted rapist Ghanat Khan, an Afghan refugee, being lashed at Bara near Pakistan's northwestern city of Peshawar. Kahn received 15 lashes in a public whipping as mandated by Islamic law. Why do some countries still impose physical punishments for crimes? Why are they sometimes carried out in public?

The "cat" got its name from the marks it left on the body, which were like the scratches of a cat. One especially cruel form of the whip, the Russian knout, was made of leather strips fitted with fishhooks. When a prisoner was whipped, the hooks would dig into the body, ripping away a proverbial "pound of flesh" with each stroke. A thorough whipping with the knout could result in death from blood loss.

Flogging was also widely used in the American colonies to enforce discipline, punish offenders, and make an example of "ne'er-do-wells" (shiftless and irresponsible individuals). As a mechanism for enforcing compliance with prison rules, flogging survived into the 20th century. As late as 1959, Harry Elmer Barnes and Negley K. Teeters were able to write, "Floggings have been prison practice down to our own times, and deaths have occurred due to over-severe whippings in southern prison camps and chain-gangs. Tying prisoners up by their hands and allowing them to hang suspended with their toes barely touching the floor or ground has been a common method of enforcing discipline." [11]

Branding

Branding, a type of mutilation, was practiced by Roman society. Criminals were branded with a mark or letter signifying their crimes. Brands, which were often placed on the forehead or another part of the face, served to warn others of an offender's criminal history.

The last documented incident of facial branding of English criminals occurred in 1699.[12] After that year, offenders were branded on the hand, since it was feared that more obvious marks would reduce employment possibilities. Branding was abolished in England during the last half of the 18th century.

The French branded criminals on the shoulder with the royal emblem. They later switched to burning onto the shoulder a letter signifying the crime of which the offender had been convicted.

Branding was also practiced in the early American colonies. The East Jersey Codes of 1668 and 1675, for example, ordered that burglars be branded on the hand with the letter *T* (for *thief*). After a second offense, the letter *R* (for *rogue*) was burned into the forehead. Maryland branded blasphemers with the letter *B* on the forehead. Women offenders were not branded but were forced to wear letters on their clothing.

Mutilation

Mutilation was another type of corporal punishment used in ancient and medieval societies. Archaeological evidence shows that the pharaohs of ancient Egypt and their representatives often ordered mutilation.[13] In ancient Rome offenders were mutilated according to the law of retaliation, or *lex talionis. Lex talionis,* as a punishment philosophy, resembles the biblical principle of "an eye for an eye and a tooth for a tooth."

Medieval justice frequently insisted that punishment fit the crime. Hence, "thieves and counterfeiters had their hands cut off, liars and perjurers had their tongues torn out, spies had their eyes gouged out, sex criminals had their genitals removed, and so forth."[14] Blasphemers sometimes had their tongues pierced or cut out and their upper lips cut away.[15]

Mutilation had a deterrent effect; the permanently scarred and disfigured offenders served as warnings to others of what would happen to criminals. Sometimes, mutilation served merely as a prelude to execution. The right hand of a murderer, for example, was sometimes cut off before he was hanged.[16]

Instant Death

According to Spierenburg, beheading, hanging, and garroting (strangulation by a tightened iron collar) were the most common means of merciful

A 1786 German woodcut depicts a public execution by burning. What purpose did such public dispensing of justice serve?

or instant death.[17] Instant death was frequently reserved for members of the nobility who had received capital sentences (usually from the king) or for previously honorable men and women who ran afoul of the law. Decapitation, especially when done by the sword, was regarded as the most honorable form of capital punishment—since a sword was a symbol that was both noble and aristocratic. Hanging, says Spierenburg, "was the standard nonhonorable form of the death penalty." For women, however, hanging was considered indecent. Garroting tended to replace hanging as a capital punishment for women.

Lingering Death

The worst fate a criminal offender—especially one convicted of heinous crimes—might meet in medieval Europe was a slow or lingering death, often preceded by torture. Some offenders were burned alive, while others were "broken on the wheel." Breaking on the wheel was a procedure that broke all of the major bones in the body. A person who had been broken on the wheel and was still alive was often killed by an executioner's blow to the heart.

Offenders who were to be hanged sometimes had their arms and legs broken first; others were whipped or burned. Burning alive, a practice used in France until the 18th century, was undoubtedly one of the period's cruelest forms of capital punishment.

The Role of Torture

A variety of other corporal punishments were employed, some of which involved torture. Pain was central to retaliatory punishments, and it was used to extract confessions and get information. "Torture," said one source, "is the twisting (torsion) from its subjects of guilty secrets."[18] The use of torture in medieval England was based on a theory that knowledge of one's own guilt, or of the guilt of others, was an offense in itself. Moreover, the theory went, such knowledge was a kind of property that rightly belonged to the state. Hence, forcing an offender to relinquish such "property," by any means necessary, was a right of the government.

Tortures of all kinds were also used during the Middle Ages in an effort to gain confessions from heretics. Heresy was considered a crime against the church and against God. At the time, there was no separation between church and state in many Western societies, and church courts were free to impose punishment as they saw fit. Believers were sure that the heretic's soul was condemned to eternal damnation and that confession would lead to salvation. As a result, torture flourished as a technique for saving souls. Some saw the suffering induced by corporal punishments as spiritually cleansing. Others compared it to the suffering of Jesus on the cross. They argued that physical pain and suffering might free the soul from the clutches of evil.

A common medieval torture was the rack—a machine that slowly stretched a prisoner until his or her joints separated. In another method of torture, red-hot pincers called *hooks* were used to pull the flesh away. Thumbscrews were used as their name implies. In *cording*, an offender's thumbs were tied tightly together behind the back by a rope that passed through a support in the ceiling. Weights were then tied to the ankles, and the person was hoisted into the air by his or her thumbs. Stones were used to crush confessions out of offenders: First a convict was covered with boards, and then suffered as one stone after another was placed on top of them.

Exile and Transportation

In a number of early societies, exile, or banishment, sometimes took the place of corporal and capital punishment. The ancient Greeks permitted offenders to leave the Greek state and travel to Rome, where they might gain citizenship. Early Roman law also established the punishment of exile. Exile was regarded as akin to a death sentence, since the banished person could no longer depend on his or her former community for support and protection. He or she could generally be killed with impunity if attempting to reenter the area.

Exile was practiced in some European communities into the 1800s. One historical study, for example, revealed that, between 1650 and 1750, 97 percent of the noncapital sentences handed down in Amsterdam included banishment.[19] Sentences of banishment drove petty offenders out of a municipality and kept known offenders out of town. But banished criminals resurfaced quickly in neighboring towns, and many communities in Europe confronted a floating population of criminals—especially petty thieves.

Though it was rarely practical to banish offenders from an entire province or nation, England practiced for more than 200 years a form of criminal exile known as *transportation*. An English law authorizing the transportation of convicts to newly discovered lands was passed in 1597. The law was intended primarily to provide galley slaves for a burgeoning English merchant fleet. Soon, however, public support grew for the transportation system as a way of ridding England of felons. As a result, large numbers of convicts were sent to America and other English colonies. One writer estimates that, by the beginning of the American Revolution, 50,000 prisoners had been sent to the New World. Most of them "were sold as indentured servants in the southern colonies, where their market value was greater than in New England."[20]

After the American Revolution, convicted felons began piling up in English jails with no place to go. Legislation was soon passed authorizing prisoners to be housed aboard floating prison ships called *hulks*. Many of these vessels were abandoned merchant ships or broken-down warships. Hulks were anchored in rivers and harbors throughout England. They were unsanitary, rat infested, and unventilated, and the keepers flogged the inmates to force them to work. Disease ran rampant in the hulks, sometimes wiping out all the prisoners on a ship, as well as the crew and nearby citizens. This "temporary" solution lasted about 80 years.

The system of hulks eventually proved impractical, and England soon began shifting its convict population to Australia, which Captain Cook had come upon in 1770. Convict transportation to Australia began in earnest in 1787,[21] with English convicts being transported to New South Wales, Norfolk Island, and Van Diemen's Land—now known as Tasmania (see Exhibit 2–1). The journey was long and demanding, and conditions on prison ships were often ghastly. Many convicts did not survive the trip. Those who did were put to work at heavy labor when they reached their destinations, helping develop the growing region.

Soon convicts who had served their sentences began to receive land grants. In 1791 the governor of New South Wales initiated a program to give released convicts up to 30 acres of land each, along with enough tools, seeds, and rations to last 18 months.

Devil's Island, the infamous French prison where many political prisoners were held. What role did transportation play in the criminal punishments of times past?

In the late 18th century, the English government began turning broken-down war vessels and abandoned transport ships into *hulks* to house prisoners. What event caused the prison overcrowding that made these hulks necessary?

English transportation of criminals began to wane in 1853, when Parliament abolished transportation for prisoners with sentences of fewer than 14 years. Opposition to transportation was especially strong among the free settlers who had begun to populate Australia and nearby regions. In 1867 the practice of transportation officially ended, although England continued to send inmates from India to its penal colony in the Andaman Islands until World War II.

France also experimented with transportation. Beginning in 1791 French authorities sent prisoners in large numbers to Madagascar, New Caledonia, the Marquesas Islands, and French Guiana. Devil's Island, in

---

EXHIBIT 2–1   **Van Diemen's Land**

Van Diemen's Land, an island off the southern coast of Australia that is known today as Tasmania, served as a destination in the English system of convict transportation during the early 1800s. The paragraphs that follow, which were written in 1832, give some historical insight into the practice.

Van Diemen's Land was discovered so long ago as the year 1642, by the Dutch navigator Tasman, who gave it the name which it still bears, in honour of his employer Anthony Van Diemen, the then governor of the Dutch possessions in India. It was not, however, till the year 1804 that the country was taken possession of by England. In the early part of that year Colonel David Collins, having been appointed Governor of the projected settlement, arrived on the island with about four hundred prisoners in charge and a force of fifty marines under his command. He was accompanied also by several gentlemen, commissioned to fill the various situations on the new government. They fixed their headquarters on the site of the present capital, to which they gave the name of Hobart Town, after Lord Hobart, the then Secretary for the Colonies. The Colony . . . being thus founded, continued to take root, although at times suffering very great hardships. . . . No sheep or cattle were imported till three years after the settlement of the island. For some time after this, indeed, the colony was looked upon merely as a place of punishment for persons convicted of crimes in New South Wales, numbers of whom accordingly continued to be sent to it every year. Governor Collins died in 1810; and in 1813 Lieutenant-Colonel Davey arrived as his successor.

From about this time the colony began to be considered in a new light. The population consisted no longer merely of the convicts and the garrison; but, besides many persons who, having been originally crown prisoners, had obtained their freedom by servitude or indolence, embraced a considerable number of settlers who had arrived in successive small parties from the neighbouring colony of New South Wales. Hitherto the only places with which Van Diemen's Land was allowed to hold any communication had been New South Wales and England: That restriction was now done away with, and the two colonies were placed, in respect to foreign commerce, on precisely the same footing. . . .

In 1817 Colonel Davey was succeeded in the government by Colonel Sorell. The first object which engaged the attention of the new governor was the suppression of an evil under which the colony had for some years been suffering, the ravages of the bush-rangers, as they were called, or prisoners who had made their escape and roamed at large in the woods. The capture and execution of the principal leaders of these marauders in a short time put an end, for the present, to their destructive inroads.

About 1821 may be said to have begun the emigration from England, which has since proceeded almost with uninterrupted steadiness. . . . In December 1825, Van Diemen's Land was declared entirely independent of New South Wales; and an executive and legislative Council were appointed as advisers to the Governor, the members of both being named by the Crown. In 1827 the island was divided into eight police districts, each of which was placed under the charge of a stipendiary magistrate.

Source: The Society for the Diffusion of Useful Knowledge, *The Penny Magazine,* vol. 1, no. 1, March 31, 1832.

the Caribbean Sea, off the coast of French Guiana, continued to function as a prison until 1951. The island was named for the horrors associated with imprisonment there. It was the site of an infamous penal colony that was used mostly for political prisoners. The island was also made famous by the Dreyfus Affair, which began in 1894 when French Captain Alfred Dreyfus (1859–1935) was convicted of treason by a court-martial, sentenced to life imprisonment, and sent to the island. Thirty-six years later, Dreyfus was exonerated after it was demonstrated that the original charges against him were the result of anti-Semitism in the French military and had no factual basis.

The only Western nation to practice transportation into the 1990s was Russia, which sent prisoners to Siberia as late as 1990. Siberia is a cold and formerly desolate region in what is now central and eastern Russia. It stretches from the Ural Mountains to the Pacific Ocean. The extensive area was annexed by Russia in stages during the 16th and 17th centuries. It was used as a place of exile for political prisoners since the early 17th century. In 1741 the Russian Count Biron was found guilty of treason, but his sentence of death by quartering was changed to exile to Siberia.[22] Hard labor in Siberia became a common sentence for criminal offenders in Czarist Russia, and it is estimated that hundreds of thousands of vagrants, felons, political prisoners, and even voluntary exiles were sent to Siberia under the Czars to force settlement of the region and to develop its natural resources. During Joseph Stalin's rule (1928–1953), Siberian prison camps forced tens of millions of victims into a vast labor system. The brutal conditions in these camps resulted in millions of deaths and have been graphically described in the works of Aleksandr Solzhenitsyn.[23] After Stalin's death the camp population greatly decreased, although detention in remote and inhospitable parts of Siberia is still used to punish criminals and dissenters.[24]

Public Humiliation

Many corporal punishments were carried out in public, primarily to deter other potential lawbreakers. Some other forms of punishment depended on public ridicule for their effect. These included the stocks and the pillory.

Found guilty of the offense of impiety in Athens in 399 B.C., Socrates chose poison over imprisonment. What was the goal of most early penalties for crimes?

Stocks held a prisoner in a sitting position, with feet and hands locked in a frame. A prisoner in the pillory was made to stand with his or her head and hands locked in place. Both devices exposed the prisoner to public scorn. While confined in place, prisoners were frequently pelted with eggs and rotten fruit. Sometimes they were whipped or branded. Those confined to the pillory occasionally had their ears nailed to the wood, and they had to rip them free when released. England abolished the pillory in 1834; according to at least one source, the pillory was still in use in Delaware in 1905.[25]

Confinement

Confinement by chaining or jailing has been a punishment since ancient times. At times, confinement served functions other than punishment for crimes. In early Greece, for example, prisons were used to punish convicted offenders, to enforce the payment of debts, to hold those awaiting other punishments, and to detain foreigners who might otherwise flee before their cases could be heard.[26] Until the 1600s and the development of prisons as primary places of punishment, prisons were used to detain people before trial; to hold prisoners awaiting other punishments, such as death or corporal punishment; to force payment of debts and fines; and to hold and punish slaves.

Early European prisons were rarely called *prisons*. They went by such names as *dungeon, tower,* and *gaol* (from which we get the modern term *jail*). Some places used as prisons had been built for other purposes. The Tower of London, for example, was originally a fortified palace that had been used as an arsenal. The French Bastille began as a fortified city gate leading into Paris. Judicial proceedings were not necessary before imprisonment in such places, nor was a formal sentence. As a result, anyone thrown into a dungeon at the behest of authorities was likely to stay there until granted clemency or until death.

INCARCERATION AS PUNISHMENT

According to Pieter Spierenburg, a Dutch justice historian, a form of punishment that emerged around the year 1500 was *penal bondage,* which included all forms of incarceration.[27] Spierenburg explained, "Courts came to use it almost as frequently as physical sanctions. Instead of being flogged or hanged, some offenders were incarcerated in workhouses or forced to perform labor in some other setting." According to Spierenburg, the word *bondage* means "any punishment that puts severe restrictions on the condemned person's freedom of action and movement, including but not limited to imprisonment."

Among the forms of penal bondage imposed on criminals, vagrants, debtors, social misfits, and others were forced labor on public works projects and forced conscription into military campaigns. Later, houses of correction also subjected inmates to strict routines.

One early form of incarceration developed in France. For at least 200 years, prisoners were regularly assigned to French warships as galley slaves. After the naval importance of galleys had declined, French naval officials continued to have custody of convicted offenders. By the mid-1700s, they had begun to put convicts to work in the shipyards of Toulon, Brest, and Rochefort. At night these prisoners were sheltered in arsenals, where they slept chained to their beds. As Spierenburg notes, "the arsenals were in fact labor camps where convicts had to remain within an enclosed space, so the penalty was more akin to imprisonment than to public works."

The public-works penalty, sometimes called *penal servitude,* became especially popular in Germany and Switzerland in the 1600s and 1700s. According to Spierenburg, "convicts dug ore in mines, repaired ramparts, built roads or houses, or went from door to door collecting human waste."[28]

The House of Correction (1550–1700)

Midway between corporal punishments and modern imprisonment stands the workhouse or the house of correction. The development of workhouses was originally a humanitarian move intended to manage the unsettling social conditions of the late 16th and early 17th centuries in England. The feudal system had offered mutual protection for land-owning nobles and for serfs, who were tied to the land. By 1550 that system was breaking down in Europe. Hordes of former serfs roamed the countryside, unable

bridewell

A workhouse. The word came from the name of the first workhouse in England.

to earn a living. Many flocked to the cities, where they hoped to find work in newly developing industries. The change from an agrarian economy to an industrial one displaced many persons, resulted in growing poverty, and increased the numbers of beggars and vagrants.

Vagrancy became a crime, and soon anyone unable to prove some means of support was imprisoned in a workhouse. The first workhouse in England was called Bridewell because it was located at St. Bridget's Well, near the town of Blackfriars. Soon, the word **bridewell** entered the language as a term for a workhouse. English Parliament ordered workhouses to be created throughout England. Parliament intended that those housed in workhouses be taught habits of industry and frugality and that they learn a trade.

At first, prisoners in workhouses were paid for the work they did. Work included spinning, weaving, clothmaking, the milling of grains, and baking. Soon, however, as the numbers of prisoners grew, the workhouse system deteriorated. As workhouses spread through Europe, they became catchall institutions that held the idle, the unemployed, the poor, debtors, insane persons, and even unruly individuals whose families could not cope with them. According to one writer, imprisonment in a workhouse could serve "as a tool of private discipline. . . . The family drew up a petition explaining why the individual should be imprisoned, and the authorities decided whether or not to consent. Usually, private offenders were confined because of conduct considered immoral."[29]

Hence, workhouses served as informal repositories for people the community regarded as "inconvenient," irresponsible, or deviant—even if their behavior did not violate the criminal law. In the midst of this large population of misfits and unwanted persons could be found a core group of criminal offenders. In 1706 the British Parliament passed legislation "permitting judges to sentence felons to the house of correction for up to two years."[30]

By the end of the 17th century, houses of correction had become mere holding cells with little reformative purpose. Nonetheless, because workhouses relied primarily on incarceration rather than corporal punishments, they provided a model for prison reformers bent on more humanitarian correctional practices.

Bridewells were penal institutions for social outcasts—ranging from vagrants to petty criminals—who were forced to work under strict discipline. What social conditions prompted governments to establish such houses of correction?

The Emergence of the Prison

Two main elements fueled the development of prisons as we know them today. The first element was a philosophical shift away from punishment of the body toward punishment of the soul or human spirit. By the late 1700s in Europe and America, a powerful movement was under way to replace traditional corporal punishments with deprivation of personal liberty as the main thrust of criminal sentencing. Michel Foucault explains the shift this way: "The punishment-body relation [was no longer] the same as it was in the torture during public executions. The body now serves as an instrument or intermediary: If one intervenes upon it to imprison it or to make it work, it is in order to deprive the individual of a liberty that is regarded both as a right and as property. The body, according to this penalty, is caught up in a system of constraints and privations, obligations and prohibitions. Physical pain, the pain of the body itself, is no longer the constituent element of the penalty."[31]

The transition from corporal punishments to denial of liberties found its clearest expression in the work of the Philadelphia Society for Alleviating the Miseries of Public Prisons. The society, established by the Pennsylvania Quakers in 1787, had as its purpose the renovation of existing prisons and jails and the establishment of the prison as the basic form of criminal punishment. Thanks largely to the widely publicized works of the society, Pennsylvania became in April 1794 the first state to abolish permanently the death penalty for all crimes except first-degree murder, and it adopted a system of fines and imprisonment in place of corporal punishments.[32] The new Pennsylvania criminal code was important because it "marked the first permanent American break with contemporary juristic savagery, was the forerunner of the reform codes of other American states, and was the essential basis of Pennsylvania criminal jurisprudence until the next systematic revision in 1860."[33]

The second element fueling the development of modern prisons was the passage of laws preventing the imprisonment of anyone except criminals. Civil commitments to prison ended, and a huge class of social misfits were removed from prisons and dealt with elsewhere. Primary among this group were debtors, who historically had been cast into jails as a result of civil rulings against them. John Howard's study of English jails found 2,437 debtors among the 4,084 prisoners he encountered.[34] Many others were vagrants who had committed no "intentional" crime.

According to Pieter Spierenburg, the Dutch were the first Europeans to segregate serious criminals from vagrants and minor delinquents, and Dutch courts were the first European courts to begin substituting imprisonment for corporal punishments.[35] The workhouse in Amsterdam, which opened in 1654, "represented the first criminal prison in Europe," says Spierenburg. By the start of the 1700s, Dutch "courts frequently imposed sentences of imprisonment. During the third quarter of the seventeenth century, the Amsterdam court did so in one-fifth of its criminal cases; a century later, it did so in three-fifths. By the 1670s the court of Groningen-City imposed imprisonment in two-fifths of criminal cases." Even so, the imprisonment of debtors persisted in Holland for another hundred years, and Dutch prisons of the period held both criminal and civil "convicts."

These ideas—that "doing time" was often the most appropriate punishment for criminal activity and that incarceration should be imposed only on criminal offenders—soon combined with a burgeoning emphasis on reformation as the primary goal of criminal sentencing. Reformation, argued many prison advocates of the time, could best be achieved by enforced solitude.

In 1776 the British philanthropist Jonas Hanway published a book titled *Solitude in Imprisonment*. Hanway's work appears to have had a significant influence on prison advocates. Hanway argued that the interruption of transportation provided a much-needed opportunity to reexamine prevailing policies for dealing with prisoners. He suggested that reformation should be the primary goal of criminal sentencing and said that it was plainly not being met by sentencing practices then in existence. Solitary confinement, said Hanway, would force the prisoner to face his or her conscience—leading to reformation: "The walls of his prison will preach peace to his soul, and he will confess the goodness of his Maker, and the wisdom of the laws of his country."[36]

THE REFORMERS

Prisons, as institutions in which convicted offenders spend time as punishment for crimes, are relatively modern. They came about largely as a

---

Talking about CORRECTIONS

SECURITY TECHNOLOGIES IN CORRECTIONS

Visit *Live Talk* at **Corrections.com** (www.justicestudies.com/talking04) and listen to the program "Security Technologies in Corrections," which relates to ideas discussed in this chapter.

THE STAFF SPEAKS

I am a psychologist for the New Hampshire Department of Corrections working in a mental health unit at a correctional institution. My job is to lead a treatment program for offenders with moderate to severe Axis 1 (illness-type) mental disorders. Correctional counselors, nurses, or other mental health employees refer inmates to my supervisor, the Chief of Mental Health. If he thinks the inmate may have a serious illness-type mental disorder, he gives the case to me. Then either I or one of my team members carefully read the inmate's offender record and medical chart, do a thorough interview, and, with the client's written permission, write for information from mental health professionals who have worked with the client. Usually, the psychiatrist on the team will see the inmate also. If we think the person does have a disorder appropriate for us to treat, we develop a treatment plan and schedule the individual for a treatment team meeting, attended by a nurse, the correctional counselor, the psychiatrist, my team members, and myself. We talk with the client about goals and interventions. These may include nonaddictive psychotropic medications, psychotherapy (individual and group), case management, and monitoring. When it's appropriate, we refer clients to other programs at the prison—for example, the sexual offender program or the substance abuse program. As the clients approach release, we do our best to set them up with mental health and other resources in the community, so that they will remain in good mental health and so that a worsening of their mental disorder does not contribute to their reoffending.

Laura Magzis
Psychologist
Mental Health Unit
New Hampshire State Prison for Men

result of growing intellectualism in Europe and America and as a reaction to the barbarities of corporal punishment.

The period of Western social thought that began in the 17th century and lasted until the dawn of the 19th century is known as the Age of Enlightenment. One author explains, "The phrase was frequently employed by writers of the period itself, convinced that they were emerging from centuries of darkness and ignorance into a new age enlightened by reason, science, and a respect for humanity."[37] The Enlightenment, also known as the Age of Reason, was more than a set of fixed ideas. Enlightenment thought implied an attitude, a method of knowing based on observation, experience, and reason.

One of the earliest representatives of the Enlightenment was the French social philosopher and jurist Charles de Montesquieu (1689–1755) whose masterwork, *The Spirit of Laws*, was published in 1748. Montesquieu wrote that governmental powers should be separated and balanced in order to guarantee individual rights and freedom. He strongly believed in the rights of individuals. His ideas influenced leaders of both the American Revolution and the French Revolution.[38]

Another celebrated philosopher of the Enlightenment was the French writer Voltaire, who satirized both the government and the religious establishment of France. Voltaire twice served time in the Bastille and chose exile in England over prison for additional offenses. Voltaire deeply admired the English atmosphere of political and religious freedom.

A number of important thinkers influenced the justice systems of Western nations and the directions the correctional enterprise would take over the next 200 years. We will now turn our attention to those individuals.

William Penn

William Penn (1644–1718), regarded as the founder of Pennsylvania, was the son of Sir William Penn, a distinguished English admiral. During his youth, Penn traveled widely throughout Europe, served in the Royal Navy, and studied law. In 1667 he converted to the Quaker faith and by the next year found himself confined in the Tower of London as punishment for promoting the faith. While imprisoned he wrote a paper titled "No Cross, No Crown." After release he was again imprisoned on a number of occasions, causing him to seek refuge in America. In 1682 Penn obtained a charter creating the Commonwealth of Pennsylvania, and naming him governor. Gathering together hundreds of Quakers, Penn set sail for the New World. The colony he founded promoted religious tolerance, and it was soon attracting persecuted minorities from England, Germany, Holland, and Scandinavia.

Penn's influence on the criminal law of this country and on the coming age of imprisonment was most visible in the "Great Act" of 1682. Through that single piece of legislation, the Pennsylvania Quakers reduced capital offenses to the one crime of premeditated murder and abolished all corporal punishments as they had existed under English code.

John Howard

John Howard (1726–1790) was born to a deeply religious English family. On a trip to Portugal as a young man, Howard was taken prisoner by pirates when the British merchant ship on which he was traveling was captured by a French privateer.[39] He and his fellow passengers were kept below deck in subhuman conditions. When they arrived in France, he was imprisoned in a French dungeon, but he was later released in exchange for a French naval officer.

In 1773, Howard was appointed high sheriff of Bedfordshire. He was shocked at the abysmal conditions that existed in English jails of the time, and he set out on a quest for prison reform. He began arguing for the abolishment of spiked collars and chains, which prisoners were made to wear, and he argued against the common practice of paying jailers for release. Within a few years, Howard had visited almost every county in England, Wales, and Scotland, traveling no fewer than 7,000 miles in 1779 alone. He also inspected prisons in a number of other countries, including France, Belgium, Holland, Italy, Germany, Spain, Portugal, Denmark, Sweden, and Russia.

Although most prisons Howard visited were like those in England, he found one—the Maison de Force in Ghent, Belgium—that embodied the highest standards of its day.

Howard's greatest legacy was his 1777 book, *The State of the Prisons in England and Wales*,[40] in which he described the abysmal state of English prisons. *The State of the Prisons* also contained descriptions of clean and well-run institutions, prisons in which the sexes were separated, and jails in which inmates were kept busy at productive work.

Howard's book promoted the notion that the fundamental business of corrections should be to reform rather than to punish, and he argued that every citizen must accept responsibility for the criminal justice system of the society in which he or she lives. *The State of the Prisons* appealed to policymakers looking for alternatives to existing systems, and it fueled the efforts of prison reformers in both Europe and America. Many of the principles described in Howard's book later became the foundation for the English Penitentiary Act of 1779.

As Randall McGowen, corrections historian at the University of Oregon, explains, "Howard's contribution was to make the prison the center of focus, shifting all other forms of punishment to the margins. He fostered a vital change of perspective at the very time that judges were sentencing greater numbers of felons to confinement. Howard's book

A plaque near London honoring John Howard, the great English prison reformer. Howard proposed the idea that the fundamental business of corrections should be to reform rather than to punish. How does his work influence corrections today?

Cesare Beccaria (1738–1794), an Italian jurist and criminologist, was one of the first to argue against capital punishment and inhumane treatment of prisoners. What writing by Beccaria influenced the criminal justice systems of Western Europe?

created the impression that the prison was the natural and inevitable shape of punishment."[41]

Howard died of the plague in Russia in 1790. At the time, he was in the midst of his sixth tour of European prisons and was about to leave on a trip to study prisons in Turkey and Asia. On his tomb are engraved these words:

whosoever Thou Art
Thou Standest at the
Grave of Thy friend

Cesare Beccaria

Cesare Beccaria (1738–1794) was born in Italy, the eldest son of an aristocratic family. By the time he reached his mid-20s, Beccaria had formed, with his close friends Pietro and Alessandro Verri, an intellectual circle called the Academy of Fists.[42] The academy took as its purpose the reform of the criminal justice system. Through the Verri brothers, Beccaria became acquainted with the work of French and British political writers such as Montesquieu, Thomas Hobbes (1588–1679), Denis Diderot (1713–1784), Claude-Adrien Helvetius (1715–1771), and David Hume (1711–1776).

In 1764 Beccaria published an essay titled *On Crimes and Punishments*. Although the work was brief, it was, perhaps, the most exciting essay on law of the 18th century. In the essay, Beccaria outlined a utilitarian approach to punishment, suggesting that some punishments can never be justified because they are more evil than any "good" they might produce. The use of torture to obtain confessions falls into that category, said Beccaria. Beccaria also protested punishment of the insane, a common practice of the times, saying it could do no good because insane people cannot accurately assess the consequences of their actions. Beccaria said that *ex post facto* laws, or laws passed after the fact, imposed punishment unfairly, since a person could not calculate the risk of acting before a law against a specific action was passed. He also argued against the use of secret accusations, the discretionary power of judges, the inconsistency and inequality of sentencing, the use of personal connections to obtain sentencing reductions, and the imposition of capital punishment for minor offenses.

Beccaria proposed that punishment could be justified only if it was imposed to defend the social contract—the tacit allegiance that individuals owe their society, and the obligations of government to individuals. It is the social contract, said Beccaria, that gives society the right to punish its members.

Beccaria also argued that punishment should be swift, since swift punishment offers the greatest deterrence. When punishment quickly follows a crime, said Beccaria, the ideas of crime and punishment are more closely associated in a person's mind. He also suggested that the link between crime and punishment would be stronger if the punishment somehow related to the crime.

Finally, said Beccaria, punishments should not be unnecessarily severe. The severity of punishment, he argued, should be proportional to the degree of social damage caused by the crime. Treason, Beccaria said, is the worst crime, since it most harms the social contract. Below treason, Beccaria listed crimes in order of declining severity, including violence against a person or his property, public disruption, and crimes against property. Crimes against property, he said, should be punished by fines.

Zaira Tena
Correctional Officer New Mexico Women's Correctional Facility Grants, New Mexico

Zaira Tena is employed by Corrections Corporation of America (CCA) as a correctional officer at the New Mexico Women's Correctional Facility in Grants, New Mexico. She started working there four years ago. This is Tena's first job in corrections. She was attracted to CCA and a career in corrections because of the benefits that CCA offered her.

Tena attended Laramie County Community College in Laramie, Wyoming, before joining CCA. The company provided additional training in interpersonal communication, special-needs inmates, crisis intervention, infectious diseases, suicide prevention, first aid, CPR, and firearms, giving her the skills she needs to ensure the health, welfare, and safety of prison employees and inmates. Since Tena especially enjoys recreation, she also coordinates the institution's recreation activities.

Tena's enthusiasm for her own career and professional development shows in her advice to people thinking about a career in corrections. Wisely, she is taking her own advice. She plans to stay in corrections and hopes one day soon to become assistant shift commander at the Grants women's facility.

> *I like my job. I like working with people. What I learned and what I'd tell someone is, be very professional, firm, fair, and consistent at all times, and be able to work under a lot of pressure.*

When his essay was translated into French and English, Beccaria became famous throughout much of Europe. Philosophers of the time hailed his ideas, and several European rulers vowed to follow his lead in the reform of their justice systems.

Jeremy Bentham

Philosopher and jurist Jeremy Bentham (1748–1832) was born in London. As a young child, he was considered a prodigy, having been found, at the age of 2, sitting at his father's desk reading a multivolume history of England.[43] He began to study Latin at the age of 3. When Bentham was 12, his father, a wealthy attorney, sent him to Queen's College, Oxford, hoping that he would enter the field of law.

After hearing lectures by the leading legal scholar of the day, Sir William Blackstone (1723–1780), young Bentham became disillusioned with the law. Instead of practicing law, he decided to criticize it, and he spent the rest of his life analyzing the legal practices of the day, writing about them and suggesting improvements.

Bentham advocated **utilitarianism,** the principle that the highest objective of public policy is the greatest happiness for the largest number of people. Utilitarianism provided the starting point for Bentham's social analysis, in which he tried to measure the usefulness of existing institutions, practices, and beliefs against a common standard. Bentham believed that human behavior is determined largely by the amount of pleasure or pain associated with a given activity. Hence, he suggested, the purpose of law should be to make socially undesirable activities painful enough to keep people from engaging in them. In this way, said Bentham, "good" can be achieved.

Bentham's idea, that people are motivated by pleasure and pain and that the proper amount of punishment can deter crime, became known

utilitarianism

The principle that the highest objective of public policy is the greatest happiness for the largest number of people.

hedonistic calculus

The idea that people are motivated by pleasure and pain and that the proper amount of punishment can deter crime.

as **hedonistic calculus**. Bentham's hedonistic calculus made four assumptions:

1. People by nature choose pleasure and avoid pain.
2. Each individual, either consciously or intuitively, calculates the degree of pleasure or pain to be derived from a given course of action.
3. Lawmakers can determine the degree of punishment necessary to deter criminal behavior.
4. Such punishment can be effectively and rationally built into a system of criminal sentencing.

Bentham is also known as the inventor of the *panopticon* (from a Greek word meaning "all-seeing")—a type of prison he proposed building in England as early as 1787. The panopticon was intended to put utilitarian ideas to work in the field of penology.

Key to the panopticon was its unique architecture, which consisted of a circular, tiered design with a glass roof and with a window on the outside wall of each cell.[44] The design made it easy for prison staff, in a tower in the center of the structure, to observe each cell (and its occupants). Within the wheel-like structure, walls separated the cells to prevent any communication between prisoners. Speaking tubes linked cells with the observation platform so that officers could listen to inmates.

The panopticon, also called an *inspection house*, was intended to be a progressive and humanitarian penitentiary. Bentham thought of it as a social experiment. The design was touted as being consistent with the ideals of utilitarianism because only a few officers would be subject to the risks and unpleasantness of the inspection role, while many prisoners would benefit from this enlightened means of institutional management.

Jeremy Bentham (1748–1832), an English philosopher and social reformer, spent his life trying to reform the law. His innovative plan for a prison, called the *panopticon,* consisted of a huge structure covered by a glass roof. A central tower allowed guards to see into the cells, which were arranged in a circle. Although the British government did not use Bentham's plan, several U.S. prisons did, including one in Joliet, Illinois, known as Stateville Correctional Center. What is the name given to Bentham's principle that the highest object of public policy is the greatest happiness for the greatest number of people?

After years of personally promoting the concept, Bentham saw his idea for an innovative penitentiary die. The panopticon was never built in England, and in 1820 government officials formally disavowed it. The concept may have fallen victim to the growing emphasis on transportation, which delayed all prison construction in England. Another significant factor in the demise of the panopticon ideal, however, was Bentham's insistence that panopticons be built near cities to deter crime among the general population. Although a number of sites were chosen for construction, nearby residents always protested plans to build any sort of prison in their neighborhoods. Despite Bentham's failure ever to construct a facility completely true to his panopticon plan, he will always be remembered for his idea that order and reform could be achieved in a prison through architectural design.

Sir Samuel Romilly

Sir Samuel Romilly (1757–1818) was an English legal reformer who worked ceaselessly to lessen the severity of existing criminal law in his home country. Romilly, once described as "the flower of the English reform movement,"[45] attacked laws that authorized capital punishment for a host of minor felonies and misdemeanors.

Romilly's dedication to his cause drew the admiration from a number of reformers. M. Dumont, once described as "the leading orator of the French Revolution," said of Romilly, "[He is] always tranquil and orderly yet has an incessant activity. He never loses a minute; he applies all his mind to what he is about. Like the hand of three watches, he never stops."[46] Another contemporary said of Romilly that "in the House of Commons he looked like Apollo surrounded by crowds of satyrs and goats. . . . This man it was who led the fight to get the gentleness of the English character expressed in its laws."[47]

Romilly entered Parliament in 1806, and in 1810 proposed a reexamination of the Penitentiary Act of 1779. As a result, the government appointed the Holford Committee to examine issues associated with penal reform. Until his early death in 1818, Romilly fought to reduce the number of English capital crimes. He succeeded in getting passed a bill abolishing the death penalty in cases of "private stealing from the person," and he won the abolition of the death penalty in cases of soldiers and sailors found absent without leave. At the time of his death, 200 offenses were still punishable by sentence of death. The movement he began, however, continued to flower. By 1840 the number of capital crimes in England had been reduced to 14, and by 1861 the number fell to 4 (treason, murder, piracy, and setting fire to arsenals).

Romilly's work and the results it produced led others to recognize the need for alternatives to capital punishment as a means of dealing with the large majority of offenders.

Sir Robert Peel

Sir Robert Peel (1788–1850) was a British parliamentary leader bent on seeing the ideas of Romilly, Bentham, and others incorporated into English law. Peel is best known in the history of criminal justice for establishing a police force that influenced the development of policing throughout much of the rest of the world. His force, the London Metropolitan Police, became known as the Met.

Prior to Peel's time, agents of law enforcement often meted out "justice" as they saw fit, sometimes apprehending the offender and punishing

Eye On Corrections

Predictions for Corrections in the 21st Century

A Compilation of Thoughts,
Trends, and Predictions for the Corrections Industry

By Michelle Gaseau

The Corrections Connection polled leaders from several aspects of corrections to find out where the profession is headed, where the challenges lie, and what workers in the field should pay attention to in the coming years, from staffing issues to the growth of professionalism to changes in how society looks at punishment. What follows are excerpts from some of their feedback.

BILL KISSEL, HEALTH DIRECTOR, GEORGIA DEPARTMENT OF CORRECTIONS

Our biggest challenges are going to be the challenges that any organization or agency that has a health care responsibility will face: handling the budgetary impact of scientific advancements especially in the area of pharmaceuticals, mental health medications, and Hepatitis C. As these scientific advancements, which are outstanding, hit us, we in correctional health care are then forced to figure out how to pay for that. It's a good guesstimate that it will only continue as new treatments become the community standard. What we're having to do is determine whether they are community standard.

Then, of course, we'll be challenged with an older population that we'll face because of mandatory sentencing. We've established within our medical prison a chronic care unit here. We have consolidated our inmates system-wide who frequently would have to be sent to a free world hospital.

For the future, in Georgia our goal is to better integrate folks into the community, especially for mental, health, Hepatitis C, and HIV. We're working with other agencies so when folks are on discharge or probation in Georgia. We can connect them to resources. We're trying to do that from a vocational perspective as well.

Then of course we'll be challenged with recruiting qualified health care professionals in physical, mental, and dental health. With a strong economy people don't want to work in prisons. My vision would be we develop partnerships with other agencies and teaching facilities where we increase opportunities for students to train in the prison environment. Hopefully some would gain interest in working in this environment.

DAVID PARRISH, COMMANDER, HILLSBOROUGH, FLORIDA, COUNTY SHERIFF'S DEPARTMENT

The most significant thing is the continuing difficulty in hiring and keeping qualified people. There's an old saying that "If only I had the right staff I could run a good prison in an old red barn." We're building lots of new facilities nationwide but if we don't have the staff we'll be in serious trouble.

I'm seeing a trend in some jurisdictions where the solution to recruiting difficulties is to lower standards. We've worked so hard to improve standards for selection and employment in this profession, I can't see going backwards. I chaired the American Jail Association's Jail Manager Certification process, and I always thought that was a significant step. That was started for jails, and now the American Correctional Association is developing a similar program for correctional staff working in prisons primarily.

If you don't set some standards for yourself, no one else will appreciate that you are professional.

BRIAN DAWE, OFFICER, CORRECTIONS USA

One of the first things we'll see is the end of prison privatization as it relates to medium and maximum security facilities. It has become pretty evident they don't save money, and they cause more problems than anything else.

We're also going to need to see some changes in the level of training and staffing numbers. We're going to need to see mandatory staffing principles.

These inmates have all day long to think up schemes. They deal nationally and internationally. Intelligence has to be shared, and it all comes down to training. We're required by law that part of our training is in firearms, we should have it, but it's rare that we use it. With physical defense [tactics], we get that once, but we see it every day.

One thing we will have to see in the system is an alternative to sentencing programs. We cannot continue to have some of these individuals behind the walls. There are a great number who would be better served and we would be better served by them being in community resource centers.

Also, there will be changes in laws and eventually a turn back of mandatory sentencing. There's a movement among the judiciary to restore some of the decision-making process to them. That's where you need the discretion back in the process. There has to be discretion. You can't build your way out of a crime problem.

ART LEONARDO, FORMER WARDEN, GREEN CORRECTIONAL INSTITUTION, NEW YORK STATE, AND CORRECTIONS CONSULTANT

In my opinion, the most important task we face in the future is to pay more attention to the men and woman who work in the correctional field. The pay in most jurisdictions is still very poor; we constantly lose good people to better status and higher benefits. Training in the field is very much improved, but we can't rest on our laurels. We all need to work on the public, legislative, and governmental perception of our workforce. They are good people doing a tough job.

Not adequately compensating our people leads to constant turnover, poor security and higher real costs. Unions, wardens, commissioners, professional organizations all need to work together to improve the overall status of our people.

In corrections you need experienced people and you need something to keep them working. It's not the easiest job in the world. My experience has been in New York where the pay and the benefits are good. Technology is fine, but people are the ones who run all of that, and consistent people are very important.

Source: "A Compilation of Thoughts, Trends, and Predictions for the Corrections Industry," Michelle Gaseau, The Corrections Connection Network News (CCNN). Eye on Corrections. www.corrections.com. January 3, 2000.

Sir Robert Peel, founder of the London Metropolitan Police. Punishment, said Peel, should not be imposed by the police, but by specialists in penology. In what other ways did Peel influence the field of corrections?

him or her on the spot. Peel and other legal reformers of the day worked to identify the fundamental function of the police as the investigation of crime and the apprehension of criminals. Peel insisted that the police should be responsible for investigation and arrest only, while the trial, defense, and conviction phase of the justice process should reside entirely in the hands of another body, the judiciary.[48] Punishment, he said, should not be imposed by the police, but by specialists in the field of penology. In Peel's words, it is necessary for the police "to recognize always the need for strict adherence to police executive functions and to refrain from even seeming to usurp the powers of the judiciary or avenging individuals or the state and of authoritatively judging guilt and punishing the guilty."

In effect, while working to formalize police administration, Peel pointed out the need for other specialists in the administration of justice such as attorneys, magistrates, and correctional personnel. Peel was also primarily responsible for legislation, Peel's Gaol Act of 1823, aimed at reforming British jails. The Gaol Act required that men and women be segregated while in jail and mandated the supervision of female prisoners by female correctional personnel.[49]

Elizabeth Fry

Elizabeth Fry (1780–1845), a strict Quaker committed to religious and philanthropic work, campaigned during the early 1800s to "expose the plight of women in prison and to promote better conditions for them."[50] While most Enlightenment era thinkers had been influenced by a belief in utilitarian principles, Fry's reformist activities grew out of her religious faith.

Fry had been strongly influenced by a delegation of American Quakers who visited London's notorious Newgate jail in 1813. Their report said that they had been horrified to find "blaspheming, fighting, dram-drinking, half-naked women" occupying part of the facility. A few months later, Fry visited the jail herself and found that women were being held in what she described as "filthy" conditions. From then on Fry campaigned for reform of the conditions under which women were confined, arguing that women should be treated "tenderly" and "with gentleness and sympathy so that they would submit cheerfully to the rules and cooperate willingly in their own reform."[51]

Fry formed the Ladies Association for the Reformation of Female Prisoners in Newgate and, later, the British Ladies Society for the Reformation of Female Prisoners. Fry's influence was also felt in the United States where concerned women banded together under the banner of prison reform in order to draw attention to the welfare of women prisoners.

Fry and her followers, including American feminist leader Dorthea Dix, believed that women are more likely than men to change and that appeals "to the heart" would be more effective with women offenders than with men. In her 1825 publication, *Observations on the Siting, Superintendence, and Government of Female Prisoners,* Fry provided concrete ideas on how women's prisons should be run. "Especially important for women," she argued, "were cleanliness, plain decent clothing, and warm, orderly surroundings."[52]

Mary Belle Harris

Another American woman reformer who was influenced by Fry was Mary Belle Harris (1874–1957). Harris, who was born in Pennsylvania, eventually became the first warden of the Federal Institution for Women in Alderson, West Virginia, when it opened in 1927. Harris had turned to a career in corrections only after already having been a teacher, social worker, and archeologist.

Harris came to Alderson after serving as superintendent of the Women's Workhouse on Blackwell Island (New York), as superintendent of the State Reformatory for Women at Clinton, New Jersey, and as assistant director of the section on Reformatories and Detention Homes for the U.S. War Department.

Known as a vocal advocate of correctional reforms and as an avid supporter of the reformation ideal, Harris believed that reformation and not punishment should be the primary focus of most correctional programs and institutions. Harris also believed that the criminality of women was largely the result of their social roles and specifically their economic dependency upon men. As a result, Harris advocated training programs that would permit women prisoners to become financially independent upon release. At Alderson, Harris oversaw the development of programs designed to break the cycle of dependency. Her work became widely known and served as a model for women's prisons throughout the nation.

Mary Belle Harris (1874–1957), the first warden of the Federal Institution for Women at Alderson, West Virginia. What historical role have women played in the development of the field of corrections?

Before retiring in 1941, Harris wrote a number of books describing her experiences in corrections. Among them are *I Knew Them in Prison* (1936) and *The Pathway of Mattie Howard to and from Prison: The Story of the Regeneration of an Ex-Convict and Gangster Woman* (1937).

Sanford Bates

Sanford Bates (1884–1972) was the first director of the Federal Bureau of Prisons (BOP), a position he held from 1930 until 1937. Before becoming the bureau's first director, Bates served in the Massachusetts state legislature, was commissioner of Penal Institutions in Boston from 1917 to 1919, and held the position of commissioner of the Massachusetts Department of Corrections. Bates became superintendent of Prisons, U.S. Department of Justice, in 1929. While in that post he prepared the legislation that established the Federal Bureau of Prisons in 1930.

During his tenure as director of the BOP, Bates authored a number of books including *Prisons and Beyond*.[53] In *Prisons*, Bates wrote that "the perplexing problem confronting the prison administrator of today is how to devise a prison so as to preserve its role of a punitive agency and still reform the individuals who have been sent there." Although the BOP began operations during the Great Depression, Bates believed in rehabilitation and in the value of inmate labor, thinking that work provided both a sense of purpose and a tool for reformation. Consequently he began Federal Prison Industries (FPI), and served as its chair from 1934 until his death in 1972. Bates created FPI programs involving work on prison farms, public lands, military bases, and highway construction, thereby largely avoiding the ire of labor unions that were seeking jobs for their

Sanford Bates (1884–1972), first director of the Federal Bureau of Prisons. Why did Bates believe in the value of inmate labor?

members. Under Bates's leadership, the U.S. federal prison system became one of the most progressive and adequately financed correctional systems in the world.

Bates believed that prisoner rehabilitation offered the best hope of protecting society from crime.[54] He also became president of the American Correctional Association and, after retiring as director of the BOP, served as executive director of the Boys Clubs of America, parole commissioner for New York State, and New Jersey state commissioner of Institutions and Industries. Today, the Sanford Bates Library, a collection of over 5,000 personal papers, books, and monographs, is housed at Sam Houston State University's George J. Beto Criminal Justice Center.

George J. Beto

Like Bates, George J. Beto (1916–1991), director of the Texas Department of Corrections from 1962 until 1972, believed in the goal of rehabilitation—promoting it as a goal to be achieved in prisons everywhere. Under Beto's leadership, the Texas prison system became known for its order and stability.

Beto began his career as a Lutheran minister, but became interested in reformation after serving on the Texas Prison Board, a volunteer organization that oversaw the entire state prison system. As a board member Beto initiated one of the earliest General Education Development (GED) testing programs for prisoners in the nation.[55] He also served for a time on the Illinois Parole Board, frequently visiting the Stateville Prison in Joliet, Illinois.

Beto drew special attention to the importance of preparing inmates for release back into society. On October 11, 1970, as he delivered the presidential address at the Centennial Congress of Correction of the American Correctional Association in Cincinnati, Beto told attendees:

> The future will bring an expanded use of pre-release programs. It is sheer folly to keep a man in prison two or three or four or five years and, at the termination of his sentence or upon parole, release him with a few dollars, a cheap suit, and the perfunctory ministrations of the dismissing officer. To an even greater degree, the future will witness programs which devote themselves to easing the inmate's transition from the most unnatural society known to man—prison society—to the free world. . . . We must blur the line between the institution and the community.[56]

George J. Beto (1916–1991), director of the Texas Department of Corrections from 1962 to 1972. What did Beto mean when he said, "We must blur the line between the institution and the community"?

During his tenure as director of the Texas Department of Corrections, Beto earned the nickname "Walking George" for his habit of showing up unannounced at prisons at any hour of the day or night and conducting on-the-spot inspections. He's best known, however, for having developed a program of prisoner management called the Texas control model. The control model built on the belief that inmates were in prison because of a lack of self-control, necessitating the need for strong external controls. The control model depended upon strict rule enforcement, and prisoners were punished for even minor infractions of prison regulations. Beto was convinced that discipline, order, and control were necessary in order to provide a safe environment for inmates to better themselves.[57] Before he left the position of director, Beto convinced the state legislature to enact a law requiring state agencies to buy prison-made goods, thereby greatly expanding opportunities for inmate labor in Texas.

The George J. Beto Criminal Justice Center at Sam Houston State University in Huntsville, Texas. How can corrections professionals benefit from academic study?

Other correctional reformers, including John Augustus, Alexander Maconochie, Sir Walter Crofton, and Zebulon Brockway, are discussed later in this text. One of the most recent innovations in corrections and criminal sentencing is the movement toward restorative justice, which is described in the Reflections on the Future piece at the end of this chapter, and in greater detail in Chapter 3.

REVIEW & APPLICATIONS

REFLECTIONS ON THE FUTURE *by Mark Umbreit*

Restorative Justice

University of Minnesota

Restorative justice is a victim-centered response to crime that provides opportunities for those most directly affected by crime—the victim, the offender, their families, and representatives of the community—to be directly involved in responding to the harm caused by the crime. Restorative justice is based upon values that emphasize the importance of providing opportunities for more active involvement in the process of offering support and assistance to crime victims; holding offenders directly accountable to the people and communities they have violated; restoring the emotional and material losses of victims (to the degree possible); providing a range of opportunities for dialogue and

problem solving among interested crime victims, offenders, families, and other support persons; offering offenders opportunities for competency development and reintegration into productive community life; and strengthening public safety through community building.

Restorative justice policies and programs are known to be developing in nearly every state, including a growing number of state and county justice systems that are undergoing major systemic change. Restorative justice is also developing in many other parts of the world, including numerous European countries, Australia, New Zealand, and South Africa. In recent years, restorative justice practices and/or policies have

been endorsed by the American Bar Association (victim–offender mediation and dialogue), the European Council, and the United Nations.

The principles of restorative justice draw upon the wisdom of many indigenous cultures from throughout the world, most notably Native American culture within the United States and Aboriginal/First Nation culture in Canada. These principles are also deeply rooted in the ancient values of Judeo-Christian culture, which have emphasized crime as being a violation against people and families, rather than the state." Many examples are found in the Old and New Testaments of the Bible of the responsibility of offenders to directly repair the harm they caused to individuals, representing a breach in the Shalom community."

Specific examples of restorative justice include crime repair crews, victim intervention programs, victim–offender mediation and dialogue; family group conferencing, peacemaking circles, victim panels that speak to offenders, sentencing circles, community reparative boards before which offenders appear, offender competency development programs, victim empathy classes for offenders, victim-directed and citizen-involved community service by the offender, community-based support groups for crime victims, and community-based support groups for offenders. As the oldest and most widely developed expression of restorative justice, with more than 25 years of experience and numerous

studies in North America and Europe, victim–offender mediation and dialogue programs currently work with thousands of cases annually through more than 300 programs throughout the United States and more than 1,200 in Europe.

There have been more than 60 empirical studies of restorative justice dialogue programs (primarily victim–offender mediation but also a smaller number of studies of family group conferencing). Findings have included high levels of victim and offender satisfaction with the process and outcome, greater likelihood of successful restitution completion by the offender, greater perceptions of fairness, reduced fear among victims, and reduced frequency and severity of further criminal behavior.

About the Author

Mark Umbreit, PhD, is a professor at the University of Minnesota, School of Social Work. He is the founding director of the Centre for Restorative Justice & Peacemaking as well as the National Restorative Justice Training Institute. Dr. Umbreit has more than 30 years of experience as a mediator, trainer, and researcher and has authored six books and more than 140 articles, book chapters, and monographs in the field of restorative justice and mediation. His most recent books are *The Handbook on Victim Offender Mediation: An Essential Guide for Practice & Research* (San Francisco: Jossey-Bass, 2001) and *Facing Violence: The Path of Restorative Justice & Dialogue* (Monsey, NY: Criminal Justice Press, 2003).

SUMMARY

1 Corporal, or physical, punishments were the most common response to crime for centuries before criminals began to be incarcerated.

2 Criminal punishments of the past generally consisted of flogging, branding, mutilation, exile, transportation, and public humiliation.

3 Torture of all kinds was used during the Middle Ages in an effort to gain confessions. Torture was justified by the belief that guilty knowledge was properly the property of the king or the state, and that exceptional means could be used to recover it.

4 Many reformers based their ideas on Enlightenment principles, including the use of reason and deductive logic to solve problems. They laid the groundwork for the use of imprisonment as an alternative to traditional punishments.

5 Beginning in the mid-1700s, a number of correctional reformers fought the use of corporal punishments and sought to introduce more humane forms of punishment. Among those reformers were Cesare Beccaria, Jeremy Bentham, and John Howard.

KEY TERMS

corporal punishments, *p. 40*
bridewell, *p. 50*

utilitarianism, *p. 55*
hedonistic calculus, *p. 56*

QUESTIONS FOR REVIEW

1 What are corporal punishments? What has been the purpose of corporal punishments throughout history? List and describe at least four corporal punishments used in the past for criminal offenders .

2 Describe the major criminal punishments used throughout history. Which ancient civilization provided the earliest evidence that physical punishment is part of Western society tradition?

3 What role did torture play in the application of corporal punishments? How was the use of torture justified?

4 What cultural developments contributed to the creation of prisons as an alternative to corporal punishments?

5 Which important thinkers discussed in this chapter adapted principles born of the Enlightenment and applied them to the field of law and corrections? Describe the contributions each made to the field.

THINKING CRITICALLY ABOUT CORRECTIONS

Corporal Punishment

In 1994 Michael Fay, an American teenager convicted of spray-painting parked cars, was flogged in Singapore. The flogging (called *caning* because it was done with a bamboo rod) sparked an international outcry from opponents of corporal punishment. In this country, however, it also led to a rebirth of interest in physical punishments—especially for teenagers and vandals.

The last official flogging of a criminal offender in the United States took place in Delaware on June 16, 1952, when a burglar was tied to a whipping post in the state's central prison and was given 20 lashes. Since then, no sentencing authority in this country has imposed whipping as a criminal punishment, and most jurisdictions have removed all corporal punishments from their statutes. Moreover, corporal punishment, other than capital punishment, is now forbidden in U.S. prisons under the Eighth Amendment. Amnesty International, however, reports that whipping is still in use in parts of the world for certain kinds of prisoners.

After the Fay flogging, lawmakers in eight states introduced legislation to institute whipping or paddling as a criminal sanction. Mississippi legislators proposed paddling graffitists and petty thieves, Tennessee lawmakers considered punishing vandals and burglars by public caning on courthouse steps, the New Mexico Senate Judiciary Committee examined the feasibility of caning graffiti vandals, and Louisiana looked into the possibility of ordering parents (or a correctional officer if the parents refused) to spank their children in judicial chambers. So far, none of the proposals has become law.

1. Would a return to corporal punishments, in the form of whipping or paddling, be justified for some offenders? Why or why not?

2. Might paddling be appropriate for some juvenile offenders? Why or why not?

3. Do you think that any state legislatures will eventually pass legislation permitting the paddling or whipping of criminal offenders? Why or why not?

Capital Punishment

Proponents frequently cite deterrence as a benefit of the death penalty. Some studies refute this contention. When confronted with such studies, proponents sometimes respond that execution "will definitely deter the executed offender." They also argue that death is the only thing that the offender really "deserves."

1. How would you respond to the proponents' first argument?

2. How would you respond to the proponents' second argument?

ON-THE-JOB DECISION MAKING

Counseling

You are a parole officer for the state corrections system. You are so burdened with paperwork that you rarely get out of the office to see any of your 200 clients—even though you are supposed to make regular home visits.

While you are shuffling papers one day, one of your clients, Bob Boynton, knocks at your door. It is time for him to make his monthly report. You tell him to have a seat, and you ask him the usual questions: "Have you been in trouble with the law since I saw you last?" "Are you still working?" "Are you paying your bills on time?"

Before you finish the interview, Boynton says, "You know, I'm never going to get anywhere this way. I need a better education. The time I spent in prison was wasted. They didn't teach me anything. I need to learn a skill so that I can make more money. If I can't earn better money I won't be able to pay my bills—and I'm afraid that I'll be tempted to get into the drug business again. I don't want to do that!"

You tell Boynton that there are a number of training schools in the area that can teach him a skill. Some of the computer classes offered at the local community college, you've heard, can lead to jobs paying decent wages. Boynton says, "I don't have a high school diploma. I can't get into the college. I'll never learn computers. I'm just too old. Besides, I need to work with my hands."

You go through the list of schools and training centers in the area, but Boynton raises an objection to each one. You sense that Boynton is trying to transfer responsibility for his success or failure to you. What should you do to get him to take responsibility for himself, yet provide support and guidance for his efforts?

Dispute Resolution

As a newly assigned assistant warden, you are responsible for discipline within your correctional facility. During your initial meeting with the warden, he said that your predecessor had a well-earned reputation among the inmate population as one who unfailingly sided with the correctional staff in all disputes between staff and inmates, no matter how egregious the staff member's behavior. Warden Cowen specifically asked you to establish yourself as a fair and impartial arbiter to reduce inmate concerns of injustice in dispute resolution.

An incident on your second day on the job presents you with a dilemma that even Solomon might be at a loss to resolve. Correctional Officer Tim Dashe is a six-year veteran with absolutely no record of abusive behavior toward inmates. In fact, during your transitional briefing into this job, your predecessor cited Dashe as one of the stalwarts on your staff, particularly praising his professionalism, maturity, good judgment, and reliability.

Inmate Deon Kussick has been incarcerated for 13 years without a single blemish on his record. Quiet, mature, and intelligent, Kussick is considered one of the "go-to" inmates when the administration needs cooperation from the prisoners to resolve a problem.

Inexplicably, Dashe and Kussick got into a fight this morning. A real knock-down drag-out, the fight is now the buzz of conversation among both the prisoner population and the correctional staff. Not surprisingly, tension is rising between the prisoners and the staff as both elements back "their" man and claim that the other man was responsible for the fight.

While it is clear that something is amiss, both Dashe and Kussick are closemouthed about the reason or reasons behind the fight. Their vague explanations are of the "It was just one of those things" variety. Obviously, though, there is a significant point of contention between the two men that, unless resolved, might lead to another confrontation. You can't resolve it, however, if you can't figure out what it is.

For you, the situation is particularly delicate, and the stakes are high. The correctional staff is waiting to see if you will back their fellow officer, the inmates are watching to see if you will be impartial in your handling of the incident, and the warden is evaluating your ability to handle a crisis. What you do will establish your reputation for loyalty (among the staff) and fairness (among the inmates) and serve as an indicator (to the warden) of your reliability and judgment.

One of the old-timers among the inmates sidled up a few minutes ago and, with a casualness that belied his intense interest, asked this simple question: "Watcha gonna do, chief?"

1. What are you going to do?

2. Why?

LIVE LINKS

at www.justicestudies.com/livelinks04

2–1 Do Criminal Punishments Prevent Unsafe Acts?

Making conduct criminal is society's ultimate condemnation. This article examines whether criminalization actually reduces the frequency of undesirable conduct.

2–2 Prison Use and Social Control

Allegations that incarceration undermines less coercive institutions of social control are largely speculative, according to this article, which reviews and evaluates the existing evidence that recent increases in incarceration have had such effects.

2–3 Preventing Crime: What Works, What Doesn't and What's Promising

This congressionally mandated evaluation of state and local crime prevention programs funded by the U.S. Department of Justice summarizes the conclusions reached by the authors in developing three separate lists of programs for which at least a minimum level of scientific evidence is available: what works, what doesn't, and what's promising.

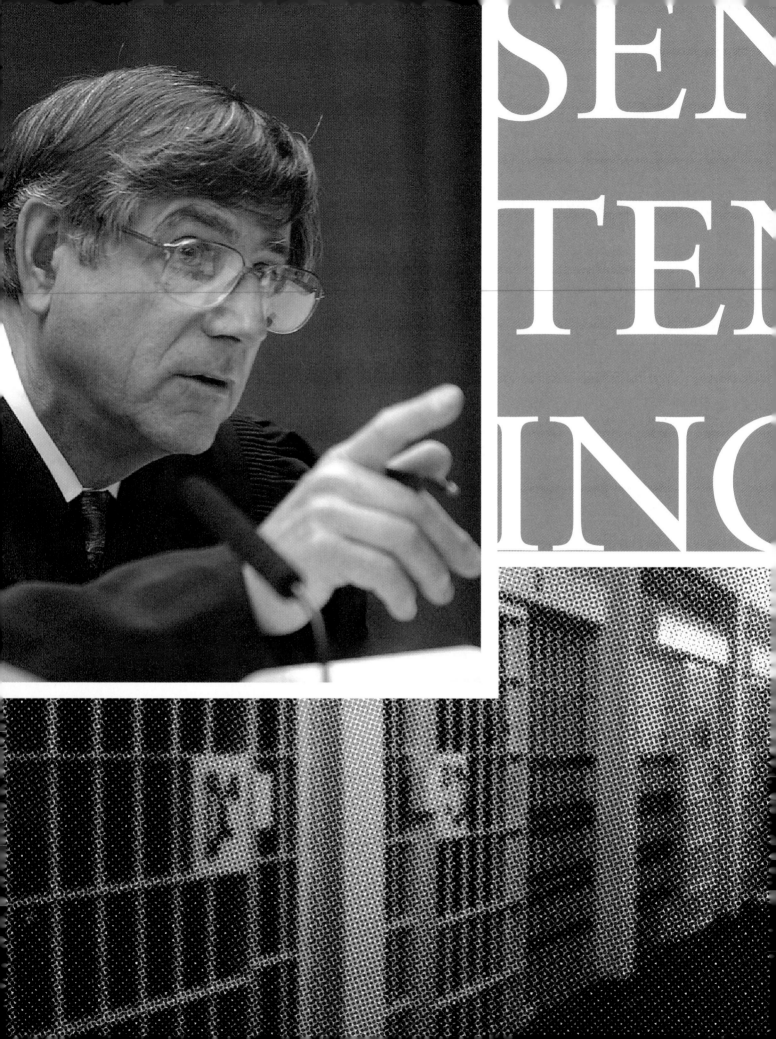

SEN
TEN
ING

SENTENCING

To Punish or to Reform?

CHAPTER OBJECTIVES

After completing this chapter you should be able to do the following:

1 Describe sentencing philosophy and identify the central purpose of criminal punishment.

2 Name the seven goals of criminal sentencing.

3 List and explain the sentencing options in general use today.

4 Explain what a model of criminal sentencing is and identify models in use today.

5 Describe three-strikes laws and their impact on the correctional system.

6 Identify and explain some major issues related to fair sentencing.

We will not punish a man because he hath offended, but that he may offend no more; nor does punishment ever look to the past, but to the future; for it is not the result of a passion, but that the same thing be guarded against in time to come.

—Seneca, the younger,
Roman Philosopher,
3 B.C.–A.D. 65

In 2004, in a decision that impacted sentencing practices in criminal cases nationwide (*Blakely v. Washington*), attorneys for Ralph Howard Blakely won a U.S. Supreme Court appeal on behalf of their client. Blakely had pled guilty to charges that he kidnapped his estranged wife, Yolanda, in 1998 and to charges of using a firearm during the commission of a felony. Yolanda was forced from her home in Grant County, Washington, by Blakely—who bound her with duct tape and forced her at knifepoint into a wooden box in the back of his pickup truck. While committing the crime, Blakely implored Yolanda to dismiss the pending divorce suit. When the couple's 13-year-old son, Ralphy, returned home from school, he encountered his father, and Blakely ordered him to follow in another car, threatening to harm Yolanda with a shotgun if he didn't. Ralphy escaped and sought help, but Blakely took Yolanda to a friend's house in Montana. He was arrested after the friend called police.

Ralph Howard Blakely in Grant County (Washington) Superior Court on March 22, 2005. Blakely, made famous for his role in the 2004 U.S. Supreme Court case of *Blakely* v. *Washington,* was sentenced to 35 years in prison for plotting to have his ex-wife and daughter murdered. What did the Court rule in *Blakely* v. *Washington?*

After Blakely pled guilty, prosecutors recommended a sentence within the standard range of 49 to 53 months, as set by sentencing guidelines in the state of Washington. Upon hearing Yolanda's description of the kidnapping, however, the judge determined that Blakely had acted with "deliberate cruelty" and sentenced him to 90 months in prison instead of the 53 months that state sentencing guidelines would have called for. Because that sentence was 37 months beyond the maximum, Blakely's lawyers objected. The judge then conducted a three-day bench hearing featuring testimony from Blakely, Yolanda, Ralphy, a police officer, and medical experts. When the hearing ended, the judge issued 32 findings of fact and concluded, "The defendant . . . used stealth and surprise, and took advantage of the victim's isolation. He immediately employed physical violence, restrained the victim with tape, and threatened her with injury and death to herself and others. He immediately coerced the victim into providing information by the threatening application of a knife. He violated a subsisting restraining order."

The judge kept the sentence at 90 months, but Blakely's attorneys appealed, claiming that the judge had sentenced their client inappropriately on the basis of facts not admitted in Blakely's guilty plea and that the judge had improperly assumed the role of a jury in determining those facts, thereby violating the Sixth Amendment to the Constitution. The U.S. Supreme Court agreed, holding, "Because the facts supporting petitioner's exceptional sentence were neither admitted by petitioner nor found by a jury, the sentence violated his Sixth Amendment right to trial by jury." The *Blakely* decision effectively invalidated sentencing plans that allow judges rather than juries to determine any factor that increases a criminal sentence, except for prior convictions. As you will learn later in this chapter, the decision necessitated revision of nearly a dozen state sentencing schemes and set the stage for a later court decision that made judicial adherence to federal sentencing guidelines largely voluntary.

A note about Blakely: In 2005 he was convicted of attempting to hire a hitman to kill his ex-wife and daughter and was sentenced to 35 years in prison by the same judge who had originally accepted his guilty plea on kidnapping charges.[1]

The Blakely case highlights the important role of sentencing in the justice process. **Sentencing** is a court's imposition of a penalty on a convicted offender. A **sentence** is the penalty imposed.

This chapter concerns itself with the nature, history, purpose, and philosophy of criminal sentencing. One of the most crucial issues surrounding sentencing is whether to punish or to reform. The punish-or-reform debate has a long history and continues to concern many people today. We turn now to an examination of the history of sentencing philosophy.

sentencing

The imposition of a criminal sanction by a sentencing authority, such as a judge.

sentence

The penalty a court imposes on a person convicted of a crime.

SENTENCING: PHILOSOPHY AND GOALS

Philosophy of Criminal Sentencing

Western society has a long tradition of punishing criminal offenders. Historically, offenders were banished, exiled, killed, or tortured. Corporal, or physical, punishments became common during the Middle Ages, replacing executions as the preferred penalty. Physical punishments such as flogging and mutilation, though severe in themselves, deterred rampant use of the death penalty. Eventually, as we shall see in later chapters, imprisonment and a variety of other sentencing alternatives replaced corporal punishments as criminal sanctions.

Contemporary sentencing of offenders is still intimately associated with historical notions of punishment. Crimes are frequently seen as *deserving* of punishment. We often hear it said that the criminal must "pay a debt to society" or that "criminals deserve to be punished." John Conrad puts it another way: "The punishment of the criminal is the collective reaction of the community to the wrong that has been done."[2] Conrad goes on to say, "It is the offender's lot to be punished."

Philosophers have long debated *why* a wrongful act should be punished. Many social scientists suggest that criminal punishment maintains and defends the **social order**. By threatening potential law violators and by making the lives of violators uncomfortable, they say, punishments reduce the likelihood of future or continued criminal behavior.

Still, one might ask, instead of punishing offenders, why not offer them psychological treatment or educate them so that they are less prone to future law violation? The answer to this question is far from clear. Although criminal sentencing today has a variety of goals, and educational and treatment programs are more common now in corrections, punishment still takes center stage in society's view. Some writers, such as Con-

social order

The smooth functioning of social institutions, the existence of positive and productive relations among individual members of society, and the orderly functioning of society as a whole.

A crowded city street. Many social scientists say that criminal punishments help maintain social order. What would a society without order be like?

revenge

Punishment as vengeance. An emotional response to real or imagined injury or insult.

rad, have suggested that society will always *need* to punish criminals because punishment is a natural response to those who break social taboos.[3] Others disagree, arguing that an enlightened society will choose instead to reform lawbreakers through humanitarian means.

The Goals of Sentencing

In July 2005, Nushawn Williams, an inmate at the Clinton Correctional Facility in Dannemora, New York, was denied parole. Williams was 22 years old in 1999 when he was sentenced to 4 to 12 years in prison for statutory rape and two counts of reckless endangerment. Williams, a convicted drug dealer from Chautauqua County, New York, had been accused of infecting as many as 103 teenage girls and young women with the AIDS virus in a series of drugs-for-sex encounters.[4] At trial, prosecutors were able to show that Williams had sex with the women while knowing he was HIV-positive. Williams, who kept a journal of his many "conquests," was originally charged with one count of reckless endangerment for each sexual encounter and with first-degree assault for each partner who subsequently became infected. The statutory rape conviction stemmed from his having had sex with a 13-year-old girl who later tested positive for the AIDS virus. During trial, prosecutor James Subjack told jurors, "It takes an individual with no regard for human life to do something like this." Williams is still in a New York prison as this book goes to press.[5]

The Williams case demonstrates a crucial component of contemporary sentencing philosophy: that people must be held accountable for their actions and for the harm they cause. From this perspective, the purpose of the criminal justice system is to identify persons who have acted in intentionally harmful ways and (where a law is in place) to hold them accountable for their actions by imposing sanctions. Seen this way, our justice system is primarily an instrument of retribution.

Sentencing, however, also has a variety of other purposes. As shown in Exhibit 3–1, the goals of sentencing are (1) revenge, (2) retribution, (3) just deserts (or the fact of deserving punishment), (4) deterrence, (5) incapacitation, (6) rehabilitation or reformation, and (7) restoration.

Revenge   One of the earliest goals of criminal sentencing was revenge. **Revenge** can be described as both an emotion and as an act in response to victimization. Victims sometimes feel as though an injury or insult requires punishment in return. When they act on that feeling, they have taken revenge.

While we think of vengeance as a primitive need, it can still play an important role in contemporary societies and even in modern justice systems. The "tit-for-tat" exchange of terrorist attacks for military incursions between the Palestinians and Israelis that is taking place as this book goes to press is one example of a highly charged emotional situation where calls for revenge seem to play an important—and sometimes guiding—role. Similarly, had the terrorists who perpetrated the 9/11 attacks been captured (instead of dying in the suicide attacks), there can be little doubt that many Americans would have sought revenge on the perpetrators through our justice system—as was done with Zacarias Moussaoui, the "twelfth highjacker," who was in jail at the time of the 9/11 attacks.

EXHIBIT 3–1	Goals of Criminal Sentencing

Goal	Rationale
Revenge	Punishment is equated with vengeance and involves an emotional response to criminal victimization.
Retribution	Punishment involves a "settling of scores" for both society and the victim.
	Victims are entitled to "get even."
Just deserts	Offenders are morally blameworthy and deserving of punishment.
	Punishment restores the moral balance disrupted by crime.
Deterrence	Punishment will prevent future wrongdoing by the offender and by others.
	Punishment must outweigh the benefits gained by wrongdoing.
Incapacitation	Some wrongdoers cannot be changed and need to be segregated from society.
	Society has the responsibility to protect law-abiding citizens from those whose behavior cannot be controlled.
Rehabilitation or reformation	Society needs to help offenders learn how to behave appropriately.
	Without learning acceptable behavior patterns, offenders will not be able to behave appropriately.
Restoration	Crime is primarily an offense against human relationships and secondarily a violation of a law.
	All those who suffered because of a crime should be restored to their previous sense of well-being.

Retribution Retribution involves the payment of a debt to both the victim and society and, thus, atonement for a person's offense. Historically, retribution was couched in terms of "getting even," and it has sometimes been explained as "an eye for an eye, and a tooth for a tooth." *Retribution* literally means "paying back" the offender for what he or she has done. Retribution is predicated on the notion that victims are *entitled* to reprisal.

Because social order suffers when a crime occurs, society is also a victim. Hence, retribution, in a very fundamental way, expresses society's disapproval of criminal behavior and demands the payment of a debt to society. It is not always easy to determine just how much punishment is enough to ensure the debt is paid.

Just Deserts Retribution is supported by many sentencing schemes today—although the concept is now often couched in terms of **just deserts** even though there is a difference between retribution and just deserts. The concept of just deserts de-emphasizes the emotional component of revenge by claiming that criminal acts are *deserving* of punishment, that offenders are *morally blameworthy,* and that they must be punished. In this way, just deserts restores the moral balance to a society wronged by crime.

Andrew von Hirsch, who identified the rationales underlying criminal punishment, says that when someone "infringes the rights of others . . . he deserves blame [and that is why] the sanctioning authority is entitled

retribution

A sentencing goal that involves retaliation against a criminal perpetrator.

just deserts

Punishment deserved. A just deserts perspective on criminal sentencing holds that criminal offenders are morally blameworthy and are therefore *deserving* of punishment.

to choose a response that expresses moral disapproval: namely, punishment."[6] Hence, from a just deserts point of view, justice *requires* that punishments be imposed on criminal law violators.

Of all the purposes of punishment that are discussed here, only retribution and just deserts are past oriented. That is, they examine what has already occurred (the crime) in an effort to determine the appropriate sentencing response.

Deterrence   A third goal of criminal sentencing is **deterrence**. Deterrence is the discouragement or prevention of crimes similar to the one for which an offender is being sentenced. Unlike retribution and just deserts, deterrence is future oriented in that it seeks to prevent crimes from occurring. Two forms of deterrence can be identified: specific and general.

Specific deterrence is the deterrence of the individual being punished from committing additional crimes. Long ago, specific deterrence was achieved through corporal punishments that maimed offenders in ways that precluded their ability to commit similar crimes in the future. Spies had their eyes gouged out and their tongues removed, rapists were castrated, thieves had their fingers or hands cut off, and so on. Even today, in some countries that follow a strict Islamic code, the hands of habitual thieves are cut off as a form of corporal punishment.

General deterrence occurs when the punishment of an individual serves as an example to others who might be thinking of committing a crime—thereby dissuading them from their planned course of action. The **pleasure-pain principle**, which is central to modern discussions of general deterrence, holds that actions are motivated primarily by the desire to experience pleasure and avoid pain. According to this principle, the threat of loss to anyone convicted of a crime should outweigh the potential pleasure to be gained by committing the crime.

For punishment to be effective as a deterrent, it must be relatively certain, swiftly applied, and sufficiently severe. *Certainty, swiftness,* and *severity* of punishment are not always easy to achieve. The crime funnel, described in Chapter 1, demonstrates that most offenses do not end in arrest, and most arrests do not end in incarceration. Although it may not be easy for all offenders to get away with crime, the likelihood that any individual offender will be arrested, successfully prosecuted, and then punished is far smaller than deterrence advocates would like it to be. When an arrest does occur, an offender is typically released on bail, and, because of an overcrowded court system, the trial, if any, may not happen until a year or so later. Moreover, although the severity of punishments has increased in recent years, modern punishments are rarely as severe as those of earlier centuries. Arguments over just how much punishment is enough to deter further violations of the criminal law rarely lead to any clear conclusion.

Incapacitation   Many believe that the huge increase in the number of correctional clients has helped lower the crime rate by incapacitating more criminals. Many of these criminals are behind bars, and others are on supervised regimens of probation and parole. **Incapacitation** restrains offenders from committing additional crimes by isolating them from free society. A recent report by the National Center for Policy Analysis, for example, observed that a "major reason for [the] reduction in crime is that crime has become more costly to the perpetrators. The likelihood of going to prison for committing any type of major crime has increased substantially."[7]

deterrence

The discouragement or prevention of crimes through the fear of punishment.

specific deterrence

The deterrence of the individual being punished from committing additional crimes

general deterrence

The use of the example of individual punishment to dissuade others from committing crimes.

pleasure-pain principle

The idea that actions are motivated primarily by a desire to experience pleasure and avoid pain.

incapacitation

The use of imprisonment or other means to reduce an offender's capability to commit future offenses.

The report claims that "the best overall measure of the potential cost to a criminal of committing crimes is *expected punishment*." Expected punishment, says the report, "is the number of days in prison a criminal can expect to serve for committing a crime." The center calculated expected punishment by multiplying the median sentence imposed for each crime by the probabilities of being apprehended, prosecuted, convicted, and sentenced. Crime rates are declining, says the report, because expected prison stays are significantly longer today than two decades ago for every category of serious crime.

According to the center, "Between 1980 and 1995, expected punishment more than doubled for murder and nearly tripled for rape. It increased by about three-fourths for burglary and larceny/theft and increased 60 percent for motor vehicle theft."

A number of studies have claimed to show that incapacitating offenders through incarceration is cost-effective. Such studies conclude that imprisoning certain types of offenders (especially career or habitual offenders) results in savings by eliminating the social costs of the crimes offenders would be likely to commit if they were not imprisoned. Those social costs include monetary loss, medical costs of physical injury, and time lost from work.

One of the most frequently cited studies attempting to quantify the net costs of incarceration was done by Edwin Zedlewski.[8] Zedlewski used a RAND Corporation survey of inmates in three states (Michigan, Texas, and California) to estimate the number of crimes each inmate would commit if not imprisoned. In the survey, the average respondent reported committing anywhere from 187 to 287 crimes annually just before being incarcerated. To calculate the cost associated with each crime, Zedlewski divided the total criminal justice expenditures in the United States by the total number of crimes committed in the United States. From this he concluded that the average crime "costs" $2,300. Multiplying $2,300 by the 187 crimes estimated to be committed annually by a felon, Zedlewski calculated that society saves $430,100 per year for each felon who is incarcerated. Figuring that incarceration costs society about $25,000 per prisoner per year, he concluded that prisons produce a cost–benefit return to society of 17 to 1 ($17 saved for every $1 spent)—leading him to strongly support increased incarceration.

Three years after Zedlewski's work, well-known criminologist John DiIulio performed a cost–benefit analysis using a survey of Wisconsin prisoners. The study, called "Crime and Punishment in Wisconsin," led to the conclusion that prisons saved taxpayers in Wisconsin approximately $2 for every dollar they cost.[9]

Studies such as those by Zedlewski and DiIulio are part of the growing field of correctional econometrics. **Correctional econometrics** is the study of the cost-effectiveness of various correctional programs and related reductions in the incidence of crime. Recent studies have identified a decreasing return associated with the expanded use of incarceration. In 2006, for example, the Washington State Institute for Public Policy conducted an econometric study of how state incarceration rates affect county crime rates in Washington. Institute researchers concluded that "a 10 percent increase (or decrease) in the incarceration rate leads to a statistically significant 3.3 percent decrease (or increase) in crime rates."[10] The study noted, however, that diminishing returns "begin to erode the crime reduction effects as incarceration rates are increased." Other research, also published in 2006, found that "the effect of prison growth on crime diminishes as the scale of imprisonment increases."[11] In fact, this second

correctional econometrics
The study of the cost-effectiveness of various correctional programs and related reductions in the incidence of crime.

THE OFFENDER SPEAKS

Well, here I am, about two and one-half years into my life sentence. The worst part so far for me has been the loneliness. I'm close to 3,000 miles away from my family. I really don't have anyone right now. I think my family is still digesting the fact that I'm in prison. I don't hear from them very often.

With all the time I have alone in my cell, my brain works overtime. I think about all the people I've hurt, whether physically, emotionally, or financially. I think about my crime every day of my life. I took a human life. What makes a man do that? I don't really know. All I can remember is the anger I felt and the hurt feelings. I can remember my heart hurting so bad that I couldn't function normally anymore. I cried all the time and I couldn't eat or sleep. At first it was all jealousy and then it was anger and pain. I guess it all came to a head that night. I had never felt that much rage before in my life. When it was over, I was holding a lifeless body in my arms. I couldn't speak or move. All I could feel was my soul leaving my body. It was an emptiness that I hope I never feel again. It was like I too had died that night.

I remember the day I was sentenced like it was yesterday. I knew ahead of time what I was getting, but it didn't make it any easier. The tears, the stares, the looks, and the glares were all

directed in court from people who were once my friends. I was sentenced to life so I couldn't hurt anyone else ever again (or at least I thought so). I called home that afternoon to let my family know that it was all over and that I was going down for life. My father told me that my mom had tried to kill herself by putting a .38 in her mouth. By a miracle of God, my dad had called home at that very moment and talked her out of it. She was so depressed about me, plus she was addicted to painkillers because she had so many back operations. I wanted so much to comfort her, but I couldn't. I didn't know how.

I remember the time I saw my father cry. It was a day I'll never forget. It was a day or two after I was arrested and a week before I was extradited to Arizona when he came to visit me in the county jail in Pennsylvania. I was so nervous. We hadn't talked in years. He didn't like me much at all because I had disappointed him so many times over the years. I couldn't blame him. I was a failure in his eyes as well as mine. I walked down the hallway to where my father was sitting. I sat down in a chair and looked at him through the glass that separated us. He looked so broken and so sad. We picked up the phones and started to talk. The tears just started to run down his face. I had a lump in

my throat so that I couldn't swallow. My heart was bleeding inside and the pain was unbearable to see a rock of a man crumble before me because of what I had done. I wanted to end my life right there. My father didn't deserve what I was putting him through. He tried so hard to be a good father. He was strict but fair. I know it wasn't easy for him. I was his stepson. All through my childhood, he never treated me like less than his own son. As I looked into my father's eyes, I wished that he could hug me and I could cry too.

I guess I should thank God for letting me live for 31 years. I tried to destroy myself so many times with drugs, alcohol, and suicide attempts. In a way, prison has saved my life. I would have died at a young age from drugs or alcohol, or maybe the suicide attempts would have worked sooner or later. I'm just thankful I was able to overcome the demons in my life. I'm a better person now. I'm responsible, caring, and able to be kind. I guess that's all part of growing up, and that's what I've done the past few years. I still have a long way to go, but it's a start.

George Killian, #82256
ASPC-Eyman Complex, Meadows Unit
Florence, Arizona

---

study stated that "when the incarceration rate reaches a certain point (the inflection point), a further increase in prison population actually produces an increase in crime."

rehabilitation

The changing of criminal lifestyles into law-abiding ones by "correcting" the behavior of offenders through treatment, education, and training.

reintegration

The process of making the offender a productive member of the community.

Rehabilitation or Reformation The goal of **rehabilitation** or reformation is to change criminal lifestyles into law-abiding ones. Rehabilitation has been accomplished when an offender's criminal patterns of thought and behavior have been replaced by allegiance to society's values. Rehabilitation focuses on medical and psychological treatments and on social skills training, all designed to "correct" the problems that led the individual to crime.

A subgoal of rehabilitation is **reintegration** of the offender with the community. Reintegrating the offender with the community means mak-

As a goal of sentencing, incapacitation restrains offenders from committing more crimes by isolating them from society. Does this threat of social isolation encourage law-abiding behavior?

ing the offender a productive member of society—one who contributes to the general well-being of the whole.

Rehabilitation, which became the focus of American corrections beginning in the late 1800s, led to implementation of indeterminate sentencing practices (soon to be discussed), probation, parole, and a separate system of juvenile justice. During the 1970s, however, rehabilitation came under harsh criticism. As American society experienced disruptions brought about by economic change, the decline of traditional institutions, and fallout from the war in Vietnam, conservatives blamed the rehabilitative ideal for being too liberal, and liberals condemned it for providing an unfair basis for coercive action against disenfranchised social groups.[12] About the same time, an influential and widely read study by Robert Martinson, which evaluated rehabilitation programs nationwide, reported that few, if any, produced real changes in offender attitudes.[13] Dubbed the "nothing works doctrine," Martinson's critique of rehabilitation as a correctional goal led some states to abandon rehabilitation altogether or to de-emphasize it in favor of the goals of retribution and incapacitation. In other states, attempts at rehabilitation continued but were often muted.

Today, some governments and private organizations are reembracing rehabilitation, emphasizing treatment and education. According to Francis T. Cullen and Paul Gendreau, it is time to give the rehabilitative ideal a second chance. They call for *reaffirming rehabilitation*. "Many [rehabilitative] programs fail to work," say Cullen and Gendreau, "because they either are ill-conceived (not based on sound criminological theory) and/or have no therapeutic integrity (are not implemented as designed)." "We would not be surprised," they write, "if young children turned out to be illiterate if their teachers were untrained, had no standardized curriculum, and met the children once a week for half an hour."[14] Until recently, contend Cullen and Gendreau, many correctional treatment programs were in such a state.

Other writers hold that continued efforts at rehabilitation are mandatory for any civilized society. "In order to neutralize the desocializing potential of prisons," says Edgardo Rotman, "a civilized society is forced into rehabilitative undertakings. These become an essential ingredient of its correctional system taken as a whole. A correctional system" with no "interest in treatment," says Rotman, "means . . . de-humanization and regression."[15]

Rehabilitation typically implies the notion of treatment, in the belief that offenders who receive appropriate counseling, psychological treatment, psychiatric intervention, or drug therapy will be less prone to repeat criminality. California's Proposition 36, officially known as the Substance Abuse Crime Prevention Act of 2000 (SACPA), is indicative of the return to rehabilitation now occurring. Passed by the state's voters in 2000, it became effective on July 1 of that year. The law's purpose, stated in Section 3(c), is to "enhance public safety by reducing drug-related crime and preserving jails and prison cells for serious and violent offenders, and to improve public health by reducing drug abuse and drug dependence through proven and effective drug treatment strategies." It seeks to accomplish that goal by mandating probation for any person convicted of a nonviolent drug possession offense, and it requires participation in, and completion of, proven and effective community-based treatment programs as a condition of probation. According to some estimates, approximately 37,000 offenders will be diverted from the California correctional system and into treatment programs as a result of the new law.[16]

restoration

The process of returning to their previous condition all those involved in or affected by crime—including victims, offenders, and society.

restorative justice

A systematic response to wrongdoing that emphasizes healing the wounds of victims, offenders, and communities caused or revealed by crime.

victim-impact statement

A description of the harm and suffering that a crime has caused victims and survivors.

Restoration   In recent years, a new goal of criminal sentencing, known as **restoration**, has developed. **Restorative justice** is based on the belief that criminal sentencing should involve restoration and justice for all involved in or affected by crime.

Advocates of restorative justice (or, as some agencies refer to it, *community justice* or *reparative justice*) believe that crime is committed not just against the state but also against victims and the community. Restorative justice is especially concerned with repairing the harm to the victim and the community. Harm is repaired through negotiation, mediation, and empowerment rather than through retribution, deterrence, and punishment. A restorative justice perspective allows judges and juries to consider **victim-impact statements** in their sentencing decisions. These are descriptions of the harm and suffering that a crime has caused victims and their survivors. Also among the efforts being introduced on behalf of victims and their survivors are victim assistance and victim compensation programs.

Advocates of restorative justice believe not only that the victim should be restored by the justice process but also that the offender and society should participate in the restoration process. To this end, efforts at restoration emphasize, as well as victims' rights and needs, the successful reintegration of offenders into the community. Another aspect of involving offenders in restoration is having them actively address the harm they have caused. The system strives to accomplish this by holding them directly accountable and by helping them become productive, law-abiding members of their community.[17] Restorative justice programs try to personalize crime by showing offenders the consequences of their behavior.

Restorative justice is based on the premise that since crime occurs in the context of the community, the community should be involved in addressing it. Particular restorative justice or community justice programs

Erich Parsons
Deputy Sheriff   Palm Beach County, Florida

Erich Parsons is deputy sheriff with the Palm Beach County Sheriff's Department in West Palm Beach, Florida. A 44-year-old Army veteran and grandfather of five, he attended Johnson Bible College in Knoxville, Tennessee, where he received a bachelor of arts degree, and has been an ordained minister since 1986. He has been with the department since 2000, working the midnight to 8 A.M. shift.

Deputy Parsons had no educational background in law enforcement. While working in his family's business in the late 1990s (as a glazier in the family glass factory), he tore his rotator cuff, and he says that during his stay in the hospital he became interested in the job.

"Part of my desire to move on to something of this caliber was the need for significance. I felt that even though I was comfortable where I was and who I was, I like challenges. I'm a kid from the streets—grew up fast. So my penchant was to reach youth, and the training I took in theology was youth ministry–specific. I felt that my greater outreach perhaps would be those individuals in the county level as opposed to the state level, that the street kids needed more than just the church setting."

On a typical day, Deputy Parsons will handle unresolved issues from the previous shift; handle new arrests, fingerprints, and photographs; "and try to maintain order as we're doing all that," he says.

I love my job," he says. "My satisfaction is to know that I've done my job the best I was able to do, with what was available to me."

Even though I see the charges as they come in on the rough arrests, I try not to judge them. I know sometimes they're in bad situations. I try to maintain the dignity of an individual. Usually they reciprocate, and say, 'Thank you for treating me human.'

might make use of any of the following: (1) victim–offender mediation, (2) victim–offender reconciliation, (3) victim-impact panels, (4) restorative justice panels, (5) community reparative boards, (6) community-based courts, (7) family group conferences, (8) circle sentencing, (9) court diversion programs, and (10) peer mediation.

Restorative justice seeks to restore the health of the community, repair the harm done, meet victims' needs, and require the offender to contribute to those repairs. Thus, the criminal act is condemned, offenders are held accountable, offenders and victims are involved as participants, and repentant offenders are encouraged to earn their way back into the good graces of society. Restorative justice principles, developed by the Restorative Justice Consortium in 1998 and modified in 2002, are shown in Exhibit 3–2.

Not only is restorative justice having an impact on U.S. sentencing practices (Exhibit 3–3), but it is also becoming influential internationally. A 2002 United Nations report on the international acceptance of restorative justice principles in 35 member countries, for example, found that the concept has received considerable international attention by both practitioners and policymakers who view it as an alternative approach to more common criminal justice practices. According to the report, restorative justice is seen as offering promising concepts and options if taken as a supplement to established criminal justice practices. In general, says the report, restorative justice principles are seen as a complement to established justice systems and practices but not as a replacement for existing systems.[18]

EXHIBIT 3–2 Restorative Justice Principles

The following principles were developed by the Restorative Justice Consortium in order to provide a working basis for particular settings involved in the practice of restorative justice, including adult criminal justice, youthful offenders, schools, the workplace, prisons, and communities.

1. Principles relating to the interests of all participants
   a. Voluntary participation based on informed choice
   b. Avoidance of discrimination, irrespective of the nature of the case
   c. Access to relevant agencies for help and advice
   d. Ongoing access to various established methods of dispute resolution
   e. Processes that do not compromise the rights under the law of the participants
   f. Commitment not to use information in a way that may prejudice the interests of any participant in subsequent proceedings
   g. Protection of personal safety
   h. Protection of and support for vulnerable participants
   i. Respect for civil rights and the dignity of persons
2. Principles relating to those who have sustained harm or loss
   a. Respect for their personal experiences, needs, and feelings
   b. Acknowledgment of their harm or loss
   c. Recognition of their claim for amends
   d. Opportunity to communicate with the person who caused the harm or loss, if that person is willing
   e. Entitlement of victim to be the primary beneficiary of reparation
3. Principles relating to those who caused the harm or loss to others
   a. The opportunity to offer reparation, including before any formal requirement
   b. Reparation appropriate to the harm done and within the person's capacity to fulfill it
   c. Respect for the dignity of the person making amends
4. Principles relating to the interests of local community and society
   a. The promotion of community safety and social harmony by learning from restorative processes and the taking of measures that are conducive to the reduction of crime or harm
   b. The promotion of social harmony through respect for cultural diversity and civil rights, social responsibility, and the rule of law
   c. Opportunity for all to learn mediation and other methods of nonviolent resolution of conflict
5. Principles relating to agencies working alongside the judicial system
   a. Settlement outside the judicial system, except when this is unworkable due to the level of harm done,

the risk of further harm, issues of public policy, or disagreement about the critical facts
   b. Avoidance of unfair discrimination by ensuring that rights under the law are not compromised
   c. Provision of a wide and flexible range of opportunities to enable those who have caused loss or harm to make amends
6. Principles relating to the judicial system
   a. A primary goal of repairing harm
   b. Restorative requirements that are fair, appropriate, and workable
   c. Opportunities for community reparation or reparation to others who have suffered harm or loss when a restorative requirement is appropriate but victims decline to participate
   d. Enforcement of community reparation when a restorative requirement is appropriate but those who have caused harm or loss decline to participate
   e. Valuing of voluntary offers to repair harm or loss by those who have caused it
   f. Privileged status of content of restorative meetings, subject to public interest qualifications
7. Principles relating to restorative justice agencies
   a. Commitment to needs-based practice
   b. Safeguarding of legal human rights
   c. The participation of restorative justice practitioners who are seen to be neutral
   d. The participation of restorative justice practitioners who act impartially
   e. Maintenance of neutrality and impartiality by restorative justice practitioners who play no other role in the case
   f. Commitment of restorative justice agencies to keep confidential the content of restorative meetings, subject to the requirements of the law
   g. Participant commitment to confidentiality about the contents of restorative meetings
   h. Facilitation of the engagement of weaker parties in negotiation
   i. Upholding of respectful behavior in restorative processes
   j. Upholding of equality of respect for all participants in restorative processes, separating this from the harm done
   k. Engagement with good practice guidelines within the restorative justice movement
   l. Commitment by the agency to the use of constructive conflict resolution in general and of internal grievance and disciplinary procedures in specific
   m. Commitment to the accreditation of training, services, and practitioners
   n. Commitment to continually improved practice

Source: Restorative Justice Principles. Copyright © Restorative Justice Consortium.

| **EXHIBIT 3-3** | **American Correctional Association** |

Sentencing Policy Statement

The American Correctional Association actively promotes the development of sentencing policies that should:

- be based on the principle of proportionality. The sentence imposed should be commensurate with the seriousness of the crime and the harm done;
- be impartial with regard to race, ethnicity, gender, age, health, and economic status as to the discretion exercised in sentencing;
- include a broad range of options for custody, supervision, and rehabilitation of offenders;
- be purpose-driven. Policies must be based on clearly articulated purposes. They should be grounded in knowledge of the relative effectiveness of the various sanctions imposed in attempts to achieve these purposes;
- encourage the evaluation of sentencing policy on an ongoing basis. The various sanctions should be monitored to determine their relative effectiveness based on the purpose(s) they are intended to have. Likewise, monitoring should take place to ensure that the sanctions are not applied based on race, ethnicity, gender, age, health, or economic status;
- recognize that the criminal sentence must be based on multiple criteria, including the harm done to the victim, past criminal history, the need to protect the public,

and the opportunity to provide programs for offenders as a means of reducing the risk for future crime;
- provide the framework to guide and control discretion according to established criteria and within appropriate limits and allow for recognition of [the] individual;
- have as a major purpose restorative justice—righting the harm done to the victim and the community. The restorative focus should be both process and substantively oriented. The victim or his or her representative should be included in the "justice" process. The sentencing procedure should address the needs of the victim, including his or her need to be heard and, as much as possible, to be and feel restored to whole again;
- promote the use of community-based programs whenever consistent with public safety; and
- be linked to the resources needed to implement the policy. The consequential cost of various sanctions should be assessed. Sentencing policy should not be enacted without the benefit of a fiscal-impact analysis. Resource allocations should be linked to sentencing policy so as to ensure adequate funding of all sanctions, including total confinement and the broad range of intermediate sanction and community-based programs needed to implement those policies.

Source: Copyright © American Correctional Association.

SENTENCING OPTIONS AND TYPES OF SENTENCES

Options

Legislatures establish the types of sentences that can be imposed. The U.S. Congress and the 50 state legislatures decide what is against the law and define crimes and their punishments in the jurisdictions in which they have control. Sentencing options in wide use today include the following:

- fines and other monetary sanctions;
- probation;
- alternative or intermediate sanctions such as day fines, community service, electronic monitoring, and day reporting centers;
- incarceration; and
- death penalty.

As punishment for unlawful behavior, fines have a long history. By the fifth century B.C., Greece, for example, had developed an extensive system of fines for a wide variety of offenses.[19] Under our modern system of justice, fines are usually imposed as punishment for misdemeanors and infractions. When imposed on felony offenders, fines are frequently combined with another punishment, such as probation or incarceration.

Fines are only one type of monetary sanction in use today. Others include the court-ordered payment of the costs of trial, victim restitution,

Eye On Corrections

Reflections on Restorative Justice in Corrections

By Keith Martin

With the shift in corrections moving more toward community involvement and inclusion, restorative justice initiatives are becoming more commonplace in agencies both in the United States and internationally. By working with citizens to take a more positive role in halting the ripple effect of crime, agencies are turning to methods that focus more on making things right than on making people pay.

"It boils down to the fact that when people see [restorative justice], they recognize it as the right thing to do and common sense," says Ron Claassen, codirector of the Center for Peacemaking and Conflict Studies at Fresno State University. "I think that when [others] look at the idea of restoration versus retribution and think about what makes people change and makes a better community, it is obvious that restoration is the way to go."

Claassen adds that there are some misunderstandings about the true nature of restorative justice endeavors in corrections. For example, if individuals think of it as purely "a victim's program," then they are missing the bigger picture. While the victim's needs and concerns are a large piece of restorative justice, they are just one aspect.

"[Restorative justice approaches] should also address the larger community concerns," he says. "I think if [it] is labeled as a 'victim's program,' it's true—it is for the victim *and* for the community *and* for offenders."

Considering restorative justice as purely a program with the victim in mind is just one of many misconceptions in corrections, however.

KEEPING IN MIND PRINCIPLES, NOT ACTIONS

While the heart of any restorative justice initiative lies in aiding the community, the offender, and the victim, it is the principles behind the initiative, not the activity itself, that set it apart from other approaches in corrections.

"The question is, 'Is it being done to repair damage and make right, or is it being done to punish?'" says Claassen. "Inmates can do community service, for example, as a way to make them miserable or to help [themselves], the victim, and the community. Also, [the question should be asked] 'Does it establish or reestablish dignity and reintegrate those harmed?'"

If the answer to the latter question is yes, he adds, then it is a restorative approach. If the activity is to punish and have others see the punished in a negative light, then the answer is no. Sometimes correctional agencies will label an activity "restorative justice" because it gives back to the community but does not take into account the true principles that should be at the heart of such an initiative.

The reason for this mislabeling is not deliberate, says Kay Pranis, restorative justice planner for the Minnesota Department of Corrections. In her opinion, it is because the level of information on the subject can vary, so people assume something like community service is restorative, when it is only if it looks past the practice itself and to the philosophy.

Source: "Reflections on Restorative Justice," Keith Martin, The Corrections Connection Network News (CCNN). Eye on Corrections. www.corrections.com. December 24, 2001.

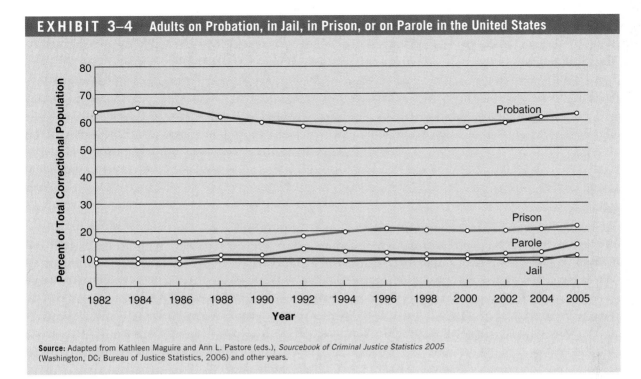

EXHIBIT 3–4 Adults on Probation, in Jail, in Prison, or on Parole in the United States

Source: Adapted from Kathleen Maguire and Ann L. Pastore (eds.), *Sourcebook of Criminal Justice Statistics 2005* (Washington, DC: Bureau of Justice Statistics, 2006) and other years.

various fees, forfeitures, donations, and confiscations. **Restitution** consists of payments made by a criminal offender to his or her victim as compensation for the harm caused by the offense. While fines are usually paid to the government, restitution may be paid directly to the victim (or paid to the court which turns it over to the victim). Some innovative courts have ordered offenders to donate specified amounts to specified charities in lieu of a fine.[20] Restitution is an example of a restorative justice sentencing option.

With a sentence of probation, the convicted offender continues to live in the community but must comply with court-imposed restrictions on his or her activity and freedom of movement. Alternative sanctions or intermediate sentencing options (which are discussed in detail in Chapters 4 and 5) usually combine probation with some other punishment, such as community service or house arrest with electronic monitoring. A sentence of incarceration, or total confinement away from the community, is used when the community needs to be protected from further criminal activity by an offender. The death penalty, or capital punishment, is the ultimate sentence. Exhibit 3–4 displays recent trends in four sentencing options.

Types of Sentences

A sentence is generally imposed by a judge. Sentencing responsibility can also be exercised by a jury or a group of judges, or it may be mandated by statute. **Mandatory sentences** are those that are required by law under certain circumstances—such as conviction of a specified crime or of a series of offenses of a specified type. Mandatory sentences may add prison time to sentences for offenders who carried weapons during the commission of their crimes, who used or possessed illegal drugs, or who perpetrated crimes against elderly victims. Such sentences allow judges no leeway in sentencing.

restitution

Payments made by a criminal offender to his or her victim (or to the court, which then turns them over to the victim) as compensation for the harm caused by the offense.

mandatory sentences

Those that are required by law under certain circumstances—such as conviction of a specified crime or of a series of offenses of a specified type.

presentence report (PSR)

A report, prepared by the probation department of a court, that provides a social and personal history as well as an evaluation of a defendant as an aid to the court in determining a sentence.

consecutive sentences

Sentences served one after the other.

concurrent sentences

Sentences served together.

model of criminal sentencing

A strategy or system for imposing criminal sanctions.

flat sentences

Those that specify a given amount of time to be served in custody and allow little or no variation from the time specified.

indeterminate sentence

A sentence in which a judge specifies a maximum length and a minimum length, and an administrative agency, generally a parole board, determines the actual time of release.

Even when there is no mandatory sentence, judges cannot impose just any sentence. They are still limited by statutory provisions. They also are guided by prevailing sentencing goals. A judge usually considers a **presentence report (PSR)**. This report, prepared by the probation department attached to a court, is a social and personal history as well as an evaluation of the offender. Finally, judges' sentencing decisions are influenced by their own personal convictions and characteristics.

Once the sentence is chosen, the judge must decide how it will be served, especially if more than one sentence is being imposed. Sentences can be consecutive or concurrent. **Consecutive sentences** are served one after the other. When a person is convicted of multiple offenses, a judge might impose, for example, a sentence of 10 years for one offense and 20 years for another. If the sentences are to run consecutively, the offender will begin serving the second sentence only after the first one expires. **Concurrent sentences** are served together. If the sentences in the example are to run concurrently, the 10-year sentence will expire when the offender has served one-half of the 20-year sentence. The offender will then need to serve the remainder of the 20-year sentence before being released. When multiple sentences are imposed, most are ordered to be served concurrently.

SENTENCING MODELS

A **model of criminal sentencing** is a strategy or system for imposing criminal sanctions. Sentencing models vary widely (see Exhibit 3–5). Over the past 100 years, a shift has occurred from what might be called a judicial model of sentencing to an administrative model. Judges generally have far less discretion in sentencing decisions today than they previously did. The majority of sentences imposed in American courts today follow legislative and administrative guidelines.

Sentencing in 19th-century America involved mostly fines, probation, and "flat" prison sentences. **Flat sentences** specify a given amount of time to be served in custody and allow little or no variation from the time specified. A typical flat sentence might be stated as "five years in prison." Flat sentences generally mean that an offender has to complete the sentence imposed and cannot earn an early release.

Indeterminate Sentencing

By the close of the 19th century, sentencing reform in the United States began replacing the flat sentence with indeterminate sentences.[21] At the time, the criminal justice system was coping with a rapidly expanding and increasingly diverse prison population, increased efficiency of police and courts, and other factors. Overcrowded prisons and the warehousing of inmates resulted.[22]

In an **indeterminate sentence**, the judge specifies a maximum length and a minimum length, within limits set by statute, and a parole board determines the actual time of release. The parole board's determination depends on its judgment of whether the prisoner has been reformed, has been cured, or has simply served enough time. An example of an indeterminate sentence is "5 to 10 years in prison." A second form of indeterminate sentencing requires the judge to specify only the maximum sentence length, with the associated minimum set by statute. Some states, for example, require an offender to serve as little as one-quarter of the sentence before becoming eligible for parole.

With an indeterminate sentence, discretion is distributed, not only among the prosecutor, defense counsel, and judge, but also to prison officials and the parole board, which have considerable influence over an offender's length of stay. Prison officials have discretion over the amount of **good time** an inmate earns, which can affect parole eligibility, the discharge date, or both. The parole board decides the actual release date for most inmates. The result is a system of sentencing in which few people understand or can predict who will be imprisoned and for how long.

Under indeterminate sentencing, punishments are made to fit the criminal rather than the crime. Proponents of indeterminate sentences assume that crime is a product of individual deviation from the norm and that rehabilitation can be achieved within a prison system designed to punish and not treat inmates. They also assume that prison personnel have the knowledge to impose treatment or to predict recidivism accurately enough to justify their discretion over when an inmate should be released. The use of indeterminate sentences has prompted numerous accusations of disparity in sentencing as well as protests from inmate groups, penologists, and other critics of the penal system. These protests have spurred a movement for sentencing reform.

good time
The number of days or months prison authorities deduct from a sentence for good behavior and for other reasons.

Determinate Sentencing

A **determinate sentence** (also known as a *fixed sentence*) specifies a fixed period of incarceration, which can be reduced for good time served. The term is generally used to refer to the sentencing reforms of the late 1970s. Determinate sentences are generally based on the incapacitation and deterrence goals of sentencing. The theory behind determinate sentencing is that criminals will be off the streets for longer periods of time. The other advantage, supporters say, is that prisoners know when they will be released. In most determinate sentencing models, parole is limited or is replaced by the use of good-time credits. With good time, inmates are able to reduce their sentences by earning credits. The amount of the reduction depends on the number of credits earned. Good-time credits can be earned by demonstrating good behavior and not being "written up" for violating prison rules. They can also be earned by participating in educational programs, community service projects, or medical experiments. The procedure for earning credits and the number that can be earned vary from state to state. Prison administrators generally favor determinate sentencing and good-time credits because they aid in controlling prison populations.

**determinate sentence
(also called *fixed sentence*)**
A sentence of a fixed term of incarceration, which can be reduced by good time.

Guideline Sentencing

As we have seen, the sentences that judges impose are regulated by law. As part of the movement to eliminate sentencing disparities, some states, as well as the federal government, have enacted sentencing guidelines for judges to follow. The guidelines fall into two categories.

Voluntary/Advisory Sentencing Guidelines Among the earliest guided sentencing innovations in the United States was the experiment with voluntary guidelines, also called *advisory guidelines*. These are recommended sentencing policies that are not required by law. Usually, they are based on past sentencing practices and serve as a guide to judges. Voluntary or advisory guidelines have had disappointing results, because they are often not enforced and are sometimes ignored. More important, the guidelines are voluntary; judges can simply ignore them. A review of

EXHIBIT 3-5   Sentencing Models

Determinate Sentencing

Sentencing to a fixed term of incarceration that may be reduced by good time. Usually, explicit standards specify the amount of punishment and a set release date, with no review by a parole board or other administrative agency. Postincarceration supervision may be part of the sentence.

Indeterminate Sentencing

Sentencing in which an administrative agency, generally a parole board, has the authority to release an incarcerated offender and to determine whether an offender's parole will be revoked for violation of the conditions of release. In one form of indeterminate sentencing, the judge specifies only the maximum sentence length (a fixed term); the associated minimum is automatically implied but is not within the judge's discretion. In the more traditional form of indeterminate sentencing, the judge specifies maximum and minimum durations within limits set by statute. The judge has discretion over the minimum and maximum sentences.

Presumptive Guidelines Sentencing

Sentencing that meets all the following conditions: (1) the appropriate sentence for an offender in a specific case is presumed to fall within a range authorized by guidelines adopted by a legislatively created sentencing body, usually a sentencing commission; (2) judges are expected to sentence within the range or provide written justification for departure; and (3) the guidelines provide for review of the departure, usually by appeal to a higher court. Presumptive guidelines may employ determinate or indeterminate sentencing structures.

Voluntary/Advisory Guidelines Sentencing

Recommended sentencing policies that are not required by law. They serve as a guide and are based on past sentencing practices. The legislature has not mandated their use. Voluntary/advisory guidelines may use determinate or indeterminate sentencing structures.

Mandatory Minimum Sentencing

A minimum sentence that is specified by statute for all offenders convicted of a particular crime or a particular crime with special circumstances (e.g., robbery with a firearm or selling drugs to a minor within 1,000 feet of a school). Mandatory minimums can be used in both determinate and indeterminate sentencing structures. Within an indeterminate sentencing structure, the mandatory minimum requires the inmate to serve a fixed amount of time in prison before being eligible for release with the approval of a parole board. Under a determinate sentence, the offender is required to serve a fixed amount of time in prison before being eligible for release.

all the major studies conducted on voluntary and advisory guidelines reveals low compliance by judges and, hence, little reduction in disparity.[23]

sentencing commission

A group assigned to create a schedule of sentences that reflect the gravity of the offenses committed and the prior record of the criminal offender.

Presumptive Sentencing Guidelines   By the early 1980s, states had begun to experiment with the use of presumptive sentencing guidelines. These models differ from determinate sentences and voluntary or advisory guidelines in three respects. First, the guidelines are developed, not by the legislature, but by a **sentencing commission** that often represents diverse interests, including private citizens as well as all segments of the criminal justice system. Second, the guidelines are explicit and highly structured, relying on a quantitative scoring instrument. Third, the guidelines are not voluntary or advisory. Judges must adhere to the sentencing system or provide a written rationale for departure.

The forces stimulating presumptive sentencing guidelines were the same as those that had driven the moves to determinate sentencing and voluntary or advisory guidelines: issues of fairness and prison crowding. These concerns provided the impetus for states to adopt guidelines, replace indeterminate sentencing with determinate sentencing, and abolish or reduce discretionary parole release. The first four states to adopt presumptive sentencing guidelines were Minnesota (1980), Washington (1981), Pennsylvania (1982), and Florida (1983).

The state of Washington's Sentencing Reform Act (SRA) of 1981 (as amended), for example, is based on a determinate sentencing model. The law mandated creation of a Sentencing Guidelines Commission, which developed a set of sentencing guidelines "to ensure that offenders who commit similar crimes and have similar criminal histories receive equivalent sentences."[24] The state's presumptive sentencing schedules, which apply to all felonies committed in the state after June 30, 1984, are structured "so that offenses involving greater harm to a victim and to society result in greater punishment." According to the Sentencing Guidelines Commission, "The guidelines apply equally to offenders in all parts of the state, without discrimination as to any element that does not relate to the crime or to a defendant's previous criminal record."

As is typically the case in presumptive sentencing states, Washington's guidelines specify a standard sentence range based on the seriousness of an offense combined with an offender's criminal history "score." In Washington State, a defendant's criminal history includes his or her prior adult felony convictions in any state or federal court or in another country and dispositions in juvenile court. Misdemeanors are not counted except when related to current convictions of felony traffic offenses (i.e., driving under the influence of alcohol or drugs may figure into a defendant's criminal history when felony convictions for crimes such as vehicular assault occur). Judges make use of forms provided by the state's sentencing commission in calculating an offender's score for sentencing purposes. Crimes representative of each "seriousness level" are shown in Exhibit 3–6.

As in other presumptive sentencing states, in Washington judges may sentence offenders outside the standard ranges found in the state's sentencing grid. Sentences that fall outside established guidelines, however, are not permitted if based solely on determinations of fact made by the sentencing judge—a limitation imposed by the U.S. Supreme Court in the 2004 case of *Blakely* v. *Washington,* with which this chapter opened. In 2005 Washington's sentencing law was changed to require that aggravating circumstances that might lead to sentencing enhancements be proved to a jury.

In 2000, Alabama became the most recent state to establish a sentencing commission. In creating the commission, the Alabama legislature identified its central functions as "establish[ing] an effective, fair, and efficient sentencing system for Alabama adult and juvenile criminal offenders which provides certainty in sentencing, maintains judicial discretion and sufficient flexibility to permit individualized sentencing as warranted by mitigating or aggravating factors, and avoids unwarranted sentencing disparities among defendants with like criminal records who have been found guilty of similar criminal conduct." "Where there is disparity," the

EXHIBIT 3–6   State of Washington: Representative Crimes by Level of Seriousness

Level of Seriousness	Representative Offense	Level of Seriousness	Representative Offense
XVI	Aggravated Murder in the First Degree[a]	V	Third Degree Child Molestation
XV	First Degree Murder Homicide by Abuse First Degree Malicious Explosion		First Degree Custodial Sexual Misconduct Domestic Violence Court Order Violation First Degree Extortion Persistent Prison Misbehavior
XIV	Second Degree Murder		Possession of a Stolen Firearm Stalking
XIII	Second Degree Malicious Explosion First Degree Malicious Placement of an Explosive	IV	Second Degree Arson Second Degree Assault
XII	First Degree Assault First Degree Rape		Bribing a Witness Counterfeiting Knowingly Trafficking in Stolen Property
XI	First Degree Manslaughter Second Degree Rape		Threats to Bomb

X	First Degree Child Molestation
	Indecent Liberties (with Forcible
	    Compulsion)
	First Degree Kidnapping
	Leading Organized Crime
		III	Third Degree Assault
			Second Degree Burglary
			Communication with a Minor for
			    Immoral Purposes
			Criminal Gang Intimidation

IX	Controlled Substance Homicide
	Inciting Criminal Profiteering
	First Degree RobberySexual Exploitation
	Vehicular Homicide, by Being Under
	    the Influence of Intoxicating Liquor or
	    Any Drug
			Harassment
			Intimidating a Public Servant
			Maintaining a Dwelling or Place for
			    Controlled Substances
			Manufacture, Deliver, or Possess with
			    Intent to Deliver Marijuana
			Patronizing a Juvenile Prostitute

VIII	First Degree Arson
	Deliver or Possess with Intent to Deliver
	    Methamphetamine
	Hit and Run—Death
	Second Degree Manslaughter
	First Degree Promoting Prostitution
	Vehicular Homicide, by the Operation of
	    Any Vehicle in a Reckless Manner
			Possession of Incendiary Device
			Possession of Machine Gun or Short
			    Barreled Shotgun or Rifle
			Tampering with a Witness

		II	First Degree Computer Trespass
			Create, Deliver, or Possess a Counterfeit
			    Controlled Substance
			Health Care False Claims
			Theft of Rental, Leased, or Lease-
			    Purchased Property (Valued at $1,500
			    or More)
			Unlicensed Practice of a Profession or
			    Business

VII	First Degree Burglary
	Drive-by Shooting
	Indecent Liberties (without Forcible
	    Compulsion)
	Involving a Minor in Drug Dealing
	Use of a Machine Gun in Commission of
	    a Felony		

VI	First Degree Incest Intimidating a Judge Intimidating a Juror/Witness Theft of a Firearm	I	Attempting to Elude a Pursuing Police Vehicle False Verification for Welfare Forged Prescription Taking a Motor Vehicle Without Permission Unlawful Use of Food Stamps

[a]Aggravated murder in the first degree is first-degree murder under certain circumstances. Among them are (a) the victim was a law enforcement officer or firefighter performing his or her official duties; (b) the defendant was serving a term of imprisonment in a state institution at the time of the homicide; (c) the defendant solicited another person to commit the crime for pay; etc. To learn the statutory elements of each of the offenses listed here, view Title 9 of the Revised Code of Washington (the state's criminal law) online at www.mrsc.org/rcw.htm. Visit the state of Washington Sentencing Guidelines Commission at www.sgc.wa.gov, where you can read the state's online adult sentencing guidelines manual. The manual contains a comprehensive list of all felonies defined by state law along with their location in the sentencing grid.

legislature noted, "it should be rational and not related . . . to geography, race, or judicial assignment."[25] In 2003, the legislature sharpened the commission's focus with passage of the Alabama SRA. The SRA called for (1) the development of voluntary sentencing guidelines; (2) the abolition of traditional parole and good-time credits for felons; and (3) the continued availability of a continuum of punishment options. The SRA tasked the commission with creating voluntary sentencing standards and presenting them to the legislature for approval—a process that has yet to be completed as this book goes to press.

Federal Sentencing Guidelines   In the early 1980s, the U.S. Congress focused its attention on disparity in sentencing.[26] Congress concluded that the sentencing discretion of federal trial judges needed boundaries. The resulting legislation, termed the Sentencing Reform Act (SRA) of 1984,[27] created the United States Sentencing Commission. The nine-member commission, first organized in October 1985, is a permanent body charged with formulating and amending national sentencing guidelines. The commission's guidelines apply to all federal criminal offenses committed on or after November 1, 1987.

Federal sentencing guidelines take into account a defendant's criminal history, the nature of the criminal conduct, and the particular circumstances surrounding the offense. Congress required that all federal trial judges follow the guidelines in their sentencing decisions. Deviations from the guidelines were permitted only when a judge provided a written justification setting forth specific reasons as to why a sentence outside of the range specified by the guidelines was appropriate.

Federal sentencing guidelines have been subject to change, and the commission may submit guideline amendments to Congress each year between the beginning of the regular congressional session and May 1. Suggested amendments automatically take effect 180 days after submission unless Congress rejects them.

Early challenges to the constitutionality of federal sentencing guidelines were resolved by the 1989 case of *Mistretta* v. *United States,* in which the U.S. Supreme Court upheld the 1984 SRA and ruled that Congress had acted properly in delegating authority to the U.S. Sentencing Commission in the creation of sentencing guidelines.

In addition to creating the U.S. Sentencing Commission, the SRA abolished parole for federal offenders sentenced under the guidelines. As a consequence, sentences imposed on convicted federal offenders today are essentially the sentences that will be served. Under federal law, however, inmates may earn up to 54 days of credit (time off their sentences) each year for good behavior.

The Legal Environment and Sentencing Guidelines   A number of U.S. Supreme Court cases focused on the authority that judges retain in deciding to depart from sentencing guidelines and on the application of **sentencing enhancements.** In 1994, in the case of *Nichols* v. *United States,* the Court held that "an uncounseled misdemeanor conviction," because no prison term was imposed, is valid when used to enhance punishment at a subsequent conviction. (An "uncounseled conviction" is one in which the defendant was not represented by an attorney.)

In the 2002 case of *United States* v. *Cotton,* the Court found that sentences imposed by a federal judge were not improper even though the judge based those sentences on a quantity of drugs that he had estimated and that had not been alleged in the original indictment brought against

sentencing enhancements

Legislatively approved provisions that mandate longer prison terms for specific criminal offenses committed under certain circumstances (such as a murder committed because of the victim's race or a drug sale near a school) or because of an offender's past criminal record.

the defendants. The *Cotton* defendants had been charged with conspiracy to distribute and to possess with intent to distribute a "detectable amount" of cocaine and cocaine base in the city of Baltimore. Under federal law, the penalty for such offenses is "not more than 20 years."[28] After the jury returned a finding of guilt, the judge made an independent finding of drug quantity (more than 500 grams of cocaine base) and then imposed enhanced penalties (up to life) as allowed under federal law. The judge's finding, the Court concluded, was based on "overwhelming and uncontroverted evidence" that the defendants "were involved in a vast drug conspiracy."

In the far-reaching case of *Apprendi* v. *New Jersey* (2000), however, the Supreme Court limited the fact-finding authority of state judges in sentencing decisions. The case involved Charles Apprendi, a New Jersey defendant who had pleaded guilty to unlawfully possessing a firearm—an offense that carried a prison term of 5 to 10 years under state law. Prior to imposing sentence, however, the judge found that Apprendi had fired a number of shots into the home of an African American family living in his neighborhood. The judge further determined that Apprendi had done so to frighten the family and to convince them to move. Statements made by Apprendi, said the judge, classified the shooting as a hate crime. The judge then applied a sentencing enhancement provision under New Jersey's hate crimes statute and sentenced Apprendi to 12 years in prison—2 years beyond the 10-year maximum authorized by statute for the weapons offense to which he had confessed. Significantly, the sentence was imposed without the benefit of a jury-based fact-finding process and with the judge alone making the determination that a hate crime had taken place. In overturning the state court's finding, the Supreme Court reasoned that Apprendi's due process guarantees were violated when the judge—and not a jury—made a factual determination that did not require proof beyond a reasonable doubt. In the words of the Court, "Under the Due Process Clause of the Fifth Amendment and the notice and jury trial guarantees of the Sixth Amendment, any fact (other than prior conviction) that increases the maximum penalty for a crime must be charged in an indictment, submitted to a jury, and proven beyond a reasonable doubt."

Blakely v. *Washington* (2004), discussed earlier in this chapter, built on the Court's holding in *Apprendi*. In *Blakely*, the Court ruled that no criminal sentence in *state* courts can be enhanced beyond the allowable maximum guideline for an offense unless the facts used to determine the enhanced sentence are found by a jury or the defendant waives the right to a jury or admits the facts in a guilty plea.

In 2007, in the case of *Cunningham* v. *California*, the U.S. Supreme Court found that California's determinate sentencing law (DSL) violated a defendant's right to trial by jury because it placed sentence-elevating fact finding within the province of judges. In that case, a judge following the requirements of the DSL had sentenced John Cunningham to a term of 16 years in prison based on a posttrial sentencing hearing in which he identified six aggravating factors and only one mitigating factor. Cunningham had earlier been found guilty of the continuous sexual abuse of a child under 14.

In 2005, in the combined cases of *United States* v. *Booker* and *United States* v. *Fanfan*, the U.S. Supreme Court turned its attention to the constitutionality of *federal* sentencing practices that made use of what it called "extra-verdict determinations of fact" in the application of sentencing enhancements. The combined cases raised two issues: (1) whether fact finding done by judges under federal sentencing guidelines violates the Sixth Amendment right to trial by jury, and (2) if so, whether the guidelines are themselves unconstitutional. Consistent with its findings in *Blakely,* the Court found that, on the first question, defendant Freddie Booker's drug trafficking sentence had been improperly enhanced under federal sentencing guidelines on the basis of facts found solely by a judge. Under a mandatory guidelines system, the Court said, a sentence cannot be increased based on facts found by a judge that were neither admitted by the defendant nor found by a jury. Consequently, Booker's sentence was ruled unconstitutional and invalidated. On the second question, the Court did not strike down the federal guidelines, as some thought might happen. Instead, it held that the guidelines could be taken into consideration by federal judges during sentencing but that they should no longer be regarded as mandatory. In effect, the combined decision in *Booker* and *Fanfan* made the federal sentencing guidelines merely advisory and gave federal judges wide latitude in imposing punishments. The result is that today federal judges must take the guidelines into account when sentencing, but they are no longer required to impose a sentence within the range prescribed by the guidelines. Congress is currently reconsidering federal sentencing law in light of *Booker.* In the meantime, some expect the federal courts to be flooded with inmates appealing their sentences.

Mandatory Minimum Sentencing

Mandatory minimum sentencing refers to the imposition of sentences required by statute for those convicted of a particular crime or a particular crime with special circumstances, such as robbery with a firearm or selling drugs to a minor within 1,000 feet of a school, or for those with a particular type of criminal history. By 1994, all 50 states had enacted one or more mandatory minimum sentencing laws,[29] and Congress had enacted numerous mandatory sentencing laws for federal offenders. Mandatory minimum sentencing rationales dominated the 1980s and early 1990s.

Many states have adopted sentence enhancements, usually the mandating of longer prison terms for violent offenders with records of serious crimes. Mandatory sentence enhancements aim to deter known and potentially violent offenders and to incapacitate persistent criminals through long-term incarceration.[30] These sentence enhancements have come to be known as *three-strikes laws* (and, in some jurisdictions, *two-strikes laws*).

Three-strikes laws vary in breadth. Some stipulate that both the prior convictions and the current offense must be violent felonies; others require only that the prior felonies be violent. Some three-strikes laws count only prior adult convictions; others permit consideration of juvenile adjudications for violent crimes. Under California's three-strikes law, an offender who is convicted of a qualifying felony and has two prior qualifying felony convictions must serve a minimum of 25 years. The law also doubles prison terms for offenders convicted of a second violent felony.[31]

Rationales Mandatory sentences have two goals—deterrence and incapacitation. The primary purposes of modest mandatory prison terms (e.g., three years for armed robbery) are specific deterrence for already-punished offenders, and general deterrence for prospective offenders. If the law increases the imprisonment rate, it also serves the goal of incapacitation, leaving fewer offenders free to victimize the population at large.

mandatory minimum sentencing
The imposition of sentences required by statute for those convicted of a particular crime or a particular crime with special circumstances, such as robbery with a firearm or selling drugs to a minor within 1,000 feet of a school, or for those with a particular type of criminal history.

Mandatory sentencing laws are often passed in reaction to public outcries against especially violent or well-publicized criminal acts. Does mandatory sentencing fulfill the goals of deterrence and incapacitation?

The intent of three-strikes (and even two-strikes) laws is to incapacitate selected violent offenders with very long terms—25 years or even life.

Mandatory sentencing laws have become highly politicized. By passing mandatory sentencing laws, legislators can convey that they deem certain crimes especially grave and that people who commit these crimes deserve, and can expect, harsh sanctions. Such laws typically are a rapid and visible response to public outcries following heinous or well-publicized crimes.

Impact Mandatory sentencing has had significant consequences that deserve close attention. Among them are its impact on crime and the operations of the criminal justice system. The possibility that the consequences will be different for different groups of people also bears examination.

Crime Evaluations of mandatory minimum sentencing have focused on two types of crimes—those committed with handguns and those related to drugs (the offenses most commonly subject to mandatory minimum penalties in state and federal courts). An evaluation of the Massachusetts law that imposed mandatory jail terms for possession of an unlicensed handgun concluded that the law was an effective deterrent of gun crime, at least in the short term.[32]

However, studies of similar laws in Michigan[33] and Florida[34] found no evidence that crimes committed with firearms had been prevented. An evaluation of mandatory sentence enhancements for gun use in six large cities (Detroit, Jacksonville, Tampa, Miami, Philadelphia, and Pittsburgh) indicated that the laws deterred homicide but not other violent crimes.[35] An assessment of New York's Rockefeller drug laws was unable to support their claimed efficacy in deterring drug crime in New York City.[36]

The Criminal Justice System The criminal courts rely on a high rate of guilty pleas to speed case processing and thus avoid logjams. Officials can offer inducements to defendants to enter these pleas. At least in the short term, mandatory sentencing laws may disrupt established plea-bargaining patterns by preventing a prosecutor from offering a short prison term (less than the new minimum) in exchange for a guilty plea. However, unless policymakers enact the same mandatory sentences for several related crimes, prosecutors can usually shift strategies and bargain on charges rather than on sentences.

Michael Tonry, a criminal justice scholar, has summarized the findings of research on the impact of mandatory sentencing laws on the criminal justice system. He concluded that mandatory sentencing laws:

- do not achieve certainty and predictability because officials circumvent them if they believe the results are unduly harsh;
- are redundant in requiring imprisonment for serious cases because the offenders in such cases are generally sentenced to prison anyway;
- are arbitrary in the sentences they require for minor cases; and
- may occasionally result in an unduly harsh punishment for a marginal offender.[37]

Most two- and three-strikes laws leave judges no discretion to deviate from the sentences dictated by legislatures. Another central feature of such laws is the extraordinary length of the prison terms they require. Offenders serving life sentences in California and North Carolina under such legislation, for example, become eligible for parole only after serving 25 years, those in New Mexico after 30 years, and those in Colorado after 40 years. Three-strikes laws in some states mandate life without the possibility of parole. Two- and three-strikes laws came about in response to public concerns about crime and the growing belief that many serious offenders were being released from prison too soon.[38] Proponents view such legislation as the best way to deal with the persistent, serious violent offender—the proverbial three-time loser.

Two- and three-strikes laws are a form of **habitual offender statute**. Although habitual offender laws have been on the books in a number of jurisdictions since at least the 1940s, the older laws were often geared to specific types of prior offenses, such as crimes of violence, sex offenses, or crimes perpetrated with guns. Moreover, most early habitual offender laws allowed enhanced sentences but did not make them mandatory as does two- and three-strikes legislation.[39]

habitual offender statute

A law that (1) allows a person's criminal history to be considered at sentencing or (2) makes it possible for a person convicted of a given offense and previously convicted of another specified offense to receive a more severe penalty than that for the current offense alone.

THREE-STRIKES MODELS— WASHINGTON AND CALIFORNIA

During the 1990s, 26 states and the federal government enacted new habitual offender laws that fell into the three-strikes category.[40] Washington State was the first of those to do so.[41] California soon followed with a considerably broader version of the three-strikes law. As those laws were being implemented, people debated the impact they would have on the criminal justice systems of those states. Proponents predicted the laws would curb crime and protect society by warehousing the worst offenders for a long time. Opponents argued that defendants facing lengthy mandatory sentences would be more likely to demand trials, slowing the processing of cases, and that more offenders would serve long terms of incarceration, ballooning prison populations already at crisis levels in many states.[42]

Although they were enacted within months of each other amid the same "three strikes and you're out" rallying cry, and they count many of the same offenses as strikes, the Washington and California laws differ in three important ways. First, in Washington all three strikes must be for felonies specifically listed in the legislation. Under the California law, only the first two convictions must be from the state's list of "strikeable" crimes (which include most violent offenses and many drug offenses); *any* subsequent felony can count as the third strike. Second, the California law contains a two-strikes provision, by which a person convicted of any felony after one prior conviction for a strikeable offense is to be sentenced to twice the term he or she would otherwise receive. There is no two-strikes provision in the Washington law. Third, the sanctions for a third strike differ. The Washington statute requires a life term in prison without the possibility of parole for a person convicted for the third time of any of the "most serious offenses" listed in the law. In California a "third-striker" has at least the possibility of being released after 25 years.[43]

California's law came under attack for the seeming ease with which offenders who commit relatively minor crimes can be sentenced to prison for a long time. The law, however, found a powerful ally in the Supreme Court. In 2001, for example, the Ninth U.S. Circuit Court of Appeals ruled in *Andrade* v. *Attorney General of the State of California*[44] that two consecutive 25-year-to-life sentences imposed on a California man who was twice caught shoplifting videotapes from a Kmart constituted cruel and unusual punishment under the Eighth Amendment to the U.S. Constitution. The offender, Leandro Andrade, 37, had been in and out of state and federal prisons since 1982. In January 1982, Andrade had been convicted of a misdemeanor theft offense and was sentenced to 6 days in jail with 12 months' probation. He was arrested again in November 1982 for multiple counts of first-degree residential burglary. He pleaded guilty to at least three of those counts, and in April of the following year he was sentenced to 120 months in prison. In 1988, Andrade was convicted in federal court of transporting marijuana, and he was sentenced to eight years in federal prison. In 1990, he was convicted in state court for a misdemeanor petty theft offense and was ordered to serve 180 days in jail. In September 1990, he was again convicted in federal court for transporting marijuana and was sentenced to 2,191 days in federal prison. In 1991, he was arrested for a state parole violation—escape from federal prison. He was formally paroled from prison in 1993.

Before his case went to trial, Andrade admitted stealing the videotapes, telling police that he had been addicted to heroin since 1977 and wanted to sell the videos so that he could buy drugs. The prosecutor decided to charge Andrade with two counts of "petty theft with a prior conviction." In California, such a charge is called a "wobbler" because it can be punishable either as a misdemeanor or as a felony. The prosecutor chose to charge Andrade with a felony, and he was convicted, resulting in the two consecutive 25-year sentences. It was that conviction and sentence that, upon appeal, led to the Ninth Circuit Court's 2001 ruling on Andrade's behalf.

On March 5, 2003, however, the U.S. Supreme Court overturned the lower court's finding and ruled that Andrade's two consecutive 25-year-to-life sentences did not violate the Eighth Amendment's proscription against cruel or unusual punishment.[45] In effect, the Court held that it is *not* cruel and unusual punishment to impose a possible life term for a conviction of a nonviolent felony committed by a defendant with a history of serious or violent convictions.

THE STAFF SPEAKS

I am a director and regional administrator for the state prison system, and I supervise nursing students in a locked ward with criminally insane clients. In addition, I'm a researcher for the National Commission on Correctional Health Care. The commission surveys prisons, jails, juvenile facilities, and immigration facilities all over the United States. I have directed teams in 29 states, in facilities ranging from 38 to 1,000 beds. Part of my job in prison is to consult with and transport clients to other countries, which have in the past included Spain, Portugal, Canada, Panama, and Venezuela.

I love this field and encourage students who want a challenge and a career that is interesting to give corrections, especially work with the criminally insane, a look. Every day and every interaction with our clients is different. No two days are alike, and no two situations are similar.

Dr. Roger Childers
Supervisor
Psychiatric Unit for the
    Criminally Insane
Bryce Hospital
Tuscaloosa, Alabama

In another 2003 case, *Ewing* v. *California*,[46] the U.S. Supreme Court upheld the conviction and sentence of Gary Ewing under California's three-strikes law. Ewing, who had a lengthy record of prior convictions, had received a 25-years-to-life sentence following his conviction for felony grand theft of three golf clubs. In writing for the Court, Justice Sandra Day O'Connor said that states should be able to decide when repeat offenders "must be isolated from society . . . to protect the public safety," even when nonserious crimes trigger the lengthy sentence.

In 2004, Californians voted down Proposition 66—a ballot initiative that would have changed the state's three-strikes law so that only specified serious or violent crimes could be counted as third strikes. Passage of the proposition would also have meant that only previous convictions for violent or serious felonies, brought and tried separately, would have qualified for second- and third-strike sentence increases.

California's three-strikes law remains firmly in place. In its current form, it punishes anyone who commits a third felony, regardless of its severity, with a mandatory sentence of 25 years to life if the first two felonies were violent or serious.

Impact on Local Courts and Jails

When three-strikes laws were first passed in Washington and California, some analysts projected a much greater impact on local criminal justice systems in California, because the California law had a much broader scope.[47] They predicted that California courts would be overwhelmed as defendants facing enhanced penalties demanded jury trials. The added time to process cases through trials and the reluctance of courts to grant pretrial release to defendants facing long prison terms, they said, would cause jail populations to explode as the number of jail admissions and the length of jail stays grew.

Early evidence from California supported these predictions. A review of 12,600 two- and three-strikes cases from Los Angeles, for example, showed that two-strikes cases took 16 percent longer to process and three-strikes cases 41 percent longer than nonstrike cases.[48] In addition, strikes cases were three times as likely to go to trial as nonstrike felonies and four times as likely as the same types of cases before the law took effect. This effect led to a 25 percent increase in jury trials as well as an

11-percentage-point rise in the proportion of the jail population awaiting trial, from 59 percent before the law was enacted to 70 percent. Furthermore, a survey of sheriff's departments showed that the pretrial detainee population in the state had grown from 51 percent of the average daily population before the three-strikes law to 61 percent by January 1, 1995.[49]

According to more recent data, however, at least some California counties are learning how to handle the changes brought about by the law. A recent survey of eight California counties with populations of more than 1 million identified several that were successfully disposing of two- and three-strikes cases early in the process.[50] In addition, data from the Los Angeles County Sheriff's Department suggest that the pace of strikes cases coming into that system may be slowing.[51]

Impact on State Prison Systems

The impact of the Washington and California laws on state corrections departments has not been as severe as projected. Planners in Washington had expected that 40 to 75 persons would be sentenced under three-strikes provisions each year. The actual numbers, however, have been much lower. During the first three years the law was in effect, only 85 offenders—not the 120 to 225 projected—were admitted to the state prison system under the three-strikes law.[52]

A similar overestimate was made of the impact the California law would have on prisons there. As of January 1, 2005, 7,574 three-strikes inmates were serving time in prisons run by the California Department of Corrections and Rehabilitation, and another 32,527 were serving time for second-strike convictions.[53] Even though the sheer number of cases affected by the law is significantly higher than that for any other state, the numbers are not as great as originally projected. Still, according to some experts, three-strikes laws may be having a real, but subtle, impact on the California prison system. Such laws, they say, funnel increasingly older persons into correctional institutions and ensure that they will remain there for a very long time. Between 1994 and 1999, for example, new felony admissions to California prisons of persons over 40 years in age increased from 15.3 percent to 23.1 percent.[54] The result is an inmate population that is getting older. The aging of America's inmate population, which has begun to concern policymakers across the country, is discussed in more detail in Chapter 12.

The Current Applicability of Three-Strikes Laws and Habitual Offender Statutes

According to the Washington, DC–based Sentencing Project, only a handful of states have convicted more than a hundred individuals using two- and three-strikes statutes—even though more than half of all states have such laws on the books. The Sentencing Project says that only Georgia, South Carolina, Nevada, Washington, and Florida are actually using three-strikes legislation "to any significant extent."[55]

There is also evidence of a movement away from mandatory minimum sentences in a number of jurisdictions where such sentences have been blamed for prison crowding and budgetary problems. In Louisiana, for example, where prison populations increased from 25,260 to 38,000 in the six years following the state's 1995 implementation of mandatory sentences, the legislature recently eliminated mandatory prison time for crimes such as residential burglary, Medicaid fraud, prostitution, theft

Talking about CORRECTIONS

SENTENCING TRENDS

Visit *Live Talk* at **Corrections.com** (www.justicestudies.com/talking04) and listen to the program "Sentencing Trends," which relates to ideas discussed in this chapter.

of a firearm, and possession of small amounts of controlled substances. "This [was] an attempt to bring under control a system that was bankrupting the state and was not reducing crime," said state senator Donald R. Cravins.

In similar legislative action, other states, including Connecticut, Indiana, and North Dakota, have eliminated some laws that required certain offenders to serve long prison terms without the possibility of parole. Likewise, in 2001, Mississippi passed a law establishing parole eligibility for nonviolent first-time offenders who have served only 25 percent of their sentences—reducing the figure from what had been a required 85 percent under previous law.[56]

The economic problems that have caused some states to use habitual offender statutes less frequently or to release repeat offenders early are present in almost all regions of the country. In 2002, for example, New York governor George Pataki proposed releasing 1,300 nonviolent drug offenders from the state's prisons. The governor said that the proposed releases would save the state of New York $28.7 million over the next fiscal year.[57] Some states have moved to release nonviolent and relatively minor drug offenders in order to address budgetary shortfalls in their correctional systems but have refused to shorten the sentences of habitual felons.

ISSUES IN SENTENCING

Many sentencing reforms have been an attempt to reduce disparity in sentencing and make the process more fair. The term **fair sentencing** or *fairness in sentencing,* has become popular in recent years. Although fair sentencing today often refers to fairness for *victims,* many suggest that any truly fair sentencing scheme must incorporate fairness for both victims and offenders. These are the issues related to fairness in sentencing:

- proportionality;
- equity;
- social debt; and
- truth in sentencing.

Proportionality

Proportionality is the sentencing principle that the severity of punishment should match the seriousness of the crime for which the sentence is imposed. To most people today, the death penalty would seem grossly disproportional to the offense of larceny—even if the offender had a history of such violations. However, this was not always the case. Larceny *was* punishable by death in medieval England. On the other hand, probation would seem disproportional to the crime of murder—although it is occasionally imposed in homicide cases.

Equity

Equity is the sentencing principle that similar crimes and similar criminals should be treated alike. The alternative to equity is *disparity,* in which similar crimes are associated with different punishments in different jurisdictions or in which offenders with similar criminal histories receive widely differing sentences. Disparity can also result from judicial discretion when judges hold widely different sentencing philosophies. In

fair sentencing
Sentencing practices that incorporate fairness for both victims and offenders. Fairness is said to be achieved by implementing principles of proportionality, equity, social debt, and truth in sentencing.

proportionality
The sentencing principle that the severity of punishment should match the seriousness of the crime for which the sentence is imposed.

equity
The sentencing principle that similar crimes and similar criminals should be treated alike.

a jurisdiction with wide leeway for judges to determine sentences, one judge might treat offenders very harshly while another may be lenient. Under such circumstances, now largely eliminated by sentencing reform, one burglar, for example, might receive a sentence of 30 years in prison upon conviction, but his partner in crime is merely put on probation simply because he appears before a more lenient judge.

As this book goes to press, the U.S. Sentencing Commission has recommended a change in federal sentencing practices because of what it perceives as a disparity in existing mandatory minimum sentences for crack and powdered cocaine.[58] Under current law, anyone convicted of possession with intent to sell 5 grams of crack cocaine receives a five-year mandatory minimum term of imprisonment—the same as someone convicted of the sale of 500 grams of cocaine powder. The federal Drug Abuse Act of 1986 created the basic framework of statutory mandatory minimum penalties currently applicable to federal drug trafficking offenses and established a 100-to-1 drug quantity ratio between powder and crack cocaine offenses for sentencing purposes. That ratio was based on beliefs that crack cocaine sales and use are associated with violent crime, that crack cocaine is highly addictive, and that children and young teens are especially attracted to crack cocaine use. Not everyone, however, agrees with those beliefs, and some point out that the 1986 law created a sentencing disparity that weighs more heavily on African Americans than other ethnic groups because African Americans are more likely to be involved in small-scale crack dealing.

To reduce what it perceives as existing disparities, the commission currently recommends increasing the drug quantity threshold for the five-year statutory minimum sentence for crack cocaine offenses from 5 grams to *at least* 25 grams. The change, if approved, would likely impact over 90 percent of crack cocaine offenders.

The commission's recommendations are controversial. Although such political heavyweights as President George W. Bush and Senators Orrin Hatch and Jeff Sessions have proposed making sentences for dealing in crack and powder more similar, the U.S. Department of Justice remains opposed to the change. The department continues to argue that crack cocaine is more dangerous than the powder form of the drug, that it is associated with urban crimes of violence, and that it is more addictive than powdered cocaine. The department also suggests that dealers in crack cocaine do more damage to society than those selling cocaine in powder form.[59]

Although only Congress can correct the disparity in the law, federal judges no longer need to blindly adhere to the 100-to-1 guideline ratio after the *Booker* case, discussed earlier in this chapter.

social debt

The sentencing principle that the severity of punishment should take into account the offender's prior criminal behavior.

Social Debt

Social debt is the sentencing principle that the severity of punishment should take into account the offender's prior criminal behavior. As we have seen, a number of laws designed to recognize social debt have recently been passed. Among them are three-strikes and two-strikes laws. Although there is considerable variation in such laws among states, the primary characteristic of these laws is that they "call for enhanced penalties for offenders with one or more prior felony convictions."[60] They require a repeat offender to serve several years in prison in addition to the penalty imposed for the current offense.

EXHIBIT 3-7 Average Prison Time Served Compared with Court Sentence in Florida, 1997–2004

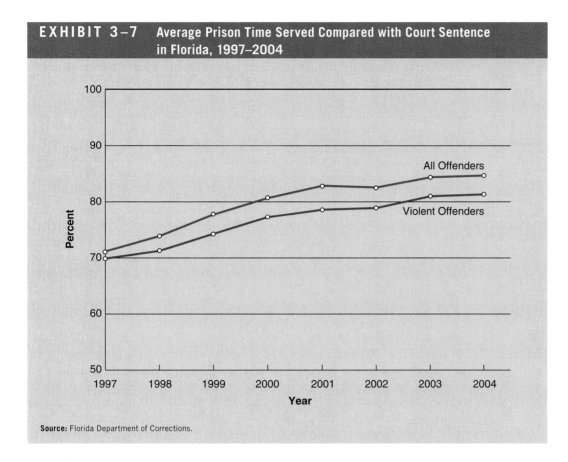

Source: Florida Department of Corrections.

Truth in Sentencing

Until the sentencing reforms of the 1970s, the laws of many states enabled convicted offenders to be released from prison long before they had served their full sentences. Inmates frequently had good time deducted from their sentences or time off for good behavior. *Gain time* could be earned for going to school, learning a trade, or doing volunteer work. Moreover, many states mandated routine parole eligibility after inmates had served one-quarter or even one-fifth of their sentences.

Recent truth-in-sentencing laws have changed such practices by requiring offenders to complete sentences very close to the ones they are given. **Truth in sentencing** requires an offender to serve a substantial portion of the sentence and reduces the discrepancy between the sentence imposed and actual time spent in prison (see Exhibit 3–7). The Violent Crime Control and Law Enforcement Act of 1994 includes a truth-in-sentencing provision. To qualify for federal aid under the act, a state must amend its laws so that an imprisoned offender serves at least 85 percent of his or her sentence before being released. Parole eligibility and good-time credits are generally restricted or eliminated in truth-in-sentencing laws.

By 1998, 27 states and the District of Columbia had met the 85 percent federal truth-in-sentencing requirement. Another 13 states had adopted truth-in-sentencing laws requiring certain offenders to serve a specified portion of their sentences.[61] Three states—Idaho, Nevada, and New Hampshire—require inmates to serve 100 percent of the minimum sentence they receive before they become eligible for release.

truth in sentencing

The sentencing principle that requires an offender to serve a substantial portion of the sentence and reduces the discrepancy between the sentence imposed and actual time spent in prison.

Broader Issues

Today's two main sentencing initiatives—guideline-based determinate sentencing and restorative justice—represent different attempts to achieve sentencing fairness. The two, however, appear to be inherently at odds with one another. That is because determinate sentencing requires a top-down approach in which an authoritative decision-making body imposes strict limits on the sentencing process, whereas restorative justice emphasizes community involvement at the grassroots level. "All this," say some experts, "suggests that, at its philosophical core, restorative justice appears to be incompatible with sentencing guidelines."[62]

One way of addressing the differences between these two approaches would be to seek greater community involvement in the development of sentencing guidelines. In fact, many states have encouraged local participation in the guideline-development process. Similarly, some guideline states encourage the use of local sentencing options such as community-based sanctions (which are discussed in more detail in Chapters 4 and 5). For example, North Carolina, a guideline state, assigns county officials the responsibility for developing and recommending local community sentencing options for certain categories of offenders.

Still, community sentencing may be appropriate only for relatively minor offenders, and traditional grid-based guidelines offer little leeway for sentencing offenders convicted of serious crimes. Some authors have suggested creation of a hybrid system of "restorative sentencing guidelines" to resolve the problem. Under the system, a new restorative sentencing option would be created and made applicable to less serious offenders. For such offenders, the traditional guideline grid, based on severity of offense and prior record, would not apply.

REVIEW & APPLICATIONS

REFLECTIONS ON THE FUTURE
America's Sentencing Future

by Richard S. Frase
University of Minnesota

Predicting the future is always a risky business, especially in the field of sentencing. Consider the revolutionary changes which have occurred in American sentencing during recent decades. Michael Tonry has observed that if a group of judges from the 1970s were able to time-travel to a national sentencing conference 25 years later, most "would be astonished at a quarter century's changes."[1] In 1970, sentencing generated little controversy or attention. There was almost universal agreement that judges and correctional authorities should have broad discretion in the imposition and execution of sentences, making highly individualized decisions based largely on assessments of the offender's need for, amenability to, and progress toward rehabilitation. By the early 1990s, political, media, legislative, and academic interest in sentencing had dramatically increased; rehabilitative goals had been abandoned or greatly de-emphasized, with sentencing based much more on the severity of the conviction offense; judicial and correctional discretion had been considerably reduced by means of sentencing guidelines, mandatory penalties, and parole abolition; and sentencing severity levels had increased dramatically. The early years of the new millennium witnessed major changes in sentencing procedures; in a series of cases the U.S. Supreme Court held that contested facts which increase the statutory maximum penalty, or which permit upward departure from the presumptive sentence under legally-enforced sentencing guidelines, must be submitted to the jury and proved beyond a reasonable doubt.[2]

What changes will the next quarter century bring? Although the particulars of future sentencing systems are difficult to predict, we can foresee changes in the fundamental elements of sentencing policy and practice which will determine—through complex interactions—each jurisdiction's sentencing future. These basic elements involve sentencing purposes, alternatives, structures, and severity. There is good reason to expect further change in each of these areas based on past changes, current trends, and the inevitable pendulum shifts in public, academic, and official thinking: We try one thing, get tired of it, and look for something new—or recycled.

Sentencing purposes will probably evolve into a hybrid approach combining elements of our current offense-based approach with greater attention to case- and offender-specific factors—in particular: (re)habilitation and (re)integration efforts, risk management, and restorative justice goals. Community-based rehabilitation programs never disappeared, and the public never stopped believing that offenders can and should be helped not to re-offend. There has recently been much greater awareness of the critical importance of integrating offenders into a stable, law-abiding life in the community—and, in particular, easing reentry of the huge number of incarcerated offenders released into the community every day. Offender risk assessment and management (in lieu of massive over-incarceration), will be facilitated by steadily improving prediction tools and behavior controls. Victim- and community-restorative justice programs will continue to enjoy broad public support. Nevertheless, offense-based sentencing goals—just deserts, general deterrence, norm-reinforcement, and sentencing uniformity—will also remain popular. The inherent conflict between offense-based and offender-based or restorative goals will be reconciled by hybrid models such as Norval Morris's theory of Limiting Retributivism: Just Deserts and other offense-based values set outer limits on maximum and minimum allowable sentencing severity, within which courts may pursue case-specific sentencing goals.[3]

Sentencing alternatives will continue to expand. Thirty years ago there were really only two alternatives: incarceration (in prison or a local jail), and probation (with few major conditions other than avoiding further crime). Since the late 1980s, more and more jurisdictions have experimented with "intermediate" sanctions such as intensive probation, day reporting centers, home detention, community service, and day fines. Since these measures are cheaper than incarceration and provide more control and punishment than probation, they are likely to be more and more heavily used. The pace of this growth will depend on whether states are willing to invest in staffing and other infrastructure to run these programs; many local jurisdictions do not have sufficient tax base and/or foresight to fund them. The specific types of intermediate sanctions used will depend in part on the development of new technologies and our willingness to employ them—not only predictive tools (including biological as well as traditional predictors), but also electronic monitoring and the blocking of chemical abuse and violence through medication or surgery.

Sentencing structures will further evolve. At present, most states still use some form of the 1970 indeterminate sentencing system described above, often combined with various mandatory penalty provisions and limited or no parole release discretion ("truth in sentencing").[4] Many states have successfully implemented guidelines (despite the unpopularity of the federal version). States have done so not only to bring greater fairness and rationality to sentencing policy and practice, but also because the increased uniformity of guideline sentencing allows states to better predict future prison populations, avoid overcrowding, set priorities in the use of limited resources, and promote the use of intermediate sanctions. Most guidelines systems implement some form of the Limiting Retributivism theory already noted, maintaining a degree of sentencing uniformity and proportionality while still leaving room, within the recommended sentence ranges or by departure or charging discretion, for sentences to reflect unusual offense details, offender characteristics, and the needs of victims and the community. Since no other existing or proposed sentencing system accommodates all of these important goals and values, it is likely that more states will create sentencing commissions to draft and implement guidelines. The additional sentencing-procedure requirements which the U.S. Supreme Court has recently imposed on legally enforced guidelines may cause some states to prefer voluntary guidelines, but other states will choose to retain or adopt the legally enforced version, since this approach seems likely to achieve more of the benefits of guidelines sentencing listed above.

Sentencing severity levels may not continue to rise so rapidly, but will probably remain high. Although adoption of a Limiting Retributive model, broader use of intermediate sanctions, or the implementation of sentencing guidelines often leads to stable or reduced overall severity levels, this result is not guaranteed—the upper limits of desert may be loosely defined, and intermediate sanctions may be targeted at low level offenders (thus *increasing* severity). In the federal system under guidelines prison populations have risen much faster than the national average, and the same is true in some states (especially those whose guidelines are voluntary or do not eliminate parole release discretion). At the close of the 20th century, the United States had the most punitive criminal justice system of any developed nation. But at least at the state level, prison population increases are slowing, and in many states they are stable or declining. More and more citizens and officials are recognizing that, particularly for non-violent drug and property offenders, the punitive binge of the 1980s and 1990s went too far. Unlike the federal government, states must balance their budgets. Moreover, correctional expenses represent a large portion of a state's budget and compete directly with popular state programs (correctional expenses are hardly even visible, in the huge federal budget). As states continue to struggle with budget crises (and gain little help from the deficit-ridden federal government), they will look for ways to reduce correctional expenditures and make better use of available resources. States will find they can achieve these goals through sentencing guidelines which reserve prison for violent and repetitive crimes, while encouraging broader use of intermediate sanctions for midlevel offenders.

NOTES

1. Michael Tonry, *Sentencing Matters* (New York: Oxford University Press, 1996), p. 6.
2. *Apprendi v. New Jersey*, 530 U.S. 466 (2000) (increased statutory maximum); *Ring v. Arizona*, 536 U.S. 584 (2002) (facts making defendant eligible for the death penalty); *Blakely v. Washington*, 542 U.S. 296 (2004) (facts permitting upward departure from guidelines sentence). See also *United States v. Booker*, 125 S. Ct. 738, 764–65 (2005) (voluntary guidelines are exempt from *Apprendi* and *Blakely* requirements).
3. Richard S. Frase, "Sentencing Principles in Theory and Practice," 22 *Crime & Justice: A Review of Research* 363 (1997).
4. Kevin R. Reitz, "Sentencing: Allocation of Authority," *Encyclopedia of Crime & Justice*, 2nd ed., Vol. 4 (New York: Macmillan Reference, 2002), p. 1400.

About the Author

Richard S. Frase is the Benjamin N. Berger professor of criminal law at the University of Minnesota Law School. He is the author or editor of 7 books and more than 60 articles, and is a frequent contributor to news stories on issues of contemporary criminal justice. His principal research interests are in the areas of sentencing and comparative criminal procedure.

SUMMARY

1 The philosophy underlying criminal sentencing is that people must be held accountable for their actions and the harm they cause. Western society has a long tradition of sentencing criminal offenders to some form of punishment. Many social scientists suggest that the central purpose of criminal punishment is to maintain social order.

2 The goals of criminal sentencing today are (1) revenge (2) retribution, (3) just deserts, (4) deterrence, (5) incapacitation, (6) rehabilitation or reformation, and (7) restoration.

3 Sentencing options in use today include fines and other monetary sanctions, probation, alternative or intermediate sentences, incarceration, and capital punishment.

4 A model of criminal sentencing is a strategy or system for imposing criminal sanctions. Sentencing models vary widely among the jurisdictions in the United States. These models include indeterminate sentences, determinate sentences, voluntary or advisory sentencing guidelines, presumptive sentencing guidelines, and mandatory minimum sentencing.

5 Recent laws have increased penalties for criminal offenses, particularly violent crimes, and for repeat offenders. Many such laws are three-strikes laws. The rationale for such laws is simple: Offenders convicted repeatedly of serious offenses should be removed from society for long periods of time. Many three-strikes laws mandate a life sentence for the third violent-felony conviction. Analysts of three-strikes laws predicted that courts would be overwhelmed as more defendants, facing enhanced penalties, demanded jury trials. The added time to process cases and the reluctance to grant pretrial release to defendants facing long prison terms, said analysts, would cause jail populations to explode as the number of admissions and the length of jail stays grew. The actual effects of the laws have been similar to the effects predicted but to a lesser extent.

6 *Fair sentencing* often refers to fairness for *victims.* Fair-sentencing advocates, however, suggest that any truly fair sentencing scheme must incorporate fairness for both victims and offenders. Issues related to fairness in sentencing are proportionality, equity, social debt, and truth in sentencing.

KEY TERMS

sentencing, *p. 71*
sentence, *p. 71*
social order, *p. 71*
revenge, *p. 72*

retribution, *p. 73*
just deserts, *p. 73*
deterrence, *p. 74*
specific deterrence, *p. 74*

general deterrence, *p. 74*
pleasure-pain principle, *p. 74*
incapacitation, *p. 74*
correctional econometrics, *p. 75*

QUESTIONS FOR REVIEW

1. Define *sentencing,* describe sentencing philosophy, and name the central purpose of criminal punishment.

2. What are the seven goals of criminal sentencing?

3. What are the major sentencing options in wide use in the United States today?

4. What is a sentencing *model*? How have American models of criminal sentencing changed over the past 100 years?

5. What are three-strikes (and two-strikes) laws? What consequences might three-strikes (and two-strikes) laws have for the criminal justice system and for the corrections subsystem?

6. What is fair sentencing? What are some of the major issues relating to fair sentencing today?

THINKING CRITICALLY ABOUT CORRECTIONS

Rehabilitation

Edgardo Rotman says, in *Beyond Punishment,* "Rehabilitation . . . can be defined tentatively and broadly as a right to an opportunity to return to (or remain in) society with an improved chance of being a useful citizen and staying out of prison."[63] Do you agree that offenders have a right to rehabilitation? Why or why not?

Mandatory Sentencing

Mandatory sentencing laws for drug possession offenses were initially hailed as the best method for toughening the government's response to the growing drug problem. Critics now complain that, in practice, mandatory sentencing rules lead to excessive punishments for many low-level offenders and to unwarranted leniency for the high-volume dealers who were the original targets of the new laws.

Further, critics contend that plea bargaining is the culprit. Faced with lengthy prison terms, many arrested bigtime dealers readily provide the names of numerous "little fish" in the drug distribution chain to prosecutors who are too quick to abandon prosecution of a single high-volume dealer in favor of procuring numerous convictions of lowlevel dealers.

Should mandatory sentencing laws be amended to prohibit plea bargaining in cases where the accused is charged with trafficking in quantities exceeding an established volume?

In view of the dramatic impact mandatory sentencing has had on prison population growth, should the sentences of current inmates be reviewed with an eye toward reducing, where appropriate, the sentences of the previously mentioned little fish?

ON-THE-JOB DECISION MAKING

Sentencing Fairness

Federal judge Max Hamlin frets over two sentences he is about to impose. Standing in front of him is Jack Edmunds. Edmunds has been convicted in federal court of selling 5 grams of crack cocaine, and federal sentencing guidelines require that he receive a mandatory minimum five-year prison sentence. Also awaiting sentencing is Richard Doggart, a defendant who has been convicted of selling 500 grams of powdered cocaine. Hamlin knows that the federal guidelines also require a minimum five-year prison term for Doggart. The judge is concerned, however, because he does not want to sentence Doggart to any more time than the mandatory minimum. However, Doggart sold 100 times as much cocaine (by weight) as Edmunds did, and the requirements of the federal sentencing law seem unfair to the judge. He knows that pharmacologists have said that there is no difference between crack and powdered cocaine. Hamlin is aware, however, that the U.S. Department of Justice says that crack is more dangerous than powder because it easily can be broken down and packaged into very small quantities—which dealers then sell to the most vulnerable members of society. Hamlin also knows that any deviation from the sentencing guidelines will require him to write a lengthy justification, and he has little time for any more writing. What should Judge Hamlin do?

Recidivism

You have spent the past six years as a counselor at a minimum-security state correctional facility. Your effectiveness has earned you a strong reputation throughout the Department of Corrections as a specialist in prerelease counseling, a program designed to prepare inmates for their return to society upon parole or completion of their sentence.

Lately, a series of highly publicized violent crimes has been committed by former inmates of the state's supermaximum-security facility. All were released recently upon completion of their sentences, and all had moved almost directly from their cell back to the criminal lifestyle that originally landed them in prison.

Hard-line correctional officers insist that because those incarcerated in the "supermax" are the worst of the worst, they cannot be trusted to behave during prerelease counseling. The safety risks such inmates represent, they say, make leaving them in their cells until the law requires they be set free the only sensible course of action. What happens after that, in the hard-liners' opinions, is both the decision and responsibility of the former inmate.

Reformers insist that immediate recidivism is the likely outcome of releasing inmates directly from a harsh, totally controlled lockdown environment. They call for significant transitional counseling as essential for helping inmates adjust to free society and also for defusing their angry urge to make society pay for the harsh life from which they are being released.

Both the governor and the commissioner of corrections face daily media demands to explain what the administration is going to do about this problem. In particular, the governor is under the gun because his opponent in the upcoming and hotly contested gubernatorial race has seized on this as an issue that demonstrates "this governor's inability, or unwillingness, to take the tough steps necessary to protect the good citizens of our state."

You have been asked to speak at a meeting to develop potential courses of action to address this problem. The meeting will be chaired by the corrections commissioner, and various wardens, assistant wardens, and senior correctional specialists from throughout the state will attend. It is likely but not yet confirmed that the governor will also attend.

1. What issues will you address?

2. How might you resolve the conflict between the need to protect counselors and staff from the often violent behavior of supermax inmates and the need to provide this critical prerelease counseling to these troubled inmates?

3. How would you respond to hard-line COs who contend that what happens after release is not their problem?

LIVE LINKS

at www.justicestudies.com/livelinks04

3–1   Thirty Years of Sentencing Reform

The purpose of this essay is to inform the debate on race, crime, and justice by critically evaluating recent empirical research examining the effect of race/ethnicity on sentence severity and by searching for clues to the contexts or circumstances in which race/ethnicity makes a difference. Forty recent and methodologically sophisticated studies investigating the linkages between race/ethnicity and sentence severity are reviewed; included are 32 studies of sentencing decisions in state courts and 8 studies of sentence outcomes at the federal level.

3–2   Reconsidering Indeterminate and Structured Sentencing

No single, widely shared vision of what sentencing and corrections should be about has emerged to replace indeterminate sentencing. This report describes the ideas of leading practitioners and scholars representing a broad cross section of points of view concerning the purposes, functions, and interdependence of sentencing and corrections policies.

3–3 Felony Sentencing in State Courts

This link provides statistics describing adults who have been convicted of felonies and sentenced in state courts. The data were collected through a nationally representative survey of 300 counties in 2002. Within the 12 reported offense categories are the number and characteristics (age, sex, race) of offenders who were sentenced to prison, jail, or probation.

PART TWO
COMMUNITY CORRECTIONS

Part Two examines what happens to con-

victed offenders, which includes diversion, probation, and intermediate sanctions. Diversion is the suspension of formal criminal proceedings before conviction in exchange for the defendant's participation in treatment, counseling, or other programs. Diversion recognizes that not all offenders should be formally prosecuted and subjected to the stigma of formal arrest, trial, and conviction.

As you will learn, diversion has its supporters and critics. Supporters believe diversion is the first opportunity to give offenders individualized assistance before they get too far down the path of crime and to resolve problems that lead to offending behavior. Critics argue that diversion tends to force people to give up some of their freedom without being tried and convicted, it violates the safeguard of due process, and it might actually produce more crime.

If diversion is not warranted or if an offender fails diversion, probation is often the next step in the correctional process. Probation is the conditional release of convicted offenders under community supervision. The degree of supervision depends on an offender's risk level. Some offenders pose no risk to the community. For them, checking in monthly at an automated probation kiosk may be all that is necessary. On the other hand, high-risk offenders require intensive face-to-face super-

vision and sometimes random drug testing, community service, and home confinement with remote-location monitoring.

Sanctions more punitive than probation but not as restrictive as incarceration are called intermediate sanctions. Drug court, economic sanctions, community service, day reporting centers, remote-location monitoring, residential centers, and boot camps are some intermediate sanctions.

Today, almost 45,000 probation officers investigate and supervise over 4.1 million adults under probation and intermediate sanctions. Probation officers are faced with enormous case investigation and supervision challenges that include increasing caseloads without new resources, deciding on what information to include in a presentence report, figuring out how to structure the report so it is read, and incorporating novel forms of technology into their day-to-day jobs.

Whether supervision is low level or intense, many probationers will violate its technical conditions. Others will commit new crimes. Tightening the offender's supervision without resorting to using an already overburdened system of incarceration is a challenge that probation officers face. The decision to revoke probation and incarcerate the offender is influenced by legal, social, political, and economic issues.

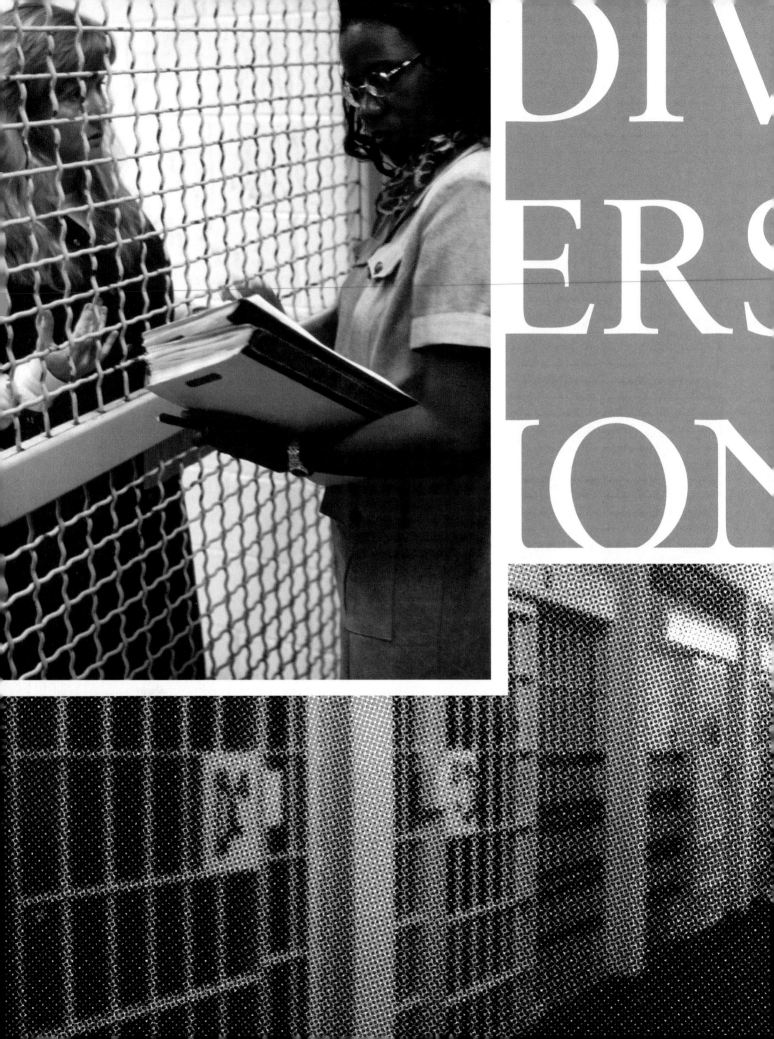

DIV
ERS
ION

DIVERSION AND PROBATION

How Most Offenders Are Punished

CHAPTER OBJECTIVES

After completing this chapter you should be able to do the following:

1 Define *diversion* and know its objectives.

2 Explain the rationales for diversion.

3 Give examples of stages at which diversion occurs in the criminal justice process.

4 Discuss diversion policy issues.

5 Define *probation* and know its goals.

6 Explain the reasons for using probation.

7 Describe some of the characteristics of adults on probation.

8 Explain the different ways that probation is administered.

9 Describe the measures used to evaluate probation.

10 Describe the investigation and supervision functions of probation officers.

11 Explain revocation hearings.

> *If all law violations were processed officially as the arrest-conviction-imprisonment model calls for, the system obviously would collapse from its voluminous caseloads and from community opposition.*
>
> —1976 National Advisory Commission on Criminal Justice Standards and Goals

On July 28, 2006, around 2:30 A.M., Oscar-winning actor-director Mel Gibson was traveling down the Pacific Coast Highway. According to a Los Angeles sheriff deputy, Gibson was traveling at speeds exceeding 85 mph. He had an open bottle of tequila at his side. A breathalyzer test showed his blood-alcohol level to be 0.12 percent (the legal limit is 0.08 percent). Gibson was charged with misdemeanor driving while having a blood-alcohol level of 0.08 percent or higher, driving with an open container of alcohol, and driving under the influence of alcohol.

As almost everyone has heard, Gibson launched into an expletive-laced rage about Jews and how they are responsible for all the wars in the world. According to the deputy, he also made crude remarks about her breasts.

Gibson later apologized for his comments and told ABC news anchor Diane Sawyer, "Now when you're loaded, you know, the balance of how you see things—it comes out the wrong way. I know that it's not as black and white as that. I know that you just can't, you know, roar about things in life. That it's wrong."[1]

Gibson was scheduled to be arraigned on September 28 but his lawyers arranged to move up his court appearance by more than a month to avoid a media frenzy with his plea. On October 17, Gibson pleaded *nolo contendere* (see Chapter 1 for the definition) to the charge of driving with an alcohol level of 0.08 percent or above. Two other misdemeanor charges, driving with an open container of alcohol and driving under the influence, were dropped as part of his plea agreement. Gibson could have been sentenced to six months in jail, but instead, Judge Lawrence Mira sentenced Gibson to three years' probation, and ordered him to attend "self-help" meetings five times a week for four and a half months and three meetings per week for another seven and a half months. Gibson was also ordered to complete a three-month alcohol education and counseling program for first offenders, and pay fines and fees totaling $1,608. Judge Mira also restricted Gibson's driver's license for 90 days. Gibson volunteered to make a public-service announcement about the hazards of drinking and driving, but Judge Mira did not make that a condition of his sentencing.

This chapter introduces two options to control offenders' behavior in the community, diversion and probation. Together they represent how most offenders are punished.

On July 28, 2006, around 2:30 A.M., actor and Oscar-winning director Mel Gibson (born Melvin Columcille Gerard Gibson on January 3, 1956) was stopped for speeding on the Pacific Coast Highway. The arresting officer found an open bottle of tequila at Gibson's side and a breathalyzer test showed his blood-alcohol level to be 0.12 percent (the legal limit is 0.08 percent). Almost three months later, Gibson pleaded *nolo contendere* to the charge of driving with an alcohol level of 0.08 or above. Two other misdemeanor charges were dropped as part of his plea agreement. Judge Lawrence Mira sentenced Gibson to three years' probation; ordered him to attend "self-help" meetings for one year and an alcohol education and counseling program for three months; ordered him to pay fines and fees totaling $1,608; and restricted his driver's license for 90 days. Is probation an effective criminal sanction?

OVERVIEW OF DIVERSION AND PROBATION

Mel Gibson's case demonstrates a number of points covered in this chapter. A majority of offenders are sentenced to probation. Conditions of probation routinely include paying fines, making restitution, counseling, and performing community service.

On January 1, 2006, 4,162,536 adults—1 of every 53 adults—were on probation in the United States.[2] The number of adults on probation is equivalent to the adult population of Wisconsin.

The typical probationer is a southern white male who has never married and has either completed high school or earned a general equivalency diploma (GED). He has been convicted of a felony and has at least one prior sentence, to probation or confinement. He has five or more probation conditions, and pays an average of $34 monthly in supervision fees plus monetary restitution to his victim. At least 40 percent of probationers are ordered to undergo substance abuse treatment.

However, the face of probation is changing. Using new laws that prohibit people from maintaining a building where drugs are sold or used, federal judges are ordering probation for companies found guilty of violating federal law. On June 13, 2001, a company called *Barbecue of New Orleans* pleaded guilty to violating federal crack-house laws. The company had leased a building known as the State Palace Theater for raves, or dance parties that feature extensive use of Ecstasy and other drugs. Since 1995, federal investigators had linked the raves held at the State Palace Theatre to numerous overdoses, and to the death of a 17-year-old girl in 1998. Drug Enforcement Administration (DEA) agents bought 13 grams of Ecstasy at eight raves at the theater in 2001. The court did not shut down the raves but ordered that the Barbecue of New Orleans be placed on probation. The company was also fined $100,000 and ordered to stop the distribution of drug paraphernalia, including pacifiers, inhalers, and dust masks, at raves on its premises.

This chapter introduces you to two areas of corrections that most offenders first experience—diversion and probation. Diversion occurs *before* trial. Probation occurs *after* a person has been convicted. Exhibit 4–1 shows how these two processes can occur in the criminal justice system. Because offenders can be diverted one or more times before they are tried, convicted, and sentenced to probation, we discuss diversion first.

DIVERSION

Diversion has been defined as "the halting or suspension, before conviction, of formal criminal proceedings against a person, [often] conditioned on some form of counterperformance by the defendant,"[3] and this is the definition we will use. **Counterperformance** is the defendant's participation, in exchange for diversion, in a treatment, counseling, or educational program aimed at changing his or her behavior. The candidate for diversion is a person who has been or could be arrested for an alleged offense and who is or could become the defendant in a criminal prosecution. Suspending the prosecution of a case is the hallmark of the diversion process.

Diversion has its roots in labeling theory, the idea that a person processed through the criminal justice system will be more stigmatized than

diversion

The halting or suspension, before conviction, of formal criminal proceedings against a person, conditioned on some form of counterperformance by the defendant.

counterperformance

The defendant's participation, in exchange for diversion, in a treatment, counseling, or educational program aimed at changing his or her behavior.

EXHIBIT 4–1   Case Flow Model for Diversion and Probation

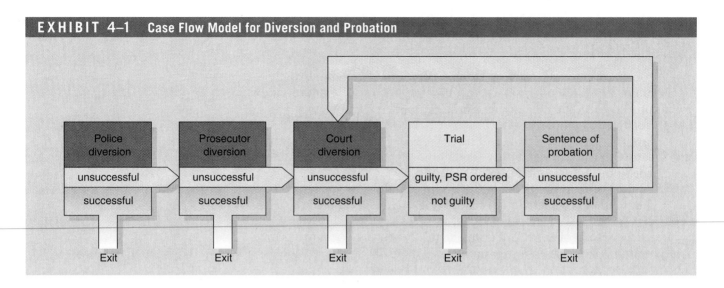

Police diversion	Prosecutor diversion	Court diversion	Trial	Sentence of probation
unsuccessful	unsuccessful	unsuccessful	guilty, PSR ordered	unsuccessful
successful	successful	successful	not guilty	successful
Exit	Exit	Exit	Exit	Exit

true diversion

A form of diversion that keeps an offender out of the system and helps him or her avoid formal prosecution and labeling.

minimization of penetration

A form of diversion that keeps an offender from going further into the system.

a person handled informally, as well as the idea that incarceration can do more damage than good. In 1967, the President's Commission on Law Enforcement and Administration of Justice recommended the establishment of services to divert offenders from the criminal justice system.

The overall goal of diversion is to reduce recidivism through rehabilitation. In the criminal justice system, diversion is used in two ways. First, it can be used to keep an offender out of the system and help him or her avoid formal prosecution and labeling. This is called **true diversion.** For example, a person caught smoking marijuana by the police could be counseled by the police and referred to Treatment Alternatives to Street Crime (TASC) without the threat of arrest and prosecution for not attending. TASC provides services to encourage diversion such as diagnosing drug problems, referring clients to community treatment programs, and monitoring progress.

Across the United States today, TASC is one of the major approaches to the diversion of drug-abusing offenders. A rigorous study of five TASC diversion programs in 1999 found that TASC was effective in delivering treatment services such as drug counseling, urinalysis to detect drug use, and AIDS education. However, there was no clear evidence of reductions in either new arrests or technical violations (technical violations are discussed later in this chapter). The research also found that the hard-core offenders benefit from TASC more than those who pose the least threat or seem the easiest to treat.

The second way of using diversion is to keep an offender from going further into the system. This is called **minimization of penetration.** For example, if you lived in Philadelphia and were charged with possession and use of a small amount of crack cocaine, you could be referred to the Philadelphia Treatment Court (PTC). PTC is a postplea diversion program that seeks to prevent future criminal activity by diverting selected defendants from criminal justice processing into community supervision and service. PTC started in 1997. It targets nonviolent offenders with drug addiction problems and offers them a chance to avoid the jail time they could face if convicted, in exchange for a guilty plea and participation in a four-phase drug court program. Of the more than 800 felony

The police, a prosecutor, a judge, or a probation officer may call for diversion. Here the police and a probation officer practice *true diversion* by counseling youth caught smoking marijuana and referring them to TASC. Do you think true diversion invites more law violation by allowing offenders to avoid prosecution?

drug arrests made each month in Philadelphia, approximately 100 cases are eligible for diversion.

If PTC participants meet all the program requirements, which generally take a year to complete, they "graduate." If a year later they haven't been arrested again, the charges are expunged from their records. But if they fail to abide by the court's strict rules (counseling, drug testing, restitution, and weekly court appearances), the judge will enter a verdict of guilty and sentence the individual accordingly.

As of May 24, 2007, 1,357 offenders—ages 18 to 70—had graduated PTC, and 90 percent had remained drug, arrest, and conviction free for one year after graduation and had their records wiped clean. The average cost per participant was $3,500, compared to $29,000 to incarcerate a prisoner for a year in Philadelphia. According to cost–benefit statistics collected by the Drug Court Clearinghouse at American University, PTC saved an estimated $3.8 million in 2000 and 2001 because participants were not in jail, they were not being tried, they were not in city hospitals, and their children and dependents didn't have to rely as much or at all on the city's welfare system to support them.[4]

Most diversion programs like TASC and the PTC share three objectives:

1. Prevent future criminal activity by diverting certain defendants from criminal justice processing into community supervision and service. This goal is based on the belief that diversion programs are more effective ways to control criminal behavior than taking offenders to court, convicting them, and sentencing them.

2. Save prosecution and judicial resources for serious crimes by offering, for less serious crimes, alternatives to the usual prosecution process. Defendants eligible for diversion are given the opportunity to avoid arrest or prosecution and to obtain medical services, counseling, and educational and vocational training.

3. Provide, where appropriate, a vehicle for restitution to communities and victims of crime.

Rationales for Diversion

Diversion has four rationales. First, the experience and the stigma of being formally arrested, tried, and convicted can actually encourage more criminal behavior. For example, having a criminal record might restrict a person's educational, vocational, and social opportunities, making the person more apt to turn to crime to survive. In addition, as a result of time spent in jail or prison, an offender may be more likely to associate with other offenders.

A second rationale for using diversion is that it is less expensive than formally processing an offender through the criminal justice system. The expense of arrest, trial, conviction, and sentence is easily justified for serious crimes. In most cities and counties across the United States today, however, police are overworked, courts are overloaded, jails and prisons are overcrowded, and probation and parole officers have caseloads that are unmanageable. Diversion is a way to reduce or at least contain these burdens, reserving formal criminal justice processing for the cases that need it the most.

A third rationale for diversion is that the public may think formal processing through the criminal justice system is inappropriate for crimes without perceived victims. These offenses involve a willing and private exchange of illegal goods or services. Examples include prostitution, certain forms of sexual behavior, gambling, and drug sales. Such offenses are called *victimless crimes* because the participants do not feel they are being harmed. Prosecution is justified on the grounds that these offenses harm society as a whole by threatening the moral fabric of the community. Since formal prosecution of these offenses is costly, offenders are often diverted to health clinics and treatment programs.

A final rationale for using diversion is to give the typical diversion client a better chance in life. Our nation's jails, lockups, prisons, and probation and parole caseloads are filled with people who are economically disadvantaged, belong to minority groups, and are young, undereducated, and chronically unemployed or underemployed. Diversion offers such persons help with some of the challenges they face, without adding to their difficulties the stigma of formal arrest, trial, and conviction.

The Process of Diversion

Diversion may occur at any point in the criminal justice process after a criminal complaint has been filed or police have observed a crime. The police, a prosecutor, or a judge may call for diversion. The accused participates voluntarily and has access to defense counsel before deciding whether to participate.

Diversion programs offer a variety of remedial responses to defendants' problems. Such responses can include drug and alcohol treatment, mental health services, employment counseling, and education and training. They may involve agencies in or outside the criminal justice system. The variety of responses often reflects a community's unique criminal justice population.

Diversion is also used for persons who are classified as mentally ill or incompetent and either are not equipped to stand trial or need a form of incarceration and treatment other than imprisonment. Such persons may be referred to an agency for voluntary treatment or civil commitment to an institution in lieu of prosecution and a prison sentence.

A study of pretrial diversion in the federal system found that between 1995 and 1999, the number of federal pretrial divertees averaged 2,000 annually.[5] Their offenses were mostly fraud, larceny, theft, and embezzlement. The conditions of their diversion emphasized restitution and community service. Divertees were more likely to be female, U.S. citizens, employed, and relatively older (average age was 36 years) and to have an education background that included at least some college. The average duration of diversion was 12 months. Across the five-year period, 88 percent of the divertees successfully completed the diversion program and their cases were not prosecuted. Data on the impact of diversion on future recidivism were not available.

Diversion Policy Issues

Diversion has its supporters and critics. Supporters believe diversion is the first opportunity to give offenders individualized assistance before they get too far down the path of crime. Diversion may thus resolve problems that lead to offending behavior. Critics argue that diversion tends to force people to give up some of their freedom without being tried and convicted. They argue that it violates the safeguard of due process. Other critics believe that diversion is "nonpunishment" and might actually produce more crime. And still others contend that diversion programs serve too small a percentage of offenders (mostly less serious crime and low-risk offenders when the real need in criminal justice is to focus on serious crime and high-risk offenders) and spend too many resources on them. To these and other issues about diversion we now turn our attention.

Legal and Ethical Issues   There is agreement that a diversion program should protect a defendant's rights. Protections include requiring an informed waiver of the right to a speedy trial, the right to a trial by jury, the right to confront one's accusers, and the privilege against self-incrimination, and informed consent to the conditions of a diversion program. For supporters, the risk of violating rights is outweighed by the chance diversion gives defendants to avoid the stigma of a criminal record and by the possibility of resolving problems that might result in future criminal behavior.

Unconditional diversion is the termination of criminal processing at any point before adjudication with no threat of later prosecution. It affords the best protection for a defendant's legal rights because dismissal of charges does not require any counterperformance. In effect, the defendant has everything to gain and nothing to lose. In unconditional diversion, treatment, counseling, and other services are offered on a voluntary basis. Many corrections leaders believe that voluntary treatment is more likely than coerced treatment to have beneficial effects. Whether that is true or not is subject to debate. Research consistently indicates that offenders' motivation for entering correctional programs (voluntary or coerced) are not as important in treatment outcome as their ultimate length of stay in treatment.[6]

Conditional diversion means that charges are dismissed if the defendant satisfactorily completes treatment, counseling, or other programs ordered by the justice system. Conditional diversion at or after arraignment, with judicial participation, affords greater protection against prosecutorial overreach and more assurance of informed voluntary decisions by the defendant than does diversion by the police or the prosecutor. In diversion programs run by the police and prosecutor, some participants may not have been prosecuted at all or might have been exonerated (cleared of blame) if they had been prosecuted. Conditional diversion

unconditional diversion

The termination of criminal processing at any point before adjudication with no threat of later prosecution. Treatment, counseling, and other services are offered and use is voluntary.

conditional diversion

Diversion in which charges are dismissed if the defendant satisfactorily completes treatment, counseling, or other programs ordered by the justice system.

does not eliminate the possibility of more severe penalties for divertees who fail the program.

Law Enforcement Issues Does diversion weaken law enforcement? Does diversion invite more widespread violation of laws by allowing offenders to avoid conviction? There is no particular evidence one way or the other. Certainly, if unconditional diversion were practiced extensively, there might be increases in violations. However, if unconditional diversion is limited to the first or second charge, then increases in violations are less likely. Conditional diversion requiring supervision and counterperformance does not seem more likely to encourage crime than the dispositions it most often replaces—fines, suspended sentences, and probation.

Economic Issues How cost-effective is diversion? What is the least costly method of diversion that will yield acceptable results? What are the trade-offs among different kinds of diversion programs? How does diversion compare in cost and effectiveness with traditional prosecution and sentencing practices?

Some argue that, in the long run, diversion can protect the community better than traditional processing can. Consider that, with diversion, treatment starts promptly after the criminal act, the social handicap of a criminal record is avoided, and exposure to criminal influences is minimized.

Presumably, diversion is less conducive to recidivism than is traditional processing. However, efforts to compare diversion with what would have happened without it have been unsuccessful. It seems safe to say that the community protection that diversion affords is at least comparable to the traditional measures that would most likely be used if prosecution were not suspended. The economic question, then, is, which approach costs less?

The costs of both diversion and its alternatives include the costs of arriving at a decision; the costs of implementing decisions; and the costs of undesired consequences of decisions, such as reinstatement of prosecution, leveling of new charges, or revocation of probation or parole because of a new charge or violation.

Diversion is not always the appropriate response to criminal behavior. When diversion fails to bring about the desired changes in an offender's behavior, probation is often the next step in the corrections process.

PROBATION

Probation has long been one of the most popular and most frequently used forms of criminal punishment (see Exhibit 4–2). It is a way to keep the offender at home in the community, avoid incarceration, and carry out sanctions imposed by the court or the probation agency. **Probation** is the conditional release of a convicted offender into the community, under the supervision of a probation officer. It is conditional because if the probationer violates the conditions of her or his probation, the judge may either set more restrictive conditions of probation, or may revoke probation and sentence the defendant to prison. Later in this chapter we discuss the impact that revoking even a small precentage of the probation population can have in the prison population.

probation

The conditional release of a convicted offender into the community, under the supervision of a probation officer. It is conditional because it can be revoked if certain conditions are not met.

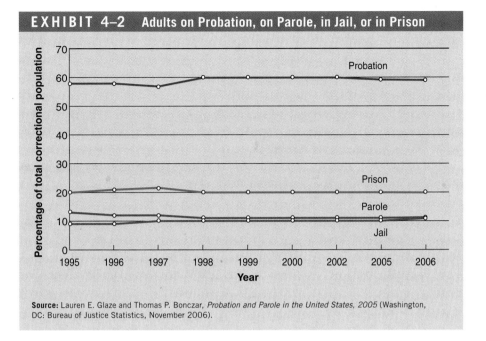

EXHIBIT 4–2   Adults on Probation, on Parole, in Jail, or in Prison

Source: Lauren E. Glaze and Thomas P. Bonczar, *Probation and Parole in the United States, 2005* (Washington, DC: Bureau of Justice Statistics, November 2006).

The judge or the probation department usually imposes a set of restrictions on the offender's freedom. For example, a survey of 4,000 probationers by the Bureau of Justice Statistics found that 82 percent of probationers are given three or more conditions, which often include monetary penalties, drug testing, employment requirements, and mandatory treatment.[7] Monetary requirements were the most common condition (84 percent): 61 percent were required to pay supervision fees; 56 percent, a fine; 55 percent, court costs; and 33 percent, victim restitution. One in 10 probationers was restricted from any contact with the victim. One in 4 was required to perform community service; 2 of every 5 were required to maintain employment or to enroll in an employment or educational program. Ten percent of the probationers were under some form of monitoring or restriction of movement. And since so many probationers were convicted of public-order offenses, especially those related to alcohol abuse, it is not surprising that 2 out of 5 probationers (40 percent) were required to enroll in substance abuse treatment. Alcohol treatment is required more frequently for misdemeanants than for felons (41 percent, compared to 21 percent), while drug treatment is required more often for felons than for misdemeanants (28 percent compared to 15 percent). Nearly one-third of all probationers were subject to mandatory drug testing. If the probationer violates any of the technical conditions of her or his probation or commits a new crime, the judge may order that the entire sentence be served in prison.

Reasons for and Goals of Probation

Probation is used for at least four reasons. First, probation permits the offender to remain in the community for reintegration purposes. Offender reintegration is more likely to occur if social and family ties are not broken by incarceration.

Second, probation avoids prison institutionalization and the stigma of incarceration. Prison institutionalization is the process of learning and adopting the norms and culture of institutional living. Living in the artificial environment of an institution does not teach prisoners how to live in the free world. Probationers do not experience prison institutionalization, nor do they have to worry about the negative effects of being treated like a prisoner, which decrease even further their ability to function as a law-abiding citizen when released.

The third reason for probation is that it is less expensive than incarceration, more humanitarian, and at least as effective as incarceration in reducing future criminal activity.

The final reason for probation is that it is fair and appropriate sentencing for offenders whose crimes do not merit incarceration. Furthermore, probation is the base from which more severe punishments can be built. Not all crimes deserve incarceration, nor do all crimes deserve probation. Probation is preferred when the offender poses no threat to community safety, when community correctional resources are available, and when probation does not unduly deprecate the seriousness of the offense. The probation risk–needs assessment and statutory sentencing guidelines help identify which offenders deserve community-based punishment and which deserve institutional punishment.

The goals of probation reflect society's values. In the 1960s, when society showed a strong interest in social welfare and offender rehabilitation, probation work reflected that emphasis. Today, probation emphasizes offender control. Most probation programs share five goals:

1. Protect the community by preparing the presentence report (PSR) to assist judges in sentencing and supervising offenders. The PSR indicates the degree of risk an offender poses to the community. It also identifies the offender's special needs. Offenders posing a threat to the community are then given secure placement, usually incarceration. Offenders who do not pose a threat to the community are given probation supervision. (We will return to the PSR later in this chapter.)

2. Carry out sanctions imposed by the court. Probation officers accomplish this by educating offenders about the orders of the court, supervising offenders, and removing them from the community when they violate the conditions of their probation.

3. Conduct a risk–needs assessment to identify the level of supervision and the services probationers need.

4. Support crime victims by collecting information that describes the losses, suffering, and trauma experienced by a crime victim or by the victim's survivors. This information is reported to the court in a written document called the *victim-impact statement*. The judge considers it when sentencing the offender. The information is particularly valuable for sentences that include restitution.

5. Coordinate and promote the use of community resources. Probation officers refer offenders to community agencies and programs that serve the offenders' needs. Such programs include drug and alcohol treatment, job training, vocational education, anger management, and life skills training.

Not all probation agencies achieve these objectives in the same way. A probation department's orientation is a function of many things, including department philosophy, leadership, the community served, and the offenders supervised. Some departments lean more toward treating the

Probation officer training and development are opportunities to learn new ideas and discuss cases within the context of the agency's goals. Most probation agencies share five goals. What are the goals of probation and what factors infuence an agency's decision to emphasize one goal over another?

offender; others lean more toward offender control. It is likely that the majority of probation departments do both, depending on the need and the situation. The American Probation and Parole Association (APPA) policy on probation is found in Exhibit 4–3.

History of Probation

Probation in America developed during the 19th century. What started as a charitable and volunteer movement took almost 125 years to become available to adults in every state across the country.

Probation Begins in America   It was in the Boston courtroom of municipal court judge Peter Oxenbridge Thatcher, in 1830, that the groundwork for probation was laid. Searching for a new way to exercise leniency and to humanize the criminal law—sentencing goals that still dominate corrections—Judge Thatcher made the first recorded use of *release on recognizance* in America, in sentencing Jerusa Chase.

> The indictment against Jerusa Chase was found at the January term of the court.... She pleaded guilty to the same and would have been pronounced at that time, but upon the application of her friends, and with the consent of the attorney of the Commonwealth, she was permitted, upon her recognizance for her appearance in this Court whenever she should be called for, to go at large.[8]

Chase's release had many of the characteristics of present-day probation: suspension of sentence, freedom to stay in the community, conditions on that freedom, and the possibility of revocation of freedom for violation of the conditions.

In 1841, when 57-year-old John Augustus,[9] a wealthy Boston shoemaker, became interested in the operation of the courts, the practice of probation began to emerge. Augustus was particularly sensitive to the problems of persons charged with violating Boston's vice or temperance

John Augustus (1785–1859) was a Boston shoemaker who invented probation in 1841 and became the first "unofficial" probation officer. He is called the founder of probation. Which aspects of Augustus's probation system are still in use today?

| **EXHIBIT 4–3** | **American Probation and Parole Association Position Statement on Probation** |

Probation

Purpose

The purpose of probation is to assist in reducing the incidence and impact of crime by probationers in the community. The core services of probation are to provide investigation and reports to the court, to help develop appropriate court dispositions for adult offenders and juvenile delinquents, and to supervise those persons placed on probation. Probation departments in fulfilling their purpose may also provide a broad range of services including, but not limited to, crime and delinquency prevention, victim restitution programs and intern/volunteer programs.

Position

The mission of probation is to protect the public interest and safety by reducing the incidence and impact of crime by probationers. This role is accomplished by:

- assisting the courts in decision making through the probation report and in the enforcement of court orders;
- providing services and programs that afford opportunities for offenders to become more law-abiding;
- providing and cooperating in programs and activities for the prevention of crime and delinquency;
- furthering the administration of fair and individualized justice.

Probation is premised upon the following beliefs:

Society has a right to be protected from persons who cause its members harm, regardless of the reasons for such harm.   It is the right of every citizen to be free from fear of harm to person and property. Belief in the necessity of law to an orderly society demands commitment to support it. Probation accepts this responsibility and views itself as an instrument for both control and treatment appropriate to some, but not all offenders. The wise use of authority derived from law adds strength and stability to its efforts.

Offenders have rights deserving of protection.   Freedom and democracy require fair and individualized due process of law in adjudicating and sentencing the offender.

Victims of crime have rights deserving of protection.   In its humanitarian tradition, probation recognizes that prosecution of the offender is but a part of the responsibility of the criminal justice system. The victim of criminal activity may suffer loss of property, emotional problems, or physical disability. Probation thus commits itself to advocacy for the needs and interests of crime victims.

Human beings are capable of change.   Belief in the individual's capability for behavioral change leads probation practitioners to a commitment to the

laws. He was a member of the Washington Total Abstinence Society, an organization devoted to the promotion of temperance. By posting bail in selected cases, he had the offenders released to his care and supervision, and so began the work of the nation's first probation officer, an unpaid volunteer. Augustus carefully screened the offenders he sought to help. Here is an entry from his journal:

> In the month of August, 1841, I was in court one morning . . . in which [a] man was charged with being a common drunkard. The case was clearly made

| EXHIBIT 4–3 | American Probation and Parole Association Position Statement on Probation—*continued* |

reintegration of the offender into the community. The possibility for constructive change of behavior is based on the recognition and acceptance of the principal of individual responsibility. Much of probation practice focuses on identifying and making available those services and programs that will best afford offenders an opportunity to become responsible, law-abiding citizens.

Not all offenders have the same capacity or willingness to benefit from measures designed to produce law-abiding citizens.   Probation practitioners recognize the variations among individuals. The present offense, the degree of risk to the community and the potential for change can be assessed only in the context of the offender's individual history and experience.

Intervention in an offender's life should be the minimal amount needed to protect society and promote law-abiding behavior.   Probation subscribes to the principle of intervening in an offender's life only to the extent necessary. Where further intervention appears unwarranted, criminal justice system involvement should be terminated. Where needed intervention can best be provided by an agency outside the system, the offender should be diverted from the system to that agency.

Punishment.   Probation philosophy does not accept the concept of retributive punishment. Punishment as a corrective measure is supported and used in those instances in which it is felt that aversive measures may positively alter the offender's behavior when other measures may not. Even corrective punishment, however, should be used cautiously and judiciously in view of its highly unpredictable impact. It can be recognized that a conditional sentence in the community is, in and of itself, a punishment. It is less harsh and drastic than a prison term but more controlling and punitive than release without supervision.

Incarceration may be destructive and should be imposed only when necessary.   Probation practitioners acknowledge society's right to protect itself and support the incarceration of offenders whose behavior constitutes a danger to the public through rejection of social or court mandates. Incarceration can also be an appropriate element of a probation program to emphasize the consequences of criminal behavior and thus effect constructive behavioral change. However, institutions should be humane and required to adhere to the highest standards.

Where public safety is not compromised, society and most offenders are best served through community correctional programs.   Most offenders should be provided services within the community in which they are expected to demonstrate acceptable behavior. Community correctional programs generally are cost-effective and they allow offenders to remain with their families while paying taxes and, where applicable, restitution to victims.

Source: American Probation and Parole Association.

out, but before sentence was passed, I conversed with him for a few moments, and found that he was not yet past all hope of reformation. . . . He told me that if he could be saved from the House of Corrections, he never again would taste intoxicating liquors; there was such an earnestness in that one, and a look of firm resolve, that I determined to aid him; I bailed him, by permission of the Court. He was ordered to appear for sentence in three weeks; at the expiration of this period of probation, I accompanied him into the courtroom. . . . The Judge expressed himself much pleased with the account we gave of the man, and instead of the usual penalty—imprisonment in the House of

Correction—he fined him one cent and costs, amounting in all to $3.76, which was immediately paid. The man continued industrious and sober, and without doubt has been by this treatment, saved from a drunkard's grave.

Augustus criticized the police, judges, and others who did not share his views. His "helping" role was not universally accepted. Law enforcement officials of the day wanted offenders punished, not helped. A newspaper of the time described him as someone who "seems to have a great itching for notoriety, and dollars . . . and takes more airs upon himself than all the judges and officers . . . and unless he conducts himself henceforth with a great deal more propriety, we shall take it upon ourself [sic] to teach him decency."

Still, Augustus persisted and, by the time of his death in 1859, he had won probation for almost 2,000 adults and several thousand children. Several aspects of his probation system are still in use. Augustus investigated the age, character, and work habits of each offender. He identified persons he thought redeemable and "whose hearts were not fully depraved, but gave promise of better things." He made probation recommendations to the court. He developed conditions of probation and helped offenders with employment, education, and housing. And he supervised offenders during their probation, which lasted, on the average, about 30 days. Until 1878, probation continued to be the work of volunteers—individuals and agencies.

Early Probation Statutes   After Augustus's death in 1859, unpaid volunteers continued his work. In 1878, the Massachusetts legislature passed the first statute authorizing probation and provided for the first paid probation officer. The law applied only to Suffolk County (Boston). It required the mayor of Boston to appoint a probation officer from the police department or citizenry and required the probation officer to report to the chief of police; but this was changed three years later so that the probation officer then reported to the state commissioners of prisons.[10] In 1880, a new law authorized probation as an option in all cities and towns in Massachusetts. But because the law remained voluntary and the probation concept was still new, few cities and towns exercised the power. In 1891, the power to appoint probation officers was transferred from the mayor to the court, in response to criticism that the mayor's appointments were influenced by political considerations. The second state to pass a probation statute was Vermont, in 1898.

As more and more states passed laws authorizing probation, probation became a national institution. On March 4, 1925, President Calvin Coolidge signed the National Probation Act. The act authorized each federal district court to appoint one salaried probation officer with an annual income of $2,600.[11] However, it wasn't until 1927 that the first eight federal probation officers were appointed to federal district courts in Georgia, Illinois, Massachusetts, New York, Pennsylvania, and West Virginia.[12]

The early laws had little in common. Some allowed probation for adults only. Others allowed it for juveniles only. (In fact, the spread of probation was accelerated by the juvenile court movement.) Some laws restricted the crimes for which probation could be granted. Still others provided for the hiring of probation officers, but neglected to provide for paying them. Training for probation officers was brief or nonexistent. Appointments were often based on politics rather than merit, and salaries were typically even lower than those of unskilled laborers. By 1925, probation was available for juveniles in every state; by 1956, it was available for adults in every state.

Characteristics of Adults on Probation

On January 1, 2006, 4,162,536 adults were on federal, state, or local probation. The increase from 1 year earlier was only 19,070 probationers (0.5%), the smallest increase in the last 26 years.[13] One out of every 54 persons age 18 or older is on probation. The average length of probation is 27 months.[14] Exhibit 4–4 shows that the majority of adults on probation are in regular caseloads, they have one face-to-face contact with their probation officers per month, and the cost of their supervision is $2.11 per day. By contrast, offenders who pose a higher risk of reoffending or who might otherwise be incarcerated are placed in intensive supervision caseloads. Each caseload averages 29 offenders, with seven face-to-face contacts with their probation officers per month, and costing approximately $9.66 per day. Without probation, the cost of jail incarceration is approximately $57 per day, and the cost of prison incarceration is approximately $74 per day. Probation is cost-effective providing it can protect the community by matching the level of supervision with the level of risk an offender poses.

Exhibit 4–5 presents selected characteristics of the 4.1 million adults on probation on January 1, 2006. For example, women made up 23 percent of the probation population. Blacks represented almost one-third of probationers, while Hispanics, who may be of any race, made up 13 percent of probationers. Less than 1 percent of probationers are on federal probation. For the first time since data collection began in 1979, probationers convicted of a misdemeanor (50 percent) accounted for a larger percentage of the population than probationers convicted of a felony (49 percent). Twenty-six percent were on probation for drug law violations and 15 percent for driving while intoxicated.

The Bureau of Justice Statistics also reported that 57 percent of probationers had a direct sentence to probation; 22 percent received a sentence to incarceration that had been suspended; and 10 percent received incarceration followed by probation, an arrangement sometimes called a *split*

EXHIBIT 4-4	**Probation Statistics**		
Case Type[1]	Average Caseload per Officer	Average Number of Face-to-Face Contacts Between Probationer and Officer per Month	Average Cost per Day per Probationer
Regular	139	1	$2.11
Intensive	29	7	9.66
Electronic	6	3	8.71
Special	45	4	4.27

1. **Regular supervision:** Supervision of a probationer according to normal/average number of visits, contacts, or reports with a probation officer. **Intensive supervision:** Supervision of a probationer that includes a greater number of visits, contacts, or reports to or from a probation officer than exists under regular supervision. Offenders who pose a higher risk of reoffending or who might otherwise be incarcerated are candidates for placement under intensive supervision.
Electronic supervision: Supervision of a probationer that includes the use of an electronic monitoring device such as an ankle bracelet, pager, or voice verification telephone that assists probation officers in ascertaining an offender's whereabouts. **Special supervision:** Supervision of a probationer that includes special programming such as boot camp, substance abuse treatment programs, sex offender treatment, or other programs or services. More about intensive, electronic, and special supervision programming is discussed in Chapter 5.
Source: Adapted from Camille Graham Camp and George W. Camp, *The Corrections Yearbook, 2000,* pp. 170, 172, 176, 177, and 187. Copyright © 2000 Criminal Justice Institute.

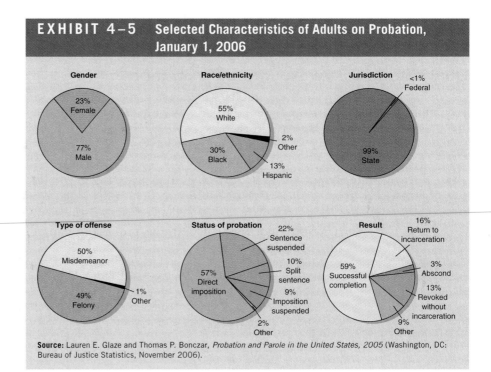

EXHIBIT 4–5   Selected Characteristics of Adults on Probation, January 1, 2006

Gender
- 23% Female
- 77% Male

Race/ethnicity
- 55% White
- 2% Other
- 30% Black
- 13% Hispanic

Jurisdiction
- <1% Federal
- 99% State

Type of offense
- 50% Misdemeanor
- 1% Other
- 49% Felony

Status of probation
- 22% Sentence suspended
- 10% Split sentence
- 9% Imposition suspended
- 57% Direct imposition
- 2% Other

Result
- 16% Return to incarceration
- 3% Abscond
- 13% Revoked without incarceration
- 59% Successful completion
- 9% Other

Source: Lauren E. Glaze and Thomas P. Bonczar, *Probation and Parole in the United States, 2005* (Washington, DC: Bureau of Justice Statistics, November 2006).

sentence. As Exhibit 4–5 shows, 59 percent of the more than 2.2 million adults discharged from probation in 2005 had successfully met the conditions of their supervision, with *successful* meaning the satisfaction of all requirements of supervision (that is, completing all proscribed visits, passing substance abuse tests, receiving counseling, and meeting other requirements that may have been in place), down 1 percent from the previous year.

The percentage of probationers discharged successfully has ranged between 62 percent (1995) and 59 percent (2005). Probationers discharged from supervision because of incarceration due to a new offense or rule violation has varied, from 21 percent in 1995 to 15 percent in 2000 to 16 percent in 2005. Another 3 percent of those discharged from probation had absconded and 13 percent had their probation revoked without incarceration.

Recently, researchers at the Department of Justice learned from hour-long interviews with active probationers that 9 percent of male probationers and 28 percent of female probationers had been physically or sexually abused before their sentence and before age 18.[15] (Prevalence estimates of child abuse in the general population are 5 to 8 percent for males and 12 to 17 percent for females.) Abused probationers told DOJ researchers that the abuser was either a family member or someone they knew intimately. Researchers are just beginning to study the link between child abuse and offending.

On January 1, 2006, 1,858 adults were on probation for every 100,000 persons age 18 and older in the United States, up from 1,297 a decade earlier. The BJS also reports that the southern states generally have the highest per capita ratio of probationers—reporting 2,067 probationers per 100,000 adults. In terms of sheer numbers of probationers, Texas has the largest adult probation population (about 430,312), followed by California (388,260). The smallest adult probation populations are in New

Hampshire (4,285) and North Dakota (3,749). Only 28,602 persons were on federal probation on January 1, 2006.

The five states that use probation the most are Massachusetts (3,350 per 100,000 adult population), Rhode Island (3,091), Minnesota (2,988), Delaware (2,828), and Ohio (2,745). The five states that use probation the least are New Hampshire (457 per 100,000 adult population), West Virginia (533), Utah (578), Nevada (709), and Kansas (723).

If probation were being used primarily as an alternative to incarceration, one might expect to find that the states that imposed more probationary sentences would have lower than average incarceration rates and vice versa. This is not the case. Southern states generally place more persons on probation at a high rate, and they generally incarcerate more than the rest of the nation, as we shall see in Chapter 7. The main reason is that there are no national guidelines for granting probation or limiting its use. The court is supposed to grant probation when the defendant does not pose a risk to society and if the granting of probation would not underrate the seriousness of the offense. Only recently have states begun to define categories of offenses that render offenders ineligible for probation. Mandatory sentencing now limits judicial discretion and the court's ability to grant probation to repeat offenders.

Who Administers Probation?

As probation spread throughout the United States in the late 19th and early 20th centuries, its organization and administration depended on local and state customs and politics. Currently, probation in the 50 states is administered by more than 2,000 separate agencies, reflecting the decentralized and fragmented character of contemporary corrections. The agencies have a great deal of common ground, but because they developed in different contexts, they also have a lot of differences in goals, policies, funding, staffing, salaries, budgets, and operation. In 2000, the average budget for probation agencies across the United States was $56 million, an increase of only 1 percent ($600,000) from 1992. Meanwhile, the number of persons on probation increased almost 37 percent from 1992 to 2000, from 2.8 to 3.8 million. Probation supporters argue that resources for probation have not kept pace with the increase in the number of persons sentenced to probation.

In an effort to offset declining budgets for probation and parole agencies and provide resources for the increased population of probationers and parolees, all but 12 states now have laws allowing authorities to collect fees from probationers and parolees who can afford to contribute to the cost of their supervision.[16] Missouri charges probationers and parolees $60 a month. In Colorado, it's $50 a month. Some states, such as Rhode Island and South Dakota, charge probationers and parolees a token amount ($15 per month), whereas other states charge considerably more. Hawaii charges felony probationers $150 a month. New Mexico law allows probation authorities to collect up to $185 a month from felony probationers. Iowa charges probationers and parolees a one-time enrollment fee of $250. Michigan imposes a fee on a sliding scale of up to 5 percent of monthly income, not to exceed a monthly total fee of $135.

Most states waive or reduce fees for probationers and parolees who are indigent. In Florida, for example, an offender who qualifies for the services of a public defender at trial is presumed to be low income and will be required to pay a fee of $50 a month, which is less than half the

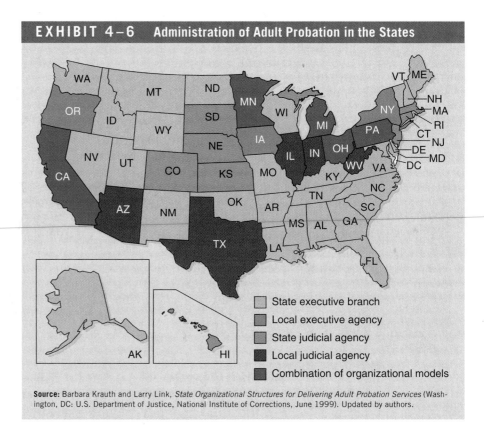

EXHIBIT 4–6   Administration of Adult Probation in the States

☐ State executive branch
☐ Local executive agency
☐ State judicial agency
☐ Local judicial agency
☐ Combination of organizational models

Source: Barbara Krauth and Larry Link, *State Organizational Structures for Delivering Adult Probation Services* (Washington, DC: U.S. Department of Justice, National Institute of Corrections, June 1999). Updated by authors.

amount charged for others on regular probation. In Pennsylvania, offenders who have poverty-level income, are students, or are collecting welfare are entitled to a reduction or a waiver of a $25 monthly supervision fee imposed on those who can afford to pay.

Probation is commonly considered a part of the correctional system, although it is technically a function of the court system. Exhibit 4–6 gives a state-by-state breakdown of how probation is administered. The map shows that the most common organizational structure for probation is for a state executive branch agency to provide probation services throughout the state.[17] In 29 states, a state or local agency in the executive branch of government delivers adult probation services. In 3 states, probation services are delivered exclusively through county or multicounty agencies in the executive branch. In 8 states, the judicial branch of state government is responsible for probation services. In 5 states, local agencies in the judicial branch deliver probation services. And in 5 states, probation services are delivered through some combination of state executive branch, local executive agencies, or local agencies in either the judicial or the executive branch (California).

Kathy Waters, past president of the American Probation and Parole Association, has worked in both executive and judicial branches of government that have the jurisdiction and responsibility for probation. She says there's nothing magical about where probation services are organized and administered.[18]

There are difficulties in both jurisdictions. . . . Probation and parole continue to change as each matures. . . . Whether under the executive branch of government (which, for some jurisdictions, works well) or under the judiciary (which seems like the only natural place for probation to be in some states), the system will have problems and frustrations that will need to be addressed. . . . Both branches provide leadership, policy establishment and the resources to fulfill their mission.

Privatizing Probation   Today there is also a movement to let the private sector administer probation supervision. Probation agencies in at least 15 states have privatized probation services to supervise low-risk offenders.[19] Colorado and Connecticut were among the first. In both states, the impetus for privatizing probation was similar: Staffing and resources were not keeping pace with increasing caseloads. Community supervision officials felt they had exhausted the use of interns and volunteers, and funding for new staff was not possible. They used risk management principles to assign staff and resources in direct proportion to the risk levels of a cases. Both states partnered with the private sector to monitor the low-risk offender population, people who generally have few needs, whose past records reflect little or no violence, and who successfully complete probation about 90 percent of the time.

In Connecticut, the privatization initiative to monitor low-risk offender populations by the private sector allowed scarce resources to be used to better monitor offenders with higher levels of risk. Private case management responsibilities in Connecticut included sending an introductory letter to the probationer, monitoring restitution payments and compliance with conditions of probation, responding to probationer's inquiries, preparing standardized reports for probation officers, providing verification of condition compliance, and providing statistical reports. Robert J. Bosco, director of Connecticut's Office of Adult Probation, says that the "success" of this privatization initiative "is in the agency's ability to use its resources to control recidivism of the highest risk offender population."[20]

The situation in Colorado was similar. When Colorado officials adopted risk management and looked at how treatment and supervision were matched with levels of risk, they found more probation officers were needed than the Colorado General Assembly would fund. The result was a directive that allowed probation departments to contract with private agencies for the supervision of low-risk probationers. Thirteen of Colorado's 22 judicial districts have entered into such contracts. The private agencies directly bill the probationers for their supervision, eliminating public expenditures for community supervision. According to Suzanne Pullen, management analyst with Colorado's Judicial Department in the Office of Probation Services, "The diversion of these low-risk offenders allows local probation departments to focus more clearly on the supervision and case management of medium- and high-risk offenders that are burdening their caseloads."[21]

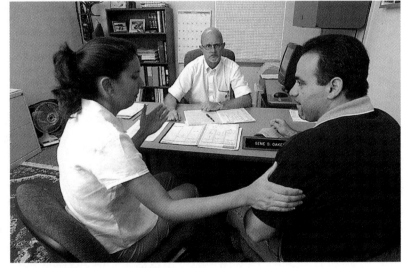

A probation officer involves an offender's spouse to help with rehabilitation. Probation officers also refer offenders to community agencies to help them overcome the problem that led to their offending behavior. What obstacles might a probation officer face in making referrals to a community agency and involving the family in offender rehabilitation?

A number of researchers and organizations have expressed reservations about turning over probation to the private sector. The American Probation and Parole Association (APPA) does not support the wholesale privatization of probation, parole, or community-based corrections, but it does recognize that the private sector offers new tools—such as

Mechael Dedeian

Senior Probation and Parole Officer (CSAC)   District 29
Adult Probation and Parole   Fairfax, Virginia

Mechael Dedeian is a senior probation and parole officer with District 29 Adult Probation and Parole in Fairfax, Virginia. She has worked there for the past 15 years, in a senior position for the past 3. Prior to that, she worked as both a jails auditor and a case manager. She earned her bachelor of science degree in elementary education from Longwood College in Farmville, Virginia. She later went on to acquire her Certified Substance Abuse Counselor (CSAC) certification.

Dedeian says she fell in love with probation while working with the jail program, and it was also in her blood to start with—her father was a juvenile probation officer. She specializes in substance abusers and individuals with mental health problems, so on any given day she sees a wide variety of challenges: getting relapsed individuals into detox, placing people in the right programs, deciding when to have someone arrested, and working with jails and others within the system. With a laugh, she describes her days as "rough . . . neverending."

"I wear many hats, and that's the one thing with a probation officer," she says. "Sometimes I'm the jailer, sometimes I get them off the street, sometimes I try to get them into the treatment program that they need. I just have to decide which hat to put on—am I the police officer? Am I the counselor? It's a case by case basis."

Although the job is tough, Dedeian loves what she does. She recalls her first parolee, when she started the job at age 24—he still calls her every now and then to tell her he's doing well. "So there are some successes," she says. "But it's not a job where you get a lot of pats on the back—you have to be a self-motivator, and you have to know that what you're doing is making a difference, even if you don't see it all the time."

> *There are days where all you do is put out a fire— sometimes they're huge fires. But when you're dealing with people that don't follow rules, this is what you get.*

expertise, specialized services, and advanced technologies with which the jurisdiction has had little experience or involvement—to assist probation departments in supervising offenders. Carl Wicklund, executive director of APPA, cautions that private companies need to be held to the same standards as public agencies. "It's not enough to do it because it is cheaper," he argues. Government jurisdictions and their representatives are ultimately accountable for the quality and care of private sector services delivered under contractual agreements. By operating within established parameters, standards, regulations, and laws, private probation providers can contribute to the ability of a probation department to protect the public and supervise offenders under its jurisdiction.

Does Probation Work?

The most common question asked about probation is, "Does it work?" In other words, do persons granted probation refrain from further crime? **Recidivism**—generally defined as *rearrest*—continues to be the primary outcome measure for probation, as it is for all corrections programs. Summaries of probation effectiveness usually report the recidivism rates of felons as if felons represented the total adult probation population,

recidivism

The repetition of criminal behavior; generally defined as *rearrest*. It is the primary outcome measure for probation, as it is for all corrections programs.

instead of just 49 percent of it. Some researchers tell us that recidivism rates are low for misdemeanant probationers, but high for felony probationers. RAND researchers found that over three-fourths of offenders on probation for a misdemeanor successfully complete their probation, but almost two-thirds of felony probationers are rearrested.[22] Recently, however, a study of the recidivism of male property offenders on felony probation showed just the opposite: a success rate of 67.7 percent, in essence the antithesis of RAND's findings.[23] According to the Department of Justice, however, the percentage of all offenders successfully completing their probation terms is falling. In 1986, 74 percent of those who exited probation successfully completed their terms. In 1995, it dropped to 62 percent. It fell again in 2006 to 59 percent.

What these data mean is open to debate. The statistics don't necessarily imply that recidivism is going up. To a considerable extent, increased probation failure rates may merely reflect tougher monitoring and enforcement policies.

Recidivism rates vary greatly from place to place, depending on the seriousness of offenses, population characteristics, average length of probation, and the amount and quality of intervention, surveillance, and enforcement. A summary of 17 studies of adult felony probationers found that felony rearrest rates ranged from 12 to 65 percent. James Gondles Jr., executive director of the American Correctional Association, argues that, by the time offenders reach probation, other institutions of social control have failed. If the offending behavior could have been controlled, families, neighborhoods, schools, and other social institutions would have controlled it. Offending behavior is not easy to correct and for that reason Gondles believes that probation systems across the United States need help.

> [Probation officers] are often held accountable for the failures of other elements of the criminal justice community. Therefore, all of us in corrections must help them by doing our own jobs better, to escape the perception that they are ineffective. We must work together to ensure that all elements of the criminal justice system receive adequate funding and that all elements of the criminal justice system work closer together to provide offenders with the services they require.[24]

The APPA, representing U.S. probation officers nationwide, argues that recidivism rates measure just one probation task while ignoring others. The APPA has urged its member agencies to collect data on other outcomes, such as the following:

- amount of restitution collected;
- number of offenders employed;
- amounts of fines and fees collected;
- hours of community service performed;
- number of treatment sessions attended;
- percentage of financial obligations collected;
- rate of enrollment in school;
- number of days of employment;
- educational attainment; and
- number of days drug free.

Advocates of measures other than recidivism tell us that probation should be measured by what offenders do while they are in probation programs, not by what they do after they leave.

The American public understands that not all criminals can be locked up. Doubts are being raised about allocating a significant proportion of tax dollars to prisons. The cost of prison construction and housing now totals nearly $30 billion annually.[25] Seeing no reduction in crime will slowly move the public to reassess attitudes toward punishment.

Research also shows that citizens are less punishment oriented than many political leaders believe. For example, in surveys conducted in Alabama, Delaware, and Pennsylvania, the Public Agenda Foundation of New York City found that "when the public is made aware of the possible range of punishments, and given information about how and with whom they are used, they support alternatives to incarceration—including punishments administered in the community—for offenders considered nonviolent and low risk."[26]

Similar findings were reported recently in Connecticut when a University of Connecticut poll found that close to 9 out of 10 (89 percent) residents supported sending nonviolent offenders with mental illness to mental health facilities instead of prison, another 84 percent supported replacing prison sentences with mandatory drug treatment and probation for people convicted of nonviolent illegal drug use, and almost two-thirds (61 percent) supported relaxing mandatory minimum sentences for first-time offenders in order to reduce prison crowding.[27]

To implement credible and effective probation programs, several steps appear necessary. Petersilia offers us five suggestions.[28]

1. Implement High-Quality Programs and Enforce Them

Experienced probation officers tell us that besides using the techniques and strategies of coercion and threats of incarceration to induce offenders to comply with the conditions of probation supervision, we should not neglect to reward cooperative behavior and compliance. When offenders respond favorably to supervision, praise and tangible rewards sustain favorable behavior. That is the practice in drug courts nationwide, for example. Reclassifying offenders, reducing their level of supervision (e.g., face-to-face contacts and drug testing), and advocating early termination are used to encourage offenders to comply and cooperate.

2. Invest Adequate Resources in Treatment *and* Surveillance

When probationers receive *both* surveillance (e.g., unannounced contact and random drug tests) and treatment, recidivism can decline by one-third.[29] Probation can become more effective by giving some offenders more intensive supervision and treatment and others less and by targeting the effort to offer precise services and meet objectives by using a standardized assessment of probationer risks and needs. This approach can help probation staff determine more reliably which clients need intensive supervision, special services, or routine probation. When appropriate interventions (e.g., residential drug treatment, outpatient treatment, urine monitoring) are used with drug-involved clients, scarce treatment resources are utilized more effectively to reduce recidivism and relapse. However, treatment, surveillance, and classifying probationers to appropriate levels of supervision cost money. Adequate funding will be available only if the public believes that new supervision conditions are punitive as well as effective in reducing crime.

3. Demonstrate That Probation Is Tough on Crime

Policymakers say they send large numbers of persons to prison because the public wants to be tough on crime. But there is a groundswell of evidence that tough punishment may no longer equate with prison.[30] Some offenders see probation as more punitive and restrictive than prison. For example, Petersilia and Deschenes found that inmates ranked five years of intensive supervision probation (ISP) as harsher punishment than one year in prison (although not as severe as three years in prison). Researchers in Texas and Oregon gave offenders the choice of serving a prison term or serving probation with mandatory drug testing, community service, employment, counseling, and frequent visits with a probation officer. In Oregon, 25 percent of those eligible for probation chose prison. In Texas, many offenders described common prison terms as less punitive than even only three to five years on probation. Prison was more attractive than the pressures of close supervision. The public must be convinced that probation sanctions can be just as punitive as prison. Of course, the choice of probation or prison should be for the judge to make, not the offender.

4. Target Drug Offenders
Drug offenders are prime candidates for tough probation programs. Research has revealed the different risks and needs of traffickers, addicts, and low-level users.[31] Even if drug offenders are coerced into treatment by the court, there is evidence that the treatment can reduce both later drug use and later crimes. The largest study of drug treatment outcomes found that criminal justice clients stayed in treatment longer than clients without involvement in the justice system and had higher than average success rates.[32] Indeed, offenders in outpatient drug treatment programs have significantly lower rates of rearrest and relapse if they stay in treatment for more than three months than if they drop out earlier.[33]

The new knowledge is resulting in different laws and punishment strategies for different kinds of drug offenders. Many Americans prefer prison sentences for drug traffickers but are willing to accept something other than prison for other drug offenders. Nationally, 17 states have either reformed their drug laws or are considering it. In 1996, the people of Arizona led the way in drug reform by passing the Drug Medicalization, Prevention and Control Act. The centerpiece of the act is the diversion of persons convicted of possession or use of a controlled substance. The act requires drug offenders to be placed on probation and participate in appropriate drug treatment (an example of conditional diversion discussed earlier in this chapter). In the second year of operation, 62 percent of the probationers complied with treatment. Probation supervision and community treatment cost approximately $1.1 million. Based on prison costs of almost $53 per day, Arizona saved an estimated $6.7 million in incarceration. Four years later, 61 percent of California voters passed Proposition 36—the Substance Abuse and Crime Prevention Act. The act allows first- and second-time nonviolent drug offenders convicted of possession, use, or transportation of drugs substance abuse treatment instead of incarceration. As of February 2002, of the 4,329 defendants sentenced to drug treatment in Los Angeles County from July 1, 2001, to December 31, 2001, 69 percent were still receiving treatment. Judges and county officials say they are pleased with the program, and preliminary reports are that the program is working. Similar ballot initiatives are being considered across the country.

5. Make Probation Research a Priority
With more than 4.1 million adults under probation supervision today, probation

research should be a priority. The suggestion is to incorporate research on causes and effective interventions into local probation programs. Furthermore, local probation departments need to conduct research into their programs to see what works best in reducing recidivism, and consult the what-works literature discussed in Chapter 1 in developing new probation programs.

It would also be useful for probation research to assess the value of revoking probation for persons who commit technical violations (which are failures to fulfill the conditions of probation—attending counseling, paying restitution, contacting the probation officer) instead of committing new offenses. Judges need assurance that probationers will be held accountable for their behavior, and the public needs assurance that probation sanctions are punitive. More research is needed on the relationship of technical violations to criminal behavior. For example, what types of conditions are imposed? How do those conditions manage offenders, encourage rehabilitation, and protect the community? What are the trends in the number of technical violators and the effect on jails and prisons? What innovative programs, policies, and statutes have emerged in other jurisdictions to deal with technical violators?

WHAT PROBATION OFFICERS DO

Probation officers (POs) are more extensively involved with offenders and their cases—often starting at arrest—than any other criminal justice professionals, for that reason their work exacts a toll in job-related stress.

Researchers at the National Institute of Justice reported recently that the major sources of probation and parole officers' stress are high caseloads, excess paper/computer work, and deadline pressures.[34] As reported later in this chapter, the average caseload of a probation officer is very high—139 cases—and computers haven't necessarily reduced the stress. In fact, even with computerized management information systems, officers still deal with hardware and software problems. And the problem with deadlines is that many of them are unexpected and cannot be controlled.

NIJ researchers found that when they asked probation and parole officers how they deal with stress in a positive way, more officers cited physical exercise than any other technique. Other positive ways include discussing cases with other officers, seeking support through religion, "venting," and talking to a family member.

On the negative side, many officers reported dealing with stress by taking extra sick days, requesting transfers, or applying for early retirement.

In addition to dealing with stress, building a relationship with the offender and developing rapport are also important. Scholars and practitioners tell us that probation officers must be aware of the cultural differences between themselves and their probationers if they are to build rapport and help change offending behavior. Recall from our earlier discussion that the majority of probationers are male and almost half are members of minority groups. Slightly more than half of the probation officers are female, and three-fourths of all POs are white. These demographic differences raise questions on how probation officers can build rapport across gender, race, and ethnicity. Without rapport, experts believe there is more likelihood that probationers will miss scheduled appointments, not follow through on referrals, violate the conditions of probation, reoffend, and end up back in the system.

Racial and cultural tensions that exist in society at large can also be present between the probationer and the probation officer. For example, interviews with juvenile probation officers in Maricopa County, Arizona, found that juvenile court staff had little understanding of culturally or gender-specific programming and often acted "based more on the perceptions they have of girls and their families than on the realities the girls face, including both individual and societal factors."[35] As a result of gender and racial/ethnic stereotypes, girls have few options for treatment and services. To lessen this tension and mistrust, experts suggest five strategies to build rapport between the probationer and probation officer.[36]

1. Sincerity is one thing that allows probationers to forgive probation officers who violate a cultural norm such as saying the wrong thing.

2. High service energy sends a message to probationers that the probation officer is in their corner. The probationers may think that less service energy has something to do with ethnic differences.

3. Knowledge of the probationers' culture increases empathy in the cross-cultural counseling relationship. For example, if the probationer speaks English as a second language, it would be helpful in building rapport for the officer to learn key words and phrases in the probationer's native language.

4. A nonjudgmental attitude increases the officer's credibility.

5. Helping probationers with needed resources facilitates rapport building and officer credibility.

The American Psychological Association (APA) underscores the importance of the officer–offender relationship in the what-works literature that we refer to in this book (see Chapter 1).[37] The APA refers to it as a **working alliance,** an effective relationship between a change agent and a client, with negotiated goals and a mutual willingness to compromise when necessary to meet the goals or to maintain a viable relationship. The APA believes that the working alliance contributes far more to the outcomes of treatment and supervision than the actual type of treatment or intervention delivered.

At least one organization, Justice System Assessment and Training (JSAT) of Boulder, Colorado, has developed a training program for probation officers that emphasizes the working alliance.[38] The program, called COMBINES, focuses on understanding the correctional client and long-term behavioral change using **cognitive-behavioral treatment,** which is problem-focused intervention that emphasizes skill training. The what-works literature has determined that cognitive-behavioral treatment is effective in reducing a wide variety of human behavior problems, including depression, anxiety, obsessive-compulsive disorder, antisocial conduct, and so on. The National Institute of Corrections says that, in general, offenders respond far better to cognitive-behavioral treatment than any other program intervention.

According to JSAT, an effective working alliance can take place only when the officer has adequate personal knowledge of the offender and a vision for effective behavior change that he or she is able to convey to the offender—a fundamental shift from simply monitoring the conditions of probation or parole. The United States Probation and Pretrial

working alliance

An effective relationship between a change agent and a client, with negotiated goals and a mutual willingness to compromise when necessary to meet the goals or to maintain a viable relationship.

cognitive-behavioral treatment

A problem-focused intervention that emphasizes skill training.

Services Charter for Excellence (similar to a code of ethics) reinforces these rapport-building strategies.

On January 1, 2000, there were 16,768 state adult probation officers, 21,466 state adult probation and parole officers, and 6,750 federal probation and parole officers in the United States. There were more female (54 percent) than male probation officers. By race and ethnicity, 72 percent were white, 21 percent were African American, 4.2 percent were Hispanic, 1.1 percent were Asian, 0.5 percent were Native American/Native Alaskan, and 1.2 percent were other races and ethnicities. Probation officers completed an average of 31 hours of in-service training in 2000 and earned over $36,000. In 22 states and the federal government, probation officers are also peace officers.[39]

Probation officers interact with many criminal justice agencies and influence many decisions affecting offenders. They do this in two major roles: through case investigation and client supervision.

Case Investigation

Investigation includes the preparation of a *presentence report (PSR)*, which the judge uses in sentencing an offender. The PSR is a report prepared by the probation department of a court, that provides a social and personal history as well as an evaluation of a defendant as an aid to the court in determining a sentence. The PSR is an integral part of the sentencing process in many jurisdictions despite the growth in mandatory sentencing laws, three-strikes laws, and truth-in-sentencing legislation, as well as the increased use of sentencing guidelines. In some states, for example, Missouri, the report is called a *sentence assessment report.*[40] As the centerpiece of Missouri's sentencing guidelines, it sets forth the recommended sentence options and the appropriate correctional resources available both in the community and in prison. While a PSR is required for sentencing purposes in many states, it remains discretionary

A probation officer interviews a defendant in preparation of the presentence report (PSR). Case investigation is the first major role of a probation officer. The PSR provides a social and personal history as well as an evaluation of the defendant as an aid to the court in determining a sentence. What questions should a probation officer ask the defendant?

ETHICS & PROFESSIONALISM

UNITED STATES PROBATION AND PRETRIAL SERVICES

Charter for Excellence

We, the members of Probation and Pretrial Services of the United States Courts, are a national system with shared professional identity, goals, and values. We facilitate the fair administration of justice and provide continuity of services throughout the judicial process. We are outcome driven and strive to make our communities safer and to make a positive difference in the lives of those we serve. We achieve success through interdependence, collaboration, and local innovation. We are committed to excellence as a system and to the principles embodied in this Charter.

We are a unique *profession*.

Our profession is distinguished by the unique combination of:

A multidimensional knowledge base in law and human behavior;

A mix of skills in investigation, communication, and analysis;

A capacity to provide services and interventions from pretrial release through post-conviction supervision;

A position of impartiality within the criminal justice system; and

A responsibility to positively impact the community and the lives of victims, defendants, and offenders.

These *goals* matter most.

Our system strives to achieve the organizational goals of:

Upholding the constitutional principles of the presumption of innocence and the right against excessive bail for pretrial defendants by appropriately balancing community safety and risk of nonappearance with protection of individual liberties;

Providing objective investigations and reports with verified information and recommendations to assist the court in making fair pretrial release, sentencing, and supervision decisions;

Ensuring defendant and offender compliance with court-ordered conditions through community-based supervision and partnerships;

Protecting the community through the use of controlling and correctional strategies designed to assess and manage risk;

Facilitating long-term, positive changes in defendants and offenders through proactive interventions; and

Promoting fair, impartial, and just treatment of defendants and offenders throughout all phases of the system.

We stand by these *values*.

Our values are mission-critical:

Act with integrity.

Demonstrate commitment to and passion for our mission.

Be effective stewards of public resources.

Treat everyone with dignity and respect.

Promote fairness in process and excellence in service to the courts and the community.

Work together to foster a collegial environment.

Be responsible and accountable.

Ethical Dilemma 4–1: Does gender or celebrity status play a role in who gets probation? For more information go to Ethical Dilemma 4–1 at www.justicestudies .com/ethics04.

Ethical Dilemma 4–2: Should probation officers be advocates for sentencing reform? Why or why not? What are the issues? For more information go to Ethical Dilemma 4–2 at www.justicestudies.com/ethics04.

Ethical Dilemmas for every chapter are available online.

in others. During 1999, more than 538,000 state and federal PSRs were written. Probation staff in Texas wrote the most (89,000), and staff in South Carolina wrote the fewest (26).

Purposes of the Presentence Report   The PSR has two main purposes. First, and most important, the PSR assists the court in reaching a fair sentencing decision. The specific content areas of the PSR vary from jurisdiction to jurisdiction, but common areas include (1) information regarding the current offense; (2) the offender's past adult and juvenile criminal record; (3) family history and background; and (4) personal data about education, health, employment, and substance abuse history. In addition, some state statutes dictate content areas such as victim-impact statements. It is not uncommon for jurisdictions to include a sentencing recommendation in the PSR. However, sentencing reforms are limiting judicial sentencing discretion so the PSR recommendation is much less important than it once was. Still, research on the relationship between the sentencing recommendation and actual sentencing outcomes is very clear: Judges follow the recommendation over 80 percent of the time when probation is recommended, and over 60 percent of the time when prison is recommended.

A recent study of 227 Utah judges, prosecutors, public defenders, and probation/parole officers found significant opposition (86 percent) to the notion of removing the sentencing recommendation from the PSR altogether.[41] Critics of the PSR have asserted that judges do not bother to read the entire report, so the Utah study asked respondents their approach to reading the PSR. The study asked, Do you (a) start at the beginning and read the entire report by section, (b) skip over most of the report and focus on the evaluative summary and sentence recommendation, or (c) skim and scan the entire report? Ninety percent of judges claimed to read the entire report from the beginning, but only 55 percent of all respondents (judges, prosecutors, public defenders, and probation/parole officers) indicated that they start at the beginning and read the entire report section by section. The rest would either skim and scan the entire report or ignore most of it and focus on the sentencing recommendation and evaluative summary sections. The authors of the study conclude, "While this finding might surprise some, we believe that it is consistent with other communications research on selective reading. As a result of time constraints, working professionals skim and scan documents and read only what they deem important. Given the pressure and time limitations confronting the various PSR user groups, there was no reason for us to assume that they would behave any differently."[42]

The second purpose of the PSR is to outline a treatment plan for the offender. During the investigation, besides determining the degree of risk the offender poses to the community, the probation officer identifies treatment needs so that the offender can receive appropriate services (counseling, treatment, education, community service, restitution, employment, and some form of supervision) during probation or in jail or prison.

In most cases, the court orders the PSR after conviction but before sentencing. The defendant reports to the probation department if released on bond pending sentencing. Otherwise, the probation officer visits the defendant in jail.

client-specific plan (CSP)

A privately prepared presentence report that supplements the PSR prepared by the probation department.

Client-Specific Plans   The defendant or defense counsel may hire a private agency to prepare a PSR in addition to the one ordered by the court. A privately prepared PSR is sometimes called a **client-specific plan**

(CSP). CSPs accomplish three things. First, they are an alternative source of information to judges. Second, they generally favor the defendant, encouraging greater use of treatment, counseling, education, community service, restitution, employment, and supervision. They may, however, call for the offender to pay a greater share of the cost of treatment. Third, they balance the PSRs prepared by government agencies.

Creating a Presentence Report   The PSR starts with an interview between the probation officer (PO) and the defendant. The interview follows a structured format for obtaining information on the offense and the offender. The PO is expected to verify, clarify, and explore any information to be presented in the PSR. Recently, researchers in Utah found that POs frequently made no attempt to verify the accuracy of the information supplied by the defendant because of the large volume of presentence reports and the time limitations placed on the POs. How widespread this assertion may be in other jurisdictions is unknown because the research is unavailable.

In the PSR, the PO is also expected to estimate the offender's degree of risk to the community. The estimate is based on the offender's lifestyle, prior criminal involvement, and experience with the criminal justice system. The PO summarizes the information gathered and, in most jurisdictions, makes a sentence recommendation. If the sentence recommended is incarceration, in most jurisdictions the length must be within guidelines set by statute (see Chapter 3). However, if the sentence recommended is probation or some other intermediate sanction (see Chapter 5), few jurisdictions have guidelines for sentence length. Only recently have some states (e.g., Delaware, North Carolina, and Pennsylvania) begun to design sentencing guidelines for nonprison sentences like probation. Copies of the PSR are filed with the court and made available to the judge, the prosecutor, and the defense attorney. Exhibit 4–7 is an example of a short-form federal PSR. Space does not allow us to include everything. Not shown here is the officer's summary of the defendant's pretrial adjustment, substance abuse history, education and vocational skills, employment record, financial condition, and necessary monthly living expenses.

Disclosure of Presentence Reports   One of the most important questions about the PSR is whether the defendant has a constitutional right to see it and challenge the statements contained in it. Judges and probation officers generally oppose disclosure for several reasons. First, they fear that persons having knowledge about the offender will refuse to give information if the defendant knows they have given information about him or her. Second, they believe that, if the defendant challenges information in the PSR, court proceedings may be unduly delayed. Third, opponents believe to give the defendant some kinds of information, such as psychological reports, might be harmful to that defendant. And fourth, they argue the PSR is a private and confidential court document. On the other hand, advocates of disclosure argue that fundamental fairness and due process demand that convicted persons should have access to the information in the PSR on which their sentence is based so they can correct inaccuracies. However, the U.S. Supreme Court has held, in *Williams* v. *Oklahoma* (1959), that unless disclosure is required by state law or court decisions, there is no denial of due process of law when a court considers a PSR without disclosing its contents to the defendant or giving the defendant an opportunity to rebut it.

EXHIBIT 4–7	Sample Presentence Report

IN THE UNITED STATES DISTRICT COURT
FOR THE NORTHERN DISTRICT OF ALABAMA

UNITED STATES OF AMERICA	)	
	)	PRESENTENCE
v.	)	REPORT
	)	
EDDIE PALMER	)	Docket No. CR 06-H-248-S

Prepared For: Honorable Casandra Phillips
U.S. District Judge

Prepared By: Noelle Koval
U.S. Probation Officer
Birmingham, AL
(205)555-0923

Offense: Count One: Possession With Intent to Distribute a Schedule II Controlled Substance (Cocaine Base), not less than 10 Years and not more than Life and/or $4,000,000 Fine. With Enhancement, Mandatory Life and/or $8,000,000 Fine.

Release Status: Released on $25,000 unsecured bond on 8/26/06
Remanded to custody on 12/14/06

Identifying Data

Date of Birth:	1/9/74
Age:	32
Race:	B
Sex:	M

Charge(s) and Conviction(s)

Eddie Palmer was indicted on two counts by the September 2006 Grand Jury for the Northern District of Alabama. Count One charged that on June 12, 2006, the defendant unlawfully possessed with intent to distribute approximately 500 grams of a mixture or substance containing a detectable amount of cocaine, Schedule II controlled substances, in violation of 21 USC § 841(a)(1). Count Two charged that on June 12, 2006, the defendant carried a firearm during the commission of a drug trafficking crime in violation of 18 USC § 924(c)(1). The October 2006 Grand Jury returned a superseding indictment in which the defendant was charged in two counts. Count One charges that on June 12, 2006, the defendant intentionally possessed with intent to distribute approximately 100 grams of a mixture or substance containing a detectable amount of cocaine base and approximately 240 grains of a mixture or substance containing a detectable amount of cocaine, Schedule II controlled subtances, in violation of 21 USC § 841(a)(1). Count Two charges that on June 12, 2006, the defendant carried a firearm during the commission of a drug trafficking crime in violation of 18 USC § 924(c)(1). On December 14, 2006, Palmer pled guilty to Count One, and Count Two was dismissed on motion of the government. Sentencing was continued generally to a later date.

However, the opposite is true in capital cases. In 1977 the Court said in *Gardner* v. *Florida* that the defendant was denied due process of law when the death penalty was imposed because he had been sentenced to death at least, in part, on the basis of information in the PSR that he had no opportunity to deny or explain because his lawyer did not request access to the full report.

The trend today is toward limited disclosure of information to the defendant's attorney. The American Bar Association favors disclosure of

EXHIBIT 4–7	Sample Presentence Report *(continued)*

SENTENCING RECOMMENDATION

UNITED STATES DISTRICT COURT
FOR THE NORTHERN DISTRICT OF ALABAMA

UNITED STATES V. EDDIE PALMER   DOCKET NO. CR 03-H-248-S

TOTAL OFFENSE LEVEL: 29
CRIMINAL HISTORY CATEGORY: III

	Statutory Provision	Guideline Provisions	Recommended Sentence
CUSTODY:	Mandatory Life	Mandatory Life	Life
PROBATION:	N/A	N/A	N/A
SUPERVISED RELEASE:	Not Less Than 10 Years	10 Years	10 Years
FINE:	$8,000,000	$15,000 to $8,000,000	$15,000
RESTITUTION:	N/A	N/A	N/A

Justification

The sentence of life is mandatory. Supervised release must be ten years. A $15,000 fine is recommended because it is incumbent upon the defendant to demonstrate that he does not have the financial ability to pay a fine. He and his attorney have not cooperated in providing information, and it appears that he does have the ability to pay the minimum fine based on his purported monthly income from trafficking in illegal drugs.

Voluntary Surrender

The defendant is in custody.

Respectfully submitted,

Noelle Koval

Noelle Koval
U.S. Probation Officer

the factual contents and conclusions of the PSR (not the sources of confidential information) and the defendant's opportunity to rebut them.[43] Federal courts require that the PSR be disclosed to the defendant, his or her counsel, and to the attorney for the government, except in three instances: when disclosure might disrupt rehabilitation of the defendant, when information disclosed in the PSR was obtained on the promise of confidentiality, and when disclosure might result in harm to the defendant or any other person. Observers note that jurisdictions that practice limited disclosure have not encountered the problems anticipated by opponents of disclosure.[44] Limited disclosure has led probation departments to analyze the offense and the offender more objectively, increase the court's reliance on the PSR, and develop a closer relationship between the offender and probation officer.

Technology and Case Investigations Today, technological innovations are affecting where and how POs do their job. Software packages can generate PSRs from data from official records and interviews entered by probation officers. The software programs can also calculate

My first PO was a man who had years of experience. He was cynical. He took his job too seriously. I cooperated and soon he trusted me. His requirements were few. I was rarely asked to report at his office, and he would call to let me know he was coming to my home for a visit.

After several months, I was assigned a female PO. I was required to give urine samples under her observation. That bothered me, because I had no history of substance abuse. The purpose of these samples seems to have been to humiliate me. I wondered why the feds wanted to be in the business of humiliating people!

Being on supervised release was no big deal, as long as I sent in my monthly reports and got permission to travel outside the district (which meant ten miles to the north and twelve miles to the west). At my request, my second PO processed the forms for my release from supervision one year ahead of schedule. My cooperation paid off.

I don't know if federal probation reduces crime. But I do think that probation should be used more often, instead of incarceration, with community service. I think most prison sentences are too long and disruptive to families. I also think that all efforts should be made to support an offender's attempts to straighten out his or her life. The entire "justice" system needs to become caring and compassionate, putting more people into treatment and job programs than into prison.

Did probation disrupt my life? Yes. But I committed a crime and accepted probation willingly. Still, I think that it was wasteful, since once the feds realized that I had paid my fine off early, had no drug problems, kept a stable work record, and was cooperative, they might have saved us all some money by letting me off even sooner than they did.

Anonymous female, previously on federal probation

---

risk assessment scores. A PO can edit the report before submitting it to the court.

The trend toward telecommuting is also affecting probation officers' case investigations. Telecommuting is usually defined as an employee working at home or other telework facility for at least one day a week during regularly scheduled business hours, supported by the necessary hardware and software. Today, between 30 and 40 million people either telecommute or work strictly from their homes.[45] Some jurisdictions are finding that presentence officers are successful telecommuters. The U.S. Probation Office in the Middle District of Florida found that presentence officers reported an increase in job satisfaction and a higher level of productivity. They reported to the office to interview defendants, meet with attorneys, attend court hearings, and perform other routine office duties. They spent the remainder of their time at their residences working on their investigations. The officers averaged 2.5 to 3.0 days a week telecommuting. Their work was transmitted electronically through a secure intranet mailing system. Telecommuting was not effective for supervision officers, however, who were needed in the probation office to handle the needs of their offenders and who had to travel in the field to meet their probationers.

supervision

The second major role of probation officers, consisting of resource mediation, surveillance, and enforcement.

Supervision

The second major role of probation officers is client supervision. Probation **supervision** has three main elements: resource mediation, surveillance, and enforcement. *Resource mediation* means providing offenders access to a wide variety of services, such as job development, substance abuse treatment, counseling, and education. *Surveillance* means monitoring the activities of probationers through office meetings, home and work visits, drug and alcohol testing, and contact with family, friends, and employers. *Enforcement* means making probationers accountable for their

When I started as a probation officer in West Virginia, Martinson's "Nothing Works" study supported the philosophy that, since rehabilitation and probation failed, the real answer to crime control was to "lock 'em up" for long periods of time. Nothing-works philosophy translated to the "truth in sentencing" perspective and widespread spending in the construction of new federal, state, and local prisons and jails. Probation and rehabilitation advocates were afraid that, if they challenged the new philosophy, they would find themselves unemployed. In the 1970s, I helped develop the West Virginia Association of Probation Officers to improve the professionalism of probation in West Virginia. One of our aims was to consolidate probation under the West Virginia Supreme Court instead of having it under the Department of Welfare, the Department of Corrections, and the local courts. Today, probation comes under the West Virginia Supreme Court. Nationally, the American Probation and Parole Association has enhanced probation and community-based programs that have proved to be successful.

Juvenile programs administered by our department include mediation and arbitration for juveniles in which volunteers help resolve conflicts between juvenile offenders, their families, victims, and others. Alternative Learning Center programs provide education for violent juvenile offenders in off-school settings. Volunteers in Probation programs provide a mentor for every juvenile placed on probation. Adult programs include community probation officers for supervision and treatment and the supervision of community service work by offenders. I can honestly say that after 27 years as a probation officer, I am more energized than I have ever been, thanks to our success in the community. And I know that the 21st century will confirm that probation and its community-based programs are an effective way to reduce crime, rehabilitate offenders, and bring peace to many households and communities.

James R. Lee
Chief Probation Officer
First Judicial Circuit
Wellsburg, West Virginia

behavior and making sure they understand the consequences of violating the conditions of probation.

Caseload The average PO in the United States supervises approximately 139 offenders.[46] On January 1, 2000, probation officers in Rhode Island had the largest probation caseload (311), followed by Georgia (279). Such large caseloads do not allow probation officers time for adequate resource mediation, surveillance, or enforcement. A number of jurisdictions are experimenting with Probation Automated Management (PAM). The PAM kiosk is similar to an ATM and allows low-risk probationers to report in 24 hours a day, seven days a week, with their fingerprints as biometric identifiers. The fingerprints are compared to the ones collected when the offender first began probation. Some kiosks also take a digital face photo. The kiosk used by the Federal District of Utah Probation and Pretrial Office is located in the lobby of the federal community corrections center.[47]

Once a match is established, the offender can interact with the kiosk by pressing buttons on the touch screen. Data are entered to verify address and employment status and to respond to questions asked by the probation officer. Advocates of probation kiosks argue that they save scarce jail beds for those offenders posing a serious risk to the community and that

Olmsted County (Rochester, Minnesota) probation officer Bernie Sizer (*right*), tests Kevin Rood for alcohol during a visit to Rood's apartment. Case supervision is the second major role of a probation officer. What are the three main elements of case supervision?

to the offender's particular crime or history. For example, a person convicted of cybercrime may be subject to the special conditions shown in Exhibit 4–10.

Talking about **CORRECTIONS**

COMMUNITY CORRECTIONS TECHNOLOGIES

Visit *Live Talk* at **Corrections.com** (www.justicestudies.com/talking04) and listen to the program "Correctional Education," which relates to ideas discussed in this chapter.

Technology and Supervision   As in case investigation, there are now software programs to help POs in client supervision. Computer programs can track fine and probation payments, alert POs when their clients are behind on payments, and help them track whether probationers have satisfied the conditions of their sentences.

Another technological innovation, one of the more interesting strategies for managing the three elements of probation supervision, is mapping technology or geographic information systems (GIS). Mapping has helped law enforcement locate hot spots of crime. Police departments used to

At the entr
jail in Roch
second-tim
drunk drivir
before the
month and
answer que
Probation k
low-risk off
face-to-fac
officer. Wh
tages do yc

EXHIBIT 4–10   Specific Probation Conditions for Computer Crime

(A = Internet Access Permitted; B = Limited or 0 Access to Internet)	A	B
You shall consent to your probation officer and/or probation service representative conducting periodic unannounced examinations of your computer(s) equipment which may include retrieval and copying of all memory from hardware/software to ensure compliance with this condition and/or removal of such equipment for the purpose of conducting a more thorough inspection; and consent at the direction of your probation officer to having installed on your computer(s), at your expense, any hardware or software systems to monitor your computer use or prevent access to particular materials. You hereby consent to the periodic inspection of any such installed hardware or software to insure it is functioning properly.	X	X
You shall not possess encryption or steganography software.	X	X
You shall provide your probation officer accurate information about your entire computer system and software; all passwords used by you; and your Internet Service Provider(s).	X	X
You shall possess only computer hardware or software approved by your probation officer. You shall obtain written permission from your probation officer prior to obtaining any additional computer hardware or software or Internet Service Provider(s).	X	X
You shall refrain from using a computer in any manner that relates to the activity in which you were engaged in committing the instant offense or violation behavior, namely_____.	X	X
You shall provide truthful information concerning your identity in all Internet or E-Mail communications and not visit any "chat rooms" or similar Internet locations/sites where minors are known to frequent.	X	
You shall maintain a daily log of all addresses you access via any personal computer (or other computer used by you), other than for authorized employment, and make this log available to your probation officer.	X	
You shall not create or assist directly or indirectly in the creation of any electronic bulletin board, Internet Service Provider, or any other public or private network without the prior written consent of your probation officer. Any approval shall be subject to any conditions set by the U.S. Probation Office of the Court with respect to that approval.	X	X
You shall not possess or use a computer with access to any "on-line" computer service at any location (including employment or education) without prior written approval of the U.S. Probation Office of the Court. This includes any Internet Service Provider, bulletin board system, or any other public or private computer network. Any approval shall be subject to any conditions set by the U.S. Probation Office or the Court with respect to that approval.		X
You shall not purchase, possess, or receive a personal computer which utilizes a modem, and/or an external mode.		X
You will have an occupational condition that you can not be employed directly or indirectly where you are an installer, programmer, or "trouble shooter" for computer equipment.	X	X

Source: Arthur L. Bowker and Gregory B. Thompson, "Computer Crime in the 21st Century and Its Effects on the Probation Officer," *Federal Probation*, vol. 65, no. 2 (September 2001), p. 21.

A probation officer interviews a crime victim. Case investigation is one of a probation officer's most important tasks. What questions would you ask a crime victim as part of the investigation?

map with pins on a "point map." Today, mapping is done electronically and affords complex and instant analyses. Probation departments use mapping as a tool for the management of offenders in the community. Mapping helps ensure that probation and parole officers are dispersed in areas with high concentrations of them.

Agencies in Wisconsin and New York are using probation mapping to enhance offender supervision. Mapping can show what kind of crime problem an area has (e.g., drug or theft) and deploy probation staff and resources appropriately. Services can be moved to areas that need them most. For example, the Wisconsin Department of Corrections found through mapping that "if you have an area with a drug usage problem, we would bring drug programming to that area. Really, our experience was we got better attendance and better completion rates with that."[50] The Center for Alternative Sentencing and Employment in New York uses mapping to monitor employment rates in areas where ex-offenders will reside and, with the assistance of community agencies, helps them find a job link upon leaving prison. Learn more about the role of technology in offender supervision, parole hearings, victim notification, and professional development in Chapters 5, 8, 11, 13, 14, and 17.

Revocation of Probation   If the offender willfully violates the conditions of his or her probation, a **revocation hearing** is usually the next step. A revocation hearing is a due process hearing that must be conducted by the court or probation authority to determine whether the conditions of probation (or parole as we will see in Chapter 8) have been violated before probation can be revoked and the offender removed from the community. **Revocation** is the formal termination of an offender's conditional freedom. During 1999, states averaged 4,400 probation revocation hearings per year.

Revocation is a serious matter for four reasons. First, the offender might lose his or her freedom to remain in the community. Second, the handling of probation violators by supervision agencies and courts consumes a significant portion of the court's time, energy, and resources. One jurisdiction estimated that, in addition to the equivalent of more than two full-time probation officers, the various stages of the probation violation process consumes the equivalent of a full-time judge, prosecutor, and

revocation hearing

A due process hearing that must be conducted to determine whether the conditions of probation have been violated before probation can be revoked and the offender removed from the community.

revocation

The formal termination of an offender's conditional freedom.

Eye On Corrections

Social Workers & Cowboys: Social Worker Finds Success

By Sarah Etter

In Kentucky, there's a saying that has motivated Lelia VanHoose, Director of Probation and Parole for the state's Department of Corrections, for years.

"We walk a fine line between being social workers and cowboys," VanHoose says.

According to VanHoose, that fine line is a necessary balance between focusing on rehabilitation and punishing offenders who continue to act out while they are on parole or probation.

"In social services, you have people who are more interested in the officer side of it, and arresting people," VanHoose explains. "Then you have people who are so dead set on social work that they forget about the times when an arrest is necessary. It's important to strike a balance between those things—and teach that balance to others."

VanHoose has constantly applied this philosophy on the job. And while working with tough cases, Van-Hoose has maintained the humane, yet firm, attitude.

"It's easy to get emotional in corrections—we're all human." VanHoose says. "There are plenty of [offenders] that are well versed at bringing forth emotions in other people. But you have to be firm, fair and consistent. You have to have a plan of where you want an offender to go, how you want them to progress, and you have to carry it out."

With a clear focus on rehabilitation, VanHoose has become a member of the state's corrections family. She is known among her peers for her outstanding relationships with everyone from judges to law enforcement officials. Described by co-workers as a "true professional," VanHoose was named the 2005 Probation and Parole Supervisor of the Year in Kentucky.

The Corrections Connection recently spoke with VanHoose and asked about her goals in corrections—and her focus on rehabilitation.

Q: How did you get involved in the corrections field?

VanHoose: I started pretty much out of college, after I earned a sociology degree. I was interested in probation and parole and criminal justice matters. I found openings in areas that I liked in Central Kentucky, where I'd gone to college. I took some tests and got into probation and parole.

Q: Why were you interested in probation and parole?

VanHoose: This is a human service field—you don't go into this to get rich or for personal awards. This almost sounds like a bad thing, but I always think this job teaches that many of us are pretty blessed. If you have a job and you can go to work every day, you are blessed. People tend to feel sorry for themselves sometimes.

But if I ever feel sorry for myself, I go out and do home visits and I realize things aren't so bad for me. That's one of the most eye opening experiences, to be in a parolee's home and see the circumstances they are surrounded by.

But I do this for the love of the work and the passion for the people—not the personal glory and the pay. It's the desire to do a good job, help the community, help the people around you and help offenders adjust to that community.

Q: What's the most rewarding part of your job?

VanHoose: There have been several times that I realized that if I just made one difference [with someone], it mattered. There was one fellow that I supervised for a murder conviction when I was 23 or 24, and he was a hardened murderer, so to speak. He came into our meeting and told me he had started using drugs again. I personally drove him, in my own vehicle, in the snow, and took him immediately to a treatment center. He stuck with the treatment plan. Now, he is a reverend that has a doctorate and he's doing amazing things in his community.

I think about another fellow I supervised that went back to college and got a Master's degree and now he's changing lives. That makes all of the difference—seeing those successes and what they are doing for others.

Q: What is your philosophy when it comes to work? What keeps you going every day?

VanHoose: I've always said that we need to work smarter, not harsher . We're working with limited budgets and limited access to some things. But we're trying to use best practices, and make sure the offenders are getting their needs met as best as possible too.

My philosophy has always been to be firm, fair and consistent. Now, I'm just in a different role to make sure we're using that philosophy. We just want to find new and better ways to do the job. We need to rehabilitate [offenders] and get them on the right track, so they don't re-offend. I would hope that anyone in a similar field would have the same focus I do.

But the goal—no matter what—is that you always treat people the way you want to be treated. When you keep that in mind, the goal is that all the success and hard work is worth it. Just to know there is one success—you've helped one person become successful; you've helped an offender, their family and even the employees. If you make one positive difference for someone along the line, it's worth it. Unfortunately, there's a lot of negative in the business we're in, so you have to keep the positives in mind.

Q: How do you feel about being recognized for your work?

VanHoose: I'm very, very pleased with the award. You always feel like you're working hard to do a good job, but the district I had gone to work in had some issues and I worked very hard to get those settled. It was a good office but we had to get it settled and back focused. I felt so pleased but I felt it was an acknowledgement of the hard work and progress that we made with that district.

It's always gratifying for anyone in any position to be recognized for hard work. You do the work and you work hard because—I'm proud to say—my parents instilled in me a work ethic that doesn't accept substandard. I have been raised with that instilled. It's just a part of doing your job well and a job well done. It's an inner satisfaction and the acknowledgement is an important part of any type of supervision—to acknowledge the good things.

Source: "Social Workers & Cowboys: Social Worker Finds Success," Sarah Etter, The Corrections Connection Network News (CCNN). Eye on Corrections. www.corrections.com. January 23, 2006.

courtroom staff.[51] Third, the cost of keeping an offender under probation supervision is much lower than that required for care and treatment in prison or jail. For example, we saw in Exhibit 4–4 that the per-day cost of probation ranges from $2.11 to $9.66, depending on the level of supervision and risk an offender poses, but it costs $56.72 per day to keep an offender in jail and $57.92 per day to keep an offender in prison. And fourth, imprisoning offenders who otherwise would have been placed on probation may force their families to go on welfare or make greater demands on community resources.

Still, revocation is the only way to protect the community from some offenders who refuse to abide by the conditions or probation. A group of leading officials in the field of probation and parole, called the Reinventing Probation Council, recently concluded that the reason probation has not been able to protect the public is lax enforcement of the probation rules. Others agree. Joan Petersilia, a criminologist at the University of California, Irvine, notes, "The result is that probationers quickly learn that failing a drug test, or violating other court-ordered conditions, has little consequence."[52] The council stresses, "All conditions of a probation sentence must be enforced. The response must be swift and sure. This does not mean that each violation will result in the revocation of probation but rather the imposition of graduated sanctions."[53]

A number of jurisdictions now recognize that revoking even a small percentage of the probation population can have a dramatic effect on the prison population. In some states (e.g., California, Oregon, and Texas), over two-thirds of prison admissions are probation or parole violators. While it is important to take action when violations are discovered, prison may not be the best response. State legislatures in Georgia, Mississippi, Oregon, and Washington are trying to reserve prison space for violent offenders by structuring the courts' response to technical violations. Georgia and Mississippi use 90-day boot camp programs for probation and parole violators. Oregon and Washington use short jail stays (two to three days). The South Carolina Department of Probation, Parole and Pardon Services was named in the American Correctional Association's Best Practices for having one of the best methods for managing probation and parole violations.[54] The agency developed violation guidelines so that the responses were appropriate, consistent, and proportional; empowered the department's internal administrative hearing officers so that they could impose intermediate sanctions and community options; ensured that the response to violations reflected the severity of the violation and the risks posed to the community; issued citations in some cases rather than a warrant in order to eliminate the need for many offenders to be housed in jails to await disposition of their violations; and created a method to evaluate the progress of these initiatives. "We're trying to establish consistency in addressing violations," said Joan Meacham, deputy director for field services, South Carolina Department of Probation, Parole and Pardon Services. "We are trying to make it simple for the caseworkers. We make sure we choose the right person to go to court because we don't want to waste anyone's time."[55]

Some probation violation sanctions that South Carolina probation and parole officers are imposing include placing an offender in a halfway house for up to 60 days, placing an offender in a residential or nonresidential treatment facility, placing offenders on home detention, and increasing reporting or drug testing. If an agent cannot resolve a violation case, the case goes to an administrative hearing, which is the last step before it goes to the court or parole board.

Corrections officials and researchers make two observations about these new responses to probation and parole violators. First, these programs increase the certainty of punishment. The offender will find the term disruptive to normal living and be deterred from further violations. Second, there is no evidence that technical violators go on to commit new offenses; therefore, commitment to prison is a wasted resource.

Violations That Trigger Revocation Revocation is triggered in one of two ways. Either offenders willfully violate the *technical* conditions of their probation, or they commit *new offenses*.

A **technical violation** is failure to comply with conditions of probation. It is not a criminal act; most revocations are the result of technical violations. According to a report published by the National Institute of Corrections (NIC) in 2001, the most likely reason for prison incarceration of probation (and parole) violators is technical violations.[56] In 1999, technical violators accounted for 68 percent of all prison admissions. The most commonly committed technical violations are positive urinalysis, failure to participate in treatment, **absconding** (fleeing without permission of the jurisdiction in which the offender is required to stay), and failure to report to the probation officer. Most probation officers do not ask the court to revoke probation for an occasional technical violation. They understand that technical violations are supervision issues and best handled by program or treatment referrals. One analyst in the NIC report commented, "If our jails and prisons are filled with offenders who are merely noncompliant, there will be no room for the dangerous offender." To ensure compliance, probation officers can tighten the offender's supervision with a reprimand, increase reporting requirements, limit travel or other privileges, increase drug/alcohol testing, make treatment/education referrals, restructure payments (for probationers who demonstrate an inability to pay in accordance with the court-established payment plan), or extend the terms of probation. A probationer who says he or she did not understand the conditions of probation could be required to spend a Friday evening attending a "reorientation" meeting at the local halfway house. The possibilities are limitless. The key to creating these types of violation responses is understanding that a violation may be the manifestation of a supervision issue. If a circumstance is discovered early enough, the need to impose sanctions may not arise. Repeated serious technical violations, however, may lead to revocation.

The revocation process is also predicated on the offender committing a *willful* or *intentional* violation. In this case it is guided by a body of court decisions. For example, if a probationer made a real effort to pay his or her court-ordered supervision fees and/or victim restitution but was unable to do so because of minimal education, few job skills, job loss, and so forth, probation may not be revoked unless alternate measures are inadequate to meet the state's interest in deterrence and punishment. However, the courts have held that, where there may be a risk to public safety, probation can be revoked even if the offender is not responsible for his or her inability to complete the conditions of probation. For example, if a sex offender is unable to complete a sex offender treatment program through no fault of his or her own, the court noted that, without treatment, the offender would present public safety risks because of the likelihood of reoffending, and it thus supported revocation.

A **new offense violation** is the arrest and prosecution for the commission of a new crime. Depending upon the seriousness of the new offense, the court may, in response to a violation of probation (or parole, see Chapter 8)

technical violation
A failure to comply with the conditions of probation.

absconding
Fleeing without permission of the jurisdiction in which the offender is required to stay.

new offense violation
The arrest and prosecution for the commission of a new crime.

based on a new offense, impose a sentence of incarceration upon revocation of probation, *plus* any new sentence of incarceration that may be imposed for the new offense. The two sentences may be imposed to run concurrently or consecutively (see Chapter 3). In the case of parole, a new offense violation may trigger return to prison to serve out the unexpired sentence, *plus* sentence for the new offense. In 1999, 32 percent of adults sentenced to prison were admitted for probation violations as well as a new felony. In 2001, NIC conducted a study of how jurisdictions respond to probation violators in Macomb County, Michigan, and Suffolk County, New York.[57] The researchers found that 12 percent of the violations for which probation officers filed motions to revoke probation were for new felonies and 4 percent were for new misdemeanors. The point to remember is that a substantial percentage of the prison population each year is probation (and parole) violators.

Revocation Hearings Revocation hearings usually begin with a violation report prepared by the probation officer. They are governed by the 1973 U.S. Supreme Court decision known as *Gagnon* v. *Scarpelli*. In this case, the Court said that there was no difference between probation and parole revocation because both of them resulted in loss of liberty. The Court extended the same rights to probationers that it granted to parolees a year earlier in *Morrissey* v. *Brewer*. The Court ruled that probation cannot be revoked without observing the following elements of due process:

1. written notice of the charge;
2. disclosure to the probationer of the evidence;
3. the opportunity to be heard in person and present evidence as well as witnesses;
4. the right to confront and cross-examine witnesses;
5. the right to judgment by a detached and neutral hearing body;
6. a written statement of the reasons for revoking probation; and
7. the right to counsel under "special circumstances" depending on the offender's competence, case complexity, and mitigating circumstances.

REVIEW & APPLICATIONS

REFLECTIONS ON THE FUTURE

by *Kathy Waters*
Arizona Supreme Court

Probation: A Status, System, and Process

In the future, probation professionals must have a clear mission and must define for all involved, including the public, what the expectations of probation will be. We must stop telling the public, legislatures, and other criminal justice professionals that we are responsible for public safety and for changing offenders' behavior. What we need to tell them is that our efforts—holding offenders accountable and enforcing court orders—contribute to the safety of the community and also help change offenders' behavior. We are enforcement agents and, it is hoped, assist offenders in changing their behavior. We do not change offenders; they change themselves with our assistance and with the help of many other professionals and the support systems in their lives.

Unless we communicate and reestablish our goals and the purpose of probation, we will continue to exist in a shadow cast from considerable doubt about the effectiveness of probation and the future use of community supervision. Today, probation is the most widely used judicial sanction and disposition that encompasses elements of both community protection and offender rehabilitation. It is a status, a system, and a process.

We continue to struggle with the ability to present grounded and credible research as to the outcomes of probation and community supervision. We talk about "what works," but do we really know? Are we able to back up these statements about our programs with facts? Evidence-based practices will need to be a requirement. We must establish ourselves as a viable sanction, and we must agree about what is the true purpose of probation. We must enlist the community to help develop and accept outcome measures, which is supported by credible research.

Finding people with the right attitudes and knowledge must drive hiring practices. Staff must demonstrate the knowledge and skills to produce effectively the outcomes we are trying to achieve. The ability of a probation officer effectively to monitor and assist an offender while enforcing the orders of the court will demand ongoing training and skill development. Resources must be available to ensure this training is available.

In summary, as prison overcrowding continues, probation has an opportunity to demonstrate its worth in the criminal justice system. We must take advantage of the current situation and focus on the core values and basics of what probation supervision was intended to be. If we do not, we will be seen as an ineffective cog in a larger failing criminal justice system.

About the Author

Kathy Waters is past president of the American Probation and Parole Association and director of Adult Services, Administrative Office of the Courts, Arizona Supreme Court. Waters received a bachelor of science in business administration and master of science in criminal justice administration from Northeastern State University, Tahlequah, Oklahoma.

SUMMARY

1 Diversion is the official halting or suspension, before conviction, of formal criminal proceedings against a person, often conditioned on some form of counterperformance, such as participation in a treatment, counseling, or educational program. Diversion is intended to (1) prevent future criminal activity by diverting certain defendants from criminal justice processing into community supervision and service, (2) save prosecution and judicial resources for serious crimes by offering alternatives to the usual prosecution process for less serious ones, and (3) provide, where appropriate, a vehicle for restitution to communities and victims of crime.

2 There are four rationales for diversion: (1) Formal processing can encourage more criminal behavior; (2) diversion is cheaper than formally processing an offender through the criminal justice system; (3) formal processing may seem inappropriate for crimes without perceived victims; and (4) formal arrest, trial, and conviction add to the burdens of certain disadvantaged groups.

3 Diversion may occur at any stage in the criminal justice process after a criminal complaint has been filed or police have observed a crime. The police, a prosecutor or judge may call for diversion.

4 Issues concerning diversion include (1) the legal and ethical issues of protecting a defendant's rights; (2) the law enforcement question whether diversion encourages violation of the law; and (3) the economic question of diversion's cost-effectiveness.

5 Probation is the conditional release of a convicted offender into the community, under the supervision of a probation officer. Most probation programs are designed to (1) protect the community by assisting judges in sentencing and supervising offenders, (2) carry out sanctions imposed by the court, (3) help offenders change, (4) support crime victims, and (5) coordinate and promote the use of community resources.

6 Probation is used for four reasons: (1) It permits offenders to remain in the community for reintegration purposes, (2) it avoids institutionalization and the stigma of incarceration, (3) it is less expensive than incarceration and more humanitarian, and (4) it is appropriate for offenders whose crimes do not necessarily merit incarceration.

7 On January 1, 2006, federal, state, and local probation agencies supervised 4.1 million adult U.S. residents, with felony convictions accounting for almost one-half. Twenty-three percent of all probationers were women, and 55 percent of probationers were white. Fifty-seven percent of adults had a direct sentence to probation.

8 In 29 states, a state or local agency delivers adult probation services. In 3 states, adult probation services are delivered exclusively through county or multicounty agencies in the executive branch. In 8 states, the judicial branch of government is responsible for adult probation services. In 5 states, local agencies in the judicial branch deliver adult

probation services. And in five states, adult probation services are delivered through some combination of state executive branch, local executive agencies, or local agencies in either the judicial or the executive branch.

9 Corrections professionals urge evaluators to collect data on outcomes other than recidivism, such as amount of restitution collected, number of offenders employed, amounts of fines and fees collected, hours of community service, number of treatment sessions completed, percentage of financial obligations collected, rate of enrollment in school, number of days employed, educational attainment, and number of days drug free.

10 Case investigation and client supervision are the two major roles of probation officers. Investigation includes the preparation of a presentence report (PSR), which the judge uses in sentencing an offender. Supervision includes the functions of resource mediation, surveillance, and enforcement.

11 A revocation hearing is a due process hearing that must be conducted to determine whether the conditions of probation have been violated before probation can be revoked and the offender is removed from the community. Probation can be revoked when offenders fail to comply with the technical conditions of probation or commit new crimes.

KEY TERMS

diversion, *p. 111*
counterperformance, *p. 111*
true diversion, *p. 112*
minimization of penetration, *p. 112*
unconditional diversion, *p. 115*
conditional diversion, *p. 115*

probation, *p. 116*
recidivism, *p. 128*
working alliance, *p. 133*
cognitive-behavioral treatment, *p. 133*
client-specific plan (CSP), *p. 135*

supervision, *p. 140*
revocation hearing, *p. 145*
revocation, *p. 145*
technical violation, *p. 149*
absconding, *p. 149*
new offense violation, *p. 149*

QUESTIONS FOR REVIEW

1 Explain diversion and its objectives.

2 Apply the rationales of diversion to a hypothetical case.

3 Distinguish the stages at which diversion occurs in the criminal justice process.

4 How would you respond to the diversion policy issues?

5 Explain probation and its goals.

6 Defend the reasons for using probation.

7 Construct a profile of the characteristics of adults on probation.

8 Summarize the different ways that probation is administered.

9 Evaluate the measures of probation.

10 Distinguish between the investigation and supervision functions of probation and provide an example of each.

11 Summarize what occurs at a revocation hearing.

THINKING CRITICALLY ABOUT CORRECTIONS

PSRs

Critics of PSRs claim that the information in them is not always verified or reliable even though the trend today is toward limited disclosure of information to the defendant's attorney. Actually, much of the information in a PSR is hearsay. Although defendants or victims may object to the contents of a PSR or the way it characterizes their behavior, they have no right to have the PSR reflect their views.

As a probation officer, how would you respond to these criticisms?

Probation Effectiveness

Recidivism is one current measure of probation effectiveness. Others include the amount of restitution collected, the number of offenders employed, the amounts of fines and fees collected, the number of hours of community service performed, the number of treatment sessions completed, the percentage of financial obligations collected, the rate of school enrollment, the level of educational attainment, the number of days employed, and the number of days drug free.

1. How important to you, as a taxpayer, is recidivism as a measure of program success?

2. Do you believe probation officers can really keep offenders from committing new crimes or violating the conditions of their probation?

3. If you were a probation officer today, by which outcome measures would you want to be judged? Why?

4. If recidivism is used as a measure of probation's effectiveness, how should it be defined?

ON-THE-JOB DECISION MAKING

Responding to Program Violations

The new diversion program in your county was developed to help first-time misdemeanor drug offenders avoid incarceration and seek help in controlling their dependency. Your job as the new diversion officer is to set the conditions of the diversion program and then monitor and enforce compliance. One of your first clients fails the required weekly drug test.

1. Should you immediately remove that person from the program?

2. Why or why not?

Probation and Recidivism

At a recent staff meeting, the chief PO reported that the department's recidivism rate exceeded the national average by 5 percent. The chief asks what can be done about it. You say, "Look at other measures besides recidivism." The chief asks you to explain. What do you say?

LIVE LINKS

at www.justicestudies.com/livelinks04

4–1 A Guide to Implementing Police-Based Diversion Programs for People with Mental Illness

This report addresses what law enforcement agencies are doing nationally to improve their response to people with mental illness—largely through partnerships with the mental health community—and explores how these agencies have overcome barriers to create and maintain effective programs.

4–2 Pretrial Services Programs

This report provides a review of issues and practices in the field of pretrial services. It describes how pretrial programs operate, discusses key policy issues, and outlines issues and challenges for the future. It pays particular attention to how pretrial services programs obtain and convey information relevant to the pretrial release/detention decision. It also describes how pretrial services agencies, the court, and other criminal justice system agencies can work together to minimize the risks of nonappearance and pretrial crime.

4–3 Stress Among Probation and Parole Officers and What Can Be Done About It

Researchers investigated the nature and scope of stress among probation and parole officers at nine sites around the country. They identified the major sources of stress (heavy caseloads, paperwork, deadlines) and what officers do to cope. They summarize key findings and provide case studies of promising stress reduction programs.

4–4 Probation and Parole in the United States, 2005

This document tracks the probation and parole population in the United States at year-end 2005. It presents data on the number of persons on probation and parole, the rate per 100,000 adult population, states with the largest and smallest populations, and characteristics of adults on probation and parole.

4–5 Trends in Probation and Parole in the States

This paper discusses six trends that characterize the efforts of probation and parole to meet their mandates and improve their effectiveness. Environmental factors that impact probation and parole are organizational structure, workload, resources and funding, and sentencing alternatives and reform. Trends that redefine the missions and organizational culture of parole and probation are collaboration and partnerships, results-driven management, the reemergence of rehabilitation, specialization, technology, and community justice.

INTERMEDIATE SANCTIONS

Between Probation and Incarceration

> Crime and bad lives are the measure of a State's failure; all crime in the end is the crime of the community.
>
> —H. G. Wells, originator of modern science fiction, 1866–1946

CHAPTER OBJECTIVES

After completing this chapter you should be able to do the following:

1 Define *intermediate sanctions* and describe their purpose.

2 Define *net widening*.

3 Describe how intensive supervision probation works.

4 Explain what drug courts are.

5 Explain how day fines differ from traditional fines.

6 Describe what a sentence to community service entails.

7 Explain what day reporting centers are.

8 Describe how remote-location monitoring works.

9 Explain what residential community centers are.

10 Identify the major features of boot camps.

11 Distinguish between a policy-centered approach and a program-centered approach to planning intermediate sanctions.

12 Define *community corrections*.

13 Explain what community corrections acts are.

In 1982, Culture Club and Boy George became the first (and still only) group since the Beatles to have at least three top 10 hits on the Billboard Hot 100 from a debut album. Born George Alan O'Dowd on June 14, 1961, Boy George's talent and androgynous style caught the attention of music executives and by 1985 he had become a household name in many countries around the world.[1]

Boy George's musical climb did not last long however. Disappointing sales on new albums, the breakup of his relationship with his drummer Jon Moss, and his addiction to heroine and cocaine caused the downward spiral of the group and they eventually disbanded in 1987. Since then Boy George has released several solo albums and pursued a career in DJing.

On October 7, 2005, 44-year-old Boy George called 911 and told the New York Police Department he thought that someone was trying to break in to his Manhattan loft. When the police arrived, they found no signs of a break-in or burglary. What they found instead was an eighth of an ounce (3.5 grams) of cocaine next to his computer. George was arrested and the Manhattan District Attorney's office charged him with possession of cocaine.

On August 14, 2006, Culture Club's Boy George started five days of community service with the New York City Department of Sanitation as part of his sentence for falsely reporting that someone was trying to break in to his Manhattan loft. The court dismissed the charge of possession of cocaine in turn for Boy George's plea agreement. He also agreed to enter a drug treatment program in England, pay a fine of $1,000 and a surcharge of $160, and avoid arrest for six months. Do you think intermediate sanctions teach offenders a lesson better than regular probation alone?

In March 2006, George accepted a plea agreement that dismissed the felony cocaine possession charge and pled guilty to a third-degree false reporting of an incident. He agreed to enter a drug treatment program in England, perform five days of community service, pay a fine of $1,000 and a surcharge of $160, and avoid arrest for the next six months.

However, by early June 2006, George did not perform the community service and did not pay the fine or surcharge. Criminal court judge Anthony Ferrara issued a warrant for George's arrest but withdrew it and ordered a hearing for June 26, 2006, on whether George violated the terms of his sentence. On that date, Judge Ferrara scolded George for not complying with the terms of his sentence. Judge Ferrara told him, "This is a simple matter. Five days of community service. It is up to you as to whether it will be an exercise in humiliation or humility." He shot down George's suggestions for fulfilling his community service duties, including holding a fashion and makeup workshop, helping teenagers make a public service announcement, and serving as a DJ at an HIV/AIDS benefit. The judge roared back, "So he'd write and produce a song for a public-service announcement? DJ for a benefit concert? Hold a special class on makeup? Do you really think that's punishment? To be a DJ?" Ferrara ordered George to report to the office that assigns court-ordered community service and complete his community service by August 28, 2006, or be jailed. George started his community service at the sanitation department on August 14 wearing a bright orange vest with yellow stripes, bearing the words "New York City Department of Sanitation." He was taken to the median of a Lower East Side street and began sweeping. However, because he was immediately swarmed by reporters and photographers, he was allowed to sweep a gated sanitation parking lot and mop office floors. He completed his community service on August 28.

Punishing the criminal behavior of George Alan O'Dowd captures the essence of this chapter. Today, judges have unlimited opportunities to order penalties that match the seriousness of a crime. The punishments given to George—enter a drug treatment program in England, perform five days of community service, pay a fine of $1,000 and a surcharge of $160, and avoid arrest for the next six months—constitute what we call **intermediate sanctions:** punishment options that fill the gap between traditional probation and jail or prison and that better match the severity of punishment to the seriousness of the crime. Intermediate sanctions fulfill the important sentencing goals discussed in Chapter 3: retribution, deterrence, just deserts, incapacitation, rehabilitation, and restoration. Because intermediate sanctions are administered outside the prison or jail and generally in the offender's community, they are a form of **community corrections.** After considering the principal intermediate sanctions in use in the United States, we will turn our attention to community corrections in general.

intermediate sanctions
New punishment options developed to fill the gap between traditional probation and traditional jail or prison sentences and to better match the severity of punishment to the seriousness of the crime.

community corrections
A philosophy of correctional treatment that embraces (1) decentralization of authority, (2) citizen participation, (3) redefinition of the population of offenders for whom incarceration is most appropriate, and (4) emphasis on rehabilitation through community programs.

INTERMEDIATE SANCTIONS

Sanctions less restrictive than prison but more restrictive than probation are not new. Variations of intermediate sanctions like many of those discussed later in this chapter (restitution, fines, and community service) were used as sentences in ancient Israel, Greece, and Rome. Other intermediate sanctions—such as drug court, remote-location monitoring, boot camps, and day fines—started in the 1980s. What is new today is the effort to bring all these sanctions together into a comprehensive sentencing system like the one suggested in Exhibit 5–1, which provides judges with an expanded menu of corrections options. Relatively less intrusive interventions proportional to the severity of a violation and the risk of the offender are to the left in Exhibit 5–1; more intrusive ones are to the right. Exhibit 5–1 is also multidimensional, creating depth for each step on the continuum. For example, if an offender on intensive supervision probation

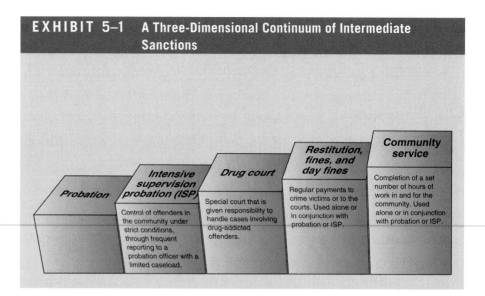

EXHIBIT 5–1   A Three-Dimensional Continuum of Intermediate Sanctions

Probation

Intensive supervision probation (ISP)
Control of offenders in the community under strict conditions, through frequent reporting to a probation officer with a limited caseload.

Drug court
Special court that is given responsibility to handle cases involving drug-addicted offenders.

Restitution, fines, and day fines
Regular payments to crime victims or to the courts. Used alone or in conjunction with probation or ISP.

Community service
Completion of a set number of hours of work in and for the community. Used alone or in conjunction with probation or ISP.

(ISP) fails to report as scheduled (whether to an ISP officer or via an automated probation machine as described in Chapter 4) and is relatively low risk, it may be appropriate to require more frequent reporting for a period of time within ISP than to move to the next higher level of intervention.

Others have taken a broader view of intermediate sanctions and called for a fundamental reshaping of sentencing systems in the United States that stresses accountability of the offender to the victim and the state, and accountability of the corrections system to the public and to other criminal justice agencies. Such a system would employ a range of sentencing options like those shown in Exhibit 5–1, and would structure the movement of offenders in and out of the corrections system, making it fairer and more cost-efficient. For example, in 1985 then-Delaware governor Pierre S. du Pont IV proposed a new sentencing system from unsupervised probation (level 1) to maximum-security imprisonment (level 10), with judges having discretion to make adjustments as needed up and down the scale of restrictiveness.[2]

However, for the most part in the United States today, sentencing systems are not structured as Governor du Pont hoped for. Most jurisdictions use intermediate sanctions as conditions of probation and have not included them in sentencing guidelines or penal codes. (Later in this chapter you will learn that other countries have sentencing systems that stress the accountability noted previously and where intermediate sanctions are available as "freestanding" sentencing options.) However, some professional organizations such as the American Jail Association believe that sentencing guidelines and penal codes that incorporate intermediate sanctions treat prison as the backstop, not the backbone, of the corrections system (see Exhibit 5–2). This type of sentencing enables criminal justice officials to reserve expensive prison and jail space for violent offenders. It gives nonviolent offenders less restrictive intermediate sanctions and restitution-focused sentences while teaching them accountability for their actions and heightening their chances for success in the community.

Intermediate sanctions are most often used for offenders considered nonviolent and low risk. They usually require the offender to lead a productive life in the community by working (finding work if unemployed) or learning new job skills; to perform unpaid community service; to pay restitution to victims; to enroll in a treatment or educational program; or sometimes to do all of these.

EXHIBIT 5–1   *continued*

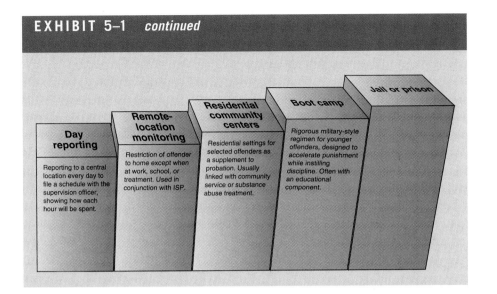

Intermediate sanctions are sometimes referred to as *front-end programs* or strategies. **Front-end programs** are options for initial sentences that are more restrictive than traditional probation but less restrictive than jail or prison. They are usually designed to limit the number of people who go to prison. In front-end programs, judges commonly sentence offenders directly to one or a combination of intermediate sanctions before requiring incarceration. **Back-end programs** are reduced restrictions for offenders who have made progress in compliance and treatment. In back-end programs, offenders are moved from higher to lower levels of control to complete the final phase of their sentences. For example, the state department of corrections may move an offender from prison to remote-location monitoring.

In between the two is what some call **trap-door** or **side-door programs.** These programs function as safety valves or emergency release options. For example, in November 2006, the Arkansas Board of Corrections invoked its Emergency Powers Act to allow early release for 687 prison inmates. Arkansas state law advances the release date for inmates by up to 90 days. The act has been used every 90 days since November 1998 to address the backlog of state inmates in county jails.[3]

Front-end programs tend to apply more to offenders who would otherwise receive less restrictive sentences than to those who would otherwise go to jail or prison. In that way, they contribute to **net widening.** Net

front-end programs
Punishment options for initial sentences more restrictive than traditional probation but less restrictive than jail or prison.

back-end programs
Sanctions that move offenders from higher levels of control to lower ones for the final phase of their sentences.

trap-door/side-door programs
Emergency release options for special docket offenders, generally used to relieve prison crowding.

net widening
Increasing the number of offenders sentenced to a higher level of restriction. It results in sentencing offenders to more restrictive sanctions than their offenses and characteristics warrant.

EXHIBIT 5–2   American Jail Association Resolution

Intermediate Punishments

WHEREAS, the American Jail Association (AJA) recognizes the detrimental impact that crowding places on local jails; and

WHEREAS, many of those who are incarcerated in jails do not pose a known danger to themselves or to society;

THEREFORE BE IT RESOLVED THAT AJA supports the expansion of intermediate punishments in states and localities throughout America for offenders who do not pose a known danger to public safety. AJA believes that intermediate punishments address real concerns of constituents.

widening is increasing the number of offenders sentenced to a higher level of restriction. As a result, many offenders may receive more restrictive sentences than their offenses and characteristics warrant. Community service, for instance, might be added to probation in a front-end program. The downside of such intermediate sanctions that provide discipline and structure for disruptive individuals is that large numbers of people will receive sanctions that will not be suitable.

Value of Intermediate Sanctions

Since January 1, 2002, the nation's jail and prison population has continued to exceed 2 million inmates. From January 1, 1996, to January 1, 2006, the number of people confined in state and federal prisons and local jails increased 34 percent, from 1.6 million to 2.2 million, an annual increase of 3.3 percent.[4] This level of increase in the nation's prisons and jails places a heavy economic burden on taxpayers. That burden includes the cost of building, maintaining, and operating prisons and jails, as well as the loss of offenders' contributions and the cost of caring for the destabilized families left behind. In addition, overcrowded jails and prisons are hard to manage and staff, and they invite disorder.

During the same period, new intermediate-sanction programs expanded rapidly across the United States, and the number of persons sentenced to them increased. The result has been an explosion in the number of persons under correctional supervision. Many intermediate sanctions were started with the goal of reducing the prison population. Though there has been no decline in the number of people sentenced to prison since these new intermediate sanctions appeared, proponents argue that, without the new programs, the number would be even larger. Other supporters say that, by increasing the surveillance, punishment, and treatment of offenders under community supervision, intermediate sanctions achieve other correctional goals.

Intermediate sanctions are valuable for a number of reasons. First, they provide a means for offenders who are not dangerous to repay their victims and their communities. Second, intermediate sanctions promote

EXHIBIT 5–3	**Average Annual Cost of Correctional Options**
Correctional Option	**Cost per Year per Participant**
Boot camp	$32,119
Prison	23,267
Jail	20,702
Halfway house	18,074
Remote-location monitoring	4,102
Intensive supervision	3,551
Day reporting	2,781
Community service	2,759
Drug court	2,500
Probation/parole	1,222
House arrest	402

Sources: Adapted from *Seeking Justice: Crime and Punishment in America* (New York: Edna McConnell Clark Foundation, 1977), p. 34; Camille Graham Camp and George M. Camp, *Adult Corrections* (Middletown, CT: Criminal Justice Institute, 2001), pp. 87, 125, 188, 198; Camille Graham Camp and George M. Camp, *Jails* (Middletown, CT: Criminal Justice Institute, 2001), p. 42; Web site of the National Association of Drug Court Professionals, www.nadcp.org/whatis/; James J. Stephen, *State Prison Expenditures, 2001* (Washington, DC: U.S. Department of Justice, Bureau of Justice Statistics, June 2004).

In January of 2001, I pled guilty to fifth-degree assault. It was a domestic-type thing. Instead of jail time, I wore a home monitor, which I wore around my ankle. I had to wear it 24/7, and I couldn't take it off until my time was up—and if you do try to tamper with it, it gives a signal and they know right away and come to arrest you. There is a little bit of discomfort—it weighed maybe a half-pound. It's not torturous by any means, but you look forward to getting the darned thing off.

I was allowed to leave for work on certain hours, so between 8 a.m. and 4 p.m. I was allowed to be gone, but I had to be home at 4 p.m. and couldn't leave after that. Could you walk out to the garage from your house? I didn't—I always called and got permission, because I didn't want to set that thing off.

You don't think it's a big deal at first, but it really makes you feel like you're a prisoner in your own home. There is some punitive feeling that you get from having to wear it. It takes away some

of your freedom. So I think it's very, very effective. It's a better alternative than going to jail, but it's still not like "Oh, you didn't do anything, you can go home." You are being punished. It's a good alternative to crowded jails—it's a great idea. Not that I liked it. I hated it. I couldn't wait to get it off.

Mike Schoffman
Spicer, Minnesota

rehabilitation—which most citizens want, but most prisons and jails find difficult to provide—and the reintegration of the offender into the community. And third, once the programs are in place, they can do these things at a comparatively low cost. Compare the lower costs of intermediate sanctions with jail and prison in Exhibit 5–3. In California alone, officials estimate that 2,120 people are serving prison time for petty theft. Sentencing them to intermediate sanctions would save the state $14 million.[5]

Intermediate sanctions should not be haphazardly planned or implemented. High-quality intermediate sanctions must be thoughtfully conceived, effectively targeted, well planned, and well staffed. Most important, intermediate sanctions must be incorporated into sentencing guidelines to achieve reasonable consistency in sentencing while allowing judges to consider meaningful differences between cases. (Delaware, North Carolina, and Pennsylvania are on the vanguard of incorporating intermediate sanctions into their sentencing guidelines.[6]) Perhaps the most important lesson learned from 20 years' experience with intermediate sanctions is "they are seldom likely to achieve their goals unless means can be found to set and enforce policies governing their use. Otherwise, the combination of officials' risk aversion and practitioners' preferences to be guided solely by their judgments about appropriate penalties in individual cases is likely to undermine program goals."[7]

Varieties of Intermediate Sanctions

The specific varieties of intermediate sanctions discussed in the following subsections include intensive supervision probation, drug courts, fines, community service, day reporting centers, remote-location monitoring (formerly known as *house arrest* and *electronic monitoring*), residential community centers, and boot camps.

Intensive Supervision Probation Probation with frequent contact between offender and probation officer, strict enforcement of conditions, random drug and alcohol testing, and other requirements is known as **intensive supervision probation (ISP)**. Estimates on the number of persons currently on ISP are not known. However, in 2001 Camp and Camp reported that approximately 5 percent (122,938) of the adult population on probation or parole was on ISP.[8] If we estimated only 5 percent of

intensive supervision probation (ISP)

Control of offenders in the community under strict conditions, by means of frequent reporting to a probation officer whose caseload is generally limited to 30 offenders.

today's probation and parole population on ISP, we're likely to find over 200,000 adults on ISP.

As a technique for increasing control over offenders in the community, ISP has gained wide popularity. It allows offenders to live at home but under more severe and more punitive restrictions than those of conventional probation. The primary purpose of such program restrictions and surveillance is to protect the community and deter the offender from breaking the law or violating the conditions of release. Requirements of ISP usually include performing community service, attending school or treatment programs, working or looking for employment, meeting with a probation officer (or team of officers) as often as five times a week, and submitting to curfews, employment checks, and tests for drug and alcohol use. Because of the frequency of contact, subjection to unannounced drug tests, and rigorous enforcement of restitution, community service, and other conditions, ISP is thought more appropriate for higher-risk offenders.

ISP was initially the most popular intermediate sanction. It emerged in the 1960s as an effort to improve offender rehabilitation by reducing probation and parole caseloads from 100 or more to 30. However, researchers soon discovered that small caseloads led to enhanced supervision and control (and more violations) but not necessarily to enhanced treatment.[9] It wasn't until ISP combined supervision and control with treatment components and skill development programs and reinforced clearly identified behaviors that it became effective.[10] Today, ISP programs exist in every state. They may be state or county programs and may be administered by parole, probation, or prison departments. As a result, it is not easy to estimate the number of ISP programs in the United States.

Research on ISP has produced two main findings. First, if ISP programs focus on offender monitoring and surveillance without offering offenders treatment services, then there is no significant improvement in recidivism rates. Offenders sentenced to surveillance-oriented ISP programs commit new crimes at about the same rate as comparable offenders receiving different sentences. Also, technical violation and revocation rates are typically higher for ISP surveillance-oriented programs because more frequent contact makes misconduct more likely to be discovered. Early proponents of surveillance-oriented ISP programs argued that ISP would reduce recidivism rates, rehabilitate offenders, and save money and prison resources. However, most evaluations suggest that the combination of net widening, high revocation rates, and costs of processing revocations makes savings unlikely.[11]

On the other hand, in 2006 when the Washington State Institute for Public Policy (see Chapter 1) assessed the effectiveness of various types of correctional programs to determine what works in corrections, it found that the average ISP program with a focus on offering offenders treatment services reduced the recidivism rate of participants by 16.7 percent[12]—what some call "extremely successful."[13] According to the editors of the *Criminal Justice Newsletter,* "The lesson from this research is that it is the treatment—not the intensive monitoring—that results in recidivism reduction."[14] Rearrests are reduced when offenders receive treatment in addition to the increased surveillance and control of ISP programs. For

An ISP officer explains court-ordered sanctions to a probationer. Frequent face-to-face contact is a condition of ISP. What other controls are used to monitor offenders on ISP?

example, the literature demonstrates that participation in drug treatment, whether voluntary or compelled, can reduce both drug use and crime by drug-using offenders. Data indicate that in many cities, one-half to three-fourths of arrested felons are drug abusers; ISP programs with a focus on offering offenders treatment services hold promise as a device for getting addicted offenders into treatment and keeping them there.[15]

To reap the benefits of ISP, what must be done is straightforward. Because recidivism rates for new crimes are no higher for ISP participants than for comparable imprisoned offenders, ISP is a cost-effective alternative to prison for offenders who do not present unacceptable risks to public safety. Cost savings are likely to depend, however, on using ISP only for offenders who would have received appreciable prison time. And technical violations require a range of responses, as Chapter 4 pointed out, not a rush to incarcerate the violator. Incarcerating all violators cancels out the initial savings of ISP.

Drug Courts Drug court is a special court that is given responsibility to handle cases involving drug-addicted offenders.[16] It is a new intermediate sanction that uses the power of the court to treat, sanction, and reward drug offenders with punishment more restrictive than regular probation but less severe than incarceration. In testimony before the Senate Judiciary Subcommittee on Youth Violence, John S. Goldcamp of Temple University's Department of Criminal Justice told the panel of senators, "The effect of the drug court movement on courts and the justice system over the last 11 years may turn out—with more historical distance—to have been one of the major justice reforms of the last part of the 20th century in the United States."[17] In fact, the *National Drug Control Strategy Update,* issued in March 2004 by the White House, hailed the creation of drug courts as "one of the most promising trends in the criminal justice system."[18]

In 1989, troubled by the devastating impact of drugs and drug-related crime on Dade County (Florida) neighborhoods and the criminal justice system, Miami judge Herbert M. Klein developed the nation's first drug court and proactively oversaw an intensive, community-based treatment, rehabilitation, and supervision program for felony drug defendants. By November 2006 over 1,600 drug courts were operating in all 50 states, the District of Columbia, Northern Marina Islands, Puerto Rico, Guam, 121 tribal courts, and another 400 were in the planning process.[19] In these jurisdictions, coalitions of judges, prosecutors, attorneys, substance abuse treatment professionals, probation officers, community-based service organization staff, law enforcement officials, and others use the coercive power of the court to force abstinence from drugs and alter the behavior of substance-abusing offenders.

In comparison with the aims of other types of courts, those of the drug court are much less punitive and more healing and restorative in nature. This new approach integrates substance abuse treatment, sanctions, incentives, and frequent court appearances with case processing to place drug-involved defendants in judicially supervised rehabilitation programs. Successful completion of the treatment program results in dismissal of the charges, reduced or set-aside sentences, lesser penalties, or a combination of these. Drug court provides a new alternative to traditional methods of dealing with the devastating impact of drugs and drug-related crime and a way to eliminate the revolving-door syndrome of substance abuse in the criminal justice system. Exhibit 5–4 is a sample drug court participation agreement.

drug court
A special court that is given responsibility to treat, sanction, and reward drug offenders with punishment more restrictive than regular probation but less severe than incarceration.

EXHIBIT 5–4   **Sample Drug Court Participation Agreement**

STATE OF ALABAMA	)	IN THE SIXTH JUDICIAL CIRCUIT COURT
	)	DRUG COURT DIVISION
VS.	)	TUSCALOOSA COUNTY, ALABAMA
	)	
_____		CASE NO. _____

DRUG COURT TREATMENT PROGRAM
PARTICIPATION AGREEMENT

I agree to the following as conditions of my participation:

1. Following assignment by the Tuscaloosa County Drug Court Judge to the Drug Court Program, I will be treated by Indian Rivers Treatment Facility. (Treatment only).

2. An assessment will be conducted to determine whether my participation in the Drug Court Treatment Program is clinically appropriate.

3. If treatment is indicated, I will begin attendance the following day or as instructed. Treatment will continue for approximately two (2) years.

4. Treatment will be in four (4) phases:

    Phase I: Attend four IOP Groups per week for two weeks and one Saturday Family Group

    Phase II: Attend three IOP Groups per week plus one Saturday Family Group or Thursday Family Group for 12 weeks, attend three (3) 12-step meetings a week (or equivalent court-approved program).

    Phase III: Attend one weekday Alumni Group per week and one Thursday Family Group (if qualified) <u>or</u> One Saturday Alumni Group per week for 12 weeks, attend four (4) 12-step meetings a week (or equivalent court approved program).

    Phase IV: Attend one weekday Alumni group per week for seventy-eight weeks, attend four (4) 12-step meetings a week for 78 weeks (Or equivalent court-approved program).

5. I agree to provide a urine specimen to be tested for the presence of drugs as follows:

    Phase I: Twice a week (minimum)

    Phases II and III: Once per week (minimum)

    Phase IV: When requested by the Court or Treatment

6. I agree to sign an individualized plan for treatment with my case manager and to participate in the accomplishment of goals and objectives as designated.

7. The Tuscaloosa County Drug Court Judge and the Case Manager will be informed of my attendance in counseling, results of urinalysis and progress in the program.

8. Failure to attend counseling, remain drug and alcohol free or demonstrate progress in treatment will result in a review of my case by the Tuscaloosa County Drug Court Judge to determine my continued participation in the Drug Court Program or the imposition of interim legal consequences, including incarceration.

9. I understand and accept the contents and ramifications of this form which I have read or have had read to me.

_____	_____
Attorney for Defendant	Defendant

Drug courts vary from one jurisdiction to another in terms of structure, scope, and target populations and this fuels the debate over the effectiveness of drug court because reported rates of recidivism from individual drug courts vary widely. The variation reflects the diversity across drug courts in the characteristics of participants (for example, in the severity of addiction, the types of drugs used, and criminal history) and in how drug courts operate (for example, program eligibility, treatment availability and quality, and court monitoring policies).

Because drug courts are developed at the local level, their design and structure reflect the unique strengths, circumstances, and capabilities of each community. Still, all drug courts share three primary goals: (1) to reduce recidivism, (2) to reduce substance abuse among participants, and (3) to rehabilitate participants. The key components of drug court that work together to achieve these goals are the following:

- incorporating drug testing into case processing;
- creating a nonadversarial relationship between the defendant and the court;
- identifying defendants in need of treatment and referring them to treatment as soon as possible after arrest;
- providing access to a continuum of treatment and rehabilitation services;
- monitoring abstinence through frequent, mandatory drug testing;
- establishing a coordinated strategy to govern drug court responses to participants' compliance;
- maintaining judicial interaction with each drug court participant;
- monitoring and evaluating program goals and gauging their effectiveness;
- continuing interdisciplinary education to promote effective drug court planning, implementation, and operations; and
- forging partnerships among drug courts, public agencies, and community-based organizations to generate local support and enhance drug court effectiveness.

Judge Sarah Smith congratulates drug court participant Bronco Anderson in her Tulsa, Oklahoma, courtroom for completing phase one and moving to phase two of the drug court program. Drug courts treat, sanction, and reward drug offenders with punishment more restrictive than regular probation but less severe than incarceration. What are the key components of drug court?

Because drug courts are relatively new, the body of research concerning them is still growing. Still, researchers agree that the thrust of findings from assorted studies is generally supportive of drug courts and points to positive results. After conducting drug court research for more than a decade, Goldcamp told the Senate Judiciary Subcommittee on Youth Violence that "drug courts can and do have an important impact on substance abuse and offending and represent an important new direction in criminal justice, drug treatment, and health."[20] In a study of two of the nation's oldest and longest operating drug courts, Goldcamp reported that drug court graduates were rearrested less frequently during one, two, and three-year follow-up periods than nongraduates overall and during each year studied.[21]

The National Association of Drug Court Professionals (NADCP) produced other positive findings:

- Drug courts provide more comprehensive and closer supervision of the drug-using offender than do other forms of community supervision.
- Drug use and criminal behavior are substantially reduced while clients are participating in drug court.
- Criminal behavior is lower after program participation, especially for graduates.
- Drug courts generate cost savings ($10 for every $1 spent on drug court) from reduced jail/prison use, reduced criminality, and lower criminal justice system costs.

- Drug courts are successful in bridging the gap between the court and the treatment/public health systems and spurring greater cooperation among the various agencies and personnel within the criminal justice system, as well as between the criminal justice system and the community.[22]

In 2001, Columbia University's National Center on Addiction and Substance Abuse (CASA) concluded an updated study of its seminal 1998 review of drug court research and evaluations.[23] It found that drug courts continue to provide the most comprehensive and effective control of the drug-using offenders' criminality and drug usage while under the court's jurisdiction.

The revised study, based on a review of 37 evaluations, finds that the results are consistent with the 1998 analysis and the 2000 update based on 48 other evaluations finding that "drug courts provide closer, more comprehensive supervision and much more frequent drug testing and monitoring during the program than other forms of community supervision" and that "drug use and criminal behavior are substantially reduced while offenders are participating in drug court." In fact, the average recidivism rate for those who complete the drug court program is between 4 and 29 percent as compared to 48 percent for those who do not participate in a drug court program.

In July 2003, the National Institute of Justice and the Drug Court Program Office produced the first estimate of recidivism among a nationally representative sample of drug court graduates.[24] Researchers identified all drug courts funded by the Drug Court Program Office that had been in operation for at least one year as of January 1, 1999, and had at least 40 program graduates. From a population of 17,000, FBI records of 2,021 drug court graduates from 95 drug courts were analyzed.

Researchers defined recidivism as any arrest and charge that carried a sentence of at least one year upon conviction. Within one year after graduation, 16.4 percent of drug court graduates had been arrested and charged with a serious offense (a success rate of 83.6 percent). Within two years, rearrests increased to 27.5 percent, lowering the success rate to 72.5 percent.

Researchers also estimated the number of serious offenses committed by drug court graduates. In the first year after graduation, drug court graduates averaged 0.23 serious crimes per person and 0.50 serious crimes per person in the first two years after graduation. Among those drug court graduates that did commit a serious crime, the average was 1.42 in the first year and 1.83 in the second year.

Researchers discovered other interesting findings about drug court. When they compared drug court recidivism to the severity of the population admitted to drug court, they found that drug courts with the highest recidivism rates tended to accept offenders who were primarily cocaine and heroin users, and who were classified by the drug courts as having "moderate" or "severe" drug problems. Researchers also found that recidivism was related to the size of the drug court. Graduates of the largest drug courts (defined as having more than 832 total graduates) had a two-year recidivism rate of 30.8 percent, compared with a two-year recidivism rate between 22.5 and 24 percent for drug courts with fewer graduates. The reason, we suggest, is large drug courts are located in the largest metropolitan areas and accept clients with the most severe drug problems.

Jurisdictions from New York to Oregon are reporting success of drug court as an intermediate sanction. In 2003, New York released the first statewide analysis of drug courts.[25] The study followed drug court participants in urban, suburban, and rural communities over a three-year period after initial arrest. The drug courts generated an average 29 percent recidivism reduction over the three-year postarrest period and an average 32 percent reduction over the one-year postprogram period. In Maryland, researchers found that drug court participants had a significantly longer time to rearrest than did a control group and experienced less drug crime failure during the two-year follow-up period. The researchers wrote, "compliance with various drug court components, particularly early and continued drug treatment attendance, reduced the risk of failure among this sample."[26] And in Oregon, researchers found that when drug courts are used as an intermediate sanction for drug-involved offenders, taxpayers realize significant savings because there is less use of jail and probation time. Drug courts saved Multnomah County (Portland) approximately $3 million in 30 months (an average savings of $5,000 for each of the almost 600 program participants in the study compared to the almost 600 who were assigned to traditional court).

And finally, two important publications on drug court effectiveness were released in 2006 that corroborate what previous research has found. In June, the National Institute of Justice published a collection of findings from recent studies in order to identify what works to practitioners and policymakers.[27] The researchers found:

1. Research indicates that drug courts can reduce recidivism and promote other positive outcomes. However, research has not uncovered which court processes affect which outcomes and for what types of offenders. The magnitude of a court's impact may depend upon how consistently court resources match the needs of the offenders in the drug court program. Teams that are educated in addiction and substance abuse theory, treatment approaches, and relapse prevention are better able to ensure that offender needs are met.

2. To address alcohol and drug problems, treatment services should (1) be based on formal theories of drug dependence and abuse, (2) use the best therapeutic tools, and (3) give participants opportunities to build cognitive skills. Treatment that applies a scattershot approach —of sometimes incompatible philosophies—may be counterproductive. In addition, ancillary services that address co-occurring mental and physical health, housing, and other needs may be helpful.

3. Compared to adults, juveniles can be difficult to diagnose and treat. Many young people referred to drug court have no established pattern of abuse or physical addiction; others have reached serious levels of criminal and drug involvement. Neither general treatment research nor drug court evaluations have produced definitive information on juveniles. Most juvenile drug court teams are still exploring whether their mission should be prevention or intervention.

4. Proper assessment and treatment of offenders is primarily the responsibility of service providers, but all drug court team members should be concerned with the integrity of treatment planning, service delivery, and performance reporting (including drug test results). Teams that are educated in addiction and substance abuse theory, treatment approaches, and relapse prevention are better able to ensure that offender needs are met.

5. Offenders report that interactions with the judge are one of the most important influences on the experience they have while in the program. They respond to the judge's interpersonal skills and ability to resolve legal problems expeditiously and provide ready access

to services. Offenders who interact with a single drug court judge, rather than multiple judges, may be more likely to comply with program demands.

6. Programs are influenced by a variety of factors that may be external (e.g., trends in drug use), internal (e.g., staff turnover), or policy-related (e.g., drug court as diversion versus postdisposition). Because the impact of these factors may change over time, studying a court over several years offers feedback on how past policies and procedures affect program outcomes.

7. The decision to allocate resources to a drug court should be based on a demonstrated benefit (such as reduced recidivism) given the costs and savings. Drug courts can estimate costs using figures found in public information sources (i.e., proxies like the average cost of incarceration). More definitive analyses examine costs incurred by every agency involved. One definitive cost–benefit evaluation estimated that the average investment per program participant was $5,928; the savings were $2,329 in avoided criminal justice system costs and $1,301 in avoided victimization costs over a 30-month period.

The second important publication on drug court effectiveness, the work of the Washington State Institute on Public Policy discussed in Chapter 1 and referenced in this and other chapters, was released in October 2006.[28] The institute found 57 evaluations of the effects of adult drug court on recidivism, and reported that the average adult drug court reduced the recidivism rate of participants by 8 percent. The Washington researchers estimated that the average investment per program participant was $4,333; the savings were $4,395 in avoided criminal justice system costs and $4,705 in avoided victimization costs. Benefits (such as avoidance of law enforcement costs—arrest, booking, jail time, and probation, and victimization costs including lost productivity and medical expenses) minus program costs were $4,767 per drug court participant.

With these national, state, and local benchmark estimates, the future of drug courts is promising. More than 300,000 adults and 12,500 juveniles have enrolled in drug courts, and 73,000 adults and 4,000 juveniles have graduated. The retention rate is 70 percent, and 30 years of treatment literature states that the longer a person stays in treatment, the better the outcome. Over three-fourths of drug court participants were previously incarcerated, a finding that lessens the problem of net widening. More than 1,000 drug-free babies have been born, and 3,500 drug-free parents have regained custody of their children. Child support payments are being made by more than 4,550 drug-free parents, and almost three-fourths of drug court graduates have obtained employment. These results; federal funding for planning, implementing, and enhancing drug courts through the U.S. Department of Justice Drug Courts Program Office; and the support of national, state, and local leaders who recognize that traditional criminal justice policies have little impact on substance abuse suggest that drug courts will play an increasingly visible role in the nation's response to drug-related crime.

fine
A financial penalty used as a criminal sanction.

Fines   A **fine** is a financial sanction requiring a convicted person to pay a specified sum of money. The fine is one of the oldest forms of punishment. It is, in practice, the criminal justice tool for punishing minor misdemeanors, traffic offenses, and ordinance violations. To be effective, fines should be proportionate to the seriousness of an offense and should have roughly similar economic impacts on persons with differing financial resources who are convicted of the same offense. In the United States, fines are rarely regarded as a tough criminal sanction. They are not taken seriously, for at least four reasons. First, judicial, legislative, and prosecutorial attitudes restrict their use to traffic offenses, minor misdemeanors, and ordinance violations. Second, a judge seldom has enough reliable information on an offender's personal wealth to impose a just fine. Third, mechanisms for collecting fines are often ineffective. Far too often the responsibility for collecting fines has been left to probation officers, who are already overburdened and have no interest in fine collection. As a result, fines are seldom paid. Fourth, many believe that fines work hardship on the poor, while affluent offenders feel no sting.

A **day fine** is a financial penalty based on the seriousness of the crime and the defendant's ability to pay. It is called a *day fine* because it is based on the offender's daily income. Day fines, also called *structured fines*, have been common in some northern and western European countries for many years. They were introduced in Sweden in the 1920s and were quickly incorporated into the penal codes of other Scandinavian countries. West Germany adopted day fines as a sentencing option in the early 1970s. Today, Sweden and Germany have made day fines the preferred punishment for most criminal cases, including those involving serious crimes. In Germany, for example, day fines are the only punishment for three-quarters of all offenders convicted of property crimes and two-thirds of offenders convicted of assaults.[29] Recently, the day fine of an heir to a family-owned sausage business in Finland was set according to Finland's day fine policy. Jussi Salonoja was caught driving 50 miles per hour (mph) in a 25-mph zone and fined $217,000. With Finnish tax records showing his wealth at $8 million, he was given a world-record speeding fine. His fine more than doubles the existing records of a $96,000 fine given in 2002 to Annssi Vanjoki, a Nokia vice president, for driving his Harley-Davidson 17 miles above the speed limit on a Helsinki street; a $31,200 fine given in 2001 to Pekka Ala-Pietila, Nokia president, for driving through a red light; and a $71,000 fine given in 2000 to Jaakko Rysola, dot-com millionaire, for zigzagging through Helsinki in his Ferrari.[30]

Day fines have been tried experimentally in some areas of the United States, including New York, Arizona, Connecticut, Iowa, and Oregon. Exhibit 5–5 is a sample notification of a structured fine program. The notice may be mailed to a defendant along with the summons or handed to the defendant when he or she appears in court.

To be effective, a day fine program must have the support of a cross section of criminal justice professionals in a jurisdiction, as well as others who have a stake in the operation of the criminal justice system. According to a Bureau of Justice Assistance report[31] on day fines, the following officials should be involved in planning a county day fine program:

- a prosecutor;
- a public defender;
- a representative of the private defense bar;
- a court administrator;
- the presiding judges of the general and limited-jurisdiction courts;
- the director of a pretrial services agency;
- the chief probation officer or the director of a community corrections agency;
- the sheriff or another jail administrator; and
- representatives of county government.

day fine
A financial penalty scaled both to the defendant's ability to pay and the seriousness of the crime.

EXHIBIT 5–5   **Sample Notification of a Structured Fine Program**

A PRELIMINARY COMPLAINT
HAS BEEN FILED CHARGING YOU WITH
AN INDICTABLE OFFENSE

IF CONVICTED, THE COURT <u>MAY</u> IMPOSE ONE OR MORE OF THE FOLLOWING SANCTIONS:

1. JAIL OR PRISON
2. PROBATION
3. A FINE

If a fine is imposed, the Court may structure the level of the fine partly according to the seriousness of the offense and partly in relation to your means or ability to pay the fine. This method of computing the amount of a "structured fine" is an effort by the Court and the Polk County Attorney's Office to equalize the impact of criminal sanctions and to reduce the number of persons who are sentenced to prison, jail, or formal probation.

In order for the County Attorney's Office to consider recommending a structured fine to the Court at the time of sentencing, you or your attorney must schedule an interview with a Structured Fines Officer at 555-1234, IMMEDIATELY. If you intend to secure an attorney to represent you on this charge, please make these arrangements prior to calling the Structured Fines Program.

Your ability to pay a structured fine as well as the length of time needed to pay the fine are based on the information you provide in the attached AFFIDAVIT OF FINANCIAL CONDITION. It is required that you and/or your attorney complete this form prior to meeting with a Structured Fines Officer. It is also required that you take to your meeting with the Structured Fines Officer verification of your income in the form of paycheck stubs, income tax returns, etc.

POLK COUNTY ATTORNEY'S OFfiCE
STRUCTURED FINES PROGRAM
POLK COUNTY COURTHOUSE, ROOM B-40
DES MOINES, IOWA 50309
555-1234

Appointments with a Structured Fines Officer are available
Monday through Friday, from 1:30 P.M. to 4:30 P.M.

The planning process for introducing day fines is unique for each jurisdiction, depending on its organizational structure, traditions, personalities, and legal culture. Every jurisdiction, however, addresses similar issues: current sentencing patterns, current fine collection operations and their effectiveness, goals and priorities for the day fine program, and potential legal challenges to the program.

Once a system for imposing day fines is put in place, the next step is to develop a structured process for setting fines. This structured process is the feature that distinguishes day fines from traditional fines. The process usually has two parts: (1) a unit scale that ranks offenses by severity and (2) a valuation scale for determining the dollar amount per unit for a given offender.

The first step in setting a day fine is to determine the number of fine units to be imposed. A portion of the unit scale used in a Staten Island, New York, day fine experiment is shown in Exhibit 5–6. The number of

EXHIBIT 5–6   **Example of a Day Fine Unit Scale**

Staten Island Day Fine Unit Scale (Selected Offense Categories)

Penal Law Charge[1]	Type of Offense[2]	Number of Day Fine Units		
		Discount	PRESUMPTIVE	premium
120.00 AM	Assault 3: Range of 20–95 DF			
	A. Substantial Injury	81	**95**	109
	Stranger-to-stranger; or where victim is known to assailant, he/she is weaker, vulnerable			
	B. Minor Injury	59	**70**	81
	Stranger-to-stranger; or where victim is known to assailant, he/she is weaker, vulnerable; or altercations involving use of a weapon			
	C. Substantial Injury	38	**45**	52
	Altercations among acquaintances; brawls			
	D. Minor Injury	17	**20**	23
110/120.00 BM	Attempted Assault 3: Range of 15–45 DF			
	A. Substantial Injury	38	**45**	52
	Stranger-to-stranger; or where victim is known to assailant, he/she is weaker, vulnerable			
	B. Minor Injury	30	**35**	40
	Stranger-to-stranger; or where victim is known to assailant, he/she is weaker, vulnerable; or altercations involving use of a weapon			
	C. Substantial Injury	17	**20**	23
	Altercations among acquaintances; brawls			
	D. Minor Injury	13	**15**	17
	Altercations among acquaintances; brawls			

1. AM = Class A Misdemeanor; BM = Class B Misdemeanor.
2. DF = Day Fines.

SOURCE: Adapted from Bureau of Justice Assistance, *How to Use Structured Fines (Day Fines) as an Intermediate Sanction* (Washington, DC: Bureau of Justice Assistance, 1996), p. 59.

units ranges from a low of 5 to a high of 120, for the most serious misdemeanors handled by the court. For example, the presumptive number of units for the offense of assault with minor injury and aggravating factors is 70; the range is from 59 to 81 units. The presumptive number is the starting point. Negotiation and consideration of individual circumstances may raise or lower the number. There is no magic in the unit scale established. What is important is to establish a scale broad enough to cover the full range of offenses handled by the courts that will use structured fines.

Once the unit scale is established, the second step is to create a valuation table. The purpose of the valuation table is to establish the dollar amount of each fine. A portion of the valuation table used in the Staten Island experiment is shown in Exhibit 5–7. Net daily incomes run down the left side, and numbers of dependents run across the top. Net daily income is the offender's income (after-tax wages, welfare allowance, unemployment compensation, etc.) divided by the number of days in a payment period. Staten Island planners also adjusted the net daily income downward to account for subsistence needs, family responsibilities, and incomes below the poverty line.

Suppose a defendant convicted of assault, with minor injury and aggravating factors, has a net daily income of $15 and supports four people,

EXHIBIT 5–7   Example of a Day Fine Valuation Table

Staten Island, New York, Valuation Table Dollar Value of One Day Fine Unit, by Net Daily Income and Number of Dependents

Net Daily Income ($)	Number of Dependents (Including Self)							
	1	2	3	4	5	6	7	8
3		1.05	0.83	0.68	0.53	0.45	0.37	0.30
4	1.70	1.40	1.10	0.90	0.70	0.60	0.50	0.40
5	2.13	1.75	1.38	1.13	0.88	0.75	0.62	0.50
6	2.55	2.10	1.65	1.35	1.05	0.90	0.75	0.60
7	2.98	2.45	1.93	1.58	1.23	1.05	0.87	0.70
8	3.40	2.80	2.20	1.80	1.40	1.20	1.00	0.80
9	3.83	3.15	2.48	2.03	1.58	1.35	1.12	0.90
10	4.25	3.50	2.75	2.25	1.75	1.50	1.25	1.00
11	4.68	3.85	3.03	2.47	1.93	1.65	1.37	1.10
12	5.10	4.20	3.30	2.70	2.10	1.80	1.50	1.20
13	5.53	4.55	3.58	2.93	2.28	1.95	1.62	1.30
14	7.85	4.90	3.85	3.15	2.45	2.10	1.75	1.40
15	8.42	5.25	4.13	3.38	2.63	2.25	1.87	1.50

Source: Adapted from Bureau of Justice Assistance, *How to Use Structured Fines (Day Fines) as an Intermediate Sanction* (Washington, DC: Bureau of Justice Assistance, 1996), p. 64.

including herself. Find the row for her net daily income. Move across the row to the column for the number of dependents. The figure there is the value of one structured fine unit for that defendant. Multiply the number of fine units to be imposed (70) by the value of a single fine unit (3.38). The product, $236.60, is the amount of the day fine to be imposed.

The National Institute of Justice (NIJ) sponsored an evaluation of the Staten Island experiment. That evaluation showed that judges used day fines for many offenses for which they had formerly used fixed fine amounts—including some property crimes, drug possession, and assault.[32] Most judges cooperated with the new, voluntary scheme throughout the yearlong experiment. Research showed that the average fine increased by 25 percent, from $206 before the experiment to $258 during the year day fines were used. If day fines had not been held low by state law, the average day fine would have been $440. The news on collections was also good. Eighty-five percent of the defendants in the day fine program paid their fines in full, compared with 71 percent in a control program using routine collection processes. Furthermore, when full payment was not made, partial payment was much more likely in the day fine cases than in cases from before the experiment or in the control group. Thus, the higher fines levied in the day fine cases did not make collection more difficult, and the new enforcement procedures independently improved collection rates.

There has been little evidence-based research on the effectiveness of fines in reducing recidivism rates. The Washington State Institute for Public Policy wrote that day fine programs are in need of additional research and development before we can conclude that they do or do not work (i.e., reduce crime outcomes).[33] However, since the use of fines could reduce the costs of courts and corrections and since day fines address problems of inequality, fines are a promising intermediate sanction. At present, most Western justice systems, except the United States, rely heavily on financial penalties. In the 21st century, U.S. jurisdictions are likely to continue their experiments with monetary penalties and to assign them even greater importance.

Community Service **Community service** is a sentence to serve a specified number of hours working in unpaid positions with nonprofit or tax-supported agencies.[34] Recall Boy George's five days of community service that introduced this chapter.

Community service is punishment that takes away an offender's time and energy. Community service is sometimes called a "fine of time." Requiring offenders to compensate victims with their time or money was customary in ancient civilizations. The desire for compensation in time or money was probably at least as common then as the urge to retaliate. In colonial Boston, drunkards were sentenced to chop wood. During World War II, youths were given the choice of going to detention or going to war.[35]

community service

A sentence to serve a specified number of hours working in unpaid positions with nonprofit or tax-supported agencies.

Community service as a criminal sanction began in the United States in 1966 in Alameda County, California. Municipal judges there devised a community service sentencing program for indigent women who violated traffic and parking laws. Too poor to pay fines, these women were likely to be sentenced to jail. But putting them behind bars imposed a hardship on their families. Community service orders (CSOs) increased sentencing options, punished the offenders, lightened the suffering of innocent families, avoided the cost of imprisonment, and provided valuable services to the community. As Alameda judges gained experience with the new sentencing option, they broadened the program to include male offenders, juveniles, and persons convicted of crimes more serious than traffic or parking violations.

The Alameda County community service program received international attention. England and Wales developed pilot projects in the 1970s, using community service as a midlevel sanction between probation and prison and as an alternative to prison sentences up to six months. By 1975, community service had become a central feature of English sentencing. The approach swept throughout Europe, Australia, New Zealand, and Canada.

However, what had begun as an American innovation atrophied in the United States.[36] Today in this country, community service is seldom used as a separate sentence. Instead, it may be one of many conditions of a probation sentence. Nor is it viewed

On March 19, 2007, British supermodel Naomi Campbell started five days of community service with the New York City Department of Sanitation. She showed up wearing an estimated $4,400 outfit including a Ralph Lauren coat and Christian Louboutin stilletto boots. Campbell pleaded guilty to misdemeanor assault for throwing her BlackBerry at her maid, Anna Scolavino, over a missing pair of jeans. Scolavino required four stitches to her head. Campbell said it was an accident because she did not intend to hit her. In an agreement negotiated with prosecutors, a Manhattan Criminal Court judge sentenced Campbell to five days of community service, to take anger management classes, and to pay $363.32 in restitution to Scolavino, as well as covering her hospital bills. Community service as a criminal sanction is valuable to the community, the victim, and the offender. How does each benefit?

as an alternative to imprisonment in the United States, as it is in other countries. Generally speaking, in the United States, public officials do not consider any sanction other than imprisonment punitive enough. Substituting community service for short prison sentences is not accepted. This is unfortunate because community service is a burdensome penalty that meets with widespread public approval,[37] is inexpensive to administer, and produces public value. Also, it can be scaled to the seriousness of the crime.

Community service can be an intermediate sanction by itself or be used with other penalties and requirements, including substance abuse treatment, restitution, or probation.[38] Proponents of community service include the American Correctional Association (see Exhibit 5–8). Offenders sentenced to community service are usually assigned to work for government or private nonprofit agencies. They paint churches; restore historic buildings; make baby blankets; maintain parks; clean roadways, public parks, and county fairgrounds; remove snow from around public buildings; perform land and river reclamation; and renovate schools and nursing homes. Offenders who are doctors may be ordered to give medical service to persons who might otherwise lack it. Traffic offenders may be ordered to serve in hospital emergency rooms to learn about

---

EXHIBIT 5–8   **American Correctional Association**

Policy on Community Service

Introduction:

Establishing a sense of community is an important part of the rehabilitation process of offenders. Whether within an institution or as part of community corrections, it is beneficial to promote community service for offenders to assist their re-entry into society.

Policy Statement:

While promoting community service, justice systems and institutions must consider factors that contribute to the success of the effort—for the offender and the public. These factors must include:

- A. protecting public safety;
- B. integrating the offender into the community;
- C. gaining public support for programs and promoting acceptance of offenders;
- D. enhancing the self-esteem of offenders by using their time, talents, and skills to benefit themselves and others;
- E. providing value to government, the community and nonprofit organizations;
- F. teaching valuable, transferable skills to offenders;
- G. contributing to principles of restorative justice; and
- H. restoring public confidence in offenders as well as the justice system.

The American Correctional Association supports community service for offenders and urges its use as consistent with correctional management principles and public safety objectives.

This Public Correctional Policy was unanimously ratified by the American Correctional Association Delegate Assembly at the Winter Conference in Nashville, Tenn. Jan. 24, 2001.

Megan Hill
Case Manager   Day Reporting Center
Boston, Massachusetts

While an undergraduate at Northeastern University, Megan Hill participated in several co-op programs, including spending six months at a day reporting center in Boston. Shortly after her experience ended, the day reporting center advertised for a case manager and hired Hill for the job. Hill credits Northeastern's co-op program with giving her the qualifications to be hired full-time before earning her degree and with providing her the opportunity to explore different aspects of the criminal justice field.

Each day, Hill's responsibilities include approving day reporting clients' daily itineraries, monitoring clients' call-in times, and visiting her clients at home and work. Daily contact, she says, helps her know her clients better, understand what they're going through, and know how to assist them. She also believes it's important to respect clients. "The more respect you give your clients, the more respect and honesty you get in return."

Hill's advice to people interested in working in corrections is to do an internship or participate in a co-op to find out if they like the work. For Megan Hill, the most important thing is to be happy with your job and to feel that you're making a difference.

Probably the best part about my job is working with individuals who are truly dedicated to their recovery and reintegration back into society. The feeling you get from seeing a client start with all the frustrations of job rejections and discrimination to seeing them attain their first legal job and actually enjoy it is pretty satisfying. I am actually helping people put their lives back together.

the injuries they risk for themselves and others. Drug offenders who are prominent sports figures may be ordered to lecture in high schools on the dangers of drugs. The service options are limited only by the imagination of the sentencing judge and the availability of personnel to ensure that the offender fulfills the terms of the sentence. To become and remain a tough criminal sanction, community service must have credible and efficient enforcement mechanisms.

By the late 1980s, some form of community service sanction was in use in all 50 states. When Congress passed the Comprehensive Crime Control Act and Criminal Fine Enforcement Act of 1984, it mandated that felons who receive a sentence (except for class A or B felony—the most serious) must be ordered to pay a fine, make restitution, and/or work in community service. The Bureau of Justice Statistics estimates conservatively that 6 percent of all felons in the United States are sentenced to perform community service, often in conjunction with other sanctions.[39]

States like Washington, Georgia, and Texas are making extensive use of community service. At least one-third of Washington's convicted felons receive sentences that include community service. Washington State sentencing guidelines permit substitution of community service for incarceration at a rate of 8 hours of work for 1 day of incarceration, with a limit of 30 days. Most jurisdictions recognize 240 hours as the upper limit for community service. Washington State also is breaking new ground in sentencing reform with the idea of *interchangeable sentences* for nonviolent or not very violent crimes against strangers. The actual sentence depends on the offender and the purposes to be served. For those with little or no income, community service may substitute for a fine. Before offenders are sentenced to community service in Washington, they complete a community service order questionnaire (see Exhibit 5–9). The questionnaire helps the state department match the offender's abilities and limitations with community service work. A community corrections officer then makes sure the offender performs the required community service.

Georgia reported that in 2001, offenders worked 1.6 million hours of community service. Their work was worth $8.6 million to the state.[40] For offenders who do not present unacceptable risks of future violent crimes, a punitive intermediate sanction such as community service—which costs much less than prison, can save other state monies, promises comparable recidivism rates, and presents negligible risks of violence by those who would otherwise be confined—has much to commend it.

Recently, a statewide survey of community service in Texas found that two-thirds of the state's 122 community supervision and corrections departments operate a specialized Community Service Restitution unit that is responsible for managing community service restitution in the department.[41] Other interesting findings from the survey are the following:

- Community service in Texas is used most often (66 percent) or always (28 percent) as a supplement to probation supervision and is more often used as an alternative to jail than as a sole punishment.
- Drug and theft offenders are most commonly ordered to probation-supervised community service.
- Community service hours range from very short terms (20 hours) to more than 600 hours.
- The typical community service order for misdemeanants is 60 hours; for felons it's 230 hours.
- In Texas, one day of jail confinement is considered served for each 8 hours of community service.
- Five million hours of community service were completed in 2000. Based on this total and the then-minimum wage of $5.15 per hour, more than $26 million worth of community services were contributed to communities across Texas.
- On average, 71 percent of offenders successfully complete their community service order hours.
- Most department administrators surveyed supported the use of community service as an alternative to jail for low-level, nonviolent offenders.
- Although administrators held positive views about community service, most commented that it was not a tough enough sanction for most offenders. Slightly less than one-half indicated that criminal justice officials do not take community service seriously.

day reporting center (DRC)

A community correctional center to which an offender reports each day to file a daily schedule with a supervision officer, showing how each hour will be spent.

Day Reporting Centers   A **day reporting center (DRC)** is a nonresidential community correctional center to which an offender reports each day to file a daily schedule with a supervision officer. The schedule shows how each hour will be spent—at work or looking for work, in class, at a support group meeting, and so on.[42] Aiming primarily to provide treatment and reduce prison crowding, DRCs typically offer numerous services to address offenders' problems, and they strictly supervise offenders in a setting that is more secure than probation but less inhibiting than

EXHIBIT 5–9 **Sample Community Service Order Questionnaire**

| STATE OF WASHINGTON | COMMUNITY SERVICE WORKER QUESTIONNAIRE |
| DEPARTMENT OF CORRECTIONS | AND RELEASE OF INFORMATION |

_____   _____

Name   DOC Number

By action of the Superior Court, or an administrative Department of Corrections action, you have been ordered to perform community service work. This work must be performed within an approved unit of government or non-profit agency. To help us find the best assignment for you, and ensure reasonable accommodation for any sensory, physical or mental limitations or disabilities that you may have, please supply the following information. You are not obligated to disclose conditions that do not relate to your ability to perform community service.

1. List your job skills.

2. Do you have a preference for a certain agency or a particular type of work that you would like to perform?
   If yes, describe:

3. List the hours and days you are available for work.

   Monday _____   Wednesday _____   Friday _____   Sunday _____

   Tuesday _____   Thursday _____   Saturday _____

4. What means of transportation do you have to get to and from the work site?

5. Do you wear contacts or glasses?   Yes   No   N/A   (circle one)

6. Are you pregnant?   Yes   No   N/A   (circle one)

7. Are you currently taking any prescription medications that have side effects that may affect your ability to perform community service work (i.e., drowsiness, slurred speech, etc.)?   Yes   No   (circle one)

   If "Yes," describe side effects:

8. Note whether you have been diagnosed as having any of the following problems:

	Yes	No		Yes	No		Yes	No
Severe Allergy Reactions			Heart Problems			Epilepsy		
Breathing Disorders			Hearing Loss			Uncorrected Vision Problems		
Balance Problems			Diabetes			Other		

   If "Yes," please describe:

9. Is there any activity or motion that is difficult for you to do (i.e., crawling, climbing, bending, lifting, etc.)?
   Yes   No   (circle one)   If "Yes," please describe:

10. Do you have any other sensory, physical and/or mental limitations or disabilities that may affect your ability to do community service?   Yes   No   (circle one)   If "'Yes," please describe:

11. You are required to provide to your Community Corrections Officer, a clearance from your health care provider, documenting any sensory/physical/mental limitations or disabilities which impact your ability to perform community service hours. This documentation is required within 30 days of today's date, and will be at your expense. Release of information is on the reverse side.

Distributions: ORIGINAL-Community Service Worker, COPY-Worksite, Community Service Coordinator, File

DOC 05-103 (REV 10/97) OCO   COMMUNITY SERVICE PROGRAM incarceration. DRCs differ from other intermediate sanctions by a marked concentration on rehabilitation. Staff members assess the offender's needs and offer her or him various types of in-house treatment and referral programs, including substance abuse treatment, education, vocational training, and psychological services. DRCs have an aura of rigor that appeals to those wanting punishment and control of offenders, and it appeals to those advocating more access to treatment for offenders.[43] While DRCs differ in the type of offenders they serve, they all have three common threads: daily reporting, significant programming to assist offenders, and offender accountability.

DRCs first developed in Great Britain in 1972. British officials noted that many offenders were imprisoned not because they posed a risk to the public but because they lacked basic skills to survive lawfully. Frequently, such offenders were dependent on drugs and alcohol. In 1986, the Hampden County Sheriff's Department in Springfield, Massachusetts, established the first DRC in the United States. Ten years later, a National Institute of Justice survey identified 114 DRCs in 22 states.[44] Most had opened after 1990. Many of the programs were concentrated in just a few states, including Connecticut, Kansas, Oregon, Texas, and Wisconsin.

DRCs provide rehabilitation for offenders through intensive programming, while retaining a punishment component by maintaining a highly structured environment. DRCs commonly require offenders to obey a curfew, perform community service, and undergo drug testing twice a week. Participants check in at the center in person once a day and telephone periodically. They are responsible for following a full-time schedule that includes a combination of work, school, and substance abuse or mental health treatment. Programs range in duration from 40 days to nine months, and program content differs. Most programs require hour-by-hour schedules of participants' activities. Some are highly intensive, with 10 or more supervision contacts per day, and a few include 24-hour remote-location or other electronic monitoring.[45] Some centers refer clients to service agencies; others provide services directly. Some focus on monitoring; others emphasize support.

There have been few evaluations of DRCs. Early evaluations were favorable, but they were based on impressions rather than validated findings. The NIJ-sponsored survey showed generally high failure rates, averaging 50 percent. A study conducted on DRCs in North Carolina in 2000 compared the outcome of offenders sentenced to DRCs *plus* intensive supervision probation to that of offenders sentenced to intensive probation alone.[46] The researchers found that the addition of a DRC to ISP did not significantly reduce the rate of rearrest. In fact, they suggested that any rehabilitative effect that DRCs may have is counterbalanced by increased surveillance. "The 'piling up' of sanctions increases the likelihood of the offender's exposure to numerous forms of control and scrutiny culminating in frequent violations of the terms of the sentence."[47] On the positive side, however, the researchers found that DRCs empower the individual offender through literacy courses, a general equivalency diploma (GED), substance abuse counseling, and anger management classes. Reasons for the lack of evaluation are, first, that the DRC is still relatively new and, second, that DRCs vary greatly in terms of target population, eligibility criteria, services offered, monitoring procedures, and termination policies.

Two recent studies of DRCs in Vigo County, Indiana,[48] and Cook County (Chicago), Illinois,[49] looked at rearrest and reincarceration and which variables were associated with program completion. In Cook County, researchers discovered that almost one-half of the DRC clients who remained in the program for at least 70 days had not been rearrested compared to only one-quarter of the control group (those in the program fewer than 10 days). Similarly, two-thirds of the DRC clients who remained in the program for at least 70 days had not been reincarcerated compared with less than one-half of the control group.

In Vigo County, Indiana, 69 percent of the 179 adult offenders who were placed on DRC during the calendar years 1998 and 1999 successfully completed the program. One-third did not. Four individual characteristics and several case characteristics predicted success or failure. The four individual characteristics were age, living arrangement, marital status, and alcohol-drug history. DRC clients over age 40, married, either living alone or with their spouse, children, or parents, and with little to no history of alcohol and drug abuse were more successful. Case characteristics that predicted success or failure were crime type, charge count and reduction, commitment type, and sentence length. DRC clients convicted of misdemeanors with only one or two counts who received no charge reduction, who were in DRC as a condition of probation, and whose sentence to DRC did not extend beyond 120 days (as opposed to more than 120 days) were more successful. The researchers showed that the number of subjects who fail to complete the program increases as the sentence to DRC increases.

As DRCs move into the 21st century, a number of policy issues will influence their development and implementation. Those issues are (1) ensuring offenders' access to services, (2) responding to violations of DRC regulations in ways that will not add to jail and prison crowding, and (3) conducting evaluation of DRC programs. Charles Bahn and James Davis conclude that "since most offenders are ultimately going to be released from incarceration, it is essential that we experiment with and evaluate innovative community-based programs [such as day reporting centers] that will enable offenders to reintegrate into society."[50]

Remote-Location Monitoring   Technologies that probation and parole officers use to monitor remotely the physical location of an offender are known as **remote-location monitoring.** For example, home-based electronic monitoring (EM) is often used by officers to monitor remotely offenders who are restricted to their homes. It is estimated that from 1994 to 1998, the number of EM programs jumped from 400 to 1,500, and the number of offenders on EM rose from 12,000 to 95,000.[51] (While it is commonplace to refer to home confinement as EM, the acronym actually refers to a technological tool for monitoring a participant's compliance with some of the rules of the overall home confinement program.)

Remote-location monitoring uses technological systems such as EM, the Global Positioning System (GPS), voice verification, and other tracking systems to verify a person's physical location, either periodically or continuously, 24 hours a day. An offender's compliance with the conditions of supervision may require him or her to schedule appointments, conduct a job search, and maintain regular employment. Location monitoring systems provide a tool to verify—in real time—a person's whereabouts for specific risk issues or court-ordered release conditions. In this way, technology aids the officer in effectively satisfying specific supervision functions.

A major benefit of remote-location monitoring is that it costs significantly less than incarceration. Another is that it allows defendants and offenders to continue to contribute to the support of their families and pay taxes. Moreover, courts may order program participants to pay all or part

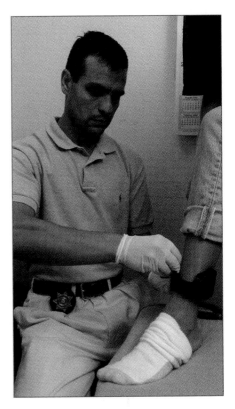

A probation officer attaches an electronic bracelet to an offender's ankle in order to monitor remotely the physical location of the offender. Remote-location monitoring technologies such as electronic monitoring, Global Positioning Systems, and voice verification provide judges with an expanded menu of corrections options. What are the pros and cons of remote-location monitoring as a probationary strategy?

remote-location monitoring

Technologies, including Global Positioning System (GPS) devices and electronic monitoring (EM), that probation and parole officers use to monitor remotely the physical location of an offender.

of the costs. Depending on the type of equipment used, the cost of remote-location monitoring ranges from approximately $9 per day for traditional EM ankle or wrist bracelets to $25 per day for the GPS tracking unit.

The GPS is a collection of 24 satellites owned and controlled by the U.S. Department of Defense that provides highly accurate, worldwide positioning and navigation information, 24 hours a day. The satellites orbit the earth every 12 hours. Each satellite transmits its precise time and position in space to receivers on earth that pick up the signals from multiple satellites simultaneously. A monitoring station determines the location of the receiver by calculating the time it takes the satellite signals to reach the receiver and the relative positions of the satellites at any particular time. This can accurately plot the receiver's position to within a few feet.

Although originally designed and developed for use in military applications, car manufacturers now install GPS units so that owners of private vehicles can plan a trip, get directions while on the road, or call for emergency assistance. GPS units are also used in fleet vehicles; public transportation systems; delivery trucks; courier services; police, fire and emergency vehicles; and even wildlife management to map, survey, and keep track of endangered animals.

Remote-location monitoring can be categorized into three risk-related areas: random/programmed contact systems, hybrid systems, and GPS or terrestrial-based systems.[52] Random/programmed contact systems are either active or passive. Active systems are typically comprised of automated telephone contact systems that require the offender to call in or receive a telephone call, followed by a process of identification and location, usually through voice verification methods that compare the spoken words or phrases to a voice template created during the system enrollment. Passive systems monitor the offender's location through a series of radio frequency signals emitted usually every 10 to 15 seconds by a tamper-resistant transmitter worn on the ankle to a receiver unit connected to the home phone. Some ankle bracelets can monitor an offender's blood-alcohol level by measuring the ethanol migrating through the surface of the skin. Normally, the participant must stay within a prescribed distance of the receiving unit. The supervising officer sees the results of active and passive systems on a computer screen. Program participants who do not comply with the conditions of their supervision may face sanctions ranging from reprimand to loss of privileges to revocation proceedings. An alternative passive system is referred to as "drive-by" interrogation. Here, a handheld portable receiver can be used by the supervision officer to determine that a subject is within the prescribed premises.

Hybrid systems combine EM and a programmed contact method such as voice or video verification. EM verifies the person's location while at home, and the programmed contact system periodically verifies the location when away from home. The programmed voice contacts substitute for the officer's telephone calls or in-person field visits to monitor the person's compliance with an approved schedule and location. Video verification calls are placed to the offender, who has a video camera in his or her home with a telephone line video adaptor. The offender is told to perform an action, such as holding up two fingers, and the picture is transmitted to the central station, where it is date and time stamped. Some hybrid systems can measure an offender's breath alcohol content. A breath alcohol analyzer is connected to the in-home receiver/dialer. Periodically, or on demand from a telephone call from the officer, the offender blows into a straw, and his or her breath alcohol level is recorded. The technology uses voice verification to ensure that it is the offender providing the sample. Other technologies take a photograph of the offender as he or she provides the sample. The sample is then reported immediately through the offender's phone line to the supervision officer.

Today, researchers are in the developmental phase of designing a ground-based tracking technology that is expected to be more accurate and cost-effective than GPS. This system is called *terrestrial-based monitoring*. The biggest difference between GPS and terrestrial-based monitoring is that the latter does not require the use of a satellite to transmit signals. There are a number of environments where GPS cannot function as designed, including indoor and underground locations as well as what are called "urban canyons" where tall buildings can block satellite signals. Terrestrial-based systems can use existing cell phone or radio towers to send and receive signals to pinpoint the location of an offender. The offender wears a small bracelet that interacts continuously with the receiving towers. Advocates also say that terrestrial-based systems will cost less than GPS because many cell phone and radio towers already exist. Towers would have to be built only in remote areas where they do not exist. In addition, the equipment being designed is smaller and weighs less than the tracking unit an offender must use with GPS. A diagram showing how some equipment manufacturers are combining terrestrial-based monitoring with GPS wireless tracking is shown in Exhibit 5–10.

EXHIBIT 5–10   Terrestrial-Based Monitoring and GPS Wireless Tracking Working Together

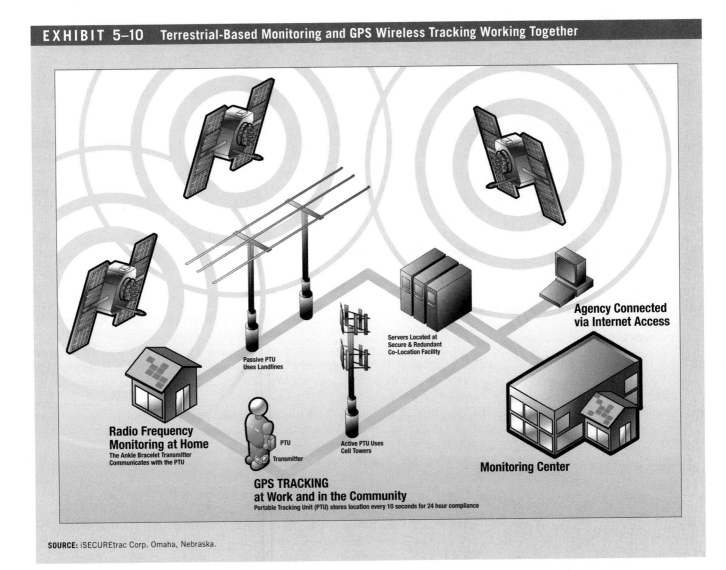

Servers Located at Secure & Redundant Co-Location Facility

Agency Connected via Internet Access

Passive PTU Uses Landlines

Radio Frequency Monitoring at Home
The Ankle Bracelet Transmitter Communicates with the PTU

PTU

Transmitter

Active PTU Uses Cell Towers

Monitoring Center

GPS TRACKING at Work and in the Community
Portable Tracking Unit (PTU) stores location every 10 seconds for 24 hour compliance

SOURCE: iSECUREtrac Corp. Omaha, Nebraska.

In theory, remote-location monitoring satisfies three correctional goals. First, it incapacitates the offender by restricting him or her to a single location. During the pretrial phase, remote-location monitoring is an alternative to detention used to ensure that individuals appear in court. In the postsentence phase, it is used as punishment, viewed as more punitive than regular probation but less restrictive than imprisonment. Second, remote-location monitoring is punitive because it forces the offender to stay home when not at work, school, counseling, or community service. Third, it contributes to rehabilitation by allowing the offender to remain with his or her family and continue employment, education, or vocational training.

There isn't a large body of scientifically produced research to support the idea that GPS monitoring deters future crime. However, there is some research that shows that offenders on active GPS monitoring commit fewer crimes. For example, recently a review of the performance of 17,000 participants in the federal home confinement program from 1988 through 1996 showed positive results.[53] Eighty-nine percent of the participants successfully completed home confinement without incident. The success rate for postsentence offenders was slightly higher than for pretrial defendants in the home confinement program (89 vs. 77 percent). The main reasons for unsuccessful termination included testing positive for illegal substances or incurring unauthorized leave violations. Only 0.7 percent of prerelease participants and 4.8 percent of postsentence participants were arrested or charged with new offenses, including misdemeanor offenses, such as driving under the influence (DUI) or shoplifting, or with more serious offenses such as theft, fraud, or drug possession.

In 1997, Florida was the first state to use GPS to monitor sex offenders on community supervision. In 2002, a survey of states' use of GPS monitoring of offenders by Kathrine Johnson, professor of criminal justice and legal studies at the University of West Florida, found that 16 states either implemented or expressed interest in pursuing the use of GPS monitoring for sex and domestic violence offenders.[54] Currently 23 states use GPS to monitor some sex offenders while they are on parole.[55] Some states such as Florida, Oklahoma, and Ohio will use this technology to monitor sex offenders who have committed specific sex crimes, particularly those against children, for the rest of their lives.[56] States not using GPS most frequently cite cost and technology as drawbacks.

In 2004, Florida evaluated its use of GPS monitoring and found that parolees fitted with GPS monitoring equipment were less likely to commit new crimes than those who were monitored by traditional means.[57] Statistics showed that the corrections department revoked the community release of 31 percent of GPS-monitored offenders because of bad behavior, but had to revoke the release of 44 percent of those monitored by other means. Six percent of offenders monitored by GPS committed new felonies or misdemeanors and 11 percent of those not electronically monitored committed new crimes.

According to Johnson, "GPS technology allows offenders to be monitored as closely, some would say more closely, as they would be in prison, at a substantial cost savings to the public."

Advocates of remote-location monitoring point to a number of advantages. Since the offender often pays to use the system, it usually pays for itself. In fact, it often generates profits for the supervising agency. Some hypothesize that, if only 10 percent of inmates were transferred to any of the three categories of remote-location monitoring, the savings would be nearly $4 billion.[58] It's tougher than routine probation. And since offenders can remain at home, keep working, maintain ties to the community, and avoid the negative influence of incarceration, it is more humane. The American Probation and Parole Association supports remote-location monitoring to assist probation and parole officers in achieving their prescribed goal of community protection.

Critics argue that when the innovation of remote-location monitoring is tested with sophisticated research designs involving comparison groups matched for offender risk, it shows no connection to program completion or recidivism, and it has a net-widening effect.[59] They also tell us that the requirement to have a telephone and pay for the monitoring equipment keeps remote-location monitoring out of reach for many offenders who would benefit from it. In addition, traditional home confinement with or without EM does not guarantee that crimes will not occur in the house. Vice crimes, domestic violence, and assaults—to name a few—occur during electronic house arrest. (*House arrest* is an intermediate sanction that requires an offender to remain in his or her house except for approved absences, such as going to work, school, or treatment programs.) And electronic monitors intrude on the privacy of the family and increase family stress.

Despite these concerns, remote-location monitoring has grown enormously throughout the United States since electronic surveillance technology was introduced in 1969. Not only is the number of offenders on remote-location monitoring increasing, but the offenders are also becoming more diverse. Initially, remote-location monitoring targeted only the traditional clients of house arrest: low-risk probationers, such as those convicted of DUI. More recently, however, it has expanded to include people awaiting trial or sentencing, offenders released from institutional and community corrections facilities, and juvenile offenders. Furthermore, whereas electronic house arrest initially gained acceptance as a response to property crimes, advances in remote-location monitoring allow probation and parole officers to set up exclusion zones (such as schools, parks, and homes) for offenders who are territory-restricted (e.g., stalkers and child molesters).

Residential Community Centers   A **residential community center (RCC)** is a medium-security correctional setting that resident offenders are permitted to leave regularly—unaccompanied by staff—for work, educational or vocational programs, or treatment in the community. Initially, such centers were called *halfway houses* and were for offenders who either were about to be released from an institution or were in the first stages of return to the community. However, as the number of halfway houses grew and new client groups (divertees, pretrial releasees, and probationers) were added, the umbrella term *residential community center* was adopted.

Halfway houses, prerelease and work release centers, and restitution centers are examples of RCCs. Some RCCs specialize in a type of client or treatment—for example, in drug and alcohol abuse, violent and sex offenders, women, abused women, or prerelease federal prisoners.

The most recent data on RCCs show that on January 1, 2000, more than 1,000 RCCs involving almost 27,000 adult residents were in operation across the United States,[60] and there is substantial diversity among them.[61] Some are public and some private. There are RCCs at all levels of government. The largest number of programs (about 40 percent) are operated by private nonprofit agencies. Those in the next largest group (about 35 percent) are run by state government. Then come those run by county government (almost 20 percent), for-profit corporations (less than 10 percent), and other agencies (less than 5 percent). RCCs range from

residential community center (RCC)
A medium-security correctional setting that resident offenders are permitted to leave regularly—unaccompanied by staff—for work, education or vocational programs, or treatment in the community.

Eye On Corrections

New Directions in Community Corrections: The Move Toward Evidence-Based Practices

By Michelle Gaseau and Meghan Mandeville

A new day is dawning for many in the community corrections field, as an emphasis on evidence-based practices is slowly, but surely, changing the way probation and parole departments do business. With an eye on reducing recidivism, many agencies have begun to embrace evidence-based practices and the systemic changes that come with them.

While research regarding "what works" for improving offender outcomes has been around for nearly two decades, community corrections agencies have, in the last few years, really started to focus in on evidence-based practices, hoping that this new approach towards supervision will have a more meaningful impact on offenders.

With many departments discussing how to put this "what works" philosophy into motion, the National Institute of Corrections and other non-profit organizations have stepped up to assist agencies that want to integrate evidence-based practices into their departments' daily routines. Multnomah County, Oregon, is one jurisdiction that has already had some success in implementing evidence-based practices. It is discussed here.

Multnomah County

Multnomah County, located in Oregon, which has been designated as a "learning site" for the NIC project, began the implementation process several years ago and the probation system has continued to reap the benefits.

The catalyst for change in Multnomah County in the 90s was a combination of budgetary issues and high caseloads for probation and parole agents. This caused county probation and parole officials to look deeper into the department's practices to see where it could be more effective and efficient.

They landed on the "what works" philosophy and evidence-based practices.

"That was going to be the framework for our changes [in the department]," said Don Trapp, What Works Program Supervisor for Multnomah County.

The principles that Multnomah County focused on included targeting of high- and medium-risk offenders, having a reliable risk assessment to evaluate offenders' risk and needs, providing a climate for offender change and using effective practices for those at low-risk.

In addition, the department lowered caseloads to 79 per probation officer as part of these changes.

"Studies show that with the low risk, the more you drag them back into the system the worse they do," said Trapp.

With this in mind the department opened a day reporting center and a secure alcohol and drug treatment facility for low-risk offenders.

Trapp said these moves have shown both community corrections officials and lawmakers that the changes were worth the effort.

"We've had some twelve month periods where the recidivism of this [low-risk] group was zero. When you talk about 10,000 [offenders] and 2,500 in the low, limited group, that's a lot of folks not committing new crimes. It allows for our field POs to pay more attention to high and medium offenders," said Trapp.

Trapp said the change process required the participation of everyone in the system, from the top on down to the officers doing the work in the field.

"What works is trying to align our practices with those that are effective and making better use of our resources and changing the climate and culture of how we talked about cases and interacted with offenders," Trapp said.

Trapp said the old style of doing business would be following a court order to the "T" but now a supervising officer may look more broadly at an offender to ensure he receives the services that will help him succeed.

In order to make these changes, the department formed a What Works Steering Committee that, from the beginning, has talked about how change should be implemented. The committee included management, line staff, trainers, research staff and others.

"This was an organizational change from top to bottom. We weren't talking about a new form or a new process for one group of offenders. This was how we were going to do business. We were charged with creating the vision, including the vision and what does case management look like and the instrumentation look like [after the vision is implemented]," said Trapp.

The steering committee was critical to implementation because it was able to identify specific changes that needed to be made in training, supervision and case management.

Trapp said the committee identified about 20 different training elements that needed to be addressed in the training curricula as well as changes to case management, such as the inclusion of the motivational interview when assessing offenders.

In order to make massive organizational changes, Trapp said a department needs to have political support. Multnomah County was lucky in that its leader at the time was well connected and respected by lawmakers and therefore was able to obtain the freedom needed to implement change.

"If you can't get the political support, you can't move forward. You have to be free to innovate or know what your limitations are," said Trapp.

Trapp said another important element to change on this level is knowing how to utilize the skills and experience of the staff.

"The approach I took was saying [to staff] 'It is a lot of things you already know and do, but we are putting it altogether into a case management system,'" he said. "My pitch was always to relate it to what people already know."

This is all key to changing the way people do their jobs in the department, he added, which is why the department also linked the changes to employee performance.

"When we do a performance appraisal. The supervisors [now] look for different things. It stopped being 'this is a great idea' to 'this is how your work will be measured.'" Trapp said "It wasn't just a suggestion or a good idea, we changed the expectations for how parole and probation officers do their work."

This is also the goal of the NIC project—to change the way community corrections agencies operate to, hopefully improve their effectiveness.

And NIC is confident that, by using an integrated approach to implementing evidence-based practices, the desired outcome will be achieved.

"If we work these principles, we're much more likely to change behaviors and prevent recidivism," said Dot Faust, a Correctional Program Specialist.

Source: "New Directions in Community Corrections: The Move Towards Evidence-Based Practices," Michelle Gasean and Meghan Mandeville, The Corrections Connection Network News (CCNN). Eye on Corrections www.corrections.com. February 21, 2005.

fewer than 10 beds to more than 200 beds. More than half are small, with fewer than 50 beds; almost 30 percent are classified as medium in size, with 50 to 100 beds; and 20 percent are large, with more than 100 beds. More than half of RCCs serve only men, 40 percent serve both men and women, and fewer than 10 percent serve only women.

The federal Bureau of Prisons (BOP) has the largest number of inmates (11,289) in RCCs, almost 6 percent of the BOP's total population. Almost 80 percent of eligible federal prisoners are released through RCCs where they spend, on average, three to four months before being released into the community.[62] Texas operates 17 restitution style RCCs with a combined bed capacity of more than 700 residents.[63] The primary purpose of the program is to serve as a cost-effective form of punishment. Residents' activities are monitored by the center's staff and by the probation department. Residents work in the community and return to the center after work. They use their wages to pay for room and board, transportation, court and probation costs, victim restitution, and child support. They also perform community service. One review of the Texas Restitution Center Program reported the following:

- An average of 61 percent of the residents successfully completed the program.
- Twelve percent are discharged for technical violations; 2 percent are discharged for new crimes, mostly misdemeanors that do not threaten public safety.
- Seventy-five percent were employed upon successful completion.
- Residents perform almost 97,000 hours of community service each year.
- Each year center residents pay approximately $96,000 in victim restitution: $75,000 for court costs, fines, and fees; $74,000 for probation fees; almost $200,000 to support dependents and into personal savings; and almost $75,000 to other financial obligations in the community.

According to Richard Lawrence, professor of criminal justice at St. Cloud State University (Minnesota) and author of the study of RCCs in Texas, "Considering the incarceration costs in the Texas Department of Corrections, the restitution center program is a success. The operating cost for Texas prisons is reported to be $37.50 per day per inmate. This figure includes only operating expenses, not the more than $50,000 per cell for new prison construction. Cost to the Texas Adult Probation Commission for operating the Restitution Center Program averages $30 per day per bed space. In addition to lower operating costs, the monetary restitution paid by the residents helps make a strong case for the program."[64]

The objectives of RCCs are community protection and offender reintegration. Community protection is achieved by screening offenders; setting curfews; administering drug or polygraph tests; confirming that when residents leave the center they go directly to work, school, or treatment; and providing a medium-security correctional setting. Reintegration is achieved by giving residents opportunities to learn and use legitimate skills, thereby reducing their reliance on criminal behavior. Staff members determine the obstacles to each resident's reintegration, plan a program to overcome those obstacles, and provide a supportive environment to help the resident test, use, and refine the skills needed.

The benefits of RCCs are many. RCCs benefit offenders by providing them with the basic necessities of food, clothing, and shelter while they find housing and employment. RCCs also offer residents emotional support to deal with the pressures of readjustment and help them obtain community services. Benefits to the community include a moderately secure correctional setting in which residents' behavior is monitored and controlled, as well as an expectation that opportunities for offenders to get on their feet will reduce postrelease adjustment problems and criminal behavior. For the criminal justice system, an RCC offers a low-cost housing alternative to incarceration of nonviolent offenders. An RCC can control offenders in the community at less cost than building and operating more secure facilities. It may also serve as an enhancement to probation and an option for dealing with probation and parole violators.

There has not been much research on the effectiveness of RCCs. An early General Accounting Office (GAO) report proposed that extensive planning and coordination of information were greatly needed for halfway houses to reach their objectives.[65] More recently, the state of Colorado conducted a statewide study of recidivism of halfway house clients.[66] The Colorado Office of Research and Statistics analyzed information on all offenders ($n = 3,054$) who terminated from 25 halfway houses during fiscal year 1997–1998 and explored why some clients failed while others succeeded. The study tracked cases for 24 months. It reported that 69 percent had no arrest within 24 months. Of the 31 percent who recidivated within 24 months, the majority of cases were drug or alcohol related. Only 3.4 percent were for violent offenses. High-risk, prior criminal history, young age, and lack of postrelease supervision predicted future offending. The report recommended that intensive treatment, therapeutic community models, and multidisciplinary approaches to deal with drug and alcohol addiction should be replicated across the state. The report stated that the criminal justice system alone cannot manage the problem of addiction and that programs following halfway house models yielded high success rates. The report also called for specific aftercare services to enhance offenders' likelihood of success, maximize public safety, and reduce recidivism. Offenders who did not receive postrelease supervision were almost twice as likely to fail as those who did (45 percent compared to 26 percent).

Recently a study of Ohio's 38 halfway houses found that residential community centers were most effective with parole violators and higher-risk offenders.[67] Furthermore, the most effective programs provided the greatest number of services targeting criminogenic needs, offered cognitive behavioral treatment, and engaged in role playing and practicing of newly learned skills.

Some researchers have concluded that "adopting more realistic outcome measures may make it possible to bridge the wide gap between public expectations for the justice system and what most practitioners recognize as the system's actual capability to control crime. By documenting what corrections programs can accomplish, we can move toward integrating programs like work release [as part of a residential community center program] into a more balanced corrections strategy. Such a strategy would successfully return low-risk inmates to the community, thereby making room to incarcerate the truly violent offenders."[68]

Boot Camps   In 1983, in an effort to alleviate prison crowding and reduce recidivism, the departments of corrections in Oklahoma and Georgia opened the first adult prison programs modeled after military boot camps. Since then, boot camp (sometimes referred to as *shock incarcera-*

boot camp

A short institutional term of confinement that includes a physical regimen designed to develop self-discipline, respect for authority, responsibility, and a sense of accomplishment.

tion, intensive confinement centers [ICCs], or *work ethic camps*[69]) has become an increasingly popular intermediate sanction. However, as you will learn, the use of correctional boot camps is on the decline and the evidence-based literature reports that the average boot camp has no effect on recidivism.[70]

Boot camp is a short institutional term of confinement, usually followed by probation, that includes a physical regimen designed to develop self-discipline, respect for authority, responsibility, and a sense of accomplishment. According to the NIJ, four characteristics distinguish boot camps from other correctional programs: (1) military drill and ceremony, (2) a rigorous daily schedule of hard labor and physical training, (3) separation of boot camp participants from the general prison population, and (4) the idea that boot camps are an alternative to long-term confinement.[71] Women represented 9 percent (723) of the adult boot camp population.

Boot camps have progressed through three phases. The first phase stressed military drill and ceremony. The second phase incorporated treatment programs such as anger management and alcohol and drug treatment. In the third phase some correctional agencies added aftercare such as postrelease supervision, remote-location monitoring, and networking boot camp graduates to community agencies to continue the treatment and services provided in boot camp. By 1995, state and local agencies operated 75 boot camps for adults and 30 for juveniles, and large counties operated 18 in local jails.

Boot camp goals were threefold: reduce recidivism, prison populations, and operating costs. However, as fast as boot camps were proliferating across the United States, research studies were showing that boot camps were not reaching their goals for at least three reasons.[72] First, when prisoners were asked to volunteer for boot camp as a back-door strategy to reduce prison crowding, many prisoners chose not to volunteer because states were also ordering the early release of nonviolent and drug-

The military-style training and drill that characterize boot camps are frequently supplemented with substance abuse education and vocational training. What aftercare programs might contribute to the effectiveness of boot camp strategies?

THE STAFF SPEAKS

We opened the Fresno County Boot Camp on December 5, 1997. We're out in a rural area, so it took us a year to pass all the red tape to open up the facility.

The main mission of our facility is to decrease the number of victims in the community, and to prepare these young men for a crime-free life. I take the things that the military model teaches, then add programs on top of that. We teach the kids to achieve and be successful. The kids that come to us are not acquainted with success—they're not acquainted with walking across the school stage and getting awards.

Our famous quote is "Do what you're told when you're told; do more than what's asked." That's the formula for success for employment. So although we come across in a very tough way, they have to have those skills to be employed. Kids don't know how to listen. So teaching them to focus on what somebody is telling them is very, very important. So we do it by setting them up for success, teaching them to listen, and teaching them how to function socially in a very appropriate manner.

Our other motto is it's a "no-fail program." Do we have kids who fail?

Absolutely. But we maintain a very high standard, and the kids rise to it. When you set a low standard—when you say, "We need to relate to them on their level" —that's the best way to keep them there.

Our ages go from 14 to 18, boys. Fourteen to 16 is our least successful population—junior high kids have problems all their own. They're not mature enough for the long-lasting effect you're looking for. Our program runs from six to eight months, and they've done a lot to get here—they may have gotten into the system at 10 or 11, so they can be pretty dysfunctional young men. Our most successful is the more mature population, 16 to 18. Most of these kids have a three-years-plus deficit in their education and usually not because they're stupid—it's because they don't go to school and haven't for years.

If a program is done right and if you're working to build experiences with kids, you can't buy that. Coming in here, these kids only know one way to be—with their gang emphasis, their bad attitude, and the way they've related to people all their lives. They come out of here a different way. Now, the challenge is, are they going to use it?

We have our kids out all over the county doing projects—they're working with the community, painting, planting trees, and these people just eat it up. They have good manners, saying, "Yes ma'am, yes sir." They go out and do color guards, they're in parades, and people come up and shake their hands and congratulate them. You can't buy that in any rehab program. We put them in all kinds of social situations, because that builds character.

Our goal is "no new victims." So even though we might have some young men not doing very well in the community, if they're not committing a crime, they're a success. But we have a tremendous number of kids going on to college. We're teaching them "How do I get myself through the day; what am I responsible for?" Right now we're running about an 82 percent success rate.

Commander Leslie Knobel
Assistant Director
The Elkhorn Correctional Facility
Fresno County, California

---

offending inmates, the target population for most boot camp programs. Inmates recognized that volunteering for boot camp as a way to reduce their sentence was unnecessary. Early release of nonviolent and drug-offending inmates meant inmates could avoid the regimentation that boot camp demanded.

Second, while military drill and ceremony and a daily schedule of hard labor and physical training were common to most boot camps and appealed to the general public, there was no conceptual model guiding implementation. Observers soon discovered that rigorous physical activity only produced physically fit offenders and did little to reduce short- and long-term recidivism, prison populations, and operating costs.

Third, there was no agreement on the role of treatment or aftercare. Some boot camp programs included them; most did not. Researchers showed that without treatment and aftercare, the benefits of boot camp were short-lived.

Most boot camps target young, first-time offenders who have been convicted of such nonviolent crimes as drug possession, burglary, or theft and who seem more open to changing their attitudes and behavior than older offenders. Most participants are males who do not have extensive criminal histories and are physically and psychologically able to complete the strict military exercise requirements. Offenders with disabilities or those with nondisabling medical conditions that limit their physical performance (e.g., being overweight) are typically excluded.

States differ in their age requirements for boot camp eligibility. For example, in California, participants must be 40 or younger; in Illinois, 17 to 29; in Kansas, 18 to 25; in Maryland, under 32; in New York, 30 or younger; in Oklahoma, under 25; and in Tennessee, 17 to 29.

Several researchers have examined boot camp programs for women.[73] Some programs integrated women with male inmates. Others were completely separate female programs. The researchers found that when boot camps combined men and women, few women were in the camp, and those women faced serious problems. They were supervised more intensely than the men, and their activities were restricted to protect them from abuse and harassment and to prevent sexual relations with male drill instructors. Combined programs did not take into consideration women inmates' physical stamina, nor did they offer therapeutic programs for the problems that many of these women faced, such as how to survive sexual assault or battering, make a successful transition into the community, or obtain job skills. Combined programs also failed to take into consideration the importance of children to women in boot camps.

Women in separate programs fared better. The separate camps were more likely to offer therapeutic programs suited to women's needs. Visitation policies were less restrictive, so the women had more opportunities to see their children while in boot camp. The researchers concluded that women should not be combined with men in boot camps designed for men. If boot camps are developed for women, they should be compatible with the needs and characteristics of women offenders.

The emergence of juvenile boot camps has been a recent and explosive trend. In 1995, MacKenzie and Rosay identified 37 juvenile boot camps operating across the United States.[74] The typical juvenile boot camp inmate was a nonviolent male between the ages of 14 and 18. Unlike most adult boot camps that exclude violent offenders from participating, however, half of the juvenile boot camps accepted offenders convicted of violent crimes. Juvenile boot camps were more likely than adult boot camps to spend more time on education and counseling. Still, when recidivism was examined in four high-quality studies involving random assignment of subjects to groups, there were no significant differences between the boot camp youths and the control groups. In one site, the youths released from the boot camp recidivated more than those in the control group. Recently, the NIJ released the findings from an evaluation of the Los Angeles County Drug Treatment Boot Camp, one of the longest-continuous-running boot camps in the United States since its inception in 1990.[75] The researchers found no difference in rearrests or convictions between juvenile boot camp graduates and a comparison group. The only significant difference they reported was that juvenile boot camp graduates were more likely to have probation revocations than the comparison group. They concluded, "The findings from this project support the conclusion from the existing literature that juvenile boot camps as a treatment model are probably not any more effective than most existing juvenile programs."

Changing the focus of juvenile boot camps is happening elsewhere. On January 5, 2006, Martin Lee Anderson, age 14, entered the Bay County (Panama City, Florida) Sheriff's boot camp, one of 82 juveniles in boot camps across Florida. Martin died the following day after he was punched, kneed, and attacked by a group of seven boot camp staff while a nurse looked on. Martin was sent to the Bay County boot camp as punishment for joyriding in his grandmother's car. The Bay County boot camp was one of the few in Florida where the use of deadly force, chemical agents, and pressure points was allowed. It also had one of the highest reoffender rates: About half of the juveniles returned to the juvenile justice system within a year of release. An initial autopsy blamed a rare blood disorder, but a second autopsy blamed the staff that choked Anderson and forced him to inhale ammonia. (The Bay County camp was closed after Anderson's death.)[76]

In April 2006, then-Florida governor Jeb Bush signed into law the Martin Lee Anderson Act. The new legislation bans the use of stun guns, pepper spray, pressure points, mechanical restraints, "harmful psychological intimidation," and the use of ammonia capsules to revive juveniles. Per diem pay for boot camp staff also increased from $80 a day to $100, because lawmakers believed low pay was attracting poorly trained staff. The new law renames Florida's boot camps STAR academies—an acronym that stands for Sheriff's Training and Respect—and clones Florida's successful boot camp in Martin County, where fewer than a quarter of juveniles commit crimes a year after release.

The bill requires juveniles to have physical exams upon entering an academy and enhances their access to medical care during their stay. Youths entering the camps will now be told of their right to outside counsel, given abuse hotline telephone numbers, and undergo physical exams that will also be performed when they exit the facilities. Boot camp staff can no longer use extreme intimidation tactics and restraint techniques such as ammonia capsules. Boot camp replacements must come under the same Department of Juvenile Justice rules as other juvenile facilities, and physical force can be used only when a child is a threat to himself on herself or others or if he or she tries to leave the camp without permission.

Critics have raised questions about using boot camps as a correctional tool. They note that correctional boot camp programs are built on a model of military basic training that the military itself has found lacking and in some cases has revised. Critics also argue that the military model was designed to produce a cohesive fighting unit and that after military boot camp there is further specialized training and career planning. That is not a goal of corrections. One analyst wrote, "If an offender can't read [or] write and is drug-involved, sending him to a 90-day boot camp that does not address his job or literacy needs will only have a short-term effect, if any, on his behavior."[77]

There is reason for both optimism and skepticism about boot camps. Although boot camps are promoted as a means of reducing recidivism rates, there is no evidence that they significantly reduce recidivism or promote socially desirable activities. A multisite evaluation of boot camps in Texas, South Carolina, and Florida showed no significant differences in reoffending rates among the different groups of offenders.[78] Research on Oklahoma's boot camp program, called the Regimented Inmate Discipline (RID) program, revealed that even when the researchers controlled for type of offense, age, and race on recidivism, boot camp graduates recidivated more frequently than either traditionally incarcerated inmates or probationers.[79] Research published in 2001 on a county-based boot camp in Florida shows similar results. The likelihood of an offender being rearrested was unaffected by his or her being sent to boot camp. Eighty-one percent of the boot camp graduates were rearrested, averaging 271 days before rearrest. Seventy-three percent of the comparison group was rearrested, averaging 290 days before rearrest.[80]

Research at the national level leads to the same conclusion: Recidivism for boot camp graduates is no better than it is for comparison groups. Recently the federal Bureau of Prisons (BOP) dealt a death blow to boot camps (called intensive confinement centers at the federal level). In January 2005, the BOP announced that it would close down the intensive confinement center program after the current group of 300 to 500 inmates completed the military-style course. Approximately 740 federal inmates each year participated in the ICC, out of a total prison population of over 183,000. In the future, ICC-bound inmates will be housed in minimum-security programs.

In making the announcement, BOP director Harley Lappin offered several reasons for the closure, including cost and program effectiveness. He explained that the closing is part of a cost-saving plan made necessary by "the very constrained budget we are facing this fiscal year."[81] He estimated that the closing will cut federal prison costs by $1.2 million. Lappin went on to say that "a substantial body of research indicated that they [ICCs] have no impact in reducing recidivism."[82]

Critics of the federal plan say they are confused by the BOP's turnaround. "Up until 2004, the BOP was touting the value of this program," said Assistant Federal Defender Timothy Hoover.[83] In 1996 the BOP estimated that it saved $9,337 for each prisoner who entered the ICC program rather than serving a 30-month sentence. Federal legislators, judges, and attorneys asked the BOP to reconsider, but Director Lappin responded,

> We recognize the concern voiced by some members of the Judiciary, especially with respect to discontinuing the ICC program. However, the fact remains that ICCs were costly to operate and no more effective in reducing recidivism than ordinary minimum-security facilities. Operating traditional minimum-security beds in lieu of ICCs requires fewer staff and allows us to confine more inmates.[84]

Some researchers have reported that boot camp graduates have higher self-esteem, have better attitudes toward family, are less likely to see themselves as victims of circumstances, and are more likely to feel in control of their future.[85] However, with limited exceptions, these positive changes didn't translate into reduced recidivism. Research into what boot camp participants say they'll do is less conclusive than research into what they've actually done.

Also disappointing is that the recidivism rates of boot camp graduates are very similar to those of other parolees.[86] One-third to one-half of front-end boot camp participants fail to complete their programs and are sent to prison as a result. In most programs, close surveillance of graduates after release leads to technical violation and revocation rates that are higher than those of comparable offenders in less intensive programs.

Boot camps are also promoted as a means of reducing prison crowding and corrections costs. Here the news is not all bad. Back-end programs, to which imprisoned offenders are transferred by corrections officials, do save money and prison space. Although they often experience high failure, technical violation, and revocation rates, those rates are no higher than those for offenders who have been kept in prison longer. If enough offenders complete boot camp and are released early from prison, the programs can reduce prison crowding. However, a number of researchers have found that most boot camps have not reduced prison crowding because the programs are designed for offenders who would otherwise be on probation, not those who would otherwise have received prison terms.[87] MacKenzie and her colleagues found in a multisite evaluation of boot camps that only two of the five boot camp programs examined appeared to save prison beds. The remaining three boot camp programs appeared to increase the need for prison beds.[88] Crowding can be reduced only if boot camp participants are selected from inmates already incarcerated and only if their participation substantially reduces their overall sentence lengths.

A number of researchers and policymakers have pointed out that the most successful boot camp programs are those that emphasize treatment over military regimen and increase postrelease supervision and support for graduates. Participants should benefit from earning a GED or learning job skills to make them more employable in the future or to encourage them to continue their education or vocational training. Successful boot camp programs also offer intensive postrelease supervision and support that helps graduates bridge the program to their neighborhood. Support is needed because boot camp graduates return to their previous environments with the same problems, such as unemployment, poverty, racial discrimination, dysfunctional families, lack of opportunities, and criminal temptations. Stinchcomb and Terry put it this way: "It is one thing to make noble commitments under closely controlled custody; it is quite another to maintain those commitments in the reality of a world where drill instructors are often replaced by drug dealers, where secure confinement is replaced by self-control, and where marching in straight lines is replaced by hanging out on street corners."[89] The programs that include continuing supervision and support are the ones that help boot camp graduates make more successful transitions back into the life of the community.[90]

Policy-Centered Approach to Developing Intermediate Sanctions

A policy is a statement of intent. It expresses *why* we are engaging in a particular set of activities. It also tells *how* we are to carry out these activities. Policy can be very general, very specific, or in between.

In recent decades, sanction options have proliferated, increasing the choices available to judges at sentencing and to governmental agencies

A drug court team meets to discuss progress of drug-involved offenders. Coalitions of judges, prosecutors, defense attorneys, substance abuse treatment professionals, probation officers, community-based service organization staff, law enforcement officials, and others represent a policy-centered approach to treat, sanction, and reward drug offenders. What are the advantages of using a policy-centered approach to devise intermediate sanctions like drug court?

policy-centered approach

A method of thinking about and planning for intermediate sanctions that draws together key stakeholders from inside and outside the corrections agency that will implement the sanction.

moving offenders from higher levels of control to lower ones. As we take stock of the contributions and limitations of the movement toward intermediate sanctions, it is important to think about such sanctions not as punishments developed in isolation from one another but rather as parts of a system of policy-driven responses to criminal behavior.

The **policy-centered approach** to intermediate sanctions emphasizes the policy that spells out the sentencing scheme and the place of each sentencing option as much as the sanctions and programs themselves. This approach draws together stakeholders from inside and outside the corrections agency that will implement the proposed sanction. The planning group often includes decision makers from all three branches of government (judicial, executive, and legislative) and all three subsystems of criminal justice (police, courts, and corrections). The group examines the overall context within which the proposed new sanction will be used and analyzes data on offenses and offenders to form sound policy. Public hearings may also be held. The policy that emerges is a statement of intent. It expresses why the group has decided to provide a particular set of sanctions and explains how those sanctions should be implemented. A good example of a policy-centered approach in intermediate sanctions is found in the experience of North Carolina and Pennsylvania. These two states developed comprehensive sentencing guidelines that incorporated confinement and nonconfinement punishment sanctions, including intermediate sanctions, for the courts to follow. The legislatures in these states drew together panels of stakeholders from law enforcement, courts, executive branches of government, and community groups to form the policies.

Program-Centered Approach to Developing Intermediate Sanctions

program-centered approach

A method of planning intermediate sanctions in which planning for a program is usually undertaken by a single agency that develops and funds the program.

Unfortunately, most intermediate sanctions are discrete local programs, devised and implemented without the participation of the decision makers who will use them. In such a **program-centered approach,** planning for an intermediate-sanction (e.g., remote-location monitoring) program is usually undertaken by a single agency that develops and funds the program. The program staff then tries to inform judges, prosecutors, defense counsel, and other corrections agencies about the program, its potential benefits, and the target population for which it is best suited.

The program-centered approach has serious limitations and often results in disappointment. It makes nationwide comparison and evaluation difficult because there is no coordination among the programs of different jurisdictions. Programs that are established this way are seldom evaluated because most local agencies lack the resources and the understanding of evaluation research. The program-centered approach often leads to many new programs that pursue multiple goals, sometimes even conflicting ones. When that happens, ambiguous and inconsistent operating policies develop. Finally, the program-centered approach tells us very little about how intermediate sanctions affect a jurisdiction's overall sentencing and imprisonment practices, very important information for most intermediate-sanction programs.

COMMUNITY CORRECTIONS

So far in this chapter, we have been discussing intermediate sanctions as strategies to control crime. Now we turn our attention from the *strategies* to the goal they are designed to achieve. That goal is community corrections. There is no consensus in the field of criminal justice on the definition of *community corrections*. Sometimes the term refers to noninstitutional programs. Sometimes it refers to programs administered by local government rather than the state. Other times, it indicates citizen involvement.

We define *community corrections* as a philosophy of correctional treatment that embraces (1) decentralization of authority from state to local levels; (2) citizen participation in program planning, design, implementation, and evaluation; (3) redefinition of the population of offenders for whom incarceration is most appropriate; and (4) emphasis on rehabilitation through community programs.

Community corrections recognizes the importance of partnership with the community in responding to crime. In short, our communities not only have a *right* to safe streets and homes but also bear *responsibility* for making them safe. All the major components of the criminal justice system have alliances today with the community. The field is experiencing many changes, including the following:

- *community policing*—a law enforcement strategy to get residents involved in making their neighborhoods safer by focusing on crime prevention, nonemergency services, public accountability, and decentralized decision making that includes the public;

- *community-based prosecution*—a prosecution strategy that uses a combination of criminal and civil tactics and the legal expertise, resources, and clout of the prosecuting attorney's office to find innovative solutions to a neighborhood's specific problems;

- *community-based defender services*—a defender strategy that provides continuity in representation of indigent defendants and helps defendants with personal and family problems that can lead to legal troubles; and

- *community courts*—a judicial strategy of hearing a criminal case in the community that is most affected by the case and including that community in case disposition.

Debate and innovation continue to reflect these themes. The Vermont Department of Corrections leads the nation in giving local citizens decision-making authority about punishment and supervision issues that directly affect the offender, the victim, and community safety. In 1995, the Vermont DOC established a network of "community-based reparative boards." Today there are more than 65 reparative boards involving 750 citizen volunteers. In 2005, these boards handled more than 1,300 cases. After conviction and referral by a judge, offenders meet with their local reparative board to review their offense and learn how it harmed the community. They must then accept the terms of what is usually a multifaceted, community-based sanction, including apologies, restitution, and community service. An evaluation of Vermont's community reparative boards was published in 2000 under a grant from the NIJ.[91] The researchers used focus groups; in-depth interviews with board members, crime victims, and offenders; and telephone surveys with randomly selected Vermonters. They found that Vermonters had more confidence in the criminal justice system after the establishment of community reparative boards than they did before the reparative boards existed. Thus, what began as an attempt to make the major components of the criminal justice system more community based now involves citizen volunteers as they strive to reinvent a supervision system to manage offender harm and repair effectively. The American Correctional Association has also em-

Talking about CORRECTIONS

EVIDENCE-BASED PRACTICES IN COMMUNITY CORRECTIONS

Visit *Live Talk* at **Corrections.com** (www.justicestudies.com/talking04) and listen to the program "Evidence-Based Practices in Community Corrections," which relates to ideas discussed in this chapter.

community corrections acts (CCAs)

State laws that give economic grants to local communities to establish community corrections goals and policies and to develop and operate community corrections programs.

braced community corrections. ACA's support of community corrections is shown in Exhibit 5–11.

Community Corrections Acts

This spirit of correctional collaboration and community partnership has led 28 states to pass **community corrections acts (CCAs)** (Exhibit 5–12). CCAs are state laws that give economic grants to local communities to

---

EXHIBIT 5–11   American Correctional Association

Public Correctional Policy on Community Corrections

Introduction:

Community corrections programs are an integral component of a graduated system of sanctions and services. They enable offenders to work and pay taxes, make restitution, meet court obligations, maintain family ties, and develop and/or maintain critical support systems with the community. To be successful, community corrections programs must promote public safety and a continuum of care that responds to the needs of victims, offenders, and the community. These programs should include a collaborative comprehensive planning process for the development of effective policies and services.

Policy Statement:

Community corrections programs include residential and nonresidential programs. Most community corrections programs require offenders to participate in certain activities or special programs that are specifically directed toward reducing their risk to the community. Those responsible for community corrections programs, services, and supervision should:

- A. seek statutory authority and adequate funding, both public and private, for community programs and services as part of a comprehensive corrections strategy;
- B. develop and ensure access to a wide array of residential and nonresidential services that address the identifiable needs of victims, offenders and the community;
- C. inform the public about the benefits of community programs and services; the criteria used to select individuals for these programs; and the requirements for successful completion;
- D. recognize that public acceptance of community corrections is enhanced by the provision of victim services, community service and conciliation programs;
- E. mobilize the participation of a well-informed constituency, including citizen advisory boards and broad-based coalitions, to address community corrections issues;
- F. participate in collaborative, comprehensive planning efforts which provide a framework to assess community needs and develop a systemwide plan for services; and
- G. ensure the integrity and accountability of community programs by establishing a reliable system for monitoring and measuring performance in accordance with accepted standards of professional practices and sound evaluation methodology.

This Public Correctional Policy was unanimously ratified by the American Correctional Association Delegate Assembly at the Winter Conference in Orlando, Fla., Jan. 20, 1985. It was reviewed and amended Jan. 29, 1997, at the Winter Conference in Indianapolis, Ind. It was reviewed and amended Jan. 14, 2002, at the Winter Conference in San Antonio, Texas.

establish community corrections goals and policies and to develop and operate community corrections programs. Most CCAs transfer some state functions to local communities, decentralizing services and engaging communities in the process of reintegrating offenders. Along with the transfer of correctional responsibility from the state to the community, CCAs provide financial incentives for counties, private citizens' groups, and private agencies to participate. The financial incentives help communities manage more of their own correctional cases. With the money, local communities design, implement, and evaluate a complete range of local sentencing options. (The intermediate sanctions discussed earlier in this chapter, for example, can be funded through a CCA.) Locally designed sanctions have a better chance of succeeding because they are based in the community where offenders' families, friends, and other social supports are. Although CCAs authorize and allow funding for a range of sanctions, including intermediate sanctions, they do more than that. CCAs implement community corrections philosophy by providing statewide structures that specify government and citizen roles and responsibilities in the planning, development, implementation, and funding of community sanctions.

In 1973, Minnesota became the first state to adopt a CCA. Minnesota officials wanted to reduce fragmentation in criminal justice service delivery, to control costs, and to redefine the population of offenders for whom state incarceration was most appropriate. Communities throughout Minnesota were willing to assume greater correctional responsibility for less serious offenders, as long as the communities were also given state subsidies and significant control over planning and service delivery. The huge success of Minnesota's CCA can be seen in Minnesota's incarceration rate, one of the lowest in the United States today. While the crime rate is not much different from those of other states, the incarceration rate is only 180 persons for every 100,000 residents. The U.S. average on

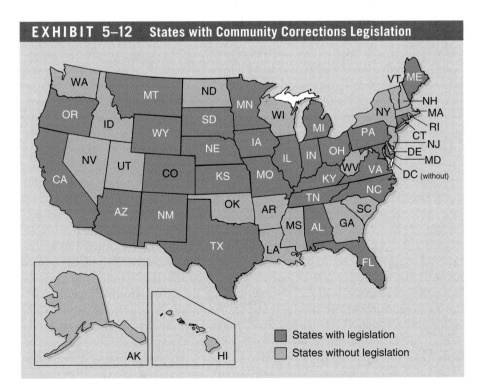

EXHIBIT 5–12   States with Community Corrections Legislation

States with legislation
States without legislation

January 1, 2006, was 491 per 100,000 residents. The majority of Minnesota's offenders are handled under the CCA.

There are tremendous differences among the CCAs in the United States. The most common goal, held in 14 states, is expansion of sanction choices. Twelve states cite the promotion of state and community partnerships as the goal. Some CCAs focus on nonviolent offenders; others merely include them. Some CCAs help communities move offenders out of local jails and into correctional programs that are less expensive and that offer reasonable community protection.

Simply having correctional programs in a community does not mean that a community corrections program exists. Consistent goals and consistent approaches to achieving those goals are the backbone of successful community corrections. Community corrections legislation can help accomplish that consistency.

REVIEW & APPLICATIONS

REFLECTIONS ON THE FUTURE

Intermediate Sanctions: Quality Programs or Stepchildren of the Correctional and Judicial Systems

By Herbert J. Hoelter
National Center on
Institutions and Alternatives

When asked to write some introductory comments on the future of intermediate sanctions, I accepted the task with enthusiasm, welcoming the opportunity to share the wisdom of my 30 years of experience in alternative and community corrections. Being an inveterate optimist, I was confident that I could put forth a piece that might enlighten and encourage those in the field of community corrections, as well as those hoping to enter the field.

However, upon reflecting on how to address most accurately the issue of the future in this field, my optimism waned. I came to realize that to be able to address the future of a particular topic, there is an inherent assumption that there is a past, or at minimum a present, in a given field. On the issue of intermediate sanctions, that assumption is misguided. Truth be known, the use of intermediate sanctions in the prison and correctional system in the United States is much more of a *concept* than a reality.

In order to begin to understand this, it is incumbent to remember how

the term *intermediate sanctions* entered the field of community corrections. It was during the early 1980s when conservatives were arguing that rehabilitation was a failure and worthless, and the liberal advocacy organizations decided that in order to "win" the argument for community corrections, rehabilitation should be downplayed (and in some cases abandoned) in favor of punishment and deterrence. The theory was that successful arguments could be made to legislators and judges that programs such as house arrest, community sanctions centers, rigorous community service, ankle bracelets, global positioning tracking, drug testing, and shameful sentencing could be effective "intermediate sanctions," bridging the gap between traditional probation and prisons, particularly for nonviolent offenders. In theory, perhaps it was an interesting idea; in practice, it has become an albatross. Probation officers have turned into foot soldiers for the prison system, and many programs originally designed to help offenders in the com-

munity have turned into mini correctional facilities.

This is not to suggest that all of the intermediate sanction programs currently in operation are somehow failures; on the contrary, there are hundreds of successful programs doing intensive supervision, effective monitoring, valuable community service, and restitution and providing treatment in the community. The point is that these are isolated, individual programs on the fringes of the prison system. They are not now, nor have they ever been, viewed as an integral part of any state or federal correctional system. Additionally, they are subject to the political ideology and budget priorities of the day.

If there is to be a future to intermediate sanctions, the challenge is to find a method and political will to move these programs firmly into the correctional and judicial systems, rather than having them be the stepchildren of those systems. In my view, and in looking at lessons learned from the past, there are three fundamental issues to address in order to move the concept of intermediate sanctions into accepted practice.

The first issue is that we must be strong in our conviction that rehabilitation of offenders is an acceptable and worthwhile process. Rehabilitation can and does work, and everybody deserves the opportunity to change.

Second, we must recognize that intermediate sanctions deserve the financial resources to do the difficult task of working with offenders in the community. We must advocate that some or all of the $22,000 spent on keeping a person incarcerated for a year gets

recommitted to the intermediate sanction serving that person.

Finally, unpopular as it may sound, we must develop a philosophy that we handle offenders in the community with the same care, concern and commitment we would expect if they were our own sons or daughters, fathers or mothers. We must insist on developing quality programs that have respect for the individuals they serve and maintain a certain dignity for all of our populations, even those that seem "undeserving."

Intermediate sanctions can and should have a future—but it must be

on these terms, not those defined by the failing prison system.

About the Author

Herbert J. Hoelter is cofounder and CEO of the National Center on Institutions and Alternatives. He is recognized as one of the country's leading experts in developing alternative programs to incarceration. Hoelter holds a master of social work degree from Marywood College in Pennsylvania and a bachelor of arts degree from the University of Buffalo. He is coeditor of *The Real War on Crime*.

SUMMARY

1 *Intermediate sanctions* is the term given to the range of new sentencing options developed to fill the gap between traditional probation and traditional jail or prison sentences, better match the severity of punishment to the seriousness of the crime, reduce institutional crowding, and control correctional costs. Punishments typically identified as intermediate sanctions include intensive supervision probation (ISP), drug courts, fines, community service, day reporting centers, remote-location monitoring, residential community centers, and boot camps.

2 *Net widening* means increasing the number of offenders sentenced to a higher level of restriction. As a result, many offenders receive more restrictive sanctions than their offenses and characteristics warrant.

3 Intensive supervision probation (ISP) is control of offenders in the community through strict enforcement of conditions and frequent reporting to a probation officer with a reduced caseload. ISP programs exist in all 50 states. They may be state or county programs and may be administered by parole, probation, or prison departments.

4 Drug courts are special courts that are given responsibility to handle cases involving drug-addicted offenders.

5 A day fine is a financial punishment scaled to the seriousness of the offense and the offender's ability to pay. A traditional fine is based on a fixed amount, without regard to the offender's ability to pay.

6 Community service is a sentence to serve a specified number of hours working in unpaid positions with nonprofit or tax-supported agencies. Research suggests that, for offenders who do not present unacceptable risks of future violent crimes, community service costs much less than prison, has comparable recidivism rates, and presents negligible risks of violence by those who would otherwise be confined.

7 A day reporting center (DRC) is a community correctional center to which an offender reports each day to file a daily schedule with a supervision officer, showing how each hour will be spent. DRCs aim to provide strict surveillance over offenders and, depending on their resources, provide treatment services, refer offenders to community social service agencies, or arrange to have community agencies offer services on site.

8 *Remote-location monitoring* refers to technologies that probation and parole officers use to monitor remotely the physical location of an offender. For example, home-based electronic monitoring (EM) is often used by officers to monitor remotely offenders who are restricted to their homes.

9 Residential community centers (RCCs) are medium-security correctional settings that resident offenders are permitted to leave regularly—unaccompanied by staff—for work, educational or vocational programs, or treatment in the community.

10 Boot camp is a short institutional term, usually followed by probation, that includes a physical regimen designed to develop self-discipline, respect for authority, responsibility, and a sense of accomplishment.

11 A policy-centered approach draws together diverse stakeholders to think about and plan for an intermediate sanction. A program-centered approach, on the other hand, is usually undertaken by a single agency that develops and funds the program in isolation from other programs.

12 Community corrections is a philosophy of correctional treatment that embraces decentralization of authority from state to local levels; citizen participation in program planning, design, implementation, and evaluation; redefinition of the population of offenders for whom incarceration is most appropriate; and emphasis on rehabilitation through community programs.

13 Community corrections acts (CCAs) are state laws that give economic grants to local communities to establish community corrections goals and policies and to develop and operate community corrections programs. CCAs decentralize services and engage communities in the process of reintegrating offenders by transferring correctional responsibility from the state to the community and by providing financial incentives for communities to manage more of their own correctional cases.

KEY TERMS

intermediate sanctions, *p. 157*
community corrections, *p. 157*
front-end programs, *p. 159*
back-end programs, *p. 159*
trap-door/side-door programs, *p. 159*
net widening, *p. 159*
intensive supervision probation (ISP),
    p. 161

drug court, *p. 163*
fine, *p. 168*
day fine, *p. 169*
community service, *p. 173*
day reporting center (DRC), *p. 176*
remote-location monitoring, *p. 179*
residential community center (RCC),
    p. 183

boot camp, *p. 188*
policy-centered approach, *p. 194*
program-centered approach, *p. 194*
community corrections acts (CCAs),
    p. 196

QUESTIONS FOR REVIEW

1 Explain intermediate sanctions and describe their purpose.

2 Apply the concept of net widening to intermediate sanctions.

3 Differentiate between intensive supervision probation and regular probation.

4 Distinguish between drug courts and other types of courts.

5 Explain the principles behind day fines.

6 Why is community service sometimes called a "fine of time"?

7 What are the features of a day reporting center?

8 For which offenders do you believe remote-location monitoring is most beneficial?

9 What criteria would you use to assess the effectiveness of residential community centers?

10 What would you predict about the future of boot camps from the literature?

11 Give an example of a policy-centered approach and a program-centered approach to planning intermediate sanctions.

12 Discuss the importance of community involvement in community corrections.

13 How do community corrections acts implement the philosophy of community corrections?

THINKING CRITICALLY ABOUT CORRECTIONS

Fines

Summarizing the results of a national survey of judges' attitudes toward fines, researchers noted that "at present, judges do not regard the fine alone as a meaningful alternative to incarceration or probation."[92] What could you tell such judges to convince them that day fines, or structured fines, are a viable sentencing option?

Policy-Centered Approach to Intermediate Sanctions

Supporters of the policy-centered approach to devising intermediate sanctions cite three advantages: (1) It avoids wasting scarce resources on the wrong category of offender; (2) it draws the support of judges, prosecutors, and defense counsel outside the sponsoring agency; and (3) it helps develop consensus on specific goals for a program. If your jurisdiction was planning a juvenile drug court, why would you argue for a policy-centered approach in the planning and operational phases of the drug court?

ON-THE-JOB DECISION MAKING

Why Day Fines?

Your state legislature recently passed a bill authorizing day fines as an intermediate sanction. Part of the bill requires each probation department to send one or more probation officers to a workshop to prepare for implementing the bill. The chief probation officer designates you. Before the workshop, you are given two questions: (1) Why are day fines a good idea? (2) What would you do with offenders who don't pay? Write a response to bring to the workshop.

Are Drug Courts Working?

Imagine you are Herbert M. Klein, founder of the nation's first drug court in Miami, Florida, in 1989. Experience tells you that drug courts provide closer, more comprehensive supervision and much more frequent drug testing and monitoring than other forms of community supervision. Yet some researchers are finding that there is no difference in arrest rates between drug court offenders and comparison group members, and if there is, it's difficult to say which of the 10 components of drug court or combinations of features are the most important for determining success. The media asks you to respond. What do you say? (Recall that in Chapter 4 we talked about outcome measures other than recidivism. You might consider searching the links on the home page of the National Association of Drug Court Professionals at www.nadcp.org/home.html for additional information.)

LIVE LINKS

at www.justicestudies.com/livelinks04

5–1 Drug Courts The Second Decade

Researchers have begun to look at the inner workings of drug courts and to investigate how key functional drug court components, singly and in combination, affect outcomes. This report summarizes six key findings.

5–2 The Future of Drug Courts

This paper examines the implementation of drug courts in four states (Louisiana, Missouri, New York, and Ohio). Topics discussed include the early years of drug courts, leadership and mavericks, the art of selling drug courts, the role of statutes in drug court growth, laws creating alternatives to incarceration, federal support, 10 key components, an operational challenge, different models, centralizing authority, building support, promoting best practices, creating infrastructure, increasing capacity, and conclusion—lessons of institutionalization.

5–3 Correctional Boot Camps: Lessons from a Decade of Research

This report presents findings from 10 years of data analyzing whether boot camps are successful in reducing recidivism, prison populations, and operating costs. The report found that although boot camps generally had positive effects on the attitudes and behaviors of inmates during confinement, these changes did not translate into reduced recidivism.

5–4 Sentencing to Service Program Review/ Assessment Report

This document discusses how Minnesota's Sentencing to Service (STS) program has proven to be both cost-efficient and effective with long-term benefits for the state and the offenders it serves.

5–5 What Future for "Public Safety" and "Restorative Justice" in Community Corrections?

Restorative justice and public safety principals are reshaping community corrections around the country. Pursuing public safety requires community corrections to take a proactive approach, to come from behind the desk into the community. This report discusses the role of restorative justice in the pursuit of public safety.

INSTITUTIONAL CORRECTIONS

Part Three examines jail, prison, and parole.

These three correctional components account for almost 3.1 million offenders daily.

How much have jail inmates, facilities, and staff changed since the country's first jail officially opened in Philadelphia in 1776? As you will learn, many of today's jails are large and some are quickly adapting high technology to their purposes. Even though only 3 percent of the nation's 3,365 locally operated jails are "mega" jails (having 1,000 or more cells), they hold over 45 percent of the jail population. And why is it that with only 95 percent of all jail capacity occupied nationwide, jail staff perceive that jails are overcrowded? Staffing has not kept up with the increase in the jail population. Are privatization and accreditation solutions? You will decide.

Prisons also first developed in Pennsylvania. In 1790, a wing of the Walnut Street Jail was devoted to long-term incarceration and served as a model for the world's first prison, the Eastern State Penitentiary, in 1829. The architecture of jails and prisons changed over the years from linear to podular. Prisoner supervision approaches also changed, from indirect to direct. Regardless of all the changes, overcrowding remains a problem.

Each day, 1,600 people will leave prison. How prepared are they to reenter society? Did they receive the educational and vocational preparation and drug treatment they need to minimize their likelihood of reoffending? Unfortunately, probably not. Prisons simply do not have the resources to rehabilitate all inmates under their care. Even after release, one of five prisoners will have no supervision because he or she served a full sentence, as a result of legislation that abolished discretionary parole board release completely or for certain violent offenses. Has the pendulum swung too far? Many think so. Offender reentry is the hot button topic in parole since President George W. Bush called for the nation to expand successful reentry efforts to help released prisoners in his 2004 State of the Union address.

JAILS

Way Stations Along the Justice Highway

CHAPTER OBJECTIVES

After completing this chapter you should be able to do the following:

1 List the purposes of jails.

2 Understand how jail populations are different from prison populations.

3 Trace briefly the development of jails in history.

4 Explain how first-, second-, third-, and fourth-generation jails differ in design and in method of inmate management.

5 Outline the characteristics of jail inmates, facilities, and staff.

6 Outline the arguments for and against privatization.

7 Discuss ways to reduce jail crowding.

8 Describe how jail vocational and educational programs affect inmate behavior and recidivism.

9 Discuss how faith-based organizations and a jail chaplain can influence jail inmates and help jail staff.

10 Discuss why jail accreditation is important.

11 Explain why it is important for jail staff to conduct themselves as professionals.

"

Informed people know that jails today have become the biggest mental hospitals in the United States with the largest three being Los Angeles County Jail system, number one, New York City Department of Corrections, number two, and Cook County Department of Corrections, Chicago, number three. Many of these inmates with mental health problems also have an addiction to alcohol/drugs, what people today refer to as co-occurring disorders.
—Ken Kerle, managing editor of *American Jails*

"

College sports are supposed to be fun. But sometimes they can be deadly. That's what 21-year-old University of Northern Colorado football starting punter Rafael Mendoza found out after his teammate and backup punter, Mitch Cozad, allegedly stabbed him in his kicking leg, leaving a five-inch gash. Mendoza was returning to his apartment in Evans, a small town south of Greeley, around 9:30 P.M. after study hall on campus on Monday, September 11, 2006.[1] The case has drawn quick comparison to the 1994 assault on Olympic figure skater Nancy Kerrigan by Shane Stint, the hitman hired by rival skater Tonya Harding's ex-husband Jeff Gilloly.

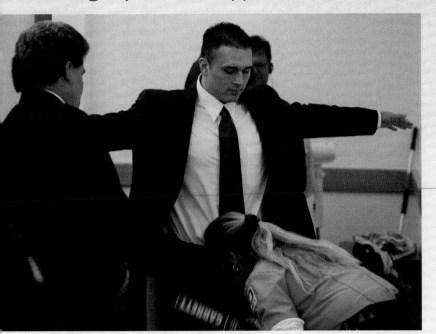

On Thursday, August 9, 2007, University of Northern Colorado football back-up punter Mitch Cozad was convicted of second-degree assault but acquitted of the more serious charge of attempted first-degree murder. Cozad was found guilty of leaving a 3- to 5-inch-deep gash in Rafael Mendoza's kicking leg during a September 11, 2006, ambush in an attempt to get the starter's position. Earlier Cozad was booked in the Weld County Jail and released following a bond hearing. Cozad faces up to 16 years in prison. What is the purpose of jail?

According to police reports, Mendoza turned to face his attacker—dressed in black sweatpants and a sweatshirt with a hood cinched around his face. Mendoza fought his attacker and then fell to the ground. Mendoza then was stabbed.

A witness saw Cozad get into a 2006 Dodge Charger with a passenger, police said. The pair sped away but were seen a few minutes later at a liquor store where the two were pulling tape off the Charger's Wyoming vanity license plate "8-KIKR." A store employee called police.

The license plate was tracked to Cozad's mother in Wheatland, Wyoming. Evans city police found Cozad in his dormitory room on the UNC campus. They interviewed him and found a black hooded sweatshirt in his closet. Cozad was arrested on a charge of second-degree assault and at 6 P.M. he was booked into the Weld County Jail. Following a bond hearing he was released on a $30,000 bond.

Police believe that Mendoza foiled an attempt on his life motivated by Cozad's desire for the starter's position. According to an arrest affidavit, Cozad wanted to play in a game against Portland State two days before the attacks and that he was upset at Mendoza for "[messing] up his kicking numbers."

On Thursday, October 19, 2006, the Weld County district attorney charged Cozad with attempted first-degree murder and second-degree assault. On Monday, October 23, 2006, Cozad surrendered to local authorities. He posted a $500,000 bond and was released. At Cozad's preliminary hearing on January 19, 2007, Kevin Aussprung, Cozad's dorm mate at UNC, told Weld County District Judge Marcelo Kopcow that Cozad offered to pay him $100 for driving the car and he had to agree to wear a black hooded sweatshirt, black sweatpants, and black shoes. On Monday, March 12, 2007, Cozad pleaded not guilty to charges of attempted murder and assault. On August 9, 2007, a jury convicted Cozad of second-degree assault but acquitted him of the more serious charge of attempted first-degree murder. Cozad faces up to 16 years in prison.

Cozad and Mendoza's story isn't much different from the thousands of men and women who enter our nation's jails each day, many with substance addictions. Most are not as economically fortunate or as athletically talented, but the offense similarities are surprising. As you'll read in this chapter, jails are often disparaged in corrections, but that image is changing. Today's jails have opportunities that were unheard of just a decade ago. Citizen advocates, community linkages, judicial oversight, and jail professionalism are changing the ways jails are operating. These windows of opportunity can leverage jails to successfully perform their functions.

PURPOSE OF JAILS

Jails are locally operated correctional facilities that confine people before or after conviction. Jails are different from prisons (the subject of Chapter 7) in a number of ways that you will learn about as you read. The fundamental difference between jail and prison is the nature of their populations.[2]

Total admission is the total number of persons admitted to jail each year, which falls between 10 million and 13 million. The **average daily population (ADP),** on the other hand, is the sum of the number of inmates in a jail or prison each day for a year, divided by the total number of days in the year. Jail ADP at midyear 2006 was 755,896. Prison total admission is currently estimated at 733,000 a year, and prison ADP on January 1, 2006, was 1,525,924 adults (see Chapter 7). The *daily* population of jails is lower than that of prisons, but the *annual* total of people incarcerated in jails is higher. Put another way, it takes almost two years for the nation's state and federal prison population to turn over once; the jail population turns over almost 15 times each year. The jail population is, thus, dynamic, and the prison population is static. The changing nature of jail populations raises significant issues and problems that form the core of this chapter.

On June 30, 2006, local jail authorities held or supervised 826,232 offenders, an increase of 1.1 percent from midyear 2005.[3] Jail authorities supervised approximately 7.3 percent of these offenders (60,222) in alternative programs outside jail facilities (see Exhibit 6–7). A total of 766,010 were housed in local jails.

Inmates sentenced to jail usually have a sentence of one year or less. Most jail inmates will spend only hours or days in jail before being released to the street or transferred to other institutions, however, an estimated 20 percent will spend at least one month, 12 percent at least two months, and 4 percent will spend more than six months.[4]

At midyear 2006, the majority of the nation's jail population (62 percent—an all-time high) was pretrial detainees.

jails
Locally operated correctional facilities that confine people before or after conviction.

total admission
The total number of people admitted to jail each year.

average daily population (ADP)
Sum of the number of inmates in a jail or prison each day for a year, divided by the total number of days in the year.

Jails also incarcerate persons in a wide variety of other categories. Jails are used to do the following:

- Receive persons awaiting court action on their current charge.
- Readmit probation and parole violators and bail-bond absconders.
- Detain juveniles until custody is transferred to juvenile authorities.
- Hold persons with mental illness until they are moved to appropriate health facilities.
- Hold individuals for the military.
- Provide protective custody.
- Confine persons found in contempt.
- Hold witnesses for the courts.
- Hold inmates about to be released after completing a prison sentence.
- Transfer inmates to federal, state, or other authorities.
- House inmates for federal, state, or other authorities because of crowding of their facilities.
- Operate some community-based programs as alternatives to incarceration.
- Hold inmates sentenced to short terms (generally under one year) of incarceration.

For all their important roles and responsibilities, jails have been a disgrace to every generation.[5] Many of the nation's 3,365 locally operated jails are old, overcrowded, poorly funded, scantily staffed by underpaid and poorly trained employees, and given low priority in local budgets. Yet a strong groundswell of support is rising for the nation's jails. Tomorrow's jail professionals have tremendous opportunities to continue that momentum. Progress is being made because of new emphases on jail education, staff selection and training, professional associations, standards, technology, accountability, and laws, among other things. Groups such as the American Jail Association (AJA) are advancing jail professionalism through training, information exchange, technical assistance, publications, and conferences. Members of the AJA include sheriffs, jail administrators, judges, attorneys, educators, correctional staff, jail inspection officials, health care providers, and clergy. The AJA mission statement is shown in Exhibit 6–1. This chapter will explore the problems of jails of the past and present and discuss direction for the 21st century.

Almost one-half of the nation's jails like the one pictured are small (less than 50 cells), holding only 4 percent of the jail population. Most small jails were built in the early part of the 20th century. What management style does this jail suggest?

JAILS IN HISTORY

It is believed that King Henry II of England ordered the first jail built, in 1166. The purpose of that jail was to detain offenders until they could be brought before a court, tried, and sentenced. From that beginning, jails spread throughout Europe but changed in scope and size over time.

THE STAFF SPEAKS

I've been on the job 15 years, and it's been wonderful—it's been an excellent career. I would tell anybody to step into it. It's so rewarding—it can be so stressful, but there are so many rewards. I'm a hands-on person; I enjoy working with people. We don't always see people coming into jail pretty—you see them at their lowest—and if you can help that person to move up, I guess that's where the reward comes in.

Prior to this, I worked at the state hospital, so I worked with the mentally challenged and the handicapped. Then I had my second child and went into day care, and I baby-sat the sheriff's grandson. I always told him, "If there's ever an opening, keep me in mind," so I went for an interview and got a position.

I have never been afraid of my position; I've never been afraid of working with individuals. I've had a wonderful captain—he always trained in the adage "Treat them as you'd like to be treated if you were behind bars." I've always used that as my outlook with the individuals that I come into contact with here. You never know; you could be falsely charged with something—it could be you behind bars.

People in the community do not know what it is like to be locked up. And in a sense, I'm locked up for eight hours a day, or if I have to stay longer. When we work the floor, we're basically prisoners too. We don't realize what it's like for somebody to be away from their family—sure, they've messed up. But if we can give them a TV or send them to a GED class or a religious class, that is taking their minds off of thoughts of suicide, thoughts of "I'm worthless." I've been through I don't know how many attempted suicides, and it's not a pretty sight. You have to step into a prisoner's eyes and see where they're at but not step down to their level.

Some people say that we're just glorified babysitters, but if you feel that way, you're in the wrong position. We're not here to find these people guilty—we're here to meet their needs while they're incarcerated.

Right now I'm in charge of the transport area—I deal a lot with probation and courts and see to it that people are transported to where they need to be. So I've got to keep the rapport good and open with probation and the court. That's one area that I really work hard at. But my work ethic is maybe different than some—because when I'm here, I'll do whatever I can to help anybody out. I love my job, and you don't hear too many people say that after so many years. You can always find something good in a person.

Terrie Butterfield
Sergeant
Kandiyohi County Jail
Wilmer, Minnesota

EXHIBIT 6-1   American Jail Association

Mission Statement

To band together all those concerned with or interested in the custody and care of persons awaiting trial, serving sentences, or otherwise locally confined; to improve the conditions and systems under which such persons are detained.

To advance professionalism through training, information exchange, technical assistance, publications, and conferences.

To provide leadership in the development of professional standards, pertinent legislation, management practices, programs, and services.

To present and advance the interests, needs, concerns, and proficiency of the profession as deemed appropriate by the membership and their representatives.

Copyright © American Jail Association.

With the development of workhouses and poorhouses in the 15th and 16th centuries in England, sheriffs took on the added responsibility of supervising vagrants, the poor, and the mentally ill. These institutions, despite their distinct names, were indistinguishable from jails. Their squalid, unhealthy conditions and the sheriffs' practice of demanding money from persons under their charge caught the attention of 18th-century Enlightenment reformers. One such reformer was the English sheriff John How-

The Walnut Street Jail, started in Philadelphia in 1776, originally housed offenders without regard to sex, age, or offense. Following its redesignation as a penitentiary in 1790, it housed only convicted felons. Which religious group's principles influenced correctional institutions in Pennsylvania?

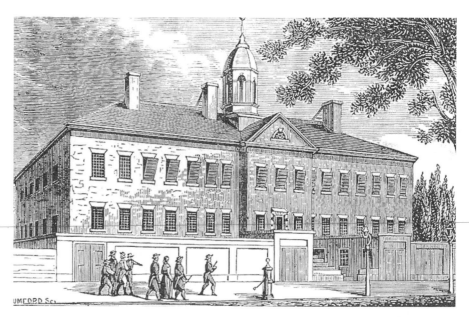

ard. In 1779, England's Parliament passed the four jail reforms that Howard proposed: secure and sanitary structures, jail inspections, elimination of fees, and an emphasis on reforming prisoners. To this day, the John Howard Association and *Howard Journal* carry Howard's ideas forward.

First Jail in America

The first jail in America was the Walnut Street Jail in Philadelphia, built in 1776. The jail housed offenders without regard to sex, age, or offense. Following the jail's opening, conditions quickly deteriorated. According to some, the jail became a "promiscuous scene of unrestricted intercourse, universal riot, and debauchery."[6] The Philadelphia Quakers had wanted the Walnut Street Jail to be a place where inmates reformed themselves through reflection and remorse. In 1790 the Philadelphia Society for Alleviating the Miseries of Public Prisons and the General Assembly of Pennsylvania designated a wing of the Walnut Street Jail a penitentiary. Implementing Quaker beliefs, the penitentiary emphasized prisoner reform through reflection and penitence and rehabilitation through good conduct. Sixteen solitary cells were added to the facility and workshops were built. Alcohol and prostitution were prohibited; prisoners were segregated by sex, age, and offense; diets were monitored; guardians were appointed to care for minors; and religious, health care, and educational services were provided. Debtors were housed separately from the general inmate population and had no such privileges. Their prison conditions were pitiful, and many debtors starved.[7]

In 1798 a fire destroyed the workshops at Walnut Street. The destruction brought about disillusionment and idleness. Rising costs crippled the jail's budget. Disciplinary problems rose with overcrowding, and escape and violence increased. The number of inmates who were destitute vagrants or debtors soared as did the incidence of disease. There were political conflicts between the religious Quakers and the non-Quaker prison board members. Prisoners rioted on March 27, 1820, and on October 5, 1835, the Walnut Street Jail closed. State prisoners were transferred to the new Eastern State Penitentiary in Philadelphia, the first institution of its kind in the world (see Chapter 7). County inmates and those awaiting trial were transferred to a new county jail.

By the close of the 19th century, most cities across the United States had jails to hold persons awaiting trial and to punish convicted felons. The sheriff became the person in charge of the jail. As crime increased and urban centers expanded, jails grew in importance, as did the sheriffs' control over jails.

American Jails in the 20th Century

On any given day, America's jails serve a variety of functions. They detain people awaiting arraignment or trial, 62 percent at midyear 2005. They confine offenders serving short sentences for less serious offenses. Jails also serve as surrogate mental hospitals, a topic we return to later in this chapter and in Chapter 12. They frequently detain people with drug or alcohol dependency. They are the first stop on the social services highway for the homeless, street people, and some with extremely poor physical health, especially those with HIV, AIDS, and tuberculosis (TB).

Some historians refer to America's jails as the "poorhouse of the twentieth century," the dumping grounds for society's problems.[8] Jails in 20th-century America evolved into institutions of social control not only for people who committed criminal acts but also for those who made up the underclass in American society.

John Irwin, former California prison inmate turned college professor, called the purpose of jails **rabble management;** that is, the control of persons whose noncriminal behavior is offensive to their communities.[9] The central purpose of the 20th-century jail was to detain the most disconnected and disreputable persons, who were arrested more because they were offensive than because they had committed crimes. They were individuals of whom all were aware yet whom society ignored: public nuisances, derelicts, junkies, drunks, vagrants, the mentally ill, and street people. One study in Las Vegas, Nevada, found that most jail inmates were incarcerated not because of their threat to society, but for their inability to post bail and pay fines, essentially making the jail a poor house.[10]

rabble management
Control of people whose noncriminal behavior is offensive to their communities.

Therefore, the purpose of America's 20th-century jails must be understood in relation to the composition of the jail population. Jails not only confined people before and after conviction but also held those who did not fit into the mainstream of American society. Moreover, since jails housed society's outcasts, there was no incentive to improve jail conditions. Today, good business practices are driving the design and operation of well-run facilities.

Architecture and Inmate Management

In an attempt to better manage and control inmate behavior, jails have progressed through four phases of architectural design. Each design is based on a particular philosophy of inmate management and control.

First-Generation Jails First-generation jails were built in a linear design that dates back to the 18th century, when prison and jail design was shifting from single-cell and religious emphasis to congregate housing and secular administration (more on the history of correctional architecture is presented in Chapter 7).

In a typical **first-generation jail,** inmates live in multiple-occupancy cells or dormitories. The cells line corridors that are arranged like spokes. Inmate supervision is sporadic or intermittent; staff must patrol the cor-

first-generation jail
Jail with multiple-occupancy cells or dormitories that line corridors arranged like spokes. Inmate supervision is intermittent; staff must patrol the corridors to observe inmates in their cells.

EXHIBIT 6–2 First-Generation Jail—Intermittent Surveillance

Cells line corridors in first-generation jails. Unable to observe all inmate housing areas from one location, prison and jail staff must patrol inmates' living areas to provide surveillance. What are the consequences of first-generation jails?

ridors to observe inmates in their cells. Contact between jailers and inmates is minimal unless there is an incident to which jailers must react. See Exhibit 6–2.

The design of such linear jails reflects the assumption that inmates are violent and destructive and will assault staff, destroy jail property, and try to escape. The facility is designed to prevent these behaviors. Heavy metal bars separate staff from inmates. Reinforced metal beds, sinks, and toilets are bolted to the ground or wall. Reinforced concrete and razor wire surround the facility.

The biggest problem with first-generation jails is the inability of an officer to see what is going on in more than one or two cells at a time. That limitation gave rise to the second-generation jails of the 1960s.

Second-Generation Jails Second-generation jails emerged in the 1960s to replace old, run-down linear jails and provide officers the opportunity to observe as much of the housing area as possible from a single vantage point.

Second-generation jails adopted a different philosophical approach to construction and inmate management. In a **second-generation jail,** staff remain in a secure control booth overlooking inmate housing areas, called *pods* (see Exhibit 6–3). Although visual surveillance increases in such jails, surveillance is remote, and verbal interaction with inmates is even less frequent than in first-generation jails. Property destruction is minimized because steel and cement continue to define the living areas. Outside, fences and razor wire continue to discourage escapes as well as unauthorized entry. Second-generation jails have been termed *podular remote-supervision facilities.*

While staff can observe activity in common areas, or *dayrooms,* they are unable to respond quickly to problems or even to interact effectively with inmates because of the intervening security control booth. In both the first- and second-generation jails, the biggest problem is that staff and inmates are separated. As David Parrish, detention commander for the Hillsborough County Sheriff's Department (Tampa, Florida) puts it, "Staff

second-generation jail

Jail where staff remain in a secure control booth surrounded by inmate housing areas called *pods* and surveillance is remote.

EXHIBIT 6-3 Second-Generation Jail—Remote Surveillance

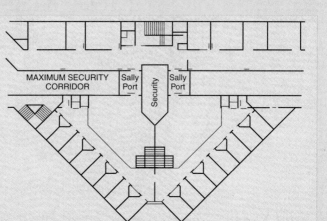

Inmate living areas are divided into pods, or modules, in which cells are clustered around dayrooms that are under remote observation by staff in a secure control room. What are the consequences of second-generation jails?

managed the hallways and control rooms, generally about 10 percent of the facility, while inmates ran the housing areas, roughly 90 percent."[11]

Third-Generation Jails Third-generation jails, also known as *direct-supervision jails*, emerged in 1974 when the Federal Bureau of Prisons opened three Metropolitan Correctional Centers (MCCs) in New York, Chicago, and San Diego. These three Federal facilities were the first jails planned and designed to be operated under the principles of unit management, which later became known as direct supervision (see Exhibit 6–4 for a list of the nine principles of direct supervision). The housing unit design of such jails is podular. Inmates' cells are arranged around a common area, or dayroom. There is no secure control booth for the supervising officer, and there are no physical barriers between the officer and the inmates. Direct supervision places a single deputy directly in a "housing pod" with between 32 and 64 inmates. The officer may have a desk or table for paperwork, but it is in the open dayroom area.

In a third-generation jail the inmate management style is direct super-

third-generation jail (also *direct-supervision jail*)

A jail where inmates are housed in small groups, or pods, staffed 24 hours a day by specially trained officers. Officers interact with inmates to help change behavior. Bars and metal doors are absent, reducing noise and dehumanization.

EXHIBIT 6-4 Nine Principles of Direct Supervision

1. *Effective control:* The unit officer is the secure perimeter.
2. *Effective supervision:* Continuous supervision is maintained by the unit officers.
3. *Competent staff:* Correctional standards guide recruitment.
4. *Staff and inmate safety:* Performance-based data are collected.
5. *Manageable and cost-effective operations:* There are more architectural choices, commercial-grade furnishings, and equipment options.
6. *Effective communication:* Direct communication exists between inmates and officers, officers and supervisors.
7. *Classification and orientation:* Know with whom you are dealing; intense supervision is maintained for the first 12–72 hours.
8. *Justice and fairness:* Unit officers exercise primary informal discipline.
9. *Ownership of operations:* Inmate policy decisions are guided by a team approach.

EXHIBIT 6-5 **Third-Generation Jail—Direct Supervision**

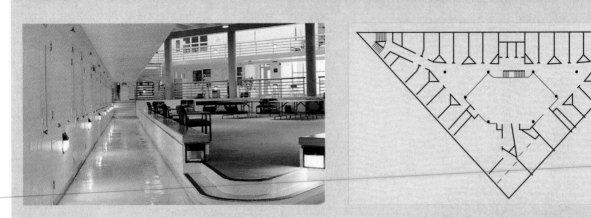

Cells are grouped in housing units, or pods. Each pod has a central dayroom. Prison staff are stationed inside the housing unit to encourage direct interaction between inmates and staff. What are the consequences of direct-supervision jails?

vision. An officer is stationed in the pod with the inmates, much like a teacher in a classroom. The officer moves about the pod and interacts with the inmates to manage their behavior. Advocates of direct supervision tell us that when correctional officers are in constant and direct contact with inmates they get to know them and can recognize and respond to trouble before it escalates into violence.

The pod contains sleeping areas, dayroom space, all necessary personal hygiene fixtures, and sufficient tables and seats to accommodate unit capacity. Officers are not separated from inmates by a physical barrier. Officers provide frequent, nonscheduled observation of and personal interaction with inmates (see Exhibit 6–5). Furnishings are used to reduce inmate stress caused by crowding, excessive noise, lack of privacy, and isolation from the outside world. Bars and metal doors are absent, reducing noise and the dehumanization common in first- and second-generation jails.

Direct-supervision jails facilitate staff movement, interaction with inmates, and control and leadership over pods. By supervising inmate activities directly, the staff can help change inmate behavior patterns, rather than simply react to them. Staff control inmate behavior through the enforcement of boundaries of acceptable behavior and the administration of consequences for violating the boundaries. Observing unacceptable behavior and administering consequences is less likely to occur in first- and second-generation jails where staff supervision is sporadic and remote.

Researchers tell us that pods and direct supervision provide a safer and more positive environment for inmates and staff than do first- and second-generation jails.[12] Still, there's an element of resistance to the concept of direct supervision, especially with local law enforcement agencies. Reasons for the skepticism include the short history of direct supervision, little supporting data, and the belief among sheriffs and jail administrators that direct-supervision facilities are not as "safe" or "strong" as remote-supervision facilities because of distance and physical separation from inmates.[13] Simply put, many agencies are not comfortable removing the "barriers" between "us and them," especially if the jail becomes overcrowded. However, one sheriff's captain with over 25 years of experience working in overcrowded remote-supervision and overcrowded direct-supervision jails recently wrote, "It is clear to me that the direct-supervision jail is superior when it comes to safety, security, and over-all operations in overcrowded conditions. . . . Those who maintain their commitment to the direct-supervision principles will maintain better con-trol and ownership of their facilities. With the current or future reality of overcrowding in our facilities, it is difficult for me to understand why anyone would choose lack of control over more control."[14] Yellowstone (Montana) County sheriff's captain Dennis McCave explained that, when his direct-supervision facility became overcrowded and the sheriff's budget was too tight to build more beds or hire more staff, his agency "Hot Podded." Inmates shared hours out of their cell in the pod day-room—only one-half of the inmates were allowed out at a time. "I've been there and I'm convinced," wrote Captain McCave. "Managing by the principles and philosophy of direct supervision is by far the superior alternative in the 'best of times and the worst of times.'"[15]

The first direct-supervision county jail in the United States was the Martinez Detention Facility in Contra Costa, California. It opened in January 1981. Today, an estimated 349 of the 3,365 local jails use direct-supervision, but as one researcher has asked, "Are they really direct-supervision jails?"[16] After receiving surveys from half of the direct-supervision jails, Christine Tartaro, professor of criminal justice at the Richard Stockton College of New Jersey, found that while many jails are being called direct supervision, few of them truly are. Only 40 percent said their facilities operate under a unit management structure, and few offered any inmate services other than recreation on the pod. The major-ity operated under traditional centralized management and a few used elements of both. Tartaro also found that half of the direct-supervision jails offered correctional officers no more than two days of communica-tion skills training even though the training requirements for learning to communicate with a diverse group of inmates is difficult and needs more than one or two days of instruction. The majority of Professor Tartaro's sample (70 percent) also identified their jail's furnishings and fixtures as vandalism resistant and half-bolted their furniture to the floor, conveying the message that inmates are expected to misbehave. (The first MCCs outfitted inmate living areas with normalized com-mercial fixtures, furnishings, and finishes.) Furthermore, because of jail crowding, the majority of the inmates in direct-supervision facilities are no longer housed in single cells. Tartaro believes that jails that are only partially implementing the direct-supervision model are not secure or well-run facilities. This risks giving a bad reputation to those that are as escapes, riots, or violence occurs in the partially implemented third-generation jails. This leads us to the newest development in archi-tectural design and philosophy of inmate management, fourth-generation jails.

Fourth-Generation Jails   Over the past few decades, architects and correctional planners have worked together to improve direct-supervision jails in two important ways, thereby introducing the next phase of jail development, **fourth-generation jails.** First, they introduced the concept of "borrowed light." Directing natural light into the dayroom where staff work and inmates spend most of their day makes them more alert and interactive with one another, and improves attitudes. In most jails, even third-generation jails, staff and inmates are isolated inside, unable to tell night from day, or experience the positive effects of daylight. In fourth-generation jails sunlight bathes the dayroom. Light passes into the sleeping

fourth-generation jail

Jail that incorporates natural light into the dayroom where staff work and inmates spend most of their day, and brings program services, staff, volun-teers, and visitors to the housing unit.

EXHIBIT 6–6   Fourth-Generation Jail—Direct Supervision, Natural Light, and Pod-Based Programming

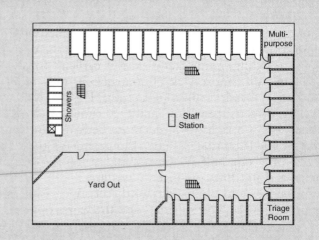

Natural light illuminates the podular design where staff work and inmates spend most of their day under the principles of direct supervision. Program services and visitation also take place on the pod.

cells through the large windows in the cell doors. On sunny days lighting can be turned down, thereby saving electricity.

The second improvement is programmatic. One problem with third-generation jails is it isolates the officer with the inmates. (Recall from Professor Tartaro's research that the majority of third-generation jails do not offer any inmate services on the housing unit other than passive recreation (for example, watching TV, reading, and playing cards and board games). The fourth-generation jail brings program services, staff, volunteers, visitors, and even vending machines to the housing unit, thereby reducing the feeling of isolation in the unit. Proponents of fourth-generation jails argue that this improvement adds significantly to the correction officer's ability to carry out the nine principles of direct supervision (see Exhibit 6–4). The only known fourth-generation jail in operation to date is the King County Regional Justice Center in Kent, Washington (see Exhibit 6–6).[17]

CHARACTERISTICS OF JAIL INMATES, FACILITIES, AND STAFF

Who is in jail? Why are they there? How many jails are there? How many people work in jail? What do we know about the operation and administration of jail facilities? To these and related questions we now turn our attention.

Jail Inmates

The characteristics of jail inmates changed slightly from mid-2005 to mid-2006. In June 2006, local jail authorities held or supervised 826,232 offenders—an increase of 1.1 percent from June 2005. Almost 7.3 percent of these offenders (60,222) were supervised outside jail facilities (see Exhibit 6–7). A total of 766,010 were housed in local jails.

Since 1970, when the first national jail statistics were collected, the number of inmates held in locally operated jails has almost quadrupled.

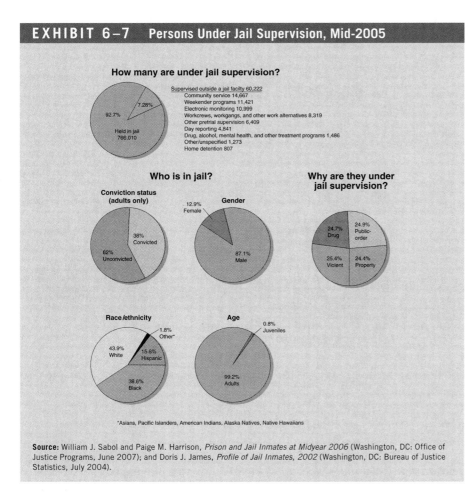

EXHIBIT 6-7   Persons Under Jail Supervision, Mid-2005

How many are under jail supervision?

7.28%

92.7%

Held in jail
766,010

Supervised outside a jail facilty 60,222
Community service 14,667
Weekender programs 11,421
Electronic monitoring 10,999
Workcrews, workgangs, and other work alternatives 8,319
Other pretrial supervision 6,409
Day reporting 4,841
Drug, alcohol, mental health, and other treatment programs 1,486
Other/unspecified 1,273
Home detention 807

Who is in jail?

Why are they under jail supervision?

Conviction status
(adults only)

38%
Convicted

62%
Unconvicted

Gender

12.9%
Female

87.1%
Male

24.7%
Drug

24.9%
Public-order

25.4%
Violent

24.4%
Property

Race/ethnicity

43.9%
White

1.8%
Other*

15.6%
Hispanic

38.6%
Black

Age

0.8%
Juveniles

99.2%
Adults

*Asians, Pacific Islanders, American Indians, Alaska Natives, Native Hawaiians

Source: William J. Sabol and Paige M. Harrison, *Prison and Jail Inmates at Midyear 2006* (Washington, DC: Office of Justice Programs, June 2007); and Doris J. James, *Profile of Jail Inmates, 2002* (Washington, DC: Bureau of Justice Statistics, July 2004).

During the 1970s, the growth was very modest—13 percent—but during the 1980s it was more than 120 percent.

Since 2000, the nation's jail population has increased an average of 3.6 percent a year. But, as we pointed out earlier, the 4.7 percent growth in 2005 was the largest annual growth since 2002. That growth, in addition to the steady percentage increase in the number of jail inmates who are pretrial detainees (62 percent in 2005, up from 44 percent in 2000), leads one of the country's most respected voices in jail issues, Dr. Ken Kerle (managing editor of *American Jails* and author of this chapter's Reflections on the Future) to write that "this is another unhappy sign that inmate processing is slowing down."[18] If more jail inmates are not being tried, convicted, or sentenced, jail resources become overburdened, crowding results, and the conditions of confinement worsen.

The Bureau of Justice Statistics has compiled a profile of inmates in local jails. That profile is shown in Exhibit 6–8. Note that at the time of arrest:

- more than half of the inmates were under supervision by the courts or corrections;
- almost one-third were on probation and almost one-eighth were on parole;
- 4 of every 10 had a criminal history;
- over 80 percent used drugs regularly;

EXHIBIT 6-8   Profile of Jail Inmates

Categories	Percentage of Jail Inmates		Categories	Percentage of Jail Inmates
Criminal Justice Status at Arrest			**Physical or Sexual Abuse (Females)**	
None	46.8%		Ever	18.2%
Status[1]	53.2		Before age 18	10.9
On probation	33.6		Age 18 or after	4.9
On parole	12.6		Physical abuse	15.1
On bail-bond	6.9		Sexual abuse	7.7
On other pretrial release	2.3			
			Employment Status	
Criminal History			Employed	71.0%
None	39.5%		Full-time	57.4
Violent recidivists	33.7		Part-time	10.9
Nonviolent recidivists	26.9		Occasionally	18.4
			Not employed	29.0
Prior Drug Use				
Never	17.8%		**Person(s) Lived with Most of the Time**	
Ever[1]	82.2		Both parents	43.6%
Regular	68.7		Mother only	39.2
In month before the offense[2]	52.6		Father only	4.4
At the time of the offense[2]	28.8		Grandparents	10.3
			Other	2.5
Alcohol at Time of Offense[2]			Homeless in past year	14.3
Not under the influence	65.5%			
Under the influence	34.5			
Substance Abuse Treatment				
Never	42.0%			
Ever[1]	58.0			
Since admission to jail	15.1			

1. Detail may add to more than total; inmates may fit more than one category.
2. Based on convicted jail inmates only.

Source: Adapted from Doris J. James, *Profile of Jail Inmates, 2002* (Washington, DC: Bureau of Justice Statistics, July 2004).

- one-third were under the influence of alcohol;
- 2 of every 10 women had been physically or sexually abused;
- almost one-third were unemployed at the time of arrest;
- more than half grew up in homes without both parents; and
- 14 percent were homeless.

The latest statistics seem to indicate that as many as 12 million people annually will come in contact with the jails in America. Given the country's population of almost 300 million, this means that 4 percent of the population will find themselves in a local jail each year.

Another way to look at the nation's jail population is to consider the rate of incarceration. Jail populations give us a count of the total number held in jail (e.g., 766,010 offenders held or supervised in mid-2006). Because of differences in total population, however, such counts do not allow for accurate comparison of jurisdictions. Rates of jail incarceration, expressed as the number of jail inmates per 100,000 residents age 18 and older, provide for a more meaningful and useful analysis of trends in incarceration. With rate data, we can compare changes over time. Exhibit 6–9 shows changes in the jail incarceration rate from 1995 through 2006. Note that the incarceration rate increased 30 percent, from 193 jail inmates per 100,000 adults in 1995 to 256 jail in-

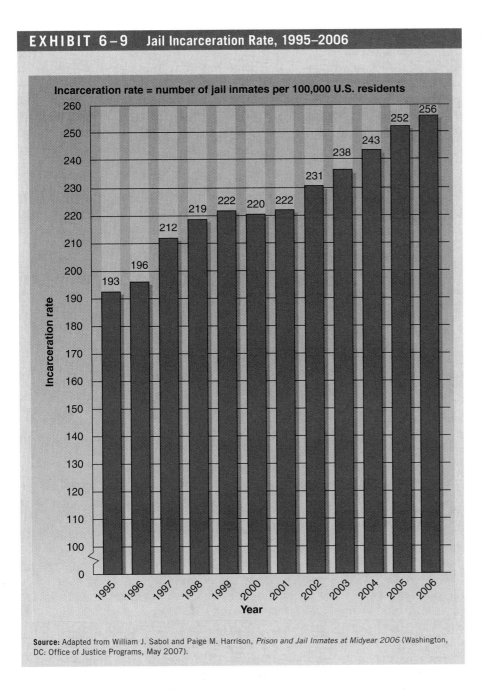

EXHIBIT 6-9   Jail Incarceration Rate, 1995–2006

Incarceration rate = number of jail inmates per 100,000 U.S. residents

Source: Adapted from William J. Sabol and Paige M. Harrison, *Prison and Jail Inmates at Midyear 2006* (Washington, DC: Office of Justice Programs, May 2007).

mates per 100,000 adults in 2006. Relative to the numbers of male and female U.S. residents, the incarceration rate of men was seven times that of women (457 per 100,000 adult population for men compared to 66 per 100,000 adult population for women) in mid-2006. The incarceration rate of blacks was nearly five times the incarceration rate of whites (815 versus 170 per 100,000 adult population, respectively) and three times the incarceration rate of Hispanics (815 vs. 283 per 100,000 adult population).

Gender and Jail Populations   There has been an upsurge in the number of women incarcerated in the United States, explained, in part, by guideline sentencing, under which gender is not considered an appropriate consideration. Though females have historically been treated more leniently than men at sentencing, guideline sentencing has tended to limit or end this practice.

The number of women in jail has more than quintupled over the past 25 years, from 19,000 in 1985 to 98,577 in mid-2006, representing 12.9 percent of the local jail inmate population in mid-2006. On average, the adult female jail population has grown 3.3 percent annually in the past 5 years, while the adult male population has grown 2.0 percent. The absolute number of women in jail is much smaller than the absolute number of men (98,577 and 661,329, respectively). However, their impact on jail operations is significant, raising concerns about the adequacy of jail facilities and the services provided.

The typical female jail inmate is poor, is a high school dropout with low skills, has held mainly low-wage jobs, is young (25 to 29), is unmarried with one to three children, and belongs to a racial minority.

Almost one-half of women and one-third of men in jail are first-time offenders (49 vs. 37 percent).[19] Almost half of the women and men in jail were under the influences of alcohol or drugs at the time of the offense. Forty-six percent had members of their immediate families sentenced to prison. Two of every 10 grew up in a home where one or both parents abused drugs, alcohol, or both. And more than one-half of the women (55 percent) and 13 percent of the men had been physically or sexually abused before age 18. Women in jail need targeted interventions that address these issues.

This profile also raises troubling concerns about the children of jailed mothers. Two-thirds of women in jail are mothers with children under age 18 who were living with them prior to detention. When mothers go to jail, children become silent victims. The children may already have been victims if their mothers used drugs during pregnancy. Young children, not yet capable of understanding why their mother is gone, where she has gone, and if or when she will return, may develop depression and feelings of abandonment. Even children who are fortunate enough to be placed with emotionally supportive caregivers must cope with seeing their mother only through a glass barrier and hearing her voice only over the phone. Studies have shown that children of incarcerated mothers have more behavioral problems at home and in school and are four times as likely to become juvenile delinquents as children from similar socioeconomic backgrounds with parents at home. Maintaining bonding with children and family is the most difficult female inmate experience.[20] Recognizing that children should not be made to suffer for the poor choices of their parents and recognizing that support for family maintenance is a societal value, some jails are establishing visitation and parenting programs that accommodate this need. Through such programs, jail administrators have the opportunity to become leaders in preserving families and reducing crime.

Some scholars believe that many women in jail do not pose a threat to public safety but are jailed because they do not have the financial resources to make bail. Seventeen percent are charged with violent offenses.[21] Most are charged with property offenses (32 percent), drug offenses (29 percent), and public-order offenses (21 percent). This suggests some differences are needed in women's facility bed space and program space from men's facility space (for example, there may need to be less high-security bed space and more substance abuse programming space).

The increase in the number of women in jail has required that local officials identify and try to meet the needs of female inmates, yet severe limitations in resources often impede the provision of programs and services for women in jail. Jails are not prepared to house and treat rapidly rising female populations. They have difficulty providing appropriate housing, bed space, programs, jobs, mental health care, and other services. Women in jail have high needs for education, job training, health care, mental health care, alcohol and drug abuse counseling, and parenting skills development. Properly classifying women according to their risks and needs is beyond the scope of most jails in the United States.[22] In 1993, the National Institute of Justice surveyed 54 jails and found that the same classification instrument was used for both male and female inmates in 50 jails. The survey found no effort to gauge women inmates' different needs, circumstances, and risk profiles.[23]

Ignoring problems relating to women in jail increases a jail's exposure to litigation and liability. The National Institute of Corrections argues against doing nothing: "The 'get tough on inmates' mood, combined with decreasing levels of accountability for maintaining some level of minimum standards, raises the specter of decreased funding for jails, corresponding cutbacks in staff and training, and the rebirth of the sorts of very brutal, barbaric, and often dangerous conditions that led to the initial wave of court intervention in the early 1970s."[24]

Women are normally housed in a "women's unit," often an afterthought built inside facilities designed for men or simply a replica of the men's facility design. Such design fails to take into account the different needs of women. For example, the traditional jail bunks and fixed-seating arrangements in the jail's dayroom or at dining room tables may present safety and comfort issues for women who are pregnant in jail. In addition, jailed women seldom have access to programs and services provided to male inmates. Special programming designed specifically for their unique needs as women and mothers is not offered.[25]

Another deficiency affecting women in jail is jail staffing. Either there are no female correctional officers or there are too few to ensure around-the-clock supervision of women in jail. The result too often is that women inmates are exploited and abused by male staff. In 1975, a North Carolina jury found Joan Little, then 20 years old, not guilty of the murder of 62-year-old Clarence Alligood, a correctional officer in the Beaufort County Jail. Alligood had entered Little's cell and sexually attacked her. She argued that she killed him in self-defense with the ice pick he had brought into her cell. Ken Kerle, managing editor of *American Jails,* argues that the best defense for a jail against female inmates' allegations of sexual harassment by male staff is to have a female officer present at all times.[26]

Recently the National Institute of Corrections released a report to help jail and prison administrators more effectively manage the women in their care.[27] According to the researchers, women offenders behave the way they do because of four factors. Understanding these factors in combination with each other will help jail administrators consider how to adjust policies and procedures and how to assess and improve services to women in their care. They are:

1. **Pathways perspective.** Women in jail often have histories of sexual and/or physical abuse and substance abuse and are consumers of mental health. These women typically are unskilled, earn low incomes, have sporadic work histories, and are single parents. Thus, understanding how women enter the criminal justice system helps jails improve their responses.

2. **Relational theory and female development.** Relational theory describes the different ways women and men develop. An important

difference suggested by the research is that women develop a sense of self and self-worth when their actions arise out of, and lead back into, connections with others even if this means establishing dysfunctional relationships. Many women offenders are drawn into criminal activity because of their relationships with others. Knowing this explains why jail staff often perceive that communicating with female offenders is more difficult and time-consuming than communicating with male inmates.

3. **Trauma theory.** Trauma is the injury done by violence and abuse and it is largely unrecognized by the women offenders themselves. Mental health services that understand past trauma and its effect on current behavior are needed to respond to trauma.

4. **Addiction theory.** When substance abuse treatment programs for women are combined with additional pathway factors (mental illness, trauma, abuse), jail-based treatment is successful.

Ethnicity and Jail Populations Whites comprise nearly 70 percent of the U.S. population but only 44 percent of the jail population. In the general population, Hispanics make up almost 16 percent, and blacks make up 12.7 percent, but in jail their populations are 16 percent and 39 percent, respectively.

From 1995 through mid-2006, the majority of local jail inmates were black or Hispanic. Blacks were nearly five times more likely than whites, nearly three times more likely than Hispanics, and over nine times more likely than people of other races to have been in jail at midyear 2005.

In November 2006, the Bureau of Justice Statistics published its seventh report on jails in Indian country in the United States.[28] (*Indian country* is a statutory term that includes all lands within an Indian reservation; dependent Indian communities; and Indian trust allotments, or lands held in trust for tribes or their members.) The bureau reported that 68 Indian country facilities held 1,546 adults and 198 juveniles, down 4 percent from the previous year when 70 Indian country facilities supervised 1,826 persons. Still, American Indians have the highest jail confinement rate of any racial group.[29] Six of the 10 largest jails in Indian country are in Arizona. In 2005, together these 10 jails held 44 percent of the total inmate population.

In 2004, the Department of the Interior inspector general delivered a report to Congress detailing the present conditions of Indian jails in the United States.[30] The inspector general wrote, "It became abundantly clear that some facilities we visited were egregiously unsafe, unsanitary, and a hazard to both inmates and staff alike. BIA's detention program is riddled with problems and, in our opinion, is a national disgrace with many facilities having conditions comparable to those found in third-world countries . . . our assessment found evidence of a continuing crisis of inaction, indifference, and mismanagement throughout the BIA detention program. . . . Our anxiety over the detention program remains heightened, however, not only because of what we found during our site visits but, more importantly, because of what we fear remains undiscovered at the sites we did not visit." [31]

To correct these deficiencies, the inspector general offered 25 recommendations that called for strong leadership, attention from senior management, regular compliance checks, alternatives to detention for intoxicated inmates, on-site medical assistance, improved recruiting and training, increased staffing, and regular meetings to encourage best practices.

On May 4, 2007, Paris Hilton was sentenced to 45 days in jail for violating her probation. Because of a state jail policy encouraging good inmate behavior, Hilton served 23 days at the Los Angeles County Sheriff's Department's Century Regional Dentention Facility for women in Lynwood. The judge's ruling excluded Hilton from serving time in a pay-to-stay jail, as some are allowed. Because of her fame, Hilton lived in the "special needs housing unit" that is reserved for police officers, public officials, celebrities, and other high-profile inmates. Should a person's status be a factor in where they are incarcerated?

Explanations for the overrepresentation of minorities in jail abound, not the least of which is how the U.S. Census Bureau defines *race*. The decennial census measures race and ethnicity differently than did the previous census. First, the census item on *race* (on which people identify themselves as white, black, or of other races and ethnicities) and the item on Hispanic identity are separate. This means that one can be both black and Hispanic. Second, for the first time in 2000, census respondents could check more than one race, an attempt by the Census Bureau to identify multiracial people. One result is that blacks and Hispanics are not two distinct groups. In 2000, about 1.7 million blacks were also estimated to be Hispanic. How does one determine which group is larger? Should blacks be deducted from the Hispanic population or the other way around? Does one grouping take precedence over the other?

Another explanation for minority overrepresentation in jail has to do with the function of jails as pretrial detention centers. The jail population is heavily influenced by bail decisions. A number of researchers have found that judges impose higher bail—or are more likely to deny bail altogether—if the defendant is a racial minority.[32] Still another reason is the impact of the war on drugs and on law enforcement strategies of racial profiling. Other researchers have argued that the war on drugs has had a particularly detrimental effect on black males.[33] Across the past two decades, more black males than white males have been detained for drug offenses. Researchers at the University of Nebraska argue that police are *reactive* in responding to crimes against persons and property but are *proactive* in dealing with drug offenses. "There is evidence," they write, "to suggest that they [police] target minority communities—where drug dealing is more visible and where it is thus easier to make an arrest—and tend to give less attention to drug activities in other neighborhoods."[34]

Juveniles and Jail Populations   Over the past 25 years, there has been a dramatic reversal in the theory and practice of punishing juveniles, as Chapter 16 will explain. In the mid-1970s, juvenile offenders were deemed to have special needs. The Juvenile Justice and Delinquency Prevention Act provided federal money to states and cities that agreed not to hold juveniles in jails where they might have regular contact with adults. By 1996, however, in the face of pressure to increase punishment for juvenile offenders, new legislation allowed cities and states to detain juvenile offenders for up to 12 hours in an adult jail before a court appearance and made it easier to house juveniles in separate wings of adult jails. That shift in philosophy and policy has increased the number of juveniles held as adults in adult jails. At midyear 1995, 76 percent of the 7,800 juveniles confined in the nation's jails were held as adults. At midyear 2000, 80 percent of juveniles in jail were held as adults. At midyear 2005, it was 85 percent. On June 30, 2006, 79 percent (4,836) of the 6,104 juveniles confined in the nation's jails were held as adults. The remainder (1,268) were held as juveniles. The transfer of juveniles to adult jails is discussed in Chapter 16.

The incarceration of juveniles in adult jails is criticized for a number of reasons. Holding juveniles in adult jails places young people at greater risk of being physically, sexually, and mentally abused by adult offenders. Juvenile girls are especially vulnerable to sexual assault. Juveniles in adult jail are almost eight times more likely to commit suicide than are juveniles in juvenile detention centers. One explanation is that juveniles are held in isolated parts of adult jails where they receive less staff support and supervision. Another is that jail staff are not trained to recognize depression in juveniles.

So why does the practice continue? Perhaps it is because there is a lack of alternatives. Or maybe it is because smaller counties believe separate facilities are cost prohibitive. Perhaps society does not know or believe there is a problem. Or maybe the public believes that jailing juveniles is necessary for public safety and to reduce crime.

Jail Facilities

Occupancy   The capacity to house jail inmates has kept pace with the jail population. For more than 10 years the nation's jail capacity has averaged only 94 percent. The occupied percentage of jail **rated capacity,** which is the number of beds or inmates a rating official assigns to a correctional facility, has remained below 100 percent since 1995. (The other ways to measure capacity are discussed in Chapter 7.)

rated capacity

The number of beds or inmates a rating official assigns to a correctional facility.

Public Versus Private   Of the nation's 3,365 jails, 47 are privately operating under contract to local governments.[35] Texas leads the nation in private jail operations with approximately one-fifth of its inmates (3,469) and facilities (eight). (We will discuss jail privatization later in this chapter.) Tennessee has the second-largest number of inmates (2,278) in privately operated jails, followed by Florida (1,931). Across the country, another 15 percent of jails are under federal court order or consent decree (most often for crowding or other confinement conditions). Another 11 percent have been ordered to limit populations.

Size, Location, and Budget   On June 30, 2006, almost 40 percent of the nation's jails had an average daily population of fewer than 50 inmates and held only 3.1 percent of the jail population. In contrast, 5.6 percent of the nation's jails, referred to as *megajails,* had average daily populations of 1,000 or more inmates.[36] Megajails held over 50 percent of the nation's jail population by midyear 2006.[37] Typically these large facilities are located in major metropolitan and urban areas. Jail operating budgets are highest in New York (almost $1.1 billion) and lowest in North Dakota ($3.5 million).[38]

Nicole Brockett, a 22-year-old bartender in Los Angeles, served 21 days for DUI at the Santa Ana City Jail, one of a dozen pay-to-stay jails in California, instead of incarceration at the nearby county jail. Brockett paid $82 per day for living conditions that the jail says are "a world away from cement and steel bars." What are the advantages and disadvantages of pay-to-stay jail?

Today a number of local jails charge inmates housing fees and medical co-pay fees. It is not known how common this is across the United States, but several states have adopted the practice. For example, more than half of the 95 jails currently operating in the state of Kansas charge a housing fee ranging from $10 to $70 a day. The average daily housing fee charged is $38. According to the researchers, the overriding reason jails assess housing fees is due to jail crowding and the need to cover operating costs (e.g., medical, food, utilities, staff, transportation, etc.).[39] However, out of concern for gender-responsive services for females, some are asking what impact medical co-pays will have on female offenders who statistically enter correctional facilities with more medical problems than do males and who will have to pay extra for something that is a result of being female.[40]

Pay-to-Stay Jail   In addition to charging inmates housing and medical co-pay fees as a way to offset jail operations, some jurisdictions have added **pay-to-stay jails,** also referred to as *self-pay jails.* Pay-to-stay jails are an alternative to serving time in a county jail and offer privileges to offenders (called clients) convicted of minor offenses such as non-drug-related offenses who pay $75 to $127 per day. Estimates are there are approximately 12 pay-to-stay jails in California.[41] Exhibit 6–10 compares five pay-to-stay jails in southern California in terms of cost per day, number of beds available, amenities, what inmates are allowed to bring in, and eligibility criteria. For example, persons convicted of DUI and sentences to 21 days in the Santa Ana City Jail will pay over $1,700 for the extra privileges. Recently an assistant sheriff of Orange County (California) was convicted of perjury and misuse of public funds. He asked the court for permission to serve his sentence of 243 days at the Fullerton City Jail. For $18,000 he will have access to a private cell, bathroom, and shower stall; may use his cell phone; and can eat food brought by his visitors or even order pizza delivery.

Offenders normally petition the court at their sentencing proceedings to serve their sentence at a pay-to-stay jail. If the court agrees and the city accepts the offender's application, the offender is housed separately

pay-to-stay jails
An alternative to serving time in a county jail. Also called *self-pay jails,* offenders convicted of minor offenses are offered privileges for a fee from $75 to $127 per day.

EXHIBIT 6–10	Comparison of Five Pay-to-Stay Jails				
	Santa Ana	**Seal Beach**	**Montebello**	**Pasadena**	**Fullerton**
Price per day	$82	$70 plus $100 application fee[1]	$75 plus $100 application fee	$127 plus $58 one-time administrative fee	First two consecutive days, $100, $75 thereafter
Beds in the program	30	30	10	20	2
What inmate gets	Work furlough, daily visitation	Work furlough, (if approved), up to 2-hour approved daily visitation	Work furlough, up to 2-hour daily visitation	Work furlough daily visitation	Visitors twice weekly
What inmate can bring	Nothing	Books, games, iPods	Books, games, iPods	A Bible or book, watch (no jewelry), and up to $20 in cash	Cell phone, reading materials, official court papers, pillow and blanket, small food deliveries
Who cannot come	Anyone who has assaulted someone in law enforcement; people who need protective custody	Violent offenders	Violent offenders	Anyone with a history of violent behavior or drug background arrest, or with serious medical problems requiring multiple medications	Drug or alcohol addicts in withdrawal, epileptics with a history of seizures, mentally deranged, those with suicidal tendencies or history of attempts, those with contagious diseases

1. $15 a day extra for GPS bracelets if required.

Source: Jennifer Steinhauer, "For $82 a Day, Booking a Cell in a 5-Star Jail," *The New York Times*, April 29, 2007, www.nytimes.com (accessed April 30, 2007).

from other inmates but may have minimal contact with the general inmate population during meal service. Most pay-to-stay jail inmates are required to work several hours a day outside their cells in food preparation, laundry, facility sanitation, vehicle washing, and so on, even if they work elsewhere in the community or attend school. The accommodations are usually cleaner and safer.

Supporters of the self-pay model argue that pay-to-stay jails benefit everyone: paying inmates generate cash for the community; taxpayers pay less to house offenders in city rather than county jails; offenders can serve their time in a smaller, nonviolent facility; and paying inmates are generally easier to deal with.

On the other hand, critics charge that pay-to-stay jails create inherent injustices, offering cleaner, safer alternatives to those who can afford it. The concept of offering a cleaner, safer jail is valid, they say, but the criterion of inmates paying for it is not. To date, there is no research to support the claims of self-pay jails or whether offenders who pay for their own jail stay are less likely to recidivate.

Inmates with Mental Illness   Chapter 12 discusses the problems of prisoners with mental illness in depth and Chapter 13 discusses prisoner violence. Here we point out that incarceration—especially jail—has become the nation's default mental health treatment.

At midyear 2005, almost two-thirds (64 percent) of all jail inmates had a mental health problem compared to about 11 percent of the general adult population.[42] The jail inmates were either told by a mental health professional that they had a mental disorder or, because of a mental health problem had stayed overnight in a hospital, used prescribed medication, or received professional mental health therapy. Today, there may be as many as eight times more people with mental illness in the nation's jails (over 478,000) than there are in mental hospitals (over 60,000).[43]

The Los Angeles County Jail is the largest psychiatric inpatient facility in the United States with more than 3,400 prisoners afflicted with mental health problems.[44] New York City's Rikers Island is second with 3,000, and Chicago's Cook County Jail is third with over 1,500. How jail became the institution of choice to manage increasing numbers of people with mental illness and what can be done about it is discussed in Chapter 12.

Suicide and Homicide   Progress in achieving inmate safety can be seen in the fact that the jail suicide rate today is about one-third of what it was 25 years ago (47 per 100,000 today compared to 129 per 100,000 in 1983). The sad news, however, is it is still over four times higher than it is for the general U.S. population (11 per 100,000).[45]

The situation for small jails is even worse. Researchers Tartaro and Ruddell found that the suicide rate for jails with 50 or fewer beds was 177 per 100,000.[46] For jails with 51 to 99 beds it was 77. The reasons are that smaller jails tend to be older and poorly staffed, are less able to provide sight and sound separation for inmates of different ages or genders, are less likely to use volunteers to deliver religious or rehabilitative programs, typically pay lower wages, find it difficult to comply with standards for physical or mental health care, use less classification, and offer less inmate supervision. Nearly half of jail suicides occur in the first week of custody.

The consequences of inmate suicide are lost lives, the devastation to families, the short- and long-term psychological effects on other inmates and correctional staff, expensive investigations and litigation, and medical care costs. Researchers call for greater use of suicide screening forms and increased annual training and awareness for jail staff.

Unlike suicide rates, homicide in the nation's jails is less than in the general population, another sign of the progress jails are achieving in the area of inmate safety.[47] During 2000–2002, the number of jail homicides averaged fewer than 20 each year, resulting in an annual rate of 3 jail homicides per 100,000 compared to the general population's rate of 6 per 100,000. Jail homicide rates have been stable for the past 25 years.

BJS reported that kidnapping offenders are most likely to be murdered in jail (15 per 100,000 inmates—five times the rate for all jail inmates), followed by violent offenders, property offenders, and then public-order offenders. Drug offenders have the lowest homicide victimization rate.

The consequences of jail homicides are as devastating as jail suicides. Jail professionals recognize that more must be done to protect jail inmates regardless of the seriousness of their offenses.

Jail Staff

Twenty years ago, staffing was cited as the number-one concern in a survey of 2,452 jails.[48] The managing editor of *American Jails*, Ken Kerle, says this is still a major problem.[49] Today, an estimated 297,600 people work in the nation's jails.[50] Women comprise one-third of all jail employees (one-fourth of all corrections officers). Sixty-six percent of all jail corrections officers are white, 24 percent are black, 8 percent are Hispanic, and 2 percent are of other races. Minority employees are underrepresented relative to their proportion among inmates.

In spite of the fact that there are more jail beds than inmates, as noted earlier, jail staff perceive that jails are overcrowded because there are not enough staff on shift to handle the workload properly. Jail staff think of a jail as overcrowded if, due to staff shortages, inmate counts, bed checks, and cell searches are not performed and inmate programs such as visitation and outdoor recreation are postponed.[51] Because most jails are

A jail correctional officer practices lifesaving skills. Professional development requires the lifelong or careerlong dedication to quality officer selection, academy training, and development of jail staff. Which inservice training programs do you believe are necessary for the professional development of jail staff?

locally funded, local politics determine how much staff a county government allocates to operate the county jail. How much is the county willing to spend on the jail compared to other county agencies such as roads, police, and fire?

Most jails spend 75 to 90 percent of their budgets on salaries. One jail post operating 24 hours a day, seven days a week requires five officers when sick time, vacation, and other leaves are factored in. This partially explains why county officials are reluctant to increase staffing to correspond with an increase in inmate population. Yet understaffing poses a threat to inmate and staff security and safety. Too often inadequate staffing leads to inmate lockdowns to prevent escape and ease the handling of prisoners. Further, without appropriate staff supervision, little can be done to protect inmates from one another in multiple-occupancy cells.

Other problems of jail staff include substandard pay compared to that of other employees in the criminal justice system, low job prestige, high turnover, and inadequate systems for recruitment, selection, and training. The National Sheriff's Association (NSA) believes that too often "warm bodies are taken off the street, put into uniform, given a set of keys, and told to go to work."[52] Concerning salaries, the NSA wrote, "Jail officer careers will never achieve the status they deserve so long as counties continue to pay jail officers less money than the officers assigned to law enforcement. . . . No person wants to make a career where the reward is lousy wages. You can't attract the people who have the potential to be the best officers by paying them wages in the poverty range."[53]

Although the Palm Beach County Sheriff's Department starts certified jail corrections officers at $41,088, not all jails can do this. Nevertheless, most jails can help officers find satisfaction in their work by setting clearly defined goals, identifying the officer's job obligations and performance expectations, and providing jail officers adequate organizational resources to perform their jobs. Recruiting and retaining jail employees depends on effective recruitment, providing meaningful preservice and inservice training and career development, and responsive management and leadership.

JAIL ISSUES

Jail administration and staff will face many important issues in the 21st century. A number of those issues such as inmates with mental illness and jail suicides and homicides were covered in this chapter. Others such as jail gangs (better known as STGs—security threat groups) will be discussed in Chapter 13. Here we cover a few more of these important issues and their effects on corrections professionals.

Privatization

Privatization is defined as a contract process that shifts public functions, responsibilities, and capital assets, in whole or in part, from the public sector to the private sector. We expand on the issue of *correctional* privatization in Chapter 13. Our focus here is on *jail* privatization.

privatization

A contract process that shifts public functions, responsibilities, and capital assets, in whole or in part, from the public sector to the private sector.

Jails can be privatized in one of three ways: through private management, private sector development, or private services provision. In private management, private firms have total responsibility for the operation of a facility. This is the most common application of the term *privatization* and the most controversial aspect of the private sector's involvement in corrections.

In private sector development, the private sector develops, designs, and finances or arranges for the financing of jails. This often involves owning the jail and leasing it back to the jurisdiction through a lease/purchase contract, which serves as an alternative to a public bond issue or outright tax increase.

In private services provision, jails contract with private vendors to run services such as health and dental care, alcohol and drug treatment, mental health services, food service, training, and programming. This is the most familiar privatization model and the least controversial.

The debate between proponents and opponents of jail privatization surfaced early and continues today. Pressures for privatization come from escalating costs and crowded jails as well as from general dissatisfaction with county government. Jail privatization is sometimes seen as a practical option when a jurisdiction needs to update facilities quickly in response to a court order for additional capacity. Advocates of privatization claim that private operators can operate facilities more efficiently and cost-effectively.

Opponents of jail privatization dismiss cost comparisons—dispute them altogether. Some insist that the fundamental point is that it is the responsibility of local governments to operate jails, not to delegate power and liability. Opponents believe that the administration of justice is a basic function of government and a symbol of state authority and should not be delegated. From this perspective, jails are, as John J. DiIulio Jr., University of Pennsylvania professor of politics, religion, and civil society, put it, "a public trust to be administered on behalf of the community and in the name of civility and justice."[54]

Opponents also fear that if we privatize jails, we risk enabling private corporations to use their political influence to continue programs not in the public interest. For example, would private contractors keep jail occupancy rates high to maintain profit? Might private contractors accept

Eye On Corrections

The Kiosks Are Coming! The Kiosks Are Coming!

By Jim Montalto

A consequence of putting men in cells and controlling their movements is that they can do almost nothing for themselves. For their various needs they are dependent on one person, their gallery officer. Instead of feeling like a big, tough guard, the gallery officer at the end of the day often feels like a waiter serving a hundred tables or like the mother of a nightmarishly large brood of sullen, dangerous and demanding children.

> CO, would you call to check the money in my commissary account?
> CO, can you find out when my disciplinary hearing is?
> CO, can you call to see why my laundry bag didn't come back?
> CO, will you call to see if they got a new package list?

(Ted Conover, in his book, *Newjack: Guarding Sing Sing*)

How many times have you or your staff felt burdened by the incessant barrage of questions posed by inmates on just one shift alone? They might come from different inmates and perhaps be asked in different ways but most usually require the same answer or same task again and again. Taking the time to address appropriate inmate requests and concerns is part of the job. But they should not distract officers so much that they prevent them from keeping their area orderly and safe.

Jan Bates, the inmate program manager at the Hillsborough County Sheriff's Office, thought so too, which is why she found a way to address CO concerns about the increasing number of inmate requests.

"We looked at our deputies to see all the redundant work they were doing, like distributing canteen order forms, and checking the day's kitchen menu. Our population keeps growing, but our staff numbers can't keep up with inmate requests," Bates says, "so we started looking for ways to become more efficient and use technology better."

Hillsborough County's Orient Road and Falkenburg Road jails are not designed like the ordinary jail cell and control room configuration. Each pod is 10,000 square feet and holds 64 beds. Within each pod, one deputy oversees between 64 and 72 inmates in a dorm-like setting. County officials say this direct supervision system creates a sense of trust and safety between inmates and deputies, which makes for a quieter and less hazardous environment compared to a typical jail setting—Bates says in the 23 years she has worked in the pod system she has not seen any major disturbances.

"However, the number of requests was overwhelming, so we decided to put a kiosk in each pod that addressed a lot of inmate concerns," she says.

Bates initially looked for turnkey cabinet solutions, but the costs were too high. So, she separately bid for the cabinets, touch screens and CPUs. As a result, she was able to keep production expenses to about $2,000 per kiosk and ensure programming flexibility with her legacy facility systems.

The cabinets, which are bolted to the floors, look like blue standing mailboxes and encase the touch screens and any necessary wiring. The CPUs, which were purchased from Dell under a state contract, are also protected inside the cabinet and provide access to just about anything inmates need from ordering bibles and canteen items to communicating with their public defender.

"This was our way of getting inmates some sort of connectivity to the questions they ask on a daily basis: When's my next court date? What are my charges? What are the menus for the daily meals? Where can I find a bail bondsman?" Horvath says.

"Through a simplified email system, called I-mail, offenders can choose from about twenty topics that can then be sent to the Public Defenders office. The attorneys then call our facility to talk with their clients," Horvath explains.

Inmates can find general information on the screens. When they log in with their booking number and password, they can review their charges and gained time awards, sign up for programs, review schedules, and request a visitation.

"I can also send out general announcements for entire the population or just to designated areas or individuals," Bates adds.

Soon, inmates will be able to request non-emergency medical assistance, obtain information on community services, submit and receive requests for the chaplain, medical facility, and law library, access classification, and read information about the Prison Rape Elimination Act. Bates says video capability could be the next upgrade, because it will address literacy issues.

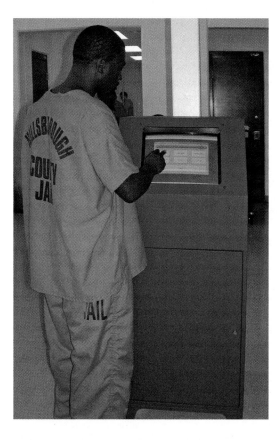

Despite the amount of information available, both Bates and Horvath stress that inmates do not have access to public or in-house computer systems. Each kiosk is stripped of Internet capabilities and any programs that do not contribute to the basic informational program. Even the I-mail is a limited feature that prevents inmates from doing much else but send a request for assistance.

The kiosks may appear to be a convenient tool for inmates, but Bates wants to be clear that they were built with the deputy in mind.

"There will be a significant reduction of numerous time-intensive, paper-based tasks that are currently submitted and manually processed," she stresses. "The purpose of the kiosks is to make processes more efficient and use less staff for these repetitive requests. By accomplishing this, deputies can concentrate on security."

Bottom Line: Mainstreaming redundant processes, by creating a kiosk or by posting frequently sought out information, can help COs stay focused on keeping themselves and inmates safe and secure.

Source: "The Kiosks Are Coming! The Kiosks Are Coming!" Jim Montalto, The Corrections Connection Network News (CCNN). Eye on Corrections, www.corrections.com. June 21, 2006.

Quentin X. Escott
Deputy Sheriff Jefferson County Birmingham, Alabama

Quentin X. Escott has been a deputy sheriff for 1½ years. He is currently assigned to the county jail booking area. His responsibilities include searching incoming prisoners, using the computer imaging system to take inmate photographs and fingerprints, recording personal property, exchanging civilian clothes for jail clothes, and assigning prisoners to housing areas based on their charge classifications.

Deputy Escott has completed almost two years at Lawson State College. He is transferring to the University of Alabama at Birmingham, where he will major in criminal justice.

His advice to persons interested in working in a jail? "Treat people like you want to be treated. Yeah, they're prisoners and they broke the law. For that they're in here for punishment. But if I'm going to like my job I have to get along with everybody, prisoners and staff. That means treating everyone with respect and hopefully getting it back in return." For Deputy Escott, the most gratifying part of the job is helping an inmate who really wants help.

When I work with an inmate and help him change his life, it's extremely gratifying. But the inmate has to want to change. He has to want help. I can't force it. A lot of prisoners want to know you'll help them and give them a chance. That's all.

only the best inmates, leaving the most troublesome for public facilities to handle?

Turning a jail over to a private corporation also raises questions about accountability. Who is responsible for monitoring the performance of the private contractor? Who will see that local laws and regulations are followed? As jail incarceration rates continue to rise, the debate over privatizing jails and the competition for new contracts will continue.

After reviewing the pros and cons of jail privatization, Chang and Tillman concluded, "It is good to have private management as a viable alternative that plays the role of checking and balancing the public sector management. Whether county jails should be privatized depends on how well jails are managed in keeping costs of operation low and preparing inmates for their after-release adaptation to mainstream society. As Kerle stated, 'A badly run jail . . . would be an inviting target for privatization.'" [55]

Professional associations have addressed jail privatization through policy statements that range from cautious (American Correctional Association) to negative (American Jail Association and the National Sheriff's Association). The American Federation of State, County and Municipal Employees has been opposed from the beginning, and the American Bar Association has urged a moratorium until more information is available.

Overcrowding

Even though by mid-2006 only 94 percent of jail capacity was occupied, overcrowding is the most critical problem in large urban jails. In 2006, 8 of the nation's 25 largest jails were operating at over 100 percent of their rated capacity.

Jail crowding has a number of causes, including mandatory arrests and sentences, overcrowding at state and federal prisons, and an overall increase in the arrest rate as politicians "get tough" on crime. Crowded jails have serious health and safety consequences for staff and inmates, including decreased quality of life; overloaded educational, vocational, and recreational programs; insufficient medical services and supplies; increased discipline problems; spread of disease; and staff and inmate assaults.

Seriously overcrowded jails can create unconstitutional conditions in violation of the Eighth Amendment prohibition against cruel and unusual punishment. If extreme enough, overcrowding can lead to a court order that necessitates early release of certain prisoners in order to bring jails into compliance with the Constitution. (We return to a discussion of early release in Chapters 8 and 13.)

Ways to Reduce Jail Overcrowding

Practices that can reduce crowding include creating a comprehensive plan for the collection, analysis, and discussion of jail data, financial and nonfinancial pretrial release, diversion, and new jail construction.

Create a Comprehensive Plan   It's a mistake to think that adopting one or two new alternatives to detention will reduce jail crowding and then be surprised that the population did not go down. To reverse this thinking, in 2002 the National Institute of Corrections raised the bar on ways to control jail crowding, from nuts and bolts approaches to analytical thinking.[56] According to NIC, the key to prevent crowding is continuously to collect, monitor, and analyze admission and length-of-stay information and then to share the results with other justice officials and with officials in leadership positions in general government such as the judiciary, the mayor, and county commissioners. Collectively, these officials control the policies and practices that determine jail admissions and length of stay. Jail administrators and sheriffs can exert a great deal of influence on the decision making of other agencies. However, only if they have the facts can they competently answer questions about how the jail population is changing and clearly demonstrate how changes in admission rates or lengths of stay can improve the administration of justice. As Mark Cunniff writes, "A county must ascertain changing jail usage and the forces at play in its jail system before it can implement effective programs and measures to alleviate jail crowding, including the construction of new jail beds."[57]

Financial Pretrial Release   Financial pretrial release programs are one alternative to the pretrial detention of accused offenders. Releasing a person upon that person's financial guarantee to appear in court is known as **release on bail**. The Eighth Amendment to the United States Constitution reads, "Excessive bail shall not be required, nor excessive fines imposed, nor cruel and unusual punishments inflicted." The Constitution does not guarantee defendants an automatic right to bail—only protection from excessive bail. The defendant has the option to post the full amount of the bail, secure the amount privately through a bail bondsman, or deposit a percentage (usually 10 percent) with the court.

release on bail
The release of a person upon that person's financial guarantee to appear in court.

Nonfinancial Pretrial Release   An alternative form of pretrial release requires only the defendant's promise to appear in court as required.

release on own recognizance (ROR)
Pretrial release on the defendant's promise to appear for trial. It requires no cash guarantee.

citation
A type of nonfinancial pretrial release similar to a traffic ticket. It binds the defendant to appear in court on a future date.

supervised pretrial release
Nonfinancial pretrial release with more restrictive conditions (for example, participating in therapeutic or rehabilitative programs, reporting to a pretrial officer, and checking in regularly).

conditional release
Pretrial release under minimal or moderately restrictive conditions with little monitoring of compliance. It includes ROR, supervised pretrial release, and third-party release.

This release without a cash guarantee is called **release on own recognizance (ROR)**. Generally, information about defendants is gathered and verified to determine the appropriateness of nonfinancial pretrial release.

Another type of nonfinancial pretrial release is a **citation**. Similar to traffic tickets, citations are issued by police in some jurisdictions for misdemeanors such as disorderly conduct. A citation binds the defendant to appear in court on a future date. It places no conditions on the released person's behavior and requires no payment to guarantee the court appearance.

In the 1960s and 1970s, a new form of nonfinancial pretrial release emerged. Called **supervised pretrial release,** it imposes more restrictive conditions on defendants. The conditions often include participating in therapeutic or rehabilitative programs, reporting to a pretrial officer, and checking in regularly. During the same period, a third-party release option developed. A third party—such as the defendant's lawyer, family, or employer or a social service agency—assumes responsibility for the defendant's appearance in court.

Programs such as ROR, supervised pretrial release, and third-party release are all forms of **conditional release.** They impose minimal or moderately restrictive conditions with little monitoring of compliance. In a number of jurisdictions across the United States today, electronic monitoring is also being used as part of conditional release.

Diversion Another way jail crowding can be reduced is through the expanded use of diversion. Diversion, as we learned in Chapter 4, means referring defendants to non-criminal-justice agencies for services instead of processing them through the criminal justice system. For example, people with substance abuse problems can be diverted to treatment centers. Jail inmates with mental disorders can be referred to mental health clinics, where they receive both treatment and custodial supervision. After accepting diversion, a defendant is required to cooperate and participate in treatment, whether or not he or she feels it is necessary. Failure to show progress may lead to reinstatement of charges.

For nearly 30 years jail diversion programs have had wide support as a way to prevent people with mental illness and substance abuse disorders from unnecessarily entering the criminal justice system, by providing more appropriate community-based treatment. What impact, however, have these programs had? Unfortunately, few systematic outcome studies have examined their effectiveness. Physicians at the University of Southern California School of Medicine studied a prebooking jail diversion program in Los Angeles to determine whether emergency outreach teams composed of police officers and mental health professionals could assess and make appropriate dispositions for psychiatric crisis cases.[58] The researchers concluded that the emergency teams benefited from shared access to mental health and criminal justice records in making disposition decisions. The trained police provided security, transportation, law enforcement field resources, and knowledge about handling violence. The mental health specialists provided knowledge about mental illness and experience in diagnosis, crisis evaluation, and interaction with psychiatric patients. Overall, the teams increased the percentage of persons with mental illness who had access to the mental health system. Other prebooking jail diversion programs in Memphis and Birmingham showed great promise for diverting people who were mentally ill from jail, keeping them in the community, and facilitating access to treatment.[59] Across all three sites, only 6.7 percent of the mental disturbance calls resulted in arrest.

Today, there are jail diversion programs all across the United States. In Broward County (Fort Lauderdale), Florida, we find a day reporting center. In Lancaster County (Lincoln), Nebraska, we find an intensive case management system to divert people with mental illness. These and many other programs like them are funded by the U.S. Department of Health and Human Services, through the Substance Abuse and Mental Health Services Administration (SAMHSA), specifically its Center for Mental Health Services (CMHS). SAMHSA makes federal funding available for programs to divert individuals with mental illness from jail to mental health treatment and appropriate support services.

In fiscal years 2002, 2003, and 2004, SAMHSA funded 20 proposals to implement prebooking and postbooking jail diversion programs.[60] SAMHSA requires jail grantees to use four strategies that are known to be effective:

1. Train service providers to implement evidence-based services. The evidence-based services include:
   - case management services;
   - community treatment;
   - medication management and access;
   - integrated mental health and co-occurring substance abuse treatment;
   - psychiatric rehabilitation;
   - life skills training;
   - housing placement;
   - vocational training;
   - educational job placement;
   - health care;
   - gender-based services for women; and
   - trauma-specific services.
2. Create service linkages between individuals and groups that serve the targeted population (mental health and substance abuse service providers and criminal justice system personnel). This includes:
   - developing partnerships and coalitions among mental health, substance abuse, and criminal justice systems to increase systems integration; and
   - developing specific linkages among key personnel in each system.

3. Undertake community outreach to communicate to the larger community the importance of mental health and the capacity of the jail diversion program to serve people with mental illness. This includes:
   - building consensus among stakeholders and potential stakeholders for the adoption, implementation, and evaluation of the jail diversion program;
   - ensuring that services are available for the target population; and
   - ensuring that the community accepts the use of the services as beneficial.

4. Engage in program evaluation and dissemination to demonstrate program outcomes and the quality and completeness of services implementation. This includes:
   - collecting required data;
   - obtaining, at minimum, an 80 percent response rate at each data collection point; and
   - disseminating program findings, include relevant materials directed to consumers, service providers, administrators, and community, state, and federal policymakers who need this type of knowledge.

New Construction New construction is another way to reduce jail crowding. Proponents of new construction argue that jail incarceration is here to stay. Because the public supports jails, we have a responsibility to build them. Opponents argue that if we continue to add new beds to the nation's jails, we will fill up all the space we create. In other words, some believe that availability drives up occupancy. They also claim that most nonviolent pretrial detainees and convicted offenders do not need to be in jail and that it wastes resources to house them there.

Jail Reentry (Begins at Entry)

reentry

The transition offenders make from prison or jail to the community.

Another solution to jail crowding is jail **reentry,** the process of transition that offenders make from prison or jail to the community. (We return to a discussion of reentry in Chapter 8.) It seems only natural to add jail reentry to the list of strategies so that fewer people, once released, return to jail.

Most jails limit their reentry efforts to basic adult and secondary education (55 percent), faith-based and drug-related counseling (70 percent), fee-for-service health care (39 percent), and mental health screening at intake and psychotropic medication (78 percent).[61] Less effort is put into vocational education (6 percent), job seeking (15 percent), or life skills (21 percent). As evidence suggests, improving inmate job skills, helping inmates find jobs upon release, and increasing inmate wage potential all have a significant impact on recidivism.[62] However, most jails suffer from several constraints that limit their ability to engage in a comprehensive reentry effort. Most jails are small, with high turnover rates; and the fact that they have inmates for only a short period means that whatever reentry efforts they provide must be done quickly. "Much of the money and attention spent on reentry efforts has focused on those offenders being released in the community from prison."[63] Exhibit 6–11 shows what some of the jails across the United States are doing in jail reentry.

Educational, Vocational, and Inmate Work Programs Many jail inmates have poor reading skills. National studies show that more than 40 percent of all jail inmates have less than a ninth-grade education.[64] They also have substance abuse problems and few job skills. They

EXHIBIT 6–11 Jail Reentry

To date, reentry policies and programs have primarily targeted people released from state and federal prison. However, jail reentry has at least as much of an impact on public safety, if not more. Although the nation's jail capacity is lower than its prison capacity—there are approximately 691,000 jail beds, compared to 1.4 million prison beds—admissions and releases from jails far exceed those from prisons. According to the forthcoming Bureau of Justice Statistics 2004 Survey of Large Jails, 20 percent of jail inmates serve at least one month, and only 4 percent serve more than six months. As a result, the jail population is continuously turning over, resulting in approximately 12 million admissions and releases per year.

The short sentences served in jail and the proximity of jails to inmates' home communities have important implications—both positive and negative—for the role of local jails in addressing the challenges of prisoner reentry, highlighted as follows:

- **Mental illness.** Sixteen percent of both jail inmates and state prisoners report a mental condition or overnight stay in a mental hospital. However, only 41 percent of inmates with mental illness receive mental health services compared to 61 percent of state prisoners with mental illness.
- **Substance abuse and dependence.** More than two-thirds (68 percent) of jail inmates are dependent on or abuse drugs or alcohol, but only 18 percent receive treatment or participate in other substance abuse programs after entering jail. Sixty-nine percent of jail inmates are regular drug users, and 29 percent of convicted jail inmates report drug use at the time of their offense.
- **Limited employability.** Fifty-seven percent of jail inmates were working full-time the month prior to their arrest. Thirty percent of all jail inmates reported personal earnings totaling less than $300 per month.
- **Extensive criminal histories.** Three-fourths of jail inmates have served a prior probation or incarceration sentence, and nearly a quarter (24 percent) have served three or more prior sentences to incarceration. More than half of all jail inmates have a current criminal justice status at the time of arrest.

Source: Adapted from Nancy G. La Vigne, Amy L. Solomon, Karen A. Beckman, and Kelly Dedel, *Prisoner Reentry and Community Policing: Strategies for Enhancing Public Safety* (Washington, DC: U.S. Department of Justice, Office of Community Oriented Policing Services, March 2006).

Jail inmates at the Onondaga County Justice Center (Syracuse, New York) take a test at their small-engine repair class. The class is divided between work, tests, and hands-on engine work. What do you believe will happen if educational and vocational programs are not available for jail inmates?

frequently cannot find jobs after they are released or can find only low-paid or temporary work. As a result, in part, they often return to a life of crime.

Too many jails simply warehouse inmates and care little about education or job skills. It costs taxpayers money to provide educational services to jail inmates—the same people who already have financially and psychologically burdened society through their crimes. Education does not guarantee that an offender will remain free of crime upon release. However, consider the alternative: More than 40 percent of defendants on pretrial release have one or more prior convictions. The cost of keeping one inmate in jail for one year ranges from $20,000 to $40,000. Studies also show that inmates who earn their GEDs while incarcerated are far less likely to return to crime. Educational and vocational programs help offenders help themselves, they boost self-esteem, and they encourage legitimate occupations upon release. Overall, it costs less to educate offenders and teach them job skills than to do nothing to change their attitudes, abilities, and outlooks. Ignoring an offender's educational and vocational deficiencies leaves the offender with fewer marketable skills or qualifications when released, increasing the chance of a return to crime.

Recently, the Orange County, Florida, Jail—one of the largest in the nation, with 3,300 beds—began an innovative strategy.[65] The entire jail—the operation, budget, and architecture—now revolves around its educational and vocational programs. The jail offers inmates a wide range of structured educational and vocational programs designed to fit inmates' short stays. The jail provides job readiness and placement services. It offers inmates valuable incentives to participate in programs and to avoid misconduct. And it uses the design and philosophy of third-generation jails, discussed earlier in this chapter, to manage inmates in a way that contains costs, promotes inmate responsibility, and creates classrooms in open areas. According to the National Institute of Justice, "Each of these features is part of a comprehensive corrections strategy that enables programming to flourish at the same time that it saves the county money, keeps inmates occupied and out of trouble, and (it is hoped) reduces recidivism."[66]

The principal steps in the Orange County Jail's educational and vocational programs are presented in Exhibit 6–12. The jail provides unusually intensive educational and vocational opportunities to most of its inmates. Five features are very important to the success of the programs: incentives for participation, direct supervision, active support by corrections officers, cooperation from schools, and programs tailored to short jail stays.

Besides Orange County, other jurisdictions tailor inmate work programs to local community needs. Joe Arpaio—the controversial sheriff of Maricopa County (Phoenix), Arizona, who makes prisoners live outside in tents, serves bologna meals twice a day, requires inmates to wear striped prison suits and pink underwear, and for entertainment requires that inmates watch C-Span—needed a shelter for animals held as evidence while court cases worked their way through the criminal justice system. He converted an old jail into an animal shelter and staffed it with female inmates who cared for the animals so they can be adopted once their cases are adjudicated. While there is no research on how effective this program is in returning fewer women to jail, it fills an important community need.

Mental Health Programs   Earlier in this chapter, former California prisoner-turned-professor John Irwin referred to the purpose of jails as

EXHIBIT 6–12   Orange County, Florida, Jail Educational and Vocational Programs

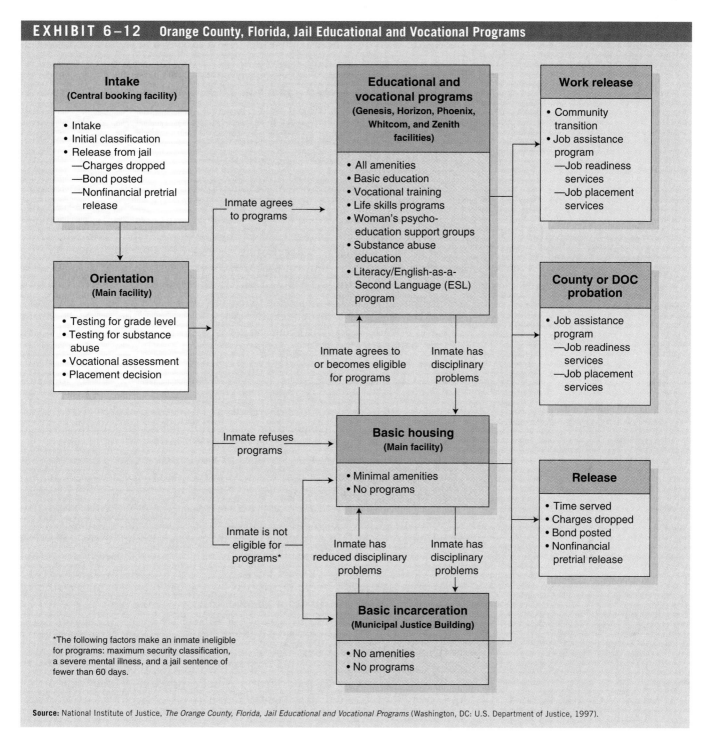

Intake
(Central booking facility)

- Intake
- Initial classification
- Release from jail
  —Charges dropped
  —Bond posted
  —Nonfinancial pretrial release

Inmate agrees to programs

Orientation
(Main facility)

- Testing for grade level
- Testing for substance abuse
- Vocational assessment
- Placement decision

Inmate refuses programs

Inmate is not eligible for programs*

Educational and vocational programs
(Genesis, Horizon, Phoenix, Whitcom, and Zenith facilities)

- All amenities
- Basic education
- Vocational training
- Life skills programs
- Woman's psycho-education support groups
- Substance abuse education
- Literacy/English-as-a-Second Language (ESL) program

Inmate agrees to or becomes eligible for programs

Inmate has disciplinary problems

Basic housing
(Main facility)

- Minimal amenities
- No programs

Inmate has reduced disciplinary problems

Inmate has disciplinary problems

Basic incarceration
(Municipal Justice Building)

- No amenities
- No programs

Work release

- Community transition
- Job assistance program
  —Job readiness services
  —Job placement services

County or DOC probation

- Job assistance program
  —Job readiness services
  —Job placement services

Release

- Time served
- Charges dropped
- Bond posted
- Nonfinancial pretrial release

*The following factors make an inmate ineligible for programs: maximum security classification, a severe mental illness, and a jail sentence of fewer than 60 days.

Source: National Institute of Justice, *The Orange County, Florida, Jail Educational and Vocational Programs* (Washington, DC: U.S. Department of Justice, 1997).

"rabble management"; that is, the control of persons whose noncriminal behavior is offensive to their communities. Nowhere is rabble management as obvious as in the incarceration of persons who are mentally ill, a topic we highlight in this chapter but discuss in depth in Chapter 12, where we introduce the problems and concerns facing special populations in corrections.

In recent surveys conducted by the Bureau of Justice Statistics and others, 56 percent of state prison inmates, 45 percent of federal prison inmates, 64 percent of those in local jails, 16 percent of probationers, and 5 to 10 percent of parolees reported either a mental condition or an overnight stay in a mental hospital.[67] Overall, the numbers are staggering: eight times more people with mental illness are in jails and prisons than in state psychiatric hospitals—over 478,000 compared to 60,000.[68] Other sources report that as many as 75 percent of persons who are mentally ill in jails and prisons suffer from co-occurring disorders, particularly substance abuse, due to the lack of health insurance and their lifestyles, which frequently include transient behavior, financial instability, and high-risk behaviors such as intravenous drug use, smoking, and multiple sex partners.[69]

Despite the large number of offenders with mental illness under correctional supervision, these individuals are not often fit subjects for retribution or punishment. Jail diversion programs are seen as a way of removing them from correctional facilities. James Gondles, executive director of the American Correctional Association, said, "The notion that the prospect of incarceration will deter an individual with a mental illness from committing a crime does not apply to a population that cannot fully comprehend the consequences of its actions, especially in cases where the crime is a direct result of an illness."[70] Other experts tell us that the criminal justice system is ill-equipped to meet the special needs of persons with mental illness who are incarcerated or on supervised release in the community.[71]

Until recently, community and institutional punishment of persons with mental illness received little public policy attention. However, the U.S. Department of Health and Human Services' SAMHSA, the Mentally Ill Offender Treatment and Crime Reduction Act of 2003, and a congressional report titled *Incarceration of Youth Who Are Waiting for Community Mental Health Services in the United States*[72] indicate that policymakers on the national level are taking notice of the burden that incarceration of persons with mental illness places on an already overcrowded criminal justice system and the tragic consequences that imprisonment of such individuals can have on families and communities. SAMHSA, the act, and the congressional report promote the diversion of individuals with mental illness from the nation's jails, collaboration between the justice system and the mental health communities, and treatment and training. We complete our discussion of the incarceration of persons who are mentally ill in Chapter 12.

Jail Ministry   Very little is written about the use and effects of jail ministry and faith-based programming in jail. Too often the topic is looked at skeptically by outsiders, who believe that inmates pretend to "find God" as a convenient way to obtain release or forgiveness. However, getting into trouble and then turning to religion is supported by the "coping" literature, which links major life events to a greater tendency to turn to spirituality or religion. What we will explore here, however, is not the research supporting the veracity of inmates' claims of conversion but instead the partnership between government and faith-based organizations to meet the nation's corrections needs. We will also consider the experiences of those who minister to jail inmates.

Religious belief can make a difference in people's lives and can assist in tackling social problems. Much crime is the result of people making the wrong moral choices. Churches and religious organizations can provide the moral and spiritual aspects to correctional programs. There are not enough correctional officers, probation or parole officers, or police to prevent every ex-offender from committing another crime, and

A faith-based organization encourages jail inmates to form a circle and ask their victims for forgiveness. Major life events like incarceration are linked to a greater tendency to turn to spirituality or religion. What do you think is the role of jail ministry?

help from other partners is needed. As President George W. Bush said, "Government cannot be replaced by charities, but it can and should welcome them as partners." Pat Nolan, vice president of Prison Fellowship Ministries writes, "The way society will be able to reduce crime is if during their time of incarceration, offenders have been transformed and internalized a moral code that allows them to exercise self-restraint and be good citizens after they are released. . . . It will be helpful to look upon local churches as partners to help teach inmates these important lessons during their incarceration and to act as mentors as they re-enter their communities."[73]

Recently researchers conducted a study to investigate the impact of religious programs on two matched groups of adult male prisoners in New York.[74] They found that inmates most actively involved in Bible studies (meaning they attended 10 or more classes over the course of 1 year) were less likely than inmates who attended fewer classes (or none) to commit institutional infractions or, if they did, the infractions were not as serious as the infractions of those who attended fewer classes (or none); and inmates most actively involved in Bible studies were less likely than inmates who attended fewer classes (or none) to be arrested during a 1-year follow-up. Subsequent research found that differences in rearrest peaked at 2 and 3 years after release. The average time to rearrest for the inmates who were most actively involved in Bible studies was 3.8 years versus 2.3 years for inmates who attended fewer classes (or none). However, differences between the two groups diminished after that and were not statistically significant in years 4 through 8. Over time, the effects of Bible study attendance are diminished in importance. Risk for arrest in years 4 through 8 was explained by other factors such as prior record, race, and age.

Those who minister to jail inmates tell us there are at least five benefits of jail chaplaincy. First, most jail chaplains believe that the cycle of crime can be broken only one life at a time. Jail inmates must experience an inner conversion before they change their behavior. Jail chaplains can assist in that conversion. Second, jail chaplains can help jail staff with their emotional and family problems. An on-site chaplain can help staff deal with problems daily, as they develop. Third, jail chaplains are in a unique position to mediate and moderate tensions and conflicts between inmates and staff before they get serious. Pleading for nonviolence is a chaplain's strong tool. Inmates usually see a jail chaplain as neutral—not as "one of them." The chaplain has the unique opportunity to speak his or her mind and be seen as someone who cares enough to confront and comfort. Fourth, the public perceives ministering to the disadvantaged as legitimate, and so such ministry helps the community remember those they would just as soon forget (recall the concept of inmates as "rabble," discussed earlier in this chapter). In the role as community liaisons, chaplains help raise the awareness about and sensitivity to jail issues and interests. The ability of chaplains to involve the public as jail volunteers is an added benefit. And fifth, jail chaplains can help inmates confront the truth about themselves and reverse the "everything is relative" attitude that offenders develop to justify their crimes.

In the following excerpt, a chaplain shares some thoughts about his two years on the job:[75]

> A chaplain occupies a unique place in an inmate's thinking. She or he is not seen as "one of them"; we are not associated so much with the institution or judicial system. That gives us unique opportunities to speak openly and be viewed not as someone who has a sinister hidden agenda, but as someone who cares enough to confront.

Jail Accreditation

accreditation

Process through which correctional facilities and agencies can measure themselves against nationally adopted standards and through which they can receive formal recognition and accredited status.

jail accreditation

Formal approval of a jail by the American Correctional Association and the Commission on Accreditation.

Accreditation is a process through which correctional facilities and agencies can measure themselves against nationally adopted standards and through which they can receive formal recognition and accredited status. We will expand on the issue of correctional accreditation in Chapter 13. The focus here is on jail accreditation.

Jail accreditation is the formal approval of a jail by the American Correctional Association (ACA) and the Commission on Accreditation. The ACA and the commission have developed standards for the services, programs, and operations they consider essential to good jail management. The standards cover administrative and fiscal concerns, staff training and development, the physical plant, safety and emergency procedures, sanitation, food service, and rules and discipline. Standards are divided into two categories. To be accredited, a jail must have 100 percent compliance with mandatory standards and 90 percent compliance with nonmandatory standards. Accreditation is valid for three years. Then the jail may apply for reaccreditation and receive another on-site audit by ACA staff and an accreditation hearing.

Very few jails followed established standards or policies before the 1960s. Several reasons for this have been suggested, including the traditional independence of sheriffs, who operate the jails in most jurisdictions, and the tendency of most sheriffs to focus on law enforcement rather than on corrections.

Although jails were slow to respond to the standards movement, their response has picked up in recent years. On April 29, 1986, and then again on May 19, 1993, the American Jail Association passed a resolution urging all jails to become involved in the accreditation process. Today, only 129 of the nation's 3,365 jails are ACA-accredited.[76]

There are several reasons jails have been slow to adopt national standards or seek national accreditation. First, accreditation is expensive and

ETHICS & PROFESSIONALISM

Code of Ethics for Jail Officers

As an officer employed in a detention/correctional capacity, I swear (or affirm) to be a good citizen and a credit to my community, state, and nation at all times. I will abstain from questionable behavior which might bring disrepute to the agency for which I work, my family, my community, and my associates. My lifestyle will be above and beyond reproach, and I will constantly strive to set an example of a professional who performs his/her duties according to the laws of our country, state, and community and the policies, procedures, written and verbal orders, and regulations of the agency for which I work.

On the job I promise to

KEEP the institution secure so as to safeguard my community and the lives of the staff, inmates, and visitors on the premises.

WORK with each individual firmly and fairly without regard to rank, status, or condition.

MAINTAIN a positive demeanor when confronted with stressful situations of scorn, ridicule, danger, and/or chaos.

REPORT either in writing or by word of mouth to the proper authorities those things which should be reported and keep silent about matters which are to remain confidential according to the laws and rules of the agency and government.

MANAGE and supervise the inmates in an evenhanded and courteous manner.

REFRAIN at all the times from becoming personally involved in the lives of the inmates and their families.

TREAT all visitors to the jail with politeness and respect and do my utmost to ensure that they observe the jail regulations.

TAKE advantage of all education and training opportunities designed to assist me to become a more competent officer.

COMMUNICATE with people in or outside of the jail, whether by phone, written word, or word of mouth, in such a way so as not to reflect in a negative manner upon my agency.

CONTRIBUTE to a jail environment which will keep the inmate involved in activities designed to improve his/her attitude and character.

SUPPORT all activities of a professional nature through membership and participation that will continue to elevate the status of those who operate our nation's jails. Do my best through word and deed to present an image to the public at large of a jail professional, committed to progress for an improved and enlightened criminal justice system.

Adopted by the American Jail Association Board of Directors on Novermber 10, 1991, Revised May 19, 1993.

Source: Copyright © American Jail Association.

Ethical Dilemma 6–1: Female offenders have

an average of 2.5 children. Rising numbers of incarcerated, pregnant, and/or parenting women being sentenced to jail have resulted in many more children being separated from their mothers. Should jail administrators concern themselves with providing services for families of jail inmates? For more information go to Ethical Dilemma 6–1 at www.justicestudies.com/ethics04.

Ethical Dilemma 6–2: Sometimes administra-

tors must make hard decisions when faced with budget cuts. As a jail administrator, you must cut one position, either a correctional officer or teacher. Which position will you cut? Why? For more information go to Ethical Dilemma 6–2 at www.justicestudies.com/ethics04.

Ethical Dilemmas for every chapter are available online.

---

time-consuming. Many jails do not have the resources to commit to it. This is especially true of small jails that are already overburdened. Approximately 2,000 U.S. jails are designed to hold fewer than 50 inmates. Second, jails hold relatively few long-term inmates. Few inmates are in a jail long enough to file a successful legal action regarding poor conditions in the jail. Knowing this, some jail administrators may not be willing to undergo the expense and burden of seeking accreditation. Third, some states have their own standards that jails must meet.

There are, however, at least four reasons for jails to have national accreditation:

1. Accreditation by the ACA and the Commission on Accreditation indicates that a jail adheres to strict standards to protect the health and safety of staff and inmates.

2. Being accredited may help a jail defend itself against lawsuits over conditions of incarceration. For example, in 1999, Thelma Grayson filed suit in federal court after her client, Gerald Collins, was found dead the day after he was arrested and transported to the Fairfax County (Virginia) Adult Detention Center. Grayson alleged that the arresting officer, the sheriff in charge of the detention center, and Fairfax County had violated Collins's constitutional rights. However, the court found that Grayson's own expert penologist conceded that the sheriff's policies met the standards of both the Virginia Board of Corrections and the American Correctional Association. At the time of the incident, the Adult Detention Center had been accredited for more than 10 years by both the American Correctional Association and the National Commission on Correctional Health Care, two organizations whose training requirements often surpass minimal constitutional standards.

3. In preparing for the accreditation review, the sheriff's office may evaluate all operations, procedures, and policies, leading to better management practices.

4. With accreditation come professional recognition and status, greater appreciation by the community, and a sense of pride in the achievement and in the hard work that went into it. As Sheriff B. J. Roberts of Hampton, Virginia, put it, "Being accredited puts legitimacy in our operation. Accreditation is an honor, not only for the Sheriff's Office but for the city of Hampton as well."[77]

Jail Staff as Professionals

Jail staff assume enormous responsibility, and we expect them to conduct themselves as professionals. Before 1970, training and education for jail officers were virtually nonexistent, for several reasons. Jail officers often aspired to be law enforcement officers, or they were using jail work as their last stop on the road to retirement. Many people also believed that education and training for jail staff were unnecessary because the work was unsophisticated and could be learned on the job.

Since 1970, however, the image of jail staff has changed. Thanks to organizations such as the American Jail Association and the American Correctional Association, national, state, and local commissions on jail issues, and studies by practitioners, consultants, and academic researchers, jail work is now recognized not only as difficult but also as a career path that is different from law enforcement and requires different attitudes and skills. Jail staff perform work that is vital, complex, and potentially hazardous, even under the best of circumstances.

To conduct themselves as professionals, jail staff must have strong communication skills, knowledge of the psychology of behavior, multicultural sophistication, ethnic and racial tolerance, human management expertise, endurance, and fitness. Even more important, they must, for their own mental well-being, be able to understand and tolerate the stress of a potentially explosive environment. The American Jail Association's Code of Ethics for Jail Officers is shown in the Ethics and Professionalism box.

The trend toward better-educated and trained jail staff is evident across the United States. There are tougher entrance requirements. Applicants must have a higher level of education, increased basic training, more experience, other related skills, and the appropriate personality. Jail staff also learn to conduct themselves as professionals.

Many departments require applicants to have completed a correctional officer training and education program. There are a number of advantages to the policy. First, a department can hire certified correctional officers without paying for training. Second, the department can ask training program staff about applicants' abilities, reliability, and other relevant issues. And third, new jail officers will have the needed skills and an essential understanding of the job.

In 1978, the ACA pioneered correctional accreditation. In 1999, it embarked on another milestone in the process of bringing professionalism into corrections by developing a national Commission on Correctional Certification (CCC) and an online Corrections Academy.

Just as accreditation provides an opportunity for facilities to be recognized, certification is an opportunity for jail staff to be recognized as qualified correctional practitioners. The ACA certification process requires applicants to meet the educational requirements of the category within which they seek certification (for example, the category of correctional executive requires a college degree; correctional managers and supervisors require an associate degree; correctional officers require a high school diploma). Next, applicants must pass a national examination developed by the National Institute of Corrections for the job tasks and related competencies associated with the job category. Third, applications enter into "candidacy status," a two-year period during which they must pass a certification examination. Those who pass the certification exam become Certified Corrections Professionals for three years. Maintaining that status involves becoming recertified and obtaining a specified number of continuing education credits. Through the efforts of the ACA's Commission on Correctional Certification, jail personnel are on the road to upgrading their public image and professional stature and achieving the status of other professions that rely on universal compliance with a self-imposed credentialing process.

REVIEW & APPLICATIONS

REFLECTIONS ON THE FUTURE

by Ken Kerle
American Jail Association

21st Century Jails

The number of inmates in American jails continues to increase on a regular basis. A glance at the first edition [1991] of *Who's Who in Jail Management* lists 2,572 of the nation's 3,353 jails in the United States with a rated capacity of fewer than 100 inmates.[1] This volume also lists 54 jail systems (mega jails) whose rated capacity exceeded 1,000.

By 2003, when the 4th edition appeared the figures had changed dramatically. The number of jails decreased to 3,276 and there were only 1,822 jails whose rated capacity was under 100 inmates, a decline of 750. The number of mega jails had risen from 54 to 155. Readers should remember that the American Jail Association defines a jail as an institution that holds a person more than 72 hours. Anything less than that is considered a lockup. There are no accurate statistics on the number of lockups or short-term holding facilities in the United States. These lockups are frequently found in some police departments who eventually transport the prisoners to county or city jails if cause is established to hold the prisoners for trial.

Jail Growth

Jail populations continue to grow according to the Bureau of Justice Statistics (BJS). In 1997 the U.S. Department of Justice issued a press release that stated that there are almost 30 times as many admissions to local jails as there are new court commitments to state and federal prisons. It is estimated that more than 11 million people a year are booked into the nation's jails. Students of corrections know that today's state and federal prison populations have eclipsed the 1.5 million mark and the jail population exceeded 740,000 with another 72,000 under community supervision by jail staff.

Allen Beck, now-Principal Deputy Director of the BJS, in an article published in *American Jails* in 2002 projected jail population growth for the first decade of the 21st century based on demographics only, demographics consistent with the 2001 rate, along with the past two- and five-year averages.[2] Beck warned of the rising number of pretrial detainees, the steady flow of inmates sentenced to jail, the length of stay of pretrial detainees and sentenced inmates which had increased in the early 1990s, the rising number of inmates held for other authorities, and the jails holding an increasing number of community supervision violators.

A large amount of those arrested and brought into the jails make bond or are released on their own recognizance. Nevertheless, it is not well understood by most citizens that many of the people brought into jail booking centers are under the influence of alcohol and drugs, are often afflicted with mental problems, and are more prone to sickness and disease when compared to the average law-abiding population. Jail staff must deal with these people, even though it may be for only a short period of time.

In contrast, individuals who are sentenced to prison have already been in jail long enough to dry out, receive medical treatment, and have experienced incarceration at the jail level. These prison-bound individuals are the same people who earlier were processed into the jails. Some often misbehaved in jail in a violent and/or unorthodox manner, much of which is related to their alcohol/drug inebriation and their mental instability. This places heavy stress on jail staff that must continually face this kind of aberrant behavior on a fairly regular ba-

sis. County governments which fail to require adequate jail training for jail staff only make matters worse since staff that are inadequately trained can increase opportunities for litigation against the county government when prisoners sue for violations of their constitutional rights.

Direct Supervision and the Failure to Train

There is no sadder example of the reluctance to emphasize jail supervisory training than what we find in direct supervision jails. Simply stated, a direct supervision jail is an institution where the jail staff is located inside the podular housing areas with the inmates. One officer may be responsible for the management of 40 to 72 inmates. The basis for the success of a direct supervision jail is grounded in the philosophical principles of direct supervision, a concept developed in the 1970s when the federal Bureau of Prisons first opened three direct supervision jails in New York City, Chicago, and San Diego. When it began the eight principles were *effective control, effective supervision, need for competent staff, staff and inmate safety, manageable and cost-effective operations, effective communication, classification and orientation,* and *justice and fairness.*[3] In 1992, the American Jail Association added a ninth principle called *staff ownership of operations.*[4] Officers in these jail pods are expected to use interpersonal communications skills that assert proactive leadership in the management of inmates.

Starting in the mid-1980s, the American Jail Association has held direct supervision symposium training each year at its annual training conference. In addition, direct supervision training is offered in regional training sessions held throughout the United States.

However, in 2006, Richard Stockton College of New Jersey criminal justice professor Christine Tartaro published an article critical of the

training provided to direct supervision staff. Professor Tartaro found that most of the jails in her survey provided only one or two days of communications skills training, a crucial element in training direct supervision jail officers.[5] Many of the direct supervision jails in the survey ignored the recommendation for a non-institutional physical environment by using porcelain toilets and commercial grade furnishings to replace the usual stainless steel objects such as toilet/washbasin combinations and picnic tables bolted to the floors. Tartaro found it puzzling that new police officers receive an average of 27.5 weeks of training but new jail officers receive considerably less.

Jail Reentry

In this century, there appears to be a renewed focus on what to do about repeat offenders. The Urban Institute in Washington, D.C. held a conference in June 2006 where practitioners and academics discussed possible solutions. If recidivism can be reduced, this will contribute to the reduction of jail populations and reduce the management pressure particularly in the jails, but also on other criminal justice agencies. A few jail systems have made significant strides in this direction. For example, the jail system in Montgomery County, Maryland, in cooperation with other county agencies, has now developed a "release card" for inmates who have finished their sentences. This allows them to use the card for free public transportation for the first 60 days to travel to job interviews and other private and government agencies when there is a need. This card also functions as a library card.

Officials in Hampden County, Massachusetts, understand the importance of having valid data on jail reentry and a commitment to staff training. The jail mandates an investment in staff with a background in research and a commitment to staff training. The jail has collected recidivism statistics since 1998. It provides some evidence as to the value of jail programs.

REFERENCES
1. American Jail Association, *Who's Who in Jail Management* (Hagerstown, MD: American Jail Association, 1991).
2. Allen J. Beck, "Jail Population Growth: National Trends and Predictors of Future Growth," *American Jails*, vol. 16, no. 2 (May/June 2002), pp. 9–14.
3. W. Raymond Nelson, *New Generation Jails: The Development of a Trend for the Future of the American Jail* (Boulder, CO: National Institute of Corrections, 1983); W. Raymond Nelson, "New Generation Jails," *Corrections Today*, vol. 45, no. 1 (March/April 1983), pp. 108–112.
4. W. Raymond Nelson and Russell Davis, "Podular Direct Supervision—The First Twenty Years, *American Jails*, vol. 9, no. 3 (July/August 1995), pp. 11–22.
5. Christine Tartaro, "Are They Really Direct Supervision Jails," *American Jails*, vol. 20, no. 5 (November/December 2006), pp. 9–17.

About the Author

Ken Kerle has been managing editor of *American Jails*, a publication of the American Jail Association, since 1986. He has visited over 900 jails and prisons in the United States and 21 foreign countries. Kerle is author of *Exploring Jail Operations* (American Correctional Association, 2004). He received his PhD from American University, and has taught a jail course using his text *Exploring Jail Operations*.

SUMMARY

1 There are 3,365 locally operated jails in the United States. Besides incarcerating people who have sentences of a year or less, jails serve a number of purposes. They hold people awaiting trial, probation and parole violators, adults and juveniles awaiting transfer, and prison inmates about to be released. Sometimes they operate community-based programs. The jail population is different from the prison population in terms of total admissions and average daily population.

2 The *daily* population of jails is lower than that of prisons, but the *annual* total of people incarcerated in jails is higher.

3 Jails emerged in Europe in the 12th century to detain offenders for trial. In the 15th and 16th centuries, the poor and unemployed were detained alongside criminals. The first jail in America was the Walnut Street Jail. Quakers designed it according to their principles of religious reflection and penance. It fell short of reaching its goals and closed in 1835.

4 American jails have progressed through four phases of architecture and inmate management: first-generation jails (linear design and sporadic supervision), second-generation jails (pod design and remote supervision), third-generation jails (pod design and direct supervision), and fourth-generation jails ("borrowed light" and less isolation).

5 By mid-2006, jails held or supervised 826,232 offenders, an increase of 1.1 percent from mid-2005. An estimated 38 percent of jail inmates are convicted offenders. Women represent 12.9 percent of the jail population; nonwhites, 56.1 percent; and juveniles, 0.8 percent. By mid-2006, 94 percent of jail capacity was occupied. Forty-seven jails are privatized. The most (eight) are in Texas. Almost 300,000 people work in jails. The increase in the jail population is outpacing the growth in jail staff. The problems of jail staff include low pay and prestige, high turnover, and inadequate systems for recruitment, selection, and training.

6 Advocates of privatization claim they can build and operate jails more efficiently than can government. Opponents argue they cannot, or they dismiss the cost issues altogether. For them, operating a jail is a basic function of government and a symbol of state authority and should not be delegated.

7 Jail crowding can be reduced by creating a process for the collection, analysis, and discussion of jail data, and through financial and nonfinancial pretrial release, diversion, and new jail construction.

8 Jail vocational and educational programs are important avenues for managing inmates and reducing recidivism. They keep inmates occupied, boost self-esteem, and help inmates find jobs after release.

9 Jails are partnering with faith-based organizations to meet the needs of jail inmates. Jail chaplaincy can influence jail inmates in five ways. First, chaplains can help inmates with the inner conversion needed to break the cycle of crime. Second, a jail chaplain can help staff deal with day-to-day problems. Third, a jail chaplain can mediate and moderate tensions and conflicts between inmates and staff. Fourth, jail chaplaincy can involve the public as jail volunteers and remind people that inmates exist. And fifth, chaplains can help inmates confront the truth about themselves.

10 Jail accreditation is important for four reasons. First, accreditation indicates that a jail adheres to strict standards. Second, accreditation may help a jail defend itself against lawsuits over conditions of incarceration. Third, through accreditation, the sheriff's office may evaluate all jail operations, procedures, and policies, leading to better management practices. And fourth, accreditation generates professional recognition and status, greater appreciation by the community, and a sense of pride.

11 It is important for jail staff to conduct themselves as professionals because jail work is difficult and carries enormous responsibility. It requires a special attitude, communication skills, knowledge of the psychology of behavior, multicultural sophistication, endurance, and fitness. Together, college education and jail training prepare jail staff to work as professionals. In 1999, the American Correctional Association established the Commission on Correctional Certification (CCC). The purpose of the CCC is to recognize jail staff as qualified correctional practitioners using a self-imposed credentialing process.

KEY TERMS

jails, *p. 207*
total admission, *p. 207*
average daily population (ADP), *p. 207*
rabble management, *p. 211*
first-generation jail, *p. 211*
second-generation jail, *p. 212*
third-generation jail, *p. 213*

direct-supervision jail, *p. 213*
fourth-generation jail, *p. 215*
rated capacity *p. 224*
pay-to-stay jail, *p. 225*
privatization, *p. 229*
release on bail, *p. 233*
release on own recognizance (ROR), *p. 234*

citation, *p. 234*
supervised pretrial release, *p. 234*
conditional release, *p. 234*
reentry, *p. 236*
accreditation, *p. 242*
jail accreditation, *p. 242*

QUESTIONS FOR REVIEW

1 Jails serve a number of purposes. Which do you believe is the most important and why?

2 Describe how jail populations are different from prison populations.

3 Summarize the history of jails.

4 Explain how first-, second-, third-, and fourth-generation jails are different.

5 What can you infer from the characteristics of jail inmates, facilities, and staff?

6 What ideas can you add to the arguments for and against jail privatization?

7 What solution is best for reducing jail overcrowding?

8 How do jail vocational and educational programs affect inmate behavior and recidivism?

9 What criteria would you use to assess the impact that faith-based organizations and jail chaplains have on jail inmates and staff?

10 What ideas can you add to the arguments for and against jail accreditation?

11 What might happen if jail staff did not conduct themselves as professionals?

THINKING CRITICALLY ABOUT CORRECTIONS

Pretrial Release

When deciding whether to grant pretrial release, a judge looks at the offense, the evidence, and the defendant's family ties, employment, financial resources, character, mental condition, length of residence in the community, and criminal record. To which of these do you think the judge should give the greatest weight? Why?

Faith-Based Organizations

President George W. Bush has said that faith-based organizations can help meet the nation's needs. What needs can they meet in jail and how?

ON-THE-JOB DECISION MAKING

Promoting a Third-Generation Jail

You are the administrator of a new county jail with the architecture and philosophy of direct supervision. The new jail replaced a jail built in 1912. Some of the senior staff have begun complaining to you about direct supervision. They say they don't like to interact with inmates. They talk about "the good old days" when inmates were "on the other side" of the reinforced glass and steel bars. There's even been a letter to the editor in the local newspaper complaining that the new jail doesn't "look like a jail."

1. What could you tell the senior staff about direct-supervision philosophy that might ease their concerns?

2. What strategies might you use to educate the public about the benefits of direct supervision?

Reducing Jail Crowding

Jail crowding is a problem across the country. Imagine you are the sheriff of a large urban county with a mega-jail (more than 1,000 beds), and your jail is overcrowded. Since you are an elected official and would like to be re-elected, you don't want to appear "soft on crime," yet you know you can't build your way out of the crowding problem. There's simply not enough money to expand the jail or build a new one. How do you argue in favor of reducing jail crowding?

LIVE LINKS

at www.justicestudies.com/livelinks04

6-1 American Indian Suicides in Jail

The results of this research suggest that suicide risk assessment protocols tailored to the cultural backgrounds of detainee populations are more effective than an impersonally administered one-size-fits-all approach.

6-2 Providing Services for Jail Inmates with Mental Disorders

This report discusses findings from an NIJ-sponsored survey and selected site visits undertaken to identify innovative policies and practices to address the needs of offenders with mental disorders detained in the nation's jails. Few jails are equipped to provide a comprehensive range of mental health services. Most jails have no policies or procedures for managing and supervising these detainees. Approximately 84 percent of survey respondents reported that mental health services were received by one-tenth or fewer of their inmates.

6-3 When Neighbors Go to Jail

The impact of incarceration rates on community disorganization and family and economic life in Leon County, Florida, is examined to determine the relationship between direct and indirect exposure to the criminal justice system and attitudes toward social control. This review reports on the attitudinal differences between people who have been exposed to incarceration and those who have not and how they alter neighborhood life.

6-4 Making Jail Mental Health a Community Issue

The implementation of Orange County Jail Oversight Commission's (JOC) recommendations regarding offenders with mental illness in jails is related. This article is comprised of the following sections: background; confronting the situation—pre-booking diversion, post-booking diversion, and in-custody services; JOC revisited; and community action.

PRISONS TODAY

Change Stations or Warehouses?

CHAPTER OBJECTIVES

After completing this chapter you should be able to do the following:

1 Explain the differences between the Pennsylvania and Auburn prison systems.

2 Outline the nine eras of prison development.

3 Describe the characteristics of today's prisoners and discuss reasons for the incarceration of women and minority prisoners.

4 Explain prisoner classification and its purposes.

5 Trace the development of faith-based correctional institutions.

6 Explain what the evidence-based literature says about prison industries.

7 Report on the availability of education, recreation, and health care programs for prisoners.

8 Compare state and federal prison organization and administration.

9 Discuss the question "Does incarceration work?"

> *When society places a person behind walls and bars, it has an obligation—a moral obligation—to do whatever can reasonably be done to change that person before he or she goes back into the mainstream of society.*
>
> —Warren Burger, former United States Supreme Court Chief Justice, 1981

On April 17, 2006, 72-year-old former Illinois pharmacist, secretary of state, lieutenant governor, and governor George Ryan was convicted of 18 counts of racketeering, mail fraud, cheating on his taxes, and lying to federal agents.[1] On September 6, 2006, Ryan was sentenced to 6½ years in federal prison and told by U.S. District Court Judge Rebecca Pallmeyer to start serving his sentence on January 4, 2007, at the Federal Correctional Institution at Oxford, Wisconsin. Pallmeyer also denied Ryan's request to remain free on bond pending his appeal. (Since the 1970s, Ryan is the third Illinois ex-governor convicted of a public corruption charge and sentenced to federal prison.)

On April 17, 2006, George Ryan, former pharmacist and Illinois governor, was sentenced to 6½ years in federal prison for racketeering, mail fraud, cheating on his taxes, and lying to federal agents. Six months later, the Seventh Circuit Court of Appeals ruled that Ryan may remain free on bond pending appeal. It's interesting that Ryan is the third Illinois ex-governor convicted on a public corruption charge and sentenced to federal prison since 1970. What's even more interesting is how George Ryan, a conservative Republican and death penalty supporter, became the poster child for the anti-death-penalty movement, a topic we return to in Chapter 15. If you were Ryan's prison case manager, what kind of prison programming would you recommend?

However, on November 28, 2006, the Seventh Circuit Court of Appeals ruled that Ryan did not have to start his 6½-year prison sentence as scheduled and may remain free on bond pending appeal. But the appeals court said in its ruling that if it upholds the racketeering and fraud conviction handed down by Pallmeyer, Ryan must report to federal prison immediately where he will be allowed to bring in his identification, legal papers, and his wedding band. In prison, 72-year-old Ryan may be seen as a father figure since the average federal inmate is 37 years old.

As you will learn later in this chapter, if the appeals court upholds the lower court's decision, Ryan will be interviewed by the prison staff and receive an orientation to the prison. He will be assigned an eight-digit number and tan coveralls with a button-down collar. Depending on where he is housed within prison, he could have up to four roommates.

As a federal inmate, Ryan will be allowed four hours of face-to-face visiting each month with family and friends and private meetings with his lawyers. He'll be able to receive an unlimited amount of mail, although each letter will be opened and inspected. The warden will first approve all of Ryan's newspapers and magazines. Ryan will have a prison job. The jobs available in federal prison include food service, orderly, plumber, painter, warehouse worker, and grounds-keeper. Ryan will be paid between 12 cents and $1 an hour.

On February 20, 2007, Ryan's lawyers and federal prosecutors argued their cases before a three-judge panel of the Seventh Circuit. The judges could rule in a couple of weeks or take months to issue a decision. If the judges fail to overturn his convictions, Ryan must immediately report to FCI Oxford, Wisconsin. If the appellate judges order a new trial, Ryan would remain free because a different set of appellate judges allowed him a rare appeal bond.

The other interesting part of Ryan's story is his stand on capital punishment, which we discuss in Chapter 15. Ryan served one term as Republican Illinois governor from 1999 to 2003. He was a staunch supporter of capital punishment but stunned the world just days before leaving office on January 13, 2003, when he commuted 164 death row inmates' sentences to life in prison, commuted 3 other death row inmates' sentences to 40 years in prison with the possibility of parole, and pardoned 4 other men. Why he did it and the impact it has had are discussed in Chapter 15.

Later in this chapter we will learn more about the federal prison system. We begin the chapter with a look at the history of American prisons. Then we will discuss the composition of the prison population, programs for prisoners, and the way America's prisons are organized and administered. We conclude with the question "Does incarceration work?"

HISTORY OF PRISONS IN AMERICA

Prisons are relatively modern social institutions, and their development is distinctly American. Until the mid-18th century, fines, banishment from the community, corporal punishment, and execution were the primary forms of punishing offenders. By the latter part of the century, incarceration was championed as a more humane form of punishment. It reflected and fueled a shift from the assumption that offenders were inherently criminal to a belief that they were simply not properly trained to resist temptation and corruption. The two prison systems that emerged in the United States—the Pennsylvania system and the Auburn system—were copied throughout the world.

The Pennsylvania and Auburn prison systems developed in the United States at the turn of the 19th century. Pennsylvania Quakers advocated a method of punishment more humane than the public corporal punishment used at the time. The Quakers shifted the emphasis from punishing the body to reforming the mind and soul. Together with an elite group of 18th-century Philadelphians, they ushered in the first **penitentiary,** a place for reform of offenders through repentance and rehabilitation. They

penitentiary

The earliest form of large-scale incarceration. It punished criminals by isolating them so that they could reflect on their misdeeds, repent, and reform.

Pennsylvania system

The first historical phase of prison discipline, involving solitary confinement in silence instead of corporal punishment; conceived by the American Quakers in 1790 and implemented at the Walnut Street Jail.

Auburn system

The second historical phase of prison discipline, implemented at New York's Auburn prison in 1815. It followed the Pennsylvania system and allowed inmates to work silently together during the day, but they were isolated at night. Eventually sleeping cells became congregate and restrictions against talking were removed.

believed prisoners needed to be isolated from each other in silence to repent, to accept God's guidance, and to avoid having a harmful influence on each other. Known as the **Pennsylvania system** or the *separate system*, this method was first used at the Walnut Street Jail, which the Quakers reorganized in 1790 as the country's first institution for punishment. The Eastern State Penitentiary, constructed in 1829, was also based on these principles. The prison was designed for solitary confinement at labor, with instruction in labor, morals, and religion. To make the isolation less severe and to help inmates prepare for employment after release, prison officials permitted inmates to work by themselves in their cells at various occupations, such as shoemaking, weaving, tailoring, and polishing marble. For the first time in American history, rehabilitation and deterrence emerged as goals of corrections.

The solitary confinement of the Pennsylvania system was expensive, and it reportedly drove prisoners insane and further hardened criminal tendencies. Reformers responded with what has been termed the **Auburn system:** regimentation, military-style drill, silence unless conversation was required in workshops, congregate working and eating, separation of prisoners into small individual cells at night, harsh discipline, shaved heads, black-and-white striped uniforms, and industrial workshops that contracted with private businesses to help pay for the institution. Prison factories in the 19th century produced shoes, barrels, carpets, engines, boilers, harnesses, clothing, and furniture—goods that could not be produced under the "solitary" system of Pennsylvania or not in quantities sufficient to make a profit. This merchandise was sold on the open market to American consumers or exported to Canada and Latin America, and the proceeds helped support prison operations. The first prison to use this system opened in Auburn, New York, in 1819. The Auburn system, congregate by day and separate by night, eventually gave way to congregate cells at night and removal of the restrictions against talking.

Prison reform in the United States caught the attention of prison officials around the world. The Pennsylvania system of isolation and silence became popular in Europe. In the United States, the two competing philosophies of prison life clashed, and the debate over which system was superior raged on for decades. Supporters of the Pennsylvania system argued that it made it easier to control prisoners and prevented prisoners from learning bad habits from each other. Supporters of the Auburn system claimed that prisoners' spirits needed to be broken before true reform could begin and that their system of harsh discipline and congregate but silent labor accomplished that. Auburn supporters also argued that their prison system was cheaper to build and that the use of contract labor would keep down costs.

A system that was congregate by day (and eventually by night as well) seemed more compatible with the political and economic tone of the time. The Pennsylvania system represented a traditional approach to production: handcrafted labor in solitary cells. In contrast, the Auburn system reflected the emerging developments of the Industrial Revolution: power machinery, factory production, and division of labor. The attractiveness of the Auburn system's perceived economic benefits as well as a belief in the rehabilitative value of hard work settled the debate. Thus, the congregate system became the preferred model of incarceration in the United States. In 1913, Eastern State Penitentiary, the epitome of the Pennsylvania system, converted to the Auburn system, ending the great debate. Congregate prisons have been the mode ever since. Today, however, new

The Eastern State Penitentiary, completed in 1829, was designed on the Quakers' principle of solitary confinement in silence, with instruction in labor, morals, and religion. What name was given to this separate system of prisoner management?

Interior view of a cellblock at Eastern State Penitentiary. Linear design and sporadic inmate supervision characterized Eastern State. What problems emerged at Eastern State that caused the demise of the Pennsylvania system?

voices are calling for a return to long-term solitary confinement in supermax prisons (one of several topics discussed in Chapter 13).

Stages of Development

Prisons in America have progressed through nine stages of development (see Exhibit 7–1). Many of these changes were influenced by cultural movements in society. As you review the historical stages, think about how the goals of imprisonment changed in each era as society changed. Remember too that old ways did not disappear when new ways emerged. Rather, new thinking challenged the thinking of previous eras and facilitated the development of new correctional policy, including the shift toward professionalism in corrections. Most often, new ideas simply developed alongside existing ones.

Penitentiary Era (1790–1825)   The first era in prison history was the penitentiary era. In 1790, the renovated Walnut Street Jail opened with a penitentiary wing that emphasized the Quakers' religious belief in prisoner reform through reflection, penitance, and rehabilitation through good conduct. From that beginning two competing prison systems merged, the Pennsylvania system of separate and silent confinement and the Auburn system of harsh discipline and congregate but silent labor. The era witnessed the demise of the Pennsylvania system and the building of 30 state prisons on the Auburn pattern of congregate by day and separate by night. This pattern eventually changed to congregate both day and night.

Mass Prison Era (1825–1876)   The second era was the mass prison era. During that period, the idea of prison as a place for punishment flourished across the United States. As a result, 35 more Auburn-system

EXHIBIT 7–1   **Stages of Prison History in the United States**

Stage	Penitentiary Era	Mass Prison Era	Reformatory Era	Industrial Era
Years	1790–1825	1825–1876	1876–1890	1890–1935
Goal	Rehabilitation and deterrence	Incapacitation and deterrence	Rehabilitation	Incapacitation
Characteristics	Separate and silent Congregate and silent	Congregate labor and living spaces without silence Contract prison labor	Indeterminate sentencing Parole	Public accounts industries Contract labor State-use labor Convict lease Public works labor
Examples of Institutions	Walnut Street Penitentiary, Philadelphia, PA Eastern State Penitentiary Cherry Hill, PA Auburn Prison, Auburn, NY	Sing Sing Prison, Ossining, NY San Quentin State Prison, San Quentin, CA	Elmira, NY Indiana Reformatory for Women and Girls, Indianapolis, IN	Most major prisons
Related Events	1819 Congregate, silent system implemented in Auburn Penitentiary, New York. 1829 Eastern State Penitentiary opens under the Pennsylvania prison model.	1841 John Augustus begins the practice of probation in Massachusetts. 1871 *Ruffin* v. *Commonwealth* establishes that convicted felons not only forfeit liberty but are slaves of the state; this provides the legal justification for courts to maintain a "hands-off doctrine." 1913 Eastern State Penitentiary converts to the Auburn prison model.	1876 The first women's prison, the Indiana Reformatory for Women and Girls, opens. 1876 Zebulon Brockway appointed warden at Elmira Reformatory and initiates first parole system in the United States. 1878 First probation law is passed in Massachusetts.	1899 First juvenile court established in Cook County (Chicago), Illinois. 1914–1918 World War I begins and ends. 1929 Hawes-Cooper Act passed to regulate interstate sale of prison-made goods. 1929 Great Depression begins. 1930 Federal Bureau of Prisons is established.

EXHIBIT 7–1	Stages of Prison History in the United States (*continued*)			
Punitive Era	**Treatment Era**	**Community-Based Era**	**Warehousing Era**	**Just Deserts Era**
1935–1945	1945–1967	1967–1980	1980–1995	1985–Present
Retribution	Rehabilitation	Reintegration	Incapacitation	Retribution
Strict punishment and custody	Medical model Emerging prisoner unrest	Intermediate sanction: halfway houses, work release centers, group homes, fines, restitution, community service	Sentencing guidelines End of discretionary parole release Serious crowding More prison riots	Just deserts Determinate sentencing Truth in sentencing Three-strikes law Serious crowding
U.S. Penitentiary, Alcatraz, CA	Patuxent Institution, Jessup, MD	Major prison riots (Attica, NY; Santa Fe, NM)	Most major prisons	Spreading through the United States
1934 Alcatraz ("Hellcatraz") opens. 1939 Great Depression ends. 1939–1945 World War II begins and ends. 1942–1945 Japanese and Japanese American relocation centers open and close.	1950 Federal Youth Corrections Act passed to create treatment for offenders under the age of 22 in the federal system. 1964 *Cooper* v. *Pate* formally recognizing the constitutional rights of prisoners. 1967 *In re Gault* U.S. Supreme Court ruling that juvenile offenders are entitled to state-provided counsel and due process guarantees. 1967 President Johnson's Commission on Law Enforcement and Administration of Justice recommends changing the criminal justice system.	1970 Massachusetts becomes first state to close down all of its juvenile reform schools. 1974 Robert Martinson's "What Works" is published and is used by politicians as reason to pull resources from prisons. 1976 Maine is first state to abolish discretionary parole board release. 1979 Prison Industry Enhancement (PIE) certification program repeals limitations on interstate commerce in prison-made goods.	1980s President Reagan declares "war on drugs." 1984 Federal Sentencing Reform Act imposes mandatory sentences for specific crimes. 1993 Three-strikes-and-you're-out laws spread across the United States. 1994 Congress passes the Violent Crime Control and Law Enforcement Act, which increases financial incentives for states to put more violent criminals in prison.	1994 Federal Bureau of Prisons opens its supermax prison. 1995 Eight states reinstate chain gangs. 1999 Number of people incarcerated in the United States exceeds 2 million for the first time. 2004 Abuse of prisoners at Abu Ghraib prison in Baghdad, Iraq, by U.S. military personnel becomes public. 2007 Evidence-based research shapes correctional practice.

The Industrial Revolution ushered in the era of the industrial prison. The era had good intentions. What were they and what happened?

public accounts system

The earliest form of prison industry, in which the warden was responsible for purchasing materials and equipment and for overseeing the manufacture, marketing, and sale of prison-made items.

contract system

A system of prison industry in which the prison advertised for bids for the employment of prisoners, whose labor was sold to the highest bidder.

convict lease system

A system of prison industry in which a prison temporarily relinquished supervision of its prisoners to a lessee. The lessee either employed the prisoners within the institution or transported them to work elsewhere in the state.

prisons were built, including Sing Sing in New York State in 1825, San Quentin in California in 1852, and Joliet in Illinois in 1858. Most were built by prisoners who quarried the stones on-site.

Reformatory Era (1876–1890) The third era was the reformatory era. Influenced by progressive beliefs that education and science were vehicles for controlling crime, the first reformatory for young men opened at Elmira, New York, in 1876. The reformatory, whose prisoners had indeterminate sentences (a sentence for which a judge specifies a maximum length and a minimum length and for which an administrative agency, generally a parole board, determines the actual time of release), used a grading system that led to early release on parole and offered academic education, vocational training, individual rehabilitation, and military instruction and discipline. During this era, 20 reformatories opened for men, as well as the first prison for women, Mount Pleasant in Ossining, New York, and the first reformatory for women, the Indiana Reformatory for Women and Girls in Indianapolis. Massachusetts passed the first probation law in 1878, extending progressive belief into community supervision as well.

Industrial Era (1890–1935) Fourth was the industrial era. During this time, inmates worked in prison industries. The first prisons had used the **public accounts system** for work. The warden at the Walnut Street Jail had determined the product, purchased materials and equipment, and overseen the manufacture, marketing, and sale of prison-made items. At Auburn, prison industries expanded to include copper, weaving, tailor, blacksmith, and shoemaking shops. However, as more states adopted the Auburn model, the **contract system** replaced the public accounts system. Under the contract system, the prison advertised for bids for the employment of prisoners, whose labor was sold to the highest bidder. The desire to increase profits for the prison and the private contractor often led to exploitation of the prisoners under this system.

During the industrial era, prisons progressed from the public accounts and contract systems of the Pennsylvania and Auburn prisons to *convict lease, state use,* and *public works* systems. Which system was used in a state depended on the region the state was in and the period in which the transition was made.

The **convict lease system** was prevalent in the post-Civil War South and functioned as a replacement for the institution of slavery. Many southern prisons had been destroyed during the war. Southern states found it easier to relinquish supervision of their prisoners to a lessee. The lessee either employed prisoners as slave labor for private businesses within a state institution or transported them to work elsewhere in the state. Railway, lumber, and coal mining companies leased the greatest numbers of inmates. Lessees housed, fed, clothed, and disciplined inmates. The convict lease system generated income for the prison and reduced overhead because the contractors were responsible for feeding and sheltering the convicts they leased. Left to the mercy of the contractors, however, leased convicts were subjected to terrible abuses of nearly unimaginable brutality.

From attempts to deal with this problem emerged the state use system. Under the **state use system,** prisoners manufactured products for use by state governments and their agencies, departments, and institutions. By putting inmates to work manufacturing products for sale exclusively to government agencies, prisons were better able to keep inmates occupied while at the same time reducing direct competition with the private sector and avoiding the exploitative character of inmate leasing. As the western states developed, a **public works system** emerged. This system used inmates to build public buildings, roads, and parks.

In time, national labor organizations saw prison industries as unfair competition and lobbied Congress to regulate prison industry. In 1929, the Hawes-Cooper Act banned the interstate shipment of prison-made goods. The Ashurst-Sumners Act of 1935 prohibited carriers from accepting prison-made goods for transportation. Ashurst-Sumners also mandated the labeling of prison-made goods. In 1940, Congress passed the Sumners-Ashurst Act, forbidding the interstate transportation of prison-made goods for private use, regardless of whether a state banned importation of prison goods (products manufactured for the federal government or other state governments were exempt). Thus, much of the private market was closed to goods made by inmates. Today, it is a violation of federal law for state prisons to sell their products in interstate commerce unless they are certified by a federal program known as Prison Industry Enhancement (PIE). Under provisions of the PIE program, inmates must be paid the same wages as free workers engaged in similar work. They must also be allowed to keep 20 percent of what they earn. The rest of their wages can be withheld to pay income taxes, child support obligations, room and board charges, and restitution to victims and to victim assistance funds.

It was also during the industrial era that the Federal Bureau of Prisons (BOP) was established in 1930. We return to a discussion of the BOP later in this chapter.

Punitive Era (1935–1945)   The closing of prison industries ushered in the punitive era, with its emphasis on strict punishment and custody. The holding of prisoners in the Big House, in complete idleness, monotony, and frustration, characterized this era. The "escape proof" federal prison on the island of Alcatraz in San Francisco Bay opened on the eve of this era. It became the prototype of the latter-day supermax prisons that we will discuss in Chapter 13. It was retrofitted with the latest security hardware then available and staffed with an elite corps of officers. It opened in 1934 to receive the toughest prisoners in the federal BOP.

Treatment Era (1945–1967)   The sixth era, treatment, emerged in response to prison riots across the United States. After World War II, the prison population exploded. Overcrowding, idleness, poor food, and other deprivations led prisoners to take matters into their own hands. Prison riots erupted in California, Colorado, Georgia, Illinois, Louisiana, Massachusetts, Michigan, Minnesota, New Jersey, New Mexico, Ohio, Oregon, Pennsylvania, Utah, and Washington. The riots aroused public support for prisoner rehabilitation.

Reform through classification, therapy, and increased use of the indeterminate sentence was the focus of the **medical model,** in which criminal behavior was regarded as a disease to be treated. If the diagnosis showed poor socialization and inadequate work skills as the factors that caused

state use system

A system of prison industry that employs prisoners to manufacture products consumed by state governments and their agencies, departments, and institutions.

public works system

A system of prison industry in which prisoners were employed in the construction of public buildings, roads, and parks.

medical model

A philosophy of prisoner reform in which criminal behavior is regarded as a disease to be treated with appropriate therapy.

a person to turn to crime, the prescription could involve a combination of social skills counseling and vocational training. Maryland's Patuxent Institution, with legions of mental health experts, promised to predict dangerousness accurately and to release only those prisoners who were no longer a threat to the community. However, Patuxent failed to keep that promise. Scholars and advocacy groups also began finding fault with the medical model. They argued that it did not have as favorable an effect on recidivism as supporters argued it would have. They also argued that the medical model encouraged inmates to give the false impression that they were rehabilitated and suitable for early release. Above all was the view that the medical model was a form of coercion and that genuine changes in human behavior could not be coerced. In addition, the social and political unrest of the 1960s had found its way into the nation's prisons. A race riot broke out at San Quentin in 1967, and protests, riots, and killings occurred in other prisons. Corrections experts believed that a new approach was needed—one in which offenders were supervised in the community rather than imprisoned in fortresslike institutions.

Community-Based Era (1967–1980) Community-based corrections mostly developed after the 1960s, although some community-based programs had begun a century earlier. New York City Quakers opened the Isaac T. Hopper Home in 1845 as a shelter for released inmates; Zebulon Brockway opened the Detroit House of Corrections in 1861 as a shelter for released women; the Philadelphia House of Industry opened in 1889; and Maude Ballington Booth opened Hope Hall, a refuge for ex-inmates in New York, in the 1890s. After that, the community-based concept lay dormant until the 1950s when church groups founded more halfway houses (St. Leonard's House in Chicago and Crenshaw House in Los Angeles) and then until 1967 when President Lyndon Johnson's crime commission came to the conclusion that the community was a source of offenders' problems. The commission recommended that offenders be rehabilitated by using community resources. More halfway houses, community corrections centers, intensive supervision probation programs, work release centers, and the like quickly spread across the United States. By the end of the 20th century, halfway houses—which were practically unknown a century earlier—were an indispensable part of corrections.

Observers soon discovered that the community-based approach did not lower the crime rate, reduce the prison population, or make the community safer. With the goals of community corrections unmet, the community-based era gave way and President Nixon ushered in the country's attitude of "get tough on crime."

Warehousing Era (1980–1995) During the warehousing era, indeterminate sentencing was replaced by determinate sentencing in all states. Discretionary parole board release was abolished in a number of states and the federal government, and the pendulum swung from rehabilitation to incapacitation. President Reagan declared "war on drugs," federal sentencing reform mandated sentences for specific crimes, and three-strikes-and-you're-out and truth-in-sentencing laws swept across the United States. Within 15 years, the number of people under correctional supervision jumped from 1.8 million to almost 6 million. Prisons were operating over capacity, and controlling prisoners in such an environment was difficult. For staff and inmates alike, the nation's prisons were dangerous places to be. Extreme crowding resulted in violent outbreaks, which further hardened the attitudes of correctional policymakers and caused them to crack down even more.

Just Deserts Era (1985–present)   Along with the get-tough policies of the warehousing era emerged a distinct but parallel vision of corrections. The just deserts philosophy focuses on punishment and provides a philosophy that supports the practice of warehousing. Chain gangs, striped uniforms, and boot camps have been resuscitated, parole has been cut back to 19th-century levels, and corrections has become as much of a political football as at any time in its history. Under the philosophy of just deserts, offenders are punished because they deserve it, the sanction used depending on the seriousness of the offense. Just deserts is not concerned with inmate rehabilitation, treatment, or reform. It separates treatment from punishment. Prisons today provide opportunities for inmates to improve themselves, but participation is not mandatory, nor is it a condition of release as it was for most of the 20th century. Change is facilitated, not coerced. Determinate sentencing, capital punishment, truth in sentencing, and three-strikes laws have grown in popularity. As we move into the 21st century, supermax and "no-frills" prisons are becoming the trend.

WHO IS IN PRISON TODAY?

On January 1, 2006, 1,525,924 adults were under the jurisdiction of state and federal prison authorities—187,618 held in federal prisons and 1,338,306 held in state prisons.[2] Almost 5 percent (73,097) of state and federal prisoners were held in local jails, a topic we return to later in this chapter.[3] In absolute numbers, there was a total increase of 28,824 prison inmates between January 1, 2005, and January 1, 2006. Overall, the nation's prison population grew 1.9 percent during that year, which was less than the average annual growth of 3.1 percent since the end of 1995. By 2010, the number of adults having ever served time in prison will have increased from 5.6 million U.S. adult residents (about 1 in every 37 U.S. adults) to 7.7 million (1 in every 29 U.S. adults).[4] Nearly 1 in 15 persons born in 2001 (6.6 percent) will go to state or federal prison during their lifetime, up from 5.2 percent in 1991, and 1.9 percent in 1974. Other estimates include that

- the lifetime chances for men going to prison (1 in 9) are six times greater than those for women (1 in 56); and
- about 1 in 3 black males, 1 in 6 Hispanic males, and 1 in 17 white males are expected to go to prison during their lifetime.

The rate of incarceration on January 1, 2006, was 491 sentenced inmates per 100,000 U.S. residents, up from 411 in 1995. The rate of incarceration ranged from 144 people per 100,000 in Maine (the lowest) to 797 people per 100,000 in Louisiana (the highest). The federal system led the country with the most inmates (187,618); North Dakota had the fewest (1,385; see Exhibit 7–2).

Since 1995, the number of sentenced inmates per 100,000 residents has risen from 411 to 491. During this period prison incarceration rates rose most in the Midwest (from 310 to 383) and West (from 358 to 431). The rate in the South rose from 483 to 539, and the rate in the Northeast

EXHIBIT 7–2　Prison Statistics Among the States and the Federal Government, January 1, 2006

Number of Inmates		Incarceration Rate per 100,000 Population		Number of Female Prisoners	
5 HIGHEST:					
Federal	187,618	Louisiana	797	Texas	13,506
California	170,676	Texas	691	Federal	12,422
Texas	169,003	Mississippi	660	California	11,667
Florida	89,768	Oklahoma	652	Florida	6,153
New York	62,743	Alabama	591	Ohio	3,260
5 LOWEST:					
North Dakota	1,385	Maine	144	Maine	129
Maine	2,023	Minnesota	180	New Hampshire	133
Wyoming	2,047	Rhode Island	189	Vermont	152
Vermont	2,078	New Hampshire	192	North Dakota	155
New Hampshire	2,530	North Dakota	208	Wyoming	222

Source: Adapted from Paige M. Harrison and Allen J. Beck, *Prisoners in 2005* (Washington, DC: U.S. Department of Justice, Bureau of Justice Statistics, November 2006).

decreased slightly from 301 to 298. If our attitudes and policies on imprisonment do not change, some believe that state and federal prisons will swell by more than 192,000 inmates over the 2006 population and the nation's incarceration rate will reach 562 sentenced inmates per 100,000 U.S. residents by 2011 (see Exhibit 7–3).

When prison and jail incarceration rates are combined, the United States imprisons 724 people per 100,000 population, up from 601 in 1995. That's more than any other country in the world. Russia is second with 611 prisoners per 100,000.[5]

States with almost identical populations and crime rates have widely different rates of incarceration. For example, in 2005, Wisconsin had a

EXHIBIT 7–3　Projected National Prison Population and Incarceration Rate, 2006–2011

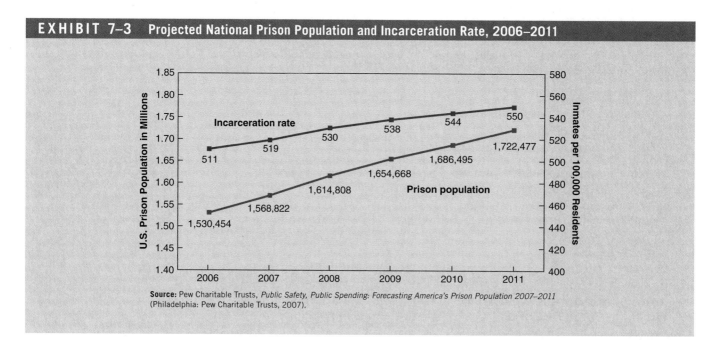

Source: Pew Charitable Trusts, *Public Safety, Public Spending: Forecasting America's Prison Population 2007–2011* (Philadelphia: Pew Charitable Trusts, 2007).

population of 5.5 million residents, a crime rate of 2,901 offenses per 100,000 population, and an incarceration rate of 380 per 100,000.[6] Minnesota had 5.1 million residents, a crime rate of 3,381 offenses per 100,000 population, and an incarceration rate of only 180 per 100,000 population. With similar population and crime rates, Wisconsin's incarceration rate was 2.1 times Minnesota's. What causes these disparities among states and their prison use? An interesting answer to this question was provided in 1993 by Bowers and Waltman. Their investigation of felony sentencing in the United States found that the preferences of the public weigh heavily on the sentencing of violent offenders. More recently, world leaders of the prison administrations of the 45 member countries of the Council of Europe concluded that levels of imprisonment are usually influenced more by political decisions than by levels of crime or rates of detection of crime. They also concluded that jurisdictions can choose to have high or low rates of imprisonment, and this choice is reflected in the sentencing patterns adopted by legislatures.[7]

State and Federal Inmates Held in Privately Operated Facilities

The issue of correctional privatization, including the pros and cons of building and operating private prisons, is discussed in depth in Chapter 13. The focus here is on the current use of privately operated correctional facilities.

On January 1, 2006, 33 states and the federal system held 107,447 prisoners in 264 privately operated prisons, up from 16,663 inmates in 110 private prisons in 1995.[8] (Seventeen states have no private prisons.)

Private facilities held 6.0 percent (80,401) of all state prisoners and 14.4 percent (27,046) of all federal inmates. The federal system (27,046), Texas (17,517), Florida (6,261), Oklahoma (5,908), and Tennessee (5,162) reported the largest number of inmates in private facilities on January 1, 2006. Five states—Alaska, Hawaii, Montana, New Mexico, Oklahoma, and Wyoming—held at least 25 percent of their prisoner population in private facilities.

The use of private prisons is concentrated in southern and western states. Overall, 8.5 percent of state inmates in the South and 7.2 percent of inmates in the West were in privately operated correctional facilities, compared to 2.1 percent in the Northeast and 1.2 percent in the Midwest.

State and Federal Inmates Held in Local Jails

On January 1, 2006, 35 states and the federal system housed 5 percent (73,097) of their prisoner populations in local jails. For many jurisdictions, housing state and federal inmates contributes to the problem of jail crowding discussed in Chapter 6. By region, most state and federal inmates are housed in jails in the South (10.0 percent), followed by the West (2.1 percent), and in the Northeast and Midwest both had 1.2 percent of their state prisoners in local jails.

Gender

Women represent the fastest-growing population in correctional facilities. Over the past decade, the number of women in prison has grown from 68,468 (in 1995) to 107,518 (in 2006), an increase of 57 percent.

COMMISSION ON SAFETY AND ABUSE IN AMERICA'S PRISONS: PREVENTING VIOLENCE

" *If you put poor, underprivileged young men together in a large institution without anything meaningful to do all day, there will be violence. If that institution is overcrowded, there will be more violence. If that institution is badly managed . . . [including] poor mental health care, there will be more violence. And if there is inadequate supervision of the staff, if there is ineffective discipline, if there is a code of silence, if there are inadequate investigations, there will be even more violence.* "

—Donald Specter, Director of the Prison Law Office in California, summarizing the driving factors of violence in his testimony to the Commission.

The ability of a correctional facility to protect prisoners and staff from physical harm is a fundamental measure of the success or failure of that institution. Corrections administrators do not want to run violent facilities. When individuals under their care are seriously hurt, administrators are likely to experience those breaches in safety as personal and professional failures. Emotions run high because lives, careers, and reputations are at stake, and because assessing levels of violence in America's prisons and jails is a very difficult thing to do.

Jack Beck, an attorney and director of the Prison Visiting Project at the Correctional Association of New York, told the commission that the lowest levels of tension and violence seem to exist in facilities where staff clearly follow policies, where there is meaningful communication between prisoners and staff, and where prisoners feel respected. All of these qualities flow from good leadership.

Witness after witness told the commission that violence in prisons and jails is not inevitable. Donald Specter, director of the Prison Law Office in California, told the commission, "Prisons don't have to be as dangerous and as violent as they are. The culture of our prisons virtually dictates the level of violence that you will have in them. And if you change that culture, you will reduce the violence."

The following six recommendations focus on preventing violence in America's prisons and jails:

Reduce Crowding
States and localities must commit to eliminating the crowded conditions that exist in many of the country's prisons and jails and work with corrections administrators to set and meet reasonable limits on the number of prisoners that facilities can safely house.

Promote Productivity and Rehabilitation
Invest in programs that are proven to reduce violence and to change behavior over the long term.

Use Objective Classification and Direct Supervision
Incorporate violence prevention in every facility's fundamental classification and supervision procedures.

Use Force, Nonlethal Weaponry, and Restraints Only as a Last Resort
Dramatically reduce the use of nonlethal weapons, restraints, and physical force by using nonforceful responses whenever possible, restricting the use of weaponry to qualified staff, and eliminating the use of restraints except when necessary to prevent serious injury to self or others.

Employ Surveillance Technology
Make good use of recording surveillance cameras to monitor the correctional environment.

Support Community and Family Bonds
Reexamine where prisons are located and where prisoners are assigned, encourage visitation, and implement home call reform.

Source: Adapted from the Commission on Safety and Abuse in America's Prisons, *Confronting Confinement* (New York: Vera Institute of Justice, 2006).
Note: The full 126-page report, *Confronting Confinement: A Report of the Commission on Safety and Abuse in America's Prisons,* can be accessed on the Internet at www.prisoncommission.org.

On January 1, 2006, 107,518 adult women were in prison, one-third in Texas, California, and federal prisons. Women represent the fastest-growing correctional population. Why do you think that's so?

On January 1, 2007, women prisoners constituted 7.0 percent of the U.S. prison population (see Exhibit 7–4).

The rate of incarceration for women was 65 per 100,000 female residents, compared with 929 men per 100,000 male residents. On January 1, 2006, California, Texas, and the federal system held more than a third of all female inmates. See Exhibit 7–2 for the jurisdictions with the highest and lowest female prison populations.

According to Beth Richie, a professor of criminal justice and women's studies at the University of Illinois at Chicago, the racial/ethnic profile of women in prison represents one of the most vivid examples of racial disparity in the United States.[9] The majority of women in prison are women of color. Two-thirds are black, Hispanic, or of other nonwhite ethnic groups. They are also young and poor. Only one-third graduated from high school or earned a GED. Two-thirds have a history of physical or sexual abuse, and 3.5 percent are HIV positive. The most recent BJS estimate of the lifetime chance of being sent to prison at least once shows that about 5 of 1,000 white women, 36 of 1,000 black women and 15 of 1,000 Hispanic women will be incarcerated during their lifetime.[10] And sadly, the corrections literature suggests that, despite the fact that some women do quite well putting their lives back together when they are released from prison, most are likely to return to the same disenfranchised neighborhoods and difficult situations without having received any services to address their underlying problems. If it is true, as the corrections literature suggests, that prior arrest history predicts postprison recidivism, then the outlook for women prisoners is bleak: 65 percent of women in prison have a history of prior convictions. One-half have three or more convictions.

Scholars debate the reasons for the increase in women's incarceration over men's. Some suggest that, as women moved into jobs from which they were formerly excluded, they gained the opportunities and skills to commit criminal acts for which incarceration was appropriate punishment. Others disagree, saying that poverty of young, female, single heads

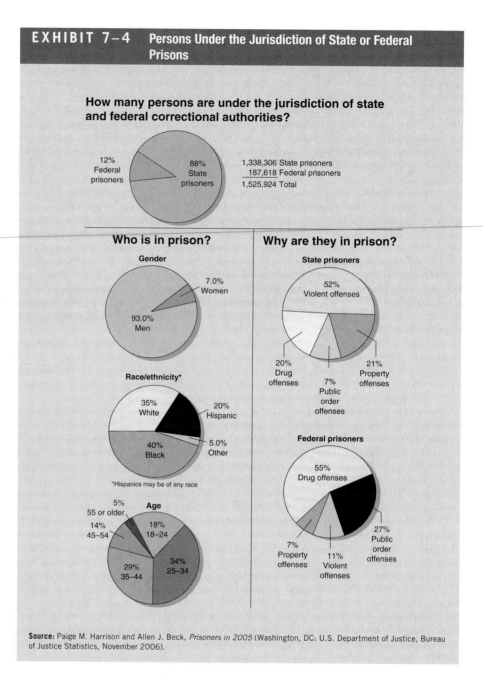

EXHIBIT 7–4   Persons Under the Jurisdiction of State or Federal Prisons

How many persons are under the jurisdiction of state and federal correctional authorities?

12% Federal prisoners

88% State prisoners

1,338,306 State prisoners
187,618 Federal prisoners
1,525,924 Total

Who is in prison?

Gender

7.0% Women

93.0% Men

Race/ethnicity*

35% White

20% Hispanic

40% Black

5.0% Other

*Hispanics may be of any race

Age

5% 55 or older

14% 45–54

18% 18–24

29% 35–44

34% 25–34

Why are they in prison?

State prisoners

52% Violent offenses

20% Drug offenses

7% Public order offenses

21% Property offenses

Federal prisoners

55% Drug offenses

7% Property offenses

11% Violent offenses

27% Public order offenses

Source: Paige M. Harrison and Allen J. Beck, *Prisoners in 2005* (Washington, DC: U.S. Department of Justice, Bureau of Justice Statistics, November 2006).

of households has contributed to the increase in women's crime and incarceration, particularly for property and drug offenses. One scholar put it this way: "The war on drugs has translated into a war on women."[11] Others think the criminal justice system is becoming more "gender blind" due to the emergence of "get tough" attitudes and sentencing policies. Instead of seeing women offenders as weaker and giving them differential, if not preferential, treatment, judges and juries now sentence women more harshly whether they are first-time drug offenders or they have committed crimes against persons or property. The combined effects of harsh drug laws, changing patterns of drug use, and mandatory sentencing policies have lead to a significant increase in women's incarceration. Almost one-third of sentenced women prisoners are serving time for nonviolent, drug-related offenses. Quite likely, the reason for the increase in women's incarceration is a product of all these theories. Whatever the reason, 1.5 million children have mothers under correctional supervision.[12] The majority of these children range between the ages of 1 and 10.[13] In Chapter 10 we will discuss the characteristics of female prisoners and the issues they face.

Race

The primary observation to be made about the prison population in the United States is that minorities are strikingly overrepresented. Although they comprise about 20 percent of the U.S. population, they make up 65 percent of all incarcerated offenders. Conversely, whites are underrepresented: over 80 percent of the general population but only 35 percent of the prison population. More black males and females are in prison than white or Hispanic males and females.

When incarceration rates are estimated separately by age groups, black males in their 20s and 30s have high rates relative to other groups. Expressed in terms of percentages, 8.1 percent of black non-Hispanic males age 25 to 29 were in prison on January 1, 2006, compared to almost 2.6 percent of Hispanic males and about 1.1 percent of white males in the same age group. For black male high school dropouts, the numbers are still worse: 41 percent between the ages of 22 and 30 are locked up.

Female incarceration rates reveal similar racial and ethnic disparities. Black non-Hispanic females were more than twice as likely as Hispanic females and over three times more likely than white non-Hispanic females to have been in prison on January 1, 2006.

As is the case with so many other criminological controversies, there is a debate over the relationship between race and crime. Official crime data indicate that minority group members are involved in a disproportionate share of criminal activity, which results in their greater rates of punishment. According to the FBI's *Crime in the United States 2006*, blacks account for about 12 percent of the U.S. population, yet they account for 41.5 percent of violent crime arrests (murder, rape, robbery, and assault)

The number of state, federal, and private prisons in the United States is 1,668. Minorities make up almost two-thirds of the prison population. Why is that so?

and 32 percent of property crime arrests (burglary, arson, theft, and motor vehicle theft). The offense with the highest number of black arrestes in 2006 was drug abuse violations (483,886).[14] Others argue that the higher arrest rates, convictions, and sentences to prison of blacks are a function of racial profiling and racism in the criminal justice system. Still others blame faulty data collection. Some argue that although discriminatory practices exist, it is improbable that criminal justice bias alone could account for the disproportionate arrest rates of blacks. They suggest the social problems of unemployment, economic deprivation, social disorganization, and social isolation of the nation's inner cities as additional causes. The inner city, the residence of most of the nation's poor, experiences by far the highest violence rates. Middle-class communities have more resources to deal with offenders, especially drug offenders, and get them into treatment. In low-income communities, those resources are not available so a drug problem is more likely to develop into a criminal justice problem. In 1998, the Department of Health and Human Services showed that black drug users are more likely to be arrested and incarcerated than white drug users: Blacks represent about 35 percent of people arrested for drug offenses and 50 percent of drug convictions.[15] These high rates may be a function of the fact that, on any given day, one of every three black males ages 20 to 29 is under the supervision of the criminal justice system—either in prison or jail or on probation or parole—making it likely that their drug use will be discovered by authorities.

Age

The nation's population is aging, and this is reflected in the prison population. Middle-aged inmates make up a growing portion of the prison population. In 1995, 57 percent of the nation's prisoners were between 18 and 34 years old, and 29 percent were between 35 and 44. In 2006, the representation of 18- to 34-year-olds had decreased to almost 52 percent and the presence of 35- to 44-year-olds held steady at 29 percent. The presence of inmates 55 and older increased from 3 to 5 percent (see Exhibit 7–4). In Chapter 12, we'll discuss older prisoners in more detail.

Most Serious Offense

Another characteristic to compare is the most serious offense of which a prisoner was convicted. On January 1, 2006, 52 percent of state prisoners were held for violent offenses, up from 46 percent in 1995. The percentage of state prisoners held for property offenses dropped from 23 percent in 1995 to 21 percent in 2006, and the percentage held for drug offenses dropped from 22 to 20 percent across the same time period. Still, the number of inmates doing time for drug violations in state and federal prison is triple what it was a decade ago. Convictions for public order offenses decreased from 9 to 7 percent across the same period.

Among federal inmates, persons sentenced for drug offenses constituted the largest group (55 percent) on January 1, 2006, similar to what it was in 1995. Immigration, weapon, and other public-order offenders made up approximately 27 percent of the federal prison population at the beginning of 2006, up from 18 percent in 1995. The percentage of violent offenders in federal prison in 2006 was 11 percent, similar to what it was in 1995. And property offenders constituted 7 percent in 2006, paralleling what it was in 1995 (see Exhibit 7–4).

PROGRAMS FOR PRISONERS

Among the most important elements of an inmate's institutional experience, whether in federal or state prison, are the programs and services available. Today there is evidence-based research supporting the success rates against recidivism for correctional programs and services in education (academic and vocational), drug and alcohol, mental health, anger management, faith-based interventions, job readiness, and other programs. Some programs and services such as recreation and personal wellness do not directly indicate a reduction in recidivism, but, as you will read later in this chapter, experts tell us that personal wellness and recreation are vehicles to promote health and prevent disease, a goal for all of us.

But what does success mean? According to one of the best reviews of the current evidence of the effectiveness of adult correctional programming by Aos and his colleagues at the Washington State Institute for Public Policy, it means reducing recidivism by 5 to 15 percent.[16] Chapter 12 discusses special prison populations. There we discuss programs for inmates who are drug offenders and mentally ill.

CLASSIFICATION

Researchers with the Pennsylvania Department of Corrections use the following analogy to make the point that criminal justice agencies often attempt to determine what is wrong with offenders by relying on subjective assessments of offenders' likelihood of reoffending:

> Imagine that a couple goes to the grocery store, fills a cart with their desired items, walks to the checkout lane, and the clerk simply eyeballs their selections and says, "looks like about $200 worth to me." They probably would not be too happy with this approach. Of course, if they felt it was an under estimate, they might be willing to let it go, but most people would expect a more systematic means of tallying the bill. Indeed, the widespread use of bar-code scanners is yet the latest attempt to take human error out of the cashier process.[17]

The analogy demonstrates the importance of classification, the principal management tool for allocating scarce prison resources efficiently and minimizing the potential for escape or violence. Prisoner **classification** is the process of subdividing the inmate population into meaningful categories to match offender needs with correctional resources. As prisons become more crowded, classification decisions play a significant role. Because classification lies at the heart of inmate programming, we emphasize it here.

Classification is based on the premise that there are wide differences among prisoners. Its purpose is to assign inmates to appropriate prison housing and to help staff understand, treat, predict, and manage prisoner behavior. Prior to the 19th century, when most prisons were privately operated (a topic we return to in Chapter 13), a detainee's financial condition determined his or her classification. For example, until the early 19th century the keeper at Newgate prison (England) was allowed to collect fees for reception, discharge, supervision, and accommodation (single vs. multiple occupancy cells).[18] It wasn't until 1832 that Newgate offenders were separated by age and offense severity.

One hundred years ago, the Elmira Reformatory in Elmira, New York, classified offenders as "specimens" and labeled them either "Mathemati-

classification

The process of subdividing the inmate population into meaningful categories to match offender needs with correctional resources.

EXHIBIT 7–5   **American Correctional Association**

Public Correctional Policy on Classification

Introduction

Proper classification of offenders promotes public, staff, and offender safety. It is a continuing process basic to identifying and matching offender needs to correctional resources. Classification also serves as a tool for identifying gaps in correctional services. This continuing process involves all phases of correctional management.

Policy Statement

Classification should balance the public's need for protection, the needs of offenders, and the efficient and effective operation of the correctional system. In developing and administering its classification system, a correctional agency should:

- A. develop written classification policies that establish criteria specifying different levels of security, supervision, and program involvement; establish procedures for documenting and reviewing all classification decisions and actions; describe the appeal process to be used by individuals subject to classification; and specify the time frames for monitoring and reclassifying cases;
- B. develop the appropriate range of resources and services to meet the identified control and program needs of the population served;
- C. base classification decisions on rational assessment of objective and valid information, including background material (criminal history, nature of offense, social history, educational needs, medical/mental health needs, etc.), as well as information regarding the individual's current situation, adjustment, and program achievement;
- D. train all personnel in the classification process and require specialized training for those directly involved in classification functions;
- E. use the classification process to assign individuals to different levels of control on the basis of valid criteria regarding risk (to self and others) and individual needs, matching these characteristics with appropriate security, level of supervision, and program services;
- F. involve the individual directly in the classification process;
- G. assign appropriately trained staff to monitor individual classification plans for progress made and reclassification needs;
- H. objectively validate the classification process and instruments, assess on a planned basis the degree to which results meet written goals, and, as needed, refine the process and instruments; and
- I. provide for regular dissemination of classification information to all levels of correctional staff and involve decision-makers outside of corrections as aids in the planning, management, and operation of the correctional agency.

Source: Copyright (c) American Correctional Association.

---

cal Dullards," "Those Deficient in Self-Control," or "Stupid."[19] Today, the classifications are more sophisticated. The belief is that "somewhere between the extremes of 'all offenders are alike' and 'each offender is unique' lies a system (or systems) of categorization along pertinent dimensions that will prove to be of value in reaching correctional goals."[20]

The American Correctional Association believes that classification is one of the most important features of an effective correctional treatment system. ACA's policy statement on classification is presented in Exhibit 7–5. What does ACA recommend a correctional agency do to balance the public's need for protection, the needs of offenders, and the efficient and effective operation of the correctional system?

Types of Classification   There are two types of prisoner classification: external and internal. **External classification** determines an inmate's security level (maximum, close, medium, minimum, or community) for *interinstitutional* placement. For example, maximum-security inmates are placed in a maximum-security facility. External classification answers the question "Where should I put this inmate?"

external classification

Interinstitutional placement of an inmate that determines an inmate's security level.

Internal classification is *intrainstitutional* placement. Once an inmate arrives at the institution, she or he undergoes a classification review. Classification staff review an inmate's behavior, personality, educational, chemical dependency, medical, and mental health needs. Staff then assign inmates to housing units or cellblocks, work, and programming based on their risk, needs, and time to serve. The Pennsylvania Department of Corrections develops a unique correctional plan for each prisoner that identifies problem areas and treatment needs to be addressed by the prisoner during incarceration (see Exhibit 7–6). In approximately two-thirds of the states, the processes of internal and external classification are done at the same time.[21] Classification staff recommend both an inmate's security level and housing assignments and programming. The remaining states defer internal classification to the facility to which the prisoner is transferred.

A survey by the National Council on Crime and Delinquency (NCCD) found that only nine states had a formal internal classification system that used structured scoring instruments, staff specialists who were formally trained to use them, and a reclassification process to update previously classified prisoners.[22] NCCD found that some kind of internal classification process exists in all prison systems to assign newly arrived inmates to housing units, work assignments, and programs, but these processes are usually informal and rely on subjective criteria. Most (86 percent) state correctional agencies use the same classification assessment criteria for both males and females.[23] However, a few states—including Idaho, Massachusetts, New York, and Ohio—have developed gender-specific classification instruments that acknowledge that the nature and extent of women's criminal behavior and the ways in which they respond to supervision and incarceration makes a difference.

Three of the best-known systems of internal classification are the Adult Internal Management System (AIMS), the Prisoner (or Client) Management Classification (PMC) system, and behavior-based systems (BBSs). AIMS is used by several facilities in the federal BOP and a number of state departments of corrections including Missouri, Ohio, South Dakota, and Washington. Its purpose is to reduce institutional predatory behavior by identifying inmates who are likely to be incompatible in terms of housing and inmates who are most likely to pose a risk to the safe and secure operation of a facility. AIMS uses personality checklists that are designed to determine an inmate's ability to be housed successfully with other inmates. Based on these scores, inmates are classified into one of five groups. Alpha I and Alpha II inmates are characterized as offenders most likely to be a threat to the safety and security of the facility. They are characterized as predators. Sigma I and Sigma II inmates are unlikely to be assaultive, but they pose other management problems, such as disregarding direct orders and disrupting the orderly operation of the institution. They are characterized as inmates at risk of being victimized. Kappa inmates are least likely to present management problems. They are neither predators nor prey.

PMC uses a semistructured attitudinal interview to assist staff in identifying potential predators and victims and those inmates who require special programs or supervision. The attitudinal items tap the inmate's attitude regarding the current offense; criminal history; family relationships; relationships with staff, inmates, and peers; and plans after release. In addition, other items assess the inmate's social status and demeanor during the interview. Based on these scores, inmates are classified into one of four groups: Limited Setting (LS) and Casework Control (CC) inmates

internal classification

Intrainstitutional placement that determines, through review of an inmate's background, assignment to housing units or cellblocks, work, and programming based on the inmate's risk, needs, and time to serve.

EXHIBIT 7–6   Pennsylvania's Prisoner Intake Process

The Intake Process

The PA DOC intake process is designed to be completed in 2 weeks, as shown in the table. However, it can take up to 4 to 6 weeks to establish medical, mental health, initial custody, and programming requirements for the prisoners.

Identifying the Prisoner

During day 1, the prisoner's identification is verified and he/she is strip searched, photographed, and fingerprinted; court documents are reviewed; and the prisoner's property is inventoried. Each prisoner bathes and receives baseline drug tests for illicit substances and medical and mental health screens. Additionally, the prisoner is interviewed by custody staff to identify potential security threat group membership and by a counselor to determine the need for separating the prisoner from other prisoners or staff members. Each prisoner also is issued a prisoner handbook in English, Spanish, or Braille. At the end of the first day, the prisoner has been identified, assigned to a cell, and has received institutional clothing and toiletries.

On day 2, a counselor provides formal orientation during which basic institutional rules and procedures are explained.

During the next 7 business days, the prisoner receives a full medical examination and takes a series of academic achievement, psychological, and substance abuse tests. As indicated by the results from the written tests, the psychologist and drug and alcohol treatment specialist conducts clinical interviews with the prisoner. In addition, the medical staff interview the prisoner about his/her medical history. DNA samples are collected from prisoners convicted of murder, stalking, and/or a sex-related offense. By the end of the 10th day at the intake center, prisoners have medical, mental health, education, and substance abuse ratings that indicate their level of need for services and/or treatment. These ratings are forwarded to classification staff for custody, facility, work, and programming assignments.

Classification

Classification staff use PACT [Pennsylvania Assessment and Classification Tool]—a fully automated classification system that synthesizes data collected throughout the intake process to establish an prisoner's custody level and to recommend housing, work detail, treatment, and programming assignments—to classify and assess the needs of prisoners. They also develop electronically a classification summary . . . that is used by staff at the long-term facility to plan with the prisoner his/her institutional program and work assignments. The facility placement recommendation considers the prisoner's custody level, separation and regionalization issues, program needs, and bedspace availability. Because PACT and the classification summary are automated, the counselor simply reviews the preliminary custody assessment, annotates any applicable administrative or discretionary overrides, recommends a preliminary custody level, and generates a form for recording the custody assessment and facility placement recommendations and decisions.

Initial Classification

Classification staff use PACT to determine the prisoner's custody level and facility placement. The initial custody level is based on seven discrete items: severity of current offense, severity of criminal history, escape history, institutional adjustment, number of prior institutional commitments, time to expected release, and stability factors (e.g., current age, marital status, and employment at arrest). A facility placement recommendation also is made during the initial classification process. It addresses custody, program, medical, and mental health needs; case management/case planning; and other specific prisoner or institution needs (e.g., electrician, maintenance technician, plumber).

Administrative overrides—based on the prisoner's legal status, current offense, and sentence—can change classification recommendations. Discretionary overrides by the case manager are permitted based on the prisoner's security threat group affiliation; escape history; nature of current offense; and behavior, mental health, medical, dental, and program needs. Information about cases for which discretionary overrides are recommended is forwarded electronically to the appropriate staff for approval. Multiple levels of review by classification supervisory staff and the central office are required for all overrides.

Reclassification

The reclassification process parallels the initial classification process. Regularly scheduled custody reassessments are conducted as part of the prisoner's annual review. Reassessments are also conducted following major misconduct reports and select minor violations, significant changes in the prisoner's program needs, time credits, escape time, sentence continuations, detainers, prerelease applications, unusual incident reports, transfer requests, and as needed to ensure the safety and security of the facility.

Reclassification is based on the severity of current offense, severity of criminal history, escape history, history of institutional violence, number and severity of misconduct reports during the previous 18 months, current age, program participation, work performance, and housing performance. As with the initial classification, these items are tallied on the PACT to create the total score. Again, mandatory and discretionary override factors are considered and reviewed.

EXHIBIT 7–6   Pennsylvania's Prisoner Intake Process (*continued*)

Overview of Pennsylvania's Prisoner Intake Process

Tasks	Conducted	Who Is Tested?	Personnel Responsible for Task	Instrument(s) and/or Process(es) Used
DAY 1				
Identification	Yes; mandatory	All prisoners	Records staff	Court orders, AFIS, and LiveScan
Medical screen within 24 hours	Yes; mandatory	All prisoners	Health care staff	Medical screen
Mental health screen	Yes; mandatory	All prisoners	Intake office and mental health staff	Mental health screen
Drug testing	Yes; mandatory	All prisoners	Health care	Urine test
Prisoner separation	Yes; mandatory	All prisoners	Security staff and counselors	Interview and court documents
Gang membership	Yes; mandatory	All prisoners		Tattoos, criminal and institutional records, and interview
DAYS 2–10				
Academic achievement	Yes; mandatory	All prisoners	Education staff	TABE and WRAT
IQ tests	Yes; mandatory	All prisoners	Psychology staff	Beta III and WAIS
Vocational aptitude	No; not required			
Substance abuse	Yes; mandatory	All prisoners	Drug treatment staff	TCUDDS
Psychological	Yes; mandatory	All prisoners	Psychology staff	PAI, GBA, and clinical interview
Physical exam	Yes; mandatory	All prisoners	Health care staff	Physical exam, blood work, and interview
DNA testing	Yes; not required	Prisoners convicted of murder, stalking, and/or a sex-related crime	Lab technicians	Blood work
DAYS 11–15				
Criminal history	Yes; mandatory	All prisoners	Records staff	NCIC, presentence investigation, DOC MIS, and court orders
Social history	Yes; mandatory	All prisoners	Classification staff	Interview and presentence investigation
Institutional adjustment	Yes; mandatory	All prisoners	Classification staff	Jail documents and DOC MIS
Custody level	Yes; mandatory	All prisoners	Classification staff	PACT
Internal classification	Yes; mandatory	All prisoners	Classification staff	Custody and needs assessments
Security level/facility	Yes; mandatory	All prisoners	Classification staff	PACT
Prisoner separation	Yes; mandatory	All prisoners	Classification and security staff	Self-reports and court documents
Victim notification	Yes; not required	Only prisoners with a victim	District attorney's office	Offense type

Source: Adapted from Patricia L. Hardyman, James Austin, and Johnette Peyton, *Prisoner Intake Systems: Assessing Needs and Classifying Prisoners* (Washington, DC: U.S. Department of Justice, National Institute of Corrections, February, 2004).

THE STAFF SPEAKS

PRIDE Enterprises is an internationally recognized general manufacturing and services company. A private, not-for-profit corporation founded in 1981, PRIDE Enterprises has experience and expertise in working in a secure prison environment providing on-the-job training, job placement, and support for ex-offenders to help them successfully transition back into society after a period of incarceration. PRIDE operates 38 diverse industries in 22 correctional institutions throughout Florida. It has received national and international attention as a model for public/private partnerships, especially regarding the privatization of government functions.

PRIDE consists of 200 employees and 2,000 inmate workers, and its products and services yield annual sales of over $60 million. The state has not provided any funds to the corporation, and since its inception PRIDE has contributed over $121 million to the State of Florida in cash, inmate wages, investment in state property, victim restitution, and job training, placement, and support services.

PRIDE's customer base is divided between state government (55%), nonstate government (22%), and private sector (23%).

Current production ranges from simple assembly to full-scale manufacturing in digital technology, custom design and production, industrial manufacturing, construction and assembly, retrofitting and refurbishing, and distribution and fulfillment.

Now in its 23rd year, PRIDE is encouraged by the current national focus on the potential of inmate workers to become an asset to America's economy.

Pamela J. Davis
President and CEO
PRIDE Enterprises of Florida
www.peol.com

---

are expected to be more aggressive and harder to control. Selective Intervention (SI) and Environmental Structure (ES) inmates are characterized as needing minimal supervision and requiring separation from LS and CC inmates. Once inmates are classified, detailed guidelines provide staff with management techniques for handling prisoners and programming approaches for inmates assigned to their designated housing units.

BBSs assess inmates according to behavioral measures as reflected by disciplinary records and work performance, in contrast to personality and attitude scales. Florida, Illinois, New Jersey, and Oregon use BBSs. Inmates are scored according to their level of aggression, which is determined by the severity and frequency of institutional misconduct and gang-related activities. Staff who use a BBS conduct a historical assessment of the inmate to achieve an understanding of an inmate's potential behavior. Staff review a host of factors such as type of disciplinary incidents, days spent in segregation, time remaining to serve, external custody level, and needs assessment. The factors are scored and placed into grids that identify the inmate's housing type, potential cellmates, and treatment and program needs.

Florida's BBS uses a system of five risk scores. Score 5 characterizes the most hostile, violent, and aggressive inmates with the potential for a high rate of disciplinary problems, fights, assaults, threats of bodily harm, and destruction of property. Score 1 means inmates are least likely to be involved with fights or assaults within prison. They have a low rate of disciplinary reports. New Jersey uses three behavioral classification systems. Highly aggressive inmates are those with a recent institutional history of aggressive, violent, or confrontational behavior. They are characterized as predators and visible agitators. Moderately aggressive inmates have less severe recent histories of violent or aggressive institutional conduct and behavior that would not threaten their potential return to society. Inmates classified as having low aggression have very limited or nonexistent histories of aggressive institutional misconduct. Often they are older and serve their sentences quietly.

My Incarceration

No one other than one who has been incarcerated can really identify with what this is like. Even those who are charged with the responsibility of keeping us on this side of the fence cannot really feel what we feel.

Because good social norms of society are missing elements in the prison setting, how can one expect antisocial behaviors to change? Incarceration forces a man to redefine what is normal. So naturally you will find us gravitating to that which we can best relate to. This can be on a peer level, a racial level, a spiritual level, or a level where we use gambling, sex, drugs, alcohol, food, television, and so on, as a way of coping. Some of us consciously use these devices to escape from reality or replace some missing aspect of our being. Others lack the cognitive ability to understand these dynamics and fall prey to the prison mentality. Thus you have a large number of offenders who, once they get out of the system, find themselves not equipped or in some cases less equipped to be productive members of society. My awareness of the so-called prison mentality can be attributed only to my relationship with my lord and savior Jesus Christ.

My Offense and Punishment

My crime is capital murder. I was sentenced to Life Without the Possibility of Parole. In other words, I was given a living death sentence. It would've been real easy for me to adapt to the prison culture and mentality if the opportunity for positive endeavors had not become available. To be honest, for a short time I did take part in the prison gambling industry. In my mind, this was the lesser of the many evils associated with prison life. I was only lying to myself. There are

so many variables to the gambling industry in prison. In some cases it could mean your life.

What the Faith-Based Restorative Justice Dorm Has Meant to Me

This brings me to October of '98, when the DOC was ordered by the prison commissioner to open up honor dorms at all its facilities. That month I made the decision to apply for the honor dorm. At the time, I wanted only to be a part of something positive. I also made a promise to my mother, shortly after coming to prison, that I would not do anything to make her cry again, as long as I could help it. So to begin with the honor dorm gave me the opportunity and the environment to keep the promise I made to my mother.

The Impact on My Life

The restorative justice community, where the definition of respect, problem solving, and normal behavior more closely emulate that in society, has been a good foundation for me to begin the work of earning my way back into society. It may be hard for those who have never been incarcerated to understand the culture and mentality of the prison environment. If one could put aside the media's portrayal of prison life, they could see that there are good things happening behind these walls. One of the most effective programs that I've had an opportunity to be a part of is the *Faith-Based Restorative Justice Honor Dorm.* The *"faith-based"* aspect of the dorm promotes and encourages spirituality both structured and nonstructured, which allows even the nonbeliever to have the opportunity of exposure to God's word and believers to practice their faith communally or individually. The dorm's guiding philosophy, *restor-*

ative justice, allows an offender to begin the work of understanding how his crime has affected the person or persons and his community that were directly harmed by his crime. For me personally, this area of focus in the dorm has helped me become an advocate for victims' rights. Coming from an offender's point of view this may seem strange, but to me, it is only a natural outcome of restorative justice. I truly am sorry for the pain I've caused those who were affected by my crime. Believe me when I say that this approach does make a difference to offenders' accountability, responsibility, and ownership of crime. I know because it has made a difference in my life. Our restorative justice community provides the physical environment that allows men to begin the work of living a life reflective of how one wants to be perceived by society. Through its class curriculums, our restorative justice community gives men the tools that are needed to be productive members in their current community and future communities outside these walls when released.

Prospects for the Future

I have seen how this restorative justice subcommunity has influenced the general population over the past five years. I envision a future where the prison mentality will be a reflection of the Faith-Based Restorative Justice community philosophy. I envision a future where positive behavior is promoted as opposed to deviant behaviors. I envision a spiritually based restorative healing mission, in an environment conducive for these concepts to be practiced, which eventually spreads throughout the entire prison.

Tony Joyce

Classification of incoming inmates is based on many factors, including medical and health care needs, custody needs, institutional risk, work skills, and educational needs. Classification serves the custody goals of a prison but tends to label prisoners. Is such labeling appropriate?

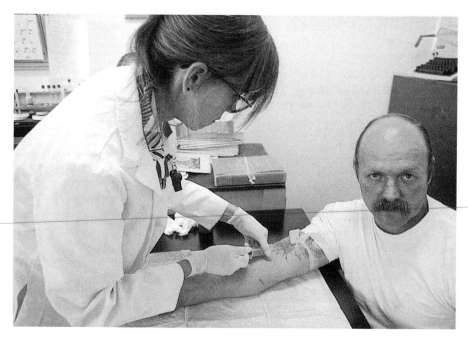

Advantages of Classification Good internal classification systems offer a number of advantages. First, separating inmates by risk level and program needs puts extremely aggressive inmates in high security, while those who require less or are at risk of being victimized are kept in low security. Within those levels of security, prisoners' needs may also be considered. Does the facility offer drug and alcohol treatment? Sex offender treatment? Anger management training? GED preparation? Such classification offers prisoners a chance for counseling, education, or vocational training, and it may keep aggressive inmates from assaulting passive inmates.

Second, a good classification system minimizes misclassification, thus promoting a safe environment for inmates and staff. When prisons are over capacity, as they are today, staff feel pressure to classify inmates quickly, which often results in misclassification. A good classification system will include safeguards against misclassification. For example, when there is not enough space in maximum-security facilities, a good system will direct staff to house only the lowest-risk high-security inmates in medium-security facilities.

Third, a good classification system more accurately places inmates and more effectively deploys staff. Without good classification, the tendency is to place inmates in more secure, more expensive prisons than necessary. Good classification controls the inmate population, assigns inmates to appropriate security levels, and better deploys staff.

Fourth, a good classification system enhances prison security by reducing tension in prison. Misclassification can jeopardize a prison's security and increase violence and escapes. A review of the major developments and trends in prisoner classification over a recent 20-year period found significant improvement in classification technology (e.g., computer software to help collect, store, and manage the data) and more sophisticated assessment of risk and of medical, mental health treatment, and education needs.[24]

Orientation to the Institution

While the process of internal classification is being conducted, state and federal prison systems provide inmates an orientation to the institution. For several weeks, as shown in Pennsylvania's prisoner intake process (Exhibit 7–6), inmates participate in an admission and orientation program. It provides an introduction to all aspects of the institution and includes screening by staff from the case management, medical, and mental health units. Inmates receive copies of the institution's rules and regulations, including the inmate discipline policy, and they are introduced to the programs, services, policies, and procedures of the facility. Increasingly prison systems such as the Louisiana State Penitentiary at Angola use inmates to orient new arrivals to prison life. According to some researchers, North Carolina conducts the most detailed orientation, which includes videos about the facility, prisoner responsibilities, and diseases as well as questionnaires about drug use, potential visitors, and family background.[25]

Unit Management and Faith-Based Honor Dorms and Prisons

Unit management is based on the idea that cooperation is most likely in small groups that have lengthy interactions.[26] A unit is a self-contained living area for 50 to 200 inmates that is managed semiautonomously within the larger institution. Third- and fourth-generation jails discussed in Chapter 6 are unit management systems.

In the federal system and in a number of states, prisons use a **unit management system**. The purpose of dividing prisons into functional units, each with its own permanently assigned staff and a unit manager who serves as a "mini warden," was largely to improve program delivery. Many units—drug treatment units, in particular—were established to focus on specific program needs. The unit team—typically composed of the unit manager, one or more case managers, two or more correctional counselors, and a unit secretary—is directly responsible for the inmates living in that unit. Unit staff receive input from other employees involved in an inmate's progress (such as work supervisors, teachers, and psychologists) and meet with the inmate on a regular basis to develop, review, and discuss the work assignments and programs the inmate should be involved in as well as any other needs or concerns.

Traditional correctional institutions make decisions through a centralized and hierarchical management structure, whereas unit management strives to decentralize decision making. When decisions are made at the unit level, they are made with better information and by staff who know the inmates better. Unit management gives inmates direct daily contact with the staff who make most of the decisions about their daily lives. It results in improved inmate access to staff and greater staff access to inmates, providing staff with an awareness of significant inmate concerns and potential problems. Unit management also means that not all units will be managed in the same way. Having different management methods is a strength because different inmates require different management approaches.

The success of unit management is affected by internal classification. Inmates who are assigned to a given institution are then assigned to a specific unit based on their risks and needs. After the processes of internal classification and initial orientation, each inmate meets with the unit team to formulate a program plan, which may include drug treatment,

unit management system
A method of controlling prisoners in self-contained living areas and making inmates and staff (unit manager, correctional counselor, and unit secretary) accessible to each other.

education, and vocational training as well as institution maintenance jobs or other work assignments. The unit team reviews the inmate's progress and makes changes in the program plan as needed. Unit management emphasizes candid, open communication between staff and inmates. Direct and frequent communication helps staff know inmates, understand their needs, and respond appropriately to those needs.

The principles of classification and unit management have produced another type of prison housing—*faith-based*—in which inmates volunteer to be housed in facilities that provide special activities and classes, religious and secular, aimed at character development and personal growth. The earliest example of faith-based prison housing can be traced to 1997 when Texas opened a rehabilitation tier of a religiously based program in one of its prison facilities.[27] In 2001, President Bush created the new White House Office of Faith-Based and Community Initiatives to focus solely on helping religious or faith-based groups compete with secular organizations for federal tax dollars to address the needs of offenders through faith-based assistance. Then in 2004 he renewed his pledge to support those efforts with $300 million in grant money available over four years for prisoner reentry initiatives, including those involving faith-based efforts. Today, nearly half of state and federal prison systems are operating or developing at least one residential faith-based program,[28] ranging from prisons and jails offering faith-based programs alone or in partnership with local agencies such as in Escambia County (Pensacola), Florida, where the sheriff's department partners with the Christian Counseling Center of Baptist Hospital's Pathways for Change Offender Reintegration Program, to one or more housing units within a prison that are faith-based, to entire prisons built around the faith-based concept, to faith-based parole and reentry initiatives.

Supporters of faith-based initiatives argue that such programs *may* reduce recidivism and improve other postrelease outcomes; are generally free or low cost because they are provided by volunteer groups (Mears cites the case in Oregon where faith volunteers contributed the equivalent of 121 full-time staff positions valued at roughly $4.5 million[29]); may improve in-prison behavior (such as more compliance with rules, participation in treatment, and physical and mental health among inmates); lessen the dehumanization of incarceration; and are unlikely to harm anyone.

On the other hand, opponents argue that faith-based programs may not be effective; may actually cost taxpayers; promote a religious orientation and hence may be unconstitutional as reported in a recent legal challenge to a taxpayer-supported prison program in Iowa run by Charles Colson's Prison Fellowship; may actually lessen offender accountability for their crimes; and may coerce some inmates into certain kinds of religious activity.

In spite of its growth, however, there have been few legal challenges to faith-based programming and only a few studies have examined its effectiveness. The few studies that have, Mears and O'Connor say, suffer from measurement problems, research design issues, and data collection and interpretation.[30] Both researchers concluded that it will be difficult to know the potential that faith-based services, lives, and interventions have to offer corrections until research improves.

Others tell us that faith-based programming in prison should not be contingent on the issue of program effectiveness for several reasons. "First, regardless of social science findings, prisoners have a right to express their religious views. . . . Second . . . the real outcome or purpose of religion in prison is not only to reduce anti-social behavior/criminal behavior or relapse into criminal activity, but also to counteract the tendency of prisons to dehumanize people and help prisoners prevent a further decline in their humanity. . . . Finally . . . [researchers] question whether we can accurately tap into the deeper religious dimensions of that person's motivations and thereby assess whether a particular individual has changed."[31]

On the legal front, in June 2006 federal judge Robert Pratt of the U.S. District Court for the Southern District of Iowa struck down a taxpayer-supported prison program in Iowa run by Charles Colson's Prison Fellowship. Judge Pratt said the Iowa program was unconstitutional since it was so intertwined with the state and funded in part by taxpayers. InnerChange Freedom Initiative operates the Newton Correctional Facility. It describes the program for inmates as "a revolutionary, Christ-centered, faith-based prison program supporting prison inmates through their spiritual and moral transformation." Judge Pratt ordered the program to shut down within 60 days and reimburse the state $1.53 million, but he stayed the order pending the expected appeals.

On June 25, 2007, the United States Supreme Court ruled in *Hein* v. *Freedom From Religion Foundation, Inc.* that taxpayers cannot challenge a White House initiative that promotes federal grants to religious charities. The Court said executive programming like President Bush's faith-based initiative, paid for with discretionary funds, are diffferent from specific programs funded by the legislature. This important ruling means that Presidents have a lot of power to spend discretionary money in favor of religion without any review by the courts.

Examples of faith-based housing units within a prison can be seen in the Offender Speaks boxes in this chapter and in Chapter 12. They were written by inmates living in a faith-based honors dorm at Alabama's Holman Correctional Facility, a maximum-security prison of 1,000 inmates, including 170 on death row. Approximately 150 inmates live in the prison's faith-based honors dorm. The dorm uses the principles of restorative justice, discussed in Chapter 3, and encourages and promotes both structured and unstructured opportunities for inmate spirituality as a foundation on which to build successful reentry initiatives.

From 1997 to 2001, Maryland converted seven inmate housing dormitories to honor dorms (each housing about 100 men) at the Maryland House of Correction (MHC), a maximum-security institution housing 1,200 inmates.[32] MHC administrators and staff isolated the violent, high-risk offenders in cell housing where their movements could be controlled at all times, thereby enabling honor dorm inmates to change their lifestyles and live out the rest of their sentences in a safe environment.

In order to be eligible for residence in an honor dorm, MHC inmates had to be infraction free for one year prior to being considered for transfer to an honor dorm. Inmates had to sign a contract promising that they would abide by the rules and have an assigned institutional job. Benefits of living in the honor dorm included an additional visit each month, additional phone time in the dorm, movies on weekends in the dorm (eliminating the need to go to the gym to view a film with hundreds of other inmates), and use of microwaves and coffee pots. According to MHC Warden James Peguese and Security Chief Robert Koppel, there was an immediate decrease in assaults on inmates (from 17 in 1997 to 6 in 2001), none on staff, and a substantial decrease in the amount of infractions committed by inmates assigned to both honor housing and cell housing.

Florida took the lead in December 2003 when it opened the country's first faith-based prison at the Lawley Correctional Institution. Lawley houses 780 male prisoners representing 30 religious denominations and faiths, as well as atheists and agnostics. Approximately 800 volunteers provide inmates access to prayer sessions, religious studies, choir practice, and religious counseling seven days a week in addition to courses in math, reading, personal integrity, mentoring, and anger and money management. Reverend William Wright, senior chaplain at Lawley, said, "I've seen faith change these men where nothing else really did." Instead of seeing grudges being settled in the prison yard, Wright said he regularly sees men walk away from fights, apologize to one another for using harsh words, and pray together.

In 2004, Florida converted the previously all-male Hillsborough Correctional Institution to the country's first faith and character correctional institution for women prisoners. The faith and character programs are aimed at facilitating inmate institutional adjustment, helping inmates assume personal responsibility, and preparing offenders for reentry and release into society. The program includes weekly worship opportunities, rituals and sacraments, religious education classes, religious holiday observation, revivals, support groups, crisis counseling, death notifications, bereavement counseling, marriage enrichment seminars, self-esteem seminars, anger management, mentoring, sacred text studies, chapel choir and library, cell to cell visitation, and literature distribution. Faith-based parole and reentry initiatives are discussed in the next chapter.

Today Florida has three faith-based prisons (two serving men and one for women), seven other prisons with faith-based/self-improvement dormitories, and in December 2006, a panel appointed by former Florida governor Jeb Bush recommended tripling the number of faith-based prisons within two years.

Daily Routine

A typical prison day begins with breakfast at 6:30 A.M. For inmates with prison jobs, work begins about 7:30 A.M. By this time, inmates are expected to have cleaned their personal living areas and made their beds. After work and the evening meal, inmates may participate in organized or individual recreation, watch television, or engage in personal hobbies. In most prisons, inmates must remain in their quarters after the 10 P.M. count. The weekend and holiday routines are somewhat more relaxed for all inmates.

Prisons regularly count inmates to ensure that all are where they are supposed to be. How often inmates are counted varies considerably. In some prisons, formal inmate counts are taken five times a day, including a morning count at 6, an afternoon count at 4, and three counts between 10 P.M. and morning. Informal counts may be conducted in program areas at various times during the day, to ensure that inmates are in the proper place. Emergency counts may be held at any time. On weekends and holidays, when routines are more relaxed, counts are still made.

After serving his four-month federal prison sentence in 2005, Baltimore Ravens running back Jamal Lewis described his daily prison routine to reporters: "I wasn't used to getting up early (4:30 A.M.) and having guards watching you every minute. And having to stand there three times a day and be counted. But you make the best of it."[33] Lewis held a job in the prison tool room, handing out equipment to work details. He told reporters that his worst problem in prison was the lack of privacy and that the thing he missed most during his incarceration was his freedom. "It's not about Jamal Lewis; it's not about the football player. You know you're just another number in the prison cell."

Work Assignments

Work is a very important part of institutional management and offender programs. Meaningful work programs are the most powerful tool prison administrators have in managing crowding and idleness, which can lead to disorder and violence. And now the news on prisoner work assignments is even better. The evidence-based reviews introduced in Chapter 1 and mentioned throughout the text show that the average prison industry program reduces the recidivism rate of participants by almost 6 percent. Some prison industries achieve better results, some worse. On average, however, researchers find that the typical prison industry can be expected to reduce recidivism by 6 percent.[34]

Prison work is generally of one of three types: operational assignments within the institution, community projects, or prison industry.

Operational Assignments   In operational assignments within the institution, inmates perform tasks necessary to the functioning of the facility or larger corrections system. Institutional maintenance assignments including farm and other agricultural activities are the largest single option for inmate work. Forty-five states, the District of Columbia, and the BOP pay inmates a wage for services rendered to the institution. The average wage range for institutional maintenance work is $0.99 to $3.98 per day. Inmates working in institutional maintenance perform the following types of work: laundry, heating and air conditioning repair, building maintenance and custodial service, landscaping and grounds maintenance, and food preparation and service.

Community Projects   Many correctional institutions allow inmates to gain work experience through community projects. Through community projects, offenders contribute their labor to benefit the community while developing job skills in a practical, nonprison setting. Community work usually takes the form of construction, landscaping, horticulture, and agriculture activities. Construction/repair of public property and parks development and maintenance are by far the most common types of community work activities. Examples of other community projects include building houses for low-income persons, painting municipal swimming pools, providing snow removal services, providing backup firefighting services, and delivering antidrug programs in schools. In South Carolina, inmates who meet the criteria for community work build playground equipment, pick up trash on state highways, maintain and clean up state parks, aid flood victims, clean up debris after storm damage, and provide skilled labor for Habitat for Humanity. Inmate work organizations also raise money for the Special Olympics and other charities.

State Prison Industries and the Prison Industry Enhancement Certification Program (PIECP)   PIECP allows private industry to establish joint ventures with state and local correctional agencies to produce goods using prison labor. PIECP exempts state and local certified departments of corrections from normal restrictions on the sale of prisoner-made goods in interstate commerce. In addition, the program lifts existing restrictions on these certified corrections departments, permitting them to sell prisoner-made goods to the federal government in amounts exceeding the $10,000 maximum normally imposed on such transactions. With the exception of PIECP programs, U.S. jail and prison inmates are prohibited by law from producing goods for sale in open markets based on the Ashurst-Summers Act of 1935.

Inmates at the Snake River Correctional Institution, Ontario, Oregon, make calls arranging business meetings for the consulting firm Perry Johnson. What are the benefits of prison industry for inmates, their families, and victims while in prison and after release, the institution, the business community, and taxpayers?

How much does the electorate support PIECP? Eighty-two percent of U.S. voters said that job training is very important for a person to reintegrate successfully into society after incarceration.[35] Their faith in prison industry programs is supported by the what-works literature introduced in Chapter 1. Of the 30 rigorous evaluations of prison industries examined by the Washington State Institute for Public Policy, an agency created by the state legislature to conduct research on policy issues, the studies showed an average 6 percent reduction in recidivism due to prison industry.

PIECP was created by Congress in 1979 to encourage states and units of local government to establish employment opportunities for prisoners that approximate private sector work opportunities. The program is designed to place inmates in a realistic working environment, pay them the local prevailing wage for similar work, and enable them to acquire marketable skills to increase their potential for successful rehabilitation and meaningful employment upon release. PIECP was first authorized under the Justice System Improvement Act of 1979, later expanded under the Justice Assistance Act of 1984, and made permanent under the Crime Control Act of 1990.

The PIE certification program has two primary objectives: First, to generate products and services that enable prisoners to make a contribution to society, help offset the cost of their incarceration, compensate crime victims, and provide inmate family support. And second, to provide a means of reducing prison idleness, increasing inmate job skills, and improving the prospects for successful inmate transition to the community upon release.

Currently, PIE certification programs operate in 37 states and 4 counties in the United States. These programs manage over 175 business partnerships with private industry.[36] By the end of 2005, 6,555 offenders were employed in the program. PIECP generated more than $34 million for victims' programs, $22 million for inmate family support, $101 million for correctional institution room and board costs, $48 million in state and federal taxes, and $14 million in mandatory inmate savings.[37]

In addition to PIE certification programs, there are hundreds of innovative prison industry programs across the United States. Inmates in

Maine, Mississippi, Nevada, Ohio, and Virginia train guide dogs to aid the visually impaired, hearing dogs to assist the deaf and hearing-impaired, and service dogs to assist individuals suffering from physical disabilities. Other Nevada inmates learn building construction, while still others learn to employ resistance-free training methods to tame and train wild horses in order to improve their adoptability. At the Louisiana State Penitentiary in Angola, a maximum-security prison, inmates built Prison View, a nine-hole golf course that is on prison property and open to the public. Although inmates cannot play, they learned landscape design, horticulture, and groundskeeping. And in Arizona, some inmates volunteer for a one-year-long rigorous Braille translation program certified by the Library of Congress. Other Arizona inmates learn to repair Braille machines.

One of the best-known prison industry programs operates at the Eastern Oregon Correctional Institution in Pendleton, Oregon, the famous mill town known for Pendleton fabrics. Here, prisoners make a line of T-shirts, jackets, and jeans known as Prison Blues®. Inside Oregon Enterprises owns the business. It operates a 47,000-square-foot factory on the prison grounds, a type of industrial park with bars. All 50 inmates working in the factory are paid prevailing industry wages, which range from a base of $7.80 to $9.58 per hour. They can also earn bonus incentives for quality and productivity.

What Impact Does PIECP Have? In June 2006, researchers at the University of Baltimore asked if PIECP inmates return to prison less frequently or enter more successful employment than inmates in traditional prison industries and those who did not work at all.[38] The researchers found that PIECP inmates became tax-paying citizens quicker and remained in that status longer than inmates who worked in traditional prison industries or not at all. Furthermore, 82 percent of PIECP inmates were not arrested in their first year following release, compared to 77 percent of inmates who worked in traditional prison industry jobs, and 76 percent of those who were not employed at all while in prison.

Although the results of the PIECP study are positive, they are not conclusive because participants in the three groups were not randomly assigned to groups. Prisoners volunteered to participate in the PIECP and traditional prison industries. Therefore, inmates who worked either in PIECP or traditional prison industries were "self-selected" and may have had different motivations and backgrounds than other inmates, which may have led to better outcomes.

Federal Prison Industries and UNICOR In the federal system, legislation authorizing the establishment of paid inmate work programs was introduced into Congress in 1934. However, the American Federation of Labor (AFL) voiced its opposition, arguing that federal prison industries have an unfair competitive advantage over the public sector because they pay their inmates less than a private company worker would be paid for carrying out similar assignments. President Franklin Roosevelt took a personal interest in the matter and called AFL president William Green

Many state correctional systems channel prison labor into industrial and commercial programs. One such program is the Prison Blues® brand of jeans, T-shirts, work shirts, and yard coats manufactured by Inside Oregon Enterprises, a division of the Oregon Department of Corrections. What benefits to inmates do such work programs provide?

Eye On Corrections

The Surprisingly Sweet Mix of Inmates and Wine

By Sarah Etter

Pruno is usually considered the most popular wine in corrections. Fermented in cellblocks, the illegal prison booze is a mix of old cafeteria fruit, sugar, and rations of fruit punch. Stored away under inmate bunks, this particular wine is something corrections officials are always on the lookout for.

At Colorado's East Canon prison complex, inmates have taken their winemaking to the next, and legal, level by creating a chardonnay blush with hints of a sweet bouquet. However, this wine will not serve as a fine accompaniment to their meals.

Across 28 acres of vineyard, East Canon inmates can be seen plucking grapes just before they ripen. Once harvested, they are shipped to the Holy Cross Abbey Winery where vintners blend a combination of white and red grapes into their own Wild Canon Harvest.

"It is a fun, sweet wine," says Abbey Winery owner Larry Oddo. "I call it my cotton candy wine; it has a scent of strawberries and cotton candy. It's a wine supported by the community, too. People love it, not because the grapes come from the inmates, but because it tastes good."

Since 2001, Abbey Winery has purchased plucked grapes from the self-funded Colorado Correctional Industries program, a division of the Colorado DOC that employs pre-release inmates.

"We are always looking for ways to put inmates to work, and for us this is a cash crop. It brings in more money every year, it's labor intensive and it keeps our offender population busy," says Steve Smith, CCI's agriculture business manager.

Typically, CCI will produce three to four tons of grapes per acre, or about 112 tons every season. Depending on the fruit's quality, each ton can be worth between $800 and $1,000. Last year, the more than 1,000 cases of Wild Canon Harvest were produced from sloped prison acreage.

In the vineyards, typically 15 to 30 inmates prune grapes for eight hour shifts. When harvesting time comes, 40 more inmates are added to the project.

"Initially, we started off with seven acres of Chardonnay, and we've recently added another 21 acres to grow white zinfandel, cabernet and merlot," Smith explains. "We're experimenting to see what works in our climate."

The vineyards are a productive and profitable venture for the CDOC and CCI, but Smith says that some grapes do not flourish in the Colorado environment.

"We're constantly training and learning. There is such a small window to prune grapes in. You can prune apples for months, but grapes can only be pruned until March," Smith explains. "The abbey has been a great help to us. They help us train the inmates and they let us know where we can improve. We realized very early on that you cannot just tell someone to prune a grape plant. It's a delicate process."

CCI's early attempts at a merlot vineyard have not been very successful, while recent growth spurts of Riesling grapes have proved profitable. In an effort to produce the best grapes possible, inmates and officials recently installed a drip irrigation system in the vineyard and this year, CCI anticipates producing more grapes than the abbey can handle.

"The irrigation system has really helped us," says Smith. "It allows us to control the amount of water each plant gets. We're really focusing on having the right slope to the ground which affects the way the grapes grow, and we've also ensured that there is a lot of drainage so the plants don't sit in water. We're focusing on quality over quantity."

As the DOC and CCI make strides to improve the quality of the wine crop, abbey officials say they have seen constant improvements in grapes over the last three years.

"We're continuing to work with the DOC to see what will work," says Oddo. "Overall, though, this partnership is working out pretty well and we're encouraging the DOC to become more involved in the industry. Obviously, this a very specialized industry, but if the DOC continues to focus on training, it could be very lucrative."

Even though the prison vineyard requires constant upkeep and care, Smith says the project is a great fit for corrections.

"I would certainly recommend this program to other states if their climate allows for it," says Smith. "If you're looking for something that puts a lot of inmates to work, this is it. Start out with five acres and see where that goes. Then you can grow into it, so to speak."

Source: "The Surprisingly Sweet Mix of Inmates and Wine," Sarah Etter, The Corrections Connection Network News (CCNN). Eye on Corrections. www.corrections.com. May 24, 2006.

Federal Prison Industries (FPI)

A federal, paid inmate work program and self-supporting corporation.

UNICOR

The trade name of Federal Prison Industries. UNICOR provides such products as U.S. military uniforms, electronic cable assemblies, and modular furniture.

and BOP director Sanford Bates to the Oval Office. Together, the three men were able to draw out Green's objections to the proposed legislation and his suggestions for improvement, and ultimately the AFL withdrew its opposition. On June 23, 1934, President Roosevelt signed the law that authorized the establishment of **Federal Prison Industries (FPI)**, and on December 11, 1934, he issued Executive Order 6917, which formally created FPI. FPI is a federal work program in which inmates are paid. Better known by its trade name, **UNICOR**, FPI is a self-supporting corporation owned by the federal government and overseen by a governing board appointed by the president.

Since 1934, FPI has operated factories and employed inmates in America's federal prisons. When the United States entered World War II in December 1941, FPI manufactured bomb fins and casings, TNT cases, parachutes, cargo nets, and wooden pallets for the military. It also handled the military's laundry and built, remodeled, and repaired military patrol boats, tugboats, and barges. FPI also contributed in another way to the war effort. It trained inmates to move directly into jobs in defense industries after release from prison. During the 1990–1991 Persian Gulf War, FPI provided Kevlar helmets, camouflage battle uniforms, lighting systems, sandbags, blankets, cables for the Patriot missile system, and night-vision eyewear for military use during Operation Desert Shield and Operation Desert Storm. Today, FPI in Tennessee sews the military vests worn by U.S. soldiers and Marines fighting in Afghanistan and Iraq. Other products manufactured by UNICOR are electronic cable assemblies, executive and modular furniture (FPI ranks ninth in such manufacture in the United States), metal pallet racks, stainless-steel food service equipment, mattresses, towels, utility bags, brooms, thermoplastics, military helmets, and government forms. UNICOR also provides services, such as data entry, sign making, and printing.

The mission of FPI is to employ and provide job skills training to the greatest practical number of inmates confined within the federal Bureau of Prisons; contribute to the safety and security of federal correctional facilities by keeping inmates constructively occupied; produce market-priced quality goods for sale to the federal government; operate in a self-sustaining manner; and minimize FPI's impact on private business and labor. In 2005, FPI operated in seven business areas: clothing and textiles, electronics, fleet management and vehicular components, industrial products, office furniture, recycling activities, and service. Virtually all of FPI's electronic sales, and the vast majority of FPI's clothing and textile sales, are in support of the Department of Defense's war effort in Iraq. In 2005, FPI had industrial operations at 106 factories located at 73 prisons and employed 19,720 medically eligible federal inmates, representing 14 percent of the total number of federal inmates. In 2005, FPI grossed almost $766 million and made a profit of $117 million.[39]

UNICOR demonstrates its contribution to the private sector in a number of ways: It purchases its products from private sector suppliers, it does business with private sector subcontractors, and it is a major employer of noninmate members in the communities where it operates factories. To ensure that UNICOR does not compete unfairly with the private sector, product guidelines require a public announcement and a hearing process for any new product it proposes. UNICOR is one of the most successful and cost-effective enterprises of the federal government.

Inmates employed by UNICOR start out earning 23 cents per hour. To advance to the maximum wage of $1.15 per hour, inmates must have a high school diploma or GED. Although wages are low in most prison industry programs, most inmates who work in them are more interested in doing something meaningful that keeps them busy and makes serving time seem to go faster. In many cases, such prisoners also learn job skills and have a better chance of staying crime free after release.

What Impact Does UNICOR Have?   In 1990, Congress mandated an independent market study of UNICOR. The accounting firm of Deloitte and Touche conducted the study. One of the principal findings was that UNICOR's impact on the private sector was negligible. UNICOR's sales amounted to only 2 percent of the federal market for the types of products and services that it provided.

At about the same time, the federal BOP released a study that compared the postrelease activities of a group of inmates who had participated in UNICOR programs with those of another group of inmates who had not. The study found that inmates employed by UNICOR were 24 percent more likely, upon release, to become employed and remain crime free for as long as 12 years after release than those who were not involved in UNICOR programs. Another study showed that inmates employed in federal prison industries had survival times (measured by the number of days before recommitment) that were 20 percent longer than those of the comparison group.[40]

UNICOR's success, however, is being questioned by Congress. Critics of UNICOR argue that because federal agencies are required to purchase products and services from UNICOR if those goods can be delivered in a timely manner and the prices are considered competitive, UNICOR does not have to compete to receive federal contracts. Critics note that UNICOR regularly ranks in the upper third among the top 100 federal contractors, behind corporate giants like Exxon Mobil, and 72nd among top Department of Defense contractors, ahead of Motorola and Tyco. Critics argue that the result is an unfair competitive advantage and the loss of jobs in the private sector. Support for abolishing UNICOR's preferential status has been gaining momentum in Congress since 2000 and several pieces of federal legislation have chipped away at UNICOR's preferential status.

Education and Recreation Programs

The majority of prisoners cannot read or write well enough to function in society. In fact, the illiteracy rate among prisoners is two and one-half times that of the U.S. adult population.[41]

According to a report by the Bureau of Justice Statistics, state and federal prison inmates, local jail inmates, and probationers differ substantially in educational attainment from persons 18 and older in the general civilian noninstitutional population.[42] An estimated 40 percent of state prison inmates, 27 percent of federal inmates, 47 percent of inmates in local jails, and 31 percent of those serving probation sentences had not completed high school or its equivalent (GED), while about 18 percent of the general population failed to attain high school graduation. This may be due in part to the higher rate of learning disabilities found among inmates.[43] An estimated 30 to 50 percent of inmates have a learning disability compared with 5 to 15 percent of the general adult population.

Researchers also found that state prison inmates without a high school diploma and those with a GED were more likely to have a prison sentence than those with a high school diploma or some college or other postsecondary courses.

And according to others, inmates' literacy is declining.[44] Fewer inmates are participating in prison education literacy programs today than

---

Talking about **CORRECTIONS**

SENTENCING TRENDS

Visit *Live Talk* at **Corrections.com** (www.justicestudies.com/talking04) and listen to the program "Correctional Education," which relates to ideas discussed in this chapter.

a decade ago. Today, only one-third of all those released from prison will have participated in education literacy programs.

However, can prison education programs rehabilitate prisoners so that they eventually contribute constructively to society upon reentry? The Correctional Education Association (CEA) believes they can. CEA is a nonprofit professional association serving educators and administrators around the world committed to educating prisoners. CEA conducted one of the nation's largest investigations on the impact of correctional education on rearrest, reconviction, reincarceration, and on employment outcomes. CEA's *Three-State Recidivism Study* compared 1,373 correctional education participants and 1,797 nonparticipants in three states—Maryland, Minnesota, and Ohio—for three years after release from prison. Key findings are:

1. For rearrest, correctional education participants had statistically significant lower rates of rearrest (48 percent) when compared to the comparison group of nonparticipants (57 percent).

2. For reconviction, correctional education participants had statistically significant lower rates of reconviction (27 percent) when compared to the control group of nonparticipants (35 percent).

3. For reincarceration, correctional education participants had statistically significant lower rates of reincarceration (21 percent) when compared to the control group of nonparticipants (31 percent).

4. Overall, there were no significant differences between the participants and nonparticipants in the types of new offenses committed. Both groups had less serious rearrest offenses compared to their original offense for which they had been in prison.

5. The findings indicated overall that both groups of study participants were in compliance with postrelease supervision requirements.

6. Only about one-fourth of the participants in either group were engaged in any postrelease program activity including education, substance abuse, counseling, or other assistance.

7. Both correctional education participants and nonparticipants had high rates of employment, with nonparticipants showing slightly higher rates (81.4 percent) of employment compared to the participants (77.3 percent). The difference, however, was not statistically significant. These high rates of employment for both correctional education participants and nonparticipants may be attributable in part to the state of the economy and the employment rates nationwide at the time the study was conducted.

8. For each of the three years wage earnings were reported, data showed that correctional education participants had higher earnings than nonparticipants.

Overall, CEA's results reveal a statistically significant correlation between participation in education and a lower rate of recidivism in each state. The results parallel the evidence-based reviews on prisoner education programs that show that the typical prison education program can be expected to reduce recidivism by 7 percent.[45] According to Laurie Robinson, former assistant attorney general for the Department of Justice's Office of Justice Programs: "While literacy alone will never be a vaccine against criminality, it is one of many skills needed to function—and function well—as a responsible and law-abiding adult in our society."[46]

Prisons vary considerably in the education programs they provide for prisoners. One hundred percent of federal prisons, 91 percent of state prisons, and 88 percent of private prisons offered some type of educational program in 2000, but only 35 percent of prisoners participated in them.

Correctional educators face substantial hurdles in delivering effective instruction. Inmates do not enter prison or jail to attend classes. They often do not see the importance of gaining an education, and many have a history of educational failure. They do not enroll in programs or participate in classes with the same enthusiasm as the noninstitutionalized population. Even negative peer pressure can discourage inmates from joining programs. Correctional educators face the challenge of motivating inmates to involve themselves in educational programming because they know that programming inside correctional facilities greatly influences what happens once inmates are released. Emphasizing the relevance of education to inmates, helping inmates experience success in learning, and developing an institutional culture that endorses the importance of education are vital components as correctional facilities work to achieve rehabilitation through education.

In December 2000, University of Kentucky sociologist Karen Lahm published the results of a study on educational and vocational prison programming in 30 states.[47] She found that general education programs are readily available across the United States, but postsecondary programming has been on the decline since President Bill Clinton's 1994 crime bill, which denied Pell grants to inmates and a wave of closings of inmate education programs by state lawmakers under political pressure to show they were being tough on crime.[48]

However, more than a decade later the share of the nation's prison population enrolled in college-level courses has rebounded. According to the Institute for Higher Education Policy (IHEP), CEA's *Three-State Recidivism Study* revived interest in offering higher education to some inmates. Forty-three state prisons reported offering higher education opportunities in the 2003–2004 academic year. However, access to higher education varies from state to state. The federal BOP and 14 states accounted for 89 percent of the 85,000 inmates enrolled in postsecondary education programs. "Offering postsecondary education to inmates seems 'less soft on crime' and more of a cost effective means to reduce recidivism and gain control of the mounting tax burden," said Jamie P. Merisotis, president of IHEP.

Lahm also found that women's prisons are still more likely to offer gender-stereotyped vocational training in technical, sales, or administrative occupations and service occupations. Some jurisdictions, however, offer unique vocational programming for women. For example, Ohio offers a program called ONOW (Orientation to Nontraditional Occupations for Women) that prepares women inmates for jobs in trade industries such as plumbing, carpentry, and electricity that require math skills, physical fitness, and blueprint reading skills.

All inmates are entitled to some form of recreation. However, the specifics about the nature and extent of recreation programming in prison and inmates' participation in such programs are not known. What is known is that recreation and organized sports can make doing time more bearable and, as a result, make the jobs of correctional officers easier. They can also be used as an incentive for good behavior, and by reducing tension, they can cut the number of prison assaults. Physical and mental health experts tell us that recreation programs can be a vehicle for teaching ways to promote health and prevent disease. Inmates who play hard are more likely to stay fit, possibly reducing health costs. Nutrition experts know that eating healthful food, participating in a regular exercise program, and stopping smoking are central to maintaining good health in prison. They also reduce the cost of prison health care.

Health Care

Good health care plays an important role in the day-to-day operations of a correctional facility. Investments in prisoner health care mean fewer correctional disturbances, disciplinary actions, and inmate injuries and less negative publicity for the institution. For the nation's one-half million correctional employees and thousands of daily visitors to prisons and jails, good health care also reduces their risk of becoming infected from inmates with communicable diseases.

The public health suffers when good health care is not provided, as it did in 1989 in New York City when 80 percent of tuberculosis cases were traced to people released from jail and prison. In Los Angeles, a meningitis outbreak in the county jail spread to surrounding neighborhoods. Thus, our policies toward prisoners have a direct impact on the public health of everyone.

Medical care remains the number-one operational expenditure for prison systems.[49] In 1999, the states and the federal government spent $2 billion to provide health care services to inmates. In 2001, they spent $3.3 billion. In 2004, the amount was $4 billion. In 2006 it was a staggering $4.4 billion.[50] The percentage allocated for medical care within the budgets of the departments of correction ranges from a low in Wisconsin of 5 percent to a high in South Dakota of almost 25 percent.

Providing inmates adequate health care is of concern to the courts and professional associations. In 1976, the U.S. Supreme Court established a constitutional standard in the Texas case of *Estelle* v. *Gamble*. Gamble claimed that prison officials had inflicted undue suffering when they failed to provide adequate health care for an injury that he sustained while working on a prison assignment. Even though the case was found in favor of the Texas Department of Criminal Justice, the Court ruled that "deliberate indifference to serious medical needs" constitutes cruel and unusual punishment, which is prohibited by the Eighth Amendment of the U.S. Constitution. Over time, the Court redefined the decision and established that inmates have the right to seek medical care, professional medical judgment, care that is ordered, informed consent, refusal of treatment, and medical confidentiality. However, the Court also made clear that such a right did not mean that prisoners have unqualified access to health care. Lower courts have held that the Constitution does not require the medical care provided prisoners to be perfect, the best obtainable, or even very good.[51] According to an excellent review of legal health care standards and the legal remedies available to prisoners, the courts support the **principle of least eligibility**: that prison conditions—including the delivery of health care—must be a step below those of the working class and people on welfare. As a result, prisoners are denied access to medical specialists, second opinions, prompt delivery of medical services, technologically advanced diagnostic techniques, the latest medications, and up-to-date medical procedures. In addition, prisoners do not have the right to sue physicians for malpractice, or if they do, the damages are lower than those awarded to people outside prison.

California, with the nation's largest correctional health care system, spent 20 percent ($974.5 million) of the state's corrections budget on inmate health care in 2004. Despite that amount of money and after 25 years of litigation, on Friday, July 1, 2005, senior U.S. district judge Thelton Henderson announced the most sweeping federal takeover of a prison

principle of least eligibility

The requirement that prison conditions—including the delivery of health care—must be a step below those of the working class and people on welfare.

health care system in the nation's history.[52] In San Francisco, Henderson said that he was taking control of California's troubled prison health care system, saying he was driven to act by "stunning testimony" that medical malpractice or negligence has been causing, on average, one death each week. Henderson said he would appoint a receiver, accountable only to him, to run the almost $1 billion-a-year medical system plagued by inadequate staffing, red tape, and personnel procedures that protect dangerous doctors and nurses. Henderson ordered immediate short-term fixes, mostly in costs for physicians, nurses, pharmacists, and top-level managers, and the installation of a new, computerized record-tracking system costing the state an extra $100 million a year. While some heralded Henderson's ruling, others expressed frustration. Lance Corcoran, vice president of the California Correctional Police Officers Association, said, "In many ways (prisoners) receive better health care than our elderly and our veterans." Still, health care professionals and inmate advocates—such as the American Medical Association and the National Commission on Correctional Health Care—insist on alleviating the pain and suffering of all people, regardless of their status. They believe that no distinction should be made between inmates and free citizens. We will return to the mental health issues of special needs inmates in Chapter 12.

PRISON ORGANIZATION AND ADMINISTRATION

All 50 states and the BOP operate prisons. In addition, four local jurisdictions in the United States operate prison systems: Cook County (Chicago), Illinois; Philadelphia; New York City; and Washington, DC. It is estimated that there are 1,668 state, federal, and private prisons: 84 federal, 1,320 state, and 264 private prisons.[53] More than 8 of every 10 prisons house men only; facilities housing women only and facilities holding both men and women each accounted for fewer than 1 out of every 10 confinement facilities.

Jurisdictions use a variety of capacity measures to reflect both the space available to house inmates and the ability to staff and operate an institution. Some use rated capacity (first introduced in Chapter 6), which is the number of beds or inmates a rating official assigns to an institution. Some use **operational capacity**, the number of inmates that a facility's staff, existing programs, and services can accommodate. Others use **design capacity**, the number of inmates that planners or architects intend for the facility. For instance, an architect might design a prison for 1,100 inmates. Administrators might add more staff, programs, and services to be able to confine 1,300 in the same space. The design capacity was 1,100, but the operational and rated capacities are 1,300. The institution is operating 18 percent above design capacity.

On January 1, 2006, the federal prison system was operating at 34 percent over capacity. Overall, state prisons were operating between 1 percent and 33 percent over capacity. We return to the issue of prison capacity and overcrowding in Chapter 13.

State Prison Systems

Organization The administration of state prisons is a function of the executive branch of government. The governor appoints the director of corrections, who in turn appoints the wardens of the state prisons. A

operational capacity
The number of inmates that a facility's staff, existing programs, and services can accommodate.

design capacity
The number of inmates that planners or architects intend for the facility.

change in governors often means a change in state prison leadership and administration.

The organization of most state prison systems involves a central authority, based in the state capital. Local communities, private contractors, or the state itself may provide prison services (from treatment and education to maintenance and repair). This method of organizational structure and delivery of services across wide geographic areas is often criticized for its fragmentation; duplication of structure, effort, and services; lack of coordination; and ambiguous goals. Still, for legal control and for maintaining an equitable distribution of resources, a centralized model has been maintained, while in other areas of corrections (e.g., community corrections and probation), services are often decentralized.

As we explained about the organization and administration of probation in Chapter 4, there is no correct way to organize corrections. Any arrangement that helps corrections reach its goals is appropriate. The organizational styles found across the United States developed over time and are the result of political interaction and accommodation among government agencies and interest groups. Today, prisons borrow consumer-oriented management techniques from private business. They periodically survey staff and inmates to identify problems and avoid confrontations. Technological improvements give prison administrators access to more information for decision making, and management training is more popular.

Size and Costs   State prison organizations vary in size. In 2006 one of the smallest was North Dakota's, with 513 employees and an annual operating budget of $49 million. The largest was California's, with almost 57,000 employees and an annual operating budget of $8.75 billion.[54] On Thursday, May 3, 2007, California governor Arnold Schwarzenegger signed a bill to allocate $7.9 billion to build space for new jail and prison beds, the largest prison construction project in the state's history.[55] More than 390,000 people work in adult correctional facilities; 260,943 are correctional officers, 50,627 are clerical, maintenance, and food service workers, 53,988 are professional/technical staff, 13,322 are educators, and 11,158 are administrators.[56] Most correctional facility staff are male (67 percent) and white (64 percent). Nineteen percent of all correctional facility staff are black, and 7 percent are Hispanic. The minimum starting salary for new correctional officers ranges from $24,091 in South Carolina to $45,549 in New Jersey.

In 2001, states spent $29.5 billion for prisons. By 2006, the amount was $35.6 billion. By 2011 researchers estimate that without policy changes by the states, the pricetag for imprisoning over 1.7 million people will be a staggering $40 billion.[57] Some states are even forecasting what it will cost now to accommodate the prison population in 2016. For example, the Iowa Board of Corrections is studying a consultant's recommendation to spend $250 million now to accommodate the expected growth in prison population from 9,056 in 2007 to 11,383 in 2016.[58]

Some ask if the money spent on state corrections encroaches on funds for higher education because the money has to come from somewhere. Is there discussion about this kind of trade-off? Jennifer Gonnerman, a reporter for the *Village Voice* writes, "When parents get a tuition bill for their kids' college education, I always think they should get a little note that says tuition went up $200 last year because we decided to build two new prisons. Then we can all decide whether we think that's a good use of our money or not."[59] Others have said, "Every additional dollar spent

EXHIBIT 7–7	States with the Highest and Lowest Reported Average Annual Operating Costs per Inmate		
Highest		**Lowest**	
Rhode Island	$44.860	Louisiana	$13,009
Massachusetts	43,026	Alabama	13,019
New York	42,202	South Carolina	13,170
Alaska	42,082	Mississippi	13,428
Maine	35,012	South Dakota	14,157

Source: Pew Charitable Trusts, *Public Safety, Public Spending: Forecasting America's Prison Population 2007–2011* (Philadelphia: Pew Charitable Trusts, 2007).

on prisons, of course is one dollar less than can go to preparing for the next Hurricane Katrina, educating young people, providing health care to the elderly, or repairing roads and bridges."[60]

According to the U.S. Department of Justice, Bureau of Justice Statistics, states spend, on average, approximately $22,650 a year to incarcerate one offender.[61] Others believe the cost is even higher, $31,073.[62] And depending on the prison security level, the capital costs of building one prison cell can be as much as $100,000.[63] States with the highest and lowest reported average annual operating costs per inmate are shown in Exhibit 7–7.

Reasons for the variation between states in the cost of operating prisons include differences in the cost of living; employees' salaries and benefits; climate; and inmate-to-staff ratios. High inmate-to-staff ratios are most common in states reporting low average costs per inmate; low inmate-to-staff ratios predominate in states with high average annual costs per inmate. For example, Maine, one of the states with the highest reported average annual operating cost per inmate ($35,012), has an inmate-to-staff ratio of 1.7:1. Louisiana, on the other hand, has one of the lowest reported average annual costs per inmate ($13,009) and an inmate-to-staff ratio of 6.8:1.

To help cover the costs of incarceration as well as teach inmates responsibility and accountability, more than half of the states now collect some sort of inmate fees in their prisons and more than 40 states have passed legislation that allows their jails to charge fees.[64]

In 1982, Michigan passed the first law in the United States allowing corrections officials to charge a medical copayment. Today, fees are generally assessed in four major areas: medical, per diem (housing food, and basic programs), other nonprogram functions (telephone, haircuts, escorts, and drug testing), and program participation (work release, electronic monitoring, education, substance abuse treatment, and medical costs). However, not all jurisdictions have begun collecting these fees, nor are there national data on how much is being collected. However, with medical copay fees ranging from $2 in Kansas, Kentucky, Louisiana, and Oklahoma to $10 in Georgia, more states are looking at changing inmate fees to help cover the cost of incarceration and teach inmates responsibility and accountability.

Connecticut enacted a law in 1998 to charge prisoners for the cost of incarceration, and in the first four years of operation collected $1.5 million. The Macomb County (Michigan) Sheriff's Office, 25 miles north of Detroit, collected $1.5 million in "pay to stay" fees from many of the 22,000 people processed into the county jail in 2003. Macomb officials bill inmates on a sliding scale of $8 to $56 a day, depending on an inmate's ability to pay. And the Davidson County (Tennessee) Sheriff's Office collects approximately $500,000 annually through its fee programs.

Inmate fees are taking on more importance as corrections budgets are cut and money is put in homeland security. State spending on adult prisons increased from $12 billion in 1986 to $29.5 billion in 2001,[65] but since the events of 9/11, state spending for corrections has been decreasing nationwide and more money is going to homeland security. Between 2003 and 2004, 11 states cut their corrections budgets, and 20 others saw just small increases.[66] Governors in Florida, Illinois, Michigan, Ohio, Utah, and Virginia are closing entire prisons. New York, Texas, and Nevada have downsized prison space by closing housing units. Oregon's budget crisis halted prison construction, and construction on two prisons in Pennsylvania was postponed in an effort to save $15 million. In 2006, states' corrections budgets lost a combined total of $310.2 million.

Many argue that taking the money away from corrections to combat terrorism is shortsighted. Corrections must be a major consideration in the national effort against terrorism. Once terrorists are arrested, prosecuted, and convicted, they are incarcerated in a jail or prison somewhere in the United States. As has been the experience with gang leaders and organized-crime members, criminal activity does not cease at the prison gates. Terrorists do not stop planning and coordinating acts of terrorism once they are behind prison walls. Allan Turner, research professor at George Mason University and former warden at the federal prison in Marion, Illinois, one of the toughest federal prisons in the nation, reminds us that "the al-Qaeda training manual devotes a lesson describing the actions to be taken when an operative is incarcerated. It specifies the need for incarcerated 'brothers' to continue to communicate with terrorists outside the prison or jail."[67] For example, Sheikh Omar Abdel Rahman, the blind sheikh who is serving a life sentence in New York for conspiring to bomb a number of New York City landmarks, was accused of sending messages from prison through visiting attorneys to members of Gama'a al-Islamiyya, Egypt's largest militant group.

According to Professor Turner, a key area for recruitment of terrorists is U.S. prisons and jails, where al-Qaeda and other organizations have found men who have already been convicted of violent crimes and have little or no loyalty to the United States. Prisoners are a captive audience, and many inmates are willing to hear how they can attack U.S. institutions. For example, there are conflicting reports about where and when Jose Padilla, the "dirty bomber," found Islam. Some believe that he was introduced to radical Islam while in prison in Florida. In 1994, Padilla formally converted to Islam and changed his name to Ibrahim. He eventually made his way to Pakistan. Once in Pakistan, Padilla changed his name once more to Abdullah al-Muhajir, which translates as "Abdullah the Immigrant." In April 2002, Padilla was captured at Chicago's O'Hare International Airport, en route to contaminate a U.S. city with a radiological bomb.

maximum- or close/ high-security prison

A prison designed, organized, and staffed to confine the most dangerous offenders for long periods. It has a highly secure perimeter, barred cells, and a high staff-to-inmate ratio. It imposes strict controls on the movement of inmates and visitors, and it offers few programs, amenities, or privileges.

Correctional facilities can be tremendous sources of information, Professor Turner tells us, but corrections officers must be professional and be trained and equipped to collect, analyze, and disseminate that intelligence.[68] They must also learn from the scandals of prisoner abuse in Abu Ghraib, Iraq, that prisoners cannot be mistreated in the name of intelligence gathering.

Security Level Prisons are classified by the level of security they provide. A **maximum- or close/high-security prison** is designed, organized, and staffed to confine the most violent and dangerous offenders for long

In these two photographs, the presence of gun towers and fences suggests the degree of violence and dangerousness of the inmates, the level of staffing, and the operating procedures. Maximum or high security is the most restrictive security level. It is characterized by gun towers. Medium-security prisons confine less-dangerous offenders and are characterized by fortified perimeters, generally rows of fencing. What factors are important in deciding an offender's prison security level?

periods. It imposes strict controls on the movement of inmates and their visitors, and custody and security are constant concerns. The prison has a highly secure perimeter with watchtowers and high walls. Inmates live in single- or multiple-occupancy barred cells. The staff-to-inmate ratio is high, routines are highly regimented, and prisoner counts are frequent. Programs, amenities, and privileges are few. There are 332 maximum- and close/high-security prisons in the United States confining 36 percent of the prisoner population.[69]

Inmates in a **medium-security prison** are considered less dangerous than those in maximum-security prisons and may serve short or long sentences. Medium-security prisons impose fewer controls on inmates' and visitors' freedom of movement than do maximum-security facilities. Outwardly, medium-security prisons often resemble maximum-security institutions, and they, too, have barred cells. The staff-to-inmate ratio is generally lower than in a maximum-security facility. Medium-security

medium-security prison

A prison that confines offenders considered less dangerous than those in maximum security, for both short and long periods. It places fewer controls on inmates' and visitors' freedom of movement than does a maximum-security facility. It, too, has barred cells and a fortified perimeter. The staff-to-inmate ratio is generally lower than in a maximum-security facility, and the level of amenities and privileges is slightly higher.

Minimum-security prisons confine the least dangerous offenders. They are sometimes referred to as open institutions because they have no fences or walls surrounding them. How are minimum-security prisons designed, organized, and staffed?

minimum-security prison

A prison that confines the least dangerous offenders for both short and long periods. It allows as much freedom of movement and as many privileges and amenities as are consistent with the goals of the facility. It may have dormitory housing, and the staff-to-inmate ratio is relatively low.

open institution

A minimum-security facility that has no fences or walls surrounding it.

prisons place more emphasis on treatment and work programs than do maximum-security prisons, and the level of amenities and privileges is slightly higher. Forty-eight percent of the prisoner population is serving time in 506 medium-security prisons.[70]

A **minimum-security prison** confines the least dangerous offenders for both short and long periods. It allows as much freedom of movement and as many privileges and amenities as are consistent with the goals of the facility while still following procedures to avoid escape, violence, and disturbance. The staff-to-inmate ratio is low, and inmates live in dormitory housing or private rooms. Some leave the institution for programming in the community. There are 370 minimum-security prisons in the United States confining 17 percent of the prisoner population.[71] They are sometimes referred to as **open institutions** because they have no fences or walls surrounding them.

Approximately 27 percent of men's prisons are maximum security. The rest are split between medium (42 percent) and minimum security (31 percent). The security level of women's prisons is approximately one-third each, minimum, medium, and maximum.[72]

Federal Bureau of Prisons

The BOP is an entirely separate system from state and local prison systems. Before the 1890s, the federal government did not operate its own prisons. Instead, the Department of Justice paid state prisons and county jails to house people convicted of committing federal crimes. The public outcry over the convict lease system, however, motivated the passage of a federal law prohibiting the leasing of federal offenders. Many state prisons and county jails subsequently became reluctant to house federal offenders because it was not economically advantageous to incarcerate inmates they could not lease. Moreover, the expansion of federal law enforcement activities and the enactment of new federal laws in the late 19th century led to an increase in the prosecution of federal lawbreakers and to overcrowding in the prisons where they were held. With a growing population of federal prisoners, and the growing reluctance of nonfederal prisons to house them, the federal government had no choice but to build prisons of its own. Congress authorized the establishment of three federal

> **EXHIBIT 7-8** Mission Statement
>
> It is the mission of the Federal Bureau of Prisons to protect society by confining offenders in the controlled environments of prison and community-based facilities that are safe, humane, and appropriately secure and that provide work and other self-improvement opportunities to assist offenders in becoming law-abiding citizens.
>
> **Source:** Federal Bureau of Prisons, July 1998.

prisons in 1891: U.S. penitentiaries at Atlanta (Georgia), Leavenworth (Kansas), and McNeil Island (Washington).

Bureau of Prisons In 1930, th BOP was established to provide more progressive and humane care for 13,000 federal inmates, to professionalize the prison service, and to ensure consistent and centralized administration of the 11 federal prisons in operation at that time. Between 1940 and 1980, the BOP held steady with approximately 25 institutions and some 25,000 inmates. Most of the BOP's growth in institutions and inmates occurred in the 1980s as a result of federal law enforcement efforts and new legislation that altered sentencing in the federal criminal justice system. From 1980 to 1989, the federal inmate population doubled, from 25,000 to more than 58,000. During the 1990s, the population doubled again as efforts to combat illegal drugs and illegal immigration contributed to increasing conviction rates. Today the federal prison population stands at 187,618.

Exhibit 7–8 shows the mission statement of the BOP. The central office in Washington, DC, six regional offices, two staff training centers, and 106 confinement and community-based correctional institutions carry out this mission. The BOP also houses the National Institute of Corrections (NIC), which advises and assists state and local correctional agencies throughout the country, primarily through technical assistance, training, and information services. The attorney general appoints the director of the BOP. Harley G. Lappin was sworn in as director of the BOP on April 4, 2003. He is the seventh director of the bureau since its establishment in 1930.

The BOP employs more than 34,000 people nationwide. Almost 30 percent of the BOP workforce is female and one-third is minority. Thirty percent of BOP personnel have completed some college. Another 30 percent have a bachelor's degree or further education.

The BOP budget for 2007 was $5.0 billion.[73] The largest portion, $2.3 billion, was for institution security and administration, including the costs of facility maintenance, motor pool operations, and other administrative functions for all BOP facilities. The second highest cost was $1.8 billion for inmate care and programs. This included the costs of all food, medical supplies, clothing, welfare services, transportation, staff salaries, academic courses, social and occupational education courses, religious programs, psychological services, and drug abuse treatment. The starting salary of a federal correctional officer is approximately $27,000. Starting federal salaries are slightly higher in areas where prevailing local pay levels are higher. The average annual cost to incarcerate an inmate was $23,429 in 2005.

Institutions and Security Level On January 1, 2006, 187,618 inmates were under the jurisdiction of the federal prison system (27,046 federal prisoners were held in privately operated facilities). The BOP

CAREER PROFILE

Rachel Anita Jung
Training Officer   Arizona Department of Corrections

Rachel Anita Jung is staff training officer for the Arizona Department of Corrections. She plans the statewide corrections staff training curriculum and coordinates staff training at the Arizona State Prison in Yuma. She joined the department in 1996. Previously, she worked as an adult probation officer and a jail case manager.

Jung received her bachelor's degree in criminal justice from California State University at San Bernardino, and her master's degree in criminal justice from the University of Alabama. She feels that a number of undergraduate courses helped her succeed in the corrections field. Constitutional law gave her an appreciation for the ethical issues in corrections. Procedural law gave her an understanding of offenders' due process safeguards. And criminological theory led her to understand that the causes of criminal behavior are complex. She says that criminological theory was "a real challenge."

Jung believes that careers in corrections can really make a difference in offenders' lives. As a corrections training officer, she believes that her work has additional influences, because she has the opportunity to develop a curriculum that influences the way staff throughout the state interact with inmates.

In the future, Jung hopes to move forward in corrections administration, possibly doing corrections research and influencing correctional policy.

> *You have to be very inquisitive. You have to know a lot about people. You have to be a good communicator. You especially have to be a good listener and develop training programs that adapt to the evolving challenges in the field.*

operates 114 confinement and community-based correctional institutions of several different security levels to confine appropriately a broad range of federal offenders. The classification of facilities by security level is based on such factors as the presence of gun towers, security barriers, or detection devices; the types of housing within the institution; internal security features; and the staff-to-inmate ratio. Each facility is placed in one of five groups—minimum security, low security, medium security, high security, and administrative:

- *Minimum-security institutions,* also known as *federal prison camps (FPCs),* have dormitory housing, a relatively low staff-to-inmate ratio, and limited or no perimeter fencing. These institutions are work and program oriented. Many are adjacent to larger institutions or on military bases, where inmates help serve the labor needs of the institution, military base, or other federal entities such as the National Park Service and U.S. Forest Service. Approximately 20 percent of BOP inmates are in minimum-security facilities.

- *Low-security federal correctional institutions (FCIs)* have double-fenced perimeters, mostly dormitory housing, and strong work and program components. The staff-to-inmate ratio in these institutions is higher than in minimum-security facilities. Approximately 39 percent of BOP inmates are in low-security facilities.

- *Medium-security FCIs* have fortified perimeters (often double fences with electronic detection systems), cell housing, and a wide variety of work and treatment programs. They have an even higher staff-to-inmate ratio than do low-security FCIs, providing even greater internal controls. Approximately 25 percent of BOP inmates are in medium-security facilities.

EXHIBIT 7-9   Institutions of the Federal Bureau of Prisons

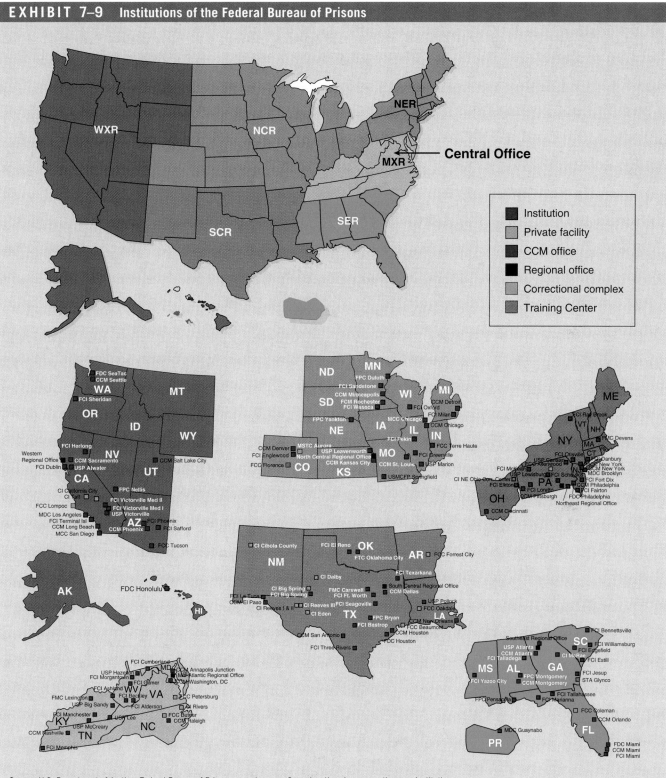

Source: U.S. Department of Justice, Federal Bureau of Prisons, www.bop.gov. Some locations have more than one institution.

- *High-security institutions,* known as *U.S. penitentiaries (USPs),* have highly secure perimeters (featuring walls or reinforced fences), multiple- and single-occupancy cell housing, close staff supervision, and strict movement controls. Approximately 11 percent of BOP inmates are in high-security facilities.

- *Administrative institutions* have special missions, such as detention of noncitizens or pretrial offenders, treatment of inmates with serious or chronic medical problems, or containment of extremely dangerous or escape-prone inmates. Approximately 6 percent of BOP inmates are in administrative facilities. Exhibit 7–9 shows the locations of all BOP facilities.

DOES INCARCERATION WORK?

After reading this chapter, you might wonder if incarceration works. Whether incarceration works depends on whom you ask and how he or she interprets the question. What does "work" mean? Does it refer to the prevention of rearrest, reconviction, or reincarceration? Should a new offense be related to previous ones? What if a new offense occurs 5 or 10 years after release from prison? Should the prison experience deter potential *and* actual offenders? Should it lower the crime rate? If so, by how much, how fast, and at what cost? What about criminological theories that link crime to forces outside the individual and over which the offender has little or no control such as his or her biology or psychological makeup, social structures, and even the more radical explanations that link crime to economic development, race, class, and gender? Politicians and researchers see the question differently. Governors and directors of corrections see the question straightforwardly: Were it not for prison, there would be more crime. Removing convicted offenders from the community ensures public safety, and the cost of incarceration is the price tag for ensuring that safety.

Researchers feel the effectiveness question can only be answered with randomly designed experiments, in which identically matched offenders are randomly assigned to prison or to other punishments. Even if such experiments were possible, there are differences between prisoners and people not sent to prison, and these differences will influence future offending.

The common expectation is that crime rates will decline as the number of persons incarcerated increases, and that crime will increase if incarceration rates fall. If you look at the relationship between the crime index and the prison population over the past 10 years, you might reach the conclusion that as the nation's prison population grew, crime fell and, therefore, the experiment in locking up more people lowered the nation's volume of crime. For example, David Muhlhausen, a policy analyst at the Heritage Foundation, argues that increasing incarceration decreases crime. "Considering that there are still about 12 million crimes a year," Muhlhausen concludes, then "maybe we're not incarcerating enough people."[74] Unfortunately, if you look at the past quarter century of prison buildup, you find that as the prison population increased, crime increased, decreased, increased, and decreased. There is simply no strong or consistent relationship between incarceration rate and crime rate.[75] Alfred Blumstein, a criminologist at Carnegie-Mellon University in Pittsburgh, believes that only about 25 percent of the drop in crime in recent years resulted from locking up more offenders. The rest resulted from other factors, including the ebbing of the crack cocaine

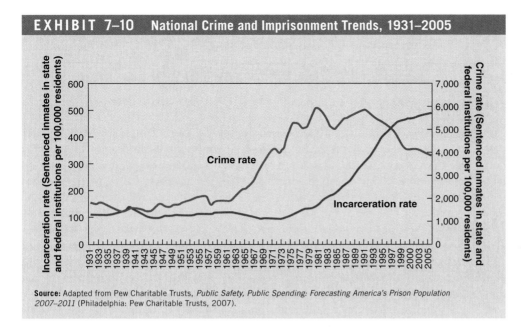

EXHIBIT 7–10   National Crime and Imprisonment Trends, 1931–2005

Source: Adapted from Pew Charitable Trusts, *Public Safety, Public Spending: Forecasting America's Prison Population 2007–2011* (Philadelphia: Pew Charitable Trusts, 2007).

epidemic, changes in policing strategies, and the strong economy of the 1990s.[76] (See Exhibit 7–10.)

In June 2002, the Bureau of Justice Statistics reported on four measures of recidivism of 272,111 prisoners discharged from 15 states and tracked for three years after their release in 1994.[77] Overall, 68 percent were rearrested within three years. More than two-thirds of the recidivism occurs within the first year after incarceration. Specifically, the study found that, within three years from their release in 1994,

- 68 percent of the prisoners were rearrested for a new offense (almost exclusively a felony or a serious misdemeanor). Released prisoners with the highest rearrest rates were robbers, burglars, larcenists, motor vehicle thieves, those in prison for possessing or selling stolen property, and those in prison for possessing, using, or selling illegal weapons. Released prisoners with the lowest rearrest rates were those in prison for homicide, rape, other sexual assault, and DWI:
- 47 percent were reconvicted for a new crime;
- 25 percent were resentenced to prison for a new crime; and
- 52 percent were back in prison, serving time for a new prison sentence or for a technical violation of their release.

BJS also found no evidence that spending more time in prison raises the recidivism rate. BJS evidence was mixed, however, regarding the question of whether spending more time in prison reduces recidivism. Specifically, BJS found that recidivism rates did not differ significantly among those released after serving 6 months or less (66 percent), those released after 7 to 12 months (65 percent), those released after 13 to 18 months (64 percent), those released after 19 to 24 months (65 percent), and those released after 25 to 30 months (68 percent). The increase in time served in prison, however, has implications for reentry (the subject of Chapter 8) in that longer prison stays may impact subsequent employment and earnings and are associated with less family contact, which, in turn, can have adverse effects on community reintegration upon release.[78] Thus, there is no indication that we have come any closer in reaching consensus on the question of whether incarceration works.

REVIEW & APPLICATIONS

REFLECTIONS ON THE FUTURE

The Future of American Corrections

By James W. Marquart,
University of Texas–Dallas

If the past is any predictor of the future, then we will see continued expansion of the American prisoner population and continued refinement in the management of prisoners. First and foremost, there will be continued growth of the prison population, particularly among women and juveniles. The crime rate will go up, it will go down, and this cycle will repeat itself, but these crime cycles will not have a dampening effect. The reason, I believe, for this increase in the prisoner population is rooted in punitiveness, in punishment. In our society, public policy is governed by incapacitation, and we will continue to see prisoners obtaining long punitive sentences—lengthy minimum sentences. Prisoner population growth coupled with incapacitation and a continued emphasis on punishment will dominate the correctional scene for decades to come.

Another issue that will continue to develop is the decline of the American welfare state. We are seeing fewer and fewer people on welfare and a restriction on the number of social programs for the poor. This shrinkage of social programs will influence prison programming. I predict that there will be a decline in state-subsidized programming for prisoners. Until the late 1980s and early 1990s, most prison systems offered a variety of programs at state expense for prisoners. Recreation, health care, college, and school programs were provided to the inmate at state expense. We have seen lately a restriction in this, and I think this is going to be a major movement within prison organizations over the next several decades. If offenders want advanced college courses, technical school, or trade school, I predict that offenders are going to have to pay for it themselves.

Coupled with the decline in programming, I think we will see continued refinement in classification procedures. As classification procedures are refined to cull out the high-risk and dangerous inmates within the inmate population, we are going to set aside special settings for their incarceration. We will see continued growth in administrative segregation and in supermaximum settings for high-risk, dangerous inmates within the prison community. No longer will there be emphasis on rehabilitation and treatment. A major emphasis is being placed on public safety, and the way to enhance public safety is through increased improvement in classification procedures to identify the most dangerous inmates. We will see little pockets of inmates within prison organizations: the young doing long sentences, the mentally ill, inmates with infectious diseases, women prisoners, sex offenders, high-risk, dangerous inmates within the prisoner population. There will be continuous segmentation of the inmate population into smaller and smaller groups for risk management purposes.

Another area where we will see growth and change will be in the staff. Staff will parallel the inmate population in terms of race and ethnicity—there will be greater minority participation within the correctional employment sector. Another issue that will continue to develop is the problem of staff having inappropriate relationships with prisoners. One of the biggest changes in terms of staff has been the desexualization of the work place—female employees can work within male prisoner institutions.

The use of technology to manage offender populations is another expanding area. We will see greater use of architecture to help prison administrators manage inmates—pod type designs coupled with a greater use of such technologies as cameras and electronics and computers to help manage the inmate population. This kind of heavy technology will be used to manage the high-risk inmates to such an extent that the social distance between or any kind of human contact between keeper and keep will be minimized. Advancements in using technology will help to manage and control inmates, to keep staff away from dangerous inmates on the inside. I think we will definitely be using chips and other electronic devices to track and follow inmates and track their movement and behavior on the outside. This will become critical and will become a civil rights issue, but I think that public safety will win out over the use of such intrusive devices. This issue will become a major civil rights issue and it will be tested in the Supreme Court, but we are going to see great advancements in technology that monitor the movement of criminal offenders in the free society. The test cases are going to be with sex offenders and how these offenders are to be monitored in the free community.

About the Author

James W. Marquart is professor of criminology in the School of Economics, Political and Policy Sciences at the University of Texas–Dallas as well as the program head of the Criminology Program. He has long-term research and teaching interests in prison organizations, capital punishment, criminal justice policy, and research methods. His current research involves an analysis of the long-term effects (i.e., prison violence, racially motivated attacks, and gang-related violence) of the in-cell racial integration policies in the California and Texas prison systems.

SUMMARY

1 The Pennsylvania and Auburn prison systems emerged in the United States at the turn of the 19th century. The Pennsylvania system isolated prisoners from each other to avoid harmful influences and to give prisoners reflection time so they might repent. The Auburn system allowed inmates to work together during the day under strict silence. At night, however, prisoners were isolated in small sleeping cells. With time, sleeping cells became congregate and restrictions against talking were removed.

2 There have been nine eras in U.S. prison history:
- Penitentiary era (1790–1825)
- Mass prison era (1825–1876)
- Reformatory era (1876–1890)
- Industrial era (1890–1935)
- Punitive era (1935–1945)
- Treatment era (1945–1967)
- Community-based era (1967–1980)
- Warehousing era (1980–1995)
- Just deserts era (1985–present)

3 On January 1, 2006, 1,338,306 people were under the jurisdiction of state correctional authorities, and 187,618 people were under the jurisdiction of the federal prison system. Of these state and federal inmates, 93 percent were male, 35 percent were white, 40 percent were black, and 20 percent were Hispanic. Reasons for the increase in women prisoners include women's presence in the U.S. labor market, which has brought about increased opportunities for crime; the increased poverty of young, female, single heads of households, which means that more women are turning to crime to support themselves and their families; changes in the criminal justice system, which no longer affords women differential treatment; and the combined effects of harsh drug laws, changing patterns of drug use, and mandatory sentencing policies. Reasons for the increase in minority prisoners include an increase in serious criminal activity that results in incarceration; racial profiling and racism by the criminal justice system; and the prevalence of social conditions that exist in the nation's inner cities, which is where most minorities in the United States regardless of race live, and the fact that large urban areas have the highest violence rates.

4 Classification is the principal management tool for allocating scarce prison resources efficiently and minimizing the potential for escape or violence. The purpose is to assign inmates to appropriate prison housing and to help staff understand, treat, predict, and manage prisoner behavior. There are two types of classification, external and internal. External classification determines an inmate's security level (maximum, close, medium, minimum, or community). Internal classification determines an inmate's assignment to housing units or cellblocks, work, and programming based on the inmate's risk, needs, and time to serve.

5 Faith-based correctional institutions can be traced back to 1997 when Texas opened a rehabilitation tier of a faith-based program in one of its prison facilities. Today, nearly half of state and federal prison systems are operating or developing at least one residential faith-based program, ranging from prison and jails offering a few religious services and programs, to one or more housing units within a prison that are faith-based, to entire prisons built around the faith-based concept, to faith-based parole and reentry initiatives.

6 The evidence-based literature on prison industries shows that the average prison industry program reduces the recidivism rate of participants by almost 6 percent.

7 General education programs are readily available across the United States, and postsecondary programming, which has been on the decline since President Clinton's 1994 crime bill denied Pell grants to inmates, is now rebounding. Occupational training is also provided in a wide variety of areas but is often limited to a few inmates. The exact nature and extent of recreation programming in prison and inmates' participation in them is not known. In 1976, the U.S. Supreme Court ruled in *Estelle* v. *Gamble* that inmates have a constitutional right to reasonable, adequate health care for serious medical needs. However, the Court also made clear that such a right did not mean that prisoners have unqualified access to health care.

8 All 50 states, the Federal Bureau of Prisons (BOP), and four local jurisdictions operate correctional institutions. State prison administration, a function of the executive branch of government, is most often organized around a central authority, operating from the state capital. There are three levels of prison security: maximum, for the most dangerous offenders serving long sentences; medium, for less dangerous offenders serving long or short sentences; and minimum, for the least dangerous offenders. Most prisons are either medium or minimum security. The BOP operates 114 federal confinement and community-based correctional facilities. The BOP operates minimum-security prisons known as *federal prison camps,* low- and medium-security facilities known as *federal correctional institutions,* high-security institutions known as *U.S. penitentiaries,* and administrative institutions with special missions, such as detention of illegal immigrants, treatment of people with chronic medical problems, and containment of extremely dangerous or escape-prone inmates. The majority of federal prisoners are confined in low- and medium-security facilities.

9 Whether incarceration works depends on whom you ask and how he or she interprets the question. Politicians and researchers see the question differently. Governors and directors of corrections see the question straightforwardly: Were it not for prison, there would be more crime. Researchers feel the question can be answered only with randomly designed experiments. There is no indication that we have come any closer to reaching consensus on the question of whether incarceration works.

KEY TERMS

penitentiary, *p. 253*
Pennsylvania system, *p. 254*
Auburn system, *p. 254*
public accounts system, *p. 258*
contract system, *p. 258*
convict lease system, *p. 258*
state use system, *p. 259*
public works system, *p. 259*

medical model, *p. 260*
classification, *p. 269*
external classification, *p. 270*
internal classification, *p. 271*
unit management system, *p. 277*
Federal Prison Industries (FPI), *p. 286*
UNICOR, *p. 286*

principle of least eligibility, *p. 290*
operational capacity, *p. 291*
design capacity, *p. 291*
maximum- or close/high-security prison, *p. 294*
medium-security prison, *p. 295*
minimum-security prison, *p. 296*
open institution, *p. 296*

QUESTIONS FOR REVIEW

1 Explain the differences between the Pennsylvania and Auburn prison systems.

2 Summarize the eras of prison development.

3 What can you infer from the characteristics of today's prisoners and the reasons for the incarceration of women and minority inmates?

4 Are there criteria you would add to prisoner classification schemes?

5 Summarize the literature and the issues on the program effectiveness of faith-based institutions.

6 Discuss the impact of the evidence-based literature on prison industries.

7 What ideas can you add to the reasons for including education, recreation, and health care programs for prisoners?

8 Evaluate the strengths and limitations of the various ways prisons are organized and administered.

9 What ideas can you add to the question "Does incarceration work?"

THINKING CRITICALLY ABOUT CORRECTIONS

Internal Classification

Review the three internal classification systems discussed in this chapter (Adult Internal Management system, Prisoner Management Classification system, and behavior-based systems). AIMS and PMC use personality and attitude measures (what inmates say they'll do—sometimes called a *casework model*) to assign inmates to housing units or cellblocks, work, and programming. BBS employs a behavioral model (how the inmate has behaved in the past) to determine internal classification. Write a list of three advantages and disadvantages of each approach (casework model of personality and attitude versus behavioral). Which method do you think is better to determine internal classification, and why?

Does Incarceration Work?

This chapter concludes with the statement, "Thus, there is no indication that we have come any closer in reaching consensus on the question of whether incarceration works." After more than 200 years of prison history, what is it about the question "Does incarceration work?" that makes it so difficult to reach consensus? Do you think there's a model muddle in corrections, meaning adult prisons set more goals than their resources can accomplish? Do you see areas where the goals of adult prisons conflict with one another and thus make it difficult to answer the question "Does incarceration work?" If you had the ability to remove the confusion, what goal(s) would you set for adult prisons and which measures of effectiveness would you employ?

ON-THE-JOB DECISION MAKING

Advantages of UNICOR

Imagine that you are chairperson of the five-member Federal Prison Industries Board of Directors appointed by the president. In 2005, FPI employed 19,720 federal prisoners, paid them between $0.23 and $1.15 an hour, generated sales in excess of $765 million (down from $802 million a year earlier), and made a profit of $117 million. (You can learn more about FPI at its Web site at www.unicor.gov.) Imagine further that it is an election year and the U.S. economy is stagnant. Organized labor and small businesses are complaining that FPI is too big and constitutes unfair competition. Search the Web site of the National Federation of Independent Business for criticism of FPI (www.nfib.com). Prepare a 30-second sound-bite on the advantages of FPI's success that the president will give when addressing a national meeting of the AFL-CIO.

Advancing Prison Education Programming

As the newly appointed director of prison education programming, you remember two things from your undergraduate corrections course: first, fewer inmates are participating in prison education programs today than a decade ago; second, while literacy alone will not prevent crime, it is one of the many skills needed to function well as a responsible and law-abiding adult in our society.

Your warden would like to create a model prison education program and asks you (1) what can be done with little or no budget increase to encourage more inmates to participate in prison education and (2) how will you know if your strategies have been effective? What will you tell the warden?

LIVE LINKS

at www.justicestudies.com/livelinks04

7–1 The Delaware Department of Correction Life Skills Program

The Delaware Department of Correction has implemented an innovative four-month Life Skills Program for prison inmates that does more than teach traditional academic and applied life skills. The program, which meets for three hours every weekday, has three major components: academics, violence reduction, and applied life skills. The core of Delaware's Life Skills Program is Moral Reconation Therapy (MRT), which is a systematic, step-by-step process of raising the moral reasoning level of prisoners through a series of moral and cognitive stages.

7–2 Objective Prison Classification

The current state of the art in prison classification is reviewed. The document includes a brief history of objective prison classification, what objective prison classification is, effective strategies, evaluations of prison classification systems, classification of women prisoners, and other special topics and issues in classification.

7–3 Prison Research at the Beginning of the 21st Century

This analysis discusses what is known and knowable about the collateral effects of imprisonment, crime-control effects of imprisonment, prisoners and prison staff, prison management, and the political economy of prisons at the beginning of the 21st century.

7–4 Classification of High-Risk and Special Management Prisoners: A National Assessment of Current Practices

Results from a survey designed to obtain information on the procedures used to classify high-risk inmates, particularly those in protective custody or administrative segregation, and inmates with mental illness or medical problems.

7–5 Developing Gender-Specific Classification Systems for Women Offenders

This report addresses the critical need for gender-specific objective classification systems. It covers the literature in classification issues for women offenders, women's classification initiatives, building blocks to effective classification of women offenders, addressing classification issues that require systemic change, and future steps. This report also has two appendixes: descriptions of seven states' women's classification initiatives (Colorado, Florida, Hawaii, Idaho, Nebraska, West Virginia, and Wisconsin); and sample initial and reclassification instruments developed by Colorado and Idaho.

PAROLE
Early Release and Reentry

CHAPTER OBJECTIVES

After completing this chapter you should be able to do the following:

1 Present a brief history of American parole development.
2 Understand the function of parole in the criminal justice system.
3 Define *parole* and explain the parole decision-making process.
4 Describe the characteristics of the parole population.
5 Explain the circumstances under which parole may be revoked.
6 Summarize current issues in parole.

> " *America is the land of the second chance, and when the gates of the prison open, the path ahead should lead to a better life.*
>
> —President George W. Bush
>
> "

Dr. Jack Kevorkian defiantly refused for nearly a decade to stop his assisted suicide crusade.[1] He claims to have assisted in at least 130 deaths in the 1990s. In each of these cases, the individuals themselves took the final action that resulted in their own deaths. Dr. Kevorkian allegedly assisted only by attaching the individual to a device that he had made. The individual then pushed a button that released the drugs or chemicals that would end his or her life.

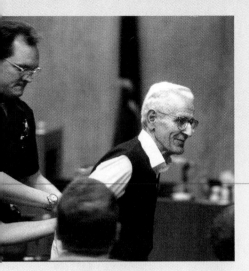

On June 1, 2007, Dr. Jack Kevorkian (dubbed "Dr. Death" by the media) was paroled by the Michigan Parole Board from the Lakeland Correctional Facility in Coldwater, Michigan, after serving 8 years and two months and earning a year and nine months off for good behavior. Kevorkian was convicted of second-degree murder for pushing the button that delivered the fatal dose of drugs to Thomas Youk because Youk was unable to press the button himself. Kevorkian was sentenced to 10 to 25 years in prison. For 2 years, Kevorkian is prohibited from being present and/or assisting in any suicide, including providing information or offering any person advice or counseling. Do you think persons who violate the conditions of parole should be reincarcerated?

But on September 17, 1998, Kevorkian pressed the button to deliver a fatal dose of drugs to Thomas Youk because Youk was unable to press the button himself. He filmed the procedure and submitted it for broadcast on *60 Minutes* two months later. Oakland County prosecutors believed that Kevorkian had crossed the assisted-suicide line and claimed that he single-handedly caused Youk's death. On March 26, 1999, Jack Kevorkian was convicted of second-degree murder and sentenced to 10 to 25 years in prison.

After serving a minimum of 8 years and two months (and earning a year and nine months off for good behavior) at the Lakeland Correctional Facility in Coldwater, Michigan, on June 1, 2007, the Michigan Parole Board granted parole to Dr. Kevorkian. The parole board determined that Kevorkian was safe for release and would not be a menace to society.

Among the conditions of his parole is an understanding that he won't be present at any assisted suicide or in any way participate in such activities, including providing operational or implementation information or offering any person advice or counseling in the matter of assisted suicide or euthanasia, said Russ Marian, spokesperson for the Michigan DOC. Kevorkian will be permitted to talk to audiences about assisted suicides, but he cannot individually counsel anyone. Kevorkian will be under supervised release for two years, during which time he can't leave the state or change his residence without written permission from his parole officer.

At 78, Kevorkian suffers from diabetes, hepatitis C, high blood pressure, hardening of the arteries in his brain, and vertigo. He plans to return to the Detroit area and live on a small pension and Social Security payments.

In 1991, Michigan suspended Kevorkian's medical license one year after he helped Janet Adkins of Portland, Oregon, become the first person to use a suicide machine developed by Kevorkian. Without a license, he could no longer buy some of the drugs he used, so he began using different techniques, including the use of carbon monoxide canisters.

Parole has been used for early release from prison for more than a century, but never before have so many individuals been released from prison. Kevorkian is one of more than 1,600 persons released from prison every day, some with only $5 to $100 in gate money. As you will learn in this chapter, nationally, about two-thirds of them will be rearrested within three years, and one-half will return to prison within that same period.

While it was once politically taboo to speak of providing resources for prisoners, these startling statistics have brought many lawmakers throughout the United States, both liberal and conservative, to the same conclusion: The nation's correctional system is correcting very little. That reality has sparked a movement to improve prisoner "reentry," a buzzword that's on the lips of politicians from coast to coast.

PAROLE AS PART OF THE CRIMINAL JUSTICE SYSTEM

People often confuse *parole, probation,* and *pardon.* All three place offenders in the community, but they are very different.

Parole is the conditional release of a prison inmate, prior to sentence expiration, with supervision in the community. A parole usually comes from authorities in the correctional system—responsibility for offenders passes from the judicial system to the correctional system upon imprisonment. Release on parole may be mandatory or discretionary. **Discretionary release** is at the paroling authority's discretion, within boundaries established by the sentence and by law. **Mandatory release** is early release after a specific period of time, as specified by law. In those states that permit discretionary release, state laws give correctional officials the authority to change, within certain limits, the *length* of a sentence. Correctional officials may also change the *conditions* under which convicted offenders are supervised—they may release offenders from prison to supervision in the community or to an outside facility. The American Probation and Parole Association (APPA), the nation's largest association of probation and parole professionals, supports discretionary parole (see Exhibit 8–1).

As we saw in Chapter 4, *probation* is a judge's sentence that allows a convicted offender to continue to live in the community, with restrictions on activities and with supervision for the duration of the sentence.

A **pardon** is an executive act that legally excuses a convicted offender from penalty. It is granted by a governor or the president. Those who are pardoned are excused from any further supervision.

parole
The conditional release of a prisoner, prior to completion of the imposed sentence, under the supervision of a parole officer.

discretionary release
Early release based on the paroling authority's assessment of eligibility.

mandatory release
Early release after a time period specified by law.

pardon
An executive act that legally excuses a convicted offender from a criminal penalty.

Historical Overview

The parole concept has its roots in an 18th-century English penal practice—indentured servitude. Judges transferred custody of physically fit condemned felons to independent contractors, paying those contractors a fee to transport the prisoners to the American colonies and sell their services, for the duration of their sentences, to the highest bidder. This practice was similar to today's parole in that the indentured servant had to comply with certain conditions to remain in supervised

EXHIBIT 8–1   **American Probation and Parole Association**

Policy Statement on Discretionary Parole

Definition

Parole can refer to both a guidelines process and a discretionary decision. Both of these methods of parole have merit. This position statement addresses only discretionary parole. Discretionary parole is a decision to release an offender from incarceration whose sentence has not expired, on condition of sustained lawful behavior that is subject to supervision and monitoring in the community by parole personnel who ensure compliance with the terms of release.

APPA Position

The American Probation and Parole Association supports discretionary parole as an integral and important part of a criminal justice system that is committed to public safety, victim and community restoration and the reintegration of offenders as law-abiding and productive citizens.

Discretionary parole decisions are based on a number of factors that weigh the need for punishment, successful community reintegration and victim and community restoration. These factors include the nature of the crime; the offender's criminal history, behavior in prison, social background and risk posed to the community; and information from crime victims and affected communities. Discretionary parole decisions enhance public safety by working to keep dangerous offenders incarcerated and that other offenders carefully selected for release receive the necessary structure and assistance to become law-abiding citizens in the community in which they reside.

Discussion

Parole is rooted in the fundamental belief that offenders can be motivated to make positive changes in their lives. Offenders are more likely to cooperate with correctional authorities if release is conditioned on good behavior, and after release the likelihood of their becoming law abiding is increased when offered assistance. The result is enhanced public safety.

Discretion is inherent at every level of the criminal justice system. Police exercise discretion when determining whom to arrest and charge. The court system uses discretion to decide whom to indict, whom to release pre-trial, whether to go to trial, and what criminal penalties to recommend. Judges use their discretion to determine the appropriate level of punishment given the circumstances of the crime and the offender's criminal history. They may sentence one offender to probation and another to prison for the same offense.

Parole boards closely examine and consider each offender's entire record, recognizing that correctional authorities can better manage inmates who have an incentive to follow institutional rules. The possibility of parole also provides inmates with an incentive to participate in programs that build competency skills. Parole boards know that the great majority of offenders sent to prison will eventually be released.

Parole boards are in a unique position to listen to and address the needs and concerns of crime victims and communities. Parole board control over offenders and communication with victims provides the framework for victim assistance and community restoration from the damage of crime.

During periods when there are an inadequate number of correctional beds, parole boards apply a rational process, targeting for release those inmates who pose the least risk to community safety. Parole boards are the only component of the criminal justice system that can weigh all of the factors and release only those offenders who can be best managed under community supervision, thus providing a powerful enhancement to public safety.

The core services offered by parole—investigations, victim advocacy, release planning, community supervision, immediate response to violations, and treatment services—provide optimum public protection. Parole is a powerful partner to both the courts and to victims. Parole boards ensure that the victim's voice is both heard and heeded, creating a natural and valuable ally for victims and victim advocacy groups.

The American Probation and Parole Association is committed to promoting discretionary parole as an integral and important part of the criminal justice system, designed to enhance the protection of victims and promotion of community safety.

Source: American Probation and Parole Association.

"freedom." This practice was discontinued with the beginning of the American Revolutionary War in 1775 because English offenders were joining colonial forces against England.

From 1775 through 1856, English offenders were sent to Australia as punishment. Those who committed further felonies in Australia were transported to England's most punitive prison on Norfolk Island, 1,000 miles off the east coast of Australia. In 1840, British Navy Captain Alexander Maconochie was appointed superintendent of the penal colony. Maconochie favored indeterminate sentences rather than fixed sentences.

He recommended, and in part implemented, a marks system to measure the prisoner's progress toward release from prison, and he urged a system of graduated release and aftercare of prisoners to resettle them in the community. He developed a "ticket of leave" system, which moved inmates through stages: imprisonment, conditional release, and complete restoration of liberty. Inmates moved from one stage to the next by earning "marks" for improved conduct, frugality, and good work habits. Although Maconochie had control over island tickets of leave, he could not control a graduated return to society in England. Maconochie's ideas did not blend well with the official English position on punishment, which was rooted in deterrence and relied on the infliction of suffering. He was removed in 1844 and the penal colony at Norfolk Island lapsed into a period of extraordinary brutality before it closed in 1856. Maconochie is referred to as the father of parole.

In 1854, Sir Walter Crofton, director of the Irish prison system, implemented a system that was based on Maconochie's ticket of leave system. Crofton's version required that, upon conditional release, a former inmate do the following:

1. Report immediately to the constabulary on arrival and once a week thereafter.
2. Abstain from any violation of the law.
3. Refrain from habitually associating with notoriously bad characters.
4. Refrain from leading an idle and dissolute life, without means of obtaining an honest living.
5. Produce the ticket of leave when asked to do so by a magistrate or police officer.
6. Not change locality without reporting to the constabulary.[2]

The former inmate who did not comply with the conditions of release was reimprisoned. Crofton's system of conditional release is considered the forerunner of modern American parole.

Use of the term *parole* for early release from prison began with a letter from Dr. S. G. Howe of Boston to the Prison Association of New York in 1846. Howe wrote, "I believe there are many [prisoners] who might be so trained as to be left upon their parole (a promise made with or confirmed by a pledge of one's honor) during the last period of their imprisonment with safety."[3]

Early American Parole Development The first legislation authorizing parole in the United States was enacted in Massachusetts in 1837, and the Elmira Reformatory in New York, which opened in 1876, was the first U.S. correctional institution to implement an extensive parole program. Zebulon Brockway, the institution's first superintendent, implemented a system of upward classification. The first grade was Brockway's personal interview with the new inmate. The second grade was the prison regime that Brockway established for the prisoner: a mix of labor (in the iron foundry or factories, on the farm, or on the maintenance crew), formal schooling, mandatory religious service, and military drill. An inmate who earned three marks each for labor, education, and behavior each month for six months in the second grade was promoted to the third grade. Six months after achieving the third-grade promotion, the inmate was granted a parole hearing before Brockway and five other Elmira staff members. Paroled inmates made their own living and work arrangements. Elmira employees and community volunteers provided parole supervision.

Captain Alexander Maconochie, who became superintendent of the British penal colony on Norfolk Island, Australia, in 1840, implemented a "ticket of leave" system to ease inmate transition from custody to freedom. Later, Sir Walter Crofton, director of the Irish prison system, implemented a system based on Maconochie's ideas. How did their systems influence current parole procedures?

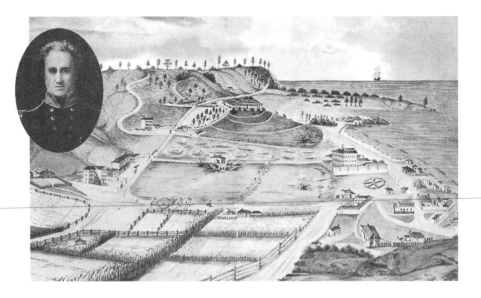

Failure to comply with conditions of parole meant parole revocation and return to Elmira's second grade.[4]

By 1889, 12 states had implemented parole programs; by 1944, all 48 states had enacted parole legislation.

Parole Development in the Early 20th Century   The 1920s and early 1930s were a turbulent period in the United States. During Prohibition, organized crime increased, street gang warfare escalated, and the media provided obsessive coverage of criminals and their activities. Prison riots erupted in response to prisoner idleness and arbitrary rules and punishment. Prisons and the parole system failed to rehabilitate offenders.

The Wickersham Commission, a commission on law enforcement and observance appointed by President Herbert Hoover, issued a report in 1931 that advocated uniformity in state parole practices by recommending that states establish centralized policymaking boards to write standards and guidelines for parole practices.[5] This report included a list of the "essential elements" of a good parole system:

1. indeterminate sentence law permitting the offender to be released (conditionally) at the time when he or she is most likely to make a successful transition back to society;

2. provision of quality release preparation—in the institution—for the offender who is reentering the community;

3. familiarity by the parole officer with the home and environmental conditions of the offender before he or she leaves the institution; and

4. sufficient staffing levels to ensure an adequate number of parole officers to supervise parolees.[6]

The Wickersham Commission reported that parole was logical because it was an inexpensive way to supervise offenders. Moreover, the commission reported, the parolee earns money, whereas the prisoner cannot support himself or herself and cannot contribute financially to his or her family. By 1944, all of the states had passed parole legislation.[7]

Despite the fact that all the states had enacted parole legislation by the mid-1940s, opposition was strong. The attitude that parole boards were turning hardened criminals loose on society sparked a series of angry attacks through national and state commissions, investigatory hearings, editorials and cartoons, press releases, and books.[8] Opponents claimed that parole had a dismal performance record, its goals were never realized, parole board members and parole officers were poorly trained, and parole hearings were little more than hastily conducted, almost unthinking interviews.

In spite of the gap between its goals and reality, parole fulfilled important functions for officials in the criminal justice system. Wardens supported parole because the possibility of earning parole served as an incentive for offenders, making it easier to keep peace. Wardens also used parole to control prison overcrowding by keeping the number of people being released on parole about equal to the number of new prisoner admissions. Legislators supported parole because it cost less than incarceration. District attorneys supported parole because they felt it helped with plea bargaining. Without parole, district attorneys argued, there was little motivation for defendants, particularly those facing long prison sentences, to plead guilty to lesser crimes. District attorneys also supported parole because parolees could be returned to prison without new trial proceedings.

Together, these groups made a claim to the public that parole actually extended state control over offenders because parolees were supervised. Eventually, the public accepted the claim that parole was tough on criminals and that abolishing parole would end state control over dangerous persons.

Parole Development in the Late 20th Century Opposition to parole resurfaced in the 1960s and 1970s, this time as part of a larger political debate about crime, the purposes of sanctioning, and the appropriateness of the unlimited discretion afforded various sectors of the criminal justice system (paroling authorities in particular). During this period, the debate on correctional policy addressed both the assumptions of the rehabilitative ideal and the results of indeterminate sentencing and parole.

In the 1970s, research indicated that prison rehabilitation programs had few positive benefits. Parolees were not rehabilitated, as parole advocates had claimed.[9] This position was supported on all sides of the political spectrum, including by those who believed that prisons "coddled" dangerous criminals and by those who questioned the ethics of coercing offenders into submitting to unwanted treatment as a condition of release.[10] These research findings led to many of the sentencing reforms of the 1970s and 1980s and helped usher in the warehousing and just deserts eras discussed in Chapter 7. During a time when supporting *parole* represented a "soft" stance on crime and when crime rates and recidivism were up, the public did not want prisoners released on parole.

In 1987, the American Probation and Parole Association voiced its support of parole and objected to efforts to abolish it. Nevertheless, in that same year, six states abolished discretionary parole board release. By the year 2000, 16 states and the federal government had abolished it, and another four states had abolished discretionary parole release for certain violent offenses or other crimes against a person. The APPA position statement on parole is presented in Exhibit 8–2.

Reentry

At the beginning of this chapter we introduced the subject of parole reentry. We expand on that here.

| EXHIBIT 8-2 | American Probation and Parole Association |

Position Statement on Parole

The mission of parole is to prepare, select, and assist offenders who, after a reasonable period of incarceration, could benefit from an early release while, at the same time, ensuring an appropriate level of public protection through conditions of parole and provision of supervision services. This is accomplished by:

* assisting the parole authority in decision making and the enforcement of parole conditions;
* providing prerelease and postrelease services and programs that will support offenders in successfully reintegrating into the community; and
* working cooperatively with all sectors of the criminal justice system to ensure the development and attainment of mutual objectives.

Source: American Probation and Parole Association.

Reentry is the use of programs targeted at promoting the effective reintegration of offenders back to communities upon release from prison and jail. Reentry has occurred since the Walnut Street Jail opened in 1776. However, the scale of offender reentry is larger today than ever before, and we face enormous challenges in managing the reentry of persons leaving prison and jail. Ninety-five percent of all prisoners will be released prior to the expiration of their sentences. In just 20 years, the number of inmates being released from prison has quadrupled. Estimates are that more than 1,600 offenders leave state and federal prison every day and according to the largest recidivism study ever conducted in the United States, two out of every three are rearrested within three years of their release and half are returned prison in that same period.[11] Why is corrections not correcting? There are many reasons. Among them are the following:

* **Parole supervision:** Most parole officers manage large caseloads and typically meet with offenders for about 15 minutes once or twice a month. Why should we expect such a small amount of contact to make a large difference?
* **Shift in parole function:** Parole has shifted from a service orientation to a surveillance-oriented, control-based strategy centered on monitoring behavior, detecting violations, and enforcing rules. Surveillance technologies such as the Global Positioning System, remote-control monitoring, and drug testing make it easier to monitor behavior and detect violations. However, what academics and practitioners have been telling us for years—that surveillance alone does not change criminal behavior—is in fact a reality. We must direct our financial resources toward developing a network of more effective and efficient community correctional options.
* **Responses to technical violations:** Violators of probation and parole represent the fastest-growing category of admissions to jail and prison. Legislators are beginning to realize that as the correctional populations swell, so do corrections budgets. American taxpayers spent almost $30 billion for corrections in 2001; by 2005, the figure had climbed to $35 billion. And, as we said in Chapter 7, by 2011 researchers estimate that the pricetag for imprisoning over 1.7 million people will be a staggering $40 billion.

Politicians on both sides of the aisle now agree that there is simply not enough money to build our way out of the problem. Why not reallocate the money in the hope of a more promising return? The growth in the correctional population must be managed, and policymakers must do a better job of ensuring that ex-offenders become productive, healthy members of families and communities after their release from jail and prison.

Talking about CORRECTIONS

HOUSING AND REENTRY

Visit *Live Talk* at **Corrections.com** (www.justicestudies.com/talking04) and listen to the program "Housing and Reentry," which relates to ideas discussed in this chapter.

- **Offender problems:** In 1984, 70 percent of parolees successfully completed their parole. But as "get tough on crime" became the political mantra throughout the 1970s, 1980s, and 1990s, by 2005, that number had dropped to 45 percent. Research shows that when people are released from jail and prison, their job prospects are dim, their chances of finding a place to live are bleak, and their health is poor. Fewer than half have a job lined up before leaving prison. Three-fourths still have a substance abuse problem. Over one-third have a physical or mental disability. Almost one in five has hepatitis C. More than half have dependent children who rely on these reentering adults for financial support. Only one-third participated in educational programs while incarcerated, and even fewer participated in vocational training.[12] (See Exhibit 8–3.) These returning prisoners are increasingly concentrated in communities that are often crime ridden and lacking in services and support systems.[13] For example, in Illinois, 51 percent of prisoners released from state correctional institutions in 2001 returned to Chicago, and 34 percent of them returned in just six of Chicago's 77 neighborhoods. And, no services were located in two of those six neighborhoods. Regrettably, parole violations and new crimes are often committed because offenders reentering the community lack the skills and support to adapt to community life. But as we will discuss later, now that we know that there are geographic concentrations of returning prisoners to a handful of neighborhoods in most large cities, we now have an opportunity to place our reentry efforts in those areas.

With such high rearrest rates, it became clear to many that simply placing an offender in prison does not deter future criminal behavior. The U.S. prison and parole systems have become a revolving door that cities and towns across the nation were not prepared to handle. Amy Solomon, a researcher with the Urban Institute, said, "A business with these kinds of results would look to reinvent itself."[14] That's exactly what is happening across the United States today.

EXHIBIT 8–3   **Service Needs of State and Federal Prisoners**

Area of Need	Prevalence (Percentage of All Prisoners)
Substance abuse	75
Physical or mental disability	83
No high school diploma	86
No diploma or GED	40
Earned less than $600/month prior to incarceration	50
Homeless before or after incarceration	10

Source: The Council of State Governments, *The Report of the Re-Entry Policy Council: Charting the Safe and Successful Return of Prisoners to the Community* (Lexington, KY: The Council of State Governments, 2005), p. 49.

Offender reentry is the hot-button topic in parole. President George W. Bush recognized the importance of improving services to those leaving the nation's prisons and jails. In his 2004 State of the Union address, he called for action "to expand job training and placement services, to provide transitional housing and to help newly released prisoners get mentoring, including from faith-based groups."

In 2003, Congress passed the Serious and Violent Offender Reentry Initiative (SVORI). That legislation provided $100 million in grants through the Department of Justice to fund all 50 states, the District of Columbia, and the U.S. Virgin Islands to develop programs to facilitate the reentry of individuals convicted of serious and violent offenses who return to their communities after prison. While the amount seems like a lot, the $100 million represents less than $200 for each of the more than 600,000 persons released to parole each year. Furthermore, the funds were spread out over three years.

Instead of expanding SVORI, in 2005, Congress passed the Prisoner Reentry Initiative and gave $20 million to the Department of Labor to manage. This legislation excludes violent offenders and focuses on employment-related issues.

More recently, Congress passed the Marriage and Incarceration Initiative. This $30 million appropriation was given to the Department of Health and Human Services to strengthen marriage and families among male correctional populations.

One person has said that every time the funding stream changes, state agencies must develop new programs to meet the objectives of the new initiative. Given the difficulties faced by returning inmates, one reentry researcher criticized the constant changes saying we don't expect the National Institutes of Health to change its approach to cancer treatment every two or three years, and we shouldn't do less on this important issue.[15]

Furthermore, researchers' understanding of who is in prison and jail, the communities to which they return, and the issues that contribute to their successes and failures in the community upon release has generated an unprecedented level of attention by legislators and correctional policymakers. Underlying all the attention is the increasing recognition that reentry is not the responsibility of corrections alone. Non-criminal-justice sectors like public health, workforce development, and housing are the foot soldiers accompanying an offender's successful reentry. Recognizing that reentering populations are part of the non-criminal-justice sector clientele, and that continuity of care is needed from prison to the community, has been at the core of a major national report on reentry by the Council on State Governments.

The Report of the Re-Entry Policy Council: Charting the Safe and Successful Return of Prisoners to the Community[16] (referred to as the *Report*) offers a comprehensive set of bipartisan, consensus-based recommendations for policymakers and practitioners interested in improving the likelihood that adults released from confinement will avoid crime and become productive members of their communities. This unprecedented project brought together nearly 100 leaders and agencies representing a wide spectrum of systems connected with prisoner reentry. The American Correctional Association's public correctional policy statement on reentry is shown in Exhibit 8–4.

The *Report* is encyclopedic. It provides a comprehensive analysis of those elements essential to improving the likelihood that adults released from prison or jail will avoid crime and become productive, healthy mem-

EXHIBIT 8–4 **American Correctional Association**

Public Correctional Policy on Re-Entry of Offenders

Introduction

Re-entry programs are in the best interest of society because they help prepare offenders for community life, help reduce future criminal behavior, remove the barriers that make it difficult for offenders to re-enter their communities, and develop necessary community support.

Policy Statement

The American Correctional Association fully supports re-entry programs and encourages the elimination of any local, state and federal laws and policies that place barriers on the offender's successful re-entry. Therefore, public and private agencies at the federal, state, and local levels should:

- A. Advocate for the review of existing laws and regulations that inhibit the successful re-entry of offenders.
- B. Initiate transitional planning, consistent with the individual needs to the offender, during intake to the facility.
- C. Provide an expedited process to obtain appropriate legal identification prior to or upon release.
- D. Assist the offender in accessing appropriate housing upon release.
- E. Provide sufficient staff to supervise offenders released to the community.
- F. Develop community partnerships and support networks for providing a seamless and timely connection between pre- and post-release programs and services.
- G. Provide information and assistance to address health care needs, such as obtaining medicaid, medical and substance abuse treatment, and other health and psychological services, to offenders in the community upon release. Provide a sufficient supply of prescription medication upon release.
- H. Provide information and assistance to offenders to gain employment upon release, such as pre-employment readiness training, job identification and retention skills training, and job placement services.
- I. Provide prerelease counseling to help reunite offenders with their families and communities.

Source: Copyright © American Correctional Association.

bers of families and communities. The 600-page report is divided into three parts and offers a total of 35 policy statements that are consensus-based principles the group believes are critical underpinnings of reentry. Taken collectively, the policy statements represent a comprehensive vision for the safe and successful transition of offenders from jail or prison to the community.

Part I ("Planning a Re-Entry Initiative") reviews the steps that policymakers and practitioners must address in order to establish a successful reentry initiative. Most important is to engage the community, especially relevant stakeholders, in the reentry initiative and develop their understanding that reentry requires serious work on multiple fronts that goes beyond running safe, secure, and humane facilities. It also details key issues that underlie the long-term sustainability and effectiveness of reentry, such as mission redefinition, funding, performance measurement, and public information.

Part II ("Review of the Reentry Process: From Admission to the Institution to Return to the Community") identifies reentry opportunities along a person's path from admission to a correctional facility to the completion of supervised release for improving the likelihood that the offender will avoid crime and become a healthy, productive member of his or her family and community. The prison programs discussed in Chapter 7 (classification, orientation, housing, work assignments, education, vocational training, and physical and mental health treatment) are windows of opportunity in the admissions process to begin planning for reentry. The policy statements in this part emphasize the need for collaboration between corrections staff both inside prison and jail and those non-criminal-justice sectors on the outside, such as public health, workforce development, housing, victims, and the community at large.

The policy statement in Part III ("Elements of Effective Health and Social Service Systems") are predicated on accessible and effective services and supports from the non-criminal-justice sectors. They explain what must occur within communities to provide housing, workforce development, substance abuse treatment, mental health services, children and family supports, and health care so that offenders have a chance at becoming productive, healthy members of families and communities.

In addition to the council's *Report,* state and federal governments are involved with reentry initiatives of their own. For example, California is showing success with its Preventing Parole Crime Program (PPCP). PPCP provides parolees with employment, substance abuse treatment and education, math and literacy, and housing services. So far, parolees who enrolled in these programs have done better than those who did not.[17]

However, as mentioned earlier, since 2003 Congress has moved funding for reentry from the Department of Justice to the Department of Labor to the Department of Health and Human Services, leaving some to draw the analogy that we don't expect the National Institutes of Health to change its approach to cancer treatment every two or three years, and we shouldn't do less with parole reentry.

In 2003, the U.S. Department of Justice in conjunction with other federal agencies funded the Serious and Violent Offender Reentry Initiative (SVORI). SVORI provides funding to develop, implement, enhance, and evaluate reentry strategies that will ensure the safety of the community and the reduction of serious, violent crime. SVORI funding supports a three-phase continuum of services that begins in prison, moves to a structured reentry phase before and during the early months of release, and continues for several years as released prisoners take on increasingly productive roles in the community. All SVORI programs share the common goals of improving a parolee's employment, education, health, housing, and criminal justice outcomes. To date, 45 adult and 13 juvenile correctional agencies and 11 state agencies such as public health departments have received SVORI funding. RTI International, a nonprofit research organization, and the Urban Institute are studying the impact of SVORI. They are conducting a longitudinal study of adult male, adult female, and juvenile male returning prisoners. To date, no data are available.[18]

Recently, the Legal Action Center (LAC) published the results of an exhaustive two-year study of legal obstacles that people with criminal records face when they attempt to reenter society and become productive, law-abiding citizens. LAC developed a report card to judge how states deal with seven roadblocks that criminals face upon reentry: employment, public assistance and food stamps, housing benefits, voting, access to criminal records, parenting, and driving. States were graded from 1 (being the best) to 10 (the worst). Scores ranged from 10 to 48. States with the lowest overall scores have the fewest barriers to reentry. State scores are shown in Exhibit 8–5.

EXHIBIT 8-5   Report Card on How States Deal with the Legal Obstacles Prisoners Face on Reentry

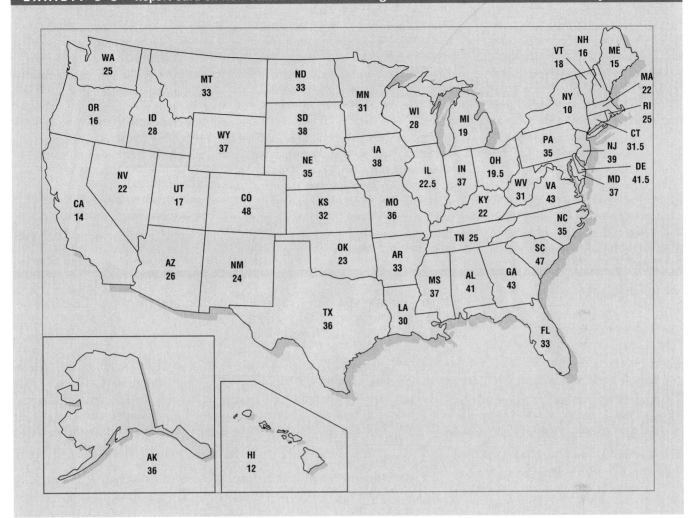

Eligibility for Reentry An inmate's eligibility for parole is determined by the sentence received from the court, as set by law. The **parole eligibility date** is the earliest date on which an inmate might be released. State statutes usually dictate parole eligibility dates and specify what portion of a sentence an offender must serve before being considered for release. Generally, state statutes apply formulas to deduct amounts of time from sentences to determine when an inmate might be eligible for release. The state statutes vary but, in general, reduce the sentence based on the number of days the inmate serves without disciplinary problems. The parole eligibility date, then, is determined by subtracting the maximum number of good-time days that could be earned from the length of the sentence. For example, a state statute might allow one day of good-time credit for every five days of good behavior. In this instance, an inmate could be eligible for parole after serving 292 days of a one-year sentence.

Granting Parole—The Paroling Authority Every jurisdiction in the United States has a paroling authority. In most states, a **paroling authority** is a correctional agency (often called a *parole board* or *parole commission*) that has statutory authority to grant parole, set conditions

The Legal Action Center's report card grades states on their legal obstacles to parole. Scores range from 10 to 48. States with the lowest scores have the fewest barriers.

parole eligibility date

The earliest date on which an inmate might be paroled.

paroling authority

A person or correctional agency (often called a *parole board* or *parole commission*) that has the authority to grant parole, revoke parole, and discharge from parole.

THE STAFF SPEAKS

I work in a city of 80,000, which currently has no supervision for parolees who have been serving sentences of two years or more in a federal facility. Currently, there are 30 to 40 such individuals in unsupervised conditions. There are also many more who are assigned to halfway houses in nearby communities, making life unnecessarily difficult on some of these individuals.

We are trying to bring a 12-bed facility into the community. We are facing strenuous resistance, including death threats—ironic, isn't it?—of both the NIMBY (not in my back yard) and the NOPE (not on planet earth) variety. Some of the resistance, I'm sure, is based on fear that we are bringing criminals into the community. One obvious answer is that many of these individuals came from the community in the first place.

One really hard question to answer is whether the local property values will be negatively affected. That's a realistic concern for everyone. Yet, the most recent material that I have been able to find is from the early 1980s. It suggests that there is no clear effect on property values and that most people on a street are unaware that such accommodations are there, once they have been there a while. Of course, if these former offenders are released into the community without any preparation or socialization, they won't have a chance, let alone a halfway chance, of following the rules and becoming a positive contributor to the community that denies them.

Linda Deutschmann
Halfway House Worker
Brookhaven, Kansas

---

of parole, supervise parolees, revoke parole, and discharge from parole. For jurisdictions with determinate sentencing and no discretion for the timing of release, the paroling authority still may determine conditions of release.

Parole boards vary in size from 3 members (Alabama, Hawaii, Montana, North Dakota, Washington, and West Virginia) to 10 or more (Michigan, 10; Connecticut, 11; Ohio, 11; Illinois, 12; Texas, 18; and New York, 19). Of the 52 jurisdictions—the 50 states, the District of Columbia, and the federal government—only 34 have full-time salaried parole board members. Minnesota's paroling authority is its Commissioner of Corrections.[19]

The paroling authority's decision to grant or deny parole is partially based on its assessment of potential risk to the community. Risk-assessment factors may include the nature and circumstance of the crime; the offender's criminal record and prison record; and input from court officials, victims, and other interested parties.

A parole board meets to consider a release candidate. While discretionary release by parole boards was at one time very common, it has been eliminated in many jurisdictions. Does parole provide offenders with an effective opportunity to reintegrate into society?

Not all parole authorities use the same release criteria. Observations of federal parole hearings, for example, suggest that an inmate's institutional behavior and program participation are given little importance in release decisions.[20] "Noncompliance with required treatment programs or poor institutional behavior may be reasons to deny parole, but completion of treatment programs and good institutional behavior are not sufficient reasons to grant parole."[21]

A national survey of parole board members said that the most important factors in the decision to grant or deny parole were the nature of the inmate's offense and the inmate's prior criminal record, attitude toward the victim, institutional adjustment (as measured by the inmate's participation in prison programs), and insight into the causes of past criminal conduct.[22] Least important are the inmate's physical health and age, prison conditions, and the public awareness of the case. Studies of parole in Colorado found that, in order to process the large volume of cases, parole boards find it necessary to develop a routine and to look for a few factors that will decide their cases for them:

> The parole board first considers the inmate's current and prior offenses and incarcerations. Parole board members also determine if the inmate's time served is commensurate with what they perceive as adequate punishment. If it is not, the inmate's institutional behavior, progress in treatment, family circumstances, and parole plan will not outweigh the perceived need for punishment.[23]

Some states use scoring instruments for risk assessment—the most commonly used are based on the U.S. Parole Commission's **salient factor score (SFS)**.[24] The salient factors are (1) number of prior convictions/adjudications, (2) number of prior commitments of more than 30 days, (3) age at current offense, (4) recent commitment-free period (three years), (5) probation/parole/confinement/escape violation at time of current offense or during present confinement, (6) heroin/opiate dependence, and (7) older age. The SFS places the offender in one of four risk categories: very good, good, fair, or poor. Parole officials consider this score in deciding whether parole is to be granted and, if so, what level of supervision will be required.

Policymakers disagree about which criteria are the most important, and each parole board member brings to the release decision a variety of assumptions, values, and views on the purpose of imprisonment (rehabilitation, incapacitation, or deterrence). The information used to make the parole decision varies significantly, depending on the goal or goals of the decision maker.[25]

State statutes also specify factors that paroling authorities must consider when making their decisions. These considerations generally include the likelihood of recidivism, the welfare of the community into which the inmate will be released, the inmate's prison conduct, and any treatment or rehabilitation plans developed for the inmate.

Parole plays a key role in criminal justice administration, and that puts a parole board in a powerful position. The majority of state parole boards determine the actual duration of incarceration and exercise discretionary release and revocation powers, specifying conditions of release and terms of supervision. The parole board's release policies can have a direct impact on institutional management. For example, parole boards can help reduce prison population by increasing the number of parolees. Lawsuits against the Alabama Department of Corrections, widespread crowding problems (with 27,000 people in prison, Alabama's prisons are about double design capacity), and voters' rejection of a tax referendum, forced Governor Bob Riley to relieve the prison crisis by granting early

salient factor score (SFS)
Scale, developed from a risk-screening instrument, used to predict parole outcome.

Kenneth Wong
State Parole Agent   California Department of Corrections and Rehabilitation

Kenneth Wong is a state parole agent with the California Department of Corrections and Rehabilitation. Before joining the San Francisco parole office in 1990, Wong worked three and one-half years as a correctional officer at the California State Prison at San Quentin and one and one-half years as an auto mechanic. Wong completed the automotive program of the College of Alameda and later enrolled in courses in human behavior at the University of California at Hayward.

As a parole officer, Wong works closely with police and social service agencies. He conducts antinarcotic testing, refers parole violators to the State Board of Prison Terms, and helps parolees make a smooth transition from prison to the community. His paramount concern is community protection.

Wong's advice to people interested in corrections is simple: "If you like working with people who've been in prison and if you have the patience to listen to their problems and make positive referrals and provide advice, then you should apply. The job is challenging, and there is always something new."

In 1996, the California Probation, Parole, and Correctional Association recognized Ken Wong as Parole Agent of the Year. The association said Wong's job performance was exemplary and that he made a significant contribution to the field of corrections.

Wong plans to spend his career with the California Department of Corrections and Rehabilitation. He would like to pursue management positions, beginning with parole unit supervisor.

> *I like being a parole agent because the job allows me to help people who got caught up in the criminal justice system and assist them with a smooth transition from prison back into society by providing a range of services. The most exciting thing about my job is I get to help parolees perform acceptably in the community and remove those who cannot.*

parole to 5,000 persons sentenced for petty theft, DUI, and drug offenses. The state legislature created a special four-member panel to hear early release cases, in addition to the state's three-member parole board. Each panel hears 40 to 50 cases a day, four days a week. At its first hearing on December 3, 2003, the parole board approved early release for 15 prisoners but denied it for 24 others.

Granting Parole—The Hearing In general, parole hearings are attended by victims, the applicant, the institutional representative, and hearing examiners or parole board members. A two-year study of 5,000 parole hearings in Colorado found that the parole board heard too many cases to allow for individualized treatment.[26] The time for a typical parole hearing was 10 to 15 minutes. Unusual cases take longer.

In today's high-tech environment, a number of states such as West Virginia are experimenting with video conferencing equipment that links that state's seven regional jails and three prisons. Instead of requiring the five parole board members to travel around the state to conduct parole hearings at each institution, the new system is expected to save on travel costs and also permit crime victims to testify without having to be in the same room as the offender.

The final decision to grant or deny parole is based on both eligibility guidelines and the interview. If parole is granted, a contract that defines the release plan is executed and the inmate is given a release date. The inmate who is conditionally released to community supervision is called a **parolee.**

parolee
A person who is conditionally released from prison to community supervision.

The trend among parole authorities is to grant or deny parole on the basis of risk to the community. If parole is denied, the common reasons are "not enough time served," "poor disciplinary record," "need to see movement to lower security and success there," and "lack of satisfactory parole program" (proposed home, work, or treatment in the community). In that case, the inmate remains in prison, and a date is set for the next review. The waiting period between hearings depends on the jurisdiction and the inmate's offense.

For example, in October 2006, the New York State Parole Board denied parole for the fourth time to Mark David Chapman, the man who shot and killed John Lennon in 1980. The panel of three board members held a 16-minute hearing and concluded that they remained "concerned about the bizarre nature of this premeditated and violent crime . . . While the panel notes your satisfactory institutional adjustment, due to the extremely violent nature of the offense, your release would not be in the best interest of the community" or his own personal safety.[27] Chapman was sentenced to 20 years to life in 1980. According to New York law, Chapman is entitled to a parole hearing every two years.

Conditions of Parole Paroling authorities set specific conditions for parole, on a case-by-case basis (see Exhibit 8–6). Parolees must comply with these conditions, which may include restitution, substance abuse aftercare, remote-electronic monitoring, and/or house arrest, among others.

Parolees are technically in state custody; they have merely been granted the privilege of living in the community instead of prison. Parole officers, who work closely with the parolee and the paroling authority, carry out the supervision of parolees, and they can return parolees to prison if they threaten community safety or otherwise violate the conditions of release. Depending on the severity of the crime and the risk presented by the offender, parole supervision can incorporate several types of contact with and "examination" of the parolee, including drug testing, setting of a curfew, remote-location monitoring, and employment verification. The paroling authority has at least three responsibilities:

1. to help a parolee with employment, residence, finances, or other personal issues that often present difficulties for a person trying to readjust to life in the community;
2. to protect the community by helping parolees avoid situations that might encourage recidivism; and
3. to expedite parole for those who meet the criteria established by the paroling authority and are unlikely to commit another crime.

The conditions under which parolees must live are very similar in form and structure to those for probationers. Sometimes the rules are established by law, but more often they are established by the paroling authority. The paroling authority can require any of the following forms of release: standard parole supervision, parole with enhanced treatment and programming conditions, halfway house placement, intensive supervision, parole with remote-electronic monitoring and/or voice and location tracking, or release with follow-up drug testing and payment of supervision fees and restitution.

Types of Parole Release on parole may be mandatory or discretionary. Discretionary parole decisions are made by a paroling authority such as a parole board or parole commission after its members review a case to determine whether they believe the prisoner is ready to be returned to

EXHIBIT 8–6   Sample Order for Release on Parole

MARYLAND PAROLE COMMISSION   No. 028239

ORDER FOR RELEASE ON PAROLE

The Parole Commission, by virtue of the authority conferred upon it by the laws of the State of Maryland, does hereby grant parole to:

(True Name)   Travis Glen Hardin, #273843, DOB November 24, 1973

(Commitment Name/s)

who was convicted of: Distribution of cocaine; Violation of probation

Court: Talbot County Circuit Court #6903

Sentenced: May 18, 2003

Term: 6 years; 2 years, 6 months

From: March 10, 2003; consecutive

Therefore, the said Commission does hereby order the release on parole of the said prisoner from

Eastern Correctional Institution

(Correctional Institution or Jail)

The Parolee, upon release, shall be deemed to remain in legal custody until the expiration of the full, undiminished term and upon violation of any condition of his parole shall be remanded to the authority from which paroled, where a hearing shall be conducted by the Parole Commission. If parole is revoked, the Commission shall determine the amount of time spent on parole, if any, which shall be credited to the parolee.

This order is subject to the rules, regulation, and conditions of this parole as set forth below and on page 2 of this agreement, and such further conditions as the Commission may impose at any time during the period of parole.

Upon being released, report to the Division of Parole and Probation office located at

301 Bay Street, Suite 302, Easton, MD 21601 (410-555-1212)

MARYLAND PAROLE COMMISSION

Parole Expiration Date: September 2011   By: Patricia K. Cushwa
                                                                        Commissioner

Special Condition(s): substance abuse therapy, supervision and drug testing fees, subject to curfew as
    directed by parole agent, community service if agent directs, employment within 30 days

                                                                        March 20, 2006
                                                                        Date

Home/Employment Plan: live with mother–Lynn Fortney, 2055 Sokol Drive,

Tilghman, MD 21671 (410-822-5555)

Anyone serving a sentence for a crime committed on or after May 1, 1991, must pay supervision and/or drug testing fees as prescribed in Article 41, Section 4.519 of the Annotated Code of Maryland.

Date(s) of Offense(s): January 6, 2003

MPC - 14 - (Revised 8/15/96)

WHITE – Parolee · PINK – Parole Commission Copy · YELLOW – Institution Copy · BLUE – Certified Copy · GREEN – Court Copy

the community. The criteria used to reach the decision vary from state to state, as discussed earlier. Discretionary parole decisions occur in jurisdictions using indeterminate sentencing.

Mandatory parole release is set by law and occurs in jurisdictions using determinate sentencing. It requires the correctional authority to grant

EXHIBIT 8–7	Comparing Discretionary Release and Mandatory Release	
	Discretionary Release	**Mandatory Release**
Release date	Decided by parole board	Determined by law
Criteria	Based on parole board guidelines	None[1]
Postrelease supervision	Yes	Maybe

1. Corrections authorities may have discretion to grant or deny good-time credits in mandatory release cases.

Source: Adapted from Jeremy Travis and Sarah Lawrence, *Beyond the Prison Gates: The State of Parole in America* (Washington, DC: Urban Institute, 2002). Copyright © 2002 The Urban Institute.

parole after the inmate serves a specific period of time, as required by law. Exhibit 8–7 compares discretionary and mandatory parole release.

Historically, most states used discretionary parole release. But over the past few decades, the balance between the two methods of parole release has shifted. In 1977, 69 percent of parolees received discretionary parole board release. States began moving away from discretionary release policies in the 1980s in favor of determinate sentences and mandatory parole release. (We will return to a discussion of this trend later in this chapter.) Consistent with the adoption of truth in sentencing and other mandatory release statutes, mandatory parole release increased from 45 percent in 1995 to 51 percent in 2005, while discretionary parole release decreased from 50 to 31 percent. Exhibit 8–8 shows how much the share of prison releases by type of parole has changed from 1977 to 2005.

Mandatory release is the most common method of release from prison today. Some argue that abandonment of discretionary release in favor of mandatory release has detrimental effects. Proponents of discretionary parole board release argue that parole boards serve a salutary function by requiring inmates to focus their efforts on successful reentry from prison to the community. Without the prospect of discretionary release,

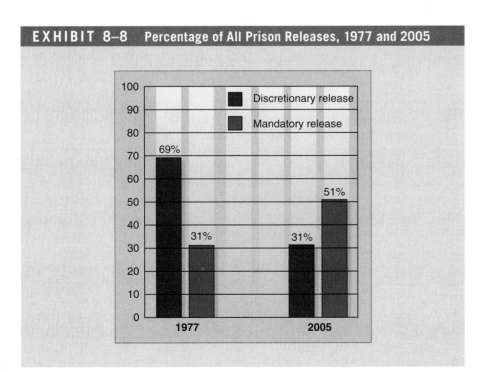

EXHIBIT 8–8   Percentage of All Prison Releases, 1977 and 2005

inmates have fewer incentives for engaging in good behavior or participating in rehabilitative programs, and prison administrators have fewer mechanisms for relieving institutional crowding.

Whether prisoners are released by mandatory or discretionary parole, nationally approximately 80 percent of all parolees are placed on community supervision after release from prison for a predetermined period of time and must adhere to certain conditions, such as those shown in Exhibit 8–6. The national statistic, however, masks the large number of prisoners being released back into the community without any parole supervision. For the past 15 years, the percentage of persons released from state prison due to the expiration of their sentence increased from 13 percent in 1990 to 19 percent in 2004. (This meant they were released from prison with no special obligations. They had no parole officer, no special legal status, and no restrictions on their behavior, except those that result from their criminal convictions such as prohibitions against voting and certain kinds of employment.) Even though the percentage of all persons released from prison unconditionally has remained relatively stable, the sheer number of people released from prison with no community supervision some say is cause for alarm and for a rethinking of the role of discretionary release, if not to benefit the individual then to protect public safety.

Reentry Issues for Women Prisoner reentry problems are magnified for women leaving prison, especially minority women. Nearly two-thirds of the women confined in jails and state and federal prisons are black, Hispanic, or of other nonwhite ethnic groups. As reported in Chapter 7, women in prison have a high rate of prior sexual or physical abuse, high rates of positive-HIV status and other sexually transmitted diseases, and high alcohol, drug use, and addiction rates at the time of arrest. "In most of their communities," writes Beth Richie of the University of Illinois at Chicago, "there are few services and very limited resources available to assist women in the process of reentry."[28] Based on a series of interviews with women three times released from prison, Richie identifies seven challenges and barriers to successful reentry for women prisoners:

1. Many women require long-term prison-based treatment for substance abuse problems and continuation of treatment after release, with attention paid to gender-specific needs such as child care and protection from sexual harassment. Such treatment and protection are related to successful reentry.

2. Most women who enter correctional facilities receive emergency medical care while they are incarcerated, but most are released with their long-term health care needs unmet. Richie learned that women on parole need help to manage the ongoing complications of HIV, asthma, diabetes, and reproductive health problems. Unless women on parole receive ongoing medical care, health problems follow women back into the community after release.

3. More than one-half of the women Richie interviewed had chronic mental health issues for which they received no treatment during and after incarceration. Mental health treatment during and after incarceration facilitates successful reintegration.

4. Community social services must remove the barriers that keep women with arrest records from receiving their services. Women on parole return to abusive relationships and high-risk communities and need support to deal with violence.

5. Without educational and employment services, women on parole experience an increased pull to return to illegal activity as they exhaust their public aid options. Most women on parole do not have academic or job-related skills or experiences to support themselves or their children. Their life histories establish an immediate need for communities to do more (not less, as argued for by politicians in favor of the no-frills movement discussed in Chapter 13) and to develop comprehensive educational and occupational programs during and after incarceration.

6. Housing that is safe, secure, and affordable is probably the most immediate need of a woman parolee. Where will she spend the night? Many have severed ties with their families because of their illegal activities. All of the women in Richie's sample had been homeless at least once for three months or more. Finding housing is related to the educational and employment opportunities already mentioned and complicated by the fact that women with criminal records are often barred from publicly funded low-income housing.

7. It is easy to believe that women on parole are not caring parents. However, Richie found that "even in those instances where the nature of the illegal activity and the situations that women found themselves in created a less than optimal environment for child rearing, most women report worrying about their children before and after they are arrested."[29] The challenge is to offer mothers in prison parental support. Even learning how to have a noncustodial relationship with their children, Richie argues, can help stabilize women as they make difficult transitions back into the community.

Women on parole face many problems. Communities can acknowledge the unique needs of such women and work to make reentry successful for them, or they can ignore them and watch as their problems follow them back into the community after release.

CHARACTERISTICS OF PAROLEES

The tremendous increase in the prison population discussed in Chapter 7 has given many people a sense of safety and security. However, the majority of the population is also unconcerned—or unaware—that at least 95 percent of those who enter prisons eventually return to the community, and most do so in about two and one-half years. Some have put it this way: More prisoners in results in more prisoners out!

More than 1,600 prisoners each day leave prison. About one in five leaves prison with no postrelease supervision because of changes in sentencing legislation that allow some prisoners to "max out" (serve their full sentences) and leave prison with no postcustody supervision as discussed previously. On January 1, 2006, 784,408 American adults were on parole—an increase of 1.6 percent (12,556 parolees) over January 1, 2005.[30] Eighty-eight percent of those adults were state parolees; the rest were federal.

The basic demographics of parolees have not changed much over the past 20 years. The typical adult parolee is a white, non-Hispanic male on mandatory parole and under active parole supervision for more than one year. The median age is 34, with an 11th-grade education. Women make up 12 percent of the parole population (see Exhibit 8–9). The region with the highest number of parolees is the South, followed by the West, Northeast, and Midwest.

EXHIBIT 8–9   **Selected Characteristics of Adults on Parole**

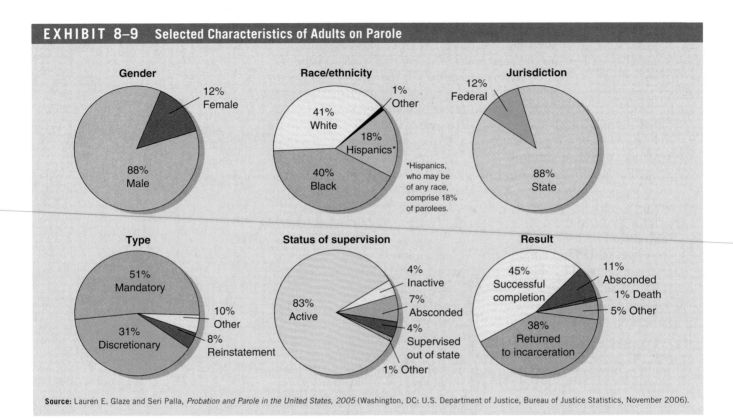

Source: Lauren E. Glaze and Seri Palla, *Probation and Parole in the United States, 2005* (Washington, DC: U.S. Department of Justice, Bureau of Justice Statistics, November 2006).

Not all who are sent to prison are released on parole. Those who are the most serious offenders (those who have life sentences or who face the death penalty) or who have disciplinary problems while incarcerated generally are not paroled. Instead, they live out their lives in prison or are released when they have served their entire sentences.

Trends in the Parole Population

The estimated number of adults under community supervision and incarceration from 1995 through 2005 is shown in Exhibit 8–10. The parole population has continually increased, averaging a growth of 1.4 percent per year. The low rate of growth in the parole population reflects changes in sentencing and parole release policies that have resulted in increasing lengths of stay in prisons and declining prison release rates. Still, according to one criminologist, "The numbers of returning offenders dwarf anything known before, the needs of released inmates are greater, and corrections has retained few rehabilitation programs." [31] Many parolees have long histories of criminal or gang involvement and few marketable skills. Most employers are also reluctant to hire ex-offenders. A survey in five major cities revealed that two of three employers would not knowingly hire an ex-offender (regardless of the offense), and one of three said they had checked the criminal records of their most recent hires. [32] Further, there are increased employment restrictions on parolees convicted of felonies who want to practice a profession that requires licensing (for example, law, real estate, medicine, nursing, physical therapy, teaching, dentistry, engineering, pharmacy, and barbering). Thirty-four states (including the District of Columbia) impose some kind of legal restriction on public employment after a felony conviction. [33]

Here's the contradiction: States spend at least $1.2 billion a year on parole, convincing offenders that they need to find legitimate employment, but then they frustrate them by barring them from many kinds of

EXHIBIT 8–10	Adults on Probation, in Jail or Prison, and on Parole, 1995–2005				
	Total Estimated Correctional Population	Probation	Jail	Prison	Parole
1995	5,342,900	3,077,861	507,044	1,078,542	679,421
2000	6,445,100	3,826,209	621,149	1,316,333	723,898
2001	6,581,700	3,931,731	631,240	1,330,007	732,333
2002	6,758,800	4,024,067	665,475	1,367,547	750,934
2003	6,936,600	4,144,781	691,301	1,392,796	745,125
2004	6,996,500	4,151,125	713,990	1,421,911	765,355
2005	7,056,000	4,162,536	747,529	1,446,269	784,408

Source: Adapted from Lauren E. Glaze and Seri Palla, *Probation and Parole in the United States, 2005* (Washington, DC: U.S. Department of Justice, Bureau of Justice Statistics, November 2006), p. 1.

jobs that could improve the level of their existence.[34] And it's not only in the employment arena that parolees have problems. Currently an estimated 4 to 5 million people in the United States have lost their voting rights as the result of a felony conviction. Although some believe that disenfranchisement of felons is an acceptable penalty for crime, others argue that denying large segments of the population the right to vote is likely to cause further alienation and make people less willing to participate in legitimate free-world activities. We return to the issue of parolees' voting later in this chapter.

Exhibit 8–11 defines parole populations among the states on January 1, 2006. California had the largest number of adults on parole, followed by Texas and Pennsylvania. Pennsylvania also had the highest rate of parole supervision (787 parolees supervised per 100,000 adult residents), which means it used parole more than any other state; Maine used parole the least (3 per 100,000 adult residents).

Does Parole Work?

Parole rates, like probation rates, should be viewed in context. Parole starts with a population of 100 failures (i.e., convicted felons). How realistic is it then to expect parole, after conviction and after the debilitating aspects of prison, to magically succeed with criminals where the home, the school, the police, and the courts have all arguably failed?

Still the most common way to answer the question "Does parole work?" is to ask what percentage of people placed on parole supervision complete their parole term successfully. There are at least four ways to view success.

The first way to view success may include those who do not return to prison. A second view may include those who are not rearrested while under parole supervision. A third may include those who do not commit any technical violations. The fourth takes a broader view and focuses on issues such as stable employment, adequate housing, and healthy family and personal relationships. Data on the first three ways of defining parole success are available and are discussed in the following text. Data on the fourth view are not routinely collected and are beyond the scope of this chapter.

Parole Success   The U.S. Department of Justice's Bureau of Justice Statistics defines parole as successful if the parolee completes a term of community supervision without returning to prison or jail or absconding. Using this definition, in 2006 45 percent of people discharged from

EXHIBIT 8-11   Selected Parole Populations Among the States, January 1, 2006

Ten States with the Largest Parole Populations	Number Supervised	Ten States with the Highest Rates of Supervision	People Supervised per 100,000 Adult U.S. Residents	Ten States with the Lowest Rates of Supervision	People Supervised per 100,000 Adult U.S. Residents
California	111,743	Pennsylvania	787	Maine	3
Texas	101,916	Arkansas	782	Florida	34
Pennsylvania	75,732	Oregon	766	Rhode Island	41
New York	53,533	Louisiana	712	North Carolina	47
Illinois	34,576	Texas	611	Nebraska	50
Louisiana	24,072	California	421	North Dakota	57
Georgia	22,851	Missouri	414	Massachusetts	73
Oregon	21,499	South Dakota	414	Virginia	78
Michigan	19,978	Wisconsin	365	Mississippi	90
Ohio	19,512	New York	364	Delaware	92

Source: Adapted from Lauren E. Glaze and Seri Palla, *Probation and Parole in the United States, 2005* (Washington, DC: U.S. Department of Justice, Bureau of Justice Statistics, November 2006), p. 3.

parole (that is, people leaving active parole supervision in the community) were successful. The percentage of persons discharged from parole who were deemed successful has been relatively stable for the past 10 years.

Researchers in Tennessee found that first-time releases to state parole do better than rereleases.[35] In every year during the 1990s, first-time releases to state parole were more successful than re-releases. In 1990, 56 percent of first-time releases were successful compared with 15 percent of rereleases. In 1999, of those exiting parole, 63 percent of first-time releases were successful, compared to 21 percent of rereleases.

The researchers also found that success on parole depends on the method of release—whether it is discretionary or mandatory. In every year between 1990 and 1999, state prisoners released by a parole board had higher success rates than those released through mandatory release. Between 1990 and 1999, the percent of successful discretionary parole board releases varied between 50 and 56 percent, while the percent of successful mandatory releases ranged between 24 and 33 percent.

When the researchers combined method of release and status of parolee (first-time vs. rerelease), first-time mandatory parole releases had a higher success rate (79 percent) than did first-time discretionary parole board releases (61 percent). However, when researchers looked at the success of parolees rereleased from state prison, they found just the opposite: Discretionary parole board releases in 1999 who had been rereleased from prison were more successful (37 percent) than were mandatory parolees (17 percent).

The research results can be an important tool for allocating resources. Knowing that method of release and status of parolee (first-time vs. rerelease) are related to success on parole may suggest different sets of parole conditions depending upon method of release and status of parolee, allowing for a better distribution of fiscal and human resources.

A parole officer questions one of his parolees about a suspected new offense violation. One reason for revoking parole is the parolee's arrest for a criminal offense. What are other reasons parole may be revoked?

Parole Failures Rates of relapse and recidivism are high, especially in the vulnerable period immediately following release. In fact, two-thirds of all parolees are rearrested within three years, typically within the first six months of release.

The number of parole violators returned to prison continues to increase. Of the nearly 503,800 parolees discharged from parole supervision in 2005, 191,800 (38 percent) were returned to prison because of either a rule violation or a new offense, up from 27,177 in 1980 and 160,000 in 1995. The numbers are so high that parole failures account for a growing proportion of all new prison admissions.

Shouldn't parole supervision produce lower recidivism? The obvious answer is yes. However, if you look at only broad national statistics on the impact of parole supervision, the data are not encouraging. For example, researchers at the Urban Institute discovered that parole supervision has little effect on the rearrest rates of released prisoners.[36] (Mandatory parolees—who represent the largest share of released prisoners—are no better off in terms of rearrest than prisoners released without supervision [inmates released at the expiration of their sentence].) Those screened by parole boards are less likely to be rearrested, but the difference is relatively small. Furthermore, this small difference may be due to factors other than supervision, given that parole boards base their decision on such factors as attitude, motivation, and preparedness for release.

The public safety impact of supervision is minimal and often nonexistent among the largest share of the release cohort—male property, drug, and violent offenders. Supervision does not appear to improve recidivism outcomes for violent offenders or property offenders released to mandatory parole. Supervision is only associated with lower rearrest rates among discretionary parolees who had been incarcerated for a property offense. In fact, for male drug offenders, mandatory release to supervision predicts higher rearrest rates than for unconditional releasees or discretionary parolees. These higher rates may reflect the fact that mandatory parolees are a higher-risk population than discretionary parolees and face heightened surveillance (such as drug testing) compared with unconditional releasees. In short, while postprison supervision may have modest effects on recidivism in some cases, it does not appear to improve rearrest rates for the largest subsets of released prisoners. The answer is to look beyond the broad sweep of national statistics and examine what impact parole supervision has on women, those with few prior arrests, public order offenders, and technical violators. When those questions are asked, we find rearrest rates as much as 16 percentage points lower than rates observed with unconditional release. In addition, persons with combinations of these characteristics (e.g., females with few prior arrests who were incarcerated for a public order offense) who were released to supervision were predicted to have even lower rearrest rates.

Once again, research results can be an important tool for allocating resources.

Why are they returning? Parole may be revoked for two reasons. A *technical violation* occurs when any of the technical conditions of parole (e.g., find and keep a job, live at home, sign no contracts, pay restitution and fees, perform community service, attend drug and alcohol abuse counseling) are violated. According to the U.S. Department of Justice, more than one-third of incoming prisoners are admitted for violating parole. Of the parole violators returned to prison, nearly one-third were returned for a new conviction and two-thirds for a technical violation. The Justice Department adds that a significant number of these are attributable to incomplete and/or inadequate release planning, imposition of unrealistic rules, and ineffective case management.[37] Other scholars tell us that technical violations are sometimes a function of clients' symptoms or their difficulties in following directions. Parolees with serious mental illness might violate the technical conditions of supervision because of cognitive impairment, delusions, confusion, or side effects of psychotropic medications.[38] And parolees with HIV/AIDS require collaborative assistance from correction departments, departments of public health, and community-based organizations that few communities can provide. Alaska's standard conditions of parole are presented in Exhibit 8–12.

The second type of violation is a *new offense violation*. This involves arrest for the commission of a new crime. A new offense violation might involve a technical violation. For example, an arrest for selling drugs and a positive test for drug use would be a violation for a new offense and a technical violation.

When a violation occurs, a revocation hearing date is set. The purpose of a revocation hearing is to determine whether the violation warrants the parolee's removal from the community. During a revocation hearing, the parolee has certain rights of due process because he or she could lose conditional freedom; but the parolee is not entitled to a full adversary hearing, as would be the case in a new criminal proceeding. If the parolee violates the conditions of parole, a revocation hearing could return the offender to prison to serve the remainder of the original sentence plus any new sentence that might be given because of new violations.[39] Returning parole violators to prison has consequences for prison crowding. Some argue that only parole violators who commit new offense violations should be returned to prison. Those who violate the technical conditions of their parole should be punished through community sanctions such as community service, remote-electronic monitoring, drug treatment, intensive parole supervision, or jail. The entire continuum of intermediate sanctions (the topic of Chapter 5), they argue, should be used before sending chronic technical violators to prison. For example, in Wyoming parole violators are sent to a 60-bed revocation center where they receive

ETHICS & PROFESSIONALISM

American Probation and Parole Association Code of Ethics

- I will render professional service to the justice system and the community at large in effecting the social adjustment of the offender.
- I will uphold the law with dignity, displaying an awareness of my responsibility to offenders while recognizing the right of the public to be safeguarded from criminal activity.
- I will strive to be objective in the performance of my duties, recognizing the inalienable right of all persons, appreciating the inherent worth of the individual, and respecting those confidences which can be reposed in me.
- I will conduct my personal life with decorum, neither accepting nor granting favors in connection with my office.
- I will cooperate with my co-workers and related agencies and will continually strive to improve my professional competence through the seeking and sharing of knowledge and understanding.
- I will distinguish clearly, in public, between my statements and actions as an individual and as a representative of my profession.
- I will encourage policy, procedures, and personnel practices, which will enable others to conduct themselves in accordance with the values, goals, and objectives of the American Probation and Parole Association.
- I recognize my office as a symbol of public faith and I accept it as a public trust to be held as long as I am true to the ethics of the American Probation and Parole Association.
- I will constantly strive to achieve these objectives and ideals, dedicating myself to my chosen profession.

Source: American Probation and Parole Association.

Ethical Dilemma 8–1: Offenders often leave prison without job skills, money, or personal coping skills. Should they be released on parole? Is parole working? What can agencies do to assist parolees? For more information go to Ethical Dilemma 8–1 at www.justicestudies .com/ethics04.

Ethical Dilemma 8–2: A woman with young children is a repeat offender who has again violated her parole. Should she remain in the community, or should she return to prison? What are the issues? Should a parolee's gender make a difference in treatment? For more information go to Ethical Dilemma 8–2 at www.justicestudies .com/ethics04.

Ethical Dilemmas for every chapter are available online.

---

intense treatment in substance abuse, education in work skills, and help with other issues needing attention. Treatment at the revocation center is carried out in a therapeutic setting that provides a supportive environment for offenders to hold each other accountable. Parole violators stay at the center from three to nine months, depending on the offender's risk and needs assessment and individual case plan.

Some jurisdictions are experimenting with incentives that encourage positive actions on the part of the offender. The belief is that sometimes we focus too much on trying to control behavior through punishment and ignore the other side of the equation—encouraging compliance with incentives and rewards. These incentives include reduced reporting requirements, allowing reports to be made through phone calls or other methods that do not involve office visits, early termination of supervision, and extensions of time to accomplish specific activities. Although using rewards to recognize positive offender accomplishments can be an important component of a violation system, to date this aspect of supervision has received much less attention than the alternative, responding to failures with disciplinary sanctions. The American Probation and Parole Association Code of Ethics reinforces these rapport-building strategies (see the Ethics and Professionalism box).

The primary difference between a criminal trial and a revocation hearing is the threshold of evidence that the hearing body needs in order

EXHIBIT 8–12 Sample State Conditions of Parole

State of Alaska

Standard Conditions of Parole

The following standard conditions of parole apply to all prisoners released on mandatory or discretionary parole, in accordance with AS 33.16.150(a).

1. REPORT UPON RELEASE: I will report in person no later than the next working day after my release to the parole officer located at the PAROLE OFFICE and receive further reporting instructions. I will reside at _____.

2. MAINTAIN EMPLOYMENT/TRAINING/TREATMENT: I will make a diligent effort to maintain steady employment and support my legal dependents. I will not voluntarily change or terminate employment without receiving permission from my parole officer to do so. If discharged or if employment is terminated (temporarily or permanently) for any reason, I will notify my parole officer the next working day. If I am involved in an education, training, or treatment program, I will continue active participation in the program unless I receive permission from my parole officer to quit. If I am released, removed, or terminated from the program for any reason, I will notify my parole officer the next working day.

3. REPORT MONTHLY: I will report to my parole officer at least monthly in the manner prescribed by my parole officer. I will follow any other reporting instructions established by my parole officer.

4. OBEY LAWS/ORDERS: I will obey all state, federal, and local laws, ordinances, orders, and court orders.

5. PERMISSION BEFORE CHANGING RESIDENCE: I will obtain permission from my parole officer before changing my residence. Remaining away from my approved residence for 24 hours or more constitutes a change in residence for the purpose of this condition.

6. TRAVEL PERMIT BEFORE TRAVEL OUTSIDE ALASKA: I will obtain the prior written permission of my parole officer in the form of an interstate travel agreement before leaving the state of Alaska. Failure to abide by the conditions of the travel agreement is a violation of my order of parole.

7. NO FIREARMS/WEAPONS: I will not own, possess, have in my custody, handle, purchase, or transport any firearm, ammunition, or explosives. I may not carry any deadly weapon on my person except a pocket knife with a 3" or shorter blade. Carrying any other weapon on my person such as a hunting knife, axe, club, etc. is a violation of my order of parole. I will contact the Alaska Board of Parole if I have any questions about the use of firearms, ammunition, or weapons.

8. NO DRUGS: I will not use, possess, handle, purchase, give, or administer any narcotic, hallucinogenic, (including marijuana/THC), stimulant, depressant, amphetamine, barbiturate, or prescription drug not specifically prescribed by a licensed medical person.

9. REPORT POLICE CONTACT: I will report to my parole officer, no later than the next working day, any contact with a law enforcement officer.

10. DO NOT WORK AS AN INFORMANT: I will not enter into any agreement or other arrangement with any law enforcement agency which will place me in the position of violating any law or any condition of my parole. I understand the Department of Corrections and Parole Board policy prohibits me from working as an informant.

11. NO CONTACT WITH PRISONERS OR FELONS: I may not telephone, correspond with, or visit any person confined in a prison, penitentiary, correctional institution or camp, jail, halfway house, work release center, community residential center, restitution center, juvenile correctional center, etc. Contact with a felon during the course of employment or during corrections-related treatment is not prohibited if approved by my parole officer. Any other knowing contact with a felon is prohibited unless approved by my parole officer. I will notify my parole officer the next working day if I have contact with a prisoner or felon.

12. CANNOT LEAVE AREA: I will receive permission from my parole officer before leaving the area of the state to which my case is assigned. My parole officer will advise me in writing of limits of the area to which I have been assigned.

13. OBEY ALL ORDERS/SPECIAL CONDITIONS: I will obey any special instructions, rules, or order given to me by the Alaska Board of Parole or by my parole officer. I will follow any special conditions imposed by the Alaska Board of Parole or my parole officer.

Source: State of Alaska Board of Parole, *Parole Handbook, Appendix II; Conditions of Parole*, June 1998.

to convict. In a criminal trial, a conviction may be obtained only if the government proves its facts *beyond a reasonable doubt*. In a revocation hearing, the panel need only find that a violation is shown *by a preponderance of the evidence*.[40] In addition, there is a more relaxed rule of what constitutes evidence—a rule that permits letters, affidavits, and reports to be presented in lieu of direct testimony.

ISSUES IN PAROLE

Over the past few decades, the face of parole has changed. This chapter concludes with a discussion of several important issues in parole, including voting rights, reentry courts, successful reintegration programs involving victims, court rulings that have changed the parole revocation process, the abolition of discretionary parole board release, prisoner reentry and community policing, and community-focused parole.

Can Parolees Vote?

Among the many issues being debated by legislators and correctional policymakers in planning for successful reentry is felon disenfranchisement, meaning depriving persons who have been convicted of felonies of the right to vote. Currently, an estimated 4 to 5 million people in the United States have lost their voting rights as the result of a felony conviction, including more than 1.4 million African American men (13 percent of the adult black male population), 500,000 U.S. veterans, and almost 700,000 women.[41] There is no federal law governing the voting rights of people who have been convicted of crimes. The U.S. Constitution, Article 1, Section 2, gives the matter of voting rights to the states.

Today, 45 states and the District of Columbia deny felons the right to vote. Only five states (California, Florida, Maine, Maryland, and Vermont) have restored the voting rights of ex-offenders. Maine and Vermont do not place any restrictions on the right of felons to vote. In Maine and Vermont prisoners vote by absentee ballot.

States' voting restrictions are as follows:

- 17 states bar felons from voting while they are incarcerated or serving parole or probation sentences: Arizona, Arkansas, Florida, Georgia, Idaho, Kansas, Louisiana, Minnesota, Missouri, New Jersey, New Mexico, North Carolina, Oklahoma, Pennsylvania, Rhode Island, South Carolina, Texas, West Virginia.

- 12 states deny voting rights to felons only while they are incarcerated: Hawaii, Indiana, Illinois, Massachusetts, Michigan, Montana, New Hampshire, North Dakota, Ohio, Oregon, South Dakota, Utah.

- 11 states have lifetime bans on voting for some or all felons convicted of crimes: Alabama, Delaware, Iowa, Kentucky, Maryland, Mississippi, Nebraska, Nevada, Tennessee, Virginia, Washington, Wyoming.

- 5 states bar felons from voting while they are incarcerated or on parole: Alaska, California, Colorado, Connecticut, New York, Wisconsin.[42]

Policies on reinstating an ex-felon's right to vote vary greatly from state to state. A few states instantly reinstate voting privileges after offenders serve their sentence, including any community supervision. Most require a reinstatement process such as review and approval by a clemency board, a waiting period after the completion of community supervision, or the

Only Maine and Vermont do not place any restrictions on the right to vote for people with felony convictions. Prisoners in Maine and Vermont vote by absentee ballot. An estimated 4 to 5 million people in the United States have lost their voting rights as a result of a felony conviction. What are the arguments for and against felon disenfranchisement?

governor's approval. No one knows for sure, but some believe that very few ex-offenders petition to regain their right to vote because the process is confusing and complex.[43]

Even local boards of elections are unclear about the reinstatement policies. Almost one-fourth of Ohio's boards of elections misinformed callers posing as people with felony convictions, telling them that they could not vote while under community supervision, although Ohio state law denies voting rights to felons only while they are incarcerated.[44] During the research, 13 of Ohio's 88 boards of elections said they did not know the state's law on whether people on probation or parole could vote.

Below we present the arguments for and against felon disenfranchisement. As you read them, remember that they have not been scientifically proved. They sound rational on the surface, but social science research has yet to validate them.

There are at least four arguments in support of felon disenfranchisement. First, inmates should be denied the right to vote as a matter of principle because they committed a felony. Second, states have the right to deny felons the right to vote as added punishment, just as they have the right to restrict felons from certain occupations. For example, today some states have exercised their right to require felons convicted of certain child sex abuse crimes to wear an electronic monitor for life. On May 2, 2005, then-Florida governor Jeb Bush signed into law the Jessica Lunsford Act. The act is named after the 9-year-old girl who was kidnapped from her bedroom and murdered by John E. Covey, a convicted sex offender. The act requires that persons convicted of certain child sex abuse crimes on children under 12 be sentenced to at least 25 years in prison and lifetime tracking by the Global Positioning System (GPS) satellite if they are ever released from prison.

Third, denying felons the right to vote sends a message about respect for the law and acts as a deterrent to crime. And fourth, felons should be denied the right to vote because they cannot be trusted to make politically informed decisions.

On the other hand, there are five arguments against felon disenfranchisement. First, voting is not a privilege but a right guaranteed by the Constitution, and states don't have the right to take it away. Second, felon disenfranchisement laws are unfair to minorities who are treated unfairly by the criminal justice system. Third, felon disenfranchisement laws are not an effective form of punishment since most ex-felons did not vote before incarceration. Fourth, removal of an inmate's right to vote is inconsistent with reentry. Offenders should be encouraged to accept more responsibility for their future roles in the community. Voting encourages inmates to view themselves as participating members of society, not as outcasts from it. And fifth, once we open the door by declaring that a certain group of people does not deserve the basic right to vote, then which group of people might be the next we attempt to restrict?

The irony in denying felony inmates, probationers, and parolees the right to vote is that they can run for Congress and in many states for governor, attorney general, sheriff, or even judge. The 1995 U.S. Supreme Court ruling in U.S. *Term Limits, Inc.* v. *Thornton* gave inmates the freedom to run for Congress. In 2002, eight-term U.S. Representative Jim Traficant (D-Ohio) was sentenced to eight years in federal prison on charges of corruption for taking campaign funds for personal use. While incarcerated in White Deer, Pennsylvania, Traficant ran as an independent candidate for another term in the House as an Ohio representative.

He received 15 percent of the vote (27,487 votes) and became one of only a handful of individuals in the history of the United States to run for a federal office from prison.

In Chicago, Percy Giles and Wallace Davis Jr. were seeking to reclaim their seats on the city council on election day, February 28, 2007. Both men were convicted on public corruption charges while in office and served time in federal prison. Illinois law bars ex-felons from running for municipal office, but nobody challenged Giles and Davis possibly because of the reform efforts they demonstrated after release from prison. (Giles became a minister and works with released offenders. Davis owns Wallace's Catfish Corner on Chicago's West Side and several other commercial properties.) On election day, however, both men received only 10 percent of the vote. Does it make sense to deny felons the right to vote if they can run for office?

In 2001, the bipartisan National Commission on Election Reform, cochaired by former presidents Gerald Ford and Jimmy Carter, concluded that ex-felons who have completed their sentences should be allowed to vote. In 2005, the American Correctional Association unanimously approved a policy on restoration of voting rights for felony offenders (see Exhibit 8–13).

EXHIBIT 8–13 **American Correctional Association**

Public Correctional Policy on Restoration of Voting Rights for Felony Offenders

Introduction

People convicted of crimes are expected to become responsible citizens after being discharged from correctional supervision. However, many individuals are excluded from exercising their civic rights because they are banned from voting in many jurisdictions. The laws that prohibit offenders from voting, even after they have been discharged from correctional supervision, frustrate the offenders in their attempts to fully reenter society successfully, reduce the voting constituency, and disproportionately exclude a large number of people from participating fully in society.

Nearly all states place some form of restriction on felon voting rights. Some states have developed processes to restore voting rights, but many felons are unaware of them, do not present the proper documentation, or the processes are often very cumbersome and have the effect of discouraging voting.

Policy Statement

The American Correctional Association affirms that voting is a fundamental right in a democracy and it considers a ban on voting after a felon is discharged from correctional supervision to be contradictory to the goals of a democracy, the rehabilitation of felons, and their successful re-entry to the community.

Therefore, ACA advocates:

- A. Restoring voting rights for felony offenders once they have been discharged from incarceration or parole;
- B. Developing protocols for federal, state, and local correctional agencies that inform inmates near their release about the means by which their voting rights will be restored and provide education and assistance to felony offenders in completing the restoration process to regain their civil rights; and
- C. Developing state election agency procedures that permit eligible felony offenders to vote in elections after completing and filing all necessary paperwork.

Source: Copyright © American Correctional Association.

A reentry court transition team meets with the parolee on a regular basis to manage and support offenders after release from prison. A reentry court manages the return to the community of individuals released from prison, using the authority of the court to apply graduated sanctions and positive reinforcement and to marshal resources to support the prisoner's reintegration. What are the core elements of reentry court?

reentry court

A court that manages the return to the community of individuals released from prison.

In recent years attempts at removing voting restrictions failed in Alabama, Arizona, and Nebraska.

Reentry Courts

It is incumbent on criminal justice policymakers who are interested in greater public safety and more efficient use of public tax dollars to consider how we might better handle the challenges of the more than 1,600 offenders who leave prison each day. Because of the potential threats that parolees pose to victims, families, children, and communities, investing in effective parole programs may be one of the best investments we make.

One of the latest innovations in helping offenders released from prison make a successful adjustment to the community is the reentry court. A **reentry court** manages the return to the community of individuals released from prison, using the authority of the court to apply graduated sanctions and positive reinforcement and to marshal resources to support the prisoner's reintegration. The U.S. attorney general has proposed that reentry courts operate like drug courts or other problem-solving courts (domestic violence court, community court, family court, gun court, and DWI court).[45] In drug court, for example, a judge is limited to managing a caseload of drug-involved offenders. The judge requires an offender to make regular court appearances and participate in drug treatment and testing. If the drug offender violates the conditions of release, the judge administers a predetermined range of graduated sanctions that do not automatically require return to prison (except for new crimes or egregious violations). Frequent appearances before the court, offers of assistance, and the knowledge of a predetermined range of sanctions for violations of the conditions of release assist the offender in getting back on track.

The U.S. Department of Justice proposes that a reentry court have six core elements:

- **Assessment and planning:** Correctional administrators and the reentry judge meet with inmates who are near release to explain the reentry process, assess inmates' needs, and begin building links to a range of social services, family counseling, health and mental health services, housing, job training, and work opportunities that support reintegration.
- **Active judicial oversight:** The reentry court sees all prisoners released into the community with a high degree of frequency, maybe once or twice a month. Also involved are the parole officer and others responsible for assessing the parolee's progress. In court, offender progress is praised, and offender setbacks are discussed.
- **Case management of support services:** The reentry court acts as a service broker and advocates on behalf of parolees for substance abuse treatment, job training, private employment, faith instruction, family member support, housing, and community services.

- **Accountability to the community:** Reentry courts appoint broad-based community advisory boards to develop and maintain accountability to the community. Advisory boards also help courts negotiate the sometimes difficult task of brokering services for parolees and advocate on their behalf.
- **Graduated sanctions:** Reentry courts establish a predetermined range of graduated sanctions for violations of the conditions of release that do not automatically require return to prison.
- **Rewarding success:** Reentry courts incorporate positive judicial reinforcement actions after goals are achieved. Examples include negotiating early release from parole or conducting graduation ceremonies similar to those used in drug courts.

Models of four reentry courts are shown in Exhibit 8–14.

According to the U.S. Department of Justice, "The successful completion of parole should be seen as an important life event for an offender, and the court can help acknowledge that accomplishment. Courts provide powerful public forums for encouraging positive behavior and for acknowledging the individual effort in achieving reentry goals."[46] The U.S. Department of Justice is promoting the idea and asking communities to experiment with it, depending upon statutory framework, caseload considerations, administrative flexibility, and levels of collaboration among the judiciary, corrections officers, parole officers, police, business community, religious institutions, community organizations, and the like. Whichever form a reentry court takes, developing new ways that communities can manage and support offenders after release from prison with assistance in securing employment, housing, substance abuse treatment, family counseling, and other services is essential to our ability to reduce crime and keep communities safe.

Research on reentry courts is still new, but already studies show that recidivism among all drug court participants has ranged between 5 and 28 percent and is less than 4 percent for program graduates.[47] The largest reentry court in operation today is in Richland County, Ohio.[48] The court accepted its first parolees in 2000. Reentry court supervision lasts a minimum of one year. During this time, parolees appear in court each month to discuss their progress. They receive an average of 12 monthly intensive supervision contacts, undergo random drug and alcohol testing, and are required to participate in remote-location monitoring. Of the initial 160 reentry clients, 34 had successfully completed the program, 22 did not, and 104 were still active in the program as of August 31, 2002. Jeffrey Spelman, professor of criminal justice at Ashland University, compared the two groups and found that being female, completing high school, holding a job, and being over age 29 distinguished those who successfully completed reentry court from those who did not.

Professor Spelman also found evidence that reentry court benefited the terminated group. Of the 22 parolees terminated, only four were rearrested for a new criminal offense. The others were terminated as a result of multiple technical violations or one serious technical violation. The contrast between the 7 percent rearrest rate in Richland County's reentry court and BJS data from a 15-state recidivism study that found a one-year rearrest rate of 44 percent suggests that reentry court is capable of making a difference in the lives of individuals even if they are terminated from the program. However, only time and further research will test the accuracy of these early results.

EXHIBIT 8–14   Models of Reentry Court

The Fort Wayne, Indiana, Reentry Program

One judge-centered Reentry Court model is operating in Ft. Wayne, Indiana, which borrows heavily from the drug court experience: that is, an ongoing, central role for a judge, a "contract" drawn up between court and offender, discretion on the judge's part to impose graduated sanctions for various levels of failure to meet the conditions imposed, and the promise of the end of supervision as an occasion for ceremonial recognition. In Ft. Wayne, the Reentry Court Judge has been vested with authority by the Indiana Parole Commission to act on the Commission's behalf in supervising released adult offenders. A transition team, comprised of treatment providers, corrections staff, law enforcement, employment trainers, and family counselors, are assigned to the offender to assist with the development, monitoring, and enforcement of the reentry plan that is implemented upon release from the institution. This plan is based on assessments (i.e., risk, educational, vocational, mental health, and substance abuse) and developed with the offender and his/her support system. This plan becomes the guide by which the offender's reentry into the community is managed. Many of the offenders have been connected with a network of mentors who help guide their transition back into the community.

With the reentry plan completed, and upon the offender's release from commitment, the offender appears before the Reentry Court Judge for formalization or ordering of the reentry plan, depending on the offender, the support system, and the agencies of government representing the community. Typically, an offender will have to remain drug free, make restitution to his victim and reparation to the community, participate in programs that had begun in commitment (work, education, emotions management, parenting classes, etc.), refrain from committing crime, and comply with any other terms and conditions of the reentry plan. The offender is also required to appear before the Reentry Court Judge on a regular basis to determine if the plan remains appropriate and effective and if the offender is in compliance.

The Ohio Reentry Court Program

The Richland County Common Pleas Court in partnership with the Ohio Department of Rehabilitation and Correction developed a comprehensive reentry program that addresses all offenders sent from prison and return to Richland County, Ohio. The Richland County Reentry Court Program began in January 2000, following its selection by the U.S. Department of Justice's call for a concept paper on establishing a reentry court to enhance accountability of offenders being released from prison with judicial oversight, stronger supervision and an emphasis on addressing issues which make reentering society difficult. The reentry court was fully operational and became a part of the judicial process January 1, 2001. Through early assessment and planning the reentry court addresses the basic issues that lead most offenders to crime and which most often resurface when they return. By establishing reentry release plans at sentencing, offenders are presented with those areas which they must address

before release back into the community. The probation and parole supervision system must also address the reentry needs of the offender prior to release, and during supervision to make pro-social reintegration more successful. Already the benefits of this collaborative process have begun to surface, not only with the increased success of offenders returning to the community, but with the closer collaborations between the criminal justice, law enforcement, social service and treatment communities to assist them.

The Iowa Reentry Program

The Iowa reentry court project is a pilot initiative and is a collaboration between the Iowa Department of Corrections, the Iowa Parole Board, and the city of Cedar Rapids and targets offenders who have mental health disorders or who have been dually diagnosed with mental health and substance abuse problems. This program in Cedar Rapids is operational. Another program is being implemented in Des Moines and focuses on the 22 percent of offenders who refuse treatment and parole, as well as paroled offenders who are not typically assigned to a parole officer. The Iowa reentry court makes use of an administrative law judge (ALJ) under the jurisdiction of the Parole Board, and relies on a Community Accountability Board that works with the ALJ. Composed of local service providers, probation and parole officers, victims, and other interested citizens, the Accountability Board identifies community service and support opportunities and develops accountability mechanisms for the successful reentry of released inmates.

A Reentry Coordinator in the Department of Corrections Offender Services Office works with institutional counseling staff who are preparing offenders for participation in the reentry process. Staff are now working to identify special needs of at-risk inmates through assessment and diagnosis in the prison setting, and will begin pre-release treatment and planning to connect them with community resources. Upon release from confinement, parolees will meet with the Community Accountability Board and ALJ at least monthly.

The West Virginia Reentry Program

The Division of Juvenile Services has implemented a juvenile reentry court initiative targeting adjudicated youth (male and female) who have been committed to the West Virginia Industrial Home for Youth and the Davis Center and who will be returning to Grant, Mineral, or Tucker counties. The Industrial Home for Youth is the state's most secure committed facility and the Davis Center is a medium secure facility. These counties are located in the panhandle region in a fairly remote part of the state. This initiative is modeled after the OJJDP-supported Intensive Community-Based Aftercare Program (IAP) currently being replicated by juvenile justice systems throughout the country. In addition to intensive case management provided to youth while in confinement and upon return to the community, collaborative partnerships

EXHIBIT 8–14   **Models of Reentry Court (*continued*)**

have been formed with the Circuit Court and Juvenile Probation, local law enforcement, faith communities, and local school systems.

Youth are oriented into the program at the time of commitment to the Industrial Home for Youth. Youth returning to Grant, Mineral, and Tucker Counties are assessed for eligibility. Upon return to the community, youth attend monthly court hearings before the Juvenile Court Judge. An aftercare case manager is immediately assigned to the case. Along with the juvenile probation officer, the aftercare case manager will provide intensive supervision and surveillance with frequent contacts in the school, at home, and at work, if applicable. Advisory boards in each of the counties have been established to allow community members to provide valuable input to the restorative justice process.

Source: "Serious and Violent Offender Reentry Initiative Appendices," U.S. Department of Labor Employment and Training Administration, www.doleta.gov/sga/sga/reentry_app.cfm (accessed September 5, 2007).

Reintegration Involving Victims

Successful reintegration programs also involve victims.[49] Victims and victim organizations can assist in the reintegration of parolees by providing parole board members and parole officers with relevant information, offering their experience and expertise, and encouraging offender accountability.

Each year, about 30 million people in America become victims of crime. Most states give victims the right to (1) be notified about parole proceedings, (2) be heard on matters relating to the offender's parole, (3) be present at parole proceedings, and (4) receive restitution as a condition of parole. These rights are designed to ensure that the views of victims are taken into account before decisions about parole are made and to help victims prepare themselves for the offender's release. Victim input can highlight the need for strict supervision or special conditions such as restitution orders, order of protection, or mandated treatment in order to discourage reoffending and encourage reintegration.

Programs involving victims operate in a number of ways. Some encourage victims to volunteer relevant information to parole officers. For example, in stalking cases, victims can tell parole officers whether offenders are in areas where they are not supposed to be. Other programs encourage victim–offender communication. In these programs, victims educate offenders about the impact of the crime and generate remorse in the hope that they can change offender behavior in the future. Whether the program features one-on-one conversation or a victim talking to an audience of imprisoned or paroled offenders, the aim is to convey to offenders the consequences of their actions in terms of the victims' pain and suffering.

Legal Decisions Affecting Parole

As we will see in Chapter 11, numerous challenges to the correctional system have brought about changes in prisoners' rights. You may recall that due process guarantees that a person has a right to be heard fairly before being deprived of liberty. Three of the most widely cited cases affecting parolees' and probationers' rights are *Morrissey v. Brewer* (1972), *Gagnon v. Scarpelli* (1973), and *Greenholtz v. Inmates of the Nebraska Penal and Correctional Complex* (1979).

In *Morrissey v. Brewer*, John Morrissey pled guilty to writing bad checks in 1967. He was sentenced to not more than seven years of confinement in the Iowa State Prison and paroled in June 1968. Seven months

THE OFFENDER SPEAKS

I was on parole for 30 months after doing 16 years straight on a very lengthy sentence. When I got out, I paroled to a place where I had never been before—everything was new to me and the only person I knew in my whole town was my wife. Starting over again was great, I made new friends, got a good job, joined the church, and integrated back into society just like I was supposed to.

Then it happened. I began to fall apart for a very simple reason—I stopped doing what my parole officer told me to do and started doing what I wanted to do. Subsequently, I was violated and returned to prison to do more time on my sentence, and that is where I sit at this writing.

There are good people and bad people in the world, and parole officers are the same. I was lucky and got a good one. From day one she told me that whether or not I succeeded was entirely up to me. She laid out a simple plan for me to follow, which I did for a while. Even when I started breaking the rules, instead of punishing me she put me in places that offered help for the issues I had. Finally, I left her no choice but to violate me, and she did just that.

Parole is a good idea because the inmate will have some of the awesome powers of the state at his disposal to help with the reintegration process. Done alone, the process can be terrifying. If the inmate does not define

and address his own situation while he is in prison, the chance of that person making it on parole is slim to none. On the other hand, if the inmate has truly applied himself and has identified and addressed the "thing" that makes him able to break the law, parole is an excellent idea.

For myself, I know this: If I would have done what I needed to do while doing 16 years in prison, I would not be sitting here now praying for the chance to be free again and live a normal life.

Anonymous

later he was arrested for parole violation and incarcerated in the county jail. One week later, at the direction of the parole officer's written report, the Iowa Board of Parole revoked his parole, and he was returned to the penitentiary.

Morrissey's complaint stated that he had received no counsel and no hearing prior to parole revocation. The Supreme Court agreed and overturned the Iowa parole board's decision. The Court ruled that due process establishes a parolee's right to a preliminary and a final hearing before parole can be revoked. According to the Court, a preliminary hearing must be held at the time of arrest and detention to determine whether there is probable cause to believe that the parolee has violated the conditions of supervision. If probable cause is established, "a more comprehensive hearing prior to making of the final revocation decision" determines guilt or innocence and extends to the parolee certain minimum due process rights: written notification of the alleged violation, disclosure of evidence, opportunity for a hearing to present witnesses and evidence, the right to confront and cross-examine adverse witnesses, a neutral hearing body, and a written statement by the hearing authority as to the evidence relied upon and the reasons for revocation.[50]

Morrissey did not extend to parolees the right to legal representation in parole revocation hearings. This issue was addressed one year later, in *Gagnon* v. *Scarpelli*. In a Wisconsin court in July 1965, Gerald Scarpelli pled guilty to a robbery charge. He was sentenced to 15 years; the judge suspended the sentence and placed him on probation for seven years. One month later, Scarpelli was arrested and charged with burglary. His probation was revoked. He was sent to the Wisconsin state reformatory to serve a 15-year prison term and was paroled after three years. Before he was paroled, however, Scarpelli filed a *habeas corpus* petition. He alleged that his right to due process had been denied—he had no access to counsel and no hearing prior to probation revocation. The Court ruled in favor of Scarpelli. It applied the fundamental due process and two-stage hearing requirements that it had laid out one year earlier in *Morrissey*, thus equating probation with parole. In *Gagnon,* the Court ruled that offenders do not have an absolute constitutional right to counsel at revocation proceedings. States may assign counsel at the hearing under "special circumstances," and decisions should be made on a case-by-case basis, depending on the offender's competence, case complexity, and mitigating evidence.

In *Greenholtz* v. *Inmates of the Nebraska Penal and Correctional Complex* (1979), a case involving a routine parole board hearing, the U.S. Supreme Court ruled that parole is a privilege, rather than a right, and the full complement of due process rights need not be afforded at parole hearings. The Court also said that the parole board is not required to specify the evidence used in deciding to deny parole. As a result of this case, states are deciding what inmate privileges are appropriate at parole hearings.

Abolition of Discretionary Parole Board Release

Earlier in this chapter we discussed that there was strong opposition to parole in the 1930s and that opponents wanted to abolish it. They argued that parole boards were turning hardened criminals loose on society, parole had a dismal performance record, its goals were never realized, parole board members and parole officers were poorly trained, and parole hearings were little more than hastily conducted, almost unthinking interviews. In spite of the gap between goals and this 1930s reality, parole fulfilled important functions for wardens, legislators, and district attorneys.

The movement to abolish discretionary parole boards resurfaced in the 1970s, when the concept of "just deserts"—the idea that offenders deserve punishment for what they do to society—was being discussed.[51] However, states did not do away with parole altogether; they restructured it. As the data in Exhibit 8–15 show, by the end of 2000, 16 states and the federal government had abolished discretionary release from prison by a parole board for all offenders. Another four states had abolished discretionary parole release for certain violent offenses or other crimes against a person. In these states, postrelease supervision still exists and is referred to as "mandatory supervised release," "controlled release," or "community control." Parole boards still have discretion over inmates who were sentenced for crimes committed prior to the effective date of the law that eliminated parole board release and the responsibility to place offenders under either conditional or supervised release, the authority to return an offender to prison for violating the conditions of parole or supervised release, and the power to grant parole for medical reasons. But how well is this working? Petersilia offers a sober thought: "In California, where more than 125,000 prisoners are released yearly, there is no parole board to ask whether the inmate is ready for release, since he or she *must* be released once his or her term has been served. Generally, a parolee must be released to the county where he or she lived before entering prison. Since the vast majority of offenders come from economically disadvantaged, culturally isolated, inner-city neighborhoods, they return there upon release."[52]

The backdrop for the debate on just deserts was an extraordinary increase in the nation's crime rate that began in the mid-1960s and continued through the 1970s. Legislatures were growing anxious about crime and were willing to try new options in correctional approaches to the

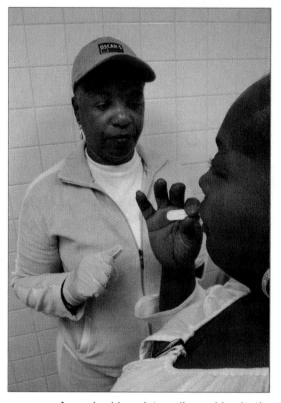

A parolee blows into a disposable plastic mouthpiece. The parole officer then attaches the mouthpiece to a portable handheld breath-testing machine that digitally registers the parolee's blood-alcohol level. Other portable alcohol technology tests urine, skin, and hair. What are the advantages of such technology in supervising parolees?

Eye On Corrections

The Housing Hunt for Released Offenders

By Michelle Gaseau

Reentry programming and services are the buzz in corrections these days as offenders receive educational programming, job skills and many now have their medical and mental health appointments set up by the time their sentences end. But one of the most critical pieces to successful reentry is more difficult for corrections departments to procure—appropriate housing.

But without a safe place to lay their heads, offenders are at high risk to fall back into their old bad habits and recidivate.

"One of the things that is tricky is people on the corrections side don't know where to start. The housing process in community systems is so complex. It's one thing to say 'We're going to do something.' But not knowing who to call or even the right [housing] language to speak is another thing," said Katherine Brown, Policy Analyst, Criminal Justice Programs for the Council of State Governments.

CSG, which operates the Re-Entry Policy Council and issued a major report last year on reentry best practices, has launched a housing initiative to help corrections and community agencies come together to find proper housing for releasing offenders. Other jurisdictions have also forged ahead on their own to create housing plans and housing goals to meet this important need.

With estimates that 10 percent of the 600,000 offenders released from prisons each year are homeless, states and local jurisdictions are beginning to realize that discharge planning efforts need to include stable housing. CSG hopes to help with that.

HOUSING RISES TO TOP OF THE LIST

States such as Georgia and Vermont have also begun to address housing issues for inmates reentering the community. For Georgia, its new Re-Entry Partnership Housing program grew out of the realization that many inmates were sitting behind bars who could be released—if they only had housing.

"This came out of housing being one of the barriers for successful reintegration once they are released [but] we also had a population within our system that had been granted parole, but parole requires they have a suitable housing plan," said A.J. Sabree, Director of Reentry for the Georgia DOC.

According to Sabree, the DOC began by speaking with faith-based organizations in the community to learn about the challenges they faced in working with recently released offenders. Sabree said the DOC learned that the first two or three months—before offenders were able to land employment—were the most difficult for both the offenders and service providers who were trying to support them.

With that information, Georgia DOC officials set out to find a solution.

"We identified some funds that were initially targeted to relieve prison bed space and we inquired to see if we could use some of that funding to help service providers on the outside to give [them] a subsidy for providing room and board, establishing mentors and helping with family reunification," said Sabree.

So far that funding that is available to community services providers would equate to $600 per offender, per month for the first two or three months they are involved with those organizations.

"We are targeting those offenders who would be released already if they had somewhere to live. We have quite a number of offenders and if we can show there is a cost savings to the taxpayer, it could [be expanded]," he said.

In order to ensure that releasing offenders receive all the services they need, the DOC has targeted service providers who have some type of home environment.

"We are looking for folks to have a program component because our goal is that these people need programs and connections to resources to help them stay out, such as job placement programs and connections with physical health services," Sabree said.

The DOC is currently accepting grant applications from community service providers who fit the criteria in five different areas of the state.

"We are looking at different types of housing. The majority of our offenders will eventually cohabitate with their families. We are looking for service providers who help with that transition," he said.

And, before those offenders are released, the DOC is also helping them to prepare. Sabree said the DOC has focused its attention in assessments for criminogenic needs and matching them to programs that will address those needs, including cognitive restructuring, educational programs, job readiness and adult basic literacy.

"A large number of people haven't had the opportunity to be self-sufficient. We are trying to address these issues with the offender at the earliest point of entry and connect them early in the process to assess their needs and also make sure they buy into an accountability plan," he added.

Although the reentry program phase in the community is just beginning, corrections officials are hopeful that it, combined with work done inside prison walls, will be successful by lowering recidivism rates.

"Our main goal is to reduce recidivism and also provide public safety by helping offenders have a successful transition to the community. Housing is one of those critical barriers that if a person doesn't have it, it contributes to their re-offending," Sabree said.

Other states, like Vermont, are facing similar situations.

And in many jurisdictions, even starting the conversation is a step in the right direction as corrections officials and community service providers begin to realize that they must work together in order to help stop the cycle of crime that leads to prison and jail overcrowding and rising costs for incarceration.

Source: "The Housing Hunt for Released Offenders," Michelle Gaseau, The Corrections Connection Network News (CCNN). Eye on Corrections, www.corrections.com. February 13, 2006.
Note: This article has been reprinted in part from CCNN. To read the article in its entirety, go to www.corrections.com.

EXHIBIT 8–15	States That Have Abolished Discretionary Release, 2000

For All Offenders	For Certain Violent Offenders
Arizona	Alaska
California[a]	Louisiana
Delaware	New York
Florida[b]	Tennessee
Illinois	
Indiana	
Kansas[c]	
Maine	
Minnesota	
Mississippi	
North Carolina	
Ohio[d]	
Oregon	
Virginia	
Washington	
Wisconsin	

a. In 1976 the Uniform Determinate Sentencing Act abolished discretionary parole for all offenses except some violent crimes with a long sentence or a sentence to life.
b. In 1995 parole eligibility was abolished for offenses with a life sentence and a 25-year mandatory term.
c. Excludes a few offenses, primarily first-degree murder and intentional second-degree murder.
d. Excludes murder and aggravated murder.

Source: Adapted from Timothy A. Hughes, Doris James Wilson, and Allen J. Beck, *Trends in State Parole, 1999–2000* (Washington, DC: U.S. Department of Justice, Bureau of Justice Statistics, October 2001).

crime problem. They felt that rehabilitation and indeterminate sentencing were not working. Their answer was determinate sentencing and abolition of discretionary parole board release.

Why did some states abolish discretionary release from prison by a parole board? There are at least four reasons.

First, scholars concluded that indeterminate sentencing and discretionary parole did not achieve offender rehabilitation, which was unfair since it was based solely on parole board judgment, without explicit standards of fairness and equity in sentencing. Studies showed that wide disparities resulted when the characteristics of the crime and the offender were taken into account, and decisions were influenced by the offender's race, socioeconomic status, and place of conviction. Second, eliminating discretionary parole appeared to be tough on crime. Third, parole boards' lack of openness in the decision-making process, in which boards made their parole decisions on a case-by-case basis without benefit of a written set of policies and procedures, prompted criticism. Fourth, state politicians were able to convince the public that parole was the cause of the rising crime problem and that abolition was the solution.

Prisoner Reentry and Community Policing

Reentry isn't just for corrections anymore for two reasons. First, the fourfold increase in the number of persons being released each year from state and federal prisons over the past two decades into crime-ridden neighborhoods that lack services and support systems is more than community corrections officers can handle. There has not been a fourfold increase in the number of community supervision officers as Chapter 4 pointed out, and for that reason probation and parole agencies are experimenting with privatization in community corrections (see Chapter 13).

Second, in spite of all the efforts being made at prisoner reform, offenders are still leaving prison unprepared for successful reentry, as this chapter has pointed out. Not enough prisoners are receiving education or vocational training. Not enough prisoners are receiving alcohol and drug treatment. Not enough prisoners are receiving life skills. These challenges not only impact prisoners, but they also threaten public safety. Prisoners who are not prepared to lead productive, law-abiding lives will reoffend. (We found earlier in this chapter that more than two-thirds are rearrested for a new crime within three years, and 51 percent are returned to prison during that same period either for a new crime or for a technical violation of the conditions of their release.) Communities that provide prisoners with the services and environment to transition successfully into the community will also protect themselves from further harm.

One way some communities are responding to the problems of prisoner reentry is to involve community policing with reentry initiatives. The argument for involving community policing in reentry is this: Since the majority of ex-offenders are rearrested within three years, making contact with former prisoners is part of the everyday business of law enforcement. In fact, researchers at the Urban Institute say that "arrest frequencies for returning prisoners are 30 to 45 times higher than for the general population. Police agencies stand to benefit from their involvement in reentry because successful efforts to reduce reoffending among released prisoners can, by definition, prevent future crimes and help improve community relations with police."[53]

The community policing approach is to analyze and understand the reasons behind repeat offending and create partnerships with local businesses, residents, government agencies, and other stakeholders to solve underlying crime problems and prevent future offending.

Joint supervision of parolees by teams of police and parole officers is the most common way that police currently contribute to prisoner reentry efforts. Team supervision usually takes the form of police accompaniment on parole home visits, parole ride-alongs on police patrols, and parole involvement in policing activities, such as attending community meetings and staffing neighborhood substations. The team approach sends the message that community corrections is not soft on crime. It also contributes additional eyes and ears to enhance surveillance and assistance to community supervision.

According to the Urban Institute, although there are numerous examples across the United States where police send returning prisoners meeting announcements, encourage them to comply with the law, share intelligence information with partner agencies, and work with prosecutors to target habitual offenders, they do not take advantage of the prisoner release process. Only 15 police agencies across the country can be identified in which community policing plays a lead or key role in prisoner reentry and demonstrates how police are proactively and centrally engaged in reentry initiatives directed toward reducing crime and disorder in their communities. Exhibit 8–16 illustrates the example of community police practice in offender reentry in the Ogden (Utah) City Police Department.

Community-Focused Parole

Earlier we said that communities that provide prisoners the services and environment to transition successfully into the community will also protect themselves from further harm. Community policing and prisoner reentry is one strategy.

Another is community-focused parole, a process of engaging the community so the community engages parole.[54] The process requires at least three changes to current parole practice.

The first is to capture a mission statement that the public understands. Some parole agencies are adopting public safety in addition to offender reform as a definition of their services. By raising their profile in the community as agencies that deliver public safety and highlighting that in their mission statement, parole agencies could decentralize parole officers into local neighborhoods (perhaps utilizing neighborhood police substations) and form collaborative partnerships with police and others similar to what community police do with local businesses, residents, government agencies, and other stakeholders to solve underlying crime problems and prevent future offending.

A second change is visibility. Unless the work of parole is made visible to the community, it will not result in the service being valued or supported. For many citizens, the issue of prisoners and their return to

EXHIBIT 8–16 | **Prisoner Reentry and Community Policing**

Ogden (Utah) City Police Department

Project T.E.A.M.

Team Enforcement and Monitoring (Project T.E.A.M.) was formed in response to crimes committed by the high number of individuals returning to a small area within Ogden City, Utah. Assessments of reentry patterns revealed that nearly 12 percent of the population in one eight-block neighborhood were under either probation or parole supervision. This high concentration of ex-offenders resulted in unmanageable caseloads for Weber County community supervision officers and restricted the amount of one-on-one contacts with clients. The goal of the Project T.E.A.M. collaborative is to improve the capacity of criminal justice agents to monitor and support reentry transitions by linking participants to social service organizations. To do so, the project has granted the police authority to act as community supervision agents. Although this authorization is contingent upon the individual signing a waiver, the incentive to participate is attractive to many releasees because it is often offered as an alternative to returning to prison for technical violations. The primary role for police includes strengthening the deterrence message communicated during the face-to-face introductory notification sessions, during which the consequences of noncompliance, especially for weapons offenses, are explained. In addition, police support supervision activities by conducting random curfew checks and home visits. This program benefits parole agents who typically have 60 to 80 offenders on their caseload, giving them extra support from the police to supervise higher risk parolees. For police, face-to-face meetings foster positive interactions with former prisoners and provide police with important context to individual circumstances of reentry.

Key Program Elements

- **Encouraging Compliance.** Individuals returning to Weber County on parole attend a meeting with police officers on the day of their release during which they are informed of the consequences of not abiding by the law. They are specifically informed that they may be federally prosecuted if they possess or use a firearm. If a parolee commits a technical violation, he or she is offered the option of joining the program instead of returning to prison. Participation in T.E.A.M. is contingent on the individual signing a contract that permits police officers to act in the capacity of parole officers and may include a curfew requirement or alcohol restrictions, among other stipulations.
- **Increasing Surveillance.** The police have the same powers that the parole officer has over the parolee, including the right to make unannounced visits and search without a warrant or consent if they believe the individual is participating in criminal activity. Twice a month a police officer joins a parole officer in conducting visits to every high-risk parolee in the county.
- **Connecting to Services.** The program offers participants opportunities to receive education and employment support, including access to general equivalency diploma classes, computer courses, and career centers. Participants are linked with relevant social service organizations in the community during notification sessions.

Note: Partners include the Ogden City Police Department, all law enforcement agencies within Weber County, the Utah Department of Corrections, the Weber County Adult Probation and Parole Office, Ogden City's Enterprise Community, Safe Haven, and the Utah Department of Workforce Services.
Source: Adapted from Nancy G. La Vigne, Amy L. Solomon, Karen A. Beckman, and Kelly Dedel, *Prisoner Reentry and Community Policing: Strategies for Enhancing Public Safety* (Washington, DC: U.S. Department of Justice, Office of Community Oriented Policing Services, March 2006).

society is met with fear. However, scientifically conducted public opinion polls show that the public supports offender job training, treatment, and education. Media relations can help create a positive image and increase visibility regarding the work of parole. Other examples are participating in local events and using a highly visible offender community service work program that involves nonprofit organizations.

The third change—building partnerships—is central to any community-oriented initiative. Strategies that raise an agency's profile and elicit support are critical to the development of a community-focused parole service. Appearances on local news shows, articles in local newspapers, meetings with neighborhood associations, and sponsoring of local events such as Relay for Life are ways that parole agencies show they care about the community and can educate the community about strategies in place to support and supervise returning prisoners.

The literature on community-oriented policing has found that proactive crime prevention strategies can yield long-term crime reduction benefits. It stands to reason then that community-focused parole can also have a positive impact on community safety.

REVIEW & APPLICATIONS

REFLECTIONS ON THE FUTURE

Parole: A System in Transition

by Jeremy Travis
John Jay College of
Criminal Justice

Parole today looks quite different from its original formulation. Parole boards are on the wane. Parole supervision has been increased. We have decoupled the release decision from the supervision decision. Parole revocations now contribute significantly to the prison populations of the states. We have created a system of backend sentencing, sending tens of thousands of people back to prison. We seem far removed from the goal of rehabilitation and confidence in official exercise of discretion.

Yet even this national picture tells only part of the story because it masks enormous state variation. Some states have retained parole boards, some have abolished them; some states place all released prisoners on supervision, some only half; some states aggressively revoke parole, others are more lenient. So, we have replaced a single, unifying American approach, indeterminate sentencing, with a patchwork quilt of state-level experiments in sentencing reforms.

What is the future of parole, given this history? It is hard to imagine a political scenario that will restore the practice of parole release to its former position of dominance. The public and the politicians they elect are too distrustful of governmental discretion, particularly when criminal sentences are involved. Yet that same political mood is likely to call for increases in the reach of parole supervision—more people on parole, for longer periods of time, with more stringent conditions; more high-tech surveillance; and consequently more parolees violated and returned to prison.

Yet there are important cross currents that may carry the day. Sentencing reformers are challenging the practice of "backend" sentencing, calling for guidelines for parole revocations. Parole administrators are promoting the principles of restorative justice, embracing the goals of community service and victim-offender reconciliation, hoping to provide a higher purpose to community supervision. Drug policy analysts, noting that a larger portion of illegal drugs is consumed by offenders under community supervision, have urged adoption of new regimes of drug testing, sanctions and treatment to break the cycle of drug use and crime. Community justice advocates, tracking the success of community policing, have called upon parole departments to create new partnerships with community institutions, essentially sharing responsibility for prisoner reintegration. The renewed interest in prisoner reentry at the turn of the 21st century has focused the attention of housing providers, health care agencies, employment developers, and others on ways to improve the chances of successful reentry, thereby forging new definitions of the parole process itself.

In the middle of this ferment, one must note the absence of a strong research base that might guide these critical policy discussions. Given the centrality of the institution of parole to the system of indeterminate sentencing, the high public safety risks posed by this population, and the enormous costs of incarceration and community supervision, one would think that these policy options would be well evaluated. Unfortunately, that is not the case. Hopefully, the next century will produce the base of knowledge that will guide parole practice, under whatever name, to a more effective future.

About the Author

Jeremy Travis is president of John Jay College of Criminal Justice. He is a former Senior Fellow at the Urban Institute, former director of United States Department of Justice's National Institute of Justice, deputy commissioner for Legal Matters of the New York City Police Department, and chief counsel to the Subcommittee on Criminal Justice of the House of Representative Committee on the Judiciary. Travis holds a JD and an MPA from New York University.

SUMMARY

1 Early English judges spared the lives of condemned felons by exiling them to America as indentured servants. Captain Alexander Maconochie, superintendent of the British penal colony on Norfolk Island, devised a "ticket of leave" system that moved inmates through stages. Sir Walter Crofton used some of Maconochie's ideas for his early release system in Ireland. In the United States, Zebulon Brockway implemented a system of upward classification.

2 Paroling authorities play powerful roles in the criminal justice system. They determine the length of incarceration for many offenders and can revoke parole. The paroling authority's policies have a direct impact on an institution's population. Paroling authorities use state laws and information from courts and other criminal justice agencies to make release decisions.

3 Parole is the conditional release of a prison inmate, prior to sentence expiration, with supervision in the community. The parole process of release begins in the courtroom when the judge sentences an offender to either a determinate or an indeterminate sentence. After serving a certain portion of his or her sentence, an offender is eligible for parole release. That portion varies from state to state. If an inmate maintains good conduct for a certain amount of time preceding the parole hearing and is granted parole, he or she must live in accordance with specified rules and regulations in the community. If a parolee violates either the technical conditions of parole or commits a new crime, he or she may have parole revoked.

4 On January 1, 2006, 784,408 American adults were on parole, representing an increase of 1.6 percent (12,556) over January 1, 2005. Eighty-eight percent are state parolees. The typical adult parolee is a white, non-Hispanic male, on mandatory parole, and under active parole supervision for more than one year. His median age is 34, and he has an 11th-grade education. Women make up 12 percent of the parole population. The region with the highest number of parolees is the South, followed by the West, Northeast, and Midwest.

5 Parole may be revoked for a technical violation (failure to comply with one of the conditions of parole) or for a new offense violation (commission of a crime). Two-thirds of all parolees are rearrested within three years, typically within the first six months of release. Of the nearly 503,800 parolees discharged from supervision in 2005, 191,800 (38 percent) were returned to prison either because of a rule violation or new offense, up from 27,177 in 1980 and 160,000 in 1995.

6 Only Maine and Vermont do not place any restrictions on the right to vote for people with felony convictions. The reentry court concept, designed to manage parolee return to the community, requires that the parolee make regular court appearances for progress assessment. Reintegration involving victims encourages victims to volunteer relevant information to parole officers and supports victim–offender communication. In these programs, victims educate offenders about the impact of the crime and generate remorse in the hope that they can change offender behavior in the future.

Three important U.S. Supreme Court decisions significantly affected parole. In *Morrissey* v. *Brewer* (1972), the U.S. Supreme Court said that parole, once granted, becomes a right and that parolees are to have certain due process rights in any revocation hearing. In *Gagnon* v. *Scarpelli* (1973), the U.S. Supreme Court held that a probationer has a limited right to counsel in a revocation hearing and that the hearing body must decide whether counsel should be provided on a case-by-case basis. In *Greenholtz* v. *Inmates* of the *Nebraska Penal and Correctional Complex* (1979), the U.S. Supreme Court ruled that parole is a privilege; therefore, the full complement of due process rights need not be afforded at parole hearings. As a result, states are deciding what inmate privileges are appropriate at parole hearings.

Today, 16 states and the federal government have abolished discretionary release from prison by a parole board for all offenders. Another 4 states have abolished discretionary parole release for certain violent offenses or other crimes against a person. In these states, postrelease supervision still exists and is referred to as "mandatory supervised release," "controlled release," or "community control."

New initiatives in parole are community policing and reentry, and community-focused parole. In the former we find joint supervision of parolees by teams of police and parole officers. The latter focuses on ways to engage the community so the community engages parole.

KEY TERMS

QUESTIONS FOR REVIEW

1 Explain the history of parole development in the United States.

2 Outline how parole functions in the criminal justice system.

3 Describe parole and the parole decision-making process.

4 What can you infer from the characteristics of the parole population?

5 What do you think about the circumstances under which parole may be revoked?

6 Critique the current issues in parole.

THINKING CRITICALLY ABOUT CORRECTIONS

Faith-Based Reentry Initiatives

After President Bush was elected in 2000, he proposed what he called a faith-based initiative that would use federal taxes to subsidize community service programs administered by faith-based organizations to combat social ills including alcoholism, drug addiction, and domestic violence. According to Professor Ethan Fishman at the University of South Alabama, there are three main objections to Bush's proposal.[55] First, since organized religions characteristically rely on evangelism in their struggle against social ills, religious congregations would be enlarged at the expense of nonbelievers.

Second, opponents are concerned about the possibility of unscrupulous religious denominations, such as Taliban marriage counseling centers and Aryan Nations Interfaith dialogues, claiming government subsidies.

Third, Bush's initiatives involve the issue of discrimination in employment. Groups that accept federal funds are prohibited from discriminating in the hiring process. Yet President Bush insisted that an exclusion be made for denominations that, for religious reasons, refuse to hire homosexuals and/or members of other faiths.

With these objections looming large, why do you believe religious institutions continue to maintain a relationship with party politics?

The Carceral Problem

In *The Prison Reform Movement* (1990), Larry Sullivan suggests that prison reforms have always failed because they never addressed the "carceral problem." That is, is it possible to instill free-society values in a caged population? What do you think about Sullivan's premise in terms of preparing prisoners for early release?

ON-THE-JOB DECISION MAKING

Responding to Technical Violations

You have just learned that one of your parolees tested positive for drugs. In your state a positive drug test is a technical violation of parole and requires a revocation hearing. You have long wished that your state had a set of guidelines for responding to such technical violations so that you could handle the violation without waiting for a hearing. In this case, you could immediately place the parolee in a substance abuse program rather than waiting for a decision that might yield the same result. Draft a proposal for such a technical violation response policy. First, formulate the basic expectations of the policy (for example, "The least restrictive response to the behavior should be used"). Then determine what components the policy should include (for example, "Define clear goals and clarify the agency's concept of supervision").

Mentors and Offender Reentry

As chief parole officer in your area, write a two-page proposal recommending the involvement of mentors in offender reentry. Include what you believe are the advantages of mentoring for offender reentry and strategies for recruiting, training, and matching mentors with parolees.

LIVE LINKS

at www.justicestudies.com/livelinks04

8–1 But They All Come Back: Rethinking Prisoner Reentry

Reentry management approaches that reintegrate offenders into the community and prevent recurring antisocial behavior are explored and the need for the judiciary to play a greater role is emphasized.

8–2 After Prison

The legal barriers ex-offenders face upon their reentry to the community are explained. Particular attention is given to what the law is, roadblocks to reentry, employment, public assistance and food stamps, voting, access to criminal records, public housing, drivers' licenses, adoptive and foster parenting, student loans, report card, and vision for the future.

8–3 Reentry Programs for Women Inmates

This essay discusses the inmate rehabilitation programs that are being developed specifically for female inmates. Specifically, it presents an evaluation of two therapeutic community drug rehabilitation programs for female prisoners in Delaware: (1) The KEY program at Baylor Women's Correctional Institute and (2) CREST, a work release program at Sussex Correctional Institute.

8–4 Residential Substance Abuse Treatment for State Prisoners: Breaking the Drug–Crime Cycle Among Parole Violators

This document examines the Residential Substance Abuse Treatment (RSAT) program at the South Idaho Correctional Institution. The program targets parole-violating inmates with substance abuse problems in an effort to reduce recidivism. Researchers conducted a 15-month evaluation of the program's process to identify strengths and weaknesses.

8–5 Responding to Parole and Probation Violations: A Handbook to Guide Local Policy Development

Policy responses to probation and parole violations that enhance the effectiveness of supervision while also improving community safety are discussed.

8–6 Prisoner Reentry and Community Policing: Strategies for Enhancing Public Safety

Police are crucial partners in the pursuit of successful prisoner reintegration whether it is coordinating community policing partnerships for the purpose of prisoner reentry, participating in prerelease reentry planning, or joining parole pursuit of successful prisoner reintegration. This report presents information on why prisoner reentry is an important issue for the policing profession, and describes with the support of examples from the field various models of police involvement in reentry.

PART FOUR
THE PRISON WORLD

Part Four explores life inside prison for in-

mates and staff, the legal challenges surrounding their roles and responsibilities, and the special needs of inmates who are elderly, infected with HIV or AIDS, or mentally or physically challenged.

Custodial staff are most directly involved in the daily work of managing the inmate population. The extent to which correctional officers share beliefs, values, and behaviors is largely a function of the correctional officer subculture and each individual's personality.

Prisoners, too, develop a subculture that helps them adjust to the self-doubt, reduced self-esteem, and deprivations they experience as a result of confinement. Inmate subculture is also based on the life experiences that prisoners bring with them when they enter confinement. One question that we try to answer is, Why does men's prisoner subculture encourage isolation while women's prisoner subculture encourages relationships?

For a century, prisoners were considered civilly dead, and prisons operated entirely without court intervention. However, in 1970, the U.S. Supreme Court declared that, if states were going to operate prisons, they would have to do so according to the dictates of the Constitution. Since then, prisoners have reclaimed many of their conditional rights under the U.S. Constitution. But today, changes in state and federal statutes have slowed the pace of prisoners' rights cases, and the U.S. Supreme Court seems to have become less sympathetic to prisoners' civil rights claims.

Special needs inmates—those who are elderly, suffer from HIV, AIDS, or other chronic diseases, or are mentally or physically challenged—present significant problems for correctional managers. Special needs inmates may be more prone toward violence and disruption. They frequently require close monitoring to reduce the risk of suicide, and they may tax scarce medical resources and become targets of abuse by other inmates.

The preprison drug use and sexual activity of many prisoners has brought HIV, AIDS, and tuberculosis into jails and prisons. Managing these problems requires training in early detection, treatment, classification, staff education, and adequate funding. These problems are compounded by the fact that many prisoners have co-occurring physical and mental health problems.

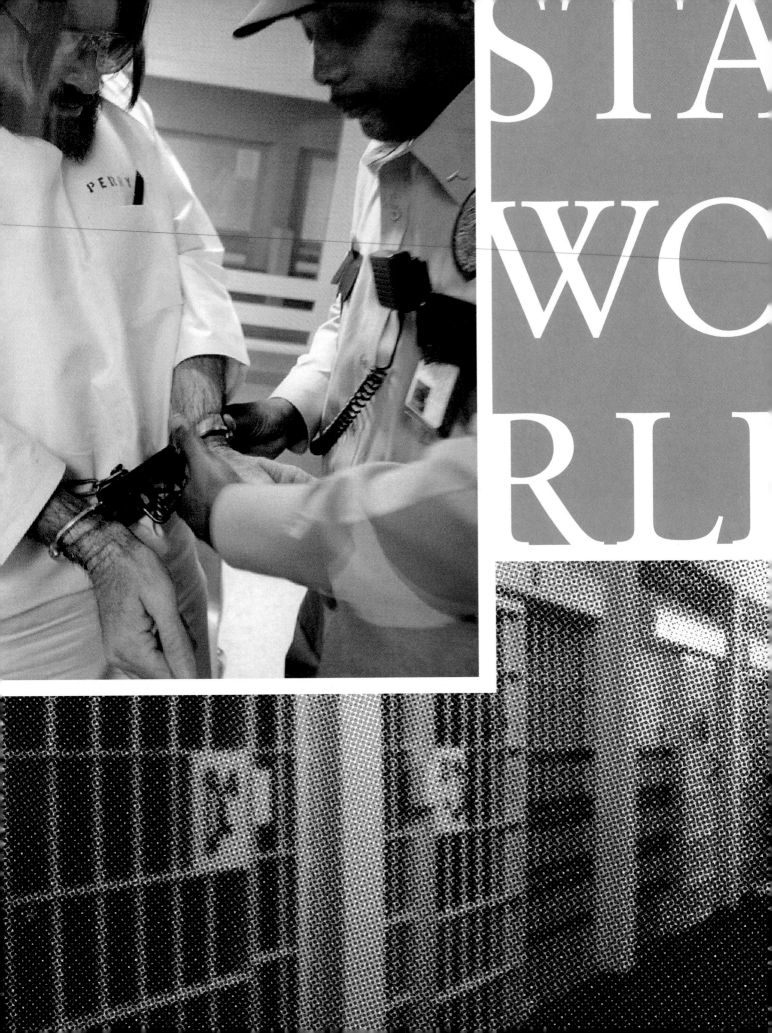

THE STAFF WORLD

Managing the Prison Population

CHAPTER OBJECTIVES

After completing this chapter you should be able to do the following:

1 List the staff roles within the organizational hierarchy of correctional institutions.

2 Define *custodial staff,* and explain the role of custody personnel.

3 Identify the types of power available to correctional officers.

4 Explain what structured conflict is and how it applies to correctional institutions.

5 Define the word *subculture* and identify some of the essential features of correctional officer subculture.

6 List and describe the most common correctional officer personality types.

7 List and describe the seven correctional officer job assignments.

8 Describe how female correctional officers tend to differ from males in their approach to the workplace.

9 Explain why stress is a problem in corrections work, and list some techniques for reducing stress.

10 List the elements that correctional administrators must consider when planning for staff safety.

11 Explain the impact that terrorism is having on prisons and on the running of correctional institutions today.

> " *Corrections is not a business where only one sex, race, religion, or type of person can succeed. It takes men and women of all races, religions, and color to create a dynamic and effective workforce to manage diverse inmates and solve the problems we face.*
>
> —Dora Schriro, former Missouri director of corrections "

In 2006, American Correctional Association (ACA) executive director James A. Gondles Jr. issued a special media statement titled *"Guard* Must Go." [1] Gondles was objecting to the use of the word *guard* by the media to describe correctional officers. "The role of correctional officers," said Gondles, "is to ensure that offenders complete their sentences in a way that sufficiently addresses the wide range of problems they often bring with them, while maintaining corrections' paramount duty—public safety."

Gondles pointed to the fact that the ACA had taken action to eliminate the word *guard* from its publications, advertisements, and announcements more than 20 years earlier, and that doing so had now become official policy. Rejecting the term *guard,* Gondles said, was necessary "because it implies that the job is inherently passive and demands nothing more than watching locked-up inmates. Nothing could be further from the truth."

In contrast, said Gondles, the term *correctional officer* "embodies the diverse skills officers employ each day—communication skills, cultural awareness, first aid, suicide prevention, emergency response preparedness, program and service delivery, and the proper use of force."

James A. Gondles Jr., American Correctional Association executive director. Why does Director Gondles reject use of the word *guard* in describing today's correctional officers?

THE STAFF HIERARCHY

Practically speaking, a prison of any size has a number of different staff roles—each with its own unique set of tasks. **Roles** are the normal patterns of behavior expected of those holding particular social positions. **Staff roles** are the patterns of behavior expected of correctional staff members in particular jobs. Eventually, many people internalize the expectations others have of them, and such expectations can play an important part in their self-perceptions.

Ideally, today's correctional staff members have four main goals:

1. to provide for the security of the community by incarcerating those who break the law;
2. to promote the smooth and effective functioning of the institution;
3. to ensure that incarceration is secure but humane; and
4. to give inmates the opportunity to develop a positive lifestyle while incarcerated and to gain the personal and employment skills they need for a positive lifestyle after release. [2]

Prison staff are organized into a hierarchy, or multilevel categorization, according to responsibilities. An institution's hierarchy generally has a warden or superintendent at the top and correctional officers at a lower level. A typical correctional staff hierarchy includes the following:

- administrative staff (wardens, superintendents, assistant superintendents, and others charged with running the institution and its programs and with setting policy);
- clerical personnel (record keepers and administrative assistants);

roles

The normal patterns of behavior expected of those holding particular social positions.

staff roles

The patterns of behavior expected of correctional staff members in particular jobs.

- program staff (psychologists, psychiatrists, medical doctors, nurses, medical aides, teachers, counselors, caseworkers, and ministers—many of whom contract with the institution to provide services);
- custodial staff (majors, captains, lieutenants, sergeants, and correctional officers charged primarily with maintaining order and security);
- service and maintenance staff (kitchen supervisors, physical plant personnel, and many outside contractors); and
- volunteers (prison ministry, speakers, and other volunteers in corrections).

Organizational charts graphically represent the staff structure and the chain of command within an institution. An organizational chart for a typical medium-to-large correctional institution is shown in Exhibit 9–1. **Custodial staff** are most directly involved in managing the inmate population, through daily contact with inmates. Their role is to control prisoners within the institution. **Program staff,** on the other hand, are concerned with encouraging prisoners to participate in educational, vocational, and

custodial staff
Those staff members most directly involved in managing the inmate population.

program staff
Those staff members concerned with encouraging prisoners to participate in educational, vocational, and treatment programs.

EXHIBIT 9–1   Organizational Chart of a Typical Midsize or Large Correctional Institution

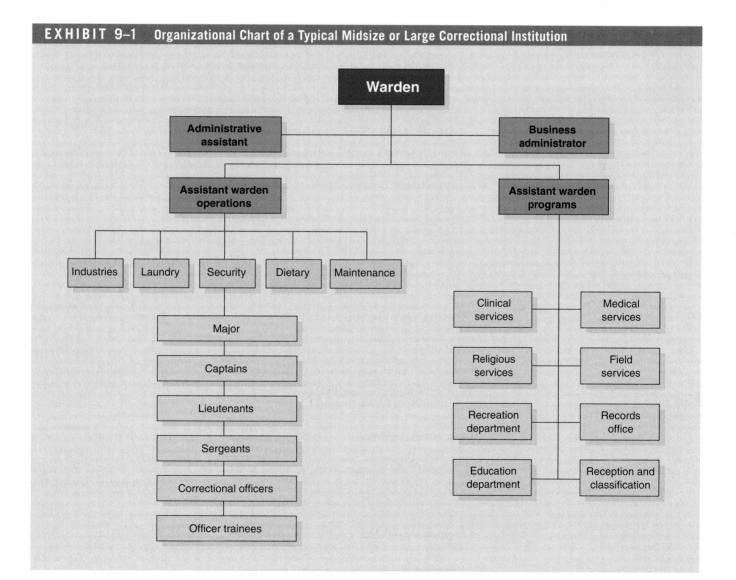

treatment programs. Custodial staff, who make up over 60 percent of prison personnel, are generally organized in a military-style hierarchy, from assistant or deputy warden down to correctional officer. Program staff generally operate through a separate organizational structure and have little in common with custodial staff.

To a great extent, prison management involves managing relationships—among employees, between employees and inmates, and among inmates. Prisons are unique in that most of the people in them (the inmates) are forced to live there according to the terms of their sentence; they really do not want to be there. Such a situation presents tremendous challenges. The people on the front lines dealing around the clock with such challenges are the correctional officers.

THE CORRECTIONAL OFFICER— THE CRUCIAL PROFESSIONAL

Although security is still the major concern, correctional officers today are expected to perform a variety of other tasks. As one commentator has said,

> Correctional officers have more responsibilities [now] than in the past and their duty is no longer to merely watch over the prisoners. They now have to play several roles in keeping prisoners in line. They have to be "psychiatrists" when prisoners come to them with their problems, and they have to be "arbitrators and protectors" when inmates have complaints or problems with each other, while still watching out for their own safety. In these situations, the wrong decision could offend someone and start a riot. This makes correctional officers "prisoners" of the daily emotional and physical moods of the inmates.[3]

Don Josi and Dale Sechrest explain it this way: "Correctional officers today must find a balance between their security role and their responsibility to use relationships with inmates to change their behavior constructively. They routinely assume numerous essential yet sometimes contradictory roles (e.g., counselor, diplomat, caretaker, disciplinarian, supervisor, crisis manager), often under stressful and dangerous conditions."[4]

Josi and Sechrest then go on to say, "These divergent and often incompatible goals can prove problematic; role conflict, role diffusion, and role ambiguity may be difficult if not impossible to avoid."[5]

Bases of Power

Correctional officers rely on a variety of strategies to manage inmate behavior. After surveying correctional officers in five prisons, John Hepburn identified five types of officers' power, according to the bases on which they rest: legitimate power, coercive power, reward power, expert power, and referent power.

Legitimate Power Correctional officers have power by virtue of their positions within the organization. That is, they have formal authority to command. As Hepburn says, "The prison guard has the right to exercise control over prisoners by virtue of the structural relationship between the position of the guard and the position of the prisoner."[6]

Coercive Power Inmates' beliefs that a correctional officer can and will punish disobedience give the officer coercive power. Many correctional officers use coercive power as a primary method of control.

Securing an inmate in preparation for a trip back to his cell. Correctional officers need to elicit inmates' cooperation to effectively carry out their custodial duties. What are some techniques officers might use?

Reward Power Correctional officers dispense both formal and informal rewards to induce cooperation among inmates. Formal rewards include assignment of desirable jobs, housing, and other inmate privileges. Correctional officers are also in a position to influence parole decisions and to assign good-time credit and **gain time** to inmates. Informal rewards correctional officers use include granting special favors and overlooking minor infractions of rules.

gain time

Time taken off an inmate's sentence for participating in certain activities such as going to school, learning a trade, and working in prison.

Expert Power Expert power results from inmates' perceptions that certain correctional officers have valuable skills. For example, inmates seeking treatment may value treatment-oriented officers. Inmates who need help with ongoing interpersonal conflicts may value officers who have conflict-resolution skills. Such officers may be able to exert influence on inmates who want their help.

Referent Power Referent power flows from "persuasive diplomacy." Officers who win the respect and admiration of prisoners—officers who are fair and not abusive—may achieve a kind of natural leadership position over inmates.

Some years before Hepburn's study, Gresham Sykes wrote that correctional officers' power can be corrupted through inappropriate relationships with inmates.[7] Friendships with prisoners, as well as indebtedness to them, can corrupt. According to Sykes, staff members who get too close to inmates and establish friendships are likely to find their "friends" asking for special favors. Similarly, officers who accept help from inmates may one day find that it is "payback time." In difficult or dangerous situations, help may be difficult to decline. In such cases, staff members must be careful not to let any perceived indebtedness to inmates influence their future behavior.

The Staff Subculture Prison life is characterized by duality. An enormous gap separates those who work in prisons from those who live in them. This gap has a number of dimensions. One is that staff members officially control the institution and enforce the rules by which inmates

A prison superintendent talks with an inmate. Effective communication is one way of overcoming the differences in beliefs, values, and behaviors between inmates and prison staff. What barriers to communication might such differences create?

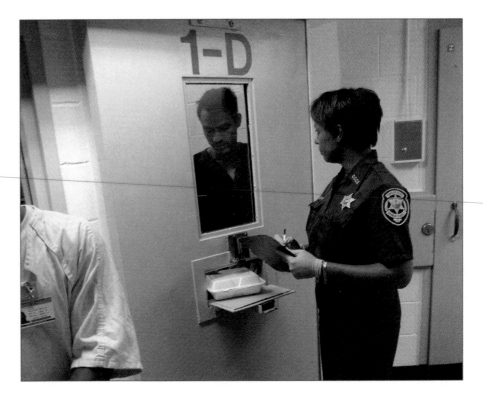

live. Other formal and informal differences exist, including differences in background, values, and culture. Primarily, however, the relationship between correctional officers and inmates can be described as one of structured conflict.[8]

Structured conflict is a term that highlights the tensions between prison staff members and inmates that arise out of the correctional setting. In one sense, the prison is one large society in which the worlds of inmates and staff bump up against one another. In another sense, however, the two groups keep their distance from each other—a distance imposed by both formal and informal rules. Conflict arises because staff members have control over the lives of inmates, and inmates often have little say over important aspects of their own lives. The conflict is structured because it occurs within the confines of an organized institution and because, to some extent, it follows the rules—formal and informal—that govern institutional life.

Both worlds—inmate and staff—have their own cultures. Those cultures are generally called *subcultures* to indicate that both are contained within and surrounded by a larger culture. One writer has defined **subculture** as the beliefs, values, behavior, and material objects shared by a particular group of people within a larger society.[9] That is the definition we will use. The subcultures of inmates and correctional officers exist simultaneously in any prison institution. The beliefs, values, and behavior that make up the **staff subculture** differ greatly from those of the inmate subculture. Additionally, staff members possess material objects of control, such as keys, vehicles, weapons, and security systems.

Kauffman has identified a distinct correctional officer subculture within prisons.[10] Those beliefs, values, and behaviors set correctional officers apart from other prison staff and from inmates. Their beliefs and values form an "officer code," which includes the following:

- Always go to the aid of an officer in distress.
- Do not "lug" drugs (bring them in for inmate use).

structured conflict

The tensions between prison staff members and inmates that arise out of the correctional setting.

subculture

The beliefs, values, behavior, and material objects shared by a particular group of people within a larger society.

staff subculture

The beliefs, values, and behavior of staff. They differ greatly from those of the inmate subculture.

- Do not rat on other officers.
- Never make a fellow officer look bad in front of inmates.
- Always support an officer in a dispute with an inmate.
- Always support officer sanctions against inmates.
- Do not be a "white hat" or a "goody two-shoes."
- Maintain officer solidarity in dealings with all outside groups.
- Show positive concern for fellow officers.

Gender and Ethnicity of Correctional Officers

The American Correctional Association (ACA) says that most correctional personnel at state and local levels are white males.[11] Two-thirds of female custodial and administrative staff members are white (see Exhibit 9–2). Thirty-two percent of corrections personnel are members of minority groups. Of these, most are black.

Ideally, the ethnic breakdown of correctional staff should closely approximate the ethnic breakdown of the population of the United States. According to the U.S. Census Bureau,[12] out of a 2000 population of about 282 million people, 34.7 million (12.3 percent) were black, 35.3 million (12.5 percent) were Hispanic, and 13.1 million (4.7 percent) were members of other minority groups. Exhibit 9–3 compares ethnic groups as a proportion of prison personnel and as a proportion of the U.S. population.

From Exhibit 9–3, it is easy to see that blacks are overrepresented among correctional personnel. Although only 12 percent of the U.S. population,

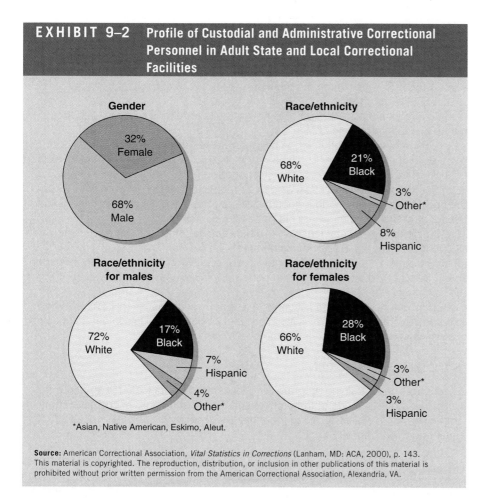

EXHIBIT 9–2   Profile of Custodial and Administrative Correctional Personnel in Adult State and Local Correctional Facilities

Gender
- 32% Female
- 68% Male

Race/ethnicity
- 68% White
- 21% Black
- 3% Other*
- 8% Hispanic

Race/ethnicity for males
- 72% White
- 17% Black
- 7% Hispanic
- 4% Other*

Race/ethnicity for females
- 66% White
- 28% Black
- 3% Other*
- 3% Hispanic

*Asian, Native American, Eskimo, Aleut.

Source: American Correctional Association, *Vital Statistics in Corrections* (Lanham, MD: ACA, 2000), p. 143. This material is copyrighted. The reproduction, distribution, or inclusion in other publications of this material is prohibited without prior written permission from the American Correctional Association, Alexandria, VA.

Eye On Corrections

On-the-Job Training: The Real Experience

By Michelle Gaseau

Training staff properly can make a huge difference in keeping staff happy and keeping them on the job. On-the-job training can be a major part of ensuring that new officers are trained right. The get-your-hands-dirty experience of the sights and smells of the cell block is, according to many, when the real training begins.

One of the main elements of making this training work is having the right officer—a field training officer—work with the new recruits for a significant period of time. "When you start trying to train adults, repetition is an [important part of it.] The field training officer process is skills based. Where [the new officer] is required to go from reading to putting [his] hands on things, tasting, touching, smelling and hearing it," said Randy McCloud, Assistant Director for Security Systems and Training for the Texas Department of Criminal Justice (TDCJ).

Texas began a new on-the-job (OJT) training program earlier this year that involves specialized field training officers in each facility. The model is based on a program supported by the National Institute of Corrections (NIC) that emphasizes on-the-job testing and evaluation of new recruits.

FIELD OFFICER TRAINING FORMALIZES ON-THE-JOB PROCESS

According to Tom Reid, Program Manager for NIC, the field officer training was created to help improve on-the-job training programs nationwide.

"We wanted to develop a formal training program for new employees to bridge the gap between the academy and the [prison.] A lot of [the programs] are too informal. [In some places] it [the training] is not well documented; it is more like partnering," said Reid.

Reid said training with an experienced officer can help new recruits transfer the information they have learned that is in their heads into actual practice.

Usually the field training officer in an institution trains new recruits in addition to performing his or her regular duties. Agencies should choose FTOs who will be good teachers, who have good writing skills, and who have good job skills. The FTO position is a good testing ground for future supervisors.

"More and more [on the job training] is very critical as people recognize what they want out of training. If you want performance on the job, you need a good translator to take the conceptual information and translate it to behavior," said Reid. That is where NIC's training comes in.

NIC strives to improve on-the-job training by teaching the field training officers in an agency how to work with a new recruit, model for them, and fairly evaluate them.

"Informal [programs] are more show and tell. Our model is very specific, and each task has a performance evaluation attached to it [as well as] an instruction period, a practice period, and testing," Reid said.

Under NIC's model, which is competency based, it could take a new recruit between 4 and 12 weeks, depending on how long he or she practices certain skills. "You want someone who is competent and confident. If it takes them 12 weeks, it develops successful employees," he said.

TEXAS REVAMPS CO TRAINING

In 2001, the TDCJ made changes to its training program for new correctional officers (COs) and modified its two-phase training process. Phase one of the training consists of 200 hours of cognitive study in the classroom. Upon graduation, COs are assigned to their unit and they begin the OJT process. OJT is phase two and involves 84 hours working with a FTO.

Each institution has an FTO. Resource trainers in firearms, chemical agents, and other specialized areas are also used to train new COs.

"The whole process is a mentoring, coaching, and a support function," said McCloud. "I want them to learn the right way the first day."

The FTO has to certify that the officer has demonstrated competency in seven skill areas, including offender escorts, cell and housing searches, and strip searches.

McCloud said the TDCJ is looking at instituting an extension of the OJT process in which the CO can call on a seasoned employee for guidance when he or she has problems on the job. "The next natural progression that relates to this process is like a lifeline. In many institutions officers are assigned to a shift mentor. "We take the employee from the safety of the academy to the FTO process and further," said McCloud.

MICHIGAN COs LEARN THE ROPES

Following academy instruction, new recruits in Michigan are assigned to two months of on-the-job training in the facility where they will be working. The department is also using the concept to help seasoned employees understand the multitude of jobs being performed inside a facility.

For new recruits, the OJT process involves additional instruction in firearms and other areas, and then they are assigned to a status officer with whom they work on morning and day shifts. The new recruits go through training in the housing unit, gun tower, visiting room, yard, and food service with the status officer.

"It is critical. We structure it so they come to the academy first and they get the basics in the classroom. After six weeks, now we are going to put [officers] in the environment and let [them] apply what [they] have learned," said Carol Frederick, Academy Operations Manager for the Michigan Department of Corrections.

During OJT the status officer fills out a weekly evaluation sheet outlining the recruit's performance in various tasks. After OJT, the new officers return to the academy for a final training and debriefing.

According to Matt Davis, spokesman for the department, the process also gives the officers a chance to see if the job is what they want to do and demonstrates how they are going to react to comments and situations.

In an adaptation of OJT, some institutions also have created job shadowing or cross-training programs for employees of all areas. "What it is trying to do is expose various staff to other types of jobs that they may not have anticipated when they first became employed and see if they might be interested or have a knack for it. It is a constantly moving group of people. To maintain the quality [of employees] it is important to get the people in the right kind of jobs," said Davis.

Staff, under the warden's direction, are able to spend up to eight hours with another staff member to see what other jobs are like. For example, COs might want to see what the records supervisor does, or a CO might work with the hearings investigator, said Davis. Frederick said the cross training helps bridge the custody and noncustody rift that seems to occur naturally in corrections. "They come with a new appreciation of the other person's job," she said.

Both this and the OJT program, which has been in place since 1983, have helped the Michigan DOC consistently fill officer positions and retain them. "[High] quality recruits will be enticed by a wide variety of options available to them. It could mean more jobs available to them [in the future,]" said Frederick.

Source: "On the Job Training: The Real Experience," Michelle Gaseau, The Corrections Connection Network News (CCNN). Eye on Corrections. www.corrections.com. March 6, 2000.
Note: This article has been reprinted in part from CCNN. To read the article in its entirety, go to www.corrections.com.

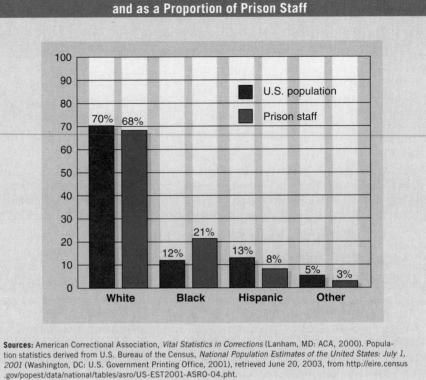

EXHIBIT 9-3   Ethnic Groups as a Proportion of the U.S. Population and as a Proportion of Prison Staff

Sources: American Correctional Association, *Vital Statistics in Corrections* (Lanham, MD: ACA, 2000). Population statistics derived from U.S. Bureau of the Census, *National Population Estimates of the United States: July 1, 2001* (Washington, DC: U.S. Government Printing Office, 2001), retrieved June 20, 2003, from http://eire.census.gov/popest/data/national/tables/asro/US-EST2001-ASRO-04.pht.

they account for 21 percent of the correctional workforce. Hispanics are underrepresented (accounting for 13 percent of the country's population and just 8 percent of the correctional workforce), as are other minorities (5 percent of the population, 3 percent of correctional staff). Whites, on the other hand, are slightly underrepresented.

Twenty-seven percent of federal Bureau of Prison employees (8,097) are female.[13] About 20 percent of correctional staff members in federal institutions are black. In juvenile facilities, females make up slightly more than 42 percent of the correctional workforce.

The American Correctional Association also says that approximately 13 percent of all correctional staff positions are supervisory (i.e., above the level of sergeant). Females hold 16 percent of all supervisory positions but fewer positions at the level of warden or superintendent.[14]

Correctional Officer Personalities

correctional officer personalities
The distinctive personal characteristics of correctional officers, including behavioral, emotional, and social traits.

The staff subculture contributes to the development of **correctional officer personalities.** Those personalities reflect the personal characteristics of the officers as well as their modes of adaptation to their jobs, institutional conditions, the requirements of staff subculture, and institutional expectations.[15] We will next explore the common personality types that have been identified.[16]

The Dictator   The dictator likes to give orders and seems to enjoy the feeling of power that comes from ordering inmates around. Correctional officers with dictator personalities are often strongly disliked by prisoners and may face special difficulties if taken hostage during a prison uprising.

First Lieutenant Gary F. Cornelius
Programs Director   Fairfax County Adult Detention Center
Fairfax County Office of the Sheriff   Fairfax, Virginia

First Lieutenant Gary Cornelius is programs director with the Fairfax County Adult Detention Center in Fairfax, Virginia. He has held this position since October of 1995 but has been with the sheriff's department since 1978.

He earned his bachelor of arts and social sciences with a focus in criminal justice from Edinboro State College in Pennsylvania in 1974. He later completed specialized police courses at the Northern Virginia Criminal Justice Academy Basic Police School as well as the U.S. Secret Service. He is a former officer of the Uniformed Division of the Secret Service.

Lieutenant Cornelius is also the author of five books, including *The Twenty Minute Trainer, The Correctional Officer: A Practical Guide,* and *The Art of the Con: Avoiding Offender Manipulation.* "Writing gives me a chance to share what I have learned and to learn new concepts through research," he says.

His duties include the development and oversight of inmate programs, ranging from recreation to rehabilitation and substance abuse. He oversees inmate education, manages volunteers and college interns, and supervises other staff members in charge of inmate recreation.

Cornelius says he enjoys watching his efforts—and the efforts of his teammates—result in positive changes. "Probably the best thing about my job is working with good people who care about both jail security and making programs work for the betterment of inmates," he says. "The most difficult aspect is convincing staff of the need for programs, rehabilitative efforts, and volunteers. And trying to get through the old-fashioned 'jailhouse mentality.'"

What are the skills that serve him best in his day-to-day affairs? "Tolerance for others' points of view, patience, not giving up, and diplomatic people skills when dealing with both civilians and sworn staff," he says.

> " *Having staff work together on an idea and watching operations improve is one of the best parts of this job.* "

The Friend The correctional officer who tries to befriend inmates is often a quiet, retiring, but kind individual who believes that close friendships with inmates will make it easier to control the inmates and the work environment. Inmates, however, usually try to capitalize on friendships by asking for special treatment, contraband, and the like.

The Merchant Merchant-personality correctional officers set themselves up as commodity providers to the inmate population. If an inmate needs something not easily obtained in prison, the merchant will usually procure it—at a cost. Often, such behavior is a violation of institutional rules, and it can lead to serious violations of the law as the merchant–correctional officer smuggles contraband into the institution for the "right price."

The Turnkey Turnkey officers do little beyond the basic requirements of their position. A turnkey usually interacts little with other officers and does the minimum necessary to get through the workday. Unmotivated and bored, the turnkey may be seeking other employment. Some turnkey officers have become disillusioned with their jobs. Others are close to retirement.

Tom Hanks as a correctional officer in *The Green Mile*. This chapter describes a variety of correctional officer personality types. Which do you think is the most common? The least?

The Climber The correctional officer who is a climber is set on advancement. He or she may want to be warden or superintendent one day and is probably seeking rapid promotion. Climbers are often diligent officers who perform their jobs well and respect the corrections profession. Climbers who look down on other officers, however, or attempt to look good by making coworkers look bad, can cause many problems within the institution.

The Reformer The reformer constantly finds problems with the way the institution is run or with existing policies and rules. He or she always seems to know better than anyone else and frequently complains about working conditions or supervisors.

The Do-Gooder The do-gooder is another type of reformer—one with a personal agenda. A devoutly religious do-gooder may try to convert other correctional officers and inmates to his or her faith. Other do-gooders actively seek to counsel inmates, using personal techniques and philosophies that are not integrated into the prison's official treatment program.

Although the personalities described here may be exaggerated, their variety suggests that correctional officer personalities result from many influences, including the following:

- general life experiences;
- biological propensities;
- upbringing;
- staff subculture;
- working conditions; and
- institutional expectations and rules.

Correctional Officer Job Assignments

Seven different correctional officer roles or job assignments have been identified.[17] They are classified by their location within the institution, the duties required, and the nature of the contact with inmates.

block officers

Those responsible for supervising inmates in housing areas.

Block Officers **Block officers** are responsible for supervising inmates in housing areas. Housing areas include dormitories, cell blocks, modular living units, and even tents in some overcrowded prisons. Safety and security are the primary concerns of block officers. Conducting counts, ensuring the orderly movement of prisoners, inspecting personal property, overseeing inmate activity, and searching prisoners are all part of the block officer's job. Block officers also lock and unlock cells and handle problems that arise within the living area. Block officers are greatly outnumbered by the inmates they supervise. Hence, if disturbances occur, block officers usually withdraw quickly to defensible positions within the institution.

work detail supervisors

Those who oversee the work of individual inmates and inmate work crews.

Work Detail Supervisors **Work detail supervisors** oversee the work of individual inmates and inmate work crews assigned to jobs within the

Ms. Eagle, a teacher in the Delaware Prison Life Skills Program, invited family members twice to come to the prison. On one occasion, she had the family members and students break into small groups—I wasn't in the same group with my mom—to discuss what various family members should do when someone comes home very late at night. Then each group reported its solutions to the whole class. In my group, a mom actually had a son who was going through this problem. The groups help each family to see how other families would solve the problem, and they also help everyone to see that everyone has the same problems.

An inmate in the Delaware Prison Life Skills Program

institution or outside it. Jobs assigned to inmates may include laundry, kitchen, and farm duties, as well as yard work and building maintenance. Work detail supervisors must also keep track of supplies and tools and maintain inventories of materials. Prison buildings are sometimes constructed almost exclusively with the use of inmate labor—creating the need for large inmate work details. On such large projects, supervising officers usually work in conjunction with outside contractors.

Industrial Shop and School Officers Industrial shop and school officers work to ensure efficient use of training and educational resources within the prison. Such resources include workshops, schools, classroom facilities, and associated equipment and tools. These officers oversee inmates who are learning trades, such as welding, woodworking, or automobile mechanics, or who are attending academic classes. Ensuring that students are present and on time for classes to begin, protecting the school and vocational instructors, and securing the tools and facilities used in instruction are all part of the job of these officers. The officers work with civilian instructors, teachers, and counselors.

Yard Officers Yard officers supervise inmates in the prison yard. They also take charge of inmates who are (1) moving from place to place, (2) eating, or (3) involved in recreational activities. Like other officers, yard officers are primarily concerned with security and order maintenance.

Administrative Officers Administrative officers are assigned to staff activities within the institution's management center. They control keys and weapons. Some administrative officers oversee visitation. As a result, they have more contact with the public than other officers do. Many administrative officers have little, if any, contact with inmates.

Perimeter Security Officers Perimeter security officers (also called *wall post officers*) are assigned to security (or gun) towers, wall posts, and perimeter patrols. They are charged with preventing escapes and detecting and preventing intrusions (such as packages of drugs or weapons thrown over fences or walls from outside). Perimeter security can become a routine job because it involves little interaction with other officers or inmates and because relatively few escape attempts occur. Newer institutions depend more heavily on technological innovations to maintain secure perimeters, requiring fewer officers for day-long perimeter observation.

industrial shop and school officers
Those who ensure efficient use of training and educational resources within the prison.

yard officers
Those who supervise inmates in the prison yard.

administrative officers
Those who control keys and weapons and sometimes oversee visitation.

perimeter security officers
Those assigned to security (or gun) towers, wall posts, and perimeter patrols. These officers are charged with preventing escapes and detecting and preventing intrusions.

relief officers
Experienced correctional officers who know and can perform almost any custody role within the institution, used to temporarily replace officers who are sick or on vacation or to meet staffing shortages.

Relief Officers **Relief officers** are experienced correctional officers who know and can perform almost any custody role in the institution. They are used to temporarily replace officers who are sick or on vacation or to meet staffing shortages.

CORRECTIONAL STAFF ISSUES

Female Officers

On a pleasant Sunday morning a few years ago, a high-custody female inmate at the Chillicothe (Missouri) Correctional Center was sitting in a dormitory, drinking her morning coffee. Having a good time, surrounded by friends, the inmate began laughing. Soon, however, the laughter turned to choking. Unable to breathe, she turned blue. Correctional officer Lisa Albin rushed to her side and found her hanging onto her bed, unable to speak. Albin remained calm as she applied the Heimlich maneuver to the inmate. After three attempts, the trapped coffee cleared the inmate's windpipe and she began breathing again. After the incident, the inmate wrote a letter of thanks to the superintendent, saying, "If it had not been for Mrs. Albin I could have very well died in that room. She literally saved my life and I will be forever grateful to her and for the training she received." [18]

Literature and films almost invariably portray correctional officers as "tobacco-chewin', reflective sunglasses-wearin', chain-gang-runnin', good ol' boys." [19] Today's officer generally defies this stereotype, and women working in corrections have helped erode this otherwise persistent myth (Exhibit 9–4).

Like most women working in male-dominated professions, female correctional officers face special problems and barriers—many of which are rooted in sexism. Prisons are nontraditional workplaces for women. As a consequence, female correctional officers—especially those working in men's prisons—often find themselves in a confusing situation. As one author explains it, "On the one hand, to be female is to be different, an outsider. On the other hand, female guards have much in common with

As the number of women who work in corrections increases, more men must confront female authority figures. What kinds of skills do female correctional officers tend to rely on to resolve problems?

and are sympathetic to their male peers as a result of their shared job experience."[20]

According to studies, female correctional officers typically say that they perform their job with a less aggressive style than men.[21] This difference in style seems due mostly to differences in life experiences and to physical limitations associated with women's size and strength. Life experiences prepare most women for helping roles rather than aggressive ones. As a consequence, women are more likely to rely heavily on verbal skills and intuition. Female correctional officers use communication rather than threats or force to gain inmate cooperation. They tend to talk out problems. Studies have also found that female correctional officers rely more heavily than male correctional officers on established disciplinary rules when problems arise. Male staff members, on the other hand, are more likely to bully or threaten inmates to resolve problems.

According to research, 55 percent of female officers indicate that their primary reason for taking a job in corrections is an interest in human service work or in inmate rehabilitation.[22] In striking contrast, only 20 percent of male officers give this as their primary reason for working in corrections.

Perhaps as a result of such attitudes, gender makes a dramatic difference in the number of assaults on correctional officers. One national survey of maximum-security prisons in 48 states, the District of Columbia, and the Federal Bureau of Prisons showed that female officers were assaulted only 27.6 percent as often as male officers.[23]

Though female correctional officers may take a different approach to their work, the skills they use complement those of male staff members. As one expert writes, "Women may humanize the workplace in small ways by establishing less aggressive relationships with inmates."[24]

Female correctional officers competently perform day-to-day custodial tasks. Are there any areas of a male prison that female correctional officers should be barred from supervising?

EXHIBIT 9–4 American Correctional Association

Employment of Women in Corrections Policy Statement

The American Correctional Association affirms the value of women employees and supports equal employment opportunities for women in adult and juvenile correctional agencies. To encourage the employment of women in corrections, correctional agencies should:

* ensure that recruitment, selection, and promotional opportunities for women are open and fair;
* assign female employees duties and responsibilities that provide career development and promotional opportunities equivalent to those provided to other employees;
* provide all levels of staff with appropriate training on developing effective and cooperative working relationships between male and female correctional personnel;
* provide all levels of staff with appropriate education and training in cross-gender supervision; and
* conduct regular monitoring and evaluation of affirmative action practices and be proactive in achieving corrective actions.

Studies also show that male officers, by and large, believe that female officers competently perform day-to-day custodial tasks. Most male staff members are "pro-woman," meaning that they applaud the entry of women into the corrections profession.[25] Many male correctional officers do express concerns about women's ability to provide adequate backup in a crisis, however. It is important to note that the need to use force in prison is relatively rare and that officers generally do not respond to dangerous situations alone. Nonetheless, some female correctional officers report that in emergencies some male officers adopt a protective, chivalrous attitude toward them. Women generally report that they resent such "special treatment," because it makes them feel more like a liability than an asset in an emergency.

Another issue concerning women in today's workplace is personal and sexual harassment. Studies show that few female correctional officers personally experience unwanted touching or other forms of sexual harassment. The forms of harassment women most commonly experience are physical (nonsexual) assaults, threats, unfounded graphic sexual rumors about them, and demeaning remarks from peers, inmates, and supervisors.[26]

A fair amount of harassment is tolerated in the correctional officer subculture. It is viewed as customary and is often accorded little significance. The response to any form of harassment, however, is determined by the officer experiencing it. He or she can tolerate it, resist it, or report it. Female correctional officers, however, express fear of being ostracized if they complain.

One writer has made the following recommendations for improving the acceptance of women as correctional officers:[27]

1. Require managers and guards to undergo training to sensitize them to the concerns of women working in prisons.
2. Establish a strong policy prohibiting sexual and personal harassment, with significant consequences for harassers.
3. Screen male job candidates for their ability and willingness to develop relationships of mutual respect with female colleagues.

Stress

stress

Tension in a person's body or mind, resulting from physical, chemical, or emotional factors.

In all occupational categories, employers estimate that more than 25 percent of all reported sick time is due to stress.[28] **Stress**—tension in a person's body or mind, resulting from physical, chemical, or emotional factors—appears to be more commonplace in prison work than in many other jobs. Nonetheless, it is often denied. As one early writer on correctional officers' stress observed, "Most officers . . . try to disguise the toll taken by the job and make the best of what is often a frustrating situation. Though not immune to the pressures of the workplace, these officers project a tough, steady image that precludes sharing frustrations with other coworkers or family members. Some of these officers may be particularly vulnerable to stress."[29]

Correctional officers frequently deny that they are under stress, fearing that admitting to feelings of stress might be interpreted unfavorably. One correctional lieutenant, an 11-year veteran, reported repeatedly observing new correctional employees succumbing to the effects of stress by becoming depressed or turning to alcohol for relief. Although she wanted to intervene, she said she "couldn't" because "no one in law enforcement is allowed to show any emotion or signs of weakness."[30]

THE STAFF SPEAKS

One of the most interesting aspects of my job as a corrections officer is the fact that it allows me to interact with people from different socioeconomic backgrounds. Some are at the top of their careers and others at the bottom, not sure who they are, or where they're going. The job has taught me respect for the law and has given me the opportunity to progress as an individual.

As a corrections officer I consider myself to be a professional. I don't think of myself as guard but as someone who has been given the responsibility of rebuilding, retraining, and restoring. Being a corrections officer takes enthusiasm, dedication, and a desire to help people overcome difficult situations. We have good listening skills and the ability to interpret and respond to changes in inmates' behavior. As a corrections officer, I work to rehabilitate inmates who have behavior problems, and to manage them by talking calmly, rather than threatening them with violence or punishment.

I'm also a field-training officer (FTO) and I teach new officers how to do the job right; be fair but firm, show compassion but not weakness, be able to react and respond quickly, treat people with respect, give the inmates someone to look up to, and finally, conduct yourself in a manner that creates and maintains respect for you and your department.

Marquis L. Westry
Corrections Corporal
Mobile County Metro Jail
Mobile, Alabama

In misguided attempts to deal with the effects of stress, many COs resort to self-medication or other tactics to deal with feelings that they may not readily admit to, even to themselves. Unfortunately, such ineffective methods do not alleviate the pressure and may instead make it worse.

Stress among correctional officers has a number of sources. Feelings of powerlessness, meaninglessness, social isolation, and self-estrangement all contribute to stress. Some authors have identified job alienation as the major source of stress among correctional officers.[31] Correctional officers rarely participate in setting the rules they work under and the policies they enforce; as a result, they may feel alienated from those policies and rules and from those who create them.

Other factors that create stress follow:

- work overload;
- family conflict;[32]
- lack of autonomy or control over one's life;
- threat of job loss;
- role conflict or role ambiguity;
- conflicts with coworkers;
- conflicts with supervisors;
- problematic organizational culture;
- difficult working environment;
- insufficient resources to reach one's goals;
- inadequate job training;
- overqualification for one's current position;
- supervisors' problematic attitudes; and
- changes in the work environment.

Symptoms of stress can be psychological, behavioral, or physical. Psychological symptoms of stress include anxiety, irritability, mood swings, sadness or depression, low self-esteem, emotional withdrawal, and hypersensitivity (to others and to what others say). Behavioral symptoms of stress include an inability to make decisions, increased interpersonal conflict, blocked creativity and judgment, poor memory, lowered

Stress is an unhappy outcome of the correctional officer's job. How does on-the-job stress arise in the correctional officer's role? How might it be reduced?

Talking about CORRECTIONS

OFFICER STRESS

Visit *Live Talk* at **Corrections.com** (www.justicestudies.com/talking04) and listen to the program "Officer Stress," which relates to ideas discussed in this chapter.

productivity, and difficulty concentrating. The physical symptoms of stress include insomnia, headaches, backaches, gastrointestinal disturbances, fatigue, high blood pressure, and frequent illnesses.

Poorer job performance and exhaustion are the results of stress. When stress reaches an unbearable level, burnout can occur. Burnout, a severe reaction to stress, is "a state of physical and emotional depletion that results from the conditions of one's occupation."[33]

Studies have shown that a person's ability to tolerate stress depends on the frequency, severity, and types of stressors confronted.[34] Stress tolerance also depends on a number of personal aspects, including past experiences, personal values and attitudes, sense of control, personality, residual stress level, and general state of health.

Authorities suggest a number of techniques for avoiding or reducing job stress. Among them are the following:[35]

1. Communicate openly. Tell people how you feel.
2. Learn not to harbor resentment, not to gossip, and to complain less often.
3. Learn to feel confident in your skills, your values and beliefs, and yourself.
4. Develop a support system. Close friends, pets, social activities, and a happy extended family can all help alleviate stress.
5. Be a good and conscientious worker, but don't become a workaholic.
6. Learn to manage your time and do not procrastinate.
7. Make it a habit to get a good night's sleep.
8. Exercise regularly.
9. Watch your diet. Avoid excessive fat, sugars, salt, red meat, and caffeine.
10. Learn some relaxation exercises such as self-affirmation, mental imaging, deep breathing, stretching, massage, or yoga.
11. Try to have fun. Laughter can combat stress quite effectively.
12. Spend time cultivating self-understanding. Analyze your feelings and your problems—and recognize your accomplishments.
13. Set goals and make plans. Both bring order and direction to your life.

One especially effective strategy for coping with job stress is to develop clear and favorable role definitions. According to J. T. Dignam and colleagues, "Officers who have more opportunities for receiving assistance and goal clarification from supervisors and coworkers [are] less likely to experience role ambiguity than those for whom such support is not available or sought. Further, the risk of burnout or other deleterious consequences of occupational stress may be reduced for those who are 'insulated' by social support."[36]

Similarly, another group of researchers found that "support from colleagues or supervisors may be one of the most important factors ameliorating stress in the workplace."[37] The same researchers also found that when correctional officers felt "rewarding companionship" with fellow

COMMISSION ON SAFETY AND ABUSE IN AMERICA'S PRISONS: CORRECTIONAL LEADERSHIP

> *What ultimately makes a correctional institution work has to do with the hearts and minds and spirits of those who people it, not with bricks and mortar, shatterproof glass, pre-fab cells or organizational charts.*
> —Sheriff Michael Ashe, Hampden County, Massachusetts

The public rarely thinks about people in prison and thinks even less often about the men and women who manage and work in these same facilities. When we do look closely, what we see is a poorly understood profession that shoulders tremendous responsibilities and faces incredible challenges, usually without adequate resources and support. Yet this labor force is responsible for operating jails and prisons that must safely and humanely accommodate an estimated 13.5 million people annually. When corrections professionals fail to meet the demands of the job, for whatever reason, they endanger prisoners and officers alike and, at the extreme, cripple entire facilities. The failures are felt beyond the facility walls when officers and prisoners return to their families and their communities.

The recommendations for reform outlined in this box are intended to acknowledge and build on the underlying strengths of the workforce and its leaders in two broad ways: by improving the institutional culture in correctional facilities and by supporting corrections professionals at every level. Progress in these areas would provide a foundation for improving the safety and effectiveness of America's prisons and jails.

The relationship between prisoners and corrections officers is at the very core of the culture of confinement. Too often, that relationship is uncaring and antagonistic, punctuated by moments of overt hostility, aggression, and physical violence.

Today there are statewide efforts in places as far apart as Oregon, Arizona, Massachusetts, and Maryland to change the fundamental culture of prisons. Corrections administrators in these states understand that an "us versus them" mentality ultimately jeopardizes the safety and health of prisoners and staff and over time harms the families and communities to which prisoners and staff belong. Their efforts at culture change should be supported, imitated, and improved upon so that no one has to live or work in a dehumanizing environment and so that our correctional facilities serve the public's interests. The culture of these institutions cannot change, however, unless efforts are made to build a highly qualified workforce and to cultivate and support great leaders.

The following three recommendations suggest ways to meet all of these goals:

Promote a Culture of Mutual Respect
Create a positive culture in jails and prisons grounded in an ethic of respectful behavior and interpersonal communication that benefits prisoners and staff.

Recruit and Retain a Qualified Corps of Officers
Enact changes at the state and local levels to advance the recruitment and retention of a high-quality, diverse workforce and otherwise further the professionalism of the workforce.

Support Today's Leaders and Cultivate the Next Generation
Governors and local executives must hire the most qualified leaders and support them politically and professionally, and corrections administrators must, in turn, use their positions to promote healthy and safe prisons and jails. Equally important, we must develop the skills and capacities of middle-level managers, who play a large role in running safe facilities and are poised to become the next generation of senior leaders.

Source: Adapted from the Commission on Safety and Abuse in America's Prisons, *Confronting Confinement* (New York: Vera Institute of Justice, 2006).

Note: The full 126-page report, *Confronting Confinement: A Report of the Commission on Safety and Abuse in America's Prisons,* can be accessed on the Internet at www.prisoncommission.org.

correctional officers, they reported fewer stressful events (even when objective measures showed an actual rise in such events). Most researchers agree that candidates need more extensive and thorough training to prepare them for the psychological and sociological consequences of becoming correctional officers.

Staff Safety

Staff safety is a major stressor for individual correctional officers and a primary management concern for correctional administrators. Safety planning must include consideration of the following elements (adapted, in part, from studies of staff safety needs in both juvenile[38] and adult[39] institutions):

- a functionally designed physical plant that limits inmate movement and incorporates technologically advanced security systems, perimeter barriers, and rooms, doors, and locks;
- a behavior management system that establishes clear guidelines for acceptable behavior, reward systems to reinforce expected behavior, and disciplinary systems to discourage unacceptable behavior;
- appropriate staff and inmate relationships (in particular, staff must be aware of, and prepared to respond to, the dangers posed by prison gangs);
- policies and procedures, published in a manual and distributed to staff and supervisors, that support consistent implementation of rules and regulations and prevent the risk of staff letdowns resulting from excessive routine;
- shift scheduling that ensures a mutually supportive balance of senior and junior staff because a sound mix of age and experience facilitates the achievement of inmate control while providing opportunities for on-the-job development of junior officers by senior officers;
- effective supervision at every level;
- comprehensive staff training that ensures all correctional officers and their supervisors know every rule, regulation, policy, and procedure that affects their particular job (if, as the saying goes, knowledge is power, such training is key to empowering the staff to maintain a controlled, safe environment); and
- development of, and training for, a sound action plan that addresses all contingencies.

In addition to advocating thorough planning as just outlined, Stewart and Brown[40] urge continuing research to identify what works, what doesn't work, and emerging trends in staff safety. In particular, they recommend development of a safety program tailored to the needs of correctional officers nationwide. It should be modeled, they suggest, on safety programs designed for police officers, probation officers, and other officers in law enforcement.

Job Satisfaction

High levels of stress reduce the satisfaction correctional officers get from their jobs. In a sad indictment of the corrections field, a 1996 study found that correctional officers were significantly different from most other groups of correctional employees. "They showed the lowest levels of organizational commitment, possessed the highest levels of skepticism about organizational change, were the least positive about careers in corrections and the rehabilitation of offenders, possessed the lowest levels of job satisfaction, were the least involved in their jobs, and were described as having the poorest work habits and overall job performance."[41] In a separate study, correctional supervisors and managers were found to have much higher levels of job satisfaction and professionalism.[42]

One reason for the difference in job satisfaction between supervisory personnel and those on the front lines of corrections work is that correctional officers often feel alienated from policymaking.[43] As one writer puts it, "when looking at the atmosphere and environment of a state or federal prison, it would seem obvious what correction personnel like least about working there: surveys of personnel who resign or quit show that their biggest problems are with supervisory personnel rather than inmates."[44]

Correctional officers' job satisfaction appears to be tied to the amount of influence they feel they have over administrative decisions and policies. Officers who feel they have some control over the institution and over their jobs seem much more satisfied than officers' who believe they have no control. Hence, it appears that correctional officers job satisfaction can be greatly enhanced by caring administrators who involve the officers in policymaking.

For some correctional officers, the perception that their profession suffers a generally poor public image[45] further reduces their job satisfaction. Compared to local and state police officers and agents of the various federal law enforcement organizations, correctional officers may be viewed as the "poor relations" of the law enforcement family. As one researcher wrote, "Most people do not know of a child who says, I want to be a correctional officer when I grow up."[46]

Media portrayals of correctional officers exacerbate the situation. Movies and television often depict COs as lowly qualified "guards" (considered a derogatory title; "guards work at Macy's and banks")[47] whose primary function seems to be abusing prisoners. Correctional officers "believe they are seen as brutes, only a shade better than the people behind bars."[48] Consequently, COs have a difficult time overcoming these images as they attempt to convey the significance and professional demands of their positions to civic leaders and the public.[49]

There is evidence, however, that job satisfaction among correctional officers is rising. The rise may be partly due to increasing awareness of what correctional officers find most important in the work environment. Recent studies have identified the most important determinants of job satisfaction among correctional officers as (1) working conditions, (2) the level of work-related stress, (3) the quality of working relationships with fellow officers, and (4) length of service.[50]

In one of the most significant studies to date, treatment-oriented correctional staff reported far higher levels of job satisfaction than did custody-oriented staff.[51] The study was of survey data collected from 428 Arizona correctional service officers (CSOs) and 118 correctional program officers (CPOs). Job satisfaction was significantly greater among the human-services-oriented CPOs than among the traditional-custody-oriented CSOs. The findings suggest that additional attention should be given to enhancing and enriching the duties of correctional officers, extending their control over and involvement in prisoners' activities, and redefining their roles more as service workers than as control agents.

Determinants of job satisfaction appear to differ for male and female correctional officers. One study found that the quality of working relationships with other officers, the amount of stress experienced at work, the length of service as a correctional officer, and educational level were all positively related to job satisfaction for males.[52] Women officers, on the other hand, appeared to place more emphasis on the quality of working relationships with all other correctional officers (not just the ones with whom they worked) and tended to be happier in prisons at lower security levels. Other studies have related higher job satisfaction among white female officers to the officers' positive evaluation of the quality of supervision. In other words, white female correctional officers tend to be happier in prisons that they believe are well run.[53]

Professionalism

On October 29, 1994, correctional officer Ken Davis was instantly catapulted to the forefront of national attention when he tackled a man shooting at the White House. Without warning, Francisco Martin Duran had leveled a Chinese-made AK-47 assault rifle at the White House from outside the iron gates and had begun firing. While most other bystanders either fled or stood stunned, Davis ran toward Duran and wrestled him to the ground, holding him until police and White House security officers arrived. Duran was later sentenced to 40 years in prison with no chance of parole on charges of attempting to assassinate President Clinton.

Davis, a correctional officer at the Victor Cullins Academy[54] in Maryland, was honored for his quick actions. During the ceremony honoring him, he noted a few lifestyle principles that could benefit all correctional officers. "Correctional officers serve and survive better," said Davis, "if they adopt the capacity for balance as a personal philosophy."[55] Balance means understanding themselves, knowing when they can handle a situation and when they cannot, and admitting when they need help. It also means having a clear sense of their roles and keeping a clear view of their purpose and their career goals. A good sense of balance, said Davis, reduces job stress and "improves officer–officer relations" by leading to good teamwork. Correctional officers need to understand the importance of positive peer relationships in maintaining high morale. Officer Davis observed that inmates look for correctional officers without a personal sense of balance and "systematically and continuously work to manipulate the human frailties of correctional officers."

"There is danger in ignorance," Davis said. "Learning is a lifelong process. True knowledge is knowing what you do not know! Don't worry about sounding stupid. Know when to call for help. Don't be afraid to say, 'I need help,' 'I don't understand this duty post,' or 'This approach seems wrong.'"

Training can enhance professionalism. As more and more prison staff develop a professional perspective, the structural organization of prisons and interactions among staff and inmates may significantly change. What kinds of training may help correctional officers adjust to a changing environment?

ETHICS & PROFESSIONALISM

International Association of Correctional Officers: The Correctional Officer's Creed

To speak sparingly . . . to act, not argue . . . to be in authority through personal presence . . . to correct without nagging . . . to speak with the calm voice of certainty . . . to see everything and to know what is significant and what not to notice . . . to be neither insensitive to distress nor so distracted by pity as to miss what must elsewhere be seen. . . .

To do neither that which is unkind nor self-indulgent in its misplaced charity . . . never to obey the impulse to tongue lash that silent insolence which in time past could receive the lash . . . to be both firm and fair . . . to know I cannot be fair simply by being firm, nor firm simply by being fair. . . .

To support the reputations of associates and confront them without anger should they stand short of professional conduct . . . to reach for knowledge of the continuing mysteries of human motivation . . . to think; always to think . . . to be dependable . . . to be dependable first to my charges and associates and thereafter to my duty as employee and citizen . . . to keep fit . . . to keep forever alert . . . to listen to what is meant as well as what is said with words and with silences.

To expect respect from my charges and my superiors yet never to abuse the one for abuses from the other . . . for eight hours each working day to be an example of the person I could be at all times . . . to acquiesce in no dishonest act . . . to cultivate patience under boredom and calm during confusion . . . to understand the why of every order I take or give. . . .

To hold freedom among the highest values though I deny it to those I guard . . . to deny it with dignity that in my example they find no reason to lose their dignity . . . to be prompt . . . to be honest with all who practice deceit that they not find in me excuse for themselves . . . to privately face down my fear that I not signal it . . . to privately cool my anger that I not displace it on others . . . to hold in confidence what I see and hear, which by telling could harm or humiliate to no good purpose . . . to keep my outside problems outside . . . to leave inside that which should stay inside . . . to do my duty.

Source: Copyright © 2000 Bob Barrington.

Ethical Dilemma 9–1: There are reports that find sexual misconduct is a problem in prisons for women. These reports state that male staff victimize women inmates. Should only female staff work in prisons for women? What are the issues? For more information go to Ethical Dilemma 9–1 at www.justicestudies.com/ethics04.

Ethical Dilemma 9–2: Stress among correctional staff is widespread, and your facility has a stress-reduction program. You are feeling very stressed, but you are afraid to take advantage of the program, thinking it may reflect poorly on you at promotion time. Do you participate in the program anyway? For more information go to Ethical Dilemma 9–2 at www.justicestudies.com/ethics04.

Ethical Dilemmas for every chapter are available online.

Davis also noted that "listening is the heart of communication. Good listening practices shape a successful officer. Effective officers strive to perfect both active and passive listening skills, by exploring innovative ways to improve communication with peers and supervisors, inmates, visitors, and the public."

"One way for officers to accomplish the achievement of their personal career goals," noted Davis, "is to constantly groom themselves early in their career for higher rank and responsibility by learning from their experienced supervisors and by keeping a journal of lessons learned. This process will provide dividends for years to come. It will give you a bank of positive experiences to draw on in future times of career decisions and in times of crisis."

The International Association of Correctional Officers has published a Correctional Officer's Creed (see the Ethics and Professionalism box), which summarizes the duties and responsibilities of a correctional officer.

Eye On Corrections

Monitoring Extremist Groups

By Michelle Gaseau

Criminal plots being hatched behind prison walls, recruitment of isolated and disenfranchised individuals, orders being given to extremists on the outside. These are serious threats to the security of both corrections facilities and society at large and their prevention is a source of frustration for many corrections administrators.

While the vast majority of inmates practicing religion in prison do so in a peaceful and constructive way, there are groups of inmates with extreme views who hide behind religion in order to commit crimes and pass on their beliefs.

"Particularly in this post-9/11 environment, analysts recognize that the prison can be a breeding ground for all kinds of security risks under the guise of being a religion and that's what is so tough—it's the balancing act [between religious rights and security threats] that corrections officials have to tackle," said Brian Levin, Professor and Director of the Center for the Study of Hate & Extremism at California State University, San Bernardino.

Levin said corrections officials need to think carefully about how they respond to these threats, recognize inmates' right of religion and, at the same time, be cognizant of, and take action against, groups that represent a threat inside or outside the prison. If they don't, then inmates may prevail either by furthering their cause or getting official status in court.

"Unfortunately [corrections officials] have to think out a possible court response, but so much of what the court relies on is situationally specific," said Levin. "It really comes down to the ability of corrections officials to show that their acts are reasonable and they are not targeting religious practices in a punitive way, but actual security threats themselves."

Many believe that the clock is ticking for corrections agencies to figure out this balance because extreme religious groups represent a legitimate threat inside the prisons that should be monitored.

UNDERSTANDING THE THREATS

Mark Pitcavage of the Anti-Defamation League says there are [important] issues surrounding extremist groups that corrections agencies should consider. He says that while corrections agencies are typically aware of gangs and their activities, extremist groups also pose some of the same problems in that they are involved in organized crime or other types of criminal activity.

Furthermore, extremists who are incarcerated want to recruit others there. One example, he says, is with the members of the Montana Freemen group who were jailed in the 90s. While in jail, Pitcavage says, they started teaching their extremist tactics to others.

Corrections should also be aware, Pitcavage says, that extremist groups on the outside view prisons as fertile ground for recruitment and, once inside, extremists will continue to direct the actions of others on the outside. . . .

The issue of monitoring extremist groups was raised in a report by the federal Office of the Inspector General published in May [2004], which questioned some of the practices within the federal Bureau of Prisons regarding the selection of Muslim religious leaders.

The report, which investigated the practices of various institutions and made recommendations for change, highlighted several deficiencies in how the BOP selected and supervised Muslim religious service providers.

Included among this list in the report were concerns that the BOP typically did not examine the doctrinal beliefs of applicants for religious service positions to determine if they were inconsistent with BOP security practices; the BOP and FBI did not adequately exchange information about the BOP's Muslim endorsing organizations; the BOP does not effectively use the expertise of its current Muslim chaplains to screen, recruit and supervise Muslim religious services providers; BOP inmates often lead Islamic religious services and are subject to intermittent supervision from BOP staff and, within the BOP's chapels, significant variations exist in the level of supervision provided by correctional officers.

According to published reports . . . , a BOP spokesman said the agency has made changes . . . to better screen religious services providers. And, in testimony before the Senate's Subcommittee on Terrorism, Technology and Homeland Security last October, BOP Director Harley Lappin said that the agency has been sharing information with the FBI, National Joint Terrorism Task Force and other intelligence agencies regarding inmates with terrorist ties.

Nevertheless, some can understand why security might have been lax around the provision of services to Muslim inmates.

"The history of [followers of] Islam in prison is they have been very orderly. They stop drinking, get in fewer fights, and therefore for most of the last several decades it has been a pretty benign influence, or it didn't have a dangerous influence. And because they didn't pose a particular threat, prison officials developed a comfortableness," says Pitcavage.

Pitcavage also recognizes that the world has changed since 9/11 and so, too, must security practices.

"After 9/11, in our prison systems, [we learned] we weren't as sensitive as we might have been to issues of radical Islamists having a presence in our systems," he said.

The incidents that have taken place since then show why a closer look at some of the practices by these groups inside prison is needed. Pitcavage said in New York and Pennsylvania, Imams with a radical view of Islam have been able to talk with prisoners and some have been able to bring radical materials into prison libraries. Still other stories, such as the one of a radical Imam in Los Angeles sending materials to inmates in Texas, show the potential threats that exist.

Those threats come from many groups, however, not just radical Islamists. The followers of the World Church of the Creator, Five Percenters and others can pose a threat to prison security as they attempt to spread their message by claiming religious status.

But as corrections officials understand the seriousness of these threats, they also struggle to find a model to follow to address them. One of the main problems in regulating radical religious groups is that there is no consistent approach in the field. One system, for example, allows inmates to lead religious services, while another allows for no unsupervised gathering of inmates for religious purposes whatsoever. . . .

BALANCING LEGAL RULINGS AND SECURITY

Some state prison systems have already had their security practices scrutinized in the courts as inmates claiming religious group membership have filed lawsuits claiming their rights have been ignored or violated.

These cases have been filed by inmates under RLUIPA, the Religious Land Use and Institutionalized Persons Act, which was signed into law in 2000 by President Clinton. The statute replaces the protections afforded inmates under the Religious Freedom Restoration Act, which was determined [to be] unconstitutional by the federal courts.

RLIUPA reads in part, "No government shall impose a substantial burden on religious exercise of a person residing in or confined to an institution . . . even if the burden results from a rule of general applicability, unless . . . it is a furtherance of a compelling governmental interest; and is the least restrictive means of furthering that compelling governmental interest.

"RLUIPA puts the burden on the government. It was designed to protect the religious rights of prisoners, which historically have been denied," said Pitcavage.

Source: "Monitoring Extremist Groups and Maintaining Religious Rights," Michelle Gaseau, The Corrections Connection Network News (CCNN). Eye on corrections. www.corrections.com. September 20, 2004.
Note: This article has been reprinted in part from CCNN. To read this article in its entirety, go to www.corrections.com.

The Impact of Terrorism on Corrections

The events of September 11, 2001, created an awareness of potential crises that could arise in correctional institutions as a result of terrorist actions. Today's prison administrators must be concerned about inmate involvement in terrorist activities, the impact of a terrorism event within the community in which their facility is located, and the threat of a terrorist act being undertaken by an inmate or inmates within their facility.

In addition, incarcerating those convicted of terrorism presents new challenges for correctional administrators. For example, Sheik Omar Abdel-Rahman, spiritual leader for many terrorists, including Osama bin Laden, is now serving a life sentence in a U.S. federal penitentiary for conspiring to assassinate Egyptian President Hosni Mubarak and blow up five New York City landmarks in the 1990s. Speculation that the sheik continues to motivate terrorist acts against the United States gained credibility when his attorney was sentenced to 28 months in prison in 2006 for passing illegal communications between Abdel-Rahman and an Egyptian-based terrorist organization known as the Islamic Group.[56] Another convicted terrorist, September 11 conspirator Zacarias Moussaoui, also known as the 20th hijacker, is serving a life sentence at the federal administrative maximum facility in Florence, Colorado. Moussaoui's fellow prisoners, housed on what has come to be known as "Bomber's Row," include al-Qaeda shoe bomber Richard Reid; Ramzi Yousef, mastermind of the 1993 World Trade Center bombing; seven of Yousef's accomplices; Ahmed Ressam, who was arrested at the Canadian border with explosives he intended to use to bomb Los Angeles International Airport; four men convicted in the 1998 bombing of U.S. embassies in Africa; and Abdul Hakim Murad, convicted in a 1995 al-Qaeda plan to bomb 12 airplanes during a two-day period.

Correctional personnel play a potentially important role in preventing future attacks of terrorism and in averting crises that could arise in correctional institutions as a result of terrorist action. The role of the correctional officer in terrorism prevention was highlighted in a speech given in 2005 by former New York City police commissioner Bernard B. Kerik. Speaking to participants at the American Correctional Association's winter conference, Kerik pointed to the crucial role of effective intelligence gathering within correctional institutions, as well as the importance of intelligence sharing between enforcement agencies. "Intelligence—that's the key to the success of this battle," Kerik said.[57] "You have to be part of that, because when we take people off the streets in this country that go to jail, they communicate and they talk, they work with other criminals, organized gangs, organized units. You've got to collect that information, you have to get it back to the authorities that need it."

Jess Maghan, former training director for the New York City Department of Corrections and now the director of the Forum for Comparative Corrections and professor of criminal justice at the University of Illinois at Chicago, points out that "the interaction of all people in a prison (staff, officers, and inmates) can become important intelligence sources."[58] Moreover, says Maghan, the flow of information between inmates and the outside world needs to be monitored in order to detect attack plans—especially when prisons house known terrorist leaders or group members. Covert information, says Maghan, can be passed through legal visits (where people conveying information may have no idea of its significance); sub-rosa communications networks in prisons that can support communications between inmates and the outside world; and prison transportation systems.

Because of their marginal social status, inmates may be particularly vulnerable to recruitment by terrorist organizations. According to Chip Ellis, research and program coordinator for the National Memorial Institute for the Prevention of Terrorism, "Prisoners are a captive audience, and they usually have a diminished sense of self or a need for identity and protection. They're usually a disenchanted or disenfranchised group of people, [and] terrorists can sometimes capitalize on that situation."[59] Ellis points out that inmates can be radicalized in a variety of ways, including exposure to extremist literature and other radical inmates, as well as through anti-U.S. sermons delivered during religious services.

The FBI says that al-Qaeda continues to actively recruit followers inside American correctional institutions. Islamic terrorists are keenly aware of the 9,600 Muslims held in the federal prison system and see them as potential converts. "These terrorists seek to exploit our freedom to exercise religion to their advantage by using radical forms of Islam to recruit operatives," says FBI counterterrorism chief John Pistole.[60] "Unfortunately," notes Pistole, "U.S. correctional institutions are a valuable venue for such radicalization and recruitment."

In 2005, the Institute for the Study of Violent Groups at Sam Houston State University charged that Wahhabism—the most radical form of Islam—was being spread in American prisons by clerics approved by the Islamic Society of North America (ISNA). ISNA is one of two organizations that the Federal Bureau of Prisons uses to select prison chaplains to serve inmates in its facilities.[61] "Proselytizing in prisons," said the institute, "can produce new recruits with American citizenship." An example might be Chicago thug Jose Padilla, aka Abdulla al-Mujahir, who converted to Islam after exposure to Wahhabism while serving time in a Florida jail. Authorities claim Padilla intended to contaminate a U.S. city with a radiological dirty bomb. In 2007, Padilla was convicted of federal terrorism charges. Similarly, convicted shoe bomber Richard Reid converted to radical Islam while in an English prison before planning his attack on an American Airlines flight from Paris to Miami.[62]

In 2004 the Office of the Inspector General of the U.S. Department of Justice released a review of the practices used by the Federal Bureau of Prisons in selecting Muslim clergy to minister to inmates in the bureau's facilities. The report concluded that the primary threat of radicalization came not from chaplains, contractors, or volunteers but from inmates. According to the report, "Inmates from foreign countries politicize Islam and radicalize inmates, who in turn radicalize more inmates when they transfer to other prisons."[63] The report also identified a form of Islam unique to the prison environment called "Prison Islam."[64] Prison Islam, the report said, is a form of Islam that is used by gangs and radical inmates to further unlawful goals. It adapts itself easily to prison values and promotes the interests of the incarcerated. Prison Islam was found to be especially common in institutions where religious services are led by lay *Mullahs* (spiritual leaders, who are often inmates)—a practice made necessary by a lack of Muslim chaplains. The report recommended that "the BOP can and should improve its process for selecting, screening, and supervising Muslim religious services providers. We recommend," said the report, that "the

Muslim prisoners at prayer in New York's Wende Correctional Facility. Radicalized inmates of any faith can represent a threat to facility security. What connection might exist between radicalized inmates and criminals or terrorist groups on the outside?

Indonesian terrorist Imam Samudra in prison in Bali awaiting execution. Samudra was convicted of masterminding terrorist bombings that killed 202 people in 2002 and sentenced to death by firing squad. While imprisoned, Samudra wrote a jailhouse manifesto on the funding of terrorism through cyberfraud. How might incarcerated terrorists constitute a threat to the facilities in which they are housed?

BOP take steps to examine all chaplains', religious contractors', and religious volunteers' doctrinal beliefs to screen out anyone who poses a threat to security." Another report, this one recently released by the Homeland Security Policy Institute (HSPI) at George Washington University and the Critical Incident Analysis Group (CIAG) at the University of Virginia, says that the First Amendment right of prisoners to practice religion makes it difficult for prison officials to prevent radicalization. The HSPI/CIAG report notes that "prison facilities bear the burden of proof if they wish to deny an inmate's request for any service or activity related to religion."[65]

In 2006, the U.S. Justice Department's Office of the Inspector General released another report—this one critical of BOP inmate mail monitoring procedures, saying that "the threat remains that terrorist and other high-risk inmates can use mail and verbal communications to conduct terrorist or criminal activities while incarcerated." The report was based on findings that three convicted terrorists had been able to send 90 letters to Islamic extremists in the Middle East in 2005, praising Osama bin Laden. The report noted the fact that the BOP does not have the needed number of translators proficient in Arabic who are able to read inmate mail, and said that budget restrictions do not allow for the reading of all incoming and outgoing mail.[66]

The threat of a terrorist act being carried out by inmates within a prison or jail can be an important consideration in facility planning and management. Of particular concern is the possibility of bioterrorism. A concentrated population such as exists within a prison or jail would be highly susceptible to rapid transmission of the ill effects from such an attack.[67]

Seemingly significant recommendations come from Y. N. Baykan, a management specialist with the Maryland Division of Correction. Baykan says that no successful strategies are being used today to control radical Islamist influences in American prisons and suggests the following:[68]

- Prison administrators must realize that the threat of transnational terrorism in American facilities is real.
- Radical Islamic groups should be seen as sophisticated social networks rather than gangs.
- Prison authorities must evaluate existing policies and strategies, looking closely at the roles and backgrounds of chaplains and volunteers and the rules governing religious conversions.
- Meetings of radicals should be closely monitored as should incoming propaganda.
- Prison staff should be taught to understand political Islam and should use information-management solutions that involve cutting-edge collection, storage, and analysis of data.
- Prison authorities must follow what is happening in other countries and learn from it.
- Threat information should be shared by all stakeholders, including state and federal systems and other law enforcement agencies.

As the United States faces more and more threats of terrorism, it is likely that the issues identified here will take on greater significance for correctional facilities throughout the nation and around the world.

REVIEW & APPLICATIONS

REFLECTIONS ON THE FUTURE
Correctional Leadership in the 21st Century

by Richard Kiekbusch
University of Texas–
Permian Basin

As we proceed into the 21st century, American corrections is in need of *leadership*—not just sound management, but *strong, purposeful leadership.*

We are a nation that makes generous use of its correctional resources. We have over 6 million adults under some form of correctional supervision, roughly 6.3 percent of America's adult population. There is certainly nothing inherently wrong with this heavy use of our broad array of institutional and community-based correctional programs. In employing these programs, however, we need to be reasonably sure that we are actually making our communities safer and not simply pandering to emotionally laced public demands and furthering the careers of "tough-on-crime" politicians. And this requires *leadership.*

Leadership, though, is an overused term, a term that is liberally employed by speakers and writers who really don't know what it means. Exactly what *does* "leadership" mean in the context of 21st century American corrections? Further, who must provide it and what should they advocate? Here are my personal thoughts.

Management and *leadership* are not synonymous. Competent correctional managers run their agencies and institutions in compliance with public policy. Forceful leaders help shape public policy. Many managers are not capable of exercising genuine leadership or even desirous of doing so. Conversely, not all leaders are effective agency or institutional managers. American corrections needs both effective managers and persuasive leaders—*but especially the latter.*

A person does not become a leader simply because he or she becomes a commissioner, director, or sheriff. There are scores of correctional executives in this country who are skill-ful managers but who do not exercise authentic leadership. Unfortunately, some of these executives actually confound corrections' need for informed, consistent, and durable public policy by accepting, or even seizing, the acclamation of "leader" and then failing to satisfy the requirements of genuine leadership.

What are those requirements? What traits characterize real correctional leaders? First and foremost, leaders stand for something. They have firm positions on major issues confronting the corrections profession (e.g., sentencing policies, the role of community-based sanctions, inmate rights, capital punishment). Those positions, furthermore, are the products of a careful consideration of varied points of view on each issue. They are not simply a thoughtless reaffirmation of politically correct and popularly fashionable public opinions. Additionally, the true leader remains open to have his or her positions altered by new information or the persuasive arguments of others.

Real correctional leaders in this country understand their serious obligation to implement public policy emanating from our partisan political arena, but they also understand their corresponding obligation, equally as serious, to inform that arena. They acknowledge their nonpartisan responsibility to ensure that political representatives who are debating and formulating corrections-related public policy clearly comprehend the implications and consequences of the laws and initiatives they are proposing. They understand that a critical component of leadership is public education.

Finally, as the leader advocates his or her positions on critical policy issues and attempts to inform the politicians and the public, he or she may tell them things they don't want to hear. The persistent correctional leader, then, runs the risk of annoying some powerful and influential people. Risk takers often pay a price for their risk taking. True correctional leaders must be willing to "pay the price"—even if that price involves the loss of an appointment or an election. Leadership, in other words, requires courage and sacrifice.

Who must provide the brand of correctional leadership that I have just described? Who must continuously educate the general public and its political policymakers on key correctional issues and demonstrate the requisite courage in doing so? Without question, the commissioners and directors of our federal and state correctional agencies must step up and meet this challenge. Another group, usually overlooked but critically important, upon whom we must be able to rely for correctional leadership are the elected sheriffs who operate the 3,000 plus jails across the country. Sheriffs, in particular, need to understand that, at this point in time, their corrections/detention responsibilities are at least as prominent as their law enforcement responsibilities.

Purposeful correctional leadership must also be supplied by the staff executives and elected officers of our principal professional associations—the American Correctional Association, the American Jail Association, and the National Sheriffs' Association at the very least.

Substantively, what policy positions should contemporary American correctional leaders take? What should they stand for? I prefer not to suggest specific policies and programs as these should be the result of informed discourse and should be tailored to meet the unique needs of particular locales and circumstances. I do suggest, however, three assumptions that should be embraced by our correctional leadership and undergird specific policy and program initiatives.

First, our correctional leaders must understand that the proper goal of the American criminal justice system is not to incarcerate as many people as possible. Rather, it is to keep our communities safe and to do so as inexpensively as possible. Incarceration is one means to that end, not an end in itself. Jail and prison beds are expensive commodities and should be used very selectively for those offenders whose supervision in noninstitutional programs would unduly compromise the safety of the communities in which those programs are located. Our correctional leadership should insist that any proposed legislation involving sentencing, good time, parole eligibility, or other mechanisms that affect institutional populations be carefully reviewed for their capital implications. Expansion or construction deemed excessive or unnecessary should be vigorously opposed. At the same time, our correctional leaders should encourage and support practicably designed and reasonably priced research projects that are intended to provide usable insights as to what types of offenders can be safely supervised in community-based programs and what types re-

quire secure incarceration. Our leaders must then press for the inclusion of the research findings in subsequent legislative discussions and debates.

Second, our correctional leaders must understand that society's principal efforts to prevent and control crime need to occur outside of the criminal justice system, not within it. We need strong families in which children receive a value-laden upbringing and a firmly entrenched sense of right and wrong. We need well-staffed and properly equipped schools that educate and not just baby-sit. And, the political incorrectness of this observation notwithstanding, we need assertive churches, synagogues, and mosques that infuse our young people with a sense of a higher moral authority. Our correctional leadership must help our legislators and other public officials to understand that correctional programs cannot serve as the primary vehicles of education and value formation. Before the institutional counselor, teacher, or chaplain arrives in a young person's life, the family, school, and church must have already been there. Our correctional leaders must understand that public policies pertaining to our families, our schools, and our churches are, in fact, crime control policies, and those leaders must establish a presence in policymaking in those areas.

And third, our correctional leaders must understand that "tough-on-

crime" fiscal conservatism and offender rehabilitation programs are not mutually exclusive. Public policymakers must come to appreciate that to have an offender under supervision for an extended period of time and not offer the offender opportunities for self-improvement during that time constitutes relative inattention to public safety and markedly poor stewardship of the public dollar. Our correctional leaders must persuade our political representatives that, if they are truly "get-tough-on-crime" fiscal conservatives, they will endorse well-run inmate rehabilitation programs.

In conclusion, as we forge ahead into the 21st century, American corrections is in need of decisive leaders who understand the proper goals of American criminal justice, who acknowledge that society's principal crime prevention and crime control efforts must occur outside of the criminal justice system, and who support well-run offender rehabilitation programs.

About the Author

Dr. Richard Kiekbusch is associate professor of criminology at the University of Texas–Permian Basin. Dr. Kiekbusch earned his degrees from the University of Notre Dame. He has over 20 years' experience in correctional administration—including work in juvenile corrections, jail administration, and private corrections.

SUMMARY

1 There is a hierarchy of staff positions, from warden (or superintendent) at the top, down to correctional officer and correctional officer trainee. A typical correctional staff includes (1) administrative staff, (2) clerical personnel, (3) program staff, (4) custodial staff, (5) service and maintenance staff, and (6) volunteers.

2 The custodial staff consists of correctional officers only—not correctional administrators, treatment or educational staff, or other staff members.

3 The types of power available to correctional officers are legitimate power, coercive power, reward power, expert power, and referent power.

4 In correctional institutions, *structured conflict* refers to the tensions between prison staff members and inmates that arise out of institutional arrangements.

5 A *subculture* is a particular group of people within a larger society who share beliefs, values, behavior, and material objects. The subculture of correctional officers reinforces group solidarity and cohesion among correctional personnel.

6 Common correctional officer personality types include (1) the dictator, (2) the friend, (3) the merchant, (4) the turnkey, (5) the climber, (6) the reformer, and (7) the do-gooder.

7 The seven correctional officer assignments are (1) block officers, (2) work detail supervisors, (3) industrial shop and school officers, (4) yard officers, (5) administrative officers, (6) perimeter security officers (also called *wall post officers*), and (7) relief officers.

8 Female correctional officers tend to be less aggressive in their approach to workplace problem solving than are male officers. They are more likely to resolve disputes through nonconfrontational means and tend to rely more heavily on verbal skills and interpersonal communication. Studies have also found that female correctional officers depend more on established disciplinary rules when problems arise.

9 Feelings of powerlessness, meaninglessness, social isolation, self-estrangement, and alienation are all sources of correctional officer stress. Techniques for reducing stress include open communication, self-confidence building, a support system, conscientious work performance, effective time management, adequate sleep, exercise, a wholesome diet, relaxation techniques, laughter, self-understanding, setting of realistic goals and plans, and avoidance of resentment.

10 Staff safety planners must consider the physical plant, behavior management processes, staff/inmate relationships, policies and procedures, age and experience in shift scheduling, supervision, staff training, and development of a sound action plan.

11 Today's prison administrators and corrections personnel must be vigilant against the threat of terrorism, and must guard against terrorist activities from within the institution and from outside.

KEY TERMS

roles, *p. 358*
staff roles, *p. 358*
custodial staff, *p. 359*
program staff, *p. 359*
gain time, *p. 361*
structured conflict, *p. 362*
subculture, *p. 362*

staff subculture, *p. 362*
correctional officer personalities,
  p. 366
block officers, *p. 368*
work detail supervisors, *p. 368*
industrial shop and school officers,
  p. 369

yard officers, *p. 369*
administrative officers, *p. 369*
perimeter security officers, *p. 369*
relief officers, *p. 370*
stress, *p. 372*

QUESTIONS FOR REVIEW

1 What staff roles does the hierarchy of a typical correctional institution include?

2 What is the role of a prison's custodial staff?

3 According to John Hepburn, what are five bases of the power that correctional officers use to gain inmate compliance?

4 What is meant by *structured conflict?* How does it apply to correctional institutions?

5 What is a subculture? What elements make up staff subculture in a correctional institution?

6 List and describe common personality types found among correctional officers.

7 What are the seven correctional officer job assignments?

8 List and explain some challenges facing women who work as correctional officers.

9 What are some sources of stress for correctional officers? How might such stress be addressed?

10 What factors should correctional administrators consider when planning for the safety of their staff members?

11 Briefly explain the impact that terrorism is having on prisons and prison administration.

THINKING CRITICALLY ABOUT CORRECTIONS

Prison Rape

James Gilligan, MD, contends that rape in prisons is "an intrinsic and universal part of the punishments that our government metes out to those whom it labels as 'criminal.'" [69] In essence, Gilligan suggests, prison administrators passively employ inmate-on-inmate rape as a management tool to control the prisoner population.

Dr. Gilligan bases his charge on three contentions:

First, the relevant legal authorities, from judges to prosecutors who send people to prison, to the prison officials who administer them, are all aware of the existence, the reality, and the near-universality of rape in the prisons. Indeed, this is one reason why many conscientious judges are extremely reluctant to send anyone to prison except when they feel compelled to, either by the violence of the crime or, as is increasingly true, by laws mandating prison sentences even for nonviolent crimes, such as drug offenses.

Second, the conditions that stimulate such rapes (the enforced deprivation of other sources of self-esteem, respect, power, and sexual gratification) are consciously and deliberately imposed upon the prison population by the legal authorities.

Third, all these authorities tacitly and knowingly tolerate this form of sexual violence, passively delegating to the dominant and most violent inmates the power and authority to deliver this form of punishment to the more submissive and nonviolent ones, so that the rapists in this situation are acting as the vicarious enforcers of a form of punishment that the legal system does not itself enforce formally or directly.

Given that rape is universally acknowledged as a crime, Dr. Gilligan's charge is tantamount to an accusation of criminal conspiracy of monumental proportions.

1. Do you believe there is merit to Gilligan's claims?

2. If so, how would you propose addressing this issue?

The Staff Subculture

The staff culture is generally instilled in correctional officer trainees by more experienced officers and by work experiences. Socialization into the staff subculture begins on the first day of academy training or the first day of work (whichever comes first). One of the most important beliefs of the staff subculture is that officers should support one another.

Some people argue that the staff subculture is dangerous because it can sustain improper and even illegal behavior, while forcing correctional officers to keep to themselves what they know about such behavior. Others, however, suggest that the staff subculture is a positive element in the correctional world. It is important to correctional officer morale, they claim. They also suggest that it "fills the gaps" in formal training by establishing informal rules to guide staff behavior and decision making in difficult situations. The staff subculture can provide informal "workarounds" when the formal requirements of a correctional officer's position seem unrealistic.

1. Do you think the staff subculture contributes to or detracts from meeting the goals of institutional corrections? Why?

2. Do you think the staff subculture benefits or harms the lives and working environment of correctional officers? Explain.

3. What functions of the staff subculture can you identify? Rate each of those functions as positive or negative for its role in meeting the goals of institutional corrections.

ON-THE-JOB DECISION MAKING

Use of Force

You are an experienced correctional officer, assigned to yard duty. As you patrol the prison yard, watching inmates milling around and talking, a fellow officer named Renée approaches you. Renée was hired only a week ago, and she has gained a reputation for being inquisitive—asking experienced correctional officers about prison work. Renée walks up and says, "You know, I'm wondering what I should do. Yesterday I saw an officer push an inmate around because the guy didn't do what he asked. I don't know if the inmate didn't hear what was being said, or if he was just ignoring the officer. Renée looks at the ground. "What am I supposed to do in a situation like that? Should I have said something right then? Should I talk to the officer privately? Should I

suggest to the officer that maybe the inmate didn't hear him? He knows we aren't supposed to use force on inmates unless it's really necessary. If I see him do this kind of thing again, should I report him?" Looking up, Renée says, "I know we're supposed to support each other in here. But what would you do?" How would you respond to Renée's questions?

Former CO Inmate

For about four years, Alex Kaminsky was one of your fellow correctional officers at the McClellan Correctional Facility. During your service together, you developed a friendship close enough to include social occasions outside the job, and your wives became good friends.

Two years ago, Kaminsky was convicted of dealing controlled substances to inmates and received a 12- to 20-year sentence. Upon your recent transfer to the Brownley Correctional Facility, you discover that Kaminsky is one of the inmates incarcerated there. He resides in one of the cell blocks that falls in your area of responsibility and works on the maintenance crew that you supervise.

1. Should you seek assignment to another area of the prison or seek to have Kaminsky transferred out, to prevent the necessity of having contact with him? Explain.

2. If Kaminsky approaches you, should you permit the reestablishment of a relationship that might (or might not) prove beneficial to his rehabilitation?

LIVE LINKS

at www.justicestudies.com/livelinks04

9–1   Census of State and Federal Correctional Facilities

This link provides information on facilities, inmates, programs, and the staff of state, federal, and private correctional facilities throughout the nation that house state or federal inmates.

9–2   A 21st-Century Workforce for America's Correctional Profession

This document summarizes the discovery phase of an extensive project titled "Building a Strategic Workforce Plan for the Corrections Profession." Five sections follow an executive summary: (1) growth of the corrections system; (2) the demographics of the correctional workforce in the United States; (3) looking ahead at the demand side; (4) looking ahead at the supply side; and (5) promising human resource practices.

9–3   Correctional Officer Recruits and the Prison Environment

This report examines the adaptation of newly hired corrections officers to the prison environment. The report focuses on the following aspects of the job: attitudes toward the correctional work, attitude toward inmates, support for rehabilitation, deterrence, and the significance of a human services orientation.

9–4   Duress Systems in Corrections Facilities

In order to respond effectively to assaults on personnel and other emergencies, corrections facilities must be able to pinpoint the location and nature of the problem within seconds of its occurrence. A duress system—typically composed of a closed network of portable and mounted transmitters and receivers linked by ultrasonic, infrared, or radio frequency waves to a command center alarm console—permits the rapid and coordinated response that can save lives and reduce institutional damage. This guide provides detailed information on nine commercially available systems, locator, and control subsystems; hardware and software used; and additional features of such alarms.

INM
WO
RL

THE INMATE WORLD

Living Behind Bars

CHAPTER OBJECTIVES

After completing this chapter you should be able to do the following:

1 Profile state inmate populations.

2 Explain what *inmate subculture* is.

3 Distinguish among *deprivation theory, importation theory,* and the *integration model* as they explain the development of inmate subculture.

4 Know what is meant by the *prison code,* and be able to list some elements of the prison code.

5 Explain what is meant by *prison argot.*

6 List some common roles that male inmates assume.

7 Describe some major differences between women's and men's prisons.

8 Compare some of the characteristics of female inmates with those of male inmates.

9 Explain how the social structure in women's prisons differs from that in men's prisons.

> " In prison, those things withheld from and denied to the prisoner become precisely what he wants most of all.
> —Eldridge Cleaver, African American author and activist
> "

In 2005, 33-year-old gang member and convicted burglar Adam Morales found himself back in a Texas prison serving 35 years for weapons offenses and escape.[1] Morales had left prison in 2002 after spending 10 years in administrative segregation—or what is popularly known as solitary confinement. Morales had been segregated from other inmates in an effort to protect him from rival gang members and to reduce threats to prison security. Unfortunately, his prison experience had not prepared him for success on the outside. "It was like being released to a dark room," Morales said, "knowing that there are steps in front of you and waiting to fall." While he was free, even trips to the Wal-Mart near his home seemed threatening. Customers noticed him walking with his back to the walls and avoiding them. "Being in isolation so long, it's hard to explain the feeling," Morales reported. "When people get close to you in prison, it's usually because they want to hurt you." A number of failed jobs and an argument with his father sent Morales on a drinking spree, and he ended up firing a handgun into the walls of his apartment. Following arrest, he tried to escape from the local jail, resulting in a heightened sentence.

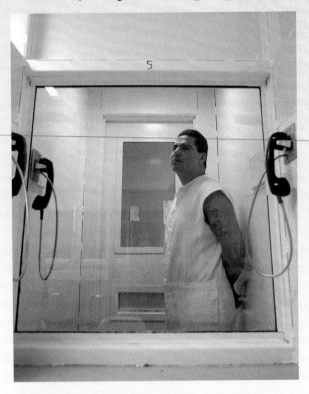

Adam Morales, 33, serving a new 35-year sentence at the Gatesville state prison in Texas.

Unlike Morales, the large majority of prison inmates do not spend long periods in segregation. Not only do most inmates routinely interact with one another, attend classes and religious services, participate in skills-training programs, and even work behind bars, but they also have relationships that extend beyond prison walls. This chapter will examine prison life, the inmate subculture, and the prison experience in general by looking first at men in prison and then at imprisoned women.

MEN IN PRISON

As we have already seen, most state inmates are male, belong to racial or ethnic minority groups, are relatively young, and have been incarcerated for a violent offense. A recent Bureau of Justice Statistics study examined social, economic, and other characteristics of state inmates nationwide.[2] Highlights of that study are shown in Exhibit 10–1.

Prisons and other total institutions are small, self-contained societies with their own social structures, norms, and rules. While not entirely isolated, prison inmates are physically, emotionally, and socially restricted from anything more than minor participation in the surrounding society. As a consequence, they develop their own distinctive lifestyles, roles, and behavioral norms.

EXHIBIT 10–1   National Profile of State Prison Inmates

57%
had a high school diploma or its equivalent

55%
had never married

43%
had lived with both parents most of the time while growing up

67%
were employed during the month before their arrest for their current crime

37%
had an immediate family member who had served time

38%
had not been incarcerated before

32%
committed their offense under the influence of alcohol

32%
committed their offense under the influence of drugs

96%
were U.S. citizens

Sources: Bureau of Justice Statistics, *Characteristics of State Prison Inmates*, retrieved February 27, 2007 from www.ojp.usdoj. gov/bjs/crimoff.htm#inmates; Allen Beck et al., *Survey of State Prison Inmates, 1991* (Washington, DC: U.S. Department of Justice, March 1993), and Christopher J. Mumola and Jennifer C. Karberg, "Drug Use and Dependence, State and Federal Prisoners, 2004" (Washington, DC: Bureau of Justice Statistics, 2006).

In his classic work *Asylums,* Erving Goffman used the phrase **total institution** to describe a place where the same people work, eat, sleep, and engage in recreation together day after day.[3] Life within total institutions is closely planned by those in control, and activities are strictly scheduled. Prisons, concentration camps, mental hospitals, and seminaries are all total institutions, said Goffman. They share many of the same characteristics—even though they exist for different purposes and house different kinds of populations. His words were echoed years later by Hans Toch, who noted that "prisons are 24-hour-a-day, year-in-and-year-out environments in which people are sequestered with little outside contact."[4]

total institution

A place where the same people work, play, eat, sleep, and recreate together on a continuous basis. The term was developed by the sociologist Erving Goffman to describe prisons and other similar facilities.

Goffman also identified a number of modes of adaptation to prison life whereby inmates attempt to adjust to the conditions around them. Some inmates, said Goffman, *convert* to life within institutions, taking on the staff's view of themselves and of institutional society. Others *withdraw*. Still others make attempts at *colonization*—meaning that they strike a balance between values and habits brought from home and those dictated by the social environment of the prison. Finally, some inmates *rebel*, rejecting the demands of their surroundings and often ending up in trouble with authorities. As Victoria R. Derosia, of Castleton State College, points out in her book *Living Inside Prison Walls*, some people "will make it through incarceration relatively unscathed and move on to a better life as a rehabilitated (or habilitated) citizen, while others will repeatedly fail at life outside prison. Offenders will successfully or poorly adjust to prison because of, or in spite of, who they were before incarceration, who they were while in prison, what they chose to do or not to do in prison, and who they want to become once released."[5]

What Is the Inmate Subculture?

Although any prison has its own unique way of life or culture, it is possible to describe a general inmate subculture that characterizes the lives of inmates in correctional institutions nationwide. The **inmate subculture** (also called the *prisoner subculture*) can be defined as "the habits, customs, mores, values, beliefs, or superstitions of the body of inmates incarcerated in correctional institutions."[6]

Prisoners are socialized into the inmate subculture through a process known as *prisonization*. The concept of **prisonization** was identified by Donald Clemmer in his book *The Prison Community*.[7] Clemmer defined *prisonization* as the process by which inmates adapt to prison society, and he described it as "the taking on of the ways, mores, customs, and general culture of the penitentiary." When the process of prisonization is complete, Clemmer noted, prisoners have become "cons."

In a further study of prisonization, Stanton Wheeler examined how prisoners adapted to life at the Washington State Reformatory.[8] Wheeler found that prisonization has greater impact with the passage of time. The prisonization of inmates, said Wheeler, can be described by a *U*-shaped curve. When an inmate first enters prison, the conventional values of the outside society still hold sway in his life. As time passes, however, he increasingly adopts the prison lifestyle. Wheeler also found that within the half-year before release, most inmates begin to demonstrate a renewed appreciation for conventional values.

In *The Society of Captives*,[9] Gresham Sykes described what he called the **pains of imprisonment**. According to Sykes, new inmates face major problems, including the loss of liberty, a lack of material possessions, deprivation of goods and services, the loss of heterosexual relationships, the loss of personal autonomy, and a reduction in personal security. These deficits, Sykes noted, lead to self-doubts and reduced self-esteem. Prison society compensates for such feelings and reduces the pains of imprisonment for the prison population as a whole. It also meets the personal and social needs induced in inmates by the pains of imprisonment. In short, said Sykes, inmate society compensates for the losses caused by imprisonment, and it offers varying degrees of comfort to those who successfully adjust to it.

The inmate subculture can vary from one institution to another. Variations are due to differences in the organizational structure of prisons.

---

inmate subculture

(also *prisoner subculture*) The habits, customs, mores, values, beliefs, or superstitions of the body of inmates incarcerated in correctional institutions; also, the inmate social world.

prisonization

The process by which inmates adapt to prison society; the taking on of the ways, mores, customs, and general culture of the penitentiary.

pains of imprisonment

Major problems that inmates face, such as loss of liberty and personal autonomy, lack of material possessions, loss of heterosexual relationships, and reduced personal security.

Maximum-security institutions, for example, are decidedly more painful for inmates because security considerations require greater restriction of inmate freedoms and access to material items. As a result, the subcultures in maximum-security institutions may be much more rigid in their demands on prisoners than those in less secure institutions.

How Does an Inmate Subculture Form?

Early students of inmate subcultures, particularly Clemmer and Sykes, believed that such subcultures developed in response to the deprivations in prison life. This perspective is called **deprivation theory.** Shared deprivation gives inmates a basis for solidarity.[10]

A more recent perspective is that an inmate subculture does not develop in prison, but is brought into prison from the outside world. Known as **importation theory,** this point of view was popularized by John Irwin and Donald R. Cressey.[11] It was further supported by the work of James Jacobs.[12] Importation theory holds that inmate society is shaped by factors outside prison—specifically, preprison life experiences and socialization patterns. Inmates who lived violent lives outside tend to associate with other violent inmates and often engage in similar behavior in prison.[13]

More realistic is the **integration model,** which acknowledges that both theories have some validity. According to the integration model, people undergo early socialization experiences. In childhood, some people develop leanings toward delinquent and criminal activity, acquiring—from peer groups, parents and other significant adults, television, movies, other mass media, and even computer and video games—values that support law-violating behavior. Those who become inmates are also likely to have experienced juvenile court proceedings and may have been institutionalized as juveniles. As a consequence, such people are likely to have acquired many of the values, much of the language, and the general behavioral patterns of deviant or criminal subcultures before entering adult prison.

The integration model also recognizes, however, the effects that the norms and behavioral standards of inmates in a particular prison have

deprivation theory
The belief that inmate subcultures develop in response to the deprivations in prison life.

importation theory
The belief that inmate subcultures are brought into prisons from the outside world.

integration model
A combination of importation theory and deprivation theory. The belief that, in childhood, some inmates acquired, usually from peers, values that support law-violating behavior but that the norms and standards in prison also affect inmates.

In some prisons, inmate subculture is fragmented as inmates form competing gangs and other groups along ethnic, racial, and geographic lines. How could the differences among such groups affect the order and stability of a prison?

on those who are imprisoned. If a new inmate has already been socialized into a criminal lifestyle, the transition into the inmate subculture is likely to be easy. For some people, however—especially white-collar offenders with little previous exposure to criminal subcultures—the transition can be very difficult. The language, social expectations, and norms of prison society are likely to be foreign to them.

Norms and Values of Prison Society

prison code

A set of norms and values among prison inmates. It is generally antagonistic to the official administration and rehabilitation programs of the prison.

Central to prison society is a code of behavior for all inmates. The **prison code** is a set of inmate rules antagonistic to the official administration and rehabilitation programs.[14] Violations of the code result in inmate-imposed sanctions, ranging from ostracism to homicide. Sykes and Messinger have identified five main elements of the prison code:[15]

1. Don't interfere with the interests of other inmates. Never rat on a con. Don't have loose lips.
2. Don't lose your head. Don't quarrel with other inmates. Play it cool. Do your own time.
3. Don't exploit other inmates. Don't steal. Don't break your word. Pay your debts.
4. Don't whine. Be tough. Be a man.
5. Don't be a sucker. Don't trust the guards or staff. Remember that prison officials are wrong and inmates are right.

Prison Argot—The Language of Confinement

prison argot

The special language of the inmate subculture.

Prison argot is the special language of the inmate subculture. *Argot* is a French word meaning "slang." Prison society has always had its own unique language, illustrated by the following argot-laden paragraph:

> The new con, considered fresh meat by the screws and other prisoners, was sent to the cross-bar hotel to do his bit. He soon picked up the reputation through the yard grapevine as a canary-bird. While he was at the big house, the goon squad put him in the freezer for his protection. Eventually, he was released from the ice-box and ordered to make little ones out of big ones until he was released to the free world. Upon release he received $100 in gate money, vowing never to be thrown in the hole or be thought of as a stool-pigeon again.[16]

Prison argot originated partly as a form of secret communication. Gresham Sykes, however, believed that it serves primarily as "an illustrative symbol of the prison community"—or as a way for inmates to mark themselves as outlaws and social outcasts.[17] Sykes's work brought prison argot to the attention of sociologists and criminologists. Since Sykes's time other authors have identified a number of words, terms, and acronyms in prison argot. Some of these terms are presented in Exhibit 10–2. Interestingly, rap musicians, many of whom have spent time in prison or deal with prison-related themes, have brought prison argot to a wider audience.

Social Structure in Men's Prisons

Inmate societies, like other societies, have a hierarchy of positions. Inmates assume or are forced into specific social roles, and some inmates—by virtue of the roles they assume—have more status and power than others.

Early writers often classified prisoners by the crimes they had committed or their criminal histories. Irwin, for example, divided prisoners into

EXHIBIT 10-2	Prison Argot: The Language of Confinement

ARGOT IN MEN'S PRISONS

ace duce: best friend

badge (or bull, hack, "the man," or screw): a correctional officer

ball busters: violent inmates

banger (or burner, shank, sticker): a knife

billys: white men

boneyard: conjugal visiting area

cat-J (or J-cat): a prisoner in need of psychological or psychiatric therapy or medication

cellie: cell mate

center men: inmates who are close to the staff

chester: child molester

dog: homeboy or friend

fag: a male inmate believed to be a natural (preprison) homosexual

featherwood: a peckerwood's "woman"

fish: a newly arrived inmate

gorilla: an inmate who uses force to take what he wants from others

hipsters: young, drug-involved inmates

homeboy: a prisoner from one's hometown or neighborhood

ink: tattoos

lemon squeezer: an inmate who has an unattractive "girlfriend"

man walking: phrase used to signal that a guard is coming

merchant (or peddler): one who sells when he should give; or one who sells goods and services to other inmates illegally

nimby: not in my back yard

peckerwood (or wood): a white prisoner

punk: a male inmate who is forced into a submissive role during homosexual relations

rat (or snitch): an inmate who squeals (provides information about other inmates to the prison administration)

real men: inmates respected by other inmates

schooled: knowledgeable in the ways of prison life

shakedown: search of a cell or a work area

shu (pronounced *shoe*): special housing unit

toughs: those with a preprison history of violent crimes

tree jumper: rapist

turn out: to rape or make into a punk

wolf: a male inmate who assumes an aggressive role during homosexual relations

ARGOT IN WOMEN'S PRISONS

cherry (or cherrie): an inmate not yet introduced to lesbian activities

fay broad: a white inmate

femme (or mommy): an inmate who plays a female role during a lesbian relationship

safe: the vagina, especially when used for hiding contraband

stud broad (or daddy): an inmate who assumes a male role in a lesbian relationship

Sources: Gresham Sykes, *The Society of Captives* (Princeton, NJ: Princeton University Press, 1958); Rose Giallombardo, *Society of Women: A Study of Women's Prison* (New York: John Wiley, 1966); Richard A. Cloward et al., *Theoretical Studies in Social Organization of the Prison* (New York: Social Science Research Council, 1960). For a more contemporary listing of prison slang terms, see Reinhold Aman, *Hillary Clinton's Pen Pal: A Guide to Life and Lingo in Federal Prison* (Santa Rosa, CA: Maledicta Press, 1996); Jerome Washington, *Iron House: Stories from the Yard* (Ann Arbor, MI: QED Press, 1994); Morrie Camhi, *The Prison Experience* (Boston: Charles Tuttle, 1989); Harold Long, *Survival in Prison* (Port Townsend, WA: Loompanics Unlimited, 1990).

such categories as thieves (those with a culture of criminal values), convicts (time doers), square johns (inmates unfamiliar with criminal subcultures), and dope fiends (drug-involved inmates).[18]

Other writers have identified **inmate roles,** defining them as prison lifestyles or as forms of ongoing social accommodation to prison life. Each role has a position in the pecking order, indicating its status in the prison society.

About a decade ago, Frank Schmalleger developed a typology of male inmate roles.[19] It is based on actual social roles found among inmates in prison, and it uses the prison argot in existence when it was created to name or describe each type. Each type can be viewed as a prison lifestyle either chosen by inmates or forced on them. Some of the types were previously identified by other writers. Although the terminology used in the typology sounds dated, the types of inmates it identifies are still characteristic of prison populations today. The thirteen inmate types are discussed in the following paragraphs.

inmate roles

Prison lifestyles; also, forms of ongoing social accommodation to prison life.

THE OFFENDER SPEAKS

Prison life is living in an insane world with insane rules. There's strength in numbers, and even the weak seem to "click up" in here. Everyone knows their own kind, it seems. Predators know one another immediately, as well as the bull queers, fags, and dudes just walking it down, keeping their nose clean. . . .

Here, these groups can set themselves apart quickly. Staff keeps track of high-profile inmates, and makes sure not to give them too much rope.

You definitely are classified by those you hang around with—labels are hard to shake in this environment. And the most important thing I've learned here is, there's plenty of dudes here who just love to hate on you and keep you here doing their digits with them. Misery loves company.

It's best to hook up with those that have the same objectives out of doing time as yourself. For me it's simply walking this time down to go home, and that's the type of dude I choose to hang with. Granted, he has to be solid, but first and foremost he has to be smart enough to choose which battles are worth dying over.

At any given time one group can have drama with another or trouble within its own ranks. So be sure that what you are willing to knuckle up over is well worth the repercussions, because you can be absolutely positive that staff will know what's happening almost as it's happening. This is a very small community—there are no secrets! Not even for staff.

You will hook up with dudes in here, and you feel some sort of bond grow between you and your bros. So you are there for them when they need you, and you can expect the same from them. Because even though this is prison, it's also where you live, and where they live.

Anonymous

The Real Man Real men do their own time, do not complain, and do not cause problems for other inmates. They see confinement as a natural consequence of criminal activity and view time spent in prison as an unfortunate cost of doing business. Real men know the inmate code and abide by it. They are well regarded within the institution and rarely run into problems with other inmates. If they do, they solve their problems on their own. They never seek the help of correctional officers or the prison administration. Although they generally avoid trouble within the institution, they usually continue a life of crime once released.

The Mean Dude Some inmates are notorious for resorting quickly to physical power. They are quick to fight and, when fighting, give no quarter. They are callous, cold, and uncaring. Mean dudes control those around them through force or the threat of force. The fear they inspire usually gives them a great deal of power in inmate society. At the very least, other inmates are likely to leave the mean dude alone.

The Bully A variation of the mean dude is the bully. Bullies use intimidation to get what they want. Unlike mean dudes, they are far more likely to use threats than to use actual physical force. A bully may make his threats in public so that others see the victim's compliance.

The Agitator The agitator, sometimes called a "wise guy," is constantly trying to stir things up. He responds to the boredom of prison life by causing problems for others. An agitator may point out, for example, how a powerful inmate has been wronged by another inmate or that an inmate seen talking to a "rat" must be a snitch himself.

The Hedonist The hedonist adapts to prison by exploiting the minimal pleasures it offers. Hedonists always seek the easy path, and they plot to win the "cushiest" jobs. They may also stockpile goods to barter for services of various kinds. Hedonists live only in the now, with little concern for the future. Their lives revolve around such activities as gambling, drug running, smuggling contraband, and exploiting homosexual opportunities.

The Opportunist The opportunist sees prison as an opportunity for personal advancement. He takes advantage of the formal self-improvement opportunities of the prison, such as schooling, trade training, and counseling. Other inmates generally dislike opportunists, seeing them as selfish "do-gooders." Staff members, however, often see opportunists as model prisoners.

The Retreatist Some inmates, unable to cope with the realities of prison life, withdraw psychologically from the world around them. Depression, neurosis, and even psychosis may result. Some retreatists attempt to lose themselves in drugs or alcohol. Others attempt suicide. Isolation from the general prison population, combined with counseling or psychiatric treatment, may offer the best hope for retreatists to survive the prison experience.

The Legalist Legalists are known as "jailhouse lawyers," or simply "lawyers," in prison argot. They are usually among the better-educated prisoners, although some legalists have little formal education. Legalists fight confinement through the system of laws, rules, and court precedent. Legalists file writs with the courts, seeking hearings on a wide variety of issues. Although many legalists work to better the conditions of their own confinement or to achieve early release, most also file pleas on behalf of other prisoners.

The Radical Radicals see themselves as political prisoners of an unfair society. They believe that a discriminatory world has denied them the education and skills needed to succeed in a socially acceptable way. Most of the beliefs held by radical inmates are rationalizations that shift the blame for personal failure onto society. The radical inmate is likely to be familiar with contemporary countercultural figures.

The Colonist Colonists, also referred to as "convicts," turn prison into home. Colonists know the ropes of prison, have many "friends" on the inside, and often feel more comfortable in prison than outside it. They may not look forward to leaving prison. Some may even commit additional offenses to extend their stay. Colonists are generally well regarded by other prisoners. Many are old-timers. Colonists have learned to take advantage of the informal opportunity structure in prisons, and they are well versed in the inmate code.

The Religious Inmate Religious inmates profess a strong religious faith and may attempt to convert both inmates and staff. Religious inmates frequently form prayer groups, request special meeting facilities and special diets, and may ask for frequent visits from religious leaders. Religious inmates are often under a great deal of suspicion from inmates and staff, who tend to think they are faking religious commitment to gain special treatment. Those judged sincere in their faith may win early release, removal from death row, or any number of other special considerations.

The Punk The punk is a young inmate, often small, who has been forced into a sexual relationship with an aggressive, well-respected prisoner. Punks are generally "turned out" through homosexual rape. A punk

Former Florida prison inmate Joe Murphy, who served time for murder, leads a prayer at the Okaloosa Correctional Institution in Crestview, Florida. What different kinds of inmates does this chapter identify?

usually finds a protector among the more powerful inmates. Punks keep their protectors happy by providing them with sexual services.

The Gang-Banger   Gang-bangers, or those affiliated with prison gangs, know that there is power in numbers. They depend upon the gang for defense and protection as well as for the procurement of desired goods and services. Gang-bangers are known by their tattoos and hand signs, which indicate gang affiliation and can be read by anyone familiar with prison society. Prison gangs, which are discussed in more detail in Chapter 13, often have links outside prison—leading to continued involvement in crime by those directing them from inside prison, and to the creation of channels for the importation into correctional facilities of banned items.

Sexuality in Men's Prisons

Violence and victimization occur in men's prisons, and a good deal of prison violence has sexual overtones. The top of the sexual hierarchy in male prisons is occupied by inmates engaged in situational homosexuality who are called, quite simply, "Men." *Men* are heterosexual inmates who feel compelled to engage in homosexual behavior by the conditions of confinement.[20] Men with the power to own and control their own "punk" rise to the top of the inmate sexual hierarchy.

Punks are "owned" by powerful inmates, who provide them protection from sexual violence and from other inmates. Many punks are forced to fill the traditional role of a wife and can often be found doing their Man's laundry, ironing, and making up the Man's bed. Although punks are usually seen as totally powerless and dependent upon their Man, punks can influence their "owners" in various ways. As one inmate observer[21] describes it, "There are punk wiles just as there are feminine wiles. A contented punk is much more desirable than a sullen and reluctant one, so there is a definite incentive for the Men to back off from a confrontation with their punks on an issue which they don't consider essential, though no Man will tolerate a rebellious punk." He adds, "A Man has a social obligation to share his wealth with his punk, much as a rich man on the outside is expected to keep his wife in furs and take her out to eat. As one Man put it: 'You punks have got it made; you don't have to fight, and you get all the dope and commissary from the men with the most money.'"[22]

The most powerful Men in prison society, cell block leaders, gang leaders, and so on, will "own" the most desirable punks. Punks, however, can be sold or given away. Once a person has become a punk, he can never again become a Man—at least not while still in prison. Not all punks, however, are outcasts. Punks belonging to Men who have high social status within the institution are treated with deference by other inmates. One rule of inmate society demands that a Man share what he has with his punk. Hence, Men will generally bestow what comforts they have accumulated in prison with their punks.

It is not uncommon for affectionate relationships to develop between Men and their punks. Some couples even "marry" in imitation ceremonies—many of which are followed by "parties" and attended by inmate "guests." As one writer explains it, "Imprisoned long enough, men can transfer any emotion they feel for women to their punks."[23]

One person who has contributed significantly to the study of sexual violence in men's prisons is Daniel Lockwood.[24] Using interviews and background data from prison files, Lockwood identified and studied 107 "targets" of aggressive sexual threats and 45 inmate "aggressors" in New York state male prisons. He also conducted a general survey that revealed that 28 percent of all male prisoners had been targets of sexual aggressors in prison at least once. Lockwood found that only one of the inmates he interviewed had actually been raped—an indication that the incidence of prison rape is quite low relative to other types of harm that may accompany sexual incidents, such as physical abuse, verbal abuse, threatening gestures, and threatening propositions.

Targets, when compared with nontargets, were found to be physically slight, young, white, nonviolent offenders from nonurban areas. They generally had a higher rate of psychological disturbance than other inmates and were more apt to attempt suicide while in prison. Exhibit 10–3 shows a note found by a new inmate in his cell at a New York state prison unit. The new inmate was young and not prison-wise. After discovering the note, the inmate asked to be moved to the prison's isolation area. His request was granted.[25]

The typical incident of sexual aggression, Lockwood found, is carried out by a group. About half the incidents Lockwood identified included physical violence, and another third involved threats. The incidents studied showed patterns of escalation from verbal abuse to physical violence.

Lockwood also found that prison rapes generally occur when gangs of aggressors circumvent security arrangements to physically control their victims. Fear, anxiety, suicidal thoughts, social disruption, and attitude changes develop in many victims of homosexual rape.

In 2003, in an effort to learn more about prison rape, Congress mandated the collection of prison rape statistics under the Prison Rape Elimination Act (PREA).[26] The PREA, which also established the federal Prison

Texas prison inmate Roderick Johnson, who claims that he was raped hundreds of times after his return to prison on charges of bouncing a $300 check while on parole for breaking and entering. In 2004, a federal lawsuit filed by Johnson, 33, an admitted homosexual, was allowed to go to trial. It names the head of the Texas Department of Criminal Justice, along with more than a dozen other officials at the James V. Allred Unit in Iowa Park, claiming that they failed to protect him from violent sexual attacks. What will the 2003 Prison Rape Elimination Act do for inmates like Johnson? Use the Internet to learn what happened to the civil suit filed on Johnson's behalf.

EXHIBIT 10–3   Inmate Note

> Yo S
> Check this out if you don't give me a peace
> of your ass I am going to take you off the
> count and that is my word.
> I be down a very long time So I need it Very
> Bad I will give you 5 Pack's of Smokes if
> you do it OK That is my word So if you
> Want to live you Better do it and get it over
> with there are Three of us who need it.
> OK. . .

Rape Commission, calls for an evaluation of issues related to prison rape as well as for the development of national standards to help prevent prison rape. In 2004, the Bureau of Justice Statistics (BJS) announced plans to implement a massive data-gathering project under the PREA focused on adult and juvenile correctional facilities. The PREA requires BJS to collect data in federal and state prisons, county and city jails, and juvenile institutions, while the U.S. Census Bureau will store the data as they are collected. Many researchers felt that pre-PREA information on prison rapes was less than reliable because it was based largely on self-reports that surveyed only small populations. Consequently, the PREA, which will ask offenders about numerous categories of sexual assault, including abusive sexual contacts, attempted nonconsensual sex acts, and completed nonconsensual sex acts, has been heralded as a way to gather accurate data on the prison rape phenomenon. The survey will also attempt to identify instances of staff-on-inmate sexual misconduct by gender. Many believe that the PREA will encourage a culture change in corrections and have likened the attention now being paid to sexual violence in prison as similar to that given to use of force in the 1980s.[27] Results from the first-ever administrative survey of sexual violence reported by correctional authorities were published by BJS in 2005 and covered 1,404 prisons and 400 jails.[28] The survey revealed an estimated 8,210 allegations of sexual violence in 2004. Of these, 2,100 incidents were substantiated by investigations. Forty-two percent of allegations involved staff sexual misconduct while 37 percent involved inmate-on-inmate nonconsensual sexual acts. Sexual harassment by staff accounted for 11 percent of the allegations, and another 10 percent was categorized as abusive sexual contact by staff. Statistically, there were 3.15 reported allegations of sexual violence per 1,000 inmates nationwide in 2004.

Official reports are unlikely to reflect the true incident of sexual violence, however. As BJS notes, "due to fear of reprisal from perpetrators, a code of silence among inmates, personal embarrassment, and lack of trust in staff, victims are often reluctant to report incidents to correctional authorities."[29] To circumvent such issues, and to gather more reliable informtion, BJS is planning a system of self-reports, to be implemented about the time this book goes to press. Data will be collected from incarcerated individuals, as well as those recently released. Completed data will likely be used to assess existing policies and practices and to modify them as appropriate.

WOMEN IN PRISON

In America today, there are far fewer women's prisons than men's prisons, and men in prison outnumber women in prison 12 to 1.[30] As noted in Chapter 7, however, the number of women in prison is increasing much faster than that of men, and women represent the fastest-growing population in correctional facilities today.

A state usually has one women's prison, housing a few hundred women. The size of a women's prison generally depends on the population of the state. Some small states house women prisoners in special areas of what are otherwise institutions for men.

Women's prisons are generally quite different from men's. Here's how one writer describes them:

> Often, there are no gun towers, no armed guards, and no stone walls or fences strung on top with concertina wire. Neatly pruned hedges, well-kept flower gardens, attractive brick buildings, and wide paved walkways greet the visitor's eye at women's prisons in many states. Often these institutions are located in rural, pastoral settings that may suggest tranquility and well-being to the casual observer.[31]

Such rural settings, however, make it hard for female inmates to maintain contact with their families, who may live far from the correctional facility.

Many prisons for women are built on a cottage plan. Cottages dot the grounds of such institutions, often arranged in pods. A group of six or so cottages constitutes a pod. Each cottage is much like a traditional house, with individual bedrooms; a day room with a television, chairs, couches, and tables; and small personal or shared bathrooms.

Security in women's prisons is generally more relaxed than in men's, and female inmates may have more freedom within the institution than their male counterparts. Practically speaking, women—even those in prison—are seen as less dangerous than men and less prone to violence or escape.

Treatment, education, recreation, and other programs in women's prisons have often been criticized as inferior to those in men's prisons. Recent research has uncovered continuing disparities in many areas.[32] For example, men's institutions often have a much wider range of vocational and educational training programs and services and larger and better-equipped law libraries. Similarly, exercise facilities—including weight rooms, jogging areas, and basketball courts—are often better equipped and larger in men's institutions today than in women's.

Prison administrators have often found it impractical to develop and fund programs at the same level in women's and men's prisons, because of differences in interest, participation, and space and the fact that relatively low numbers of women prisoners don't allow for the same econo-

Although there are far fewer women in prison than men, the number of women behind bars is growing steadily. What might account for the rising number of imprisoned women?

Jack Osborn
Custody Utility Officer
Jefferson City Correctional Center
Jefferson City, MO

Jack Osborn is a custody utility officer at the Jefferson City Correctional Center in Missouri. As a utility officer, he may be assigned to any area or department that needs an additional staff member. Before becoming a correctional officer, Osborn was a deputy sheriff for 10 years. He has completed two years of community college coursework.

Osborn advises knowing the inmates and being able to interpret behavioral changes. "Know what silence means. Communicate—listen," he says. "Learn who runs drugs and gambling, who the punks are. That's where your trouble will come from." Osborn believes that if you follow this advice and know the mechanics of the job, you should have a great career in corrections.

What makes a good custody officer? Being firm, fair, and consistent—clear, concise actions with the inmates and the other prison staff. Being honest goes far. If you don't know the answer, say so. If you say you will find out, do it. Learn to say no, too. You can change it to a yes easier than changing a yes to a no.

---

mies of scale found in men's institutions. Nonetheless, it is important to strive for parity of opportunity as an ideal. The American Correctional Association, for example, through its Guidelines for Women's Prison Construction and Programming,[33] insists that the same level of services and opportunities be available in women's prisons as in men's prisons in the same jurisdiction.

In some instances, women may be placed in an institution housing inmates with a range of security levels. Consequently, women who are low security risks may have less personal freedom than their male counterparts. Women may also not have the opportunity to transfer to a less secure institution as their risk level drops.

Overcrowding, violence, and poor conditions are not unknown in prisons for women. By 2002 the Julia Tutwiler Prison for Women in Wetumpka, Alabama, for example, was home to more than 1,000 women. Built in 1942 with a capacity of only 364 inmates, it became the focus of a federal lawsuit brought by inmates to address extreme crowding.[34]

Due largely to overcrowded conditions, the facility did not have the ability to separate dangerous prisoners from one another; nor did it have the resources to safely care for and separately house prisoners with mental illness and those with serious diseases. Meaningful programs for inmates were practically nonexistent, and most of the female prisoners spent endless idle hours in terribly hot dormitories crammed full of beds, sleeping pallets, and bunks.

The severe beating of a correctional officer in July 2002 brought problems with understaffing and crowded dorms into the spotlight. At the time there were, on average, only 12 officers at any given time responsible for supervising more than 1,000 prisoners—and at one point, there were as few as nine officers on duty. Ninety-one assaults were recorded within the institution in 2002, making Alabama's only women's prison the most violent institution in the state.

The prisoner-brought lawsuit asked for, among other things, a reduction in crowding and the hiring of more corrections officers. Finally, under pressure from a federal judge, the state reduced the population at Tutwiler, sending hundreds of women to prisons out of state through contracts for prison space. Today, a population of around 700 remains at Tutwiler, and many of the previously unsafe conditions have been eliminated.

Characteristics of Women Inmates

Many of our conceptions of female inmates derive more from myth than reality. Recent BJS surveys provide a more realistic picture of female inmates.[35] At the start of 2006, women comprised 7.0 percent of sentenced prisoners in the nation. Since 1995, the female prison population has grown 57 percent,[36] a significantly higher rate of growth than experienced in the male prison population, which saw a 33 percent increase during the same period. As of January 1, 2006, there were 107,518 women under the jurisdiction of state and federal prison authorities.[37]

Female prisoners largely resemble male prisoners in race, ethnic background, and age. However, they are substantially more likely to be serving time for a drug offense and less likely to have been sentenced for a violent crime. Women are also more likely than men to be serving time for larceny or fraud.

Female inmates have shorter criminal records than male inmates. They generally have shorter maximum sentences than men. Half of all women receive a maximum sentence of 60 months or less, while half of all men are sentenced to 120 months or less.

Significantly, more than 4 in 10 of the women prisoners responding to BJS surveys reported prior physical or sexual abuse. One of the major factors distinguishing male inmates from female inmates is that the women have experienced far more sexual and physical abuse than the men. Interviews with incarcerated women have found that 70 percent of them report the occurrence of sexual molestation or severe physical abuse in childhood at the hands of parents or adolescent caregivers.[38] Fifty-nine percent report some form of sexual abuse in childhood or adolescence, and 75 percent of those interviewed report having been severely abused by an intimate partner as adults.

A 2003 report by the National Institute of Corrections found that women enter correctional institutions through different "pathways" than men. According to the report, most women offenders are typically nonviolent and their crimes are less threatening to community safety than those committed by male offenders. "Women's most common pathways to crime," said the report, "result from abuse, poverty, and substance abuse"—all of which, according to the report, are interconnected.[39] Exhibit 10–4 is a comparison of selected characteristics of female and male state prisoners.

Offenses of Incarcerated Women

Drug offenses account for the incarceration of a large percentage of the women behind bars. Two-thirds of all women in federal prisons are serving time on drug charges.[40] Some sources estimate that drug crimes and other crimes indirectly related to drug activities together account for the

EXHIBIT 10–4	Characteristics of Women and Men in State Prisons

WOMEN IN PRISON

Criminal offense

35% are in prison for violent offenses

29% are in prison for drug offenses

30% are in prison for property offenses

5% are in prison for public-order offenses

1% other offenses

Criminal history

46% are nonviolent recidivists

28% have no previous sentence

26% are violent recidivists

Family characteristics

78% have children

42% lived with both parents most of time growing up

33% had a parent/guardian who abused alcohol or drugs

17% were married at the time they committed the offense for which they were incarcerated

45% have never married

47% have a family member who had been incarcerated

Drug and alcohol use

59% used drugs in the month before the current offense
36% were under the influence of drugs at the time of the offense

12% were under the influence of alcohol at the time of the offense

MEN IN PRISON

Criminal offense

53% are in prison for violent offenses

20% are in prison for property offenses

19% are in prison for drug offenses

7% are in prison for public–order offenses

1% other offenses

Criminal history

50% are violent recidivists

31% are nonviolent recidivists

19% have no previous sentence

Family characteristics

64% have children

43% lived with both parents most of time growing up

26% had a parent/guardian who abused alcohol or drugs

18% were married at the time they committed the offense for which they were incarcerated

56% have never married

37% have a family member who had been incarcerated

Drug and alcohol use

56% used drugs daily in the month before the current offense

31% were under the influence of drugs at the time of the offense

18% were under the influence of alcohol at the time of the offense

Sources: Paige M. Harrison and Allen J. Beck, *Prisoners in 2005* (Washington, DC: Bureau of Justice Statistics, U.S. Department of Justice, November 2006); Allen Beck et al., *Survey of State Prison Inmates, 1991* (Washington, DC: U.S. Department of Justice, March 1993); and Christopher J. Mumola and Jennifer C. Karberg, "Drug Use and Dependence, State and Federal Prisoners, 2004" (Washington, DC: Bureau of Justice Statistics, 2006).

imprisonment of around 95 percent of today's women inmates. In short, drug use and abuse, or crimes stimulated by the desire for drugs and drug money, are what send most women to prison. This has been true for at least a decade. According to an ACA report, the primary reasons incarcerated women most frequently give for their arrest are (1) trying to pay for drugs, (2) attempts to relieve economic pressures, and (3) poor judgment.[41]

According to the BJS, before arrest, women in prison use more drugs than men and use those drugs more frequently.[42] About 54 percent of imprisoned women have used drugs in the month before the offense for which they were arrested, compared with 50 percent of the men. Female inmates are also more likely than male inmates to have used drugs regularly (65 percent vs. 62 percent), to have used drugs daily in the month preceding their offense (41 percent vs. 36 percent), and to have been under the influence at the time of the offense (36 percent vs. 31 percent). Nearly one in four female inmates surveyed reported committing the offense to get money to buy drugs, compared with one in six males.

Female inmates who used drugs differed from those who did not in the types of crimes they committed. Regardless of the amount of drug use, users were less likely than nonusers to be serving a sentence for a violent offense.

Social Structure in Women's Prisons

As might be expected, the social structure and the subcultural norms and expectations in women's prisons are quite different from those in men's prisons. Unfortunately, however, relatively few studies of inmate life have been conducted in institutions for women.

One early study of women at the Federal Reformatory for Women in Alderson, West Virginia, was an effort to compare subcultural aspects of women's prisons with those of men's. Rose Giallombardo reached the conclusion that "many of the subcultural features of the institution are imported from the larger society."[43] Giallombardo believed that male and female inmate subcultures are actually quite similar, except that women's prisons develop "a substitute universe," a world "in which inmates may preserve an identity which is relevant to life outside the prison."

Giallombardo was unable to find in the women's prison some of the values inherent in a male inmate subculture, such as "Do your own time." The inmate subculture in a women's prison, she said, tends to encourage relationships rather than isolation. Hence, women are expected to share their problems with other inmates and to offer at least some support and encouragement to others. On the other hand, she observed, women prisoners tend to see each other as conniving, self-centered, and scheming. Hence, a basic tenet of the inmate subculture in a women's prison is "You can't trust other women." As Giallombardo put it, women prisoners tend to believe that "every woman is a sneaking, lying bitch."

Giallombardo concluded that the social structure of women's prisons and the social role assumed by each inmate are based on three elements:

1. the individual woman's level of personal dependence and her status needs (which are said to be based upon cultural expectations of the female role);
2. the individual's needs arising from incarceration, combined with the institution's inability to meet female inmates' emotional needs; and
3. needs related to the individual's personality.

A more recent study was of inmates in the District of Columbia Women's Reformatory at Occoquan, Virginia.[44] Esther Heffernan identified three roles that women commonly adopt when adjusting to prison. According to Heffernan, women's roles evolve partly from the characteristics the women bring with them to prison and depend partly on the ways the women choose to adapt to prison life. The roles she described are discussed in the following paragraphs.

The Cool Inmate Cool women usually have previous records, are in the know, are streetwise, and do not cause trouble for other inmates while in prison. Cool women are seen as professional or semiprofessional criminals who work to win the maximum number of prison amenities without endangering their parole or release dates.

The Square Inmate Square women are not familiar with criminal lifestyles and have few, if any, criminal experiences other than the one for which they were imprisoned. They tend to hold the values and roles of conventional society.

The Life Inmate   Life inmates are habitual or career offenders and are generally well socialized into lives of crime. They support inmate values and subculture. Life inmates typically have been in and out of prison from an early age and have developed criminal lifestyles dedicated to meeting their political, economic, familial, and social needs outside conventional society.

Recently, California State University (Fresno) criminologist Barbara Owens studied the culture of imprisoned women at Central California Women's Facility in Chowchilla, California, and found a "prison culture that is itself complex and diverse across numerous dimensions."[45] Owens identified a central component of that culture that she refers to as "the mix."

The mix, according to Owens, "is any behavior that can bring trouble and conflict with staff and other prisoners." It consists of fighting, doing drugs, prison-based lesbian activity ("homo-secting," in Owens's terms), and making trouble for the staff. It also involves continuing the kinds of behaviors that brought women to prison. Consequently, the mix is to be avoided by those who want to leave prison and not return. New women coming into the institution, Owens found, were advised to "stay out of the mix." The mix, says Owens, is also a state of mind, a way of thinking like a troublemaker.

One writer, summarizing the results of studies such as those discussed here, found that two primary features distinguish women's prisons from men's prisons:[46]

1. The social roles in women's prisons place greater emphasis on homosexual relations as a mode of adaptation to prison life.
2. The mode of adaptation a female inmate selects is best assessed by studying the inmate's preinstitutional experiences.

Pseudofamilies and Sexual Liaisons

pseudofamilies

Familylike structures, common in women's prisons, in which inmates assume roles similar to those of family members in free society.

A unique feature of women's prisons is pseudofamilies. **Pseudofamilies** are familylike structures, common in women's prisons, in which inmates assume roles similar to those of family members in free society. Pseudofamilies appear to provide emotional and social support for the women who belong to them. Courtship, marriage, and kinship ties formed with other women inmates provide a means of coping with the rigors of imprisonment. One inmate has explained pseudofamilies this way: "It just happens. Just like on the outside, you get close to certain people. It's the same in here—but we probably get even closer than a lot of families because of how lonely it is otherwise."[47]

Some authors suggest that pseudofamilies are to women's prisons what gangs are to men's.[48] Men establish social relationships largely through power, and gang structure effectively expresses such relationships. Women relate to one another more expressively and emotionally. Hence, family structures are one of the most effective reflections of women's relationships in prison, just as they are in the wider society. At least one study of prison coping behavior found that new female inmates, especially those most in need of support, advice, and assistance in adjusting to the conditions of incarceration, are the women most likely to become members of prison pseudofamilies.[49]

To a large extent, the social and behavioral patterns of family relationships in prison mirror their traditional counterparts in the community. Families in women's prisons come in all sizes and colors. They can be

The kinship of substitute families plays a major role in the lives of many female inmates, who take the relationships very seriously. How might these relationships supplant values such as "do your own time" commonly found in the subculture of men's prisons?

virtual melting pots of ethnicity and age. A member of a family may be young or old and may be black, white, or Hispanic. As in families in free society, there are roles for husbands and wives, sisters, brothers, grandmothers, and children. Roles for aunts and uncles do not exist, however.

"Stud broads," in prison argot, assume any male role, including that of husband and brother. Other inmates think of them as men. "Men" often assume traditional roles in women's prisons, ordering women around, demanding to be waited on, expecting to have their rooms cleaned and their laundry done, and so forth. Most women who assume masculine roles within prison are said to be "playing" and are sometimes called "players." Once they leave, they usually revert to female roles. A "femme" or "mommy" is a woman who assumes a female role in a family and during homosexual activity.

Most women in prison, including those playing masculine roles, were generally not lesbians before entering prison. They resort to lesbian relations within prison because relationships with men are unavailable.

Though gender roles and family relationships within women's prisons appear to have an enduring quality, women can and sometimes do change role genders. When a woman playing a male role, for example, reverts to a female one, she is said to have "dropped her belt." A stud broad who drops her belt may wreak havoc on relationships within her own family and in families related to it.

Special Needs of Female Inmates

Rarely are the special needs of imprisoned women fully recognized—and even less frequently are they addressed. Many of today's prison administrators and correctional officers still treat women as if they were men. Nicole Hahn Rafter, for example, says that many prisons have an attitude akin to "just add women and stir."[50]

THE STAFF SPEAKS

Oftentimes, my prison clients tell me that prison rehab providers like myself have few clues about the needs of people in prison rehabilitation programs. I think that many prisoners believe that educated people who have never used drugs have difficulty in developing and implementing drug rehab programs that really work. Many of my clients say they would design the program differ- ently. I usually listen to their ideas, and sometimes I incorporate some of their thoughts in my work. But I realize that they would water a program down so much that other inmates who want to save themselves wouldn't have an opportunity to do so. Sometimes these clients argue that drug rehab provid- ers should be former addicts—as if any knowledge gained in school, many years of experience, and dedication to helping others are worthless. I don't say that to them, but I do remind them that dentists don't need rotten teeth to be good dentists.

John McNerney
Correctional Counselor
Willard-Cybulski Correctional Institution
Enfield, Connecticut

A 2003 report by the National Institute of Corrections (NIC) called for criminal justice agencies to acknowledge the "many differences between male and female offenders," and for the implementation of gender-responsive programming for treating the problems of imprisoned women.[51] *Gender-responsiveness* can be defined as "creating an environment . . . that reflects an understanding of the realities of women's lives and addresses the issues of the women."[52] Gender-responsive programming might, for example, strengthen policies against staff sexual misconduct in institutions that house women; provide more "safe and nurturing" drug treatment programs; and help inmate mothers to maintain strong relationships with their children. The NIC report concluded that "gender-responsive practice can improve outcomes for women offenders by considering their histories, behaviors, and life circumstances."[53]

Susan Cranford is division director of the Community Justice Assistance Division of the Texas Department of Criminal Justice. Rose Williams is warden of Pulaski State Prison in Hawkinsville, Georgia. Recently, Cranford and Williams suggested that "correctional staff should keep the unique needs of women offenders in mind."[54] They say that the effective running of a women's prison requires consideration of those needs.

A critical difference between male and female prisoners, say Cranford and Williams, is "the manner in which they communicate." Female offenders, they note, are usually much more open, more verbal, more emotional, and more willing to share the intimacies of their lives than men are. Male prisoners, like most men in free society, are guarded about the information they share and the manner in which they share it. "For men, information is power. For women, talking helps establish a common ground, a way to relate to others."

Gender-specific training is vital for COs who work in women's prisons, say Cranford and Williams. Proper training, they write, can head off the development of inappropriate relationships (especially initiated by male staff members), which could lead to sexual misconduct. Moreover, staff members who work with women should receive additional training in negotiating and listening skills.

An example of effective gender-specific training is the task-oriented curriculum titled *Working with the Female Offender*, developed by Florida's Department of Corrections.[55] The program addresses unique aspects of managing female inmates and provides correctional staff training in the behaviors, actions, needs, and backgrounds presented by female offenders. A special segment examines how female offenders relate to supervision in various institutional or community corrections settings.

Moreover, say Cranford and Williams, it is important to realize that a woman's children are usually very important to her and that many imprisoned women have children on the outside. Hence, parenting skills should be taught to imprisoned mothers, since most will rejoin and be with their children during critical stages in the children's development.

There are, however, those who feel that gender-responsive strategies won't work. The reason, they say, is because more and more women are being "convicted of crimes for which they would not previously have received a custodial sentence," and are being sent to prison "not because of the seriousness of their crimes, but mainly to receive psychological programming and reintegration training when, in fact, their main problems have stemmed from inadequate housing, poverty, and abusive men."[56] In other words, gender-responsive strategies assume that imprisonment can make a positive difference in women's lives, something that may not be true since such strategies often do little to address the problems women will again face upon release.

Mothers in Prison

According to one BJS study,[57] an estimated 6.7 percent of black women, 5.9 percent of Hispanic women, and 5.2 percent of white women are pregnant at the time of incarceration.

An estimated 4,000 women prisoners give birth each year, even though most women's prisons have no special facilities for pregnant inmates.[58] Some experts recommend that women's prisons should routinely make counseling available to pregnant inmates, and that they should fully inform these women of the options available to them, including abortion and adoption.[59]

The ACA[60] recommends that institutions provide counseling for pregnant inmates, that "prenatal care" should be offered, and that deliveries should be made at community hospitals.[61] Similarly, the American Public Health Association's standards for health services in correctional institutions say that pregnant inmates should be provided with prenatal care, including medical exams and treatment, and that pregnant prisoners should be allowed a special program of housing, diet, vitamin supplements, and exercise.

Once inmates give birth, other problems arise—including the critical issue of child placement. Some states still have partial civil death statutes, which mean that prisoners lose many of their civil rights upon incarceration. In such states, women may lose legal custody of their children. Children either become wards of the state or are placed for adoption.

Although there is some historical precedent for allowing women inmates to keep newborns with them in the institutional setting, very few women's prisons permit this practice. Overcrowded prisons lack space for children, and the prison environment is a decidedly undesirable environment for children. A few women's prisons allow women to keep newborns for a brief period. Most, however, arrange for foster care until the mother is able to find relatives to care for the child or is released. Others work with services that put prison-born infants up for adoption. Some facilities make a special effort to keep mother and child together. Even relatively progressive prisons that allow mother–child contact usually do so only for the first year.

Talking about CORRECTIONS

INSTITUTIONAL CULTURE IN CORRECTIONS

Visit *Live Talk* at **Corrections.com** (www.justicestudies.com/talking04) and listen to the program "Institutional Culture in Corrections," which relates to ideas discussed in this chapter.

Many women are already mothers when they come to prison. BJS statistics[62] show that more than three-quarters of all women in prison in the United States have young children (i.e., under the age of 18). Black (69 percent) and Hispanic (72 percent) female inmates are more likely than white (62 percent) female inmates to have young children. Also, black women are more likely than other women to have lived with their young children before being imprisoned.

The children of 25 percent of women inmates with children under age 18 live with the other parent. More than a third of white female inmates report that their children are living with the children's fathers, compared to a quarter of Hispanic women and less than a fifth of black women. Regardless of race, grandparents are the most common caregivers: 57 percent of imprisoned black mothers look to grandparents for child care, as do 55 percent of imprisoned Hispanic mothers and 41 percent of imprisoned white mothers. Nearly 10 percent of the inmate mothers reported that their children are in a foster home, agency, or institution.

Worry about children affects female inmates' physical and emotional well-being. Although 78 percent of mothers (and 62 percent of fathers) report having at least monthly contact with their children, only 24 percent of mothers (and 21 percent of fathers) report personal visits from their children at least monthly.[63] A majority of both mothers (54 percent) and fathers (57 percent) report never having had a personal visit with their children since their imprisonment began.

According to BJS, nearly 90 percent of women with children under age 18 have had contact with their children since entering prison. Half of all women inmates surveyed have been visited by their children, four-fifths have corresponded by mail, and three-quarters have talked with children on the telephone. Female inmates with children under age 18 are more likely than those with adult children to make daily telephone calls to their children.

Understandably, inmate mothers frequently express concern about possible alienation from their children due to the passage of time associated with incarceration. They often worry that their children will develop strong bonds with new caretakers and be unwilling to return to them upon release.[64]

Finally, it is important to note that a number of women's prisons operate programs designed to develop parenting skills among inmates. Included are the Program for Caring Parents at the Louisiana Correctional Institute for Women; Project HIP (Helping Incarcerated Parents) at the Maine Correctional Center; and Neil J. Houston House, a program for nonviolent female offenders in Massachusetts.[65]

In a BJS Special Report published in 2000,[66] Christopher Mumola estimated that 721,500 state and federal inmates were the parents of 1,498,800 children under age 18. Cranford and Williams reported that these children are about eight times as likely to become criminals as are the children of nonoffenders.

In the federal population, 63.4 percent of male prisoners and 58.8 percent of female prisoners have minor children. The state data reverse this distribution, with 65.3 percent of female inmates and 54.7 percent of male inmates having minor children.

It is noteworthy that male inmates are, for the most part, rarely provided with any special assistance for maintaining contact with their children during their incarceration. During the past decade, however, administrators in women's institutions across the country have implemented measures to foster stronger bonds between incarcerated mothers and their children. Ranging from the establishment of prison nurseries to the development of special visitation areas, these measures seek to facilitate the continued family contact that appears to be so important to female offenders.[67]

With 1 in 12 inmates pregnant at the time of admission[68] and 22 percent of all minor children with a parent in prison being under 5 years old,[69] correctional administrators need to address the unique problems presented by pregnant offenders and those with very young children. Some institutions have opted to create nurseries on site. At Nebraska's Correctional Center for Women, for example, inmates due for release before their children are 18 months old may keep the children with them in a specially designated floor of a standard prison building. The mothers are provided parenting and child-care classes, and they work only part time. While they work, other trained inmates provide child care.

Another example of programs designed to facilitate family bonding is the Ohio Reformatory for Women's annual three-day weekend camp, which brings children ages 6 to 12 from all over the state to spend days with their inmate mothers. Originally pioneered at Bedford Hills Correctional Facility, New York's maximum-security prison for women, such camping visits have become more common in other facilities as well. Some states even allow overnight camping trips, both on and off the prison grounds.

Inmates apply for the program in January each year. Local churches and other community service groups support the program.[70] Selection criteria include a review of inmates' disciplinary records during incarceration, and those whose crimes involved their children are prohibited from participating. During the weekend, activities such as storytelling, softball, crafts, and meals facilitate bonding between mother and child. The inmates return to the prison to sleep at night, but the children "camp out" in sleeping bags at a local church.

Another innovative effort is Florida's "Reading Family Ties: Face to Face" program.[71] Begun in February 2000, it uses high-speed videoconferencing technology to permit weekly family visits between incarcerated mothers in two rural institutions and their children in the Miami area. Inmate mothers may sit before an Internet-linked camera to read to their children. Logistical limitations, of course, are significant, but administrators plan to expand the program to other major cities in Florida.

Perhaps the most family-centered efforts are being tried in California. Oakland's Project Pride[72] permits mothers convicted of nonviolent offenses to serve the last portion of their sentences in residential community settings with their preschool-age children. Under the Family Foundations Program in Santa Fe Springs (CA),[73] sentencing of convicted mothers with substance abuse histories can include treatment in residential centers where they can live with their children.

Some hard-liners might decry such programs as unjustified coddling of convicted offenders. Few, however, can argue the benefits such programs provide to the children of incarcerated parents. Meanwhile, it remains to be seen whether the programs

Most children of incarcerated mothers have little contact with their mothers. The lack of contact often upsets their emotional development. How might prisons contribute to the development of positive relationships between incarcerated mothers and their children?

Eye On Corrections

Serving Women Well in Corrections

By Michelle Gaseau

Not too long ago, women's issues among the offender population were an afterthought for many corrections administrators. Women made up a small proportion of the total inmate numbers for one thing, and for another, there was little research available on what women needed in terms of programming and care while in prison or jail.

Today all that has changed. There's plenty of work being done by researchers to outline the specific needs of the female inmate population nationwide and, the number of women being sentenced to prison or jail is climbing—good reasons for the approach towards women offenders to change.

"Unless you can relate to the issues that bring women into the system in the first place, you can't develop an appropriate response to improve outcomes. Our approach has been gender neutral for so long and many of our opinions of gender neutral [actually] mean focusing on males. It's important to identify the reasons why women come into the criminal justice system so that we can prevent this cycle from continuing and we can also prevent the intergenerational cycle," said Barbara Bloom, Associate Professor, Department of Criminal Justice Administration at Sonoma State University and an author on the subject of women offenders.

Programmatically, according to Bloom, there's much that corrections officials need to consider when serving the female offender population. In [a] study she co-authored, *Gender Responsive Strategies,* six major principles were identified relating to female offenders that should be used to guide decisions about them: gender, environment, relationships, services and supervision, socioeconomic status and community.

"They are broad principles that can be adapted by agencies in the community, [and] people working in jails and prisons. We intend for them to be general enough so that whatever jurisdictions that were interested could use them," she said.

First and foremost, according to Bloom, officials need to acknowledge that gender makes a difference in almost every aspect of how a woman comes to a criminal justice facility.

"If you look at the relationship between past abuse and trauma [for example] and that so many women are survivors of trauma and then you look at some of the standard operating procedures, like the use of restraints or the use of isolation, then you also have to look at how those procedures impact women," Bloom said.

Other major themes that illustrate the distinction between male and female offenders are the participation level in the crimes they commit, their levels of motivation to commit those crimes and the types of crimes they commit.

There are also differences in the levels of harm caused by crimes committed by men and women, she said.

Beyond this, agency heads and officials need to consider the differences between men and women in relation to how they are classified, where they are housed and what programs and treatment they need.

Bloom said that she has started to see a slow attitudinal shift among corrections agencies to include some of these principles.

"It used to be we believed all people in the criminal justice system should be treated the same, but over time, people have found that there are unique differences and they come into the system requiring different approaches," Bloom said.

CONSIDERING CLASSIFICATION

As research has increased regarding the different programming requirements of female offenders, so too has work been done to examine the classification issues surrounding female offenders.

In the study *Developing Gender-Specific Classification Systems for Women Offenders,* researchers Patricia Hardyman and Patricia Van Voorhis looked at how current classification practices could unfairly impact female offenders.

Also as part of the study, Hardyman, Senior Associate with the Criminal Justice Institute, and Van Voorhis of the Center for Criminal Justice Research at the University of Cincinnati, examined classification practices in seven states and made recommendations for improvements throughout the corrections field.

"Agencies will readily admit that managing women offenders is totally different than working with male offenders, but not all realize this needs to translate into a different classification system for women offenders," said Hardyman.

Among the recommendations for agencies are to ensure the validity of the classification systems for women offenders, to avoid overclassifying women offenders and to modify current risk factors to reflect differences between men and women.

Hardyman explains that the criteria and standards designed to predict men's behavior in prisons do not translate into predictors of women offenders' behavior and, if used with female offenders, will tend to overclassify them in security levels that are inappropriate.

The report suggests that housing a woman at custody levels that are too high is unethical and has an effect on their ability to program in a facility.

"Women might behave differently but also their criminal history and the current offense that brings them in [differs]. They may be a co-defendant where they were a partner and the other person was the leader or they might be led by another person," said Hardyman.

In the study, the researchers found that in Idaho, certain property offenses—such as forgery or a bad check—that are typically considered low-risk for men, tended to be correlated with institutional misconduct for women.

In addition, Hardyman said there are a whole host of other factors that contribute to a women's behavior in prison.

"Also important are the issues associated with stability factors. Some jurisdictions will consider substance abuse, current age, education, employment at time of arrest, women tend to have different pathways to getting into crime, it looks different," she said.

Substance abuse, for example, plays a different role in the assessment of men and women. Hardyman said that it is so common for female offenders to have a substance abuse problem that it can't really be a predictor of behavior.

"If everyone has it, it doesn't tell much different about one person over another," she said.

Beyond these factors, children play a major role in stability for female offenders. Hardyman suggests that if something is wrong with their children on the outside or there is a concern about their children, it will affect their behavior inside the prison.

"It creates stress factors and they tend to act out or have problems. Some different jurisdictions will look at the stress factors going on for women offenders [on a periodic basis,]" said Hardyman. And that is what they should be doing, she adds. . . .

Source: "Serving Women Well In Corrections," Michelle Gaseau, The Corrections Connection Network News (CCNN). Eye On Corrections. www.corrections.com. August 2, 2004.
Note: This article has been reprinted in part from CCNN. To read this article in its entirety, go to www.corrections.com.

will serve to sustain family relationships, ease prisoners' return to the family environment after release, and, ultimately, reduce recidivism rates.

Cocorrectional Facilities

In 1971, a disturbance at the federal women's prison at Alderson, West Virginia, led to calls for ways to expand incarceration options for women. The Federal Bureau of Prisons responded by moving low-security female prisoners from the crowded Alderson institution to a federal minimum-security prison at Morgantown, West Virginia. The Morgantown facility had been built for young men but had not reached its design capacity. With this move, the modern era of coed prisons, or cocorrections, was born.

A **coed prison** is a facility housing both men and women, and **cocorrections** is the incarceration and interaction of female and male offenders under a single institutional administration.[74] It is estimated that as many as 52 adult correctional institutions in the United States are coed and that they confine almost 23,000 men and 7,000 women.[75]

Since its inception, cocorrections has been cited as a potential solution to a wide variety of corrections problems. The rationales in support of cocorrections are that it:

1. reduces the dehumanizing and destructive aspects of incarceration by permitting heterosocial relationships;
2. reduces problems of institutional control;
3. creates a more "normal" atmosphere, reducing privation;
4. allows positive heterosocial skills to emerge;
5. cushions the shock of release;
6. increases the number of program offerings and improves program access for all prisoners; and
7. expands career opportunities for women.

An examination of the cocorrections literature from 1970 to 1990, however, found no evidence that cocorrections benefits female prisoners.[76] A former warden of a coed prison contends that "going coed" has often been done to appease male egos and smooth the running of men's prisons. Warden Jacqueline Crawford tells us that most women in prison have generally been exploited by the men in their lives. A coed prison, she says, furthers this experience because male prisoners continue the abuse women have come to expect from men.[77]

Others have found that some women's prisons have been turned into coed prisons, thus limiting correctional options for women. Overall, researchers have concluded, "Cocorrections offers women prisoners few, if any, economic, educational, vocational, and social advantages."[78] Whether prisoners released from coed prisons adjust better to the community or experience less recidivism has not been sufficiently studied.

Although literature related to single-sex prisons[79] has repeatedly shown poor overall performance in prisoner rehabilitation and public safety, correctional decision makers, policymakers, legislators, and the public are not calling for an end to one-sex imprisonment. If cocorrections is to become more than window dressing, however, it requires more attention to planning, implementation, and evaluation. Despite some early claims of success, coed prisons are not a quick fix for problems of prison administration.

coed prison

A prison housing both female and male offenders.

cocorrections

The incarceration and interaction of female and male offenders under a single institutional administration.

REVIEW & APPLICATIONS

REFLECTIONS ON THE FUTURE

By Tara Gray
New Mexico State University

Living Behind Bars: Fear and Boredom

Police officers sometimes say their job is 99 percent boredom and 1 percent sheer terror. Inmates could easily say the same.

If there is one word that characterizes inmate life, it is probably the word, "boredom." To understand the extent of the boredom, lock yourself in your bathroom for one weekend. Before you lock yourself in, place a sleeping roll on the floor. Pack sack lunches sufficient to last you through two days and two nights. As you pack your lunches, imagine the food available to inmates in prison. Pack any reading materials you want with you, including homework, but know you won't have a telephone, television, computer, or any electronic device in your "cell." Tell your roommate that he or she is free to talk with you through the door.

Congratulations. By going through two days "behind the bars," you have just had a taste of giving up your freedom. It won't be quite like incarceration of course because you choose the date and the length of stay, which was considerably less than the average prison stay of 23 months. You also had more control over the food, the reading materials, and the roommate than most inmates have. But still, you couldn't help noticing you were living in a very small room—a toilet! You wanted to eat something besides the food that was issued! You wanted to call someone! You wanted to go somewhere!

Congratulations again. You tried to experience what it is like to leave everyone and everything you ever knew behind you and give up some important elements of freedom. You have had some important insights about what life is like behind bars. You have experienced the boredom but missed out on the other negative of inmate life: sheer terror.

What **is** the terror like for inmates? It depends greatly on the prison or jail. Some institutions resemble the violence of the ghetto or barrio. Others are relatively peaceful. In the most violent institutions, "watching your back" is a full time job. Everyone is to be feared, including every other inmate and some correctional officers. Assaults are frequent and deadly. Rapes are common for both women and men. Don't get too bored: Watch out.

About the Author

Tara Gray teaches criminal justice at New Mexico State University. Prisons are her passion, and she remains convinced that prisons can be places of hope instead of places of terror and despair. One of her three books is *Exploring Corrections: A Book of Readings* (Allyn & Bacon, 2002). The book includes readings about living in prison and jail for men, women, and juveniles, as well as living with the threat of rape, with AIDS, in the "hole," on psychotropic drugs, or on death row. The book includes futuristic models of prison administration that show what is possible in a prison and how to keep hope alive.

SUMMARY

1 Most state inmates are male, belong to racial or ethnic minority groups, are relatively young, and have been incarcerated for a violent offense.

2 Prison inmates live their daily lives in accordance with the dictates of the inmate subculture. The inmate subculture consists of the customs and beliefs of those incarcerated in correctional institutions.

3 Deprivation theory holds that prisoner subcultures develop in response to the pains of imprisonment. Importation theory claims that inmate subcultures are brought into prisons from the outside world. A more realistic approach might be the integration model, which uses both theories to explain prisoner subcultures.

4 An important aspect of the male inmate subculture is the prison code. The prison code is a set of norms for the behavior of inmates. Central elements of the code include notions of loyalty (to prison society), control of anger, toughness, and distrust of prison officials. Because the prison code is a part of the inmate subculture, it is mostly opposed to official policies.

5 The inmate subculture also has its own language, called *prison argot.* Examples of prison argot are "fish" (a new inmate), "cellie" (cell mate), and "homeboy" (a prisoner from one's hometown).

6 Inmate roles are different prison lifestyle choices. They include the real man, the mean dude, the bully, the agitator, the hedonist, the opportunist, the retreatist, the legalist, the radical, the colonist, the religious inmate, the punk, and the gang-banger.

7 There are far fewer women's prisons than men's in the United States. Women's prisons often have no gun towers or armed guards and no stone walls or fences topped by barbed wire. They tend to be more attractive and are often built on a cottage plan. Security in most women's prisons is more relaxed than in institutions for men, and female inmates may have more freedom within the institution than do their male counterparts in their institutions. Other gender-based disparities favoring male prisoners exist. A lack of funding and inadequate training have been cited to explain why programs available to women inmates are often not on a par with those available to male prisoners.

8 Female prisoners largely resemble male prisoners in race, ethnic background, and age. However, they are substantially more likely to be serving time for drug offenses and less likely to have been sentenced for violent crimes.

9 While there are many similarities between men's and women's prisons, the social structure and the subcultural norms and expectations of women's prisons differ from those of men's prisons in a number of important ways. One important difference is that the prisoner subculture in a women's prison tends to encourage relationships rather than isolation. As a consequence, pseudofamilies arise, with fully developed familial relationships and roles.

KEY TERMS

total institution, *p. 393*

inmate subculture, *p. 394*

prisoner subculture, *p. 394*

prisonization, *p. 394*

pains of imprisonment, *p. 394*

deprivation theory, *p. 395*

importation theory, *p. 395*

integration model, *p. 395*

prison code, *p. 396*

prison argot, *p. 396*

inmate roles, *p. 397*

pseudofamilies, *p. 408*

coed prison, *p. 416*

cocorrections, *p. 416*

QUESTIONS FOR REVIEW

1 Describe the characteristics of the inmate population in state prisons.

2 What is the *inmate subculture,* and how is it central to understanding society in men's prisons?

3 Explain how inmate subcultures develop, according to deprivation theory, importation theory, and the integration model.

4 What is the *prison code?* What are some of its key features? How does it influence behavior in men's prisons?

5 What is *prison argot?* Give some examples.

6 Explain what is meant by *inmate roles,* and give some examples.

7 In what ways do women's prisons differ from men's prisons?

8 Compare female and male inmates by their criminal histories, their family characteristics, and the offenses for which they are incarcerated.

9 How does the social structure of women's prisons differ from that in men's prisons? What are *pseudofamilies,* and why are they important to the society of women's prisons?

THINKING CRITICALLY ABOUT CORRECTIONS

Prison Birth

A woman who gives birth in prison may lose her child to state authorities or may have her parental rights severely restricted. In most cases, the child is removed from the inmate mother shortly after birth. Do you think this is fair? Why or why not?

Housing Assignments

Not surprisingly, state policies differ significantly on the question of housing assignments for prisoners. Some permit inmates to choose their cell mates, while others enforce random cell assignments. What are the advantages and disadvantages of each policy style? Which style do you think is best?

ON-THE-JOB DECISION MAKING

Male Officers in Women's Prisons

You are a correctional officer assigned to a women's prison. Six months ago, the superintendent of your institution ordered an investigation to determine the proper role of male officers within the facility. The investigation centered on charges by a handful of inmates that they had been sexually harassed by male COs. The alleged harassment included requests for sexual favors in return for special privileges, observation of female inmates in various states of undress while in their rooms and in shower facilities, and inappropriate touching during cell and facility searches (policy allows only female COs to conduct body searches).

Although the investigation was inconclusive, the activities of male COs have been restricted. They are no longer permitted to have any physical contact with inmates unless an emergency demands that they restrain or search inmates. They have been reassigned to areas of the facility where they cannot view shower and toilet facilities. They are expected to announce their presence in living areas, and they have been ordered to take special classes on staff-inmate interaction.

Unfortunately, however, there are not enough female COs for all of the reassignments required by the recent shift in policy. As a result, the routines of female officers are being significantly disrupted. Female officers are being asked to work shifts that are inconvenient for their personal lives (many are mothers or college students and had come to count on predictable shift work). Most female COs also feel that their workload has increased, since they have to cover areas of the institution and assume tasks that male officers would previously have handled.

A few female COs have already left for jobs elsewhere, citing difficulties created in the work environment by the new policies. The talk among the correctional staff is that many of the remaining female staff members might also soon leave. If more female COs leave the facility, it will be impossible for those who remain to keep the facility running under the new rules.

1. Did the superintendent make the right decision in limiting the activities of male COs? Why or why not?

2. Might there be other ways to resolve the issues raised by the investigation into sexual harassment? If so, what might they be?

Same-Sex Relationships

You are a chaplain working in a large state-run correctional facility. You take pride in your reputation among the inmates as a fair and reasonable counselor who treats them with courtesy and respect and never judges them for past transgressions or present problems.

Ronald, an inmate whom you know well, comes to you with a special request. He wants to marry Lawrence, another inmate, and he wants you to perform the ceremony in private. He also tells you that he knows that the "marriage" will have no legitimacy on the outside but says that the ceremony will be deeply moving for him and for Lawrence. Ronald's incarceration record is sterling. His disciplinary record shows no infractions, and there are numerous positive annotations regarding the obvious sincerity of his efforts to rehabilitate himself in preparation for his return to free society.

You are concerned that Ronald may actually be straight, and that his relationship with Lawrence may arise more from the pains of imprisonment than from any innate sexual orientation. You are uncertain what prison regulations might say about such a ceremony, but you suspect that, were you to inquire, the ceremony would be officially disallowed. Additionally, church elders in your denomination have condemned same-sex marriages like the one you are being asked to perform. Still, you think that Ronald is well-meaning in his efforts to form a more stable relationship with Lawrence, and you believe that such a relationship can help him adjust to the stresses of prison life.

1. What do you do? Is this an issue that you need time to think about, or do you answer right away?

2. Would you consider counseling Ronald in order to better assess his "true" sexual orientation?

3. Is his "true" sexual orientation an important consideration?

4. Would you further consider counseling Ronald and Lawrence, individually and jointly, regarding their desire to formalize their relationship?

5. Would you take the issue to the prison superintendent?

LIVE LINKS

www.justicestudies.com/livelinks04

10–1   Prisons Research at the Beginning of the Twenty-First Century

This report on the collateral effects of imprisonment suggests that policymakers have been flying blind, making decisions costing billions of dollars and affecting millions of lives without adequate knowledge of the nature and costs of the unintended consequences of imprisonment. The writer advocates a more reasoned and empirical approach to criminal justice sentencing policy.

10–2   Sexual Violence Reported by Correctional Authorities

This report presents data from the Survey on Sexual Violence, an administrative records collection of incidents of inmate-on-inmate and staff-on-inmate sexual violence reported to correctional authorities. It provides counts of sexual violence by type and includes tables on reporting capabilities, how investigations are handled, and characteristics of victims and perpetrators of sexual violence.

10–3   Caught in the Net: the Impact of Drug Policies on Women & Families

The rate of imprisonment of women for drug crimes has far outpaced that of men—but why? This report suggests that either we have turned a blind eye or we simply misunderstand women's experiences with drugs. Jointly published by the ACLU, Break the Chains: Communities of Color and the War on Drugs, and the Brennan Center for Justice at NYU School of Law, this report intends to open a new dialogue on questions about women and drugs, and existing laws and policies.

10–4   Gender-Responsive Strategies: Research, Practice, and Guiding Principles for Women Offenders

This document attempts to identify critical differences between male and female inmates and to define the implications of those differences for improving correctional management and services for women offenders.

THE LEGAL WORLD

Prisoners' Rights

CHAPTER OBJECTIVES

After completing this chapter you should be able to do the following:

1 Explain what is meant by the *hands-off doctrine.*

2 Identify the sources of prisoners' rights.

3 Recite the central question raised by the concern with the rights of prisoners.

4 List the five ways in which inmates can challenge their conditions of confinement.

5 Describe the major changes that took place during the prisoners' rights era.

6 List and explain the four amendments to the U.S. Constitution on which most prisoners' claims are based.

7 Explain how the development of rights for female prisoners has differed from that of rights for male prisoners.

> *All persons under any form of detention or imprisonment shall be treated in a humane manner and with respect for the inherent dignity of the human person.*
>
> —United Nations General Assembly Resolution 43/173, December 9, 1988

In 1871, in the case of *Ruffin* v. *Commonwealth*, a Virginia judge declared the following: "A convicted felon . . . punished by confinement in the penitentiary instead of with death . . . is in a state of penal servitude to the State. He has, as a consequence of his crime, not only forfeited his liberty, but all his personal rights except those which the law in its humanity accords to him. He is for the time being the slave of the State. He is *civiliter mortuus*; and his estate, if he has any, is administered like that of a dead man. The Bill of Rights is a declaration of general principles to govern a society of freemen, and not of convicted felons and men civilly dead."

The judge in *Ruffin* was voicing what had long been believed: that prisoners had no rights. It was this kind of thinking that long supported a "hands-off" approach to prisoners' rights. If inmates were really civilly dead, the federal government and the federal courts certainly had no cause to tell the states how to run their prisons.

The Bill of Rights, which provides criminal defendants with a number of due process rights, also forms the basis of a number of inmate rights. What rights should inmates have?

THE HANDS-OFF DOCTRINE

hands-off doctrine

A historical policy of American courts not to intervene in prison management. Courts tended to follow the doctrine until the late 1960s.

Under the **hands-off doctrine,** American courts for many decades avoided intervening in prison management. The doctrine was based on two rationales: (1) that under the *separation of powers* inherent in the U.S. Constitution, the judicial branch of government should not interfere with the running of correctional facilities by the executive branch and (2) that judges should leave correctional administration to correctional experts.[1] For a very long time in our nation's history, states ran their prisons as they saw fit. Prison inmates were thought of as "nonpersons," and rights pertained only to persons. Pleas from prisoners based on allegations of deprivations of their rights were ignored.

The hands-off doctrine and the philosophy of the prisoner as a slave of the state began to change in the mid-1900s. Public attitudes about punishment versus rehabilitation changed, and more and more people became aware that inmates had *no* rights. As a result, the courts began to scrutinize the correctional enterprise in America.

Decline of the Hands-Off Doctrine

The 1941 case of *Ex parte Hull* began a dismantling of the hands-off doctrine. Prior to *Hull*, it had been common for corrections personnel to screen inmate mail, including prisoner petitions for writs of *habeas corpus*. Corrections officials often confiscated the petitions, claiming they were improperly prepared and not fit to submit to court. In *Hull*, the Supreme Court ruled that no state or its officers may interfere with a prisoner's right to apply to a federal court for a writ of *habeas corpus*.

San Quentin State Prison in Marin County, California. Opened in 1852, it is one of the state's oldest and best-known correctional institutions. Under the hands-off doctrine, American courts long refused to intervene in prison management. When did the hands-off doctrine end?

Thus, court officials, not corrections officials, have the authority to decide whether such petitions are prepared correctly.

Though this seemed like a small step at the time, it would facilitate a major leap in prisoners' rights. Three years later, in *Coffin* v. *Reichard* (1944) the Sixth Circuit Court of Appeals extended *habeas corpus* hearings to consideration of the conditions of confinement. Even more important, the *Coffin* case was the first in which a federal appellate court ruled that prisoners do not automatically lose their civil rights when in prison.[2] In the words of the Court, a prisoner "retains all the rights of an ordinary citizen except those expressly, or by necessary implication, taken from him by law."

Another important development occurred in 1961, with the Supreme Court's ruling in *Monroe* v. *Pape.* Prior to *Pape*, it was believed that the phrase "under color of state law" in the Civil Rights Act of 1871 meant that a Section 1983 suit (explained in greater detail on page 427) could involve only actions authorized by state law. In *Pape*, however, the Court held that for activities to take place *under color* of state law, they did not have to be *authorized* by state law. The statute, said the Court, had been intended to protect against "misuse of power, possessed by virtue of state law and made possible only because the wrongdoer is clothed with the authority of state law."

Officials "clothed with the authority of state law" seemed to include state corrections officials. Thus, state corrections officials who violated an inmate's constitutional rights while performing their duties could be held liable for their actions in federal court, regardless of whether state law or policy supported those actions.[3]

A third important case establishing inmates' rights to access the courts was *Cooper* v. *Pate* (1964). In *Cooper*, a federal circuit court clarified the *Pape* decision, indicating that prisoners could sue a warden or another correctional official under Title 42 of the U.S. Code, Section 1983, based on the protections of the Civil Rights Act of 1871.

Commenting on the importance of *Cooper*, one observer noted,

Just by opening a forum in which prisoners' grievances could be heard, the federal courts destroyed the custodian's absolute power and the prisoners'

The case of *Holt* v. *Sarver* brought the hands-off era to a close and opened a new era of prisoners' rights. What were the issues involved in that case?

isolation from the larger society. The litigation itself heightened prisoners' consciousness and politicized them.[4]

With prisoners' access to the courts now established, cases challenging nearly every aspect of corrections were soon filed. The courts, primarily the federal district courts, began to review prisoners' complaints and intervene on prisoners' behalf.

The hands-off era is said to have ended in 1970, when a federal district court, in *Holt* v. *Sarver*, declared the entire Arkansas prison system "so inhumane as to be a violation of the Eighth Amendment bar on cruel and unusual punishment." Robert Sarver, the Arkansas commissioner of corrections, admitted that "the physical facilities at both [prison units named in the suit] were inadequate and in a total state of disrepair that could only be described as deplorable." Additionally, he testified that inmates with trustee status, some of them serving life or long-term sentences, constituted 99 percent of the security force of the state's prison system.

Commissioner Sarver continued, testifying that "trustees sell desirable jobs to prisoners and also traffic in food, liquor, and drugs. Prisoners frequently become intoxicated and unruly. The prisoners sleep in dormitories. Prisoners are frequently attacked and raped in the dormitories, and injuries and deaths have resulted. Sleep and rest are seriously disrupted. No adequate means exist to protect the prisoners from assaults. There is no satisfactory means of keeping guns, knives, and other weapons away from the prison population."

The *Holt* court declared in 1970,

> The obligation . . . to eliminate existing unconstitutionalities does not depend upon what the Legislature may do or upon what the Governor may do. . . . If Arkansas is going to operate a Penitentiary System, it is going to have to be a system that is countenanced by the Constitution of the United States.

Prisoner litigation had brought sad conditions to light, and the court had intervened to institute reforms for the prisoners in Arkansas.

PRISONERS' RIGHTS

Legal Foundations

prisoners' rights

Constitutional guarantees of free speech, religious practice, due process, and other private and personal rights as well as constitutional protections against cruel and unusual punishments made applicable to prison inmates by the federal courts.

Prisoners' rights have four legal foundations: the U.S. Constitution, federal statutes, state constitutions, and state statutes. Most court cases involving prisoners' rights have involved rights claimed under the U.S. Constitution, even though state constitutions generally parallel the U.S. Constitution and sometimes confer additional rights. State legislatures and Congress can also confer additional prisoners' rights.

constitutional rights

The personal and due process rights guaranteed to individuals by the U.S. Constitution and its amendments, especially the first 10 amendments, known as the Bill of Rights. Constitutional rights are the basis of most inmate rights.

The U.S. Constitution   The U.S. Constitution is the supreme law of our land. At the heart of any discussion of prisoners' rights lies one question: What does the Constitution have to say? As scholars began to search the Constitution, they could find no requirement that prisoners give up all of their rights as American citizens (and human beings) after conviction.

It is important to remember, however, that **constitutional rights** are not absolute. Does freedom of speech mean that you have a protected right to stand up in a crowded theater and yell "fire"? It does not (at least not unless there *is* a fire). That is because the panic that would follow such an exclamation would probably cause injuries and would needlessly put members of the public at risk of harm. Hence, the courts have held that, although freedom of speech is guaranteed by the Constitution, it is not an absolute right; in other words, there are limits to it (*Schenck* v. *United States*, 1919).

So, the central question raised by those interested in prisoners' rights seems to be, to what degree does a person retain constitutional rights when convicted of a criminal offense and sentenced to prison? Answering that question has become a job of the courts. The answers are dependent upon the courts' interpretation of the U.S. Constitution, state constitutions, and federal and state laws. Generally speaking, the courts have recognized four legitimate **institutional needs** that justify some restrictions on the constitutional rights of prisoners:

1. maintenance of institutional *order*;
2. maintenance of institutional *security*;
3. *safety* of prison inmates and staff; and
4. *rehabilitation* of inmates.

According to the courts, *order* refers to calm and discipline within the institution, *security* is the control of individuals and objects entering or leaving the institution, *safety* means avoidance of physical harm, and *rehabilitation* refers to practices necessary for the health, well-being, and treatment of inmates.[5]

Federal Statutes Laws passed by Congress can confer certain rights on inmates in federal prisons. In addition, Congress has passed a number of laws that affect the running of state prisons. The Civil Rights Act of 1871, for example, was enacted after the Civil War to discourage lawless activities by state officials. Section 1983 reads as follows:

> Every person who, under color of any statute, ordinance, regulation, custom, or usage, of any State or Territory, subjects, or causes to be subjected, any citizen of the United States or other person within the jurisdiction thereof to the deprivation of any rights, privileges, or immunities secured by the Constitution and laws, shall be liable to the party injured in an action at law, suit in equity, or other proper proceeding for redress.

This section imposes **civil liability** (but not criminal blame) on any person who deprives another of rights guaranteed by the U.S. Constitution. The Civil Rights Act of 1871 allows state prisoners to challenge conditions of their imprisonment in federal court. Most prisoner suits brought under this act allege deprivation of constitutional rights. Another important piece of legislation is the Civil Rights of Institutionalized Persons Act (CRIPA),[6] which is discussed in more detail in Chapter 12.

State Constitutions Most state constitutions are patterned after the U.S. Constitution. However, state constitutions tend to be longer and more detailed than the U.S. Constitution and may contain specific provisions regarding corrections. State constitutions generally do not give prisoners more rights than are granted by the U.S. Constitution, except in a few states such as California and Oregon. Inmates in such states may challenge the conditions of their confinement in state court under the state's constitutional provision.

State Statutes Unlike the federal government, state governments all have inherent police power, which allows them to pass laws to protect the health, safety, and welfare of their citizens. A state legislature can

institutional needs
Prison administration interests recognized by the courts as justifying some restrictions on the constitutional rights of prisoners. Those interests are maintenance of institutional *order,* maintenance of institutional *security, safety* of prison inmates and staff, and *rehabilitation* of inmates.

civil liability
A legal obligation to another person to do, pay, or make good something.

A writ of *habeas corpus* is a court order requiring that a prisoner be brought before the court so that the court can determine whether the person is being legally detained. What is required of a state prisoner who wants to bring a *habeas corpus* action in federal court?

writ of *habeas corpus*

An order that directs the person detaining a prisoner to bring him or her before a judge, who will determine the lawfulness of the imprisonment.

tort

A civil wrong, a wrongful act, or a wrongful breach of duty, other than a breach of contract, whether intentional or accidental, from which injury to another occurs.

pass statutes to grant specific rights beyond those conferred by the state constitution. Often such legislation specifies duties of corrections officials or standards of treatment for prisoners. Prisoners who can show failure of officials to fulfill state statutory obligations may collect money damages or obtain a court order compelling officials to comply with the law.

Mechanisms for Securing Prisoners' Rights

Inmates today have five ways to challenge the legality of their confinement, associated prison conditions, and the practices of correctional officials: (1) a state *habeas corpus* action, (2) a federal *habeas corpus* action after state remedies have been exhausted, (3) a state tort lawsuit, (4) a federal civil rights lawsuit, and (5) a petition for injunctive relief.[7]

Writ of *Habeas Corpus* A **writ of habeas corpus** is an order from a court to produce a prisoner in court so that the court can determine whether the prisoner is being legally detained. *Habeas corpus* is Latin for "you have the body." A prisoner, or someone acting for a prisoner, files a *habeas corpus* petition asking a court to determine the lawfulness of the imprisonment. The petition for the writ is merely a procedural tool. If a writ is issued, it has no bearing on any issues to be reviewed. It guarantees only a hearing on those issues.

Federal and state prisoners may file *habeas corpus* petitions in federal courts. State prisoners must first, however, exhaust available state *habeas corpus* remedies. In 2000, of 11,880 petitions that inmates filed in *federal* courts, 3,870 (33 percent) were *habeas corpus* actions; of 46,371 petitions that inmates filed in *state* courts, 21,345 (46 percent) were *habeas corpus* actions.[8]

Tort Action in State Court State inmates can file a tort action in state court. A **tort** is a civil wrong, a wrongful act, or a wrongful breach of duty, other than a breach of contract, whether intentional or accidental, from which injury to another occurs. In tort actions, inmates commonly claim that a correctional employee, such as the warden or a correctional officer, or the correctional facility itself failed to perform a duty required by law regarding the inmate. Compensation for damages is the most common objective. Tort suits often allege such deficiencies as negligence, gross or wanton negligence, or intentional wrong.

Federal Civil Rights Lawsuit Federal and state inmates can file suit in federal court alleging civil rights violations by corrections officials. Most of these suits challenge the conditions of confinement, under Section 1983 of the Civil Rights Act of 1871, which is now part of Title 42 of the U.S. Code. Lawsuits may claim that officials have deprived inmates of their constitutional rights, such as adequate medical treatment, protection against excessive force by correctional officers or violence from other inmates, due process in disciplinary hearings, and access to law libraries. According to the Bureau of Justice Statistics, 1 of 10 civil cases filed in U.S. district courts is Section 1983 litigation, as it is commonly called.

When such suits seek monetary damages from federal agents for violation of constitutional rights, they are often referred to as *Bivens* actions, recalling the 1971 case in which the U.S. Supreme Court articulated inmates' entitlement to sue. In subsequent rulings (e.g., *FDIC* v. *Meyer*, 1994), the Court specified that "a *Bivens* action may only be maintained against an individual," not the federal agency by which he or she is employed, and it declined to extend the damage action authority of *Bivens* to permit suits against private entities operating correctional facilities under federal contract (*Correctional Services Corporation, Petitioner* v. *John E. Malesko*, 2001).

If inmates are successful in their civil suits, in state or federal courts, the courts can award three types of damages. **Nominal damages** are small amounts of money that may be awarded when inmates have sustained no actual damages, but there is clear evidence that their rights have been violated.

Compensatory damages are payments for actual losses, which may include out-of-pocket expenses the inmate incurred in filing the suit, other forms of monetary or material loss, and pain, suffering, and mental anguish. Some years ago, for example, a federal appeals court sustained an award of $9,300 against a warden and a correctional commissioner. The amount was calculated by awarding each inmate $25 for each day he had spent in solitary confinement (a total of 372 days for all the inmates) under conditions the court found cruel and unusual (*Sostre* v. *McGinnis*, 1971).

Punitive damages are awarded to punish the wrongdoer when the wrongful act was intentional and malicious or was done with reckless disregard for the rights of the inmate.

Request for Injunctive Relief   An **injunction** is a judicial order to do or refrain from doing a particular act. A request for an injunction might claim adverse effects of a health, safety, or sanitation procedure and might involve the entire correctional facility. It is important for anyone working in corrections to realize that a lack of funds cannot justify failure to comply with an injunction (*Smith* v. *Sullivan*, 1977).

The Criminal Court System   There is a dual court system in the United States; the federal and state court systems coexist (see Exhibit 11–1). The federal court system is nationwide, with one or more federal courts in each state. These courts coexist with state court systems. Whether a defendant is tried in a federal court or a state court depends on which court has jurisdiction over the particular case.

The **jurisdiction** of a court is the power or authority of the court to act with respect to a case before it. The acts involved in the case must have taken place or had an effect in the geographic territory of the court, or a statute must give the court jurisdiction.

District courts are the trial courts of the federal system. They have original jurisdiction over cases charging defendants with violations of federal criminal laws. Each state has at least one United States district court, and some, like New York and California, have as many as four. There are also federal district courts in Puerto Rico, the District of Columbia, and the U.S. territories. There are currently 11 United States courts of ap-

nominal damages

Small amounts of money a court may award when inmates have sustained no actual damages, but there is clear evidence that their rights have been violated.

compensatory damages

Money a court may award as payment for actual losses suffered by a plaintiff, including out-of-pocket expenses incurred in filing the suit, other forms of monetary or material loss, and pain, suffering, and mental anguish.

punitive damages

Money a court may award to punish a wrongdoer when a wrongful act was intentional and malicious or was done with reckless disregard for the rights of the victim.

injunction

A judicial order to do or refrain from doing a particular act.

jurisdiction

The power, right, or authority of a court to interpret and apply the law.

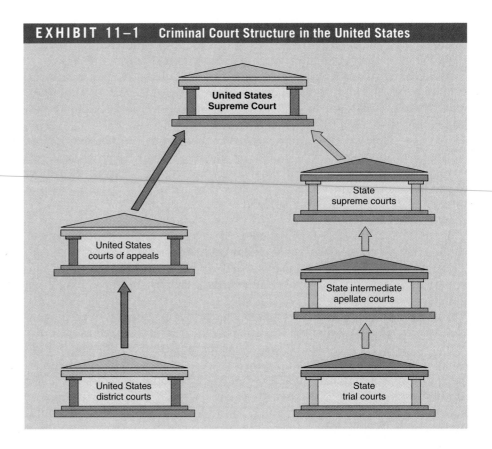

EXHIBIT 11–1   Criminal Court Structure in the United States

peals, arranged by circuit, a District of Columbia circuit, and one federal circuit—see Exhibit 11–2).

Each state has its own court system. Most state court structures are similar to the federal court structure—with trial courts, intermediate appellate courts, and a top appellate court. In most states, the trial courts are organized by county.

Though federal offenses are prosecuted in federal court and state offenses are prosecuted in state courts, the federal courts have supervisory jurisdiction over the administration of criminal justice in the state courts. The U.S. Supreme Court has ruled that constitutional requirements for criminal procedure in federal courts also apply to the states. Violation of these constitutional requirements can be the subject of both state appeals and federal suits by prisoners.

Inmate Grievance Procedures

Inmate grievance procedures are formal institutional processes for hearing inmate complaints. Grievance procedures, which typically employ internal hearing boards, are the method most frequently used by inmates to enforce the protections afforded to them by law.[9] Most inmate grievances concern discipline, program assignments, medical issues, personal property, and complaints against staff members. Only about 1 in 12 inmate grievances is approved or results in some action being taken by prison administrators to correct the problem.

The creation of formal mechanisms for the hearing of inmate grievances was encouraged by the comptroller general of the United States following the riot at New York's Attica Prison. The comptroller's report, published in 1977,[10] listed a number of reasons for establishing grievance

EXHIBIT 11–2	United States Courts of Appeal
Court of Appeals	**District Courts Included in Circuit**
Federal Circuit	United States
District of Columbia Circuit	District of Columbia
First Circuit	Maine, Massachusetts, New Hampshire, Rhode Island, and Puerto Rico
Second Circuit	Connecticut, New York, and Vermont
Third Circuit	Delaware, New Jersey, Pennsylvania, and the Virgin Islands
Fourth Circuit	Maryland, North Carolina, South Carolina, Virginia, and West Virginia
Fifth Circuit	Louisiana, Mississippi, and Texas
Sixth Circuit	Kentucky, Michigan, Ohio, and Tennessee
Seventh Circuit	Illinois, Indiana, and Wisconsin
Eighth Circuit	Arkansas, Iowa, Minnesota, Missouri, Nebraska, North Dakota, and South Dakota
Ninth Circuit	Alaska, Arizona, California, Hawaii, Idaho, Montana, Nevada, Oregon, Washington, Guam, and the Northern Mariana Islands
Tenth Circuit	Colorado, Kansas, New Mexico, Oklahoma, Utah, and Wyoming
Eleventh Circuit	Alabama, Florida, and Georgia

mechanisms, including (1) promoting justice and fairness, (2) providing opportunities for inmates to voice complaints, (3) reducing the number of court cases filed by inmates, (4) assisting correctional administrators in the identification of institutional problems, and (5) reducing violence.

Today, most correctional systems use a three-step process for resolving grievances. First, a staff member or committee in each institution receives complaints, investigates them, and makes decisions. Second, if a prisoner is dissatisfied with that decision, the case may be appealed to the warden. Third, if the prisoner is still dissatisfied, the complaint may be given to the state's commissioner of corrections or the state's corrections board. This three-step procedure satisfies the requirements for U.S. Department of Justice certification.

THE PRISONERS' RIGHTS ERA (1970–1991)

Many refer to the era following *Holt* v. *Sarver* (1970) as the *prisoners' rights era*. As some have observed, "The prisoners' rights movement must be understood in the context of a 'fundamental democratization' that has transformed American society since World War II, and particularly since 1960."[11] Over the past 40 years, an increasing number of once-marginal groups, including African Americans, Hispanics, gays, and those who are economically disenfranchised and physically and mentally challenged, have acquired social recognition and legal rights that were previously unavailable to those outside of the American social mainstream. Seen in this context, the prisoners' rights era was but a natural outgrowth of an encompassing social movement that recognized the existence and potential legitimacy of a wide number of group grievances.

Eye On Corrections

Prisoner Rights in the 21st Century

An interview with Bill Collins, one of the country's most experienced correctional law attorneys

By Michelle Gaseau

I think that over the last 30 years, litigation and the threat of litigation have probably had the greatest impact on corrections as any other force, and I would say it was a positive impact. There have been some cases where the court involvement has been extraordinarily painful, but the overall impact has been one that has forced positive change.

What I see happening now, and will probably continue to happen for the next few years, is that the threat of being held accountable by a court is diminishing because of a variety of factors. Supreme Court decisions going back 15 years or more have increasingly reduced inmate substantive rights but have discouraged courts from getting involved [as well].

The passage of the Prison Litigation Reform Act has also cut down on the number of filings. It discourages involvement by the courts and reduces the attorney fees, which discourages private attorneys from getting involved.

There will be fewer cases being brought and fewer courts getting aggressively involved. The positive impact has been that corrections has made huge advances in its professionalism. Standards, policies, and procedures have been universally adopted. [Many feel] that corrections doesn't need court oversight any more and can make advances on its own.

The negative spin is that big organizations, like DOCs, and smaller ones, like jails, when you take away external oversight and accountability, tend not to continue to advance. They tend to slow down and relax their standards. I think we're more likely to see a gradual deterioration of the operation of institutions combined with the fact that legislators can trim corrections budgets and get rid of training for officers and frills for inmates and so on. In years past, if we didn't get that money for training, we could get sued. Now the legislature can say, "I don't think that's going to happen."

I'm a little concerned that we will see an eroding of some of the gains in recent years. Facilities will look better, but we may have some problems developing around operations.

In time we may hear about inmates getting the short end of the stick, and then the pendulum may swing the other way.

There will be some big cases from time to time. The thing I hope corrections agencies can continue to do is look at the human side of what they do. We have increasing amounts of technology, but I hope we don't lose sight of the human side we're dealing with.

Source: "The Future of Prisoner Rights," Michelle Gaseau, The Corrections Connection Network News (CCNN). Eye on Corrections. www.corrections.com. January 3, 2000.

Inmate lawsuits are common. However, with the advent of more advanced grievance systems, the number of lawsuits drops, because through the grievance system some disputes can be resolved. But we still have lawsuits, and some of them are pretty outlandish. Just because someone files a lawsuit doesn't mean that it ever goes to trial.

We see quite a few filings or attempts at lawsuits on our grooming policy. It's pretty strict, because of our fears of inmates being able to change their appearance and being able to hide contraband in long hair. So male inmates have to have their hair above their collar and above their ears and no facial hair except if there are medical reasons. Males may have a neatly trimmed mustache. Females can have their hair shoulder length.

We get people saying that they have taken a vow of the Nazarite and that having a razor or scissors touch their hair would violate their beliefs. So far they have yet to prevail in court, because we have a genuine security interest. And inmates are always going to challenge issues of confinement, and some of those get pretty outlandish. We had one inmate file a lawsuit because he wanted to wear women's underwear. He did not win.

A couple of years ago we instituted a ban on all tobacco products, because of the fears of secondhand smoke and the cost of our health care. There have been some filings regarding that. They think it's their freedom—pursuit of happiness—and that it's cruel and unusual punishment not to have tobacco products. Those cases haven't gone anywhere yet either.

If a lawsuit is truly frivolous, it won't get to court—the judge will stop them before they get to that. Lawsuits I see without merit? Most of them.

Generally inmates have to exhaust the grievance process before they can file—which is good. It gives them a voice—last year we had more than 49,000 grievances filed by inmates in this system. Of those, about 1,300 were found to have merit, which is a small percentage—but it's still 1,300 cases where something wasn't quite right. And if that's the case, we need to know.

Dina Tyler
Assistant to the Director
Arkansas Department of Correction

Although the phrase *prisoners' rights era* might give the impression that prisoners won virtually every case brought during that period, such is not the case. Although prisoners did win some significant court battles, it was the turnaround in legal attitudes toward prisoners that was most remarkable. As we shall see, courts went from practically ignoring prison systems to practically running those systems. It might be more appropriate to refer to the period as the "court involvement era." We will now review some of the most important cases won *and* lost by inmates, presented in order of the constitutional amendments on which they were based.

When we speak of prisoners' rights, we are generally speaking of the rights found in four of the amendments to the U.S. Constitution. Three of these—the First (free expression), Fourth (privacy), and Eighth Amendments (cruel and unusual punishment)—are part of the Bill of Rights (the first 10 amendments to the Constitution). The fourth is the Fourteenth Amendment (deprivation of life, liberty, and property). Keep in mind that what we call inmates' rights today are largely the result of federal court decisions that have interpreted constitutional guarantees and applied them to prisons and prison conditions. Often such a case sets a **precedent**, serving as an example or authority for future cases. Rulings in cases that find violations of inmates' rights must be implemented by the administrators of affected correctional systems and institutions. (See Exhibit 11–3 for more U.S. Supreme Court cases involving prisoners' rights.)

precedent
A previous judicial decision that judges should consider in deciding future cases.

First Amendment

Congress shall make no law respecting an establishment of religion, or prohibiting the free exercise thereof; or abridging the freedom of speech, or of the press; or the right of the people peaceably to assemble, and to petition the government for a redress of grievances.

First Amendment guarantees are important to members of a free society. It is no surprise, then, that some of the early prisoners' rights cases con-

EXHIBIT 11-3   Selected U.S. Supreme Court Cases Involving Prisoners' Rights

Case Name	Year	Decision
U.S. v. Georgia	2006	Under the Americans with Disabilities Act, a state may be liable for rights deprivations suffered by inmates who are disabled held in its prisons.
Johnson v. California	2005	This case invalidated the California Department of Corrections and Rehabilitation's unwritten policy of racially segregating prisoners in double cells each time they entered a new correctional facility.
Wilkinson v. Austin	2005	This case upheld an Ohio policy allowing the most dangerous offenders to be held in "supermax" cells following several levels of review prior to transfer.
Overton v. Bazzetta	2003	This case upheld the Michigan Department of Corrections' visitation regulation that denies most visits to prisoners who commit two substance abuse violations while incarcerated.
Porter v. Nussle (Eighth Amendment)	2002	The "exhaustion requirement" of the Prison Litigation Reform Act of 1995 (PLRA) applies to all inmate suits about prison life, whether they involve general circumstances or particular episodes and whether they allege excessive force or some other wrong.
Hope v. Pelzer (Eighth Amendment)	2002	The Court found an Eighth Amendment violation in the case of a prisoner who was subjected to unnecessary pain, humiliation, and risk of physical harm.
Booth v. Churner (Eighth Amendment)	2001	This case upheld a requirement under the PLRA that state inmates must "exhaust such administrative remedies as are available" before filing a suit over prison conditions.
Lewis v. Casey	1996	Earlier cases do not guarantee inmates the wherewithal to file any and every type of legal claim. All that is required is "that they be provided with the tools to attack their sentences."
Sandin v. Conner (Fourteenth Amendment)	1995	Perhaps signaling an end to the prisoners' rights era, this case rejected the argument that disciplining inmates is a deprivation of constitutional due process rights.
Wilson v. Seiter (Eighth Amendment)	1991	This case clarified the totality of conditions notion, saying that some conditions of confinement "in combination" may violate prisoners' rights when each would not do so alone.
Washington v. Harper (Eighth Amendment)	1990	An inmate who is a danger to self or others as a result of mental illness may be treated with psychoactive drugs against his or her will.
Turner v. Safley (First Amendment)	1987	A Missouri ban on correspondence between inmates was upheld as "reasonably related to legitimate penological interests."
O'Lone v. Estate of Shabazz (First Amendment)	1987	An inmate's right to practice religion was not violated by prison officials who refused to alter his work schedule so that he could attend Friday afternoon services.

cerned those rights. For example, in 1974, in *Pell* v. *Procunier*, four California prison inmates and three journalists challenged the constitutionality of regulation 415.071 of the California Department of Corrections and Rehabilitation (CDCR). That regulation specified that "press and other media interviews with specific individual inmates will not be permitted." The rule had been imposed after a violent prison episode that corrections authorities attributed at least in part to a former policy of free face-to-face prisoner-press interviews. Such interviews had apparently resulted in a relatively small number of inmates gaining disproportionate notoriety and influence with other prisoners.

The U.S. Supreme Court held that "in light of the alternative channels of communication that are open to the inmate appellees, [regulation] 415.071 does not constitute a violation of their rights of free speech." Significantly, the Court went on to say, "A prison inmate retains those

EXHIBIT 11–3		Selected U.S. Supreme Court Cases Involving Prisoners' Rights (*continued*)
Case Name	**Year**	**Decision**
Whitley v. *Albers* (Eighth Amendment)	1986	The shooting and wounding of an inmate was not a violation of that inmate's rights, since "the shooting was part and parcel of a good-faith effort to restore prison security."
Ponte v. *Real*	1985	Inmates have certain rights in disciplinary hearings.
Hudson v. *Palmer* (Fourth Amendment)	1984	A prisoner has no reasonable expectation of privacy in his prison cell that entitles him to protections against "unreasonable searches."
Block v. *Rutherford* (First Amendment)	1984	State regulations may prohibit inmate union meetings and use of mail to deliver union information within the prison. Prisoners do not have a right to be present during searches of cells.
Rhodes v. *Chapman* (Eighth Amendment)	1981	Double-celling of inmates is not cruel and unusual punishment unless it involves the wanton and unnecessary infliction of pain or conditions grossly disproportionate to the severity of the crime committed.
Ruiz v. *Estelle* (Eighth Amendment)	1980	The Court found unconstitutional conditions in the Texas prison system—including overcrowding, understaffing, brutality, and substandard medical care.
Cooper v. *Morin*	1980	Neither inconvenience nor cost is an acceptable excuse for treating female inmates differently from male inmates.
Jones v. *North Carolina Prisoners' Labor Union, Inc.* (First Amendment)	1977	Inmates have no inherent right to publish newspapers or newsletters for use by other inmates.
Bounds v. *Smith*	1977	This case resulted in the creation of law libraries in many prisons.
Estelle v. *Gamble* (Eighth Amendment)	1976	Prison officials have a duty to provide proper inmate medical care.
Wolff v. *McDonnell* (Fourteenth Amendment)	1974	Sanctions cannot be levied against inmates without appropriate due process.
Procunier v. *Martinez* (First Amendment)	1974	Censorship of inmate mail is acceptable only when necessary to protect legitimate governmental interests.
Pell v. *Procunier* (First Amendment)	1974	Inmates retain First Amendment rights that are not inconsistent with their status as prisoners or with the legitimate penological objectives of the corrections system.
Cruz v. *Beto* (First Amendment)	1972	Inmates have to be given a "reasonable opportunity" to pursue their religious faiths. Also, visits can be banned if such visits constitute threats to security.
Johnson v. *Avery*	1968	Inmates have a right to consult "jailhouse lawyers" when trained legal assistance is not available.
Monroe v. *Pape*	1961	Individuals deprived of their rights by state officers acting under color of state law have a right to bring action in federal court.

first amendment rights that are not inconsistent with his status as prisoner or with the *legitimate penological objectives* of the corrections system" (emphasis added). **Legitimate penological objectives** are the permissible aims of a correctional institution. They include the realistic concerns that correctional officers and administrators have for the integrity and security of the correctional institution and the safety of staff and inmates. The *Pell* ruling established a **balancing test** that the Supreme Court would continue to use, weighing the rights claimed by inmates against the legitimate needs of prisons.

Freedom of Speech and Expression Visits to inmates by friends and loved ones are forms of expression. But prison visits are not an absolute right. In *Cruz* v. *Beto* (1972), the Supreme Court ruled that all visits

legitimate penological objectives
The realistic concerns that correctional officers and administrators have for the integrity and security of the correctional institution and the safety of staff and inmates.

balancing test
A method the U.S. Supreme Court uses to decide prisoners' rights cases, weighing the rights claimed by inmates against the legitimate needs of prisons.

Tammy Waldrop
Inspector of Correctional Facilities   Palm Beach County, Florida

Tammy Waldrop is an inspector with the Palm Beach County (Florida) Sheriff's Office, assigned to Corrections Administration. She has been in the position for almost one year. Quarterly, Waldrop inspects all four correctional facilities in Palm Beach County to verify that each one complies with agency, local, state, and American Correctional Association standards. She investigates staff and inmate grievances and works with the Legal Advisors' office to resolve conflicts.

Waldrop received her bachelor's degree in criminal justice from Florida Atlantic University in Boca Raton. She remembers that the undergraduate course that influenced her the most was a sociology course titled "Social Conflict." She says, "This course changed my perspective on life and my views on crime. It was the best preparation for my current job. It helped me understand the importance of changing conflict into occasions for problem solving."

In the future, Waldrop would like to build on her present career, attend law school, concentrate on corrections law, and work in the Legal Advisors' office.

In corrections, the words care, custody, *and* control *are repeatedly stated as your primary tasks. But remember three additional words in your interactions with inmates:* fair, firm, *and* consistent. *If you build your officer reputation on this foundation, you will not have any problems. Treat everyone with respect and the respect will come back to you. And never, never lie to an inmate.*

---

can be banned if they threaten security. Although *Cruz* involved short-term confinement facilities, the ruling has also been applied to prisons.

Another form of expression is correspondence. As a result of various court cases, prison officials can (and generally do) impose restrictions on inmate mail. Inmates receive mail, not directly from the hands of postal carriers, but from correctional officers. They place their outgoing mail, not in U.S. Postal Service mailboxes, but in containers provided by the correctional institution.

Corrections officials often read inmate mail—both incoming and outgoing—in an effort to uncover escape plans. Reading inmate mail, however, is different from censoring it. In 1974, in *Procunier* v. *Martinez*, the U.S. Supreme Court held that the censoring of inmate mail is acceptable only when necessary to protect legitimate government interests. The case turned upon First Amendment guarantees of free speech.

Under a 1979 federal appeals court decision, in *McNamara* v. *Moody*, prison officials may not prohibit inmates from writing vulgar letters or those that make disparaging remarks about the prison staff. Similarly, while correctional administrators have a legitimate interest in curbing inmates' deviant sexual behavior, courts have held that viewing nudity is not deviant sexual behavior. Hence, prison officials may not ban mailed nude pictures of inmates' wives or girlfriends (*Peppering* v. *Crist*, 1981), although restrictions against posting them on cell walls have generally been upheld. Similarly, officials may not prevent inmates from receiving, by mail direct from publishers, publications depicting nudity unless those publications depict deviant sexual behavior (*Mallery* v. *Lewis*, 1983).

In 1989, in the case of *Thornburgh* v. *Abbott*, in an effort to clear up questions raised by lower court rulings concerning mailed publications, the U.S. Supreme Court ruled as follows:

> Publications which may be rejected by a warden include but are not limited to publications which meet one of the following criteria: (1) it depicts or describes procedures for the construction or use of weapons, ammunition, bombs, or incendiary devices; (2) it depicts, encourages or describes methods of escape from correctional facilities or contains blueprints, drawings, or similar descriptions of Bureau of Prisons institutions; (3) it depicts or describes procedures for the brewing of alcoholic beverages or the manufacture of drugs; (4) it is written in code; (5) it depicts, describes, or encourages activities which may lead to the use of physical violence or group disruption; (6) it encourages or instructs in the commission of criminal activities; (7) it is sexually explicit material which by its nature or content poses a threat to the security, good order, or discipline of the institution or facilitates criminal activity.

Unless at least one of these standards is met, restrictions on the receipt of published materials—especially magazines and newspapers that do not threaten prison security—are generally not allowed. In the 2006 U.S. Supreme Court case of *Beard* v. *Banks*, however, the justices held that Pennsylvania prison officials could legitimately prohibit the state's most violent inmates from having access to newspapers, magazines, and photographs. Prison officials had argued that the policy helped motivate better behavior on the part of particularly difficult prisoners. The Court agreed, noting that "prison officials have imposed the deprivation only upon those with serious prison-behavior problems; and those officials, relying on their professional judgment, reached an experience-based conclusion that the policies help to further legitimate prison objectives."

Similarly, in the case of *Turner* v. *Safley* (1987), the Supreme Court upheld a Missouri ban on correspondence among inmates. Such a regulation is valid, the Court said, if it is "reasonably related to legitimate penological interests." *Turner* established that officials had to show only that a regulation was reasonably *related* to a legitimate penological interest. No clear-cut damage to legitimate penological interests had to be shown.

The U.S. Supreme Court sided with corrections officials in its 1977 decision in *Jones* v. *North Carolina Prisoners' Labor Union, Inc.* In *Jones*, the Court upheld regulations established by the North Carolina Department of Correction that prohibited prisoners from soliciting other inmates to join the union and barred union meetings and bulk mailings concerning the union from outside sources. Citing *Pell* v. *Procunier*, the Court went on to say, "The prohibition on inmate-to-inmate solicitation does not unduly abridge inmates' free speech rights. If the prison officials are otherwise entitled to control organized union activity within the confines of a prison, the solicitation ban is not impermissible under the

Inmate rights are not absolute, but are limited by legitimate penological objectives. What does the phrase "legitimate penological objectives" mean?

438   PART 4   The Prison World

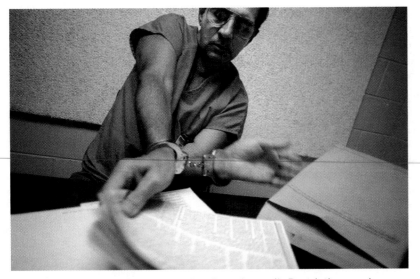

Inmates have limited rights to send and receive mail. Restrictions on inmates' mail focus on maintaining institutional security. Judicial interpretations of which constitutional amendment have led to inmates' rights to send and receive mail?

First Amendment, for such a prohibition is both reasonable and necessary."

Freedom of Religion Lawsuits involving religious practices in prison have been numerous for at least 40 years. In 1962, for example, in *Fulwood* v. *Clemmer*, the court of appeals for the District of Columbia ruled that the Black Muslim faith must be recognized as a religion and held that officials may not restrict members of that faith from holding services.

In 1970, the U.S. Supreme Court refused to hear an appeal from inmate Jack Gittlemacker, who wanted the state of Pennsylvania to provide him with a clergyman of his faith. The Court held that although states must give inmates the opportunity to practice their religions, they are not required to provide clergy for that purpose.

In *Cruz* v. *Beto* (mentioned earlier), the Supreme Court also decided that inmates had to be given a "reasonable opportunity" to pursue their religious faiths. Later federal court decisions expanded this decision, requiring officials to provide such a "reasonable opportunity" even to inmates whose religious faiths were not traditional.

In 1975, the U.S. Court of Appeals for the Second Circuit ruled in *Kahane* v. *Carlson* that an Orthodox Jewish inmate has the right to a kosher diet unless the government can show good cause for not providing it. Similarly, the courts have held that "Muslims' request for one full-course pork-free meal once a day and coffee three times daily is essentially a plea for a modest degree of official deference to their religious obligations" (*Barnett* v. *Rodgers*, 1969).

On the other hand, courts have determined that some inmate religious demands need not be met. In the 1986 Fifth Circuit Court of Appeals case of *Udey* v. *Kastner*, for example, Muslim prisoners had requested raw milk, distilled water, and organic fruits, juices, vegetables, and meats. The special diet was so costly that a federal court allowed the prison to deny the inmates' request.

In 1986, a federal court of appeals considered the appeal of Herbert Dettmer, an inmate at Powhatan Correctional Center in Virginia. Beginning in 1982, Dettmer had studied witchcraft through a correspondence course provided by the Church of Wicca. Within a year, he was holding private ceremonies for meditation as described in the course. Dettmer decided that he needed certain items to aid him in these ceremonies. Those items included a white robe with a hood, sea salt or sulfur to draw a protective circle on the floor around him, and candles and incense to focus his thoughts. Late in 1983, Dettmer requested permission to order the items he felt he needed for meditating. The prison property officer refused permission because the prison rules did not list the items as "authorized personal property." The Supreme Court concluded that "the security officer's concern about inmates' unsupervised possession of candles, salt, and incense is reasonable."

In 2000, the Religious Land Use and Institutionalized Persons Act (RLUIPA) became law. RLUIPA says, "No government shall impose a substantial burden on the religious exercise of a person residing in or confined to an institution even if the burden results from a rule of general applicability, unless the government demonstrates that imposition of the burden on that person (1) is in furtherance of a compelling governmental interest; and (2) is the least restrictive means of furthering that compelling governmental interest." Because RLUIPA is a federal law, it is especially relevant to prison programs and activities that are at least partially supported with federal monies. In 2005, in the case of *Benning* v. *State*, the Eleventh Circuit Court of Appeals found in favor of a Georgia state prison inmate who claimed that RLUIPA supported his right as a "Torah observant Jew" to eat only kosher food and wear a yarmulke (or skullcap) at all times. Also in 2005, in the case of *Cutter* v. *Wilkinson*, the U.S. Supreme Court ruled in favor of past and present Ohio inmates who claimed that the state's correctional system failed to accommodate their non-mainstream religious practices.

Fourth Amendment

> The right of the people to be secure in their persons, houses, papers, and effects, against unreasonable searches and seizures, shall not be violated, and no Warrants shall issue, but upon probable cause, supported by Oath or affirmation, and particularly describing the place to be searched, and the persons or things to be seized.

The right to privacy is at the heart of the Fourth Amendment. Clearly, unreasonable searches without warrants are unconstitutional. Does this mean that an inmate has a right to privacy in his or her cell? When is it reasonable to search a cell without a warrant? Some suggest that the needs of institutional security prohibit privacy for inmates. Others argue that a prison cell is the equivalent of an inmate's house. Over the years, the courts have been fairly consistent in deciding that the privacy rights implied in this amendment must be greatly reduced in prisons to maintain institutional security.

Correctional officers preparing for a cell search at Rikers Island Jail in New York City. One of the officers is carrying an electric stun shield for protection from aggressive inmates. Prisoners do not retain the right to privacy in their cells or possessions because institutional interests of safety and security supersede constitutional guarantees of privacy. Under which amendment to the Constitution falls the right to be free from unreasonable searches and seizures?

THE OFFENDER SPEAKS

My name is Brian Pierce. I'm an ex-con.

Let me tell you about myself. I grew up in a small southern Minnesota river town. In an effort to bring our family closer together, my parents purchased a small family-run tourist business they hoped we could eventually run as a family. My parents have always been hard workers and Christians. I am not sure what got me started really, but by the time I was 14 I was using drugs heavily and starting to spin the revolving door of Minnesota's illustrious correctional system.

First, I was court-ordered into a drug treatment center called the Cannon Valley Center in Cannon Falls, Minnesota. From there I went to a halfway house in Winona named the East House. When the county ran out of funding, they told me I could leave, despite the fact that the counselors did not think I was ready. Not long after getting home I was on the way to the Minnesota Correctional Facility at Red Wing, the end of the line for juveniles in Minnesota.

When I turned 18, I was moving too fast to slow down and was soon on my way to the Minnesota Correctional Facility at St. Cloud. I was sentenced to 38 months for third-degree burglary and received two shorter sentences that ran concurrently for theft charges. Under Minnesota's guidelines, I had to serve two-thirds of that sentence inside and the remaining one-third on parole.

St. Cloud is relatively old and made predominately out of dark gray granite. The wall is solid granite and somewhere around 20 feet high and several feet thick. It encompasses over 50 acres, including several cell houses, factories, maintenance facilities, and a yard for recreation. There are armed guard towers spaced evenly around the top of the wall.

Like most of my friends there, I got out and quickly got back into the same old routine. An Olmstead County judge gave me the option of pleading guilty to possession of a controlled substance but getting a stay of adjudication pursuant to Minnesota Statute Section 152.18 and being sentenced to treatment rather than a prison term. If I completed the recommended treatment, follow-up, and aftercare, the charge would not appear on my record. Although it sounded good, I had already been in prison once and thought I would screw it up in the treatment program and end up doing the time anyway. I asked to have my sentence executed.

A few months after being released from St. Cloud for the second time in four years, I jumped my parole and began wandering around the country with a group of misfits selling Dunn-EZ, a homemade chemical cleaner, to small businesses. Eventually, we ended up in Atlanta, Georgia, where I met my wife. She was a single mother with two young boys and was as wild as I was. Together, my wife, the boys, and I traveled the country treading water for the next several months until we found ourselves in the Lowndes County, Georgia, jail for credit card fraud. It was the most miserable time I have ever had in jail—first, because the woman I loved was in with me and, second, because the conditions were unbelievable. I slept on the floor of a very small one-man cell with two other guys. At night the guards would come by and for a Little Debbie snack or two, they would sell you a full bottle of Nyquil. One of my cell mates would drink it and get high.

With the help of my parents, my new wife and I rode the Greyhound back to Minnesota. I had to finish up about 30 days' worth of my last Minnesota sentence so that my parole would expire. Because the time left on my sentence was so short, Minnesota refused to extradite me from Georgia for the parole violation (leaving the state) but was ready and willing to incarcerate me for every day I had coming if I returned to Minnesota.

Once released and working odd jobs, I enrolled in the University of Minnesota, Duluth. I received my B.A. *magna cum laude* in criminology, with a minor in psychology, almost four years later. Graduating from college felt so unbelievably good to me. I was energized and committed to going on to law school. I applied to the University of Minnesota's law school, where I received my Juris Doctorate *cum laude,* May 10, 1997. Midway through my first year I hooked up with a law professor interested in computers, as I was. Together we created the Human Rights Library on the World Wide Web.

I completed a one-year judicial clerkship with a judge on the Court of Appeals, and I am currently clerking for my second year with the Chief Judge of the Court of Appeals. In addition, I develop Web sites for law firms and nonprofit human rights organizations, and I am writing a book. I also do public speaking about drugs, crime, corrections, and rehabilitation.

Brian Pierce

In *United States* v. *Hitchcock* (1972), an inmate claimed that his Fourth Amendment rights had been violated by a warrantless search and seizure of documents in his prison cell. Previously, courts had generally held that "constitutionally protected" places—such as homes, motel rooms, safe-deposit boxes, and certain places of business—could not be searched without a warrant. In *Hitchcock*, however, the U.S. Court of Appeals for the Ninth Circuit created a new standard: "first, that a person have exhibited an actual (subjective) expectation of privacy and second, that the expectation be one that society is prepared to recognize as reasonable." The court concluded that, although Hitchcock plainly expected to keep his documents private, his expectation was not reasonable. In the words of the court,

> It is obvious that a jail shares none of the attributes of privacy of a home, an automobile, an office, or a hotel room. In prison, official surveillance has traditionally been the order of the day. . . . [Hence], we do not feel that it is reasonable for a prisoner to consider his cell private.

In *Hudson* v. *Palmer* (1984), a Virginia inmate claimed a correctional officer had unreasonably destroyed some of his permitted personal property during a search of his cell. The inmate also claimed that under the Fourth Amendment, the cell search was illegal. Echoing *Hitchcock*, the U.S. Supreme Court ruled that "a prisoner has no reasonable expectation of privacy in his prison cell entitling him to the protection of the Fourth Amendment against unreasonable searches." Similarly, in *Block* v. *Rutherford* (1984), the Court ruled that prisoners do not have the right to be present during searches of their cells.

In 1985, the Ninth Circuit Court of Appeals decided a case involving inmates at San Quentin State Prison (*Grummett* v. *Rushen*). The inmates had brought a class action lawsuit against prison administrators, objecting to the policy of allowing female correctional officers to view nude or partly clothed male inmates. Women officers, complained the inmates, could see male inmates while they were dressing, showering, being strip-searched, or using toilet facilities. Such viewing, said the inmates, violated privacy rights guaranteed by the U.S. Constitution.

At the time of the suit, approximately 113 of the 720 correctional officers at San Quentin were female. Both female and male correctional officers were assigned to patrol the cell block tiers and gun rails. Both were also assigned to supervise showering from the tiers and from the gun rails, but only male officers were permitted to accompany inmates to the shower cells and lock them inside to disrobe and shower. Female officers were allowed to conduct pat-down searches that included the groin area.

The court found that prison officials had "struck an acceptable balance among the inmates' privacy interests, the institution's security requirements, and the female guards' employment rights." According to the court,

> The female guards are restricted in their contact with the inmates, and the record clearly demonstrates that at all times they have conducted themselves in a professional manner, and have treated the inmates with respect and dignity. . . . Routine pat-down searches, which include the groin area, and which are otherwise justified by security needs, do not violate the Fourteenth Amendment because a correctional officer of the opposite gender conducts such a search.

Eighth Amendment

Excessive bail shall not be required, nor excessive fines imposed, nor cruel and unusual punishments inflicted.

Many prisoners' rights cases turn upon the issue of **cruel and unusual punishment.** Defining such punishment is not easy. A working definition, however, might be "punishments that are grossly disproportionate to the offense as well as those that transgress today's broad and idealistic

cruel and unusual punishment
A penalty that is grossly disproportionate to the offense or that violates today's broad and idealistic concepts of dignity, civilized standards, humanity, and decency (*Estelle* v. *Gamble,* 1976, and *Hutto* v. *Finney,* 1978). In the area of capital punishment, cruel and unusual punishments are those that involve torture, a lingering death, or unnecessary pain.

consent decree

A written compact, sanctioned by a court, between parties in a civil case, specifying how disagreements between them are to be resolved.

deliberate indifference

Intentional and willful indifference. Within the field of correctional practice, the term refers to calculated inattention to unconstitutional conditions of confinement.

concepts of dignity, civilized standards, humanity, and decency."[12] Cases concerning constitutional prohibition of cruel and unusual punishment have centered on prisoners' need for decent conditions of confinement. In one case, *Ruiz* v. *Estelle* (1980), the conditions of confinement in the Texas prison system were found unconstitutional, and a **consent decree** was imposed on the system. Inmate rights cases involving the Eighth Amendment cover areas as diverse as medical care, prison conditions, physical insecurity, psychological stress, and capital punishment.

Medical Care   In 2006, James A. Gondles Jr., executive director of the ACA, told a national audience that "inmates are the only group of Americans with the constitutional right to adequate health care, while more than 45 million Americans have no health insurance."[13] The history of inmates' rights in the health care area can be traced to the 1970 case of *Holt* v. *Sarver* in which a federal district court declared the entire Arkansas prison system inhumane and found that it was in violation of the Constitution's Eighth Amendment's ban on cruel and unusual punishment.

In a related case, medical personnel in state prisons had given inmates injections of apomorphine without their consent, in a program of "aversive stimuli." The drug caused vomiting, which lasted from 15 minutes to an hour. The state justified it as "Pavlovian conditioning." The federal courts, however, soon prohibited the practice (*Knecht* v. *Gillman*, 1973).

Another decision, that of *Estelle* v. *Gamble* (1976), spelled out the duty of prison officials to provide inmates with medical care. The Court held that prison officials could not lawfully demonstrate **deliberate indifference** to the medical needs of prisoners. In the words of the court, "Deliberate indifference to serious medical needs of prisoners constitutes the 'unnecessary and wanton infliction of pain' proscribed by the Eighth Amendment." A serious medical condition is one that "causes pain, discomfort, or threat to good health" (*Rufo* v. *Inmates of Suffolk County Jail*, 1992). The mental health needs of prisoners are governed by the same constitutional standard of deliberate indifference as those described in court opinions dealing with the physical health of inmates.[14]

A Newark, NJ, prison inmate takes tuberculosis medication as a nurse watches. A number of Eighth Amendment cases have established that prison officials have a duty to provide adequate medical care to inmates in their charge. How does the concept of "deliberate indifference" relate to that requirement?

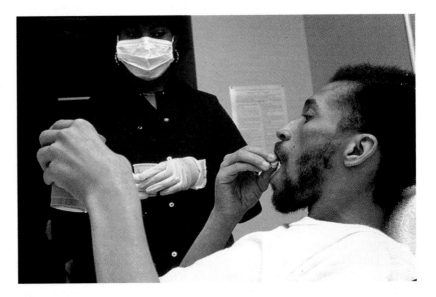

Prison Conditions The 1976 federal court case of *Pugh* v. *Locke* introduced the **totality of conditions** standard. That standard, said the court, is to be used in evaluating whether prison conditions are cruel and unusual. The *Pugh* court held that "prison conditions [in Alabama] are so debilitating that they necessarily deprive inmates of any opportunity to rehabilitate themselves or even maintain skills already possessed." The totality-of-conditions approach was also applied in a 1977 federal case, *Battle* v. *Anderson*, in which officials in overcrowded Oklahoma prisons had forced inmates to sleep in garages, barbershops, libraries, and stairwells. Oklahoma prison administrators were found to be in violation of the cruel and unusual punishment clause of the U.S. Constitution.

The U.S. Supreme Court ruled on the use of solitary confinement in *Hutto* v. *Finney* (1978). The Court held that confinement in Arkansas's segregation (solitary confinement) cells for more than 30 days was cruel and unusual punishment. It then went on to exhort lower courts to consider the totality of the conditions of confinement in future Eighth Amendment cases. Where appropriate, it said, a court should specify the changes needed to remedy the constitutional violation.

In the 1991 case of *Wilson* v. *Seiter*, the U.S. Supreme Court clarified the totality-of-conditions standard. The Court noted,

> Some conditions of confinement may establish an Eighth Amendment violation "in combination" when each would not do so alone, but only when they have a mutually enforcing effect that produces the deprivation of a single, identifiable human need such as food, warm th, or exercise—for example, a low cell temperature at night combined with a failure to issue blankets. . . . To say that some prison conditions may interact in this fashion is a far cry from saying that all prison conditions are a seamless web for Eighth Amendment purposes. Nothing so [shapeless] as "overall conditions" can rise to the level of cruel and unusual punishment when no specific deprivation of a single human need exists.

Several rulings have addressed inmate claims that overcrowding was cruel and unusual punishment. A U.S. Supreme Court case, *Rhodes* v. *Chapman* (1981), decided the issue of double-celling (housing two inmates in a cell designed for one) in long-term correctional facilities. In response to rising prison populations, Ohio authorities had begun double-celling. There was no evidence that Ohio authorities had wantonly inflicted pain through the practice, and double-celling had not resulted in food deprivation, a lower quality of medical care, or a decrease in sanitation standards. For those reasons, the Court denied the inmates' claims.

In *Rhodes*, the Court also emphasized that the Eighth Amendment prohibition of cruel and unusual punishment is a fluid concept that "must draw its meaning from the evolving standards of decency that mark the progress of a maturing society." In other words, what is considered cruel and unusual changes as society evolves.

In 1982, the U.S. Court of Appeals for the Seventh Circuit ruled, in *Smith* v. *Fairman*, that double-celling in a short-term facility (a jail) was not cruel and unusual punishment. The court said that government officials did not intend to punish inmates by double-celling. The double-celling was innocent overcrowding required by circumstances.

totality of conditions

A standard to be used in evaluating whether prison conditions are cruel and unusual.

The Eighth Amendment's prohibition of cruel and unusual punishment has been tied to prisoners' need for decent conditions of confinement. In determining if conditions such as overcrowding and inadequate diet constitute a denial of such protection, courts have used the concept of totality of conditions. What is meant by the *totality of conditions*?

Many conditions of confinement that violate prisoners' Eighth Amendment rights can be remedied by changes in prison rules, by special training for correctional personnel, or by educational programs for prisoners. The remedies can be implemented through everyday administrative policies in the prison, once prisoners' court petitions have brought violations to light. Relief of overcrowding, however, is not always within the power of prison administrators. Prison officials have little control over the sizes of their prisons or the numbers of inmates the courts assign to them. New prison facilities are expensive and take time to build.

Fourteenth Amendment

No State shall make or enforce any law which shall abridge the privileges or immunities of citizens of the United States; nor shall any State deprive any person of life, liberty, or property, without due process of law; nor deny to any person within its jurisdiction the equal protection of the laws.

When the Constitution and the Bill of Rights became law, the people of many states thought the document applied only to federal courts and to federal law. This attitude prevailed at least until the end of the Civil War. After the war, to clarify the status of the newly freed slaves and to apply the Bill of Rights to state actions, the Fourteenth Amendment was passed. The just-quoted portion of the Fourteenth Amendment is relevant to our discussion.

Most cases involving prisoners' rights and the Fourteenth Amendment deal with issues of **due process.** Due process requires that laws and legal procedures be reasonable and that they be applied fairly and equally. The right to due process is a right to be fairly heard before being deprived of life or liberty.

By 1987, long after the hands-off doctrine had eroded, U.S. Supreme Court justice Sandra Day O'Connor summarized the thrust of earlier opinions, holding that "prison walls do not form a barrier separating prison inmates from the protections of the Constitution" (*Turner* v. *Safley*). Without access to the courts, inmates have no due process opportunities.

To bring their cases to court, however, prisoners need access to legal materials, and many of them need legal assistance. What if one inmate understands how to file cases with the court, but a second inmate does not? Does the second inmate have a right to enlist the aid of the first? "Yes," said the U.S. Supreme Court in *Johnson* v. *Avery* (1968). Inmates have a right to consult "jailhouse lawyers" (other inmates knowledgeable in the law) when trained legal advisers are not available.

The case of *Wolff* v. *McDonnell* (1974) expanded the concept of due process by applying it to disciplinary actions within prisons. Prior to *Wolff*, prison administrators had the discretion to discipline inmates who broke prison rules. Disciplinary procedures were often tied to vague or nonexistent rules of conduct and were exercised without challenge. A prisoner might be assigned to solitary confinement or might have goodtime credits reduced because of misconduct. Because the prisoner was physically confined and lacked outside communication, there was no opportunity for the prisoner to challenge the charge. The *Wolff* Court concluded that sanctions (disciplinary actions) could not be levied against inmates without appropriate due process, saying,

[The state of Nebraska] asserts that the procedure for disciplining prison inmates for serious misconduct is a matter of policy raising no constitutional issue. If the position implies that prisoners in state institutions are wholly

due process

A right guaranteed by the Fifth, Sixth, and Fourteenth Amendments to the U.S. Constitution and generally understood, in legal contexts, to mean the expected course of legal proceedings according to the rules and forms established for the protection of persons' rights.

without the protection of the Constitution and the Due Process Clause, it is plainly untenable. Lawful imprisonment necessarily makes unavailable many rights and privileges of the ordinary citizen, a retraction justified by the consideration underlying our penal system. . . . But though his rights may be diminished by the needs and exigencies of the institutional environment, a prisoner is not wholly stripped of constitutional protections when he is imprisoned for a crime.

The *Wolff* Court imposed minimal due process requirements on prison disciplinary proceedings that could lead to solitary confinement or reduction of good-time credits. The requirements included (1) advance notice by means of a written statement of the claimed violation, (2) a written statement by an impartial fact finder of the evidence relied on and the reasons for imposing punishment, and (3) an opportunity to testify and call witnesses unless the fact finder concluded such proceedings would undermine institutional security.

In 1976, inmates lost three due process appeals. First, in *Baxter* v. *Palmigiano*, the Supreme Court decided that due process for an inmate in a disciplinary hearing does not include a right to counsel, even when the consequences are potentially "serious." In a second opinion issued that year (*Meacham* v. *Fano*), the Court held that prisoners have no right to be in any particular prison and therefore have no due process protections before being transferred from one prison to another. A third case (*Stone* v. *Powell*) denied prisoners the right in most instances to seek federal review of state court Fourth Amendment search-and-seizure decisions.

Inmates' right to legal materials was formally recognized in 1977, in the U.S. Supreme Court decision in *Bounds* v. *Smith*. In *Bounds* the Court held,

The fundamental constitutional right of access to the courts requires prison authorities to assist inmates in the preparation and filing of meaningful legal papers by providing prisoners with adequate law libraries or adequate assistance from persons trained in the law.

As a result of the *Bounds* decision, law libraries were created in prisons across the nation.

As we saw in Chapter 9, one challenge facing corrections personnel is to find safe, humane ways to manage inmate populations. Inmates often have grievances regarding conditions of confinement or disciplinary actions for infractions. Those grievances must be dealt with to maintain the safety and security of the institution. The Supreme Court's decision in *Jones* v. *North Carolina Prisoners' Labor Union, Inc.* (1977) required prisons to establish and maintain formal opportunities for the airing of inmate grievances. *Ponte* v. *Real* (1985) required prison officials to explain to inmates why their requests to have witnesses appear on their behalf at disciplinary hearings were denied.

The due process clause protects against unlawful deprivation of life or liberty. When a prisoner sued for damages for injuries (*Daniels* v. *Williams*, 1986), the Supreme Court ruled that prisoners could sue for damages in federal court only if officials had inflicted injury intentionally. According to the Court, "The due process clause is simply not implicated by a negligent act of an official causing unintended loss or injury to life, liberty, or property."

A 2001 ruling by a panel of federal judges in the case of *Gerber* v. *Hickman* addressed a unique claim of unlawful deprivation of life. Gerber wanted to impregnate his wife. He was, however, serving a life sentence

Inmates must be allowed access to the courts and assistance in preparing their cases. To meet that requirement, most states stock law libraries in each correctional institution. Under which clause of the Fourteenth Amendment does inmates' access to the courts fall?

in a California Department of Corrections and Rehabilitation (CDCR) prison, and CDCR regulations prohibit conjugal visits for life-term prisoners. Consequently, the Gerbers could not employ the usual method for creating the child they desired.

Undeterred, Gerber sought permission to artificially inseminate his wife. CDCR officials denied his request, citing the facts that (1) impregnating his wife was not medically necessary for Gerber's physical wellbeing and (2) Gerber had failed to show that denial of the request would violate his constitutional rights.

In a civil suit, however, Gerber alleged that the CDCR regulation violated the due process clause by denying him his constitutional right to procreate. On a defendant's motion, the suit was dismissed in federal district court. Gerber appealed to the U.S. Court of Appeals for the Ninth Circuit where a three-judge panel initially held "that the right to procreate survives incarceration." The panel reversed the district court's dismissal and reinstated Gerber's claim, mandating further review of the case. Upon review, however, the full Ninth Circuit Court of Appeals ruled that prison inmates do not have a constitutional right to fatherhood. The appellate court's majority opinion cited the 1984 U.S. Supreme Court case of *Hudson* v. *Palmer* (mentioned earlier in this chapter), which held that "while persons imprisoned . . . enjoy many protections of the Constitution, it is also clear that imprisonment carries with it the . . . loss of many significant rights."

As we have seen, federal and state inmates can file suits in federal court alleging civil rights violations by corrections officials. In 1988, the U.S. Supreme Court (in *West* v. *Atkins*) decided that private citizens who contracted to do work for prisons could be sued for civil rights violations against inmates. The Court found that such contractors were acting "under color of state law," as required by Section 1983 of the Civil Rights Act of 1871.

As a result of Supreme Court decisions, most prisons now have rules that provide for necessary due process when prisoners appear before disciplinary committees. The makeup of disciplinary committees varies among institutions. The committees may include both inmates and free citizens.

End of the Prisoners' Rights Era

By the late 1980s, the prisoners' rights era was drawing to a close. Following a change in the composition of the Supreme Court, the justices sitting on the Court had become less sympathetic to prisoners' civil rights claims. As discussed earlier, the 1986 case of *Daniels* v. *Williams* helped establish the notion that due process requirements were intended to prevent abuses of power by correctional officials, not to protect against mere carelessness. Further, judicial and legislative officials began to realize that inmates frequently abused what had previously been seen as their right of access to the courts. As state costs of defending against **frivolous lawsuits** by inmates began to grow, federal courts began to take a new look at prisoners' rights.

Examples of abuse of the court system by prison inmates abound. One inmate sued the state of Florida because he got only one bread roll with dinner. He sued two more times because he did not get a salad with lunch and because prison-provided TV dinners did not come with drinks. He sued yet again because his cell was not equipped with a television. Another inmate claimed prison officials were denying him freedom of religion. His religion, he said, required him to attend prison chapel services in the nude. Still another inmate, afraid that he could get pregnant through homosexual relations, sued because prison officials would not give him birth control pills.

As early as 1977, the U.S. Supreme Court refused to hear an appeal from Henry William Theriault, founder of the Church of the New Song (or CONS).[15] Theriault, an inmate at the federal penitentiary in Atlanta, had a mail-order divinity degree. Members of CONS celebrated communion every Friday night. They claimed that prison officials must supply them with steak and Harvey's Bristol Cream sherry for the practice. Although "Bishop Theriault" admitted that he had originally created CONS to mock other religions, he claimed that he became a serious believer as the religion developed and acquired more followers. The U.S. Supreme Court dismissed that argument and held that the First Amendment does not protect so-called religions that are obvious shams.

The Cases   One of the important cases setting the stage for a review of prisoners' claimed rights was that of *Turner* v. *Safley*, decided in 1987. In *Turner*, the U.S. Supreme Court established a four-pronged test for determining the reasonableness of prison regulations. In order for a prison regulation to be acceptable, said the Court, there must first be a "valid, rational connection" between the prison regulation and the "legitimate governmental interest" offered to justify it. A second factor relevant in determining the reasonableness of a prison restriction, especially one that limits otherwise established rights, is whether alternative means of exercising that right remain available to prison inmates. If they do, then the restriction is more acceptable. A third consideration is the impact that accommodating an asserted constitutional right would have on officers and other inmates and on the allocation of scarce prison resources. If accommodation makes the job of correctional officers more dangerous or if it is unduly expensive, then it need not be granted. Finally, the fourth prong holds that prisoners have no recourse if there are no readily available al-

frivolous lawsuits
Lawsuits with no foundation in fact. They are generally brought for publicity, political, or other reasons not related to law.

ternatives that might permit exercise of claimed rights without compromising penological goals. In other words, if inmates or their attorneys cannot suggest a workable alternative to meet an asserted right, then accommodations need not be made.

In *Wilson* v. *Seiter* (1991), the U.S. Supreme Court sided with prison officials in a way uncharacteristic of the previous two decades. In *Wilson*, the Court found that overcrowding, excessive noise, insufficient locker space, and similar conditions did not violate the Constitution if the intent of prison officials was not malicious. The Court ruled that the actions of officials did not meet the "deliberate indifference" standard defined in *Estelle* v. *Gamble* (1976).

After *Wilson*, inmates won very few new cases. The courts either reversed themselves or tightened the conditions under which inmates could win favorable decisions. Decisions supporting freedom of religion had been among the earliest and most complete victories during the prisoners' rights era. Even in that area, however, things began to change. The courts held that crucifixes and rosaries could legally be denied to inmates because of their possible use as weapons (*Mark* v. *Nix*, 1993, and *Escobar* v. *Landwehr*, 1993). Although some jurisdictions had previously allowed certain Native American religious items within prisons (*Sample* v. *Borg*, 1987), the courts now ruled that prohibiting ceremonial pipes, medicine bags, and eagle claws did *not* violate the First Amendment rights of Native American inmates (*Bettis* v. *Delo*, 1994).

In the 1992 Supreme Court case of *Hudson* v. *McMillan*, the "deliberate indifference" standard was interpreted as requiring both actual knowledge *and* disregard of the risk of harm to inmates or others. This tighter definition allowed federal courts to side more easily with state prison officials in cases in which prisoners claimed there was deliberate indifference. In 1994, in the case of *Farmer* v. *Brennan*, the Supreme Court ruled that even when a prisoner is harmed and even when prison officials knew that the risk of harm existed, officials cannot be held liable if they took appropriate steps to mitigate that risk.

If there was any question that the prisoners' rights era had ended, that question was settled in 1995 by the case of *Sandin* v. *Conner*. In *Sandin*, the Supreme Court rejected the argument that, by disciplining inmates, a state deprived prisoners of their constitutional right not to be deprived of liberty without due process. "The time has come to return to those due process principles that were correctly established and applied in earlier times," said the Court. A year later, the decision in *Lewis* v. *Casey* overturned portions of *Bounds* v. *Smith*. The *Bounds* case had been instrumental in establishing law libraries in prisons. The Court in *Lewis* held, however, that "*Bounds* does not guarantee inmates the wherewithal to file any and every type of legal claim but requires only that they be provided with the tools to attack their sentences."

In *Edwards* v. *Balisok* (1997), the Supreme Court made it even harder to successfully challenge prison disciplinary convictions. The Court held that prisoners cannot sue for monetary damages under Section 1983 of the U.S. Code for loss of good-time credits until they are able to sue successfully in state court to have their disciplinary conviction set aside.

Finally, in 2003, in the case of *Overton* v. *Bazzetta*, the Court upheld visitation regulations established by the Michigan Department of Corrections that denied most visits to prisoners who had committed two substance abuse violations while incarcerated. In its ruling, the Court said that "the regulations bear a rational relation to legitimate penological interests [sufficient] to sustain them." Wording taken directly from the

EXHIBIT 11–4 *Overton v. Bazzetta* (2003)

Responding to concerns about prison security problems caused by the increasing number of visitors to Michigan's prisons and about substance abuse among inmates, the Michigan Department of Corrections (MDOC) promulgated new regulations limiting prison visitation. . . .

The fact that the regulations bear a rational relation to legitimate penological interests suffices to sustain them regardless of whether respondents have a constitutional right of association that has survived incarceration. This Court accords substantial deference to the professional judgment of prison administrators, who bear a significant responsibility for defining a corrections system's legitimate goals and determining the most appropriate means to accomplish them. The regulations satisfy each of four factors used to decide whether a prison regulation affecting a constitutional right that survives incarceration withstands constitutional challenge.

First, the regulations bear a rational relationship to a legitimate penological interest. The restrictions on children's visitation are related to MDOC's valid interests in maintaining internal security and protecting child visitors from exposure to sexual or other misconduct or from accidental injury. They promote internal security, perhaps the most legitimate penological goal, by reducing the total number of visitors and by limiting disruption caused by children. It is also reasonable to ensure that the visiting child is accompanied and supervised by adults charged with protecting the child's best interests. Prohibiting visitation by former inmates bears a self-evident connection to the State's interest in maintaining prison security and preventing future crime. Restricting visitation for inmates with two substance-abuse violations serves the legitimate goal of deterring drug and alcohol use within prison.

Second, respondents have alternative means of exercising their asserted right of association with those prohibited from visiting. They can send messages through those who are permitted to visit, and can communicate by letter and telephone. Visitation alternatives need not be ideal; they need only be available.

Third, accommodating the associational right would have a considerable impact on guards, other inmates, the allocation of prison resources, and the safety of visitors by causing a significant reallocation of the prison system's financial resources and by impairing corrections officers ability to protect all those inside a prison's walls.

Finally, [complainants] have suggested no alternatives that fully accommodate the asserted right while not imposing more than a [minimum] cost to the valid penological goals.

SOURCE: *Overton v. Bazzetta*, 539 U.S. 126 (2003), Syllabus.

Court's opinion is shown in Exhibit 11–4. It provides a summary of the factors used by the courts to decide whether prison regulations meet constitutional requirements.

The Legal Mechanisms Changes in state and federal statutes have also slowed the pace of prisoners' rights cases. In 1980, Congress modified the Civil Rights of Institutionalized Persons Act.[16] It now requires a state inmate to exhaust all state remedies before filing a petition for a writ of *habeas corpus* in federal court. In effect, a state prisoner must give the state an opportunity to correct alleged violations of its prisoners' federal rights (*Duncan v. Henry*, 1995). Inmates in federal prisons may still file *habeas corpus* petitions directly in federal court. In their petitions, federal inmates are now required to show (1) that they were deprived of some right to which they were entitled despite the confinement and (2) that the deprivation of this right made the imprisonment more burdensome.

The Prison Litigation Reform Act of 1995[17] (PLRA) was another legislative response to the ballooning number of civil rights lawsuits filed by prisoners. It restricts the filing of lawsuits in federal courts by:

1. requiring state prisoners to exhaust all local administrative remedies prior to filing suit in federal court;
2. requiring inmates to pay federal filing fees unless they can claim pauper status;[18]
3. limiting awards of attorneys' fees in successful lawsuits;
4. requiring judges to screen all inmate lawsuits and immediately dismiss those they find frivolous;
5. revoking good-time credit toward early release if inmates file malicious lawsuits;
6. barring prisoners from suing the federal government for mental or emotional injury unless there is an accompanying physical injury;
7. allowing court orders to go no further than necessary to correct the particular inmate's civil rights problem;
8. requiring some court orders to be renewed every two years or be lifted; and
9. ensuring that no single judge can order the release of federal inmates for overcrowding.

In May 2001, the U.S. Supreme Court further restricted inmate options under the PLRA. The ruling mandates that inmates must complete prison administrative processes that could provide some relief before suing over prison conditions, even if that relief would *not include a monetary payment* (*Booth* v. *Churner*, 2001).

A 2005 study of the PLRA's effectiveness, conducted by the National Council for State Courts (NCSC), found that the PLRA "achieved its intended effects" and significantly lowered the number of frivolous filings by inmates in federal courts.[19]

FEMALE INMATES AND THE COURTS

The prisoners' rights movement has been largely a male phenomenon. While male inmates were petitioning the courts for expansion of their rights, female inmates frequently had to resort to the courts simply to gain rights that male inmates already had.

The Cases

One early state case, *Barefield* v. *Leach* (1974), demonstrated that the opportunities and programs for female inmates were clearly inferior to those for male inmates. In that case, a court in New Mexico spelled out one standard for equal treatment of male and female inmates. The court said that the equal-protection clause of the Constitution requires equal treatment of male and female inmates but not identical treatment. *Barefield*, however, was a state case—not binding on other states or the federal government.

In 1977, in *State, ex rel. Olson* v. *Maxwell*, the Supreme Court of North Dakota ruled that a lack of funds was not an acceptable justification for unequal treatment of male and female prisoners. Although this decision also came in a state court case, it would later be cited as a legal authority in a similar federal court case.

In *Glover* v. *Johnson* (1979), a U.S. district court case, a group of female prisoners in the Michigan system filed a class action lawsuit claim-

Many claims of female inmates have focused on the failure of correctional institutions to provide them with educational opportunities and medical care comparable to those provided male inmates. The equal protection clause of which amendment guarantees female inmates conditions of confinement comparable to those of male inmates?

ing that they were denied access to the courts and constitutional rights to equal protection. The prisoners demanded educational and vocational opportunities comparable to those for male inmates. At trial, a prison teacher testified that, although men were allowed to take shop courses, women were taught remedial courses at a junior high school level because the attitude of those in charge was "Keep it simple, these are only women." The court found that "the educational opportunities available to women prisoners in Michigan were substantially inferior to those available to male prisoners." Consequently, the court ordered a plan to provide higher education and vocational training for female prisoners in the Michigan prison system. *Glover* was a turning point in equal treatment for imprisoned women. Since 1979, female inmates have continued to win the majority of cases seeking equal treatment and the elimination of gender bias.

In the 1980 case of *Cooper* v. *Morin*, the U.S. Supreme Court accepted neither inconvenience nor cost as an excuse for treating female jail inmates differently from male inmates. Female inmates at a county jail in New York had alleged that inadequate medical attention in jail violated their civil rights. Later that same year, a federal district court rejected Virginia's claims that services for female prison inmates could not be provided at the same level as those for male inmates because of cost-effectiveness issues (*Bukhari* v. *Hutto*, 1980). Virginia authorities said that the much smaller number of women in prison raised the cost of providing each woman with services. The appellate court ordered the state of Virginia to provide equitable services for inmates, regardless of gender.

An action challenging the denial of equal protection and the conditions of confinement in the Kentucky Correctional Institution for Women was the basis of *Canterino* v. *Wilson*, decided in U.S. district court in 1982. The district court held that the "levels system" used to allocate privileges to female prisoners, a system not applied to male prisoners, violated both the equal-protection rights and the due process rights of female inmates. The court also held that female inmates in Kentucky's prisons must have the same opportunities as men for vocational education, training, recreation, and outdoor activity.

In 1982, in *McMurray* v. *Phelps*, a district court in Louisiana ordered an end to the unequal treatment of female inmates in that state's jails. (Recall that the federal courts have supervisory jurisdiction over state courts.) The next year, the Seventh Circuit Court of Appeals found that strip searches of female misdemeanor offenders awaiting bond in a Chicago lockup were unreasonable under the Fourth Amendment (*Mary Beth G.* v. *City of Chicago*, 1983). In addition, the court found that a policy of subjecting female arrestees to strip searches while subjecting similarly situated males only to hand searches violated the equal-protection clause of the Constitution.

In 1994, in a class action suit by female inmates, a federal district court held the District of Columbia Department of Corrections liable under the Eighth Amendment for inadequate gynecological examinations and testing, inadequate testing for sexually transmitted diseases, inadequate health education, inadequate prenatal care, and an inadequate overall prenatal protocol (*Women Prisoners of the District of Columbia Department of Corrections* v. *District of Columbia*, 1994).

Court oversight of ob-gyn services at the District of Columbia Department of Corrections ended in 2004, following an agreement in which the department promised to continue to provide adequate services for women inmates. The agreement ended 33 years of court oversight of the DC department—involving a total of 15 class action lawsuits filed by inmate groups or their representatives during that time.[20]

Also in 2004, U.S. district judge Myron Thompson approved a settlement in a class action lawsuit centered on concerns about medical care and general conditions at three Alabama women's prisons. Thompson said that the settlement, which required lowering the number of prisoners held at three locations, would not make the facilities "comfortable or pleasant" but would "afford class members the basic necessities mandated by the United States Constitution."[21] Affected were the Julia Tutwiler Prison for Women, the Tutwiler Annex, and the Birmingham Work Release Facility—all operated by the Alabama Department of Corrections. The lawsuit, filed by the Southern Center for Human Rights, had complained of "intensely overcrowded" and "unbearably hot and poorly ventilated dormitories." Tutwiler Prison had been built in the 1940s to hold no more than 364 inmates but was filled with over 1,000 inmates at the time of the lawsuit. Under the agreement, the population was lowered to 700 by sending some inmates to prisons in Louisiana and by releasing others under community supervision.

REVIEW & APPLICATIONS

REFLECTIONS ON THE FUTURE

Corrections and Technologies

By Thomas J. Cowper

Police Futurists International

The 21st century promises to be an era of rapid and dynamic change for society and for its public servants. New and amazing technologies are emerging almost daily, bringing with them capabilities for people and organizations that could hardly be imagined even as recently as the last decade of the 20th century. Computers and the Internet are only the tip of a technological iceberg that will emerge over the next few decades and advance at exponential rates. Radical new fields like nanotechnology, genetic engineering, and neurotechnology will give people new and expanded physical and cognitive powers, while fostering smaller, more powerful, and more pervasive computing devices that will be woven directly into the fabric of our lives, our human relationships, and our governmental processes. Wireless networks, wearable computers, and augmented reality systems will allow us to process, retrieve, and transmit information at unprecedented speeds, making it possible for one person to accomplish tomorrow what it takes three people to accomplish today. Biometric identification systems, radio frequency identification (RFID) chips (potentially implantable in people and most products), and data-mining technologies will improve homeland security and help reduce crime in our communities. Artificial intelligence, cybernetics, and robotics will dramatically improve the human-machine interface and accelerate the way people collectively exchange and utilize information.

The technological benefits from these advances, while immense, bring with them dangers and problems as well. The employment of new technologies by government agencies carries with it the tremendous responsibility to do so in a way that does not erode our fundamental constitutional guarantees even as we use it to protect the innocent from criminal predators. In the 21st century the public sector must employ new technologies in creative ways to deter, identify, capture, and incarcerate criminals and terrorists because those same social predators will undoubtedly exploit new technological capabilities to perpetrate age-old and innovative offenses against government institutions and civilians. This technological balancing act between effective use of technology to constrain criminals and restraint in the way public servants use it so as not to undermine civil liberties means that public sector professionals must fully understand the capabilities, implications, and political nuances of technology before they set about procuring it. The balancing act is further complicated as technology becomes

more powerful and the complexities of procuring it increase. Missteps in implementing a new and powerful capability because of technological ignorance or naïveté may generate a public backlash that delays or prevents that capability from being used by the government no matter how effective or beneficial to society the technology may be.

Technology, along with becoming exponentially more powerful, is also getting smaller, more user friendly, less expensive, and, therefore, more available to everyone. Surveillance technologies, RFID, biometries, and wireless communication are becoming commonplace and can be used both for beneficial and malicious purposes. As micro- and nanotechnologies reduce the size and detectable signature of these devices, their use by criminals inside correctional institutions is inevitable. Correction officers and administrators not only have to be capable of using technology to secure the institutions they serve but they also have to be able to think creatively in order to anticipate how inmates might use new technologies to commit crimes inside their facilities.

At the same time it appears that the American prison population will continue to rise along with the expense of physical incarceration in "brick and mortar" facilities. Like most governmental processes, it is becoming increasingly evident that with the help of emerging technology new and innovative correctional philosophies and methodologies must be conceived and developed so as to maximize the use of taxpayer dollars in keeping dangerous criminals off our streets. Correctional institutions and their methods must become more efficient while remaining highly secure, and there are a number of emerging technologies, used correctly, that may greatly improve correctional efficiencies, reducing the overall number of incarcerated individuals and the number of correctional officers necessary for safe and effective operation.

For example, the Defense Advanced Research Projects Agency (DARPA)

augmented cognition program is working to dramatically improve the way humans interact with computers in an effort to (1) enhance human cognitive abilities in stressful operational environments, (2) increase a person's situational and context awareness, and (3) empower one person to do the work of three or more individuals. The U.S. Navy intends to use this kind of advanced technology to reduce staffing levels on future combat ships, allowing today's 300-person vessels to be operated effectively in the future by a crew of 90. Robotics, telepresence, and cybernetic advances may decrease those numbers even further.

Similar efficiencies should be possible within correctional institutions of the future, providing increased facility security and officer safety while lowering the overall cost of correctional services. It cannot be done, however, by forcing Information Age technologies into Industrial Age business models. Emerging technologies bring with them unique and extraordinary capabilities, many of which cannot be realized or even conceived within current organizational mindsets, methodologies, and policies. It is not technology that is the central issue facing correctional services of the future; it is the way correctional professionals think about technology and accept the resulting changes. Over the next decade the exponential increases in technological advancement and the social, political, and cultural turmoil that will result demand that correctional officers and their institutions change, not just their business models and methodologies but also the way they think about themselves, their inmates, and the public they serve.

Correctional services, a critical component in maintaining a free democracy, must actively participate in the development of technology necessary to create a peaceful and prosperous society. Creation of the right technology program and systems within correctional facilities for the right reasons; training officers to employ technology correctly, ethically, and legally within the correctional environment;

and envisioning and fostering the kind of future correctional system necessary to overcome tomorrow's Information Age criminal justice and social problems are complex and difficult challenges that require today's supervisors, managers, and administrators to be well versed in both progressive correctional methodology and emerging technology. It requires knowledge and innovation; visionary leadership coupled with effective managerial insight. The way in which corrections professionals think about technology and how they implement it within correctional systems, structures, and organizations will be a major component of their success or failure in the coming years of the 21st century.

About the Author

Thomas J. Cowper is a 24-year police veteran with extensive experience in patrol, patrol supervision, and SWAT assignments. For the last 14 years he has been involved in the procurement, implementation, and management of law enforcement technologies. Cowper is on the board of directors of the Society of Police Futurists International (PFI) (www.policefuturists.org) and is a member of the FBI Futures Working Group, a collaborative partnership between the FBI and the PFI to study and strategize about the future of law enforcement. He is a graduate of the FBI National Academy, has a bachelor of science degree in mechanical engineering technology from LeTourneau University, and has a master's degree in public administration from Marist College. He has been a firearms, defensive tactics, and leadership instructor and is a published author and regular speaker regarding emerging technologies and their impact on law enforcement, government, and society.

SUMMARY

1 The hands-off doctrine was a working philosophy of the courts in this country until 1970. It allowed corrections officials to run prisons without court intervention. The hands-off doctrine existed because courts were reluctant to interfere with activities of the executive branch and because judges realized that they were not experts in corrections.

2 The sources of prisoners' rights are the U.S. Constitution, federal statutes, state constitutions, and state statutes.

3 The central question about prisoners' rights is not whether prisoners have them, but rather, to what extent they retain or forfeit them by virtue of incarceration.

4 Inmates can challenge the legality of their confinement, associated prison conditions, and the practices of correctional officials through (1) a state *habeas corpus* action, (2) a federal *habeas corpus* action, (3) a state tort lawsuit, (4) a federal civil rights lawsuit, and (5) an injunction to obtain relief.

5 During the prisoners' rights era (1970–1991), inmates won many court cases based on claims that conditions of their confinement violated their constitutional rights. Court decisions affected inmate rights to freedom of expression, including free speech; personal communications; access to the courts and legal services; religion; assembly and association; the voicing of grievances about disciplinary procedures; protection from personal and cell searches; health care, including diet and exercise; protection from violence; adequate physical conditions of confinement; and rehabilitation.

6 Most prisoners' claims focus on denial of constitutional rights guaranteed by the First (freedom of expression and religion), Fourth (freedom from unlawful search and seizure), Eighth (freedom from cruel and unusual punishment), and Fourteenth (due process and equal protection of the law) Amendments.

7 The prisoners' rights movement has been largely a male phenomenon. Female inmates have had to petition the courts to gain rights that male inmates already had.

KEY TERMS

hands-off doctrine, *p. 424*
prisoners' rights, *p. 426*
constitutional rights, *p. 426*
institutional needs, *p. 427*
civil liability, *p. 427*
writ of *habeas corpus, p. 428*
tort, *p. 428*
nominal damages, *p. 429*

compensatory damages, *p. 429*
punitive damages, *p. 429*
injunction, *p. 429*
jurisdiction, *p. 429*
precedent, *p. 433*
legitimate penological objectives, *p. 435*
balancing test, *p. 435*

cruel and unusual punishment, *p. 441*
consent decree, *p. 442*
deliberate indifference, *p. 442*
totality of conditions, *p. 443*
due process, *p. 444*
frivolous lawsuits, *p. 447*

QUESTIONS FOR REVIEW

1 Why was the hands-off doctrine so named? What was the basis for the doctrine?

2 What are the key legal sources of prisoners' rights?

3 What is the central question identified by this chapter with regard to prisoners' rights?

4 What are the legal mechanisms through which inmates can challenge the legality of their confinement and associated prison conditions?

5 What rights were won by inmates during what the book calls the prisoners' rights era?

6 What constitutional amendments are most often cited by prisoners claiming rights? What claimed rights are associated with each of these amendments?

7 Do the rights accorded male inmates correspond to the rights of female inmates? Why or why not?

THINKING CRITICALLY ABOUT CORRECTIONS

Freedom of Nonverbal Expression

The right to freedom of nonverbal expression is said to be implied in the First Amendment. Hence, how people wear their hair and how they dress are expressions that some believe are protected by the First Amendment.

1. Might there be modes of dress that interfere with a correctional institution's legitimate goals?

2. If so, what might they be?

Checks and Balance

On January 11, 2003, in a dramatic legal move shortly before leaving office, former Illinois governor George Ryan commuted the sentences of every one of the state's 167 death row inmates. Four of the sentences were reduced to 40-year terms; the remaining 163 sentences were commuted to life in prison. Governor Ryan based his action on his de-termination of inherent arbitrariness and unfairness in the application of capital punishment and on the high risk of executing an innocent person.

While the scope of his action is unusual, the commutations typify the power placed in the hands of each state's chief executive. Essentially, this means that, within the respective states and based solely on personal opinion, a single individual is empowered to overturn sentencing decisions and attendant legal rulings on those decisions made at any level up to and including the nation's most powerful court, the U.S. Supreme Court.

1. Should this be the case?

2. Does the lack of a legal mechanism to counter a governor's decision regarding a pardon or a commutation violate the principle of checks and balances so intricately woven into America's state and federal governmental structures?

ON-THE-JOB DECISION MAKING

Inmate Communications

You are a prison administrator. The prison where you work has a rule that inmates may write letters in English only. This rule seems sensible. After all, if inmates could write in languages not understood by correctional officers, they could discuss plans to escape, riot, or smuggle drugs or weapons into the prison. The courts allow the censoring of outgoing inmate mail; what good is that power if corrections personnel cannot read the mail?

It occurs to you, however, that inmates who cannot write in English will have difficulty communicating with the outside world and with their families. Inmates unable to write in English will not even be able to write to their attorneys. You also wonder what might happen if an inmate can write in English but his parents can read only a for-eign language. If the inmate and his parents cannot afford long-distance phone calls, they will not be able to communicate with each other at all. You begin to consider how the English-only rule might be changed to facilitate wholesome communications while still preventing communications that might endanger the safety of the institution and the inmate population.

1. Can the English-only rule be amended to meet the inmate needs discussed here while still being consistent with legitimate institutional concerns? If so, how?

2. Does an inmate have a constitutionally protected right to communicate with his or her parents?

3. What if that right conflicts with prison policy?

Law Libraries

The Supreme Court's ruling in *Bounds* v. *Smith* (1977) led to the establishment of law libraries for prisoner use in correctional facilities throughout the nation. Numerous subsequent prisoner civil suits resulted in follow-on rulings mandating the need to maintain these libraries with up-to-date reference materials in serviceable condition.

You are an advisor on correctional issues on the staff of your state's attorney general. In the past few weeks, she has repeatedly complained that these rulings impose excessive financial demands on the state's already nearly impoverished correctional system. In particular, she says, routine vandalism by inmates who tear pages from law books and take the pages back to their cells—or simply discard them—is especially costly. It also creates a circumstance wherein another inmate could threaten another civil suit upon finding a book to be "unserviceable" when attempting to use it, a threat to which the system can respond only by immediately purchasing a replacement book.

This, the attorney general says, typifies a cycle that causes an extraordinary drain on limited financial resources. She rants about the "ludicrous" fact that the reference material in her own office is so out of date as to be virtually unusable, but she cannot fix the problem because she spends that portion of her budget on repeatedly restoring the prisoners' law libraries in the various institutions throughout the state.

The attorney general has tasked you to resolve this issue.

1. What will you do?

2. Might advances in information technology be the key to a solution?

LIVE LINKS

at www.justicestudies.com/livelinks04

11–1 *Pell* v. *Procunier*, 417 U.S. 817 (1974)

The link provides the full text of this court opinion. In this case the U.S. Supreme Court ruled that "so long as [a] restriction operates in a neutral fashion, without regard to the content of the expression, it falls within the 'appropriate rules and regulations' to which 'prisoners necessarily are subject,' and does not abridge any First Amendment freedoms retained by prison inmates."

11–2 *Cruz* v. *Beto*, 405 U.S. 319 (1972)

The link provides the full text of this court opinion. In this case the U.S. Supreme Court held that a complaint that challenged restrictions on an inmate's practice of Buddhism established a claim upon which relief could be granted, ruling that "reasonable opportunities must be afforded to all prisoners to exercise the religious freedom guaranteed by the First and Fourteenth Amendments without fear of penalty."

11–3 *Estelle* v. *Gamble*, 429 U.S. 97 (1976)

The link provides the full text of this court opinion. In this case the U.S. Supreme Court held that deliberate indifference to serious medical needs is prohibited whether the indifference is manifested by prison doctors in their response to the prisoner's needs or by prison guards in intentionally denying or delaying access to medical care or intentionally interfering with the treatment once prescribed.

11–4 *Wolff* v. *McDonnell*, 418 U.S. 539 (1974)

The link provides the full text of this court opinion. In this case the U.S. Supreme Court expanded due process standards to govern the imposition of discipline upon prisoners. But since prison disciplinary proceedings are not part of a criminal prosecution, the full rights of a defendant are not extended to prisoners.

11–5 *Wilson* v. *Seiter*, 501 U.S. 294 (1991)

The link provides the full text of this court opinion. In this case the U.S. Supreme Court held that any pain and suffering endured by a prisoner that is not formally a part of his sentence—no matter how severe or unnecessary—will not be held violative of the Cruel and Unusual Punishments Clause unless the prisoner establishes that some prison official intended the harm.

SPECIAL PRISON POPULATIONS

Prisoners Who Are Elderly, Mentally Challenged, and Who Have HIV/AIDS

> "
>
> *The democratic principle that 'all men are created equal' implies that persons with disabilities are entitled like everyone else to equal access and fair treatment appropriate to their context, whether the context is a prison, church, or place of employment.*
>
> —Marca Bristo, former chairperson, National Council on Disability, letter to the editor of the *Washington Times*, July 27, 1998
>
> "

CHAPTER OBJECTIVES

After completing this chapter you should be able to do the following:

1 Define the term *special-needs inmate*.

2 Report on the management needs of special population inmates.

3 Report on the impact of substance abusers on the corrections system.

4 Discuss why treating HIV in prison is difficult.

5 Discuss the five essential elements of cost-effective management of HIV/AIDS inmates.

6 Explain why there are so many inmates with mental illnesses.

7 Describe ways to divert persons with mental illness from the criminal justice system.

8 List the cost and health issues associated with older inmates.

9 Review the legal issues surrounding special population inmates.

By 2010, elderly prisoners are expected to constitute one-third of the U.S. prison population. That statistic is creating a new phenomenon in correctional policy—*an over 50 institution* to house older inmates, provide round-the-clock nursing care, and offer hospice care for dying prisoners.

Since 1995, there has been an 85 percent increase in elderly prisoners. Herb Hoelter, author of Reflections on the Future in Chapter 5, believes that the issue of elderly inmates is a hidden problem that is going to grow into a dinosaur soon. Consider these cases.[1]

Dennis Whitney was condemned to die when he was 17 for a double murder. He spent 12 years on death row at the Florida State Prison (renamed Union Correctional Institution in 1973) near Raiford. His sentence was commuted to life in prison in 1972 when the U.S. Supreme Court declared Florida's death penalty law unconstitutional. Today about 800 of the 1,550 beds at Union Correctional Institution are set aside for older inmates.

By age 61, Whitney had undergone two angioplasties at state expense to clear blocked blood vessels, and he still needed a third. The first two cost $9,000. Whitney was denied parole every time he appeared before the Florida parole commission. "If they turn me down, I'm just going to let the state take care of me for the rest of my life. I'm well-fed, well-clothed, and well taken care of." Whitney died a prisoner in 2005.

Sixty-seven-year-old Robert Doyle is also serving a life sentence at Union Correctional Institution. He describes his prison experience as struggling to survive. There is "absolutely nothing for us to do," Doyle told a reporter. "You see people go downhill. They actually give up. This is a warehousing institution."

Today, elderly prisoners have an average of three chronic illnesses (an illness or condition that affects an individual's well-being for an extended interval, is usually not curable, but can be controlled to provide a reasonable level of physical and psychological functioning) and incarcerating one elderly prisoner costs taxpayers an estimated $80,000 per year. What can or should correctional policymakers do about elderly prisoners? This chapter raises the issue of prisoners who are elderly, mentally ill, drug addicted, or afflicted with a communicable disease. Such prisoners are special-needs inmates, and corrections professionals are responding to their incarceration in unique and innovative ways as this chapter explains.

Dennis Whitney, shown here at age 61, had been incarcerated for 44 years in Florida for the 1960 murder of seven people. During his time in prison Whitney received two angioplasties at state expense to clear blocked blood vessels. He was eligible for parole after serving 30 years but the Florida Parole Commission turned him down. Just before his last parole hearing in 2004 Whitney said, "If they turn me down, I'm just going to let the state take care of me for the rest of my life. I'm well fed, well clothed and well taken care of." And that is what happened. Whitney died a prisoner in 2005. Today the elderly are the fastest-growing segment of the prison population. By the year 2010, elderly prisoners are expected to constitute one-third of the U.S. prison population. Do elderly prisoners threaten public safety? Could they be paroled? Should they be held in nursing-home-like facilities away from the general population? What are the implications for housing an elderly prisoner population?

SPECIAL-NEEDS INMATES

Increasingly, prisons and jails are dealing with a growing population of special-needs inmates. **Special-needs inmates** are "those prisoners who exhibit unique physical, mental, social, and programmatic needs that distinguish them from other prisoners and for whom jail and prison management and staff have to respond to in nontraditional and innovative ways." [2] These special populations suffer from mental illness; chemical dependency (drug or alcohol); communicable diseases (especially HIV/AIDS and tuberculosis); chronic diseases (e.g., diabetes, heart disease, seizures, and detoxification); the general problems of the elderly; the special concern of managing young female offenders in correctional settings; the problems that arise when youthful offenders are housed in adult institutions; and the issues arising from sexual identity, prisoner victimization, transgender prisoners, and the management of sex offenders within correctional settings.

Such inmates present operational and administrative problems for correctional staff—it is often difficult for the staff to know what they are observing or, once they recognize an inmate's special needs, how to address the situation. However, society benefits when correctional administrators and health professionals work together to provide regular medical care and better prevention programs.

A statewide research study on jail management in New Mexico indicated that special-needs inmates require extra attention from jail staff. [3] For example, they must be watched closely for possible suicide. Almost 9 of 10 such inmates disrupt normal jail activities; 7 of 10 require an excess of scarce medical resources; 4 of 10 engage in acts of violence; and almost 3 of 10 are abused by other inmates. The characteristics of special-needs inmates, the treatment programs offered, and the policies for dealing with those inmates depend on the type of special need.

The American Correctional Association urges correctional agencies to develop and adopt procedures for the early identification of special-needs inmates, to provide the services that respond to those needs, and to monitor and evaluate the delivery of services in both community and institutional settings (see Exhibit 12–1). This chapter reviews the management and treatment of the five largest groups of special-needs inmates: substance-abusing inmates, HIV-positive and AIDS inmates, inmates with mental illness, inmates with tuberculosis, and older inmates.

Substance-Abusing Inmates

Alcohol and other drug problems are the common denominator for most offenders in the criminal justice system and untreated substance-abusing offenders are more likely to relapse to drug abuse and return to criminal behavior. A **substance-abusing inmate** is an incarcerated person suffering from dependency on one or more substances including alcohol and a wide range of drugs.

Substance abuse takes a toll on users, the community, and the criminal justice system. In October 2002, the National Center on Addiction and Substance Abuse at Columbia University (CASA) released its findings on substance abuse and the prison population. [4] According to this study, 83 percent of America's jail and prison population—some 1.7 million prisoners at the end of 2000, up from 80 percent at the end of 1996—had seriously abused or were addicted to drugs and/or alcohol. Some had been arrested for offenses connected with drugs and alcohol (drug sales, DWI, etc.).

special-needs inmates

Those prisoners who exhibit unique physical, mental, social, and programmatic needs that distinguish them from other prisoners and for whom jail and prison management and staff have to respond to in nontraditional and innovative ways.

substance-abusing inmate

An incarcerated individual suffering from dependency on one or more substances including alcohol and a wide range of drugs.

The Corrections Connection®
N E T W O R K   N E W S

Eye On Correction

Meeting Anthony

By Sarah Etter

Anthony isn't afraid to tell me exactly what's on his mind as we sit at a table at the Massachusetts Bridgewater Treatment Center for sex offenders.

"I'm here because I drugged and raped young girls," Anthony says looking me straight in the eye. "But I've come to recognize what was wrong with me when I acted like that."

Anthony is a 39-year-old resident at the center and doesn't go into much more detail about his offense. Instead, he shuffles through paperwork on the table until he comes to a page filled with his handwriting. Phrases like "she deserved it" and "she wanted me to do it" are scrawled on lines in the pamphlet.

"These are my validations," he explains. "These are the things I used to say to myself when I committed my crimes. These are the justifications I used to make it ok."

Anthony is currently enrolled in the center's Core Program, a pre-release curriculum that every sex offender completes during their last 24 months of incarceration. Each offender is here for a different reason; some are pedophiles, some rapists; some are civilly committed, while others volunteered to be [in] this environment. Yet, every offender strives toward a common goal; rehabilitation.

Core is an intense process. Once placed in the program, offenders work through a rigorous daily schedule of support meetings with loved ones, and group and individual counseling with a goal-oriented staff of therapists.

Currently, 78 inmates are in the program. A typical day begins with an inmate count, and then breakfast, followed by therapy and classes. Offenders also take psychological education classes that help them focus on their sexual triggers.

Anthony says those triggers weren't always easy to identify.

"This place really makes you aware of the red flags," he says. "But being here, I know which thoughts are dangerous. I'll never be fully finished with this program, but this is the essential part of my recovery; recognizing I have a problem and addressing it."

Those preparing for release have created somewhat of a community. In quiet rooms dotted with white, round tables, Core participants tutor each other and hold impromptu discussions about things they are struggling with. They attend Alcoholics Anonymous and Narcotics Anonymous meetings, and learn more about themselves by interacting with others.

"I like the community here," Anthony says in a hushed voice. "Solitude can make you think too much. Here, I'm learning exactly who I am, and I'm learning that my life is not over. I used drugs as a tool to fulfill my desires, and I surrounded myself with negative social influences."

He takes a breath and looks at me again.

"I never want to create another victim."

Core programmers spend a majority of their time learning about themselves. Anthony says the program clarified the particular feelings he had that brought about more problems. He felt unloved and inadequate, so he became reckless about what he did or whom he hurt. He knows better now, he says.

"I never understood what an emotional collapse was before I came here. I realized now that it is a big deal. It is my trigger to act out."

By identifying certain triggers, people like Anthony are able to improve their chance for success once released. Despite the many social stigmas that exist about sex offenders, Anthony refuses to let them hold him back.

"The center has changed everything for me. Much of society isn't informed about people like me. There really can be a change."

Source: "Meeting Anthony," Sarah Etter, The Corrections Connection Network News (CCNN). Eye on Corrections. www.corrections.com. October 16, 2006.

EXHIBIT 12-1   **American Correctional Association**

Public Correctional Policy on Offenders with Special Needs

Introduction

The provision of humane and gender responsive programs and services for the accused and adjudicated requires addressing the special needs of juvenile, youthful, and adult offenders. To meet this goal, correctional agencies should develop and adopt procedures for the early identification of offenders with special needs. Agencies should provide the services that respond to those needs and monitor and evaluate the delivery of services in both confined and community settings.

Policy Statement

Correctional systems should assure provision of specialized services, programs, and conditions of confinement to meet the special needs of offenders. To achieve this, they should:

A. identify the categories of juvenile, youthful, and adult offenders who will require special care or programs. These categories include:

1. offenders with psychological needs, mental retardation, psychiatric disorders, behavior disorders, disabling conditions, neurological impairments, and substance abuse;
2. offenders who are physically disabled or chronically or terminally ill;
3. older offenders;
4. offenders with social and/or educational deficiencies, learning disabilities, or language barriers;
5. offenders with special security or supervision needs;
6. sex offenders;
7. adolescents; and
8. female offenders.

B. provide services and programs in a manner consistent with professional standards and nationally accepted exemplary practices. Such services and programs may be provided within the correctional agency itself, or by referral to another agency that has the necessary specialized program resources, or by contracting with private or voluntary agencies or individuals that meet professional standards;

C. maintain appropriately trained staff and/or contractors for the delivery of care, programs, and services;

D. maintain professionally appropriate record keeping of the services and programs provided;

E. evaluate the quality and effectiveness of services provided; and

F. provide leadership and advocacy for legislative and public support to obtain the resources needed to meet these special needs.

Note: This Public Correctional Policy was ratified by the American Correctional Association Delegate Assembly at the Congress of Correction in San Antonio, Texas, August 23, 1984. It was reviewed and amended January 16, 1991, at the Winter Conference in Louisville, Kentucky. It was reviewed August 21, 1996, at the Congress of Correction in Nashville, Tennessee, without change. It was reviewed and amended at the Congress of Correction in Philadelphia, August 15, 2001.
Source: Copyright © American Correctional Association.

Others had been under the influence of drugs or alcohol when they were arrested for other offenses.

Drug Use and Dependence   If inmates are any indication, the war on drugs is not affecting persons who commit prison-bound offenses. In October 2006, the U.S. Department of Justice reported its findings on drug use and dependence among state and federal prisoners in 1997 and

2004.[5] That survey found that in 1997 and 2004, nearly one-third of state inmates and one-fourth of federal inmates committed their offenses under the influence of drugs. Drug use in the month before the offense by state prisoners remained unchanged from 1997 (stable at 56–57 percent), but drug use in the month before the offense by federal prisoners rose from 45 to 50 percent. The actual number of drug offenders in state and federal prisons is estimated to be 330,000, an increase of 57,000 inmates over 1997.

Drug Use Among state inmates, one-third said they had committed their current offense while under the influence of drugs. Most reported using marijuana, hashish, cocaine, heroine, and other opiates. However, more than one-half reported using drugs in the month before their offense. The profile of a state prisoner using drugs in the month before the offense is male (56 percent), white (58 percent), and 24 years old or younger (66 percent).

Among federal inmates, one-fourth said they had committed their current offense while under the influence of drugs. Most reported using marijuana, hashish, cocaine, heroine, and stimulants including amphetamines and methamphetamines. In the month before their offense, one-half (up from 45 percent in 1997) reported drug use. The profile of a federal prisoner using drugs in the month before the offense is either male or female (female use jumped from 37 percent in 1997 to 48 percent in 2004), white (58 percent), and 24 years old or younger (62 percent).

The survey also reported that state drug offenders reported more serious criminal records than federal prisoners. Among state drug offenders, 50 percent were on probation, parole, or escape at the time of their arrest, 78 percent had a prior sentence to incarceration or probation, 22 percent had a prior violent offense, and 16 percent reported that all prior sentences were for drug offenses. Among federal prisoners only 24 percent were on a criminal justice status at the time of their arrest, 62 percent had a prior sentence, 16 percent had a prior violent offense, and 15 percent reported prior sentences only for drug offenses.

An interesting finding in the government's survey is that prior drug use grew most quickly among middle-aged inmates. Although drug use in the month before the offense is still highest among the youngest inmates (24 or younger), the largest increase in prior drug use since 1997 was reported by middle-aged inmates. Among state prisoners ages 45 to 54, drug use in the month before the offense rose from 40 to 47 percent.

Drug Dependence and Abuse The same Department of Justice survey reported on drug dependence and abuse among state and federal prisoners, and compared those results with drug dependence and abuse in the U.S. adult resident population. Overall, 53 percent of state inmates, 46 percent of federal inmates, and 48 percent of jail inmates met the criteria for drug dependence or abuse. The national prevalence of drug dependence or abuse in the U.S. adult resident population is 2 percent. These statistics signal the importance of drug treatment for inmates. Yet, as this chapter will show, only 13 percent of prisoners who need drug treatment actually receive it.

Abuse symptoms included repeated drug use in hazardous situations such as driving, swimming, or using machinery, or recurrent occupational, educational, legal, or social problems related to drug use. Recurrent social problems (for example, arguments or physical fights with spouse, intimate, family, or friends) due to drug use were the most

Over 80 percent of America's jail and prison inmates need some sort of substance-abuse treatment, but only 13 percent receive it while incarcerated. What should jails and prisons do to control the revolving door of drug and alcohol abusers and addicts in and out of prison?

commonly reported abuse symptom (45 percent of state and 34 percent of federal inmates).

Drug dependence covered a range of symptoms including greater tolerance for drugs and more drug use, compulsive use, bad after-effects from cutting down or stopping drug use, neglect of work, school, and family activities, and continued use even though it was causing emotional or psychological problems. Continued use even though it was causing emotional or psychological problems was the most common symptom reported by both state and federal inmates (36 and 28 percent, respectively), followed by increasing tolerance (34 percent state and 28 percent federal).

According to the National Institute of Justice's Arrestee Drug Abuse Monitoring Program (ADAM), which tracks drug use among arrestees in 35 cities, the percentage of men testing positive for drugs when arrested ranges from 49 percent in Laredo, Texas, to 84 percent in Chicago. Among women, percentages range from 35 percent in Laredo to 81 percent in New York City.[6]

Drug Treatment Programs Why should prisoners receive drug treatment? According to Jeremy Travis, president of John Jay College of Criminal Justice, former senior fellow at the Urban Institute, director of the National Institute of Justice, and author of Reflections on the Future in Chapter 8, there are two powerful reasons.[7]

First, drug offenders consume a staggering volume of illegal drugs, and any reduction in their drug use represents a significant reduction in the nation's demand for illegal drugs. About 60 percent of the cocaine and heroin consumed by the entire nation in a year is consumed by individuals arrested in that year. Drug treatment has the potential for significantly reducing the nation's demand for illegal drugs.

Second, we now know that we can reduce drug use in the offender population. Drug abuse treatment improves outcomes for drug-abusing offenders and has beneficial effects for public health and safety. There is ample, consistent, and cumulative evidence that substance abuse treatment for incarcerated populations is an effective intervention for drug abusers, even if the motivation for entering treatment is coerced.[8] The National Treatment Improvement Evaluation Study found that prison-based treatment programs produced reductions in criminal behavior and in arrests.[9] Participation in correctional substance abuse treatment is also associated with enhanced mental health and physical health. Ideally treatment programs should begin the moment a person enters prison. Research shows that treatment programs that start nine months to a year before prison release, provide community-based aftercare services (housing, education, employment, and health care), attract and retain staff who demonstrate concern for the offender's welfare, and give offenders a clear understanding of the program's rules and the penalties for breaking them provide the greatest chances for success.[10] Such programs have success rates as high as 80 to 90 percent. Community aftercare services are particularly important for substance abusers because they tend to have medical problems such as cirrhosis of the liver, diabetes, and HIV/AIDS.

The criminal justice system has become the largest source of mandated, or coerced, drug treatment in the United States.[11] Contrary to what some believe, research consistently indicates that offenders' motivations for entering drug treatment (voluntary or coerced) are not as important in treatment outcome as their ultimate length of stay in treatment. The longer inmates participate in treatment, the more likely they are to adopt prosocial attitudes and overcome their initial resistance. (Generally, better outcomes are associated with treatment that lasts longer than 90 days, with the greatest reductions in drug abuse and criminal behavior occurring to those who complete treatment.) This point is important because treatment in a prison always involves an element of coercion.

With thousands of inmates returning to the general population each month, correctional health and public health are becoming increasingly intertwined. Health care and disease prevention in correctional facilities must become a top priority for correctional managers and all correctional personnel.

Officials estimate that 83 percent of prison and jail inmates need some sort of substance abuse treatment but only 13 percent receive it while incarcerated.[12] It is estimated that of the 60 percent of prisoners serving sentences for drug offenses, about one-third have moderate to severe substance abuse problems that urgently need care. Most state institutions do not have the staff or the resources to provide treatment to every inmate who needs it.

The National Center on Addiction and Substance Abuse at Columbia University (CASA) is concerned about the low priority given to dealing with inmates' drug/alcohol addictions. From 1990 to 1999, the number of inmates who needed substance abuse treatment climbed from 551,608 to 948,769.[13] In 1990, an estimated 13 percent of inmates needing treatment received it; in 1999, the figure remained 13 percent. And, according to CASA, alcohol is linked more closely with violent crimes than are drugs. More widely available than illegal drugs, alcohol is connected with rape, assault, child and spouse abuse, and most homicides arising from disputes or arguments. Twenty percent of state inmates convicted of a violent offense were under the influence of alcohol—and no other substance—when they committed their crimes; in contrast, only 4 percent of violent offenders were under the influence of drugs at the time of their crimes.

CASA also reports a link between alcohol abuse and addiction and property crime. Among state prisoners, 16 percent of property offenders were under the influence of alcohol (and no other substance) at the time of their crime; among federal prisoners, it was 5 percent.

CASA estimates that states spend 5 percent of their prison budget on drug/alcohol treatment; the BOP spends less than 1 percent. Treatment

Many inmates enter prison addicted to illegal drugs. Although there's evidence that drug and alcohol treatment in prison reduces recidivism, only 13 percent of inmates who need substance abuse treatment actually receive it. Should correctional facilities be required to provide substance abuse treatment? What are the benefits of substance abuse treatment?

need far outstrips treatment availability, and much treatment is either short term or not intensive enough to address inmates' needs. "Considering the depth of the typical inmate's addiction," writes Dr. Lana Harrison, associate director of the Center for Drug and Alcohol Studies at the University of Delaware, "self-help or drug education programs are unlikely to effect long-lasting change. Nor is prison time, because 77 percent of state and 62 percent of federal inmates had served prior sentences."[14]

Drug treatment programs provide evidence that rehabilitation is more likely to succeed for those offenders who complete drug treatment programs, and reducing drug-seeking behavior aids in management of jail facilities. A recent NIJ-sponsored research study found that the greatest benefit of drug treatment programs in jails was that they provided a "behavioral management tool" that controlled inmates' behavior and helped lower the incidence of inmate violence.[15]

The study evaluated five drug treatment programs in California and New York. At all five sites, substance abuse inmates in drug treatment programs had lower rates of serious physical violence and other behavioral problems (e.g., insubordination and possession of nondrug contraband) than those not in the programs. During a one-year follow-up 83 percent of the inmates in drug treatment and 77 percent of the control group were not convicted of another offense.

therapeutic community (TC)

A residential treatment program in which substance abuse inmates are housed in a separate unit within a prison or jail facility.

Therapeutic Community   One successful prison-based substance treatment program is the therapeutic community. A **therapeutic community (TC)** is a residential treatment program in which inmates are housed in a separate unit within a prison or jail facility, characterized by highly structured treatment involving resocialization, intensive counseling, and an increasing level of responsibility as the inmate progresses through the program. TC relies on interactions within the peer group to help members confront their addictions and to commit to lifestyle changes that will enable them to remain drug free and crime free. Prison-based TCs first appeared in the 1980s. By 2000, over 300 TCs were operating in 47 states.[16]

Postrelease Outcomes   Evaluations of prison-based TC programs conducted in several states and the federal prison system have provided empirical support for the effectiveness of these programs in reducing recidivism and relapse to drug use, especially when combined with continuity of care in the community following release from prison to parole.

In September 2000, the federal BOP published the results of a three-year evaluation of its residential drug abuse treatment programs that are designed for inmates with moderate to severe substance abuse problems.[17] The study assessed the postrelease outcomes of 1,842 men and 473 women released from 20 different federal prisons with residential drug treatment programs between August 1992 and December 1997. The evaluation revealed that male inmates who completed residential drug abuse treatment were 16 percent less likely to be rearrested or have their supervision revoked than were inmates who did not receive such treatment; the comparable figure for female inmates was 18 percent. This reduction in recidivism was coupled with a 15 percent reduction in drug use by male participants and an 18 percent reduction in drug use by female participants. The study also found improved employment for women after release. The research strongly suggests that residential drug abuse treatment can make a significant difference in the lives of inmates following their release from prison and return to the community. Similar results have been reported in Delaware where researchers conducted a longitudinal study of inmates who completed in-prison and work-release TC treatment.[18] They were more drug free and arrest free than their control groups at 18-month and three- and five-year follow-up periods. The Delaware research demonstrates the importance of treatment continuing during the transition stage to work and the free community.

In 2004, the White House Office of National Drug Control Policy estimated that the cost to society of drug abuse was $180.9 billion.[19] Almost $108 billion was associated with drug-related crime, including criminal justice system costs and costs borne by victims of crime. The cost of treating drug abuse (including research, training, and prevention) was estimated to be $15.8 billion, a fraction of these overall costs.

Drug abuse treatment is cost-effective in reducing drug abuse and bringing about associated health care, crime, and incarceration cost savings. Positive net economic benefits are consistently found for drug abuse treatment across various settings and populations.[20] The largest economic benefit of treatment is seen in avoided costs of crime (incarceration and victimization costs), with greater economic benefits resulting from treating offenders with co-occurring mental health problems and substance use disorders. Residential prison treatment, such as the therapeutic communities discussed earlier in this chapter, is more cost-effective if offenders continue to attend treatment after incarceration, according to research. Drug courts (see Chapter 5) also convey positive economic benefits, including participant-earned wages and avoided incarceration and future crime costs.

What Works? Principles of Drug Abuse Treatment for Criminal Justice Populations
Controlling the revolving door of drug and alcohol abusers and addicts in the criminal justice population is an important aspect of management for corrections officials. The National Institute on Drug Abuse (NIDA) looked at all the research that had been published on

California Proposition 36 requires that first- and second-time nonviolent simple drug possession offenders be placed on probation instead of being sentenced to time behind bars. On Wednesday, June 27, 2001, California state senate president pro tem John Burton held a news conference on the Lindesmith Center Drug Policy Foundation's grading of how 11 counties plan to implement Proposition 36. How do such new laws save taxpayers' money and rehabilitate drug offenders?

drug abuse treatment for the last 40 years and discovered 13 principles that constitute effective drug treatment.[21] They are:

1. Scientists have found that drug addiction is a brain disease that affects behavior, the brain's anatomy and chemistry, and that these changes can last for months or years after the individual has stopped using drugs.

2. Effective drug abuse treatment engages participants in a therapeutic process, retains them in treatment for an appropriate length of time, and helps them learn to maintain abstinence over time.

3. Effective drug abuse treatment must last long enough to produce stable behavioral changes. Individuals with severe drug problems and co-occurring disorders typically need longer treatment (no less than three months) and more comprehensive services.

4. A comprehensive assessment of the nature and extent of an individual's drug problems and mental health evaluation is the first step in effective drug abuse treatment.

5. Tailoring services to fit the needs of the individual is an important part of effective drug abuse treatment because individuals differ in terms of age, gender, ethnicity, problem severity, recovery stage, and level of supervision needed.

6. Effective drug abuse treatment programs carefully monitor drug use because individuals trying to recover from drug addiction may experience a relapse, or return, to drug use. Monitoring drug use through urinalysis or other objective methods provides a basis for assessing and providing feedback on the offender's treatment progress. It also provides opportunities to determine rewards and sanctions to facilitate change and modify treatment plans.

7. Effective drug abuse treatment programs target feelings that are associated with criminal behavior. These can include feeling entitled to have things one's own way; feeling that one's criminal behavior is justified; failing to be responsible for one's actions; and constantly failing to anticipate or appreciate the consequences of one's behavior.

8. Effective drug abuse treatment programs incorporate treatment planning for drug-abusing offenders, and treatment providers are aware of correctional supervision requirements as treatment goals. Ongoing collaboration ensures that offenders meet correctional supervision requirements as well as the offender's changing needs such as housing, child care, medical, employment, and so on.

9. Effective drug abuse treatment programs recognize that continuity of care is essential for drug abusers reentering the community. Continuity of care helps offenders deal with problems at reentry, such as learning to handle situations that could lead to relapse, learning how to live drug free in the community, and developing a drug-free peer support network.

10. Effective drug abuse treatment programs recognize that a balance of rewards and sanctions encourages prosocial behavior and treatment participation. These programs are experimenting with incentives that encourage positive actions on the part of the offender such as recognition for progress, reduced reporting requirements, allowing reports to be made through phone calls or other methods that do not involve office visits, and early termination of supervision.

11. Effective drug abuse treatment programs recognize that high rates of mental health problems are found in persons under correctional

supervision and those with substance abuse problems. Offenders with co-occurring drug abuse and mental health problems require an integrated approach that combines drug abuse treatment with psychiatric treatment, including the use of medication to address depression, anxiety, and other mental health problems.

12. Effective drug abuse treatment programs recognize that medications are an important part of treatment for many drug-abusing offenders and can be instrumental in enabling offenders with co-occurring mental health problems to function successfully in society.

13. Effective drug abuse treatment programs understand that rates of infectious diseases such as tuberculosis and HIV/AIDS are higher in drug abusers, incarcerated offenders, and those under community correctional supervision than in the general population. Effective drug abuse treatment programs are using that knowledge to develop strategies for drug-abusing offenders who are living in or reentering the community.

Probation Programs Drug offenders are prime candidates for tough probation programs. There is evidence that even coerced treatment programs can reduce both later drug use and later crimes.[22] The largest study of drug treatment outcomes found that criminal justice clients stayed in treatment longer than did clients without involvement in the justice system and had higher-than-average success rates.[23] Indeed, for offenders in outpatient drug treatment programs, rates of rearrest and relapse are significantly lower if they stay in treatment for more than three months than if they drop out earlier.[24]

Research has revealed the different risks and needs of traffickers, addicts, and low-level users.[25] Many Americans prefer prison sentences for drug traffickers but are willing to accept something other than prison for other drug offenders. Seventeen states have either reformed their drug laws or are considering doing so. In 1996, the people of Arizona led the way in drug reform by passing the Drug Medicalization, Prevention and Control Act. The centerpiece of the act is the diversion of persons convicted of possession or use of a controlled substance. The act requires drug users to be placed on probation and to participate in appropriate drug treatment. In the second year of operation, 62 percent of the probationers complied with treatment. Probation supervision and community treatment cost approximately $1.1 million. Based on prison costs of almost $53 per day, Arizona saved an estimated $6.7 million in incarceration.[26] Four years later, 61 percent of California voters passed Proposition 36—the Substance Abuse and Crime Prevention Act. The act requires that first- and second-time nonviolent drug offenders convicted of possession, use, or transportation of drugs be offered substance abuse treatment instead of incarceration. As of February 2002, of the 4,329 defendants sentenced to drug treatment in Los Angeles County from July 1, 2001, to December 31, 2001, 69 percent were still receiving treatment.[27] Judges and county officials say they are pleased with the program, and preliminary reports are that the program is working. Similar ballot initiatives are being considered across the country.

HIV-Positive and AIDS Inmates

HIV is the acronym for **human immunodeficiency virus,** which is any of a group of retroviruses that infect and destroy helper T cells of the immune system. When enough of a person's T cells have been destroyed by

HIV (human immunodeficiency virus)
A group of retroviruses that infect and destroy helper T cells of the immune system, causing the marked reduction in their numbers that is diagnostic of AIDS.

AIDS (acquired immunodeficiency syndrome)

A disease of the human immune system that is characterized cytologically, especially by reduction in the numbers of CD4-bearing helper T cells to 20 percent or less of normal, rendering a person highly vulnerable to life-threatening conditions. the disease is caused by infection with HIV commonly transmitted in infected blood and bodily secretions (as semen), especially during sexual intercourse and intravenous drug use.

HIV, he or she is diagnosed with **AIDS,** or **acquired immunodeficiency syndrome.** The AIDS virus attacks the body's natural immune system, making it unable to fight off diseases. In this state, a person is highly vulnerable to life-threatening conditions, which people with healthy immune systems can fight off easily.

There are at least four reasons why corrections professionals should be concerned with treating communicable diseases in the inmate population:

1. Sexually transmitted diseases, HIV/AIDS, hepatitis B and C, and tuberculosis can be transmitted to other inmates.

2. Correctional employees and prison visitors are at risk of becoming infected from inmates with communicable diseases if appropriate precautions are not implemented.

3. Over 1,600 prisoners are released every day from prison. Unless they are effectively treated, they may transmit their diseases into the community, threatening public health.

4. Unless prisoners are treated in prison, they become a financial burden on community health care systems.[28]

Although the numbers of inmates suffering from these diseases remain large, the numbers continue to decline. On January 1, 2005, 1.9 percent of state prison inmates and 1.1 percent of federal prison inmates were known to be infected with HIV. Correctional authorities report that 21,336 state inmates and 1,680 federal inmates were HIV-positive, down from a total of 23,663 one year earlier.

Of those known to be HIV-positive in all U.S. prisons on January 1, 2005, the estimated number of AIDS cases was 6,027, up from 5,944 one year earlier. The prevalence of AIDS among inmates is three times greater than it is among the general U.S. population. About 50 in every 10,000 inmates had confirmed AIDS, compared to 15 in 10,000 persons in the U.S. general population. However, due to advances in medical science, fewer inmates are advancing to AIDS or dying of AIDS (see Exhibit 12–2).

HIV-positive inmates have been concentrated in a small number of jurisdictions. California, Florida, Georgia, New York, Texas, and the federal system housed nearly two-thirds of all HIV-positive prisoners in 2004. State prisons in the South held the most HIV-positive prisoners (10,691), followed by prisons in the Northeast (6,756), Midwest (2,025), West (1,894), and the Federal Bureau of Prisons (1,680).

Treating HIV in prison is difficult for at least five reasons.[29] The first is the issue of privacy. People infected with HIV usually do not want to disclose their condition. The therapeutic regimen often involves taking multiple drugs several times a day, and going to the prison medication line often compromises a prisoner's privacy and increases the risk of stigmatization by other inmates and staff. Stigmatization can range from isolation and shunning to more overt forms of abuse. This is true even when high-quality health care is available. Anti-retroviral therapies (ART) can effectively treat HIV, but only if corrections officials help inmates overcome the obstacles to obtaining the treatment.

A second reason involves the frequency of taking medication and the prison routine. Some drugs must be taken with food and others in a fasting state. As the therapeutic regimen increases to five or six times a day, it strains the routine of most prisons to dispense medication frequently and to provide food as required.

EXHIBIT 12-2	HIV and AIDS in Correctional Institutions, 2005

HIV-Positive Prison Inmates				Percentage of Population with Confirmed AIDS		
Year End	Number	Percentage of Custody Population	Year	U.S. General Population	State and Federal Prisoners
1995	24,256	2.3%	1995	0.08%	0.51%
2000	25,088	2.0	2000	0.13	0.53
2001	24,147	1.9	2001	0.14	0.57
2002	23,864	1.9	2002	0.14	0.48
2003	23,663	1.9	2003	0.15	0.51
2004	23,046	1.8	2004	0.15	0.50

HIV-Positive Prison Inmates			Number of Confirmed AIDS Cases		
Jurisdiction	Number	Percentage of Custody Population	Year	Reported Number	Estimated Number
New York	4,500	7.0%	1995	5,099	5,157
Florida	3,250	3.9%	2000	5,528	6,520
Texas	2,405	1.7%	2001	5,754	6,286
Federal system	1,680	1.1%	2002	4,898	5,643
California	1,212	0.7%	2003	5,227	5,944
Georgia	1,109	2.2%	2004	5,483	6,027

Number AIDS-Related Deaths Among State and Federal Prisoners and Jail Inmates			
Year End	State	Federal	Jails
1995	1,010	—	—
2000	185	21	58
2001	256	22	55
2002	215	17	42
2003	213	14	—
2004	128	18	—

Sources: Adapted from Laura M. Maruschak, *HIV in Prisons, 2004* (Washington, DC: U.S. Department of Justice, Bureau of Justice Statistics, November 2006); Laura M. Maruschak, *HIV in Prisons and Jails, 2002* (Washington, DC: U.S. Department of Justice, Bureau of Justice Statistics, December 2004).

The third reason is distrust of the medical and legal system. Not surprisingly, many inmates do not trust the legal and health care systems. This may be especially true for women and minorities who have a documented history of being experimented on without consent and being denied appropriate legal and medical care.

The fourth reason is fear of side effects. The HIV drug regimen is known to make patients feel worse than they already do. Consequently, inmates will be less likely to adhere to the strict dosages and timing.

The final reason is that the courts have rejected the idea that the level and quality of health care available to prisoners must be the same as is available to society at large.[30] This falls under the principle of least eligibility—the belief that prison conditions, including the delivery of health care, be a step below those of the working class and people on welfare. Thus, prisoners are denied access to medical specialists, timely delivery of medical services, technologically advanced diagnostic techniques, the

THE OFFENDER SPEAKS

I am serving a life without parole sentence under Alabama's Habitual Offender Act. All 17 years of my incarceration have been spent here at W. C. Holman Correctional Facility in Atmore, Alabama. When I first came to Holman prison, life was hard. There was a lot of violence and very little hope. Most of my effort was spent just trying to get through each day with my sanity intact. The institution offered little if any opportunity for self-betterment. The guilt for my crime and the feelings for the people I had hurt, both my victim and my family, weighed heavily upon me.

The stress of prison life, however, gave me little time to reflect upon these areas. Consequently, I gave in to the temptation of doing drugs and gambling as a means of dealing with prison life. This ultimately led me down a path that left me more depressed and guilt ridden than I was to begin with. Facing life without parole and turning 40 years old caused me to ask some serious questions of myself. I wanted my life to be worth something, even if I never was allowed to reenter society.

That is why restorative justice is such a refreshing concept to me. It puts crime back into a human perspective and believes that all the parties involved are worthwhile and important. When the honor dorm was started at Holman, I was skeptical at first, but the chaplain convinced me that I should give it a try. Since becoming a part of the dorm, I have learned to live in a community setting where positive growth and respect for others is promoted. This has been such a drastic change here at Holman because there has never been a program or movement like the honor dorm before now.

With the implementation of restorative justice principles, I have learned a new way to deal with conflict. I have had the opportunity to focus on the crime that brought me to prison and reflect on its impact to my victim and my family, from whom I've been separated. My experience in the dorm allows me to take on responsibility and feel as if my life is of more value. It helps me to have a sense that the choices I make in life are important because I can see how they affect others in a community environment.

If I am to expect society to trust me again as a citizen, then I must earn that trust and what better way to do that than to work hard, help others, and believe that the time I'm spending in prison is meaningful and not wasted.

Anonymous

---

latest medication and drug therapies, up-to-date surgical procedures, and second opinions.[31]

Overcoming these obstacles will not be easy. If an inmate undergoes complex drug therapy in prison but cannot obtain the same therapy upon release, his or her health is compromised. In addition, he or she may transmit the virus to others. The key is developing trust between HIV-infected prisoners and the prison health care team, extending the regimen when inmates are discharged, and building collaboration between correctional institutions and public health agencies.

Cost-effective management of such inmates with HIV has at least five essential elements:

1. early detection and diagnosis through medical and mental health screening of each new jail inmate upon admission;
2. medical management and treatment by health specialists, including regular reevaluation and assessment;
3. inmate classification and housing to discourage intravenous drug use and homosexual intercourse or to provide private rooms for terminally ill inmates;
4. education and training of staff and inmates in the cause of AIDS, the stages of the disease, transmission methods, preventive measures, available treatment and therapies, testing issues and policies, confidentiality issues and policies, classification and program assignment policies, and supervision issues, including transportation and inmate movement; and
5. adequate funds to provide increasingly costly treatment to inmates with HIV or AIDS.

Dealing with HIV/AIDS Inmates Most correctional systems test their inmates for HIV, but testing policies vary widely:

- All states (except Iowa), the District of Columbia, and the Federal Bureau of Prisons test inmates if they have HIV-related symptoms or if the inmates request a test.
- Forty states and the federal BOP test inmates after they are involved in an incident.
- 15 states test inmates who belong to specific "high-risk groups."
- 19 states test all inmates who enter their facilities.
- 3 states (Alabama, Nevada and Missouri) and the federal BOP test inmates upon their release.
- 5 states (Arkansas, Georgia, Mississippi, Nevada, and South Carolina) test all inmates currently in custody.
- 3 states (New York, Oregon, and Virginia) and the federal BOP test inmates selected at random.[32]

Today's corrections professionals need a network of medical experts—university medical school faculty, state health department staff, federal health officials, and local health care providers—to consult about HIV and AIDS. Such consultation will give corrections professionals reliable information and familiarize the noncorrectional medical community with the problems facing jails. The ACA recommends that all correctional staff adopt universal precautions when dealing with inmates. This means the staff should assume that all inmates are carrying the virus because, without testing, there is no way to know who is infected and who is not.[33]

Education and Prevention Education and prevention programs are becoming more common in correctional facilities. Incarceration offers opportunities for high-risk inmates to learn basic disease information, safer sex practices, tattooing risks, and triggers for behavior relapse, and they may develop more accurate risk self-perceptions. Such programs benefit not only the inmate but also the health and well-being of the community to which the inmate returns. (Canadian officials estimate that 45 percent of inmates acquire a tatoo while in prison. Believing that stopping tatooing isn't going to happen, Canadian correctional officials set up safe tattoo studios in 6 of its 51 federal prisons.)[34]

The types of education and prevention programs provided vary among correctional systems but may include instructor-led programs, pretest/posttest counseling, multisession prevention counseling, and audiovisual and written materials.

Another method of reducing high-risk behavior among incarcerated populations is peer-led counseling. Besides providing information about HIV/AIDS in formal settings, the informal interactions that incarcerated peer educators have with other inmates in the yard or other locations around the institution offer opportunities for ongoing dialogue about HIV/AIDS. Peer-led counseling is also cost-effective because most peer educators are volunteers and therefore provide HIV/AIDS education to others at no additional cost to the correctional facility.

Research on peer-led counseling has shown that peer educators report significant improvement in their self-esteem, may become paid employees of community-based organizations following release from prison as a result of the skills acquired in peer education training, and are influential in encouraging other inmates to volunteer for HIV testing. However, only 13 percent of state and federal prisons and 3 percent of jails in the United

Talking about CORRECTIONS

MENTAL HEALTH REENTRY

Visit *Live Talk* at **Corrections.com** (www.justicestudies.com/talking04) and listen to the program "Mental Health Reentry," which relates to ideas discussed in this chapter.

HIV/AIDS is a serious problem for our nation's correctional facilities. To overcome the taboo that prevents at-risk people from testing themselves for HIV, the Reverend Jesse Jackson took an HIV test with Cook County (Chicago) jail inmates. Should HIV-positive inmates be treated any differently from other inmates? Should they be isolated?

States offer peer-led HIV/AIDS education programs.

Some say that among the 50 states, HIV and AIDS care is most extensive in New York.[35] With the highest proportion (7.6 percent) of HIV-positive inmates—almost 5,000 of its 63,000 inmate population,[36] New York is one of the few states that has all 11 FDA-approved HIV drugs in all 69 state prisons as well as a state-wide standard of care, established by the New York State AIDS Institute. Available programs include confidential testing, education, support services, one-on-one and group counseling, and transitional and prerelease counseling.

A little bit of charm and persuasion also works. In August 2001, the Reverend Jesse Jackson visited the Cook County Jail in Chicago. He, along with 177 jail inmates and 25 ministers, took a two-minute HIV test.[37] "We're here to save your lives," Reverend Jackson told the inmates. He talked with them about the psychological barrier, the "taboo," that prevents at-risk people from testing themselves for HIV infection. He told the inmates, "Regardless of the results, people who take the test can't lose. Those who test negative should view themselves as lucky—they can get out of the way of AIDS through their knowledge, behavior, and commitment. HIV-positive detainees, on the other hand, can take solace in the fact that early detection leads to correction." Results were reported within two weeks, with only two tests coming back positive. Those persons received counseling and referrals.

Inmates with Mental Illness

Mental health is fundamental to a person's overall health, indispensable to personal well-being, and instrumental in leading a balanced and productive life. Every day, our nation's 3,365 local jails face the challenge of dealing with offenders who are not only suffering from schizophrenia, bipolar disorders, and major depression, among other illnesses, but also suffering from co-occurring substance abuse and dependence disorders and require close monitoring, medication, and other services. It is estimated that 16 percent of the nation's incarcerated are mentally ill and their per-inmate cost is twice that of the rest of the jail and prison population, and that is only for security, not treatment.[38] Jails are the largest provider of mental health services in the United States.

At midyear 2005, more than half of all prison and jail inmates had a mental health problem such as schizophrenia, major depression, bipolar disorder, or posttraumatic stress disorder.[39] (Mental health problems were defined by two measures: a recent history or symptoms of a mental health problem, and its occurrence in the past 12 months.) Significant as these numbers are, many mental health experts believe that due to underreporting by people who do not want to disclose the information or are unaware of their illness, the numbers are actually higher.[40]

As special needs inmates, people who are mentally ill do not do well in prison. They are perceived as disruptive, unpredictable, and sometimes dangerous. They are stigmatized, neglected, and easy prey for inmate assaults and robberies. Behaviors that are characteristic of mental illness such as neglecting personal hygiene, ignoring orders, screaming, and banging against walls oftentimes are met with discipline, which can mean being placed in isolation where the conditions worsen.

A recently reached agreement in a lawsuit against the state of New York will provide a "heightened level of care" to inmates in solitary confinement, increase mental health staff, add new beds to treatment units, build a new residential mental health building, limit the circumstances under which inmates can be put into isolation, limit the duration of isolation to no more than four days, limit the circumstances under which inmates are kept in isolation without clothing to where there is a specific safety and security need, and increase the in-cell and out-of-cell contact with mental health specialists.[41] Dr. Michael Hogan, Commissioner of the New York State Office of Mental Health, believes that New York will now have the strongest prison mental health care system in the United States.

Is corrections being asked to shoulder the burden of the nation's failure to diagnose properly and care for those with mental or emotional disorders? You be the judge: It is estimated that there are nearly eight times more people who are mentally ill in the nation's jails and prisons (nearly 478,000) than there are in mental hospitals (60,000).[42] Six to 8 percent of the 10 to 12 million people who enter the nation's jails annually have severe mental illness. The three largest de facto psychiatric hospitals in the United States are now the Los Angeles County Jail, Rikers Island Jail in New York City, and Cook County Jail in Chicago. Approximately 28 percent of the male inmates and 31 percent of the female inmates booked into the L.A. County Jail in 1998 had a mental disorder.[43] The L.A. County Jail spends $10 million a year on psychiatric medication!

Suggesting that these facilities replace mental hospitals altogether overstates their treatment capacity and the function of these facilities—the mental health care required is far beyond what most correctional facilities are equipped to offer. Correctional officers are not therapists and correctional facilities are not mental hospitals. Corrections personnel are not trained to facilitate mental health treatment and, according to Dr. David Satcher, U.S. surgeon general from 1998 to 2002, "they should not have to."[44]

All jails have a constitutional mandate to provide at least minimum mental health or psychiatric care to detainees, yet 2 of 10 jails have no access to mental health services, 8 of 10 jail officers receive little or no training in mental health issues, and record numbers of jail inmates with mental illness are released into the community without any discharge planning, increasing the probability they will relapse and return to incarceration. Dr. Satcher noted that treating mental health rather than incarcerating those affected by mental illness could save $3 billion.

Why So Many? Why are there so many people who are mentally ill in the nation's jails? The reasons include failure to differentiate who should be in jail and who shouldn't, failure to treat people before they enter the criminal justice system, deinstitutionalization (moving the mentally ill from hospitals to nonsecure residential community settings), stricter commitment laws, less stringent discharge criteria, reductions or curtailment of public funding, lack of adequate insurance coverage, and three-strikes laws because those with mental illness may, when the illness is not effectively treated, be less able to follow the rule of law.[45] Former mental patients as well as people whose bizarre behavior might have landed them in a hospital bed a few years ago are now being arrested and are ending

THE STAFF SPEAKS

About 13 years ago, we began what's called the Maryland Community Criminal Justice Treatment Program. I developed this in partnership with the Maryland Correctional Administrators Association, because we were seeing numbers of people with mental illness coming into the local detention centers. So we developed comprehensive programs that provided each detention center—there are 23—with mental health services case management. The case managers' role is to try to connect people to community services upon release.

As we started understanding the population more, we started seeing that it wasn't just about mental health and corrections—it was about poverty and homelessness and substance abuse. So we had to try to develop community-based systems of support that brought together all of the different publicly based entities. We're very holistic—housing is crucial. You're not going to get someone to leave and "be compliant" while they're living under a bridge. We all start with "what would we want? What would we need?"

It's never just one thing. Our latest thing we're seeing is pregnant women—pregnant, incarcerated women. What started out as a program to meet the needs of mentally ill folks in the jail has branched into this program that addresses needs across the board.

Our project is an interesting blend of federal, state, and private money. With the leadership of both correctional administration and mental hygiene coming together, you realize these are all of our folks, and just because they rotate from system to system doesn't mean we drop them. We also believe these are the highest users of public services. You look at how many of them go into jails, how many of them are using the ER without insurance, using homeless shelters, using court time—it's a myriad of different public services that separately, at different times, provide for their needs. We believe if we can have one co-ordinated effort, we're not only serving the client better but reducing the need for them to be rotating from system to system.

Recidivism? Last year we only had 4.9 percent go back to jail.

Joan Gillece
Director of Special Needs Populations
Maryland Mental Hygiene Administration

---

up in jail. While 40 state mental hospitals have closed in the last decade, more than 400 new prisons have opened,[46] state spending for treatment of people who are mentally ill is one-third less today than it was in 1950,[47] and changes in mental health laws have made involuntary commitment more difficult. As a result, jails and prisons have become the institutions most likely to house those with mental illness.

In addition, offenders often live as transients or in crowded conditions, increasing their levels of stress which can precipitate mental illness. Offenders also tend to be economically disadvantaged, meaning they are less likely to get mental health treatment. Finally, they have high rates of substance abuse, which is correlated with mental illness.

A family whose child stops taking medication calls county mental health professionals who tell the family they cannot do anything until the child becomes "dangerous." When the child deteriorates to the point at which she or he is dangerous, the mental health professionals are no longer the ones who respond; sheriffs' deputies and police take over, and encounters between such children and law enforcement often turn deadly. According to Thomas Faust, executive director of the National Sheriff's Association, justified killings by law enforcement involving people with mental illness are four times greater than such killings involving mentally healthy people.[48]

Correctional facilities have an opportunity to provide prevention and treatment interventions to a seriously underserved and needy population. Policies and programs for prisoners help them return to our communities as better citizens, in better health, under treatment for their medical and mental health conditions, and better equipped and motivated to protect themselves and others, while possibly reducing the cost to taxpayers of future health care and reincarceration. Good health care is also an integral part of institutional security. Investments in prisoner health care result in fewer correctional disturbances, disciplinary actions, and inmate injuries and in less negative publicity for the institution.[49]

The key to curbing recidivism of people who are mentally ill is to expand public health services into the jails and prisons so that inmates can begin therapy the moment they walk into custody. When that happens, correctional institutions can provide offenders a better "hand off" from the institution to the community. Unless correctional policy moves in this direction, mental illness will continue to worsen in isolation and, for some inmates, lead to suicide.

What will it take for corrections policy to shift in that direction? Dean Aufderheide, director of Mental Health Services for the Florida Department of Corrections, believes we need to think of mental illness as a chronic illness. When we do that, we'll develop new strategies for dealing with it in prison and after release. He wrote, "By conceptualizing mental illness as a chronic illness, one that waxes and wanes, and like diabetes, is the manifestation of dynamic combinations of genetic and congenital vulnerabilities, environmental influences, and individual behavior, public health and safety officials can collaborate in seizing the opportunity to develop more and effective and efficient strategies for managing inmates with mental illness in prison and after release."[50]

Innovative Alternatives There are many successful and innovative ways to divert persons with mental illnesses from the criminal justice system, including the creation of law enforcement–mental health liaison programs, increased training of law enforcement personnel, and a general improvement in the funding and effectiveness of community mental health services. Three innovative strategies are presented below.

The Memphis Police Crisis Intervention Team (CIT) has won widespread national acclaim for the cooperative relationships that developed between the police and the mental health system. CIT officers, dispatchers, and other key police personnel receive intensive training about the signs and symptoms of serious mental illnesses, crisis intervention and deescalation techniques, and community mental health resources and options. A specialized mental health triage unit at the University of Memphis medical center was created to respond specifically to individuals referred by the police. Memphis police now know they have options available to them other than arrest and incarceration. So far there have been fewer arrests, better treatment outcomes, and reduced officer injuries.[51] CIT has been emulated in more than 50 communities across the United States, and other communities have developed alternative law enforcement–mental health triage capabilities.

A second innovative strategy for keeping people with mental illness out of jail and prison is mental health court, an extremely recent phenomenon. The term *mental health court* is most often used to refer to a specialized docket for defendants with mental illness that provides the opportunity to participate in court-supervised treatment. A court team, composed of a judge, court personnel, and treatment providers, defines the terms of participation, provides ongoing status assessments with individualized sanctions and rewards, and determines resolution of cases upon successful completion of court-ordered treatment plans. In 1997, there were four mental health courts in the United States. By January 2004 the number had risen to 70 in 29 states. As of February 2005, there were 107 mental health courts in 34 states.[52] Two rationales underlie mental health courts: (1) to protect the public by addressing the mental

Jon Wood
Family Counselor
Kandiyohi County Community Corrections
Kandiyohi, Minnesota

Jon Wood is a family counselor with the Kandiyohi County Community Corrections office in Kandiyohi, Minnesota. He has held that position for the past five years, after working in a similar position as a contractor for two years. Prior to that he received a master's degree in community counseling and a bachelor's degree in applied psychology from St. Cloud State University in St. Cloud, Minnesota.

Wood says the bulk of his time is spent providing counseling to first-time offenders, either in a one-on-one capacity or in a family setting. He specializes in dealing with juveniles with mental health issues, many of which are just emerging or have not even been diagnosed yet. He also works with schools, collaborates with other mental health professionals who might be dealing with the same individuals, and deals with social service agencies and probation agents.

Most of his clients are very young—according to Wood, the problems start to show up around age 10. "They're showing some behaviors at school, and I try to coordinate treatment with psychologists and psychiatrists, so we can figure out what to do for them," he says. "And a big challenge is trying to talk parents into making it happen, given the stigma that is attached to mental health issues."

Wood says his goal is to help both parents and children understand the illnesses that they are facing and help them develop methods of dealing with them. This means developing new cognitive skills and learning problem solving and negotiation skills. "It's trying to help them find other ways to think," he says, "so they don't have to always be fighting each other or some authority figure.

"About once every two years I'll get a letter from a parent saying thanks. It doesn't happen very often but once in a while. And every now and then I'll run into an old client in a grocery store, and he tells me that he's going to college. So I know that something that we talked about made sense to him."

> **"**
>
> *So often parents who are dealing with the juvenile justice system get to a point where they freak out, they don't want to have anything to do with it, and they throw their hands up in the air and give up.*
>
> **"**

illness that contributed to the criminal act, thereby reducing recidivism, and (2) to recognize that criminal sanctions, whether intended as punishments or deterrents, are neither effective nor morally appropriate when mental illness is a significant cause of the criminal act. Very little research is available on the effectiveness of mental health courts, but early findings on such courts in Broward County, Florida, point to relative success. Defendants were twice as likely to receive services for their mental illness and were no more likely to commit a new crime, despite spending 75 percent fewer days in jail than did comparable defendants.[53] Congress has promoted the development of mental health courts with the passage of the Law Enforcement and Mental Health Project Act in 2000, which makes federal funds available to local jurisdictions seeking to establish or expand mental health courts and diversion programs, and the Mentally Ill Offender Treatment and Crime Reduction Act of 2004, which authorizes federal funds for jail diversion, mental health treatment for inmates with mental illnesses, community reentry services, and training. The acts recognize that states and communities are best able to develop their own innovative approaches to reduce the criminalization of people with mental illnesses.

There are eight times more people with mental illness in jail and prison than there are in mental hospitals. What are some ways the needs of women correctional clients with mental disorders can be met?

A third strategy to keep people who are mentally ill out of jail and prison is the Assertive Community Treatment (ACT) Program. ACT programs are teams of social service professionals who provide a broad and integrated range of services to individuals diverted from jails or reentering communities following incarceration with severe and persistent mental illnesses. The services include medication and medication management, housing assistance, case management, substance abuse treatment, vocational supports, and mobile crisis management. ACT teams emphasize preventing people in crisis from "falling through the cracks." Today there are approximately 15 ACT programs in the United States, 3 of them in the Ohio Department of Rehabilitation and Corrections, for individuals with severe and persistent mental illnesses reentering their communities after completing prison sentences.

The American Association for Community Psychiatrists Committee on the Mentally Ill Behind Bars developed a list of recommendations to keep people with mental illness out of jail:[54]

1. Address the lack of access to community mental health and other diagnostic services in order to improve early diagnosis and treatment.

2. Create alternatives to incarceration for as many nonviolent offenders with mental illness as possible. For example, have a center to which police can take people who are experiencing a mental crisis.

3. Improve jail conditions that have negative effects on the mental health of inmates. For example, researchers are finding that serious bullying is a cause of suicide.[55] Suicide is the leading cause of death in jail and ranks third in prison.[56]

4. Establish vigorous programs designed to reintegrate inmates with mental illness into the community, with specific attention paid to their housing needs.

5. Create oversight boards to prevent human rights abuses and to guarantee that adequate physical and mental health services are available upon release.

tuberculosis (TB)
A highly variable communicable disease that is characterized by toxic symptoms or allergic manifestations that in humans primarily affect the lungs.

Inmates with Tuberculosis

Jails are at great risk for the spread of **tuberculosis (TB)**.[57] This is due to very close living quarters, overcrowding, poor sanitation, and the large number of inmates with a high risk of having TB, such as HIV-positive detainees, intravenous drug users, and immigrants. This was underscored by the 1999–2001 institutional outbreak of TB among 33 HIV-infected inmates in a segregated housing unit for HIV-infected inmates in South Carolina. In fact, TB is reported to be more than three times as prevalent in jails and prisons as it is in the general U.S. population and it is considered to be the most common cause of death among the world's prisoners.[58] When a person who has TB coughs, sneezes, or laughs, tiny droplets of fluid containing TB bacteria are released into the air, which are then inhaled by others. The TB germ becomes active in people when their immune system becomes weak. It multiplies and causes active TB. If left untreated, active TB can cause the infected person to literally waste away. TB was once the leading cause of death among Americans.

Experts concerned about TB in jails have indicated that the most important issues for jail professionals are to understand the causes and control of TB, to implement appropriate and cost-effective screening programs, and to develop close working relationships with local health authorities. Public health departments can provide correctional facilities access to expert TB medical consultation and laboratory services. Health department staff can also train correctional personnel in performing, interpreting, and recording tuberculin skin tests, identifying signs and symptoms of tuberculosis disease, initiating and observing therapy, monitoring medication side effects, collecting specimens, educating inmates, and maintaining record systems.

Older Inmates

Bureau of Justice Statistics figures for 2005 indicate that there were nearly 2.2 million inmates in the nation's prisons and jails, representing an increase of 2.6 percent (56,400) over the previous 12 months. Problems that were manageable two decades ago now threaten to overwhelm state and federal corrections systems. One issue that is being addressed by administrators across the nation is the aging of the prison population, the issue we turn to next in this chapter.

The Aging of the Prison Population   Most of us imagine prisoners as young and aggressive. However, *elderly* and *passive* describe a significant portion of the prison population. The definition of *elderly* is subject to debate. Some define *elderly* as 65 years of age and older, some suggest 60 years, others suggest 55, and still others 50. There are some who do not consider chronological age at all. Rather, they believe that, because of the impact of prison lifestyle, including lower socioeconomic status and limited access to medical care, a prisoner's physiological age may be higher than his or her chronological age. In addition, some say that a lengthy prison stay can age an inmate 10 years beyond chronological age.

Despite the differences among definitions of *elderly*, it is possible to establish a common chronological starting point to define *older* inmates for purposes of comprehensive planning, programming, evaluation, and research within and among prison systems. After careful study of the issue, the National Institute of Corrections recommended that correctional agencies nationwide adopt age 50 as the chronological starting point for defining *older inmates*.[59]

COMMISSION ON SAFETY AND ABUSE IN AMERICA'S PRISONS: HEALTH CARE

> " *Much of the public imagines jails and prisons as sealed institutions, where what happens inside remains inside. In the context of disease and illness, which can travel naturally from one environment to another, that view is clearly wrong. Protecting the public health, reducing human suffering, fulfilling our constitutional obligation to those we incarcerate, and addressing the financial cost of untreated illness depends on good and adequately funded correctional health care.* "
>
> — The Commission on Safety and Abuse in America's Prisons

Every year, more than 1.5 million people are released from jail and prison carrying a life-threatening infectious disease. At least 300,000 to 400,000 prisoners have a serious mental illness—a number three times the population of state mental hospitals nationwide. And prisoners on average require significantly more health care than most Americans because of poverty, substance abuse, and because they most often come from underserved communities.

Many corrections leaders are struggling to provide quality care without adequate resources and often without frontline staff who understand and share their goal. The consequences for individuals and families can be tragic. In California, where control of health care in state prisons has been ceded to a federal judge, one prisoner was dying needlessly from medical malpractice or neglect every six to seven days as recently as October 2005.

Correctional facilities have a constitutional obligation to provide health care—and some fulfill that obligation with vigor. They also have a tremendous opportunity: to protect the public health and to use precious health care resources efficiently through disease prevention, early detection, and appropriate treatment. But corrections cannot do this alone, and legislatures chronically underfund correctional health care.

The following six recommendations suggest ways to improve correctional health care:

Partner with Health Providers from the Community

Departments of corrections and health providers from the community should join together in the common project of delivering high-quality health care that protects prisoners and the public.

Build Real Partnerships Within Facilities

Corrections administrators and officers must develop collaborative working relationships with those who provide health care to prisoners.

Commit to Caring for Persons with Mental Illness

Legislators and executive branch officials, including corrections administrators, need to commit adequate resources to identify and treat prisoners who are mentally ill and, simultaneously, to reduce the number of people with mental illness in prisons and jails.

Screen, Test, and Treat for Infectious Disease

Every U.S. prison and jail should screen, test, and treat for infectious diseases under the oversight of public health authorities and in compliance with national guidelines and ensure continuity of care upon release.

End Copayments for Medical Care

State legislatures should revoke existing laws that authorize prisoner copayments for medical care.

Extend Medicaid and Medicare to Eligible Prisoners

Congress should change the Medicaid and Medicare rules so that correctional facilities can receive federal funds to help cover the costs of providing health care to eligible prisoners. Until Congress acts, states should ensure that benefits are available to people immediately upon release.

Source: Adapted from the Commission on Safety and Abuse in America's Prisons, *Confronting Confinement* (New York: Vera Institute of Justice, 2006). Note: The full 126-page report, *Confronting Confinement: A Report of the Commission on Safety and Abuse in America's Prisons,* can be accessed on the Internet at www.prisoncommission.org.

Because researchers have not universally adopted this recommendation, a research focal point has not emerged, making trends in prison population aging difficult to identify and analyze, eliminating the possibility of generating point-by-point comparisons, and yielding confusing and potentially misleading results. For example, Neeley and colleagues project that, by the year 2010, inmates over the age of 50 will constitute 33 percent of the total prison population.[60] The most current age data gathered by federal agencies, however, is arrayed in age brackets 45–54 and 55 or older.[61] These data show that on January 1, 2006, the 270,100 inmates over the age of 45 accounted for 17.7 percent of the number of sentenced prisoners under state and federal jurisdiction; only 4.4 percent (66,500) were 55 or older.

Older inmates represent the fastest-growing group in the general population of state and federal prisoners. From 1995 to 2006, the number of prisoners under state and federal jurisdiction over age 45 jumped from 108,100 to 270,100 or about 150 percent. The number over age 55 doubled from 32,600 to 66,500 an increase of almost 104 percent. During the same period the total number of prisoners under state and federal jurisdiction increased by only 41 percent.

Are populations of older inmates increasing at a rate that makes Neeley's projections accurate? Do these current data indicate that the rate is accelerating or slowing? What percentage of the 270,100 inmates above the age of 45 are actually above the age of 50? How would that information affect interpretation of the data? Policymakers and researchers need clarity of information. The existing situation, however, renders such clarity impossible.

In an examination of the impact of California's three-strikes law,[62] Ryan King and Marc Mauer of The Sentencing Project found that the law has significantly altered the demographics of that state's prison population in just the 7 years since its inception. They estimate that, within 25 years, 30,000 prisoners will be incarcerated in California under sentences of 25 years to life. King and Mauer project this burgeoning population of older prisoners will place an extraordinary burden on the penal system's resources. Of particular concern is the increased cost of housing older inmates, who typically have greater need of costly medical care.

Geriatric Prison Facilities   An increasing number of states are beginning to provide long-term-care needs for a prison population that has quadrupled during the past 30 years. Alabama, Arizona, Georgia, Illinois, Kansas, Kentucky, Maryland, Michigan, Minnesota, Mississippi, North Carolina, New Jersey, Ohio, Pennsylvania, South Carolina, Tennessee, Texas, Virginia, West Virginia, and Wisconsin have special prisons for the elderly, often called "aged/infirm," "medical/geriatric," "disabled," or simply "geriatric." The facility itself accommodates special needs of the elderly. Few stairs, reduced distances, more crafts and leisure activities, and staff trained in gerontological issues make these facilities unique. The majority confine only elderly male prisoners. Older female prisoners, who constitute only a small percentage of the total elderly prisoner population, are generally kept in a state's only women's prison.

hospice
An interdisciplinary, comfort-oriented care facility that helps seriously ill patients die with dignity and humanity in an environment that facilitates mental and spiritual preparation for the natural process of dying.

Prison Hospice Programs   Before the onset of AIDS and the increased numbers of elderly prisoners, few prisoners died while incarcerated. Inmate deaths occur more frequently now, and correctional administrators have taken measures to address the unique problems associated with helping terminally ill prisoners through their passing. A **hospice** is an interdisciplinary, comfort-oriented care facility that helps seriously ill patients die with dignity and humanity in an environment that facilitates mental and spiritual preparation for the natural process of dying. Hospice programs provide a wide array of services, including pain management, spiritual support, and psychological counseling, as well as grief counseling for bereaved families. As of August 2004, 30 prison hospice programs have been initiated nationwide.

Often, one of the challenges in starting a prison hospice is educating the prison staff in caring for terminally ill prisoners and making a psychological adjustment to get over the resentment that prisoners are getting this level of care. According to Elizabeth Craig, executive director of the National Prison Hospice Association (NPHA) in Boulder, Colorado, "In my view, inmates are being punished by being incarcerated; we don't need to create more suffering for them."[63]

The nation's best-known prison hospice program is the one at the Louisiana State Penitentiary (LSP) at Angola. LSP Angola is the nation's largest state prison. Of its nearly 5,200 inmates, over 90 percent are expected to die while incarcerated.[64]

LSP Angola's hospice program has five core goals:

1. Provide quality end-of-life care irrespective of a patient's criminal charge or personal history.
2. Honor the patient's support system, including his family (as defined by him).
3. Address the patient's needs holistically, with emphasis on palliation of physical, social, spiritual, and emotional suffering.
4. Assist the patient with activities that he considers life-affirming.
5. Maintain an end-of-life care system consistent with "free world" standards.

A fundamental part of hospice care at LSP Angola is the emphasis on family. Each inmate patient is allowed to designate two inmates from Angola's general prisoner population as "family," and within the constraints of security, these inmates are treated like the inmate's biological family members. Angola's staff provides whatever considerations are possible within the constraints of security to ensure that the patient's final days are as meaningful as possible for all involved.

Health Issues The physical, mental, and medical health care needs of older inmates have implications for prison policymakers, administrators, and staff. Older, sicker inmates challenge health care systems.

It is estimated that an elderly prisoner suffers from an average of three chronic illnesses. Almost 70 percent of the geriatric women incarcerated in California in 2004 said that at least one prison activity was very difficult for them: 59 percent reported difficulties hearing orders, 57 percent said it was very difficult for them to drop to the floor for alarms, 35 percent said it was very difficult for them to stand in line for head counts, 14 of the 35 women who were assigned to upper bunks said it was very difficult for them to climb on and off a top bunk, and 61 percent said they had been given jobs that were too difficult to perform, including janitorial and yard crew work.[65] Incarcerating older prisoners with impaired eyesight, physical disabilities, cancer, arthritis, diabetes, heart disease, hypertension, or Alzheimer's disease and treating these illnesses raise many concerns. For example, how ethical is it for prisons to provide surgery, physical therapy, and daily medication to elderly prisoners when people outside prison are unable to afford similar medical treatment?

Get-tough-on-crime policies have led to an increased number of inmates serving longer periods of time behind bars. The Colorado Territorial Correctional Facility in Cañon City includes a 32-bed infirmary for elderly prisoners with cancer, heart disease, diabetes, and respiratory problems and highlights the public health costs associated with elderly prisoners. What are some of the special needs of geriatric inmates?

syphilis

A sexually transmitted disease caused by the bacteria *Treponema pallidum*. If left untreated, syphilis can cause serious heart abnormalities, mental disorders, blindness, other neurological problems, and death. Syphilis is transmitted when an infected lesion comes in contact with the soft skin of the mucous membrane.

gonorrhea

The second most common sexually transmitted disease. Often called *the clap,* gonorrhea is caused by the *Neisseria gonorrhea* bacteria found in moist areas of the body. Infection occurs with contact to any of these areas.

Another issue that must be considered is the effect of health-related legislation. For example, the Americans with Disabilities Act (ADA) affects not only mainstream society, but also prisons and jails. Designing prison spaces that are accessible for elderly prisoners, with ramps, handrails, good lighting, and subtle grades, is now law under ADA. In *U.S.* v. *Georgia* (2006), the Supreme Court ruled that prisoners with disabilities may sue for monetary damages if the violation of ADA is so serious as to also constitute a violation of civil rights.[66]

Cost Issues   The economic consequences of incarcerating older prisoners are huge. The estimated national cost per year to confine an inmate over 55 years old is $70,000.[67] In North Carolina it costs $37,000 per year to keep elderly prisoners at the McCain Correctional Facility. The average annual cost for such an inmate in Maryland is $69,000. In California, it is $80,000.

Could elderly prisoners who are considered harmless be released early to go back to their families or to independent care living and thereby save prisons money? Systematic research on how elderly prisoners adapt after prison release is sketchy, although it is known that recidivism drops with age: According to the U.S. Parole Commission, older federal prisoners show lower recidivism rates. The U.S. Department of Justice reported that only 2 percent of inmates who are 55 or older when paroled return to prison.[68] It is doubtful that, when mandatory sentencing laws, three-strikes laws, and truth-in-sentencing laws were enacted, the economic impact of incarcerating elderly prisoners for long periods of time was actually considered. Unless legislatures give courts and prison administrators more leeway to interchange prison sentences with community sentences, states will find themselves in economic crises as they attempt to provide for the 33 percent of the inmate population that is projected to be elderly by the year 2010.

SEXUALLY TRANSMITTED DISEASES IN JAIL

Most studies on infectious diseases in correctional facilities focus on prison. The problem of sexually transmitted diseases (STDs) in jail is addressed less frequently even though some believe that STDs are more common in jail than in prison.[69] However, rapid turnover and frequent movement of inmates make jails difficult settings in which to study the prevalence of various diseases. But recently, the Society of Correctional Physicians published a report by Dr. Karl Brown, infectious disease supervisor at New York City's Rikers Island Jail, on the increase of STDs in jail and the difficulties diagnosing and treating four of the most common STDs found in jail today: syphilis, gonorrhea, chlamydia, and genital herpes. **Syphilis** is caused by the bacterium *Treponema pallidum*. Syphilis is passed from person to person through direct contact with a syphilis sore. Transmission of the bacterium occurs during sexual contact. **Gonorrhea** is caused by *Neisseria gonorrhea*, a bacterium that grows and multiplies in mucous membranes of the body. Gonorrhea bacteria grows in the warm, moist areas of the reproductive tract, including the cervix, uterus, and fallopian tubes in women, and in the urethra (urine canal) in women and men. The bacteria can also grow in the mouth, throat, and anus. Gonorrhea is spread through sexual contact. **Chlamydia** is the most frequently reported STD in the United States. It is caused by the bacterium *Chlamydia trachomatis*. Chlamydia is transmitted through sexual contact. **Genital herpes** is a lifelong infection caused by the herpes simplex viruses type 1 (HSV-1) and type 2 (HSV-2). A person can get HSV-1 by coming into contact with the saliva of an infected person. HSV-1 causes infections of the mouth and lips, so-called "fever blisters." A person almost always gets HSV-2 infection during sexual contact with someone who has a genital HSV-2 infection. According to Brown, after declining for many years, the rates of syphilis, gonorrhea, and chlamydia began increasing in jails and juvenile detention centers in 2000, especially among female prisoners.

The jail environment may be the key to controlling STDs, but less than half of the nation's jails have a policy of routine screening, and even in those jails with routine screening, less than half of the inmates were tested for syphilis, gonorrhea, or chlamydia. Brown also found another problem: Approximately half of arrestees were released within 48 hours, but most jails received the inmates' test results more than 48 hours after admission.

The type of screening for STDs in jail should be based on the prevalence of STDs as measured by the population served. For example, gonorrhea and chlamydia are four times higher in northern Florida than they are in northern California. The key to controlling STDs is to continuously collect, monitor, and analyze information and then to discuss the results with public health officials. Diagnosis also requires a thorough nonjudgmental sexual history and a careful genital exam.

LEGAL ISSUES

Providing inmates adequate health care is of concern to the courts and professional associations. In 1976, the U.S. Supreme Court ruled in *Estelle* v. *Gamble*[70] that inmates have a constitutional right to reasonable, adequate health services for serious medical needs. However, the Court also made clear that such a right did not mean that prisoners have unqualified access to health care. Lower courts have held that the Constitution does not require that medical care provided to prisoners be perfect, the best obtainable, or even very good.[71] According to an excellent review of legal health care standards and the legal remedies available to prisoners, the courts support the principle of least eligibility (defined in Chapter 7). Prisoners do not have the right to sue physicians for malpractice, or if they do, the damages are lower than those awarded to people outside prison. Nevertheless, health care professionals and inmate advocates—such as the American Medical Association, the American Correctional Health Services Association, and the National Commission on Correctional Health Care—insist on alleviating the pain and suffering of all persons, regardless of their status. They believe that no distinction should be made between inmates and free citizens.

Another important piece of legislation affecting inmate health care is the Civil Rights of Institutionalized Persons Act (CRIPA).[72] This law places prisoners in a class with others confined in government institutions, such as people with disabilities and elderly people in government-run nursing homes. Enacted in 1980, CRIPA evolved from the U.S. Department of Justice's Civil Rights Division's *amicus curiae* ("friend of the court") intervention in a 1972 lawsuit brought by parents, volunteer organizations, and individual residents at the Willowbrook State School for the Mentally Retarded. The suit alleged that the State of New York and school administrators were negligent in permitting abominable conditions to exist at the school. Ongoing problems at the site included severe crowding (65 percent above capacity), faulty plumbing, general filth, lack of adequate medical

chlamydia

The most common sexually transmitted disease. Caused by the bacteria *Chlamydia trachomatis,* it can affect the eyes, lungs, or urogenital (urinary-genital) area, depending on the age of the person infected and how the infection is transmitted.

genital herpes

A sexually transmitted disease caused by the herpes simplex virus, or HSV. It is one of the most common STDs in the United States.

personnel, and failure to control residents, resulting in more than 1,300 incidents of injury, assaults, or fights within one eight-month period.

The Civil Rights Division helped the parents and others prove that the civil rights of the residents were being violated. Coupled with an admission by the deputy commissioner of the State of New York that conditions at Willowbrook were "a major tragedy," the Civil Rights Division's efforts forced a settlement and ultimate correction of the appalling conditions at the school.

The case became the impetus for CRIPA by publicizing conditions that were all too common in facilities run by government agencies at the time. The passage of CRIPA protects all institutionalized persons, including prisoners, by providing them an established avenue of relief. However, some believe CRIPA has not had a significant effect on prison conditions or on prisoners' rights.

Inmates with Disabilities

Inmates with special needs face numerous difficulties. Consider the case of Ronald Yeskey. Yeskey was sentenced to 18 to 36 months in a Pennsylvania correctional facility. He was recommended for a motivational boot camp, which would have shortened his sentence to six months. He was, however, refused admission to the boot camp because of a physical disability—hypertension. He sued, claiming that the **Americans with Disabilities Act (ADA)** of 1990 prohibits any "public entity" from discriminating against a "qualified individual with a disability" because of that disability.

In 1998 in a unanimous opinion, the U.S. Supreme Court held that state prisons fall squarely within the ADA's definition of a "public entity."[73] Reacting to the decision, Yeskey's attorney noted, "The court's ruling means that prison officials cannot discriminate against prisoners with disabilities and must make reasonable modifications to prison operations so that these prisoners will have reasonable access to most prison programs;"[74] otherwise, prisoners can sue for monetary damages.

Inmates with HIV/AIDS

Most suits by prisoners with HIV/AIDS are claims that officials have violated a prisoner's rights by revealing the condition or by segregating the prisoner because of the condition. In 1988, officials in Erie County, New York, placed an HIV-positive female prisoner in a segregated prison wing reserved for inmates with mental illness. They also placed on her possessions red stickers revealing her HIV-positive status. The inmate sued, claiming denial of her rights to privacy and due process. The district court agreed (*Nolley* v. *County of Erie*, 1991). In the same year, however, the Eleventh Circuit Court of Appeals held that an Alabama policy of isolating all HIV-positive inmates did not violate the Fourth or Eighth Amendments (*Harris* v. *Thigpen* and *Austin* v. *Pennsylvania Dept. of Corr.*).

Other legal issues relate to the work assignments of HIV/AIDS inmates. In 1994, in *Gates* v. *Rowland*, the Ninth Circuit Court of Appeals ruled that California correctional officials could continue to bar HIV-positive inmates from working in prison kitchens. The court made it clear that its decision was based more on the anticipated reactions of prisoners receiving the food than on any actual risk of infection. The court agreed that food service "has often been the source of violence or riots" because inmates "are not necessarily motivated by rational thought and frequently have irrational suspicions or phobias that education will not modify"

Americans with Disabilities Act (ADA)
Public Law 101-336, enacted July 26, 1990, which prohibits discrimination and ensures equal opportunity for people with disabilities in employment, state and local government services, public accommodations, commercial facilities, and transportation. It also mandates the establishment of TDD/telephone relay services.

Prisoners in wheelchairs, and others with special needs, place an extraordinary strain on prison resources. Inmates with disabilities are protected under the federal Americans with Disabilities Act (ADA) of 1990. What does the act require of correctional facilities? What are the alternatives to incarceration for inmates with disabilities?

and because prisoners "have no choice of where they eat." Correctional officials had based their policy, the court said, on "legitimate penological concerns."

Inmates with Mental Illness

The federal courts have recognized the right of inmates who are mentally ill to treatment. According to a district court in Illinois, this right is triggered when it becomes reasonably certain that (1) the prisoner's symptoms demonstrate a serious mental disease or brain injury, (2) the disease or injury is curable or at least treatable, and (3) delaying or denying care would cause substantially more harm to the inmate (*Parte* v. *Lane*, 1981). In 1990, in *Washington* v. *Harper*, the U.S. Supreme Court ruled that inmates who are dangerous to themselves or others as a result of mental illness may be treated with psychoactive drugs against their will. Such involuntary drug treatment, however, has to be in the best interest of the inmate's mental health, not just for the convenience of the correctional institution.

REVIEW & APPLICATIONS

REFLECTIONS ON THE FUTURE

Correctional Health Care: An Integral Component of Public Health

by Edward A. Harrison

president, National Commission on Correctional Health Care

The cost of running correctional facilities is a tremendous and growing strain for many of our states and communities, and a principal cause is health care. Between 1985 and 1998 health care costs per prison inmate more than doubled (primarily because of more effective but more costly pharmaceuticals), while at the same time departments of corrections' medical budgets increased more than five-fold[1] (because of increased pharmacy costs and the growing inmate population). These rates of increase are far higher than those seen for other costs of incarceration.

Given that inmates have a constitutional right to necessary health care, provision of such care will become onerously expensive for taxpayers in the years ahead. For example, correctional facilities must contend with diseases, such as HIV and hepatitis C, that are both pervasive among inmates and costly to treat. Our urban jails

have become the nation's largest mental health facilities and thus are burdened with the associated costs of treatment. As well, prisons must care for an aging inmate population (the result of longer sentences being served) and its greater need for health services. Clearly, the economics of correctional health care will help determine its future.

While the importance of inmate health care is something too many Americans still do not accept, that attitude—as well as public policy—is beginning to change. In 1988, Surgeon General designate David Satcher became the first Surgeon General to state publicly his desire to include inmates in the nation's public health strategy. Four years later Surgeon General Richard Carmona, himself once a jail physician, said that correctional health care would be a priority of his administration.

Melding public health and correctional health is an important

step. According to NCCHC's seminal report "The Health Status of Soon-to-Be-Released Inmates: A Report to Congress,"[2] undiagnosed and underdiagnosed diseases in inmates, as well as untreated or undertreated illness, are threats to the nation's health and economy. Many inmates with undiagnosed and untreated diseases do not or cannot utilize community health services after they are released, and with millions of inmates released every year from all correctional facilities, the magnitude of the problem is potentially vast.

Fortunately, correctional health care presents a unique opportunity to reduce health risks and financial costs to the community. When treatment and prevention services are provided in the correctional setting, not only are they cost-effective or even cost-saving, but they also help protect the larger public health.

Closer collaboration between public health systems and correctional systems in our communities is what lies ahead. This will reduce wasteful duplication of services and improve patient care. Correctional systems and public health systems will share the costs associated with treating chronic health conditions. And by rectifying gaps in prevention, screening and treatment services in prisons and jails, communities can take advantage of a tremendous opportunity to improve public health by reducing the problems associated with untreated inmates returning to the community.

NOTES
1. Correctional Health Care: Guidelines for the Management of an Adequate Delivery Systems, Anno, B.J., 2001, National Commission on Correctional Health Care, Chicago, and National Institute of Corrections, Washington, DC.
2. The Health Status of Soon-to-Be-Released Inmates: A Report to Congress, 2002, National Commission of Correctional Health Care, Chicago.

About the Author

Edward A. Harrison is president of the National Commission on Correctional Health Care (NCCHC). NCCHC is the recognized national standards-setting body for correctional health care and for certifying correctional health professionals. Harrison received a bachelor of arts in communication from the University of Illinois and a master of business administration from Northwestern University.

SUMMARY

1 Some inmates require special treatment or care because they suffer from mental illness, chemical dependency, a communicable disease, or typical problems associated with elderly people. These inmates present unique problems for correctional staff and administrators.

2 Special-needs inmates present significant management problems because they are typically more violent and prone to be disruptive, require close monitoring as suicide risks, tax scarce medical resources, and are often targets of abuse by other inmates.

3 A tenfold increase in prison populations over the past 25 years caused a commensurate increase in the number of inmates with substance abuse problems. These inmates tremendously drain finite resources, are disruptive to daily life within the walls, and create unique management problems in all areas of prison life.

4 Special difficulties related to HIV/AIDS among prison populations include privacy issues, disruption of the prison routine due to the frequency of taking medication, inmate distrust of the medical and legal systems, fear of side effects, and the legal dilemma embodied in the principle of least eligibility.

5 The five essential elements of cost-effective management of HIV/AIDS inmates are early detection and diagnosis, medical management and treatment, inmate classification and housing, education and training of staff and inmates, and funding.

6 The increase in the number of inmates with mental illness is attributable to several factors: the deinstitutionalization of persons who are mentally ill to nonsecure residential environments; stricter commitment laws; failure to know who should and should not be in jail; failure to treat them before they enter the criminal justice system; less stringent discharge criteria; reduction or elimination of public funding; lack of adequate insurance coverage; and three-strikes laws because those with mental illness may, when the illness is not effectively treated, be less able to follow the rule of law.

7 Ways to divert persons with mental illnesses from the criminal justice system include the creation of law enforcement–mental health liaison programs, increased training of law enforcement personnel, and a general improvement in the funding and effectiveness of community health services.

8 Estimates are that, on average, each older inmate is afflicted with three chronic illnesses that require ongoing and expensive medical treatment. Some question the equity of providing such free treatment to criminal offenders when the same free treatment is not provided to the public at large. The annual cost of incarcerating an elderly inmate is significantly higher than the average per-inmate cost of incarceration.

9 Inmates with disabilities, infectious diseases, and/or mental illness present unique legal and moral dilemmas for correctional administrators and the courts. The legal issues threaten to overwhelm the court systems with suits brought by prisoners. Meanwhile, the moral issues frequently mandate compassion, flexibility, and creativity among staff and administrators in navigating the daily routine of prison life.

KEY TERMS

special-needs inmates, *p. 461*
substance-abusing inmate, *p. 461*
therapeutic community (TC), *p. 468*
HIV (human immunodeficiency
   virus), *p. 471*

AIDS (acquired immunodeficiency
   syndrome), *p. 472*
tuberculosis (TB), *p. 482*
hospice, *p. 484*
syphilis, *p. 486*

gonorrhea, *p. 486*
chlamydia, *p. 487*
genital herpes, *p. 487*
Americans with Disabilities Act
   (ADA), *p. 488*

QUESTIONS FOR REVIEW

1 What is a *special-needs inmate?*

2 Summarize the management problems that special-needs inmates pose for corrections officials.

3 What criteria would you use to assess the impact that substance abusers have on the corrections system?

4 How would you design a system that makes it easier to treat HIV in prison?

5 What ideas can you add to the five essential elements of providing cost-effective management of HIV/AIDS inmates?

6 What evidence explains why there are so many inmates with mental illness in prison?

7 Suggest additional strategies for diverting persons with mental illness from the criminal justice system.

8 What should corrections do about the cost and health issues associated with older inmates?

9 Why is it important to understand the legal issues surrounding special population inmates?

THINKING CRITICALLY ABOUT CORRECTIONS

Aging Prison Population and Costs

As the prison population ages, the costs of incarcerating large numbers of older inmates will skyrocket. This, in turn, will strain correctional budgets and adversely impact correctional administrators' ability to provide essential services to the general prisoner population. Should elderly inmates be released from incarceration? Could services provided by other public agencies be tapped to meet the needs of elderly inmates? If so, which services might be invoked?

The Principle of Least Eligibility

Discussions of the principle of least eligibility invariably fire emotions. Should inmates rate free medical care that is not available to law-abiding citizens? Why or why not? Would you support a ballot proposal to formalize the principle of least eligibility as law in your state? Why or why not? If such a law were adopted, do you think it would withstand challenge through the state and federal court systems? Why or why not?

ON-THE-JOB DECISION MAKING

How to Use Personal Experience to Advance Correctional Training in HIV/AIDS

You are the warden of a state prison and on record as a supporter of the principle of least eligibility. Walter Edmunds is one of your most dependable correctional officers. Mature, calm, and unfailingly professional, Edmunds can be counted on in every crisis. You have come to rely on his leadership as a positive element among the correctional staff. Unfortunately, Edmunds has a young son dying of AIDS, which he contracted through a blood transfusion during an appendectomy.

Yesterday, your medical staff conducted training for your correctional officers on procedures for handling inmates

suffering from HIV and AIDS. About 10 minutes into the training session, Edmunds apologized for interrupting and then asked why the prisoners received top-notch medical treatment for free, treatment that ordinary law-abiding citizens can't afford.

From that single question, things quickly deteriorated, and Edmunds became increasingly agitated. Before long, the training room was in turmoil, as Edmunds's questions and angry comments whipped up the sympathy and anger of his fellow correctional officers.

Clearly out of his depth, the medical officer canceled the remainder of the training session and then bolted to your office. By the time he finished relating the incident, one of your correctional lieutenants appeared to report that the unionized correctional staff was in an uproar and threatening to walk off the job. What would you do to defuse this situation? Once you contained the crisis, how would you handle Edmunds?

Deciding Legitimate Penological Concerns

You are a correctional lieutenant at a state prison that has a conjugal visitation program. Carl Packard, one of your inmates, was recently diagnosed as HIV-positive. During an interview with a member of the medical staff, Packard acknowledged recent illicit drug use during which he shared a needle with other inmates. He and the medic believe this needle sharing to be the source of Packard's HIV infection.

Yesterday, Packard applied for a conjugal visit with his wife. You summoned him to your office and asked if he had advised his wife of his infection. Packard stated he had not and that he had no intention of "tellin' that bitch nothin'." This morning, you sought guidance from the prison's legal advisor and the warden. They informed you that infection with HIV did not prohibit an inmate's participation in the conjugal visitation program and that privacy policies prohibit you from informing Mrs. Packard of her husband's physical condition. You strongly believe that the threat to Mrs. Packard's health and safety outweighs what you consider to be ill-advised rules and policies.

1. What do you do?
2. What is your reasoning?

LIVE LINKS

at www.justicestudies.com/livelinks04

12–1   Mental Health Problems of Prison and Jail Inmates

The report compares the characteristics of offenders with a mental health problem to those without, including current offense, criminal record, sentence length, time expected to be served, co-occurring substance dependence or abuse, family background, and facility conduct since current admission. It presents measures of mental health problems by gender, race, and age. The report describes mental health problems and mental health treatment among inmates since admission to jail or prison. Findings are based on the Survey of Inmates in State and Federal Correctional Facilities, 2004, and the Survey of Inmates in Local Jails, 2002. Highlights include the following: Nearly a quarter of both state prisoners and jail inmates who had a mental health problem, compared to a fifth of those without, had served three or more prior incarcerations; female inmates had higher rates of mental health problems than male inmates (state prisons: 73 percent of females and 55 percent of males; federal prisons: 61 percent of females and 44 percent of males; local jails: 75 percent of females and 63 percent of males); over one in three state prisoners, one in four federal prisoners, and one in six jail inmates who had a mental health problem had received treatment since admission.

12–2   Crossing the Bridge: An Evaluation of the Drug Treatment Alternative-to-Prison (DTAP) Program

DTAP is a program that offers prosecutors the same kind of effective alternative to prison that has proved so successful for judges in drug courts. Significantly, DTAP shows that coerced treatment can work for a most difficult population: drug-addicted offenders, including sellers, who have as many as five prior felony convictions and who have spent an average of 49 months in prison. The National Center on Addiction and Substance Abuse (CASA) evaluation found that individuals participating in the DTAP program, including those who did not graduate, were less likely to be rearrested, reconvicted, and reincarcerated. DTAP participants remained in treatment six times longer than the overall median of individuals in long-term residential drug treatment programs. DTAP graduates are at least three times more likely to be employed than they were before their arrest.

12–3   Telemedicine Can Reduce Correctional Health Care Costs

Telemedicine, the remote delivery of health care through telecommunications, is promising for prison use. This report examines how prisons can use telemedicine to reduce health care costs and decrease security risks. Demonstrations of telemedicine in four federal prisons indicate that, in addition to cost savings, remote telemedical consultations can provide access to new specialists and improve the quality of care delivered to prison populations.

12–4   Correctional Health Care Addressing the Needs of Elderly, Chronically Ill, and Terminally Ill Inmates

This report discusses the management of aging and infirm prisoners. It focuses on what we know about elderly, chronically ill, and terminally ill inmates; effective evaluation for identifying the special needs of inmates; program, housing, and treatment considerations; ethical and policy considerations for the care of elderly and infirm inmates; and conclusions.

12–5 Dignity Denied: The Price of Imprisoning Older Women in California

The impact of incarceration on elderly female offenders is investigated. Sections following an executive summary are introduction; findings regarding activities of daily life, housing, work and programming, health care, abuse, support, surviving, and thriving, and growing old behind bars; responding to the crisis; geriatric prisons—not a solution; and recommendations. The "primary recommendation of this report centers on reducing the number of older prisoners in California through a combination of early release programs and expansion of community-based alternatives to incarceration."

PART FIVE
ISSUES IN CORRECTIONS

Part Five focuses on some of the most con-

troversial debates in contemporary corrections. Prison overcrowding became a problem shortly after a wing of the Walnut Street Jail was converted into the world's first prison in 1790, and it continues to be a problem today. When prisons are overcrowded, safety is compromised and conditions ripen for disturbances and riots.

One way to control prison overcrowding is to build more prisons. Today, the federal government and some states are building supermax prisons to deal with inmates whose violent behavior makes it impossible for them to live among the general prison population. Other options to control prison overcrowding are accreditation, which mandates acceptable staff-inmate ratios; privatization, the goal of which is to turn institutions into cost-effective private businesses; and technology, which can reduce the number of people required to supervise a given inmate population.

The increase in attention to victims' rights has also changed the corrections landscape. Today, all states and the federal government have laws that establish, protect, and enforce victims' rights. However, as you will learn, victims' rights laws are unevenly applied and sometimes partially ignored. Would a constitutional amendment, as recommended by Congress and the president, result in more even application and enforcement?

Possibly no other corrections issue has received more attention than capital punishment. The watershed U.S. Supreme Court case *Furman* v. *Georgia* (1972) changed the way judges and juries impose the death penalty. Since 1977, 1,096 people have been executed in the United States, and 3,350 are on death row today. New research on defendant–victim racial characteristics, execution of the innocent, and social consensus is sharpening the debate over capital punishment.

The face of juvenile corrections is also changing. The first juvenile court established in Cook County (Chicago, Illinois) in 1899 had high hopes for controlling and preventing delinquency. However, today society's response to rare yet high-profile juvenile offending means that the needs of the vast majority of juveniles who are arrested for nonviolent offenses are virtually ignored. There is no magic bullet to prevent delinquency, but there are correctional strategies and "best practices" that work. Implementing them will be up to you, the next generation of correctional professionals.

The final chapter in Part Five expands on the theme of professionalism in corrections first introduced in Chapter 1. Here we discuss the challenges facing the development of professionalism in corrections and answer the questions of how one fosters professionalism, how professionalism impacts the correctional environment, and what a correctional administrator can do to ensure that professionalism will be maintained.

PRI
SON
ISS

PRISON ISSUES AND CONCERNS

Security, Privatization, Technology, and Accreditation

CHAPTER OBJECTIVES

After completing this chapter you should be able to do the following:

1 List the four main reasons prisons are overcrowded.

2 Identify six methods of controlling prison overcrowding.

3 Explain how prisons control the influence of security threat groups (STGs).

4 Identify five causes of prison riots.

5 Describe what can be done to prevent prison riots.

6 Outline the emergence of supermax housing and its impact on prisoners and staff.

7 Describe "no-frills" jails and prisons and their impact on corrections.

8 List the reasons correctional agencies and facilities should be accredited.

9 List the arguments for and against privatization.

10 Discuss the impact of technology on corrections.

A flip of the switch activated the electromagnetic field between the inmates' metallic boots and the prison floor and stopped the prison disturbance in the film *Face/Off* starring John Travolta and Nicolas Cage. Sound far out? It may not be that unimaginable. Imagine reporting a crime to a "software agent" police officer at your local police department via the Internet. Imagine probation officers monitoring electronically transmitted smells to keep track of the lifestyles of convicted drug offenders. Imagine virtual courtrooms, digitally displayed evidence, and virtual tours of crime scenes. You do not even have to imagine. The technology is already here.

But what are the issues and concerns of the prison environment today? In this chapter, we shall consider seven aspects of the prison environment: overcrowding, riots and violence, supermax housing, "no-frills" prisons and jails, accreditation, privatization, and technocorrections.

Detection technology, like the magnetic field and the principles of geographical information systems that stopped the prison disturbance in *Face/Off,* starring Nicolas Cage and John Travolta, is changing corrections. How can technology address correctional health, safety, and security issues?

OVERCROWDING

In the past, a prison was often referred to as "the big house." Today, however, a more appropriate description is "the full house." Over the past 25 years, prison population has increased sixfold—from 240,000 to more than 1.5 million. Some say that prisons are "capacity driven"; that is, if you cut the ribbon, they are full. Saying exactly how full, though, is difficult because each state has its own method for measuring prison capacity. Four jurisdictions use rated capacity only (the number of beds in a facility), 9 use operational capacity only (the number of inmates that can be accommodated based on a facility's staff and existing programs and services), and 3 use design capacity only (the number of inmates that planners intended the facility to house).[1] The problem is compounded because 32 jurisdictions use more than one definition, and some have their own definitions. In spite of the differences, by any measure today's prisons are overcrowded.

On January 1, 2006, state prisons taken as a whole were operating between full capacity and 33 percent above capacity, while federal prisons were operating at 34 percent above capacity.[2] That would suggest that as many as 441,640 (33 percent) of the 1,338,306 persons held in state prison and 63,790 (34 percent) of the 187,618 persons held in federal prison were housed in overcrowded facilities. Eliminating the present overcrowding would require building 339 new prisons at a cost of more than $22 million (assuming that each has a capacity of 1,300 cells and each cell costs conservatively $50,000 to build) and then staffing and maintaining the new facilities at an average cost of $26 million each per year. Even if this were possible, the relief from overcrowding would be short term because the prisoner population grows continually. Future prison growth is difficult to predict due to declining crime rates and changing federal, state, and local criminal justice policies. If the prisoner population continued the growth it experienced in 2004 (28,824 new inmates in 2005), keeping up with the increased number of inmates would require spending $1.1 billion a year to build 22 new prisons plus at least $26 million each per year for operating costs.

Why Are Prisons Overcrowded?

There are four main reasons prisons are overcrowded. The first is a continuous increase in the number of people sent to prison. In 1995, 1,078,542 persons were in state and federal prisons. On January 1, 2006, that number increased to over 1.5 million. Nearly 1 of every 140 people in the United States is incarcerated. Probation and parole violators represent a significant percentage of the number of people admitted to prison each year. As we discussed in Chapter 8, technical violators accounted for 68 percent of all prison admissions in 2004.[3] This indicates that the concerns that emerged in the 1980s about admissions to prisons as a result of reduced tolerance for parole condition violations and their impact on the prison population are still well-founded.

The second reason is that offenders now serve a larger portion of their sentences. The amount of time served has increased from an average of 22 months for prisoners released in 1990 to 30 months for those released in 2002. Even the amount of time served by offenders given life sentences increased from an average of 21 years in 1991 to 29 years in 1997.[4] Sentencing laws changed, reducing the difference between the sentence imposed and the actual time served and restricting the possibility of early release from prison. Jurisdictions began to depart from the prevailing approach, known as *indeterminate sentencing* (broad authorized sentencing ranges, parole release, and case-by-case decision making), in the mid-1970s (see Chapter 3). Today, the trend in many jurisdictions is toward determinate sentencing—a fixed term of incarceration and no possibility of parole. In addition, most jurisdictions have adopted one or more of the following sentencing approaches: mandatory minimum sentences, three-strikes laws, or truth-in-sentencing laws requiring offenders to serve mandated percentages of imposed sentences (see Chapter 3). As a result, between 1995 and January 1, 2006, the number of sentenced offenders under the jurisdiction of state and federal correctional authorities grew annually by an average of 3.1 percent.

The third reason prisons are overcrowded is that many incoming prisoners are drug users, not the drug dealers the tougher drug laws were designed to capture. The goal of tougher drug laws was to arrest and convict drug dealers, thereby reducing drug use and the drug-related crime rate. This goal has not been achieved. At least 55 percent of the federal prison population consists of nonviolent drug offenders. Today, over 300,000 people are behind bars for drug crimes. According to an article in *The New York Times,* Americans do not use more drugs than people in other nations, but the United States is virtually alone among Western democracies in choosing the path of incarceration for drug offenders.[5]

The fourth reason prisons are overcrowded is a trend some people call the "prison industrial complex." Private corporations have a real estate

THE STAFF SPEAKS

Do you want to know why Louisiana has the highest incarceration rate in this country? Our sentences are too long, our sentences are too tough! You're doing more time for every crime than you do in most any other state. The problem with Louisiana? We don't ever let 'em go. Once you break the law, you don't get another chance. If it were up to me I'd say let's not keep dying old men in prison. They're too old to pull an armed robbery or be a ski-mask rapist. They ought to do about 20 years on most any serious crime and when they turn about 50 years old—when those two come together on a graph—they pretty well should have a good shot at going free.

Burl Cain
Warden
Louisiana State Penitentiary at Angola

---

investment in the prisons they build and operate. Correctional officers' unions are expanding in many states and securing the use of incarceration into the future. Rural communities such as Del Norte, California—a remote, impoverished county in the northwest corner of the state with an unemployment rate of more than 20 percent and all of its industries severely depressed since the 1980s—negotiated successfully with the California Department of Corrections to build Pelican Bay State Prison, one of the nation's largest state prisons (inmate population 4,000). States have an incentive to incarcerate, because the 1994 crime bill provides matching funds to states to keep violent offenders in prison longer by denying them parole and requiring they serve at least 85 percent of their sentence. There is no reason to believe that the nation's prison population will decrease even though crime has declined every year since 1991. To quote Dr. Allen Beck, the Department of Justice's lead statistician on criminal justice issues, "We've got crime going in one direction (down), and prison policy going in the other (up)."

How Can Prison Overcrowding Be Controlled?

In most jurisdictions across the United States today, we find at least six methods of controlling prison overcrowding:

1. Reduce the number of people going to prison.
2. Release the less dangerous to make room for the more dangerous.
3. Change prison or jail sentences to community-related sentences.
4. Increase the number of releases.
5. Expand existing prison capacity or build new prisons.
6. Implement an overall program of structured sentencing.

The first four methods are referred to as *front-end, trap-door, side-door,* and *back-end* strategies, respectively (see Chapter 5).

The fifth method of controlling prison overcrowding is the most commonly considered—build more prisons. For the past 25 years, political leaders have addressed public concerns about crime by devoting unprecedented financial resources to the construction of prisons. The number of prisons increased from 1,160 in 1995 to over 1,600 today. In 1990, the nation's prisons cost $12 billion.[6] In 2005, the cost was $35 billion.[7] As we pointed out in Chapter 7, by 2011 researchers estimate that without policy changes by the states, the price tag for incarceration will be $40 billion.

In spite of the new resources, however, prison overcrowding continues to worsen. Some experts believe that legislators will one day have to choose between new prison construction and funding for other areas, such as health care or education. In November 2006 Texas Republican state senator Jerry Madden told the *Houston Chronicle* that after two decades of the biggest construction boom in U.S. history, Texas has run out of prison beds and is forced to rent beds from private and county facilities.[8] Instead of more prisons, Madden and others are calling for more rehabilitation, treatment, and parole for nonviolent offenders. Almost 60 percent of Texas prisoners are chemically dependent but only 5 percent receive treatment. Madden said the 5,500 repeat drunken drivers in prison across Texas should be in minimum-security facilities and offered treatment, not housed with violent offenders without treatment.

Not all agree with Madden. The Houston-based victim advocacy group, Justice For All, said unless Texas builds more prisons, the parole board will have no alternative but to parole more offenders and that will lead to a revolving door.

The sixth method of controlling prison overcrowding is the use of sentencing guidelines that are designed to save prison beds for more serious crimes and violent offenses. Structured sentencing is a compromise between indeterminate sentencing and mandatory determinate sentencing (see Chapter 3). Guidelines were conceived as a way to guide judicial discretion in sentencing.

Under **structured sentencing,** a commission creates a set of guidelines that consider both the severity of a current offense and a few personal characteristics of the offender (notably, a prior criminal record). Sentencing commissions take a wide range of forms, from mere advisory panels to bodies that have the full, legislatively delegated force of law to establish a state's sentencing guidelines. The commissions gather facts and figures on whom their states are incarcerating, why, and for how long. The stronger commissions use the information to develop guidelines and grid charts that seek to prioritize prison bed space for the most serious offenders and require judges to spell out their reasons if they depart from the sentencing recommendations.

Some states are moving to sentencing guidelines as a way to reduce prison overcrowding and avoid lawsuits. For example, California's corrections secretary James Tilton said in November 2006 that after rejecting the idea of establishing a sentencing commission seven times between 1984 and 1998, the time has come to create a sentencing commission and avoid a court decision ordering California to change its sentencing law.[9] California's 33 prisons are currently filled to more than twice their designed capacity, holding more than 170,000 inmates on January 1, 2006. Without waiting for legal motions to limit the prisoner population, Tilton imposed a de facto limit of his own. By summer 2007 Tilton said he will run out of every inch of space to house incoming prisoners. At that point he said he will accept inmates from counties only as space becomes available—one out, one in. Today 22 states, the federal government, and the District of Columbia have sentencing commissions.

A jurisdiction establishing structured sentencing might consider implementing nonprison options such as interchangeability of punishments, also called **exchange rates.** A sentencing commission might, for example, decide that three days under house arrest or 40 community service hours is equivalent to one day of incarceration or that three years under intensive supervision is equivalent to one year in prison.

What Are the Consequences of Prison Overcrowding?

Researchers and prison administrators routinely observe the consequences of prison overcrowding. These include increases in idleness, drug traffick-

Although new prison facilities are being built, crowding continues to be an issue in many places. The auditorium of the Deuel Vocational Institution in Tracy, California, is converted into a dormitory to house prisoners. The prison has a design capacity of 1,681 but an operating capacity of 3,748. How can prison crowding be controlled?

structured sentencing

A set of guidelines for determining an offender's sentence.

exchange rates

An approach to sentencing that emphasizes interchangeability of punishments; for example, three days under house arrest might be considered equal to one day of incarceration.

ing, predatory sexual behavior, safety risks, gang confrontations, arguments, fights, assaults, murders, suicides, riots, medical and mental health problems, staff turnover, and stress. Other consequences include decreases in program opportunities, inappropriate housing assignments, judicial intervention to counteract illegal conditions, fines by state governments for operating over capacity, excessive wear and tear on prison facilities and equipment, and negative publicity about conditions in overcrowded facilities. Researchers have also linked overcrowding to higher rates of recidivism.[10] Two consequences described below are court intervention and inmate assaults.

Prisons Under Court Order   At midyear 2000, almost one-fourth (357) of all state, federal, and private prisons were under a court order to correct one or more conditions of confinement.[11] The total included 324 state prisons (down from 364 in 1995), and 33 private prisons (up from 15 in 1995). No federal prisons were under court order at midyear 2000.

Among the reasons prisons are under court order are to reduce crowding (105 prisons), improve inmate visiting, mail and telephone privileges (104 prisons), accommodate prisoners who are physically challenged (95), permit religious expression (93), and offer mental health treatment (91). Fifty-nine prisons were under court order for improving the totality of prison conditions.

Inmate Assaults   Another serious consequence of prison overcrowding is sexual violence, which includes nonconsensual sexual acts (considered the most serious form of sexual assault), abusive sexual assault, staff sexual misconduct and staff sexual harassment. In 2006, correctional authorities reported an estimated 6,528 allegations of sexual violence, up slightly from 6,241 in 2005. Staff sexual misconduct accounted for 36 percent of the reported allegations; inmate-on-inmate nonconsensual acts for 34 percent; staff sexual harassment for 17 percent; and inmate-on-inmate abusive sexual contact for 13 percent. Fifty-five percent of the allegations were unsubstantiated due to insufficient evidence, 29 percent were determined not to have occurred, and 15 percent were proven to have occurred.[12] BJS reported that following sexual misconduct, staff were discharged or resigned in 77 percent of substantiated incidents. Staff were also arrested or referred for prosecution in 56 percent of incidents.[13]

Overcrowding also affects staff. Inmate assaults on staff rose approximately 27 percent, from about 14,200 in 1995 to 18,000 in 2000, most occurring in maximum security prisons. The number of staff killed in such attacks was fewer in 2000 (5) than in 1995 (14).

PRISON SECURITY

For prisoners, staff, and their families on the outside, nothing is more frightening than a prison gang confrontation, a prison riot, or a natural disaster involving a prison.

Prison Gangs—Security Threat Groups

Prison gangs are one of the most significant developments in American prisons since the existence of the Gypsy Jokers Motorcycle Club was first recorded at the Walla Walla, Washington, penitentiary in 1950. To eliminate any publicity that gang members may draw about their gang or its activities and to describe accurately how these gangs negatively impact the security of prison operations, experts refer to them as **security threat groups (STGs)**. An STG is an inmate group, gang, organization, or

security threat groups (STGs)
The current term for prison gangs.

association that has a name or identifying signs, colors, or symbols and whose members or associates engage in a pattern of gang activity or departmental rule violation to pose a threat to the staff, to public safety, to the secure and orderly operation of a correctional institution, or to other inmates. Most STGs were founded along racial and ethnic lines to offer inmates protection, but today many of them have joined alliances with other STGs to conduct organized criminal activity such as drug trafficking, prostitution, assault, or extortion. Recently, Mark Pitcavage, a historian and expert on race-based STGs, conducted a study of contemporary prison STGs. His interview with the Southern Poverty Law Center's *Intelligence Report* is presented in Exhibit 13–1.

In 2002, the National Major Gang Task Force (NMGTF) surveyed all adult prison systems in the United States, Guam, Puerto Rico, the U.S. Virgin Islands, and Canada. With almost 80 percent responding, NMGTF identified over 1,600 STGs with a total estimated membership of almost 114,000 inmates.[14]

There are six major STGs in the United States that are recognized nationally for their participation in organized crime and violence. They are:[15]

1. *Aryan Brotherhood:* Originated in 1967 in California's San Quentin Prison, its racial makeup is white.
2. *Black Guerilla Family:* Founded in 1966 at San Quentin Prison and considered the most politically oriented of the major state prison STGs, its racial makeup is black.
3. *Mexican Mafia:* Formed in the late 1950s in California's youth facility at Duel, its racial makeup is Mexican American/Hispanic.
4. *La Nuestra Familia:* Originated in the California state prison at Soledad in the mid-1960s, its racial makeup is Mexican American/Hispanic.
5. *Neta:* Established in 1970 in the Rio Piedras Prison, Puerto Rico, its racial makeup is Puerto Rican American/Hispanic.
6. *Texas Syndicate:* Originated in California's Folsom prison in the early 1970s in direct response to the other California prison gangs (notably the Aryan Brotherhood and the Mexican Mafia), which were attempting to prey on native Texas inmates, its racial makeup is Mexican American/Hispanic.

New among the STGs is an influx of street gangs, such as Miami's "112 Avenue Boys" and Boston's "Franklin Field Pistons," that have less national organization than traditional STGs and do not easily fit into standard prison gang categories because of their smaller numbers, less cohesive ties, and less organized methods of operation.

STGs have a profound impact on prison security, and many prisons today have a Security Threat Group Unit that is responsible for the identification and overall coordination of all STG-related information at their facilities. STG members are five times more likely to incite or be involved in prison violence than are nonmembers.[16] In an attempt to control STG influence, some prison administrators transferred known STG members from one institution to another only to find that this practice actually increased STG organization and activity—it extended the STG's influence throughout a state's prison system. Other states enacted "gang enhancement" statutes that imposed severe sentences on STG activity. Today, many states are adopting a new strategy, segregating known STG members to highly restrictive supermax housing, correctional facilities that are designed to house the "worst of the worst" prisoners under

Here a California inmate with the Aryan Brotherhood shows off typical tatoos. How are STG members identified?

EXHIBIT 13–1 **"Behind the Walls: An Expert Discusses the Role of Race-Based Gangs in America's Prisons"**

An interview with Mark Pitcavage

Intelligence Report (IR): Why do prisoners join gangs?

Mark Pitcavage (MP): Prison gangs offer protection—and money and drugs. Some offer ideology, racial or otherwise, but protection is the key.

IR: Is virtually every prisoner affiliated?

MP: No, no. A lot of prisoners never become affiliated. It all depends on the prison. If you're talking about a minimum-security prison, you're not going to see much of that. In maximum security prisons, you see much more gang activity.

In state prisons, where many inmates are serving long sentences, there is a great deal of gang activity. There are gangs in federal prisons, too. Some gangs even have federal and state prison chapters. But even in state prison, where there is generally more activity, a minority of prisoners will belong.

IR: What are the largest prison gangs?

MP: The most prominent white supremacist gangs are the Aryan Brotherhood, the Aryan Circle, the Nazi Low Riders, and the Peckerwoods. There are racist black groups, like the Black Guerilla Family, the Five Percenters, and the Moorish Science Temple. And major Hispanic gangs include the Mexican Mafia (known as "la eme," for its first letter) and La Nuestra Familia. And basically apolitical street gangs like the Crips and the Bloods are inside the prisons, too.

IR: Did something occur to help promote these gangs' growth?

MP: Many prison populations were desegregated during the 1960s, and one result was that many inmates felt they had to join a race-based gang for protection. If white prisoners and black prisoners were separated, then that would not be an issue. [*IR Editor's note: Some states have actually resegregated certain cell blocks as a security measure meant to weaken race-based gangs.*]

But the key to the Aryan Brotherhood—and the key to understanding virtually all prison gangs—is that ideology often takes a back seat to organized criminal activity. The Aryan Brotherhood is an organized crime group—that is the primary dynamic behind it. It's all about drugs, protection rackets, prostitution, extortion, witness intimidation, assaults, etc.

In many prisons, the Aryan Brotherhood actually makes alliances with gangs of other races. If they were ideological white supremacists, they wouldn't do that. That is why a lot of people who join race-based prison gangs while in prison don't stay with them once they're out or join other white supremacist groups. They just aren't primarily ideologically motivated.

IR: There was a major federal bust of 40 members of the Aryan Brotherhood, 30 in prison and 10 on the outside, in October 2002. A central allegation was that members killed or attempted to kill people inside and outside the prisons in order to control drug trafficking, gambling, and extortion. How do prisoners reach outside the walls to control or influence activity that involves the free world?

MP: There are a lot of ways you can pass on information from the prisons. Wives and girlfriends of prisoners often play an important role. The Aryan Circle, for example, uses its female supporters on the outside, who they call *sisters*, to conduct business operations and spread racist propaganda. And you can always meet privately with your attorney, who may be willing to carry messages to someone else on the outside. There are ways. If you are in a maximum-security prison or in administrative isolation, it obviously is more difficult.

IR: You note in your report that the men who murdered James Byrd Jr. in the Jasper, Texas, truck-dragging incident had developed their racial beliefs while behind bars. What is the link between incarceration and politicization?

MP: Exactly what dynamic occurs varies with each particular individual, but there are some universals. Prisoners have a lot of time on their hands, and as a result they are desperate for reading materials. They are desperate for stimulation. Some of them are just fine with pumping weights, but others aren't and seek out extremist publications as well as nonextremist publications. You see prisoners asking for free subscriptions, for correspondence, for people to send them materials, anything. They may not be ideological at that point, but they want something—and the material they get can lead to their politicization.

Another thing is that many prisoners want to justify or rationalize what they have done or what has happened to them. They don't want to say they did something wrong or deserved what they got. This is true whether you are black or white. By adopting a particular ideological slant, you can rationalize that you are not a simple criminal, that you are in jail for political reasons.

Left-wing extremists have rationalized bank robberies as expropriations from the state. A right-wing prisoner rationalizes his crime as fighting back against ZOG [or "Zionist Occupied Government," a term used by many neo-Nazis]—and he will be backed up morally by white supremacist publications.

The ideologies offer an excuse and a sense of empowerment that allows someone in jail to be transformed from a criminal into a "prisoner of war" or "political prisoner."

IR: Are there other benefits for prisoners?

MP: If you join a movement, you can receive all kinds of benefits from outside people in the movement. A lot of left-wing groups do serious prisoner support, sending you gifts or money, raising funds for your defense. They may write you letters, put up Web pages about you, and so on. Many right-wing groups do the same, setting up "prison ministries." Often young women are encouraged to write to male prisoners, something that is seen as a terrifically important benefit.

This can play out well for prisoners who get out. They enter a world where they are heroes. They are ex-"POWS," liberated "political prisoners" who can tell the youngsters outside what it's all about. As such, they have access to women, drugs, all kinds of things.

EXHIBIT 13-1 *(continued)*

IR: How do outside groups recruit in the prisons?

MP: Sending materials and writing letters are the most common ways. Sometimes visits are used. Prisoners are lonely and have often been abandoned by their friends and family. Extremists capitalize on those feelings.

IR: Who decides what literature gets into prison?

MP: They're called security threat group analysts. The federal level has a whole bunch of them. On the state level, they may be substantial or sometimes just a few who monitor activities in all the prisons in a given state. They look at all the materials coming in and out of prison to see if they are allowable or if they are linked to extremism, street gangs, organized crime, violence and so on. If they identify a prisoner as a member of one of these groups, they may be able to take additional measures against him, such as placing him in administrative segregation. They have fairly wide latitude.

IR: Is there a relationship between getting recruited into these racist groups and then committing hate crimes or other violence after leaving prison?

MP: My suspicion is that there is probably not a huge link, because a lot of these people just join the gangs while they are in prison, and then leave them when they get out. But the fact is that some prisoners do get genuinely politicized, and on top of that, prison gives them an education in violence. It's a mess. I think that is what happened in Texas (with the murderers of James Byrd Jr.), and the result was one of the most inhumane acts ever perpetrated in modern America.

IR: Is there a significant distinction between those who come into prison without much racial awareness, like the men who killed James Byrd, and extremists who enter prison already highly politicized?

MP: People who are already ideologically extreme don't stop their activities in prison—some of them see prison as a great opportunity for recruiting. Take Leroy Schweitzer, the Montana Freeman (a form of "sovereign citizen") leader who's in federal prison in South Carolina serving a 22-year sentence for various financial scams. He's teaching prisoners how to engage in "paper terrorism," how to file bogus liens against public officials, attorneys, and others. He even showed one jewel dealer serving a 40-year sentence on money laundering charges how to file a (bogus) $1.5 billion lien against the judge in his case.

Other imprisoned ideologues try to influence followers outside of prison. Craig "Critter" Marshall, environmental extremist serving a five-year sentence for conspiracy to commit arson, told *Earth First!* readers last year that the only form of solidarity he wants is more arsons. He wrote something like, "When someone picks up a bomb, instead of a pen, is when my spirits really soar."

IR: How much of a threat do these gangs pose to prison staff?

MP: Prisons are dangerous. I don't know whether the violence from gang members is greater than that of nongang members, although obviously there is a greater potential for planned or organized violence. But there is a lot of training for this sort of thing now—prisons in general have better control mechanisms, whether it is cameras, doors that can automatically shut, or special training. But that doesn't stop prisoners from killing each other all the time—and it doesn't stop guards from being assaulted. Let's face it, prisons are nasty places.

Source: Excerpt from Mark Pitcavage, "Behind the Walls: An Expert Discusses the Role of Race-Based Gangs in America's Prisons," *Intelligence Report,* Winter 2002, Vol. 108, pp. 24–27. Copyright © 2002 Southern Poverty Law Center.

complete lockdown and total isolation. Advocates of this approach contend that removing STG leaders from the general prison population reduces the amount of control that STG leaders exert. Critics of the approach argue that violence actually may increase because conditions within supermax housing are so harsh that they emotionally damage inmates who may one day be returned to the general prison population or released or paroled into the community.

Two explanations for STG development are deprivation and importation. As we saw in Chapter 10, the basic premise of deprivation theory is that inmates develop a social system as a way to adapt to the pains of imprisonment. Because inmates are deprived of liberty, autonomy, goods and services, sexual relations, and security, they develop a culture that helps them get back what imprisonment has taken away. Importation theory, on the other hand, emphasizes that inmates' preprison attitudes and values guide their reactions and responses to the internal conditions

Eye On Corrections

Corrections Emerges Strong Following Hurricane Katrina

By Michelle Gaseau

Shoeless, soaked, tired and hungry, displaced inmates from Louisiana's hurricane-ravaged counties arrived at correctional facilities across the state. And the institutions that received them were ready and waiting.

Some facilities receiving prisoners—such as Washington Correctional Institute—operated via emergency generators and had no functioning phone lines, but were still able to provide for the incoming offenders and shelter staff and their families who had lost everything. And in the decimated New Orleans and Jefferson Parish areas, correctional, probation and parole staff have evacuated thousands of offenders and helped bring private citizens to safety.

"It's amazing. We moved more than 8,000 inmates and no one was injured. We were lifting kids over scaffolding; I really felt like I was back in Vietnam with the helicopters. A lot of people stepped up to the plate [during the storm]. I think our evacuation was a success," said Warden Jimmy LeBlanc of Dixon Correctional Institute, which also took in evacuees from Hurricane Katrina.

PREPARATION AND LESSONS LEARNED

While help is needed and pouring in, hindsight following the storm has shown corrections officials that their preparation plans may have helped avert a worse outcome.

According to Warden Jimmy LeBlanc evacuation plans and protocols worked well.

"Two things in my mind were so important: to know we had buses and vans and places to put [inmates]. It's so important," he said.

Evacuation plans assigned specific duties to certain staff members and the plans were coordinated through a central command, which helped keep the evacuation moving forward.

"At times I had 2,000 inmates on the interstate. The buses kept showing up and we knew relief was coming," said LeBlanc.

Leblanc said officials will take some lessons from the evacuation and recovery effort.

"For the most part I really feel good about what we did. The biggest issue was a complete collapse of the criminal justice system. All agencies should look at that," he said. "We need to come together with a plan. We had to get into the law enforcement business because we had to set up the jail."

Leblanc explained that officials from the parish jail do not have arresting power in New Orleans, so when the evacuation of the jail happened it created a vacuum of power and the New Orleans Police Department was not at full strength.

For corrections, having handled similar evacuations before and having emergency response plans in place helped operations run well.

"There's no question that having the plans in place helped us. We are able to concentrate in one area and that helps us too whereas outside corrections it's such a large area of response it makes it difficult for other agencies to come in," said Leblanc.

Leblanc said he watched in amazement as boats, firemen, ambulances and every kind of emergency vehicle wanted to come in to New Orleans to help but no one knew what to do or where to go.

Orleans Parish Police (New Orleans, Louisiana) officials watch over inmates who were evacuated from their prison to the interstate due to Hurricane Katrina's high water on September 1, 2005. Planning for natural disasters and terrorist activity is an important component of prison security. What do you think a correctional officer's toughest job is in a situation like this?

"You talk about organized confusion; it made it so chaotic," he said.

Leblanc said many corrections officials remembered and benefited from the experience of an evacuation during a severe storm in the early 90s. Facilities lost generators and jails had to be evacuated. The only difference this time, was they could not drive to the jail, they had to use a boat.

One other lesson that Leblanc expects will be discussed is mandatory evacuation prior to a large storm. Orleans and Jefferson parish officials opted not to evacuate their inmates prior to the storm, but Leblanc expects this will change.

"We knew it was headed there. We need to have contraflow emergency evacuation plans for corrections. Jefferson and St. Barnard Parishes started the evacuation for citizens 48 hours prior, then New Orleans happened 24 hours after that. We need a contra corrections flow. The storm didn't make a turn this time; it bit us," he said.

But despite these difficulties, corrections officials in Louisiana, Mississippi and other affected areas have seen their staff do what they do best—respond in crisis with a clear head and an open heart.

Source: "Corrections Emerges Strong Following Hurricane Katrina," Michelle Gaseau, The Corrections Connection Network News (CCNN). Eye on Corrections. www.corrections.com. September 12, 2005.

of prison. Both theories are valid; most major STGs can be traced to pre-prison attitudes and values, but prison conditions influence when and to what extent STG activity and violence occur.

Jail Gangs—Security Threat Groups

Most of our knowledge about STGs is based on research conducted in state or federal prisons. Comparatively little is known about the extent of STGs in jails and for that reason we report on it here.

In 2004, researchers from California State University, Chino, University of Missouri, St. Louis, and the National Youth Gang Center examined the perceptions of jail administrators about the problems that STG members cause in their facilities, the prevalence of these populations, methods of classifying gang membership, and approaches that may reduce the disruption or violence associated with these groups.[17] In spite of the methodological limitations of the study (e.g., jails in the northeast and small jails were underrepresented), the results shed some light on the influence of STGs in jails.

Jail administrators said designation of gang membership by another law enforcement agency was commonly used to define STG membership along with tattoos, clothing/gang colors, hand signs, and an individual's self-declaration. They estimated STG membership at 13.2 percent. Extrapolating this estimate to the June 2005 national jail population (747,529), for example, would result in 98,673 STG members held in jail on any given day.

When asked about the problems that STG members cause in their facilities, jail administrators reported that gang members are less disruptive than inmates with severe mental illnesses but are more likely to assault other inmates. Their most important tools to control STG harm were the gathering and dissemination of gang intelligence within the facility and to other law enforcement agencies. Segregation of STG members was also effective in large jails, but small jails are unlikely to have the ability or resources to segregate inmates.

According to Ruddell, Decker, and Egley, the benefits of controlling STGs in jails are twofold. First, jails will be safer and as a result there will be less need for inmates to join gangs in search of safety. And second, information sharing may enhance the effectiveness of prison-based STG intervention.

Prison Riots and Disturbances

Each prison disturbance and riot is unique. The precipitating conditions, resolutions, and aftermath are shaped by the characteristics of the institution, its staff, its administration, and its inmate population, as well as the state or federal agency to which it belongs. No amount of comprehensive planning can prevent all disturbances and riots, because, as one expert contends, some have no root causes.[18] It is impossible to predict where and when they will occur. Still, understanding prison disturbances and riots can help correctional administrators avoid some problems, take steps to prevent certain events from launching into full-fledged riots, limit the extent of damage, and terminate disturbances and riots in the least costly way.

In May 2002 and again in July/August 2006, the ACA published the results of a survey of prison disturbances, riots, assaults, and escapes. ACA defined **disturbance** as an altercation involving three or more inmates, resulting in official action beyond summary sanctions, and for

disturbance

An altercation involving three or more inmates, resulting in official action beyond summary sanctions and for which there is an institutional record.

which there is an institutional record. Most prison disturbances were fights, stabbings, assaults, shouting obscenities at staff, refusal to follow orders (e.g., clean cell area and return to cell), hostage taking, and cell extraction. A **riot** is any action by a group of inmates that constitutes a forcible attempt to gain control of a facility or area within a facility.

ACA recorded 2,674 disturbances in 2000 and 2,392 in 2001. (Tennessee with its own particular method of defining disturbances accounted for 2,454 of the total disturbances in 2000 and 2,153 of them in 2001.) In 2006, 405 disturbances were reported.

ACA reported a similar decrease in riots from 2000 to 2006. In 2000 there were 2 riots. In 2001, there were 19. In 2006, there were no riots.[19] From 2000 to 2006, there were also decreases in the number of inmates killed by inmates and staff, staff and officers assaulted, inmate suicide attempts and deaths, inmates injured by staff, and escapes and walkaways.

What some states call a *riot*, others downplay and call a *disturbance*. For example, in 1993 there were more than 186 disturbances in 21 corrections systems—but only 7 were classified as riots.[20] In Connecticut, a gang fight involving more than 300 inmates and causing over $100,000 in damage was called a *riot*. At Leavenworth, a racial fight involving 427 inmates that caused significant damage to the prison's auditorium, chapel, and industry buildings was called a *disturbance*. Correctional administrators label most incidents *disturbances* because the term is less sensational.

How many prison riots have there been in the United States? Nobody knows for sure. Not only do we have different opinions as to what constitutes a riot, but wardens and state officials are reluctant to publicize loss of control. Scholars estimate that almost 500 prison riots have taken place in the United States since 1855.[21]

Prison violence and riots are as old as prisons themselves. There were riots and mass escapes at the Walnut Street Jail in Philadelphia, at Newgate Prison in New York, and almost everywhere from the beginning of prisons in this country. One particularly eventful year was 1952, when riots erupted in 25 of the 152 U.S. prisons. Although no lives were lost, prison staff and inmates were in danger, and damage ran into the millions. Reasons for the riots included absence of inmate programs and work, idleness, unqualified staff who were poorly trained and poorly paid, old facilities (one-third were more than 70 years old), absence of procedures for hearing inmate grievances, overcrowding, insufficient prison budgets, absence of inmate classification, philosophical conflicts about the nature of prisoners (treat them as human beings who will one day rejoin society or "treat them rough"), and the presence of a new generation of prisoners.[22]

In 1954, reformers advocated overhauling and modernizing prison programs, replacing old prisons, hiring more and better staff, and developing an integrated state system. They advocated the creation of:

- professionally staffed classification centers;
- prisons no larger than 500 beds;
- professionally trained, well-paid correctional officers;
- inmate self-governance;
- procedures that allow inmate grievances to be aired;
- prison work programs with fair wages paid to prisoners;
- periodic review of sentencing patterns and parole board decisions;
- dissemination of statistics on commitments and releases;

riot

Any action by a group of inmates that constitutes a forcible attempt to gain control of a facility or area within a facility.

Corrections and law enforcement officers use their weapons to stop a riot. Prison riots can be costly in terms of human suffering, lost lives, and property destruction. What are some of the causes of prison riots, and how can they be prevented?

- prerelease orientation and job-finding assistance for discharged prisoners; and
- statewide prison leadership headed by nonpolitical, nationally recruited, and professionally trained individuals.[23]

Despite reformers' calls for overhauls of prison programs and management, violence-provoking conditions continue to exist in many prisons. One might wonder if anything has changed since the storm of prison riots in 1952. Three of the bloodiest and most violent prison riots in the United States occurred in severely overcrowded prisons in New York in 1971, in New Mexico in 1980, and in Ohio in 1993.

In the 1971 riot at the Attica Correctional Facility, New York, where 2,225 inmates were incarcerated in a prison designed for 1,200, 43 lives were lost: Four inmates were killed during the riot as part of inmate "justice," and when police stormed in to retake the prison, they killed 10 civilian hostages and 29 prisoners. The New York State Special Commission that investigated the riot wrote, "With the exception of Indian massacres in the late 19th century, the State Police assault which ended the four-day prison uprising was the bloodiest one-day encounter between Americans since the Civil War."[24]

In the 1980 riot at the Penitentiary of New Mexico in Santa Fe, where 1,136 inmates were confined in space designed for 900 inmates, the taking of human life was brutal. Thirty-three inmates were tortured, dismembered, decapitated, burned alive, and killed by fellow inmates. Although staff were held hostage, none were killed.

The longest prison riot in U.S. history occurred at the Southern Ohio Correctional Facility in Lucasville in 1993, where 1,820 inmates were held in a prison built for 1,540. Inmates killed nine of their fellow inmates and one correctional officer in the 11-day siege.

The riot at Lucasville cost an estimated $15 million in property damage. At Santa Fe, the estimate was $28.5 million. At Attica, the cost was more than $3 million. A new chapter in the cost of prison riots was written on August 28, 2000, when, after three decades of waiting, federal district court judge Michael A. Telesca accepted New York State's agreement to set aside $12 million (the largest amount ever in a prisoners' rights case) to compensate more than 500 inmates and relatives for the abuse that the prisoners suffered. Four million dollars was set aside for lawyer fees, and $8 million was divided among 502 inmates and relatives of the inmates who died in the uprising. After the riot ended, inmates were stripped naked and threatened with castration, forced to crawl naked in the mud with an X on their backs as if to make them a target, severely beaten, and shot. After hearing the inmates' stories, Judge Telesca described the aftermath as littered with "brutal beatings and acts of torture" and unlimited racial epithets.

Causes of Prison Riots According to sociology professor Burt Useem at the University of New Mexico, there are five theoretical explanations for the causes of prison riots.[25]

The first is random chance. Useem says that some prison riots have no root causes. It is impossible to predict where and when they will occur.

The second explanation is bad conditions. This explanation tells us that overcrowding, antiquated facilities, low staffing levels, insufficient staff training, lack of programs for inmates, lack of funding, and poor implementation of correctional policy account for prison riots. Overcrowding is the most important of these. It causes heightened prison tension and potential violent disruption. Overcrowding is responsible for curtailing or even eliminating opportunities for education, vocational training, and recreation. When the ratio of correctional officers to inmates becomes too low, something has to give. At Attica, Santa Fe, and Lucasville, overcrowding raised tensions, interfered with prisoner classification, reduced living space, and restricted access to programs. Restlessness and boredom grew.

The third explanation is rebellious inmates and racial antagonism. This includes gang members and violent or aggressive inmates. Riots tend to occur in higher-security facilities. Outside prison the ratio of racial minorities to whites is about one to five. In prison, however, whites are the minority. That different ratio, in addition to overcrowding, close living quarters, and lack of space, adds to racial antagonism. Antagonism is heightened when inmates separate themselves along racial or ethnic lines for self-protection. Researchers have discovered that as inmates' perception of overcrowding increases, their antagonism toward other racial and ethnic groups also increases. Prisoners at Attica, Santa Fe, and Lucasville were young, violence-prone, and poorly classified. Most were undereducated, underemployed, and uncommitted to society's means for achieving social goals. The racial and ethnic minority imbalance, together with these individual factors, prompted many inmates to adopt tough attitudes and join STGs for self-protection.

The fourth explanation focuses on institutional structure and readiness. Riots occur when a prison's infrastructure wears thin and authorities fail to plan and prepare. Riot readiness serves as a deterrent and prevents a situation from turning into a riot. At Attica, a faulty weld joint in a metal gate gave way and allowed prisoners access to most areas of the institution. At Santa Fe, inmates pounded on "shatterproof" glass with a fire extinguisher until the glass fell out of the frame. At Lucasville, inmates collected master keys from staff hostages and opened cell doors.

The fifth explanation focuses on administrative factors. Poor prison management and administration are linked to prison riots. Poor management can result from frequent staff turnover, low correctional officer qualifications, inadequate training, poor staff–inmate communication, and low staff pay. At Attica, Santa Fe, and Lucasville, inmates' complaints about living conditions, lack of programs, and officers' excessive use of force and harassment went unheard by administration. Rumors of riots were not taken seriously.

Preventing Prison Riots   Prison violence provokes more violence. Measures to prevent prison riots must become a national priority, and change must occur. Three years before the Attica riot, the U.S. National Advisory Commission on Civil Disorders (the Kerner Commission) warned that the only effective way to prevent riots, whether in or out of prison, was to eliminate sources of tension by making good "the promises of American democracy to all citizens, urban and rural, white and black, Spanish surname, American Indian, and every minority group." [26] While that change is long range, corrections officials can implement immediate measures to reduce the likelihood of inmate aggression, including the following:

- formal inmate grievance procedures;
- ombudsmen to mediate disputes;
- an improved classification system;
- smaller institutions;
- meaningful prison school and work programs;
- alternatives to incarceration;
- professional corrections staff who are trained and well paid;
- administrators who are visible and available to staff and inmates; and
- clearly written and understood policies on the use of force when necessary.

To ensure that the use of force is appropriate and justifiable, the ACA recommends establishing polices and procedures that govern its use (see Exhibit 13–2).

SUPERMAX HOUSING AND "NO-FRILLS" PRISONS AND JAILS

In an effort to control the behavior of violence-prone inmates, two new types of prisons are emerging—supermax housing and "no-frills" prisons and jails. Both alter the conditions of confinement for thousands of U.S. prisoners, raising important issues for the prisoners and staff who must live and work in them and the society that must accept the prisoners when they are released.

Supermax Housing

Prison systems have always needed a way to deal with inmates whose violent behavior makes it impossible for them to live with the general prison population. Generally such measures involve separating such inmates and are called *segregation* or *solitary confinement*. Prisoners who are dangerous or chronically violent, have escaped or attempted to escape from a high-security correctional facility, have incited or attempted to incite disruption in a correctional facility, or who have preyed on weaker inmates are removed from the general population. You may recall from Chapter 7 that, in 1829, the Eastern State Penitentiary in Cherry Hill, Pennsylvania, was built on the principle of solitary confinement. However, in 1913 the Pennsylvania legislature dropped "solitary" from sentencing statutes, and housing arrangements at Eastern State became congregate. From that point forward, specialized housing units were developed for management and control of troublesome inmates.

Correctional officers walk along the fence at the supermax federal prison in Florence, Colorado, where more than 25 percent of the prisoners will remain in confinement for the rest of their lives. What kinds of inmates should not be held in such facilities?

The Federal Bureau of Prisons (BOP) returned to the idea of controlling the most violent and disruptive inmates in indefinite solitary confinement when it opened Alcatraz in 1934. Alcatraz, which had a capacity of 275, did not offer any treatment program; its sole purpose was to incarcerate and punish the federal prison system's most desperate criminals and worst troublemakers. Alcatraz was "America's Devil's Island, it was 'Hellcatraz'—a place where convicts slowly went insane from the tedium and hopelessness of endless years on 'the Rock.' "[27] By

| EXHIBIT 13–2 | Public Correctional Policy on Use of Force |

Introduction

Correctional agencies are responsible for ensuring the safety in correctional programs. To achieve this goal, it may be necessary for correctional staff to use legally authorized force in certain situations.

Policy Statement

Correctional agencies are committed to exercising an appropriate use of force consistent with statutory requirements and the needs of the situation. Use of force consists of physical contact with an offender in a confrontational situation to promote safety, control behavior and enforce order. Use of force includes use of restraints (other than for routine transportation and movement), chemical agents, electronic devices, and weapons. Force is justified only when required to maintain or regain control, or when there is imminent danger of escape, injury to self, others or damage to property. To ensure that the use of force is appropriate and justifiable, correctional agencies should establish and maintain policies and procedures that:

A. Establish strategies to reduce and prevent the necessity of use of force, that authorize force only when no reasonable alternative is possible, that advocate the minimum force necessary, and that prohibit the use of force as a retaliatory or disciplinary measure;

B. Define the range of methods for and alternatives to the use of force, and that specify the conditions under which each is permitted. These policies must assign responsibility for authorizing the use of force; outline the steps for appropriate implementation of the use of force; provide for close monitoring of the person while in restraints; and require proper documentation, administrative review, investigation and remedial action;

C. Establish and maintain procedures that limit the use of deadly force to those instances where it is legally authorized and where there is an imminent threat to human life or to public safety;

D. Prohibit restraint techniques which cause or could cause partial or complete impairment of respiratory exchange (positional asphyxia) such as the hogtie position or certain restraints on the neck, or those that cause or could cause partial or complete paralysis;

E. Whenever possible, assure that age, gender, health and mental health status are considered prior to initiating the use of force and that the least restrictive and/or least likely type to cause impairment/harm is utilized. Electronic devices, chemical agents and other types of restraints should not be used on pregnant offenders or those with respiratory and other debilitating conditions;

F. Provide ongoing specialized staff training designed to teach staff to anticipate, stabilize and diffuse situations that might give rise to conflict, confrontation and violence and that ensures staff's competency in the use of all methods and equipment in the use of force.

Source: Copyright © American Correctional Association.

1963, Alcatraz was judged an expensive failure; it symbolized a penal philosophy that was outdated in an era that espoused rehabilitation, not punishment, as the goal of incarceration. Alcatraz closed in the early 1960s under orders from U.S. Attorney General Robert Kennedy. During the era of rehabilitation that followed the Alcatraz closing, prison officials used the *dispersal model*—problem prisoners were distributed to a number of prisons. Prison officials hoped that dispersal among populations of generally law-abiding inmates would dilute the influence of problem prisoners. Inmates from Alcatraz were moved to federal prisons in Atlanta and Leavenworth.

By the 1970s, the goal of incarceration had shifted back to punishment. Disturbances, violence, and riots at state and federal prisons convinced the BOP to try again to control the most troublesome federal inmates in one location. The BOP reverted to the *concentration model*—all problem prisoners would be housed together in a separate facility. The federal prison at Marion, Illinois, was chosen for this purpose. The construction features at Marion, however, made it difficult for staff to maintain complete control over recalcitrant inmates. Open cell fronts were a major limitation in Marion's design to control the toughest prisoners. Through their cell bars, inmates threw trash, urine, and feces at corrections officers; passed contraband; set fires; and verbally harassed and lunged at staff and other prisoners as they walked by. Tension, hostility, violence, and murder were all too common. On October 23, 1983, a state of emergency was declared, and the Marion facility was placed on lockdown status. Over the next few years, the BOP conceived plans to build a supermax facility that would implement construction features for controlling difficult inmates.

In 1994, the BOP opened its first **supermax housing** facility at Florence, Colorado, (officially known as Administrative Maximum—ADX), for the 450 most dangerous, violent, escape-prone, and STG federal inmate leaders. More than 25 percent will never be released from federal custody and will remain in confinement for the rest of their lives. Among the prisoners at ADX are Zacarias Moussaoui, confessed 9/11 conspirator, Olympic Park bomber Eric Rudolph, "Unabomber" Ted Kaczynski, Oklahoma City bombing conspirator Terry Nichols, would-be "shoe bomber" Richard Reid, and 1993 World Trade Center bombing conspirator Ramzi Yousef.

Construction cost totaled $60 million ($150,000 per cell). Annual operating cost per cell per year is another $40,000, or $19.2 million total annually. According to Mears and Watson, a low-end estimate of the typical life course of a supermax prison (35 years) is close to $1 billion.[28]

Supermax prisons are significantly more expensive to build than traditional prisons due in part to the enhanced and extensive high-security features on locks, doors, and perimeters; heavily reinforced walls, ceilings, and floors; and incorporation of advanced electronic systems and technology. Providing meals and other services at individual cell fronts, having multiple-officer escorts, and maintaining elaborate electronic systems contribute to the high cost. Cell design at the federal supermax prison in Florence, Colorado, resists vandalism. Each prisoner's concrete bed, desk, stool, and bookcase are made of reinforced concrete and anchored in place. Each 7 by 12 foot cell has a shower stall with flood-proof plumbing and a 12-inch black-and-white television set. Cell windows deny prisoners all views of the outside except the sky above. A simple hole-in-the-wall apparatus for lighting cigarettes has replaced matches and cigarette lighters. Meals are dispensed through cell slots in separate heated trays from airline-style carts pulled by small tractors. Cells are staggered so that inmates cannot make eye contact with other inmates. There are no congregate activities of any kind. Each cell has a double-entry door; an interior barred cage door backed up by a windowed steel door that prevents voice contact among prisoners. Visits are noncontact and inmates are allowed out of their cells for an hour a day of solitary exercise.

The new prison has 1,400 electronically controlled gates, 168 television monitors, and three mirrored-glass gun towers. The 400 cells are subdivided among nine units—each unit is self-contained and includes a sick-call room, law library, and barber chair. After three years of good behavior, an inmate gradually regains social contact. "What puts a man

supermax housing
A freestanding facility, or a distinct unit within a facility, that provides for management and secure control of inmates who have been officially designated as exhibiting violent or serious and disruptive behavior while incarcerated.

in is his behavior, and what gets a man out is his behavior," said John M. Vanyur, the associate warden.[29]

This type of super-controlled environment is taking hold across the United States. Forty states, the District of Columbia, and the BOP now operate one or more supermax prisons that collectively house more than 25,000 inmates.[30] Others report as many as 70,000. Despite the fact that supermax prisons typically cost two to three times more to build and operate than traditional maximum-security prisons, the facilities are politically and publicly attractive. "Supermax prisons have become political symbols of how 'tough' a jurisdiction has become." [31]

California opened Pelican Bay State Prison in Crescent City in 1990 for 1,600 inmates in an X-shaped windowless bunker. Construction cost was $133,653 per cell. All inmates are denied access to prison work and group exercise yards. Pelican Bay, like the federal supermax housing facility in Florence, Colorado, is entirely automated. Inmates in the supermax housing unit have no face-to-face contact with staff or other inmates. Cell doors are solid stainless steel with slots for food trays. Cell doors open and close electronically. Officers can talk with or listen in on inmates through a speaker system. These inmates do not work. They have no recreational equipment. They do not mix with other inmates. They are not permitted to smoke. They eat all meals in their cells. They leave their cells only for showers and 90 minutes of daily exercise in small cement areas enclosed by 20-foot cement walls. Visits with family and friends are noncontact behind glass partitions. Prisoners are strip-searched and handcuffed whenever they are removed from their cells and placed in full shackles with waist and hobble chains.

The National Institute of Corrections (NIC) studied supermax prisons nationwide in 1997 and published a follow-up report in 1999. In 1999, it described the supermax prison as "a highly restrictive, high-custody housing unit within a secure facility, or an entire secure facility, that isolates inmates from the general population and from each other due to grievous crimes, repetitive assaultive or violent institutional behavior, the threat of escape or actual escape from high-custody facility(s), or inciting or threatening to incite disturbances in a correctional institution." Supermax housing does not include maximum or close custody facilities that are designated for routine housing of inmates with high-custody needs, inmates in disciplinary segregation or protective custody, or other inmates requiring segregation or separation for other routine purposes. In fact, NIC opined that as comforting as it might be to prison staff to send nuisance inmates who continuously test the limits, frequently break minor rules, consume an inordinate amount of staff time, are situationally assaultive, or cannot control their behavior due to mental illness to supermax facilities, it is inappropriate to do so. Use of extended control housing for nuisance inmates is inefficient, consumes expensive high-security beds, has little overall operational impact, and is arguably overkill.

NIC found that a universal definition of supermax housing is problematic. The many states that provided information had different reasons and needs for supermax housing. Some supermax prisons house inmates who could not be controlled in traditional administrative segregation units, including prisoners who are uncontrollable due to mental illness. Others are an extension or expansion of segregation and house protective custody and/or disciplinary segregation inmates. Still others house inmates who would reside in close custody among the general population in most other jurisdictions. As these prisons have increased in number, been reported on by the media, and gained popularity with the public, a variety of names have emerged to describe them: *special housing unit, extended control unit, maxi-maxi, maximum control facility, secured housing unit, intensive housing unit, intensive management unit,* and *administrative maximum penitentiary.* The term *supermax* is the one heard most frequently in the media and in the field of corrections. Yet, as learned from the NIC survey, the term is applied to a wide variety of facilities and programs handling an equally wide variety of inmate populations. NIC's conclusion is, "Supermax as defined in the survey may exist in relatively few agencies."

To date, data relevant for evaluating supermax prisons are scarce. However, criminologists, psychiatrists, lawyers, and the courts who have studied the effects of long-term solitary confinement report evidence of acute sensory deprivation, paranoid delusion belief systems, irrational fears of violence, resentment, little ability to control rage, and mental breakdowns.[32] The vast majority of inmates in long-term solitary confinement remain anxious, angry, depressed, insecure, and confused. Some commit suicide. For example, 69 percent of the 41 suicides committed in California prisons in 2005 occurred in units where inmates are isolated for 23 hours a day. Most of the 24 prisoner suicides in Texas in 2005 were in some form of solitary confinement, leaving many to link the increase in prisoner suicides to the rising number of inmates kept in solitary confinement.[33]

Some will have been so deprived of human contact that it will be hard for them to cope with social situations. If the correctional staff cannot confidently assess what the inmate will do when supermax restrictions are lifted, the risks that have been avoided by placing an inmate in a supermax facility are revisited when the inmate is released, either back into the general prison population or into society. Some say we must consider this concern and ask if we want these inmates back in our communities in the same, better, or worse condition than when they left.[34] In 1995, *60 Minutes* reporter Mike Wallace asked Lt. Al Dienes, Pelican Bay's Information Officer, "Does Pelican Bay make society safer?" Dienes replied, "I can't answer your question; it's beyond us." Ten years later Texas took 1,458 inmates out of isolation, walked them to the prison gates, and took off the handcuffs.[35]

The impact of supermax facilities on staff is also a subject of much discussion. Having to deal on a daily basis with inmates who have proven to be the most troublesome—in an environment that prioritizes human control and isolation—presents staff with extraordinary challenges. Correctional administrators with experiences in operating supermax prisons talk about the potential for creating a "we/they syndrome" between staff and inmates. The nature and reputation of the inmate and frequently the inmate's behavior, combined with ultra-control and rigidity, magnify the tension between inmates and staff. When there is little interaction except in control situations, the adversarial nature of the relationships tends to be one of dominance and, in return, resistance on both sides. Stuart Grassian, a physician and expert on prison control units, believes that people who work in supermax facilities lose their capacity to be shocked by the kinds of things they see. "It may put money in your pocket," Dr. Grassian notes, "but over time it destroys you psychologically and brings out rage and sadism and violence and brutality."[36]

One of the few pieces of academic research to examine what the goals of supermax prison are, how they ought to be assessed, what the

"Supermax" prisons are ultra-high-security correctional facilities. Here, an empty day room at the Northern Correctional Institution at Somers, Connecticut (Connecticut's only level 5 maximum-security) can be seen with prisoner cells above as a correctional officer escorts a prisoner out of a shower, top left. What kinds of inmates should be held in such facilities?

COMMISSION ON SAFETY AND ABUSE IN AMERICA'S PRISONS: LIMITING SEGREGATION

"

Separating dangerous or vulnerable individuals from the general prison population is a necessary part of running a safe correctional facility. In some systems around the country, however, the drive for safety, coupled with public demand for tough punishment, has had perverse effects: Prisoners who should be housed at safe distances from particular individuals or groups of prisoners end up locked in their cells 23 hours a day, every day, with little opportunity to engage in programming to prepare them for release. People who pose no real threat to anyone and also the mentally ill are languishing for months or years in high-security units and supermax prisons. And in some places, the environment in segregation is so severe that people end up completely isolated, living in what can only be described as torturous conditions. There is also troubling evidence that the distress of living and working in this environment actually causes violence between staff and prisoners.

"

—The Commission on Safety and Abuse in America's Prisons

On June 30, 2000, when the federal Bureau of Justice Statistics last collected data from state and federal prisons, approximately 80,000 people were confined in segregation units. BJS also found that from 1995 to 2000 the growth rate in the number of prisoners housed in segregation outpaced the growth rate of the overall prison population, 40 percent compared to 28 percent. There are no similar data for local jails.

The commission concluded that the overreliance on and inappropriate use of segregation hurts individual prisoners and officers. Furthermore, the misuse of segregation works against the process of rehabilitating people and threatens public safety.

Walter Dickey, former secretary of the Wisconsin Department of Corrections, told the commission that his state's supermax prison was filled with the wrong people, "the young, the pathetic, the mentally ill," and at twice the cost of incarceration in a maximum-security prison.

The following three recommendations focus on limiting segregation in America's prisons and jails:

Make Segregation a Last Resort and a More Productive Form of Confinement, and Stop Releasing People Directly from Segregation to the Streets

Tighten admissions criteria and safely transition people out of segregation as soon as possible. And go further: To the extent that safety allows, give prisoners in segregation opportunities to fully engage in treatment, work, study, and other productive activities, and to feel part of a community.

End Conditions of Isolation

Ensure that segregated prisoners have regular and meaningful human contact and are free from extreme physical conditions that cause lasting harm.

Protect Prisoners Who Are Mentally Ill

Prisoners with a mental illness that would make them particularly vulnerable to conditions in segregation must be housed in secure therapeutic units. Facilities need rigorous screening and assessment tools to ensure the proper treatment of prisoners who are both mentally ill and difficult to control.

Source: Adapted from the Commission on Safety and Abuse in America's Prisons, *Confronting Confinement* (New York: Vera Institute of Justice, 2006). Note: The full 126-page report, *Confronting Confinement: A Report of the Commission on Safety and Abuse in America's Prisons,* can be accessed on the Internet at www.prisoncommission.org.

unintended effects are, and what political, moral, and economic factors enter the decision to build or not, was published in 2006.[37] Mears and Watson reviewed the literature; visited three supermax prisons where they conducted focus groups and interviews with corrections policymakers, officials, and practitioners; and interviewed similar individuals in eight other states. They concluded, "no solid empirical foundation exists to say with confidence that they [supermax prisons] are either effective or ineffective." The fact that Mears and Watson found a wide range of goals and impacts from increasing prison safety and order to controlling and improving prisoners' behavior, reducing the influence of gangs, increasing public safety, and increasing efficiencies throughout correctional systems makes cross-state evaluations of supermax prisons a challenge, and how goals should be measured remains unclear.

Mears and Watson's analysis also pointed to a wide range of potential unintended impacts, some positive (for example, increasing the quality of life among general population prison staff and inmates and improving the economy in the communities where supermax prisons are located) and some negative (for example, decreasing the quality of inmate–staff relations and increasing mental illness among supermax-confined inmates). But how common these unintended impacts are, nobody knows; and until we do know, we can't conclude that supermax prisons merit support.

Some inmates in supermax housing facilities have challenged the conditions of their confinement and the selection procedures by which inmates are transferred to supermax prison.

In 1995, inmates at Pelican Bay's supermax unit challenged the constitutionality of extreme isolation and environmental deprivation. They claimed that the degree of segregation was so extreme and the restrictions so severe that the inmates confined there were psychologically traumatized and, in some cases, deprived of sanity. The federal court agreed. The court ruled in *Madrid* v. *Gomez* (1995) that "conditions in security housing unit did impose cruel and unusual punishment on mentally ill prisoners" and "those who were at particularly high risk for suffering very serious or severe injury to their mental health." [38] The court declared that the state of California could not continue to confine inmates who were already mentally ill or those who were at an unreasonably high risk of suffering serious mental illness in the supermax unit. The court also appointed a **special master** (a person appointed to act as the representative of the court) to work with the state of California to develop a satisfactory remedial plan and provide a progress report to the court. In 2005, the U.S. Supreme Court ruled on a case from Ohio that challenged the constitutionality of the "process" by which inmates were sent to supermax prison. The Court said in *Wilkinson* v. *Austin* that Ohio's revised classification process that gave the inmate advanced notice of the impeding action, an informal administrative hearing where the inmate speaks on his or her behalf, and a statement of reasons after the decision is made provided the basic elements of due process that were sufficient to protect inmates against arbitrary or erroneous placement in supermax conditions. [39] What the Supreme Court said in *Wilkinson* is that because supermax conditions are so much more stringent than those in more "typical" prisons, inmates have a liberty interest in not being sent there and must, therefore, be afforded procedural protections before that decision is made.

special master

A person appointed by the court to act as its representative to oversee remedy of a violation and provide regular progress reports.

No-Frills Prisons and Jails

The image of prisons and jails as "country clubs" and "mini-resorts" is not new and it continues to make for great speeches, but it is erroneous. It ignores the harsh realities of imprisonment. Having only the information that appears on television and in newspapers and magazines, the public still believes that inmates are living the good life, lounging on recliners and channel surfing. In 1995, an NBC television poll found that 82 percent of Americans felt that prison life was too easy. [40] In March 1998, the *Atlanta Journal-Constitution* published a story on the elimination of sports from Georgia's prisons. [41] The article said the reason that sports programs in prison were cut back was public resentment toward criminals who have it too easy behind bars. However, there has been very little systematic empirical evidence to support this claim. Available research shows that public views on prison amenities are not as harsh as many assume. The public does not want luxurious prisons, but they want prisons to be productive, humane places that try to improve inmates during their incarceration. The public is willing to provide and retain amenities if these items are useful for inmate management and rehabilitation.[42]

Public perception has influenced reality, as corrections reform has focused on the conditions of confinement. **No-frills prisons and jails** that take away prisoner amenities and privileges are part of the corrections landscape. New policies are designed to make jail and prison life as unpleasant as possible in the belief that such conditions deter even the most hardened criminals.

no-frills prisons and jails
Correctional institutions that take away prisoner amenities and privileges.

Proponents of no-frills jails and prisons argue that the only incentives offenders should have is the opportunity to straighten out their lives. They further argue that incentives such as smoking, use of weight equipment and electronic equipment, and wearing personal clothing only encourage offenders to fake their way through incarceration to get the privileges. Pleasures of any kind, they claim, contribute to the crime rate by making prison a tolerable way of life. Reducing or eliminating amenities and privileges is what inmates deserve. It is not vindictive revenge—the offender committed a serious crime that warrants incarceration, and incarceration is meant to be punitive.

From Alaska to Mississippi to Massachusetts, states are gearing up to pass no-frills legislation. Alaska passed the No-Frills Prison Act in 1997, which removed or prohibited premium cable television, cassette tape players, tobacco use, pornographic material, and weight-lifting equipment. Alaska senator Dave Donley sponsored the bill and defended the legislation by observing that "this law will make people think twice before committing a crime in Alaska."[43] In Mississippi, Representative Mark McInnis said it clearly: "The people who run the prisons want happy prisoners. I want prisoners to be so miserable that they won't even think of coming back."[44] And in April 1998, former Massachusetts governor William Weld said that life in prison should be "akin to a walk through the fires of hell," where inmates should learn only the joys of busting rocks.[45] At the federal level, the No-Frills Prison Act was enacted in 1996. It prohibits in-cell television viewing (except for prisoners who are segregated from the general population for their own safety), coffee pot, hot plate, or heating element; R-, X-, or NC-17 rated movies; boxing, wrestling, judo, Karate, or any other martial art; any bodybuilding or weight-lifting equipment; and use or possession of any electric or electronic musical instrument in all federal prisons.

Oftentimes the public favors taking away prison amenities because it assumes they are paid for by tax dollars. States that permit in-cell television and electric equipment do not pay for them. They are purchased by the inmates or their families. Political rhetoric contributes to the public misconception regarding who pays for prison amenities. Would the public be more supportive of prison amenities if it knew the inmates paid for them? According to a citizens' survey in Tampa Bay, Florida, the answer is yes. "Respondents who were informed that prisoners pay for their privileges were more likely to support inmate access to all of the amenities except air-conditioning than were those who were told tax dollars are used to finance inmate privileges. . . . It is only when citizens are informed that taxpayers absorb the cost that they become unsupportive. . . .

No-frills prisons and jails take away prisoner amenities and privileges. What are the arguments for and against no-frills prisons and jails?

This finding suggests that educating people that inmates pay for the more "luxurious" items will result in higher levels of support for them."[46]

Arguably, proponents of no-frills jails and prisons have a point. Privileges, if not handled properly, can undermine rehabilitation. On the other hand, without privileges, offenders may not take advantage of the opportunity for rehabilitation in the first place. In a perfect world, prison would make offenders realize that their mistakes have caused them pain and deprived them of their freedom, and they would gratefully volunteer for rehabilitation programs to gain back their freedom. However, in a perfect world, these people would most likely not be incarcerated to start with because they would have realized that their behaviors were causing them unwanted consequences and would have taken corrective measure outside prison. Most offenders do not think this way; they do not think about the consequences beforehand. They think they will never get caught. The eventual consequences for their lack of responsibility are arrest and incarceration.

In August 2002, *Corrections Compendium*, the peer-reviewed journal of the American Correctional Association, published the results of a survey on inmate privileges in U.S. and Canadian prison systems.[47] Comparing the results of that survey with one taken four years earlier, the *Compendium* concluded, "The trend for decreased privileges has continued for a variety of reasons [to reduce the coddling of inmates, to control the problems of overcrowding and lack of resources, or for practical reasons such as elimination of secondhand smoke] . . . and will likely continue in the future."[48] Some of the results of the survey follow:

1. Smoking is prohibited in 53 percent of U.S. prisons. In Canada, only Saskatchewan is smoke free.

2. Free weights are prohibited in 38 percent of U.S. and 56 percent of Canadian prisons. Most systems that prohibit free weights have replaced them with weight machines or exercise courses.

3. Electronic equipment (for example, television, radio, CD or cassette players, calculators, electric shavers, typewriters, coffee/hot pots, clocks, musical instruments, fans, desk lamps, hair dryers/curlers, and video games) is prohibited in the District of Columbia in the United States and in New Brunswick, Nova Scotia, and Ontario, Canada. All other facilities attach restrictions to their use.

4. R-rated movies are prohibited in 58 percent of U.S. facilities and in 56 percent of Canadian prisons.

5. Books and magazines are restricted everywhere by content, quantity, space considerations, who sends them, and custody level. For example, prisoners in New Mexico may keep one book and one magazine at a time. Iowa prisoners may keep three publications at a time, but none may be older than three months.

CAREER PROFILE

Tammie Booker
Chief   Escambia County, Florida
Department of Community Corrections

Tammie Booker is the chief for the Escambia County Department of Community Corrections. She serves as second in command to the director of the department for 53 employees. She has been employed with the department since 1984. Over the last 23 years, Booker has worked in various positions within the department: probation assistant, probation officer, senior probation officer, criminal justice program coordinator, and pre-trial services administrator. She is a member of numerous professional and community organizations, and has received numerous awards and recognition for leadership and public speaking. She also supervises internship placements for local colleges and universities.

Booker received her bachelor of science degree from the College of Arts and Sciences at Alabama State University, and her master of criminal justice degree from the University of Alabama. She attributes her professional leadership style to the quality and relevance of the course curriculum provided by those universities. Booker is a strong advocate for continued learning and achievement. It is her desire to take advantage of every excellent learning opportunity, and she shares this sentiment with her staff. She encourages the employees within her department to attend available and applicable training sessions and workshops. She also notes that knowledge of community resources, professional networking, and staying abreast of technological advances and research are imperative in order for rehabilitation and/or punishment to be effectively and efficiently implemented.

Booker's desire is to continue to exhibit a style of leadership and management that will inspire others to work with open and free-flowing communication, to exhibit commitment to their criminal justice profession, and to provide consistency in implementing a fair and just decision-making process for the customers whom they serve. She believes that a teamwork approach in the workplace coupled with integrity and professionalism allow the staff to willingly support the department's mission.

> **"**
>
> *My philosophy can be summed up with the three C's:* communication, commitment, *and* consistency.
>
> **"**

To date, no court case has been heard on no-frills prisons and jails. Unless the eliminated or reduced amenity or privilege results in serious harm to the inmate, the no-frills movement will continue.

At present, there is no evidence that making prisons and jails more unpleasant has any effect on crime. Legislators claim that inmates will not want to be incarcerated or reincarcerated under such harsh conditions. However, more than 200 years of prison history has not proved that making a prison austere deters offenders. State wardens, corrections experts, and attorneys do not believe that eliminating privileges will reduce crime.[49] They cringe at the idea of trying to maintain civility without amenities and privileges. "What some outside the corrections profession perceive as privileges, we in the profession see as vital prison and jail management tools to insure the safety of the facility," said Bobbie Huskey, former president of the ACA.[50]

Others have wondered what impact no-frills incarceration may have on institutional security. Eliminating frills might "increase disturbances, either in the short term if inmates react violently to the loss or in the long term if inmates have more idle time, resent the perceived vindictiveness of corrections managers, or conclude they have nothing more to lose by misbehaving."[51] A corrections official in Florida concluded, "From a correctional administrator's standpoint, there is a point at which further reductions create an undue risk to a safe and orderly operation." A 27-year veteran corrections administrator in the New Jersey Department of Corrections fears that the "take-back trend," as he calls it, might result in inmate retaliation on staff.[52] Sufficient time has not passed to study the long-term impact of no-frills incarceration. However, there is concern that eliminating privileges (such as weight-lifting, television, and recreation) that keep inmates busy may encourage inmates to spend more time planning or causing trouble.

If privileges are eliminated, what positive incentives will correctional staff have with which to motivate appropriate inmate behavior? A survey of 823 wardens of state adult prisons indicates that programs and amenities serve a critical control function.[53] Correctional officers can grant access to privileges and amenities in exchange for adherence to rules and restrict access as punishment for rule violation. "The entire prison disciplinary structure is founded on punishments that amount to restriction of privileges," report the survey's authors. Chances are, prison administrators will not completely eliminate or abolish privileges or amenities; they will curtail availability and offer the privileges or amenities as reward for good behavior.

ACCREDITATION

We introduced the issue of accreditation in Chapter 6. Here, we expand on that discussion. Accreditation is a process through which correctional facilities and agencies can measure themselves against nationally adopted standards and through which they can receive formal recognition and accredited status. Besides accreditation, some correctional agencies use the evidence-based standards introduced throughout this text. However, here the focus is on accreditation.

ACA standards are the national benchmark for the effective operation of correctional systems throughout the United States and are necessary to ensure that correctional agencies and facilities operate professionally. The ACA administers the only national accreditation program for all components of adult and juvenile corrections. For that reason, the federal courts have increasingly relied on ACA's standards to decide if correctional agencies and facilities meet constitutional standards. The ACA's policy on accreditation is shown in Exhibit 13–3.

Founded in 1870 as the National Prison Association, the ACA is the oldest association specifically developed for practitioners in the corrections profession. Today, the ACA has more than 20,000 active members. The ACA initiated correctional accreditation in 1974 when it created the Commission on Accreditation for Corrections (CAC). CAC continually revises the standards based on changing practices, current case law, and agency experience. CAC is governed by 25 corrections professionals, architects, doctors, and legal experts who are elected/appointed from the following categories:

EXHIBIT 13–3   **American Correctional Association**

Public Correctional Policy on Standards and Accreditation

Introduction

Correctional agencies should provide community and institutional programs and services that offer a full range of effective, just, humane, and safe dispositions and sanctions for accused and adjudicated offenders. To assure accountability and professional responsibility, these programs and services should meet accepted professional standards and obtain accreditation. The use of standards and the accreditation process provides a valuable mechanism for self-evaluation, stimulates improvement of correctional management and practice, and provides recognition of acceptable programs and facilities. The American Correctional Association and the Commission on Accreditation for Corrections have promulgated national standards and a voluntary system of national accreditation for correctional agencies. The beneficiaries of such a process are the staff of correctional agencies, offenders, and the public.

Policy Statement

All detention and correctional facilities, institutional services, and community programs should be operated in accordance with the standards established by the American Correctional Association. These facilities and programs should be accredited through the Commission on Accreditation for Corrections. To fulfill this objective, correctional agencies should:

- **A.** implement improvement to comply with appropriate correctional standards;
- **B.** seek and maintain accreditation through the process developed by the Commission on Accreditation for Corrections in order that, through self-evaluation and peer review, necessary improvements are made, programs and services come into compliance with appropriate standards, and professional recognition is obtained.

Source: Copyright © American Correctional Association.

- National Association of Juvenile Correctional Agencies (1);
- Council of Juvenile Correctional Administrators (1);
- Association of State Correctional Administrators (2);
- National Sheriffs' Association (2);
- American Jail Association (1);
- North American Association of Wardens and Superintendents (1);
- International Community Corrections Association (1);
- American Probation and Parole Association (1);
- Association of Paroling Authorities International (1);
- National Juvenile Detention Association (1);
- American Bar Association (1);
- National Association of Counties (1);
- American Institute of Architects (1);
- Correctional Health (physician) (1);
- Juvenile Probation/Aftercare (1);
- Adult Probation/Parole (1);
- At-Large (6); and
- Citizen At-Large (not in corrections) (1).

Correctional accreditation is available for 21 different kinds of juvenile and adult correctional agencies and facilities, including institutions and community residential programs for adults and juveniles, jails and detention centers, probation and parole agencies, health care programs, and remote-location monitoring. The standards cover administrative and fiscal concerns, staff training and development, the physical plant, safety and emergency procedures, sanitation, food service, and rules and discipline. Standards are divided into two categories. To be accredited, an agency or facility must have 100 percent compliance with *mandatory* standards and 90 percent compliance with *nonmandatory* standards. Today, more than 500 of the 1,208 adult correctional institutions and 129 of the 3,365 local jails have been awarded ACA accreditation. The state of Illinois is a leader in the accreditation movement. Currently 42 of its 44 correctional facilities have been accredited by ACA, and two new facilities are under accreditation review.

Why Should Correctional Agencies and Facilities Be Accredited?

There are at least eight reasons correctional agencies and facilities should be accredited:[54]

1. Accreditation improves staff training and development.

Accreditation requires written policy and procedures to establish a training and staff development program for all categories of personnel. The training requirements address all preservice, inservice, and specialized training curricula with clear timelines and considers the institution's mission, physical characteristics, and inmate populations. The professional growth of employees is developed through training plans that annually identify current job-related training needs in relation to position requirements, current correctional issues, new theories, techniques, and technologies.

2. Accreditation assesses program strengths and weaknesses.

Accreditation assesses correctional administration and management, the physical plant, institutional operations and services, and inmate programs. It also assesses issues and concerns that may affect the quality of life at a facility such as staff training, adequacy of medical services, sanitation, use of segregation and detention, incidents of violence, crowding, offender activity levels, programs, and provisions of basic services that may impact the life, safety, and health of inmates and staff.

3. Accreditation is a defense against lawsuits.

Accredited agencies and facilities have a stronger defense against litigation through documentation and the demonstration of a "good faith" effort to improve conditions of confinement. For example, in *Grayson* v. *Peed* (1999), the Court said, "The appellant's own expert penologist conceded that [Sheriff] Peed's policies met the standards of both the Virginia Board of Corrections and the American Correctional Association. . . . Appellant's claims that [Sheriff] Peed provided inadequate training for his employees must also fail. At the time of the incident, the jail had been accredited for more than ten years . . . by the American Correctional Association . . . whose training requirements often surpass minimal constitutional standards."

4. Accreditation establishes measurable criteria for upgrading operations.
Through the standards and accreditation process agencies continuously review agency policy and procedure and have the ability to make necessary improvements when deficiencies are recognized.

5. Accreditation improves staff morale and professionalism.
Accreditation is awarded to the "best of the best" in the corrections field. Staff have a better understanding of policies and procedures, and this contributes to improved working conditions for staff.

6. Accreditation offers a safer environment for staff and offenders.
Staff and offenders benefit from increased accountability and attention to physical plant issues and security procedures. Whether for an agency or facility, the accreditation process ensures assessment of strengths and weaknesses.

7. Accreditation reduces liability insurance costs.
As an incentive for agencies willing to participate in ACA's national accreditation program, insurance companies offer a reduction on liability insurance premiums to accredited agencies and facilities. Adherence to nationally recognized standards for fire, safety, health, and training reduces claim expenses, allowing up to a 10 percent credit on liability insurance premiums. In most cases, the resulting savings on insurance premiums more than offset the agency's or facility's cost of accreditation.

8. Accreditation offers performance-based benefits.
Performance-based standards provide data that can be used to gauge the day-to-day management of the facility, thereby providing agencies with a cost-effective, proactive approach to offender care. They can also be used to justify requests for additional funding.

Traditionally, correctional agencies have sought accreditation for one of three reasons: first, to ensure that the organization is in compliance with national standards; second, to demonstrate to interested parties that the organization is operating at acceptable professional levels; and third, to comply with court orders.

PRIVATIZATION

According to Malcolm Feeler, the involvement of the private sector in corrections began shortly after the first English colonists arrived in Virginia in 1607.[55] Convicted felons were transported by private entrepreneurs to America, as a condition of pardon, to be sold into servitude. During the 18th century, jails and prisons emerged in the American colonies as alternatives to servitude or the death penalty. Privately operated facilities copied from English custom became popular. Private contractors claimed they could both manage prisons and employ convicts in labor, arguing that the practice would be both rehabilitative and financially rewarding. San Quentin was the first U.S. prison constructed and operated by a private provider in the 1850s. However, after a number of major scandals surfaced surrounding the mismanagement of the facility by the private

More than 107,000 adults are held in 264 private prisons across the United States. Still the debate over privatization continues. Why do state governments contract with for-profit companies for such services?

provider, California turned San Quentin prison over to the control of state government. By 1885, 13 states had contracts with private enterprises to lease out prison labor.

As discussed in Chapter 6, privatization is defined as a contract process that shifts public functions, responsibilities, and capital assets, in whole or in part, from the public sector to the private sector. In corrections, privatization is generally one of two types.

The first type is the "contracting out" of specific services that entails a competition among private bidders to perform governmental activities such as providing medical and mental health services, educational and vocational programming, food preparation, maintenance, work, and industry. This type of privatization emerged in the 17th century. Under these circumstances, the correctional agency remains the financier and continues to manage and maintain policy control over the type and quality of services provided. Contracts for specialized services generate little controversy.

The second type of privatization is full-scale private management of jails and prisons. Because it involves government transfer of assets, commercial enterprises, and management responsibilities to the private sector, it is controversial. In 1976, RCA Services assumed control of the Weaversville Intensive Treatment Unit in North Hampton, Pennsylvania, marking the modern beginning of privatization in corrections. The trend toward privately operated correctional institutions has continued with 107,447 adults now housed in 264 privately operated confinement and community-based correctional facilities and more than 15,000 adults in 163 privately operated halfway houses and residential drug treatment centers in 30 states, Puerto Rico, and the District of Columbia.[56] Texas has the most facilities (43), followed by California (24), Florida (10), and Colorado (9). The largest privately managed detention facility in the world is the Reeves County Detention Complex in Pecos, Texas. The facility is managed by the GEO Group, Inc. It houses 3,556 Federal Bureau of Prison inmates.[57]

Outside the United States, 31 private facilities operate in Australia, Canada, England, Netherlands Antilles, New Zealand, Scotland, and South Africa. Total revenues allocated to private corrections in 2001 were estimated at more than $4 billion.

The catalyst for privatizing correctional institutions today is prison overcrowding. As noted earlier state prisons, taken as a whole, were operating between full capacity and 33 percent above capacity, while federal prisons were operating at 34 percent above capacity. Other reasons for the growth in private corrections are the public's lack of confidence in the ability of correctional services provided by federal, state, and local governments to rehabilitate offenders and a reluctance to provide more funding for rising correctional costs. The enthusiasm for privatization is fueled by the prospect for more innovative, cost-effective prison management, including the involvement of the private sector in the financing of new prison construction. This enthusiasm is not shared by all, however.

The Debate

Largely because there has been no conclusive research, arguments continue to rage over the merits of privately run correctional facilities. The overriding reason supporting privatization in corrections is the desire of state and local governments to rapidly increase bed space, save taxpayers money by providing correctional services traditionally supplied by government at less cost, improve the quality of correctional services, and reduce crime and recidivism. For example, one private provider built a

350-bed detention center in Houston, Texas, for the Bureau of Immigration and Customs Enforcement, the first government agency to use private prisons. The project was completed within six months at a cost of $14,000 per bed. ICE calculated that government construction would have taken almost three years at a cost of $26,000 per bed. Estimates of rebuilding prisons in the District of Columbia say it would take the public sector five to six years, whereas it would take the private sector three to four years.

Most advocates of privatization also suggest that allowing facilities to be operated by the private sector could result in cost reductions of 20 percent. Most studies, however, report more modest savings. In fact, researchers at the University of Cincinnati looked at 33 cost-effectiveness evaluations of public and private prisons and concluded that prison size, age, and security level, not prison ownership (public vs. private), predict prison costs: "Relinquishing the responsibility of managing prisons to the private sphere is unlikely to alleviate much of the financial burden on state correctional budgets."[58] There are very few studies comparing the quality of inmate confinement between public and privately operated correctional institutions. Some report that private prisons outperform their public counterparts. Others do not.

In possibly the most carefully controlled comparative recidivism study of releasees from private and public prisons, Lonn Lanza-Kaduce and colleagues at the University of Florida matched 198 inmates from private prisons with 198 inmates from public prisons on the basis of offense, race, age, and prior record.[59] The researchers tracked the inmates for 12 months after each inmate's respective date of release and recorded any new rearrest, any technical violation, resentencing, and reincarceration. The researchers also measured the severity of recidivism (technical violation, misdemeanor offense, drug or weapon possession felony, property felony, or violent or personal felony). Releasees from private prisons had lower recidivism rates than did their public prison matches for all indicators of recidivism except technical violations. In the 12 months following release, 19 (10 percent) of the private facility releasees were rearrested, whereas 38 (19 percent) of the public releasees were rearrested. Only 11 (6 percent) of the private releasees were resentenced for a new offense compared with 20 (10 percent) of their public matches. Of the private prison releasees, 20 (10 percent) were reincarcerated within 12 months, but 28 (14 percent) of the public prison releasees were reincarcerated. Overall, 34 (17 percent) of the private facility releasees recidivated, whereas 47 (24 percent) of the public releasees recidivated. When the researchers analyzed seriousness of reoffending, they found that private prison releasees were more likely to return on technical violations. Public releasee recidivists were more likely to commit drug/weapon possession offenses, property offenses, or violent offenses in the year after release. In the aggregate, the recidivism of private releasees was less serious than that of public releasees. The researchers also found that, within the first three months of release, fewer private releasees recidivated than did public releasees. After 90 days, however, time to rearrest was similar for both groups.

Proponents also argue that public prisons are not without their problems, and unlike state and federal governments, private firms are free from politics, cumbersome bureaucracies, and costly union contracts. Proponents also suggest that privately run correctional facilities can be economic boons for the areas in which they are located, providing many jobs and feeding public coffers with increased tax revenues. Among groups supporting privatization are the ACA and the President's

Talking about CORRECTIONS

PRIVATIZATION SAVINGS OR NOT?

Visit *Live Talk* at **Corrections.com** (www.justicestudies.com/talking04) and listen to the program "Privatization Savings or Not?" which relates to ideas discussed in this chapter.

| EXHIBIT 13–4 | **American Correctional Association** |

Public Correctional Policy on Private Sector Involvement in Corrections

Introduction

Historically correctional programs have been operated by public agencies, but there is ongoing use of public-nonprofit and/or profit partnerships (hereafter referred to as the private sector). Private sector organizations may have resources for the delivery of services that often differ from the public correctional agency.

Policy Statement

Government has the ultimate authority and responsibility for corrections. For its most effective operation, corrections should use all appropriate resources, both public and private. Government should consider use of private sector correctional services and programs only when such programs or services:

- are needed;
- meet professional standards;
- ensure necessary public safety;
- provide the best value to the taxpayer; and
- are, at minimum, equivalent to those offered by the public sector.

While government retains the ultimate responsibility, authority and accountability for the offenders under its jurisdiction as well as for actions of private agencies and individuals under contract, it is consistent with good correctional policy and practice to consider:

- **A.** enhancing service delivery systems by contracting with the private sector when justified in terms of cost, quality, and ability to meet program objectives;

- **B.** using private sector organizations to develop, fund, build, operate, and/or provide services, programs, and facilities when such an approach has a cost benefit and is safe and consistent with the public interest and sound correctional practice;

- **C.** using the private sector to gather information and provide independent evaluation of process and performance measures of programs and services provided by or contracted for by public agencies; and

- **D.** using the private sector to enhance staff development, competency, and professionalism through training, certification, and continuing education of correctional practitioners.

Correctional agencies also should:

- **A.** continue to engage members of the private sector in an advisory role in the development and implementation of correctional programs and policies;

- **B.** ensure the appropriate level of service delivery and compliance with recognized standards through professional contract preparation and vendor selection, as well as effective evaluation and monitoring by the responsible government agency;

- **C.** indicate clearly in any contract for services, facilities, or programs the responsibilities and obligations of both government and contractor, including but not limited to liability of all parties, performance bonding, and causal factors and procedures for contract termination;

- **D.** share information about successful public-private sector partnerships with other corrections practitioners; and

- **E.** evaluate the effectiveness of services, facilities and programs.

Source: Copyright © American Correctional Association.

Commission on Privatization. ACA's support of private sector involvement in corrections is shown in Exhibit 13–4.

Opponents of privatization, on the other hand, build their arguments on mostly philosophical grounds. One writer says that the fundamental issue is a moral one: Should private parties make a profit from inflicting pain on others?[60] Will private prisons, in their pursuit for profits, find ways to keep cells filled, prison construction booming, and more offenders under private supervision? The notion that convicted offenders should be the responsibility of private entrepreneurs motivated by profit is contradictory to the public function of offender apprehension and conviction. Most opponents of privatization argue that the practice is inherently flawed by the profit motive of private corporations.[61] The corporate interest in maximizing profits, they claim, can have numerous negative consequences for inmates, correctional employees, and society. Some claim, for example, that the need to maintain healthy profit margins may preclude the cost of rehabilitation and recreational programs for inmates. Other opponents of privatization say that privately run companies save money by paying lower wages and benefits than states do.[62] Among the groups opposing privatization are the American Jail Association, the National Sheriffs' Association, and the American Federation of State, County, and Municipal Employees.

Recently, the National Council on Crime and Delinquency (NCCD) reviewed the literature on privatization and conducted a national survey of private correctional management firms. NCCD found that, rather than the projected 20 percent savings, the average saving from privatization was only about 1 percent, and most of that was achieved through lower labor costs.[63] "In summary," wrote NCCD, "the cost benefits of privatization have not materialized to the extent promised by the private sector. Although there are examples of cost savings, there are other examples in which such benefits have not been realized. Moreover, it is probably too early to determine if the initial cost savings can be sustained over a long time period."[64]

Some critics note that, although the administration of punishment may be delegated in part to the private sector, the government retains ultimate responsibility for it. Indeed, the courts have held government responsible for actions taken by a private provider that violate an inmate's constitutional rights or that put the prison staff, inmates, or surrounding community in harm's way. Today, private–public contracts include performance standards and monitoring procedures. Writing a good, clear contract that outlines the roles, responsibilities, and consequences for the private provider and government sector is key. Proponents note that governments almost always renew contracts with private operators—proving such contracts worthwhile. In spite of the arguments for and against privatization, "The core theme is that properly conceptualized, properly managed, and properly monitored privatization initiatives can serve the public interest."[65] Exhibit 13–5 summarizes the reasons to accept or reject the privatization concept.

A number of private companies operate prisons and jails. Exhibit 13–6 shows the market shares held by the major providers of private prison and jail management. Some are well known and even offer shares of their companies to the public.

Privatizing Community Supervision

There is also movement toward privatization in community corrections, including offender assessment, drug testing and treatment, electronic monitoring, halfway house management, and probation field services. Two states—Connecticut and Colorado—have successfully privatized community supervision. In both states, the impetus for privatizing community supervision was similar: Staffing and resources were not keeping pace with increasing caseloads. Community supervision officials felt they had exhausted the use of interns and volunteers, and funding for new staff was not possible. They used risk management principles to assign staff and resources in direct proportion to the risk level of a case. Both states partnered with the private sector to monitor the low-risk offender population, a group that generally has few needs, whose past records reflect little or no violence, and that successfully completes probation about 90 percent of the time.

In Connecticut, the privatization initiative to monitor low-risk offender populations by the private sector allowed scarce resources to be

EXHIBIT 13-5	Arguments for and Against Private Prisons

For Private Prisons

1. Private operators can provide construction financing options that allow the government client to pay only for capacity as needed in lieu of accumulating long-term debt.

2. Private companies offer modern state-of-the-art correctional facility designs that are efficient to operate and that are built according to value-engineering specifications.

3. Private operators typically design and construct a new correctional facility in half the time required for a comparable government construction project.

4. Private vendors provide government clients with the convenience and accountability of one entity for all compliance issues.

5. Private corrections management companies are able to mobilize rapidly and to specialize in unique facility missions.

6. Private corrections management companies provide economic development opportunities by hiring locally and, to the extent possible, purchasing locally.

7. Government can reduce or share its liability exposure by contracting with private corrections companies.

8. The government can retain flexibility by limiting the contract function and by specifying facility mission.

9. Adding other service providers injects competition among both public and private organizations.

Against Private Prisons

1. There are certain responsibilities that only the government should meet, such as safety and environmental protection. To provide incarceration, the government has legal, political, and moral obligations. Major constitutional competition among both public and private issues revolves around the deprivation of liberty, discipline, and preserving the constitutional rights of inmates. Related issues include the use of force, loss of time credit, and segregation.

2. Few private companies are available from which to choose.

3. Private operators may be inexperienced with key correctional issues.

4. Operators may become monopolies through political ingratiation, favoritism, and so on.

5. Government may lose the capability to perform the function over time.

6. The profit motive will inhibit the proper performance of duties. Private prisons have financial incentives to cut corners and offer lower wages, pensions, benefits, and staffing levels.

7. The procurement process is slow, inefficient, and open to risks.

8. Creating a good, clear contract is a daunting task.

9. Lack of enforcement remedies in contracts leaves only termination or lawsuits as recourse.

Source: Dennis Cunningham, *Public Strategies for Private Prisons,* paper presented at the Private Prison Workshop, January 29–30, 1999, at the Institute on Criminal Justice, University of Minnesota Law School.

EXHIBIT 13-6	Slicing up the Market

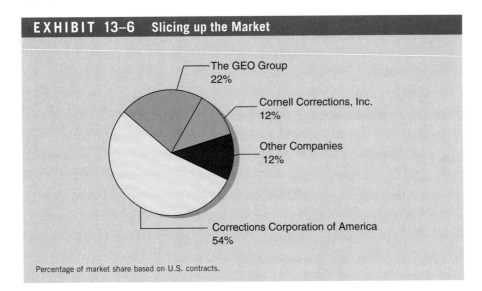

The GEO Group 22%

Cornell Corrections, Inc. 12%

Other Companies 12%

Corrections Corporation of America 54%

Percentage of market share based on U.S. contracts.

used to better monitor offenders with higher levels of risk. Private case management responsibilities in Connecticut included sending an introductory letter to the probationer, monitoring restitution payments and compliance with conditions of probation, responding to probationer's inquiries, preparing standardized reports for probation officers, providing verification of conditional compliance, and providing statistical reports. Robert J. Bosco, director of Connecticut's Office of Adult Probation, says that the "success" of this privatization initiative "is in the agency's ability to use its resources to control recidivism of the highest-risk offender population."[66]

The situation in Colorado was similar. When Colorado officials adopted risk management and looked at how treatment and supervision were matched with levels of risk, they found more probation officers were needed than the Colorado General Assembly would fund. The result was a directive that allowed probation departments to contract with private agencies for the supervision of low-risk probationers. Thirteen of Colorado's 22 judicial districts have entered into such contracts. The private agencies directly bill the probationers for their supervision services, eliminating public expenditures for community supervision. According to Suzanne Pullen, management analyst with Colorado's Judicial Department, Office of Probation Services, "The diversion of these low-risk offenders allows local probation departments to focus more clearly on the supervision and case management of medium- and high-risk offenders that are burdening their caseloads."[67]

Future Trends

According to Reginald A. Wilkinson, former director of the Ohio Department of Rehabilitation and Correction,

> The next ten years will reveal whether the privatization of prisons will succeed. If so, the evolution from public to private management may prove to be painful to correctional traditionalists. Debate on the pros and cons, rights and wrongs, of "punishment for profit" will rage back and forth. In the end, the profit margin and public opinion may be the determining factors on how much of the corrections profession will be outsourced to for-profit providers.[68]

Other trends may include the following:

1. The number of private prisons is likely to increase but not at the pace exhibited during the past two decades.
2. The number of companies operating privatized prisons is likely to decrease as competition and the costs of doing business increase, thus forcing a consolidation of firms within the industry.
3. Important inroads can be expected for the geriatric inmate population.

TECHNOCORRECTIONS

The technological forces that made the use of cell phones commonplace is converging with corrections to create "technocorrections." Technological changes have impacted communication, offender and officer tracking and recognition, and detection. "While technology alone cannot overcome the myriad challenges (facing corrections), it will most certainly play a major role."[69]

Communication

Information is crucial to a well-run correctional system. Knowing what is happening gives correctional administrators the power not only to react to problems promptly, but also to anticipate and prevent them. In recent decades, communication technology has undergone significant changes. Correctional officers can now keep in touch by e-mail and can share information in electronic databases in management information systems, and on Web pages on the Internet. The majority of corrections departments now have online searchable prisoner registries, including photographs, and some post schedules of upcoming parole hearings on the Internet. Communication technology has also brought about videoconferencing and telemedicine.

Videoconferencing Videoconferencing is another way to share thoughts and ideas in the correctional community. Meetings and lectures that once required expensive travel can now be "attended" from the comfort of one's office or from a local teleconference site. In addition, satellite TV and video technology have enhanced distance learning for both officers and inmates.

Prison systems across the country are using videoconferencing for arraignments, interrogations, and visitation. One of the largest videoconferencing correctional facilities in the United States is the Douglas County Corrections Center in Omaha, Nebraska. Taylor Dueker, one of the center's architects, reports that the videoconference visitation facility has already produced a number of benefits for staff, inmates, and family and friends of prisoners, including:

- increasing the number of visitations conducted each day;
- reducing staff time in checking in visitors;
- reducing the staff time previously needed to escort inmates to a centralized visitation area or courtroom for arraignments and other preliminary proceedings;
- reducing inmate movement, thereby increasing safety for staff and inmates;
- reducing space requirements and construction and operating costs on visitation areas; and
- eliminating contraband that was formerly passed by visitors in face-to-face contact.[70]

Videoconferencing can be especially helpful in high-profile cases where security is tighter and exposure to the public needs to be minimized. Dueker sees the day where equipped with a simple Web cam, visitation will take place from the comfort of home under certain supervisory conditions.

Telemedicine Telemedicine, one of the newest and most exciting advances in medicine, is providing prisoners with adequate, cost-effective health care. Taking a prisoner to a specialist outside the prison poses a danger to correctional officers and the community by giving the prisoner an opportunity to escape or to have contact with other people in a less-controlled environment. Telemedicine allows physicians to consult with on-site medical personnel through videoconferencing and compatible medical devices, such as medical microcameras. Health care in correctional settings is improved, and the substantial savings on in-prison

I got out of prison April 22, 1996, after being locked up for 10 years for robbing a bank at gunpoint. For three weeks, I just hung out, reacclimating to society. I got restless the fourth week and tried to get a job, but nobody called me back.

My parole officer kept asking me, "Have you gone to RIO yet?" I thought the program would get me only menial jobs, like heavy cleanup work, but finally I went just to appease my parole officer. After I completed RIO's five-day job preparation

course I got the first job I interviewed at, a sales agent at a hotel.

Project RIO Participant
RIO (Reintegration of Offenders) is a job-placement program for offenders.

consultations and on trips to local providers can offset the costs of introducing this technology. The Ohio State prison system's use of telemedicine consultations through television monitors and computer networking increased from 129 episodes in 1995 to more than 5,000 in 2000. According to Dr. Hagop Mekhjan, director of the Ohio State University Medical Center, the Ohio Department of Rehabilitation and Correction has probably saved millions of dollars in transportation costs and overtime labor.[71] Today, almost one-half of the states and the Federal Bureau of Prisons use telemedicine technology for medical and psychiatric services.[72]

Offender and Officer Tracking and Recognition

Automated kiosks, also discussed in Chapter 5, are on the way to replacing routine visits to probation and parole officers. Offenders are instructed to report to a kiosk at a specified location. There they are electronically interviewed and in some cases tested for alcohol by means of a breath analysis attachment. Using the kiosks, offenders can also e-mail their parole officers to schedule personal meetings. The system identifies the offender by reading a magnetic card and using a biometric fingerprint scanner. **Biometrics** is the automated identification or verification of human identity through measurable physiological and behavioral traits such as iris, retinal, and facial recognition; hand and finger geometry; fingerprint and voice identification; and dynamic signature. The biometrics of the future are body odor, ear biometrics, facial thermography, and thermal imagery.

biometrics
The identification or verification of human identity through measurable physiological and behavioral traits.

Remote-location monitoring of offenders, discussed in Chapter 5, is steadily improving and is likely to be used far more in the future. However, remote-location monitoring is not just for inmates. Correctional officers can also wear personal alarm and location units that allow a computer to track their locations and respond to distress signals by sending the closest officers to the site of the emergency.

Fairly new in the field of corrections is the Global Positioning System (GPS). Already used in airplanes and automobiles, GPS is now also used for monitoring offenders under community supervision. The GPS tracking unit worn by an offender allows computers to pinpoint the offender's location at any time to the precise street address. In the field of inmate monitoring, there is also some discussion about implanting chips in offenders' bodies that would alert officials to unacceptable behavior. In some cases, when criminal activity was detected, the chip might give an electric shock that would temporarily shut down the offender's central nervous system.

Prison medical staff videoconference with an offsite physician about a prisoner's physical health. Advances in technology have helped make prisons and jails safer and more secure, while facilitating innovations like telemedicine. What promises might tomorrow's technologies hold for correctional institutions?

Administrators are also relying on new telecommunications technology to help track inmates and former inmates. Speaker ID technology identifies a speaker even if he or she has a cold, just awoke from a deep sleep, or has a poor telephone connection. Systems using speaker ID can be used to keep track of who calls inmates in prison and to monitor criminal activity such as escape plans, gang activity, and smuggling of contraband. Speaker ID can also be used for low-risk offenders granted early parole as an alternative to incarceration. The system can make random calls and positively identify the speaker from his or her response. The offenders never know when or how they will receive calls. When no one answers the phone or the speaker is not identified, the system alerts authorities to a possible violation.

To increase the efficiency of inmate monitoring and cut administrative costs, a smart card, a plastic card embedded with a computer chip, can be used to store all types of information about the inmate, from medical care to meals eaten.

The use of facial recognition technology is also on the increase in corrections. All 300 employees of the Prince George County Correctional Center in Upper Marlboro, Maryland, swipe picture-image ID cards across a scanner. The swipe alerts the system that an employee is entering the facility. The system verifies the image from a database, and using the biometrics of the employee's face, compares it to the one captured by the camera. Eventually, Prince George County will use biometric-based access control technology to screen visitors to determine if they are ex-inmates.

The principles of geographic information systems (GISs) are also changing corrections.[73] GIS links graphics with tabular information to produce a graphical, layered, spatial interface or map that can help prison management in many ways. For example, in 2004 Congress approved $3 million for a high-tech prison training program known as SPECAT (Simulated Prison Environment Crisis Aversion Tools), whose aim is to help corrections officials deal with inmate disturbances by providing a three-dimensional computer modeling of prison interiors, along with preparation for confronting particular scenarios.[74]

Proponents foresee a time when corrections mapping can be used to do the following:

1. Track and display inmate location and movement via electronic monitoring devices.
2. Indicate whether a housing unit is balanced with regard to religion, group affiliation, age, race, and ethnicity.
3. Pinpoint the locations of gang members and link them to each inmate's behavioral and criminal history, as well as the inmate's rank in the hierarchy of the group.
4. Pinpoint areas in a prison that are potentially dangerous such as hallways or blind corners where a number of assaults may have occurred.
5. Incorporate aerial photos of a facility to check for possible security breaches and potential escape routes.
6. Provide a basis for proactive investigation and enforcement. For example, the flow of money in and out of prison might be mapped

and then linked with data about visitation, telephone calls, and correspondence addresses to show a potential drug problem.

7. Link inmate data with the names, telephone numbers, and addresses of all the people the inmate had contact with during incarceration, in case of an escape.

Detection

To maintain prison security, researchers have developed new detection technologies. One is ground-penetrating radar (GPR), which can be used to locate underground escape tunnels. Another is heartbeat monitoring. Using the same technology employed by geologists to detect earthquakes, geophone machines can detect the heartbeat of an inmate trying to escape in a laundry or trash truck leaving the prison. In 1999, heartbeat monitoring prevented the escape of a prisoner in Tennessee. X-rays and magnetic resonance imaging scan the body for concealed weapons, eliminating the necessity for a physical search. Noninvasive drug detection technology places a swab or patch on the skin, which absorbs perspiration, and signals the presence of illegal drugs. Pupillometry (a binocular-like device that flashes a light to stimulate pupil contraction) can also measure drug or alcohol use. Another technological tool for drug testing has inmates look through a viewfinder. Ion scans can also detect drug particles on visitors to correctional facilities.

Implementation

Despite the growth of this technology, there are still obstacles to be overcome. Corrections personnel have been slow to embrace new technology, in part because new systems are unreliable, are difficult to maintain, and exhibit high life-cycle costs. Ethical concerns about the rights of offenders might be another barrier to implementing new technology. Through a program sponsored by the Department of Justice—Staff and Inmate Monitoring (SAINT)—the Navy's Space and Naval Warfare System Center in Charleston, South Carolina, is systematically addressing biometric and smart card technology through development, testing, and evaluation of a prototype system in the Navy Consolidated Brig in Charleston.[75] There is no question, however, that new technologies are playing an increasingly important role in correctional institutions as a means to address critical health, safety, and security issues.

REVIEW & APPLICATIONS

REFLECTIONS ON THE FUTURE

Supermax Prisons

by Morris L. Thigpen, Sr.
National Institute of
Corrections, United States
Department of Justice

In 1997, the National Institute of Corrections (NIC) conducted a national survey entitled "Supermax Housing." The definition used in that survey is generally accepted by most correctional administrators: "A freestanding facility, or a distinct unit within a freestanding facility, that provides for the management and secure control of inmates who have been officially designated as exhibiting violent or seriously disruptive behavior while incarcerated."

Our knowledge and use of supermax housing has become more sophisticated in the last five or six years, and I believe we will continue to see the use of supermax facilities until we invent a better method of managing the seriously disruptive and violent inmate. We do run the risk of the courts intervening, even with their reduced involvement in prison operations cases, if we are not cautious in several areas.

The process by which inmates are placed in supermax should be carefully examined. It can be easily abused. To avoid the abuse, the classification process should involve a team approach with staff from various disciplines such as medical, psychology, programs, as well as correctional officers. Final approval should come from the executive staff. If sufficient controls are not in place, inappropriate placements will take place such as nuisance inmates or those who have only infrequently been assertive.

The violent mentally ill inmate who can be controlled by other means is not a proper placement for supermax. It is imperative that all inmates placed in supermax be fully aware of how they can work their way out. There should be opportunities to demonstrate positive behavior patterns through program participation, not just through avoidance of negative acting-out behavior. This is obviously impossible if the policy for supermax is to deny any opportunity to demonstrate positive behavior.

The role of the supermax facility as defined in the overall correctional plan can significantly impact the type and operation of the facility. Staff who lead, manage, and operate the facility will have significant impact on the philosophy and culture developed in the facility. Staff assigned to supermax should be among the best, highly trained staff available. They should have demonstrated their ability to work in a hostile environment, maintain self-control, and relate in a positive manner with difficult inmates. The nature of supermax is ripe for abuse by staff that are not prepared and trained for this assigned duty.

The supermax prison will continue to exist for a number of reasons. It is a status symbol of "tough on crime." It has political value. States without supermax facilities are seen as outside of current correctional practices. This type of facility is very expensive to build and exceedingly expensive to operate. Once it exists, it will continue to be used as a supermax unit whether it is needed or not. The majority of correctional staff will support the continued need as they view it now as a necessary component to ensure the ability to control the serious and violent offender as well as to ensure staff safety in managing the predatory inmates.

Several factors will continue to provide a stream of candidates for supermax. Sentencing changes leading to longer time to be served for violent offenders in an environment void of program and treatment interventions, along with increased idleness and gang activities, will not have any tendency to decrease the number of those inmates likely to do time in supermax facilities.

Finally, it will be up to those of you who will be the future leaders in corrections to evaluate supermax facilities, define their purposes, shape their policies, and manage the populations that they serve, hopefully in a manner that will lead to positive, changed behavior.

About the Author

Morris Thigpen is director of the National Institute of Corrections (NIC)—a position to which he was appointed in June 1994 by then–U.S. attorney general Janet Reno. NIC is an agency within the U.S. Department of Justice, Federal Bureau of Prisons, Thigpen holds a BS degree from Millsaps College, Jackson, Mississippi, and an MEd degree from Mississippi State University. He has served as commissioner of corrections in Alabama and as Mississippi's deputy administrator of the Department of Human Services.

SUMMARY

1 Prisons are overcrowded for four main reasons. First, over the past decade there has been an increase in imprisonment. Second, changes in federal and state sentencing laws require more offenders to serve longer periods. Third, there has been an increase in imprisonment for drug and violent offenses. Fourth, a prison industrial complex has emerged.

2 This chapter examined six methods of controlling prison overcrowding. First, reduce the number of people who go to prison by making more use of *front-end strategies* such as diversion, community corrections, and intermediate sanctions. Second, put a cap or ceiling on the prison population, sometimes called a *trap-door strategy.* Third, use what are called *side-door strategies,* such as giving sentenced offenders the opportunity to apply to the sentencing court for release to intensive community corrections programs, usually six months after imprisonment. Fourth, use more parole and halfway houses, called *back-door strategies.* Fifth, build more prisons and/or expand existing facilities. Sixth, use structured sentencing guidelines that are designed to save prison space for serious crimes and violent offenses, while using community corrections and intermediate sanctions for lesser offenses.

3 Prisons control the influence of security threat groups by referring to them as STGs rather than "gangs." Some prisons have Security Threat Group Units that are responsible for the identification and overall coordination of all STG-related information at their facilities. Some prisons transfer known STG members from one institution to another. Some states enacted "gang enhancement" statutes that impose severe sentences on STG activity. And some states have built super-max prisons that house STG members in complete lockdown and isolation.

4 Prison riots occur for a number of reasons. Sometimes they are a result of spontaneous outburst. Most experts believe that the primary causes of prison riots are bad conditions (overcrowding, antiquated facilities, low staffing levels, insufficient staff training, lack of programs for inmates, lack of funding, and poor implementation of correctional policy), rebellious inmates and racial antagonism, institutional structure and readiness, and administrative factors (for example, frequent staff turnover, low correctional officer qualifications, inadequate training, poor staff–inmate communication, and low staff pay).

5 Preventing prison riots requires changes both outside and inside the prison. Outside prison it is important for other social institutions to reduce sources of tension that contribute to crime. Inside prison experts recommend formal inmate grievance procedures, ombudsmen, improved classification systems, smaller institutions, meaningful educational and work programs, alternatives to incarceration, professional prison staff who are well trained and well paid, and clearly written and well-understood policies on the use of force.

6 A supermax housing facility is a freestanding facility, or a distinct unit within a facility, that provides for management and secure control of inmates who have been officially designated as violent or who exhibit serious and disruptive behavior while incarcerated. It is not yet known what impact conditions of extreme isolation have on a prisoner or on the public when prisoners released from these facilities return to the community. However, criminologists, psychiatrists, lawyers, and the courts who have studied the effects of long-term solitary confinement report evidence of acute sensory deprivation, paranoid delusion belief systems, irrational fears of violence, resentment, little ability to control rage, and mental breakdowns. Supermax prisons also present extraordinary challenges for staff, possibly creating a "we/they syndrome" and magnifying tensions between inmates and staff.

7 No-frills prisons and jails eliminate prisoner privileges and amenities in the belief that this process will deter criminals from future criminal activity. It appears, however, that no-frills correctional facilities may actually produce the results they were designed to avert, thereby increasing the number of prison disturbances and making it difficult for corrections staff to motivate appropriate inmate behavior. Corrections professionals tell us that what outsiders perceive as privileges and amenities, they consider to be important management tools. Research from Florida shows that public views on prison amenities are not as harsh as many assume. The public is willing to provide and retain amenities if they are useful for inmate management and rehabilitation.

8 Correctional facilities and agencies should be accredited for eight reasons. Accreditation improves staff training and development, assesses program strengths and weaknesses, is a defense against lawsuits, establishes measurable criteria for upgrading operations, improves staff morale and professionalism, offers a safer environment for staff and offenders, reduces liability insurance costs, and offers performance-based benefits.

9 Arguments in favor of privatization include construction financing options that allow government clients to pay only for capacity as needed in lieu of accumulating long-term debt; modern state-of-the-art correctional facility designs that are efficient to operate; less time to build than comparable government construction projects; convenience and accountability of one entity for all compliance issues; rapid mobilization and specialization in unique facility missions; and economic development opportunities from hiring and purchasing locally. Reasons not to privatize include the moral issue of the government's responsibility for public safety; a lack of private companies from which to choose; private contractor inexperience with corrections issues; the potential for private vendors to become a monopoly through political ingratiation and favoritism; the potential for government to lose the capability to perform the function over time; the potential for the profit motive to inhibit proper performance of duties; slow procurement processes that are open to risks; the difficulty of creating a contract with a private vendor; and the potential for a lack of enforcement to result in termination or expensive lawsuits as the only recourse.

10 Technology has affected corrections in the areas of communication, offender and officer tracking and recognition, and detection.

KEY TERMS

structured sentencing, *p. 501*

exchange rates, *p. 501*

security threat groups (STGs), *p. 502*

disturbance, *p. 508*

riot, *p. 509*

supermax housing, *p. 514*

special master, *p. 518*

no-frills prisons and jails, *p. 519*

biometrics, *p. 533*

QUESTIONS FOR REVIEW

1 Debate the four reasons why prisons are overcrowded.

2 Which method of controlling prison crowding do you believe is most important?

3 What do you believe is the most effective solution for controlling the influence of security threat groups (STGs)?

4 Rank order the five causes of prison riots from most to least important.

5 Speculate what can be done to prevent prison riots.

6 Summarize the emergence of supermax housing and its impact on prisoners and staff.

7 What do you think about no-frills jails and prisons and their impact on corrections?

8 What ideas can you add to the reasons correctional agencies and facilities should be accredited?

9 Critique the arguments for and against privatization.

10 Debate the pros and cons of using technology in corrections.

THINKING CRITICALLY ABOUT CORRECTIONS

The Politics of Defining Prison Overcrowding

Think about the three ways to discuss prison overcrowding. Which definition of *capacity* is the most conservative? Which one is the most liberal? Explain. If you were a warden of a prison operating at the national average of 33 percent over capacity but you didn't believe your prison was overcrowded in the strict sense of the word, and a reporter asked you if your facility was overcrowded, which definition would you offer and why? How do the politics of corrections, your job, and the definition of *overcrowding* influence your response and shape the public debate on prison overcrowding?

No-Frills Jails and Prisons and the Politics of Misinformation

The public favors taking away prison amenities in part because it believes they are paid for by tax dollars. However, in this chapter you learned that a survey of Orlando, Florida, residents supported inmate access to prison amenities when they learned that the prisoners, not the tax payers, paid for their privileges. If most jurisdictions require inmates to pay for their amenities, why is the public misinformed? Can the politics of misinformation both harm and help corrections? Explain.

ON-THE-JOB DECISION MAKING

Overcoming Opposition to Privatization

It is 2012 and you are the director of your state's Department of Corrections and Rehabilitation. Your predecessors contracted with several private vendors to perform government activities such as food preparation and inmate programming. You signed contracts for full-scale private management of two state prisons. So far, your experience with privatization has been successful. Predictions from a decade ago that your state would not privatize the entire state department of corrections might be wrong. Your prisons continue to operate above capacity and you believe you spend more time in court than you do in your office. You need more bed space, but the public refuses to spend more on prisons. You are thinking seriously about a proposal that would turn over the management of all your state's adult prisons to the private sector. How will you overcome the opposition of your state's correctional officer association?

What Inmates Need to Know to Work Their Way out of Supermax Prison

In this chapter's Reflections on the Future, Morris Thigpen, director of the National Institute of Corrections, tells us, "It is imperative that all inmates placed in supermax be fully aware of how they can work their way out." Assume your state is planning a supermax prison. You remember Thigpen's words. What will you propose as opportunities for inmates to demonstrate positive behavior to work their way out?

LIVE LINKS

at www.justicestudies.com/livelinks04

13–1   Biometrics Catalog Online

The Biometrics Catalog is a U.S. government–sponsored database of information about biometric technologies including research and evaluation reports, government documents, legislative text, news articles, conference presentations, and vendors/consultants.

13–2   Supermax Prisons and the Constitution

This monograph discusses the liability issues in operating supermax prisons. It covers the background of supermax prisons and related litigation, and it takes a close look at case law, prison policies and practices, and "lessons learned" in operational areas that give rise to litigation.

13–3   Implementing Telemedicine in Correctional Facilities

Telemedicine uses telecommunications equipment that allows health care providers to see and diagnose inmates in prisons located far from health care providers' offices. The experiment reported on here showed that prisons could improve inmate health care by providing remote access to more medical specialists while reducing prisoner transport costs and related security management costs. This report provides a model for estimating the relative costs of telemedicine under varying conditions in a correctional setting.

13–4   Resolution of Prison Riots

This research discusses how eight state and federal prisons have dealt with riots and what strategies and procedures are effective during the stages of a prison riot. Safety of prison employees, inmates, and residents of the area in which the facility is located, plus the financial cost of prison riots makes their prevention and containment a critical issue. Factors that must be addressed include such criminal justice issues as how prisons are administered (and how command is divided during riots), race relations in prisons, how prisons are built and renovated, how prisons are staffed, and how staff are utilized and augmented during riots. On the basis of an in-depth examination of eight disturbances, the study concludes that proactive planning and preparation along with reactive problem solving is the most effective approach to prison riot resolution.

THE VICTIM

Helping Those in Need

CHAPTER OBJECTIVES

After completing this chapter you should be able to do the following:

1 Briefly summarize the history of America's victims' rights movement.

2 Identify and describe important federal victims' rights legislation.

3 Understand why a victims' rights amendment to the U.S. Constitution may be considered necessary.

4 List and describe crime victims' costs.

5 Understand how corrections agencies participate in meeting victims' needs, and list victim services provided by correctional agencies.

6 Explain how crime victim compensation programs work.

7 List the three avenues available to victims to recover financial losses due to crime.

8 Understand the nature of victim impact statements, and explain why they are useful.

"

As a victim you're amazed that no one will ask you about the crime, or the effect that it has on you and your family. You took the . . . defendant's blows, heard his threats, listened to him brag that he'd 'beat the rap' or 'con the judge.' No one ever hears these things. They never give you a chance to tell them.

—A victim

"

More than a decade ago, 15-year-old Mary Vincent became the surviving victim of one of the most gruesome crimes of the 20th century.[1] Vincent, who had been hitchhiking on a trip to her grandfather's house in Corona, California, was attacked and raped by Larry Singleton—an innocuous-looking 51-year-old man who offered her a ride. In an act of sadistic violation, Singleton hacked off Vincent's forearms with a hatchet and left her for dead on a hillside. She survived, and was found the next morning wandering near a road holding the stubs of her arms in the air to prevent blood loss.

Although victims' advocates argued for a lengthy prison term for Vincent's attacker, an apparently unrepentant Singleton was paroled after serving only eight years in prison. He took up residence in Florida, and Vincent lived in constant fear that he would attack her again. Vincent's concern finally abated in 1997 when Singleton was arrested and charged with the murder of 31-year-old Roxanne Hayes, a supposed prostitute. A year later he was convicted of first-degree murder. Singleton died of cancer in 2001 while on death row at Florida's Union Correctional Institution. Today, a recovered Vincent leads a full and active life in the Pacific northwest.

Violent crime survivor Mary Vincent throws the first pitch during the Giants "Resolve to Stop the Violence Project Day," in 1999 at 3Com Park, in San Francisco. Vincent was brutally raped by Larry Singleton—who cut off her forearms with a hatchet when she was 15 years old. Singleton's release, after only eight years in prison, came to symbolize the lack of attention to the plight of crime victims that had once been characteristic of the American criminal justice system. How has the situation of crime victims changed?

A BRIEF HISTORY OF AMERICA'S VICTIMS' RIGHTS MOVEMENT

According to the Federal Bureau of Prisons (BOP), a **victim** is "someone who suffers direct or threatened physical, emotional, or financial harm as the result of the commission of a crime. The term 'victim' also includes the immediate family of a minor or homicide victim."[2]

Victims were rarely recognized in the laws and policies that govern our nation until the 1970s. From a legal perspective, crimes were considered offenses against the state (since the state made the law), not against the individual. Victims merely set the wheels of justice in motion (by filing charges) and, if necessary, helped carry out justice (by testifying in court). The victim had little or no status within the justice system, and victims' rights were virtually nonexistent.[3]

Tremendous strides have since been made in **victims' rights** legislation and victims' services. Few movements in American history have achieved as much success in prompting legislative response as did victims' rights activists' campaigns through the 1980s and 1990s.

The 1980 enactment of Wisconsin's victims' Bill of Rights, the nation's first state bill of rights for crime victims, launched an era of dramatic progress in the victims' rights movement.[4] Passage of the federal Victim and Witness Protection Act of 1982[5] (VWPA) and release of the *Final Report* by the President's Task Force on Victims of Crime in the same year brought national visibility to crime victims' concerns.

The VWPA and the *Final Report* were catalysts for a decade of significant advances in victims' rights. By the date of release of the *Final Report,* four states had legislated victims' basic rights.[6] Today, all states have laws, modeled after the VWPA, that establish, protect, and enforce victims' rights. There are now more than 27,000 victim-related state statutes and 29 state victims' rights constitutional amendments.

Most states' victims' bills of rights include basic provisions for treatment with dignity and compassion, ongoing access to information about the status of the case and the offender, notification of hearing and trial dates, permission to attend related judicial proceedings, input at sentencing and parole hearings (through victim impact statements), and restitution. (See Exhibit 14–1.)

Most states have legislated victims' rights to notification of events and proceedings at various stages of the judicial process; 39 have legislated victims' rights to attend criminal justice proceedings;[7] and 24 constitutionally protect these rights.[8] All states permit consideration of victim impact information at sentencing, with most permitting victim presentation of the information during the sentencing hearing. The majority of states require that victim impact information be included in the presentencing report, and at least half require that the court consider this information in its sentencing decision.

Despite the advances in victims' rights legislation, there remain serious deficiencies in those laws and in their implementation. Crime victims' rights, which vary significantly at the state level, are often ignored, and many victims are still denied the right to participate in the justice process. Implementation of state-enacted constitutional victims' rights is often arbitrary and based on judicial preference. Many states make no provision for victims' rights in cases involving juvenile offenders.

victim

Someone who suffers direct or threatened physical, emotional, or financial harm as the result of the commission of a crime. The term *victim* also includes the immediate family of a minor or homicide victim.

victims' rights

The fundamental rights of victims to be represented equitably throughout the criminal justice process.

EXHIBIT 14–1   **Victims' Rights**

- THE RIGHT TO INFORMATION about the case as it progresses through the justice system;
- THE RIGHT TO NOTIFICATION of many different types of justice proceedings;
- THE RIGHT TO PARTICIPATE in court proceedings related to the offense;
- THE RIGHT TO BE REASONABLY PROTECTED from the accused offender;
- THE RIGHT TO INFORMATION about the conviction, sentencing, imprisonment, and release of the offender; and
- THE RIGHT TO RECEIVE RESTITUTION from the offender.

Source: Office for Victims of Crime.

Legislation

Congressional concern for crime victims was evident in the VWPA; its stated purpose was "to enhance and protect the necessary role of crime victims and witnesses in the criminal justice process; to ensure that the federal government does all that is possible to assist victims and witnesses of crime, within the limits of available resources, without infringing on the constitutional rights of the defendant; and to provide model legislation for state and local governments."[9]

A subsection of the Crime Control Act of 1990,[10] known as the Victims' Rights and Restitution Act of 1990 (Victims' Rights Act), established a Bill of Rights for federal crime victims.[11] The Victims' Rights Act requires that federal law enforcement officials use their "best efforts" to ensure that victims receive basic rights and services. The **best efforts standard** made the federal law weaker than many state victims' rights laws in which provision for victims' rights and services is mandatory. The basic rights and services that officials must use their best efforts to provide include the following:

- fair and respectful treatment by authorities;
- reasonable protection from the accused;
- notification of court proceedings;
- presence at public court proceedings unless the court specifies otherwise;
- conference with the prosecutor;
- restitution; and
- updates to information about the offender, including conviction, sentencing, imprisonment, and release.

The Violent Crime Control and Law Enforcement Act,[12] passed in 1994, established new rights for victims of sexual assault, domestic violence, sexual exploitation, child abuse, and telemarketing fraud. This legislation also designated significant funding for combating domestic violence and

best efforts standard

A requirement of the federal Victims' Rights and Restitution Act of 1990 (also known as the Victims' Rights Act) that mandates that federal law enforcement officers, prosecutors, and corrections officials use their best efforts to ensure that victims receive basic rights and services during their encounter with the criminal justice system.

An assault victim arriving at the Macomb County, Michigan, Prosecutor's Office Crime Victims Rights Unit is greeted by victim advocate Kay McGuire. The unit's staff assists victims of violent crimes during the investigation, trial, presentencing, and postsentencing phases of their victimization and advises victims regarding compensation entitlements under Michigan's Crime Victim Compensation Act. What other kinds of agencies have traditionally provided help to crime victims?

sexual assault, placed more than 100,000 community police officers on the street, and launched a number of other crime prevention initiatives.

In 1996, the federal Community Notification Act, known as Megan's law, was enacted to ensure community notification of the locations of convicted sex offenders.[13]

In the Victims' Rights Clarification Act of 1997, Congress asserted victims' rights to attend proceedings and deliver victim impact statements within the federal system. This act was passed to ensure that victims and survivors of the Alfred P. Murrah Federal Building bombing in Oklahoma City, Oklahoma, could observe the trial and provide input at sentencing.

Exhibit 14–2 summarizes federal victims' rights legislation.

EXHIBIT 14–2	Federal Victims' Rights Legislation
Legislation	**Provisions**
Crime Victims' Rights Act, 2004	Established statutory rights for victims of federal crimes and gave them the necessary legal authority to assert those rights in federal court.
Unborn Victims of Violence Act (also known as Laci and Conner's law), 2004	Made it a separate federal crime to "kill or attempt to kill" a fetus "at any stage of development" during an assault on a pregnant woman.
Victims' Rights Clarification Act, 1997	Ensured that victims of federal crimes had the right both to attend proceedings and to deliver or submit a victim impact statement.
Mandatory Victim Restitution Act, 1996	Made restitution mandatory on the federal level in all violent crime cases and in certain other cases.
Community Notification Act (also known as Megan's law), 1996	Ensured that communities are notified of the release and location of convicted sex offenders.
Violent Crime Control and Law Enforcement Act, 1994	Created new rights for victims of sexual assault, domestic violence, sexual exploitation, child abuse, and telemarketing fraud.
Victims' Rights and Restitution Act (also called the Victims' Rights Act), 1990	Created the first federal bill of rights for victims of crime and required federal law enforcement officers, prosecutors, and corrections officials to use their *best efforts* to ensure that victims receive basic rights and services.
Victims of Crime Act (VOCA), 1984	Established the federal Office for Victims of Crime (OVC) to provide federal funds in support of victim assistance and compensation programs around the country and to advocate for the fair treatment of crime victims. Also established the federal Crime Victims' Fund to assist states in paying victim benefits.
Victim and Witness Protection Act (VWPA), 1982	Enacted a set of basic rights for crime victims and became a national model for state victims' rights laws.

Eye On Corrections

Office for Victims of Crime Guides Services in Corrections

By Michelle Gaseau

Although ensuring public safety is typically part of a corrections agency's mission, many organizations are only beginning to make solid overtures to the victims of crime. Those agencies that have connected with the victims of crime have done so by notifying them of offender hearings and parole or release dates and by encouraging restitution and restorative justice initiatives.

Since 1988 the federal Office for Victims of Crime (OVC) has supported victim assistance and compensation programs but has also been interested in improving the relations that corrections agencies have with victims. To that end, the office seeks out and promotes promising practices in the field that bridge the gap for victims between the crime and the release of the offender.

"The victim is where everything begins. While [the offenders] are in the institution the victim does feel some relief, and it lessens the anxiety. At the time of release the anxiety goes up again, and victims begin to not have as much confidence in the system. That is where it is important for corrections probation and parole [agencies] to maintain that confidence," said John W. Gillis, Director of the Office for Victims of Crime.

Involving victims in a variety of areas in the field helps to engage the community, fosters a better understanding of the criminal justice system, and builds trust in the system. These services can take place at the community corrections level but also in the facility. The OVC has offered a number of recommendations to corrections agencies to help them focus on victims and include them in the system when they wish to be involved.

OVC RECOMMENDATIONS

As a first step, the OVC recommends that every state department of corrections and paroling authority establish a victim advisory committee that includes not only victims, but also service providers to guide and support victim-related policies, programs, and services. These committees review victim notification policies, victim-offender programming, and informational materials for victims.

Staff should also be designated for a variety of responsibilities related to victims' services. A specific staff liaison should be appointed to victims and service providers in the community.

"Direct service to the victim is something that we will try to [encourage]," said Gillis, who was recently confirmed to direct the OVC. "We're looking for programs that help in that area, and we're trying to make the victim as close to whole as possible."

According to the OVC, victim notification is important to support victim safety. Agencies should notify victims upon their request of any change in the status of offenders, including pardon or clemency, that would give them access to the community. Timely notice also gives victims the ability to exercise their rights to submit a victim impact statement or attend and/or testify at a parole hearing. Changes in an offender's status such as release for a funeral or a medical emergency, less restrictive classification, death, or pardon should also be communicated to victims.

Additional responsibilities associated with victim notification include providing the name, address, and phone number of the parole or probation officer assigned to an offender; the name of the offender if it has changed at all; the address, city, and county where the offender will be released or supervised; a recent picture and a general description of the offender upon release; assistance with a safety plan for the victim if authorities believe the release of the offender may threaten the victim or family; and notification of the offender's conditions of release. Agencies should also consider making information accessible to victims by toll-free number, in printed material, and in multiple languages.

Other recommendations by the OVC include collection and distribution of restitution payments as well as restorative justice mediation between victims and offenders when appropriate, such as with a property crime.

"In most organizations like corrections or criminal justice it has to come from the top down. That is important to the organization. When it does, it has a better chance of working. These are the people who can make it happen and, if not, it is left to the whim of those on the line as to whether or not to participate," said Gillis.

EFFORTS ON ALL SIDES

Organizations have developed a variety of victim-related programs and, according to Gillis, this programming should take place both in the community corrections setting and at the facility level.

"They are doing a lot of things in the area of victims. It does a lot of things. It cuts down on the amount of calls to the police departments, which increases the demand for services and the number of officers needed in the field. There are a lot of areas that are affected in parole and probation," he said.

Gillis, a victim of crime himself, said agencies should be cognizant of victims' rights to defer participation in these programs as well. "Victims don't want to come to the institution. There are some programs that want to encourage victims to come to the institution, and they [victims] are saying they don't want to do that," he added.

Gillis said that, in his own experience as a former commissioner on the California Board of Corrections, offenders sentenced to life in prison soon learn that showing remorse can benefit them at parole hearings later.

"After two or three parole hearings the lifers start to realize they should express remorse and accept responsibility. They want to send letters to victims and request that information be passed onto the victims. But victims don't want that contact," Gillis said.

Corrections agencies should be careful about the type of contact they champion but still support appropriate victim-offender programs. "There are a lot of dedicated people out there. At OVC we want to get in touch with those people and encourage them," Gillis said.

Source: "Office for Victims of Crime Guides Services," Michelle Gaseau, The Corrections Connection Network News (CCNN). Eye on Corrections. www.corrections.com. December 10, 2001.

On October 9, 2004, the U.S. Senate passed the Crime Victims' Rights Act[14] as part of the Justice for All Act of 2004. The Crime Victims' Rights Act establishes statutory rights for victims of federal crimes and gives them the necessary legal authority to assert those rights in federal court. The act grants the following rights to victims of federal crimes:

1. the right to be reasonably protected from the accused;
2. the right to reasonable, accurate, and timely notice of any public proceeding involving the crime or of any release or escape of the accused;
3. the right to be included in any such public proceeding;
4. the right to be reasonably heard at any public proceeding involving release, plea, or sentencing;
5. the right to confer with the federal prosecutor handling the case;
6. the right to full and timely restitution as provided by law;
7. the right to proceedings free from unreasonable delay; and
8. the right to be treated with fairness and with respect for the victim's dignity and privacy.

The legislation also requires federal courts to ensure that these enumerated rights are afforded to victims. Similarly, federal law enforcement officials are required to make their "best efforts to see that crime victims are notified of, and accorded," these rights.

The Proposal for a Federal Victims' Rights Constitutional Amendment

The 1982 President's Task Force on Victims of Crime made 68 recommendations for protection of victims' rights, including a recommendation that the Sixth Amendment to the U.S. Constitution be amended to guarantee specific rights to crime victims. Although the recommendation has not yet been implemented, the National Organization for Victim Assistance (NOVA), Mothers Against Drunk Driving (MADD), the National Center for Victims of Crime (NVC—formerly the National Victim Center), and other national victims' organizations joined together in 1987 to create the National Victims' Constitutional Amendment Network (NVCAN).[15] NVCAN spent the next decade assisting state legislators in their efforts to pass amendments. Efforts to pass state constitutional amendments produced impressive results. Each of the 33 state victims' rights amendments passed by an overwhelming majority—80 to 90 percent in most states.[16]

The proposal to adopt a federal constitutional amendment gained momentum in April 2002, when President George W. Bush announced his support of the bipartisan Crime Victims' Rights Amendment authored by Senators Feinstein and Kyl.[17] As proposed, the amendment would provide specific constitutionally protected rights to crime victims but could not be used as grounds for a new trial or in support of a claim for damages. Exhibit 14–3 documents advances in victims' rights and services since 1965. Keep up-to-date on the status of the proposed victims' rights constitutional amendment via the National Victims' Constitutional Amendment Passage (NVCAP) Network at www.nvcap.org.

EXHIBIT 14–3	Crime Victims' Rights in America: A Timeline

2006
- The Violence Against Women Act of 2005 is signed into law by President George W. Bush.

2005
- The U.S. Department of Justice launches its National Sex Offender Public Registry Web site (www.nsopr .gov). The site allows users to search existing public state and territory sex offender registries.

2004
- Congress passes the Justice for All Act of 2004, which includes the Crime Victims' Rights Act of 2004, providing substantive rights for crime victims and mechanisms to enforce them.

2003
- Congress passes the PROTECT Act of 2003—also known as the Amber Alert law—which creates a national AMBER network (America's Missing: Broadcast Emergency Response) to facilitate rapid law enforcement and community response to kidnapped or abducted children.
- The American Society of Victimology (ASV) is established at the first American Symposium on Victimology, held in Kansas City, Kansas.
- In July, Congress passes the Prison Rape Elimination Act, designed to track and address the issue of rape in correctional institutions and develop national standards aimed at reducing prison rape.
- The National Domestic Violence Hotline receives its millionth call.

2002
- The National Association of VOCA Assistance Administrators (NAVAA) is created. With OVC support, NAVAA provides technical assistance and training to state VOCA assistance administrators.
- By the end of 2002, all 50 states, the District of Columbia, U.S. Virgin Islands, Puerto Rico, and Guam have established crime victim compensation programs.

2001
- Congress responds to the terrorist acts of September 11 with a host of new laws, providing funding for victim assistance, tax relief for victims, and other accommodations and protections for victims.

2000
- In October, the Violence Against Women Act of 2000 is signed into law by President Clinton, extending VAWA through 2005 and authorizing funding at $3.3 billion over the five-year period.
- In October, Congress passes the Trafficking Victims Protection Act of 2000 to combat trafficking in persons and to protect such victims.

1999
- On January 19, 1999, the federal victims' rights constitutional amendment (Senate Joint Resolution 3, identical to SJR 44) is introduced in the 106th Congress.

1998
- Senate Joint Resolution 44, a new bipartisan version of the federal victims' rights constitutional amendment, is introduced in the Senate by Senators Jon Kyl and Dianne Feinstein.
- Four new states pass state victims' rights constitutional amendments, bringing the total to 33.
- Congress enacts the Child Protection and Sexual Predator Punishment Act of 1998, providing for numerous sentencing enhancements and other initiatives addressing sex crimes against children.
- Congress passes the Crime Victims with Disabilities Act of 1998, representing the first effort to systematically gather information about the extent of victimization of individuals with disabilities.
- In October, the Identity Theft and Deterrence Act of 1998 is signed into law.

1997
- A federal victims' rights constitutional amendment is reintroduced in the opening days of the 105th Congress with strong bipartisan support.
- In March, Congress passes at historic speed the Victims' Rights Clarification Act of 1997 to clarify existing federal law allowing victims to attend a trial and to appear as "impact witnesses" during the sentencing phase of both capital and noncapital cases. President Clinton immediately signs the act.
- Congress enacts a federal antistalking law.
- *New Directions from the Field: Victims' Rights and Services for the 21st Century* is published by OVC. It assesses the nation's progress in meeting the recommendations set forth in the *Final Report* of the 1982 President's Task Force on Victims of Crime, and issues over 250 new recommendations from the field for the next millennium.

1996
- Federal victims' rights constitutional amendments are introduced in both houses of Congress with bipartisan support.
- Both presidential candidates and the attorney general endorse the concept of a federal victims' rights constitutional amendment.
- The Community Notification Act, known as Megan's law, provides for notifying communities of the location of convicted sex offenders by amendment to the national Child Sexual Abuse Registry law.

EXHIBIT 14-3	Crime Victims' Rights in America: A Timeline (*continued*)

- President Clinton signs the Antiterrorism and Effective Death Penalty Act, making restitution mandatory in violent crime cases and expanding compensation and assistance services for victims of terrorism both at home and abroad, including victims in the military.
- The Mandatory Victims' Restitution Act makes restitution in federal cases mandatory, regardless of the defendant's ability to pay.
- The National Domestic Violence Hotline is established to provide crisis intervention information and referrals to victims of domestic violence and their friends and family.

1995
- The National Victims' Constitutional Amendment Network (NVCAN) proposes the first draft of language for a federal victims' rights constitutional amendment.

1994
- President Clinton signs a comprehensive package of federal victims' rights legislation as part of the Violent Crime Control and Law Enforcement Act. The act includes the Violence Against Women Act (VAWA) and establishes a National Child Sex Offender Registry.

1993
- Congress passes the Child Sexual Abuse Registry Act, establishing a national repository for information about child sex offenders.
- Twenty-two states pass antistalking statutes, bringing the total number of states with antistalking laws to 50, plus the District of Columbia.

1992
- *Rape in America: A Report to the Nation* is published by the National Crime Victims Research and Treatment Center and the National Victim Center and clarifies the scope and devastating effect of rape in America.
- The Association of Paroling Authorities International (APAI) establishes a Victim Issues Committee to examine victims' needs, rights, and services in parole processes.
- Congress reauthorizes the Higher Education Bill, which includes the Campus Sexual Assault Victims' Bill of Rights.

1991
- Representative Ilena Ros-Lehtinen (R-FL) files the first Congressional Joint Resolution to place victims' rights in the U.S. Constitution.
- The American Probation and Parole Association (APPA) establishes a Victim Issues Committee to examine victims' issues and concerns related to community corrections.
- The New Jersey legislature passes a victims' rights constitutional amendment, which is ratified by voters in November. By the end of 1991, seven states have incorporated victims' rights into their constitutions.

1990
- The U.S. Congress passes the Hate Crime Statistics Act requiring the U.S. attorney general to collect data of incidence of crimes motivated by prejudice based on race, religion, sexual orientation, or ethnicity.
- The Student Right-to-Know and Campus Security Act, requiring institutions of higher education to disclose murder, rape, robbery, and other crimes on campus, is signed into law by President George Bush.
- Congress passes the Victims of Child Abuse Act, which features reforms to make the federal criminal justice system less traumatic for child victims and witnesses.
- The Victims' Rights and Restitution Act of 1990 incorporates a Bill of Rights for federal crime victims and codifies services that should be available to victims of crime.

1987
- The National Victims' Constitutional Amendment Network (NVCAN) is formed.
- The American Correctional Association establishes a Task Force on Victims of Crime.
- NCADV establishes the first national toll-free domestic violence hotline.

1985
- The National Victim Center (renamed the National Center for Victims of Crime in 1998) is founded to promote the rights and needs of crime victims.
- The United Nations General Assembly adopts the Declaration of Basic Principles of Justice for Victims of Crime and Abuse of Power that serves as the basis for victim service reform throughout the world.

1984
- The passage of the Victims of Crime Act (VOCA) establishes the Crime Victims Fund, made up of federal criminal fines, penalties, and bond forfeitures, to support state victim compensation and victim service programs.

EXHIBIT 14–3	Crime Victims' Rights in America: A Timeline (*continued*)

- President Reagan signs the Justice Assistance Act, which establishes a financial assistance program for state and local government and funds 200 new victim service programs.
- The National Center for Missing and Exploited Children (NCMEC) is created. Passage of the Missing Children's Assistance Act provides a congressional mandate for the center.
- Congress passes the Family Violence Prevention and Services Act, which earmarks federal funding for programs serving victims of domestic violence.
- Victim-witness coordinator positions are established in the U.S. attorneys' offices within the U.S. Department of Justice.

1983
- The Office for Victims of Crime (OVC) is created by the U.S. Department of Justice within the Office of Justice Programs to implement recommendations from the President's Task Force on Victims of Crime.
- The International Association of Chiefs of Police adopts a Crime Victims' Bill of Rights and establishes a Victims' Rights Committee to emphasize the needs of crime victims by law enforcement officials nationwide.

1982
- President Reagan appoints the Task Force on Victims of Crime. The Task Force's *Final Report* offers 68 recommendations that become the framework for the advancement of new programs and policies.
- The federal Victim and Witness Protection Act of 1982 brings "fair treatment standards" to victims and witnesses in the federal criminal justice system.
- California voters overwhelmingly pass Proposition 8, which guarantees restitution and other statutory reforms to crime victims.

1980
- Mothers Against Drunk Driving (MADD) is founded.
- Wisconsin passes the first Crime Victims' Bill of Rights.
- In October, the First National Day of Unity is established by NCADV to honor all who have worked to defeat domestic violence. This day leads to Domestic Violence Awareness Week in 1987.

1979
- Frank G. Carrington, considered by many to be the founder of the victims' rights movement, creates the Crime Victims' Legal Advocacy Institute, Inc. The nonprofit organization was renamed VALOR, the Victims' Assistance Legal Organization, in 1981.
- The World Society of Victimology is formed to promote research of victims and victim assistance.

1976
- The National Organization for Women (NOW) forms a task force to examine the problem of battering.

1975
- Citizen activists from across the country unite to expand victim services and increase recognition of victims' rights through the formation of the National Organization for Victim Assistance (NOVA).

1974
- The federal Law Enforcement Assistance Administration (LEAA) funds its first victim-witness programs.

1972
- The first three victim assistance programs are created in St. Louis, Missouri, San Francisco, California, and Washington, DC.

1965
- The first crime victim compensation program is established in California.

Source: Adapted from Office for Victims of Crime, "Crime Victims' Rights in America: a Historical Overview," www.ovc.gov/ncvrw/2006/ (accessed July 4, 2006).

THE COSTS AND CONSEQUENCES OF VICTIMIZATION

According to a two-year National Institute of Justice (NIJ) study,[18] personal crimes result in costs of about $105 billion annually for medical expenses, lost earnings, and public victim assistance programs. For

President George W. Bush speaks at the 2002 National Crime Victim Service Awards Ceremony at the Department of Justice in Washington, DC. The president used the occasion to announce his support for a crime victims' rights amendment to the U.S. Constitution. What provisions might such an amendment contain?

tangible losses

Costs such as medical expenses, lost wages, and property losses that accrue to crime victims as a result of their victimization.

intangible losses

Costs such as fear, pain, suffering, and reduced quality of life that accrue to crime victims as a result of their victimization.

victims, crime costs may include (1) out-of-pocket expenses, such as for medical bills and property replacement; (2) reduced productivity at work, home, or school; and (3) nonmonetary losses, such as fear, pain, suffering, and reduced quality of life.

Unlike **tangible losses** (such as medical expenses or lost wages), **intangible losses** (such as pain, suffering, and reduced quality of life) do not have a market price and cannot be bought or sold. Nevertheless, these losses are real and can be valued in dollars—victims would pay dearly to avoid them.

Tangible losses do not represent the true cost of victimization. Intangible losses, including pain, suffering, and reduced quality of life, place the annual cost of crime at an estimated $450 billion (see Exhibit 14–4). Violent crime (including drunk driving) accounts for $426 billion of this total; property crime, $24 billion. These estimates exclude several other types of crime such as white collar crime, personal fraud, and drug crime. Exhibit 14–4 shows the annual cost of crime in the United States.

The cost of crime victimization is far greater when its impact on society is considered. Such costs include (1) monies spent by the criminal justice system to find, prosecute, and confine offenders; (2) social costs associated with fear of crime (e.g., changed behavior, the fear of being outside at night, moving to a safer neighborhood); (3) mental health costs associated with healing "scars" from victimization; (4) private security expenditures by the general population concerned about crime; (5) monies spent by employers to train temporary or new employees; (6) the costs of lost productivity borne by employers; (7) insurance claims processing costs (for example, life insurance claims for fatalities and workers' compensation claims); (8) workers' compensation and disability payments, especially those made to workers victimized while on the job; and (9) legal expenses incurred in recovering productivity losses from offenders and insurance companies (e.g., drunk drivers and their insurers). The National Crime Victimization Survey (NCVS) data include estimates of the

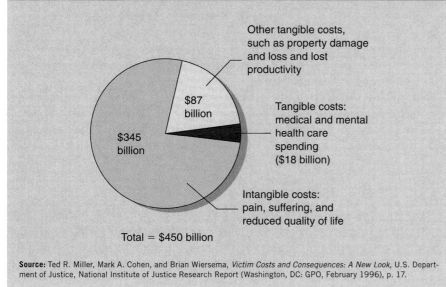

EXHIBIT 14–4 Annual Cost of Crime in the United States

Other tangible costs, such as property damage and loss and lost productivity

$87 billion

Tangible costs: medical and mental health care spending ($18 billion)

$345 billion

Intangible costs: pain, suffering, and reduced quality of life

Total = $450 billion

Source: Ted R. Miller, Mark A. Cohen, and Brian Wiersema, *Victim Costs and Consequences: A New Look,* U.S. Department of Justice, National Institute of Justice Research Report (Washington, DC: GPO, February 1996), p. 17.

number of hours of work and earnings lost due to medically related problems associated with victimization. Some specifics from the NIJ study follow:

- Violent crime necessitates 3 percent of all U.S. medical spending and 14 percent of all injury-related medical spending.
- Violent crime results in wage losses equivalent to 1 percent of American earnings.
- Violent crime is a significant factor in mental health care usage. As much as 10 to 20 percent of mental health care expenditures in the United States may be attributable to crime, primarily for victims treated as a result of their victimization.
- Personal crime reduces the average American's quality of life by 1.8 percent. Violence alone causes a 1.7 percent loss. These estimates include only costs to victimized households, ignoring the broader impact of crime-induced fear on our society.

NIJ also reports the estimated total annual cost of crime to victims in the United States, including the value of intangible losses and victim losses due to crimes.

Who Pays the Bill?

Victims and their families pay the bill for some crimes, while the public largely pays the bill for others. Insurers pay $45 billion in crime-related claims annually.[19] That is $265 per American adult. The government pays $8 billion annually for restorative and emergency services to victims, plus about one-fourth of the $11 billion in health insurance claim payments.

Taxpayers and insurance purchasers cover almost all the tangible victim costs of arson and drunk driving. They cover $9 billion of the $19 billion in tangible nonservice costs of larceny, burglary, and motor vehicle theft.

Victims pay about $44 billion of the $57 billion in tangible nonservice expenses for violent crimes—murder, rape, robbery, assault, and abuse and neglect. Employers pay almost $5 billion because of these crimes, primarily in health insurance bills. (This estimate excludes sick leave and disability insurance costs other than workers' compensation.) Government bears the remaining costs, through lost tax revenues and Medicare/Medicaid payments. Crime victim compensation accounts for 38 percent of homeowner insurance premium costs and 29 percent of automobile insurance premium costs.

Criminologists and public policy researchers are now using crime cost estimates to help assess the desirability of various policy options. Reported costs can be used to assess the wisdom of early offender release and diversion programs.

THE ROLE OF CORRECTIONS

In the past, correctional agencies were viewed only as facilities for punishing and rehabilitating offenders. Today, they also serve crime victims—protecting them from intimidation and harassment, notifying them of offender status, providing avenues for victim input into release decisions, and collecting restitution.[20] Public safety consultant Anne Seymour calls corrections-based victim services a "specialized discipline" within the field of victims' rights and services.[21]

Crimes are costly both emotionally and financially. Brendan Costin, the 14-year-old son of murder victim Michael Costin, delivers a victim impact statement about his deceased father on the witness stand at the sentencing hearing of Thomas Junta on January 25, 2002, in Cambridge, Massachusetts. Junta was sentenced to 6 to 10 years in prison for beating Costin to death at their sons' hockey practice. What purpose do victim impact statements serve?

Correctional agencies are also beginning to recognize the important role that victims can play in helping them develop policies, procedures, and programs that consider victims as well as correctional staff and offenders. Across the nation, crime victims are being asked to join advisory committees and agency boards, become official members of parole commissions, and serve as teachers in innovative classes that sensitize offenders to the impact of their offenses.

Correctional agencies are beginning to acknowledge victims' needs in their mission statements. In Oregon, for example, the state board of parole recently issued the following statement: "The Board's mission is to work in partnership with the Department of Corrections and local supervisory authorities to protect the public and reduce the risk of repeat criminal behavior through incarceration and community supervision decisions based on applicable laws, victims' interests, public safety, and recognized principles of offender behavioral change." Many state corrections departments have now issued similar mission statements, and the American Correctional Association's Policy Statement on Crime Victims is shown in Exhibit 14–5).

Crime victims' involvement with correctional agencies helps ensure priority for victim safety and services within correctional agencies (see Exhibit 14–6). Victim advisory committees now exist in a number of correctional agencies for that purpose.

Victim Notification

Victim notification of the release or pending release of convicted offenders is an important service. Without notification, victims are denied an opportunity to take precautions to ensure their own safety.

EXHIBIT 14–5   American Correctional Association

Victims of Crime Policy Statement

Victims have the right to be treated with respect and compassion, to be informed about and involved in the criminal and juvenile justice process as it affects their lives, to be protected from harm and intimidation, and to be provided necessary financial and support services that attempt to restore a sense of justice to them. Although many components of the criminal justice and juvenile justice systems share in the responsibility of providing services to victims of crime, the corrections community has an important role in this process and should:

- support activities that advocate for the rights of the victims;
- promote local, state, and federal legislation that emphasizes victims' rights and the development of victim services;
- support efforts by federal, state, and local units of government to increase the present level of funding and better use existing resources to support victim services and programs;
- advocate for the development of programs in which offenders provide restitution to victims, compensation and service to the community and, whenever possible, hold offenders financially responsible for their crimes;
- promote active participation of victims in the criminal justice and juvenile justice processes, including the opportunity to be heard and to participate in and/or attend juvenile and adult institutional release and/or parole release hearings and to receive advance notification of institutional release or escape; additionally, to provide separate waiting areas for victims and their families where offenders and victims may be present at the same hearing;
- educate, with sensitivity to language and disability needs, crime victims and victim service providers about correctional practices and involve correctional personnel in victim advocacy activities;
- train justice officials for both juvenile and adult offenders on victim program services, the impact of crime on victims, and promote sensitivity to victims' rights;
- operate those victims' assistance programs that appropriately fall within the responsibility of the field of corrections. Correctional agencies should, at a minimum but not limited to:
  - designate personnel in each correctional agency to respond to questions and concerns of victims and to ensure that appropriate victim notification and assistance procedures are implemented;
  - develop and distribute materials describing the correctional system and specific victims' rights within that system;
  - support and facilitate the use of victim impact statements in sentencing, post-conviction review, and programming processes; and
  - recognize correctional staff who are assaulted or held hostage as crime victims and develop new approaches for responding to their victimization.
- promote the use of existing community resources and community volunteers to serve the needs of victims.

Source: Copyright © American Correctional Association.

The importance of providing offender release information to crime victims has long been recognized. In 1982, it was one of the primary recommendations of the President's Task Force on Victims of Crime. In the *Final Report,* the Task Force recommended that parole boards notify victims and their families in advance of parole hearings if victims provide the paroling authority with their names and addresses. In addition, the task force called on parole boards to allow victims of crime, their

victim notification

Notification to victims of the release or pending release of convicted offenders who have harmed them.

THE OFFENDER SPEAKS

There is no such thing as a victimless crime. In my particular situation, the victim of my crime is my brother. I literally stole his identity. I used that identity to obtain cash, credit cards, and debit cards to pay bills, pay for medication, and pay for things that were needed daily. My crimes destroyed my brother's credit and his credibility with lenders and investors.

I knew what I was doing was wrong when I did it. I knew and understood that there was a reasonable chance that I would get caught. I knew that what I was doing would most likely land me in prison. In my situation, prison was not a deterrent. At the time I committed my crime, I did not feel as though I had a choice. The crime itself seemed to me to be the lesser of two evils.

When I think of my brother, my victim, the first thing I think of is all of the pain that I have put him through. I put him and the family through a great deal of pain. I feel shame. I can only hope that, someday, my brother will find it in his heart to forgive me. I feel sorrow, because my crime has placed an enormous gulf between us.

Anonymous

families, or their representatives to attend parole hearings and to provide information about the impact of the crime. According to the National Victim Services Survey, marked improvements have occurred in this area since 1985.[22]

There is, however, no consistent victim notification procedure. Some correctional agencies notify victims of only certain types of inmate releases (such as the release of sex offenders). Others notify victims of changes in offender classification. Some notify victims of an inmate's escape, while others notify victims of an inmate's clemency or death. At the federal level, the BOP has created one of the nation's first comprehensive victim notification programs, which has served as a model to the states for over a decade. The BOP notifies victims of any major change in an inmate's status.

Innovative technologies have emerged in recent years that augment victim access to notification and information. At least 10 state correctional agencies utilize automated voice notification systems that place telephone calls to victims, if requested, and inform them of offenders' pending release or release hearings. Victims can also contact a centralized call center, 24 hours a day, seven days a week. Call center operators confirm offender status and provide referrals to community-based victim services. Many state correctional agencies are following the example of the Illinois Department of Corrections, which provides current updates on inmate status and location and relevant upcoming hearings to victims and the general public via the Internet.[23]

In most jurisdictions, victims must request certain types of notification. Many victims do not request notification simply because they have not been informed that they have a right to do so.

Victim and Witness Protection

Every day in the United States, victims and witnesses are harassed, intimidated, and retaliated against by incarcerated offenders, through intimidating phone calls, mail, or threatened visits from friends and associates. Many correctional agencies have responded creatively to this problem. Today, when such problems occur, 37 states revoke an offending inmates' privileges, 36 transfer the inmate to a more restrictive level, 28 allow the filing of a new criminal charge, and 21 allow enhancement of

EXHIBIT 14-6 **Department of Justice**

Crime Victim Treatment Improvement Plan

Many people believe that much more needs to be done to involve victims and the community in the correctional process. A recent plan proposed by the Department of Justice to improve the treatment of crime victims recommended these specific steps:

- Every state department of corrections and every parole authority should establish an advisory committee of victims and service providers to guide and support victim-related policies, programs, and services.
- Correctional agencies should designate staff to provide information, assistance, and referrals to victims of crime.
- Mission statements of correctional agencies should recognize victims as an important constituency and should address victims' rights and services.
- A correctional agency should notify victims of any change in the offender's status that would allow the offender access to the community or to the victims.
- A correctional agency should place a high priority on ensuring victims' safety from intimidation, threats, or harm by offenders.
- Information about offender status and victims' rights should be accessible in several languages through toll-free numbers and printed materials.
- Correctional agencies should collect and distribute restitution payments as ordered by the court, and wage-earning opportunities should be increased for inmates, wards, and parolees who owe restitution.
- Victims' input should be sought for all decisions affecting the release of adult and juvenile offenders.
- Victim-impact awareness should be a basic component of the education and treatment programs of correctional agencies.
- Protected, supported, mediated dialogue between victim and offender should be available upon the victim's request.
- A crime victim should be notified of any violation of the conditions of the offender's probation or parole and should be allowed to comment before or during the violation hearing.
- Uniform practices should be developed and implemented for notification of a sex offender's release.

Source: Adapted from Office of Justice Programs, *New Directions from the Field: Victims' Rights and Services for the 21st Century* (Washington, DC: U.S. Department of Justice, 1998).

the inmate's sentence. In addition, 40 state correctional agencies document such harassment and threats in the offender's case file, 35 recommend investigation for additional prosecution, and 31 recommend revocation of parole when a parolee harasses, intimidates, or attempts retaliation.[24] California authorities are using an innovative method to stop the increasing number of instances in which inmates use telephones or letters to threaten and harass victims. The California Department of Corrections and Rehabilitation has created a program to block victims' phone numbers from inmate access and check inmates' outgoing mail.

In managing offenders who are ordered by the court to community supervision or released early from prison with supervision, probation and parole officers need to ensure the safety of victims and the public. Officers will generally use surveillance to identify offenders who pose a continued threat and make monitoring efforts such as checking with contacts at the offender's home and place of employment and with

Mary Achilles
Victim Advocate   Commonwealth of Pennsylvania

Mary Achilles heads the Office of the Victim Advocate for the Commonwealth of Pennsylvania, where she supervises a staff of 16. The office was formed in 1995 as an independent agency to provide services to both corrections and parole.

She began her career in 1979 as a prosecution assistant in the district attorney's office in Philadelphia, where she worked for 14 years. She moved to the department of corrections in 1993 and worked to establish the state's victim notification program. She holds a bachelor's degree in criminal justice and a master's degree in public administration.

On a daily basis, Achilles deals with victims and allows them to provide input into the release process. Her office files petitions to the board of probation and parole on behalf of victims to deny release or set supervision conditions and also selects victims to view executions if they desire to do so.

Achilles says she was drawn to her current role while working in the district attorney's office. "Helping prepare cases for trial, I started to see the inconvenience and the draw that they had on the victim," she says.

"Our philosophy is that we have to work with victims to prepare them for the fact that the offender will be released," she adds. "We'll petition the board to deny their release, but the reality is that 90 percent of all offenders will be released again."

"The challenge for us is that we work in agencies that are about the managing of offenders. Those agencies by design are about the movement of offenders through the process, and to get those agencies to be sensitive to the individual victim is always a battle."

Despite the challenges, Achilles is enthusiastic about her job. "It is incredible to see the strength of the human spirit. Since we mostly deal with state-level offenders, we're talking murders and rapes and serial rapes, the horrible stuff people don't want to talk about. It's amazing to me how people can triumph over tragedy—how much stronger they can be as a result of it."

> **"**
>
> *Victims raise a variety of issues—'I don't want him near my child's school or in my community.' I'm always engaging decision makers about what's best for the victim, the offender, and the community at large.*
>
> **"**

neighbors to ensure that the offender is meeting the conditions of probation or parole.

Just as there are special units in law enforcement and prosecutors' offices, probation and parole departments have begun to establish special units, such as sex offender and domestic violence units, to provide intensive probation or parole to reduce the safety risks to victims and society as a whole. Agents in these units have smaller caseloads and have received specialized training in intensive supervision.

Correctional agencies also use intermediate sanctions to ensure victim safety. Such sanctions include electronic monitoring, house arrest, random alcohol and drug testing, parole to a location other than the victim's community, mandatory restitution, and increased surveillance.

Community Notification

Most states have passed laws that either provide for community notification of sexual offender releases or authorize the general public or certain individuals or organizations to access sexual offender registries (see Exhibit 14–7). Often referred to as Megan's laws, in memory of seven-

EXHIBIT 14–7 **Online Sex Offender Registry**

The home page of sexoffender.com—a commercial site that combines sex offender information from many states. The U.S. Department of Justice's National Sex Offender Public Registry can be accessed at www.nsopr.gov. Community notification laws frequently result in the posting of online offender databases. How do such databases help victims?

Source: © Sexoffender.com

year-old Megan Kanka, who was murdered by a twice-convicted sex offender paroled to her New Jersey neighborhood, community notification laws recognize that a community has a compelling interest in being informed of offenders' whereabouts. In 1996, a federal Megan's law was enacted that requires states to release relevant registration information when necessary to protect the public.[25] In the mid-1990s, in rapid succession, every state enacted a Megan's law of its own.

Most state community notification laws impose a registration requirement on a sex offender at the time he or she is released on parole or probation, and the requirement typically remains in force for the duration of the parole or probation period.[26] A few states, including Alaska, California, Michigan, Montana, and South Carolina, impose a lifetime registration requirement for sex offenders against children, while other states have established a fixed registration period of 15 or 25 years. Approximately 30 states have provisions for some type of DNA testing or registration for genetic identification purposes.

To be truly effective, **community notification** laws require coordination among law enforcement officials, courts, correctional agencies, victim service providers, the news media, and other key stakeholders. Correctional agencies play a major role in providing this service by determining when and to where sex offenders will be paroled and by conducting community outreach and public education projects. Concerns, however, have been expressed over reported vigilantism (threats and acts of violence) in connection with community notification provisions, and with the inability of released offenders to find housing and to live peacefully in the community.

A promising practice in planning and implementing community notification programs emerged in 1990 in the state of Washington.[27] The

community notification

Notification to the community of the release or pending release of convicted offenders.

The entrance to the federal Office for Victims of Crime (OVC). OVC has developed model programs for assisting crime victims—including victimized correctional staff. What forms of criminal victimization might correctional staff experience?

Washington approach considers the rights and interests of victims, the community, and offenders. The strategy incorporates the following elements: establishing requirements for registration, requiring registration information for offenders, implementing guidelines for failure to register, implementing guidelines for a preliminary offender risk assessment, compiling offender information packets for distribution to the prosecutor of the county where the offender plans to reside, distributing special bulletins to law enforcement agencies, developing notification policies, creating guidelines concerning who should have access to sex offender registry information, and conducting community outreach efforts that involve victims and address their rights and needs.

Crime Impact Classes

Over the past decade, the number of educational programs in correctional institutions that involve both offenders and victims has greatly increased. The purpose of such programs is to help offenders understand the devastating impact their crimes have on victims and their families and friends, on their communities, and on themselves and their own families. For victims, participation in programs with offenders is useful because, although the harm they have suffered cannot be undone, they may prevent others from being victimized. Studies also show that participation in impact panels helps heal victims' emotional scars.[28]

Notable among victim–offender programs is the Impact of Crime on Victims (IOC) program, initiated by the California Youth Authority in 1986. The program has been replicated in more than 20 juvenile and adult correctional agencies and numerous diversion programs. IOC programs include a 40-hour curriculum that is designed to educate offenders about how different crimes affect victims and society.[29]

The U.S. Department of the Navy's Corrections and Programs Division took an important step in integrating victims into its corrections process when it issued guidelines in 1996 instructing U.S. Naval correctional facilities to implement impact-of-crime classes for prisoners before releasing them from custody. Information from inmates and correctional staff indicate that, after completing the classes, offenders have a greater understanding of the impact of their criminal conduct.

The passage of protective legislation represents a meaningful first step. But National Center for Victims of Crime surveys indicate that enforcement is generally lacking.[30] The NCVC reports that less than 40 percent of surveyed local criminal justice professionals knew their states had such legislation, and that rates of required victim notifications range as low as 30 percent. Criminal justice officials cite lack of funding as the most common reason for their inability to meet these responsibilities.[31]

Victim–Offender Dialogue

During the past two decades, a number of victim–offender dialogue programs have been developed in juvenile and criminal justice agencies, predominantly in juvenile probation agencies. These programs, primarily used in property crime cases, give victims an opportunity to engage in a structured dialogue with their offenders, who have already admitted their guilt or been convicted/adjudicated. When conducted with sensitivity to the victim and with care to ensure that participation by both victim and offender is voluntary, the victim–offender dialogue process can be very effective in helping victims overcome feelings of trauma and loss.[32] The program, which is closely linked to restorative justice initiatives discussed in earlier chapters, gives victims greater satisfaction with the justice system, increases their likelihood of being compensated, and reduces fear of future victimization.

In recent years, correctional agencies have begun to experiment with victim–offender dialogue in violent crime cases. In 1995, for example, the Texas Department of Criminal Justice initiated a victim–offender mediation/dialogue program for victims of severe violence and their incarcerated offenders. Under this program, the victim initiates the contact.

The Victimization of Correctional Staff

Correctional agencies have begun to recognize the impact of victimization on their employees. Correctional professionals are exposed to a wide range of victimization, including verbal harassment by inmates, sexual harassment by inmates or colleagues, physical or sexual assaults, hostage situations, and murder. To lessen the acute and chronic trauma this violence has on employees, many adult correctional agencies have developed written policies and procedures to respond to staff victimization and critical incidents.[33]

Most institutions have standard procedures for dealing with correctional staff victimization that focus on prevention. Many prison management departments, including California, South Carolina, and Texas, have developed procedures for helping victimized staff. Guidelines for response to employee victimization have also been developed under a national training and technical project funded by the Office for Victims of Crime (OVC).[34] The OVC project provides a comprehensive model for correctional agencies that is based on victims' rights laws, either state or federal.

VICTIM COMPENSATION

Victims generally have three options for recovering crime-related financial losses: (1) state-sponsored compensation programs; (2) court-ordered restitution; and (3) civil remedies, or lawsuits against offenders. **Victim compensation** programs, which exist in every state, may pay for medical care, mental health counseling, lost wages or loss of support, funeral and burial expenses, and/or crime scene cleanup.[35]

Restitution, the subject of the next section in this chapter, can be ordered in juvenile and criminal courts as a way to hold offenders financially accountable for their crimes.[36] The financial as well as preventative remedies that crime victims can seek through the civil justice system are not discussed in this text, but you should know that they represent one more avenue that victims can pursue in order to be compensated financially for their injuries. At the very least, correctional offices should consider implementing a policy of informing victims and victim service providers of the legal rights of crime victims to pursue reparations through the civil justice system.

The first victim compensation programs were established in New Zealand and Great Britain in 1964. These programs were based on a concept suggested by British Magistrate Margery Fry in the late 1950s. The first victim compensation program established in the United States was California's, created in 1965. By the time the President's Task Force on

victim compensation

A form of victim assistance in which state-funded payments are made to victims to help them recover financial losses due to crime.

THE STAFF SPEAKS

As government has become increasingly centralized, a major source of citizen frustration is the inability to define what is being achieved by the justice system, both on an individual case basis and from the perspective of the community. As the media focus on the spectacular failures and the extremes of the normal spectrum, government is caught between overwhelming case-loads of minor criminals and the need to target resources to protect the public from the dangerous ones. In the rush to efficiency, the government bypasses the most effective agents, the community and the family, instead focusing on the individual cases that squeak the loudest.

In the Reparative Probation program, ordinary citizens of the State of Vermont make sentencing decisions about adult criminal offenders from their community. Board members meet with offenders and victims, resolving their disputes by providing the offenders with the opportunity to acknowledge their wrongdoing, apologize to their victims, and make amends to their community. The offenders are sentenced by the court, having pled guilty to a nonviolent crime. The sentence is then suspended, pending their completion of a reparative agreement.

Direct involvement in decision making about individual cases forces citizens to look at the offenders not as strangers, not as numbers, and not as monsters. The offenders are forced to confront the reality of their offense and its impact on the community and their victims. This confrontation, with a restorative outcome, shifts the paradigm from punishment to reintegration. The offender is held accountable, the victim is restored, and the community is repaired. Perhaps even more important, the dispute is resolved by the community, and the community is empowered.

John G. Perry
Director of Planning
Vermont Department of Corrections

Victims of Crime released its *Final Report* in 1982, 36 states had victim compensation programs.[37] Today, all 50 states, the District of Columbia, the U.S. Virgin Islands, Guam, and Puerto Rico operate victim compensation programs.[38]

Victim compensation programs provide assistance to victims of almost all types of violent crime: rape, robbery, assault, sexual abuse, drunk driving, and domestic violence. These programs, as a rule, pay expenses but do not pay for lost, stolen, or damaged property. Eligibility and specific benefits vary from state to state.

In a typical year, state compensation programs pay approximately $240 million to more than 110,000 victims nationwide.[39] The amounts paid by each state vary considerably. Ten states pay less than $500,000 annually, and about 15 pay more than $3 million. The two states with the largest programs, California and Texas, pay nearly one-half of the total benefits paid in the United States.

Benefit maximums, which also vary from state to state, generally range from $10,000 to $25,000, although maximums are lower or higher for a few states. For example, California, Maryland, Minnesota, Ohio, Texas, and Wisconsin allow benefits of $40,000 to $50,000. Some states, such as New York, set no limit on payment of medical expenses; other states, such as Washington, pay medical expenses up to a predetermined maximum. Many states also set limits for other types of expense, such as funerals and mental health counseling. Nationally, the average amount paid to each victim applying for compensation is about $2,000.

President's Task Force on Victims of Crime

In 1982 the President's Task Force recommended federal funding to help support state victim compensation programs. It also documented problems in several state victim compensation programs: absence of a system for emergency compensation to cover immediate need for food, shelter, and/or medical assistance; insufficient maximum reimbursement levels; lack of coverage for domestic violence; and differences in residency requirements for eligible crime victims. Many of these problems have since been remedied through federal and state legislation and increased federal and state funding.

State-operated victim compensation programs have improved dramatically since 1982, in benefits provided and in recipients. However, some of the concerns raised by the President's Task Force, such as emergency compensation and insufficient maximums, have not been fully addressed by all states.

Victims of Crime Act

The task force's recommendation for federal support of state victim compensation programs was implemented through the Victims of Crime Act (VOCA),[40] passed in 1984. VOCA established the federal Office for Victims of Crime, which administers the federal Crime Victims' Fund, reimbursing states for up to 40 percent of victim compensation payments and providing technical assistance to state compensation programs.

All 50 states and the U.S. territories also receive annual VOCA victim assistance grants to support their victim assistance programs. A $500,000 base allocation is awarded to each state, the District of Columbia, the U.S. Virgin Islands, and Puerto Rico. The Northern Mariana Islands, Guam, and American Samoa each receive a $200,000 base allocation. Additional awards beyond the base allocation are distributed based on population. These awards support approximately 6,100 annual grants for crisis intervention, counseling, emergency shelter, criminal justice advocacy, and emergency transportation programs.[41] More than $2.3 billion in VOCA victim assistance grants was awarded between FY 1986 and FY 2001.[42]

Victims must apply for compensation in the state where the crime occurs. Prior to VOCA, many states' programs provided compensation only to residents unless a reciprocal agreement had been made with a victim's state of residence. States are now required, by federal law, to cover residents, nonresidents, and victims of federal crimes. Two states still restrict eligibility to U.S. citizens.

Recent Trends

Due to increases in publicity concerning victim compensation programs and new laws mandating that rights, services, and information be provided to victims, the number of victims applying for financial assistance has grown. As a result, many victim compensation program budgets were inadequate, and victims did not receive the compensation that they should have. Today, although a few states are still unable to pay all eligible claims, most do.

Eligibility Requirements

Each state has victim eligibility requirements for compensation benefits. Although states' requirements vary, most programs require that the victim do the following:

- Report the crime promptly, usually within 72 hours. A few states allow more time or less, but most have "good cause exceptions" that apply to children, incapacitated victims, and others with special circumstances.
- Cooperate with law enforcement agencies in investigation and prosecution of the crime.

- Submit a timely application for compensation, generally within one year. Again, a few states allow more time or less, and most may waive the deadline under certain circumstances.
- Provide other information, as needed by the program.
- Not file claims for compensation of victimization that resulted from claimant criminal activity or misconduct.

The VOCA Victim Compensation Final Program Guidelines encourage state compensation program staff members to meet with victims and victim service providers; to review state statutes, program guidelines, and policies for responsiveness to crime victims' needs; and to identify potential barriers to victim cooperation with law enforcement agencies, such as apprehension about personal safety and fear of offender retaliation. Victims tend to be reluctant to cooperate if offenders threaten violence or death. Age and psychological, cultural, or linguistic barriers may also influence the amount of victim cooperation. For instance, a young child, senior citizen, or foreign national may have difficulty communicating. Embarrassment or shame may delay or prevent reporting of a sexual assault.

Compensation programs are the victim's last resort. All other potential sources, such as the offender's insurance or public benefits, must be exhausted before state victims' compensation may be paid. If, however, payment from another source is delayed, the program may provide funds to the victim, which must be repaid if and when the victim receives other payment.

The victim cannot have been engaged in criminal activity. Dependents' eligibility depends largely on the victim's eligibility. Dependents or relatives of a homicide victim, for example, who was committing a crime at the time of death are generally not eligible for benefits.

Benefit Criteria

All compensation programs cover the same major expenses, although limits vary. The primary costs covered by all states are medical expenses, mental health counseling, wages lost as a result of a crime-related injury, lost support (for dependents of homicide victims), and funeral expenses. Nationwide, medical fees represent well over half of all compensation awards, with lost wage and support payments comprising the next highest payment percentage. In a few states, 20 to 40 percent of awards are for counseling; compensation payment in this area is increasing rapidly throughout the country. Of claim payment recipients, 25 to 30 percent are children age 17 and under.[43]

Many compensation programs also may pay for the following:

- moving or relocation expenses, when a victim may be in danger or relocation becomes medically necessary as a result of victimization;
- transportation for medical services when the provider is located far from the victim's residence or when other special circumstances exist;
- services, such as child care and/or housekeeping, that the victim cannot perform due to a crime-related injury;
- essential lost or damaged personal possessions (11 states pay for medically necessary equipment, such as eyeglasses or hearing aids, but only a few cover other such items);

- crime-scene cleanup—securing or restoring a home to its precrime condition; and
- rehabilitation—physical or job therapy, ramps, wheelchairs, and/or home or vehicle modification and/or driving instruction.

Restitution

Restitution is repayment to the victim, by the offender, for losses, damages, or expenses that result from a crime. Restitution is a form of victim compensation that holds the offender liable for the victim's financial losses. Restitution is generally seen, not as a punishment or an alternative to fines or sanctions, but as a debt owed.[44]

Criminal courts often order restitution to compensate victims for expenses that are the direct result of a crime. It is most often ordered in cases of property crime, such as a burglary. It may also be ordered to reimburse victims for expenses related to physical and/or mental health recovery and, for survivors of homicide victims, to make up for loss of support. Restitution is also common for cases of theft of services (e.g., restaurant bills), fraud, forgery, and traffic or vehicle law violation. Judges have also begun to order community restitution in which convicted offenders pay back the community through service.

Restitution, as a significant remedy for crime victims, was first imposed on the federal level in 1982, when the VWPA required federal judges to order full restitution in criminal cases or state on the record their reasons for not doing so.[45] That same year, the *Final Report* of the President's Task Force on Victims of Crime reinforced the VWPA by recommending that judges order restitution in all cases in which the victim suffered financial loss or state compelling reasons for a contrary ruling in the case record.[46]

The importance of restitution was emphasized in 1994, with enactment of the federal Violent Crime Control and Law Enforcement Act, which made restitution mandatory in cases of sexual assault or domestic violence. In 1996, the Mandatory Victim Restitution Act made restitution mandatory in all violent crime cases and in certain other cases on the federal level.[47]

In the decade that followed VWPA, every state enacted statutes that addressed restitution, most following the lead of the federal model. However, states continue to amend their statutes, creating a patchwork of financial reparations for victims across the country. As of 1995, 29 states had mandated restitution in all cases. Today, some states mandate restitution only in cases involving violent crimes, while others mandate restitution only in cases involving property crimes. A number of states require that offenders be on probation or parole before victims may collect restitution, and many do not require restitution from juvenile offenders. Probationers who fail to make restitution payments may have their probation revoked.

Despite developments in legislation, restitution remains one of the most underenforced of victims' rights in terms of ordering and monitoring, collecting, and dispersing payments. A recent DOJ study of recidivism among probationers reported that, of 32 counties surveyed,[48] only half required restitution in at least one-third of all felony probation cases. Of felony probationers who had completed their sentences, only 54 percent had fully satisfied restitution orders.[49]

All in all, the NCVC reports a poor record nationwide for ordering and collecting restitution from convicted offenders.[50] Even so, national research studies indicate that restitution is one of the most significant factors affecting the satisfaction of victims with the criminal justice process.[51]

Collecting Restitution in Institutions   Many correctional agencies encourage inmates to fulfill restitution obligations. These agencies increase collections by offering incentives (such as increased visitation and prison commissary services or priority enrollment in education programs) for compliance and by denying privileges for failure or refusal to participate.

The California Department of Corrections (CDC) has implemented an Inmate Restitution Fine Collections System, supported by state law, that allows deduction of up to 50 percent of inmate wages for payment of court-ordered restitution. These funds are transferred to the State Board of Control Restitution Fund for disbursement. This system collected over $9 million from its inception in November 1992 through early 1998. CDC's Victim Services Program staff coordinate voluntary inmate and parolee restitution payments as well.

Community Restitution   Offenders who are truly indigent may be given the option to perform community service in lieu of monetary restitution. According to OVC, however, this option should be offered only with victim consent. Some victims prefer that the monetary restitution order stand until such time, if any, the offender is able to fulfill it. Other victims may feel somewhat compensated if they participate in the decision about the type and location of the service to be performed. Payment of victim restitution does not necessarily preclude an order for community restitution. In many instances the offender has done damage not only to the victim but also to the community.

THE OFFICE FOR VICTIMS OF CRIME

Established by VOCA, OVC's official mission is to enhance the nation's capacity for assisting crime victims and to provide leadership in changing attitudes, policies, and practices to promote justice and healing for all victims.[52] OVC has five divisions that manage specific program areas, as follows:

- **Federal Assistance Division (FAD):** This division, which includes American Indian and Alaska Native initiatives, works to enable victims of federal crimes to fully participate in the criminal justice process. FAD distributes funds to nonprofit organizations, federal and military criminal justice agencies, and American Indians and Alaska Natives to support both training for service providers and direct services for victims, including crisis counseling, temporary shelter, and travel expenses incurred in going to court. FAD also supports services for U.S. citizens who are victims of federal crimes in foreign countries. In addition, the Children's Justice Act allows FAD to sponsor programs to improve the investigation and prosecution of child abuse in Indian country. These include establishing and training multidisciplinary teams to handle child sexual abuse cases.
- **Program Development and Dissemination Division (PDD):** PDD develops national-scope training and technical assistance, demonstration programs, and initiatives to respond to emerging issues in the victim assistance field. It is also responsible for coordinating public outreach and awareness. PDD provides information and assistance on highly technical victims' issues,

including services for trafficking victims, victims with disabilities, and victims of offenders who are mentally ill.

- **State Compensation and Assistance Division (SCAD):** SCAD administers federal grant programs for state crime victim compensation and state-administered local **victim assistance programs.**
- **Training and Information Dissemination Division (TID):** TID oversees the design, development, and dissemination of training and technical assistance on program development and implementation issues. The division coordinates the dissemination of training and technical assistance efforts with OVC divisions, manages the OVC professional development and state scholarship programs, and manages educational and training initiatives—such as the National Victim Assistance Academy and the State Victim Assistance Academies (SVAAs).
- **Terrorism and International Victim Assistance Services Division (TIVAS):** TIVAS was created to address emerging issues related to serving victims of violent crime, mass victimization, and terrorism both in the United States and abroad. TIVAS develops programs and initiatives to respond to victims of terrorism, mass violence, commercial exploitation, international trafficking of women and children, and other crimes involving U.S. and foreign nationals. TIVAS also coordinates OVC resources and funding for victims of terrorism and transnational crimes and administers the Antiterrorism and Emergency Assistance Program.

The Office for Victims of Crime has emerged as an invaluable support agency for state and territorial agencies, as well as for crime victims themselves. Its effective administration of victim compensation and assistance grant programs enables states and territories to provide greatly improved services to crime victims. Meanwhile, its *Fact Sheet* and *Help Series* publications provide crime victims with timely and comprehensive informational materials. A typical example[53] includes guidance to victims on their fundamental rights and an up-to-date listing of compensation and assistance program contact points within each state and U.S. territory. OVC makes these materials readily available through its well-designed and superbly maintained Web site at www.ojp.usdoj.gov/ovc.

VICTIM IMPACT STATEMENTS

Victim impact statements are assertions—by a victim and/or friends or relatives of the victim—about the crime's impact on the victim and the victim's family. Victim impact statements, now permitted at all sentencing hearings,[54] may be verbal or written, depending on the jurisdiction. Many states and the federal government now require that victim impact statements be included in presentencing reports (see Exhibit 14–8). The Crime Control and Law Enforcement Act of 1994 gave federal victims of violent crime or sexual assault a federal **right of allocution**—the right to make a statement at sentencing. Another federal law, the Child Protection Act of 1990, provides that victim impact statements from young children be allowed to take the form of drawings or models.

Victim impact statements typically include a tally of the physical, financial, psychological, and emotional impact of crime. As such, they provide information for courts to use in assessing the human and social cost of crime. Of equal significance, they also provide a way for victims

victim assistance program
An organized program that offers services to victims of crime in the areas of crisis intervention and follow-up counseling and that helps victims secure their rights under the law.

right of allocution
A statutory provision permitting crime victims to speak at the sentencing of convicted offenders. A federal right of allocution was established for victims of federal violent and sex crimes under the Violent Crime Control and Law Enforcement Act of 1994.

EXHIBIT 14–8   Sample Victim Impact Statement

VICTIM IMPACT STATEMENT

If you need more space to answer any of the following questions, please feel free to use as much paper as you need, and simply attach these sheets of paper to this impact statement. Thank you.

Your Name

Defendant's Name(s)

1. How has the crime affected you and those close to you? Please feel free to discuss your feelings about what has happened and how it has affected your general well-being. Has this crime affected your relationship with any family members, friends, co-workers, and other people? As a result of this crime, if you or others close to you have sought any type of victim services, such as counseling by either a licensed professional, member of the clergy, or a community-sponsored support group, you may wish to mention this.

2. What physical injuries or symptoms have you or others close to you suffered as result of this crime? You may want to write about how long the injuries lasted, or how long they are expected to last, and if you sought medical treatment for these injuries. You may also want to discuss what changes you have made in your life as a result of these injuries.

3. Has the crime affected your ability to perform your work, make a living, run a household, go to school, or enjoy any other activities you previously performed or enjoyed? If so, please explain how these activities have been affected by this crime.

Talking about CORRECTIONS

VOLUNTEERING IN CORRECTIONS

Visit *Live Talk* at **Corrections.com** (www.justicestudies.com/talking04) and listen to the program "Volunteering in Corrections," which relates to ideas discussed in this chapter.

to take part in the justice process. In most states, the right to make an impact statement is available to the direct victim, to family members of homicide victims, to the parents or guardians of a victimized minor, and to the guardian or legal representative of an incompetent or incapacitated victim.

According to OVC, the first victim impact statement was made in 1976 in Fresno County, California, by James Rowland,[55] who was then the county's chief probation officer. Rowland's contributions, which detailed the harm suffered by victims in that case, led Fresno County to make victim impact statements a part of all presentence reports.

In 1991, the U.S. Supreme Court case of *Payne* v. *Tennessee*[56] upheld the constitutionality of victim impact statements. Additionally, the *Payne* decision specifically permitted victim impact statements in cases involving potential application of the death penalty.

Victim impact statements are also frequently provided by victims or their survivors to parole hearing bodies. Statements are sometimes made in person; at other times they are submitted on audiotape or videotape, by teleconferencing, via computerized forms of communication, or in writing. Such statements give the paroling authority crucial information about the financial, physical, and emotional impact of crime upon the individuals most affected by it. In the past two decades, the passage of laws requiring victim input at parole has been seen as one of the greatest advances in victims' rights, with 43 states now providing this right.[57] This right loses its meaning, however, if paroling authorities do not notify victims of crime and their families of hearings in advance or do not schedule time during the hearing to allow them to describe the impact of crime on their lives.

THE FUTURE OF VICTIMS' RIGHTS

The OVC report, *New Directions from the Field*,[58] summarizes hundreds of recommendations from the field and from listening to victims, their advocates, and allied professionals who work with crime victims throughout the nation. In the course of compiling those many recommendations, certain key ideas emerged. The following five global challenges for responding to victims of crime in the 21st century form the core of the ideas and recommendations presented in the report:

- Enact and enforce consistent, fundamental rights for crime victims in federal, state, juvenile, military, and tribal justice systems and administrative proceedings.
- Provide crime victims with access to comprehensive, quality services regardless of the nature of their victimization, age, race, religion, gender, ethnicity, sexual orientation, capability, or geographic location.
- Integrate crime victims' issues into all levels of the nation's educational system to ensure that justice and allied professionals and other service providers receive comprehensive training on victims' issues as part of their academic education and continuing training in the field.
- Support, improve, and replicate promising practices in victims' rights and services built upon sound research, advanced technology, and multidisciplinary partnerships.
- Ensure that the voices of crime victims play a central role in the nation's response to violence and those victimized by crime.

REVIEW & APPLICATIONS

REFLECTIONS ON THE FUTURE

by Leslie W. Kennedy
Rutgers University

Victims in Context: Current and Future Perspectives

As a consequence of increased concerns about the rights of victims, many changes have been introduced into the criminal justice system to improve the experience of victims and to better represent their needs. These initiatives include compensation programs, police-based victim services units, and victim impact statements in offender sentencing. Many of these innovations have emerged from pressure brought to bear on legislators by interest groups representing victims.

In support of their claims, victim advocates rely heavily on research that has documented the incidence and distribution of crimes, particularly violence, from the point of view of victims. Researchers have shown that multiple victimization is a problem far beyond what was originally imagined. Individuals who are victims once are much more likely to be victimized again than are those who have never before been victimized. This revictimization appears to concentrate among groups that are particularly vulnerable because of their age, gender, lifestyle, or where they live. Further, researchers report evidence that large numbers of crimes have not been reported or have attracted little attention from the police. Crimes against women and children in domestic situations are of particular concern, as proponents in the victims' rights movement want not only to extend power to identifiable victims but also to give voice to those who find themselves unable or afraid to get help.

In addressing the needs of victims, major changes in police practice empower and protect victims, encouraging them to come forward to report crimes that previously have been kept from public scrutiny. Most noteworthy of these initiatives is mandatory arrest in domestic violence cases, where the onus for initiating an arrest is shifted from the victim (in cases where the police do not witness the assault) to the police (where they must arrest the assailant when there is physical evidence, upon arriving on the scene, that an assault has taken place). This change in police practice has been widely praised as a major improvement in the ways in which police respond to family violence cases. Previously, they may have ignored an assault or simply removed the offender for a short period to allow a cooling-off period, only to have a recurrence of the offense shortly thereafter.

There are times when the complexity of social relationships makes even something as straightforward as mandatory arrest produce surprising and unintended results, however. For example, mandatory arrest rules in cases of domestic violence have meant that either or both parties in a dispute must be arrested if the police officer determines that an assault had taken place. So, if the police conclude that a husband and wife have been in a fight and she physically injures him, she must be arrested. This occurs even if she is the one who calls the police, defining herself as a victim of longstanding abuse. The most extreme example of this is provided by the cases in which women who have suffered longstanding domestic violence shoot their husbands. If it is determined by the courts that this homicide is not clearly a case of self-defense (the spouse is not in imminent danger at the time of the killing), she is guilty of murder. There have been cases in which this murder conviction has been overturned based on the "battered woman defense," which argues that women in abusive relationships perceive themselves to be constantly in danger and that striking out is an act of self-defense. This defense suggests that we need to look beyond the specific factors that operate in the incident that is defined as criminal to its precursors, understanding that crime occurs in context and is part of a larger social event.

It is also the case that changes in the law create the situation in which the victim of a physical assault cannot decide against the arrest if the attending officer determines, based on physical evidence, that an assault has taken place. Extending rights to victims, then, has not translated into giving them a free hand in determining the disposition of a case. Other principles pertain. The rights of the victim must be considered in light of the demands by society that victims are protected both from physical injury and from coercive attempts to shield the offender from punishment at the hands of the State.

How we view victims is influenced by public perceptions of crime, personal safety, and the willingness and effectiveness of the criminal justice system to respond to crime. A great deal of the momentum that built up in support for victim rights had been fueled by constantly rising crime rates. There has been a recent downturn in the number of crimes, however. Further, there is a renewed interest in offenders' rehabilitation and their return to the community. It is not yet clear what these trends will mean for victims and victims' rights. The drop in crime rates may translate into a decrease in resources for victim support, with an overall decline in money allocated to public safety. However, there is the new concern that the return of offenders to communities after release from prison may translate into increased levels of crime. Will these crimes be adequately addressed through victims' services where victims are protected from repeat offenders?

Serious efforts are under way to implement a victims' rights amendment to the Constitution to provide victims the same protection under the law afforded criminal defendants. Whatever comes of this and other legislative initiatives, it is clear that victims' rights are now an integral part of the adjudication process. Increasingly, victims recognize the importance of increasing their involvement in defining reasonable punishment for offenders. Victims as well play an important role in rehabilitation, as has been demonstrated in experiments with sentencing circles used in Native American communities and through victim offender reconciliation programs (VORPs). While these approaches are in their infancy, they acknowledge the role of victims in the context of crime. They address the need to help victims understand the reasons for their experience and to confront offenders with the harm done as a consequence of their actions.

About the Author

Leslie W. Kennedy, a professor at the Rutgers School of Criminal Justice, was dean from 1998 to 2007. He received his BA from McGill University, his MA from the University of Western Ontario, and his PhD from the University of Toronto. Dr. Kennedy has published extensively in the areas of fear of crime, victimology, and violence. Among his published works, he is coauthor with Vince Sacco of *The Criminal Event*, appearing in its fourth edition this year, in which he advocates a holistic approach to the study of crime in social context. In addition, he has published extensively on spatial and temporal analysis of crime patterns.

Dr. Kennedy's current research in public security builds upon his previous research in event analysis and understanding the social contexts in which hazards to society are identified and deterred. He is currently director of the Rutgers Center for the Study of Public Security. RCSPS's primary focus is to conduct original analytical, objective research on how risk assessment can be applied to the study of security and to inform public policy discussions in this area. He is also coauthor with E. Van Brunschot of *Risk Balance and Security*.

SUMMARY

1 Victims were rarely recognized in the laws and policies that govern our nation until the 1970s. Since then, tremendous strides have been made in victims' rights legislation and victim services.

2 The 1980 enactment of Wisconsin's Victims' Bill of Rights, the nation's first state bill of rights for crime victims, began an era of dramatic progress in the victims' rights movement. Passage of the federal Victim and Witness Protection Act (VWPA) of 1982 brought national visibility to crime victims' concerns. In 1990, the Victims' Rights and Restitution Act (Victims' Rights Act) established a bill of rights for federal crime victims. The Violent Crime Control and Law Enforcement Act of 1994 established new rights for victims of sexual assault, domestic violence, sexual exploitation, child abuse, and telemarketing fraud. In 1996, the Community Notification Act, known as Megan's law, was enacted to ensure community notification of the locations of convicted sex offenders. In 1997, the Victims' Rights Clarification Act of 1997 asserted victims' rights to attend proceedings and deliver victim impact statements.

3 Many believe that a victims' rights amendment to the U.S. Constitution is needed to establish clear rights for crime victims and to protect those rights to the same degree that the rights of criminal suspects are already protected.

4 The costs that crime victims suffer can be divided into two major categories: (1) tangible losses, including medical bills, lost property, and lost wages; and (2) intangible losses, such as lost quality of life, fear, pain, and suffering.

5 Correctional agencies play an important role in meeting victims' needs. Services provided by correctional agencies include (1) victim and community notification of offender release or change in status; (2) victim and witness protection services; (3) classes for offenders on the impact of crime; and (4) opportunities for victim–offender dialogue.

6 Crime victim compensation programs pay for medical and mental health care, lost wages, funeral expenses, and crime-scene cleanup.

7 The three options available to victims for recovering crime-related financial losses are compensation, restitution, and civil remedies.

8 Victim impact statements are assertions by victims and/or friends or relatives of victims about the crime's impact on the victim and the victim's family. These statements are considered by judicial authorities in decisions regarding sentencing and parole.

KEY TERMS

victim, *p. 543*

victims' rights, *p. 543*

best efforts standard, *p. 544*

tangible losses, *p. 552*

intangible losses, *p. 552*

victim notification, *p. 555*

community notification, *p. 559*

victim compensation, *p. 561*

victim assistance program, *p. 567*

right of allocution, *p. 567*

QUESTIONS FOR REVIEW

1 Briefly outline the history of the American victims' rights movement.

2 Explain and date five federal laws that have significantly impacted victims' rights.

3 Why do some people consider a victims' rights amendment to the U.S. Constitution necessary?

4 What costs do crime victims suffer as a result of their victimization?

5 What can correctional agencies do to assist crime victims?

6 What are crime victim compensation programs, and what do they do?

7 What three avenues are available to victims to recover financial losses due to crime?

8 Describe victim impact statements. In what ways are they useful?

THINKING CRITICALLY ABOUT CORRECTIONS

Constitutional Amendment

In 1996, resolutions were introduced in the U.S. House and Senate to amend the Constitution to include crime victims' rights. A proposed federal constitutional amendment was reintroduced in modified form in 1999 with bipartisan support. In 2002, President George W. Bush announced his support for such an amendment. A federal constitutional amendment for victims' rights, say supporters, is needed for many different reasons, including to establish consistency in the rights of crime victims in every state and at the federal level; to ensure that courts engage in careful balancing of the rights of victims and defendants; to guarantee crime victims the opportunity to participate in criminal justice proceedings; and to further enhance the participation of victims in the criminal justice process. Do you agree or disagree that the U.S. Constitution should be amended to include victims' rights? Why?

The Focus of Correctional Agencies

While correctional services for victims exist today in many correctional agencies and institutions across the country, some people believe that correctional agencies have enough to do without worrying about victims. Dealing with offenders is a full-time job, say such critics, and the time and expense required to meet the needs of victims are just not available. Besides, they say, corrections is about controlling and rehabilitating offenders, not about making victims "whole again."

1. Should correctional agencies and correctional personnel be involved in victims' support programs? Why or why not?

2. If you were a corrections professional, how would you feel about being called upon to assist crime victims?

ON-THE-JOB DECISION MAKING

Restitution

You are director of a victim's advocacy program in your community. A criminal justice professor at a local university has asked you to participate in a public forum panel discussion addressing programs for restitution to crime victims. You decide to accept the invitation.

Upon arriving at the meeting the following week, you are surprised to find a significant turnout. The audience is larger than you expected, and the local news media are out in force. You did not anticipate this much interest.

As the meeting begins, it quickly becomes apparent that much of the audience consists of former offenders or offenders' family members. To your discomfort, you find yourself repeatedly faced with answering the same question over and over: How am I supposed to succeed in my efforts to live a noncriminal life when the bulk of my earnings get seized to repay my victim?

One particularly articulate offender conveys his dilemma: I am genuinely sorry, he says, for the suffering I caused. And while I know that nothing I do can erase my victim's painful memories of my crime, I truly want to repay her for the losses I caused, if only as a token of my genuine remorse.

But the reality, he says, is this: An unskilled ex-con's employment opportunities are limited. They are not going to get a "position" at the upper end of the pay scale. The work they find will be just "a job." It won't pay much, and it is unlikely that they will earn benefits. As a result, their weekly net pay will probably be insufficient to cover housing, feeding, and clothing themselves and their families.

When a significant percentage of that net pay is diverted to a restitution payment, he says, former offenders simply will not have enough left to meet their basic needs. It will not take long for the pressure to build. Under those circumstances, that pressure may generate a willingness to consider returning to the "easy money" available through crime. He says that makes the restitution program counterproductive because it contributes to defeating a primary aim of the rehabilitation effort: to encourage rejection of the criminal lifestyle.

1. How would you respond to the points this former offender has presented?

2. How do you answer the offender's question of "How am I supposed to succeed in my efforts to live a non-criminal life when the bulk of my earnings get seized to repay my victim?"

Offenders Meet Victims

You work in a state correctional facility. A month ago you were promoted from yard supervisory work into a program position that tasks you with conducting classes for offenders and their victims. Classes are held within the institution, and usually about five or six victims show up at each session to confront inmates. Many of the victims come from a local victims' rights group and, although they have all been victims of violent crime, they are not the people who have been victimized by the inmates involved in the class. Classes usually involve victims telling inmates about the personal impact of their crimes and about the personal burdens crime places upon victims everywhere.

What strategies could you implement to ensure that inmates express true remorse for what they have done and that victims do not use the class as an opportunity to demean inmates?

LIVE LINKS

at www.justicestudies.com/livelinks04

14–1 The Rights of Crime Victims—Does Legal Protection Make a Difference?

This survey of more than 1,300 crime victims, the largest of its kind, was conducted by the National Center for Victims of Crime to find out whether state constitutional amendments and other legal measures designed to protect crime victims' rights have been effective.

14–2 Repairing the Harm: A New Vision for Crime Victim Compensation in America

Financial compensation for victims is a critical ingredient in repairing the harm caused by crime. After the terrorist attacks of September 11, 2001, the nation responded immediately with a remarkable level of private and government support for the thousands of victims left behind. This article reflects on the government's approach to compensating the 9/11 victims and explores how best to provide financial assistance to all crime victims.

14–3 Analyzing Repeat Victimization

This report helps police identify and understand patterns of repeat victimization for a range of crime and disorder problems. It describes the concept of repeat victimization and its relationship to other patterns in public safety problems, such as hot spots and repeat offenders.

DEATH

The Ultimate Sanction

> Whatever you think about the death penalty, a system that will take life must first give justice.
>
> —John J. Curtin Jr., president, American Bar Association, 1990–1991

CHAPTER OBJECTIVES

After completing this chapter you should be able to do the following:

1 Discuss the history of capital punishment in the United States.

2 Describe the characteristics of people executed in the United States since 1977 and on death row today.

3 Discuss the politics influencing capital punishment.

4 List and summarize the major U.S. Supreme Court decisions that influenced capital punishment legislation.

5 Summarize the arguments for and against the death penalty.

6 Describe the five ways capital punishment jurisdictions weigh aggravating and mitigating circumstances to determine if a death sentence is appropriate.

7 Describe the death penalty appeals process.

8 Summarize Liebman's findings on the frequency of errors in capital punishment cases.

9 Discuss the Supreme Court's reasoning for banning the execution of offenders with mental retardation and juveniles.

the United States suffered through Prohibition and the Great Depression in the 1930s, there were more executions, an average of 167 per year, than in any other decade in American history.

By 1950, as prosperity followed World War II, public sentiment for capital punishment faded. The number of executions dropped. Support for capital punishment was at its lowest in 1966 (42 percent), and constitutional challenges were starting to surface. In the late 1960s, the Court began "fine-tuning" the way the death penalty was administered. In 1968 in *U.S.* v. *Jackson*[4] the Court held that the provision of the federal kidnapping statute requiring that the death penalty be imposed only upon the recommendation of a jury was unconstitutional because it encouraged defendants to waive their right to a jury trial to ensure they would not receive a death sentence. Later that year in *Witherspoon* v. *Illinois*,[5] the Court held that a potential juror's mere reservations about the death penalty were insufficient grounds to prevent that person from serving on the jury in a death penalty case. Jurors could be disqualified only if the prosecutors showed that the juror's attitude toward capital punishment would prevent him or her from making an impartial decision about punishment. The watershed case in capital punishment took place in 1972 when the Court decided *Furman* v. *Georgia*.[6] In brief, the Court held that Georgia's death penalty statute, which gave the sentencing authority (judge or trial jury) complete sentencing discretion without any guidance as to how to exercise that discretion, could result in arbitrary sentencing and was therefore in violation of the Eighth Amendment's ban against cruel and unusual punishment.

On June 29, 1972, the Court voided 40 death penalty statutes because they were no longer valid. Four years later, in *Gregg* v. *Georgia*, the Supreme Court upheld guided discretionary capital statutes, opining that "such standards do provide guidance to the sentencing authority and thereby reduce the likelihood that it will impose a sentence that fairly can be called capricious and arbitrary." Thirty years later the trends in capital punishment are these: Death sentences are down, executions are down, and public support for capital punishment is falling. This chapter will explore these issues.

Capital Punishment Around the World

In 2005 (the last year for which international execution data are available), there were at least 2,148 executions in 22 countries around the world. China, Iran, Saudi Arabia, and the United States were responsible for 94 percent of these known executions.

The following countries executed defendants in 2005:

- China (at least 1,770 executions)
- Iran (at least 94)
- Saudi Arabia (at least 86)
- United States (60)
- Pakistan (31)
- Yemen (24)
- Vietnam (21)
- Jordan (11)

Amir Karbalaei, right, Payam Amini, center, and Majid Qasemi, left, are seen hanging with ropes around their necks before huge crowds in the northeastern Lavizan district of Tehran, Iran, on Sunday, September 29, 2006, five days after their death verdict was approved by the Iranian Supreme Court. The men were convicted of abducting, raping, and robbing women. How would you describe the international use of capital punishment?

- Mongolia (8)
- Singapore (6)

As of March 2007, the majority of countries (123) had abolished the death penalty in law or in practice.[7] Seventy-three countries still retain it. Retentionist and abolitionist countries are shown in Exhibit 15–1.

EXHIBIT 15–1 | Countries With and Without the Death Penalty

Retentionist Countries

Afghanistan	India	Saint Christopher and Nevis
Antigua and Barbuda	Indonesia	Saint Lucia
Bahamas	Iran	Saint Vincent and Grenadines
Bangladesh	Iraq	Saudi Arabia
Barbados	Jamaica	Sierra Leone
Belarus	Japan	Singapore
Belize	Jordan	Somalia
Botswana	Kazakstan	Sudan
Burundi	Korea (North)	Swaziland
Cameroon	Korea (South)	Syria
Chad	Kuwait	Taiwan
China	Kyrgyzstan	Tajikistan
Comoros	Laos	Tanzania
Congo (Democratic Republic)	Lebanon	Thailand
Cuba	Lesotho	Trinidad and Tobago
Dominica	Libya	Uganda
Egypt	Malaysia	United Arab Emirates
Equatorial Guinea	Mongolia	United States of America
Eritrea	Nigeria	Uzbekistan
Ethiopia	Oman	Vietnam
Gabon	Pakistan	Yemen
Ghana	Palestinian Authority	Zambia
Guatemala	Philippines	Zimbabwe
Guinea	Qatar	
Guyana	Rwanda	

Abolitionist Countries (Countries whose laws do not provide for the death penalty for any crime)

Andorra	Czech Republic	Italy
Angola	Denmark	Kiribati
Armenia	Djibouti	Liberia
Australia	Dominican Republic	Liechtenstein
Austria	East Timor	Lithuania
Azerbaijan	Ecuador	Luxembourg
Belgium	Estonia	Macedonia (former Yugoslav
Bhutan	Finland	Republic)
Bosnia-Herzegovina	France	Malta
Bulgaria	Georgia	Marshall Islands
Cambodia	Germany	Mauritius
Canada	Greece	Mexico
Cape Verde	Guinea-Bissau	Micronesia (Federated States)
Colombia	Haiti	Moldova
Costa Rica	Honduras	Monaco
Cote D'Ivoire	Hungary	Mozambique
Croatia	Iceland	Namibia
Cyprus	Ireland	Nepal

EXHIBIT 15–1 **Countries With and Without the Death Penalty (*continued*)**

Netherlands	Samoa	Sweden
New Zealand	San Marino	Switzerland
Nicaragua	Sao Tome and Principe	Turkmenistan
Niue	Senegal	Turkey
Norway	Serbia and Montenegro	Tuvalu
Palau	Seychelles	Ukraine
Panama	Slovak Republic	United Kingdom
Paraguay	Slovenia	Uruguay
Poland	Solomon Islands	Vanuatu
Portugal	South Africa	Vatican City State
Romania	Spain	Venezuela

Abolitionist for "Ordinary Crimes" Only (Countries whose laws provide for the death penalty only for exceptional crimes such as crimes under military law or crimes committed in exceptional circumstances)

Albania	Brazil	El Salvador
Argentina	Chile	Fiji
Bolivia	Cook Islands	

Abolitionist in Practice (Countries that retain the death penalty for ordinary crimes such as murder, but can be considered abolitionist in practice in that they have not executed anyone during the past 10 years and are believed to have a policy or established practice of not carrying out executions)

Algeria	Kenya	Niger
Bahrain	Madagascar	Papua New Guinea
Benin	Malawi	Russian Federation
Brunei Darussalam	Maldives	Sri Lanka
Burkina Faso	Mali	Suriname
Central African Republic	Mauritania	Togo
Congo (Republic)	Morocco	Tonga
Gambia	Myanmar	Tunisia
Grenada	Nauru	

Source: Death Penalty Information Center, www.deathpenaltyinfo.org (accessed March 20, 2007).

CAPITAL PUNISHMENT IN THE UNITED STATES

The face of capital punishment is changing in the United States. Although 38 states, the U.S. military, and the federal government allow capital punishment and 12 states and the District of Columbia do not (see Exhibit 15–2), public opinion, grassroots lobbying, political and legislative changes, and judicial rulings are reshaping the capital punishment debate. As you will read later in this chapter, the broadest attack on the death penalty in decades happened when former Illinois governor George Ryan cleared the nation's eighth-largest death row by commuting 167 death row inmates' sentences to life in prison and granting pardons to four others. Illinois was the first state to establish a moratorium on the death penalty. Other states either established a moratorium or are considering legislation to impose one (Arizona, Colorado, Connecticut, Kansas, Kentucky, Maryland, Missouri, Montana, Nebraska, New Hampshire, New Jersey, New Mexico, New York, South Dakota, Tennessee, Texas,

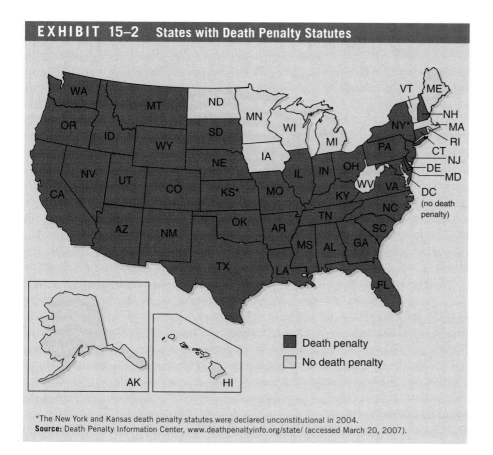

EXHIBIT 15–2   States with Death Penalty Statutes

Death penalty

No death penalty

*The New York and Kansas death penalty statutes were declared unconstitutional in 2004.
Source: Death Penalty Information Center, www.deathpenaltyinfo.org/state/ (accessed March 20, 2007).

and Washington). Five states are considering legislation to expand the death penalty (Georgia, Missouri, Texas, Utah, and Virginia).

Although research on executions in the United States has been hampered by a lack of official records, over 15,000 executions, beginning in the 1600s and continuing through 2003, have been confirmed.[8]

Executions were halted in 1968, pending a U.S. Supreme Court decision on the constitutionality of certain aspects of capital punishment. By 1977 the Court had ruled that capital punishment itself was not unconstitutional and did not violate the Eighth Amendment to the U.S. Constitution, thus paving the way for executions to resume. The first person to be executed after the moratorium ended was Gary Gilmore, who gave up his right to appeal and was executed by firing squad on January 17, 1977, by the State of Utah.

The number of executions from 1976 through 2006 is shown in Exhibit 15–3.

Today in the United States, what constitutes a **capital crime**—a crime that is punishable by death—is defined by law. This definition varies among jurisdictions. In Louisiana, for example, first-degree murder, aggravated rape of a victim under age 12, and treason are capital crimes. In Nevada, first-degree murder with at least 1 of 15 aggravating circumstances is a capital crime. In Texas, criminal homicide with one of nine aggravating circumstances is a capital offense.[9]

capital crime

A crime for which the death penalty may but need not necessarily be imposed.

The Federal Death Penalty

The Constitution of the United States does not mention the death penalty, but it does permit the federal government to deprive citizens of

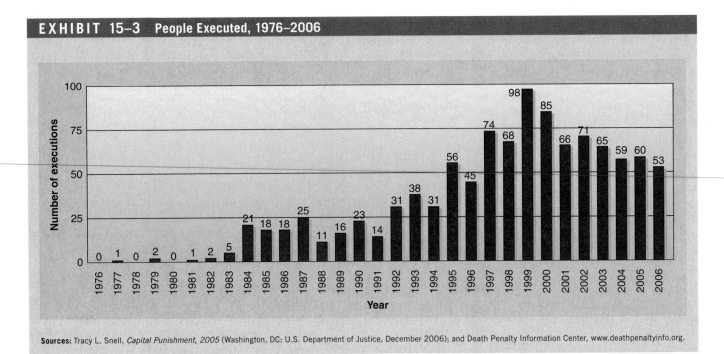

EXHIBIT 15–3   People Executed, 1976–2006

Sources: Tracy L. Snell, *Capital Punishment, 2005* (Washington, DC: U.S. Department of Justice, December 2006); and Death Penalty Information Center, www.deathpenaltyinfo.org.

life after giving due process. In 1790, the first Congress mandated the death penalty for several offenses, including treason, willful murder on federal property, forgery, piracy, counterfeiting, and several crimes on the high seas, and the first federal death penalty was used on June 25, 1790, when Thomas Bird was hanged for murder in Maine. By the end of the 19th century, the number of federal capital crimes had expanded to include kidnapping, spying, all murders, and arson of a dwelling or a fort.

Since 1790 the federal government has executed 336 men and 4 women. Of these 134 (39 percent) were white, 118 (35 percent) were black, 63 (19 percent) were Native American, and 25 (7 percent) were Hispanic or Unknown. Methods of execution in federal cases have included hanging, electrocution, and the gas chamber. Today the federal government uses lethal injection.

From 1972, the year of the Supreme Court's *Furman* decision (discussed later in this chapter), until the late 1980s, federal capital prosecutions were rare. In 1988, President Reagan signed the Anti–Drug Abuse Act, which authorized capital punishment for murder committed by people involved in certain drug trafficking activities.

In 1994, President Clinton signed into law the Violent Crime Control and Law Enforcement Act. Title VI is the Federal Death Penalty Act. It dramatically expanded the number of federal offenses punishable by death (see Exhibit 15–4).

In addition to incorporating the Supreme Court law ban on execution of offenders with mental retardation and juveniles, the Federal Death Penalty Act also exempts women while they are pregnant. The act permits federal employees who oppose the death penalty to opt out of participating in executions, and it restricts the federal government's ability to seek the death penalty for Native Americans whose offense occurred within the boundaries of Indian country.

EXHIBIT 15-4 Federal Laws Providing for the Death Penalty

- Assassination or kidnapping resulting in the death of the president or vice president
- Bank-robbery-related murder or kidnapping
- Civil rights offenses resulting in death
- Death resulting from aircraft hijacking
- Death resulting from offenses involving transportation of explosives, destruction of government property, or destruction of property related to foreign or interstate commerce
- Destruction of aircraft, motor vehicles, or related facilities resulting in death
- Espionage
- First-degree murder
- Genocide
- Mailing of injurious articles with intent to kill or resulting in death
- Murder by a federal prisoner
- Murder by an escaped federal prisoner already sentenced to life imprisonment
- Murder by the use of a weapon of mass destruction
- Murder committed at an airport serving international civil aviation
- Murder committed by the use of a firearm during a crime of violence or a drug-trafficking crime
- Murder committed during a drug-related drive-by shooting
- Murder committed during an offense against maritime navigation
- Murder committed during an offense against a maritime fixed platform

- Murder committed in a federal government facility
- Murder during a hostage taking
- Murder during a kidnapping
- Murder for hire
- Murder involved in a racketeering offense
- Murder involving torture
- Murder of a court officer or juror
- Murder of a federal judge or law enforcement official
- Murder of a foreign official
- Murder of a member of Congress, an important executive official, or a Supreme Court Justice
- Murder of a state correctional officer
- Murder of a state or local law enforcement official or other person aiding in a federal investigation
- Murder of a U.S. national in a foreign country
- Murder related to a carjacking
- Murder related to rape or child molestation
- Murder related to sexual exploitation of children
- Murder related to the smuggling of aliens
- Murder related to a continuing criminal enterprise or related murder of a federal, state, or local law enforcement officer
- Murder with the intent of preventing testimony by a witness, victim, or informant
- Retaliatory murder of a member of the immediate family of law enforcement officials
- Retaliatory murder of a witness, victim, or informant
- Terrorist murder of a U.S. national in another country
- Treason
- Willful wrecking of a train resulting in death

Source: Adapted from Tracy L. Snell, *Capital Punishment, 2005* (Washington, DC: U.S. Department of Justice, December 2006), p. 13.

The last three federal executions were:

- Timothy McVeigh, white, executed June 11, 2001;
- Juan Raul Garza, Hispanic, executed June 19, 2001; and
- Louis Jones Jr., black, executed March 18, 2003.

Procedures in Federal Capital Cases Federal prosecutors who wish to file capital charges are required by the Department of Justice to first obtain authorization from the attorney general. The request is reviewed by the assistant attorney general, by the deputy attorney general, and ultimately by the attorney general.

For example, on Monday, November 17, 2003, lawyers for serial bomber Eric Rudolph met with then attorney general John Ashcroft's death penalty committee. The committee's job was to listen, review evidence, and recommend to the attorney general whether Rudolph should be added to the list of 124 people tried under the federal death law since it was reinstated in 1988. On Friday, December 13, 2003, the attorney general authorized prosecutors to seek the death penalty against Rudolph.

The new Federal Death Penalty Act changes an offender's right to counsel in three ways. First, it requires that a minimum of two lawyers be appointed to represent federal capital defendants. Second, at least one of the two lawyers must have experience in capital work. And third, the federal court must consider the federal public defender's recommendation regarding which counsel are qualified for appointment in capital cases.

Federal Death Row Federal death row is at the United States Penitentiary, Terre Haute, Indiana. It is called the Special Confinement Unit (SCU). It opened in 1999 because of the increasing number of federal defendants sentenced to death. On June 15, 2007, 53 people were on federal death row in Terre Haute, Indiana.

SCU is a two-story renovated housing unit. It includes 120 single cells, upper-tier and lower-tier corridors, an industrial workshop, indoor and outdoor recreation areas, a property room, a food preparation area, attorney and family visiting areas, and a video-teleconferencing area that is used to facilitate inmate access to the courts and to their attorneys.

When Timothy McVeigh was executed in 2001 for the murder of 168 people in the Oklahoma City bombing, the United States Department of Justice instituted an elaborate process to handle any last-minute legal interruptions that might prevent or delay his execution. Two hours before McVeigh's execution, prison officials ended his visiting privileges to give him one final opportunity to seek a stay from the courts or President Bush. Forty-five minutes before the execution—and again at 10 minutes before the execution—the White House was contacted by telephone. In the event of a delay, a United States marshal was ready to instruct the executioner to step away from the execution equipment and to notify McVeigh and everyone present that the execution had been delayed or stayed. McVeigh received no stays.

Race and the Federal Death Penalty In 2000 the Justice Department released its findings on the question of racial and geographic disparities in federal death penalty prosecutions forwarded to the Justice Department for review between 1995 and 2000. It reported that 80 percent of the defendants were minority.[10] The study found that minorities are overrepresented in the federal death penalty system, as both victims and defendants, relative to the general population. Then attorney general Janet Reno said, "This should be of concern to all of us."

The study confirmed a personal Justice Department report on racial disparities that found that between 1988, when President Reagan signed the Anti–Drug Abuse Act into law, and October 1993, the attorney general authorized federal prosecutors to seek the death penalty against 30 defendants. Over 70 percent were black, and one-half of the remaining defendants were Mexican American.[11] Later in this chapter we will examine the debate over such statistics.

DEATH ROW TODAY

Characteristics of People Executed Since 1977

As of June 15, 2007, 1,079 people have been executed in the United States since Gary Gilmore's execution in January 1977. The peak year was 1999, when 98 people were executed. By 2006 the number of executions had declined to 53. Thirty-seven percent (394) of all executions have taken place in Texas. Has the death penalty affected the murder rate in Texas? You be the judge: From 1995 through 2005 (the last year for which complete *Uniform Crime Reports* data are available), the murder

Few issues generate more public controversy than the death penalty. In some states there are movements to end the death penalty, while in others the move is to speed up death row appeals and complete the sentence of execution. Do demonstrations such as these influence the public policy implemented by state legislatures?

rate in the United States averaged 6.2 per year per 100,000 population. In Texas, the average was 6.7 per year per 100,000 population, 0.08 percent more than the national average. In states without the death penalty the average was 2.9 per year per 100,000 population, less than half the national average.

Since 1977, the South leads the United States in executions with 883. In 2006, 75 percent of the executions took place in the South. Only 1.0 percent of all the people executed since 1977 have been female; 57 percent were white, 34 percent black, 7 percent Hispanic, and 2 percent other.[12] A total of 1,619 people had been killed by those who were executed.

Characteristics of Prisoners Under Sentence of Death

On January 1, 2007, 40 jurisdictions (38 states, the federal government, and the U.S. military) held a total of 3,350 prisoners under sentence of death, an increase from 3,344 one year earlier. At the time of Gary Gilmore's execution on January 17, 1977, there were 423 people on death row. Ten years later the number was 1,984. In 1997, there were 3,335. After more than 20 years of continued growth in the number of people sentenced to die in the United States, the size of death row leveled off in 2000 (3,593) and decreased to 3,581 in 2001, 3,557 in 2002, 3,374 in 2003, 3,315 in 2004, 3,254 in 2005, and 3,344 in 2006. Today, U.S. juries are imposing fewer death sentences than they did on average during the 1990s. In the 1990s, an average of 300 people were sentenced to death each year. That rate has dropped by two-thirds. In 2006, there were 114 death sentences issued, the fewest since 1977, when the Supreme Court reinstated the death penalty.

Forty-three percent of the nation's death row population is in three states: California (660), Florida (397), and Texas (393). Exhibit 15–5 shows additional characteristics of inmates under sentence of death.

Inmates executed in 2005 had been on death row an average of 12 years and 3 months.[13] Prisoners may leave death row by means other than execution. Between 1973 and 2005, 327 people on death row died;

Chris Summers
Chaplain
W. C. Holman Correctional Facility
Atmore, Alabama

I received an M.A. degree in Christian Theological Studies from the University of Mobile. I am an evangelical Christian, ordained Southern Baptist, and believe in the saving grace of Jesus Christ by faith.

The maximum-security prison where I now work is W. C. Holman Correctional Facility in Atmore, Alabama. I have worked with the Alabama Department of Corrections for 24 years. I began working in this system in 1981 as a full-time Chaplain's Assistant through a Christian mission organization. I was hired by the state as a full-time Chaplain in 1990. In 1997 I began work at W. C. Holman Correctional Facility, where death row is housed and sentences are carried out. This is where I began my early work in prison ministry and have known many men on death row and those who have mitigated sentences from the death penalty since 1981.

At W. C. Holman Correctional Facility I minister to the entire institution, which includes a 680-man population, 200 single-cell segregation unit, and 170-man death row unit. I am also a regional chaplaincy coordinator who is a member of the Religious Activities Review Committee, which develops policies and confirms acceptable religious expressions within the state correctional institutions of Alabama.

Among many other chaplaincy programming responsibilities, I weekly perform duties on the death row unit. Some of my responsibilities are to visit each man once a week, administrate and coordinate weekly volunteer services, and schedule periodic special events. During a two-week period prior to an execution, my responsibilities involve close practical and spiritual engagement with the offender's family and friends and the execution team officers and spiritual assistance or direct spiritual guidance for the offender. In the execution chamber as the sentence is being carried out, I am the only person in the room with the condemned. This responsibility was created and detailed by the current Warden, Grantt Culliver. The offender then has the spiritual assistance and personal comfort of the Chaplain available while the sentence is being carried out. I oftentimes hold the offender's hand and pray with him until the first stage of execution, sleep, is performed. On several occasions, responsibilities of death row ministry include the privilege of conducting funerals for the aged or those executed.

At this time, I have witnessed 24 executions, 10 by electrocution and 14 by lethal injection. In 2002 Alabama first employed the use of lethal injection and still has the option of electrocution according to the offender's preference.

Out of my experience, it is my belief that restorative justice epistemology and practice is the answer to our current criminal justice crisis. I use every given opportunity to communicate its practical and viable application, even for those victims and offenders who incur *Death: the Ultimate Sanction*. It has been my message to the men on death row and my experience that true closure for wrongs committed come through restorative accountability for all involved in the harms of crime.

> *It has been my message to the men on death row and my experience that true closure for wrongs committed come through restorative accountability for all involved in the harms of crime.*

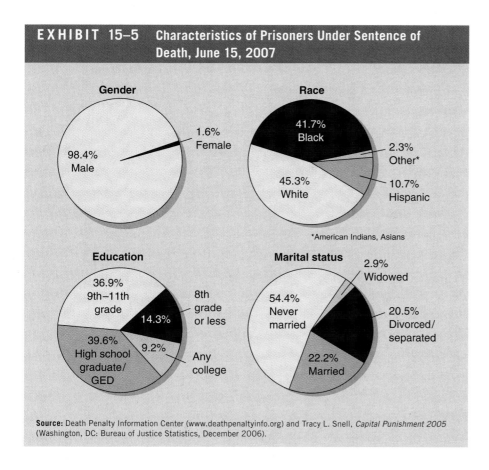

EXHIBIT 15–5   Characteristics of Prisoners Under Sentence of Death, June 15, 2007

Gender
- 98.4% Male
- 1.6% Female

Race
- 41.7% Black
- 2.3% Other*
- 10.7% Hispanic
- 45.3% White

*American Indians, Asians

Education
- 36.9% 9th–11th grade
- 14.3% 8th grade or less
- 39.6% High school graduate/GED
- 9.2% Any college

Marital status
- 2.9% Widowed
- 54.4% Never married
- 20.5% Divorced/separated
- 22.2% Married

Source: Death Penalty Information Center (www.deathpenaltyinfo.org) and Tracy L. Snell, *Capital Punishment 2005* (Washington, DC: Bureau of Justice Statistics, December 2006).

2,702 had their convictions or sentences overturned; and 341 were granted **clemency** and received a **commutation,** meaning that the severity of their punishment was lessened.[14] Exhibit 15–6 shows the clemency process by state.

Victim Race and Gender and the Death Penalty

Defendant–victim racial combinations have been the subject of considerable debate.[15] Recognizing that whites and blacks are murder victims in approximately equal numbers, why is it that 79 percent of the victims in cases resulting in executions since 1977 have been white? This disparity is confirmed even in studies that control for similar crimes by comparing defendants with similar backgrounds. In 2006, 3 of 24 white persons were executed for the murder of a black person. Does it imply that white victims are considered more important by the criminal justice system? Former U.S. attorney general John Ashcroft argued that blacks and Hispanics are more likely than whites to be sentenced to death and executed because they are more likely to be arrested on facts that can support a capital charge and because whites are more likely to negotiate plea bargains that spare their lives. Others disagree, citing consistent patterns of racial bias.[16] A study of all homicide cases in North Carolina from 1993 to 1997 in which a death sentence was possible found that those who killed white people were three and one-half times more likely to get the death penalty than those who killed nonwhites. Almost 12 percent of nonwhite defendants charged with murdering white victims were sentenced to die. In contrast, 6.1 percent of whites charged with murdering

clemency

Kindness, mercy, forgiveness, or leniency, usually relating to criminal acts.

commutation

A change of a legal penalty to a lesser one (e.g., from death to life imprisonment).

EXHIBIT 15-6 Clemency Process by State

States in Which the Governor Has Sole Authority (14)

Alabama	New Jersey	South Carolina
California	New Mexico	Virginia
Colorado	New York	Washington
Kansas	North Carolina	Wyoming
Kentucky	Oregon	

States in Which the Governor Must Have the Recommendation of Clemency from a Board or Advisory Group (8)

Arizona	Louisiana	Pennsylvania
Delaware	Montana	Texas
Florida[1]	Oklahoma	

States in Which the Governor Receives a Nonbinding Recommendation of Clemency from a Board or Advisory Group (10)

Arkansas	Mississippi	South Dakota
Illinois	Missouri	Tennessee
Indiana	New Hampshire	
Maryland	Ohio	

States in Which a Board or Advisory Group Determines Clemency (3)

Connecticut	Georgia	Idaho

States in Which the Governor Sits on a Board or Advisory Group That Determines Clemency (3)

Nebraska	Nevada	Utah

Note: For federal death row inmates, the president alone has pardon power.
1. Florida's governor must have the recommendation of the board on which he or she sits.
Source: National Coalition to Abolish the Death Penalty, "Executive Clemency Process and Execution Warrant Procedure In Death Penalty Cases" (1993), with updates by the Death Penalty information Center.

whites and 4.7 percent of nonwhites charged with murdering nonwhites received the death penalty. Similar studies have been conducted in Georgia, Kentucky, and other states.[17]

More recently, researchers at Bowling Green State University examined the data on almost 6,000 homicides in Ohio that occurred between 1981 and 1997 and found that even after controlling for several legally relevant factors, analyses revealed that homicides with white female victims were more likely to result in a death sentence than others. "In fact," the researchers wrote, "homicides with white female victims are the only statistically distinct victim dyad. This is consistent with the view that black female victims do not have the same status as white female victims. In other words, it appears that decision making in homicides is not influenced by the same factors in all cases, and that white female victim homicides may be substantively unique."[18]

Methods of Execution

Five methods of execution are used in the United States: (1) lethal injection, (2) electrocution, (3) lethal gas, (4) hanging, and (5) firing squad. As

Reporters observe the execution chair in which Gary Gilmore sat when facing a Utah firing squad on January 17, 1977. Upper right on the chair back are the bullet holes. Draped over the back of the chair is the corduroy material hood that Gilmore wore during the execution. On March 15, 2004, Utah repealed its use of the firing squad, leaving lethal injection as the only option. Should condemned inmates be permitted to choose the method of their execution if, when they were sentenced to die, state law allowed the choice?

you can see in Exhibit 15–7, lethal injection is the predominant method of execution, used in 37 states. In 1977, Oklahoma became the first state to adopt lethal injection as a means of execution. Five years later, Charles Brooks became the first person executed by that method, in Texas. Today 9 states authorize electrocution; 4 states, lethal gas; 3 states, hanging; and 2 states, firing squad. On March 15, 2004, Utah governor Olene Walker signed legislation that repealed Utah's firing squad, calling it a relic of Utah's territorial days and saying it would deny publicity seeker killers the chance to "go out in a blaze of glory." [19] The last execution by firing squad in Utah was in 1996. Only one state—Nebraska—uses the electric chair as the sole method of execution. Seventeen states authorize more than one method—lethal injection and an alternative method, generally at the election of the condemned person. However, 5 of the 17 states stipulate which method must be used according to the date of sentencing. For example, Arizona uses lethal injection for people sentenced after November 15, 1992; those sentenced before that date may select lethal injection or lethal gas. Oklahoma authorizes electrocution if lethal injection is ever held unconstitutional and firing squad if both lethal injection and electrocution are held unconstitutional. The federal government authorizes a different method of execution under each of two different laws; the method of execution for federal prisoners prosecuted under the *Code of Federal Regulations,* Volume 28, Part 26, is lethal injection; for those offenses prosecuted under the Violent Crime Control and Law Enforcement Act of 1994, the method used is that in the state in which the person was convicted. If the state has no death penalty, the inmate is transferred to another state.

When lethal injection is used, the condemned person is strapped to a gurney, and several heart monitors are positioned on his or her chest. Two needles (one is a backup) are inserted into arm veins. Long tubes connect the needle through a hole in a wall to several intravenous drips. The first is a saline solution that is started immediately. At the warden's signal, a curtain is raised, exposing the inmate to the witnesses in an adjoining room. The inmate is then injected with 60 cc of sodium thiopental or pentothal to cause unconsciousness. Next flows 60 cc of pavulon or

EXHIBIT 15-7   Method of Execution, by State, 2005

Lethal Injection			Electrocution	Lethal Gas	Hanging	Firing Squad
Alabama[a]	Kentucky[a,d]	Ohio	Alabama[a]	Arizona[a,b]	Delaware[a,g]	Idaho[a]
Arizona[a,b]	Louisiana	Oklahoma[a]	Arkansas[a,c]	California[a]	New Hampshire[a,i]	Oklahoma[f]
Arkansas[a,c]	Maryland	Oregon	Florida[a]	Missouri[a]	Washington[a]	Utah[k]
California[a]	Mississippi	Pennsylvania	Kentucky[a,d]	Wyoming[a,e]		
Colorado	Missouri[a]	South Carolina[a]	Nebraska			
Connecticut	Montana	South Dakota	Oklahoma[f]			
Delaware[a,g]	Nevada	Tennessee[a,h]	South Carolina[a]			
Florida[a]	New Hampshire[a]	Texas	Tennessee[a,h]			
Georgia	New Jersey	Utah[a]	Virginia[a]			
Idaho[a]	New Mexico	Virginia[a]				
Illinois	New York[j]	Washington[a]				
Indiana	North Carolina	Wyoming[a]				
Kansas[j]						

Note: The method of execution of federal prisoners is lethal injection, pursuant to 28 CFR, Part 26. For offenses under the Violent Crime Control and Law Enforcement Act of 1994, the method is that of the state in which the conviction took place, pursuant to 18 U.S.C. 3596. If the state has no death penalty, the inmate is transferred to another state.

a   Authorizes two methods of execution.
b   Authorizes lethal injection for people whose capital sentence was received after 11/15/92; those sentenced before that date may select lethal injection or lethal gas.
c   Authorizes lethal injection for those whose capital offense occurred on or after 7/4/83; those whose offense occurred before that date may select lethal injection or electrocution.
d   Authorizes lethal injection for those sentenced on or after 3/31/98; those sentenced before that date may select lethal injection or electrocution.
e   Authorizes lethal gas if lethal injection is ever held to be unconstitutional.
f   Authorizes electrocution if lethal injection is ever held to be unconstitutional and firing squad if both lethal injection and electrocution are held unconstitutional.
g   Authorizes lethal injection for those whose capital offense occurred after 6/13/86; those whose offense occurred before that date may select lethal injection or hanging.
h   Authorizes lethal injection for those whose capital offense occurred after 12/31/98; those whose offense occurred before that date may select lethal injection or electrocution.
i   Authorizes hanging only if lethal injection cannot be given.
j   In 2004, death penalty statutes were found to be unconstitutional in New York and Kansas.
k   Utah ended use of the firing squad on March 15, 2004, but allowed it for four death row inmates who had already requested it.

Source: Tracy L. Snell, *Capital Punishment, 2005* (Washington, D.C.: U.S. Department of Justice, Bureau of Justice Statistics, December 2006).

pancuronium bromide (a drug now banned in 19 states for euthanasia of animals), which paralyzes the entire muscle system and stops the inmate's breathing. Finally, the flow of 60 cc of potassium chloride stops the heart. The three injections are delivered separately and the lines cleaned out with saline solution after each drug injection; otherwise, the chemicals could become erosive and damage the IV lines. Death results from anesthetic overdose and respiratory and cardiac arrest while the condemned person is unconscious.[20]

As of January 1, 2007, executions were put on hold in nine states because of questions over lethal injection. Courts and legislatures will continue to grapple with tough questions about how much pain the condemned feel as they die and what role, if any, medical professionals should play in executions. (The American Medical Association's Code of Ethics prohibits physicians from participating in a lethal injection, and some contend that leaves a lot of room for error.)

What was seen as a more humane alternative to the gas chamber, electric chair, firing squad, or gallows now faces serious challenges in more than a dozen states and led to at least temporary halts to executions in 2006 in Arkansas, California, Delaware, Florida, Kentucky, Louisiana, Maryland, Missouri, and South Dakota.

Those challenging the procedure say when health professionals administer sodium thiopental before surgery, they administer tests to ensure the patient is unconscious. That doesn't happen in an execution room because corrections officials, not medical practitioners, administer the drugs. If the first chemical is not properly administered, critics charge that an inmate may remain conscious and die an excruciating death from the other two chemicals.

Two weeks before leaving office on January 2, 2007, Florida governor Jeb Bush suspended all executions until a state commission reviews the state's lethal injection process. Bush formed the commission after the December 13, 2006, execution of Angel Diaz, 55, took 34 minutes—twice the normal time—and required a second dose of lethal drugs because the first needle was improperly inserted.

On March 1, 2007, the commission released its report to Florida governor Charlie Crist. The commission found that the execution team made several errors, that the protocol for executing prisoners is itself flawed, and that members of the execution team were not adequately trained. The commission recommended:

- The development of a written protocol for executions that clearly establishes the chain of command in the injection process so that the warden has final decision-making authority;
- The development of procedures for documenting each step in the execution process as it occurs;
- A formal debriefing process after each execution that is documented in a written record; and
- Training to ensure that persons who participate in executions are suitably qualified

California's lethal injection process was ruled unconstitutionally cruel and unusual on December 15, 2006. U.S. District Judge Jeremy Fogel suspended executions until California overhauls its lethal injection procedures. The judge cited a British medical journal report that 21 inmates executed in Texas and Virginia had such low levels of the anesthetic thiopental in their blood that they probably were awake but unable to move or scream when the fatal potassium chloride was injected. After four days of hearings and a visit to the execution chamber in San Quentin, Fogel concluded it was impossible to determine whether inmates executed in California were unconscious before the fatal shot. Governor Schwarzenegger released a statement on December 18 saying, "My administration will take immediate action to resolve court concerns which have cast legal doubt on California's procedure for carrying out the death penalty."[21]

What Is Death Row Like?

Prisoners who are sentenced to death are held on **death row,** a prison within a prison. All states except Missouri and Tennessee segregate death row inmates from the general prison population. According to George Lombardi, director of the Missouri Department of Corrections, mainstreaming death row prisoners with the general population saves money; provides death row inmates more access to recreation, visitation, and prison programs and services; benefits non-death-row inmates because, before mainstreaming, even non-death-row prisoner movement was restricted due to security concerns over the segregated death row unit; and facilitates staff management of prisoners because recreation, visitation, and prison programs and services are seen as privileges that can be taken away. Mainstreaming in Missouri has also decreased inmate violence and disciplinary actions that surface when inmates feel they have nothing to lose.[22] Otherwise, according to Lombardi and others, the conditions among death rows in the majority of states are virtually indistinguishable.

death row
A prison area housing inmates who have been sentenced to death.

Prisoners who are sentenced to death are held on death row. Do most death-sentenced prisoners need to be separated from the general prison population? Why or why not?

Inmates receive few, if any, rehabilitation, treatment, or work programs, and they leave their individual cells for an average of one hour a day. About one-half of the states allow contact visitation; the other half restrict it to inmates' attorneys. For that reason, death row existence has been called "living death" to convey a prisoner's loneliness, isolation, boredom, and loss of privacy.[23]

What many people forget is that a death row inmate's living environment is a correctional officer's workplace. The concrete and steel construction materials and furnishings that guarantee security and durability in death row amplify normal sounds within its hard walls. It takes little effort to imagine what effect shouting, flushing toilets, opening and closing steel doors, janitorial work, the blaring of televisions and radios, and voices wailing has not only on those who live there but also on those who work there. In summer the oppressive heat and in winter the freezing cold are trapped by walls of steel and concrete. The quality of life experienced by inmates depends on the work environment created by the corrections officers who guard them, but even the corrections officers are affected by the surroundings.

Death row cells usually have steel bunks, toilets, and sinks. These are bolted to concrete floors and cinder-block walls. Small lockers or wall shelves hold prisoners' personal property, which may include toiletries, books, pictures, a clock, and usually a television. The television is the death row inmate's most valued possession, not only because of its entertainment value but also because it makes available the world that the death row inmate has lost. Revoking television or telephone privileges is sometimes used by correctional officers as a threat to control behavior on death row. However, corrections officers say that death row inmates seldom exhibit disciplinary problems. One death row warden described death row inmates as "the group who causes the least trouble."[24] Researchers in Indiana examined the disciplinary records of 39 death row inmates who were transferred to the general prison population following modification of their sentences from death to capital life between 1972 and 1999. The researchers found that, despite the heinousness of their capital offenses, the majority of these former death row inmates did not commit acts of serious violence on death row or after their transfer to the general prison population. Most presented little persistent disciplinary management difficulty in the general prison population.[25] The reasons, researchers suggest, are aging, prior adjustment to institutionalization while on death row, restrictive death row conditions, and higher levels of supervision.

Most death row inmates spend 22 to 23 hours a day in five-by-eight- or six-by-nine-foot cells. They are counted once an hour. They receive their meals through slots in the cell doors. Generally twice a week, they are handcuffed, escorted to, and locked in shower stalls for 5- or 10-minute showers. In some jurisdictions, death row inmates may visit the prison library; in others, books are taken to them. In Florida, death row inmates may receive mail every day except holidays and weekends. They may have cigarettes, snacks, radios, and a 13-inch television in their cells. They do not have cable television or air-conditioning and they are not allowed to be with each other in a common room. They can watch religious services on closed-circuit television. They wear orange t-shirts and blue pants.

Most death row inmates slowly lose their ties with the outside world. Although some states permit contact visits, most allow only noncontact

I am definitely sorry for all of the suffering I've caused people, especially the victims; I just wish there was a way to make things right. I wish I could let people know how genuinely I've had to deal with it for the eight years I've been in prison and had to look in the mirror every day. . . . I want to continue to help troubled teens, as I once was, and I presently get the opportunity to be in a Youth Enlightenment Program

(Y.E.P.) that we have here at this prison. . . . I came to death row a very messed up, drug-addicted, 17-year-old runaway that had to grow up here in the worst of prison realities. I've had to wake up every day facing the pain and suffering I've caused others.

Christopher Simmons
Christopher Simmons, a 17-year-old Missouri youth convicted of murder and sentenced to die, wrote this when he was on death row. On March 1, 2005, his case persuaded the United States Supreme Court that the Eighth and Fourteenth Amendments forbid the execution of offenders who were under the age of 18 when their crimes were committed.

---

visits. Every time death row inmates leave death row for visits—whether contact or noncontact—they are strip-searched before and after. Over the years, visitors and mail come less frequently, and they sometimes cease altogether. Corrections officers assigned to death row are instructed not to establish relationships with inmates because it may make it more difficult to carry out their duties. Pennsylvania's policy manual for death row corrections officers reads, "Employees must not be too familiar or discuss personal items of interest with the inmates."[26]

Preparing for an execution is a correctional officer's toughest job. "We begin to dread electrocutions weeks before they take place," says former corrections officer Lynch Alford Sr. "We're almost glad when someone is commuted, regardless of what crime he committed. We just sit around and wait. We drink coffee. We don't talk about anything. We don't talk about the electrocution. We just get it over with as soon as possible and then go home immediately." A death row inmate who refuses to walk to the death chamber is carried by corrections officers, sometimes screaming and kicking. "Guards have been known to go all to pieces during episodes such as these. Their nerves just don't hold up. In my opinion it is something you never become accustomed to. It's the most gruesome job I've come in contact with during my 35 years with the department. The more you see, the more you hate it."[27] Texas law governing execution is presented in Exhibit 15–8.

Public Opinion, Politics, and Capital Punishment

According to the Gallup Poll public support for capital punishment in the United States was at its lowest in 1966, when only 42 percent of Americans supported it. It reached its highest level (80 percent) in 1994. Most recently, the USA Today/Gallup polls found that the U.S. public still favors the death penalty by a 65 to 30 percent margin over the last three years.[28] However, as the number of innocent people released from death row increases and news of their innocence makes headlines, the empirical evidence demonstrates that capital punishment is changing in the United States. An eight-year decline in death sentences (from 283 in 1999 to 114 in 2006), a 46 percent drop in executions (from 98 in 1999 to 53 in 2006), a shrinking death row population (from 3,625 in 1999 to 3,366 in 2006), and waning support for capital punishment have marked a significant turnaround in the use of the death penalty.

Death penalty researchers across the country are finding that while the public may accept the use of capital punishment, it may actually prefer

EXHIBIT 15–8   Capital Punishment in Texas

Execution of Convict

Whenever the sentence of death is pronounced against a convict, the sentence shall be executed at any time after the hour of 6 P.M. on the day set for the execution, by intravenous injection of a substance or substances in a lethal quantity sufficient to cause death and until such convict is dead, such execution procedure to be determined and supervised by the Director of the institutional division of the Texas Department of Criminal Justice.

Warrant of Execution

Whenever any person is sentenced to death, the clerk of the court in which the sentence is pronounced, shall within ten days after the court enters its order setting the date for execution, issue a warrant under the seal of the court for the execution of the sentence of death, which shall recite the fact of conviction, setting forth specifically the offense, the judgment of the court, the time fixed for his execution, and directed to the Director of the Department of Corrections at Huntsville, Texas, commanding him to proceed, at the time and place named in the order of execution, to carry the same into execution, as provided in the preceding Article, and shall deliver such warrant to the sheriff of the county in which such judgment of conviction was had, to be by him delivered to the said Director of the Department of Corrections, together with the condemned person if he has not previously been so delivered.

Taken to Department of Corrections

Immediately upon the receipt of such warrant, the sheriff shall transport such condemned person to the Director of the Department of Corrections, if he has not already been so delivered, and shall deliver him and the warrant aforesaid into the hands of the Director of the Department of Corrections and shall take from the Director of the Department of Corrections his receipt for such person and such warrant, which receipt the sheriff shall return to the office of the clerk of the court where the judgment of death was rendered. For his services, the sheriff shall be entitled to the same compensation as is now allowed by law to sheriffs for removing or conveying prisoners under the provisions of Section 4 of Article 1029 or 1030 of the Code of Criminal Procedure of 1925, as amended.

Upon the receipt of such condemned person by the Director of the Department of Corrections, the condemned person shall be confined therein until the time for his or her execution arrives, and while so confined, all persons outside of said prison shall be denied access to him or her, except his or her physician, lawyer, and clergyperson, who shall be admitted to see him or her when necessary for his or her health or for the transaction of business, and the relatives and friends of the condemned person, who shall be admitted to see and converse with him or her at all proper times, under such reasonable rules and regulations as may be made by the Board of Directors of the Department of Corrections.

Executioner

The Director of the Texas Department of Corrections, shall designate an executioner to carry out the death penalty provided by law.

Place of Execution

The execution shall take place at a location designated by the Texas Department of Corrections in a room arranged for that purpose.

Present at Execution

The following persons may be present at the execution: the executioner, and such persons as may be necessary to assist him in conducting the execution; the Board of Directors of the Department of Corrections, two physicians, including the prison physician, the spiritual advisor of the condemned, the chaplains of the Department of Corrections, the county judge and sheriff of the county in which the Department of Corrections is situated, and any of the relatives or friends of the condemned person that he may request, not exceeding five in number, shall be admitted. No convict shall be permitted by the prison authorities to witness the execution.

Body of Convict

The body of a convict who has been legally executed shall be embalmed immediately and so directed by the Director of the Department of Corrections. If the body is not demanded or requested by a relative or bona fide friend within forty-eight hours after execution then it shall be delivered to the Anatomical Board of the State of Texas, if requested by the Board. If the body is requested by a relative, bona fide friend, or the Anatomical Board of the State of Texas, such recipient shall pay a fee of not to exceed twenty-five dollars to the mortician for his services in embalming the body for which the mortician shall issue to the recipient a written receipt. When such receipt is delivered to the Director of the Department of Corrections, the body of the deceased shall be delivered to the party named in the receipt or his authorized agent. If the body is not delivered to a relative, bona fide friend, or the Anatomical Board of the State of Texas, the Director of the Department of Corrections shall cause the body to be decently buried, and the fee for embalming shall be paid by the county in which the indictment which resulted in conviction was found.

Source: Excerpted from Texas Code of Criminal Procedure, Chapter 43, Articles 43.15–43.26.

other punishment options such as life without the possibility of parole (LWOP) when given the opportunity. There is now a significant body of research showing that support for the death penalty drops considerably when alternative sentencing options are available to respondents.[29]

National surveys, polls of U.S. Catholics, and surveys in Maryland, New Jersey, New York, and Texas of persons who say they support capital punishment find that Americans are closely divided on the appropriate punishment for those convicted of murder. A small majority now believe that life without the possibility of parole is an acceptable substitute for the death penalty (48 percent in national polls, 52 percent of the Nation's Catholics, 63 percent in Maryland, 56 percent in New York, and 64 percent in Texas).[30]

Since very little is known about death penalty proponents who support LWOP, researchers from California State University at Long Beach compared death penalty supporters who favor LWOP with death penalty supporters who oppose it.[31] Of all the characteristics they studied (sex, age, race/ethnicity, education, income, religious belief, religious activity, and political ideology), they found that people with higher incomes were more likely to oppose LWOP than people with lower incomes. This is consistent with earlier research on the death penalty: income is a leading predictor of punitiveness. People with higher incomes are more likely to support capital punishment than people with lower incomes. The researchers suggest that the explanation rests in the very reason(s) why someone believes in capital punishment in the first place. People with higher incomes view a life sentence as an "unjust" punishment for murder. On the other hand, people with lower incomes view life imprisonment as sufficient deterrence and incapacitation for certain types of murder. The explanation may also have something to do with the fact that people with higher incomes are better represented at trial, less likely to get the death penalty, and more likely to hold different views of punishment for the majority of people on death row who are poor. People with lower incomes, on the other hand, may view trial and punishment as operating against them and, hence, be more likely to support LWOP.

Similar shifts are taking place in the judicial and political arenas. Jurors and judges are now imposing fewer death penalties. The number of persons sentenced to die dropped by two-thirds in the past decade, from an average of 300 each year in the 1990s to 114 in 2006.

In January 2000, Illinois released its 13th person from death row after investigators found that he was innocent. Five of the 13 were released after postconviction DNA testing proved their innocence. The fact that more people have been released from death row for mistaken convictions than have been executed in Illinois prompted former Republican governor (and supporter of capital punishment) George Ryan to impose a moratorium on capital punishment due to mounting evidence that the death penalty was not being applied fairly. On January 11, 2003, Governor Ryan commuted 164 death row inmates' sentences to life in prison

George H. Ryan
Governor, State of Illinois

NORTHWESTERN

In January 2003, Illinois governor George Ryan commuted 164 death row inmates' sentences to life in prison, commuted 3 other death row inmates' sentences to 40 years in prison, and pardoned 4 other death row inmates because of mounting evidence that the death penalty was not being applied fairly in Illinois. Wrongful convictions and executions not only harm the accused, but also the victim, the family and friends of the accused and the victim, the criminal justice system, and society. How can we prevent the wrongful conviction and execution of innocent people?

THE STAFF SPEAKS

The men in the red jumpsuits—dead men walking! I don't judge them, I don't disrespect them, I just protect them from other inmates and themselves. I work on death row and have for a lot of years. Death row inmates sleep in cell blocks which consist of 16 individual cells with solid electronic steel doors. Some talk to everybody all the time, some don't talk to anyone, and others act as if they have multiple personalities. If they aren't talking, they're playing cards or checkers or doing push-ups.

They get outside two times a day to exercise. Law says they can't work.

Some act like they are your buddies, and some act as if they can't stand you. For the most part, the ones that act like your buddy are usually trying to get you to do something for them. As a group, they are very manipulative in every exchange they have with everyone, including each other.

Most of the inmates say they are innocent. A few say they actually committed the crime, and others say they

were framed. I know a lot about most of their cases and it seems to me that they belong here—on death row. But a few of the cases seem questionable. That's a private thought, and I don't let it change the way I deal with these offenders in red jumpsuits.

John Juehrs
Correctional Officer
Death Row
Central Prison
Raleigh, North Carolina

---

exoneration

To clear of blame and release from death row.

and commuted three other death row inmates' sentences to 40 years in prison with the possibility of parole. A day earlier, Ryan pardoned four other men. Ryan asked, "How many more cases of wrongful convictions have to occur before we can all agree that this system in Illinois is broken?" To date, 18 of the 124 **exonerations** (cleared of blame and released from death row) have been in Illinois, second only to Florida with 22 exonerations.

On March 9, 2000, Ryan appointed a blue ribbon commission to determine what reforms, if any, would ensure that the Illinois capital punishment system was fair, just, and accurate. In April 2002, the commission presented its findings. Its 85 recommendations include the creation of a statewide panel to review prosecutors' requests for the death penalty, banning death sentences for juveniles, significantly reducing the number of death eligibility factors, videotaping interrogations of homicide suspects, and controlling the use of testimony by jailhouse informants. See this chapter's Reflections on the Future for a listing of the commission's recommendations. Following Ryan's departure from office, the new governor, Rod Blagojevich, promised to continue the moratorium on executions, and the legislature overwhelmingly enacted one-third of the reforms recommended and continues to consider the implementation of other reforms.

Professional organizations and the judiciary are also weighing in on the question of capital punishment. Earlier in this chapter we discussed the American Medical Association's ban on physician participation in capital punishment. Here we discuss the American Bar Association's position on capital punishment.

At its February 1997 midyear meeting, the ABA's House of Delegates called for a death penalty moratorium until jurisdictions implement policies and procedures that ensure that death penalty cases are administered fairly and impartially, in accordance with due process, and with minimum risk of executing innocent people. In July 2000, ABA president Martha Barnett reiterated the call for a moratorium on executions, citing racial bias, racial profiling, execution of juveniles, inadequate counsel, and lack of due process.[32] On February 10, 2003, the ABA House of Delegates approved national standards of practice to ensure due process and minimize the risk of executing the innocent. In the majority of states that authorize capital punishment, we find today legislative bills considering death penalty moratoriums, funding study of capital punishment, granting death row inmates access to DNA testing, affording extra assistance to lawyers handling capital cases, raising the amount of financial compensation that states provide innocent people found to have been convicted erroneously, allowing prosecutors to seek life without parole instead of the death penalty, and barring the execution of juveniles.

Furthermore, the 2004 Justice for All Act—signed by President George W. Bush on October 30, 2004, and referred to in this chapter's opening story about Kirk Bloodsworth (the first person to be exonerated by DNA testing)—will help states improve the quality of legal representation in capital cases. The act also includes a section that expresses Congress's will that states provide reasonable compensation to any person found to have been unjustly convicted of an offense against the state and sentenced to death.

Voices from the bench are also speaking out. "If statistics are any indication," said former U.S. Supreme Court justice Sandra Day O'Connor, "the system may well be allowing some innocent defendants to be executed." She suggested that "perhaps it's time to look at minimum standards for appointed counsel in death cases and adequate compensation for appointed counsel when they are used." Justice Ruth Bader Ginsburg added that she has "yet to see a death penalty case among the dozens coming to the Supreme Court on eve-of-execution stay applications in which the defendant was well-represented at trial" and that "people who are well represented at trial do not get the death penalty." Others agree. Recently retired Florida Supreme Court chief justice Gerald Kogan said, "There are several cases where I had grave doubts as to the guilt of a particular person. . . . If one innocent person is executed along the way, then we can no longer justify capital punishment."[33] And in 1994, when the U.S. Supreme Court denied review in the Texas death penalty case of Bruce Edwin Callins, Justice Harry A. Blackmun wrote in his dissent opinion, "From this day forward, I no longer shall tinker with the machinery of death. For more than 20 years I have endeavored to develop rules that would lend more than the mere appearance of fairness to the death penalty endeavor. Rather than continue to coddle the court's delusions that the desired level of fairness has been achieved, I feel obligated simply to concede that the death penalty experiment has failed."[34]

The American Correctional Association (ACA), in its Policy Statement on Capital Punishment (see Exhibit 15–9), encourages corrections professionals to support and participate in the debate about capital punishment. There are many arguments favoring capital punishment and many arguments opposing it. Some of the arguments—pro and con—are summarized in Exhibit 15–10. Where do you stand?

THE COURTS AND THE DEATH PENALTY

"Death is different [from other punishments]," said U.S. Supreme Court justice William Brennan. For that reason, every phase of a capital crime proceeding, from jury selection to sentencing instructions, has been influenced by court rulings. The legal history of today's death penalty can be traced through several landmark cases. In the June 29, 1972, decision in *Furman* v. *Georgia*,[35] the U.S. Supreme Court ruled by a vote of five to four that the death penalty, as imposed and carried out under the laws of Georgia, was cruel and unusual punishment in violation of the Eighth and Fourteenth Amendments. According to the Court, Georgia's death

> ### EXHIBIT 15–9   American Correctional Association
>
> #### Public Correctional Policy on Capital Punishment
>
> **Introduction**
>
> Correctional agencies administer sanctions and punishment imposed by courts for unlawful behavior. In some jurisdictions the law permits capital punishment, and correctional officials have the final responsibility to carry out these executions. Opinions about capital punishment are strongly held, based upon fundamental values about public safety and human life.
>
> There is no uniformity of position about such a controversial issue as capital punishment, either within the corrections profession or as a matter of public opinion at large. A single position for or against capital punishment would not be a fair or candid representation of the range of strongly held and thoughtfully considered positions that exist within the profession.
>
> **Policy Statement**
>
> Corrections professionals have a fundamental responsibility to support participation in the public dialogue concerning capital punishment, and to make available to the public and their policy-makers the unique perspectives of persons working in the profession. Toward this end, correctional agencies should:
>
> **A.** Support conducting research on capital punishment, to inform the public debate with accurate information about all aspects of capital punishment.
>
> **B.** Support full public discussion of capital punishment, focusing on the morality, purposes and efficacy of this form of punishment.
>
> **C.** Accept and encourage a diversity of opinion within the field, ensuring that employment, promotion and retention are never affected by the expression of an opinion either in support of or in opposition to capital punishment.
>
> **D.** Select staff who are involved with carrying out executions on a voluntary basis, and carefully screen them and train them in execution procedures. In addition, post-execution interventions must be available to staff who participate in or are affected by the execution process.
>
> **Source:** Copyright © American Correctional Association.

mandatory death penalty

A death sentence that the legislature has required to be imposed upon people convicted of certain offenses.

guided discretion

Decision making bounded by general guidelines, rules, or laws.

penalty statute gave the sentencing authority (judge or trial jury) complete freedom to impose a death or life imprisonment sentence without standards or guidelines; the death penalty had been imposed arbitrarily, discriminatorily, and selectively against minorities. The Supreme Court voided 40 death penalty statutes, thereby commuting the death sentences of all 629 death row inmates around the United States, and suspended the death penalty because existing statutes were no longer valid. It is important to note that the Court majority did not rule that the death penalty itself was unconstitutional, but only the way in which it was administered at that time.

States responded to the *Furman* decision by rewriting their capital punishment statutes to limit discretion and avoid arbitrary and inconsistent results. The new death penalty laws took two forms. Some states imposed a **mandatory death penalty** for certain crimes, and others permitted **guided discretion,** which sets standards for judges and juries to use when deciding whether to impose the death penalty.

In 1976, the U.S. Supreme Court rejected mandatory death penalty statutes in *Woodson* v. *North Carolina* and *Roberts* v. *Louisiana*, but it

EXHIBIT 15–10   **Arguments Favoring and Opposing the Death Penalty**

PRO

- It deters people from crime through fear of punishment; it exerts a positive moral influence by stigmatizing crimes of murder and manslaughter.
- It is a just punishment for murder; it fulfills the "just deserts" principle of a fitting punishment; life in prison is not a tough enough punishment for a capital crime.
- It is constitutionally appropriate; the Eighth Amendment prohibits cruel and unusual punishment, yet the Fifth Amendment implies that, with due process of law, one may be deprived of life, liberty, or property.
- It reduces time spent on death row to reduce costs of capital punishment and the attendant costs of postconviction appeals, investigations, and searches for new evidence and witnesses.
- It protects society from the most serious and feared offenders; it prevents the reoccurrence of violence.
- It is more humane than life imprisonment because it is quick; making the prisoner suffer by remaining in prison for the rest of his or her life is more torturous and inhumane than execution.
- It is almost impossible for an innocent person to be executed; the slow execution rate results from the process of appeals, from sentencing to execution.

CON

- It does not deter crime; no evidence exists that the death penalty is more effective than other punishments.
- It violates human rights; it is a barbaric remnant of an uncivilized society; it is immoral in principle; and it ensures the execution of some innocent people.
- It falls disproportionately on racial minorities; those who murdered whites are more likely to be sentenced to death than are those who murdered blacks.
- It costs too much; $2 million to $5 million are poured into each execution, while other criminal justice components such as police, courts, and community corrections lack funding.
- It boosts the murder rate; this is known as the *brutalizing effect*; the state is a role model, and when the state carries out an execution, it shows that killing is a way to solve problems.
- Not everyone wants vengeance; many people favor alternative sentences such as life without parole.
- It is arbitrary and unfair; offenders who commit similar crimes under similar circumstances receive widely differing sentences; race, social and economic status, location of crime, and pure chance influence sentencing.

approved guided discretion statutes in *Gregg* v. *Georgia* and two companion cases.[36] When the U.S. Supreme Court held that the death penalty could be constitutional in *Gregg* v. *Georgia*, it indicated that jurors' sentencing discretion "must be suitably directed and limited so as to minimize the risk of wholly arbitrary and capricious action."[37]

In *Gregg*, the Court approved automatic appellate review, a proportionality review whereby state appellate courts compare a sentence with those of similar cases, and a **bifurcated trial,** or special two-part trial. The first part of a bifurcated trial, the *guilt phase*, decides the issue of guilt. If the defendant is found guilty, the second part of the trial, the *penalty phase*, takes place. The penalty phase includes presentation of facts that mitigate or aggravate the circumstances of the crime. **Mitigating circumstances** are factors that may reduce the culpability of the offender (make

bifurcated trial

Two separate hearings for different issues in a trial, one for guilt and the other for punishment.

mitigating circumstances

Factors that, although not justifying or excusing an action, may reduce the culpability of the offender.

EXHIBIT 15–11 The Florida Death Penalty Statute

921.141 Sentence of death or life imprisonment for capital felonies; further proceedings to determine sentence.

(1) SEPARATE PROCEEDINGS ON ISSUE OF PENALTY. Upon conviction or adjudication of guilt of a defendant of a capital felony, the court shall conduct a separate sentencing proceeding to determine whether the defendant should be sentenced to death or life imprisonment as authorized by s. 775.082. The proceeding shall be conducted by the trial judge before the trial jury as soon as practicable. If, through impossibility or inability, the trial jury is unable to reconvene for a hearing on the issue of penalty, having determined the guilt of the accused, the trial judge may summon a special juror or jurors as provided in chapter 913 to determine the issue of the imposition of the penalty. If the trial jury has been waived or if the defendant pleaded guilty, the sentencing proceeding shall be conducted before a jury impaneled for that purpose, unless waived by the defendant. In the proceeding, evidence may be presented as to any matter that the court deems relevant to the nature of the crime and the character of the defendant and shall include matters relating to any of the aggravating or mitigating circumstances enumerated in subsections (5) and (6). Any such evidence that the court deems to have probative value may be received, regardless of its admissibility under the exclusionary rules of evidence, provided the defendant is accorded a fair opportunity to rebut any hearsay statements. However, this subsection shall not be construed to authorize the introduction of any evidence secured in violation of the Constitution of the United States or the Constitution of the State of Florida. The state and the defendant or his counsel shall be permitted to present argument for or against sentence of death.

(2) ADVISORY SENTENCE BY THE JURY. After hearing all the evidence, the jury shall deliberate and render an advisory sentence to the court, based upon the following matters:

(a) whether sufficient aggravating circumstances exist as enumerated in subsection (5);

(b) whether sufficient mitigating circumstances exist that outweigh the aggravating circumstances found to exist; and

(c) based on these considerations, whether the defendant should be sentenced to life imprisonment or death.

(3) FINDINGS IN SUPPORT OF SENTENCE OF DEATH. Notwithstanding the recommendation of a majority of the jury, the court, after weighing the aggravating and mitigating circumstances, shall enter a sentence of life imprisonment or death, but if the court imposes a sentence of death, it shall set forth in writing its findings upon which the sentence of death is based as to the facts:

(a) that sufficient aggravating circumstances exist as enumerated in subsection (5), and

(b) that there are insufficient mitigating circumstances to outweigh the aggravating circumstances.

In each case in which the court imposes the death sentence, the determination of the court shall be supported by specific written findings of fact based upon the circumstances in subsections (5) and (6) and upon the records of the trial and the sentencing proceedings. If the court does not make the findings requiring the death sentence, the court shall impose sentence of life imprisonment in accordance with s. 775.082.

(4) REVIEW OF JUDGMENT AND SENTENCE. The judgment of conviction and sentence of death shall be subject to automatic review by the Supreme Court of Florida within 60 days after certification by the sentencing court of the entire record, unless the time is extended for an additional period not to exceed 30 days by the Supreme Court for good cause shown. Such review by the Supreme Court shall have priority over all other cases and shall be heard in accordance with rules promulgated by the Supreme Court.

(5) AGGRAVATING CIRCUMSTANCES. Aggravating circumstances shall be limited to the following:

(a) The capital felony was committed by a person under sentence of imprisonment or placed on community control.

(b) The defendant was previously convicted of another capital felony or of a felony involving the use or threat of violence to the person.

(c) The defendant knowingly created a great risk of death to many people.

d) The capital felony was committed while the defendant was engaged, or was an accomplice, in the commission of, or an attempt to commit, or flight after committing or attempting to commit, any robbery, sexual battery, arson, burglary, kidnapping, or aircraft piracy or the unlawful throwing, placing, or discharging of a destructive device or bomb.

(e) The capital felony was committed for the purpose of avoiding or preventing a lawful arrest or effecting an escape from custody.

(f) The capital felony was committed for pecuniary gain.

(g) The capital felony was committed to disrupt or hinder the lawful exercise of any governmental function or the enforcement of laws.

(h) The capital felony was especially heinous, atrocious, or cruel.

(i) The capital felony was a homicide and was committed in a cold, calculated, and premeditated manner without any pretense of moral or legal justification.

(j) The victim of the capital felony was a law enforcement officer engaged in the performance of his official duties.

(k) The victim of the capital felony was an elected or appointed public official engaged in the performance of his official duties if the motive for the capital felony was related, in whole or in part, to the victim's official capacity.

EXHIBIT 15–11 *(continued)*

(6) MITIGATING CIRCUMSTANCES. Mitigating circumstances shall be the following:

(a) The defendant has no significant history of prior criminal activity.

(b) The capital felony was committed while the defendant was under the influence of extreme mental or emotional disturbance.

(c) The victim was a participant in the defendant's conduct or consented to the act.

(d) The defendant was an accomplice in the capital felony committed by another person and his participation was relatively minor.

(e) The defendant acted under extreme duress or under the substantial domination of another person.

(f) The capacity of the defendant to appreciate the criminality of his conduct or to conform his conduct to the requirements of law was substantially impaired.

(g) The age of the defendant at the time of the crime.

(7) VICTIM IMPACT EVIDENCE. Once the prosecution has provided evidence of the existence of one or more aggravating circumstances as described in subsection (5), the prosecution may introduce, and subsequently argue, victim impact evidence. Such evidence shall be designed to demonstrate the victim's uniqueness as an individual human being and the resultant loss to the community's members by the victim's death. Characterizations and opinions about the crime, the defendant, and the appropriate sentence shall not be permitted as a part of victim impact evidence.

(8) APPLICABILITY. This section does not apply to a person convicted or adjudicated guilty of a capital drug trafficking felony under s. 893.135.

Source: Florida Statute 921.141.

the defendant less deserving of the death penalty). **Aggravating circumstances** are factors that may increase the offender's culpability (make the defendant more deserving of death). Florida's death penalty statute, including its list of mitigating and aggravating circumstances (subsections 5 and 6), is shown in Exhibit 15–11.

Florida, along with 11 other states (Arizona, Colorado, Idaho, Illinois, Mississippi, Montana, Nebraska, Nevada, New Hampshire, North Carolina, and Washington) and the federal death penalty statutes use what's called a "sufficiency" standard by which the judge and jury weigh mitigating and aggravating circumstances to determine if a death sentence is appropriate. Under this standard, the aggravating circumstances must sufficiently outweigh mitigating circumstances. In Florida, the jury must determine (1) whether sufficient aggravating circumstances exist, (2) whether sufficient mitigating circumstances exist that outweigh aggravating ones, and (3) based on these considerations whether to impose death or life imprisonment.

The other "weighing" processes used by states can be divided into four categories:

1. *Aggravating outweighs mitigating by a preponderance of the evidence:* Two states (Delaware and Maryland) require the jury to find that aggravating circumstances outweigh mitigating ones by a preponderance of the evidence.

2. *Aggravating outweighs mitigating beyond a reasonable doubt:* Six states (Arkansas, New Jersey, New York, Ohio, Tennessee, and Utah) require the jury to find that aggravating circumstances outweigh mitigating ones beyond a reasonable doubt. In New York, the aggravating circumstances must substantially outweigh mitigating ones beyond a reasonable doubt.

3. *At least one aggravating circumstance exists:* In six states (Georgia, Kentucky, Missouri, South Carolina, South Dakota, and Wyoming), the jury cannot impose the death penalty unless it finds at least one aggravating circumstance beyond a reasonable doubt. The

aggravating circumstances

Factors that may increase the culpability of the offender.

jury must consider mitigating evidence, but the statute does not specify weighing.

In New Mexico, the jury must find at least one aggravating circumstance beyond a reasonable doubt to impose the death penalty. It must weigh aggravating and mitigating circumstances, weigh them against each other, consider both the defendant and the crime, and determine whether it should impose death. But on review to the state supreme court, the court must overturn a death sentence if mitigating circumstances outweigh aggravating ones.

In Louisiana, the jury must find at least one aggravating circumstance beyond a reasonable doubt and, after considering mitigating circumstances, determine that death should be imposed. The sentencing hearing focuses on the circumstances of the offense, the character and propensities of the offender and the victim, and the impact of the victim's death on family, friends, and associates.

4. *Different sentencing structures exist:* Three states structure their sentencing hearings and require consideration of mitigating evidence in a different way. In Oregon, the jury must consider (1) if the defendant acted deliberately and with reasonable expectation of causing death, (2) whether there is a probability that the defendant would commit violent criminal acts that would be a continuing threat to society, (3) whether the defendant acted unreasonably in response to provocation, and (4) whether to impose a death sentence. To decide whether to impose a death sentence, the jury must consider aggravating and mitigating evidence concerning any aspect of the defendant's character or background, circumstances of the offense, and any victim impact evidence. The state must prove each issue beyond a reasonable doubt, and the court cannot impose a death sentence if at least one juror believes that it should not be imposed.

In Texas, the jury must decide beyond a reasonable doubt whether there is a probability that the defendant would commit violent crimes and be a continuing threat to society. It must consider all of the evidence, including the defendant's character and background and the circumstances of the offense, that mitigates imposing the death penalty. If all jurors agree that the defendant is a continuing threat, they must then decide whether there are sufficient mitigating circumstances to warrant life imprisonment rather than a death sentence. All jurors must agree to impose a death sentence after considering all of the evidence including the circumstances of the offense and the defendant's character, background, and personal moral culpability. The Texas statute defines *mitigating evidence* as evidence that a juror might regard as reducing the defendant's moral blameworthiness.

In Virginia, the prosecution must prove beyond a reasonable doubt that (1) there is a probability based on evidence of the defendant's prior history or the circumstances surrounding the offense that the defendant would commit violent crimes that would be a continuing serious threat to society or (2) the defendant's conduct in committing the offense was outrageously or wantonly vile, horrible, or inhuman, in that it involved torture, depravity of mind, or aggravated battery to the victim. The jury must consider mitigation, but the statute does not specify weighing.

In 2002, the U.S. Supreme Court handed down another decision that shaped capital sentencing. In *Ring* v. *Arizona*,[38] the Court held that only juries, not judges, can determine the presence of "aggravating factors" to be weighed in the capital sentencing process. Although judges may still reduce sentences, the Court held that a defendant may not receive a penalty that exceeds the maximum penalty that he or she would have received if punished according to the facts in the jury verdict. Two years later in *Schriro* v. *Summerlin*[39] the U.S. Supreme Court determined that its 2002 decision in *Ring* v. *Arizona* was not retroactive, thereby denying new sentencing hearings for dozens of death row inmates in Arizona, Idaho, Montana, and Nebraska whose sentences were originally handed down by judges, but whose cases are older and not in the first stages of their appeals. With their decision in *Summerlin,* the Justices decided that their original 7–2 decision in *Ring* was a procedural rule and thus was not retroactive.

Appealing the Death Penalty

Death penalty cases may pass through as many as 10 courts, across three stages: trial and direct review, state postconviction appeals, and federal *habeas corpus* appeals (see Exhibit 15–12).

In stage one, trial and direct review, a death sentence is imposed. As a consequence of the *Furman* decision, the laws of all states require that legal issues about the trial and sentence automatically be appealed to the state appellate courts. Alabama and Ohio have two rounds of appeals in the direct review process; this means that the legal issues may be heard first in the state court of criminal appeals (court 1) before reaching the state supreme court (court 2). These courts evaluate the trial for legal or constitutional errors and determine if the death sentence is consistent

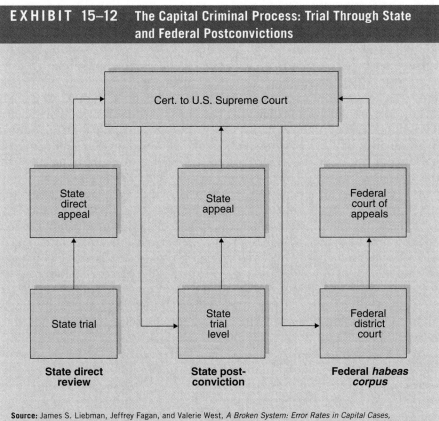

EXHIBIT 15–12   The Capital Criminal Process: Trial Through State and Federal Postconvictions

Cert. to U.S. Supreme Court

State direct appeal

State appeal

Federal court of appeals

State trial

State trial level

Federal district court

State direct review

State post-conviction

Federal *habeas corpus*

Source: James S. Liebman, Jeffrey Fagan, and Valerie West, *A Broken System: Error Rates in Capital Cases, 1973–1995* (New York: Columbia University School of Law, 2000), p. 23.

serious error

Error that substantially undermines the reliability of the guilt finding or death sentence imposed at trial.

with sentences imposed in similar cases. State appellate courts seldom overturn a conviction or change a death sentence. The defendant then petitions the U.S. Supreme Court (court 3) to grant a petition for a writ of *certiorari*—a written order to the lower court whose decision is being appealed to send the records of the case forward for review. About five years—half of the time required for the entire appeals process—is consumed by stage one, direct review. Nationally, the rate of **serious error** (error that substantially undermines the reliability of the guilt finding or death sentence imposed at trial) discovered on direct review is 41 percent. States with the highest rate of serious error found on direct review are Wyoming (67 percent), Mississippi (61 percent), North Carolina (61 percent), Alabama (55 percent), and South Carolina (54 percent).

If the defendant's direct appeals are unsuccessful and the Supreme Court denies review, stage two—state postconviction appeals—begins. At this point, many death row inmates allege ineffective or incompetent trial counsel, and new counsel is engaged or appointed. The new counsel petitions the trial court (court 4) with newly discovered evidence; questions about the fairness of the trial; and allegations of jury bias, tainted evidence, incompetence of defense counsel, and prosecutorial or police misconduct. If the trial court denies the appeals, they may be filed with the state's appellate courts (either directly to the state supreme court or, if there exists a dual level of appellate review, through a petition first to the state court of criminal appeals (court 5) followed by a petition to the state supreme court (court 6). Most often, the state appellate courts deny the petition. Defendant's counsel then petitions the U.S. Supreme Court (court 7). If the U.S. Supreme Court denies the petition for a writ of *certiorari*, stage two ends and stage three begins. The rate of serious error found on state postconviction appeals is 10 percent. State postconviction reversals are highest in Maryland (52 percent), Wyoming (33 percent), Indiana (25 percent), Utah (23 percent), and Mississippi (20 percent).

In stage three, the federal *habeas corpus* stage, a defendant files a petition in U.S. district court (court 8) in the state in which the defendant was convicted and is incarcerated and alleging violations of constitutional rights. Such rights include the right to due process (Fourteenth Amendment), prohibition against cruel and unusual punishment (Eighth Amendment), and effective assistance of counsel (Sixth Amendment). If the district court denies the petition, defense counsel submits it to the U.S. court of appeals (court 9) for the circuit representing the jurisdiction. If the court of appeals denies the petition, defense counsel asks the U.S. Supreme Court (court 10) to grant a writ of *certiorari*. If the U.S. Supreme Court denies *certiorari*, the office of the state attorney general asks the state supreme court to set a date for execution. Federal courts find serious error in 40 percent of the capital cases they review. The highest rate of serious error is found in California (80 percent), Montana (75 percent), Mississippi (71 percent), Idaho (67 percent), and Georgia (65 percent). The Eleventh Circuit—the nation's most active capital appeals circuit with jurisdiction over Alabama, Georgia, and Florida—finds serious error in 50 percent of the death cases it reviews.

In 1996, in an effort to reduce the time people spend on death row and the number of federal appeals, the U.S. Congress passed the Anti-Terrorism and Effective Death Penalty Act (AEDPA). The AEDPA defines filing deadlines and limits reasons for second, or successive, federal appellate reviews to (1) new constitutional law, (2) new evidence that could not have been discovered at the time of the original trial, or (3) new facts that, if proven, would be sufficient to establish the applicant's innocence. Under the AEDPA, if the U.S. Supreme Court denies the petition for a writ of *certiorari* in the final federal *habeas corpus* appeal, defense counsel may once again petition the federal courts; however, before a second, or successive, application for a writ of *habeas corpus* may be filed in U.S. district court, defense counsel must petition the appropriate U.S. court of appeals for an order authorizing the district court to consider the application. The petition to the U.S. court of appeals is decided by a three-judge panel; the panel must grant or deny the authorization to file the second, or successive, application within 30 days after the petition is filed. If the panel approves the petition, the district court must render a decision regarding the application within 180 days. If the motion is appealed to the court of appeals representing the jurisdiction, the court must render its decision within 120 days. If the petition is filed with the U.S. Supreme Court, the Court may grant the petition for *certiorari* or let the lower court's decision stand.

Why did inmates executed in 2005 spend an average of 12 years and 3 months on death row, and why does judicial review of capital overturned cases take so long? In short, judicial review takes so long because capital sentences are "persistently and systematically fraught with error that seriously undermines their reliability."[40] The high rate of error found at each of the three stages of appeal confirms the need for more, not less, judicial review.

DEATH PENALTY ISSUES IN THE 21ST CENTURY

Of all the reforms that capital punishment has gone through since *Furman,* perhaps none have been as significant as those that have occurred in the 21st century. Here we discuss the three most important issues and reforms that are shaping the debate on capital punishment at the beginning of the 21st century: wrongful convictions and the banning of executions of offenders who have mental retardation and juveniles.

Wrongful Convictions: The Liebman Study

According to some scholars, Americans seem to be of two minds about the death penalty. One is the fear that capital trials put people on death row who do not belong there. The other is that capital appeals take too long. The two sides are not as oppositional as it might appear, however. It may be that capital sentences spend too much time under appellate review and they are fraught with unacceptable levels of error. At least that is the conclusion of one of the most controversial studies of appellate reviews of capital sentences ever undertaken in the United States known as the Liebman study.

Possibly owing to the fact that four times as many people had their death sentences overturned or received clemency than were executed since 1977, the Judiciary Committee of the United States Senate asked Columbia law professor James Liebman to calculate the frequency of error in capital cases.[41] Liebman and his colleagues studied 4,578 appeals between 1973 and 1995. Their conclusion is powerful: The overall rate of prejudicial error in the American capital punishment system is 68 percent. More than two of every three capital judgments reviewed by the courts during the 23-year study period were found to be seriously flawed. Ten states (Alabama, Arizona, California, Georgia, Indiana,

On Friday, January 19, 2003, former Illinois death row inmate LeRoy Orange was pardoned by Governor George Ryan after spending 19 years on death row for a crime he did not commit. Since 1983, 124 persons have been released from death row and news of their innocence has set off a new debate over capital punishment in the United States. How has the Liebman report shaped the debate?

Maryland, Mississippi, Montana, Oklahoma, and Wyoming) have overall error rates of 75 percent or higher. Almost 1,000 of the cases sent back for retrial ended in sentences less than death, and 87 ended in *not guilty* verdicts.

Liebman and his colleagues found two types of serious error. The first is incompetent defense lawyering (accounting for one-third of all state postconviction appeals). The second is prosecutorial suppression of evidence that the defendant is innocent or does not deserve the death penalty (accounting for almost 20 percent). When the errors were corrected through the stages already discussed, 8 of 10 people on retrial were found to deserve a sentence less than death and 7 percent were found innocent of the capital crime. Exhibit 15–13 shows the flow of 100 death sentences imposed and reviewed between 1973 and 1995. It shows that for every 100 death sentences imposed, 41 were turned back at the trial and direct review phase because of serious error. Of the 59 that passed to the state postconviction stage, 10 percent—6 of the original 100—were turned back due to serious flaws. Of the 53 that passed to the next stage of federal *habeas corpus,* 40 percent—an additional 21 of the original 100—were turned back because of serious error. Together, 68 of the original 100 were thrown out after 9 to 10 years had passed because of serious flaws. Of the 68 individuals whose death sentences were overturned for serious error, 82 percent (56) were found on retrial not to deserve the death penalty, including 5 who were found innocent of the offense. According to the Death Penalty Information Center, since 1973, 124 people in 25 states have been released from death row with evidence of their innocence.[42] Each one spent an average of nine years and two months on death row.

Recently another researcher who studied 82 cases in Arizona, Florida, Georgia, Illinois, and Texas, where prisoners were exonerated and released from death row because of doubts about their guilt and a matched group of inmates were executed, discovered that the combination of the race of the defendant and the race of the victim predicted whether the person was exonerated or executed.[43] Cases involving a minority defendant and a white victim were most likely to lead to exoneration. Why? Because there is increased pressure on the police to solve a murder case where the suspect is minority and the victim is white.[44] "There is a rush

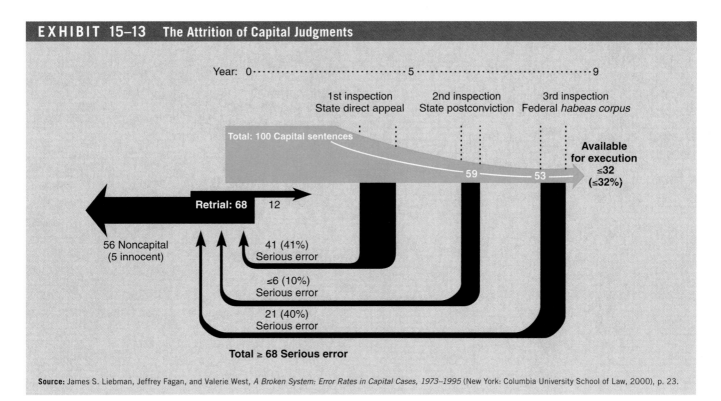

EXHIBIT 15–13   The Attrition of Capital Judgments

Year: 0 ··· 5 ··· 9

1st inspection
State direct appeal

2nd inspection
State postconviction

3rd inspection
Federal *habeas corpus*

Total: 100 Capital sentences

Available
for execution
≤32
(≤32%)

59 ——— 53 ——→

Retrial: 68   12

56 Noncapital
(5 innocent)

41 (41%)
Serious error

≤6 (10%)
Serious error

21 (40%)
Serious error

Total ≥ 68 Serious error

Source: James S. Liebman, Jeffrey Fagan, and Valerie West, *A Broken System: Error Rates in Capital Cases, 1973–1995* (New York: Columbia University School of Law, 2000), p. 23.

to point the finger at a suspect based on less evidence, thus leading to an increased chance for error."[45]

What if a death sentence is imposed today in the United States? What could the defendant, relative, lawyer, or judge expect? Liebman and his colleagues answer this way: "The capital conviction or sentence will probably be overturned due to serious error. It'll take 9 or 10 years to find out, given how many other capital cases being reviewed for likely error are lined up ahead of this one. If the judgment is overturned, a lesser conviction or sentence will probably be imposed."[46]

If death sentences are not reliable and persons are wrongfully convicted and sentenced, the error has serious consequences for the wrongly convicted, for the family of the victim whose search for justice is incomplete, for the family of the person wrongly convicted in terms of the prolonged and distorted grief they suffer, for subsequent victims of the real offender still at large, and for the public in terms of lost confidence in the criminal justice system. A report in the *Chicago Tribune* on October 26, 2003, revealed that police and prosecutors rarely pursue new leads and suspects after a wrongly convicted defendant has been released from death row.[47] The actual perpetrators remain in society to commit additional crimes, and many death row exonerees remain under a cloud of police suspicion because law enforcement failed to find the true offender.

Another consequence of wrongful convictions not often discussed is the cost of serious errors. A capital trial, incarceration, and execution average $2.5 to $5 million, compared to about $1 million for life in prison without parole. Florida reports $3.2 million and Tennessee $1 to $2 million, five capital trials in New York cost $68 million, and Kansas officials found that the average cost of a death penalty trial and appeals was $1.26 million while non-death-penalty cases cost an average of $740,000.[48] In November 2005, a study released in New Jersey found that the death penalty cost state taxpayers at least $253 million since 1982, even though no one

EXHIBIT 15–14	When Justice Fails: Compensating the Exonerated

State	Statute	Time Limits for Filling	Maximum Awards	When Passed
AL	AL Act #2001 659	2 years after exoneration or dismissal	Minimum of $50K for each year of incarceration, but legislature must appropriate the funds	2004
CA	Cal Penal Code §§ 4900 to 4906	6 months after acquittal, pardon, or release and 4 months before new legislative meeting	$100 per day of incarceration	Amended 8/28/00
DC	DC Code §§ 1-1221 to 1-1225	Available to any person released after 1979	No maximum No punitive damages	1981
IL	Ill Rev Stat ch. 705 § 505/8		≤5 yrs., $15K max, ≤14 yrs., $30K max, >14 yrs., $35K max, with COLA increase for each year since 1945	1945
IA	Iowa Code Ann § 663A.1	2 years	$50 per day & lost wages up to $25K/yr. & attorney's fees	1997
LA	R.S.15:572.9 & Code Civ. Pro. Art. 87	2 years from vacatur of conviction or for cases pending when statute was passed, by September 2007	$15K/yr. with a maximum award of $150K. Court may award costs of job/skills training for one year, and medically necessary medical and counseling services for three years; as well as tuition expenses at a community college or unit of the state university system	2005
MA	Ann L. MA. Gen'l Laws, ch. 258D §1-9	2 years	A maximum of $500K may be awarded and the Court may order services—physical and/or emotional, educational services at any state or community college—and expungement of the record of conviction	2004
ME	14 Me Rev State Ann 8241–8244	2 years from pardon	$300K, no punitive damages	1993
MD	Md State Fin & Proc § 10-501	Not specified	Actual damages	1963
MT	Mont Code Ann § 53-1-214	Not specified	Provides educational aid to wrongfully convicted persons exonerated by post-conviction DNA testing	2003

has been executed since 1963.[49] Most of the money—$7.8 million—went to prosecution costs above and beyond what would have been spent if state laws since 1982 had provided for life in prison without parole for certain crimes instead of death. Another $2.6 million per year went to defense costs. There have been 197 capital trials in New Jersey since 1982 and 60 death sentences, but 50 of the sentences have been reversed. Today, only 9 inmates are on New Jersey's death row.

Wrongful convictions add still more costs in terms of multimillion-dollar settlements. On January 25, 2005, a federal jury in Chicago found two FBI agents liable for framing Steve Manning, former Chicago po-

| | EXHIBIT 15–14 | When Justice Fails: Compensating the Exonerated (*continued*) |

State	Statute	Time Limits for Filling	Maximum Awards	When Passed
NH	NH Stat § 541-B: 14	3 years	$20K cap	1977
NJ	NJ State Ann §§ 52:4C-1 to 4C-6	2 years from release or pardon	Twice the amount of claimant's income in the year prior to incarceration or $20K/yr. of incarceration, whichever is greater	1997
NY	NY Ct. of Claims Act § 8-b	2 years	No limit	1984
NC	NC Gen Stat §§ 148-82 to 148-84	5 years	$20K/yr. Max. of $500K	1947 Amended 2001
OH	Ohio Rev Code Ann § 2305.02 & § 2743.48	2 years	$25K/yr. and lost wages, costs, and attorney's fees	1986 Amended 2002
OK	51 Okl. St. § 154	No time limit	$175K (no punitive damages)	2004
TN	Tenn Code Ann § 9-8-108	1 year	$1 million	1984 Amended 2004
TX	Tex Code Ann § 103.001	2 years release from custody or discovery of evidence substantiating claim	$25K/yr. to a max of $500K	Amended 2001
VA	8.01-195.10	Not specified	90% of the VA per capita personal income for up to 20 yrs. Tuition worth $10K in the VA Community College system	2004
US (Fed)	28 USC § 1495 & § 2513		$50K/yr. in noncapital cases and $100K/yr. in capital cases	1948
WV	W Va Code § 14-2-13(a)	2 years after pardon or dismissal	"Fair and reasonable damages"	1987
WI	Wis Stat § 775.05	Not specified	$5K/yr., max $25K but board may petition legislature for additional funds	1913

Source: Adapted from Adele Bernhard, "When Justice Fails: Indemnification for Unjust Conviction," *University of Chicago Law School Roundtable 73.* Updated by the author.

lice officer.[50] Jurors said the FBI agents induced witnesses to make false statements against Manning in the murder investigation of trucking firm owner James Pellegrino and awarded Manning $6.6 million. Manning was convicted of the murder and sent to Illinois' death row in 1993. He was exonerated and released from death row in 2000. Illinois death row inmate Dennis Williams received $13 million from Cook County (Chicago) after he was exonerated. Eighteen states and the federal government have passed laws that compensate people wrongfully convicted (see Exhibit 15–14). Nobody knows the exact amount that has been paid out, but it is reasonable to believe that prejudicial error is costly. It includes money lost on education, health and human services, community protection, and economic growth and development.

How can we reduce serious capital error? Liebman identifies two options. The first is to end the death penalty entirely. The second is to curb the scope of the death penalty to reach only the small number of offenses on which there is broad social consensus that only the death penalty will serve. The reforms he suggests follow:[51]

1. Require proof beyond any doubt that the defendant committed the capital crime.
2. Require that aggravating factors substantially outweigh mitigating ones before a death sentence may be imposed.
3. Bar the death penalty for people with extenuating circumstances such as juveniles.
4. Make life imprisonment without parole an alternative to the death penalty and clearly inform juries of the option.
5. Abolish judge overrides of jury verdicts imposing life sentences.
6. Use comparative review of murder sentences to identify what counts as the "worst of the worst."
7. Base charging decisions in potentially capital cases on full and informed deliberations.
8. Make all police and prosecution evidence bearing on guilt versus evidence and on aggravation versus mitigation available to the jury at trial.
9. Insulate capital sentencing and appellate judges from political pressure.
10. Identify, appoint, and compensate capital defense counsel in ways that attract an adequate number of well-qualified lawyers to do the work.

Banning the Juvenile Death Penalty

The first recognized juvenile execution in the United States occurred in 1642 when Thomas Graunger was hanged in Plymouth, Massachusetts, for committing the crime of buggery (having sex with an animal) when he was 16 years old.[52] Since then, the United States has executed 365 people for offenses they committed when children. In the current era of capital punishment (1976 through March 2, 2005), 22 people were executed for offenses they committed as juveniles.[53] The last was Scott Allen Hain on April 3, 2003, by lethal injection in Oklahoma. Four months after his 17th birthday, Hain and an accomplice committed murder. He was sentenced to die in May 1988.

The U.S. Supreme Court first addressed the constitutionality of applying the death penalty to juvenile offenders in 1988 in *Thompson* v. *Oklahoma*.[54] The Court ruled in a 5–4 opinion that it was unconstitutional to sentence a 15-year-old to death. The following year, in *Stanford* v. *Kentucky*[55] and *Wilkins* v. *Missouri*,[56] the Court held that the Eighth Amendment's prohibition against cruel and unusual punishment did not forbid imposition of the death penalty for crimes committed by people at 16 and 17 years of age. Justice Scalia's majority opinion reasoned that, since a majority of the 37 states that had death penalty statutes at the time allowed capital punishment for juveniles, the practice did not violate evolving standards of decency.

However on March 2, 2005, the U.S. Supreme Court, by a narrow 5–4 vote in *Roper* v. *Simmons*,[57] reversed itself and said that it was unconstitutional and in violation of the Eighth Amendment's ban on cruel and unusual punishment to execute people for crimes they committed before turning age 18. The Court's ruling vacated the death sentences of 72 people on death rows across the United States. Most of these offenders will wind up with life sentences, many without parole.

In deciding *Roper* v. *Simmons* the justices reasoned several things. First, since their 1987 decisions in *Stanford* v. *Kentucky* and *Wilkins* v. *Missouri,* 5 states banned capital punishment for juveniles, making the practice illegal in 30 states. The justices said that the trend toward banning capital punishment for juveniles reflected "evolving standards of decency that mark the progress of a maturing society."

Second, the justices cited scientific literature from the American Academy of Child and Adolescent Psychiatry, the American Medical Association, and the American Psychological Association showing that adolescents lack mature judgment, are less aware of the consequences of their decisions and actions, are more vulnerable than adults to peer pressure, and have a greater tendency toward impulsiveness and lesser reasoning skills, regardless of how big they are or how tough they talk. Or, as one person put it, "They may look like, talk like, act like and even shoot like adults, but they think like kids. . . . Juveniles are not the same as adults even though the crimes might be the same." [58]

Third, the justices cited overseas legal practices and pointed out that the death penalty for juvenile offenders has become a uniquely American practice. The death penalty for juveniles has been abandoned by nations everywhere else in large part due to the express provisions of the United Nations Convention on the Rights of the Child and of several other international treaties and agreements. Since 1990, juvenile offenders are known to have been executed in only eight countries: China, Democratic Republic of Congo, Iran, Nigeria, Pakistan, Yemen, Saudi Arabia, and the United States. The justices said that the United States' practice of executing juvenile criminals was out of line with other developed countries.

On March 2, 2005, Christopher Simmons's case led the U.S. Supreme Court to bar the execution of juveniles for crimes they committed before turning age 18 as cruel and unusual punishment prohibited by the Eighth Amendment. Simmons and 71 others on death row will wind up receiving life sentences. What were the court's rationales in deciding *Atkins* and *Simmons*?

Banning the Execution of People with Mental Retardation

In 1989, the U.S. Supreme Court held that executing people with mental retardation was not a violation of the Eighth Amendment. But on June 19, 2002, the Court held in *Atkins* v. *Virginia* that execution of offenders with mental retardation is cruel and unusual punishment prohibited by the Eighth Amendment. The Court argued that a national consensus has developed against executing this group of people. Aside from the 12 states that ban executions altogether, beginning in 1988 Arizona, Arkansas, Colorado, Connecticut, Florida, Georgia, Indiana, Kansas, Kentucky, Maryland, Missouri, Nebraska, New Mexico, New York, North Carolina, South Dakota, Tennessee, Washington, and the federal government passed statutes banning their execution. The Court argued that it was not so much the number of states that passed similar statutes but the consistency of the direction of change. In the words of the Court, "Given the well-known fact that anticrime legislation is far more popular than legislation providing protections for persons guilty of violent crime, the large number of states prohibiting the execution of people with mental retardation (and the complete absence of states passing legislation reinstating the power to conduct such executions) provides powerful evidence that today our society views these offenders as categorically less culpable

Talking about CORRECTIONS

TELEVISING McVEIGH'S EXECUTION (WHY IS PHOTOGRAPHING AN EXECUTION A CRIME?)

Visit *Live Talk* at **Corrections.com** (www.justicestudies.com/talking04) and listen to the March 2007 program "Televising McVeigh's Execution (Why Is Photographing an Execution a Crime?)" which relates to ideas discussed in this chapter.

Eye On Corrections

The Future of Lethal Injection

By Sarah Etter

Clarence Hill lay on a gurney with IV [intravenous] lines sewed into his veins. Sentenced to death for the murder of a Florida police officer more than 24 years ago, Hill was prepared to receive his final punishment by lethal injection. He was not, however, willing to suffer the pain the chemicals would cause as they coursed through his body to kill him.

The Supreme Court believed he shouldn't bear that pain either as it blocked Hill's execution mere minutes before the toxic cocktail was injected into his arms. Hill's defense attorneys had filed a brief questioning whether or not lethal injection was cruel and unusual punishment.

Currently used in 37 of the 38 states utilizing capital punishment, lethal injection has been, until recently, considered the most humane way to execute an inmate. Recent media attention of difficult executions have made death row inmates, doctors and Supreme Court Justices question the process altogether.

"[This] procedure would be prohibited if it applied to dogs and cats," said Supreme Court Justice John Paul Stevens while debating the Hill case.

In June, the Supreme Court will first rule on the legal route a death row inmate must follow to file a lawsuit that claims lethal injection is cruel and unusual.

However, the future of lethal injection might fall on the shoulders of the medical community.

"There are likely to be major changes in the execution process," says Richard Dieter, executive director of the Death Penalty Information Center. "The doctor problem is the biggest part of the issue. Lethal injection is a medical procedure, but there are ethical guidelines that say doctors cannot participate in executions."

One doctor does, in fact, have a history of involvement with the death penalty. In 1977, Dr. Stanley Deutsch created the lethal injection method. By Deutsch's method, inmates are hooked to an IV to receive sodium thiopental, a barbiturate that induces unconsciousness. A second drug, the muscle relaxant pancuronium bromide, is administered next to paralyze the entire body. Finally, potassium chloride is injected to induce cardiac arrest.

"The big mystery is how much pain these inmates feel," says Dr. Jonathan Groner, associate professor of surgery at Ohio State University and the director of Trauma Programs at Ohio's Children's Hospital. "In a hospital setting, you would be assessed after you were given the first drug to ensure you were unconscious. That doesn't always happen in an execution room."

This is why inmate defense attorneys are now questioning this procedure. They say it cannot be proven that inmates are fully unconscious before the last two drugs take effect. Typically, doctors use machines and small tests to decipher a patient's unconscious state. These tests, however, are not performed by corrections officials.

Lethal injection has become a contested issue in the medical community as well. Many medical experts claim the procedure requires medical oversight for it to be correctly administered.

"Issues like finding veins and dosage control will always be a problem during executions—but that means you have to involve a doctor in the execution," says Groner.

Finding a vein is sometimes the biggest issue for officials during an execution. In two recent cases, officials struggled to find veins of inmates who previously abused intravenous drugs. Some doctors believe they should be present at times like this to ensure that the execution is as painless as possible. According to Groner, this concerns the medical profession so much, that some allegedly aid executions anonymously in states like Missouri.

"This is a medical procedure, certainly," says Groner. "But it is against American Medical Association guidelines for doctors to participate in executions. Moreover, if I participated in an execution as a doctor, would you want me to treat your child? I believe the answer would be 'no'. It's degrading to the profession of medicine if even one doctor participates in executions."

Even though doctors can correctly administer lethal injection, many believe that their profession's ethics limits what they can do.

If the Supreme Court decides that lethal injection is cruel and unusual, corrections officials might be forced to find another method to carry out capital punishment.

"On one hand, it seems like a fixable problem: We just come up with a new mix of chemicals," says Dieter.

This still doesn't change the AMA's code of ethics prohibiting physicians from participating.

"On the other hand, if all doctors refuse to participate, it might cause a large crisis for the death penalty issue because there is no other method used. I don't think we're going back to the electric chair," says Dieter.

Groner sees a similar future.

"If all the doctors and nurses stepped up and said 'Hey, this is ethically wrong and we won't do it,' we would have to think about another way to execute people," Groner predicts. "That's what is going to come of this: a new way, an old way, or no way to conduct executions."

As the Supreme Court prepares to release a ruling on the legal road inmates should take to file suit against the practice of lethal injection, corrections officials and doctors across the country prepare to re-examine execution themselves and possibly discover a new way to administer capital punishment.

Source: "The Future of Lethal Injection," Sarah Etter, The Corrections Connection Network News (CCNN). Eye on Corrections. www.corrections.com, May 22, 2006.

Daryl Atkins, whose case led the U.S. Supreme Court on June 19, 2002, to bar the execution of people with mental retardation as cruel and unusual punishment prohibited by the Eighth Amendment, sits in a York-Poquoson Courtroom in Yorktown, Virginia. Atkins remains on death row. If a jury finds mental retardation, he will be taken off death row. If jurors don't think he has mental retardation, he'll remain on death row. What are the criteria to prove mental retardation?

than the average criminal. The evidence carries even greater force when it is noted that the legislatures that have addressed the issue have voted overwhelmingly in favor of the prohibition."[59]

In spite of the Supreme Court's ruling, Daryl Renard Atkins, the Virginia inmate whose case persuaded the U.S. Supreme Court to exclude murderers with mental retardation from executions, remains on death row as of January 1, 2007. Atkins, who has an IQ of 59 (a score of 70 or below is generally considered an indicator of mental retardation), still must prove he has mental retardation in state court before he can leave death row and get a life sentence. In its 2002 ruling, the Supreme Court left it to the states to define mental retardation and returned Atkins's case to the Virginia Supreme Court, which then passed it down to the York County Circuit Court. According to the Virginia attorney general's office, nobody in Virginia has successfully appealed a death sentence based on the Atkins decision.[60] Virginia's definition of mental retardation requires "significant subaverage intellectual functioning" at the onset of adulthood. Richard Bonnie, director of the University of Virginia's Institute of Law, Psychiatry and Public Policy, said borderline cases such as Atkins will eventually provide the guidance missing in the Court's decision. "What is going to have to emerge," said Bonnie, "are standards of forensic practice—the kinds of records people will have to obtain, the kinds of tests they have to employ" to prove that someone has mental retardation.[61]

Recently the California Supreme Court said that offenders must meet three criteria in order to prove mental retardation: significant subaverage general intellectual functioning, which means an IQ score that is approximately 70 or below; proof of significant deficits in adaptive behavior (everyday functioning); and proof that these deficits arose before age 18. Today 30 of California's almost 650 death row inmates are asking the state Supreme Court to review their cases according to these criteria.[62]

REVIEW & APPLICATIONS

REFLECTIONS ON THE FUTURE

One State's Approach to Establishing a Fair System of Capital Punishment

Report of the Illinois Governor's Commission on Capital Punishment—State of Illinois

On March 9, 2000, shortly after declaring a moratorium on executions in Illinois, Governor George Ryan appointed the Commission on Capital Punishment to determine what reforms, if any, would ensure that the Illinois capital punishment system was fair, just, and accurate. The commission members are uniform in their belief that the body of recommendations as a whole would, if implemented, answer the governor's call to enhance

significantly the fairness, justice, and accuracy of capital punishment in Illinois.

The following is a summary of the commission's recommendations, ordered according to the procedural stage to which they apply.

A. *Investigation:* We recommend videotaping all questioning of a capital suspect conducted in a police facility and repeating on tape, in the

presence of the prospective defendant, any of his statements alleged to have been made elsewhere.

Recognizing an increasing body of scientific research relating to eyewitness identification, we propose a number of reforms regarding significant revisions in the procedures for conducting lineups.

B. *Eligibility for the death penalty:* The Commission unanimously concluded that the current list of 20 factual circumstances under which a defendant is eligible for death sentence should be eliminated in favor of a simple and narrower group of eligibility criteria. A majority of the Commission agrees that the death penalty should be applied only in cases where the defendant has murdered two or more persons, or where the victim was either a police officer or a firefighter or an officer or inmate of a correctional institution, or was murdered to obstruct the justice system, or was tortured in the course of the murder.

We also have recommended that the death penalty be barred in certain instances because of the character of the evidence or the defendant. We recommend that capital punishment not be available when a conviction is based solely upon the testimony of a single eyewitness, or of an in-custody informant, or of an uncorroborated accomplice, or when the defendant is mentally retarded.

C. *Review of the prosecutorial decision to seek the death penalty:* In order to ensure uniform standards for the death penalty across the state, we recommend that a local state's attorney's decision to seek the death penalty be confirmed by a statewide commission, comprised on the Attorney General, three prosecutors, and a retired judge.

D. *Trial of capital cases:* We have proposed a number of additional measures to augment the reforms already adopted by the Illinois Supreme Court to enhance the training of trial lawyers and judges in capital cases. Included are our suggestions for increased funding.

We have offered several recommendations aimed at intensifying the scrutiny of the testimony of in-custody informants, including a pretrial hearing to determine the reliability of such testimony before it may be received in a capital trial.

To allow for future audits of the functioning of the capital punishment system, we also suggest that a designated array of information about the nature of the defendant and the crime be collected by the trial court.

E. *Review:* We recommend that, when a jury determines that death is the appropriate sentence in a case, the trail judge, who has also heard the evidence, must concur with that determination or else sentence the defendant to natural life.

We recommend that, as in several other states, the Illinois Supreme Court review each death sentence to ensure it is proportionate; that is, consider whether both the evidence and the offense warrant capital punishment in light of other death sentences imposed in the state.

About the Authors

The members of the Commission on Capital punishment are Judge Frank McGarr, chair; Senator Paul Simon, co-chair; Thomas P. Sullivan, co-chair; Deputy governor Matthew R. Bettenhausen; Kathryn Dobrinic; Rita Fry; Theodore Gottfried; Donald Hubert; William J. Martin; Thomas Needham; Roberto Ramirez; Scott Turow; Mike Waller; Andrea Zopp; Judge William H. Webster, special advisor to the commission; and Jean M. Templeton, research director. This excerpt is from the *Report of the Governor's Commission on Capital Punishment* (Springfield: State of Illinois, April 2002).

SUMMARY

1 Capital punishment has been imposed throughout history, for crimes ranging from horse stealing and witchcraft to crimes against humanity and murder. Before the 18th century, torture often preceded death. In the 18th century, use of the death penalty diminished as philosophers argued that punishment should fit the crime. After World War I, states reinstated use of the death penalty to deter threats to capitalism, and criminologists argued that capital punishment was a necessary social measure. After World War II, however, sentiment for capital punishment faded, and constitutional challenges surfaced, culminating in the Supreme Court decision of *Furman* v. *Georgia* in 1972.

2 As of June 15, 2007, 1,079 people had been executed in the United States since Gary Gilmore's execution in January 1977. The peak year was 1999, when 98 people were executed. Thirty-seven percent (394) of all executions have taken place in Texas. The South leads the United States with 883 executions. Only 1.0 percent of all the people executed since 1977 were female; 57 percent were white, 34 percent black, and 1 percent Hispanic. Today, 3,350 prisoners are on death row. Forty-three percent of the nation's death row population is in three states: California (660), Florida (397), and Texas (393). Ninety-nine percent of all prisoners on death row are male, with whites predominating (45 percent). Inmates executed in 2005 had been on death row an average of 12 years and 3 months.

3 Among the influences on capital punishment are public opinion; executive, legislative, and judicial changes; and professional organizations. Public opinion continues to support capital punishment, with more people choosing life imprisonment as an option. In the wake of the Illinois moratorium on capital punishment in 2000, professional organizations and legislatures across the country are calling for death penalty moratoriums, funding study of capital punishment, granting death row inmates access to DNA testing, affording extra assistance to lawyers handling capital cases, raising the amount of financial compensation that states provide innocent people found to have been erroneously convicted, allowing prosecutors to seek life without parole instead of the death penalty, and barring the execution of juveniles and offenders with mental retardation. In 2004, President George W. Bush signed into law the Justice for All Act aimed at reducing the risk that innocent persons may be executed.

4 The landmark cases that influenced capital punishment were *Furman* v. *Georgia* (1972), *Gregg* v. *Georgia* (1976), *Ring* v. *Arizona* (2002), *Atkins* v. *Virginia* (2002), and *Roper* v. *Simmons* (2005). In *Furman* v. *Georgia,* the U.S. Supreme Court ruled that capital punishment, as imposed by Georgia, constituted cruel and unusual punishment—Georgia's death penalty statute gave the sentencing authority (judge or trial jury) complete freedom to impose a death sentence without standards or guidelines. As a result of the *Furman* ruling, state death penalty statutes took two forms—mandatory death penalty or sentencing based on guided discretion. In *Woodson* v. *North Carolina* and *Roberts* v. *Louisiana,* the Court rejected mandatory statutes. However, in *Gregg* v. *Georgia,* the Court ruled that Georgia's new guided discretion death penalty legislation was not unconstitutional. In *Ring* v. *Arizona,* the Court held that only juries, not judges, can determine the presence of aggravating factors to be weighed in the capital sentencing process. The Court held that a defendant may not receive a penalty that exceeds the maximum penalty that he or she would have received if punished according to the facts in the jury verdict. In *Atkins* v. *Virginia* (2002) and *Roper* v. *Simmons* (2005) the Court ruled that it was unconstitutional to execute persons with mental retardation or who commit capital crimes before turning age 18.

5 Arguments in favor of the death penalty include the following: It deters rational people from becoming habitual killers; it is "just" punishment for taking someone's life; it is constitutional as long as it is achieved with due process of law; it reduces the amount of time a person spends on death row; it protects society from feared offenders; it is more humane than life imprisonment; and it is almost impossible for an innocent person to be executed. Arguments against the death penalty include the following: It violates human rights; it does not deter violent crime; it is implemented arbitrarily and unfairly; it falls disproportionately on racial minorities; it actually boosts the murder rate by promoting homicides in the months following an execution; not everyone wants vengeance; and it costs too much to support a capital trial, appeals, and execution.

6 There are five ways capital punishment jurisdictions weigh aggravating and mitigating circumstances to determine if a death sentence is appropriate: (1) The judge and jury may weigh mitigating and aggravating circumstances by what is known as the "sufficiency" standard; (2) aggravating circumstances may outweigh mitigating circumstances by a preponderance of the evidence; (3) aggravating circumstances may outweigh mitigating circumstances beyond a reasonable doubt; (4) at least one aggravating circumstance may be found to exist; and (5) different sentencing structures that exist in Oregon, Texas, and Virginia may be used.

7 Death penalty cases may pass through as many as 10 courts and across three stages: trial and direct review, state postconviction appeals, and federal *habeas corpus* appeals.

8 Liebman found that the frequency of errors in capital punishment cases is 68 percent. More than two of every three capital judgments reviewed by the courts during a 23-year study period were found to be seriously flawed. Ten states (Alabama, Arizona, California, Georgia, Indiana, Maryland, Mississippi, Montana, Oklahoma, and Wyoming) had overall error rates of 75 percent or higher. Almost 1,000 of the cases sent back for retrial ended in sentences less than death, and 87 ended in *not guilty* verdicts.

9 In 2002, the Court held in *Atkins* v. *Virginia* that execution of offenders with mental retardation is cruel and unusual punishment prohibited by the Eighth Amendment because a national consensus has developed against executing these offenders. In 2005, the Court held in *Roper* v. *Simmons* that execution of persons for crimes they committed before turning age 18 was also unconstitutional and in violation of the Eighth Amendment. The Court's reasoning in both cases was similar: The large number of states banning the execution of people with mental retardation and of persons who committed capital crimes before turning age 18 provided evidence that our society views offenders with mental retardation and juveniles as categorically less culpable than the average criminal.

KEY TERMS

capital punishment, *p. 577*
capital crime, *p. 581*
clemency, *p. 587*
commutation, *p. 587*

death row, *p. 591*
exoneration, *p. 596*
mandatory death penalty, *p. 598*
guided discretion, *p. 598*

bifurcated trial, *p. 599*
mitigating circumstances, *p. 599*
aggravating circumstances, *p. 601*
serious error, *p. 604*

QUESTIONS FOR REVIEW

1 Trace the history of capital punishment in the United States noting, in particular, the number of jurisdictions with and without the death penalty, the changes brought on by former Illinois governor George Ryan, the Supreme Court rulings that first halted and then resumed executions, the number of persons executed since 1977, and the definition of what constitutes a capital crime.

2 What are the characteristics of people executed in the United States since 1977 and on death row today?

3 Illustrate the politics influencing capital punishment.

4 What major U.S. Supreme Court decisions influenced capital punishment legislation?

5 Prioritize the arguments for and against the death penalty.

6 Differentiate among the five ways that capital punishment jurisdictions weigh aggravating and mitigating circumstances to determine if a death sentence is appropriate.

7 Evaluate the death penalty process.

8 Debate Liebman's findings on the frequency of errors in capital punishment cases.

9 What is the Supreme Court's reasoning for banning the execution of juveniles and offenders with mental retardation?

THINKING CRITICALLY ABOUT CORRECTIONS

Murder Rates and the Death Penalty

According to the Death Penalty Information Center, in 2005, death penalty states recorded higher murder rates than non-death-penalty states. The average murder rate among death penalty states was 5.3 per 100,000 population; for non-death-penalty states, the rate was 2.8. The South executes the largest percentage of offenders who are convicted of a capital crime (82 percent) and records the highest murder rate (6.6 murders per 100,000 people); the Northeast executes the fewest (less than 1 percent) and records the lowest murder rate, 4.4. What conclusions might you draw from these data?

Cost of Execution

Research shows that execution costs more than life imprisonment. Do you think there is a point at which the economic consequence of execution outweighs its value to the public? Explain.

ON-THE-JOB DECISION MAKING

Should the Cost of a Capital Trial Be a Factor in a Prosecutor's Decision to Seek the Death Penalty?

Capital murder trials are longer and more expensive at every step than other murder trials. The irreversibility of the death sentence requires courts to follow heightened due process in the preparation and course of the trial. Defen-

dants are much more likely to insist on a trial when they are facing a possible death sentence. Crime investigations, pretrial preparations and motions, expert witness investigations, jury selection, and the necessity for two trials—one on guilt and one on sentencing—make capital cases extremely costly, even before the appeals process begins. After conviction, there are constitutionally mandated appeals that involve both prosecution and defense costs. Even if a jury recommends life over death or ends as a hung jury or if the condemned person's sentence is commuted after he or she has served time on death row, the state has already paid the cost of a capital trial. Assume that you are the prosecuting attorney in a rural county of 7,500 people in a southern state. A capital case is coming up for trial. Estimates of costs for the case begin at $500,000. How will you justify paying for the prosecution of the case?

Does Maintaining Innocence Put Innocent People at Risk?

Why would a person confess to a crime he or she didn't commit and possibly face the death penalty? Professor Saul Kassin wrote an interesting article on the psychology of confessions. His thesis is innocence puts people at risk. Innocence does not protect people in a number of critical stages in criminal justice. In interrogation, police presume suspects are guilty. However, innocent people believe that everyone can see the transparency of their innocence and will naively waive their rights. Because their resistance to admitting guilt is seen as resistance and further evidence of their guilt, interrogations become more confrontational. Torture techniques like those used in the Abu Ghraib prisoner torture scandal show, for example, that extreme tactics such as excessive interrogation time and no rest is accompanied by the suspect's stress, fatigue, and feeling of helplessness.

Read Kassin's article "On the Psychology of Confessions: Does Innocence Put Innocents at Risk?" *American Psychologist*, vol. 60, no. 3, pages 215–228. (If you're not sure how to access *American Psychologist* online at your library, consult your librarian.)

Think about the issues Kassin outlines. How can we prevent these harms to innocent people?

LIVE LINKS

at www.justicestudies.com/livelinks04

15–1   Convicted by Juries, Exonerated by Science

This research report discusses a study, initiated in June 1995, to identify and review cases in which convicted persons were released from prison as a result of posttrial DNA testing of evidence.

15–2   The Future of Forensic DNA Testing

The National Commission on the Future of DNA Evidence was created by the U.S. attorney general. This report identifies the technical advances through 2010 and assesses the expected impact of these on forensic DNA (deoxyribonucleic acid) analysis.

15–3   Getting to Death

Researchers investigated the hypothesis that the more a jurisdiction used the death penalty, the greater the number of sentences that would be found legally invalid and overturned. Error rates were computed within states from 1973, when capital punishment was reinstated in the United States (following the Supreme Court decision in *Furman* v. *Georgia*), through 1995. The study found that heavy use of the death penalty created a significantly higher risk that reversible mistakes will occur. It was also concluded that the particular conditions pressuring states to overuse the death penalty (and thus increase the risk of unreliability and error) include race, politics, and poorly performing law enforcement systems. Error was also linked to overburdened and underfunded state courts. Policy options and reforms are discussed as well.

15–4   *Furman* v. *Georgia*, 408 U.S. 238 (1972)

In its decision in *Furman* v. *Georgia* in 1972, the U.S. Supreme Court invalidated all then-existing death penalty laws, determining that the death penalty was applied in an "arbitrary and capricious" and unreliable manner that violated Eighth Amendment protections against cruel and unusual punishment. In 1976 the high court ruled in *Gregg* v. *Georgia* that, on its face, Georgia's new "guided discretion" capital-sentencing procedures appeared to have reduced the problem of arbitrary, capricious, and unreliable death verdicts that had led the Court to invalidate prior capital statutes in *Furman* v. *Georgia*.

JUVENILE CORRECTIONS

End of an Era?

CHAPTER OBJECTIVES

After completing this chapter you should be able to do the following:

1 Explain *parens patriae.*

2 Describe houses of refuge, reform schools, and industrial schools.

3 Discuss the history of the juvenile court.

4 Summarize six U.S. Supreme Court cases that changed modern-day juvenile court proceedings.

5 Discuss the two types of juvenile crime.

6 List the characteristics of the typical juvenile delinquent.

7 List and explain the three stages of the juvenile justice process.

8 List disposition options for adjudicated juvenile offenders.

9 List and explain four teen court models.

10 Explain how youth gangs affect juvenile correctional institutions.

> " The vast majority of youth are good citizens who have never been arrested for any type of crime.
>
> —Shay Bilchik, executive director, Child Welfare League of America
>
> "

Here is a portion of a story that recently appeared in a midwestern city newspaper.[1]

A youthful offender is welcomed to boot camp by officers in a Montana facility. Can juveniles be more easily reformed than adults?

A teenager accused of killing his father and stepmother disliked his stepmother and used disparaging terms to describe her to his buddies, one of the youth's friends testified yesterday.

"Brandon never really liked Becky," Trevor Howe said during a hearing in Hardin County Juvenile Court. "He also called her the 'B' word."

Howe, 16, testified at a hearing to determine whether Brandon Grigaliunas, 16, should be tried as an adult for the October slayings of his father, Scott, 39, and stepmother, Rebecca, 42, in their home in Kenton, about 50 miles northwest of Columbus.

Grigaliunas is charged with two delinquency counts each of aggravated murder and murder. In juvenile court, the most serious penalty he could face is juvenile detention until age 21. As an adult, he could face life in prison.

He was 15 at the time of the shootings, and county prosecutor Lora Manon made the request to have him tried as an adult.

Ultimately, prosecutor Manon's motion for an adult trial was granted. In a subsequent plea agreement that prevented the possibility of life imprisonment, Grigaliunas pleaded guilty to two counts of voluntary manslaughter and was sentenced to a 10-year prison term.[2]

Although most juvenile offenders are charged with property offenses rather than violent offenses, the majority of juvenile offenses reported by the media involve violent crime, which overstates the violence issue and unduly alarms the public. High-profile juvenile violence—such as juvenile-perpetrated high school shootings—is changing juvenile corrections from treatment to punishment. As a result, attention and scarce resources focus on a small portion of juvenile offenders, neglecting the vast majority.

Juvenile justice will face other challenges in its second century of existence. The U.S. Congress, the Department of Justice, the American Bar Association, the National Association for the Advancement of Colored People (NAACP), think tanks, academic researchers, and others are revealing a juvenile justice system that disproportionately arrests, prosecutes, and sentences minority youth. Data from several sources show that minority youth are more likely than white youth who commit comparable crimes to be arrested, be referred to juvenile court, be detained, face trial as adults, be jailed with adults, and be sentenced to correctional institutions.

Some argue that minority youth are victims of racial bias built into the justice system. Others maintain that juvenile justice policies discriminate against low-income youth, who are overwhelmingly minority, those from single-parent homes, or those in foster care. Still others claim that overrepresentation simply means that minority youth are committing more crimes or more serious crimes. Whatever the explanation, significant change is under way. In 1992, the U.S. Congress strengthened its commitment to end disproportionate juvenile minority confinement by elevating the issue as a core requirement in federal juvenile justice legislation. The Office of Juvenile Justice and Delinquency Prevention (OJJDP) has taken the lead in developing solutions in partnership with the states.

HISTORY OF THE JUVENILE JUSTICE SYSTEM

The historical origins of America's juvenile justice system can be traced to early England, where the English Poor Laws, beginning with the Statute of Laborers in 1349, regulated the lives of the working and nonworking poor. A law passed in 1536 said that children older than 5, but less than 14, who lived in idleness and had taken to begging "may be put to service" under government authority.

By 1601 the English Poor Laws had evolved so that a child whose parents were unable to provide for his or her care could be taken away from them and sent to a facility where they would be made an apprentice to a craftsperson and provided with work. Under English law, abandoned and neglected children became the responsibility of the monarch, and the Commonwealth became their guardian.

Bridewells (the first houses of corrections) confined both children and adults until 1704, when John Howard brought to England a model of a Roman institution for juvenile offenders (see Chapter 2). Colonists took these ideas with them to America, and reformers tailored the ideas to their experiences, creating houses of refuge, reform schools, and industrial schools for juveniles. Both the English and American juvenile justice systems utilize the doctrine of *parens patriae,* which means literally "parent of his country." According to *parens patriae,* the state has the power to act as guardian for minors and for people who are mentally incompetent.

parens patriae
A Latin term that refers to the state as guardian for minors and for people who are mentally incompetent.

The first known application of *parens patriae* in America occurred in 1636 when Bridget Fuller was ordered by the governor of Plymouth Colony to take Benjamen Eaton, keep him in school for two years, and keep him employed.[3] By the end of the 19th century, every American state had affirmed its right to act as guardian of minors.

Houses of Refuge

The New York House of Refuge, the first legally chartered American custodial institution for juvenile offenders, was founded in 1825 by penal reformer Thomas Eddy, educational reformer John Griscom, and the

Society for the Prevention of Pauperism. Its purpose was to provide poor, abused, and orphaned youths with food, clothing, and lodging in exchange for hard work, discipline, and study. The concept spread, and houses of refuge were established throughout America.

Living conditions in houses of refuge were not as generous as the term *refuge* might imply. Administrators of these institutions subjected juveniles to hard physical labor and were known to use corporal punishment. Residents were expected to earn their keep and comply with strict institutional rules. Guards and superintendents, substitutes for parents or guardians, exhibited little tolerance or understanding.

Despite the path-breaking role the house of refuge played in the development of the American juvenile justice system, such institutions were short-lived. The movement as a whole died out by the middle of the 19th century.

Reform Schools

reform school

A penal institution to which especially young or first-time offenders are committed for training and reformation.

The nation's first state-sponsored **reform school** opened in Massachusetts in 1848. Named the Lyman School, for Theodore Lyman, a former mayor of Boston, the institution resembled a prison. The school was designed to house 300 boys. Because of liberal admissions policies and unregulated commitment procedures, the reformatory was filled within a few years. The Massachusetts legislature authorized an addition, doubling the structure's capacity.

In the late 1800s, with the school again becoming overcrowded, a ship in Boston Harbor was designated an annex to it. Any boy under age 14 could be committed to either Lyman School or its Nautical Branch. Boys who were housed at the Nautical Branch were trained in navigation and the duties of seamen and then transferred to passing vessels that needed cabin boys or young laborers.

Because the Lyman School housed only boys, the Massachusetts legislature voted to create a separate institution for girls. Belief that the physical and emotional makeup of girls was inherently more delicate than that of boys led reformers to focus on a new European model for the girls school.

European-style reform schools introduced a small residential arrangement, breaking down structural barriers so that staff and inmates could interact, providing a more intimate setting for treatment. Advocates of the European-style reform school believed that personal contact with youth was the cornerstone of the rehabilitative effort. Under the new design, as many as 30 inmates with similar personality traits were placed in separate small homes or cottages and supervised by paid "cottage parents." Residents of each house or cottage lived, worked, and attended school together, meeting with inmates in other living quarters only infrequently.

The first of the European-style reform schools was the Lancaster Industrial School for Girls in Massachusetts, established in 1854. The Lancaster cottages had features associated with both school and home and provided academic classes and domestic training programs. Lancaster's cottage plan gained national attention as prison reform advocates encouraged adoption of this system for youthful offenders throughout the United States.

Industrial Schools

After the Civil War, state welfare services expanded and began to require that juvenile reform schools and adult penal institutions help pay operating costs by contracting inmate labor to local manufacturers. The use of juvenile contract labor hindered the growth of reform schools. Manufacturers controlled the children during working hours, and exploitation and brutality were common. Some reform schools were converted into housing units to better serve manufacturers' labor needs.

Concerned citizens and elected officials recognized the inadequacies of reform schools. Public efforts were made to improve institutional life and to reduce the number of children being incarcerated. Special state committees investigated abuses in contract labor systems, and reform schools were added to the list of public institutions that were subject to annual inspection by regulatory agencies.

The First Juvenile Court

The movement toward establishing a separate juvenile court began in 1870, when the Illinois Supreme Court heard *People ex rel. O'Connell* v. *Turner.*[4] Daniel O'Connell was committed to the Chicago Reform School for vagrancy. His parents protested the confinement and petitioned the court for Daniel's release. In its decision, which ordered Daniel's release, the Illinois Supreme Court:

The Gardner/Betts Juvenile Justice Center in Travis County, Texas. The juvenile court movement of the late 1800s gave rise to the juvenile justice system that we know today. Why are juveniles held separately from adult prisoners?

- recognized that Daniel's parents genuinely wanted to care for their son;
- held that vagrancy was a matter of misfortune, not a criminal act;
- viewed Daniel's commitment to the Chicago Reform School as a punishment, not merely as a placement in a school for troubled children; and
- deemed Daniel's incarceration imprisonment, meaning that the doctrine of *parens patriae* did not apply and formal due process protections were required.

By the end of the 19th century, debate about juvenile facilities had established the need for differentiating between juveniles and adults in court procedures. Some states had even established children's aid societies to represent juveniles in court and to supervise them in the community.

The first completely separate juvenile court was established in Illinois in 1899. The Illinois legislature passed a law called "An Act to Regulate the Treatment and Control of Dependent, Neglected and Delinquent Children," which established a juvenile court in Cook County that had jurisdiction over any youth who committed an act that would be a crime if committed by an adult. However, young criminal offenders were not the only juveniles who needed help or supervision—the legislation was revised also to give the juvenile court jurisdiction over

> any child who for any reason is destitute or homeless or abandoned; or dependent on the public for support; or has not proper parental care or guardianship; or who habitually begs or receives alms; or who is found living in any house of ill fame or with any vicious or disreputable person; or whose home, by reason of neglect, cruelty or depravity on part of its parents, guardian or other person in whose care it may be, is an unfit place for such a child; and any child under the age of eight years who is found peddling or selling any article or singing or playing any musical instrument upon the street or giving any public entertainment.[5]

The intent of the new legislation was to give the juvenile court jurisdiction when the child's best interests would be served.

The Illinois act was a prototype for legislation in other states, and juvenile courts were quickly established in Wisconsin (1901), New York (1901), Ohio (1902), Maryland (1902), and Colorado (1903). By 1945, all states had established separate juvenile courts. New terminology accompanied the establishment of the juvenile court, to differentiate it from adult criminal court. Juvenile offenders are "delinquents" rather than "criminals," they are "taken into custody" rather than "arrested"; a "petition" rather than a "charge" is filed; juveniles are "held on petition" rather than "indicted"; there is an "adjudicatory hearing" rather than a "trial"; the court returns a "finding" rather than a "verdict" and imposes a "disposition" rather than a "sentence"; and the offender is "adjudicated" rather than "convicted," sent to a "training school" rather than a "prison," and put on "aftercare" rather than "parole."

THE U.S. SUPREME COURT AND THE JUVENILE JUSTICE SYSTEM

For most of the 20th century, all juvenile hearings were considered civil proceedings—rules of criminal procedure did not apply. Juveniles had no constitutional protections, and there were no challenges to the admissibility of evidence or the validity of testimony. Six landmark U.S. Supreme Court decisions dramatically changed the juvenile justice system, establishing due process rights for juvenile offenders. These and other significant cases affecting juvenile justice are shown in Exhibit 16–1.

Kent v. *United States* (1966)

In 1959, Morris A. Kent Jr., age 14, was taken into custody in Washington, DC, on a petition alleging burglary and attempted purse snatching. He was placed on juvenile probation and returned to his mother's custody. In September 1961, an intruder entered a woman's apartment, raped her, and stole her wallet. Police found Kent's fingerprints at the crime scene. Kent, now age 16 and still on probation, was taken into custody and charged with rape and robbery. He confessed to these offenses and several similar incidents. Kent's mother retained an attorney, who, anticipating that the case would be transferred to an adult criminal court, filed a motion to oppose the transfer.

The juvenile court judge did not rule on this motion; instead, he waived jurisdiction and remanded Kent to the jurisdiction of the adult criminal court system. Kent was tried in U.S. district court, found guilty of six counts of housebreaking, and found "not guilty by reason of insanity" on the rape charge. He received indeterminate sentences of 5 to 15 years on each count of housebreaking.

Kent's lawyer appealed the conviction, citing that the juvenile court judge failed to hear motions filed on Kent's behalf before waiving the case to adult criminal court and that Kent's due process rights had been denied. The U.S. Supreme Court heard the case, and Kent's conviction was reversed.

In *Kent*,[6] the Court ruled that, in a case involving transfer of jurisdiction, the juvenile defendant is entitled to certain essential due process rights: (1) a hearing; (2) representation by an attorney; (3) access to records involved in the transfer; and (4) a written statement of reasons for the transfer.

EXHIBIT 16–1 Significant U.S. Supreme Court Decisions Affecting Juvenile Justice

2005 —

Roper v. Simmons (2005)

Minimum age for the death penalty raised to age 18 (i.e., offenders who were younger than 18 when they committed their crimes may not be punished by death).

2000 —

Illinois v. Montanez (1996)

Voluntary confessions made by juvenile suspects may be admissible in court even when not made in the presence of a parent or another "concerned adult."

1995 —

1990 —

Stanford v. Kentucky (1989)

Thompson v. Oklahoma (1988)

Minimum age for death penalty is set at 16.

1985 —

Schall v. Martin (1984)

Preventive "pretrial" detention of juveniles is allowable under certain circumstances.

Eddings v. Oklahoma (1982)

Defendant's youthful age should be considered a mitigating factor in deciding whether to apply the death penalty.

1980 —

Smith v. Daily Mail Publishing Co. (1979)

Oklahoma Publishing Co. v. District Court (1977)

The press may report juvenile court proceedings under certain circumstances.

1975 —

Breed v. Jones (1975)

Waiver of a juvenile to criminal court following adjudication in juvenile court constitutes double jeopardy.

McKeiver v. Pennsylvania (1971)

Jury trials are not constitutionally required in juvenile court hearings.

1970 —

In re Winship (1970)

In delinquency matters, the state must prove its case beyond a reasonable doubt.

In re Gault (1967)

In hearings that could result in commitment to an institution, juveniles have four basic constitutional rights.

Kent v. United States (1966)

1965 —

Courts must provide the "essentials of due process" in transferring juveniles to the adult system.

In re Gault (1967)

On June 8, 1964, Gerald F. Gault, age 15, was taken into custody for making a crank telephone call to an adult neighbor and taken to a detention home by the sheriff of Gila County, Arizona. At the time, Gault was on juvenile probation for involvement in the theft of a woman's wallet in February 1964.

The complainant was not present at the juvenile court hearing on the following day. No one was sworn at the hearing, no transcript or recording of the proceedings was made, and no decision was issued. Gault was returned to the detention home—where he remained for several days—and then released. At a second hearing, on June 15, the judge committed Gault to the Arizona State Industrial School "for the period of his minority." Gault's attorney filed a petition for a writ of *habeas corpus* that was heard by the U.S. Supreme Court in December 1966.

In its May 1967 *Gault*[7] decision, the U.S. Supreme Court ruled that, in proceedings that might result in commitment to an institution, juveniles have the right to (1) reasonable notice of charges; (2) counsel; (3) question witnesses; and (4) protection against self-incrimination.

In re Winship (1970)

Samuel Winship, age 12, was charged with stealing $112 from a woman's purse. Winship's attorney argued that there was "reasonable doubt" of Winship's guilt. The court agreed, but, because New York juvenile courts operated under the civil court standard of "preponderance of the evidence," it adjudicated Winship delinquent and committed him to a training school for 18 months.

The U.S. Supreme Court in *Winship*[8] ruled that the reasonable doubt standard should be required in all delinquency adjudications.

McKeiver v. Pennsylvania (1971)

Joseph McKeiver, age 16, was charged with robbery, larceny, and receiving stolen property in Philadelphia, when he and 20 or 30 other juveniles took 25 cents from three boys. McKeiver had no prior arrests, was doing well in school, and was employed. McKeiver's attorney requested a jury trial; his request was denied, and McKeiver was adjudicated and put on probation.

McKeiver's attorney appealed to the state supreme court on the grounds that the juvenile court violated the Sixth Amendment's guarantee of the right to an impartial jury and the Seventh Amendment's guarantee of the right to a trial by jury. The state supreme court affirmed the lower court, arguing that, of all due process rights, a trial by jury is the one most likely to destroy the traditional nonadversarial character of juvenile court proceedings.

The U.S. Supreme Court in *McKeiver*[9] held that the due process clause of the Fourteenth Amendment did not require jury trials in juvenile court (although a state could provide a jury trial if it wished), that juries are not necessarily more accurate than judges, and that juries could be disruptive and therefore adversarial to the informal atmosphere of the juvenile court.

Breed v. Jones (1975)

In February 1971, Gary S. Jones, age 17, was charged with armed robbery and adjudicated delinquent in a Los Angeles juvenile court. The judge deferred disposition, pending receipt of a predisposition report and a recommendation from the probation department. Jones was returned to detention. When the court reconvened for the disposition hearing, the judge waived jurisdiction to adult criminal court. Counsel for Jones filed a petition for a writ of *habeas corpus*, arguing that waiver to criminal court violated the double jeopardy clause of the Fifth Amendment. The U.S. district court denied the petition, saying that Jones had not been tried twice because juvenile adjudication is not a trial. Jones was tried in adult criminal court, convicted of robbery, and committed to the California Youth Authority for an indeterminate period.

The U.S. Supreme Court in *Breed*[10] ruled that juvenile adjudication for violation of a criminal statute is equivalent to a criminal court trial; therefore, the double jeopardy clause applied. The Court ordered that Jones be released or remanded to the original juvenile court for a disposition hearing. Jones, now over 18, was released.

Schall v. *Martin* (1984)

Gregory Martin, age 14, was arrested and charged with robbery, assault, and possession of a weapon. Facts in the case showed that he and two other teenagers hit a boy on the head with a loaded gun and stole the boy's jacket and sneakers. Martin was held pending adjudication under a New York preventive detention statute because the court found there was a "serious risk" that he would commit another crime if released. Martin's attorney challenged the fairness of preventive detention, arguing that pretrial detention is essentially punishment and that many juveniles detained before trial are released before, or immediately after, adjudication. Martin was adjudicated delinquent, and his case eventually reached the U.S. Supreme Court, which upheld the constitutionality of the preventive detention statute. The Court ruled that preventive detention serves a legitimate government objective in protecting both the juvenile and society from pretrial crime and is not intended to punish the juvenile.

Impact on Juvenile Court

The U.S. Supreme Court's decisions in these cases affirmed juvenile due process rights. As a result, the "best interest of the child" is no longer the only concern for juvenile courts; they also are required to protect the juvenile's constitutional rights.

THE CONTEMPORARY JUVENILE JUSTICE SYSTEM

Every state has at least one court with juvenile jurisdiction. In most states, however, it is not actually called "juvenile court."[11] The names of the courts with juvenile jurisdiction vary by state—district, superior, circuit, county, family, or probate court, to name a few. Often the court of juvenile jurisdiction has a separate division for juvenile matters. Courts with juvenile jurisdiction generally have jurisdiction over delinquency, status offenses, and abuse/neglect matters and may also have jurisdiction in other matters such as adoption, termination of parental rights, and emancipation. Whatever their name, courts with juvenile jurisdiction are generically referred to as *juvenile courts*.

State statutes define age limits for juvenile court jurisdiction. In most states, the juvenile court has original jurisdiction over all youths under age 18 at the time of offense (see Exhibit 16–2).[12]

EXHIBIT 16–2	Oldest Age for Original Juvenile Court Jurisdiction in Delinquency Matters

Age	State
15	Connecticut, New York, North Carolina
16	Georgia, Illinois, Louisiana, Massachusetts, Michigan, Missouri, New Hampshire, South Carolina, Texas, Wisconsin
17	Alabama, Alaska, Arizona, Arkansas, California, Colorado, Delaware, District of Columbia, Florida, Hawaii, Idaho, Indiana, Iowa, Kansas, Kentucky, Maine, Maryland, Minnesota, Mississippi, Montana, Nebraska, Nevada, New Jersey, New Mexico, North Dakota, Ohio, Oklahoma, Oregon, Pennsylvania, Rhode Island, South Dakota, Tennessee, Utah, Vermont, Virginia, Washington, West Virginia, Wyoming

Juvenile Crime

Annually, U.S. law enforcement agencies take approximately 1.6 million juveniles into custody.[13] According to the Federal Bureau of Investigation (FBI), juveniles accounted for 15.3 percent of all 2006 arrests and 15.8 percent of all 2006 violent crime arrests. Most juvenile arrests were for property crime offenses (see Exhibit 16–3).

More than 90 percent of the cases handled by juvenile courts are for **delinquent offenses**—acts committed by a juvenile that, if committed by

delinquent offenses

Acts committed by juveniles that, if committed by adults, could result in criminal prosecution.

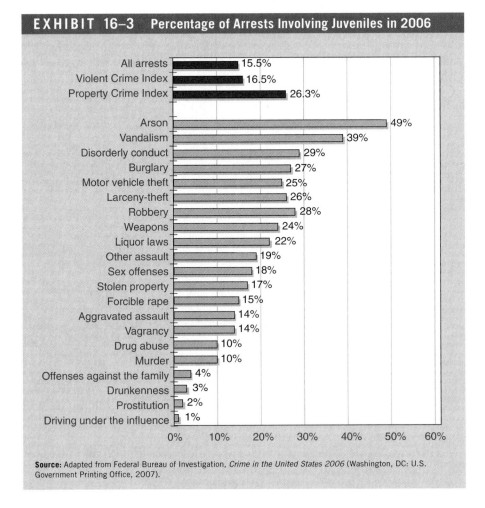

EXHIBIT 16–3   Percentage of Arrests Involving Juveniles in 2006

- All arrests — 15.5%
- Violent Crime Index — 16.5%
- Property Crime Index — 26.3%
- Arson — 49%
- Vandalism — 39%
- Disorderly conduct — 29%
- Burglary — 27%
- Motor vehicle theft — 25%
- Larceny-theft — 26%
- Robbery — 28%
- Weapons — 24%
- Liquor laws — 22%
- Other assault — 19%
- Sex offenses — 18%
- Stolen property — 17%
- Forcible rape — 15%
- Aggravated assault — 14%
- Vagrancy — 14%
- Drug abuse — 10%
- Murder — 10%
- Offenses against the family — 4%
- Drunkenness — 3%
- Prostitution — 2%
- Driving under the influence — 1%

Source: Adapted from Federal Bureau of Investigation, *Crime in the United States 2006* (Washington, DC: U.S. Government Printing Office, 2007).

an adult, could result in criminal prosecution. The remaining cases are for **status offenses**—acts that are considered offenses only when they are committed by juveniles (e.g., running away, truancy, ungovernability, and liquor law violations). Liquor law violations account for 28 percent of status offense cases; truancy, 24 percent; running away, 16 percent; ungovernability, 12 percent; and miscellaneous other status offenses, 20 percent.[14]

Profile of the Juvenile Delinquent

Some experts see many of today's children as poorly integrated into the societal mainstream, and as isolated from meaningful involvement in positive opportunities—a condition that may significantly contribute to delinquency. A publication of the American Prosecutors Research Institute, for example, depicts the position of children in today's society as follows:

> As society evolves, juveniles find themselves with ever increasing amounts of unsupervised time on their hands. The lack of parental supervision, coupled with televisions behind closed bedroom doors, music players with headphones, personal electronic games with headphones, and the anonymity of computer chat rooms and instant messaging, encourage isolation. Many children feel no real emotional connection to their environment, their neighborhoods, or their schools. The government, the criminal justice system, and the police are faceless entities that have no relevance to their lives.[15]

Of the estimated 1,615,400 delinquency cases handled by U.S. juvenile courts annually:

- 58 percent involve a juvenile age 15 or younger;
- 74 percent involve boys;
- 67 percent involve white or Hispanic juveniles and 29 percent involve black juveniles;
- 12 percent are drug, 39 percent are property, and 25 percent are public order offenses;
- 24 percent involve offenses against the person, such as robbery, assault, battery, or sexual offenses; and
- close to 935,000 cases are petitioned (handled formally by the court).[16]

THE JUVENILE JUSTICE PROCESS

Juvenile offenders are processed through one or more of three phases of the juvenile justice process: intake, adjudication, and disposition. Juvenile courts throughout the United States process more than 1.6 million delinquency cases every year.[17] Exhibit 16–4 shows the flow of events in the U.S. juvenile justice system, and Exhibit 16–5 shows the number of juveniles who were adjudicated delinquent and their subsequent disposition. Juvenile courts also process approximately 160,000 status offense cases annually, none of which fall into the "delinquency" category.[18] Typically, 60 percent of status offense cases are adjudicated, and probation is ordered in almost 60 percent of the cases.

Intake

In the first phase of the juvenile justice process, **intake,** cases that are referred to juvenile court (by law enforcement agencies, social agencies,

status offenses

Acts that are law violations only for juveniles, such as running away, truancy, or ungovernability (sometimes referred to as *incorrigibility* or *being beyond parental control*).

intake

The first stage of the juvenile justice process. A court-appointed officer reviews the case and recommends a course of action—dismissal, informal disposition, formal disposition, or transfer to adult criminal court.

EXHIBIT 16–4 The Flow of Events in the Juvenile Justice System

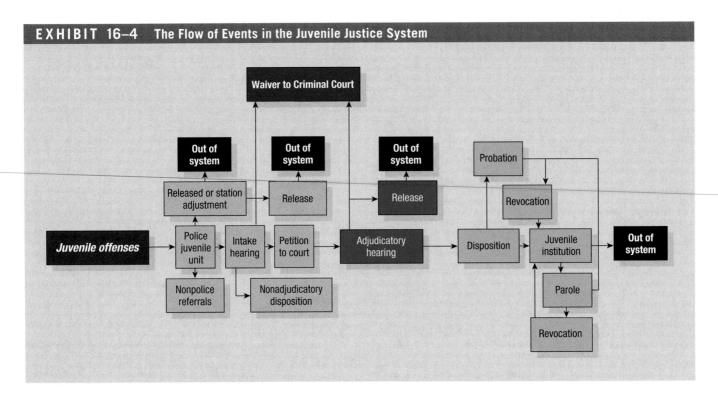

school personnel, parents or guardians, probation officers, or victims) are reviewed by a court-appointed officer (usually a prosecutor or probation officer), who recommends a course of action. The intake officer recommends that the case be (1) dismissed, (2) resolved informally (no petition is filed with the court), (3) resolved formally (a petition for an adjudication hearing is filed with the court), or (4) transferred to adult criminal court. The juvenile court establishes guidelines for the intake officer. Criteria considered in the decision in many jurisdictions include severity of the alleged offense, any prior history of delinquent behavior, attitude, age, and emotional stability.

Informal Disposition In cases that are resolved informally, disposition is decided by the intake officer, and the case goes no further. The disposition imposed is usually informal probation or some form of diversion—requiring the youth to make restitution or referring the youth to a local social service agency. Diversion is generally an option only for status offenders or low-risk delinquent offenders.

Formal Disposition In cases that are to be resolved formally, the intake officer files a petition for an adjudicatory hearing and decides whether the youth should be confined while awaiting the hearing.

juvenile detention facility

A facility for keeping juvenile offenders in secure custody, as necessary, through various stages of the juvenile justice process.

detention hearing

A judicial review of the intake officer's detention decision.

Detention Hearing If the intake officer decides that secure placement is advisable, the youth is taken to a **juvenile detention facility.** In general terms, a juvenile detention facility serves to keep juvenile offenders in secure custody through various stages of the juvenile justice process, to protect the community and the juvenile, and to ensure appearance at scheduled hearings.

A juvenile who is placed in a detention facility by an intake officer must have a **detention hearing,** usually within 48 hours. During this hearing,

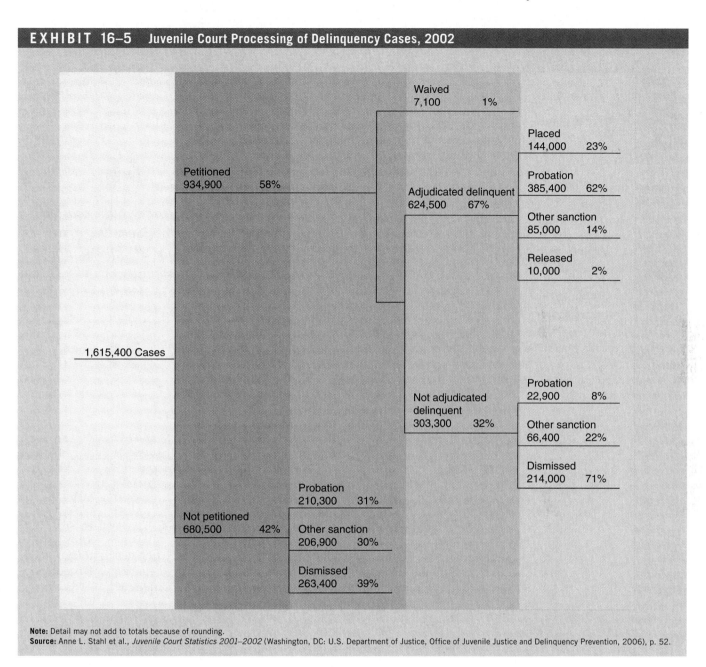

EXHIBIT 16–5 Juvenile Court Processing of Delinquency Cases, 2002

1,615,400 Cases

Petitioned
934,900 58%

Not petitioned
680,500 42%

Waived
7,100 1%

Adjudicated delinquent
624,500 67%

Not adjudicated
delinquent
303,300 32%

Placed
144,000 23%

Probation
385,400 62%

Other sanction
85,000 14%

Released
10,000 2%

Probation
22,900 8%

Other sanction
66,400 22%

Dismissed
214,000 71%

Probation
210,300 31%

Other sanction
206,900 30%

Dismissed
263,400 39%

Note: Detail may not add to totals because of rounding.
Source: Anne L. Stahl et al., *Juvenile Court Statistics 2001–2002* (Washington, DC: U.S. Department of Justice, Office of Juvenile Justice and Delinquency Prevention, 2006), p. 52.

the court reviews the intake officer's confinement decision and orders either release or continued detention pending adjudication and disposition.

Also during the detention hearing, the court determines whether the youth has legal representation and, if not, appoints defense counsel. The court may also appoint a **guardian** *ad litem,* who serves as a special guardian for the youth throughout the court proceedings. In many jurisdictions, defense counsel also serves as guardian.

Adjudication

In the second phase of the juvenile justice process, adjudication, a juvenile court hears the case. A **juvenile court** is any court that has original jurisdiction over matters involving juveniles.

guardian *ad litem*

A person appointed by the juvenile court, often defense counsel, to serve as a special guardian for the youth being processed through the juvenile justice system.

juvenile court

Any court that has jurisdiction over matters involving juveniles.

Sophia Nelson
Drug Counselor and Parent Educator
West Palm Beach, Florida

Sophia Nelson is a drug counselor and parent educator in West Palm Beach, Florida. She's been in her job for four years. As a drug counselor, she carries a caseload of 55 clients and conducts intake assessments and provides treatment. As a parent educator, Nelson facilitates group counseling for children and single mothers, and assists the children in her groups in improving their communication and interaction skills and building confidence. She helps single mothers improve their life skills and develop and acquire the knowledge, skills, and attitudes they need to maintain strong family ties, find and keep good jobs, manage their finances, and lead productive lives.

Nelson graduated from Bethune-Cookman College in Daytona Beach, Florida, with a degree in criminal justice. The courses she recalls enjoying the most were those in which there was significant classroom discussion, especially courses in prisoners' rights, correctional counseling, and social policy. She says she knew from these courses that she wanted a career working with people. Now that she's a drug counselor and parent educator, she feels she contributes to her community by helping people avoid drugs and develop healthier lifestyles. She says, "I see lives change each day."

For now, Nelson wants to keep working with drug offenders and teaching life skills to parents and children. But one day she hopes to be a prison warden and influence correctional policy on a large scale.

Be ready for a roller-coaster ride of emotions. Every day your clients are up and down. Your personality has to be able to adjust to that for you to be successful.

Adjudicatory Hearing During the adjudicatory hearing, attorneys typically present physical evidence, examine and cross-examine witnesses, and argue on behalf of their clients. If, after hearing arguments, the court rules that the evidence supports the allegations, a predisposition report is ordered and a disposition hearing scheduled.

Disposition

In the third phase of the juvenile justice process, the juvenile court decides on a **disposition**.

Predisposition Report The court's disposition decision is based on its review of the intake report (information regarding the current offense and any previous delinquent behavior; crime severity and prior adjudication greatly influence the decision) and the **predisposition report,** a document usually prepared by a probation officer, similar to the PSR (presentence report) discussed in Chapter 4. A predisposition report typically includes (1) medical and psychological background; (2) educational history; (3) information gathered from interviews with the juvenile, family members, and other people who know the youth; (4) availability of appropriate placement options; and (5) recommendations for suitable disposition. Any treatment "needs" of the youth are also considered.

Disposition Hearing At the disposition hearing the court imposes the appropriate sanction. In some jurisdictions, the youth is remanded

disposition
The third stage of the juvenile justice process in which the court decides the disposition (sentence) for a juvenile case.

predisposition report
A report that documents (1) the juvenile's background; (2) his or her educational history; (3) information gathered from interviews with the juvenile, family members, and others; (4) available placement options; and (5) recommended dispositions.

THE STAFF SPEAKS

Working with teens is especially challenging for me because—being a recent college graduate—I am not that much older than youths who are expected to do what I tell them, whether they want to or not. There are a lot of situations that can get sticky. When they do, I just remind myself to be patient and that I am many of these kids' last hope.

Most of these kids are 180-day expulsion cases from their high schools. If I give up on them, the only alternative is dropping out altogether. Each time I think of giving up I ask myself, "If this student dropped from school today could my conscience be clear that I did everything within my power to work with them?" You know what? I have not had the answer be yes yet.

Julie Judge
Teacher
Alternative Learning Center
Florissant, Missouri

---

either to the state correctional system or to a social service agency. Many juvenile courts ensure that adjudicated juveniles receive an appropriate disposition by establishing predefined sanctions based on type of offense, past delinquency, effectiveness of previous interventions, and assessment of special treatment, counseling, or training needs. Some of the more widely used sanctions are juvenile probation and commitment to group homes, residential treatment centers, boot camps, and juvenile correctional institutions.

If the sanction imposed is probation, the youth is permitted to remain in the community under the supervision of a court services officer. Exhibit 16–6 shows a supervision agreement used by the juvenile court of Topeka, Kansas.

If a youth poses a threat to public safety but incarceration is not warranted, the court may impose intensive supervised probation (ISP). The major differences between regular probation and ISP are (1) more rigid conditions and (2) more frequent contact between the probation officer and the probationer—more face-to-face interaction, closer monitoring of the juvenile's activities, and more frequent evaluation of the juvenile's progress.

Another sanction that may be imposed is referral to a **group home.** Group homes are operated by private agencies, under contract with local or state government, or by the public corrections unit, under direction of the juvenile court. Typically, group homes accommodate 15 to 30 residents. They provide living quarters, recreational and leisure areas, kitchen and dining room, and meeting room space. Youths attend school in the community, participate in field trips, and may be granted special passes to visit family, attend religious services, or participate in activities. The range of services provided by the group home often depends on the type of offender usually referred. Some group homes are treatment oriented, providing individual and/or group counseling to youths with problems such as substance abuse or lack of self-control.

Another community-based program is the **residential treatment center.** Residential treatment centers often provide long-term care and intensive treatment services.

group home
A nonsecure residential facility for juveniles.

Juvenile probation officers play an important role in the juvenile justice process, beginning with intake and continuing through the period in which a juvenile is under court supervision. Why is writing the predisposition report such an important part of the probation officer's responsibilities?

EXHIBIT 16–6   Sample Juvenile Court Supervision Agreement

SUPERVISION AGREEMENT

Name   Andrea Johnson   Case Number   00JV2751

In accordance with authority conferred by the laws of the state of Kansas, you have been placed under the supervision of Court Services. It is the order of the Court that you comply with any special conditions, programs, or counseling as set forth by the supervision Court Services Officer.

The following conditions will apply:

X   1.   You will attend all regularly scheduled appointments with the Court Services Officer and comply with their directions. If you are ill, it is your responsibility to make other arrangements.

X   2.   You will obey all laws of the State and ordinances of the City. You are to immediately report any contacts with law enforcement to your Court Services Officer.

X   3.   You are to obey the rules of your home. Persistent disobedience will be considered a violation of your supervision.

X   4.   You are not to leave the state of Kansas nor change residence without permission of your Court Services Officer. You are to notify the officer of any change in address prior to moving. You will reside in the home of your parent(s) or approved guardian and will not be permitted to spend the night away from home without prior permission of said parent(s) or guardian.

X   5.   You will attend school every day and obey all school regulations. Suspension, truancies, and tardies could result in further court action. If you are home due to illness or school suspensions, you are to consider yourself on a form of house arrest. This means if you are ill, you are only permitted to leave to attend verifiable doctors appointments. If you are on suspension, you are not to leave your home unless you are with a parent or guardian.

_____   6.   If you have been excused from attending school, you will obtain employment (get a job) and work faithfully at that job in order to maintain it. You will not quit any job without first discussing it with your Court Service Officer. If you are fired or laid off from a job, you are required to report that fact to your Court Service Officer by the end of the next business day.

X   7.   You will neither possess nor carry firearms or other weapons.

X   8.   You will neither use nor possess any alcohol, narcotics, or other controlled substances.

_____   9.   You are to submit to chemical tests of blood, breath, or urine.

X   10.   You have a curfew. If you are under the age of 15, your curfew is 9:00 p.m. Sunday through Thursday, and 10:30 p.m. Friday and Saturday. If you are 15 or older, your curfew is 10:00 p.m. Friday and Saturday. If you are 15 or older, your curfew is 10:00 Sunday through Thursday, and 12:00 midnight Friday and Saturday, Curfew means that you will be inside your own residence by the stated time, With parent or guardian's permission, you may attend a school or church sponsored function at the school or church you attend, but must be home not later than 30 minutes after the end of the event.

X   11.   It will be considered a violation of your supervision if you display clothing or insignia indicating membership in a gang, or carry a beeper, pager, or cellular telephone equipment.

X   12.   You will not be discharged from supervision until all costs, fees, and restitution has been paid in full.

Traffic/City Ordinance   District Court   Guardian Ad Litem
Fines: _____   Costs: _$25.00_   Fees: _____   Restitution: _$299.95_

X   Payment Plan   _$54.16/month for 6 months_____

X   I will complete _20_ hours Community Service Work (X) in addition to, or ( ) in lieu of the above.

EXHIBIT 16-6 *(continued)*

SPECIAL CONDITIONS:

_X_ a). Do not go into Electronics Plus for 6 months.

_X_ b). Within two weeks, write a letter of apology to Ms. Valerie Carte, owner of Electronics Plus.

_X_ c). Do not quit your weekend job at Bruno's grocery store until court costs and restitution are paid.

_X_ d). Write a three page paper on why shoplifting is wrong and hand deliver it to Judge Gray in three weeks.

I have read, understood, initialed and agreed to abide by all terms and special conditions of my supervision as explained by the assigned Court Services Officer. I understand fully that my failure to comply could result in the imposition of additional condition, revocation and/or out of home placement.

DATE: <u>February 1, 2008</u>

SIGNED <u>*Andrea Johnson*</u>
Respondent

<u>*Rosalind Johnson*</u>
Parent or Guardian

<u>*Gary Bayens*</u>
Court Services Officer

cc: Working File
Respondent
Parent or Guardian

Today, most states have juvenile boot camps. Boot camp programs vary in size, requirements, and structure. For the most part, juvenile corrections officials have been slow to accept the boot camp concept; they consider the amount of time devoted to military drill, ceremony, and exercise an encroachment on the time available for education or rehabilitation programs.

A few states have responded to violent juvenile crime by enacting **blended sentencing** legislation in which the juvenile court may impose both a juvenile sentence and an adult criminal sentence. In 1996, the Kansas legislature passed a blended sentencing law that created a new category referred to as "extended jurisdiction juvenile prosecution," for serious and violent offenders.[19] Under this legislation, two sentences are imposed, but the adult criminal sentence is waived if the juvenile offender does not violate any of the provisions of the juvenile sentence.

Juvenile Correctional Facilities

In 2007, the Council of Juvenile Correctional Administrators (CJCA) reported the results of its annual survey of juvenile corrections throughout the United States.[20] The survey, which includes information from 45 state and territorial (including Puerto Rico) youth correctional agencies, found

residential treatment center

A residential facility that provides intensive treatment services to juveniles.

blended sentencing

A two-part (juvenile and adult) sentence in which the adult sentence may be waived if the offender complies with all provisions of the juvenile sentence.

that 18 states operate free-standing juvenile correction agencies, 12 place the responsibility for juvenile corrections within a child welfare/social service system, 11 operate distinct youth correction agencies under a human services umbrella, and 10 (including Puerto Rico) place the responsibility for juvenile corrections within an adult corrections agency. Five state agencies were responsible for all juvenile services, while 3 (including Puerto Rico) were responsible only for juveniles confined in facilities. Three-quarters of the responding agencies were charged with the responsibility for juvenile corrections to include postrelease community-based reentry programs.

Operating budgets for the agencies surveyed ranged from $642 million (Florida) to about $10 million (North Dakota). On average, more than 80 percent of operating budgets were allocated to residential placements—including institutions, training schools, detention centers, assessment centers, group homes, camps, and shelters.

Nationwide, according to OJJDP-funded research, the number of delinquency cases involving detention increased 42 percent between 1985 and 2002, from 231,400 to 329,800. The largest relative increase was for drug offense cases (140 percent), followed by person cases (122 percent) and public-order cases (72 percent). In contrast, the number of property offense cases declined 12 percent during this same period.[21]

Consistent with those data, the CJCA survey determined that a total of 219,335 youths were under correctional supervision in 2006, including those housed in secure institutional treatment facilities, nonsecure residential facilities, and nonresidential community programs like probation and parole. Of this number, 38 percent were white; 38 percent were black; 20 percent were Hispanic; less than 1 percent were Alaskan Native/Pacific Islander; 1 percent were American Indian; 1 percent were Asian; and 2 percent of the youths weren't classified by ethnicity (see Exhibit 16–7).

Of the more than 200,000 youths under correction supervision throughout the nation, 14 percent were placed in the most restrictive settings, such as training schools and detention centers, while 66 percent were placed in community-based programs like probation, day treatment, and outreach programs. The remainder were served in nonsecure residential settings and reception/diagnostic centers, or were placed out of state. Medical, mental health, education, life skills, and recreation programs were offered to all supervised juveniles in all jurisdictions—while some

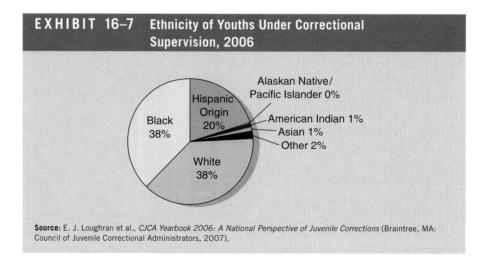

EXHIBIT 16–7 **Ethnicity of Youths Under Correctional Supervision, 2006**

Source: E. J. Loughran et al., *CJCA Yearbook 2006: A National Perspective of Juvenile Corrections* (Braintree, MA: Council of Juvenile Correctional Administrators, 2007).

jurisdictions also offered specialized vocational, sex offender treatment, family therapy, substance abuse treatment, and other programs. Twenty-seven of the jurisdictions included in the survey results reported having at least one specialized unit designated for youths with identifiable mental health problems.

When speaking of youths in custody, a distinction should be made between *detained* and *committed* youths. Detained youths are those held prior to adjudication or disposition awaiting a hearing in juvenile or criminal court, or after disposition awaiting placement elsewhere. Committed offenders are those who have been adjudicated delinquent, and who have been ordered held under correctional supervision by a judicial authority as a result of case disposition.

Youths who have either been adjudicated delinquent or been taken into custody because of alleged delinquent behavior account for approximately 95 percent of both detained and committed offenders. Compared with the detained population, however, the committed juvenile population shows a greater proportion of youths held for sexual assault, burglary, and theft; and fewer youths held for technical violations of probation or parole. The committed population also demonstrates proportionally more youths held for being ungovernable, and fewer youths held for running away from home.

The number of committed delinquents held in public or private facilities as part of a court-ordered disposition was 28 percent greater in 2003 than in 1991. The public facility committed population was 11 percent greater in 2003 than in 1991; and the private facility committed population was 77 percent greater.[22]

Data on juvenile correctional facilities gathered through the OJJDP's second Juvenile Residential Facility Census (JRFC), and published in 2006, identified 3,534 juvenile facilities throughout the United States, 2,964 of which held a total of 102,388 offenders younger than 21 years of age.[23] The number of juvenile correctional facilities, both public and private, by state, is shown in Exhibit 16–8.

The JRFC survey found that group homes or halfway houses made up 38 percent of all facilities and held 12 percent of all committed or detained juvenile offenders. Facilities identifying themselves as detention centers (26 percent) were the second most common type of facility, and detention centers held 40 percent of all juvenile offenders in residential facilities.

The survey also found that most residential facilities were small, with fewer than 50 residents, but that most offenders were in large facilities. Large facilities were most likely to be state operated, and very few state-operated facilities held 10 or fewer residents. In contrast, the JRFC survey found that 46 percent of private facilities were that small.

Although state-operated facilities made up just 17 percent of all facilities surveyed, they accounted for 66 percent of facilities holding more than 200 residents. Private facilities, on the other hand, made up 60 percent of all facilities, but they accounted for 80 percent of facilities holding 10 or fewer residents.

Security in Juvenile Facilities   One-third of all juvenile detention facilities reported that they lock youths in their sleeping rooms to confine them. Very few private facilities locked youths in sleeping rooms at least some of the time. Among public facilities, 73 percent of local facilities and 58 percent of state facilities reported locking youths in sleeping rooms. Of those, three-quarters said that they took such action when

EXHIBIT 16–8   Number of Juvenile Correctional Facilities in the United States, by State

State	Juvenile Facilities			Juvenile Offenders			State	Juvenile Facilities			Juvenile Offenders		
	Total	Public	Private	Total	Public	Private		Total	Public	Private	Total	Public	Private
U.S. total[1]	2,964	1,182	1,773	102,388	70,243	31,992	Missouri	72	60	12	1,559	1,332	227
Alabama	48	12	36	1,539	827	712	Montana	24	7	15	308	177	99
Alaska	23	7	16	402	303	99	Nebraska	19	5	14	732	513	219
Arizona	51	16	32	1,892	1,488	320	Nevada	18	10	8	1,159	861	308
Arkansas	35	9	26	733	211	522	New Hampshire	8	2	6	234	137	97
California	288	122	164	17,294	15,561	1,733	New Jersey	49	42	7	2,043	1,972	71
Colorado	65	12	52	2,063	928	1,131	New Mexico	27	18	9	803	698	105
Connecticut	26	4	22	665	244	421	New York	221	51	170	4,455	2,328	2,127
Delaware	6	4	2	271	243	28	North Carolina	66	27	39	1,286	870	416
Dist. of Columbia	13	2	11	280	183	97	North Dakota	11	4	7	246	131	115
Florida	181	53	128	8,508	3,043	5,465	Ohio	97	66	31	4,480	4,023	457
Georgia	53	30	23	2,681	2,224	457	Oklahoma	56	14	41	1,010	634	351
Hawaii	5	2	3	112	99	13	Oregon	45	26	19	1,473	1,262	211
Idaho	22	14	8	466	402	64	Pennsylvania	179	33	146	5,080	1,262	3,818
Illinois	45	25	20	2,921	2,539	382	Rhode Island	14	1	13	345	233	123
Indiana	95	42	53	3,433	2,386	1,047	South Carolina	38	14	24	1,461	966	495
Iowa	65	16	49	941	376	566	South Dakota	22	8	12	598	334	256
Kansas	56	17	39	1,114	809	306	Tennessee	58	26	32	1,559	830	829
Kentucky	50	32	18	965	814	171	Texas	129	78	51	8,371	6,726	1,645
Louisiana	62	21	41	2,363	1,830	533	Utah	47	17	30	1,073	472	601
Maine	14	2	12	278	242	36	Vermont	5	1	4	51	27	34
Maryland	43	10	33	1,216	611	606	Virginia	71	63	8	2,635	2,448	187
Massachusetts	68	18	50	1,400	452	948	Washington	40	30	10	1,931	1,759	172
Michigan	94	37	57	2,856	1,353	1,503	West Virginia	23	6	17	394	281	113
Minnesota	100	24	76	1,699	886	813	Wisconsin	81	25	56	1,784	1,182	602
Mississippi	17	15	2	688	600	68	Wyoming	21	2	19	417	141	276

Note: State is the state where the facility is located. Offenders sent to out-of-state facilities are counted in the state where the facility is located, not the state where their offense occurred.

1. U.S. total includes 153 offenders in 9 tribal facilities. These tribal facilities were located in Arizona, Colorado, Montana, Oklahoma, and South Dakota.

Source: Adapted from Melissa Sickmund, *Juvenile Residential Facility Census, 2002: Selected Findings* (Washington, DC: Office of Juvenile Justice and Delinquency Prevention, 2006), p. 2.

youths were out of control, and one-quarter did so when youths were thought to be suicidal. Locking youths in their rooms during shift changes was found to be fairly common (in 43 percent of facilities). More than half (54 percent) said they locked sleeping rooms whenever youths were in them. Locking sleeping rooms at night was more common (87 percent). Just over one-quarter said youths were locked in their sleeping rooms part of each day, and a few facilities said they locked youths in their rooms most of each day (1 percent) or all of each day (1 percent). Six percent said they rarely locked youths in sleeping rooms and had no set schedule for doing so.

Facilities participating in the JRFC survey were asked whether they used various types of locked doors or gates to confine youths within the facility or to keep intruders out. Nearly half of all facilities said that they had one or more confinement features other than locked sleeping rooms. Among public facilities, the proportion was 78 percent.

About 90 percent of detention centers and training schools said they had one or more confinement features other than locked sleeping rooms, but less than 20 percent of group homes and ranch or wilderness camps used locked doors or gates. The use of fences, walls, and surveillance equipment is increasingly common in juvenile facilities, although security hardware is generally not as elaborate as that found in adult jails and prisons. National accreditation standards for juvenile facilities express a preference for relying on staff, rather than on hardware, to provide security. The guiding principle is to house juvenile offenders in the "least restrictive placement alternative." Staff security measures include periodically taking counts of the youths held, using classification and separation procedures, and maintaining an adequate ratio of security staff to juveniles.

Facilities responding to the JRFC survey reported that daytime locks confined 8 in 10 juvenile offenders at least some of the time. This represents an increase over 1997, when 7 in 10 offenders were housed in facilities with locked arrangements. Most youths in facilities with daytime locks were in facilities that held all youths under the same security arrangements. Overall, a larger proportion of committed juveniles than detained juveniles were determined to be held in facilities that relied primarily on staff security.

Juveniles in residential placement for homicide, sexual assault, robbery, aggravated assault, arson, and technical violations were the most likely to be held behind locked doors or gates. Compared with juveniles held for delinquency offenses, those in residential placement for status offenses were more likely to be confined under staff-secure arrangements (19 vs. 32 percent). Facilities indicated whether they had various types of locked doors or gates intended to confine youths within the facility. Nearly half of all facilities that reported security information said they had one or more confinement features (other than locked sleeping rooms).

Among group homes and ranch or wilderness camps, fewer than 2 in 10 facilities said they had locked doors or gates to confine youths. A facility's staff, of course, also provides security. In some facilities, remote location is a security feature that also helps keep youths from leaving. Overall, 16 percent of facilities reported external gates in fences or walls with razor wire. This arrangement was most common among detention centers (39 percent), training schools (37 percent), and boot camps (32 percent).

Crowding   JRFC data show that crowding is a problem in a significant number of residential facilities, and in 2002, 30 percent of the facilities reported residential populations at the limit of available beds, while 6 percent had more residents than standard beds.

Thirty-six percent of facilities said that the number of residents they held on the 2002 census date put them at or over the capacity of their standard beds or that they relied on some makeshift beds. Overall, these facilities held more than 39,300 residents, the vast majority of whom were offenders younger than 21. A large proportion of private facilities (39 percent) said they were operating at 100 percent capacity.

Females in Custody   Male offenders dominate the juvenile system. This is especially true of the custody population. Females account for a small proportion of the juvenile custody population, but their numbers have increased recently. The 14,590 female offenders held in 2003 accounted for 15 percent of offenders in residential placement, an increase of 2 percent since 1991. The female proportion was greater among status offenders held (40 percent) than among delinquents (14 percent), and greater for detained (18 percent) than for committed (12 percent) delinquents.

Detention centers held the largest proportion of female offenders, and long-term secure facilities (e.g., training schools) held about one-quarter of female offenders, while group homes and halfway houses held about one-tenth.

Staff in Juvenile Correctional Facilities

The CJCA survey found that 35,598 direct care staff members served the needs of the juvenile correctional population in the jurisdictions surveyed. *Direct care staff* was defined to include staff members at secure and nonsecure residential facilities who have routine contact with youths under correctional supervision—including youth care staff, teachers, counselors, nurses, chaplains, food care workers, and temporary or contractual employees who supervise youths.

Almost three-quarters of all jurisdictions reported having education prerequisites for staff members to include high school or GED-level completion, while three jurisdictions (Colorado, Rhode Island, and the state of Washington) require an associate's degree, and two (Missouri and North Dakota) require a bachelor's degree or its equivalent.

Transfer to Adult Criminal Court

All states and the District of Columbia allow adult criminal prosecution of juveniles under certain circumstances. Juveniles may be transferred to adult criminal court under one of three provisions: waiver, direct file, or statutory exclusion. Under **waiver provisions**, the juvenile court orders transfer of the case to adult criminal court. In all but four states (Massachusetts, Nebraska, New Mexico, and New York), a juvenile court judge is authorized to waive the juvenile court's original jurisdiction over cases that meet certain criteria and to refer them to criminal court for prosecution. Under **direct file provisions**, the prosecutor determines whether to initiate a case against a juvenile in juvenile court or in adult criminal court. Fifteen states have statutes that specify circumstances in which the prosecutor may make the transfer decision. Under **statutory exclusion provisions**, state law specifies adult criminal court jurisdiction for certain juvenile cases. An increasing number of states (28 in 1998) automatically exclude from juvenile court any cases that meet specific age and offense criteria. Fifteen states (in 1998) permit certain juvenile cases to be filed directly in criminal court. In 1998, 8,100 juvenile cases were transferred to adult criminal court. Of these, 36 percent involved a crime against a person, 40 percent involved property crime, 16 percent involved a drug law violation, and 8 percent involved a public order offense.[24]

waiver provisions

Provisions under which the juvenile court orders transfer of the case to adult criminal court.

An officer greets a new arrival at a boot camp for juveniles in Forsythe County, Georgia. Boot camp facilities for juveniles are meant to shock young offenders by reorienting them toward productive goals. What other kinds of programs might do the same thing?

Teen Courts

Teen courts, also called peer and youth courts, have become a popular alternative to the traditional juvenile court for relatively young or first-time offenders. The teen court was first used in Grand Prairie, Texas, in 1976.[25] Since then the number of teen courts has grown to an estimated 1,150 nationwide.[26] Teen courts handled approximately 125,000 cases in 2005.[27]

In youth court, youth volunteers work with adults to conduct sentencing hearings and trials for young offenders. The primary purpose of youth courts is to effectively divert juvenile delinquents from the formal juvenile or criminal justice system. Adults and youth volunteers work as colleagues to achieve the goals of restoring justice to the victims, the respondents, and the community. Most important, young offenders learn that their peers will work with them to ensure that justice is served and that there are consequences for their delinquent behavior.

All teen courts are diversion processes. These programs may handle crimes and offenses that would otherwise be eligible for prosecution in juvenile court, adult court, traffic court, or a school's disciplinary process. Without a youth court, in some cases juvenile offenders would not be held accountable for their antisocial, delinquent, and criminal behavior because of the backlog in the juvenile system. Youth courts provide a measured response for youths who violate the law.

Depending on which of the many teen court models is followed, young people may take on the roles of judge, prosecutor, defense attorney, community or victim advocate, respondent or youth advocate, juror, presiding juror, bailiff, or clerk.

Teen courts generally use one of four models: Adult Judge, Youth Judge, Youth Tribunal, or Peer Jury. In the Adult Judge model, an adult serves as judge, ruling on legal terminology and courtroom procedure, and youths serve as attorneys, jurors, clerks, bailiffs, and so on. The Youth Judge model parallels the Adult Judge model, with the exception that a youth serves as judge. In the Youth Tribunal model, youth attorneys present the case to a panel of three youth judges. The Peer Jury model uses no attorneys—the case is presented to a youth jury by a youth or adult and the jury questions the defendant directly. Forty percent of teen courts use the Adult Judge model, 26 percent the Peer Jury, 8 percent the Youth Tribunal, and 17 percent the Youth Judge. The remaining 9 percent use a combination of two or more of these models.[28]

In the majority of cases, young defendants admit their wrongdoing or plead no contest to be eligible for teen court. A few teen courts (less than 8 percent) will allow a youth to plead not guilty in youth court. In those programs the teen court can conduct a trial to determine guilt or innocence. If the young person is found guilty, he or she is sentenced by the youth court. Young people must give informed consent to participate in all youth courts. In most teen courts, parents or guardians must also give consent.

Teen courts turn peer pressure into a positive tool: Youth volunteers tell respondents clearly that their behavior is wrong. However, the underlying philosophy of youth courts is not merely to punish respondents. Instead, youth volunteers work through creative ways to make respondents understand in concrete terms that their behavior has harmed specific individuals and the community. This balanced and restorative approach provides respondents with opportunities to repair the harm that they caused and to give back to their community in a meaningful way. Specific needs of the respondents are identified, and the sentence (or disposition) is directed at building strengths and skills in the respondents.

direct file provisions
Provisions under which the prosecutor determines whether to initiate a case against a juvenile in juvenile court or in adult criminal court.

statutory exclusion provisions
Provisions under which adult criminal court jurisdiction for certain juvenile cases is established by state law.

teen courts
Courts in which youths adjudicate and impose disposition for a juvenile offense.

Eye On Corrections

Jailing Juveniles: Managing a Special Population

By Michelle Gaseau and Meghan Mandeville

They may commit adult crimes, but serious juvenile offenders are not your typical adult inmate and there's no consensus on how they should be handled in the corrections environment.

Juvenile rights advocates want juvenile offenders to be housed separately from adults—no matter their offense—from the get-go. But depending on the state and the county, a juvenile could share a cell with an adult for something as mild as stealing a bicycle.

Some say that this lack of consistency—and ultimately a lack of leadership on this issue—will cause big problems down the road.

"I think there should be a ban on jailing kids with adults and I don't see that happening yet. It's one of those areas where [corrections says] we run the hotel and you tell us how many guests to put in it. But this is an area where the corrections field should take some strong positions," said Vincent Schiraldi; Executive Director of the Justice Policy Institute, a Washington D.C.–based research and public policy organization focusing on criminal justice issues.

Concerns about a juvenile's vulnerability around adult offenders, including the possibility of being sexually abused, are high among the reasons child advocates tout for having separate facilities for pre-trial and sentenced youthful offenders.

"The odd thing is less seems to have been done at the pre-trial stage than after adjudication," Schiraldi said.

He reasons that ultimately few serious youthful offenders even end up receiving sentences to adult prisons so why, then, should they be housed with adults pre-trial. . . .

Some adult jurisdictions, including many jails, have come to the realization that it is no picnic housing juveniles in [ADULT] facilities and some have pushed for legislation to have them held elsewhere. Still others in state corrections have decided that youthful offenders with adult charges need their own facilities. Although this movement is not across the board, there are some changes being made.

Officials in Prince George's County, Maryland are among this group.

STARTING FROM SCRATCH IN PRINCE GEORGE'S COUNTY

Prince George's County officials put some thought into creating a program for juveniles just in the nick of time—right before the American Civil Liberties Union contacted them to suggest that they provide some type of services to the juveniles they were housing in their adult detention facility.

At that point—in 1999—Barry Stanton, Director of the county's Department of Corrections, was already in the process of creating a task force to examine various programs around the country and bring back some ideas about how to address the needs of the juvenile offenders in the jail. Prior to Stanton's efforts, there were basically no services for the young male and female offenders who typically spend between six and eight months in the Prince George's County Correctional Center.

"I told [the ACLU] 'Give me a year. You can come back in a year and I will promise you that we will have a program up and running,'" said Stanton.

When the rights' activists returned in 2000, they were amazed by the county's progress, Stanton said. In a year's time, he had created a program that targets juveniles' healthcare, nutritional, rehabilitative and educational needs.

Prince George's County task force members had traveled to adult jails that housed juveniles in Washington State, Pennsylvania and Florida to garner information about the kinds of services that best suited this population.

"[I told the task force], 'Don't worry about cost. Don't worry about staffing. Just tell me what is the best program we can do based on the information you got,'" Station said. "And that's what we did."

Stanton started to build a program by improving healthcare services for the juveniles.

"I think it's very important that you provide appropriate healthcare assessments, including mental health," he said. "[Since] you are dealing with juveniles, you have to pay closer attention to their physical needs and their mental health needs."

After bringing a contractor on board to handle the medical evaluations and mental health assessments, Stanton set his sights on creating some type of educational programming for these offenders, which proved to be a more difficult task than tweaking healthcare procedures.

"The educational piece was a little tougher because we didn't have any teachers," said Stanton, who spent two years working with the Prince George's County school system to get them to provide teachers for the juveniles at the jail.

While it took some time for the educational portion of the program to come together, Stanton was able to implement new nutritional guidelines immediately.

"What I did was I went to the state school board and said 'How can we be part of a breakfast and lunch program?'" Stanton said.

Once he obtained the criteria for meals from the school board, he said it was easy to adjust the juveniles' food servings to meet the system's caloric requirement. But, Stanton even went a step beyond conforming to public school standards; he also tried to cut down on the juveniles' sugar intake.

"Based on research, I felt it was important to reduce sugar and candy in the commissary," Stanton said. "What I found is sweets were making the juveniles a little more aggressive."

Beyond a change in nutritional requirements and the addition of educational classes for the juveniles, Stanton also added other programs to help them rehabilitate, like religion, anger management, substance abuse and self-awareness programs.

But one of the most important aspects of the program was the creation of a juvenile coordinator position to ensure that all of these services were running smoothly.

"Getting a staff person was big," Stanton said. "I felt it was very important to the success of the program."

Another vital element that contributed to the program's success was developing training for existing staff members, who often viewed the juveniles as troublesome and disrespectful.

"[The corrections officers] didn't want to do anything special with [the juveniles] because they were violent and disruptive," Stanton said.

To help staff overcome their issues with juveniles, Stanton trained officers to work with this [special] offender population and kept the same staff members assigned to the juvenile unit.

"It worked out pretty well," Stanton said. "It improved discipline. It improved control. It improved respect," he added. "The corrections officers running the unit felt like they were really their mothers and their fathers."

The staff training, combined with the other elements of the program, paid off, said Stanton, noting that violent incidents involving the juveniles are down 35–40 percent and there have been no assaults on corrections officers by juveniles in the last three years. . . .

Source: "Jailing Juveniles: Managing a Special Population," Michelle Gaseau and Meghan Mandeville, The Corrections Connection Network News (CCNN). Eye on Corrections. www.corrections.com. August 23, 2004.

Teen courts allow youths to adjudicate peers accused of minor law violations and to impose a reasoned disposition on juveniles who come before them. Why might such courts be more effective than "traditional" juvenile courts?

Quite commonly, a teen court disposition requires a respondent to serve on the youth court as a juror or bailiff in a subsequent youth court case. This means that respondents are not excluded from the circle of their law-abiding peers but are included once more within the community and have a chance to see the law from both sides. This requirement also helps ensure that the youth court reflects the diversity of the community.

Failure to complete the disposition imposed by the youth court generally will result in referral back to the original agency. For example, youths failing to complete their disposition for crimes will be referred back to the referring agency; youths failing to complete their disposition for violating school rules will be referred back to the school disciplinary process.

Youth courts have quietly emerged as the most replicated—and fastest growing—juvenile intervention program in the United States. Estimates are that teen courts could be handling as many as 25 percent of all juvenile arrests by 2015.

According to the OJJDP, community service was the most common disposition imposed in teen court cases in the year 2000.[29] Other dispositions included victim apology letters, apology essays, teen court jury duty, drug/alcohol classes, and monetary restitution.

Tammy Hawkins, teen court coordinator for Odessa, Texas, says that teen court makes quite an impact when you give a teenaged jury sole discretion in handing down sentences. "The juvenile defendant receives this sentence from his peers and sees that they are saying, 'We as your peers do not agree with your actions and breaking the law is not acceptable.' A child is more likely to listen to one of their own, as opposed to an adult or the system. After all, as one defendant put it, 'Your peers are the ones that you want to accept you.'"[30]

YOUTH GANGS

In the 2004 National Youth Gang Center (NYGC) survey—a survey that is conducted annually by OJJDP—2,296 law enforcement agencies responded to requests for information about gang activity in their communities.[31] Eighty percent of agencies serving a population of 50,000 or more reported gang-related problems in their areas, while only 12 percent of rural agencies reported such problems. Based on survey results, the NYGC estimates that approximately 760,000 gang members and 24,000 gangs were active in the United States in 2004.

In responding to the NYGC 2004 survey, 173 big city law enforcement agencies (i.e., those serving populations of 100,000 or more) reported a gang problem along with gang homicide data. In two cities, Los Angeles and Chicago, more than half of all homicides were thought to be gang related. Moreover, the number of gang homicides reported in those cities in 2004 was 11 percent higher than the previous eight-year average.

The youth gang problem is one of the most important issues for juvenile corrections today. Many of the youths confined for serious crimes commit violent acts as gang members. For some correctional institutions, a primary housing consideration is a youth's gang affiliation—rival gang members must be housed separately. Juvenile correctional personnel regularly deal with problems that stem from gang-related activity

I am a 33-year-old female who has been involved in both the juvenile and adult system. I was in the juvenile system for truancy and running away.

I feel that the juvenile justice system was effective due to the peer culture in the group home that I was ordered into. At first, I had a male probation officer that was too authoritative. I started responding to supervision better when I was transferred to a female probation officer. I felt she was more understanding.

My male juvenile P.O. had the attitude of "Do what I say, this is the way it is, no option or choices, just authority." When I was transferred to the female I started to make more progress. I think a female probation officer should have been assigned to me right away. However, the juvenile justice system was not effective in that I got too many chances.

I learned that even juveniles can't get away with too much. I learned the lesson to respect myself. I came from a very dysfunctional family, and the juvenile system taught me to not rely on family a lot and take care of myself.

The juvenile justice experience was not fun, but it was helpful.

Anonymous

---

within the institution: extortion, violence, and attempts to smuggle in contraband.

One of the more pressing gang-related issues facing today's juvenile corrections agencies is identification of youth gangs. According to the FBI, a **gang** is "a criminal enterprise having an organizational structure, acting as a continuing criminal conspiracy, which employs violence and any other criminal activity to sustain the enterprise." [32] Members of the group need not wear similar clothing ("colors") or tattoos or use hand signs (called "throwing") or initiation rituals, and the group might not even have a specific name (e.g., "Crips" or "Bloods"). Participation in criminal activity is what distinguishes community groups or social clubs from gangs. Other terms that have been used to distinguish among types of gangs are *street gang* and *youth gang*. The term **youth gang** tends to emphasize the age of a gang's members and is usually applied to gangs consisting of members between the ages of 12 and 24. According to the OJJDP, the phrase **street gang** refers to an organized group of people on the street, often engaged in significant illegitimate or criminal activity. [33]

gang
A criminal enterprise having an organizational structure, acting as a continuing criminal conspiracy, that employs violence and any other criminal activity to sustain itself.

youth gang
A gang whose membership generally comprises people between the ages of 12 and 24.

street gang
An organized group of people on the street often engaged in significant illegitimate or criminal activity.

Members of the infamous Mara Salvatrucha 13 gang at the Tonacatepeque detention center for minors in El Salvador. Mara Salvatrucha, which has been called "America's most deadly gang," is made up predominately of Salvadorans. It originated in the Los Angeles area, not El Salvador, but the gang was later exported back to that country. What can be done to stop the spread of street gangs?

647

The membership age of street gangs varies, says OJJDP, while some street gangs are more street based than others.[34]

Police departments tend to view gangs somewhat differently than our definitions might indicate. According to a recent survey of police agencies nationwide, the most important distinguishing characteristic of a youth gang is that its members commit crimes together.[35] The fact that the gang has a name and that its members "hang out together" is somewhat less important. See Exhibit 16–9 for additional information on the criteria used by law enforcement agencies to distinguish youth gangs from other types of organizations.

Graffiti is a common method of communication for gangs.[36] It serves as the gang "newspaper" or "bulletin board," communicating many messages, including challenges, warnings, and pronouncements. Juvenile corrections professionals must become familiar with gang language, graffiti, and symbols to be able to deal with gang power and control. A partial listing of gang slang is shown in Exhibit 16–10, and the names of some of the gangs currently operating in the United States are given in Exhibit 16–11.

One reason that gangs successfully recruit members within the correctional setting is that the transition to a confined existence can be traumatic. Residents often challenge new arrivals, usually within the first few days, threatening physical harm to intimidate and exploit the youth. A youth who is the object of such an encounter may believe that joining a gang is the only way to survive.

Another reason that incarcerated juveniles join gangs is boredom. Their typical daily routine includes eating meals, exercise, and schoolwork. Leisure activities, family visitation, social programs, and other special services are intermittent and are permitted only if the juvenile complies with institution rules. Involvement in gang activity may represent excitement and adventure for confined juveniles.

THE AMERICAN CORRECTIONAL ASSOCIATION AND JUVENILE JUSTICE REFORM

In 2005, Chad Sokolowski, a sociology and criminal justice instructor at Ohio University–Eastern and Belmont Technical College, became the

EXHIBIT 16–9	**Criteria Used by Law Enforcement Agencies to Define a Youth Gang**	
	Agencies Selecting as Most Important Criterion	
Gang Characteristic	**Number**	**Percentage**
Commits crimes together	613	50%
Has a name	228	19
Hangs out together	119	10
Claims a turf or territory of some sort	104	9
Displays/wears common colors or other insignia	101	8
Has a leader or several leaders	89	7

Note: Number of observations was 1,221.
Source: Office of Juvenile Justice and Delinquency Prevention, *National Youth Gang Survey* (Washington, DC: U.S. Department of Justice, November 2000), Table 45.

EXHIBIT 16–10	Selected Terms Commonly Associated with Gangs
100-proof	The real thing
5-0	The police
13	Same as Sur
A-K	An assault rifle
All that	Something that possesses good qualities
Ay yo trip	To gain another's attention
Bag up	To be arrested by the police
Baller	A gang member who makes money
Bama	A person who can't dress
Bang	To fight to kill
Battle	To compete (i.e., as in freestyle rapping)
Blood	A member of a Los Angeles gang whose color is red
Blunt	A marijuana cigarette
Crab	A derogatory name for a Crip
Crip	A member of a Los Angeles gang whose color is blue
Cuz	A greeting, primarily used for Crip members
Down	To meet expectations
Five-0	The police
Fly girl	A very attractive female
Gangbanging	To participate in gang activity
Gat	A gun
Hay shen	A term for crack cocaine
Head up	To fight one-on-one
Hezee	A home or house
Highroller	A Crip term for someone in the gang who makes much money
Homeboy/homie	Someone from the neighborhood or gang
Hood	The neighborhood or turf
Jet	To go or leave
Jumped in	To be initiated into a gang, usually by getting beaten up
Kickin' it	To hang out with the gang
Knockin boots	To have sex
Loco	A crazy person
No diggity	To accept as the truth
OG	An original gangster; a designation awarded when someone has killed someone
Peel	To kill
Rifa	To rule
Salty (you)	To think you know everything
Set	An individual gang
Smoke	To kill
Snaps	A term for money
Sur	South or southside
Tecato	Heroin addict
Tray-eight	A .38-caliber handgun
Whadup dawg	A way of greeting friends
Yash	A greeting used on the telephone to attract attention

Sources: Adapted from several online sources, including Gang Busters, Inc., "Gangs Terminology" www.gang-busters.com/terms/html/terms.html; Mike Carlie, "Into the Abyss: Journey into the World of Street Gangs," courses.smsu.edu/ mkc096f/gangbook; Robert Walker, Gangs OR Us, www.gangsorus.com/slang.html; www.velocity.net/~acekc/ gangslang.htm.

EXHIBIT 16-11	Names of Some Youth Gangs Operating in the United States

3-D Kings	Insane Ganger Disciples
10th Street Thugs	Latin Counts
Asian Boyz	Latin Disciples
Asian Family	Latin Eagles
Asian Gangsters	Latin Force
Baby Demons	Latin Kings
Bad Boys	Locos
Black Angels	Maniac Latin Disciples
Black Gangster Disciples	Mara Salvatrucha
Bloods	Masters of Destruction
Born to Kill	Mexican Mafia
Brown Mexican Pride	Midnight Crypts
Crips	Natoma
Devil Boys	Nazi Low Riders
Dogg Pound	Playboy Gangster Crips
Fourth World Mafia	T-Dogs
Gangster Disciples	Toy Soldiers
Gaylords	Vice Lords
Hmong Nation	Young Bloods
Hollywood Criminals	West Side Crips
Imperial Vice Lords	Wetback Power
Insane Cobras	

Note: Some of the groups listed here also contain adult members, although youth "branches" consist primarily of members ages 12 to 24.
Sources: Adapted from Florida Department of Corrections, "Security Threat Groups in Florida," retrieved June 20, 2005, from www.dc.state.fi.us/pub/gangs/fi.html; Massachusetts Department of Corrections, "Gang Security Threat Group Information," retrieved June 20, 2005, from www.state.ma.us/doc/gang/Ganglist.htm; and Robert Walker, "Gangs in the United States," retrieved June 20, 2005, from www.gangsorus.com/usgangs.html.

Talking about CORRECTIONS

JUVENILE JUSTICE PROGRAMMING

Visit *Live Talk* at **Corrections.com** (www.justicestudies.com/talking04) and listen to the program "Juvenile Justice Programming," which relates to ideas discussed in this chapter.

first ACA-certified corrections executive in the newly created juvenile corrections specialization area.[37] ACA now offers specialized juvenile certification in four categories: (1) Certified Corrections Executive/Juvenile (CCE/Juv); (2) Certified Corrections Manager/Juvenile (CCM/Juv); (3) Certified Corrections Supervisor/Juvenile (CCS/Juv); and (4) Certified Corrections Officer/Juvenile (CCO/Juv). According to Ania Dobrzansak, the juvenile justice grant manager for the ACA's Professional Development Department, "The public image of juvenile corrections has evolved considerably. What was once viewed as a punitive warehousing operation is now recognized as a multifaceted specialization that involves in-depth knowledge of the juvenile offender's personality and behavior; and on the part of the juvenile corrections worker, interpersonal communication skills, motivation, commitment to teamwork and integrity."[38]

Since it was founded in 1870, the ACA has advocated juvenile justice reform. In a recent campaign for juvenile justice reform, the ACA called for:

- legislative and community action to fund and operate early-intervention strategies;
- support of continued research and responsible action based on the results of research already available on prevention programs that work;
- support of system reforms that allow juvenile justice officials, family, social, educational, and other agencies and institutions to relate to a specific child and to work together for the best interests of the child, including accountability or shared use of confidential information about children at risk;

- support of programs that address the causes of violent and delinquent activity in communities;
- opposition to efforts to establish automatic certification of juvenile offenders to adult status for certain offenses;
- opposition to determinate sentencing for juvenile offenders; and
- support of the use of confidential systems for information sharing about juvenile offenders.[39]

EXHIBIT 16–12 **American Correctional Association**

Juvenile Justice Policy Statement

Introduction

The juvenile justice system must provide a continuum of services, programs, and facilities that ensure maximum opportunity for rehabilitation. These should place a high priority on providing individualized care and rehabilitative services to juvenile offenders throughout the juvenile justice system. To implement this policy, juvenile justice officials and agencies should:

- educate the public on the reasons it is in their best interest to promote, support, participate in, and fund those programs that have proven effective in preventing delinquency and producing healthy, positive, and socially responsible children and adolescents;
- establish and maintain effective communication with those who can have an impact on the juvenile to achieve the fullest possible cooperation in making appropriate decisions in individual cases and in providing and using services and resources;
- provide a range of non-residential and residential programs and services in the least restrictive manner, consistent with the needs of individual offenders and the protection of the public;
- engage the family, whenever practical, in the development and implementation of the juvenile's treatment plan;
- operate a juvenile classification system to identify the risk and needs of the juvenile offender, and develop an individualized treatment plan based on this assessment;
- advocate for the separation of status offenders from adjudicated delinquent offenders in the same facilities;
- provide a range of non-secure and secure short-term detention pending adjudication;
- advocate for the separation of adjudicated from pre-adjudicated youth in the same housing units;
- provide planned re-entry services for youth returning from residential placement;
- establish written policies and procedures that will protect the rights and safety of the juvenile, the victim, and the public in as balanced a manner as possible;
- establish procedures to safeguard the accuracy and use of juvenile records and support limitations on their use according to approved national standards, recognizing that the need to safeguard the privacy and rehabilitative goals of the juvenile should be balanced with concern for the protection of the public, including victims;
- develop performance outcome measures from which program effectiveness and system operations can be assessed; and
- implement research and evaluation initiatives that will measure the effectiveness of juvenile justice programs.

Source: Copyright © American Correctional Association.

Cambodian gang members in Long Beach, California. Juvenile gangs are a national problem, but they also permeate correctional settings—where they are called security threat groups, or STGs. How can the influence of STGs be reduced inside facilities such as detention centers?

Juvenile justice officials and the courts rely on the ACA for guidance. The ACA responds to more than 20,000 members, disseminating information, establishing advisory standards for juvenile corrections, providing technical assistance, and training juvenile corrections personnel (Exhibit 16–12).

REVIEW & APPLICATIONS

REFLECTIONS ON THE FUTURE

The Increasing Problem of Juvenile Crime: Resources and Knowledge to Reduce Delinquency

by Alan C. Youngs, Lakewood Colorado, Police Department (retired)

Juvenile victimization, violence, and crime are some of the most critical issues of the 21st century.

Instances of youth-violence have been widely publicized, such as the April 20, 1999, Columbine High School shootings. In the wake of recent and highly visible incidents of youth violence, many communities have begun youth service improvement initiatives. Schools, law enforcement agencies, and communities have started to form partnerships to curtail youth violence. Juvenile justice organizations are planning with victim services

agencies, mental health organizations, parks and recreation departments, human and social services agencies, child welfare offices, and private industry to address youth problems. The improvement initiatives are often based on thorough assessments of the problems of troubled youth and work by inventorying the best practices in the nation for serving youth.

If funding of problems is a predictor, then the Office of Juvenile Justice and Delinquency Prevention's (OJJDP) "Best Practices in Juvenile Accountability Overview"[1] provides a look

into the future. It states that the following community goals should be funded:

- Develop and administer accountability-based sanctions for juvenile offenders.
- Hire additional juvenile judges, probation officers, and court-appointed defenders and fund pretrial services for juveniles.
- Hire additional prosecutors so cases can be prosecuted and backlogs reduced.
- Provide funding to enable prosecutor to effectively address problems

related to drugs, gangs, and youth violence.

- Provide funding for technology, equipment, and training to assist prosecutors in identifying violent juvenile offenders and expediting their prosecution.
- Provide funding to enable juvenile courts and probation offices to be more effective in reducing recidivism.
- Establish court-based juvenile justice programs that target young firearms offenders through the creation of juvenile gun courts.
- Establish drug court programs to provide continuing judicial supervision over juvenile offenders with substance abuse problems.
- Establish and maintain interagency information-sharing programs that enable the juvenile and criminal justice systems, schools, and social services agencies to make more informed decisions regarding the early identification, control, supervision, and treatment of juveniles

who repeat serious delinquent or criminal acts.

- Establish and maintain accountability-based programs that work with juvenile offenders who are referred by law enforcement agencies or programs that are designed in cooperation with law enforcement officials.

A juvenile justice system given the resources and knowledge to match juveniles with appropriate treatment programs while holding them accountable for their behavior can have a positive and lasting impact on the reduction of delinquency.

According to OJJDP, the organizations with the best practices for the future will recognize each youth's developmental stage and build on each youth's developmental stage and build on each youth's individual strengths. They will combine restorative restitution and community service with victim input. They will teach juvenile offenders how to make positive choices and resolve disputes and help them

understand how their actions affected their victims. They will use flexible, graduated sanctions and empower families to support positive activities for youth and success in school. Finally, they will connect youth with prosocial peers and conduct program activities in neighborhoods for all youth including those coming back to the community after confinement.[2]

NOTES
1. Juvenile Accountability Incentive Block Grants Program, *Best Practices in Juvenile Accountability: Overview* (Washington, DC: JAIBG, April 2003).
2. Adapted from J. Robert Flores, Administrator, "Best Practices in Juvenile Accountability: Overview," *JAIBG Bulletin*, April 2003.

About the Author

Alan C. Youngs is a retired division chief from the Lakewood, Colorado, Police Department, where he served for 33 years. He is currently a practicing attorney involving Police Civil Liability and Immigration Law. He is president of The Youngs Group, based in Denver, Colorado.

SUMMARY

1 *Parens patriae* is a legal philosophy that is used to justify intervention in children's lives when their parents are unwilling or unable to care for them.

2 Houses of refuge, the first legally chartered custodial institutions for juvenile offenders, were established in the early 19th century. Reform schools, which were established in the middle of the 19th century, sought to reform rather than punish young offenders through vocational (especially trade and industrial), physical, and military education. Reform schools for girls used "cottagelike" residential units. Industrial schools emerged in the latter part of the 19th century and emphasized vocational training for youthful offenders.

3 The first completely separate juvenile court in the United States was established in Cook County (Chicago), Illinois, in 1899 and had jurisdiction over youths who committed acts that would be crimes if they had been committed by adults and over youths who were in danger of growing up to be paupers or in need of supervision. By 1945, separate juvenile courts had been established in all states.

4 Six U.S. Supreme Court decisions established due process rights for juvenile offenders:

- *Kent* v. *United States* (1966)—a juvenile who is to be transferred to adult criminal court is entitled to a hearing, representation by an attorney, access to records being considered by the juvenile court, and a statement of reasons for the transfer.

- *In re Gault* (1967)—in a proceeding that might result in commitment to an institution, a juvenile is entitled to reasonable notice of charges, counsel, questioning of witnesses, and protection against self-incrimination.

- *In re Winship* (1970)—proof beyond a reasonable doubt, not simply a preponderance of the evidence, is required during the adjudicatory stage for a delinquent offense.

- *McKeiver* v. *Pennsylvania* (1971)—trial by jury is not a constitutional requirement for juvenile adjudication.
- *Breed* v. *Jones* (1975)—transfer to adult criminal court after juvenile court adjudication constitutes double jeopardy.
- *Schall* v. *Martin* (1984)—preventive pretrial detention of juveniles is allowable under certain circumstances.

5 Most cases handled by the juvenile courts are for delinquent offenses—acts committed by a juvenile that if they had been committed by an adult could result in criminal prosecution. The remaining cases are for status offenses—acts that are offenses only when committed by juveniles. Such offenses include running away, truancy, ungovernability, and liquor law violations.

6 Juvenile delinquents are young people, usually under age 18, who commit acts that if they had been committed by an adult could result in criminal prosecution. The typical juvenile offender is a 16-year-old white male property offender.

7 The three stages of the juvenile justice process are intake, adjudication, and disposition. During the intake stage, a court-appointed officer recommends a course of action—dismissal, informal disposition, formal disposition, or, in some instances, transfer to adult criminal court—for a juvenile who has been referred to the juvenile court. Adjudication is judicial determination of guilt or innocence. Disposition is judicial imposition of the most appropriate sanction.

8 Disposition for the majority of juvenile offenders is probation. Other dispositions include placement in group homes, residential treatment centers, juvenile boot camps, or juvenile correctional institutions.

9 Teen court, an alternative to the traditional juvenile court, operates under one of four models: Adult Judge (an adult serves as judge); Youth Judge (a youth serves as judge); Tribunal (youth attorneys present the case to youth judges); or Peer Jury (a youth or adult presents the case to a youth jury). Common teen court dispositions are apologies, educational and/or counseling programs, restitution, and community service.

10 A gang is a group of individuals involved in continuing criminal activity. Youth gangs are a serious problem for juvenile correctional professionals. For some juvenile institutions, gang affiliation is an important consideration in housing arrangements.

KEY TERMS

parens patriae, p. 623
reform school, p. 624
delinquent offenses, *p. 630*
status offenses, *p. 631*
intake, *p. 631*
juvenile detention facility, *p. 632*
detention hearing, *p. 632*

guardian *ad litem, p. 633*
juvenile court, *p. 633*
disposition, *p. 634*
predisposition report, *p. 634*
group home, *p. 635*
residential treatment center, *p. 637*
blended sentencing, *p. 637*

waiver provisions, *p. 642*
direct file provisions, *p. 643*
statutory exclusion provisions, *p. 643*
teen courts, *p. 643*
gang, *p. 647*
youth gang, *p. 647*
street gang, *p. 647*

QUESTIONS FOR REVIEW

1 Explain the principle of *parens patriae.*

2 Distinguish among houses of refuge, reform schools, and industrial schools.

3 Where and when was the first completely separate juvenile court established?

4 What significant U.S. Supreme Court rulings established due process rights for juveniles? What impact did each have on juvenile court proceedings?

5 What is a *delinquent offense?* A *status offense?*

6 What is the typical juvenile delinquent's age? Gender? Race?

7 Identify and explain the three stages of the juvenile justice process.

8 What are the three provisions for transferring juveniles to adult criminal court?

9 Describe the four teen court models discussed in this chapter.

10 How do youth gangs impact correctional facilities for juveniles?

THINKING CRITICALLY ABOUT CORRECTIONS

Sentencing Project

The Sentencing Project reports that abuse (physical and sexual) and suicide rates are higher for children who serve time in adult correctional institutions than for those held in juvenile correctional institutions—youths held in adult institutions are 7.7 times more likely to commit suicide, 5 times more likely to be sexually assaulted, twice as likely to be beaten by staff, and 50 percent more likely to be attacked with a weapon.[40] What conclusions might you draw from this report?

Public Access to Juvenile Court Proceedings

Juvenile court proceedings are becoming more accessible to the public. At least 21 states now permit open juvenile court proceedings for serious or violent crime charges or repeat offenses. In 1995, Georgia passed a law allowing the public admission to adjudicatory hearings for youths who have been charged with delinquent offenses.

1. Do you think juvenile court proceedings should be open to the public?

2. Why or why not?

ON-THE-JOB DECISION MAKING

Youth Violence

In recent months, there has been a spate of violent crimes committed by youthful offenders in your community, including numerous murders, assaults, rapes, and armed robberies. Gang violence, in particular, seems to be escalating.

Josh McFadden, a crusading journalist in your town, has been whipping up public sentiment for the inclusion of a "get-tough" referendum on the upcoming ballot. In daily newspaper articles and during frequent guest appearances on local television programs, McFadden beats the same old drum: It's time to treat all criminals as criminals, no matter what their age, he says. His strident calls for abolition of delinquency laws and automatic waiver to adult court of all juveniles who commit violent felonies seem to be touching a nerve.

You are a juvenile probation officer. You and your co-workers truly believe juveniles need special handling that is different from what they would receive in the adult criminal justice system.

In recent weeks, you have been flooded with requests to appear on various discussion panels. Your supervisor has been reluctant to enter the fray but authorizes you to participate in an upcoming panel discussion to be televised within the community. Josh McFadden will be on the panel.

1. What issues would you present to support retention of the current procedures for handling juvenile offenders?

2. How would you address the waiver of jurisdiction to adult court question?

Teen Court

Read the following case:

IN THE MATTER OF: BETH LEONARD

CHARGES: Three (3) counts of retail theft.

Hoover police were summoned to the Hoover Mall branch store of Fancy This on March 17, 2000, at 11:20 A.M. regarding a shoplifter. Beth Leonard, a 16-year-old high school honor student, was arrested at 11:52 A.M. for three (3) counts of retail theft.

An employee noticed Beth entering the dressing room with a blue short outfit and a swimsuit. Beth exited the dressing room carrying only her purse. After a quick scan of the room, the attendant, unable to locate the clothes, called security. Beth was led to the manager's office, where she confessed to putting the items on under her clothing and attempting to leave.

When the police arrived, they asked for identification and discovered a bottle of Spring Musk Perfume bearing a new, undamaged sales sticker in Beth's purse. Upon prompting, Beth admitted that she had taken this item from the Perfumeria, a mall perfume store.

A further search of Beth's purse revealed two pairs of earrings with sales stickers from Carter's, a mall accessory shop. Beth admitted to taking these items without purchasing them.

While searching Beth's purse, the officer located her wallet and found $85 in cash. When asked why she didn't just pay for the items, Beth stated she was planning to purchase a gift for her parents' wedding anniversary.

A conference was later held between Beth, her parents, and the arresting officer. During this conference, Beth stated that all her girlfriends did this and they never got caught. She was dared by one to bring certain items to her with the sales tags still intact to prove that she had not paid for them. It was dumb, but she did it, and she was sorry.

1. If you were the intake officer handling this case, would you recommend that a teen court handle it?

2. Why or why not?

LIVE LINKS

at www.justicestudies.com/livelinks04

16–1 A Century of Juvenile Justice

This document examines multiple forces that have substantially impacted the juvenile justice system during the 20th century. An examination of shifts in policy and practice over time provides a valuable foundation for envisioning justice for youths in the 21st century. First, the document describes the development of the juvenile justice system, underscoring major eras in its evolution. It then examines trends in four broad areas that have shaped the juvenile justice system: (1) social constructions of childhood and delinquency; (2) the role of criminological theory and measurement; (3) juvenile crime patterns as represented primarily in official reports; and (4) general social, economic, and cultural trends, including patterns of change in the larger criminal justice system. Finally, there is an examination of the possibilities for at least ameliorating some of the seemingly intractable dilemmas of justice for youths.

16–2 Into the Abyss: A Personal Journey into the World of Street Gangs

This groundbreaking Web-based work on the youth gang subculture provides access to more than 2,300 useful links to gang-related information.

16–3 Brick by Brick: Dismantling the Border Between Juvenile and Adult Justice

This chapter reviews the origins of juvenile justice in the United States, summarizes the legislative and policy changes that are essentially dismantling the juvenile–criminal border, and examines research on the impact of such policies. The discussion concludes with a review of issues that should be prominent in any debate about the future viability of the juvenile justice–criminal justice boundary.

PRO
FES
SIO

PROFESSIONALISM IN CORRECTIONS

" "

Professionals have a love for their work that is above that of employment merely to receive a paycheck.

—Judge Arlin Adams, United States Court of Appeals, 1989

CHAPTER OBJECTIVES

After completing this chapter you should be able to do the following:

1 List the pressures that corrections faces as a result of the expansion of prison construction.

2 List the ways that advances in technology help corrections.

3 Discuss the impact of 9/11 on corrections budgets.

4 Outline the results of the Correctional Education Association's three-state recidivism study of education.

5 Discuss why it is difficult to recruit correctional staff.

6 Discuss professionalism among the execution team.

7 Discuss the nature of professionalism.

8 Describe the differences between a professional and a nonprofessional.

9 Describe the ways a correctional leader can foster professionalism.

10 Explain what professional development is and list three ways it can be achieved in corrections.

This chapter was contributed by William Sondervan, EdD, CCE, with the assistance of Ania Dobrzanska, MS, CCM. Dr. Sondervan is Professor and Director of Criminal Justice, Investigative Forensics and Legal Studies at the University of Maryland. From 2003 to 2006, he served as director of Professional Development at the American Correctional Association. In 1999, Dr. Sondervan was appointed commissioner of the Maryland Division of Corrections. He served as commissioner until 2003. Dr. Sondervan earned a BS in business administration from the College of New Jersey, an EdM in counseling psychology from Boston University, an MPA in criminal justice from Jacksonville State University, and an EdD in adult education and human resource development from Virginia Polytechnic Institution and State University. Dobrzanska is Program Coordinator with the Moss Group, Inc., Washington, DC. She earned a BA in psychology and administration of justice from Rutgers University, and an MS in justice, law, and society at American University.

William Sondervan, EdD, CCE, Professor and Director of Criminal Justice, Investigative Forensic and Legal Studies, University of Maryland, previously served as director of Professional Development at the American Correctional Association and commissioner of the Maryland Division of Corrections. Given the opportunity, what questions about correctional professionalism would you ask Dr. Sondervan?

This discussion supplements the previous chapters of *Corrections in the 21st Century*.[1] It is intended to provide insight into many of the topics and issues outlined earlier in the text as they relate to professionalism in corrections. The material should prove relevant and valuable to individuals preparing for a career in corrections and, hopefully, will provide guidelines to aid in answering three key questions:

1. What is professionalism in corrections?
2. How does one foster professionalism, and how does it impact the correctional environment?
3. What can a correctional administrator do to ensure that professionalism will be maintained?

To begin to answer these questions, one must understand the unique climate of the correctional environment and, more importantly, the current issues and challenges facing corrections today.

Corrections work is stressful, hazardous, and always challenging. Faced with staggering budget cuts and burgeoning prison populations, correctional administrators struggle to balance limited resources to meet management and treatment demands.

After 50 years of relative stability in the proportion of people incarcerated, the prison population doubled in size between 1970 and 1982; between 1982 and 1999, it increased threefold.[2] With over 2 million Americans behind bars in the nation's prisons and jails, corrections faces pandemic overcrowding, frustrating density, the arrival of younger offenders with more serious needs, and greater numbers of female inmates. Further, corrections must deal with limited resources for inmate programs, high turnover rates, and difficulty in recruiting and training correctional workers.

TODAY'S CHALLENGES

The Expansion of Prison Construction

More than half of all the prisons in the United States have been built within the past 20 years.[3] With an average of four prisons being constructed every month, we are building more prisons than schools. "The United States has a higher per capita incarceration rate than any other industrialized democracy."[4]

This continuing growth has resulted in our nation's prisons and jails being taxed to near breaking-point levels in many areas. For the first time in history, prison construction—estimated at $6 billion a year—has appeared as a public investment opportunity listed on the stock exchange. Scott Christianson found that in Texas, the competition for prison construction during the early 1990s grew so fierce that some communities offered free country club memberships and other perks to prison officials as an incentive to get them to make the right siting decision.[5] To keep up with the rapid prison growth, corrections faces tremendous pressure to recruit, hire, train, and maintain quality staff to run these facilities in a professional manner.

Overcrowding, one of the most pressing problems, has created the dilemma of having to admit more inmates than there is available space. Obviously, overcrowding places enormous strain on classification, housing assignments, food, medical services, and the already limited spaces for treatment programs. This causes tension among inmates and places more pressure on the staff charged with maintaining order within the institutions. Every potential outbreak of violence must be detected and prevented to preserve staff and inmate safety.

Who Is Entering Our Jails and Prisons?

As society changes over time, corrections must stay on top of the game and keep up with the changes in the characteristics of the growing prison population. Today, prisoners with more serious needs are entering the system, and their needs are often unmet. Women have been the fastest-growing prison population segment. The number of women in U.S. prisons and jails is now about 10 times greater than the number of women incarcerated in all of western Europe.[6] Today, 60 percent of all women in the nation's prisons are serving time for either drug or property offenses. The increase in the women's population creates expensive demands for programs and amenities to meet gender-specific needs such as gynecological services.

Increasing budget cuts make it more and more difficult to meet the treatment needs of shifting population trends. Prisons are increasingly taking in disproportionate numbers of minority inmates—unskilled, uneducated, poor, city-raised blacks and Hispanics.

Research shows that 75 percent of the total prison population serves time for nonviolent sentences. The number of Americans incarcerated for drug-related offenses has skyrocketed. Special populations (i.e., offenders who are elderly, mentally ill, and physically disabled) have significantly increased. One out of six inmates coming into the system is mentally ill. With limited resources and greater budget cuts, corrections is under tremendous pressure to provide inmate programs and train staff to stay current about the more complex needs of the incoming prison population.

New Technology

The overwhelming growth in prison and jail populations has yielded an increase in the rates of violence in our prisons and jails. Coupled with the crowding and density, this violence has made it more difficult to manage the facilities. Not known for its innovative use of technology, corrections struggles to effectively perform its work with the limited resources available. Whereas U.S. corporations and industries have flourished as a result of technological advances, corrections has, for the most part, fallen well behind.

In many cases, fiscal resources simply are not available to provide the equipment needed. In situations where hardware and software are available, little has been done to blend the myriad databases into a smoothly flowing information system. Consequently, corrections faces problems in records accuracy and in both internal and external information exchange—problems that can critically impact public safety.

New technology is being implemented within the correctional field, but the process remains slow. Advances in technology help correctional staff communicate, observe, detect contraband, document, evaluate, interrogate, and perform all aspects of business at faster speeds and with greater accuracy. While this helps staff members keep pace with increasing management demands, it brings with it new requirements, such as training in the use of new technologies and the need to shift limited dollars from inmate programs and security. Although technology systems allow jobs to be performed faster, safer, and more effectively, they also result in high maintenance costs, labor relations conflicts, inmate climate issues, and political concerns.

In addition to meeting the technological challenges, correctional staff must deal with complex issues that have become more prominent in recent years. There are more gangs in prisons and jails. Gangs emerged with new power and influence in many jurisdictions, challenging the ability of the prison administration to control the prison environment.[7] For example, correctional officers trying to crack down on inmate drug use may receive death threats, necessitating appropriate preventive measures.

Terry L. Stewart, former director of the Arizona Department of Corrections (ADC), is a victim of an ongoing death threat against him and his family. In 1997, Director Stewart implemented a special management policy as a control measure for gang activity within the ADC prison system. When ADC inmates became aware of the department's new strategy for managing violent gang activity, the Aryan Brotherhood, a major prison gang, set forth the first known assassination plot to kill Stewart.

Two years later, in 1998, there were two separate attempts to assassinate Stewart by *La EME* (the Mexican Mafia). The Phoenix Police Department, in cooperation with the ADC, indicted several EME gang members. In 2001, members of the Aryan Brotherhood conspired to have Stewart assassinated by means of an explosive device. Today, law enforcement intelligence indicates that Stewart remains a priority target for gang assassination. The ADC has recovered two separate hit lists from different Mexican Mafia associates; both have Stewart listed as "Kill on Sight."

The Effects of 9/11

Incarceration has always been an expensive proposition, but the economic downturn brought about by the terrorist attacks of September 11, 2001, has made the situation even more critical. In preparation for attacks by terrorists, more funding has been allocated to homeland security, at great cost to prison systems nationwide. Funding to various correctional agencies has been significantly cut, forcing several states to postpone prison construction, downsize prison space by closing housing units, and, in some states, close entire prisons. Correctional organizations already operating on slim budgets continue to face pressure to maintain secure facilities and offer programming to rehabilitate inmates.

The Public Image of Corrections

Although correctional administrators continually work toward meeting ever-growing demands, their efforts often go unnoticed or are misunderstood. Much of the public has a negative view of corrections. Prison administrators have been burdened by the weight of stereotypes of corrections, and labels such as "garbage bins of society," "human warehouses," "human dumping grounds," "storage bins," and "schools of crime" are often associated with our nation's prisons.

Prisons are frequently subject to public scrutiny. Media distortion in the coverage of crime, prisons, prison administration, custody, and prisoners is not uncommon. Accordingly, the practice of corrections has been mischaracterized and misrepresented. Public perceptions about who is a criminal come, in part, from television or newspapers. But the media fail to fully explore the operations of prison and frequently paint a picture that closely mirrors stereotypical views.

Numerous articles appeared in prominent publications following the scandal at the military's Abu Ghraib prison in Iraq. Unfortunately, however, prisons and prison administrators in this country have been unjustly linked to the events in the Iraqi military prison. Several of the articles claimed that the American public should not be surprised by the events at Abu Ghraib because similar incidents routinely occur in American prisons and jails.

As a result, correctional officers became the victims of the stereotype of correctional officers as corrupt, unprofessional, abusive, and inhumane. On May 4, 2004, a *New York Times* article cited several examples of physical and sexual abuse of prisoners, specifically naming the states that were involved. Such reports served to reinforce a negative view of corrections. Overwhelmingly, correctional staff members are highly qualified, properly trained professionals. Incidents of mistreatment are rare. When they do occur, corrective action is typically firm and swift.

Prisons, like most other public institutions, are not perfect, but change and improvement have been ongoing over the last 30 years:

> There are fewer conditions of confinement lawsuits, staff are better trained, prisoner health services are greatly improved, national standards have been promulgated, prisons have become accredited, and the number of homicides has dropped—in fact, the likelihood of dying in a prison is substantially less than the likelihood of dying outside a prison.[8]

The field of corrections is improving. The process, however, remains slow and difficult, primarily because the necessary funding is simply not available. This directly impacts correctional administrators' ability to recruit quality employees, provide essential intensive training, encourage continuous professional development learning efforts, and, ultimately, foster professionalism.

Safety First

Despite these disheartening economic realities, the demands placed on correctional leaders and staffs continue to grow. Corrections administrators need to find ways to decrease costs without sacrificing security.

Corrections administrators do not promote a culture of violence. They see the mission of a professional correctional system as delivery of safe and secure corrections services. To that end, proper disciplinary actions are taken in response to incidents of violence. "People are sent to prison as punishment, not for punishment."[9] Corrections practitioners feel obligated to keep prisons a safe environment that encourages inmates to rehabilitate themselves and staff to facilitate the inmates' rehabilitative efforts.

Inmate Programs Second

With severe correctional budget cuts, prisons struggle to obtain money for inmate programs. With few rehabilitative, treatment, vocational, and educational programs, prisons have not done nearly enough to ensure decreased recidivism. Reentry, as it stands, is one of the most pressing problems we face as a nation. Every day, 1,600 ex-offenders walk out of prison with minimal skills and education, no savings, debt, no unemployment benefits, few employment prospects, and low ties to the community.[10] National statistics indicate that 7 of every 10 prisoners function at the two lowest levels of literacy.[11] Simply put, at that literacy level, they are not able to fill out a job application.

An officer pays his respect to Illinois Department of Corrections' most recent fallen hero, Anthony "Tony" Lee, who was killed in a traffic accident April 12, 2007, while transporting industry products from Illinois River Correctional Industries to Hill Correctional Industries. What threats to life does a correctional officer face on a daily basis?

Today, the needs of ex-offenders are more serious than ever before. Due to the scarcity of programs, however, those needs are often unmet. The majority of ex-offenders need substance abuse treatment, yet only a small fraction have the opportunity to receive it. A greater number of offenders with mental illness are coming through the system; one out of six inmates takes psychotropic medications for mental disorders. Upon release, without adequate health care, they are unable to receive and pay for prescribed psychotropic medications and often relapse, returning to prison.

Within three years, 67 percent of released ex-offenders recidivate; 75 percent recidivate within five years, and the literature shows that only one out of four ex-offenders remains a law-abiding citizen. The importance of inmate programs cannot be overstated. If recidivism is to decrease, reentry planning must begin from the first day of incarceration—a difficult task to accomplish in light of the dwindling resources. It is essential that we find ways to reintegrate ex-offenders into society, because each and every one of us has a stake in what comes out of our prisons.

performance-based funding

A method of allocating money for programs that present reliable and valid data that they work.

With decreased funding and a post-Martinson skepticism about rehabilitation (see Chapter 3), states became focused on **performance-based funding**, allocating money for the programs that presented reliable and valid data that they work. Research and evaluation should automatically be a part of any correctional program effort and should be considered an essential element of any budget.[12] Institutions must find not only *what works* but also *how it works* and *for whom* it is effective.

Correctional education is one inmate program that does work. Although education has played a role in the mission of the prison throughout its history, that role has been affected by the systemic conflict between security and treatment.

Presently, correctional education is the product of scattered attempts to offer prisoners an opportunity to construct meaningful lives both in prison and following release. In the early 1970s, correctional education administrators considered the need for funds to expand programs and staff, purchase educational materials and technology, and provide additional vocational training opportunities for the offender to be their top priority.[13] Studies have documented the need for instructional materials, a lack of funds, and a shortage of books and other teaching aids. Most states had neither a full-time curriculum specialist nor a media specialist on their staff. Unfortunately, we have not seen much progress since then. Those needs are still not being met.

With greater emphasis on performance-based funding, the Correctional Education Association (CEA), with funding from the U.S. Department of Education, conducted a three-year, three-state recidivism study.[14] The Three-State Recidivism Study of Correctional Education compared correctional education participants and nonparticipants in Maryland, Minnesota, and Ohio to assess the impact of correctional education on recidivism and postrelease employment. The study consisted of a 3,099-inmate cohort, making it one of the most comprehensive studies ever conducted in correctional education. The participants were mostly male (87 percent).

The study found strong support for educating incarcerated offenders. The Three-State Recidivism Study confirmed that correctional education significantly reduced long-term recidivism for inmates released in late 1997 and early 1998. For each state the measures of recidivism—rearrest, reconviction, and reincarceration—were significantly lower. Correctional education participants had statistically significant lower rates of rearrest

(48 percent) compared to nonparticipants (57 percent) and had reincarceration rates (21 percent) lower than those of nonparticipants (31 percent).

Recruitment

With the prison boom, the number of correctional employees has doubled since the 1980s:

> The corrections system now employs more than 716,000 persons, with a total monthly payroll of $2.1 billion. The total number of U.S. citizens employed by the justice system has increased so rapidly relative to the entire U.S. population that approximately 1.5 percent of the nation's entire labor force now works in the justice system.[15]

Despite the needed increase of correctional staff, the corrections profession remains in critical status because the turnover rate remains high.

Recognizing the critical status of the correctional workforce, the American Correctional Association embarked on a project titled "Building a Strategic Workforce Plan for the Corrections Profession." Although still under way, the study's initial data clearly show the difficulty of recruiting and retaining personnel, especially correctional officers.

Cast in a negative light, correctional administrators feel additional pressure to perform their jobs efficiently. Adding to this quandary is the increasing difficulty of attracting and retaining qualified personnel. As noted, funds to support salary enhancements have become all too scarce. The entry pay for corrections officers in adult facilities in 2007 varied from $20,124 in West Virginia to $45,549 in New Jersey.[16] Inadequate pay for corrections officers, as compared to law enforcement personnel and others recruited from the same workforce pool, is widely blamed for the continuing recruiting and retention difficulties. Individuals possessing associate and bachelor's degrees or even high school diplomas are unwilling to accept the low starting wage offered by prisons and jails, particularly when other fields of endeavor offer a more comfortable and safer work environment with greater compensation.

Other frequently cited causes of recruiting difficulties include burdensome hours and shift work, a shortage of qualified applicants, and the undesirable location of some corrections facilities. Individuals who do enter the corrections field, even those satisfied with their jobs, often leave as raises and other incentives continue to dry up. High rates of turnover among corrections officers result mainly from demanding hours and shift work, inadequate compensation, stress and burnout, poor initial selection of candidates, competition from other law enforcement and security agencies, poor career prospects, and poorly qualified supervisors. Consequently, there is constant pressure for continuous recruitment to replace departing officers. System growth, due to growing inmate populations, compounds the recruitment problem.[17]

The Importance of Training

Faced with staggering budget cuts and a spurt in prison population growth, corrections is struggling to utilize available limited resources to balance management with treatment. Simply put, training, leader development, salary enhancements, infrastructure repairs, drug treatment, education, and so on have been sacrificed so that prisons and jails could continue to operate in an efficient manner. The importance of training cannot be overstated. Lack of proper training may result in poor decision making, and the consequences may be problematic (e.g., the scandal at the Abu Ghraib prison).

For example, lack of proper-use-of-force training may result in poor decision making at a critical moment where a life or lives may be in jeopardy. Correctional administrators ensure development of and adequate staff training in appropriate policies and procedures. With limited resources, it is challenging for corrections administrators to recruit qualified staff and skilled field training officers, introduce new technology, and train staff in vital skills such as communication. Officers must be trained to initially respond verbally to a situation that requires potential use of force. Without proper equipment (i.e., cameras) and funding for training, everyone is at risk.

Execution Teams

Executioners are not a popular topic. We think of executioners as grisly, cold-blooded men and may wonder how they sleep at night. Our image of the executioner is often misleading and misunderstood.

Executions are complex and very difficult processes that require a high level of training and professionalism. Candidates who volunteer to serve on the execution team are carefully screened to weed out those who may experience adverse reactions to performing execution duties.

Correctional officers on execution teams are typically very serious and solemn and highly professional. Their files are carefully studied, and their backgrounds are thoroughly checked. They are then interviewed by the warden, psychologically screened by a clinical psychologist, and, ultimately, approved by the members of the execution team. The team is a close-knit family that functions as a source of support—a unity that must be trusted. To cope with the experience, a clinical psychologist is assigned to work with the team throughout the entire process.

Well-trained officers who can "keep cool" are selected to join the execution team, and from there they are trained for the execution. "They participate in the execution process not for monetary benefit but due to a sense of professionalism and commitment." Countless rehearsals are meant to produce a confident group that is capable of fast and accurate performance under pressure.[18] At the end, the job is carried out with precision, humility, and teamwork.

Everyone must have and understand a shared purpose. The team members must have a good leader, be encouraged to utilize psychological services to assist in coping with the execution process, and, most important, be able to trust one another. The assignment is broken down into a series of tasks, and each executioner is assigned a task in which he or she will specialize (e.g., strapping the right leg).

Despite the common myth that today's executions are carried out by emotionless executioners, those who take part in the process are affected by the psychological burden. The process may run smoothly, efficiently, and professionally, yet, despite moral beliefs, it remains a difficult act with which everyone must learn to cope.

> When I got back home after [execution], I went to bed and stayed there for a month. During that month I lost thirty pounds. As soon as I was able to get out of bed, I went to the Adirondacks to recover my strength. But a change had come over me. I was oppressed by a feeling of anxiety and menace. I did not realize the trend of my subconscious thoughts until duty took me to the death chamber again and I stood on the edge of the rubber mat, within reach of the chair. On that occasion, just after I had given the signal for the current to be

turned on—while the man in the chair was straining against the straps as the load of 2,200 volts shot through his body—I felt for the first time a wild desire to extend my hand and touch him.[19]

Even officers with military combat service may have difficulties dealing with executions. As a retired military officer with combat experience, Dr. Sondervan was affected by an execution even though he did not expect himself to be. Shortly after the execution process, Commissioner Sondervan was committed to a hospital to undergo knee surgery. In the preparation process, a nurse inserted a needle into his arm. This automatically evoked a flashback of the execution by lethal injection. The feeling was overwhelming and frightening.

Professionalism is required in the execution process. The officers are well trained to ensure that the execution itself is done professionally. The goal is to carry out the execution as uneventfully as possible to avoid media sensationalism. The condemned are not dragged or weeping, but they seem to submit to it with some level of acceptance. No one on the execution team seeks to inflict suffering. The execution process is carried out as humanely as possible, without any room for abuse.

In the eyes of the executioner, the execution process is not killing, nor is it a vengeful act. It is a job to be done, a lawful sanction. Officers who volunteer to be on the execution team are committed to the process, working hard to carry it out in a professional and humane manner that will be least painful to all.

Inmates

Prisoner reentry is one of the most pressing problems we face as a nation. Most released prisoners are rearrested and return to prison.[20] The reality is that 95 percent of prisoners will be released at some point. Our goal should be to ensure that those released from prison do not return to a criminal lifestyle. According to a recent study by the Bureau of Justice Statistics, 30 percent of released prisoners (or nearly one in three) were rearrested in the first six months, 44 percent within the first year, and 67 percent within three years of release from prison.[21] Comparing these recidivism rates with a nearly identical study conducted in 1983,[22] rearrest rates increased by 5 percent.[23]

Ex-offenders have difficulty finding services such as housing, employment, and child care assistance. Upon release, they often find that the criminal lifestyle is the only alternative to homelessness and hunger. Helping ex-prisoners successfully return to society can greatly improve their chances of staying out of trouble. We must adopt a goal of reintegration, not exclusion. Rehabilitation and reintegration processes must start on day one, the day the inmate is convicted.

Once the facility is running safely and security is maintained, inmate programs must be made available. Today, reentry is more problematic because, while inmate populations are increasing, inmate programs are being cut back due to the unavailability of funding. Inmates participate in fewer programs because fewer programs are available. Low participation rates are likely a symptom of program availability, not a lack of interest or need.[24]

We must conduct inmate programs to prepare inmates to return to communities as law-abiding citizens. Inmate programs not only keep inmates busy but also help them acquire and maintain skills necessary for law-abiding life on the outside. It is easy to deny inmates free programs such as education, but we must recognize that we need to invest in what is going on in our nation's prisons because every single one of us has a very high stake in what comes out of these prisons.

PROFESSIONALISM

The Need for Professionalism

Concomitant with the rise of imprisonment, corrections became pressured to recruit qualified staff to manage prisons, maintain safety, and facilitate rehabilitation. Corrections is pressured to weed out unsatisfactory recruits as soon as possible, hire and train staff, correct operational deficiencies, offer programs to meet inmate needs, and effectively contribute to the reduction of recidivism, starting from day one.

How many COs did it take to push the inmate down the stairs? None—he fell by himself.[25]

Stories about correctional officers seem to reinforce a brutal stereotype. Despite the myth, the overwhelming majority of officers have a desire to improve the system. There are officers who believe that their role is to correct inmates and are motivated to facilitate rehabilitation. On the other hand, there are a few who think that rehabilitation is not their job. Consequently, it is imperative that corrections adopts a goal of professionalism and works on instilling proper values in its employees, not only fostering professionalism but also encouraging staff to strive for it.

What Is Professionalism?

The correctional environment is formidable. However, despite the stressors and pressures, the need to focus on changing the climate has become even more critical. Such change must begin with the most important element of the correctional environment—the staff. A spirit of professionalism must be cultivated and perpetuated among correctional personnel if correctional facilities are to operate efficiently and fulfill their function of maintaining public safety.

Professionalism is commitment to a set of agreed-upon values aimed toward the improvement of the organization while maintaining the highest standards of excellence and dissemination of knowledge. In addition to having knowledge and skills, professionals must present humanistic qualities: selflessness, responsibility and accountability, leadership, excellence, integrity, honesty, empathy, and respect for coworkers and prisoners.

Professional correctional organizations have qualified and well-trained employees, well-run professional development departments, and well-developed standards of conduct. Such organizations carry out all functions necessary to achieve a fair system, document and address inmate and employee conduct, and define common sets of values that set the tone and climate. They deliver a safe and secure corrections system, free of gangs and corruption, and value inmate programs to promote positive behavior change. To ensure quality inmate programs, the organization conducts empirically tested analyses on all programs for prisoners seeking rehabilitation.

The principal value of the professional correctional organization is professionalism. The vision of the professional organization is confidence that employees will be professional and will have integrity, respect, the ability

---

ETHICS & PROFESSIONALISM

IACTP's Trainers' Code of Ethics

The International Association of Correctional Training Personnel (IACTP) enhances public safety and the fair and humane treatment of offenders by promoting organizational and individual excellence in the profession of training. The Association affirms its responsibility to develop the spirit of professionalism within its membership, and to increase awareness of ethical principles in public service by example. To this end, we, the members of IACTP, commit ourselves to the following principles:

I Service

Serve correctional staff and the public, above self-interest.

IACTP members are committed to:

II Dignity

Demonstrate the highest standards in all activities to inspire confidence and trust in training.

III Professional Excellence & Competency

Strengthen individual capabilities and encourage the professional development of others.

IV Respect

Respect and support trainees and colleagues in the promotion of the field of training.

Ethical Dilemma 17–1: Why do corrections officers need a Code of Ethics that is somewhat distinct from that of traditional law enforcement officers? How do the ethical challenges of being a uniformed police officer compare with those of being a corrections officer? What are some of the ethical challenges that confront corrections officers that are not generally a concern for uniformed police? For more information, go to Ethical Dilemma 17–1 at www.justicestudies.com/ethics04.

Ethical Dilemma 17–2: In what way does the job of corrections officer require more professionalism than it did fifty years ago? What can be done to help foster more professionalism within the ranks of corrections officers? For more information, go to Ethical Dilemma 17–2 at justicestudies.com/ethics04.

Ethical Dilemmas for every chapter are available online.

Source: International Association of Correctional Training Personnel.

---

to engage in teamwork, the motivation for continued learning, and commitment to the profession. Professional organizations teach employees to be honest and accountable and to lead by example. Staff must recognize and value differences and act in a humane manner. It is important to trust coworkers, support each other, communicate effectively, and work together toward a common purpose—to ensure a safe, professional environment that encourages rehabilitation. The administration must offer and encourage training, building, and improving through continuous learning and research.

> To become a good officer requires much more knowledge and experience than is generally supposed; and it is a long time after a new officer enters upon his duty, before he becomes, even under the most favorable circumstances, fully competent to discharge it. It is not like a man's driving a herd of oxen or working a piece of machinery, the whole mechanism of which he can learn in a short time. But it is controlling the minds of men, no two of which are alike—it is curbing their tempers, whose manifestations are infinitely various—it is directing their motives which are as diverse as their personal appearance or physical conformation. And it requires an intimate knowledge, if not of human nature at large, at least of the habits, tempers and dispositions of the men immediately under their charge . . . under such circumstances, the most gifted man would be the better for experience, and less gifted would be more valuable than him, if he had experience enough.[26]

A common difference between a professional and a nonprofessional is that a professional learns every aspect of the job, whereas a nonprofessional avoids the learning process and often considers it a waste of time. Professionals seek to prevent mistakes at all costs, but if they occur, the professional does not let them slide; nonprofessionals tend to ignore or hide them. A professional tries to be great, whereas a nonprofessional just tries to get by at what he or she does.

How to Foster Professionalism

To foster professionalism in corrections, the organization must establish the following basic elements:

purpose

The reason an organization exists.

mission

That which is done to support the purpose.

vision

The future direction of an organization.

- **purpose**—the reason the organization exists;
- **mission**—what is done to support the purpose; and
- **vision**—the future direction.

Together, the purpose, mission, and vision provide a roadmap for the organization. (If you don't know where you are going, how will you know when you get there?) With these statements in place, each employee should know how his or her duties tie into the organizational direction.

These statements were developed for the Maryland Division of Correction through strategic planning that included input from all employees. By giving employees a level of control over the development of the standards, the employees were motivated to follow the standards, rising to their own expectations.

The standards must be living documents. They must be periodically reviewed and updated to remain relevant. Everyone must be familiar with the standards, and the expectations must be routinely reinforced. The organization may include the standards in a circulating newsletter. Wardens should be aware of the standards and be held accountable for incoming employees' training. Standards should be a part of the initial process, and the code of conduct should be reviewed routinely at roll call.

Exhibit 17–1 depicts the formal mission, vision, and goals of the Maryland DOC. Exhibit 17–2 lists the values and beliefs that support the division's mission and vision statements.

Relationships

Quality relationships with key external stakeholders are essential for any correctional organization to grow and thrive. They must be actively cultivated and nurtured. Some of the stakeholders important to a corrections commissioner include the governor, the legislature, the media, unions, local police organizations, and the local community. Without their support it may be impossible to move the organization in a positive direction.

Governor: There must be a clear correctional philosophy and course of action that can be agreed upon. There must be agreement on the direction of and the level of emphasis on management (e.g., safety) and treatment (e.g., inmate programs). The governor's support will be paramount in the course of business.

Legislature: The legislature has to approve many of the programs and all legislative bills necessary to effect positive change. The legislature also has to approve the budget, which, in most cases, accounts for hundreds of millions of dollars. There will be intense scrutiny as most states are looking for ways to trim the budget.

COMMISSION ON SAFETY AND ABUSE IN AMERICA'S PRISONS: CULTURE AND PROFESSION

The public rarely thinks about people in prison and thinks even less often about the men and women who manage and work in these same facilities. When we do look closely, what we see is a poorly understood profession that shoulders tremendous responsibilities and faces incredible challenges, usually without adequate resources and support. Yet this labor force is responsible for operating jails and prisons that must safely and humanely accommodate an estimated 13.5 million people annually. When corrections professionals fail to meet the demands of the job, for whatever reason, they endanger prisoners and officers alike and, at the extreme, cripple entire facilities. The failures are felt beyond the facility walls when officers and prisoners return to their families and their communities. This is a tough profession.

—The Commission on Safety and Abuse in America's Prisons

For all their troubles and achievements, corrections professionals receive little positive recognition and are denigrated in the news and popular media. As Lance Corcoran, chief of governmental affairs for the California Correctional Peace Officers Association, told the commission, "After a lifetime, 35 years working, you look back on your life's work and it's very difficult to take pride in what you've done. Society or the newspapers or whatever has told you that this is an awful profession."

Today there are statewide efforts in places as far apart as Oregon, Arizona, Massachusetts, and Maryland to change the fundamental culture of prisons. Corrections administrators in these states understand that an "us versus them" mentality ultimately jeopardizes the safety and health of prisoners and staff and over time harms the families and communities to which prisoners and staff belong. Their efforts at culture change should be supported, imitated, and improved upon so that no one has to live or work in a dehumanizing environment and so that our correctional facilities serve the public's interests. The culture of these institutions cannot change, however, unless efforts are made to build a highly qualified workforce and to cultivate and support great leaders.

The following three recommendations suggest ways to improve the corrections culture and profession.

Promote a Culture of Mutual Respect
Create a positive culture in jails and prisons grounded in an ethic of respectful behavior and interpersonal communication that benefits prisoners and staff.

Recruit and Retain a Qualified Corps of Officers
Enact changes at the state and local levels to advance the recruitment and retention of a high-quality, diverse workforce and otherwise further the professionalism of the workforce.

Support Today's Leaders and Cultivate the Next Generation
Governors and local executives must hire the most qualified leaders and support them politically and professionally, and corrections administrators must, in turn, use their positions to promote healthy and safe prisons and jails. Equally important, we must develop the skills and capacities of middle-level managers, who play a large role in running safe facilities and are poised to become the next generation of senior leaders.

Source: Adapted from the Commission on Safety and Abuse in America's Prisons, *Confronting Confinement* (New York: Vera Institute of Justice, 2006). Note: The full 126-page report, *Confronting Confinement: A Report of the Commission on Safety and Abuse in America's Prisons*, can be accessed on the Internet at www.prisoncommission.org.

When Dr. Sondervan was first appointed commissioner of corrections, he met with each senator and delegate on the respective budget committees. With each legislative member, he discussed his vision and the issues as he saw them, and asked about any specific concerns the member or his or her constituents had. This turned out to be a very worthwhile endeavor because he developed a personal relationship with each key person. He and the members had numerous follow-up calls and discussions,

EXHIBIT 17–1   **Maryland Division of Correction**

Mission, Vision, and Goals

Mission

The professional and dedicated staff of the Maryland Division of Correction enhances public safety through the safe, secure and humane confinement of inmates, while providing opportunities to aid their successful transition back into society. This is achieved in a manner that promotes safe communities and recognizes victims' rights.

Vision

The Division of Correction will be an integrated, well-managed and technologically progressive organization. Our well-trained workforce will achieve excellence in providing effective and efficient programs that offer opportunities for inmates to change. We will continue to promote security and community partnerships for a safer Maryland.

Goals

- Improved and enhanced security operations.
- Increased pre-service, in-service, academy and out-service training opportunities for staff development and career ladders.
- Improved and enhanced programs in the areas of commitment, case management and volunteer/religious services.
- Improved organizational structure.
- Enhanced agency image.

EXHIBIT 17–2   **Maryland Division of Correction**

Values

Integrity	We are a principle-based organization. We recognize and respect the dignity of all individuals. We strive for and expect honesty, truth and respect in our service to customers and stakeholders.
Dedication	We are committed to fulfilling our mission by serving our customers and stakeholders with concern and sensitivity under challenging circumstances.
Teamwork & Communication	We value results-oriented teamwork as an essential tool to accomplish our mission. We encourage open, effective communication throughout the Division to efficiently integrate our internal and external partnerships.
Public Trust & Confidence	We value public trust and confidence. We strive to assure our citizens that we are good stewards of the public's resources entrusted to us. Through community outreach, we hope to inspire public confidence in the **P**rofessional **R**esults **I**n **D**aily **E**fforts (**PRIDE**) we take in our duties.
Professionalism	We value effective leadership and strive for impartiality and fairness in the workplace. We encourage personal and professional development. We recognize and reward dedication and commitment to competence and the highest standards of achievement.

and he received positive feedback simply because he took the time and paid the courtesy to speak with them. The relationships became very important during budget hearings and in times of crisis when their support was required.

Participation in the Larger Corrections Community

A professional corrections organization has an obligation to participate in its national community. Involvement in the larger community will assist the organization with discussion and debate on current issues, facilitate the sharing of relevant empirical research and influence where grant money goes, increase networking, and distribute current knowledge of issues and solutions.

The corrections field is fortunate to have several professional organizations that offer much valuable support. The following examples are among the many local and national organizations available to enhance correctional professionalism. The list is not inclusive; correctional personnel should seek the organization that best suits their needs.

The American Correctional Association (ACA)   The ACA is the oldest and largest membership organization dedicated to the improvement of corrections. As part of its mission, the ACA conducts workshops, seminars, exhibits, and networking opportunities. It also hosts two annual conferences that bring correctional personnel from the United States and countries around the world together for a variety of activities.

The ACA's Professional Development Department offers a variety of educational opportunities. One of the most valuable programs is the Corrections Certification Program (described in Chapters 6 and 13). It was first administered to correctional personnel in the summer of 2000, and Dr. Sondervan was among the initial group of candidates. Although Sondervan had been in the field for many years, he found the examination to be extremely challenging. Taking the exam affirmed that there is a body of knowledge associated with corrections, knowledge that both separates it from other fields of endeavor and distinguishes it as a true profession.

The Maryland DOC executive team became the first in the nation to consist of a fully certified staff. All wardens and managerial staff were encouraged to sit for the exams. Certification information packets were sent to each facility and each staff member. The number of certified staff steadily increased during Sondervan's five years as commissioner, with Maryland ranking second in the nation as far as the number of certified professionals.

It should be noted that the Corrections Certification Program, like those in other fields, requires individual recertification after a period of three years. To do so, the individual must participate in various learning activities and complete a specified number of contact training/education hours. Moreover, the recertification process documents that corrections is a bonafide profession requiring not only the possession but the ongoing enhancement of knowledge and skills throughout one's career.

The ACA's Standards and Accreditation Department develops national standards and accredits prisons and jails (as defined in Chapter 6). To be accredited by ACA, facility staff must carefully review their policies and procedures to ensure compliance with the established standards. The facility must undergo a stringent audit process and meet specified percentages of compliance with both mandatory and nonmandatory standards.

Among the many advantages of being accredited is the sense of pride and accomplishment the staff experiences. A commissioner must strongly support and encourage facilities to apply for accreditation. Commissioner Sondervan was fortunate to witness the first two successful accreditation attempts by facilities in Maryland. At a celebration ceremony held by one facility, he was overwhelmed by the emotion shown by staff as they realized their achievement. Without question, earning accreditation provided a real sense of purpose and meaning. It also served to strengthen the connection between the basic underlying principles of correctional practice and the day-to-day responsibilities of working in a prison environment.

The Association of State Correctional Administrators (ASCA) The ASCA, comprising all state correctional administrators, is dedicated to the improvement of correctional services by promoting:

- the exchange of ideas and philosophies at the top administrative levels;
- public support for the understanding of the corrections systems;
- research in correctional practices;
- the development of correctional standards and accreditation;
- the fostering of appropriate legislation; and
- the exchange of information with international correctional organizational agencies.

The ASCA also conducts training for new directors that helps them survive and excel as they begin their assignments.

National Institute of Corrections (NIC) The NIC, part of the U.S. Department of Justice Federal Bureau of Prisons, provides a variety of services including training, technical assistance, information services, and policy and program development assistance. The NIC also provides leadership to influence professional correctional policy and practice nationwide.

Professional Development

professional development
The lifelong or career-long dedication to quality selection, training, and development of employees.

Professional development is the lifelong or career-long dedication to quality selection, training, and development of employees. A well-planned, well-executed professional development program is at the core of creating a professional corrections organization. However, it is often neglected in state and county governments because of fiscal issues. This is especially true in times of severe budget constraints.

Correctional leaders must take a systems approach to professional development. System components should include recruitment of quality employees, a well-run training academy, a field training officer program, inservice training, and leadership development. Quality training and development starts from the first day on the job and continues until retirement.

Recruiting is immensely important. Corrections needs individuals with the proper character, background, and temperament for the profession. A considerable amount of time and money is devoted to new employee selection and training. Because turnover is very costly, it is essential to carefully select employees. Components of the recruitment program include:

- a comprehensive application;
- a written examination;

5 It is difficult to recruit correctional staff because the turnover rate is high, corrections is cast in a negative light, it is difficult to attract and retain qualified personnel, salary and enhancements are inadequate, the hours are burdensome, and some prisons are in undesirable locations.

6 Candidates who volunteer to serve on the execution team require a high level of training and professionalism. They are carefully screened and interviewed by the warden, psychologically screened by a clinical psychologist, and, ultimately, approved by the members of the execution team. The officers are well trained to ensure that the execution itself is done professionally. The goal is to carry out the execution as uneventfully as possible to avoid media sensationalism.

7 Professionalism is commitment to a set of agreed-upon values aimed toward the improvement of the organization while maintaining the highest standards of excellence and dissemination of knowledge. In addition to having knowledge and skills, professionals must present humanistic qualities: selflessness, responsibility and accountability, leadership, excellence, integrity, honesty, empathy, and respect for coworkers and prisoners.

8 A common difference between a professional and a nonprofessional is that a professional learns every aspect of the job, whereas a nonprofessional avoids the learning process and often considers it a waste of time. Professionals seek to prevent mistakes at all costs, but if they occur, the professional does not let them slide; nonprofessionals tend to ignore or hide them. A professional tries to be great, whereas a nonprofessional just tries to get by at what he or she does.

9 Correctional leaders can foster professionalism by efficiently managing rapidly growing, complex institutions to maintain safe environments and facilitate inmate rehabilitation. They can further foster professionalism by clearly defining the organization's purpose, mission, and vision. Additionally, the organization must form and maintain political relationships (e.g., with governor, legislature) and participate in the larger correctional community (e.g., ACA, ASCA, NIC).

10 Professional development is the lifelong or career-long dedication to quality selection, training, and development of employees. It can be achieved in corrections through college education, rotational assignments and collateral duties, and leader development specific training.

KEY TERMS

performance-based funding, *p. 664*
purpose, *p. 670*

mission, *p. 670*
vision, *p. 670*

professional
development, *p. 674*

QUESTIONS FOR REVIEW

1 Rank-order the pressures that corrections face as a result of prison construction. Defend your rank-order and propose what can be done to overcome the pressures.

2 Defend the ways that advances in technology help corrections.

3 Speculate on the consequences of cutting the corrections budget as a result of budget reallocation after 9/11.

4 If the inmate cohort in the Correctional Education Association's Three-State Recidivism Study of Cor-

rectional Education was evenly split between participants and nonparticipants, calculate the number who were not rearrested and not reincarcerated.

5 Rate the reasons why it is difficult to recruit correctional staff from most important to least important.

6 Argue why it is important to have professionalism in the execution team.

7 What are the features of professionalism?

8 How does a professional compare and contrast with a nonprofessional?

9 Propose how purpose, mission, and vision can foster professionalism in a correctional organization.

10 Provide examples of the three ways that professional development can be achieved in corrections.

THINKING CRITICALLY ABOUT CORRECTIONS

Today's Challenges

The field of corrections today faces many obstacles as it moves toward greater professionalism. This chapter outlined 11 major challenges. Separate the 11 challenges into two lists: what can be done now versus what can be done in 5 to 10 years. Identify at least one strategy to correct each short-range and long-range challenge that can facilitate the movement toward enhanced professionalism in corrections.

Fostering Professionalism

Professional development is the lifelong or career-long dedication to quality selection, training, and development of employees. Attending professional conferences, workshops, and seminars, reading professional literature, and obtaining continuing education credits play an important role for educators, physicians, lawyers, nurses, engineers, and others.

Think about the role that professional correctional *organizations* (for example, your state department of corrections or the American Correctional Association) play in a person's professional development. Then develop a top-five list of ways that a professional correctional organization can contribute to the professional development of its staff.

ON-THE-JOB DECISION MAKING

The Public Image of Corrections and Recruitment

When you were an intern at the local jail you enjoyed the experience. You got along well with the staff, including the jail warden. When the jail warden heard that you spoke a foreign language, she asked you to translate basic jail processing information for staff and inmates. You even got to teach the staff how to say the phrases. Before you left, the warden sat down with you and told you how much the jail staff appreciated what you did. She encouraged you to apply for a Corrections Officer I position after graduation. She seemed really sincere when she talked with you about professional development and the opportunities the jail could provide you. You were flattered when she said, in a serious voice, that you could be warden one day, or even state corrections commissioner. But after graduation you aren't sure you want to go back to the jail full-time. It seems that the negative public image of corrections is affecting you as well.

Assume now that you are the warden. You call your former intern a week after graduation. You tell the person that the personnel board has approved three CO I openings and ask if he or she is still interested. You hear the hesitation in your former intern's voice. As a seasoned corrections professional, you anticipate the intern's concern over the image of corrections in the community and the fact that a college degree is not required for the CO I position, the salary is minimal, and sometimes the shift hours are burdensome. Yet if corrections is to continue down the path of professionalism, you know you can't give up on this person. He or she is precisely the kind of person your jail needs.

Role-play with another student and present strong arguments why the intern should apply for the CO I position.

Correctional Budgets

Post-9/11 corrections budgets have not grown proportionately with the continued increase in the correctional population. With the advent of homeland security, what would at one time have been divided up among X number of agencies is now divided among $X + 1$. That means less for corrections.

You and your staff study your agency needs carefully, thinking of areas where you can scale back. One staff member raises the question of cutting back on the organization's financial support for staff professional development. You are concerned that reducing the budget for professional development will contradict your message of enhancing the organization's commitment to professional development. However, after all the options are presented and their consequences discussed, reducing the budget for professional development is agreed on.

Think about how you will present this information to your staff. Are there less expensive ways to continue the organization's commitment to professional development that you can present in order to demonstrate that your commitment to professional development does not depend solely on increasing budgets?

LIVE LINKS

at www.justicestudies.com/livelinks04

17–1 New Approaches to Staff Safety

Staff safety training issues for community corrections agencies are discussed, including use-of-force continuum, crisis prevention, self-defense and physical fitness, oleoresin capsicum, body protection, safety in the office, protection from disasters, arrest, search, and seizure, field work, canine considerations, scenario training, and critical incidents.

17–2 Correctional Officers Professional Orientation Scales

A review of tools utilized in assessing correctional officer attitudes is presented. Scales considered are organized into three groups: offender-related scales, orientation to correctional work scales, and attitudes toward corrections scales. Each entry includes a brief description of the scale, corresponding items, and psychometric properties to be derived from scale use.

17–3 Who Will Control the Jails Beyond 2000?

A discussion of how to succeed at jail management. Topics include how to know when there's a problem, direct supervision, mission and philosophy, and correctional leadership.

17–4 Correctional Leadership Competencies for the 21st Century

Characteristics that result in the best performance of executive- and senior-level leaders are identified along with the key skills, knowledge, and attributes of effective and successful leaders, which are then linked to sets of specific behaviors.

APPENDIX

CAREERS IN CORRECTIONS

Career development experts tell us that career development is a lifelong process that involves continual and consistent maintenance. Your interests, skills, and preferences change throughout your life. Thus, it is important that you know the steps involved in career planning, developing employability and job readiness, and finding the right job.[1]

CAREER PLANNING

Successful career planning is a continual process of self-assessment, occupational research, decision making, contacting potential employers, working at a job, and reevaluating your situation (see Exhibit A–1).

Self-Assessment

Career planning begins with **self-assessment**—learning who you are and what you can and want to do by evaluating your interests, skills, and values. Self-assessment tools, which pose a series of questions and identify potential career choices based on your answers, are available from most college and university career counselors as well as in bookstores and on the Internet. The questions involved pertain to (1) personal information—education, experience, achievements, personality factors, and interest in various activities; (2) skills—abilities in such areas as athletics, analysis, management, communication, and persuasion; and (3) values—ranking work-related issues (such as job location, pressure, security, responsibility, teamwork, and wages) in order of importance.

In addition, for a position in corrections, certain personal and physical attributes will be required by your employer. The California Department of Corrections (www.cdc.state.ca.us), for example, requires that a correctional officer candidate have a "history of law-abiding behavior" and "emotional maturity and stability, . . . leadership ability, tact, . . . alertness, integrity, dependability, good judgment, and the ability to work cooperatively with others." The Texas Department of Criminal Justice (www. tdcj.state.tx.us) requires, among other qualifications, that candidates in addition to not having any felony convictions not have had Class A or B misdemeanor convictions within the past five years.

In general, correctional officer applicants must:

- be at least 18 years old (in some states 21 years old);
- be a U.S. citizen;

self-assessment

Learning who you are and what you can and want to do by evaluating your interests, skills, and values.

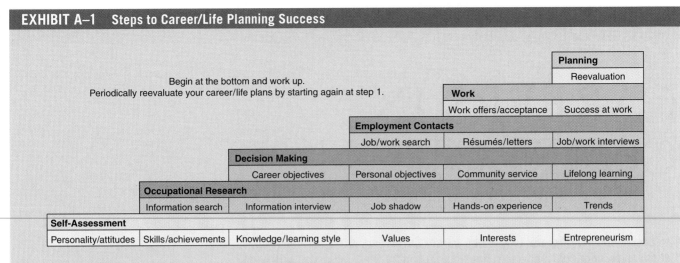

EXHIBIT A–1   Steps to Career/Life Planning Success

Begin at the bottom and work up.
Periodically reevaluate your career/life plans by starting again at step 1.

Planning	
Reevaluation	

Work	
Work offers/acceptance	Success at work

Employment Contacts		
Job/work search	Résumés/letters	Job/work interviews

Decision Making			
Career objectives	Personal objectives	Community service	Lifelong learning

Occupational Research				
Information search	Information interview	Job shadow	Hands-on experience	Trends

Self-Assessment					
Personality/attitudes	Skills/achievements	Knowledge/learning style	Values	Interests	Entrepreneurism

You may need to move from an upper step to a lower one (e.g., from step 4 to step 2) should a lack of openings in a particular field require research into a different one.

Source: Used by permission of Co-operative Education & Career Services, University of Waterloo, Waterloo, Ontario, Canada. May not be reprinted without express written permission. Individuals may access full text of *Career Development Manual* at www.cdm.uwaterloo.ca.

- have a high school diploma or general equivalency certificate (GED); and
- have no felony convictions.

Occupational Research

The second step in career planning is research. Make a list of the potential career choices identified by your self-assessment, as well as any additional careers that you would like to know more about. Other jobs in corrections besides officer positions include health service and information science jobs. See Exhibit A–2 for a list of typical jobs at a state department of corrections. Research job requirements, job characteristics, working conditions, duties, employment outlook, salary, and methods of entry for each of the career alternatives. Read everything you can find and talk to people.

Reading   The best source for information on careers and job opportunities is the Internet. See Exhibit A–3 for a list of sources on the Internet for criminal justice jobs. Information is also available in libraries (public, school, and special) and at the career development centers at your school. Among others, three U.S. Department of Labor publications—*Dictionary of Occupational Titles, Occupational Outlook Handbook,* and *Guide for Occupational Exploration*—provide information on more than 20,000 jobs and cross-reference each career field with others that are similar in nature. The U.S. Department of Labor also publishes two periodicals, *Occupational Outlook Quarterly* and *Monthly Labor Review,* that are excellent sources of information about occupational trends and salaries.

Talking to People   Networking is meeting new people (often through people that you know) who can give you information about careers, the job market, and specific positions. Broadening your acquaintance base to

networking

Meeting new people who can give you information about careers, the job market, and specific positions. It is often done through people you know.

EXHIBIT A-2   Typical Department of Corrections Positions

The following is a list of some types of positions that may be found in major institutions, field units, probation and parole offices, detention centers, work centers, day reporting centers, regional offices, or central offices.

Accountant	Office manager
Administrative assistant	Office services assistant
Agriculture supervisor	Office services specialist
Assistant warden	Operations officer
Boiler operator	Personnel analyst
Building grounds superintendent	Physician
Building/grounds supervisor	Plumber steamfitter
Business manager	Postal assistant
Buyer	Probation officer
Carpenter	Program support technician
Corrections lieutenant	Programmer/analyst
Corrections major	Psychologist
Corrections nurse technician	Radiologic technologist
Corrections officer	Recreation supervisor
Corrections sergeant	Regional administrator
Dental assistant	Regional director
Dental hygienist	Regional program manager
Dentist	Registered nurse
Electrician	Rehabilitation counselor
Electronics technician	Safety specialist
Executive secretary	Secretary senior
Fiscal assistant	Store clerk
Fiscal technician	Store operations manager
Food service supervisor	Storekeeper
H_2O/treatment plant operator	Surveillance officer
Human resource officer	Treatment plant operator
Human rights advocate	Treatment program supervisor
Inmate hearings officer	Warden
Investigator	Warehouse supervisor
Nurse clinician	Welder
Nurse practitioner	

include solid professional contacts through networking builds long-term professional relationships that facilitate job hunting and professional development and enhance personal growth.

Developing a network is an integral part of job hunting; in some fields, networking is considered the most effective method of job searching and is the number-one way people obtain jobs. It has no time limit, nor does it end when you secure a position. Start developing contacts before you begin your career planning, and keep in touch with those contacts—they might hear of a job opening for you. Continue to keep in touch after you get a job—you may need to use your network again.

How do you begin networking? How do you establish contacts if you do not have any? Anyone can be a contact: the student who sits next to you in class, your parents' next-door neighbor, your doctor, your professor, previous supervisors, people with whom you have something in common (attending the same school, working out at the same gym, belonging to the same professional association, etc.). Join organizations and participate in local programs that are related to your area of interest.

EXHIBIT A–3	Job Information Web Sites of Criminal Justice Agencies and Other Groups

American Correctional Association Job Bank www.aca.org/jobbank

Bureau of Alcohol, Tobacco, Firearms and Explosives (ATF) job information www.atf.gov/careers/index.html

Central Intelligence Agency (CIA) job information www.odci.gov/employment/index.html

Correctional Service of Canada job information www.csc-scc.gc.ca//text/employment_e.shtml

Drug Enforcement Administration (DEA) job information www.usdoj.gov/dea/job/agent/page-01.htm; www.usdoj.gov/06employment/index.html

Federal Bureau of Investigation (FBI) job information https://fbijobs.com

Federal Bureau of Prisons (BOP) job information www.bop.gov/jobs/index.jsp

Federal Jobs Digest http://jobsfed.com

USA Jobs www.usajobs.com

U.S. Customs Service www.customs.ustreas.gov; www.customs.ustreas.gov/xp/cgov/careers/

U.S. Department of Justice Career Opportunities Search http://jobsearch.usajobs.opm.gov/a9dj.asp

U.S. Citizenship and Immigration Services http://uscis.gov

U.S. Marshals Service www.usdoj.gov/marshals

One of the key elements of networking is talking to people about your career interests and goals. Most people are more than willing to share information; in fact, the majority are flattered by the attention and truly want to help. Talk to the people you meet about what they do, their backgrounds, and their perspectives on the job market for their specialties, and ask if they know anyone else with whom you might speak. Take advantage of any and every opportunity to build your network—talk to people while you are waiting in line, riding the bus, attending a seminar, or playing golf. The other key element is follow-up—keep your contacts apprised of your career status; let them know about your latest career move or your progress in a new job.

informational interviewing

Talking to people who are currently employed in a career field of interest.

Informational interviewing, talking to people who are currently employed in a career field that you are interested in exploring, is an excellent means of researching a particular job or position. Introduce yourself to the person you wish to talk to, either by calling or writing, and ask if you might have 30 minutes of time to discuss the job or position. Explain that you are gathering career information and ask for an appointment. An informational interview can provide:

- an accurate portrayal of the career field you are investigating;
- specifics about necessary skills, entry-level positions, employment trends, and so on;
- information about related volunteer, part-time, or internship opportunities;
- additional professional contacts;
- increased confidence in interacting with professionals;
- information about possible job openings; and
- information about concerns that should not be discussed in a job interview (e.g., salaries, hours, and minority issues).

Decision Making

The third step in career planning is making your career decision. Carefully review all of the information that you have gathered. For which of the corrections careers that you researched are you best qualified emotionally, physically, and academically? Which are most appealing? Which

EXHIBIT A–4 Job Search Checklist

JOB SEARCH CHECKLIST

✔ Establish specific goals. Determine two or three potential career areas that are compatible with your values, skills, and interests.

✔ Prepare your search tools. Write a résumé and sharpen your interviewing skills. Are you ready for your interview?

✔ Identify and research potential employers by utilizing different resources, such as the following:

- Career development center
- Professional associations
- Newspaper classifieds
- Internet sites
- Deans/professors/other advisors
- Trade organizations
- Career library resources/texts
- State/county employment offices

✔ Conduct informational interviews, which differ from job interviews—they provide you with an excellent opportunity to meet with individuals in a specific career field and obtain up-to-date information on that field. This can help your career decision making and develop a network of contacts.

✔ Initiate contact with employers. Establish a mailing list of potential employers within the targeted fields you identified from your earlier research. Mail your résumé with a focused cover letter and then follow up with telephone calls to request interview appointments.

✔ Follow up with each contact. Remember, follow-up is your responsibility.

✔ Get organized, and stay on schedule. Devote at least 20 hours a week to your job search. Develop a schedule and create a list of organizations, contact people, contact dates, and outcomes.

✔ Accept an offer—consider these factors when offered a position:

- size of the organization
- job security
- travel/relocation requirements
- hours
- formal training arrangements
- people you met with
- advancement potential
- entry level salary
- salary potential
- geographical factors
- education/fringe benefits
- name recognition of employer

are most likely to enhance your career development? List career choices in order of preference. Then begin your job search (see Exhibit A–4).

SEEKING EMPLOYMENT

Finding a job can be a tough process that requires an overwhelming amount of thought, time, and energy. Make the job search part of your everyday routine; decide how much time you will devote to the search and when, and stick with that decision.

Be creative in your job search; use all of the resources available to you—classified ads, Internet ads, professional associations, advisors, employment services (local and Internet), and so on—to identify available positions. One of the best sources of information on careers in corrections is the Internet. Your state's department of corrections will most likely list employment opportunities on its Web site. Federal or private corrections positions can also be researched on the Internet.

According to the U.S. Department of Justice National Institute of Corrections (www.nicic.org), people interested in a career in corrections should contact the federal, state, or local agency in which they would like to work or contact a private correctional services provider.

- For the Federal Bureau of Prisons, go to www.bop.gov.
- For links to state corrections department Web sites, go to www .corrections.com/state.html#state_DOC_online.
- For links to county sheriffs offices, go to www.corrections.com/ county.html.

Once you have narrowed your search and found a position to which you would like to apply, the next step is to submit a résumé or an application. Many civil service jobs (i.e., county, state, or federal government jobs in which hiring and promotion are determined by competitive examinations) do not require a résumé; all applicants instead complete a detailed application.

Submitting an Application

The first step in applying for a correctional officer position and many other positions in corrections is to submit an application, either by mail, in person, or online. Check with the agency to see where these applications can be obtained. In some states, applications can be obtained at any state Employment Development Department office. Make a copy of the application for yourself before you submit it.

Writing Your Résumé

The job to which you are applying may require that you submit a résumé. The state of Minnesota, for instance, requires that an application and a résumé be submitted for civil service positions.

A good **résumé**, or list of your job and other related experiences and education, may not necessarily get you the job, but a bad résumé can ensure that you do not get the job. Your résumé is not meant to convey your complete life history. Through your résumé, you convey your capability for a particular position; it must be clear, directed, and persuasive—its objective is to secure an interview. Your résumé should (1) support a career direction and (2) be selective. Career direction gives the résumé focus; all of the information included in the résumé should support the career direction that you are trying to convey. Career guidance experts tell us, "You should make yourself as attractive as possible on paper so that the employer feels as though she would be missing out by not interviewing you."[2] Your résumé should project you as someone who produces, accomplishes, and is results oriented. Use active verbs and descriptive terms; that is, write "researched and drafted reports" rather than "responsible for research and reports." What works best today is a conservative style and a focus on key achievements—particularly those that relate to the position for which you are applying; find out as much as you can about the prospective employer and then modify the résumé to highlight those items that will most benefit the company or organization. The most effective résumé is one that is tailored to a specific job; the results are well worth the extra effort. According to Tom Jackson, "The Perfect

résumé

A list of your job and other related experiences and education.

Résumé is a written communication that clearly demonstrates your ability to produce results in an area of concern to selected employers, in a way that motivates them to meet you." [3]

When creating your résumé, keep the following in mind:

- Follow the "one-page rule"—one page is ideal; two are acceptable (however, do not add a second page simply to expand content); three are unacceptable.
- Your résumé should be scanned easily: It must be organized effectively to carry the reader's eye from major point to major point (a prospective employer will look for words and phrases that convey the necessary qualifications).
- The eye should be drawn to eye-catching type; use **bold**, CAPITAL, or *italic* text to emphasize a particular item, but do not overdo it.
- Use bullets to break job and skill descriptions into easy-to-read component parts that begin with eye-catching verbs.
- Highlight talents, skills, and experience to some extent, but do not overdo it.
- Word processing allows great flexibility in the selection of fonts, but choose something simple. Avoid ornateness and avoid combining several fonts.
- Employers want employees who can set goals and complete tasks; present yourself as someone who gets things done.
- Identify your strengths and convey them on paper, this is not arrogance or boasting. The person who is reading your résumé wants to know that you are exceptional.
- Always honestly summarize your work experience and skills, including any technologies you are familiar with (spreadsheet or database software, computer hardware, telephone systems, word processing, etc.).
- Do not use personal pronouns; "I" is implied.
- Complete sentences are not necessary.
- Avoid abbreviations.

Your résumé can be a primary tool in obtaining more attractive positions, thus, extra time spent on its preparation is a good investment. All résumés should be accurate and truthful, but each should highlight different strengths, as they relate to the potential job. The résumé should go through several stages of drafting and editing until it is as perfect as it can be.

Résumé Format

The selected résumé format should establish a natural flow of information that simplifies the review process and should incorporate a consistent pattern of information placement, allowing the reader to anticipate where certain information will be found. An employer usually reviews information on the left side first—names of employers, job titles, and so on should be placed on the left. Less important information (dates, locations, etc.) should be placed on the right. No résumé format is universally preferred, although the chronological résumé and the functional résumé are the most widely used (see Exhibits A–5 and A–6.)

Chronological Résumé   The **chronological résumé** format is the most widely accepted and preferred résumé style. It is most effectively

chronological résumé

A résumé that organizes information in reverse time sequence and emphasizes work history.

EXHIBIT A–5   Chronological Résumé Format

Derrick A. Salyer
1555 Campus Lake Drive, Orlando, FL 32765
(407) 555-1212

OBJECTIVE

To secure a position as a juvenile court probation officer.

EDUCATION

Bachelor of Science, May 2007
University of Central Florida
Major: Criminal Justice
GPA: 3.20/4.00
Dean's List, Distinguished Undergraduate Award

Associate of Arts, December 2005
Pensacola Junior College, Pensacola, FL
Major: Criminal Justice

Self-financed 50% of education through work, loans, and scholarships

EXPERIENCE

Intern, January–May 2007
Florida Department of Juvenile Justice, Pensacola, FL
—Assisted department staff with hosting of three live national
  satellite videoconferences
—Served as liaison to downlink sites
—Attended all planning sessions

Intern, August–December 2006
Escambia County Juvenile Court Services, Pensacola, FL
—Assisted intake officer with presentence report investigation and
  writing
—Attended detention and adjudication hearings
—Answered questions relating to the presentence report

Sales Associate, March 2003–July 2006
Just For Feet, University Mall, Pensacola, FL
—Coordinated sales associates' schedules
—Managed evening cashier sales associates
—Achieved and maintained Best Shift/Least Checkout Errors monthly in 2004

ACTIVITIES

Criminal Justice Student Association, 2006 President, 2005
Vice President
Alpha Phi Sigma (Criminal Justice Honor Society) Spirit
Award, 2005

REFERENCES

Available upon request.

used by people who have established or are establishing credentials within a particular field or whose credentials show career growth and direction within one particular employment environment. To be effective, the chronological résumé should project a sense of quality by emphasizing skills and accomplishments, and it should be organized carefully (in terms of layout) to present most effectively a particular background. In this format, your education and work experience are presented in reverse

EXHIBIT A–6 Functional Résumé Format

Tanisha Williams
1500 Maplewood Drive, Palmdale, CA 93510
(213) 555-1212

CAREER INTERESTS:
Correctional industry management

SKILLS:
PLANNING/ORGANIZATION

- Successfully established and operated a T-shirt design shop
- Developed market/trade survey programs to determine customer interest
- Initiated radio T-shirt give-away contests
- Established connection with local homeless shelter to employ the homeless

ADMINISTRATION/MANAGEMENT/SALES MARKETING

- Supervised team of 20 sales associates
- Hired and delegated supervision of 18-person T-shirt design shop to two associate managers
- Approved corporate sales contracts
- Increased corporate sales 32%
- Managed commercial sales advertisements—three radio, one television, and one newspaper—averaging $32,000 annually

EMPLOYMENT EXPERIENCE

OWNER AND OPERATOR	2005–Present
TANISHA'S SHIRTS AND DESIGNS	
Lancaster, California	

SALES ASSOCIATE AND MANAGER	2003–2005
HUTTON'S TEES	
Lancaster, California	

EDUCATION

BACHELOR OF SCIENCE, CRIMINAL JUSTICE ADMINISTRATION, 2007
California State University
Northridge, California

REFERENCES AVAILABLE UPON REQUEST

time sequence, with the most recent degrees and jobs appearing first. In developing a chronological résumé,

- deemphasize history for the sake of content;
- devote more space to the most recent position;
- fully describe the three or four positions most supportive of the career direction—summarize other work experience unless it is exceptionally meaningful;
- avoid excessive repetition in detail and substance; and
- emphasize career growth.

functional résumé
A résumé that emphasizes abilities over work history, organizing information according to skills, results, contributions, or functions.

Functional Résumé   The **functional résumé** emphasizes abilities over work history by organizing information according to skills, results, contributions made, or functions successfully performed. It is best used by those who are changing careers or have been out of the workforce for some time. In developing a functional résumé,

- select functions that describe job-related abilities (versatile abilities, if possible);
- list functions in order of importance and relevance to your career direction, emphasizing accomplishment and achievement while illustrating specific abilities; and
- avoid including employment detail (employer names, dates of employment, job titles) within the functional descriptions; include a work history section that sets forth this information.

What to Include   Regardless of which résumé format you use, your résumé should include the following:

1. Identification—name (first, middle initial, last), address (permanent and/or present), telephone numbers (work and/or home, fax), and e-mail address (if applicable). Accurate information is critical; a prospective employer who is unable to reach you with the information provided is not likely to try to verify contact information. If the information changes, correct your résumé and reprint it.

2. Objective/Career Interest—the type of work you want to do, the position you want, or the skills/attributes you anticipate using and the employment sector in which you wish to establish a career. A career interest statement is a broader, long-range career direction that simply lists the field or occupation in which you wish to be employed.

3. Education—schools attended, degrees received, dates of graduation, majors and other concentrations of study, and academic achievement (class rank and grade point average for an undergraduate or graduate program). The education section can also include extracurricular activities of particular significance and academic honors and awards.

4. Skills/Accomplishments/Qualifications—descriptions, grouped by major functional skill area. Choose three to five functional skill areas that correspond to your career objective.

5. Experience—for a chronological résumé, list experience in reverse chronological order, beginning with your current or most recent position.

6. Optional—personal statements (relatively neutral comments about personal interests such as a foreign language, community activity, travel, sports, public speaking, unique hobbies, and military experience); honors and awards (academic honors, memberships in national honor societies, scholarships, etc.); curricular and cocurricular activities (those that demonstrate leadership), community activities, or volunteer experiences (demonstrates personal work habits, leadership potential, and level of motivation/commitment); professional associations and licenses; and publications.

References should always be listed on a separate page, not on the résumé. Do not approach the selection of references casually; your references are critical to the strength of your employment credentials.

The résumé copy should be meticulously reviewed before it is forwarded to a potential employer (you might have a friend or a qualified professional critique it).

The Cover Letter

If your prospective employer requires a résumé, a cover letter (see Exhibits A–7 and A–8) should always accompany it. Like the résumé, the cover letter should be direct, persuasive, descriptive, and attractive. Remember, the cover letter is specific to the potential employer; it should emphasize credentials and experience that apply to the position. Your cover letter can differentiate you significantly from others competing for the same position. The following is the basic format for the cover letter:

1. First paragraph—serves to get the attention of the person receiving the letter and answers the question "Why are you writing?" This can be as simple as stating that you are "a graduating student seeking employment at [name of employer]" or that you are "responding to a job posting from [name of source]." If (in the ideal situation) you are referred by a professional or personal contact, use it to your advantage—begin your letter with "Karen Davis recommended that I contact you regarding employment."

2. Second paragraph—details your interest in and your fit with the company or organization. Keep in mind that employers are more interested in what you can do for them than in what they can give you. Answer implied questions, such as the following:

   a. "Why are you interested in working for this firm or organization?" This part need only be a sentence or two but should include reference to specifics about the organization—its mission, type of work, geographic location, size, reputation in the community, and/or types of positions available. Employers' hiring decisions are often based not only on qualifications, but also on level of interest in the firm or organization. Be genuine. This is an opportunity to show that you researched the employer.

   b. "Why are you the right person for the job?" In two or three sentences, tell the prospective employer what skills you will bring to the job without reiterating details included in your résumé. Give specific examples of skills and accomplishments related to this position that you emphasized in your résumé. You might consider a wrap-up sentence commenting on how the organization might benefit from your skills and experience.

3. Last paragraph—expresses appreciation for the prospective employer's time and consideration and provides details about what you plan to do next: how you will follow up (e.g., with a telephone call) and when (either a specific date or within a certain number of weeks; wait at least one week). If you do not know whom to call to follow up, you might ask the employer to contact you at a particular telephone number or by e-mail. If a job listing says "No phone calls, please," state in the cover letter that you look forward to hearing from the employer soon.

The Examination Process: Testing and Background Investigation

If you have applied for a correctional officer position, once your application has been submitted, the next step will be a written examination.

EXHIBIT A–7   Tips on Writing Cover Letters

WRITING A COVER LETTER

Your Street Address
City, State Zip Code
Today's Date

Contact Person's Name
Contact Person's Title (if applicable)
Company/Organization Name
Street Address
City, State Zip Code

Dear (Contact Person's Name, or Contact Person's Title if name is unknown):

OPENING PARAGRAPH: Clearly state why you are writing, name the position or type of work for which you are applying, and mention how you heard of the opening. If you are writing without prior knowledge of an available opening, say that you are interested in openings that may currently be available.

MIDDLE PARAGRAPH: Explain why you are interested in working for this employer, and/or your reasons for desiring this type of work. Describe applicable experience, achievements, or other qualifications in this environment or type of employment.

MIDDLE PARAGRAPH: Refer the reader to your enclosed resume, which positively illustrates your training, skills, and experience. DO NOT DUPLICATE RESUME INFORMATION IN THE COVER LETTER—"highlight," and elaborate on how you can make a tangible contribution to this company/organization.

CLOSING PARAGRAPH: Use a closing appropriate to acquiring an interview. If you know the contact person's name and telephone number, use a proactive strategy—say that you will call to request an appointment in the very near future. If you do not know the contact person's name, ending your letter with a question often encourages a response (e.g., May we meet soon to discuss this matter further?).

Sincerely,

Your signature

Your Full Name (typewritten)

Enclosure

Most state and federal agencies will send you a letter after your application has been processed. The letter will give you a scheduled test date. In general, to be hired as a correctional officer, candidates must:

- pass a written exam;
- pass a psychological exam;

EXHIBIT A–8   **Sample Cover Letter**

1500 Maplewood Drive
Palmdale, CA 93510
January 12, 2008

Ms. Caroline Butterworth
Human Resources
State of California
Department of Corrections
Sacramento, CA 94283-0001

Dear Ms. Butterworth:

I am applying for the position of Supervisor of Correctional Industries in your Southeast Region. I am a graduate of California State University, Northridge, with a bachelor's degree in criminal justice administration. I believe that my work experience and education make me a strong candidate for this position.

My degree in criminal justice administration has given me an excellent understanding of the criminal justice field, particularly institutional corrections and the corrections industry. I completed a 15-week internship at the Chino, California, Institution for Men, where I gained considerable insight into prison industry operations—especially security—and the importance of helping prisoners develop and maintain job skills prior to release.

My work experience spans 10 years, which includes self-employment (in T-shirt design and sales—I hired and supervised a staff of 20) and industry organization and management.

I look forward to speaking with you about utilizing my business skills and criminal justice qualifications in the position of Supervisor of Correctional Industries. I will contact you next week to arrange an interview. Please call me if you have questions.

Sincerely,

Tanisha Williams

Tanisha Williams

Enclosure

- have good vision (with glasses or contact lenses), including no colorblindness, and good hearing (with or without a hearing aid);
- be able to perform the essential functions of a correctional officer, with or without reasonable accommodation (i.e., be in good physical health and of sound mental and emotional condition, demonstrated by passing a physical abilities test);
- pass a drug test;
- undergo a background investigation and be fingerprinted;
- pass a medical exam; and
- be eligible to carry a firearm.

EXHIBIT A–9   State of Illinois Examination Information for Corrections Officers

Three examinations are required of all applicants: the Test of Adult Basic Education (TABE), the Inmate Disciplinary Report Written Exam (IDR), and the Physical Agility Test (PAT). Applicants must meet the minimum standards on each examination to be eligible for hire. Upon completion of these examinations, an oral interview is conducted with each applicant. Applicants have the opportunity to earn up to a total of 100 screening points and are placed on eligibility lists in rank order. Institutions hire applicants based on scores.

Weighted values are assigned to each of the following dimensions based on its relationship to successful job performance.

1. *Test of Adult Basic Education (TABE):* The Department of Corrections requires that all applicants for security positions successfully complete a written reading comprehension and vocabulary examination. Applicants must receive a minimum score equivalent to the 10th-grade reading level. Applicants meeting this criterion can move on to the next phase in the screening process. The TABE is used to establish a baseline for reading comprehension. No screening points are awarded for its successful completion.

2. *Written Examination:* This written examination consists of the viewing of a videotaped incident after which the applicant is required to answer 30 multiple choice questions regarding the video. This examination measures an individual's ability to observe and interpret information.

3. *Physical Agility Test:* Since being in good physical shape is a prime consideration for being a correctional officer/youth supervisor trainee, applicants are required to successfully complete a physical agility test to be eligible for hire. The test is comprised of four exercises designed to measure an applicant's ability to perform the job duties required of a correctional officer/youth supervisor trainee. Applicants must complete all four of the exercises to continue in the screening process. No screening points are awarded for successful completion of the Physical Agility Test.

4. *Oral Interview:* Applicants are interviewed by a team of two Department of Corrections officials using a standardized interview questionnaire. Upon conclusion of the interview, the officials independently rate the applicant based on the six categories. An applicant can receive from 0 to 5 points in each category for a total of 30 possible points. The average of the scores is calculated to determine each applicant's total interview score.

Source: From the Illinois Correctional Industries.

Written Exam   The written exam most likely will test your skills in grammar, spelling, punctuation, reading comprehension, and basic mathematics (see Exhibit A–9).

Physical Abilities Test and Vision Test   After successful completion of all written examinations, you will be scheduled for a physical abilities test and possibly a visual acuity test.

Background Check   A background investigation will be conducted by the agency. It may include fingerprinting, photos, and a background interview. This investigative phase includes a thorough check of police records, personal, military, and employment histories; and reference checks. The criteria for the background investigation are respect for the law, honesty, mature judgment, respect for others, employment and military

EXHIBIT A–10	Fifty Questions Most Often Asked by Employers During an Interview

1. Tell me about yourself.
2. What personal goals, other than those related to your occupation, have you established for yourself for the next 10 years?
3. What do you see yourself doing 5 years from now?
4. What do you really want to do in life?
5. What are your short-range and long-range career objectives?
6. How do you plan to achieve your career goals?
7. What are the most important rewards you expect in your career?
8. What do you expect to be earning in 5 years?
9. Why did you choose the career for which you are preparing?
10. Which is more important to you, the money or the type of job?
11. What do you consider your greatest strengths and weaknesses?
12. How would you describe yourself?
13. How do you think a friend or professor who knows you well would describe you?
14. What motivates you to put forth your greatest effort?
15. How has your college experience prepared you for your career?
16. Why should I hire you?
17. What qualifications do you have that makes you think that you will be successful in this environment/setting?
18. How do you determine or evaluate success?
19. What do you think it takes to be successful in an organization like ours?
20. In what ways do you think you can make a contribution to this organization?
21. What qualities should a successful supervisor possess?
22. Describe the relationship that should exist between a supervisor and those reporting to him or her?
23. What two or three accomplishments have given you the most satisfaction? Why?
24. Describe your most rewarding college experience.
25. If you were hiring a graduate for this position, what qualities would you look for?
26. Why did you select your college or university?
27. What led you to choose your field or major?
28. What college subjects did you like best? Why?
29. What college subjects did you like least? Why?
30. If you could do so, how would you plan your academic study differently?
31. What changes would you make in your college or university? Why?
32. Do you have plans for continued study? An advanced degree?
33. Do you think that your grades are a good indication of your academic achievement/ability?
34. What have you learned from participation in extracurricular activities?
35. In what kinds of environments are you most comfortable?
36. How do you work under pressure?
37. In what part-time or summer job have you been most interested? Why?
38. How would you describe the ideal job for you following graduation?
39. Why did you decide to seek a position with this organization?
40. What do you know about this organization?
41. What three things are most important to you in your career/job?

EXHIBIT A–10	Fifty Questions Most Often Asked by Employers During an Interview (*continued*)

42. Are you seeking employment in an organization of a certain size? Why?
43. What criteria are you using to evaluate the organization/employer for which you hope to work?
44. Do you have a geographical preference? Why?
45. Will you relocate? Do relocations bother you?
46. Are you willing to travel?
47. Are you willing to spend at least six months in training?
48. Why do you think you might like to live in the area in which our organization is located?
49. Describe a major problem you have encountered and how you dealt with it.
50. What have you learned from your mistakes?

record, financial record, driving record, and use of drugs and intoxicants. Background investigations may take a few months to complete.

The Job Interview

job interview
A meeting with a prospective employer in which a job applicant projects his or her most impressive qualities.

The **job interview** plays a very important role in your job search. To interview successfully, you must understand the interview process and prepare well. Do not assume that the interview is or should be one-sided. During an interview, you must *project* your most impressive qualities. In other words, you must sell yourself to the prospective employer. As part of the evaluation process, the interviewer will be deciding how you will function as an employee. Therefore, it is essential to demonstrate how your skills, knowledge, and experience match the requirements of the position for which you are interviewing.

It is essential that you speak confidently (not arrogantly) about your skills, knowledge, and experience. In preparing, take time to think about answers to potential interview questions (see Exhibit A–10). When the interviewer asks a question for which you are unprepared, think before you speak; take a second or two and organize your thoughts. Then answer as best you can.

Reread your résumé or the copy of your application before every interview—chances are the interviewer did just that, too. In addition, review your résumé or application for possible questions you might be asked. Formulating answers ahead of time will allow you to be more relaxed and articulate during the interview. If you applied for a civil service job, review the examination bulletin and know the duties and responsibilities of the classification for the position. Job interview attire can be summed up in two words: *conservative* and *businesslike*. Proper dress will give you confidence and enhance your professional image. For most professional-level jobs, the standard dark suit is appropriate for both men and women; less formal clothing may be more appropriate for some jobs. Use common sense. College faculty and career planning counselors can help, as well as someone you may know who is employed in the same field as the position for which you are interviewing. Keep perfume or cologne and jewelry to a minimum. Do not chew gum or other food during the interview.

Take with you to the interview copies of your résumé or application, your list of references (or reference letters), any other relevant documents such as your Social Security card and driver's license, and your transcripts. (A civil service interview panel, however, may not ask to see any

EXHIBIT A–11   *Sample Job Screening Questionnaire*

SUPPLEMENTAL QUESTIONNAIRE
SELF-SCREENING
PROBATION AND PAROLE OFFICER I

The following requirements are needed by all candidates for this position. If you answer "yes" to all requirements listed, sign below and return this form with your completed application. If you answer "no" to any of the requirements, do not complete the rest of the form and do not submit an application. An answer "no" in any one area will result in a rating of "not qualified" for this position.

1. Are you willing and able to cope with unmotivated and hostile individuals who have committed all types of crimes?

    Yes _____   No _____

2. Are you willing to do field checks knowing that you will be going into areas where you may be subject to threats or physical danger?

    Yes _____   No _____

3. Are you willing to testify before the court, parole board, and other judicial hearings to answer questions, present progress reports, and make recommendations?

    Yes _____   No _____

4. Are you willing to be trained in the use of firearms and deadly force?

    Yes _____   No _____

5. Are you willing to be trained in the use of defensive tactics that involve physical contact?

    Yes _____   No _____

6. Are you willing to participate in the arrest of criminal offenders?

    Yes _____   No _____

The answers I have given are true and correct to the best of my knowledge, and I understand that I must be willing and able to perform tasks requiring physical strength and agility.

SIGNATURE _____   **DATE** _____

of these documents.) It is also a good idea to bring a pen or pencil and notebook and a list of questions.

For some positions, two interviews are required. A typical first job interview usually lasts 30 to 60 minutes, although it may run longer. Often called a *screening interview,* the first interview is used to shorten a long list of candidates. You also may be asked to complete a job-related questionnaire that may serve to shorten the list of candidates (see Exhibit A–11).

An oral interview with a civil service panel for a position in corrections may be structured or unstructured. It may include questions regarding your personal history; problem-solving abilities; ability to work effectively with other people, including supervisors, peers, and a diverse public; ability to communicate effectively; and personal qualities including motivation, integrity, and self-discipline. If the interview is for a civil service position, note the names of the panel members who are conducting the interview. An interview for a civil service job may be tape recorded. The recording is in your best interest. It can be used to verify the discussion that took place on either the part of the interviewee or the panel if an appeal is filed.

Remain alert for indications that you are on track. If the interviewer seems relaxed, is following closely, and encouraging you with comments and nods, you are probably on target. If the interviewer appears puzzled, stop and restate your reply. If the interviewer has obviously lost interest, try getting back on track by asking if you covered the point adequately. Maintain eye contact when answering questions, but do not be afraid to avert your eyes when thinking about an answer. A firm handshake will end the interview on a positive note. Thank the interviewer or panel members.

A prospective employer may request a second interview, either because initial interviews indicated that more than one of the applicants might qualify for the position or because others are involved in the hiring decision. Keep in mind when preparing for the second interview that you may now be in direct competition with others whose qualifications are as appropriate as yours. Prepare carefully by doing the following:

- Engage in a more extensive study of the organization to gain in-depth knowledge.
- Evaluate your skills, knowledge, and experience and how they are applicable to the position for which you are applying.
- Review general interview skills.
- Gather appropriate documents, such as résumés, references, and transcripts.
- Compare your personal agenda with the organization's agenda.
- Make additional copies of pertinent records.
- Prepare a list of questions.

Remember, interviewing is a two-way street. Not only is it an opportunity for the organization to ask questions of you; it is also your opportunity to learn more about the organization. Get answers to your questions; this information will help you decide which of the job offers you receive you should accept, and asking the same question of different individuals will allow you to compare responses. Whatever the outcome of any job interview, bear in mind that the employer is thinking first of organizational needs, not of you. Do not let rejections weaken your self-confidence.

The Thank-You Letter

A thank-you letter should always immediately follow a job interview. In fact, you should start thinking about the thank-you letter as soon as the interview is over and mail it within 24 hours of the interview. The thank-you letter is not just "a nice thing to do"; it is also a sales opportunity—another opportunity for you to "sell" yourself. The thank-you letter should be simple; the following is the basic format:

1. First paragraph—thank the reader for the interview and restate the position for which you are applying and your interest in it.
2. Second paragraph—restate your qualifications and reiterate what you have to offer to the company. Refer to specific points discussed during the interview.
3. Last paragraph—restate the first paragraph.

REEVALUATION

Because your interests, skills, and preferences change, you should periodically reevaluate your career choice to determine if you could more effectively use your skills, abilities, and talents in a different occupation or at a different organization. Correspond with your contacts on a fairly regular basis and investigate available positions, but be careful not to take steps that may jeopardize your present position—you may find that it is still the best job for you.

KEY TERMS

self-assessment, *p. A-1*
networking, *p. A-2*
informational interviewing, *p. A-4*
résumé, *p. A-6*

chronological résumé, *p. A-7*
functional résumé, *p. A-10*
job interview, *p. A-16*

ENDNOTES

Chapter 1

1. Details in this paragraph come from the *Oz* homepage on HBO.com, www.hbo.com/oz/index.shtml (accessed July 15, 2005).
2. Public Safety Performance Project of the Pew Charitable Trusts, *Public Safety, Public Spending: Forecasting America's Prison Population 2007–2011* (Washington, DC: Pew Charitable Trusts, 2007).
3. Fox Butterfield, "Crime Keeps on Falling, but Prisons Keep on Filling," *New York Times* News Service, September 28, 1997.
4. John P. Conrad, "The Pessimistic Reflections of a Chronic Optimist," *Federal Probation*, vol. 55, no. 2 (1991), p. 4.
5. Ibid., p. 8.
6. See, for example, Jory Farr, "A Growth Enterprise," www.press-enterprise.com/focus/prison/html/agrowthindustry.html (accessed March 28, 2002).
7. Timothy A. Hughes et al., *Trends in State Parole, 1990–2000* (Washington, DC: U.S. Department of Justice, 2001).
8. Margaret Werner Cahalan, *Historical Corrections Statistics in the United States, 1850–1984* (Washington, DC: U.S. Department of Justice, 1986).
9. Paige M. Harrison and Allen J. Beck, *Prisoners in 2005* (Washington, DC: Bureau of Justice Statistics, 2006).
10. Lauren E. Glaze and Thomas P. Bonczar, *Probation and Parole in the United States, 2005* (Washington, DC: Bureau of Justice Statistics, 2006).
11. Cahalan, *Historical Corrections Statistics*.
12. American Correctional Association, *Vital Statistics in Corrections* (Lanham, MD: American Correctional Association, 2000).
13. Kristen A. Hughes, *Justice Expenditure and Employment in the United States, 2003* (Washington, DC: Bureau of Justice Statistics, 2006), p. 6.
14. Uniform Crime Reporting statistics in this chapter come from FBI, *Crime in the United States, 2006* (Washington, DC: U.S. Department of Justice Office, 2007).
15. Some of the material in this section is adapted from Bureau of Justice Statistics, *The Nation's Two Crime Measures* (Washington, DC: U.S. Department of Justice, November 1995).
16. Shannan M. Catalind, *Criminal Victimization, 2005* (Washington, DC: Bureau of Justice Statistics, August 2006).
17. The figure may be somewhat misleading, however, because an offender who commits a number of crimes may be prosecuted for only one.
18. Much of the following material is adapted from Bureau of Justice Statistics, *Report to the Nation on Crime and Justice*, 2nd ed. (Washington, DC: Bureau of Justice Statistics, 1988), pp. 56–58.
19. President's Commission on Law Enforcement and Administration of Justice, *The Challenge of Crime in a Free Society* (Washington, DC: U.S. Government Printing Office, 1967), p. 159.
20. National Advisory Commission on Criminal Justice Standards and Goals, *Corrections* (Washington, DC: U.S. Government Printing Office, 1975), p. 2.
21. Bureau of Justice Statistics, *Correctional Populations in the United States, 1995* (Washington, DC: U.S. Government Printing Office, 1997).
22. Bob Barrington, "Corrections: Defining the Profession and the Roles of Staff," *Corrections Today*, August 1987, pp. 116–120.
23. Arlin Adams, *The Legal Profession: A Critical Evaluation*, 93 Dick. L. Rev. 643 (1989).
24. Harold E. Williamson, *The Corrections Profession* (Newbury Park, CA: Sage, 1990), p. 79.
25. Adams, *The Legal Profession*.
26. Williamson, *The Corrections Profession*, p. 20.
27. P. P. Lejins, "ACA Education Council Proposes Correctional Officer Entry Tests," *Corrections Today*, vol. 52, no. 1 (February 1990), pp. 56, 58, 60.
28. Mark S. Fleisher, "Teaching Correctional Management to Criminal Justice Majors," *Journal of Criminal Justice Education*, vol. 8, no. 1 (Spring 1997), pp. 59–73.
29. See Robert B. Levinson, Jeanne B. Stinchcomb, and John J. Greene III, "Corrections Certification: First Steps Toward Professionalism," www.aca.org/development/doc_certification firststeps.pdf (accessed March 23, 2003).
30. See the ACA's Professional Certification Program Web page at www.corrections.com/aca/development/certification.htm for more information.
31. The AJA defines a jail manager as "a person (sworn or civilian) who directs, administers, and/or is in charge of the operations of an adult jail facility, division, bureau, department, program, and/or shift; and/or a person (sworn or civilian) who supervises the work and performance of an employee or employees in an adult jail facility." See AJA, *CJM: Handbook for Candidates*, www.corrections.com/aja/cjm_handbook.pdf (accessed March 25, 2007).
32. Michale Omi and Howard Winant, *Racial Formation in the United States: From the 1960s to the 1980s* (New York: Routledge and Kegan Paul, 1986), p. 145.
33. National Center for Women and Policing, *Equality Denied: The Status of Women in Policing, 2001* (Beverly Hills, CA: NCWP, 2002), p. 11.
34. Dianne Carter, "The Status of Education and Training in Corrections," *Federal Probation*, vol. 55, no. 2 (June 1991), pp. 17–23.
35. Williamson, *The Corrections Profession*.

Chapter 2

1. *Gazette d'Amsterdam*, April 1, 1757. Cited by Michel Foucault, *Discipline & Punish: The Birth of the Prison*, trans. Alan Sheridan (New York: Vintage Books, 1995).
2. Edward M. Peters, "Prison Before the Prison: The Ancient and Medieval Worlds," in Norval Morris and David J. Rothman

(eds.), *The Oxford History of the Prison* (New York: Oxford University Press, 1995), p. 6.

3. James Hastings et al., *Dictionary of the Bible*, vol. 1 (New York: Scribner 1905), pp. 523 ff. Cited in Arthur Evans Wood and John Barker Waite, *Crime and Its Treatment: Social and Legal Aspects of Criminology* (New York: American Book Company, 1941), p. 462.

4. Foucault, *Discipline & Punish*, p. 8.

5. See Peters, "Prison Before the Prison," pp. 14–15.

6. Wood and Waite, *Crime and Its Treatment*, p. 462.

7. Pieter Spierenburg, "The Body and the State: Early Modern Europe," in Norval Morris and David J. Rothman (eds.), *The Oxford History of the Prison* (New York: Oxford University Press, 1995), pp. 52–53.

8. Ibid., p. 53.

9. Harry Elmer Barnes and Negley K. Teeters, *New Horizons in Criminology*, 3rd ed. (Englewood Cliffs, NJ: Prentice Hall, 1959), p. 290.

10. Some of the information in this section comes from Harry Elmer Barnes, *Story of Punishment* (Montclair, NJ: Patterson Smith, 1930) and George Ives, *A History of Penal Methods* (London: Stanley Paul, 1914).

11. Barnes and Teeters, *New Horizons*, p. 349.

12. Ives, *A History of Penal Methods*, p. 53.

13. Henry Burns Jr., *Corrections: Organization and Administration* (St. Paul, MN: West, 1975), p. 86.

14. Barnes and Teeters, *New Horizons*, p. 292.

15. Ives, *A History of Penal Methods*, p. 56.

16. John Howard, *The State of the Prisons* (London: J. M. Dent, 1929).

17. Spierenburg, "The Body and the State," p. 53.

18. Burns, *Corrections*, p. 87.

19. Spierenburg, "The Body and the State," p. 62.

20. See Abbott Emerson Smith, *Colonists in Bondage* (Chapel Hill: University of North Carolina Press, 1947).

21. For a good account of the practice, see Robert Hughes, *The Fatal Shore: The Epic of Australia's Founding* (Vintage Books, 1988).

22. James Trager, *The People's Chronology* (Henry Holt, 1994).

23. See Aleksandr Solzhenitsyn, *The Gulag Archipelago, 1918–1956* (1974) and *The Gulag Archipelago 2 and 3* (1975, 1978).

24. "Siberia," *Microsoft Encarta 96 Encyclopedia* (Redmond, WA: Microsoft Corporation, 1995).

25. Barnes and Teeters, *New Horizons*, p. 293.

26. Peters, "Prison Before the Prison," p. 7.

27. Spierenburg, pp. 49–77.

28. Ibid., p. 67.

29. Ibid., p. 72.

30. Randall McGowen, "The Well-Ordered Prison," in Norval Morris and David J. Rothman (eds.), *The Oxford History of the Prison* (New York: Oxford University Press, 1995), p. 83.

31. Foucault, *Discipline & Punish*, p. 11.

32. See Wood and Waite, *Crime and Its Treatment*, p. 463.

33. Harry Elmer Barnes, *The Repression of Crime* (New York: Doran, 1926), p. 101.

34. John Howard, *The State of the Prisons in England and Wales* (London: William Eyres, 1777).

35. Spierenburg, "The Body and the State," pp. 49–77.

36. McGowen, "The Well-Ordered Prison," p. 86.

37. "Enlightenment, Age of," *Microsoft Encarta 96, CD-ROM* (Redmond, WA: Microsoft Corporation, 1995).

38. Ibid.

39. Some of the information in this section comes from The Nanaimo Region John Howard Society (of Canada) at www.island.net/~ccampbel/index.html (accessed May 30, 2003).

40. Howard, *The State of the Prisons*.

41. Randall McGowen, "The Well-Ordered Prison: England 1780–1865," in Norval Morris and David J. Rothman (eds.), *The Oxford History of the Prison* (New York: Oxford University Press, 1995), p. 87.

42. Some of the information in this section comes from *The Internet Encyclopedia of Philosophy*, www.utm.edu/research/iep/ (accessed June 26, 2007).

43. Some of the information in this section comes from the Bentham Project at University College, London, www.ucl.ac.uk/Bentham-Project/jb.htm (accessed June 25, 1999).

44. For further information, see Frank E. Hagan, "Panopticon," in Marilyn D. McShane and Frank P. Williams III (eds.), *Encyclopedia of American Prisons* (New York: Garland, 1996), pp. 341–342.

45. Wood and Waite, *Crime and Its Treatment*, p. 456.

46. From "The Secret of Great Workers," *The Penny Magazine*, vol. 1, no. 1 (March 31, 1832), citing M. Dumont, "Recollections of Mirabeau."

47. See Margaret Wilson, *The Crime of Punishment* (New York: Harcourt Brace, 1931), p. 165.

48. See the All Saints Project, www.drsoft.com/allsaints/ pnotes.htm (accessed July 30, 2003). This site includes input from the Royal Canadian Mounted Police and the Nova Scotia Crime Prevention Association.

49. See Lucia Zedner, "Wayward Sisters: The Prison for Women," in Norval Morris and David J. Rothman (eds.), *The Oxford History of the Prison* (New York: Oxford University Press, 1995).

50. Ibid., p. 333.

51. Ibid., p. 336.

52. Ibid.

53. Sanford Bates, *Prisons and Beyond* (New York: Macmillan, 1936).

54. Rodney Henningson, "Sanford Bates," in Marilyn D. McShane and Frank P. Williams (eds.), *Encyclopedia of American Prisons* (New York: Garland, 1996), pp. 51–53.

55. David M. Horton and George R. Nielsen, *Walking George: The Life of George John Beto and the Rise of the Modern Texas Prison System* (Denton: University of North Texas Press, 2006).

56. Dan Richard Beto, review of Jeremy Travis and Michelle Waul (eds.), *Prisoners Once Removed: The Impact of Incarceration and Reentry on Children, Families, and Communities* (Washington, DC: Urban Institute Press, 2003), in *Federal Probation*, vol. 68, no. 2 (2004), www.uscourts.gov/fedprob/ September_2004/bookshelf.html (accessed January 10, 2007).

57. Charles Jeffords and Jan Lindsey, "George J. Beto," in Marilyn D. McShane and Frank P. Williams (eds.), *Encyclopedia of American Prisons* (New York: Garland, 1996), pp. 58–61.

Chapter 3

1. Brad W. Gary, "Blakely Gets 35 Years," *Columbia Basin Herald Online*, March 23, 2005, www.columbiabasinherald.com/articles/2005/03/23/news/news02.prt (accessed July 5, 2005).

2. John P. Conrad, "The Pessimistic Reflections of a Chronic Optimist," *Federal Probation*, vol. 55, no. 2 (1991), p. 7.

3. Sigmund Freud, *Totem and Taboo*, trans. and ed. by James Strachey (New York: Norton, 1990).

4. Lisa Kennedy, "The Miseducation of Nushawn Williams," *POZ online*, August 2000, www.poz.com/archive/ august2000/inside/nushawnwilliams.html (accessed June 20,

2002); Jackie Cooperman, "AIDS Scare Triples in Scope," ABCNEWS.com, October 28, 1997.

5. "'AIDS Monster' Denied Parole in New York," *Austin Chronicle*, August 31, 2001, www.austinchronicle.com/issues/dispatch/2001-08-31/cols_aboutaids.html (accessed June 20, 2002).

6. Andrew von Hirsch, *Doing Justice: The Choice of Punishments* (New York: Hill and Wang, 1976), pp. 48–49.

7. Morgan O. Reynolds, *The Reynolds Report: Crime and Punishment in the U.S.*, NCPA Policy Report No. 209 (Dallas, TX: National Center for Policy Analysis, 1997), www.public-policy.org/~ncpa/studies/s209/s209.html (accessed August 30, 2007).

8. Edwin Zedlewski, *Making Confinement Decisions*, Research in Brief (Washington, DC: National Institute of Justice, 1987).

9. John J. DiIulio, "Crime and Punishment in Wisconsin," *Wisconsin Policy Research Institute Report*, vol. 3, no. 7 (1990), pp. 1–56; see also William Barr, *The Case for More Incarceration* (Washington, DC: U.S. Department of Justice, Office of Policy Development, 1992).

10. Washington State Institute for Public Policy, *Evidence-Based Public Policy Options to Reduce Future Prison Construction, Criminal Justice Costs, and Crime Rates* (Olympia, WA: The Institute, October 2006), p. 10. For a national overview of such data see William Spelman, "What Recent Studies Do (and Don't) Tell Us about Imprisonment and Crime," in Michael Tonry (ed.), *Crime and Justice: A Review of Research*, vol. 27 (Chicago: University of Chicago Press, 2002), p. 422.

11. R. A. Liedka and B. Useem, "The Crime-Control Effect of Incarceration: Does Scale Matter?" *Criminology and Public Policy*, vol. 5, no. 2 (2006), pp. 245–276. Cited in Howard N. Snyder and Jeanne B. Stinchcomb, "Do Higher Incarceration Rates Mean Lower Crime Rates?" *Corrections Today*, vol. 68 (October 2006), p. 92.

12. Francis T. Cullen and Paul Gendreau, "Assessing Correctional Rehabilitation: Policy, Practice, and Prospects," in Julie Horney (ed.), *Criminal Justice 2000*, vol. 3 (Washington, DC: National Institute of Justice, 2000).

13. Robert Martinson, "What Works? Questions and Answers About Prison Reform," *Public Interest*, vol. 35 (Spring 1974), pp. 22–54.

14. Cullen and Gendreau, "Assessing Correctional Rehabilitation."

15. Edgardo Rotman, *Beyond Punishment: A New View on the Rehabilitation of Criminal Offenders* (Westport, CT: Greenwood, 1990), p. 11.

16. California Proposition 36 Steering Committee, *Impact Analysis*, February 28, 2001, www.dph.sf.ca.us/Prop36/Meetings/Minutes/2-28%20SteerComm.pdf (accessed June 18, 2007).

17. Marty Price, "Crime and Punishment: Can Mediation Produce Restorative Justice for Victims and Offenders?" www.vorp.com/articles/crime.html (accessed February 9, 1999).

18. United Nations, *Restorative Justice: Report of the Secretary-General* (Vienna, Austria: United Nations Commission on Crime Prevention and Criminal Justice, 2002).

19. Graeme Newman, *The Punishment Response* (Philadelphia: Lippincott, 1978), p. 104.

20. See, for example, Andrew R. Klein, *Alternative Sentencing: A Practitioner's Guide* (Cincinnati, OH: Anderson, 1988).

21. Much of what follows is derived from Bureau of Justice Assistance, *National Assessment of Structured Sentencing* (Washington, DC: Bureau of Justice Assistance, 1996).

22. S. A. Shane-DuBow, A. P. Brown, and E. Olsen, *Sentencing Reform in the U.S.: History, Content and Effect* (Washington, DC: U.S. Department of Justice, 1985).

23. J. Cohen and M. H. Tonry, "Sentencing Reforms and Their Impacts," in A. Blumstein et al. (eds.), *Research on Sentencing: The Search for Reform* (Washington, DC: National Academy Press, 1983), pp. 305–459.

24. State of Washington, Sentencing Guidelines Commission, *Adult Sentencing Manual 2000*, www.sgc.wa.gov/adult_sentencing_manual_2000.htm (accessed June 20, 2007).

25. Code of Alabama, 12-25-2. The commission was established by executive order on August 30, 1999.

26. The materials in this section are derived from the Web site of the United States Sentencing Commission, www.ussc.gov.

27. Title II of the Comprehensive Crime Control Act of 1984; 18 U.S.C. § 3551–3626 and 28 U.S.C. § 991–998.

28. 21 U.S.C. 841(b)(1)(C).

29. M. Tonry, *Sentencing Matters* (Oxford, UK: Oxford University Press, 1995).

30. U.S. Department of Justice, *Mandatory Sentencing* (Washington, DC: Office of Justice Programs, 1997).

31. In 1999, California's three-strikes law was upheld by the U.S. Supreme Court in the case of *Riggs v. California*, 525 U.S. 1114 (1999) cert. denied.

32. G. L. Pierce and W. J. Bowers, "The Bartley-Fox Gun Law's Short-Term Impact on Crime in Boston," *Annals of the American Academy of Political and Social Science*, vol. 455 (1981), pp. 120–132.

33. C. Loftin, M. Heumann, and D. McDowall, "Mandatory Sentencing and Firearms Violence: Evaluating an Alternative to Gun Control," *Law and Society Review*, vol. 17 (1983), pp. 287–318.

34. C. Loftin and D. McDowall, "The Deterrent Effects of the Florida Felony Firearm Law," *Journal of Criminal Law and Criminology*, vol. 75 (1984), pp. 250–259.

35. D. McDowall, C. Loftin, and B. Wierseman, "A Comparative Study of the Preventive Effects of Mandatory Sentencing Laws for Gun Crimes," *Journal of Criminal Law and Criminology*, vol. 83, no. 2 (Summer 1992), pp. 378–394.

36. Joint Committee on New York Drug Law Evaluation, *The Nation's Toughest Drug Law: Evaluating the New York Experience*, a project of the Association of the Bar of the City of New York, the City of New York, and the Drug Abuse Council, Inc. (Washington, DC: Government Printing Office, 1978).

37. Michael Tonry, *Sentencing Reform Impacts* (Washington, DC: U.S. Department of Justice, National Institute of Justice, 1987).

38. Much of what follows is taken from John Clark, James Austin, and D. Alan Henry, *Three Strikes and You're Out: A Review of State Legislation* (Washington, DC: National Institute of Justice, 1997).

39. Bureau of Justice Assistance, *National Assessment of Structured Sentencing* (Washington, DC: U.S. Department of Justice, February 1996).

40. Elizabeth A. King, "Inter Alia," *Corrections Compendium*, April 2002, p. 22.

41. Several states have had such laws on the books for many years. For example, South Dakota has had three-strikes–type legislation since 1877.

42. James Austin, "'Three Strikes and You're Out': The Likely Consequences on the Courts, Prisons, and Crime in California and Washington State," *St. Louis University Public Law Review*, vol. 14, no. 1 (1994).

43. The Washington law does permit the governor to grant a pardon or clemency, but it also recommends that no person sentenced under this law to life in prison without parole be granted clemency until he or she has reached 60 years of age and is judged no longer a threat to society.

44. *Andrade* v. *Attorney General of the State of California,* 270 F.3d 743 (2001).
45. *Lockyer* v. *Andrade,* 538 U.S. 63 (2003).
46. *Ewing* v. *California,* 538 U.S. 11 (2003).
47. Austin, "'Three Strikes and You're Out.'"
48. Countywide Criminal Justice Coordination Committee, *Impact of the "Three Strikes Law" on the Criminal Justice System in Los Angeles County* (Los Angeles: CCJCC, November 15, 1995). The number of inmates the jail system can house is limited by a federal court order and the sheriff's budget. Therefore, the use of early-release mechanisms for lower-risk offenders has been accelerated to make room for the growing number of two- and three-strikes cases. This policy has not increased the size of the jail population, but it has changed its composition.
49. California Sheriff's Association, *Three Strikes Jail Population Report* (Sacramento: California Sheriff's Association, 1995).
50. Center for Urban Analysis, Santa Clara County Office of the County Executive, *Comparing Administration of the "Three-Strikes Law" in the County of Los Angeles with Other Large California Counties* (Santa Clara, CA: Center for Urban Analysis, Santa Clara County Office of the County Executive, May 1996).
51. Los Angeles County Sheriff's Department, *"Three Strikes" Law—Impact on Jail: Summary Analysis* (Los Angeles: Los Angeles County Sheriff's Department, August 31, 1996).
52. John Clark et al., *Three Strikes and You're Out: A Review of State Legislation* (Washington, DC: National Institute of Justice, 1997).
53. *Second and Third Strikers in the Institution Population* (Sacramento: California Department of Corrections, Data Analysis Unit, March, 2005), p. 2.
54. Ryan S. King and Marc Mauer, *Aging Behind Bars: "Three Strikes" Seven Years Later* (Washington, DC: Sentencing Project, 2001).
55. Ibid.
56. Fox Butterfield, "States Easing Stringent Laws on Prison Time," *The New York Times,* September 2, 2001.
57. "Crime Spree Blamed on Early Release," Associated Press, March 12, 2003.
58. See U.S. Sentencing Commission, *Report to Congress: Cocaine and Federal Sentencing Policy* (Washington, DC: U.S. Sentencing Commission, 2002), www.schmalleger.com/pubs/cocaine2002.pdf.
59. See "Justice Department Fights to Maintain Crack/Powder Cocaine Sentencing Disparities," DRCNet, March 22, 2002, www.drcnet.org/wol/230.html#sentencingcommission (accessed June 26, 2002).
60. Edith E. Flynn et al., "Three-Strikes Legislation: Prevalence and Definitions," in National Institute of Justice, *Task Force Reports From the American Society of Criminology* (Washington, DC: National Institute of Justice, 1997).
61. Paula M. Ditton and Doris J. Wilson, *Truth in Sentencing in State Prisons* (Washington, DC: Bureau of Justice Statistics, 1999), p. 1.
62. Robin I. Lubitz and Thomas W. Ross, "Sentencing Guidelines: Reflections on the Future," *Sentencing and Corrections: Issues for the 21st Century,* no. 10 (Washington, DC: National Institute of Justice, 2001).
63. Edgardo Rotman, *Beyond Punishment: A New View on the Rehabilitation of Criminal Offenders* (Westport, CT: Greenwood Press, 1990), p. 3.

Chapter 4

1. Associated Press, "Mel Gibson Points to Movie Criticism as a Reason for Tirade," *Mobile Press-Register,* October 15, 2006, p. 5A.
2. Lauren E. Glaze and Thomas P. Bonczar, *Probation and Parole in the United States, 2005* (Washington, DC: U.S. Department of Justice, Bureau of Justice Statistics, November 2006).
3. B. J. George, "Screening, Diversion and Mediation in the United States," *New York Law School Law Review,* vol. 29 (1984), pp. 1–38.
4. M. Douglas Anglin, Douglas Longshore, and Susan Turner, "Treatment Alternatives to Street Crime: An Evaluation of Five Programs," *Criminal Justice and Behavior,* vol. 26, no. 2 (1999), pp. 168–195; "Another Chance, Instead of Jail," *The Philadelphia Inquirer,* May 26, 2005, www.philly.com/mld/inquirer/2005/05/26/news/local/11740649.htm (accessed June 19, 2005); Melissa Nann, "Philadelphia Drug Treatment Court Continues to Win Recognition," *The Legal Intelligencer,* June 23, 2004, p. 3; John S. Goldcamp, Doris Weiland, and James Moore, *The Philadelphia Treatment Court, Its Development and Impact: The Second Phase (1998–2000)* (Philadelphia: Crime and Justice Research Institute, August 2001); see also Julie Shaw, "Drug Court Deals Them a Ticket to Recovery: 10 Years of Goodbye, Jail, & Hello, Treatment," *Philadelphia Daily News,* May 24, 2007, www.philly.com (accessed May 29, 2007).
5. Thomas E. Ulrich, "Pretrial Division in the Federal Court System," *Federal Probation,* vol. 66, no. 3 (December 2002), pp. 30–38.
6. M. D. Anglin and Y. Hser, "Treatment of Drug Abuse," in Michael Tonry and James Q. Wilson (eds.), *Drugs and Crime: Crime and Justice: A Review of Research,* vol. 13 (Chicago: University of Chicago Press, 1990), pp. 393–460; D. N. Nurco, T. W. Kinlock, and T. E. Hanlon, "The Nature and Status of Drug Abuse Treatment," *Maryland Medical Journal,* vol. 43 (January, 1994), pp. 51–57; D. D. Simpson et al., "A National Evaluation of Treatment Outcomes for Cocaine Dependence," *Archives of General Psychiatry,* vol. 56, no. 6 (1999), pp. 507–514.
7. Edward W. Sieh, "A Theoretical Basis for Handling Technical Violations," *Federal Probation,* vol. 67, no. 3 (December 2003), pp. 28–33.
8. John Augustus, *A Report of the Labors of John Augustus, for the Last Ten Years, in Aid of the Unfortunate* (Boston: Wright and Hasty, 1852); reprinted as *John Augustus, First Probation Officer* (New York: National Probation Association, 1939), p. 26.
9. Ibid., pp. 4–5, 78–79.
10. Robert Panzarella, "Theory and Practice of Probation on Bail in the Report of John Augustus," *Federal Probation,* vol. 66, no. 3 (December 2002), pp. 38–43.
11. Sanford Bates, "The Establishment and Early Years of the Federal Probation System," *Federal Probation,* vol. 14 (1950), pp. 16–21; Joel R. Moore, "Early Reminiscences," *Federal Probation,* vol. 14 (1950), pp. 21–29; Richard A. Chappell, "The Federal Probation System Today," *Federal Probation,* vol. 14 (1950), pp. 30–40.
12. Richard A. Chappell, "Looking Back at Federal Probation: Recollections of Early Years," *Federal Probation,* vol. 34, no. 4 (December 1975), pp. 26–30.
13. Glaze and Bonczar, *Probation and Parole in the United States,* 2005.
14. Camille Graham Camp and George M. Camp, *The Corrections Yearbook, 2000: Adult Corrections* (Middletown, CT: Criminal Justice Institute, Inc., 2001), p. 178.

15. Caroline Wolf Harlow, *Prior Abuse Reported by Inmates and Probationers* (Washington, DC: Department of Justice, Bureau of Justice Statistics, April 1999).

16. "States Imposing More Fees on Inmates and Probationers," *Corrections Journal*, January 23, 2006, p. 7.

17. Barbara Krauth and Larry Link, *State Organizational Structures for Delivering Adult Probation Services* (Washington, DC: U.S. Department of Justice, National Institute of Corrections, June 1999), pp. 3–5.

18. Kathy L. Waters, "Probation, Parole and Community Corrections: A Difficult Topic to Understand?" *Corrections Today*, vol. 65, no. 1 (February 2003), p. 10.

19. Institute for Court Management, *Private Probation in Georgia: A New Direction, Service and Vigilance* (Atlanta: Administrative Office of Courts, May 2001), pp. 24–37.

20. Robert J. Bosco, "Connecticut Probation's Partnership with the Private Sector," *Topics in Community Corrections: Privatizing Community Supervision* (Longmont, CO: National Institute of Corrections, 1998), p. 12.

21. Ibid., p. 15.

22. Joan Petersilia et al., *Granting Felons Probation: Public Risks and Alternatives* (Santa Monica, CA: RAND, 1985).

23. W. R. Benedict and L. Huff-Corzine, "Return to the Scene of the Punishment: Recidivism of Male Property Offenders on Felony Probation," *Journal of Research in Crime and Delinquency*, vol. 34 (1997), pp. 237–252.

24. James A. Gondles Jr., "The Probation and Parole System Needs Our Help to Succeed," *Corrections Today*, vol. 65, no. 1 (February 2003), p. 8.

25. Jenni Gainsborough and Marc Mauer, *Diminishing Returns: Crime and Incarceration in the 1990s* (Washington, DC: Sentencing Project, September 2000), p. 3.

26. William H. DiMascio, *Seeking Justice: Crime and Punishment in America* (New York: Edna McConnell Clark Foundation, 1997), p. 43.

27. "The Uconn Poll: Prison Crowding," University of Connecticut, Center for Survey Research and Analysis, March 8, 2004.

28. Joan Petersilia, "Probation in the United States," in Michael Tonry, *Crime and Justice: A Review of Research*, vol. 22 (Chicago: University of Chicago Press, 1997), pp. 149–200.

29. Paul Gendreau, "The Principles of Effective Intervention with Offenders," in Alan Harland (ed.), *Choosing Correctional Options That Work: Defining the Demand and Evaluating the Supply* (Thousand Oaks, CA: Sage, 1996).

30. See, for example, Joan Petersilia and Susan Turner, *Evaluating Intensive Supervision Probation/Parole: Results of a Nationwide Experiment* (Washington, DC: National Institute of Justice, 1993); Ben Crouch, "Is Incarceration Really Worse? Analysis of Offenders' Preferences for Prison Over Probation," *Justice Quarterly*, vol. 10 (1993), pp. 67–88; Joan Petersilia and Elizabeth Piper Deschenes, "Perceptions of Punishment: Inmates and Staff Rank the Severity of Prison Versus Intermediate Sanctions," *The Prison Journal*, vol. 74 (1994), pp. 304–328; Peter B. Wood and H. G. Grasmick, "Toward the Development of Punishment Equivalencies: Male and Female Inmates Rate the Severity of Alternative Sanctions Compared to Prison," *Justice Quarterly*, vol. 16 (1999), pp. 19–50; Randy R. Gainey, Sara Stean, and Rodney L. Engen, "Exercising Options: An Assessment of the Use of Alternative Sanctions for Drug Offenders," *Justice Quarterly*, vol. 22, no. 4 (2005), pp. 488–520.

31. Stanley W. Hodge and Victor E. Kappler, "Can We Continue to Lock up the Nonviolent Drug Offender?" in Charles B. Fields (ed.), *Controversial Issues in Corrections* (Boston: Allyn & Bacon, 1999), pp. 137–151.

32. Institute of Medicine, Committee for the Substance Abuse Coverage Study, "A Study of the Evolution, Effectiveness, and Financing of Public and Private Drug Treatment Systems," in D. R. Gerstein and H. J. Harwood (eds.), *Treating Drug Problems*, vol. 1 (Washington, DC: National Academy Press, 1990).

33. R. Hubbard et al., "Treatment Outcome Prospective Study (TOPS): Client Characteristics and Behaviors Before, During, and After Treatment," DHHS Publication No. (ADM) 84-1349, in F. Tims and J. Ludford (eds.), *Drug Abuse Treatment Evaluation: Strategies, Progress and Prospects* (Rockville, MD: National Institute on Drug Abuse, 1984), pp. 29–41.

34. Peter Finn and Sarah Kuck, *Stress Among Probation and Parole Officers and What Can Be Done About It* (Washington, DC: U.S. Department of Justice, National Institute of Justice, 2005).

35. Emily Gaarder, Nancy Rodriguez, and Marjorie Zatz, "Criers, Liars, and Manipulators: Probation Officers' Views of Girls," *Justice Quarterly*, vol. 21, no. 3 (September 2004), p. 572.

36. Mark Sanders, "Building Bridges Instead of Walls: Effective Cross-Cultural Counseling," *Corrections Today*, vol. 65, no. 1 (February 2003), pp. 58–59.

37. Kathleen M. Carroll, Charla Nich, and Bruce J. Rounsaville, "Contribution of the Therapeutic Alliance to Outcome in Active Versus Control Psychotherapies," *Journal of Consulting and Clinical Psychology*, vol. 65, no. 3 (1997), pp. 510–514.

38. Brad Bogue, *The Framework Behind the COMBINES Curriculum* (Boulder, CO: unpublished manuscript).

39. Camp and Camp, *The Corrections Yearbook, 2000* pp. 199–200, 205–206.

40. "Missouri Considers New Sentencing System," *Corrections Compendium*, vol. 29, no. 6 (November/December 2004), p. 39.

41. Michael D. Norman and Robert C. Wadman, "Probation Department Sentencing: Recommendations in Two Utah Counties," *Federal Probation*, vol. 64, no. 2 (December 2000), pp. 47–51.

42. Michael D. Norman and Robert C. Wadman, "Utah Presentence Reports: User Group Perceptions of Quality and Effectiveness," *Federal Probation*, vol. 64, no. 1 (June 2000), pp. 8–9.

43. American Bar Association, *Standards Relating to Sentencing Alternatives and Procedures* (Chicago: American Bar Association, n.d.).

44. Paul F. Cromwell, Rolando V. del Carmen, and Leanne F. Alarid, *Community-Based Corrections*, 5th ed. (Belmont, CA: Wadsworth, 2002).

45. Cecil E. Greek, "The Cutting Edge: A Survey of Technological Innovation," *Federal Probation*, vol. 65, no. 1 (June 2001), p. 51.

46. Finn and Kuck, *Stress Among Probation and Parole Officers.*

47. Thomas G. Ogden, "Pagers, Digital Audio, and Kiosk: Office Assistants," *Federal Probation*, vol. 65, no. 2 (September 2001), pp. 35–37.

48. American Probation and Parole Association, *Caseload Standards for Probation and Parole* (Lexington, KY: APPA, September 2006), www.appa-net.org (accessed January 17, 2007).

49. Patricia M. Harris, Raymond Gingerich, and Tiffany A. Whittaker, "The 'Effectiveness' of Differential Supervision," *Crime & Delinquency*, vol. 50, no. 2 (April 2004), pp. 235–271.

50. Michelle Gaseau, *Mapping to Improve Supervision and Community Corrections*, October 23, 2000, www.corrections.com (accessed November 10, 2003); Jaishankar Karuppan-

nan, "Mapping and Corrections: Management of Offenders with Geographic Information Systems," *Corrections Compendium*, vol. 30, no. 1 (January/February 2005), pp. 7–9, 31–33.

51. Peggy Burke, "Probation and Parole Violations: An Overview of Critical Issues," in Madeline M. Carter (ed.), *Responding to Probation and Parole Violators* (Washington, DC: National Institute of Corrections, April 2001), p. 6.

52. Petersilia, "Probation in the United States," p. 151.

53. "Leading Officials Issue Plan for 'Reinventing' Probation," *Criminal Justice Newsletter*, vol. 30, no. 7 (April 1, 1999), pp. 1–2.

54. Meghan Fay, "Effective Ways to Manage Parole and Probation Violations," The Corrections Connection Network News (CCNN), Eye on Corrections, June 19, 1999, www.corrections.com (accessed June 24, 2005).

55. As cited in Fay, "Effective Ways to Manage Parole."

56. Burke, "Probation and Parole Violations," pp. 5–6.

57. Becki Ney and Donna Reback, "Developing Baseline Information: Understanding Current Policy and Practice," in Madeline M. Carter (ed.), *Responding to Probation and Parole Violators* (Washington, DC: National Institute of Corrections, April 2001), p. 33.

Chapter 5

1. Sources consulted include "Boy George," *Wikipedia, the Free Encyclopedia*, http://en.wikipedia.org/wiki/Boy_George#Personal_life (accessed September 13, 2006); "Boy George on US Cocaine Charge," BBC NEWS, http://news.bbc.co.uk/1/hi/entertainment/4786814.stm (accessed September 13, 2006).

2. Herbert A. Johnson, *History of Criminal Justice* (Cincinnati, OH: Anderson, 1988); Pierre S. DuPont IV, *Expanding Sentencing Options—A Governor's Perspective* (Washington, DC: U.S. Department of Justice, National Institute of Justice, 1985).

3. Associated Press, "Board Approves Early Parole for 687 Inmates," November 27, 2006, www.todaysthv.com (accessed December 1, 2006).

4. Paige M. Harrison and Allen J. Beck, *Prison and Jail Inmates at Midyear 2005* (Washington, DC: National Institute of Justice, Bureau of Justice Statistics, May 2006); Paige M. Harrison and Allen J. Beck, *Prisoners in 2005* (Washington, DC: U.S. Department of Justice, Bureau of Justice Statistics, November 2006).

5. "California Lawmakers Battle Over Prison Budget," *Corrections Today*, vol. 65, no. 3 (June 2003), p. 20.

6. Michael Tonry, "Intermediate Sanctions in Sentencing Guidelines," in Michael Tonry (ed.), *Crime and Justice: A Review of Research*, vol. 23 (Chicago: University of Chicago Press, 1998), pp. 199–253.

7. Michael Tonry and Mary Lynch, "Intermediate Sanctions," in Michael Tonry (ed.), *Crime and Justice: A Review of Research*, vol. 20 (Chicago: University of Chicago Press, 1996), pp. 102–103.

8. Camille Graham Camp and George M. Camp, *Adult Corrections Yearbook* (Middletown, CT: Criminal Justice Institute, 2001), p. 170.

9. Betsy A. Fulton, Susan Stone, and Paul Gendreau, *Restructuring Intensive Supervision Programs: Applying What Works* (Lexington, KY: American Probation and Parole Association, 1994).

10. Doris Layton MacKenzie, "Evidence-Based Corrections: Identifying What Works," *Crime & Delinquency*, vol. 46, no. 4 (October 2000), pp. 457–472.

11. Joan Petersilia, Arthur J. Lurigio, and James M. Byrne, "Introduction," in James M. Byrne, Arthur J. Lurigio, and Joan Petersilia (eds.), *Smart Sentencing: The Emergence of Intermediate Sanctions* (Newbury Park, CA: Sage, 1992), pp. ix–x; Elizabeth Deschenes, Susan Turner, and Joan Petersilia, *Intensive Community Supervision in Minnesota: A Dual Experiment in Prison Diversion and Enhanced Supervised Release* (Washington, DC: National Institute of Justice, 1995); Joan Petersilia and Susan Turner, *Evaluating Intensive Supervision Probation/Parole: Results of a Nationwide Experiment* (Washington, DC: National Institute of Justice, May 1993).

12. Steve Aos, Marna Miller, and Elizabeth Drake, *Evidence-Based Public Policy Options to Reduce Future Prison Construction, Criminal Justice Costs, and Crime Rates* (Olympia, WA: State Institute for Public Policy, 2006).

13. "Washington State Researchers Rates What Works in Treatment," *Criminal Justice Newsletter*, September 1, 2006, p. 2.

14. Ibid.

15. Doris Layton MacKenzie and J. W. Shaw, "Inmate Adjustment and Change During Shock Incarceration: The Impact of Correctional Boot Camp Programs," *Justice Quarterly*, vol. 7 (1990), pp. 125–150; Joan Petersilia and Susan Turner, "Intensive Probation and Parole," in Michael Tonry (ed.), *Crime and Justice: A Review of Research*, vol. 17 (Chicago: University of Chicago Press, 1993), pp. 281–335.

16. National Association of Drug Court Professionals, www.nadcp.org/whatis/ (accessed April 12, 2002).

17. John S. Goldcamp, "What We Know About the Impact of Drug Courts: Moving Research from 'Do They Work?' to 'When and How They Work,'" testimony before the Senate Judiciary Subcommittee on Youth Violence, October 3, 2000, p. 1.

18. The White House, *National Drug Control Strategy, Update* (Washington, DC: The White House, March 2004), www.state.gov/documents/organization/30228.pdf (accessed December 29, 2006).

19. Drug Court Clearinghouse, www.spa.american.edu/justice/drugcourts.php (accessed March 5, 2007).

20. Goldcamp, "What We Know," p. 4.

21. Ibid., p. 7.

22. www.nadcp.org/whatis/ (accessed December 29, 2006).

23. Ibid.

24. John Roman, Wendy Townsend, and Avinash Singh Bhati, *Recidivism Rates for Drug Court Graduates: Nationally Based Estimates, Final Report* (Washington, DC: National Institute of Justice, July 2003).

25. Michael Rempel et al., *The New York State Adult Drug Court Evaluation: Policies, Participants and Impacts* (New York: Center for Court Innovation, October 2003), www.courtinnovation.org/publications.html#drug-courteval (accessed June 10, 2005).

26. Duren Banks and Denise C. Gottfredson, "Participation in Drug Treatment Court and Time to Arrest," *Justice Quarterly*, vol. 21, no. 3 (September 2004), pp. 637–658; Doris Wells and Janice Munsterman, "Drug Court May Reap Big Savings for Corrections and Taxpayers," *Corrections Today*, vol. 67, no. 4 (July 2005), pp. 24–25, 111.

27. National Institute of Justice, *Drug Courts: The Second Decade* (Washington, DC: U.S. Department of Justice, National Institute of Justice, June 2006).

28. Aos, Miller, and Drake, *Evidence-Based Public Policy Options*.

29. Bureau of Justice Assistance, *How to Use Structured Fines (Day Fines) as an Intermediate Sanction* (Washington, DC: Department of Justice, November 1996).

30. "Finn's Speed Fine Is a Bit Rich," MSNBC online, http://news.bbc.co.uk/2/hi/business/3477285.stm (accessed June 10, 2005).

31. Bureau of Justice Assistance, *How to Use Structured Fines.*
32. Ibid.
33. Aos, Miller, and Drake, *Evidence-Based Public Policy Options,* p. 9.
34. Morris and Tonry, *Between Prison and Probation,* p. 152.
35. Julie C. Martin, "Community Service for Offenders," in Tara Gray (ed.), *Exploring Corrections* (Boston: Allyn & Bacon, 2002), pp. 311–318.
36. Michael Tonry, "Parochialism in U.S. Sentencing Policy," *Crime & Delinquency,* vol. 45, no. 1 (1999), p. 58.
37. DiMascio, *Seeking Justice,* pp. 43–45.
38. Warren Young, *Community Service Orders* (London: Heinemann, 1979); Gill McIvor, *Sentenced to Serve: The Operation and Impact of Community Service by Offenders* (Aldershot, UK: Avebury, 1992); Peter J. O. Tak, "Netherlands Successfully Implements Community Service Orders," *Overcrowded Times,* vol. 6 (1995), pp. 16–17.
39. DiMascio, *Seeking Justice,* p. 37.
40. *FY 2001 Annual Report* (Atlanta: Georgia Department of Corrections, Probation Division, 2002).
41. Gail A. Caputo, "Community Service in Texas: Results of a Probation Survey," *Corrections Compendium,* vol. 39, no. 2 (March/April, 2005), pp. 8–9, 35–37.
42. Dale G. Parent, "Day Reporting Centers: An Evolving Intermediate Sanction," *Federal Probation,* vol. 60, no. 4 (December 1996), pp. 51–54; George Mair, "Day Centres in England and Wales," *Overcrowded Times,* vol. 4 (1993), pp. 5–7.
43. Charles Bahn and James R. Davis, "Day Reporting Centers as an Alternative to Incarceration," *Journal of Offender Rehabilitation,* vol. 27, no. 3/4 (1998), pp. 139–150.
44. Dale G. Parent et al., *Day Reporting Centers* (Washington, DC: National Institute of Justice, 1995).
45. Dale Parent, "Day Reporting Centers: An Emerging Intermediate Sanction," *Overcrowded Times,* vol. 2 (1991), pp. 6, 8; Jack McDevitt and Robyn Miliano, "Day Reporting Centers: An Innovative Concept in Intermediate Sanctions," in James M. Byrne, Arthur J. Lurigio, and Joan Petersilia (eds.), *Smart Sentencing: The Emergence of Intermediate Sanctions* (Newbury Park, CA: Sage, 1992).
46. Liz Marie Marciniak, "The Addition of Day Reporting to Intensive Supervision Probation: A Comparison of Recidivism Rates," *Federal Probation,* vol. 64, no. 1 (June 2000), pp. 34–39.
47. Ibid., p. 37.
48. Roy Sudipto, "Adult Offenders in a Day Reporting Center—A Preliminary Study," *Federal Probation,* vol. 66, no. 1 (June 2002), pp. 44–51.
49. Christine Martin, Arthur J. Lurigio, and David E. Olson, "An Examination of Rearrests and Reincarcerations Among Discharged Day Reporting Center Clients," *Federal Probation,* vol. 67, no. 1 (June 2003), pp. 24–31.
50. Bahn and Davis, "Day Reporting Centers," p. 149.
51. Interview with Joe Russo, program manager at the National Law Enforcement and Corrections Technology Center, in Dana Razzano, "Strides Made in Electronic Monitoring: Improving Accuracy and Lowering Price," Corrections.com, www.corrections.com (accessed April 17, 2002).
52. Darren Gowen, "Remote Location Monitoring—A Supervision Strategy to Enhance Risk Control," *Federal Probation,* vol. 65, no. 2 (September 2001), pp. 38–41.
53. Darren Gowen, "Overview of the Federal Home Confinement Program, 1988–1996," *Federal Probation,* vol. 64, no. 2 (December 2000), pp. 11–18; see also Brian K. Payne and Randy R. Gainey, "The Electronic Monitoring of Offenders Released from Jail or Prison: Safety, Control, and Comparisons to the Incarceration Experience," *The Prison Journal,* vol. 84, no. 4 (December 2004), pp. 413–435.
54. Kathrine Johnson, "States' Use of GPS Offender Tracking Systems," *Journal of Offender Monitoring,* vol. 15, no. 2 (Summer/Fall 2002), pp. 15, 21–22, 26.
55. Katharine Mieszkowski, "Tracking Sex Offenders with GPS," www.salon.com/news/feature/2006/12/19/offenders/index_np.htm (accessed December 31, 2006).
56. Jim McKay, "Electronic Tether," www.govtech.net/magazine/story.php?id=98310&issue=2:2006 (accessed December 31, 2006).
57. Florida Department of Corrections, *A Report on Community Control, Radio Frequency (RF) Monitoring and Global Positioning Satellite (GPS) Monitoring* (Tallahassee, FL: Bureau of Community and Institutional Programs, Office of Program Services, December, 2004).
58. Dan M. Bowers, "Home Detention Systems," *Corrections Today,* July 2000, pp. 102–106.
59. James Bonta, Suzanne Wallace-Capretta, and Jennifer Rooney, "Can Electronic Monitoring Make a Difference? An Evaluation of Three Canadian Provinces," *Crime & Delinquency,* vol. 46, no. 1 (January 2000), pp. 61–75.
60. Camp and Camp, *Adult Corrections Yearbook,* p. 124.
61. Kay Knapp, Peggy Burke, and Mimi Carter, *Residential Community Corrections Facilities: Current Practice and Policy Issues* (Longmont, CO: National Institute of Corrections, August 1992).
62. "Director Addresses Change Within BOP," *The Third Branch,* vol. 38, no. 3 (March 2006), www.uscourts.gov/ttb/03-06/interview/index.html (accessed January 1, 2007).
63. Richard Lawrence, "Restitution Programs," in Tara Gray (ed.), *Exploring Corrections* (Boston: Allyn & Bacon, 2002), pp. 319–320.
64. Ibid., p. 320.
65. General Accounting Office, *Federal Guidance Needed If Halfway Houses Are to Be a Viable Alternative to Prison* (Washington, DC: U.S. Government Printing Office, 1975).
66. Division of Criminal Justice, Office of Research and Statistics, *Executive Summary: 2000 Community Corrections Study Results* (Denver: State of Colorado, Division of Criminal Justice, Office of Research and Statistics, March 22, 2001), www.cdpsweb.state.co.us/ors/docs.htm (accessed May 18, 2001).
67. Christopher T. Lowenkamp and Edward J. Latessa, "Developing Successful Reentry Programs: Lessons Learned from the 'What Works' Research," *Corrections Today,* vol. 67, no. 2 (April 2005), pp. 72–77.
68. U.S. General Accounting Office, *Federal Guidance,* p. 12.
69. Kurt D. Siedschlaw and Beth A. Wiersma, "Costs and Outcomes of a Work Ethic Camp: How Do They Compare to a Traditional Prison Facility?" *Corrections Compendium,* vol. 30, no. 6 (November/December 2005), pp. 1–5, 28–30.
70. Aos, Miller, and Drake, *Evidence-Based Public Policy Options.*
71. Doris L. MacKenzie and Eugene E. Hebert (eds.), *Correctional Boot Camps: A Tough Intermediate Sanction* (Washington, DC: National Institute of Justice, 1996).
72. Dale G. Parent, *Correctional Boot Camps: Lessons from a Decade of Research* (Washington, DC: U.S. Department of Justice, National Institute of Justice, June 2003).
73. Doris Layton MacKenzie et al., "Boot Camps as an Alternative for Women," in Doris L. MacKenzie and Eugene E. Hebert (eds.), *Correctional Boot Camps: A Tough Intermediate Sanction* (Washington, DC: National Institute of Justice, 1996).

74. Doris L. MacKenzie and A. Rosay, "Correctional Boot Camps for Juveniles," in *Juvenile and Adult Boot Camps* (Laurel, MD: American Correctional Association, 1996).

75. Sheldon X. Zhang, *Evaluation of the Los Angeles County Juvenile Drug Treatment Boot Camp, Executive Summary* (Washington, DC: U.S. Department of Justice, National Institute of Justice, 2000).

76. Carol Marbin Miller and Marc Caputo, "Troubled Boot Camp to Close," *The Miami Herald,* February 22, 2006, http://web.lexis-nexis.com (accessed January 17, 2007); Marc Caputo and Carol Marbin Miller, "In Wake of Death, Juvenile Boot Camp System Is Scrapped," *The Miami Herald,* April 27, 2006, http://web.lexis-nexis.com (accessed January 17, 2007), Marc Caputo, "Act May Prevent Other Parents 'Pain,'" *The Miami Herald,* June 1, 2006, http://web.lexis-nexis.com (accessed January 17, 2007); Dara Kam, "7 Guards Charged in Death at Camp Teen's Death," *Palm Beach (FL) Post,* November 29, 2006, http://web.lexis-nexis.com (accessed January 17, 2007).

77. Merry Morash and Lila Rucker, "Critical Look at the Ideal of Boot Camp as Correctional Reform," *Crime & Delinquency,* vol. 36 (1990), pp. 204–222; DiMascio, *Seeking Justice,* p. 41.

78. Doris L. MacKenzie and J. W. Shaw, "The Impact of Shock Incarceration on Technical Violations and New Criminal Activities," *Justice Quarterly,* vol. 10, no. 3 (1993), pp. 463–486.

79. Dionne T. Wright and G. Larry Mays, "Correctional Boot Camps, Attitudes, and Recidivism: The Oklahoma Experience," *Journal of Offender Rehabilitation,* vol. 28, no. 1/2 (1998), pp. 71–87.

80. Jeanne B. Stinchcomb and W. Clinton Terry III, "Predicting the Likelihood of Rearrest Among Shock Incarceration Graduates: Moving Beyond Another Nail in the Boot Camp Coffin," *Crime & Delinquency,* vol. 47, no. 2 (April 2001), pp. 221–242.

81. As cited in Dan Herbeck, "Schumer Urges Ashcroft to Reconsider Closure of Shock Prison Camps," *Buffalo News,* January 16, 2005, p. A12.

82. Ibid.

83. As cited in Nora A. Jones, "Alternative Incarceration Program Discontinued by Bureau of Prisons," *The Daily Record of Rochester,* February 16, 2005.

84. Dan Herbeck, "Local Judge, Lawyers Decry Elimination of Federal Shock Incarceration Program," *Buffalo News,* January 8, 2005, p. D1; see also "Director Addresses Change Within BOP," *The Third Branch,* vol. 38, no. 3 (March 2006), www.uscourts.gov/ttb/03-06/interview/index.html (accessed February 20, 2007).

85. See, for example Cheryl L. Clark and David W. Aziz, "Shock Incarceration in New York State: Philosophy, Results, and Limitations," in Doris L. MacKenzie and Eugene E. Hebert, (eds.), *Correctional Boot Camps: A Tough Intermediate Sanction* (Washington, DC: National Institute of Justice, 1996), pp. 38–68; MacKenzie and Hebert, *Correctional Boot Camps;* Parent, *Correctional Boot Camps.*

86. Dale Parent, "Boot Camps Failing to Achieve Goals," *Overcrowded Times,* vol. 5 (1994), pp. 8–11; Doris Layton MacKenzie, "Boot Camps: A National Assessment," *Overcrowded Times,* vol. 5 (1994), pp. 14–18; Philip A. Ethridge and Jonathan R. Sorensen, "An Analysis of Attitudinal Change and Community Adjustment Among Probationers in a County Boot Camp," *Journal of Contemporary Criminal Justice,* vol. 13, no. 2 (May 1992), pp. 139–154.

87. W. J. Dickey, *Evaluating Boot Camp Prisons* (Washington, DC: National Institute of Justice, 1994); Peter Katel and Melinda Liu, "The Bust in Boot Camps," *Newsweek,* February 21, 1994, p. 26; Parent, "Boot Camps Failing to Achieve Goals."

88. Doris L. MacKenzie and Claire Souryal, *Multi-Site Evaluation of Shock Incarceration: Executive Summary* (Washington, DC: National Institute of Justice, 1994); see also Doris L. MacKenzie and A. Piquero, "The Impact of Shock Incarceration Programs on Prison Crowding," *Crime & Delinquency,* vol. 40 (1994), pp. 222–249.

89. Stinchcomb and Terry, "Predicting the Likelihood of Rearrest," pp. 239–240.

90. Velmer S. Burton et al., "A Study of Attitude Change Among Boot Camp Participants," *Federal Probation,* vol. 57, no. 3 (1993), pp. 46–52; see also Michael W. Osler, "Shock Incarceration: Hard Realities and Real Possibilities," *Federal Probation,* vol. 55, no. 1 (1991), pp. 34–42.

91. Judith Greene and John Dobble, *Attitudes Toward Crime and Punishment in Vermont: Public Opinion About an Experiment with Restorative Justice* (Washington, DC: U.S. Department of Justice, National Institute of Justice, 2000); see also David R. Karp, "Harm and Repair: Observing Restorative Justice in Vermont," *Justice Quarterly,* vol. 18, no. 4 (December 2001), pp. 727–757, for an analysis of the decision-making process for negotiating "thin" versus "thick" reparative contracts with offenders.

92. George F. Cole et al., *The Practice and Attitudes of Trial Court Judges Regarding Fines as a Criminal Sanction* (Washington, DC: National Institute of Justice, 1987).

Chapter 6

1. Pat Graham, "Northern Colorado Punter Accused of Stabbing Rival in Kicking Leg," *Associated Press State and Local Wire,* September 13, 2006, http://web.lexis-nexis.com (accessed January 15, 2007); Deborah Frazer, "Former UNC Punter Surrenders," *Rocky Mountain (Denver) News,* October 24, 2006, http://web.lexis-nexis.com (accessed January 15, 2007); Mike Peters, "Evans Police Honors Citizens, Officers," *The Tribune (Greeley, Co),* January 12, 2007, www.greeleytribune.com/article/2007112/News/101110099 (accessed January 15, 2007); Pat Graham, "Ex-backup Punter in Court Tuesday Morning to Review Evidence," *Associated Press State and Local Wire,* February 6, 2007, http://web.lexis-nexis.com (accessed February 20, 2007).

2. Michael O'Toole, "Jails and Prisons: The Numbers Say They Are More Different Than Generally Assumed," *American Jails,* www.corrections.com/aja/mags/articles/toole.html (accessed May 9, 2003); see also Daron Hall, "Jails vs. Prisons," *Corrections Today,* vol. 68, no. 1 (February 2006) p. 8.

3. Paige M. Harrison and Allen J. Beck, *Prison and Jail Inmates at Midyear 2005* (Washington, DC: Bureau of Justice Statistics, May 2006) and Vanessa St. Gerard, "New Study Proves Jails Are an Important Component of the Reentry Equation," *On the Line,* vol. 28, no. 2 (March 2005).

4. Doris J. James, *Profile of Jail Inmates, 2002* (Washington, DC: U.S. Department of Justice, Bureau of Justice Statistics, July 2004).

5. National Advisory Commission on Criminal Justice Standards and Goals, *Corrections* (Washington, DC: U.S. Government Printing Office, 1973), p. 273.

6. Marilyn D. McShane and Frank P. Williams III (eds.), *Encyclopedia of American Prisons* (New York: Garland, 1996), p. 494.

7. Ibid., p. 496.

8. Ronald L. Goldfarb, *Jails: The Ultimate Ghetto* (Garden City, NY: Doubleday, 1975), p. 29.

9. John Irwin, *The Jail: Managing the Underclass in American Society* (Berkeley: University of California Press, 1986).

10. Randall G. Shelden and William B. Brown, "Correlates of Jail Crowding: A Case Study of a County Detention Center," *Crime & Delinquency,* vol. 37, no. 3 (1991), pp. 347–362.

11. David M. Parrish, "The Evolution of Direct Supervision in the Design and Operation of Jails," *Corrections Today,* www .corrections.com/aca/cortoday/october00/parrish.html (accessed October 26, 2000).

12. Linda Zupan, *Jails: Reform and the New Generation Philosophy* (Cincinnati, OH: Anderson, 1991); see also Richard Wener, "The Invention of Direct Supervision," *Corrections Compendium,* vol. 30, no. 2 (March/April, 2005), pp. 4–7, 32–34.

13. Dennis McCave, "Testing the Seams: When the Limits Are Pushed in Direct Supervision," *American Jails,* vol. 16, no. 1 (2002), pp. 51–56.

14. Ibid., p. 56.

15. Ibid.

16. Peter Perroncello, "Direct Supervision: A 2001 Odyssey," *American Jails,* vol. 15, no. 6 (2001), p. 25. See also Constance Clem et al., *Direct Supervision Jails: 2006 Sourcebook* (Longmont, CO: National Institute of Corrections Information Center, September 2006); Christine Tartaro, "Are They Really Direct Supervision Jails? A National Study," *American Jails,* vol. 20, no. 5 (November/December 2006), pp. 9–17.

17. Ray Coleman, former facility commander of the King County Regional Justice Center in Kent, Washington, and past president of the American Jail Association, and Chuck Oraftik, director of justice architecture at Hellmuth, Obata, and Kassabaum, San Francisco, CA (personal communication, December 15, 2006).

18. Ken Kerle, "Jail Statistics: The Need for Public Education," *American Jails* (September/October 2006), p. 5.

19. Doris J. James, *Profile of Jail Inmates, 2002* (Washington, DC: U.S. Department of Justice, Bureau of Justice Statistics, July 2004).

20. James Austin, Luiza Chan, and Williams Elms, *Women Classification Study—Indiana Department of Corrections* (San Francisco, CA: National Council on Crime and Delinquency, 1993).

21. James, *Profile of Jail Inmates, 2002:* see also Gail Elias and Kenneth Ricci, *Women in Jail: Facility Planning Issues* (Washington, DC: U.S. Department of Justice, National Institute of Corrections, March 1997).

22. Tim Brennan and James Austin, *Women in Jail: Classification Issues* (Washington, DC: U.S. Department of Justice, National Institute of Corrections, March 1997).

23. Merry Morash, Timothy S. Bynum, and Barbara A. Koons, *Women Offenders: Programming Needs and Promising Approaches* (Washington, DC: U.S. Department of Justice, National Institute of Justice, August 1998).

24. William C. Collins and Andrew W. Collins, *Women in Jail: Legal Issues* (Washington, DC: U.S. Department of Justice, National Institute of Corrections, December 1996).

25. Linda Zupan, "The Persistent Problems Plaguing Modern Jails," in Tara Gray (ed.), *Exploring Corrections* (Boston: Allyn & Bacon, 2002), pp. 37–62.

26. Kenneth Kerle, "Women in the American World of Jails: Inmates and Staff," *Margins: Maryland's Law Journal on Race, Religion, Gender, and Class,* vol. 2, no. 1 (Spring 2002), pp. 41–61.

27. Barbara Bloom, Barbara Owen, and Stephanie Covington, *Gender-Responsiveness Strategies Research, Practice, and Guiding Principles for Women Offenders* (Washington, DC:

U.S. Department of Justice, National Institute of Corrections, June 2003).

28. Todd D. Minton, *Jails in Indian Country, 2004* (Washington, DC: U.S. Department of Justice, Bureau of Justice Statistics, November 2006).

29. Lawrence A. Greenfield and Steven K. Smith, *American Indians and Crime* (Washington, DC: U.S. Department of Justice, Bureau of Justice Statistics, February 1999).

30. U.S. Department of the Interior, Office of Inspector General, *Neither Safe Nor Secure—An Assessment of Indian Detention Facilities* (Washington, DC: U.S. Department of the Interior, Office of Inspector General, September 2004).

31. Ibid., pp. 1–2.

32. Samuel Walker, Cassia Spohn, and Miriam DeLone, "Corrections: A Picture in Black and White," in Tara Gray (ed.), *Exploring Corrections* (Boston: Allyn & Bacon, 2002), pp. 13–24.

33. Michael Tonry, *Malign Neglect* (New York: Oxford University Press, 1995).

34. Walker, Spohn, and DeLone, "Corrections," p. 16.

35. James J. Stephan, *Census of Jails, 1999* (Washington, DC: U.S. Department of Justice, Bureau of Justice Statistics, August 2001).

36. William J. Sabol and Paige M. Harrison, *Prison and Jail Inmates at Midyear 2006* (Washington, DC: U.S. Department of Justice, Bureau of Justice Statistics, June 2007).

37. Ibid.

38. American Correctional Association, *Vital Statistics in Corrections,* p. 26.

39. Michael L. Birzer and Delores Craig-Moreland, "Why Do Jails Charge Housing Fees?" *American Jails,* vol. 20, no. 1 (March/April 2006), pp. 63–68.

40. Joann Brown Morton, "Providing Gender-Responsiveness Services for Women and Girls," *Corrections Today,* vol. 69, no. 4 (August 2007), pp. 6, 12.

41. Jennifer Steinhauer, "For $82 a Day, Booking a Cell in a 5-Star Jail," *The New York Times,* April 29, 2007, www .nytimes.com (accessed April 30, 2007); Jennifer Steinhauer, "Some Jails Let Prisoners Pay to Stay in Nicer Surroundings," *The San Diego Union-Tribune,* April 29, 2007, www .signonsandiego.com (accessed April 30, 2007); Larry Welborn and Eric Carpenter, "Jaramillo Wants to Pay for Jail," *The Orange County Register,* March 3, 2007, www.ocregister .com (accessed May 10, 2007). See also the Web sites of the Huntington Beach (CA) police department, Torrence (CA) police department, and Santa Ana (CA) police department.

42. Doris J. James and Lauren E. Glaze, *Mental Health Problems of Prison and Jail Inmates* (Washington, DC: U.S. Department of Justice, Bureau of Justice Statistics, September 2006).

43. Ibid.; see also Liz Lipton, "Few Safeguards Govern Elimination of Psychiatric Beds," *Psychiatric News,* vol. 36, no. 15 (August 3, 2001), p. 9, http://pn.psychiatriconline.org/cgi/ content/full/36/15/9 (accessed January 13, 2007).

44. Sally Satel, "Out of the Asylum, Into the Cell," *The New York Times,* November 1, 2003, www.psychlaws.org/General Resources/article199.htm (accessed January 13, 2007); Bazelon Center for Mental Health Law, "Lawsuit Alleges Civil Rights Violations in Cook County Jail," August 12, 2003, www.bazelon.org/newsroom/archive/2003/8-12-03cook county (accessed January 13, 2007).

45. Christopher G. Mumola, *Suicide and Homicide in State Prisons and Local Jails* (Washington, DC: U.S. Department of Justice, Bureau of Justice Statistics, August 2005).

46. Christina Tartaro and Rick Ruddell, "Trouble in Mayberry: A National Analysis of Suicides and Attempts in Small Jails,"

American Journal of Criminal Justice, vol. 31, no. 1 (2006), pp. 81–100; see also Rick Ruddell and G. Larry Mays "Expand or Expire: Jails in Rural America," *Corrections Compendium,* vol. 31, no. 6 (November/December 2006) pp. 1–2, 4–5, 20–21, 27.

47. Christopher J. Mumola, *Suicide and Homicide in State Prisons and Local Jails.*

48. National Sheriff's Association, *The State of Our Nation's Jails, 1982* (Washington, DC: National Sheriff's Association, 1982).

49. Kerle, "Women in the American World of Jails."

50. Stephan, *Census of Jails, 1999.*

51. National Sheriff's Association, *The State of Our Nation's Jails.*

52. Ibid., p. 231.

53. Ibid., p. 151.

54. As cited in National Institute of Corrections, *Briefing Paper: Trends in Jail Privatization* (Boulder, CO: National Institute of Corrections Information Center, February 1992).

55. Semoon Chang and Jack S. Tillman, "Should County Jails Be Privatized?" *American Jails,* vol. 16, no. 4 (September/October 2002), p. 48.

56. Mark A. Cunniff, *Jail Crowding: Understanding Jail Population Dynamics* (Washington, DC: U.S. Department of Justice, National Institute of Corrections, January 2002).

57. Ibid., p. 21.

58. Richard H. Lamb et al., "Outcome for Psychiatric Emergency Patients Seen by Outreach Police–Mental Health Team," *Psychiatric Services,* vol. 46, no. 12 (December 1999), pp. 1267–1271.

59. As referenced in Henry J. Steadman et al., "A SAMSHA Research Initiative Assessing the Effectiveness of Jail Diversion Programs for Mentally Ill Persons," *Psychiatric Services,* vol. 15, no. 12 (December 1999), pp. 1620–1623.

60. Substance Abuse and Mental Health Services Administration, www.samsha.gov/index.aspx (accessed June 14, 2005).

61. Mark Nadler, "Reentry for a Jail Audience," *American Jails,* vol. 19, no. 4 (September/October 2005), pp. 13–24.

62. Richard P. Seiter and Karen R. Kadela, "Prisoner Reentry: What Works, What Does Not, and What Is Promising," *Crime & Delinquency,* vol. 49, no. 3 (2003), pp. 360–388.

63. Michelle Gaseau, "Challenges of Jail Reentry," www.corrections.com/news/article.aspx?articleid=4611 (accessed January 14, 2007).

64. Caroline Wolf Harlow, *Profile of Jail Inmates, 2002,* p. 3.

65. National Institute of Justice, *The Orange County, Florida, Jail Educational and Vocational Programs* (Washington, DC: U.S. Department of Justice, 1997).

66. Ibid., p. 3.

67. Paula M. Ditton, *Mental Health and Treatment of Inmates and Probationers* (Washington, DC: U.S. Department of Justice, Bureau of Justice Statistics, July 1999), p. 1; Allen J. Beck and Laura M. Marusehak, *Mental Health Treatment in State Prisons, 2000* (Washington, DC: U.S. Department of Justice, Bureau of Justice Statistics, July 2001); Risdon N. Slate et al., "Training Federal Probation Officers as Mental Health Specialists," *Federal Probation,* vol. 68, no. 3, pp. 9–15; "Pretrial Services Officers as Mental Health Specialists," *Federal Probation,* vol. 67, no. 3 (December 2003), pp. 13–20; Doris J. James and Lauren E. Glaze, *Mental Health Problems of Prison and Jail Inmates.*

68. Thomas N. Faust, "Shift the Responsibility of Untreated Mental Illness Out of the Criminal Justice System," *Corrections Today,* April 2003, pp. 100–103; see also Lipton, "Few Safeguards Govern Elimination of Psychiatric Beds"; James and Glaze, *Mental Health Problems of Prison and Jail Inmates.*

69. Lance Couturier, Frederick Maue, and Catherine McVey, "Releasing Inmates with Mental Illness and Co-occurring Disorders into the Community," *Corrections Today,* vol. 67, no. 2 (April 2005), pp. 82–85.

70. James A. Gondles, "The Mentally Ill Don't Belong in Jail," *Corrections Today,* vol. 67, no. 2 (April 2005), p. 6.

71. Couturier, Maue, and McVey, "Releasing Inmates with Mental Illness."

72. United States House of Representatives, Committee on Government Reform—Minority Staff Special Investigations Division, *Incarceration of Youth Who Are Waiting for Community Mental Health Services in the United States* (Washington, DC: U.S. House of Representatives, July 2004).

73. Pat Nolan, "Prison Fellowship and Faith-Based Initiatives," *On the Line,* vol. 25, no. 5 (November 2002), p. 2.

74. Bryon R. Johnson, David B. Larson, and Timothy C. Pitts, "Religious Programs, Institutional Adjustment, and Recidivism Among Former Inmates in Prison Fellowship Programs," *Justice Quarterly,* vol. 14, no. 1 (March 1997), pp. 145–166; Bryon R. Johnson, "Religious Programs and Recidivism Among Former Inmates in Prison Fellowship Programs: A Long-Term Follow-Up Study," *Justice Quarterly,* vol. 21, no. 2 (June 2004), pp. 329–354.

75. Sheldon Crapo, "Breaking the Cycle of Crime . . . One Life at a Time," *American Jails,* vol. 11, no. 1 (March/April 1997), p. 24.

76. Correspondence from Jonathan Walls, American Correctional Association, June 11, 2005.

77. As posted on the American Correctional Association Web site, www.aca.org/standards/testimonials (accessed June 15, 2005).

Chapter 7

1. Mike Robinson, "Ryan, Now Facing Years Behind Bars, Takes the News Without Tears (or) Whining," *Associated Press State and Local Wire,* April 18, 2006; Matt O'Connor and Rudolph Bush, "Ryan Gets 6 1/2 Years: Ex-Governor Regrets Conviction but Doesn't Admit to Wrongdoing," *Chicago Tribune,* September 7, 2006, http://web.lexis-nexis.com (accessed March 3, 2007); Mike Robinson, "Ryan Lawyers Say Jury Turmoil Made Fair Verdict Impossible," *Associated Press State and Local Wire,* February 20, 2007.

2. Paige M. Harrison and Allen J. Beck, *Prisoners in 2005* (Washington, DC: U.S. Department of Justice, Bureau of Justice Statistics, November 2006).

3. Ibid.

4. Thomas P. Bonczar, *Prevalence of Imprisonment in the U.S. Population, 1974–2001* (Washington, DC: U.S. Department of Justice, Bureau of Justice Statistics, August 2003), p. 7.

5. Roy Walmsley, *World Prison Population List* (London: Kings College, University of London, January 2007), www.prisonstudies.org (accessed February 4, 2007).

6. Federal Bureau of Investigation, "Crime in the United States 2005" (Washington, DC: Federal Bureau of Investigation, 2006), www.fbi.gov (accessed February 4, 2007); Harrison and Beck, op. cit.

7. Andrew Coyle, "The Use and Abuse of Prison Around the World," *Corrections Today* (December 2004), pp. 64–67; see also David A. Bowers and Jerold L. Waltman, "Do More Conservative States Impose Harsher Felony Sentences? An Exploratory Analysis of 32 States," *Criminal Justice Review,* vol. 18, no.1 (Spring 1993), pp. 61–70.

8. Harrison and Beck, *Prisoners in 2005;* and James J. Stephen and Jennifer C. Karberg, *Census of State and Federal Cor-*

rectional Facilities, 2000 (Washington, DC: U.S. Department of Justice, Bureau or Justice Statistics, August 2003).

9. Beth R. Richie, "Challenges Incarcerated Women Face as They Return to Their Communities: Findings from Life History Interviews," *Crime & Delinquency*, vol. 47, no. 3 (July 2001), pp. 368–389.

10. Bureau of Justice Statistics, *Special Report: Women Offenders* (Washington, DC: U.S. Department of Justice, 1999).

11. Meda Chesney-Lind, "Putting the Breaks on the Building Binge," *Corrections Today*, vol. 54, no. 6 (August 1992), p. 30.

12. Richie, "Challenges Incarcerated Women Face."

13. The Urban Institute, *Families Left Behind: The Hidden Costs of Incarceration and Reentry* (Washington, DC: Urban Institute Press, 2003).

14. Federal Bureau of Investigation, *Crime in the United States 2006* (Washington, DC: U.S. Department of Justice, 2007), www.fbi.gov (accessed September 26, 2007).

15. Jennifer Gonnerman, "An Expert Analyzes the Prison Population Boom," *Village Voice*, February 22, 2000, p. 56.

16. Steve Aos, Marna Miller, and Elizabeth Drake, *Evidence-Based Public Policy Options to Reduce Future Prison Construction, Criminal Justice Costs, and Crime Rates* (Olympia, WA: State Institute for Public Policy, 2006).

17. Kathleen A. Gnall and Gary Zajac, "Assessing for Success in Offender Reentry," *Corrections Today*, vol. 67, no. 2 (April 2005), p. 94.

18. Niyi Awofeso, "Evolution of Prisoner Classification Systems," *American Jails* (September/October 2006), pp. 87–91.

19. Carl B. Clements, "The Future of Offender Classification: Some Cautions and Prospects," *Criminal Justice and Behavior*, vol. 8 (1981), pp. 15–16.

20. Carl B. Clements, "Offender Classification: Two Decades of Progress," *Criminal Justice and Behavior*, vol. 23 (1996), p. 123.

21. Patricia L. Hardyman, James Austin, and Johnette Peyton, *Prisoner Intake Systems: Assessing Needs and Classifying Prisoners* (Washington, DC: U.S. Department of Justice, National Institute of Corrections, February 2004), p. viii.

22. J. Alexander et al., *Internal Prison Classification Systems: A Field Test of Three Approaches* (San Francisco, CA: National Council on Crime and Delinquency, 1997).

23. Ibid., p. ix.

24. Clements, "Offender Classification."

25. Ibid.

26. Robert B. Levinson, *Unit Management in Prisons and Jails* (Lanham, MD: American Correctional Association, 1999).

27. Melvina Sumter, "Editorial Introduction: Faith Based Prison Programs," *Criminology & Public Policy*, vol. 5, no. 3 (August 2006), pp. 523–528.

28. National Institute of Corrections, *Report of the National Institute of Corrections Advisory Board Hearings: Faith-Based Approach to Correctional Issues* (Washington DC: U.S. Department of Justice, National Institute of Corrections, June 2005).

29. Daniel P. Mears, "Faith-Based Reentry Programs: Cause for Concern or Showing Promise," *Corrections Today*, vol. 69, no. 2 (April 2006), p. 32; see also D. P. Mears et al., "Faith-Based Efforts to Improve Prisoner Reentry: Assessing the Logic and Evidence," *Journal of Criminal Justice*, vol. 34, no. 4 (2006), pp. 351–367.

30. Thomas P. O'Connor, "What Works, Religion as a Correctional Intervention: Part II," *Journal of Community Corrections*, vol. 14 (2005), pp. 4–6, 20–26; "Faith-Based Prison Program Struck Down by Federal Judge," *Criminal Justice Newsletter*, June 1, 2006, pp. 1–2; and Mears, "Faith-Based

Reentry Programs," and Mears et al., "Faith-Based Efforts to Improve Prisoner Reentry."

31. As discussed in Sumter, "Editorial Introduction."

32. Jeff Brumley, "Governor Shepherding Faith Groups into State Services," *Florida Times-Union*, March 21, 2005, p. A-1; Joyce Howard Price, "Prison Operative, Ministry Teaming Up," *Washington Times*, March 16, 2004, www.washtimes.com/national/20040315-102202-8251r.htm (accessed July 13, 2005); James Pequese and Robert Koppel, "Managing High-Risk Offenders in Prison Dormitory Settings," *Corrections Today*, vol. 65, no. 4 (July 2003), pp. 82–84.

33. Camille Powell, "Ravens' Lewis Out of Prison," *The Washington Post*, June 4, 2005, p. E5; Bill Montgomery, "Pro Football: Freed, Lewis Has No Bitter Feelings," *The Atlanta Journal-Constitution*, June 4, 2005, p. 8.

34. Aos, Miller, and Drake, *Evidence-Based Public Policy Options*.

35. Barry Krisberg and Susan Marchionna, *Attitudes of U.S. Voters Toward Prisoner Rehabilitation and Reentry Policies* (San Francisco CA: National Council on Crime and Delinquency, April 2006), www.nccd-crc.org (accessed February 11, 2007).

36. Bureau of Justice Assistance, *Prison Industry Enhancement Certification Program*, www.ojp.usdoj.gov/BJA/grant/piecp.html (accessed February 11, 2007).

37. Marilyn C. Moses and Cindy J. Smith, "Factories Behind Fences: Do Prison 'Real Work' Programs Work?" *National Institute of Justice Journal*, vol. 257 (June 2007), pp. 32–35.

38. Cindy J. Smith et al., *Correctional Industries Preparing Inmates for Re-entry: Recidivism and Post-Release Employment* (Washington, DC: U.S. Department of Justice, June 2006).

39. *U.S. Department of Justice, Federal Prison Industries, Inc., FY 2004 Annual Report* (Washington, DC: U.S. Department of Justice, Federal Bureau of Prisons, www.unicor.gov (accessed February 11, 2007).

40. W. Saylor and G. Gaes, *Study of "Rehabilitating" Inmates Through Industrial Work Participation, and Vocational and Apprenticeship Training* (Washington, DC: Federal Bureau of Prisons, 1996); Joseph Summerill, "Congress Continues to Dismantle UNICOR," *Corrections Today*, vol. 67, no. 4 (July 2005) pp. 26–27, 30.

41. Karl O. Haigler et al., *Executive Summary of Literacy Behind Prison Walls: Profiles of the Prison Population from the National Adult Literacy Survey* (Washington, DC: U.S. Department of Education, National Center for Education Statistics, 1994).

42. Caroline Wolf Harlow, *Education and Correctional Populations* (Washington, DC: U.S. Department of Justice, Bureau of Justice Statistics, January 2003).

43. Anne F. Parkinson and Stephen J. Steurer, "Overcoming the Obstacles in Effective Correctional Instruction," *Corrections Today*, vol. 66, no. 2 (April 2004), pp. 88–91.

44. Joan Petersilia, "Hard Time: Ex-Offenders Returning Home After Prison," *Corrections Today*, vol. 67, no. 2 (April 2005), pp. 66–71.

45. Aos, Miller, and Drake, *Evidence-Based Public Policy Options;* see also Wendy Erisman and Jeanne Bayer Contardo, *Learning to Reduce Recidivism: A 50-State Analysis of Post-secondary Correctional Education Policy* (Washington, DC: Institute for Higher Education Policy, November 2005).

46. Quoted in "Prisoners Less Educated, Less Literate, Study Finds," press release, U.S. Department of Education, Office of Public Affairs, December 2, 1994, www.ed.gov/PressReleases/12-1994/pris.html; Stephen J. Steuer, Alice Tracy, and Linda Smith, *Three State Recidivism Study* (Lan-

ham, MD: Correctional Education Association, 2001).

47. Karen F. Lahm, "Equal or Equitable: An Exploration of Educational and Vocational Program Availability for Male and Female Offenders," *Federal Probation*, vol. 64, no. 2 (December 2000), pp. 39–46.

48. Peter Schmidt, "College-Level Programs for Prisoners Rebound After 1990s Cuts, A New Study Finds," *The Chronicle of Higher Education Today's News*, http://chronicle.com/daily/2005/11/2005110303m.htm (accessed November 3, 2005).

49. "Inmate Health Care," *Corrections Compendium*, vol. 29, no. 6 (November/December, 2004), p. 10; see also National Commission on Correctional Health Care, *The Health Status of Soon-to-Be-Released Inmates, Volumes I and II* (Chicago: National Commission on Correctional Health Care, March 2002 and April 2002, respectively).

50. "Inmate Health Care and Communicable Diseases," *Corrections Compendium*, vol. 31, no. 5 (September/October 2006), pp. 10–34.

51. Michael S. Vaughn and Leo Carroll, "Separate and Unequal: Prison Versus Free-World Medical Care," *Justice Quarterly*, vol. 15 (1998), pp. 3–40.

52. Claire Cooper, "Federal Judge Takes over State Prisons' Health Care System," *The Press Democrat*, July 1, 2005, pp. A1, A13.

53. James J. Stephan and Jennifer C. Karberg, *Census of State and Federal Correctional Facilities, 2000* (Washington, DC: U.S. Department of Justice, Bureau of Justice Statistics, August 2003, rev. October 15, 2003).

54. Excerpted from California and North Dakota's departments of corrections Web sites, www.bdcorr.ca.gov/Communications Office/facts_figures.asp, www.state.nd.us/docr/docr/biennial reports.htm (accessed February 14, 2007); see also Andy Furillo, "State Considers Sentencing Commission," *Sacramento Bee*, November 20, 2006, www.contracostatimes.com/mid/cctimes/news/state/1605 (accessed February 14, 2007).

55. Andy Furillo, "Governor Signs Prison Building Bill," *The Press Democrat* (Santa Rosa, CA), May 4, 2007, p. B6.

56. Stephan and Karberg, *Census of State and Federal Correctional Facilities*, p. 12.

57. James J. Stephan, *State Prison Expenditures, 2001* (Washington, DC: U.S. Department of Justice, Bureau of Justice Statistics, June 2004); see also Pew Charitable Trusts, *Public Safety, Public Spending: Forecasting America's Prison Population 2007–2011* (Philadelphia: Pew Charitable Trusts, 2007).

58. William Petroski, "Prison Upgrade to Cost Millions, *Des MoinesRegister.com*, http://desmoinesregister.com (accessed April 15, 2007).

59. Gonnerman, "An Expert Analyzes," p. 56.

60. Pew Charitable Trusts, *Public Safety, Public Spending*.

61. James Stephens, *State Prison Expenditures 2001* (Washington, DC: U.S. Department of Justice, Bureau of Justice Statistics, June 2004).

62. Equal Justice Initiative of Alabama, *Criminal Justice Reform in Alabama: A Report and Analysis of Criminal Justice Issues in Alabama, Part One: Sentencing, Probation, Prison Conditions and Parole* (Montgomery: Equal Justice Initiative of Alabama, March 2005).

63. Pew Charitable Trusts, *Public Safety, Public Spending.*

64. See "More States Now Billing Inmates," *Corrections Today*, vol. 66, no. 6 (December 2004), p. 18; Karla Crocker, "Inmates Fees for Service," *Corrections Today*, vol. 66, no. 4 (July 2004), pp. 82–85.

65. Stephan, *State Prison Expenditures, 2001.*

66. Allan Turner, "More Terrorists, Less Resources: Confronting One of the Most Critical Challenges in Corrections History," *Corrections Today*, vol. 66, no. 4 (July 2004), pp. 52–54.

67. Ibid., p. 53.

68. Ibid.

69. Stephan and Karberg, *Census of State and Federal Correctional Facilities*, p. 7.

70. Ibid.

71. Ibid.

72. Ibid.

73. Shawn Mansfield, Federal Bureau of Prisons, Research and Evaluation (personal communication, February 22, 2007).

74. Scott Shane, "U.S. Tops World in Prison Population; Overtakes Russia for Dubious Honor," *Arizona Republic*, June 8, 2003, p. A 14.

75. See, for example, series of three articles in *Criminology & Public Policy*, vol. 5, no. 2 (2006), pp. 213–298.

76. Shane, "U.S. Tops World."

77. Patrick A. Langan and David J. Levin, *Recidivism of Prisoners Released in 1994* (Washington, DC: Bureau of Justice Statistics, June 2002).

78. Christine Lindquist, Jennifer Hardison, and Pamela K. Lattimore, *Reentry Courts Process Evaluation (Phase I), Final Report* (Washington, DC: U.S. Department of Justice, National Institute of Justice, April 2003).

Chapter 8

1. Kathy Barks Hoffman, "Assisted Suicide Advocate Jack Kevorkian to Be Paroled in June," Associated Press State and Local Wire, December 13, 2006, http://web.lexis-nexis.com (accessed March 3, 2007); "A Timeline of Dr. Jack Kevorkian's Assisted-Suicide Campaign," Associated Press State and Local Wire, December 13, 2006, http://web.lexis-nexis.com (accessed March 3, 2007); Kathleen Gray, "Early Out For Kevorkian Unlikely," *Detroit Free Press*, February 1, 2007, http://web.lexis-nexis.com (accessed March 3, 2007).

2. Charles L. Newman, *Sourcebook on Probation, Parole and Pardons*, 3rd ed. (Springfield, IL: Charles C Thomas, 1970), pp. 30–31; see also Norval Morris, *Maconochie's Gentlemen: The Story of Norfolk Island and the Roots of Modern Prison Reform* (New York: Oxford University Press, 2002).

3. Philip Klein, *Prison Methods in New York State* (New York: Columbia University Press, 1920), p. 417. Cited in U.S. Department of Justice, *Attorney General's Survey of Release Procedures*, vol. 4 (Washington, DC: U.S. Government Printing Office, 1939–1940), p. 5.

4. M. W. Calahan, *Historical Corrections Statistics in the United States, 1850–1984* (Washington, DC: Bureau of Justice Statistics, 1986).

5. G. W. Wickersham, *Reports of the United States National Commission on Law Observance and Enforcement: Wickersham Commission, Report on Penal Institutions, Probation and Parole* (Washington, DC: U.S. Government Printing Office, 1930–1931), p. 324.

6. Ibid., p. 325.

7. Edwin H. Sutherland and Donald R. Cressey, *Principles of Criminology* (Chicago: Lippincott, 1955), p. 568.

8. David J. Rothman, *Conscience and Convenience: The Asylum and Its Alternatives in Progressive America* (Boston: Little, Brown, 1980), pp. 159–161.

9. Douglas R. Lipton, Robert Martinson, and Judith Wilks, *The Effectiveness of Correctional Treatment: A Survey of Treatment Evaluation Studies* (New York: Praeger, 1975).

10. Peggy McGarry, *Handbook for New Parole Board Members* (Philadelphia: Center for Effective Public Policy, 1989), p. 4.

11. Patrick A. Langan and David J. Levin, *Recidivism of Prisoners Released in 1994* (Washington, DC: U.S. Department of Justice, Bureau of Justice Statistics, July 2002); see also Pew

Charitable Trusts, *Public Safety, Public Spending: Forecasting America's Prison Population 2007–2011* (Philadelphia: Pew Charitable Trusts, 2007).

12. The Council of State Governments, *The Report of the Re-Entry Policy Council: Charting the Safe and Successful Return of Prisoners to the Community* (Lexington, KY: The Council of State Governments, 2005).

13. Nancy G. La Vigne et al., *Prisoner Reentry and Community Policing Strategies for Enhancing Public Safety* (Washington, DC: Urban Institute, 2006).

14. Quoted in "Parole Has Only Slight Effect on Rearrest Rates, Report Says," *Corrections Journal*, March 22, 2005, p. 7.

15. Pamela K. Lattimore, "The Challenges of Reentry," *Corrections Today*, vol. 69, no. 2 (April 2007), p. 90.

16. The Council of State Governments, *The Report of the Re-entry Policy Council*.

17. Sheldon X. Zhang, Robert E. L. Roberts, and Valerie Callanan, "Multiple Services on a Statewide Scale: The Impact of the California Preventing Parolee Crime Program," *Corrections Compendium*, vol. 30, no. 6 (November/December 2005), pp. 6–7, 30–35.

18. RTI International and Urban Institute, *The Multi-site Evaluation of the Serious and Violent Offender Reentry Initiative*, www.svori-evaluation.org (accessed February 26, 2007).

19. Camille Graham Camp and George M. Camp, *The Corrections Yearbook 1997* (Middletown, CT: Criminal Justice Institute, 1997), p. 181.

20. A. M. Heinz et al., "Sentencing by Parole Boards: An Evaluation," *Journal of Criminal Law and Criminology*, vol. 67 (1976), pp. 1–31.

21. Mary West-Smith, Mark R. Pogrebin, and Eric D. Poole, "Denial of Parole: An Inmate Perspective," *Federal Probation*, vol. 64, no. 2 (December 2000), p. 5.

22. Ronald Burns et al., "Perspectives on Parole: The Board Members' Viewpoint," *Federal Probation*, vol. 63, no. 1 (June 1999), pp. 16–22.

23. West-Smith, Pogrebin, and Poole, "Denial of Parole."

24. Peter B. Hoffman and Lucille K. DeGostin, "Parole Decision-Making: Structuring Discretion," *Federal Probation*, vol. 38, no. 4 (1974), pp. 24–28.

25. McGarry, *Handbook for New Parole Board Members*, p. 4.

26. West-Smith, Pogrebin, and Poole, "Denial of Parole."

27. "Lennon's Killer Denied Parole for 4th Time," CBC News, www.lexis-nexis.com (accessed June 15, 2007).

28. Beth E. Richie, "Challenges Incarcerated Women Face as They Return to Their Communities: Findings from Life History Interviews," *Crime & Delinquency*, vol. 47, no. 3 (July 2001), p. 370.

29. Ibid., p. 379.

30. Lauren E. Glaze and Seri Palla, *Probation and Parole in the United States, 2004* (Washington, DC: U.S. Department of Justice, Bureau of Justice Statistics, November 2005).

31. Joan Petersilia, *When Prisoners Return to the Community: Political, Economic, and Social Consequences* (Washington, DC: U.S. Department of Justice, National Institute of Justice, November 2000).

32. Harry J. Holzer, *What Employers Want: Job Prospects for Less Educated Workers* (New York: Russell Sage Foundation, 1996).

33. Devah Pager, "Evidence-Based Policy for Successful Prisoner Reentry," *Criminology & Public Policy*, vol. 5, no. 3 (August 2006), pp. 505–514.

34. Estimated from American Correctional Association, *Vital Statistics in Corrections* (Lanham, MD: American Correctional Association, 2002), pp. 6–9.

35. Robert F. Kronick, Dorothy E. Lambert, and E. Warren Lambert, "Recidivism Among Adult Parolees: What Makes the Difference?" *Journal of Offender Rehabilitation*, vol. 28, no. 1–2 (1998), pp. 61–69.

36. Amy L. Solomon, Vera Kachnowski, and Avinash Bhati, *Does Parole Work? Analyzing the Impact of Postprison Supervision on Rearrest Outcomes* (Washington, DC: Urban Institute, March 2005).

37. "FY 2000 Cooperative Agreement: Transition from Prison to the Community," *Federal Register*, May 12, 2000.

38. Arthur J. Lurigio, "Effective Services for Parolees with Mental Illnesses," *Crime & Delinquency*, vol. 47, no. 3 (July, 2006), p. 457.

39. Peggy B. Burke, *Abolishing Parole: Why the Emperor Has No Clothes* (Lexington, KY: American Probation and Parole Association, 1995).

40. U.S. Parole Commission, *Notes and Procedures Manual* (Chevy Chase, MD: U.S. Government Printing Office, 1989), p. 143.

41. Joey R. Weedon, "Voting Rights Restored," *Corrections Today*, vol. 66, no. 6 (December 2004), p. 50.

42. The Council of State Governments, *The Report of the Re-Entry Policy Council*.

43. Weedon, "Voting Rights Restored."

44. Vanessa St. Gerard, "Voting Eligibility Rules Cause Confusion in Ohio," *Corrections Compendium*, vol. 29, no. 5 (September/October 2004), p. 35.

45. *Reentry Courts: Managing the Transition from Prison to Community* (Washington, DC: Office of Justice Programs, September, 1999).

46. Ibid., p. 9.

47. Ibid., p. 5.

48. Jeffrey Spelman, "An Initial Comparison of Graduates and Terminated Clients in America's Largest Re-Entry Court," *Corrections Today*, vol. 65, no. 2 (August 2003), pp. 74–83.

49. Susan Herman and Cressida Wasserman, "A Role for Victims in Offender Reentry," *Crime & Delinquency*, vol. 47, no. 3 (July 2001), pp. 428–445.

50. Edward J. Latessa and Harry E. Allen, *Corrections in the Community*, 2nd ed. (Cincinnati, OH: Anderson, 1999), p. 221.

51. Andrew von Hirsch, *Doing Justice: The Choice of Punishments, Report of the Committee for the Study of Incarceration* (New York: Hill and Wang, 1976).

52. Petersilia, *When Prisoners Return to the Community*, p. 2.

53. La Vigne, Solomon, Beckman, and Dedel, *Prisoner Reentry and Community Policing*, p. 16.

54. Donald G. Evans, "Community-Focused Parole," *Corrections Today*, vol. 68, no. 7 (December 2006), pp. 90–91.

55. Ethan Fishman, "Jefferson's Wall v. Moore's Monument," *Journal of Contemporary Thought* (Summer and Winter, 2004), pp. 83–103.

Chapter 9

1. James A. Gondles Jr., "*Guard* Must Go," *Corrections Today*, August 2006, p. 9.

2. See Sylvia G. McCollum, "Excellence or Mediocrity: Training Correctional Officers and Administrators," *The Keeper's Voice*, vol. 17, no. 4 (Fall 1996).

3. Anthony R. Martinez, "Corrections Officer: The 'Other' Prisoner," *The Keeper's Voice*, vol. 18, no. 1 (Spring 1997).

4. Don A. Josi and Dale K. Sechrest, *The Changing Career of the Correctional Officer: Policy Implications for the 21st Century* (Boston: Butterworth-Heinemann, 1998), p. 11.

5. Ibid., p. 12.

6. John Hepburn, "The Exercise of Power in Coercive Organizations: A Study of Prison Guards," *Criminology,* vol. 23, no. 1 (1985), pp. 145–164.

7. Gresham Sykes, *The Society of Captives* (Princeton, NJ: Princeton University Press, 1958).

8. See, for example, James B. Jacobs and Lawrence J. Kraft, "Integrating the Keepers: A Comparison of Black and White Prison Guards in Illinois," *Social Problems,* vol. 25, no. 3 (1978), pp. 304–318.

9. Adapted from John J. Macionis, *Society: The Basics,* 2nd ed. (Englewood Cliffs, NJ: Prentice Hall, 1994), p. 405.

10. Kelsey Kauffman, *Prison Officers and Their World* (Cambridge, MA: Harvard University Press, 1988), pp. 85–86.

11. American Correctional Association, *Vital Statistics in Corrections* (Lanham, MD: ACA, 2000), p. 143; James J. Stephan and Jennifer C. Karberg, *Census of State and Federal Correctional Facilities, 2000* (Washington, DC: Bureau of Justice Statistics, 2003).

12. U.S. Bureau of the Census, *The Population Profile of the United States: 2000 (Internet Release),* www.census.gov/population/www/pop-profile/profile2000.html (accessed June 29, 2002).

13. ACA, *Vital Statistics in Corrections.*

14. Ibid.

15. See, for example, E. Poole and R. M. Regoli, "Work Relations and Cynicism Among Prison Guards," *Criminal Justice and Behavior,* vol. 7 (1980), pp. 303–314.

16. Adapted from Frank Schmalleger, *Criminal Justice Today: An Introductory Text for the 21st Century,* 9th ed. (Upper Saddle River, NJ: Prentice Hall, 2007).

17. Lucien X. Lombardo, *Guards Imprisoned: Correctional Officers at Work,* 2nd ed. (Cincinnati, OH: Anderson, 1989).

18. Adapted from Dora B. Schriro, "Women in Prison: Keeping the Peace," *The Keeper's Voice,* vol. 16, no. 2 (Spring 1995).

19. Ibid.

20. M. I. Cadwaladr, "Women Working in a Men's Jail," *FORUM,* vol. 6, no. 1 (1994).

21. Ibid.

22. N. C. Jurik and J. Halemba, "Gender, Working Conditions, and the Job Satisfaction of Women in a Non-Traditional Occupation: Female Correctional Officers in Men's Prisons," *Sociological Quarterly,* vol. 25 (1984), pp. 551–566.

23. Joseph R. Rowan, "Who Is Safer in Male Maximum Security Prisons?" *The Keeper's Voice,* vol. 17, no. 3 (Summer 1996).

24. Ibid.

25. See, for example, Stephen Walters, "Changing the Guard: Male Correctional Officers' Attitudes Toward Women as Coworkers," *Journal of Offender Rehabilitation,* vol. 20, no. 1 (1993), pp. 47–60.

26. Cadwaladr, "Women Working in a Men's Jail."

27. Ibid.

28. Public Service Commission (of Canada), "Stress and Executive Burnout," *FORUM,* vol. 4, no. 1 (1992). Much of the material in this section is taken from this work.

29. B. M. Crouch, "The Guard in a Changing Prison World," in B. M. Crouch (ed.), *The Keepers: Prison Guards and Contemporary Corrections* (Springfield, IL: Charles C Thomas, 1980).

30. Shannon Black, "Correctional Employee Stress & Strain," *Corrections Today,* October 2001, p. 99.

31. Lombardo, *Guards Imprisoned.*

32. Eric G. Lambert, "Work-Family Conflict: An Unexplored Stressor for Correctional Staff," *Corrections Compendium,* vol. 26, no. 5 (May 2001).

33. Public Service Commission, "Stress and Executive Burnout."

34. For an excellent overview of the literature on correctional officer stress, see Tammy L. Castle and Jamie S. Martin, "Occupational Hazard: Predictors of Stress Among Jail Correctional Officers," *American Journal of Criminal Justice,* vol. 31, no. 1 (Fall 2006), pp. 65–80.

35. "Not Stressed Enough?" *FORUM,* vol. 4, no. 1 (1992). Adapted from C. C. W. Hines and W. C. Wilson, "A No-Nonsense Guide to Being Stressed," *Management Solutions,* October 1986, pp. 27–29.

36. J. T. Dignam, M. Barrera, and S. G. West, "Occupational Stress, Social Support, and Burnout Among Correctional Officers," *American Journal of Community Psychology,* vol. 14, no. 2 (1986), pp. 177–193.

37. M. C. W. Peeters, B. P. Buunk, and W. B. Schaufeli, "Social Interactions and Feelings of Inferiority Among Correctional Officers: A Daily Event-Recording Approach," *Journal of Applied Social Psychology,* vol. 25, no. 12 (1995), pp. 1073–1089.

38. Jessie W. Doyle, "6 Elements That Form a Context for Staff Safety," *Corrections Today,* October 2001, pp. 101–104.

39. Terry L. Stewart and Donald W. Brown, "Focusing on Correctional Staff Safety," *Corrections Today,* October 2001, pp. 90–93.

40. Ibid.

41. David Robinson, Frank Porporino, and Linda Simourd, "Do Different Occupational Groups Vary on Attitudes and Work Adjustment in Corrections?" *Federal Probation,* vol. 60, no. 3 (1996), pp. 45–53. See also Francis T. Cullen et al., "How Satisfying Is Prison Work? A Comparative Occupational Approach," *The Journal of Offender Counseling Services and Rehabilitation,* vol. 14, no. 2 (1989), pp. 89–108.

42. Timothy J. Flanagan, Wesley Johnson, and Katherine Bennett, "Job Satisfaction Among Correctional Executives: A Contemporary Portrait of Wardens of State Prisons for Adults," *Prison Journal,* vol. 76, no. 4 (1996), pp. 385–397.

43. Lombardo, *Guards Imprisoned.*

44. Martinez, "Corrections Officer."

45. Thomas Gillan, "The Correctional Officer: One of Law Enforcement's Toughest Positions," *Corrections Today,* October 2001, p. 113.

46. Black, "Correctional Employee Stress & Strain," p. 99.

47. Andrew Metz, "Life on the Inside: The Jailers," in Tara Gray (ed.), *Exploring Corrections* (Boston: Allyn & Bacon, 2002), p. 65.

48. Ibid., p. 64.

49. Black, "Correctional Employee Stress & Strain," p. 99.

50. Stephen Walters, "The Determinants of Job Satisfaction Among Canadian and American Correctional Officers," *Journal of Crime and Justice,* vol. 19, no. 2 (1996), pp. 145–158.

51. John R. Hepburn and Paul E. Knepper, "Correctional Officers as Human Services Workers: The Effect on Job Satisfaction," *Justice Quarterly,* vol. 10, no. 2 (1993), pp. 315–337.

52. Stephen Walters, "Gender, Job Satisfaction, and Correctional Officers: A Comparative Analysis," *The Justice Professional,* vol. 7, no. 2 (1993), pp. 23–33.

53. Dana M. Britton, "Perceptions of the Work Environment Among Correctional Officers: Do Race and Sex Matter?" *Criminology,* vol. 35, no. 1 (1997), pp. 85–105.

54. The Victor Cullins Academy is a facility operating under contract with the Youth Services Division of the state of Maryland.

55. The material in this section comes from Jess Maghan, "Ken Davis: The Complete Correctional Officer," *The Keeper's Voice,* vol. 16, no. 2 (Spring 1995).

56. "Lawyer Sentenced to 28 Months in Prison on Terrorism Charge," *Court TV News*, October 16, 2006, www.courttv.com/news/2006/1016/cynne_Stewart_ap.html.

57. American Correctional Association, "Opening Session: Kerik Emphasizes the Importance of Corrections' Protective Role for the Country," www.aca.org/conferences/Winter05/ Updates5.asp#2.

58. Jess Maghan, *Intelligence-Led Penology: Management of Crime Information Obtained from Incarcerated Persons,* paper presented at the Investigation of Crime World Conference, 2001, p. 6.

59. Quoted in Meghan Mandeville, "Information Sharing Becomes Crucial to Battling Terrorism Behind Bars," Corrections.com, December 8, 2003, http://database.corrections.com/news/results2.asp?ID_8988 (accessed August 1, 2005).

60. "FBI: Al-Qaida Recruiting in U.S. Prisons," United Press International wire service, January 7, 2004, http://database.corrections.com/news/results2.asp?ID_9148 (accessed August 1, 2005).

61. Institute for the Study of Violent Groups, "Land of Wahhabism," *Crime and Justice International,* March/April 2005, p. 43.

62. Office of the Inspector General, *A Review of the Federal Bureau of Prisons' Selection of Muslim Religious Services Providers* (Washington, DC: U.S. Department of Justice, 2004).

63. Ibid., p. 8.

64. Ibid.

65. "Radicalization of Prisoners Is a Terror Threat, Report Says," *Corrections Journal,* September 22, 2006, p. 3.

66. U.S. Department of Justice, Office of the Inspector General, *The Federal Bureau of Prisons' Monitoring of Mail for High-Risk Inmates* (Washington, DC: U.S. Government Printing Office, 2006).

67. Keith Martin, *Corrections Prepares for Terrorism* (Corrections Connection News Network, January 21, 2002, www.corrections.com (accessed July 10, 2005).

68. Y. N. Baykan, "The Emergence of Sunni Islam in America's Prisons," *Corrections Today,* February 2007, pp. 49–51.

Chapter 10

1. Details for this story come from Kevin Johnson, "After Years in Solitary, Freedom Hard to Grasp," *USA Today,* June 9, 2005, p. A1.

2. Allen Beck et al., *Survey of State Prison Inmates, 1991* (Washington, DC: U.S. Department of Justice, March 1993), www.ojp.usdoj.gov/bjs/pub/ascii/sospi91.txt.

3. Erving Goffman, *Asylums: Essays on the Social Situation of Mental Patients and Other Inmates* (Garden City, NY: Anchor Books, 1961).

4. Hans Toch, *Living in Prison: The Ecology of Survival,* reprint ed. (Washington, DC: American Psychological Association, 1996), p. xv.

5. Victoria R. DeRosia, *Living Inside Prison Walls: Adjustment Behavior* (Westport, CT: Praeger, 1998).

6. "Inmate Subculture," in Virgil L. Williams (ed.), *Dictionary of American Penology: An Introductory Guide* (Westport, CT: Greenwood, 1979).

7. Donald Clemmer, *The Prison Community* (Boston: Holt, Rinehart & Winston, 1940).

8. Stanton Wheeler, "Socialization in Correctional Communities," *American Sociological Review,* vol. 26 (October 1961), pp. 697–712.

9. Gresham M. Sykes, *The Society of Captives: A Study of a Maximum Security Prison* (Princeton, NJ: Princeton University Press, 1958).

10. Stephen C. Light, *Inmate Assaults on Staff: Challenges to Authority in a Large State Prison System,* dissertation, State University of New York at Albany (Ann Arbor, MI: University Microfilms International, 1987).

11. John Irwin and Donald R. Cressey, "Thieves, Convicts and the Inmate Culture," *Social Problems,* vol. 10 (Fall 1962), pp. 142–155.

12. James Jacobs, *Stateville: The Penitentiary in Mass Society* (Chicago: University of Chicago Press, 1977).

13. Miles D. Harer and Darrell J. Steffensmeier, "Race and Prison Violence," *Criminology,* vol. 34, no. 3 (1996), pp. 323–355.

14. John M. Wilson and Jon D. Snodgrass, "The Prison Code in a Therapeutic Community," *Journal of Criminal Law, Criminology, and Police Science,* vol. 60, no. 4 (1969), pp. 472–478.

15. Gresham M. Sykes and Sheldon L. Messinger, "The Inmate Social System," in Richard A. Cloward et al. (eds.), *Theoretical Studies in Social Organization of the Prison* (New York: Social Science Research Council, 1960), pp. 5–19.

16. Peter M. Wittenberg, "Language and Communication in Prison," *Federal Probation,* vol. 60, no. 4 (1996), pp. 45–50.

17. Sykes, *The Society of Captives.*

18. John Irwin, *The Felon* (Englewood Cliffs, NJ: Prentice Hall, 1970).

19. Adapted from Frank Schmalleger, *Criminal Justice Today,* 7th ed. (Upper Saddle River, NJ: Prentice Hall, 2003).

20. See, for example, Donald Tucker, *A Punk's Song: View from the Inside* (AMS Press, 1981), from which some of the information here is adapted.

21. Ibid.

22. Ibid.

23. Ibid.

24. Daniel Lockwood, *Sexual Aggression Among Male Prisoners,* dissertation, State University of New York at Albany (Ann Arbor, MI: University Microfilms International, 1978); Daniel Lockwood, "Issues in Prison Sexual Violence," *The Prison Journal,* vol. 58, no. 1 (1983), pp. 73–79.

25. Adapted from Toch, *Living in Prison,* p. 274.

26. Pub. L. No. 108-79.

27. Michelle Gaseau, "PREA Activities Under Way," Corrections Connection Network News, November 1, 2004, http://database.corrections.com/news/results2.asp?ID=11778 (accessed July 30, 2005).

28. Allen J. Beck and Timothy A. Hughes, *Sexual Violence Reported by Correctional Authorities, 2004* (Washington, DC: Bureau of Justice Statistics, 2005).

29. Ibid.

30. Paige M. Harrison and Allen J. Beck, *Prisoners in 2005* (Washington, DC: Bureau of Justice Statistics, 2006), p. 1.

31. Phyllis J. Baunach, "Critical Problems of Women in Prison," in Imogene L. Moyer (ed.), *The Changing Roles of Women in the Criminal Justice System* (Prospect Heights, IL: Waveland Press, 1985), pp. 95–110.

32. See John W. Palmer and Stephen E. Palmer, *Constitutional Rights of Prisoners,* 6th ed. (Cincinnati, OH: Anderson, 1999).

33. American Correctional Association, *Standards for Adult Correctional Institutions* (Lanham, MD: ACA, 1990).

34. The information in this section comes from the Commission on Safety and Abuse in America's Prisons, *Confronting Confinement* (New York: Vera Institute, 2006), p. 26.

35. Lawrence A. Greenfeld and Tracy L. Snell, *Women Offenders,* Bureau of Justice Statistics Special Report (Washington, DC: Bureau of Justice Statistics, December 1999, revised October

3, 2000); Paige M. Harrison and Allen J. Beck, *Prisoners in 2006,* Bureau of Justice Statistics Bulletin (Washington, DC: Bureau of Justice Statistics, 2007).

36. Harrison and Beck, *Prisoners in 2006.*

37. Ibid.

38. Angela Browne, Brenda Miller, and Eugene Maguin, "Prevalence and Severity of Lifetime Physical and Sexual Victimization Among Incarcerated Women," *International Journal of Law and Psychiatry,* vol. 22, no. 3–4 (1999), pp. 301–322.

39. Bloom et al., *Gender-Responsive Strategies: Research, Practice, and Guiding Principles for Women Offenders* (Washington, DC: National Institute of Corrections, 2003).

40. Bureau of Justice Statistics, "Comparing Federal and State Prisoners," press release, October 2, 1994.

41. American Correctional Association, *Female Offenders: Meeting Needs of a Neglected Population* (Laurel, MD: ACA, 1993).

42. Tracy Snell, *Women in Prison* (Washington, DC: Bureau of Justice Statistics, 1994).

43. Rose Giallombardo, *Society of Women: A Study of a Women's Prison* (New York: John Wiley, 1966).

44. Esther Heffernan, *Making It in Prison: The Square, the Cool, and the Life* (New York: Wiley-Interscience, 1972).

45. Barbara Owens, "The Mix: The Culture of Imprisoned Women," in Mary K. Stohr and Craig Hemmens (eds.), *The Inmate Prison Experience* (Upper Saddle River, NJ: Prentice Hall, 2004). pp. 152–172.

46. Williams, "Inmate Subculture." p. 109.

47. Kathryn Watterson, *Women in Prison: Inside the Concrete Tomb,* 2nd ed. (Boston: Northeastern University Press, 1996), p. 291.

48. For example, see John Gagnon and William Simon, "The Social Meaning of Prison Homosexuality," in David M. Petersen and Charles W. Thomas (eds.), *Corrections: Problems and Prospects* (Englewood Cliffs, NJ: Prentice Hall, 1980).

49. Doris Layton MacKenzie, James Robinson, and Carol Campbell, "Long-Term Incarceration of Female Offenders: Prison Adjustment and Coping," *Criminal Justice and Behavior,* vol. 16, no. 2 (1989), pp. 223–238.

50. Nicole Hahn Rafter, *Partial Justice: Women, Prisons and Social Control* (New Brunswick, NJ: Transaction, 1990).

51. Bloom et al., *Gender-Responsive Strategies.*

52. Barbara Bloom and Stephanie Covington, *Gendered Justice: Programming for Women in Correctional Settings,* paper presented at the American Society of Criminology annual meeting, San Francisco, November 2000, p. 11.

53. Bloom et al., *Gender-Responsive Strategies.*

54. Susan Cranford and Rose Williams, "Critical Issues in Managing Female Offenders," *Corrections Today,* vol. 60, no. 7 (December 1998), pp. 130–135.

55. John DeBell, "The Female Offender: Different . . . Not Difficult," *Corrections Today,* vol. 63, no. 1 (February 2001), pp. 56–61.

56. Pat Carlen, "Analyzing Women's Imprisonment: Abolition and Its Enemies," *Women, Girls & Criminal Justice,* vol. 7, no. 6 (October/November 2006), p. 85.

57. Tracy L. Snell, "Women in Prison," *Bureau of Justice Statistics Bulletin* (Washington, DC: Bureau of Justice Statistics, March 1994).

58. As estimated by Vesna Markovic, "Pregnant Women in Prison: A Correctional Dilemma?" *The Keepers' Voice,* Summer 1995.

59. Ibid.

60. American Correctional Association, *Standards for Adult Correctional Institutions,* 3rd ed. (ACA, January 1990).

61. Gerald Austin McHugh, "Protection of the Rights of Pregnant Women in Prison and Detention Facilities," *New England Journal of Prison Law,* vol. 6, no. 2 (Summer 1980), pp. 231–263.

62. Snell, "Women in Prison."

63. National Institute of Corrections, *Services for Families of Prison Inmates* (Washington, DC: NIC, 2002), p. 3.

64. Phyllis Jo Baunach, "Critical Problems of Women in Prison," in Imogene L. Moyer (ed.), *The Changing Roles of Women in the Criminal Justice System* (Prospect Heights, IL: Waveland Press, 1985), p. 16.

65. John J. Sheridan, "Inmates May Be Parents, Too," *Corrections Today,* vol. 58, no. 5 (August 1996), p. 100.

66. Christopher J. Mumola, *Incarcerated Parents and Their Children,* Bureau of Justice Statistics Special Report (Washington, DC: Bureau of Justice Statistics, August 2000).

67. Kelsey Kauffman, "Mothers in Prison," *Corrections Today* (February 2001), pp. 62–65.

68. Harrison and Beck, *Prisoners in 2006.*

69. Mumola, *Incarcerated Parents,* p. 1.

70. Suzanne Hoholik, "Weekend Camp Lets Mother, Kids Bond," *The Columbus Dispatch,* July 22, 2000, pp. A1–A2.

71. Rini Bartlett, "Helping Inmate Moms Keep in Touch," *Correctional Compass* (Tallahassee, FL: Department of Corrections, February 2001), www.dc.state.fl.us/pub/compass/0102/page07.html (accessed June 2, 2007).

72. Kauffman, "Mothers in Prison," p. 62.

73. Ibid., p. 63.

74. John Ortiz Smykla, "Coed Prison: Should We Try It (Again)?" in Charles B. Fields (ed.), *Controversial Issues in Corrections* (Boston: Allyn & Bacon, 1999), pp. 203–218.

75. John Ortiz Smykla and Jimmy J. Williams, "Co-Corrections in the United States of America, 1970–1990: Two Decades of Disadvantages for Women Prisoners," *Women & Criminal Justice,* vol. 8, no. 1 (1996), pp. 61–76.

76. Ibid.

77. Jacqueline K. Crawford, "Two Losers Don't Make a Winner: The Case Against the Co-correctional Institution," in John Ortiz Smykla (ed.), *Coed Prison* (New York: Human Sciences Press, 1980), pp. 263–268.

78. Smykla and Williams, "Co-corrections in the United States," p. 61.

79. Lawrence W. Sherman et al., *Preventing Crime: What Works, What Doesn't, What's Promising* (Washington, DC: NIJ, 1997).

Chapter 11

1. Frances Cole, "The Impact of *Bell* v. *Wolfish* Upon Prisoners' Rights," *Journal of Crime and Justice,* vol. 10 (1987), pp. 47–70.

2. Ibid.

3. D. J. Gottlieb, "The Legacy of *Wolfish* and *Chapman:* Some Thoughts About 'Big Prison Case' Litigation in the 1980s," in I. D. Robbins (ed.), *Prisoners and the Law* (New York: Clark Boardman, 1985).

4. James B. Jacobs, *New Perspectives on Prisons and Imprisonment* (Ithaca, NY: Cornell University Press, 1983).

5. Todd Clear and George F. Cole, *American Corrections,* 4th ed. (New York: Wadsworth, 1997).

6. Civil Rights of Institutionalized Persons Act, 42 U.S.C. § 1997 et seq. (1976 ed., Supp. IV), as modified 1980. (Current through P.L. 104-150, approved June 3, 1996.)

7. R. Hawkins and G. P. Alpert, *American Prison Systems: Punishment and Justice* (Englewood Cliffs, NJ: Prentice Hall, 1989).

8. John Scalia, *Prisoner Petitions Filed in U.S. District Courts, 2000, with Trends 1980–2000* (Washington, DC: U.S. Department of Justice, December 2001).

9. Florida Department of Corrections, Office of the Inspector General, *Annual Report 1994–1995*, www.dc.state.fl.us/pub/IGannual/19941995/page6.html (accessed May 30, 2002).

10. *Report of the Comptroller General of the United States: Grievance Mechanisms in State Correctional Institutions and Large-City Jails* (Washington, DC: U.S. Government Printing Office, June 17, 1977), Appendix I.

11. James B. Jacobs, "The Prisoners' Rights Movement and Its Impacts," in Edward J. Latessa, Alexander Holsinger, James W. Marquart, and Jonathan R. Sorensen, *Correctional Contexts: Contemporary and Classical Readings*, 2nd ed. (Los Angeles: Roxbury, 2001), p. 211. Reprinted from James B. Jacobs, *Crime and Justice*, vol. II (Chicago: University of Chicago Press, 1980).

12. See *Estelle v. Gamble*, 429 U.S. 97 (1976), and *Hutto v. Finney*, 437 U.S. 678 (1978).

13. James A. Gondles Jr., "You Ought to Thank Us," *USA Today* (editorial), June 12, 2006, p. 12A.

14. American Civil Liberties Union, *ACLU Position Paper: Prisoners' Rights* (Fall 1999), www.aclu.org/library/PrisonerRights.pdf (accessed June 10, 2002).

15. In 1977, Theriault's appeal to the U.S. Supreme Court was denied (see 434 U.S. 953, November 14, 1977).

16. In Section 1997e, Congress created a specific, limited exhaustion requirement for adult prisoners bringing actions pursuant to section 1983.

17. Prison Litigation Reform Act, Pub. L. No. 104-134, § 801-10, 110 Stat. 1321 (1995).

18. If a prisoner wishes to proceed as an indigent on appeal, the prisoner must file in the district court, with the notice of appeal, a motion for leave to proceed as an indigent, a certified copy of a prison trust account statement, and Form 4 from the Appendix of Forms found in the *Federal Rules of Appellate Procedure*.

19. Fred L. Cheesman, Brian J. Ostrom, and Roger A. Hanson, *A Tale of Two Laws Revisited: Investigating the Impact of the Prison Litigation Reform Act and the Antiterrorism and Effective Death Penalty Act* (Williamsburg, VA: National Center for State Courts, 2005).

20. "Court Intervention Ends for D.C. DOC," *Corrections Today*, December 2004, p. 12.

21. "Judge Approves Settlement in Alabama Prison Lawsuit," *Corrections Journal*, August 9, 2004, p. 1.

Chapter 12

1. Excerpted from Ron Word, "Elderly Inmates Swell Nation's Prisons," www.angelfire.com/fl13/starke/elderlyswell.html (accessed October 3, 2006).

2. Stan Stojkovic (ed.), *Managing Special Populations in Jails and Prisons* (Kingston, NJ: Civic Research Institute, 2005), p. xv.

3. G. Larry Mays and Daniel L. Judiscak, "Special Needs Inmates in New Mexico Jails," *American Jails*, vol. 10, no. 2 (1996), pp. 32–41.

4. National Center on Addiction and Substance Abuse, *Trends in Substance Abuse and Treatment Needs Among Inmates* (New York: National Center on Addiction and Substance Abuse, Columbia University, October 2002).

5. Christopher J. Mumola and Jennifer C. Karberg, *Drug Use and Dependence, State and Federal Prisoners, 2004* (Washington, DC: U.S. Department of Justice, Bureau of Justice Statistics, October 2006).

6. National Institute of Justice, *Annualized Site Reports 2001* (Washington, DC: U.S. Department of Justice, National Institute of Justice, June 2003).

7. Jeremy Travis, *Framing the National Agenda: A Research and Policy Perspective*. Speech to National Corrections Conference on Substance Abuse, April 23, 1997.

8. M. D. Anglin and Y. Haer, "Treatment of Drug Abuse," in Michael Tonny and James Q. Wilson (eds.), *Drugs and Crime: Crime and Justice: A Review of Research*, vol. 13 (Chicago: University of Chicago Press, 1990), pp. 393–460; D. N. Nurco, T. W. Kislock, and T. E. Hanlon, "The Nature and Status of Drug Abuse Treatment," *Maryland Medical Journal*, vol. 43 (January 1994), pp. 51–57; D. D. Simpson et al., "A National Evaluation of Treatment Outcomes for Cocaine Dependence," *Archives of General Psychiatry*, vol. 56, no. 6 (1999), pp. 507–514.

9. Center for Substance Abuse Treatment, *NTIES: The National Treatment Improvement Study—Final Report* (Rockville, MD: U.S. Department of Health and Human Services, Substance Abuse and Mental Health Services Administration, 1997).

10. Marcia R. Chaiken, *Prison Programs for Drug-Involved Offenders* (Washington, DC: National Institute of Justice, October 1989); D. A. Andrews et al., "Does Correctional Treatment Work? A Clinically Relevant and Psychologically Informed Meta-Analysis," *Criminology*, vol. 28, no. 3 (1990), pp. 369–404; Donald Lipton and Frank Pearson, *The CDATE Project: Reviewing Research on the Effectiveness of Treatment Programs for Adults and Juvenile Offenders*, paper presented at the annual meeting of the American Society of Criminology, Chicago, IL, 1996.

11. Lana D. Harrison, "The Revolving Prison Door for Drug-Involved Offenders: Challenges and Opportunities," *Crime & Delinquency*, vol. 47, no. 3 (July 2001), pp. 462–485.

12. National Center on Addiction and Substance Abuse, *Trends in Substance Abuse and Treatment Needs Among Inmates*. See also Candice Byrne, Jonathan Faley, Lesley Flaim, Francisco Pinol, and Jill Schmidtlein, *Drug Treatment in the Criminal Justice System* (Washington, DC: Executive Office of the President, Office of National Drug Control Policy, August 1998).

13. Ibid., pp. 24–25.

14. Lana D. Harrison, "The Revolving Prison Door for Drug-Involved Offenders: Challenges and Opportunities," pp. 465–466.

15. Sandra Tunis et al., *Evaluation of Drug Treatment in Local Corrections* (Washington, DC: U.S. Department of Justice, 1997).

16. Steven S. Martin, James A. Inciardi, and Daniel J. O'Connell, "Treatment Research in *Oz*—Is Randomization the Ideal or Just Somewhere Over the Rainbow?" *Federal Probation*, vol. 67, no. 2 (September 2003), pp. 53–60.

17. Bernadette Pelissier et al., *TRIAD Drug Treatment Evaluation Project Final Report of Three-Year Outcomes: Part I* (Washington, DC: Federal Bureau of Prisons, Office of Research and Evaluation, September 2000).

18. James A. Inciardi et al., "An Effective Model of Prison-Based Treatment for Drug-Involved Offenders," *Journal of Drug Issues*, vol. 27, no. 2 (Spring 1997), pp. 261–278; James A. Inciardi, Steven S. Martin, and Clifford A. Butzin, "Five-Year Outcomes of Therapeutic Community Treatment of Drug-Involved Offenders After Release from Prison," *Crime & Delinquency*, vol. 50, no. 1 (January 2004), pp. 88–107.

19. John J. Gibbons and Nicholas de B. Katzenbach, *Confronting Confinement: A Report of the Commission on Safety and Abuse in America's Prisons* (New York: Vera Institute, 2006).

20. Steve Aos, Marna Miller, and Elizabeth Drake, *Evidence-Based Public Policy Options to Reduce Future Prison Construction, Criminal Justice Costs, and Crime Rates* (Olympia, WA: State Institute for Public Policy, 2006).

21. National Institute on Drug Abuse, *Principles of Drug Abuse Treatment for Criminal Justice Populations—A Research-Based Guide* (Washington, DC: U.S. Department of Health and Human Services, 2006).

22. Douglas Anglin and Yih-Ing Hser, "Treatment of Drug Abuse," in Michael Tonry and James Q. Wilson (eds.), *Drugs and Crime and Justice: A Review of Research,* vol. 13 (Chicago: University of Chicago Press, 1990); Michael Tonry and Mary Lynch, "Intermediate Sanctions," in Michael Tonry (ed.), *Criminal Justice: A Review of Research,* vol. 20 (Chicago: University of Chicago Press, 1996), p. 137.

23. Institute of Medicine, Committee for the Substance Abuse Coverage Study, "A Study of the Evolution, Effectiveness, and Financing of Public and Private Drug Treatment Systems," in D. R. Gerstein and H. J. Harwood (eds.), *Treating Drug Problems,* vol. 1 (Washington, DC: National Academy Press, 1990).

24. R. Hubbard et al., "Treatment Outcome Prospective Study (TOPS): Client Characteristics and Behaviors Before, During, and After Treatment," in F. Tims and J. Ludford (eds.), *Drug Abuse Treatment Evaluation: Strategies, Progress and Prospects* (Rockville, MD: National Institute on Drug Abuse, 1984), pp. 29–41.

25. Stanley W. Hodge and Victor E. Kappler, "Can We Continue to Lock Up the Nonviolent Drug Offender?" in Charles B. Fields (ed.), *Controversial Issues in Corrections* (Boston: Allyn & Bacon, 1999), pp. 137–151.

26. Administrative Office of Courts, *Drug Treatment and Education Fund, Annual Report, Fiscal Year 1999,* Arizona Supreme Court, November 2001.

27. Anna Gorman, "Judges Say New Drug Law Is Working," *Los Angeles Times,* February 5, 2002, www.mapinc.org/newsprop/v02/n193/a06.htm (accessed February 19, 2002).

28. National Commission on Correctional Health Care, *The Health Status of Soon-to-Be-Released Inmates: A Report to Congress,* Vol. I (Washington, DC: U.S. Department of Justice, September 2004), p. ix.

29. *Management of the HIV-Positive Prisoner* (New York: World Health CME, no date).

30. Michael S. Vaughn and Leo Carroll, "Separate and Unequal: Prison Versus Free-World Medical Care," *Justice Quarterly,* vol. 15, no. 1 (March 1998), pp. 3–40.

31. Ibid., pp. 31–32.

32. Laura M. Maruschak, *HIV in Prisons and Jails, 2002* (Washington, DC: U.S. Department of Justice, Bureau of Justice Statistics, December 2004).

33. American Correctional Association, *Managing Special Needs Offenders* (Lanham, MD: American Correctional Association, 2004).

34. Theodore M. Hammett, Cheryl Roberts, and Sofia Kennedy, "Health-Related Issues in Prisoner Reentry," *Crime & Delinquency,* vol. 47, no. 3 (July 2001), pp. 390–409; Abe Macher, "Clinical Management of HIV Disease in Correctional Facilities," in Stan Stojkovic (ed.), *Managing Special Populations in Jails and Prisons,* pp. 4–1 to 4–57; "Jailhouse Tatooing" (New York: Civic Reaserch Institute, 2006), *American Jails,* vol. 20, no. 4 (September/October 2006), pp. 96–98.

35. Nina Siegal, "Lethal Lottery," in Tara Gray (ed.), *Exploring Corrections* (Boston: Allyn & Bacon, 2002), pp. 122–126.

36. Maruschak, *HIV in Prisons and Jails, 2002.*

37. Jaime Shimkus, "Side by Side, Ministers and Detainees Test for HIV Infection," *CorrectCare,* Fall 2001, p. 16.

38. Mike Israel, *Criminal Justice Washington Letter,* October 15, 2004.

39. Doris J. James and Lauren E. Glaze, Mental *Health Problems of Prison and Jail Inmates* (Washington, DC: U.S. Department of Justice, Bureau of Justice Statistics, September 2006).

40. As reported in Fox Butterfield, "Experts Say Study Confirms Prison's New Role as Mental Hospital," *The New York Times,* July 12, 1999.

41. "Agreement Reached in Lawsuit on Inmates' Mental Health Needs," *Criminal Justice Newsletter,* April 16, 2007, pp. 3–4; "Mental Health in Prison," *The New York Times* (June 11, 2007), www.nytimes.com (accessed June 11, 2007).

42. Thomas N. Faust, "Shift the Responsibility of Untreated Mental Illness out of the Criminal Justice System," *Corrections Today,* April 2003, pp. 6–7; see also Liz Lipton, "Few Safeguards Govern Elimination of Psychiatric Beds," *Psychiatric News,* vol. 36, no. 15 (August 3, 2001), p. 9, http://pn.psychiatriconline.org/cgi/content/full/36/15/9 (accessed January 13, 2007); James and Glaze, *Mental Health Problems of Prison and Jail Inmates.*

43. Michael P. Maloney, Michael P. Ward, and Charles M. Jackson, "Study Reveals That More Mentally Ill Offenders Are Entering Jail," *Corrections Today,* April 2003, pp. 100–103.

44. Phillip Comey, "Health Care and Prisons: Considering the Connection," *On the Line* (Lanham: MD. American Correctional Association, November 2005), p. 1.

45. Risdon N. Slate et al., "Doing Justice for Mental Illness and Society: Federal Probation and Pretrial Service Officers as Mental Health Specialists," *Federal Probation,* vol. 67, no. 3 (December 2003).

46. Maloney, Ward, and Jackson, "Study Reveals."

47. The Bazelon Center for Mental Health Law, *Position Statement on Involuntary Commitment, 1999.* As cited in The Sentencing Project, *Mentally Ill Offenders in the Criminal Justice System: An Analysis and Prescription* (Washington, DC: The Sentencing Project, January 2002), p. 4.

48. Faust, "Shift the Responsibility of Untreated Mental Illness."

49. John M. Greacen, "Then & Now: Reflections on 25 Years of Correctional Health Care," *CorrectCare,* vol. 16, no.1 (Winter 2002), pp. 9, 22.

50. Dean H. Aufderheide, "The Mentally Ill in America's Prisons," *Corrections Today,* vol. 67, no. 1 (2005), pp. 30–33.

51. Randy M. Bourn et al., "Police Perspectives on Responding to Mentally Ill People in Crisis: Perceptions of Program Effectiveness," *Behavioral Sciences and the Law,* vol. 16, no. 4 (1998), pp. 393–402.

52. The number of mental health courts in the United States is documented in the National Survey of Mental Health Courts (www.mentalhealthcourtsurvey.com), maintained by the Council of State Governments, the National GAINS Center, and the National Alliance for the Mentally Ill.

53. Roger A. Boothroyd et al., "The Broward Mental Health Court: Process, Outcomes and Service Utilization," *International Journal of Law and Psychiatry,* vol. 26 (2003), pp. 55–71.

54. American Association for Community Psychiatrists, *Position Statement on Persons with Mental Illness Behind Bars, 1999,* www.wpic.pitt.edu/aacp/finds/mibb.html (accessed May 16, 2003). See also Arthur J. Lurigio, "Effective Services for

Parolees with Mental Illnesses," *Crime & Delinquency,* vol. 47, no. 3 (July 2001), pp. 446–461.

55. Eric Blaauw, Frans Willem Winkel, and Ad J. F. M. Kerkhof, "Bullying and Suicidal Behavior in Jails," *Criminal Justice and Behavior,* vol. 28, no. 3 (June 2001), pp. 279–299.

56. J. Richard Goss, "Characteristics of Suicide Attempts in a Large Urban Jail System with an Established Suicide Prevention Program," *Psychiatric Services,* vol. 53 (2002), pp. 574–579; Lance Couturier and Frederick R. Maue, "Suicide Prevention Initiatives in a Large Statewide Department of Corrections: A Full Court Press to Save Lives," *Jail Suicide/ Mental Health Update,* vol. 9, no. 4 (2000), pp. 1–8.

57. Mason R. Goodman, "An Overview of Tuberculosis in Jails in the United States for Health Care and Administrative Corrections Professionals," *American Jails,* vol. 10, no. 4 (1996), pp. 45–50.

58. American Correctional Association, *Managing Special Needs Offenders;* Abe Macher, "Tuberculosis in Correctional Facilities," in Stan Stojkovic (ed.), *Managing Special Populations in Jails and Prisons* (New York: Civic Research Institute, 2006), pp. 6–1 to 6–55.

59. Joann B. Morton, *An Administrative Overview of the Older Inmate* (Washington, DC: National Institute of Corrections, August 1992), www.nicic.org.

60. Connie L. Neeley, Laura Addison, and Delores Craig-Moreland, "Addressing the Needs of Elderly Offenders," *Corrections Today,* vol. 59, no. 5 (August 1997), pp. 120–124.

61. Paige M. Harrison and Allen J. Beck, *Prisoners in 2005* (Washington, DC: U.S. Department of Justice, Bureau of Justice Statistics, November 2006), p. 8.

62. Ryan S. King and Marc Mauer, *Aging Behind Bars: "Three Strikes" Seven Years Later* (Washington, DC: The Sentencing Project, August 2001).

63. Anne Seidlitz, "National Prison Hospice Association Facilities Deal with Inmate Deaths," *CorrectCare,* vol. 12, no. 1 (Spring 1998), p. 10; see "Appendix" in Statement of Professor Jonathan Turley before a Joint Hearing of the Senate Subcommittee on Aging and Long Term Care, Senate Committee on Public Safety, and Senate Select Committee on the California Correctional System, February 25, 2003.

64. Michael J. Osofeky, Philip J. Zimbardo, and Burl Cain, "Revolutionizing Prison Hospice: The Interdisciplinary Approach of the Louisiana State Penitentiary at Angola," *Corrections Compendium,* vol. 29, no. 4 (2004), pp. 5–7.

65. Ronald H. Aday, "Golden Years Behind Bars: Special Programs and Facilities for Elderly Inmates," *Federal Probation,* vol. 58, no. 2 (June 1994), pp. 47–54; Brie A. Williams et al., "Being Old and Doing Time: Functional Impairment and Adverse Experiences of Geriatric Female Prisoners," *Journal of the American Geriatric Society,* vol. 54, no. 2 (April 2006), pp. 702–707.

66. *Goodman & United States v. Georgia,* 546 U.S. 126 (2006).

67. Jurgen Neffe, "The Old Folks' Slammer: Aging Prison Population in the United States," *World Press Review,* vol. 44, no. 6 (June 1997), pp. 30–32; Irina R. Soderstrom and W. Michael Wheeler, "Is It Practical to Incarcerate the Elderly Offender? Yes and No," in Charles B. Fields (ed.), *Controversial Issues in Corrections* (Boston: Allyn & Bacon, 1999), pp. 72–89; Patricia S. Corwin, "Senioritis—Why Elderly Federal Inmates Are Literally Dying to Get Out of Prison," *Journal of Contemporary Health, Leisure and Policy,* vol. 17 (2001), pp. 687–688; Barry Holman, "Old Men Behind Bars," *Washington Post,* July 25, 1999, p. 88.

68. Alexandra Pelosi, "Age of Innocence: A Glut of Geriatric

Jailbirds," *The New Republic,* vol. 216, no. 18 (May 5, 1997), pp. 15–18.

69. Karl Brown, "Managing Sexually Transmitted Diseases in Jails," *HEPP Report,* vol. 6, no. 9 (September 2003), pp. 1–3.

70. *Estelle* v. *Gamble,* 429 U.S. 97 (1976).

71. Vaughn and Carroll, "Separate and Unequal," pp. 3–40.

72. Civil Rights of Institutionalized Persons Act, 42 U.S.C. 1997 et seq. (1976 ed., Supp. IV), as modified 1980. (Current through P.L. 104-150, approved June 3, 1996.)

73. *Pennsylvania Department of Corrections* v. *Yeskey,* 524 U.S. 206 (1998).

74. Associated Press, "Supreme Court Upholds Rights of Disabled Inmates," June 15, 1998; *Goodman & United States v. Georgia.*

Chapter 13

1. Paige M. Harrison and Allen J. Beck, *Prisoners in 2005* (Washington DC: U.S. Department of Justice, Bureau of Justice, Statistics, November 2006).

2. Ibid.

3. Lauren E. Glaze and Thomas P. Bonczar, *Probation and Parole in the United States, 2005* (Washington, DC: U.S. Department of Justice, Bureau of Justice Statistics, November 2006).

4. Christine Lindquist, Jennifer Hardison, and Pamela K. Lattimore, *Reentry Courts Process Evaluation (Phase I) Final Report* (Research Triangle Park, NC: RTI International, April 2003), p. 2; "Life Sentences on the Rise in the United States," *Corrections Today,* vol. 66, no. 4 (July 2004), p. 17; Harrison and Beck, *Prisoners in 2005,* p. 8.

5. Timothy Egan, "Less Crime, More Criminals," *The New York Times,* March 7, 1999.

6. James J. Stephan, *State Prison Expenditures, 1996* (Washington, DC: U.S. Department of Justice, Bureau of Justice Statistics, August 1999).

7. Pew Charitable Trusts, *Public Safety, Public Spending: Forecasting America's Prison Population 2007–2011* (Philadelphia: Pew Charitable Trusts, 2007).

8. "More Prisons Not Answer, 2 Texas Lawmakers Insist," *Houston Chronicle,* November 27, 2006, www.chron.com (accessed December 1, 2006).

9. Andy Furillo, "State Considers Sentencing Commission," *Sacramento Bee,* November 20, 2006, www.contracostatimes .com (accessed December 6, 2006).

10. David P. Farrington and C. P. Nuttal, "Prison Size, Overcrowding, Prison Violence, and Recidivism," *Journal of Criminal Justice,* vol. 8, no. 4 (1980), pp. 221–231.

11. James J. Stephan and Jennifer C. Karberg, *Census of State and Federal Correctional Facilities, 2000* (Washington, DC: U.S. Department of Justice Statistics, August 2003), p. 9.

12. Allen J. Beck, Paige M. Harrison, and Devon B. Adams, *Sexual Violence Reported by Correctional Authorities, 2004* (Washington, DC: U.S. Department of Justice, August 2007).

13. Ibid.

14. Keith L. Martin, "Staying Ahead of Gangs/STGs in Corrections," *Corrections.com,* www.corrections.com/news/feature/ index.html (accessed October 29, 2002).

15. Excerpted from Florida Department of Corrections, "Gang and Security Threat Group Awareness," www.dc.state.fl.us/ pub/gangs/prison.html (accessed March 30, 2003).

16. Mary E. Pelz, "Gangs," in Marilyn D. McShane and Frank P. Williams III (eds.), *Encyclopedia of American Prisons* (New York: Garland, 1996), p. 213.

17. Rick Ruddell, Scott H. Decker, and Arlen Egley Jr., "Gang Intervention in Jails: A National Analysis," *Criminal Justice Review*, vol. 31, no. 1 (March 2006), pp. 33–46.

18. Burt Useem and Peter Kimball, *States of Siege: U.S. Prison Riots, 1971–1986* (New York: Oxford University Press, 1991).

19. "Prison Violence and Escapes," *Corrections Compendium*, vol. 31, no. 4 (July/August 2006); "Riots, Disturbances, Violence, Assaults and Escapes," *Corrections Compendium*, vol. 27, no. 5 (May 2002); American Correctional Association, "Riots, Disturbances, Violence, Assaults and Escapes," *Corrections Compendium*, vol. 27, no. 5 (May 2002), pp. 6–19.

20. J. Lillis, "Prison Escapes and Violence Remain Down," *Corrections Compendium*, vol. 19, no. 6 (1994), pp. 6–21.

21. Vernon B. Fox, *Violence Behind Bars: An Explosive Report on Prison Riots in the United States* (New York: Vantage, 1956); Reid H. Montgomery Jr., "Bringing the Lessons of Prison Riots into Focus," *Corrections Today*, vol. 59, no. 1 (February 1997), pp. 28–33.

22. "Prison Riots . . . Why?" *The Prison Journal*, vol. 33, no. 1 (April 1953); "Aftermath of Riot," *The Prison Journal*, vol. 34, no. 1 (April 1954).

23. Negley K. Teeters, "The Dilemma of Prison Riots," *The Prison Journal*, vol. 33, no. 1 (April 1953), pp. 19–20.

24. New York State Special Commission on Attica (McKay Commission), *Attica: The Official Report of the New York State Special Commission on Attica* (New York: Bantam, 1972), p. xi; for a good discussion of prison violence, see James M. Byrne, Don Hummer, and Faye S. Taxman, *The Culture of Violence* (Boston, MA: Pearson, 2008).

25. As cited in Susan L. Clayton and Gabriella M. Daley, "Mock Riot," *Corrections Today*, July 2000, pp. 128–131.

26. U.S. National Advisory Commission on Civil Disorders (Kerner Commission), *Report* (Washington, DC: Kerner Commission, 1968), p. 2.

27. David A. Ward and Allen F. Breed, *The U.S. Penitentiary, Marion, Illinois: Consultants' Report Submitted to the Committee on the Judiciary, U.S. House of Representatives, Ninety-Eighth Congress, Second Session* (Washington, DC: U.S. Government Printing Office, 1985), p. 1.

28. Daniel P. Mears and Jamie Watson, "Towards a Fair and Balanced Assessment of Supermax Prisons," *Justice Quarterly*, vol. 23, no. 2 (June 2006), pp. 231–270.

29. As quoted in Francis X. Clines, "A Futuristic Prison Awaits the Hard-Core 400," *The New York Times*, October 17, 1994, p. A1.

30. Estimates of the number of supermax prisons vary. See David Lovell et al., "Who Lives in Supermaximum Custody? A Washington State Study," *Federal Probation*, vol. 64, no. 2 (December 2000), pp. 33–39; Corey Weinstein, "Even Dogs Confined to Cages for Long Periods of Time Go Beserk," in John P. May and Khalid R. Pitts (eds.), *Building Violence* (Thousand Oaks, CA: Sage, 2000), pp. 118–124; Chase Riveland, *Supermax Housing: Overview and General Considerations* (Washington, DC: National Institute of Corrections, January 1999), p. 1; Laura Sullivan, "In U.S. Prisons, Thousands Spend Years in Isolation," *National Public Radio*, July 26–28, 2006.

31. Riveland, *Supermax Housing*, p. 5. See also Gerald Berge, Jeffrey Geiger, and Scot Whitney, "Technology Is the Key to Security," *Corrections Today*, July 2001, pp. 105–109.

32. See, for example, Richard H. McCleery, "Authoritarianism and the Belief System of Incorrigibles," in Donald R. Cressy (ed.), *The Prison: Studies in Institutional Organization and Change* (New York: Holt, Rinehart & Winston, 1961), pp. 260–306; *Wright v. Enomoto* (July 23, 1980), pp. 5, 15;

Madrid v. Gomez, 889 F. Supp. 1146 (N.D. Cal. 1995); Craig Haney, "Infamous Punishment: The Psychological Consequences of Isolation," *National Prison Project Journal* (Spring 1993).

33. Kevin Johnson, "Inmate Suicides Linked to Solitary," *USA Today*, December 28, 2006, p. 1A.

34. Stephen J. Ingley, "Corrections Without Correction," in John P. May and Khalid R. Pitts (eds.), *Building Violence* (Thousand Oaks, CA: Sage, 2000), pp. 18–22.

35. Laura Sullivan, "In U.S. Prisons, Thousands Spend Years in Isolation," *National Public Radio*, July 26, 2007, www.npr.org.

36. As quoted in Weinstein, "Even Dogs Confined to Cages," p. 122.

37. Mears and Watson, "Towards a Fair and Balanced Assessment of Supermax Prisons."

38. *Madrid v. Gomez*, 889 F. Supp. 1146 (N.D. Cal. 1995).

39. *Wilkinson v. Austin*, 545 U.S._(2005).

40. Mark Curriden, "Hard Time: Chain Gangs Are In and Exercise Rooms Are Out in the Prisons of the 90s," *ABA Journal*, vol. 81 (July 1995), pp. 72–76.

41. "Sports in Prison," *Atlanta Journal-Constitution*, March 22, 1998, pp. E9–E12.

42. Brandon K. Applegate, "Penal Austerity: Perceived Utility, Desert, and Public Attitudes Toward Prison Amenities," *American Journal of Criminal Justice*, vol. 25, no. 2 (2001), pp. 253–268.

43. Nygel Lenz, "'Luxuries' in Prison: The Relationship Between Amenity Funding and Public Support," *Crime & Delinquency*, vol. 48, no. 4 (October 2002), p. 501.

44. As quoted in Garry Boulard, "What's Tough Enough?" *State Legislatures*, vol. 21, no. 10 (December 1995), p. 26.

45. Keynote speech, U.S. Attorney General's Summit on Corrections, April 27, 1998.

46. Lenz, "'Luxuries' in Prison," p. 519.

47. "Inmate Privileges and Fees for Service," *Corrections Compendium*, vol. 27, no. 8 (August 2002), pp. 4–26.

48. Ibid., pp. 8–9.

49. "5 Florida County Jails Make It Real Hard Time: No Television," *The New York Times*, August 14, 1994, p. L27; Richard Tewksbury and Elizabeth Ehrhardt Mustaine, "Insiders' Views on Prison Amenities: Beliefs and Perceptions of Correctional Staff Members," *Criminal Justice Review*, vol. 30, no. 2 (September 2005), pp. 174–188.

50. As quoted in Brett Pulley, "Always a Good Sound Bite: The 'Good Life' Behind Bars," *The New York Times*, September 22, 1996, Section 13, p. 2.

51. "5 Florida County Jails."

52. John J. Rafferty, "Prison Industry: The Next Step," *Corrections Today*, vol. 60, no. 4 (July 1998), p. 22.

53. W. Wesley Johnson, Katherine Bennett, and Timothy J. Flanagan, "Getting Tough on Prisoners: Results from the National Corrections Executive Survey, 1995," *Crime & Delinquency*, vol. 43, no. 1 (January 1997), pp. 24–41.

54. Adapted from the Web site of the American Correctional Association, www.corrections.com/aca/standards/benefits.htm (accessed June 15, 2002).

55. Malcolm M. Feeler, "The Privatization of Prisons in Historical Perspective," *Criminal Justice Research Bulletin*, vol. 6, no. 2 (1991), pp. 1–10.

56. Stephan and Karberg, *Census of State and Federal Correctional Facilities*, p. 1; see also Harrison and Beck, *Prisoners in 2005*.

57. "Public Bonds," www.publicbonds.org (accessed March 12, 2007).

58. Travis C. Pratt and Jeff Maahs, "Are Private Prisons More Cost-Effective Than Public Prisons? A Meta-Analysis of Evaluation Research Studies," *Crime & Delinquency,* vol. 45, no. 3 (July 1999), pp. 358–371.

59. Lonn Lanza-Kaduce, Karen F. Parker, and Charles W. Thomas, "A Comparative Recidivism Analysis of Releases from Private and Public Prisons," *Crime & Delinquency,* vol. 45, no. 1 (January 1999), pp. 28–47.

60. David Shichor, *Punishment for Profit: Private Prisons/Public Concerns* (Thousand Oaks, CA: Sage, 1995).

61. Joel Caplan, "Policy for Profit: The Private-Prison Industry's Influence over Criminal Justice Legislation," *ACJS Today,* vol. 26, no. 1 (January/February 2003).

62. Maeve McMahon, review of *Punishment for Profit: Private Prisons/Public Concerns,* by David Shichor, *Canadian Journal of Criminology,* vol. 39, no. 1 (January 1997), p. 115.

63. James Austin and Gary Coventry, *Emerging Issues on Privatized Prisons* (Washington, DC: U.S. Department of Justice, Bureau of Justice Statistics, February 2001).

64. Ibid., p. 29.

65. Charles W. Thomas, *Testimony Regarding Correctional Privatization,* presented before the Little Hoover Commission of the State of California, Sacramento, CA, 1997. As quoted in Austin and Coventry, *Emerging Issues on Privatized Prisons,* p. 21.

66. Robert J. Bosco, "Connecticut Probation's Partnership with the Private Sector," in National Institute of Corrections, *Topics in Community Corrections: Privatizing Community Supervision* (Washington, DC: National Institute of Justice, 1998), p. 12.

67. Suzanne Pullen, "An Evaluation of Private Probation Supervision and Case Management in Colorado," in National Institute of Corrections, *Topics in Community Corrections: Privatizing Community Supervision,* p. 15.

68. Reginald A. Wilkinson, "The Future of Adult Corrections," *Corrections Management Quarterly,* vol. 1, no. 1 (Winter 1997).

69. James A. Gondles Jr., "A Changing Reality," *Corrections Today,* vol. 65, no. 4 (July 2003), p. 6.

70. Taylor T. Dueker, "Video Visitation a Boom in Omaha," *American Jails,* vol. 18, no. 5 (November/December 2004), pp. 65–67.

71. "Telemedicine Expanding in Ohio Prison System," *TECHbeat,* Spring 2002, p. 10.

72. "Inmate Health Care," *Corrections Compendium,* vol. 29, no. 6 (November/December, 2004), pp. 11, 28–29.

73. "CORMAP It," *TECHbeat,* Summer 2002, p. 5.

74. Sean Reilly, "Earmarking Doles Out Pork in Billions," *Mobile Register,* August 15, 2004, pp. 1A, 6A.

75. Christopher A. Miles and Jeffrey P. Cohn, "Tracking Prisoners in Jail with Biometrics: An Experiment in a Navy Brig," *NIJ Journal,* no. 253 (January 2006), pp. 6–9.

Chapter 14

1. Details for this story come from Glen Puit, "1978 Mutilation: Family Relieved by Singleton's Death," *Las Vegas Review-Journal,* January 6, 2002.

2. Federal Bureau of Prisons, Program Statement number 1490.03, December 14, 1994.

3. Much of the material in this chapter is adapted from Office for Victims of Crime, *New Directions from the Field: Victims Rights and Services for the 21st Century* (Washington, DC: U.S. Department of Justice, 1998).

4. National Organization for Victim Assistance, *1988 NOVA Legislative Directory* (Washington, DC: National Organization for Victim Assistance, 1988), p. 191.

5. Victim and Witness Protection Act of 1982, Pub. L. No. 97-291.

6. Office of Justice Programs, *President's Task Force on Victims of Crime: Four Years Later* (Washington, DC: U.S. Government Printing Office, May 1986), p. 4.

7. Office for Victims of Crime, *The Crime Victim's Right to Be Present* (Washington, DC: OVC Legal Series Bulletin no. 3, November 2001).

8. National Victim Center, *1996 Victims' Rights Sourcebook: A Compilation and Comparison of Victims' Rights Laws* (Arlington, VA: National Victim Center, 1997).

9. Victim and Witness Protection Act of 1982, Pub. L. No. 97-291, Section 2(b).

10. Crime Control Act of 1990, Pub. L. No. 101-647.

11. Ibid., Title V, Section 502–503.

12. Violent Crime Control and Law Enforcement Act of 1994, Pub. L. No. 103-322.

13. Megan's Law amendment to the Jacob Wetterling Crimes Against Children and Sexual Violent Offender Act, 42 U.S.C. Section 14071.

14. S.2329.

15. NVCAN was created following a meeting sponsored by the National Organization for Victim Assistance (NOVA) and Mothers Against Drunk Driving (MADD) in 1985.

16. See the National Victims' Constitutional Amendment Network (NVCAN), *1996 Constitutional Amendment Action Kit.*

17. National Victims' Constitutional Amendment Network, *President Bush Announces Support for Bi-partisan Victims' Rights Amendment,* www.nvcan.org/home.htm (accessed June 24, 2002).

18. National Institute of Justice, *Victim Costs and Consequences: A New Look* (Washington, DC: NIJ, January 1996).

19. Ibid.

20. Much of the material in this section comes from Office for Victims of Crime, *New Directions.*

21. Anne Seymour, "Promoting Victim Justice Through Corrections-Based Victim Services," *Corrections Today,* July 2000, pp. 140–142.

22. A. Seymour, *National Victim Services Survey of Adult and Juvenile Correctional Agencies and Paroling Authorities, 1996* (Arlington, VA: National Victim Center, April 1997).

23. Office for Victims of Crime, *New Directions.*

24. Seymour, *National Victim Services Survey,* p. 5.

25. Megan's Law, Pub. L. No. 104-145, 110 Stat. 1345.

26. Information in this paragraph comes from the National Center for Victims of Crime Public Policy Issues page, www.ncvc.org/law/issues/community.htm (accessed November 25, 2007).

27. See Office for Victims of Crime, *New Directions.*

28. See Dorothy Mercer, R. Lord, and J. Lord, *Sharing Their Stories: What Are the Benefits? Who Is Helped?* paper presented at the Annual Meeting of the International Society for Traumatic Stress Studies, Chicago, IL, November 8, 1994.

29. Office for Victims of Crime, *New Directions.*

30. Dean G. Kilpatrick, David Beatty, and Susan Smith Howley, *The Rights of Crime Victims—Does Legal Protection Make a Difference?* (Washington, DC: NIJ, December 1998).

31. Ibid.

32. Office for Victims of Crime, *New Directions.*

33. Seymour, *National Victim Services Survey.*

34. Seymour, *Promising Practices and Strategies for Victim Services in Corrections* (Washington, DC: Office for Victims of Crime, 1999).

35. Office for Victims of Crime, *State Crime Victim Compensa-*

tion and Assistance Grant Programs (Washington, DC: OVC Fact Sheet, January 2002).

36. Office for Victims of Crime, *New Directions.*

37. President's Task Force on Victims of Crime, *Final Report* (Washington, DC: U.S. Government Printing Office, December 1982), p. 39.

38. National Association of Crime Victim Compensation Boards, *Crime Victim Compensation: An Overview* (Washington, DC: National Association of Crime Victim Compensation Boards, 1997), p. 1; Office for Victims of Crime, *State Crime Victim Compensation and Assistance Grant Programs.*

39. Office for Victims of Crime, *Nationwide Analysis, Victims of Crime Act: 1996 Victims of Crime Act Performance Report, State Compensation Program* (Washington, DC: U.S. Department of Justice, Office of Justice Programs, Office for Victims of Crime, April 14, 1997).

40. Victims of Crime Act of 1984, Pub. L. No. 104-235.

41. Office for Victims of Crime, *Victims of Crime Act Crime Victims Fund* (Washington, DC: OVC Fact Sheet, January 2002).

42. Office for Victims of Crime, *State Crime Victim Compensation and Assistance Grant Programs.*

43. President's Task Force on Victims of Crime, *Final Report.*

44. Much of the material in this section is taken from the Office for Victims of Crime fact sheet, www.ncjrs.org/ovcfs.htm (accessed September 1, 2003).

45. Victim and Witness Protection Act of 1982, Pub. L. No. 97-291, Sec. 4.

46. President's Task Force on Victims of Crime, *Final Report* (Washington, DC: U.S. Government Printing Office, December 1982), p. 72.

47. The Mandatory Victim Restitution Act, Title II of the Antiterrorism and Effective Death Penalty Act of 1996, Pub. L. No. 104-132 (1996), 18 U.S.C. Section 3663A (1996).

48. P. A. Langan and M. A. Cunniff, *Recidivism of Felons on Probation, 1986–89* (Washington, DC: U.S. Department of Justice, Bureau of Justice Statistics, February 1992).

49. R. L. Cohen, *Probation and Parole Violators in State Prison, 1991* (Washington, DC: Bureau of Justice Statistics, 1995).

50. Kilpatrick, Beatty, and Howley, *The Rights of Crime Victims,* p. 5.

51. Cohen, *Probation and Parole Violators.*

52. Office for Victims of Crime, *OVC Fact Sheet: What Is the Office for Victims of Crime?* (Washington, DC: OVC, 2004), from which much of the material in this section is taken.

53. Office for Victims of Crime, *What You Can Do If You Are a Crime Victim* (Washington, DC: OVC Fact Sheet, April 2002).

54. The National Victim Center, "INFOLINK: Victim Impact Statements," www.nvc.org/infolink/info72.htm (accessed January 2, 1999).

55. See Ellen K. Alexander and Janice Harris Lord, *Impact Statements: A Victim's Right to Speak, A Nation's Responsibility to Listen* (Washington, DC: Office for Victims of Crime, 1994).

56. *Payne* v. *Tennessee,* 501 U.S. 808, 111 S. Ct. 2597, 115 L. Ed. 2d 720.

57. National Victim Center, *1996 Victims' Rights Sourcebook.*

58. Office for Victims of Crime, *New Directions.*

Chapter 15

1. www.deathpenaltyinfo.org (accessed June 15, 2007); "Why DNA Exonerations May Get Rarer," *Time,* vol. 166, no. 14 (October 3, 2005), p. 18.

2. Excerpted from Susan Levine, "10 Years After Being Freed by DNA Evidence, His Life Is Still Trying," *Pittsburgh Post-Gazette,* March 2, 2003, p. A-12.

3. Details for this story come from Edward Connors et al., *Convicted by Juries, Exonerated by Science: Case Studies in the Use of DNA Evidence to Establish Innocence after Trial, Issues in Child Abuse Accusations,* vol. 10 (1998), www.ipt-forensics.com/journal/volume10/j10_3_6_2.htm (accessed March 20, 2007).

4. *U.S.* v. *Jackson,* 390 U.S. 570 (1968).

5. *Witherspoon* v. *Illinois,* 391 U.S. 510 (1968).

6. *Furman* v. *Georgia,* 408 U.S. 238 (1972).

7. www.deathpenaltyinfo.org (accessed June 15, 2007).

8. M. Watt Espy and John Ortiz Smykla, "Executions in the U.S. 1608–2003: The Espy File" (Inter-University Consortium for Political and Social Research, 1994).

9. Tracy L. Snell, *Capital Punishment, 2005* (Washington, DC: U.S. Department of Justice, Bureau of Justice Statistics, December 2006).

10. United States Department of Justice, *The Federal Death Penalty System: A Statistical Survey* (Washington, DC: U.S. Department of Justice, September 12, 2000).

11. www.deathpenaltyinfo.org (accessed June 15, 2007).

12. Ibid.

13. Snell, *Capital Punishment,* p. 10.

14. Ibid., p. 16.

15. Robert M. Bohm, *Deathquest III: An Introduction to the Theory and Practice of Capital Punishment in the United States,* 3rd ed. (Cincinnati, OH: Anderson, 2007); Raymond Paternoster, Robert Brame, and Sarah Bacon, *The Death Penalty: America's Experience with Capital Punishment* (New York: Oxford University Press, 2008).

16. John Boger, "Landmark North Carolina Death Penalty Study Finds Dramatic Racial Bias," www.deathpenaltyinfo.org (accessed April 1, 2005).

17. See summary of studies in Bohm, *Deathquest.*

18. Jefferson E. Holcomb, Marion R. Williams, and Stephen Demuth, "White Female Victims and Death Penalty Disparity Research," *Justice Quarterly,* vol. 21, no. 7 (December 2004), pp. 877–902.

19. Ashley Broughton and Carey Hamilton, "Walker Puts Option of Firing Squad to Death," *The Salt Lake Tribune,* March 17, 2004, p. 4.

20. J. Weisberg, "This Is Your Death," *The New Republic,* July 1, 1991.

21. Howard Mintz, "Schwarzenegger Orders Prison Officials to Fix Execution Problems," *San Jose Mercury News,* December 18, 2006, http://web.lexis-nexis.com (accessed March 24, 2007).

22. George Lombardi, Richard D. Sluder, and Donald Wallace, *The Management of Death-Sentenced Inmates: Issues, Realities, and Innovative Strategies,* paper presented at the annual meeting of the Academy of Criminal Justice Sciences, Las Vegas, Nevada, March 1996.

23. Robert Johnson, "Under Sentence of Death: The Psychology of Death Row Confinement," *Law and Psychology Review,* vol. 5 (Fall 1979), pp. 141–192.

24. As quoted in Bonnie Bartel Latino and Bob Vale, "Welcome to Death Row," *The Birmingham News,* January 16, 2000, pp. 1C, 4C.

25. Thomas J. Reidy, Mark D. Cunningham, and Jon R. Sorensen, "From Death to Life: Prison Behavior of Former Death Row Inmates in Indiana," *Criminal Justice and Behavior,* vol. 28, no. 1 (February 2001), pp. 62–82.

26. Mark Costanzo, *Just Revenge: Costs and Consequences of the Death Penalty* (New York: St. Martin's Press, 1997), p. 51.

27. As quoted in John Ortiz Smykla, "The Human Impact of Capital Punishment," *Journal of Criminal Justice,* vol. 15, no. 4 (1987), pp. 331–347.

28. Summaries of recent poll findings can be found on the Web site of the Death Penalty Information Center, www.deathpenaltyinfo.org (accessed March 26, 2007). See also "Death Penalty: Lethal Injection on Trial," www.stateline.org (accessed March 26, 2007); "Public Support for Death Penalty May Be Waning," *Corrections Today* (February 2006), p. 15; James D. Unnever, Francis T. Cullen, and Julian V. Roberts, "Not Everyone Strongly Supports the Death Penalty," *American Journal of Criminal Justice,* vol. 29, no. 2 (2005), pp. 187–216.

29. For example, see John K. Cochran, Denise Paquette Boots, and Kathleen M. Heide, "Attribution Styles and Attitudes Toward Capital Punishment for Juveniles, the Mentally Incompetent, and the Mentally Retarded," *Justice Quarterly,* vol. 20, no. 1 (March 2003), pp. 65–93; J. A. Fox, M. L. Radelet, and J. L. Bonsteel, "Death Penalty Opinion in the Post-Furman Years," *New York University Review of Law and Social Change,* vol. 28 (1991), pp. 499–528; M. Sandys and E. F. McGarrell, "Attitudes Toward Capital Punishment Among Indiana Legislators: Diminished Support in Light of Alternative Sentencing Options," *Justice Quarterly,* vol. 11 (1994), pp. 651–677; H. Zeisel and A. Gallup, "Death Penalty Sentiment in the United States," *Journal of Quantitative Criminology,* vol. 5 (1989), pp. 285–296.

30. For Texas, see Scott Vollum, Dennis R. Longmire, and Jacqueline Buffington-Vollum, "Confidence in the Death Penalty and Support for Its Use: Exploring the Value-Expressive Dimensions of Death Penalty Attitudes," *Justice Quarterly,* vol. 21, no. 3 (September 2004), pp. 521–546. For national opinion poll data as well as results of surveys of U.S. Catholics and residents of Maryland, New Jersey, and New York, see the Web site of the Death Penalty Information Center, www.deathpenaltyinfo.org (accessed June 15, 2007).

31. Brenda L. Vogel, "Support for Life in Prison Without the Possibility of Parole Among Death Penalty Proponents," *American Journal of Criminal Justice,* vol. 27, no. 2 (Spring 2003), pp. 263–275.

32. As cited in Robert M. Bohm, "The Future of Capital Punishment in the United States," *ACJS Today,* vol. 22, no. 4 (November/December 2000), p. 4.

33. *Washington Post,* December 25, 1998.

34. *Callins v. Collins,* 510 U.S. 1141 (1994).

35. *Furman v. Georgia,* 408 U.S. 238 (1972).

36. *Woodson v. North Carolina,* 428 U.S. 280 (1976); *Roberts v. Louisiana,* 428 U.S. 325 (1976); *Gregg v. Georgia,* 428 U.S. 153 (1976); *Jurek v. Texas,* 428 U.S. 262 (1976); *Proffitt v. Florida,* 428 U.S. 242 (1976).

37. *Gregg v. Georgia,* p. 189.

38. *Ring v. Arizona,* 122 U.S. 2428 (2002).

39. *Schriro v. Summerlin,* 542 U.S. 348 (2004).

40. James Liebman, Jeffrey Fagan, and Valerie West, *A Broken System: Error Rates in Capital Cases, 1973–1995* (New York: Columbia University School of Law, 2000), p. i.; Barry Latzer and James N. G. Cauthen, *Justice Delayed? Time Consumption in Capital Appeals: A Multistate Study* (Washington, DC: U.S. Department of Justice, March 2007). The authors found a median of 966 days to complete direct appeals across 14 states from 1992 to 2002. Processing direct appeals was fastest in Virginia (295 days) and slowest in Ohio, Tennessee, and Kentucky (1,388, 1,350, and 1,309 days, respectively).

41. Ibid. See also Timothy G. Poveda, "Estimating Wrongful Convictions," *Justice Quarterly,* vol. 18, no. 3 (September 2001), pp. 689–708; Talia Roitberg Harmon, "Predictors of Miscarriages of Justice in Capital Cases," *Justice Quarterly,* vol. 18, no. 4 (December 2001), pp. 949–968.

42. www.deathpenaltyinfo.org (accessed June 15, 2007).

43. Talia Roitberg Harmon, "Race for Your Life: An Analysis of the Role of Race in Erroneous Capital Convictions," *Criminal Justice Review,* vol. 29, no. 1 (Spring 2004), pp. 76–96.

44. S. R. Gross, "Risks of Death: Why Erroneous Convictions Are Common in Capital Cases," *Buffalo Law Review,* vol. 44 (1966), pp. 469–500.

45. Roitberg Harmon, "Race for Your Life," p. 77.

46. Liebman, Fagan, and West, *A Broken System,* p. 18.

47. Steve Mills and Maurice Possley, "After Exonerations, Hunt for Killer Rare," *Chicago Tribune,* October 27, 2003, p. 1A. www.deathpenaltyinfo.org (accessed June 15, 2007).

48. www.deathpenaltyinfo.org (accessed April 30, 2005).

49. "New Jersey Suspends Death Penalty Pending a Task Force Review," *Criminal Justice Newsletter,* January 17, 2006, p. 8.

50. Matt O'Connor, "Jury Believes Ex-Chicago Cop Framed by FBI," *Chicago Tribune,* January 25, 2005.

51. James S. Liebman et al., *A Broken System, Part II: Why There Is So Much Error in Capital Cases, and What Can Be Done About It* (New York: Columbia University School of Law, 2002), pp. 391–428.

52. Espy and Smykla, "Executions in the U.S."

53. Does not include Jose High, executed November 6, 2001, in Georgia. He may have been 17 years old at the time of the crime. Records concerning his age are disputed.

54. *Thompson v. Oklahoma,* 487 U.S. 815 (1988).

55. *Stanford v. Kentucky,* 492 U.S. 361 (1989).

56. Consolidated with *Stanford.*

57. *Roper v. Simmons,* 543 U.S._(2005).

58. James Alan Fox as cited in Meghan Mandeville, "Supreme Court Puts an End to Juvenile Death Penalty," *Juvenile Info Network* online, www.juvenilenet.org/news.html (accessed March 22, 2005).

59. *Atkins v. Virginia,* 536 U.S. (2002).

60. Chris Kahn, "Inmate in Retardation Case Remains on Death Row," *The Birmingham News,* November 29, 2003, p. 8A.

61. Ibid.

62. Richard Gonzales, "Death-Row Inmates Seek Low-IQ Exception," *National Public Radio,* March 21, 2005.

Chapter 16

1. Excerpt from Tom Sheehan, "Buddy Testifies Teen Didn't Like His Stepmother," *The Columbus Dispatch,* February 2, 2000, p. 1B. Copyright © 2000 Columbus Dispatch, used with permission.

2. "Teen Admits Killing Father, Stepmother," *The Cincinnati Enquirer,* Tristate Digest, March 25, 2000, http://enquirer.com/editions/2000/03/25/loc_tristate_digest.html (accessed June 13, 2003).

3. Ken Wooden, *Weeping in the Playtime of Others* (New York: McGraw-Hill, 1976), pp. 23–24.

4. *People ex rel. O'Connell v. Turner,* 55 Ill.280, 8 Am. Rep. 645.

5. R. M. Mennel, *Thorns and Thistles: Juvenile Delinquency in the United States, 1825–1940* (Hanover, NH: University Press of New England, 1973), p. 131.

6. *Kent v. United States,* 383 U.S. 541 (1966).

7. *In re Gault,* 387 U.S. 1, 55 (1967).

8. *In re Winship,* 397 U.S. 358 (1970).

9. *McKeiver* v. *Pennsylvania*, 403 U.S. 528 (1971).

10. *Breed* v. *Jones*, 421 U.S. 519 (1975).

11. This paragraph is adapted from Howard N. Snyder and Melissa Sickmund, *Juvenile Offenders and Victims: 1999 National Report* (Washington, DC: Office of Juvenile Justice and Delinquency Prevention, 1999), p. 99.

12. Melissa Sickmund, *Juveniles in Court* (Washington, DC: Office of Juvenile Justice and Delinquency Prevention, June 2003), p. 5.

13. FBI, *Crime in the United States, 2006* (Washington, DC: U.S. Department of Justice, 2007).

14. Charles Puzzanchera et al., *Juvenile Court Statistics 2000* (Washington, DC: Office of Juvenile Justice and Delinquency Prevention, December 2004).

15. Adapted from Caren Harp et al., *Juvenile Delinquency and Community Prosecution: New Strategies for Old Problems* (Alexandria, VA: American Prosecutors Research Institute, 2004).

16. Ibid.

17. Puzzanchera et al., *Juvenile Court Statistics*, p. 2.

18. Ibid., p. 9.

19. Gerald Bayens, *Assessing the Impact of Judicial Waiver Laws in Kansas: Implications for Correctional Policy* (Ann Arbor, MI: University Microfilms International, 1998).

20. E. J. Loughran et al., *CJCA Yearbook 2006: A National Perspective of Juvenile Corrections* (Braintree, MA: Council of Juvenile Correctional Administrators, 2007), from which parts of this section are derived.

21. Anne L. Stahl et al., *Juvenile Court Statistics 2001–2002* (Pittsburgh, PA: National Center for Juvenile Justice, 2005).

22. Howard N. Snyder and Melissa Sickmund, *Juvenile Offenders and Victims: 2006 National Report* (Washington, DC: Office of Juvenile Justice and Delinquency Prevention, 2006), from which some of the material in this section is adapted.

23. Melissa Sickmund, *Juvenile Residential Facility Census, 2002: Selected Findings* (Washington, DC: Office of Juvenile Justice and Delinquency Prevention, 2006), p. 2.

24. Charles M. Puzzanchera, *Delinquency Cases Waived to Criminal Court, 1989–1998* (Washington, DC: Office of Juvenile Justice and Delinquency Prevention, September 2001).

25. Tammy Hawkins, personal communication, September 21, 1998.

26. Youth Court Guidebook Advisory Committee, *Youth Cases for Youth Courts: Desktop Guide* (Chicago: American Bar Association, 2005), from which a number of the paragraphs that follow have been adapted.

27. Sarah S. Pearson and Sonia Jurich, *Youth Court: A Community Solution for Embracing At-Risk Youth—A National Update* (Washington, DC: American Youth Policy Forum, 2005).

28. Ibid., p. 13.

29. Jeffrey A. Butts and Janeen Buck, *Teen Courts: A Focus on Research* (Washington, DC: Office of Juvenile Justice and Delinquency Prevention, October 2000).

30. Tammy Hawkins (personal communication, September 21, 1998).

31. Arlen Egley Jr. and Christina E. Ritz, *Highlights of the 2004 National Youth Gang Survey* (Washington, DC: Office of Juvenile Justice and Delinquency Prevention, 2006).

32. Federal Bureau of Investigation, Kids Crime Prevention Page, www.fbi.gov, 2002 (accessed June 20, 2003).

33. Candice M. Kane, *Prosecutor: Technical Assistance Manual* (Washington, DC: OJJDP, 1992).

34. Ibid.

35. Office of Juvenile Justice and Delinquency Prevention, *1998 National Youth Gang Survey* (Washington, DC: U.S. Department of Justice, November 2000).

36. Jeff Ferrell, "Criminological Verstehen: Inside the Immediacy of Crime," *Justice Quarterly*, vol. 14, no. 1 (1997), pp. 3–23.

37. Ania Dobrzanska, "ACA's Certification Program Extends to Juvenile Corrections," *Corrections Today*, June 2005, pp. 20–21.

38. Ibid., p. 20.

39. James Turpin, "Juvenile Justice in the Spotlight," *Corrections Today*, vol. 59, no. 3 (1997), p. 124.

40. *Briefing Paper: Prosecuting Juveniles in Adult Court* (Washington, DC: The Sentencing Project, 1999).

Chapter 17

1. This chapter was contributed by William Sondervan, EdD, CCE, with the assistance of Ania Dobrzanska, MS, CCM. Dr. Sondervan is director of Criminal Justice, Investigative Forensics and Legal Studies at the University of Maryland University College. From 2003 to 2006 Sondervan served as director of Professional Development at the American Correctional Association. In 1999, Dr. Sondervan was appointed Commissioner of the Maryland Division of Corrections. He served as commissioner until 2003. Dr. Sondervan earned a BS in business administration from the College of New Jersey, an EdM in counseling psychology from Boston University, an MPA in criminal justice from Jacksonville State University, and an EdD in adult education and human resource development from Virginia Polytechnic Institution and State University. Dobrzanska is Program Coordinator with the Moss Group in Washington, DC. She earned a BA in psychology and administration of justice from Rutgers University, and an MS in justice, law, and society at American University.

2. Marc Mauer and Meda Cheskey-Lind (eds.), *Invisible Punishment: The Collateral Consequences of Mass Imprisonment* (New York: New Press, 2002).

3. Michael Tonry and Joan Petersilia (eds.), *Prisons: Crime and Justice: A Review of Research*, Vol. 28 (Chicago: University of Chicago Press, 1999).

4. Joan Petersilia, *When Prisoners Come Home: Parole and Prisoner Reentry* (New York: Oxford University Press, 2003).

5. Ibid.

6. Mauer and Chesney-Lind, *Invisible Punishment*.

7. Tonry and Petersilia, *Prisons: Crime and Justice*.

8. "Correctional Administrators Speak Out," Association of State Correctional Administrators, www.asca.net/press release.html (accessed May 14, 2004).

9. Ibid.

10. Petersilia, *When Prisoners Come Home*.

11. Karl O. Haigler et al., *Literacy Behind Prison Walls* (Washington, DC: U.S. Department of Education, National Center for Education Statistics, 1994).

12. Stephen Steurer and Linda Smith, *Education Reduces Crime: Three-State Recidivism Study* (Lanham, MD: Correctional Education Association, 2003).

13. A. R. Roberts and D. O. Coffey, *ACA State of the Art Survey for a Correctional Education Network* (Lanham, MD: American Correctional Association, 1976).

14. Steurer and Smith, *Education Reduces Crime*.

15. Petersilia, *When Prisoners Come Home*.

16. American Correctional Association, *A 21st Century Workforce for America's Correctional Profession* (Indianapolis, IN: Workforce Associates, Inc., 2004). Updated with information

from state web sites accessed June 15, 2007.

17. Workforce Associates, Inc., *A 21st Century Workforce for America's Correctional Profession* (Workforce Associates, Inc.: Indianapolis, IN, May 15, 2004).

18. Robert Johnson, *Death Work: A Study of the Modern Execution Process* (Belmont, CA: Wadsworth, 1990).

19. Ted Conover, *Newjack: Guarding Sing Sing* (New York: Random House, 2000).

20. Petersilia, *When Prisoners Come Home.*

21. Patrick A. Langan and David J. Levin, *Recidivism of Prisoners Released in 1994* (Washington, DC: U.S. Department of Justice, Bureau of Justice Statistics, June 2002).

22. Allen J. Beck and Bernard E. Shipley, *Recidivism of Prisoners Released in 1983* (Washington, DC: U.S. Department of Justice, Bureau of Justice Statistics, April 1989).

23. Petersilia, *When Prisoners Come Home.*

24. Ibid.

25. Conover, *Newjack.*

26. Ibid.

Appendix

1. John Barker and Jim Kellen, *Career Planning: A Developmental Approach* (Upper Saddle River, NJ: Merrill, 1998).

2. Ibid., p. 75.

3. Tom Jackson, *The Perfect Resume* (New York: Doubleday, 1990).

GLOSSARY

Numbers in parentheses indicate the pages on which the terms are defined.

A

absconding Fleeing without permission of the jurisdiction in which the offender is required to stay. (149)

accreditation The process through which correctional facilities and agencies can measure themselves against nationally adopted standards and through which they can receive formal recognition and accredited status. (242)

adjudication The process by which a court arrives at a final decision in a case; or the second stage of the juvenile justice process in which the court decides whether the offender is formally responsible for (guilty of) the alleged offense. (17)

administrative officers Those who control keys and weapons and sometimes oversee visitation. (369)

aggravating circumstances Factors that may increase the culpability of the offender. (601)

AIDS (acquired immunodeficiency syndrome) A disease of the human immune system that is characterized cytologically, especially by reduction in the numbers of CD4-bearing helper T cells to 20 percent or less of normal, rendering a person highly vulnerable to life-threatening conditions. The disease is caused by infection with HIV commonly transmitted in infected blood and bodily secretions (as semen), especially during sexual intercourse and intravenous drug use. (472)

Americans with Disabilities Act (ADA) Public Law 101-336, enacted July 26, 1990, which prohibits discrimination and ensures equal opportunity for people with disabilities in employment, state and local government services, public accommodations, commercial facilities, and transportation. It also mandates the establishment of TDD/telephone relay services. (488)

arraignment An appearance in court prior to trial in a criminal proceeding. (17)

Auburn system The second historical phase of prison discipline. It followed the Pennsylvania system and allowed inmates to work silently together during the day but remain isolated at night. Implemented at New York's Auburn prison in 1815, eventually sleeping cells became congregate and restrictions against talking were removed. (254)

average daily population (ADP) The sum of the number of inmates in a jail or prison each day for a year, divided by the total number of days in the year. (207)

B

back-end programs Sanctions that move offenders from higher levels of control to lower ones for the final phase of their sentences. (159)

balancing test A method the U.S. Supreme Court uses to decide prisoners' rights cases, weighing the rights claimed by inmates against the legitimate needs of prisoners. (435)

best efforts standard A requirement of the federal Victims' Rights and Restitution Act of 1990 (also known as the Victims' Rights Act) that mandates that federal law enforcement officers, prosecutors, and corrections officials use their best efforts to ensure that victims receive basic rights and services during their encounter with the criminal justice system. (544)

bifurcated trial Two separate hearings for different issues in a trial, one for guilt and the other for punishment. (599)

biometrics The automated identification or verification of human identity through measurable physiological and behavioral traits. (533)

blended sentencing A two-part (juvenile and adult) sentence in which the adult sentence may be waived if the offender complies with all provisions of the juvenile sentence. (637)

block officers Those responsible for supervising inmates in housing areas. (368)

boot camp A short institutional term of confinement that includes a physical regimen designed to develop self-discipline, respect for authority, responsibility, and a sense of accomplishment. (188)

bridewell A workhouse. The word came from the name of the first workhouse in England. (50)

C

capital crime A crime for which the death penalty may but need not necessarily be imposed. (581)

capital punishment Lawful imposition of the death penalty. (577)

certification A credentialing process, usually involving testing and career development assessment, through which the skills, knowledge, and abilities of correctional personnel can be formally recognized. (26)

chlamydia The most common sexually transmitted disease. Caused by the bacteria *Chlamydia trachomatis*, it can affect the eyes, lungs, or urogenital (urinary-genital) area, depending on the age of the person infected and how the infection is transmitted. (487)

chronological résumé A résumé that organizes information in reverse time sequence and emphasizes work history. (A-7)

citation A type of nonfinancial pretrial release similar to a traffic ticket. It binds the defendant to appear in court on a future date. (234)

civil liability A legal obligation to another person to do, pay, or make good something. (427)

classification The process of subdividing the inmate population into meaningful categories to match offender needs with correctional resources. (269)

clemency Kindness, mercy, forgiveness, or leniency, usually relating to criminal acts. (587)

client-specific plan (CSP) A privately prepared presentence report that supplements the PSR prepared by the probation department. (135)

cocorrections The incarceration and interaction of female and male offenders under a single institutional administration. (416)

coed prison A prison housing both female and male offenders. (416)

cognitive-behavioral treatment A problem-focused intervention that emphasizes skill training. (133)

community corrections A philosophy of correctional treatment that embraces (1) decentralization of authority, (2) citizen participation, (3) redefinition of the population of offenders for whom incarceration is most appropriate, and (4) emphasis on rehabilitation through community programs. (157)

community corrections acts (CCAs) State laws that give economic grants to local communities to establish community corrections goals and policies and to develop and operate community corrections programs. (196)

community notification Notification to the community of the release or pending release of convicted offenders. (559)

community service A sentence to serve a specified number of hours working in unpaid positions with nonprofit or tax-supported agencies. (173)

commutation A change of a legal penalty to a lesser one (e.g., from death to life imprisonment). (587)

compensatory damages Money a court may award as payment for actual losses suffered by a plaintiff, including out-of-pocket expenses incurred in filing the suit, other forms of monetary or material loss, and pain, suffering, and mental anguish. (429)

concurrent sentences Sentences served together. (84)

conditional diversion Diversion in which charges are dismissed if the defendant satisfactorily completes treatment, counseling, or other programs ordered by the justice system. (115)

conditional release Pretrial release under minimum or moderately restrictive conditions with little monitoring or compliance. It includes ROR, supervised pretrial release, and third-party release. (234)

consecutive sentences Sentences served one after the other. (84)

consent decree A written compact, sanctioned by a court, between parties in a civil case, specifying how disagreements between them are to be resolved. (442)

constitutional rights The personal and due process rights guaranteed to individuals by the U.S. Constitution and its amendments, especially the first 10 amendments, known as the Bill of Rights. Constitutional rights are the basis of most inmate rights. (426)

contract system A system of prison industry in which the prison advertised for bids for the employment of prisoners, whose labor was sold to the highest bidder. (258)

convict lease system A system of prison industry in which a prison temporarily relinquished supervision of its prisoners to a lessee. The lessee either employed the prisoners within the institution or transported them to work elsewhere in the state. (258)

corporal punishments Physical punishments, or those involving the body. (40)

correctional clients Prison inmates, probationers, parolees, offenders assigned to alternative sentencing programs, and those held in jails. (9)

correctional econometrics The study of the cost-effectiveness of various correctional programs and related reductions in the incidence of crime. (75)

correctional officer personalities The distinctive personal characteristics of correctional officers, including behavioral, emotional, and social traits. (366)

corrections All the various aspects of the pretrial and post-conviction management of individuals accused or convicted of crimes. (19)

corrections professional A dedicated person of high moral character and personal integrity who is employed in the field of corrections and takes professionalism to heart. (26)

counterperformance The defendant's participation, in exchange for diversion, in a treatment, counseling, or educational program aimed at changing his or her behavior. (111)

crime A violation of the criminal law. (5)

crime index An annual statistical tally of major crimes known to law enforcement agencies in the United States. (10)

crime rate The number of major crimes reported for each unit of population. (10)

criminal justice The process of achieving justice through the application of the criminal law and through the workings of the criminal justice system. Also, the study of the field of criminal justice. (14)

criminal justice system The collection of all the agencies that perform criminal justice functions, whether these are operations or administration or technical support. The basic divisions of the criminal justice system are police, courts, and corrections. (14)

criminal law (also called *penal law*) That portion of the law that defines crimes and specifies criminal punishments. (20)

cruel and unusual punishment A penalty that is grossly disproportionate to the offense or that violates today's broad and idealistic concepts of dignity, civilized standards, humanity, and decency (*Estelle v. Gamble*, 1976, and *Hutto v. Finney*, 1978). In the area of capital punishment, cruel and unusual punishments are those that involve torture, a lingering death, or unnecessary pain. (441)

custodial staff Those staff members most directly involved in managing the inmate population. (359)

D

day fine A financial penalty scaled both to the defendant's ability to pay and to the seriousness of the crime. (169)

day reporting center (DRC) A community correctional center to which an offender reports each day to file a daily schedule with a supervision officer, showing how each hour will be spent. (176)

death row A prison area housing inmates who have been sentenced to death. (591)

deliberate indifference Intentional and willful indifference. Within the field of correctional practice, the term refers to calculated inattention to unconstitutional conditions of confinement. (442)

delinquent offenses Acts committed by juveniles that, if committed by adults, could result in criminal prosecution. (630)

deprivation theory The belief that inmate subcultures develop in response to the deprivations in prison life. (395)

deserts See **just deserts**.

design capacity The number of inmates that planners or architects intend for the facility. (291)

detention hearing A judicial review of the intake officer's detention decision. (632)

determinate sentence (also called *fixed sentence*) A sentence of a fixed term of incarceration, which can be reduced by good time. (85)

deterrence The discouragement or prevention of crimes through the fear of punishment. (74)

direct file provisions Provisions under which the prosecutor determines whether to initiate a case against a juvenile in juvenile court or in adult criminal court. (643)

direct-supervision jail See **third-generation jail**. (213)

discretionary release Early release based on the paroling authority's assessment of eligibility. (311)

disposition The third stage of the juvenile justice process in which the court decides the disposition (sentence) for a juvenile case. (634)

disturbance An altercation involving three or more inmates, resulting in official action beyond summary sanctions and for which there is an institutional record. (508)

diversion "The halting or suspension, before conviction, of formal criminal proceedings against a person, conditioned on some form of counter performance by the defendant." (111)

drug court A special court that is given responsibility to treat, sanction, and reward drug offenders with punishment more restrictive than regular probation but less severe than incarceration. (163)

due process A right guaranteed by the Fifth, Sixth, and Fourteenth Amendments to the U.S. Constitution and generally understood, in legal contexts, to mean the expected course of legal proceedings according to the rules and forms established for the protection of persons' rights. (444)

E

equity The sentencing principle that similar crimes and similar criminals should be treated alike. (97)

Evidence-based corrections See **evidence-based penology**. (22)

evidence-based penology (also called *evidence-based corrections*) The application of social scientific techniques to the study of everyday corrections procedures for the purpose of increasing effectiveness and enhancing the efficient use of available resources. (22)

exchange rates An approach to sentencing that emphasizes interchangeability of punishments; for example, three days

under house arrest might be considered equal to one day of incarceration. (501)

exoneration To clear of blame and release from death row. (596)

external classification Interinstitutional placement of an inmate that determines an inmate's security level. (270)

F

fair sentencing Sentencing practices that incorporate fairness for both victims and offenders. Fairness is said to be achieved by implementing principles of proportionality, equity, social debt, and truth in sentencing. (97)

Federal Prison Industries (FPI) A federal, paid inmate work program and self-supporting corporation. (286)

felony A serious criminal offense; specifically, one punishable by death or by incarceration in a prison facility for more than a year. (9)

fine A financial penalty used as a criminal sanction. (168)

first-generation jail Jail with multiple-occupancy cells or dormitories that line corridors arranged like spokes. Inmate supervision is intermittent; staff must patrol the corridors to observe inmates in their cells. (211)

fixed sentence See **determinate sentence**. (85)

flat sentences Those that specify a given amount of time to be served in custody and allow little or no variation from the time specified. (84)

folkways Time-honored ways of doing things. Although they carry the force of tradition, their violation is unlikely to threaten the survival of the social group. (20)

fourth-generation jail Jail that incorporates natural light into the dayroom where staff members work and inmates spend most of their day, and brings program services, staff, volunteers, and visitors to the housing unit. (215)

frivolous lawsuits Lawsuits with no foundation in fact. They are generally brought for publicity, political, or other reasons not related to law. (447)

front-end programs Punishment options for initial sentences more restrictive than traditional probation but less restrictive than jail or prison. (159)

functional résumé A résumé that emphasizes abilities over work history, organizing information according to skills, results, contributions, or functions. (A-10)

G

gain time Time taken off an inmate's sentence for participating in certain activities such as going to school, learning a trade, and working in prison. (361)

gang A criminal enterprise having an organizational structure, acting as a continuing criminal conspiracy, that employs violence and any other criminal activity to sustain itself. (647)

general deterrence The use of the example of individual punishment to dissuade others from committing crimes. (74)

genital herpes A sexually transmitted disease caused by the herpes simplex virus or HSV. It is one of the most common STDs in the United States. (487)

gonorrhea The second most common sexually transmitted disease. Often called *the clap*, gonorrhea is caused by the *Neisseria gonorrhea* bacteria found in moist areas of the body. Infection occurs with contact to any of these areas. (486)

good time The number of days or months prison authorities deduct from a sentence for good behavior and for other reasons. (85)

group home A nonsecure residential facility for juveniles. (635)

guardian *ad litem* A person appointed by the juvenile court, often defense counsel, to serve as a special guardian for the youth being processed through the juvenile justice system. (633)

guided discretion Decision making bounded by general guidelines, rules, or laws. (598)

H

habitual offender statute A law that (1) allows a person's criminal history to be considered at sentencing or (2) makes it possible for a person convicted of a given offense and previously convicted of another specified offense to receive a more severe penalty than that for the current offense alone. (93)

hands-off doctrine A historical policy of the American courts not to intervene in prison management. Courts tended to follow the doctrine until the late 1960s. (424)

hedonistic calculus The idea that people are motivated by pleasure and pain and that the proper amount of punishment can deter crime. (56)

HIV (human immunodeficiency virus) Any of a group of retroviruses that infect and destroy helper T cells of the immune system, causing the marked reduction in their numbers that is diagnostic of AIDS. (471)

hospice An interdisciplinary, comfort-oriented care facility that helps seriously ill patients die with dignity and humanity in an environment that facilitates mental and spiritual preparation for the natural process of dying. (484)

I

importation theory The belief that inmate subcultures are brought into prison from the outside world. (395)

incapacitation The use of imprisonment or other means to reduce an offender's capability to commit future offenses. (74)

indeterminate sentence A sentence in which a judge specifies a maximum length and a minimum length, and an administrative agency, generally a parole board, determines the actual time of release. (84)

industrial shop and school officers Those who ensure efficient use of training and educational resources within the prison. (369)

informational interviewing Talking to people who are currently employed in a career field of interest. (A-4)

infraction A minor violation of state statute or local ordinance punishable by a fine or other penalty but not by incarceration, or by a specified, usually very short term of incarceration. (9)

injunction A judicial order to do or refrain from doing a particular act. (429)

inmate roles Prison lifestyles; also, forms of ongoing social accommodations to prison life. (397)

inmate subculture (also called *prisoner subculture*) The habits, customs, mores, values, beliefs, or superstitions of the body of inmates incarcerated in correctional institutions; also, the inmate social world. (394)

institutional corrections That aspect of the correctional enterprise that "involves the incarceration and rehabilitation of adults and juveniles convicted of offenses against the law, and the confinement of persons suspected of a crime awaiting trial and adjudication." (18)

institutional needs Prison administration interests recognized by the courts as justifying some restrictions on the constitutional rights of prisoners. Those interests are maintenance of institutional *order,* maintenance of institutional *security, safety* of prison inmates and staff, and *rehabilitation* of inmates. (427)

intake The first stage of the juvenile justice process. A court-appointed officer reviews the case and recommends a course of action—dismissal, informal disposition, formal disposition, or transfer to adult criminal court. (631)

intangible losses Costs such as fear, pain, suffering, and reduced quality of life that accrue to victims as a result of their victimization. (552)

integration model A combination of importation theory and deprivation theory. The belief that, in childhood, some inmates acquired, usually from peers, values that support law-violating behavior but that the norms and standards in prison also affect inmates. (395)

intensive supervision probation (ISP) Control of offenders in the community under strict conditions, by means of frequent reporting to a probation officer whose caseload is generally limited to 30 offenders. (161)

intermediate sanctions New punishment options developed to fill the gap between traditional probation and traditional jail or prison sentences and to better match the severity of punishment to the seriousness of the crime. (157)

internal classification Intrainstitutional placement that determines, through review of an inmate's background, assignment to housing units or cellblocks, work, and programming based on the inmate's risk, needs, and time to serve. (271)

J

jail accreditation Formal approval of a jail by the American Correctional Association and the Commission on Accreditation. (242)

jails Locally operated correctional facilities that confine people before or after conviction. (207)

job interview A meeting with a prospective employer in which a job applicant projects his or her most impressive qualities. (A-16)

jurisdiction The power, right, or authority of a court to interpret and apply the law. (429)

just deserts Punishment deserved. A just deserts perspective on criminal sentencing holds that criminal offenders are morally blameworthy and are therefore *deserving* of punishment. (73)

juvenile court Any court that has jurisdiction over matters involving juveniles. (633)

juvenile detention facility A facility for keeping juvenile offenders in secure custody, as necessary, through various stages of the juvenile justice process. (632)

L

legitimate penological objectives The realistic concerns that correctional officers and administrators have for the integrity and security of the correctional institution and the safety of staff and inmates. (435)

M

mandatory death penalty A death sentence that the legislature has required to be imposed upon people convicted of certain offenses. (598)

mandatory minimum sentencing The imposition of sentences required by statute for those convicted of a particular crime or a particular crime with specific circumstances, such as robbery with a firearm or selling drugs to a minor within 1,000 feet of a school, or for those with a particular type of criminal history. (91)

mandatory release Early release after a time period specified by law. (311)

mandatory sentences Those that are required by law under certain circumstances—such as conviction of a specified crime or of a series of offenses of a specified type. (83)

maximum- or close/high-security prison A prison designed, organized, and staffed to confine the most dangerous offenders for long periods. It has a highly secure perimeter, barred cells, and a high staff-to-inmate ratio. It imposes strict controls on the movement of inmates and visitors, and it offers few programs, amenities, or privileges. (294)

medical model A philosophy of prisoner reform in which criminal behavior is regarded as a disease to be treated with appropriate therapy. (260)

medium-security prison A prison that confines offenders considered less dangerous than those in maximum security, for both short and long periods. It places fewer controls on inmates' and visitors' freedom of movement than does a maximum-security facility. It has barred cells and a fortified perimeter. The staff-to-inmate ratio is generally lower than that in a maximum-security facility, and the level of amenities and privileges is slightly higher. (295)

minimization of penetration A form of diversion that keeps an offender from going further into the system. (112)

minimum-security prison A prison that confines the least dangerous offenders for both short and long periods. It allows as much freedom of movement and as many privileges and amenities as are consistent with the goals of the facility. It may have dormitory housing, and the staff-to-inmate ratio is relatively low. (296)

misdemeanor A relatively minor violation of the criminal law, such as petty theft or simple assault, punishable by confinement for one year or less. (9)

mission That which is done to support the purpose. (670)

mitigating circumstances Factors that, although not justifying or excusing an action, may reduce the culpability of the offender. (599)

model of criminal sentencing A strategy or system for imposing criminal sanctions. (84)

mores Cultural restrictions on behavior that forbid serious violations—such as murder, rape, and robbery—or a group's values. (20)

N

net widening Increasing the number of offenders sentenced to a higher level of restriction. It results in sentencing offenders to more restrictive sanctions than their offenses and characteristics warrant. (159)

networking Meeting new people who can give you information about careers, the job market, and specific positions. It is often done through people you know. (A-2)

new offense violation Arrest and prosecution for the commission of a new crime by someone on parole or probation. (149)

no-frills prisons and jails Correctional institutions that take away prisoner amenities and privileges. (519)

nolo contendere A plea of "no contest." A no-contest plea may be used by a defendant who does not wish to contest conviction. Because the plea does not admit guilt, it cannot provide the basis for later civil suits. (17)

nominal damages Small amounts of money a court may award when inmates have sustained no actual damages, but there is clear evidence that their rights have been violated. (429)

noninstitutional corrections (also called *community corrections*) That aspect of the correctional enterprise that includes "pardon, probation, and miscellaneous [activities] not directly related to institutional care." (19)

O

open institution A minimum-security facility that has no fences or walls surrounding it. (296)

operational capacity The number of inmates that a facility's staff, existing programs, and services can accommodate. (291)

P

pains of imprisonment Major problems that inmates face, such as loss of liberty and personal autonomy, lack of material possessions, loss of heterosexual relationships, and reduced personal security. (394)

pardon An executive act that legally excuses a convicted offender from a criminal penalty. (311)

parens patriae A Latin term that refers to the state as guardian of minors and of people who are mentally incompetent. (623)

parole The conditional release of a prisoner, prior to completion of the imposed sentence, under the supervision of a parole officer. (311)

parole eligibility date The earliest date on which an inmate might be paroled. (321)

parolee A person who is conditionally released from prison to community supervision. (324)

paroling authority A person or correctional agency (often called a *parole board* or *parole commission*) that has the authority to grant parole, revoke parole, and discharge from parole. (321)

pay-to-stay jail (also called *self-pay jails*) An alternative to serving time in a county jail and offers privileges to offenders (called clients) convicted of minor offenses such as non-drug related offenses who pay $75 to $127 per day. (225)

penal law See **criminal law.** (20)

penitentiary The earliest form of large-scale incarceration. It punished criminals by isolating them so that they could reflect on their misdeeds, repent, and reform. (253)

Pennsylvania system The first historical phase of prison discipline involving solitary confinement in silence instead of corporal punishment; conceived by the American Quakers in 1790 and implemented at the Walnut Street Jail. (254)

performance-based funding A method of allocating money for programs that present reliable and valid data that they work. (664)

perimeter security officers Those assigned to security (or gun) towers, wall posts, and perimeter patrols. These officers are charged with preventing escapes and detecting and preventing intrusions. (369)

pleasure-pain principle The idea that actions are motivated primarily by a desire to experience pleasure and avoid pain. (74)

policy-centered approach A method of thinking about and planning for intermediate sanctions that draws together key stakeholders from inside and outside the corrections agency that will implement the sanction. (194)

precedent A previous judicial decision that judges should consider in deciding future cases. (433)

predisposition report A report that documents (1) a juvenile's background; (2) the juvenile's educational history; (3) information gathered from interviews with the juvenile, family members, and others; (4) available placement options; and (5) recommended dispositions. (634)

presentence report (PSR) A report prepared by the probation department of a court that provides a social and personal history as well as an evaluation of a defendant as an aid to the court in determining a sentence. (84)

principle of least eligibility The requirement that prison conditions—including the delivery of health care—must be a step below those of the working class and people on welfare. (290)

prison A state or federal confinement facility that has custodial authority over adults sentenced to confinement. (5)

prison argot The special language of the inmate subculture. (396)

prison code A set of norms and values among prison inmates. It is generally antagonistic to the official administration and rehabilitation programs of the prison. (396)

prisoner subculture See **inmate subculture.** (394)

prisoners' rights Constitutional guarantees of free speech, religious practice, due process, and other private and personal rights as well as constitutional protections against cruel and unusual punishments made applicable to prison inmates by the federal courts. (426)

prisonization The process by which inmates adapt to prison society; the taking on of the ways, mores, customs, and general culture of the penitentiary. (394)

privatization A contract process that shifts public functions, responsibilities, and capital assets, in whole or in part, from the public sector to the private sector. (229)

probation The conditional release of a convicted offender into the community, under the supervision of a probation officer. It is conditional because it can be revoked if certain conditions are not met. (116)

profession An occupation granted high social status by virtue of the personal integrity of its members. (22)

professional associations Organizations of like-minded individuals who work to enhance the professional status of members of their professional group. (26)

professional development The lifelong or career-long dedication to quality selection, training, and development of employees. (674)

program-centered approach A method of planning intermediate sanctions in which planning for a program is usually undertaken by a single agency that develops and funds the program. (194)

program staff Those staff members concerned with encouraging prisoners to participate in educational, vocational, and treatment programs. (359)

property crime Burglary, larceny-theft, motor vehicle theft, and arson as reported by the FBI's Uniform Crime Reporting Program. (9)

proportionality The sentencing principle that the severity of punishment should match the seriousness of the crime for which the sentence is imposed. (97)

pseudofamilies Familylike structures, common in women's prisons, in which inmates assume roles similar to those of family members in free society. (408)

public accounts system The earliest form of prison industry, in which the warden was responsible for purchasing materials and equipment and for overseeing the manufacture, marketing, and sale of prison-made items. (258)

public works system A system of prison industry in which prisoners were employed in the construction of public buildings, roads, and parks. (259)

punitive damages Money a court may award to punish a wrongdoer when a wrongful act was intentional and malicious or was done with reckless disregard for the rights of the victim. (429)

purpose The reason an organization exists. (670)

R

rabble management Control of people whose noncriminal behavior is offensive to their communities. (211)

racism Social practices that explicitly or implicitly attribute merits or allocate value to individuals solely because of their race. (29)

rated capacity The number of beds or inmates a rating official assigns to a correctional facility. (224)

recidivism The repetition of criminal behavior; generally defined as rearrest. It is the primary outcome measure for probation, as it is for all corrections programs. (128)

reentry The use of programs targeted at promoting the effective reintegration of offenders back to communities upon release from prison and jail. (236)

reentry court A court that manages the return to the community of individuals released from prison. (340)

reform school A penal institution to which especially young or first-time offenders are committed for training and reformation. (624)

rehabilitation The changing of criminal lifestyles into law-abiding ones by "correcting" the behavior of offenders through treatment, education, and training. (76)

reintegration The process of making the offender a productive member of the community. (76)

release on bail The release of a person upon that person's financial guarantee to appear in court. (233)

release on own recognizance (ROR) Pretrial release on the defendant's promise to appear for trial. It requires no cash guarantee. (234)

relief officers Experienced correctional officers who know and can perform almost any custody role within the institution, used to temporarily replace officers who are sick or on vacation or to meet staffing shortages. (370)

remote-location monitoring Technologies, including global positioning system (GPS) devices and electronic monitoring (EM), that probation and parole officers use to monitor remotely the physical location of an offender. (179)

residential community center (RCC) A medium-security correctional setting that resident offenders are permitted to leave regularly—unaccompanied by staff—for work, education or vocational programs, or treatment in the community. (183)

residential treatment center A residential facility that provides intensive treatment services to juveniles. (637)

restitution Payments made by a criminal offender to his or her victim (or to the court, which then turns them over to the victim) as compensation for the harm caused by the offense. (83)

restoration The process of returning to their previous condition all those involved in or affected by crime—including victims, offenders, and society. (78)

restorative justice A systemic response to wrongdoing that emphasizes healing the wounds of victims, offenders, and communities caused or revealed by crime. (80)

résumé A list of your job and other related experiences and education. (A-6)

retribution A sentencing goal that involves retaliation against a criminal perpetrator. (73)

revenge Punishment as vengeance. An emotional response to real or imagined injury or insult. (72)

revocation The formal termination of an offender's conditional freedom. (145)

revocation hearing An administrative review to determine whether a violation of the conditions of probation or parole warrants removal from the community. (145)

right of allocution A statutory provision permitting crime victims to speak at the sentencing of convicted offenders. A federal right of allocution was established for victims of federal violent and sex crimes under the Violent Crime Control and Law Enforcement Act of 1994. (567)

riot Any action by a group of inmates that constitutes a forcible attempt to gain control of a facility or area within a facility. (509)

roles The normal patterns of behavior expected of those holding particular social positions. (358)

S

salient factor score (SFS) A scale, developed from a risk-screening instrument, used to predict parole outcome. (323)

second-generation jail Jail where staff remain in a secure control booth surrounded by inmate housing areas called *pods* and surveillance is remote. (212)

security threat groups (STGs) The current term for prison gangs. (502)

self-assessment Learning who you are and what you can and want to do by evaluating your interests, skills, and values. (A-1)

sentence The penalty a court imposes on a person convicted of a crime. (71)

sentencing The imposition of a criminal sanction by a sentencing authority, such as a judge. (71)

sentencing commission A group assigned to create a schedule of sentences that reflect the gravity of the offenses committed and the prior record of the criminal offender. (86)

sentencing enhancements Legislatively approved provisions that mandate longer prison terms for specific criminal offenses committed under certain circumstances (such as a murder committed because of the victim's race or a drug sale near a school) or because of an offender's past criminal record. (89)

serious error Error that substantially undermines the reliability of the guilt finding or death sentence imposed at trial. (604)

social debt The sentencing principle that the severity of punishment should take into account the offender's prior criminal behavior. (98)

social order The smooth functioning of social institutions, the existence of positive and productive relations among individual members of society, and the orderly functioning of society as a whole. (71)

special master A person appointed by the court to act as its representative to oversee remedy of a violation and provide regular progress reports. (518)

special-needs inmates Those prisoners who exhibit unique physical, mental, social, and programmatic needs that distinguish them from other prisoners and for whom jail and prison management and staff have to respond in nontraditional and innovative ways. (461)

specific deterrence The deterrence of the individual being punished from committing additional crimes. (74)

staff roles The normal patterns of behavior expected of correctional staff members in particular jobs. (358)

staff subculture The beliefs, values, and behavior of staff. They differ greatly from those of the inmate subculture. (362)

state use system A system of prison industry that employs prisoners to manufacture products consumed by state governments and their agencies, departments, and institutions. (259)

status offenses Acts that are law violations only for juveniles such as running away, truancy, or ungovernability (sometimes referred to as *incorrigibility* or *being beyond parental control*). (631)

statutory exclusion provisions Provisions under which adult criminal court jurisdiction for certain juvenile cases is established by state law. (643)

street gang An organized group of people on the street often engaged in significant illegitimate or criminal activity. (647)

stress Tension in a person's body or mind, resulting from physical, chemical, or emotional factors. (372)

structured conflict The tensions between prison staff members and inmates that arise out of the correctional setting. (362)

structured sentencing A set of guidelines for determining an offender's sentence. (501)

subculture The beliefs, values, behavior, and material objects shared by a particular group of people within a larger society. (362)

substance-abusing inmate An incarcerated individual suffering from dependency on one or more substances including alcohol and a wide range of drugs. (461)

supermax housing A free-standing facility, or a distinct unit within a facility, that provides for management and secure control of inmates who have been officially designated as exhibiting violent or serious and disruptive behavior while incarcerated. (514)

supervised pretrial release Nonfinancial pretrial release with more restrictive conditions (for example, participating in therapeutic or rehabilitative programs, reporting to a pretrial officer, and checking in regularly). (234)

supervision The second major role of probation officers, consisting of resource mediation, surveillance, and enforcement. (140)

syphilis A sexually transmitted disease caused by the bacteria *Treponema pallidum*. If left untreated, syphilis can cause serious heart abnormalities, mental disorders, blindness, other neurological problems, and death. Syphilis is transmitted when infected lesions come in contact with the soft skin of the mucous membrane. (486)

T

tangible losses Costs such as medical expenses, lost wages, and property losses that accrue to crime victims as a result of their victimization. (552)

technical violation A failure to comply with the conditions of probation or parole. (149)

teen courts Courts in which youths adjudicate and impose disposition for a juvenile offense. (643)

therapeutic community (TC) A residential treatment program in which substance-abuse inmates are housed in a separate unit within a prison or jail facility. (468)

third-generation jail (also called *direct-supervision jail*) A jail where inmates are housed in small groups, or pods, staffed 24 hours a day by specifically trained officers. Officers interact with inmates to help change behavior. Bars and metal doors are absent, reducing noise and dehumanization. (213)

tort A civil wrong, a wrongful act, or a wrongful breach of duty, other than a breach of contract, whether intentional or accidental, from which injury to another occurs. (428)

total admission The total number of people admitted to jail each year. (207)

total institution A place where the same people work, play, eat, sleep, and recreate together on a continuous basis. The term was developed by the sociologist Erving Goffman to describe prisons and other facilities. (393)

totality of conditions A standard to be used in evaluating whether prison conditions are cruel and unusual. (443)

trap-door/side-door programs Emergency release options for special docket offenders, generally used to relieve prison crowding. (159)

true diversion A form of diversion that keeps an offender out of the system and helps him or her avoid formal prosecution and labeling. (112)

truth in sentencing The sentencing principle that requires an offender to serve a substantial portion of the sentence and reduces the discrepancy between the sentence imposed and actual time spent in prison. (99)

tuberculosis A highly variable communicable disease that is characterized by toxic symptoms or allergic manifestations that in humans primarily affect the lungs. (482)

U

unconditional diversion The termination of criminal processing at any point before adjudication with no threat of later prosecution. Treatment, counseling, and other services are offered and use is voluntary. (115)

UNICOR The trade name of Federal Prison Industries. UNICOR provides such products as U.S. military uniforms, electronic cable assemblies, and modular furniture. (286)

unit management system A method of controlling prisoners in self-contained living areas and making inmates and staff (unit manager, case manager, correctional counselor, and unit secretary) accessible to each other. (277)

utilitarianism The principle that the highest objective of public policy is the greatest happiness for the largest number of people. (55)

V

victim Someone who suffers direct or threatened physical, emotional, or financial harm as the result of the commission of a crime. The term *victim* also includes the immediate family of a minor or homicide victim. (543)

victim assistance program An organized program that offers services to victims of crime in the areas of crisis intervention and follow-up counseling and that helps victims secure their rights under the law. (567)

victim compensation A form of victim assistance in which state-funded payments are made to victims to help them recover financial losses due to crime. (561)

victim-impact statement A description prepared by victims or friends and relatives of the loss, trauma, and suffering that a crime has caused them. The judge considers it when sentencing the offender. (78)

victim notification Notification to victims of the release or pending release of convicted offenders who have harmed them. (565)

victims' rights The fundamental rights of victims to be represented equitably throughout the criminal justice process. (543)

violent crime Interpersonal crime that involves the use of force by offenders or results in injury or death to victims. In the FBI's Uniform Crime Reports, violent crimes are murder, forcible rape, robbery, and aggravated assault. (10)

vision The future direction of an organization. (670)

W

waiver provisions Provisions under which the juvenile court orders transfer of the case to adult criminal court. (642)

work detail supervisors Those who oversee the work of individual inmates and inmate work crews. (368)

working alliance An effective relationship between a change agent and a client, with negotiated goals and a mutual willingness to compromise when necessary to meet the goals or to maintain a viable relationship. (133)

writ of *habeas corpus* An order that directs the person detaining a prisoner to bring him or her before a judge, who will determine the lawfulness of the imprisonment. (428)

Y

yard officers Those who supervise inmates in the prison yard. (369)

youth gang A gang whose membership generally comprises people between the ages of 12 and 24. (647)

TEXT CREDITS

Corrections Connection Network News (CCNN). Eye on Corrections. www.corrections.com. May 24, 2006. Copyright © 2006, all rights reserved, The Corrections Connection Network News (CCNN), a division of J.S. Noonan, LLC. Reprinted with permission. **p. 293**, Exhibit 7-7, States with the Highest and Lowest Reported Average Annual Operating Costs per Inmate from *Public Safety, Public Spending: Forecasting America's Prison Population 2007-2011.* Published by The Pew Charitable Trusts, 2007. Reprinted with permission of The Pew Charitable Trusts and The JFA Institute. **p. 301**, Exhibit 7-10, National Crime and Imprisonment Trends, 1931-2005 from *Public Safety, Public Spending: Forecasting America's Prison Population 2007-2011.* Published by The Pew Charitable Trusts, 2007. Reprinted with permission of The Pew Charitable Trusts and The JFA Institute.

Chapter 8: p. 312, Exhibit 8-1, American Probation and Parole Association Policy Statement on Discretionary Parole. Reprinted with permission of American Probation and Parole Association. **p. 316,** Exhibit 8-2, American Probation and Parole Association Position Statement on Parole. Reprinted with permission of American Probation and Parole Association. **p. 317,** Exhibit 8.3, Service Needs of State and Federal Prisoners from *The Report of the Re-Entry Policy Council: Charting the Safe and Successful Return of Prisoners to the Community.* Copyright © 2005. Reprinted by permission of The Council of State Governments. **p. 319,** Exhibit 8-4, American Correctional Association Public Correctional Policy on Re-Entry of Offenders. Copyright © American Correctional Association. Reprinted with permission. **p. 327,** Exhibit 8-7, Comparing Discretionary Release and Mandatory Release from *Beyond the Prison Gates: The State of Parole in America* by Jeremy Travis & Sarah Lawrence. Copyright © 2002 The Urban Institute. Reprinted with permission. **p. 335,** Ethics & Professionalism, American Probation and Parole Association Code of Ethics. Reprinted with permission of American Probation and Parole Association. **p. 339,** Exhibit 8-13, American Correctional Association Public Correctional Policy on Restoration of Voting Rights for Felony Offenders. Copyright © American Correctional Association. Reprinted with permission. **pp. 346-347,** CCNN Eye on Corrections: "The Housing Hunt for Released Offenders," Michelle Gaseau, The Corrections Connection Network News (CCNN). Eye on Corrections. www.corrections.com. February 13, 2006. Copyright © 2006, all rights reserved, The Corrections Connection Network News (CCNN), a division of J.S. Noonan, LLC. Reprinted with permission.

Note: This article has been reprinted in part from CCNN. To read this article in its entirety, go to www.corrections.com.

Chapter 9: p. 363, Exhibit 9-2, Profile of Custodial and Administrative Correctional Personnel in Adult State and Local Correctional Facilities from American Correctional Association, *Vital Statistics in Corrections* (Lantham, MD: ACA, 2000), p. 143. This material is copyrighted. The reproduction, distribution, or inclusion in other publications of this material is prohibited without prior written permission from the American Correctional Association, Alexandria, VA. Reprinted with permission. **pp. 364-365,** CCNN Eye on Corrections: "On-the-Job Training: The Real Experience," Michelle Gaseau, The Corrections Connection Network News (CCNN). Eye on Corrections. www.corrections.com. March 6, 2000. Copyright © 2000, all rights reserved, The Corrections Connection Network News (CCNN), a division of J.S. Noonan, LLC. Reprinted with permission. **p. 371,** Exhibit 9-4, American Correctional Association Employment of Women in Corrections Policy Statement. Copyright © American Correctional Association. Reprinted with permission. **p. 375,** Commission on Safety and Abuse in America's Prisons: Correctional Leadership. Excerpts from *Confronting Confinement: A Report of the Commission on Safety and Abuse in America's Prisons* by John J. Gibbons and Nicholas de B. Katzenbach, June 2006. Copyright © 2006, Vera Institute of Justice. Reprinted by permission of the Vera Institute of Justice. **p. 379,** Ethics & Professionalism, International Association of Correctional Officers: The Correctional Officer's Creed. Copyright © 2000 Bob Barrington. Used by permission of the International Association of Correctional Officers. **pp. 380-381,** CCNN Eye on Corrections: "Monitoring Extremist Groups," from "Monitoring Extremist Groups and Maintaining Religious Rights," Michelle Gaseau, The Corrections Connection Network News (CCNN). Eye on Corrections. www.corrections.com. September 20, 2004. Copyright © 2004, all rights reserved, The Corrections Connection Network News (CCNN), a division of J.S. Noonan, LLC. Reprinted with permission. Note: This article has been reprinted in part from CCNN. To read this article in its entirety, go to www.corrections.com.

Chapter 10: pp. 414-415, CCNN Eye on Corrections: "Serving Women Well in Corrections," Michelle Gaseau, The Corrections Connection Network News (CCNN). Eye on Corrections. www.corrections.com. August 2, 2004. Copyright © 2004, all rights reserved, The Corrections Connection

Network News (CCNN), a division of J.S. Noonan, LLC. Reprinted with permission. Note: This article has been reprinted in part from CCNN. To read this article in its entirety, go to www.corrections.com.

Chapter 11: p. 432, CCNN Eye on Corrections: "Prisoner Rights in the 21st Century," an interview with Bill Collins, noted corrections attorney, by Michelle Gaseau. The Corrections Connection Network News (CCNN). Eye on Corrections. www.corrections.com. January 3, 2000. Copyright © 2000, all rights reserved, The Corrections Connection Network News (CCNN), a division of J.S. Noonan, LLC. Reprinted with permission.

Chapter 12: pp. 462-463, CCNN Eye on Corrections: "Meeting Anthony," Sarah Etter, The Corrections Connection Network News (CCNN). Eye on Corrections. www.corrections.com. October 13, 2006. Copyright © 2006, all rights reserved, The Corrections Connection Network News (CCNN), a division of J.S. Noonan, LLC. Reprinted with permission. **p. 464,** Exhibit 12-1, American Correctional Association Public Correctional Policy on Offenders with Special Needs. Copyright © American Correctional Association. Reprinted with permission. **p. 483,** Commission on Safety and Abuse in America's Prisons: Health Care. Excerpts from *Confronting Confinement: A Report of the Commission on Safety and Abuse in America's Prisons* by John J. Gibbons and Nicholas de B. Katzenbach, June 2006. Copyright © 2006, Vera Institute of Justice. Reprinted by permission of the Vera Institute of Justice.

Chapter 13: pp. 504-505, Exhibit 13-1, Behind the Walls: An Expert Discusses the Role of Race-Based Gangs in America's Prisons, an Interview with Mark Pitcavage, *Intelligence Report,* Winter 2002, Vol. 108, pp. 24-27. Copyright © 2002 Southern Poverty Law Center. Used with permission. **pp. 506-507,** CCNN Eye on Corrections: "Corrections Emerges Strong Following Katrina," Michelle Gaseau, The Corrections Connection Network News (CCNN). Eye on Corrections. www.corrections.com. September 12, 2005. Copyright © 2005, all rights reserved, The Corrections Connection Network News (CCNN), a division of J.S. Noonan, LLC. Reprinted with permission. Note: This article has been reprinted in part from CCNN. To read this article in its entirety, go to www.corrections.com. **p. 513,** Exhibit 13-2, American Correctional Association Public Correctional Policy on Use of Force. Copyright © American Correctional Association. Reprinted with permission. **p. 517,** Commission on Safety and Abuse

PHOTO CREDITS

CASE INDEX

SUBJECT INDEX